THE MASTER A

IAIN McGILCHRIST is a former fellow of All Souls College, Oxford, where he taught literature before training in medicine. He is an Associate Fellow of Green Templeton College, Oxford, a Fellow of the Royal College of Psychiatrists, a Fellow of the Royal Society of Arts, a Consultant Emeritus of the Bethlem and Maudsley Hospital, London, and has researched in neuroimaging at Johns Hopkins University, Baltimore. He now lives on the Isle of Skye, where he continues to write, and lectures worldwide.

IAIN MCGILCHRIST

THE
MASTER
AND HIS
EMISSARY

THE DIVIDED BRAIN AND THE
MAKING OF THE WESTERN WORLD

NEW EXPANDED EDITION

YALE UNIVERSITY PRESS
NEW HAVEN AND LONDON

For information about this and other Yale University Press publications, please contact:
U.S. Office: sales.press@yale.edu   yalebooks.com
Europe Office: sales@yaleup.co.uk   yalebooks.co.uk

Set in Minion Pro by IDSUK (DataConnection) Ltd
Printed in the United States of America.

Library of Congress Control Number: 2018960775

ISBN 978-0-300-24592-9

ISBN 978-0-300-18837-0 (2012 pbk)
ISBN 978-0-300-16892-1 (2010 pbk)
ISBN 978-0-300-14878-7 (hbk)

A catalogue record for this book is available from the British Library.

1 0 9 8

CONTENTS

ILLUSTRATIONS

Illustrations within the text

Plate section

ACKNOWLEDGEMENTS

Charles II apologised that he had been 'an unconscionable time a-dying'. This book has been an unconscionable time in coming to birth. The intellectual debts I have incurred during the twenty years I have been gestating it are many, and I can mention only a few. First and foremost, as will be obvious to many readers, I am hugely indebted to the ground-breaking work of John Cutting, especially to his *Principles of Psychopathology*, which was a revelation to me, but also to much else of his thought, research and conversation over the years, all of which has helped me more than I can say; and of Louis Sass, particularly his *Madness & Modernism* and *The Paradoxes of Delusion*. Their massively important work stands behind every page I have written; and, whether or not I have been able to make much of the view, they are the giants on whose shoulders I stand. Both have been generous in their encouragement, and Louis Sass has given liberally of his time in reading various versions of this book, in the process making many valuable suggestions, for which I am deeply grateful.

I should like particularly to thank others that have helped through their comments on parts or all of the manuscript at some stage, including Alwyn Lishman, Sir Geoffrey Lloyd, David Lorimer, David Malone, John Onians, Christopher Pelling, Andrew Shanks, Martin Sixsmith, and Nicholas Spice; and I owe a very special debt of gratitude to John Wakefield for his careful attention to succeeding drafts and for his unstinting support throughout. His rare ability to combine tact with a shrewd incisiveness has made a huge difference and saved me from many errors. I have benefitted from correspondence with Milton Brener, whose book *Faces* I found stimulating and original. I am also indebted to Edward Hussey for advice on Greek, and to Catherine Baxter, Lotte Bredt, and Martin Sixsmith for advice on French, German and Russian respectively. It goes without saying that the faults, and errors, that remain are entirely my own.

I am very grateful for the constant support and enthusiastic commitment of Anthony Goff at David Higham, and of my editor, Phoebe Clapham, whose advice and suggestions have proved extremely helpful, as well as to Yale University Press as a whole for believing in this book from the outset. I should also mention my apparently omniscient copy-editor, Jenny Roberts, but there are many others at Yale who have contributed in different ways.

I owe much to the generosity of the Warden and Fellows of All Souls College, Oxford. My first election there more than thirty years ago enabled me to explore many things at my own pace, and my subsequent re-election in the 1990s enabled me to maintain a link with academe during years crammed with other commitments. Their forbearance in offering me a further Fellowship in 2002–4 enabled me to host a conference there on phenomenology and brain lateralisation in 2004, which played an important part in bringing this book to birth. I am also very much indebted to the unfailing kindness and good humour of my clinical colleagues, especially my dear friends Jeremy Broadhead and David Wood, who have so willingly taken care of my patients during the periods of enforced solitude that writing this book has entailed; as well as to my patients themselves for their understanding, and for the constant source of inspiration and instruction that they have afforded me.

Iain McGilchrist
April 2012

PREFACE TO THE NEW EXPANDED EDITION

'Psychiatrist debunks the left brain/right brain myth,' the headline proclaims. Always interested to learn more, I read on, only to discover that the psychiatrist in question is – myself.

This puts its finger on the nub of the matter. I don't believe in the left brain/right brain myth: I believe in discovering the truth about hemisphere difference. There can be no question that it would be foolish to believe most of what has passed into popular culture on the topic of hemisphere differences. And yet it would be just as foolish to believe that therefore there are no important hemisphere differences. There are massively important ones, which lie at the core of what it means to be a human being. It's just that we've been barking up the wrong tree.

When people object that each hemisphere is involved in everything we do, they are right. When they assume that means there are no differences, they are wrong. It is not *what* each hemisphere does, but *how* it does it that matters. Each hemisphere is involved in everything, true enough; just in a quite different way.

When *The Master and His Emissary* came out in November 2009, I was hoping that a handful of people might find its thesis truly interesting. I even hoped that they might feel inspired to take the ideas further. But I anticipated that otherwise it would be largely ignored.

Partly this was because of its topic. My colleagues and mentors in the world of psychiatry and neurology had, from the very outset some thirty years ago, counselled me against getting involved in laterality research, since it was stigmatised within the neuroscience world due to its appropriation by pop psychology. They also warned me, correctly, that it would involve going back to the drawing board. All the things we thought we knew about hemisphere difference had been shown, one by one, to be either wrong or, at best, half-truths. That had led – in a somewhat defeatist fashion, I have to say – to its being given up as a bad job. And those who gave up reconciled themselves to the lost time and effort by proclaiming loudly their own myth: that there are no significant hemisphere differences.

I knew enough, however, to realise that there were fascinating intellectual puzzles here that were simply too important to neglect, whatever the cost in terms of career. They demanded further investigation. For example, every known creature with a neuronal system, however far down the evolutionary tree one goes and however far back in time, has a system that is asymmetrical. Why on earth would that be, given that the world they are interacting with is not asymmetrical? I was already involved in neuroimaging research on the loss of normal brain asymmetry in schizophrenia that was clearly bearing fruit. So I couldn't help seeing the topic as potentially of some significance.

When after twenty years of research I arrived at the point of publication of this book, I believed I would face a hostile establishment. With a few exceptions, that has not been the case, and, thankfully, some of the best-known names in neuroscience are on record as engaging seriously with the book's thesis. I also expected, of course, the usual faction of self-appointed 'myth debunkers', who would feel comfortably one-up on the gullible masses by professing that there was 'nothing in it' without the bore of acquainting themselves with the evidence before pronouncing. I imagine there have been plenty of those, but that is neither here nor there.

The other reason I did not expect the book to be widely read was because it is, I admit, demanding. I took pains to write it as clearly as I could without, I hope, ever talking down to my audience, instead meeting them on a level footing to get to grips with issues in neuroscience and philosophy, though without presuming any prior knowledge. I aimed to explain what I saw in terms that any interested non-specialist reader should be able to understand. But neuropsychology and phenomenological philosophy probably aren't everyone's idea of an easy read.

Ten years on, I have been genuinely astonished by the completely unforeseen extent to which this book has been taken up by people in every discipline, and from every walk of life. It has already sold over 100,000 copies, and has readers all over the world. I think the reason for this must be that the structural and functional differences between the brain hemispheres which I describe have, as indeed they must, their correlates in the mind; and that we are intuitively aware of these structural and functional differences within our consciousness – but only, it seems, once they are pointed out.

One of the most common reactions from readers has been: 'You articulated ideas that I knew to be true, but for which I had never found words. You told me something that was immediately compelling because I was, at some level, already aware of the patterns you were revealing and the associations you were making.' This cannot be due to such readers simply being familiar with the popular left brain/right brain story, because the picture that emerges from this book is quite different from anything they would have come across previously. And it cannot be simply because there are philosophical distinctions here with which they were already familiar, regardless of any brain correlates, because the pattern of differences is not the same as those found in any conventional philosophical debate, though parts of it certainly have their reflections at different points in the history of ideas – the theme of the second half of the book.

Just how different this picture is from the familiar left brain/right brain story can be judged from the simplest of observations. It is, for instance, just not true that the left hemisphere is unemotional, perhaps a bit boring, but at least down-to-earth and reliable: in fact the left hemisphere is more likely than the right to get angry or dismissive, jump to conclusions, become deluded or get stuck in denial. Equally it's not true that the right hemisphere has no language (it usually has no speech, a different matter): it understands many of the subtlest and most important elements of language better than the left. Nor is it true that the left hemisphere cannot deal with visual imagery: in certain respects it very clearly can. Maths and science are not primarily dependent on the left hemisphere, but draw in different respects on both hemispheres. And, no, the left brain is not male, nor is the right brain female.

The hemisphere hypothesis transcends and replaces, and is not a perpetuation of, the old dichotomies: reason v. feeling, rationality v. intuition, 'system I v. system II', male brain v. female brain. Each hemisphere plays its part on either side of each of those dichotomies.

Trawl the internet and you will find all kinds of misinformation. Some of it is on popular 'teach yourself psychology' websites, some on the websites of management gurus. One of my favourites is this list, a slide I sometimes use in lectures with the health warning in the title: 'Right and . . . WRONG!'

LEFT BRAIN FUNCTIONS	RIGHT BRAIN FUNCTIONS
uses logic	uses feeling
detail oriented	"big picture" oriented
facts rule	imagination rules
words and language	symbols and images
present and past	present and future
math and science	philosophy & religion
can comprehend	can "get it"
knowing	believes
acknowledges	appreciates
sees order/pattern	spatial perception
knows object name	knows object function
reality based	fantasy based
forms strategies	presents possibilities
practical	impetuous
safe	risk taking

Although there is nothing unusual here, and it is actually one of the more nuanced such summaries on the web, the nuances don't help – because they are wrong.

There is only one pairing here that is broadly correct. All the others are false, sometimes so badly that they represent the inverse of what is known to be the case.

And as for conventional philosophical debate, just how different the thesis of this book is, taken as a whole, from any existing patterns can be gauged from the fact that no one to my knowledge has even seen, let alone forged, a philosophical position on the basis of the commonalities between, for example, realism, the appreciation of uniqueness, music and time, a sense of humour, a capacity for reading body language, sustaining attention and the fight-or-flight mode; or between unreasonable optimism, manipulation, disembodiment, literalism, and preoccupations with detail, theory and body parts. Put like that, they sound improbably random assortments of characteristics, not corresponding to any pre-existing philosophical world views. Yet, after reading the book, and once the bigger picture is painted, the reader will, I hope, see exactly how these elements go to form a coherent picture, one that falls into two coherent parts; a picture that also illuminates our situation here in the West today, as those who have read the book seem readily to understand.

This suggests to me that since the patterns that emerge from the neuroscience behind the book seem familiar to readers, they can do so for one reason only: namely, that they correspond to intuitions that the human mind has about its own way of working, and its consequent structuring of reality.

Nor are the elements ones that I would or could have come up with according to any preconceived theory of my own that I might have had. They simply came of immersing myself for twenty years in the field and its literature and pondering what emerged. In order to see the pattern, I needed to take in the broadest range of material; in order to examine and substantiate the detail, I needed to look closely at myriad discrete findings.

The sheer variety of people who have responded to and taken up my ideas also helps, at least in my own mind, to support the thesis that the world is structured according to hemisphere differences, since, if I am right, it ought to apply to human experience across the board. So, as well as many positive responses from the world of neurology, psychiatry, psychology and philosophy, I have had enthusiastic responses from some areas which initially surprised me (only in the sense that I know relatively little about them), such as the worlds of economics, finance and the law; and I have been delighted, but less surprised, by warm responses from artists, musicians and therapists, and from the world of teachers, priests and doctors.

Occasionally, people who ought to know better make sweepingly dismissive pronouncements on the whole topic of hemisphere difference. What they are attacking, however, when one looks more closely, are what they themselves describe as 'caricatures', 'popular beliefs', and so on. After one such gleeful romp, the authors accept that

> the left and right halves of the brain do function in some different ways, but these differences are more subtle than is popularly believed. (For example, the left side processes small details of things you see, the right processes the overall shape.)[1]

Ah, yes – indeed. But why should 'subtle' mean unimportant? Indeed, why would processing 'small details of things' versus processing the overall shape not have a whole raft of consequences? And, of course, it does. The quote, by the way, comes from publicity surrounding a book called *Top Brain, Bottom Brain*, which involved a number of caricatures of its own, so one can understand the drive to get the inconvenient hemisphere story out of the way.

The real story of hemisphere difference is indeed a subtle and complex one, hence the scope of this book, but it is one that is entirely coherent. I am confident that claims that there is little difference between the hemispheres will soon appear not just dated and out of touch, but quite simply untenable. In the last decade, there has been a plethora of findings that further substantiate the hemisphere hypothesis, some of it in areas where there were only hints at the time this book was written. The growth of such literature is gratifying, and it is impossible to ignore. More studies now are reporting results in terms of lateralisation, so awareness is increasing, though it certainly could increase further and faster with advantage. Some kinds of research can be misleading: for a range of reasons, as one research team reflects, 'neuroimaging studies may especially fail to shed light on hemispheric lateralisation'.[2] That is because they may fail to find real differences by not adequately discriminating or by aggregating data in certain ways. But a coherent body of some 5,000 independent pieces of research that I am now aware of does shed light on hemispheric lateralisation in such a way as to support the hypothesis advanced in this book.

One development over the ten years since publication has been an increasing respect for the capacities of the right hemisphere. It is no longer treated as having cognitive skills 'vastly inferior to those of a chimpanzee', as one of the giants in the field, Michael Gazzaniga, once put it.[3] In fact, recent research from Gazzaniga's own lab shows it to be the more reliable and insightful partner, and another recent study collating the areas of damage associated with a drop in IQ following a stroke showed them to be almost entirely in the right hemisphere of the brain.[4]

I don't want it to be possible, after reading this book, for any intelligent person ever again to see the right hemisphere as the 'minor' hemisphere, as it used to be called – still worse the flighty, impetuous, fantastical one, the unreliable but perhaps fluffy and cuddly one – and the left hemisphere as the solid, dependable, down-to-earth hemisphere, the one that does all the heavy lifting and is alone the intelligent source of our understanding. I might still be to some extent swimming against the current, but there are signs that the current may be changing direction.

There are a number of points I could wish to have made more clearly in this book had I been aware at the time of writing of the potential for misconception. Let me address them briefly now.

I do not mean to suggest that the brain *causes* human experience. Clearly there is a correlation between the brain and human experience. A discussion of what we can know of the nature of that correlation would take me too far from the purposes of this preface. However, my position in brief is that the nature and structure of the brain must be reciprocally related to the nature and structure of consciousness, but does not necessarily give rise to it (rather than, say, transduce it). It might, or it might not.

I also did not mean to imply that the changes in cultural balance were due to there having been gross changes in our brains over the time periods in question (the last 2,500 years). Given that we are evolving creatures, it is bound to be true that our brains have changed at some level, since our brains both mould and are in turn moulded by the culture in which we live. But that is not my point. What I suggest is that nowadays we use – draw on the potential of – our brains differently from the way in which we have used them at different periods in the past, periods which also differ from one another in this same respect. An analogy might be this. For a considerable while I might find myself listening to a selection of radio stations. If, with time, I find I am listening to one radio station only, that does not imply my having a new radio set, just that I am using the options made possible by the existing set in a more limited way.

Nor do I suggest that the causes of such cultural shifts can be reduced to neuroscience. There are many causative factors in play when cultures change, including sociological, psychological, environmental, epigenetic, technological, economic and political factors, all of which are interconnected. In a causal nexus one can privilege one over the rest if one wishes to do so, and interpret the changes in one way or another. However, I am not attempting to answer the question of what *causes* changes: just of what patterns are discernible when such changes occur, and how those patterns relate to the possible takes on the world afforded to us by the brain's bihemispheric structure. Doing so gives us insight into those situations – I believe we are in one now – where the balance is lost. It helps us see what it is we are missing.

An argument sometimes brought against the existence of hemisphere difference is that under normal circumstances each hemisphere is always active to some extent. This seems to me scarcely an argument at all – no one could dispute the fact for an instant. It does not, however, prove that the two hemispheres' roles are the same. Both the scrub nurse and the surgeon are important members of the surgical team, and work together, at the same time, on the same task: an operation becomes hazardous in the absence of one, and impossible in the absence of the other. They work well together not because they have the same role, but precisely because they have different ones.

Naturally a hemisphere is not an undifferentiated whole, but encompasses many regions of interest: there is a lot of detail about localisation in the book (often, for simplicity's sake, in the endnotes) for those who wish to know more. And differences between frontal and posterior cortex, as I point out, are particularly important. But, equally, we now realise we need to think much more in terms of widely distributed networks, rather than, as we used to do, primarily in terms of 'modules'. The hemispheres are vastly more connected within themselves than they are connected to one another, though of course interhemispheric information transfer is still important. Each hemisphere forms a complex system, and all parts of each hemisphere are prolifically interconnected, so that a change in a part can alter the whole. The greatest division in the brain is that between the two hemispheric systems, which leads to their capacity for relatively independent function. So, as in life, we need both to focus on detail and yet see the whole.

I do say clearly in the book that differences between hemispheres are not absolute, but since I have been misunderstood on the point, perhaps I should emphasise it again. Very few differences ever are absolute, especially in the living world. There is overlap, but that does nothing to undermine the essential difference. On that point, I find the example of Indonesia and Iceland helpful, two countries that are very different from one another in a host of ways, many of which can be linked in part to differences of temperature. Yet it is still true that the warmest annual temperature recorded in Iceland is higher than the lowest annual temperature recorded in Indonesia. There is, in other words, overlap: we should not expect absolute differences in order for the differences to be substantial, even dramatic, as in the case of those two countries.

A couple of related points are worth making. I have heard it said that 'the hemispheres are more like than they are unlike'. It's hard to know exactly what this phrase means; but whatever it means, sometimes in life it is the differences that count. Donald Trump and Albert Einstein are undoubtedly 'more like than they are unlike'. An old banger and a new Ferrari are both cars, with internal combustion engines, and are in that sense much more alike than not. But when I am buying one, I am interested in their differences.

Nor am I 'dichotomising'. Nature got there before me, beginning with a remarkable physical division at the core of the brain, which she has since made more robust through mechanisms of interhemispheric inhibition. Some dichotomies are valid, such as those between plants and animals (despite there being at the microscopic level some overlap). Others, between, say, good and bad drivers, are not: that is not a true dichotomy, just a continuous spectrum. Recognising valid differences between two elements of a system is not to 'dichotomise'. Some people fear dichotomies are simplistic. But it is also simplistic to reject a perfectly valid dichotomy just because you happen to have a thing against dichotomies when they occur.

It has been commented that the hemispheres work 'in the same way', referring to neural pathways. But this is to neglect phenomenological experience. The visual systems of the cat and the mouse are highly similar, but they each 'see' the world in a different way. Thus the visual pathways of each human brain hemisphere are technically similar, though their 'vision' of the world phenomenologically is not. There are significant differences between Fox News and Al Jazeera, but if we focus on the mechanics of studio lighting, cabling, cameras, TV signal transmission, cathode ray tubes, plasma/LED screens, etc., we are looking in the wrong place. We will find no differences and solemnly conclude there are none. Wrongly.

Finally, some people feel that I have gone 'well beyond the facts', that I have somehow simply 'gone too far'. Whether I have taken things too far depends on many things, including the extent of the various hemisphere differences, whether there is any pattern or overall meaning to those differences, and the context in which you view them. If you don't know the extent of the differences (and very few people do), and if at the same time you can't see the overall picture (viewing the differences as just so much lab data, not something with significance for what it means to be a living person), then – yes, it's been taken too far. If you *do* know the extent – then it is scarcely far enough. My experience has been that, where this objection has been made, the problem lies in my having dared to link brain science with the history of ideas. This may simply express a discomfort felt by too many scientists at 'straying' into the realms of philosophy and cultural history. But until about seventy years ago, scientists would have been educated in, and seen science as part of, a whole world picture in which it played just one part; it would have seemed obviously distorted to them to view science in isolation from the rest of human endeavour. In any case, when science is dealing with how consciousness brings the experienced world into being, it is simply not possible to avoid philosophy, including the history of cultures and ideas. They must be an important part of the picture.

So much for the use I have made of the data I have presented. But there is a further legitimate concern to be addressed: the extent and representativeness of the data themselves. It has been said by one or two critics that I 'must' have 'cherry-picked' the data, in other words ignored or passed over data that do not suit my argument. This is not an unreasonable suspicion to have when confronting any large work that presents a coherent overall picture. It is also the easiest of things to say and the hardest of things to counter, since it cannot be disproved; the only response must be, 'All right, you look at the same extent of evidence that I did, and show me *where* you think I have cherry-picked – then we can have a sensible conversation. We might still disagree, but if I missed something that changes the story I am happy to take it into account.' This is one reason I have been as careful as I could to give chapter and verse for every assertion I make, and why the bibliography is an important part of the book; I am grateful to Yale for reinstating it in full, as it was in the original hardback, in this new edition. In science you can be as perfunctory as you like as long as you are saying what everyone else is saying, but if you are saying something different, you need, reasonably enough, to be as explicit about your evidence and as empirically based as possible. That way you are open to challenge, and that is how science progresses.

Incidentally, I could have no interest whatever in a picture I had made up myself. That would mean I had not made contact with a reality outside myself, but simply created a pointless fantasy. I have sought to be true to whatever *is*. I have been impassioned to discover the picture that is already there, given in the structure of our selves, our brains and our minds. If I have got it wrong, and I may well have in places, it will not be because I have knowingly misrepresented the data. Many times the data have led me to change an assumption or expand a view, to reconfigure the picture and to become aware of something I otherwise would never have seen. Anomalies are often the path to a new understanding. I have also come across some anomalies that do not outweigh the other evidence available in the field. Every scientist has this to contend with, especially in the life sciences, where there will never be 100 per cent agreement on anything. The question must always be, does an 'aberrant' finding force a rethink, or would that be to lose a grip on what the rest of the findings suggest?

In writing the book I drew on a vast body of literature. Not even a team of researchers could easily have provided a comprehensive review, detailing every single study, in just one part of it, unless that part were fairly limited, never mind across the whole field. To be fair, no one has suggested I should have drawn on *more* literature, and some kind of selection is agreed to be inevitable. The question then becomes, how unrepresentative are the inevitably incomplete data? When it comes to the human brain, things are rarely if ever cut and dried, and people will differ in what they would have chosen to emphasise. However, I have tried always to be true to an emerging consensus in any one area, though no consensus is ever absolute; and where there was considerable support for an opposing view, I indicated it. Originally such moments of qualification were in the text itself, but my editor wisely thought I should put most such excursus into the endnotes, for fear of the reader losing the thread of the argument. I think this was good advice. I have carried on reading and discussing with colleagues for a further ten years, and nothing I have read leads me to change the substance, or even, except in one or two small points, the detail of what I wrote. New evidence continues to fit with the hypothesis. None of the many pieces of evidence can be by itself conclusive, but their convergence across a variety of aspects of human psychology has become increasingly persuasive. Much of this material is incorporated in my current writing, in which I am providing, at least in certain limited areas (which is all that can be humanly achieved), a more nearly comprehensive review of the literature.

Is there a value in trying to view hemisphere difference, not just as a mass of unrelated technical details, but as a coherent picture, at the level of human meaning? This seems to me the important question. To sustain any coherent vision requires one to make an attempt to span fields of knowledge, and as human knowledge expands exponentially, the task becomes *ipso facto* more difficult. Should we therefore abandon the attempt? Certainly we must conclude that attempting such a synthesis is something that scientists with respectably constrained vision can from now on never attempt. However, with luck, some will be foolhardy enough to try, since the constrained vision is not – absolutely not – a feature of science, but of the nature of the contemporary science establishment. As no less a figure than the great evolutionary biologist and palaeontologist George Gaylord Simpson, one of the founders of the so-called modern synthesis of Darwinian evolution with Mendelian genetics, the crowning achievement of twentieth-century biology, wrote:

> Science, truly to be such, must centre not on descriptions and names but on principles – that is, generalisations, theories, relationships, interconnections, explanations about and among the facts.[5]

Although I am not aware of having been criticised on these grounds, I should forestall a possible misunderstanding. I could understand someone reasonably enough expressing the view that this is a hypothesis that cannot be falsified. That is, however, not the case. While it cannot be falsified by any one experiment, it can certainly be falsified. Parts of it could be more easily falsified than the whole, but even the whole could be falsified.

It might be helpful, simply for the purposes of argument, to contrast here the theories of Freud with those of Darwin. Both had hypotheses that have proved enormously influential on subsequent thought. Neither of their hypotheses can be straightforwardly falsified, but for different reasons.

Freud has provided us with a body of concepts and a manner in which they are related that is not falsifiable at all, because no empirical observations could distinguish between his theory and any competing theory: the status of his work, then, is like that of a philosophy, in that it provides a more or less convincing account of experience, and does not depend on scientific data one way or the other to carry that conviction. You take it or leave it, depending on whether it makes better sense of your experience than any competing model – which *doesn't* mean that it is not valuable: we may find that it reconfigures our knowledge in a way that is richer than the one to which we are accustomed, and leads to the explanation of otherwise puzzling observations.

Darwin, by contrast, has provided us with a hypothesis that relates intimately to observations in relation to which empirical data are indeed relevant, notwithstanding the fact that no single experiment can possibly prove or disprove his hypothesis. To quote the Darwinian George Gaylord Simpson again:

> The most striking example [of a theory that cannot be definitively proved or disproved] is the most important of all biological theories: that of organic evolution. Although some quite limited predictions can be deduced from the theory, the theory was not in fact established by prediction and is not sufficiently tested by it. An enormous number of observations enormously varied in kind are all consistent with this theory, and many of them are consistent with no other theory that has been proposed. We therefore can and, if we are rational, must have an extremely high degree of confidence in the theory . . .[6]

Of course, I make no claim to be a Freud or a Darwin, but I do see clearly that my hypothesis is in this respect more like Darwin's than Freud's. It certainly can act as a philosophical model that reconfigures our knowledge in a way that I believe is richer. But it is derived from, and can be tested against, empirical, experimental observations. The hypothesis could be seen as an aggregate of more local hypotheses, each of which can be tested against empirical evidence and which can each be abandoned if they do not stand up to the findings. Enough such negative findings would invalidate the overall hypothesis, at least in its current form. Alternatively, it might turn out that at least some observations 'enormously varied in kind are consistent with this theory, and many of them are consistent with no other theory that has been proposed'. That is my belief.

What might be examples of such observations, in the case of the theory explained in this book? Let's start from some really basic questions about the brain, that, fundamental as they are, have not to my knowledge been satisfactorily addressed by any other theory. Why is the brain, an organ that exists *only* to make connections, divided? Why is it asymmetrical in so many measurable respects, both structural and functional, and why does its functioning seem to *depend* on its being asymmetrical? And why is the major connection between the two cerebral hemispheres, the corpus callosum, getting proportionately smaller, and function-ally more inhibitory, rather than larger, and functionally more facilitatory, with evolution? These indisputable observations are not addressed as satisfactorily by any alternative theories of which I am aware. But far more important than any of these, important as they nonetheless are, is that *there is no alternative theory that makes sense as a whole of a large number of established hemisphere differences.* We have no overarching theory that covers so many of the facts. They are otherwise simply treated as a random assortment of findings, inviting a shrug when the ques-tions why such individual differences exist, and how they make sense together, are asked. But, to me, for a scientist not to ask precisely these questions betrays an astonishing lack of intellectual curiosity, to say the least.

The explanatory power of the hemisphere hypothesis is greater than any alter-native I know of; and, as for the difference-deniers, they can't even get to first base. When a better theory is developed that covers as many findings, I will be the first to welcome it. That is how understanding evolves.

I take comfort from the words of Max Planck:

New scientific ideas never spring from a communal body, however organised, but rather from the head of an individually inspired researcher who struggles with his problems in lonely thought and unites all his thought on one single point which is his whole world for the moment.[7]

I caused some confusion by remarking at the end of the book that, while I thought it unlikely I would be shown to be wholly wrong, it would be remarkable if I were shown to be right in every respect. I followed that commonplace observation with words to the effect that, in the worst possible case, the hemisphere distinction at least provided a valuable metaphor, metaphor being how we come to understand the world. That has led some literal-minded people to assume that I do not believe in my own thesis, and that I think the decades spent investigating the neuroscience were irrelevant. It will hardly surprise you to learn that I am not of that view at all.

I have, though, sometimes been asked how essential brain science is to a critique of the modern world picture which is valid in its own terms. There are a number of answers to that point.

First, in place of a list of unconnected observations about a culture or society, and a series of problems requiring a comparable list of unconnected solutions, the recognition of hemispheric differences provides for the first time a way of seeing the picture as a coherent whole. It shows the problems as necessarily interconnected consequences of espousing a certain 'take' on the world. Incidentally, if I am right that we are currently in thrall to the left hemisphere's view, one of the consequences would be, precisely, an inability to see the whole rather than a heap of disparate elements, together with a relative inability to understand what is happening, rather than simply document it, and attempt, as best one can, to find a series of *ad hoc* solutions.

Second, and following from this, it suggests that the best way to *address* such shortcomings as we identify will be not so much by piecemeal strategies, necessary as they are bound to become at some level, as by opening our eyes to the limitations of the view of the world which underlies them, the view which, as a society, we appear to adopt as our default. It is the aim of this book to do precisely that. We don't need a lot more quick fixes. We need a shift in the paradigm.

Third, by showing that the left hemisphere, which underwrites the fragmented vision, is both literally more limited in what it can see, and less capable of understanding what it *does* see, than the right – and, to cap it all, is less aware of its own limitations – the book gives the reader good reason to reappraise the left hemisphere's world view, wherever it can be identified as such.

But there exists a fourth, most important, consideration. The book is not just a societal critique, but aims to achieve more: to add to an understanding of brain function, and to add thereby to our understanding of our own minds; to give us a means of evaluating ways of thinking that although apparently equally rational may sometimes be in conflict. It aims to help us better understand one aspect of what it is to be a human being – not, I repeat, in offering a *causative* mechanism as such, but in offering a descriptive, phenomenological model anchored in the science of the brain.

Understanding hemisphere difference offers a perspective on the structure of mind which is not available merely by introspection. If in everyday life we were aware of the discrepancies in the view, or 'take', on the world each hemisphere offers, it would render the immediate business of survival impracticable. For this reason, nature has taken care that these discrepancies should not be part of our everyday awareness. Even on sustained introspection, we can be only indirectly aware of the fact that reality is constructed from two incompatible world views.

This fact becomes manifest, however, in the disputes of philosophers and theologians over the ages about the very nature of reality. By such indirect routes we become aware of fundamental irreconcilables in the world, irreconcilables so marked that they have led philosophers, time and again, to conclude that we are 'citizens of two worlds' – though those worlds were never fully articulated. The last fifty years have brought the means to carry out painstaking observations of brain function and the changes in the lived world of the individual whose function is altered. With that comes the knowledge that those 'two worlds' the philosophers intuited are each underwritten by one hemisphere of the brain.

Finally, it would appear to be a literal truth that, as a society, we are becoming more like individuals with right hemisphere deficits. Anecdotal evidence from the teaching profession suggests that between a quarter and a third of children aged as old as five to seven are now having to be taught how to read the human face, something that until recently would have been necessary only in the case of children with autism. And about a third of all children now have difficulty carrying out tasks that a decade ago virtually every child in a mainstream school would have been able to do easily – tasks that depend on sustained attention. Add to that research suggesting that young people today are less empathic than children thirty to forty years ago. If a neuropsychologist had to choose three things to characterise most clearly the functional contribution of the right hemisphere, they would most probably be the capacity to read the human face, the capacity to sustain vigilant attention, and the capacity to empathise.

I am sometimes asked why, if the left hemisphere 'take' on the world is less insightful, it has come to dominate the way we think. And if this has happened not just once, but three times, as I believe, in Western history, how do I account for that fact? These are good questions.

I think there are, again, several reasons why this characteristic entrenchment occurs, and indeed is likely to occur whenever a civilisation passes its peak. All of them, to some degree, illustrate the self-reinforcing, recursive nature of the left hemisphere's world, a world subject to positive feedback.

First, the left-hemisphere view is designed to aid you in grabbing stuff. Its purpose is utility and its evolutionary adaptation lies in the service of grasping and amassing 'things'. As such it is seductive. It is probably for this reason that Eastern cultures which used to be more balanced in their outlook are now adopting the current Western model of the world with such enthusiasm, and appear set, very sadly, on outdoing the West at its own pernicious game. It is my view that we should be learning from them, not they from us. In the case of the Greeks, the Romans and the post-Enlightenment West, the decline of civilisation has been associated, not just with more left-hemisphere ways of thinking, but appropriately with forms of military or economic imperialism, and a consequent overextension of administration, a coarsening of values, and a failure of vitality, vision and integrity.

Second, the left-hemisphere view offers simple answers. Its mode of thinking prizes consistency above all, and claims to offer the same mechanistic models to explain everything that exists. This thinking is common to those who espouse naïve reductionist science ('scientism'), enthusiasts for technological solutions to what are complex human problems, and designers and implementers of bureaucratic systems. When this sort of thinking encounters a problem in reconciling apparent irreconcilables – for example, matter and consciousness – it simply denies that one element or the other exists. That's very convenient.

Third, the left hemisphere's world view is easier to articulate. The left hemisphere is the speaking hemisphere: the right hemisphere has literally no voice. The attempt to make the implicit explicit radically alters its nature; as a result, finding the language to put across the way of being of the right hemisphere is simply harder than doing so for the naturally explicit left hemisphere. The left hemisphere relies on concatenations of serial propositions and the literal aspects of language to make meaning explicit; by contrast, metaphor and narrative are often required to convey the implicit meanings available to the right hemisphere, and in a left-hemisphere-dominated culture, metaphors and narratives are disregarded as myths and fables or, at worst, downright lies. We live in an era where articulating and making explicit are of increasing importance and are treated as a mark of truth, and their inverse treated with increasing suspicion. Partly this is another sign of the 'move to the left hemisphere' that I am describing, but that is not the only reason for it: it is also necessitated by large-scale movements of populations with different languages and cultures, as well as the sheer size of modern urban societies in which one can no longer rely on much that was once taken for granted in smaller and more closely knit communities. The implicit has, now, to be made explicit. The catch is that in becoming explicit it is no longer the same thing at all.

Fourth, since the Industrial Revolution, but particularly in the last fifty years, we have created a world around us which, in contrast to the natural world, reflects the left hemisphere's priorities and its vision. Today all the available sources of intuitive life – the natural world, cultural tradition, the body, religion and art – have been so conceptualised, devitalised and 'deconstructed' (ironised) by self-consciousness, explicitness and the systems and theories used to analyse them, that their power to help us see intuitively beyond the hermetic world that the left hemisphere has set up has been largely drained from them. For many, TV screens and computers supplant direct face-to-face experience of reality. The cerebral and the abstract – for example, management and its systems – have become more highly valued than the hands-on task that management exists to serve, with the odd effect that the higher you rise in your craft, skill or profession, the more you will be removed from its performance in order to manage it. A century ago, the physical environment was for most of humanity that of the natural world, with its rhythms and cycles, its organic, ever-growing and ever-changing interdependent life, a world to which it seemed intuitively obvious that we belong; now it has been replaced for many by an unyielding, inert, confrontational environment of non-living surfaces, straight lines, concrete masses and largely generic shapes, which are widely experienced as alienating. The result is that the left hemisphere's world has become externalised, so that when the counterbalancing tendency of the right hemisphere to check with the real world of experience is brought into play, it is already subverted: the world 'out there' is already colonised by the left hemisphere's vision. There is a self-reflexive hall of mirrors at work, where logic seems to lead back to a solution within the system itself, rather than a need to break out of it.

Fifth, built into the relationship between the hemispheres is that they have a different take on everything – *including on their own relationship*. Neurological research reveals a consistent picture of how the two hemispheres contribute to the richness of experience. Essentially this is that the right hemisphere tends to ground experience; the left hemisphere then works on it to clarify, 'unpack' and generally render the implicit explicit; and the right hemisphere finally reintegrates what the left hemisphere has produced with its own understanding, the explicit once more receding, to produce a new, now enriched, whole. Note that the two ways of attending are both necessary and, strictly speaking, incompatible, at least at the same level and at the same time.

This could be thought of as similar to the way a performer learns a piece of music. First, he or she is attracted to the piece as a whole and has a sense of how it works overall; then the piece is taken apart, its harmonic structure analysed, certain passages of notes practised repeatedly, and so on; but, finally, all that must be banished from the performer's mind if the performance is not to be hobbled and stilted. This is not to deny the importance of the left hemisphere's contribution, just to make clear that it works its necessary effects at an *intermediate* stage. Problems arise when this is treated as the *end* stage. In terms of the metaphor of the Master and his emissary, the Master realises the need for an emissary to do certain work on his behalf (which he, the Master, must not involve himself with) and report back to him. That is why he appoints the emissary in the first place. The emissary, however, knowing less than the Master, thinks he knows everything and considers himself the real Master, thus failing to carry out his duty to report back. The right hemisphere's view is inclusive, 'both/and', synthetic, integrative; it realises the need for both. The left hemisphere's view is exclusive, 'either/or', analytic and fragmentary – but, crucially, *unaware of what it is missing*. It therefore thinks it can go it alone.

Sixth, a culture that exemplifies the qualities of the left hemisphere's world attracts to itself, in positions of influence and authority, those whose natural outlook is similar. People with certain autistic traits will be attracted to, and be deemed especially suitable for, employment in the areas of science, technology and administration which have, during the last hundred years, been immensely influential in shaping the world we live in, and are if anything even more important today. Thus a culture which already has some prominent autistic characteristics attracts to positions of influence individuals who will help it ever further down the same path. This is not the only vicious circle involved. Increasing technologisation and bureaucratisation of life help to erode the more integrative modes of attention to people and things which might help us resist the advances of technology and bureaucracy, so that in this way they aid their own replication. They make us more like themselves.

Finally, though the 'takes' of the two hemispheres are made to work together below the level of conscious awareness, they are not strictly compatible. This is most obvious when, as in our society, our thinking is no longer embodied in the practices, traditions and rituals of a community, but is developed in explicit, public, often political debate, where much of its subtlety, and tolerance of necessary ambiguity, gets lost. Once dragged into the light of day and scrutinised, the hemisphere 'takes' are seen often to pull in opposite directions. The catch is that in such a society as ours, any apparent inconsistency is treated as a sign of error or intellectual muddle. Ambiguity is no longer a strength, given that truth is known to be complicated and many-layered; it is a weakness, since truth is thought of as single and straightforward. It is therefore easier to accept the left hemisphere's point of view, which is easily articulated and unambiguous and simply stands in contradiction to the right hemisphere's view, than to accept that of the right hemisphere, which is more multifaceted and harder to articulate, and is already inclusive of the apparently incompatible left hemisphere's point of view. This virtue makes it immediately vulnerable to the charge of inconsistency, and it is therefore dismissed.

Since writing this book, I have begun to think more than ever about the philosophical implications for how we see ourselves, the planet and our relation to it. In this I have been immensely helped by the reactions of readers and discussions with colleagues. It seems to me that we face very grave crises indeed, and that, if we are to survive, we need not just a few new measures, but a complete change of heart and mind. I know from the moving correspondence I receive that this book has helped individuals, far more than I could have hoped or expected, to change their outlook on the world and even to change their lives in important respects: to do better at work, to save their marriages, to re-evaluate their goals in life. That has been a revelation to me, since I did not foresee the potential for it to have the direct therapeutic effect it apparently has. Societal change, however, is another matter. It would be good to hope that in some way the thesis of this book could play a small part in such a shift, but no one solution can be found to what are agreed to be complex, perhaps intractable, problems.

However, in an era where truth seems to be up for grabs, the question of what we can rely on as true seems ever more pressing. In particular, I believe that reductionism has become a disease, a viewpoint lacking both intellectual sophistication and emotional depth, which is blighting our ability to understand what is happening and what we need to do about it. My current thoughts are directed towards illuminating what I see as a truer picture, a more helpful and, I believe, a more hopeful way of seeing our situation here on this planet, while we still have time.

This is the theme of my current thinking and writing. There are, it seems to me, four main pathways to the truth: science, reason, intuition and imagination. I also believe strongly that any world view that tries to get by without paying due respect to all four of these is bound to fail. Each on its own has its virtues and its vices, its gifts and its inherent dangers: only by respecting each and all together can we learn to act wisely. And each is a blend of elements contributed by either hemisphere.

However, the same proviso applies in each case, namely that for each to be successful, what the left hemisphere can offer must be used in service of what the right hemisphere knows and sees, not the other way round. This is as important in the case of science as in that of imagination, in the case of reason as in that of intuition. The left hemisphere is a wonderful servant, but a very poor master.

We also need to be aware of the sheer extent to which the left hemisphere is, in the most down-to-earth, empirically verifiable way, less reliable than the right – in matters of attention, perception, judgment, emotional understanding, and indeed intelligence as it is conventionally understood. And that means that we should be appropriately sceptical of the left hemisphere's vision of a mechanistic world, an atomistic society, a world in which competition is more important than collaboration; a world in which nature is a heap of resource there for our exploitation, in which only humans count, and yet humans are only machines – not even very good ones, at that; a world curiously stripped of depth, colour and value. This is not the intelligent, if hard-nosed, view that its espousers comfort themselves by making it out to be; just a sterile fantasy, the product of a lack of imagination, which makes it easier for us to manipulate what we no longer understand. But it is a fantasy that displaces and renders inaccessible the vibrant, living, profoundly creative world that it was our fortune to inherit – until we squandered our inheritance.

Time is running out, and the way we think, which got us into this mess, will not be enough to get us out of it. Please read and I hope enjoy this book, and, if its message should speak to you, take it forward into the world. We need, I believe, to see the world with new eyes, for, as Henry Thoreau put it, 'The question is not what you look at, but what you see.'[8]

INTRODUCTION

THE MASTER AND HIS EMISSARY

THIS BOOK TELLS A STORY ABOUT OURSELVES AND THE WORLD, AND ABOUT HOW WE got to be where we are now. While much of it is about the structure of the human brain – the place where mind meets matter – ultimately it is an attempt to understand the structure of the world that the brain has in part created.

Whatever the relationship between consciousness and the brain – unless the brain plays *no* role in bringing the world as we experience it into being, a position that must have few adherents – its structure has to be significant. It might even give us clues to understanding the structure of the world it mediates, the world we know. So, to ask a very simple question, why is the brain so clearly and profoundly divided? Why, for that matter, are the two cerebral hemispheres asymmetrical? Do they really differ in any important sense? If so, in what way?

The subject of hemisphere differences has a poor track record, discouraging to those who wish to be sure that they are not going to make fools of themselves in the long run. Views on the matter have gone through a number of phases since it was first noticed in the mid-nineteenth century that the hemispheres were not identical, and that there seemed to be a clear asymmetry of function related to language, favouring the left hemisphere. At first, it was believed that, apart from each hemisphere obviously having sensory and motor responsibility for, and control of, the opposite (or 'contralateral') side of the body, language was the defining difference, the main specific task of the left hemisphere. The right hemisphere was considered to be essentially 'silent'. Then it was discovered that, after all, the right hemisphere appeared better equipped than the left hemisphere to handle visual imagery, and this was accepted as the particular contribution it made, its equivalent to language: words in the left hemisphere, pictures in the right. But that, too, proved unsatisfactory. Both hemispheres, it is now clear, can deal with either kind of material, words or images, in different ways. Subsequent attempts to decide which set of functions are segregated in which hemisphere have mainly been discarded, piece after piece of evidence suggesting that every identifiable human activity is actually served at some level by both hemispheres. There is, apparently, vast redundancy. Enthusiasm for finding the key to hemisphere differences has waned, and it is no longer respectable for a neuroscientist to hypothesise on the subject.

This is hardly surprising, given the set of beliefs about the differences between the hemispheres which has passed into the popular consciousness. These beliefs could, without much violence to the facts, be characterised as versions of the idea that the left hemisphere is somehow gritty, rational, realistic but dull, and the right hemisphere airy-fairy and impressionistic, but creative and exciting; a formulation reminiscent of Sellar and Yeatman's immortal distinction (in their parody of English history teaching, *1066 and All That*) between the Roundheads – 'Right and Repulsive' – and the Cavaliers – 'Wrong but Wromantic'. In reality, both hemispheres are crucially involved in reason, just as they are in language; both hemispheres play their part in creativity. Perhaps the most absurd of these popular misconceptions is that the left hemisphere, hard-nosed and logical, is somehow male, and the right hemisphere, dreamy and sensitive, is somehow female. If there is any evidence that could begin to associate each sex with a single cerebral hemisphere in this way, it tends to indicate, if anything, the reverse – but that is another story and one that I will not attempt to deal with in this book. Discouraged by this kind of popular travesty, neuroscience has returned to the necessary and unimpeachable business of amassing findings, and has largely given up the attempt to make sense of the findings, once amassed, in any larger context.

Nonetheless it does not seem to me likely that the ways in which the hemispheres differ are simply random, dictated by purely contingent factors such as the need for space, or the utility of dividing labour, implying that it would work just as well if the various specific brain activities were swapped around between hemispheres as room dictates. Fortunately, I am not alone in this. Despite the recognition that the idea has been hijacked by everyone from management trainers to advertising copywriters, a number of the most knowledgeable people in the field have been unable to escape the conclusion that there is something profound here that requires explanation. Joseph Hellige, for example, arguably the world's best-informed authority on the subject, writes that while both hemispheres seem to be involved in one way or another in almost everything we do, there are some 'very striking' differences in the information-processing abilities and propensities of the two hemispheres.[1] V. S. Ramachandran, another well-known and highly regarded neuroscientist, accepts that the issue of hemisphere difference has been traduced, but concludes: 'The existence of such a pop culture shouldn't cloud the main issue – the notion that the two hemispheres may indeed be specialised for different functions.'[2] And recently Tim Crow, one of the subtlest and most sceptical of neuroscientists researching into mind and brain, who has often remarked on the association between the development of language, functional brain asymmetry and psychosis, has gone so far as to write that 'except in the light of lateralisation nothing in human psychology/psychiatry makes any sense.'[3] There is little doubt that the issues of brain asymmetry and hemisphere specialisation are significant. The question is only – of what?[4]

I believe there is, literally, a world of difference between the hemispheres. Understanding quite what that is has involved a journey through many apparently unrelated areas: not just neurology and psychology, but philosophy, literature and the arts, and even, to some extent, archaeology and anthropology, and I hope the specialists in these areas will forgive my trespasses. Every realm of academic endeavour is now subject to an explosion of information that renders those few who can still truly call themselves experts, experts on less and less. Partly for this very reason it nonetheless seems to me worthwhile to try to make links outside and across the boundaries of the disciplines, even though the price may be that one is always at best an interested outsider, at worst an interloper condemned to make mistakes that will be obvious to those who really know. Knowledge moves on, and even at any one time is far from certain. My hope is only that what I have to say may resonate with the ideas of others and possibly act as a stimulus to further reflection by those better qualified than myself.

I have come to believe that the cerebral hemispheres differ in ways that have meaning. There is a plethora of well-substantiated findings that indicate that there are consistent differences – neuropsychological, anatomical, physiological and chemical, amongst others – between the hemispheres. But when I talk of 'meaning', it is not just that I believe there to be a coherent pattern to these differences. That is a necessary first step. I would go further, however, and suggest that such a coherent pattern of differences helps to explain aspects of human experience, and therefore *means* something in terms of our lives, and even helps explain the trajectory of our common lives in the Western world.

My thesis is that for us as human beings there are two fundamentally opposed realities, two different modes of experience; that each is of ultimate importance in bringing about the recognisably human world; and that their difference is rooted in the bihemispheric structure of the brain. It follows that the hemispheres need to co-operate, but I believe they are in fact involved in a sort of power struggle, and that this explains many aspects of contemporary Western culture.

THE STRUCTURE OF THIS BOOK

This book is divided, like the brain it describes, into two parts.

In Part I, I will focus on the brain itself, and what it can tell us. I will look at the evolution of the brain, its divided and asymmetrical nature, the implications of the development of music and language, and what we know about what goes on in each side of the brain. What is it they do that is so different? Well, I will argue, nothing much: it is quite true that almost everything we once thought went on in one or other hemisphere alone is now known to go on in both.[5] So where does that leave the pursuit of hemisphere differences? Right on track. The whole problem is that we are obsessed, because of what I argue is our affiliation to left-hemisphere modes of thought, with 'what' the brain does – after all, isn't the brain a machine, and like any machine, the value of it lies in *what it does*? I happen to think this machine model gets us only some of the way; and like a train that drops one in the middle of the night far from one's destination, a train of thought that gets one only some of the way is a liability. The difference, I shall argue, is not in the 'what', but in the 'how' – by which I don't mean 'the means by which' (machine model again), but 'the manner in which', something no one ever asked of a machine. I am not interested purely in 'functions' but in ways of being, something only living things can have.

Did the important semantic speech centres of the brain simply end up in the left hemisphere by accident? And if it's so important to keep a complex function such as language all in one place, then why does language also depend on the right hemisphere? Is music really just a useless spin-off from language, or something more profound? Why do we have language anyway? For communicating? For thinking? If not, for what purpose, then? Why are we right-handed (or left-handed), rather than ambidextrous? Is the body essential to our way of being, or just a useful fuelling and locomotor system for the brain? Is emotion really just an aid to cognition, helping us to weigh our decisions correctly, or is it something a bit more fundamental than that? Why does it matter if one hemisphere tends to see things in their context, while the other as carefully removes them from it?

One of the more durable generalisations about the hemispheres has been the finding that the left hemisphere tends to deal more with pieces of information in isolation, and the right hemisphere with the entity as a whole, the so-called *Gestalt* – possibly underlying and helping to explain the apparent verbal/visual dichotomy, since words are processed serially, while pictures are taken in all at once. But even here the potential significance of this distinction has been over-looked. Anyone would think that we were simply talking about another relatively trivial difference of limited use or interest, a bit like finding that cats like to have their meat chopped up into small bits, whereas dogs like to wolf their meat in slabs. At most it is seen as helpful in making predictions about the sort of tasks that each hemisphere may preferentially carry out, a difference in 'information processing', but of no broader significance. But if it is true, the importance of the distinction is hard to over-estimate. And if it should turn out that one hemisphere understands metaphor, where the other does not, this is not a small matter of a quaint literary function having to find a place *somewhere* in the brain. Not a bit. It goes to the core of how we understand our world, even our selves, as I hope to be able to demonstrate.

What if one hemisphere is, apparently, attuned to whatever is new? Is that, too, just a specialised form of 'information processing'? What role does imitation play in releasing us from determinism (a question I return to in different forms throughout the book)? I am not, of course, the first to ask such questions, and they undoubtedly admit of more than one answer, and more than one type of answer. But, while only a fool would claim to have definitive answers, I shall make some suggestions that I hope may encourage others to think differently about ourselves, our history and ultimately our relationship with the world in which we live.

Things change according to the stance we adopt towards them, the type of attention we pay to them, the disposition we hold in relation to them. This is important because the most fundamental difference between the hemispheres lies in the type of attention they give to the world. But it's also important because of the widespread assumption in some quarters that there are two alternatives: either things exist 'out there' and are unaltered by the machinery we use to dig them up, or to tear them apart (naïve realism, scientific materialism); or they are subjective phenomena which we create out of our own minds, and therefore we are free to treat them in any way we wish, since they are after all, our own creations (naïve idealism, post-modernism). These positions are not by any means as far apart as they look, and a certain lack of respect is evident in both. In fact I believe there *is* something that exists apart from ourselves, but that we play a vital part in bringing it into being.[6] A central theme of this book is the importance of our disposition towards the world and one another, as being fundamental in grounding *what it is that we come to have a relationship with*, rather than the other way round. The kind of attention we pay actually alters the world: we are, literally, partners in creation. This means we have a grave *responsibility*, a word that captures the reciprocal nature of the dialogue we have with whatever it is that exists apart from ourselves. I will look at what philosophy in our time has had to say about these issues. Ultimately I believe that many of the disputes about the nature of the human world can be illuminated by an understanding that there are two fundamentally different 'versions' delivered to us by the two hemispheres, both of which can have a ring of authenticity about them, and both of which are hugely valuable; but that they stand in opposition to one another, and need to be kept apart from one another – hence the bihemispheric structure of the brain.

How do we understand the world, if there are different versions of it to reconcile? Is it important which models and metaphors we bring to bear on our reality? And, if it is, why has one particular model come to dominate us so badly that we hardly notice its pervasiveness? What do these models tell us about the words that relate us to the world at large – 'know', 'believe', 'trust', 'want', 'grasp', 'see' – that both describe and, if we are not careful, prescribe the relationship we have with it? This part of the book will conclude with some reflections on one particular relationship, that between the two hemispheres. It seems that they coexist together on a daily basis, but have fundamentally different sets of values, and therefore priorities, which means that over the long term they are likely to come into conflict. Although each is crucially important, and delivers valuable aspects of the human condition, and though each needs the other for different purposes, they seem destined to pull apart.

Part II of the book looks at the history of Western culture in the light of what I believe about the hemispheres. These thoughts are inevitably contingent, to some extent fragmentary and rudimental. But if the world is not independent of our observation of it, attention to it, and interaction with it, and if the mind is at least mediated by the brain, it seems a reasonable bet that the brain will have left its mark on the world that we have brought about. I hope to draw attention to those aspects of this cultural history which resonate with the findings about the brain which gave rise to it, beginning with the development of writing and currency in Ancient Greece, and the extraordinary flowering of both science and the arts, especially theatre, at that time. In brief I believe this is related to the development, through enhanced frontal lobe function, of what might be called 'necessary distance' from the world, which in turn demanded increased independence of the hemispheres, allowing each hemisphere to make characteristic advances in function, and for a while to do so in harmony with its fellow. I believe that over time there has been a relentless growth of self-consciousness, leading to increasing difficulties in co-operation. The resultant instability is evidenced by alternations between more extreme positions; and, although there have been swings in the pendulum, the balance of power has shifted where it cannot afford to go – further and further towards the part-world created by the left hemisphere. The switchbacks and reverses of this progress are followed over time, looking at the main shifts that have been conventionally identified in Western culture from the Renaissance onwards, until we reach the present era.

The particular relevance to us at this point in history is this. Both hemispheres clearly play crucial roles in the experience of each human individual, and I believe both have contributed importantly to our culture. Each needs the other. Nonetheless the relationship between the hemispheres does not appear to be symmetrical, in that the left hemisphere is ultimately dependent on, one might almost say parasitic on, the right, though it seems to have no awareness of this fact. Indeed it is filled with an alarming self-confidence. The ensuing struggle is as uneven as the asymmetrical brain from which it takes its origin. My hope is that awareness of the situation may enable us to change course before it is too late.

The Conclusion, therefore, is devoted to the world we now inhabit. Here I suggest that it is as if the left hemisphere, which creates a sort of self-reflexive virtual world, has blocked off the available exits, the ways out of the hall of mirrors, into a reality which the right hemisphere could enable us to understand. In the past, this tendency was counterbalanced by forces from outside the enclosed system of the self-conscious mind; apart from the history incarnated in our culture, and the natural world itself, from both of which we are increasingly alienated, these were principally the embodied nature of our existence, the arts and religion. In our time each of these has been subverted and the routes of escape from the virtual world have been closed off. An increasingly mechanistic, frag-mented, decontextualised world, marked by unwarranted optimism mixed with paranoia and a feeling of emptiness, has come about, reflecting, I believe, the unopposed action of a dysfunctional left hemisphere. I will have some concluding thoughts about what, if anything, we can do – or need *not* to do – about it.

Because I am involved in redressing a balance, I may at times seem to be scep-tical of the tools of analytical discourse. I hope, however, it will be obvious from what I say that I hold absolutely no brief for those who wish to abandon reason or traduce language. The exact opposite is the case. Both are seriously under threat in our age, though I believe from diametrically opposed factions. The attempt by some post-modern theoreticians to annex the careful anti-Cartesian scepticism of Heidegger to an anarchic disregard for language and meaning is an inversion of everything that he held important. To say that language holds truth concealed is not to say that language simply serves to conceal truth (though it certainly can do), or, much worse, that there is no such thing as truth (though it may be far from simple). But equally we should not be blind to the fact that language is also traduced and disregarded by many of those who never question language at all, and truth too easily claimed by those who see the subject as unproblematic. It behoves us to be sceptical. Equally this book has nothing to offer those who would undermine reason, which, along with imagination, is the most precious thing we owe to the working together of the two hemispheres. My quarrel is only with an excessive and misplaced rationalism which has never been subjected to the judgment of reason, and is in conflict with it. I hope it will not be necessary for me to emphasise, too, that I am in no sense opposed to science, which, like its sister arts, is the offspring of both hemispheres – only to a narrow materialism, which is not intrinsic to science at all. Science is neither more nor less than patient and detailed attention to the world, and is integral to our understanding of it and of ourselves.

WHY IS THE STRUCTURE OF THE BRAIN IMPORTANT?

It might seem reductive to link the highest achievements of the human mind, in philosophy and the arts, to the structure of the brain. I believe it is not. For one thing, even if it were possible for mind to be 'reduced', as we say, to matter, this would necessarily and equally compel us to sophisticate our idea of what matter is, and is capable of becoming, namely something as extraordinary as mind. But leaving that aside, the way we experience the world, and even what there is of the world to experience, is dependent on how the brain functions: we cannot escape the fact, nor do we need to try. At the most basic, some things that we know to be potential objects of experience – sounds at particularly high or low frequencies, for example – are not available to us, though they may be to bats and bears; and that's simply because our brains do not deal with them. We know, too, that when parts of the brain are lost, a chunk of available experience goes with them. But this is not to hold that all that exists is in the brain – in fact, it demonstrates that that cannot be the case; nor is it to say that mental experience is *just* what we can observe or describe at the brain level.

OK, but if my purpose is to understand the world better, why do I not just deal with mind, and forget about the brain? And in particular why should we be concerned with the brain's structure? That may be of academic interest to scientists, but as long as it carries on working, does it really matter? After all, my pancreas is doing fine, without my being able to remember much about its structure.

However one conceives the relationship of mind and brain – and especially if one believes them to be identical – the structure of the brain is likely to tell us something we otherwise could not so easily see. We can inspect the brain only 'from the outside' (even when we are probing its innermost reaches), it is true: but we can inspect the mind only 'from within' (even when we seem to objectify it). Seeing the *brain's* structure is just easier. And since structure and function are closely related, that will tell us something about the nature of our mental experience, our experience of the world. Hence I believe it does matter. But I should emphasise that, although I begin by looking at brain structure in relation to the neuropsychological functions that we know are associated with each hemisphere, my aim is purely to illuminate aspects of our experience.

Freud anticipated that making connections between experience and the structure of the brain would be possible once neuroscience became sufficiently evolved. A neurologist first and foremost, he believed that the mental entities that he described, and whose conflicts shaped our world – the id, the ego and the superego – would one day be more precisely identified with structures within the brain.[7] In other words he believed that the brain not merely mediated our experience, but *shaped* it too.

When we look at our embodied selves, we look back into the past. But that past is no more dead than we are. The past is something we perform every living day, here and now. That other founding father of psychoanalysis, Jung, was acutely aware of this, and surmised that much of our mental life, like our bodies, has ancient origins:

> Just as the human body represents a whole museum of organs, with a long evolutionary history behind them, so we should expect the mind to be organized in a similar way ... We receive along with our body a highly differentiated brain which brings with it its entire history, and when it becomes creative it creates out of this history – out of the history of mankind ... that age-old natural history which has been transmitted in living form since the remotest times, namely the history of the brain structure.[8]

The brain has evolved, like the body in which it sits, and is in the process of evolving. But the evolution of the brain is different from the evolution of the body. In the brain, unlike in most other human organs, later developments do not so much replace earlier ones as add to, and build on top of, them.[9] Thus the cortex, the outer shell that mediates most so-called higher functions of the brain, and certainly those of which we are conscious, arose out of the underlying subcortical structures which are concerned with biological regulation at an unconscious level; and the frontal lobes, the most recently evolved part of the neocortex, which occupy a much bigger part of the brain in humans than in our animal relatives, and which grow forwards from and 'on top of' the rest of the cortex, mediate most of the sophisticated activities that mark us out as human – planning, decision making, perspective taking, self-control, and so on. In other words, the structure of the brain reflects its history: as an evolving dynamic system, in which one part evolves out of, and in response to, another.

I think we would accept that the conflicts that Freud helped identify – between will and desire, between intention and action, and broader disjunctions between whole ways of conceiving the world in which we live – are the proper concern, not just of psychiatrists and psychologists, but of philosophers, and of artists of all kinds, and of each one of us in daily life. Similarly, understanding the way in which the brain's structure influences the mind is of relevance not just to neuroscientists, or psychiatrists, or philosophers, but to everyone who has a mind or a brain. If it turns out that there is after all coherence to the way in which the correlates of our experience are grouped and organised in the brain, and we can see these 'functions' forming intelligible wholes, corresponding to areas of experience, and see how they relate to one another at the brain level, this casts some light on the structure and experience of our mental world. In this sense the brain is – in fact it has to be – a metaphor of the world.

THE IMPORTANCE OF BEING TWO

Although the brain is extraordinarily densely interconnected within itself – it has been estimated that there are more connections within the human brain than there are particles in the known universe – it is none the less true, as might be imagined, that the closest and densest interconnections are formed within localities, between immediately adjacent structures. Thus the brain can be seen as something like a huge country: as a nested structure, of villages and towns, then districts, gathered into counties, regions and even partly autonomous states or lands – a conglomeration of nuclei and ganglia at one level, organisational foci and broader functional regions within specific gyri or sulci (the folds of the cortex) at another, these then forming lobes, and those lobes ultimately forming part of one or other cerebral hemisphere. If it is true that consciousness arises from, or at any rate is mediated by, the sheer density and complexity of neuronal interconnections within the brain, this structure has some important consequences for the nature of that consciousness. The brain should not be thought of as an indiscriminate mass of neurones: the structure of that mass matters. In particular it has to be relevant that at the highest level of organisation the brain, whether mediator or originator of consciousness, is divided in two.

The great physiologist, Sir Charles Sherrington, observed a hundred years ago that one of the basic principles of sensorimotor control is what he called 'opponent processors'.[10] What this means can be thought of in terms of a simple everyday experience. If you want to carry out a delicate procedure with your right hand that involves a very finely calibrated movement to the left, it is made possible by using the counterbalancing, steadying force of the left hand holding it at the same time and pushing slightly to the right. I agree with Marcel Kinsbourne that the brain is, in one sense, a system of opponent processors. In other words, it contains mutually opposed elements whose contrary influence make possible finely calibrated responses to complex situations. Kinsbourne points to three such oppositional pairings within the brain that are likely to be of significance. These could be loosely described as 'up/down' (the inhibiting effects of the cortex on the more basic automatic responses of the subcortical regions), 'front/back' (the inhibiting effects of the frontal lobes on the posterior cortex) and 'right/left' (the influence of the two hemispheres on one another).[11]

I am concerned mainly with exploring just one of these pairs of oppositions: that between the two cerebral hemispheres. I will at times deal with the other oppositions – 'up/down' and 'front/back' – as they undoubtedly impinge on this, more especially since the hemispheres differ in the relationship each has with the underlying subcortical structures, and even with the frontal lobes: they are in this, as in so many other respects, asymmetrical. But it is the primary duality of the hemispheres that forms the focus of the book. It is this, I believe, that underlies a conflict that is playing itself out around us, and has, in my view, recently taken a turn which should cause us concern. By seeing more clearly what is happening we may be in a better position to do something about it.

We are nearly ready to begin our examination of the brain. Before doing so, however, I need to enter a couple of caveats, without which I risk being misunderstood.

DIFFERENCES ARE NOT ABSOLUTE, BUT EVEN SMALL DIFFERENCES GET TO BE AMPLIFIED

When I say the 'left hemisphere does this', or 'the right hemisphere does that', it should be understood that in any one human brain at any one time both hemispheres will be actively involved. Unless one hemisphere has been surgically removed, or otherwise destroyed, signs of activity will be found in both. Both hemispheres are involved in almost all mental processes, and certainly in all mental states: information is constantly conveyed between the hemispheres, and may be transmitted in either direction several times a second. What activity shows up on a scan is a function of where the threshold is set: if the threshold were set low enough, one would see activity just about everywhere in the brain all the time. But, *at the level of experience*, the world we know is synthesised from the work of the two cerebral hemispheres, each hemisphere having its own way of understanding the world – its own 'take' on it. This synthesis is unlikely to be symmetrical, and the world we actually experience, phenomenologically, at any point in time is determined by which hemisphere's version of the world ultimately comes to predominate. Though I would resist the simplistic idea of a '(left or right) hemisphere personality' overall, there is evidence I will look at later that, certainly for some kinds of activities, we consistently prefer one hemisphere over the other in ways that may differ between individuals, though over whole populations they tend to cohere.

For two reasons, even small differences in potential between the hemispheres at quite a low level may lead to what are large shifts at a higher level.

For one thing, as Ornstein has suggested, at the level of moment-to-moment activity the hemispheres may operate a 'winner takes all' system – that is, if one hemisphere is 85 per cent as efficient at a task as the other, we will not tend to divide the work between them in a ratio of 0.85:1.00, but consistently use whichever is better to do the whole job.[12] On those occasions where the 'wrong' hemisphere does get in first, however, and starts to take control, at least for not very demanding tasks, it will most probably continue to trump the other hemisphere, even if the other hemisphere would have been a better choice at the outset – possibly because the time costs of sharing or transferring control are greater than the costs of continuing with the current arrangement.[13] I will consider the working relationship of the hemispheres in detail in the last chapter of Part I.

The other is that, though such winner-takes-all effects may still be individually small, a vast accumulation of many small effects could lead ultimately to a large bias overall, especially since repeated preference for one hemisphere helps to entrench still further an advantage that may start out by being relatively marginal. To the extent that a process goes on usefully in one hemisphere, it reinforces the sending of information preferentially to that hemisphere in the future. 'Small initial differences between the hemispheres could compound during development, ultimately producing a wide range of functional asymmetries, via a "snowball" mechanism.'[14] The hemispheres are thus involved in differentiating themselves.

Equally this lack of absolutism affects the way we need to understand the data. A finding can be perfectly valid, and even of the greatest significance overall, and yet admit of contrary findings. The average temperatures in Iceland and Indonesia are clearly very different, which goes a long way to explain the wholly different characteristics of the vegetation, animal life, landscape, culture and economy of these two regions, as well as no doubt much else that differentiates their 'feel' and the ways of life there. But it is still true that the lowest average annual temperature in Indonesia is *lower* than the highest average annual temperature in Iceland – and of course the average temperature varies considerably from month to month, as well as, less predictably, from day to day, and indeed from place to place within each region. The nature of generalisations is that they are approximate, but they are nonetheless of critical importance for understanding what is going on. A misplaced need for certainty may stop the process altogether.

This also implies that generalisations can never be rules. As far as the hemispheres go, there is almost certainly nothing that is confined entirely to one or the other. I want to stress that, because I really do not wish to encourage simplistic dichotomising. The differences that I hope to establish are too nuanced to be encapsulated in a few words or simple concepts, but, I believe, they are nonetheless important for that. Descartes was a great dualist. He thought not only that there were two types of substance, mind and matter, but that there were two types of thinking, two types of bodily movement, even two types of loving; and, sure enough, he believed there were two types of people: 'the world is largely composed of two types of minds . . .'[15] It has been said that the world is divided into two types of people, those who divide the world into two types of people, and those who don't. I am with the second group. The others are too Cartesian in their categorisation, and therefore already too much of the party of the left hemisphere. Nature gave us the dichotomy when she split the brain. Working out what it means is not in itself to dichotomise: it only becomes so in the hands of those who interpret the results with Cartesian rigidity.

BRAIN ORGANISATION VARIES FROM INDIVIDUAL TO INDIVIDUAL

Then there is the question of individual difference in hemisphere dominance and laterality. I will speak throughout of 'the right hemisphere' and 'the left hemisphere' as though these concepts were universally applicable. Clearly that cannot be the case. The terms represent generalisations about the human condition. Handedness is related to such organisation, but not in any straightforward way: for this reason, I will have little to say about handedness, fascinating as it is, in this

book – except where it seems legitimately to reflect evidence of hemisphere preference.[16] In talking about any biological variable, one is making some sort of
generalisation. Men are taller than women, but the fact that some women are
taller than some men doesn't render the point invalid. Handedness is one such
variable. The situation is complicated by the fact that handedness is not a single
phenomenon; there are degrees of handedness in different individuals for
different activities (and different 'footedness', 'earedness', and 'eyedness', for that
matter). However, in the West at present, about 89 per cent of people are broadly
right-handed, and the vast majority of these have speech and the semantic
language centres in the left hemisphere – let's call this the standard pattern.[17]

In the other 11 per cent, who are broadly left-handed, there will be variable
conformations, which logically must follow one of three patterns: the standard
pattern, a simple inversion of the standard pattern, or some rearrangement. The
majority (about 75 per cent) of this 11 per cent still have their speech centres in
the left hemisphere, and would appear to follow broadly the standard pattern.[18] It
is, therefore, only about 5 per cent of the population overall who are known not
to lateralise for speech in the left hemisphere. Of these some might have a simple
inversion of the hemispheres, with everything that normally happens in the right
hemisphere happening in the left, and vice versa; there is little significance in this,
from the point of view of this book, except that throughout one would have to
read 'right' for 'left', and 'left' for 'right'. It is only the third group who, it has been
posited, may be truly different in their cerebral organisation: a subset of left-
handers, as well as some people with other conditions, irrespective of handedness,
such as, probably, schizophrenia and dyslexia, and possibly conditions such as
schizotypy, some forms of autism, Asperger's syndrome and some 'savant' conditions, who may have a *partial* inversion of the standard pattern, leading to brain
functions being lateralised in unconventional combinations. For them the normal
partitioning of functions breaks down. This may confer special benefits, or lead to
disadvantages, in the carrying out of different activities.

Dealing with these anomalous situations, intriguing and important as they are,
lies beyond the scope of this book. But one point is worth making in relation to this
last group, those with unconventional alignments of functions within either hemisphere. If it should turn out that the development of the semantic and syntactic
language centre in the left hemisphere is a key determinant of the way of seeing the
world associated with that hemisphere as a whole, its translocation to the other
hemisphere – or alternatively, the translocation into the left hemisphere of normally
right-hemisphere functions – could have widely different, even opposing, effects in
different cases. The point is this: does the coexistence in the *same hemisphere,* be it
right or left, of language and what are normally right-hemisphere functions, lead to
language being 'reinterpreted' according to the characteristic mode of a normal
right hemisphere, or does it lead to the opposite effect – the other functions going
on in that hemisphere being transformed by (what would be normally) a left-
hemisphere way of seeing things? To put it simply, does placing a maths professor
in a circus troupe result in a flying mathematician, or a bunch of trapeze artists who

can no longer perform unless they have first calculated the precise trajectory of their leap? Probably both scenarios are realized in different individuals, leading to unusual talents, and unusual deficits. This may be the link between cerebral lateralisation and creativity, and it may account for the otherwise difficult to explain fact of the relatively constant conservation, throughout the world, of genes which, at least partly through their effects on lateralisation, result in major mental illnesses, such as schizophrenia and manic-depressive psychosis (now known as bipolar disorder), and developmental disorders, such as autism and Asperger's syndrome. It may also be associated with homosexuality, which is thought to involve a higher than usual incidence of abnormal lateralisation. Such genes may, particularly in the case of mental illness, be highly detrimental to individuals, and have an impact on fertility for the population at large – and would therefore have been bred out long ago, if it were not for some hugely important benefit that they must convey. If they also, through their effects on lateralisation, in some cases led to extraordinary talents, and if particularly they did so in relatives, who have some but not all of the genes responsible, then such genes would naturally be preserved, on purely Darwinian principles.

Whether that is the case or not, we need to understand better the nature of the normal left and right hemispheres. In this book, therefore, I propose to deal only with the typical cerebral organisation, the one that has greater than 95 per cent currency and which, by the same 'winner takes all' argument, has universal applicability to the world in which we live for now.

ESSENTIAL ASYMMETRY

'The universe is built on a plan, the profound symmetry of which is somehow present in the inner structure of our intellect.'[19] This remark of the French poet Paul Valéry is at one and the same time a brilliant insight into the nature of reality, and about as wrong as it is possible to be.

In fact the universe has no 'profound symmetry' – rather, a profound *asymmetry*. More than a century ago Louis Pasteur wrote: 'Life as manifested to us is a function of the asymmetry of the universe . . . I can even imagine that all living species are primordially, in their structure, in their external forms, functions of cosmic asymmetry.'[20] Since then physicists have deduced that asymmetry must have been a condition of the origin of the universe: it was the discrepancy between the amounts of matter and antimatter that enabled the material universe to come into existence at all, and for there to be something rather than nothing. Such unidirectional processes as time and entropy are perhaps examples of that fundamental asymmetry in the world we inhabit. And, whatever Valéry may have thought, the inner structure of our intellect is without doubt asymmetrical in a sense that has enormous significance for us.

As I have said, I believe that there are two fundamentally opposed realities rooted in the bihemispheric structure of the brain. But the relationship between them is no more symmetrical than that of the chambers of the heart – in fact, less so; more like that of the artist to the critic, or a king to his counsellor.

There is a story in Nietzsche that goes something like this.[21] There was once a wise spiritual master, who was the ruler of a small but prosperous domain, and who was known for his selfless devotion to his people. As his people flourished and grew in number, the bounds of this small domain spread; and with it the need to trust implicitly the emissaries he sent to ensure the safety of its ever more distant parts. It was not just that it was impossible for him personally to order all that needed to be dealt with: as he wisely saw, he needed to keep his distance from, and remain ignorant of, such concerns. And so he nurtured and trained carefully his emissaries, in order that they could be trusted. Eventually, however, his cleverest and most ambitious vizier, the one he most trusted to do his work, began to see himself as the master, and used his position to advance his own wealth and influence. He saw his master's temperance and forbearance as weakness, not wisdom, and on his missions on the master's behalf, adopted his mantle as his own – the emissary became contemptuous of his master. And so it came about that the master was usurped, the people were duped, the domain became a tyranny; and eventually it collapsed in ruins.[22]

The meaning of this story is as old as humanity, and resonates far from the sphere of political history. I believe, in fact, that it helps us understand something taking place inside ourselves, inside our very brains, and played out in the cultural history of the West, particularly over the last 500 years or so. Why I believe so forms the subject of this book. I hold that, like the Master and his emissary in the story, though the cerebral hemispheres should co-operate, they have for some time been in a state of conflict. The subsequent battles between them are recorded in the history of philosophy, and played out in the seismic shifts that characterise the history of Western culture. At present the domain – our civilisation – finds itself in the hands of the vizier, who, however gifted, is effectively an ambitious regional bureaucrat with his own interests at heart. Meanwhile the Master, the one whose wisdom gave the people peace and security, is led away in chains. The Master is betrayed by his emissary.

PART ONE

THE DIVIDED BRAIN

CHAPTER 1

—◆—

ASYMMETRY AND THE BRAIN

THE TOPIC OF THE DIFFERENCE BETWEEN THE HEMISPHERES, THEIR fundamental asymmetry, has fascinated people for a very long time indeed. In fact speculation on the subject goes back more than two millennia: Greek physicians in the third century BC held that the right hemisphere was specialised for perception, and the left hemisphere for understanding – which, if nothing else, shows a remarkably interesting train of thought.[1]

In more modern times, the physician Arthur Wigan published his thoughtful study, *The Duality of the Mind*, in 1844, prompted by his fascination with a handful of cases he stumbled across where an individual who had remained apparently unremarkable in life was found at post mortem to have one cerebral hemisphere destroyed by disease. Over a period of 20 years Wigan collected further instances, concluding that each hemisphere on its own could support human consciousness, and that therefore we 'must have two minds with two brains', with mental disease resulting when they are in conflict.[2] But he did not make any suggestions as to how they differed, and appears to have assumed that they are largely interchangeable – a sort of 'belt and braces' approach by evolution to the possibility of one hemisphere being irremediably damaged.

WHY TWO HEMISPHERES?

That leads us to a good first question: why are there two cerebral hemispheres at all? After all, there is no necessity for an organ whose entire function, as it is commonly understood, is to make connections, to have this almost wholly divided structure. Over the course of the long evolution of *homo sapiens sapiens* there could have been developments towards a unified brain, which might on the face of it offer enormous advantages. It is true that the brain's embryological origins lie in two distinct halves. But this cannot be the answer, not only because, earlier still, the primitive hemispheres themselves arise from a single midline structure, the prosencephalon, at about five weeks' gestation (see Figure 1.1), but because midline structures and connections between the halves of the brain *do* develop later in fetal development at some levels, even though the hemispheres themselves remain deeply divided.

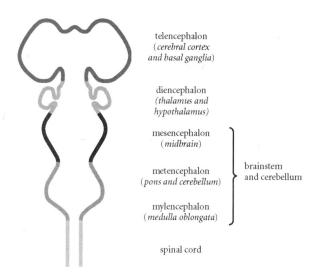

telencephalon
(*cerebral cortex
and basal ganglia*)

diencephalon
(*thalamus and
hypothalamus*)

mesencephalon
(*midbrain*)

metencephalon
(*pons and cerebellum*)   brainstem
                                 and cerebellum

mylencephalon
(*medulla oblongata*)

spinal cord

Fig. 1.1 Embryonic origins of the cerebral hemispheres and other brain regions.

And the cranium which encases the brain starts off, embryologically speaking, in several pieces on either side of the brain, but ends as a fused whole – so why not the brain itself? Instead what we see is a tendency positively to enhance the anatomical separation.

For a long time the function of the corpus callosum, the main band of neural tissue that connects the two hemispheres at their base (see Figure 1.2), was unknown. At one stage it was believed to be no more than a kind of bolster, a supportive structure that stopped the two hemispheres from sagging. Now we know that it is there to allow the hemispheres to communicate. But in what sense? What is the communication like?

The corpus callosum contains an estimated 300–800 million fibres connecting topologically similar areas in either hemisphere. Yet only 2 per cent of cortical neurones are connected by this tract.[3] What is more, the main purpose of a large number of these connections is actually to inhibit – in other words to stop the other hemisphere interfering. Neurones can have an excitatory or inhibitory action, excitatory neurones causing further neuronal activity downstream, while inhibitory neurones suppress it. Although the majority of cells projecting to the corpus callosum use the facilitatory neurotransmitter glutamate, and are excitatory, there are significant populations of nerve cells (those that use the neurotransmitter gamma-amino butyric acid, or GABA for short) whose function is inhibitory. Even the excitatory fibres often terminate on intermediary neurones, or 'interneurones', whose function is inhibitory.[4] Inhibition is, of course, not a straightforward concept. Inhibition at the neurophysiological level does not necessarily equate with inhibition at the functional level, any more than letting your foot off the brake pedal causes the car to halt: neural inhibition may set in train a sequence of activity,

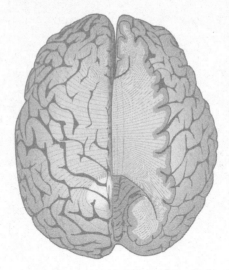

Fig. 1.2 The brain viewed from above, with right hemisphere displaced to reveal the corpus callosum.

so that the net result is functionally permissive. But the evidence is that the primary effect of callosal transmission is to produce *functional* inhibition.[5] So much is this the case that a number of neuroscientists have proposed that the whole point of the corpus callosum is to allow one hemisphere to inhibit the other.[6] Stimulation of neurones in one hemisphere commonly results in an initial brief excitatory response, followed by a prolonged inhibitory arousal in the other, contralateral, hemisphere. Such inhibition can be widespread, and can be seen on imaging.[7]

Clearly the corpus callosum does also have excitatory functions – the transfer of information, not just prevention of confusion, is important – and both this and the inhibitory role are necessary for normal human functioning.[8] But it sets one thinking about the virtues of division, and the degree to which each hemisphere can deal with reality on its own. Severing the corpus callosum altogether produces surprisingly little effect. The surgeons who performed the first so-called 'split-brain' procedures for the treatment of epilepsy, in which the corpus callosum is severed, were amazed to discover quite how normally their recovering patients functioned in everyday life, almost (with some interesting exceptions that I will explore later) as if nothing had happened.

You might think that as brains evolve to become larger, the interhemispheric connections would increase in tandem. But not at all: they actually decrease relative to brain size.[9] The bigger the brain, the less interconnected it is. Rather than taking the opportunity to increase connectedness, evolution appears to be moving in the opposite direction. And there is a close relationship between the separation of the hemispheres on the one hand and the development of something that keeps cropping up in this unfolding story: the asymmetry of the hemispheres. Because it turns out that the greater the brain *asymmetry*, too, the smaller the corpus callosum, suggesting that the evolution both of brain size and of hemisphere asymmetry went hand in hand with a reduction in interhemispheric connectivity.[10] And, in the ultimate case of the modern human brain, its twin hemispheres have been characterised as two *autonomous* systems.[11]

So is there actually some purpose in the division of neuronal, and therefore, mental processes? If so, what could that be?

I have mentioned the view of Kinsbourne that, following the physiological principle of opponent processors, duality refines control. I believe that is right, as far as it goes. But the story goes a long, long way further than that, because the brain is not just a tool for grappling with the world. It's what brings the world about.

The mind–brain question is not the subject of this book, and it is not one I have the skill or the space to address at any length. The argument of the book does not depend on holding one view or another. But it is nonetheless legitimate to ask where the author of a book like this stands on it. Hence this very brief diversion.

One could call the mind the brain's experience of itself.[12] Such a formulation is immediately problematic, since the brain is involved in constituting the world in which, alone, there can be such a thing as experience – it helps to ground experience, for which mind is already needed. But let's accept such a phrase at face value. Brain then necessarily gives structure to mind. That would not, however, equate mind and brain. It is sometimes assumed so, because of the tendency when using a phrase such as 'the brain's experience of itself' to focus on the word 'brain', which we think we understand, rather than on the troublesome word 'experience', which we don't.

All attempts at explanation depend, whether explicitly or implicitly, on drawing parallels between the thing to be explained and some other thing that we believe we already understand better. But the fundamental problem in explaining the experience of consciousness is that there is nothing else remotely like it to compare it with: it is itself the ground of all experience. There is nothing else which has the 'inwardness' that consciousness has. Phenomenologically, and ontologically, it is unique. As I will try to show, the analytic process cannot deal with uniqueness: there is an irresistible temptation for it to move from the uniqueness of something to its assumed non-existence, since the reality of the unique would have to be captured by idioms that apply to nothing else.[13]

Is consciousness a product of the brain? The only certainty here is that anyone who thinks they can answer this question with certainty has to be wrong. We have only our conceptions of consciousness and of the brain to go on; and the one thing we do know for certain is that everything we know of the brain is a product of consciousness. That is, scientifically speaking, far more certain than that consciousness itself is a product of the brain. It may be or it may not; but what is an undeniable fact is the idea that there is a universe of *things*, in which there is one thing called the brain, and another thing called the mind, together with the scientific principles that would allow the one to emerge from the other – these are all ideas, products of consciousness, and therefore only as good as the particular models used by that consciousness to understand the world. We do not know if mind depends on matter, because everything we know about matter is itself a mental creation. In that sense, Descartes was right: the one undeniable fact is our consciousness. He was wrong, however, most would now agree, to think of mind and body as two separate substances (two 'whats'). This was, I believe, a typical product of a certain way of thinking which I suggest is characteristic of the brain's left hemisphere, a concern with the 'whatness' of things. Where it was so obviously a matter of two 'hownesses' in the same thing, two different modes of being (as the right hemisphere would see it), he could formulate this only as two whatnesses, two different *things*. Equally it is a misplaced concern with the whatness of things that leads to the apparently anti-Cartesian, materialist, idea that the mind and body are the same *thing*. We are not sure, and could never be sure, if mind, or even body, is a thing at all. Mind has the characteristics of a process more than of a thing; a becoming, a way of being, more than an entity. Every individual mind is a process of interaction with whatever it is that exists apart from ourselves according to its own private history.

The type of monism represented by the scientific materialism most often espoused by neuroscientists is not radically distinct from the Cartesian dualism to which it is often thought to be opposed. Its solution to the problem has been simply to 'explain away' one part of the duality, by claiming to reduce one to the other. Instead of two whatnesses, there is just one: matter. But Descartes was honest enough to acknowledge that there is a real problem here, one he wrestled with, as is clear from the passage in Meditation VI where he writes:

> . . . I am not merely present in my body as a sailor is present in a ship, but . . . am very closely joined and, as it were, intermingled with it, so that I form with it a single entity.[14]

Phenomenologically speaking, there is here both a unity, a 'single entity', and the most profound disparity; and any account that fails to do full justice to both the unity and disparity cannot be taken seriously. There may be just one whatness here, but it has more than one howness, and that matters. Though (according to the left hemisphere) a thing, a quantity, a whatness, can be reduced to another – that is to say, accounted for in terms of its constituents – one way of being, a quality, a howness, cannot be reduced to another.[15]

THE FRONTAL EXPANSION

Let's leave the divided nature of the brain for a moment and take a slightly closer look at the brain as a whole (see Figure 1.3). The next thing one notices, after the interhemispheric divide, is the extraordinary expansion of the human frontal lobes, the most lately evolved part of the brain.

Whereas the frontal lobes represent about 7 per cent of the total brain volume of a relatively intelligent animal such as the dog, and take up about 17 per cent of the

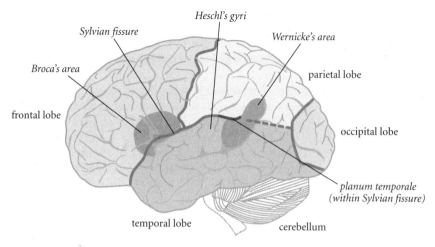

Fig. 1.3 The brain viewed from the left side, showing main language regions and landmarks.

brain in the lesser apes, they represent as much as 35 per cent of the human brain. In fact it's much the same with the great apes, but the difference between our frontal lobes and those of the great apes lies in the proportion of white matter.[16] White matter looks white because of the sheath of myelin, a phospholipid layer which in some neurones surrounds the axons, the long processes of the nerve cell whereby outgoing messages are communicated. This myelin sheath greatly speeds transmission: the implication of the larger amount in human frontal lobes is that the regions are more profusely interconnected in humans. Incidentally, there's also more white matter in the human right hemisphere than in the left, a point I will return to.[17]

The defining features of the human condition can all be traced to our ability to stand back from the world, from our selves and from the immediacy of experience. This enables us to plan, to think flexibly and inventively, and, in brief, to take control of the world around us rather than simply respond to it passively. This distance, this ability to rise above the world in which we live, has been made possible by the evolution of the frontal lobes.

Clearly we have to inhabit the world of immediate bodily experience, the actual *terrain* in which we live, and where our engagement with the world takes place alongside our fellow human beings, and we need to inhabit it fully. Yet at the same time we need to rise above the landscape in which we move, so that we can see what one might call the *territory*. To understand the landscape we need both to go out into the felt, lived world of experience as far as possible, along what one might think of as the horizontal axis, but also to rise above it, on the vertical axis. To live headlong, at ground level, without being able to pause (stand outside the immediate push of time) and rise (in space) is to be like an animal; yet to float off up into the air is not to live at all – just to be a detached observing eye. One needs to bring what one has learned from one's ascent back into the world where life is going on, and incorporate it in such a way that it enriches experience and enables more of whatever it is that 'discloses itself' to us (in Heidegger's phrase) to do just that. But it is still only on the ground that it will do so, not up in the air.

There is an optimal degree of separation between our selves and the world we perceive, if we are to understand it, much as there is between the reader's eye and the page: too much and we cannot make out what is written, but, equally, too little and we cannot read the letters at all.[18] This 'necessary distance', as we might call it (it turns out to be crucial to the story unfolding in this book), is not the same as detachment. Distance *can* yield detachment, as when we coldly calculate how to outwit our opponent, by imagining what he believes will be our next move. It enables us to exploit and use. But what is less often remarked is that, in total contrast, it also has the opposite effect. By standing back from the animal immediacy of our experience we are able to be more empathic with others, who we come to see, for the first time, as beings like ourselves.

The frontal lobes not only teach us to betray, but to trust. Through them we learn to take another's perspective and to control our own immediate needs and desires. If this necessary distance is midwife to the world of Machiavelli, it also delivers the world of Erasmus. The evolution of the frontal lobes prepares us at the same time to be exploiters of the world and of one another, and to be citizens one with another and guardians of the world. If it has made us the most powerful and destructive of animals, it has also turned us, famously, into the 'social animal', and into an animal with a spiritual dimension.

Immediately we can see the problem here. In order to stay in touch with the complexity and immediacy of experience, especially if we are to empathise with, and create bonds with, others, we need to maintain the broadest experience of the world as it comes to us. We need to be going out into the experiential world along the horizontal axis, if you like. By contrast, in order to control or manipulate we need to be able to remove ourselves from certain aspects of experience, and in fact to map the world from the vertical axis – like the strategy map in a general's HQ – in order to plan our campaigns. Might this in itself give us a clue to the question of why the brain is divided?

Yes and no. For one thing the explanation cannot simply have to do with human brains, for the obvious reason that the brains of animals and birds are also divided. But it might very well give a clue as to a way in which the already divided brain might become useful to its human possessor. Before going on to consider that further, let us move a step closer in our look at the overall structure of the brain.

STRUCTURAL ASYMMETRY

When most people think of differences in the structure of the hemispheres, the first thing that springs to mind is the now familiar fact that the brain is asymmetrically larger on the left side. In fact this difference is not so obvious as it probably sounds, though the difference is there all right. It had been known since the middle of the nineteenth century that the faculty of speech was associated with the left frontal area, a region now named, probably unjustly, after Paul Broca, a French physician whose observations were anticipated some quarter of a century earlier by his compatriot, Marc Dax.[19] They had both noticed that those who suffered a stroke or other damage to this part of the brain tended to lose their faculty of speech. Later the Prussian neurologist Carl Wernicke discovered, through similar observations, that the comprehension of language was distinct from that of speech, and was located further back in the left hemisphere, in the posterior superior temporal gyrus, a region that now bears his name.[20] It was the association with language which led to the left hemisphere being referred to as 'dominant', since it did all the talking.

Not long after, two Austrian anatomists, Richard Heschl and Oscar Eberstaller, independently observed that there are visible asymmetries in this region, Heschl lending his name to the transverse gyri in the left superior temporal lobe where incoming auditory information is processed.[21] After that things went quiet for a while until, in the 1930s, Richard Pfeifer found that the planum temporale, a region just posterior to Heschl's gyrus within the Sylvian fissure, and again involved with language and auditory function, was larger on the left. This finding was confirmed and expanded by Geschwind and Levitsky in the 1960s, who reported that in 65 per cent of cases the planum temporale is on average some 30 per cent larger on the left than on the right.[22] Subsequently analysis of skulls and brain scans revealed that there is a generalised enlargement of the posterior part of the left hemisphere in the region of the parietal lobe, known as the left petalia (the term *petalia* was originally applied to the impression left on the inner surface of the skull by protrusions of one hemisphere relative to the other, but is now applied to the protrusion itself).[23]

But that is not all. It is not just the left hemisphere that has its area of expansion. The normal brain appears to have been twisted about its central axis, the fissure between the cerebral hemispheres. The brain is not only wider on the left towards the back, but also wider on the right towards the front; as well as extending further back on the left, even a little under the right hemisphere, it extends further forward on the right, even a little overlapping the left. It is as though someone had got hold of the brain from below and given it a fairly sharp tweak clockwise. The effect is subtle, but highly consistent, and is referred to by neuroscientists as Yakovlevian torque (see Figure 1.4).[24]

What on earth is this about? Why is the brain asymmetrical in this way? If the higher brain functions were just distributed in the brain according to the dictates of space, there would be no reason for local deformities of this kind, rather than an overall diffuse and symmetrical expansion of brain capacity, especially given that the skull that contains it starts out symmetrical.

It has been accepted since the days of the great anatomist John Hunter that structure is at some level an expression of function, an idea reinforced in the early twentieth century by the work of D'Arcy Thompson.[25] The relationship of anatomical asymmetries to functional ones is of great theoretical interest.[26] Although larger size does not always equate to greater functional capacity, it most commonly does so.[27]

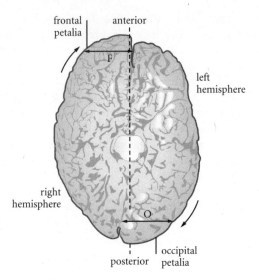

Fig. 1.4 Yakovlevian torque (brain viewed from below).

Function is reflected in volume throughout the central nervous system, in cerebrum, cerebellum and spinal cord.[28] A nice example, which not only illustrates the point, but suggests that brain areas in individuals may actually grow in response to use, is the fact that the right posterior hippocampus, the area of the brain which stores complex three-dimensional maps in space, is larger in London cabbies, taxi drivers with extensive navigational experience.[29] Another vivid demonstration of the principle comes from the left hemisphere of songbirds, which expands during the mating season, and then shrinks again once the mating season is over.[30] And there is specific evidence that these particular asymmetrical expansions of the cerebral cortex in which we are interested are likely to be related to function.[31]

The conventional explanation of the best-known anatomical asymmetry in the brain has been that, since, in Aristotle's famous phrase, man is the social animal, he needs language, and language is a complicated system, which requires a lot of brain space. Since it makes sense that language should be housed in one place, one hemisphere or the other was going to have to specialise in language, displacing other functions, and this just happened to be the left hemisphere, which has, appropriately, expanded in the 'language region' of the posterior left hemisphere to accommodate this function. Language is what separates us from the other animals: it is what gives us the power to communicate and to think. Surely it is obvious that it must have been the drive to language that caused this expansion of the left hemisphere?

As I hope to show in due course, I believe every part of this proposition is wrong, though the reasons why, as well as the reasons we make the assumptions we do, are profoundly revealing of the nature of the brain itself. And obviously it goes no way to account for an expansion in the right frontal lobe.

THE ASYMMETRY OF FUNCTION

These questions about the meaning of structure have answers, but in order to understand them, we need to take a closer look at function.

In fact the phenomenon of functional differences between the hemispheres goes a long way down the tree of phylogeny, far further than anything like language or handedness. And that is what we would expect from the fact that the structurally divided, bihemispheric brain, is not a new invention: bihemispheric structure must have offered possibilities that were adaptive. Lateralisation of function is widespread in vertebrates.[32] It is even true that some of the same neuroendocrine differences that characterise the human brain – differences in neurotransmitters or neurohormonal receptors between the hemispheres – are already present in the brains of rats.[33] We have merely taken this whole process much further. So what is the advantage to birds and animals?

Animals and birds may not have the problems posed by our frontal lobes to deal with, but they do already experience competing needs. This can be seen at one level in terms of the types of attention they are required to bring to bear on the world. There is a need to focus attention narrowly and with precision, as a bird, for example, needs to focus on a grain of corn that it must eat, in order to pick it out from, say, the pieces of grit on which it lies. At the same time there is a need for open attention, as wide as possible, to guard against a possible predator. That requires some doing. It's like a particularly bad case of trying to rub your tummy and pat your head at the same time – only worse, because it's an impossibility. Not only are these two different exercises that need to be carried on simultaneously, they are two quite different *kinds* of exercise, requiring not just that attention should be divided, but that it should be of two distinct types at once.

If we pull back a bit from this same distinction between focussed attention and open attention, we could see it as part of a broader conflict, expressed as a difference in context, in what world we are inhabiting. On the one hand, there is the context, the world, of 'me' – just me and my needs, as an individual competing with other individuals, my ability to peck that seed, pursue that rabbit, or grab that fruit. I need to use, or to manipulate, the world for my ends, and for that I need narrow-focus attention. On the other hand, I need to see myself in the broader context of the world at large, and in relation to others, whether they be friend or foe: I have a need to take account of myself as a member of my social group, to see potential allies, and beyond that to see potential mates and potential enemies. Here I may feel myself to be part of something much bigger than myself, and even existing in and through that 'something' that is bigger than myself – the flight or flock with which I scavenge, breed and roam, the pack with which I hunt, the mate and offspring that I also feed, and ultimately everything that goes on in my purview. This requires less of a wilfully directed, narrowly focussed attention, and more of an open, receptive, widely diffused alertness to whatever exists, with allegiances outside of the self.

These basic incompatibilities suggest the need to keep parts of the brain distinct, in case they interfere with one another. There are already hints here as to why the brain may need to segregate its workings into two hemispheres. If you are a bird, in fact, you solve the conundrum of how to eat and stay alive by employing different strategies with either eye: the right eye (left hemisphere) for getting and feeding, the left eye (right hemisphere) for vigilant awareness of the environment. More generally, chicks prioritise local information with the right eye (left hemisphere), and global information with the left eye (right hemisphere). And it turns out, not surprisingly, that chicks that are properly lateralised in this way are able to use these two types of attention more effectively than are those in whom, experimentally, lateralisation has not been permitted to develop.[34] Many types of bird show more alarm behaviour when viewing a predator with the left eye (right hemisphere),[35] are better at detecting predators with the left eye,[36] and will choose to examine predators with their left eye,[37] to the extent that if they have detected a predator with their right eye, they will actually turn their head so as to examine it further with the left.[38] Hand-raised ravens will even follow the direction of gaze of a human experimenter looking upwards, using their left eye.[39] For many animals there are biases at the population level towards, again, watching out for predators with the left eye (right hemisphere).[40] In marmosets, individual animals with more strongly lateralised brains are better able, because of hemisphere specialisation, to forage and remain aware of predators.[41] There are shorter reaction times in cats that have a lateralised paw preference.[42] Lateralised chimps are more efficient at fishing for termites than unlateralised chimps.[43] Even individual human brains that are, for one reason or another, less 'lateralised' than the norm appear to show global deficits.[44] In a word, lateralisation brings evolutionary advantages, particularly in carrying out dual-attention tasks.[45] As one researcher has put it succinctly: asymmetry pays.[46]

In predatory birds and animals, it is the left hemisphere that latches on, through the right eye and the right foot, to the prey.[47] It is certainly true of familiar prey: in toads, a novel or unusual choice of prey may activate the right hemisphere, until it becomes familiar as an object of prey, when it once again activates the left.[48] In general, toads attend to their prey with the left hemisphere, but interact with their fellow toads using the right hemisphere.[49]

The advantages accrue not only to the individual: being a more lateralised species at the population level carries advantages in social cohesion.[50] That may be because the right hemisphere appears to be deeply involved in social functioning, not just in primates, where it is specialised in the expression of social feelings, but in lower animals and birds as well.[51] For example, chicks preferentially use the left eye (right hemisphere) for differentiating familiar members of the species from one another, and from those who are not familiar, and in general for gathering social information.[52] Chicks approach their parents or an object on which they have imprinted using their left eye (right hemisphere),[53] as do Australian magpies.[54] Though black-winged stilts peck more, and more successfully, at prey using the right eye (left hemisphere), males are more likely to direct courtship displays to females that are seen with their left eye (right hemisphere).[55] The right hemisphere is the main locus of early social experience in rats.[56] In most animal species, intense emotional responses are related to the right hemisphere and inhibited by the left.[57]

Perhaps it is just a nice coincidence that the wry-billed plover, a native of New Zealand, which uses its beak to search for food under stones, has a bill which is curved to the right, so that it will be of most use to its manipulative left hemisphere.[58] No doubt there may be counterexamples. But there does seem to be a consistent thread running all the way through. Speech is in the left hemisphere in humans: what then about the instrumental vocalisations of other species? They arise also in the left hemisphere, in such diverse creatures as frogs, passerine birds, mice, rats, gerbils, and marmosets.[59] Similarly there is a strong right eye (left hemisphere) bias for tool manufacture in crows, *even where using the right eye makes the task more difficult.*[60] This has, as we will see when we come to consider the human situation, some important resonances for the nature of our own world. But when it comes to mediating new experience and information it is already the right hemisphere, in animals as in humans, not the left, that is of crucial importance.[61]

The consistent differences go further than this, differences that again foreshadow differences in humans. Look at the more subtle discriminatory functions. The right hemisphere in birds, as in humans, is associated with detailed discrimination and with topography;[62] while the left hemisphere of many vertebrate animals, again as in humans, is specialised in categorisation of stimuli and fine control of motor response.[63] Pigeons can, remarkably enough, categorise pictures of everyday scenes depending on the content. Still more remarkable, however, is the fact that each hemisphere apparently adopts its own strategy, with the pigeon's left hemisphere using a 'local' strategy – grouping the images according to particular features that must be invariably present – whereas its right hemisphere relies more on a 'global' strategy, taking account of the thing as a whole and comparing it with an ideal exemplar.[64] The full significance of that finding will become apparent only when we come to look at the human brain.

In general terms, then, the left hemisphere yields narrow, focussed attention, mainly for the purpose of getting and feeding. The right hemisphere yields a broad, vigilant attention, the purpose of which appears to be awareness of signals from the surroundings, especially of other creatures, who are potential predators or potential mates, foes or friends; and it is involved in bonding in social animals. It might then be that the division of the human brain is also the result of the need to bring to bear two incompatible types of attention on the world at the same time, one narrow, focussed, and directed by our needs, and the other broad, open, and directed towards whatever else is going on in the world apart from ourselves.

In humans, just as in animals and birds, it turns out that each hemisphere attends to the world in a different way – and the ways are consistent. The right hemisphere underwrites breadth and flexibility of attention, where the left hemisphere brings to bear focussed attention. This has the related consequence that the right hemisphere sees things whole, and in their context, where the left hemisphere sees things abstracted from context, and broken into parts, from which it then reconstructs a 'whole': something very different. And it also turns out that the capacities that help us, as humans, form bonds with others – empathy, emotional understanding, and so on – which involve a quite different kind of attention paid to the world, are largely right-hemisphere functions.

THE NATURE OF ATTENTION

Attention is not just another 'function' alongside other cognitive functions. Its ontological status is of something prior to functions and even to things. The kind of attention we bring to bear on the world changes the nature of the world we attend to, the very nature of the world in which those 'functions' would be carried out, and in which those 'things' would exist. Attention changes *what kind of* a thing comes into being for us: in that way it changes the world. If you are my friend, the way in which I attend to you will be different from the way in which I would attend to you if you were my employer, my patient, the suspect in a crime I am investigating, my lover, my aunt, a body waiting to be dissected. In all these circumstances, except the last, you will also have a quite different experience not just of me, but of yourself: you would feel changed if I changed the type of my attention. And yet nothing *objectively* has changed.

So it is, not just with the human world, but with everything with which we come into contact. A mountain that is a landmark to a navigator, a source of wealth to the prospector, a many-textured form to a painter, or to another the dwelling place of the gods, is changed by the attention given to it. There is no 'real' mountain which can be distinguished from these, no one way of thinking which reveals the true mountain.

Science, however, purports to be uncovering such a reality. Its apparently value-free descriptions are assumed to deliver *the* truth about the object, onto which our feelings and desires are later painted. Yet this highly objective stance, this 'view from nowhere', to use Nagel's phrase, is itself value-laden. It is just one particular way of looking at things, a way which privileges detachment, a lack of commitment of the viewer to the object viewed. For some purposes this can be undeniably useful. But its use in such causes does not make it truer or more real, closer to the nature of things.

Attention also changes who *we* are, we who are doing the attending. Our knowledge of neurobiology (for example, of mirror neurones and their function, which I will touch on later) and of neuropsychology (for example, from experiments in association-priming, which again we will have time to consider in due course) shows that by attending to someone else performing an action, and even by thinking about them doing so – even, in fact, by thinking about certain sorts of people at all – we become objectively, measurably, more *like* them, in how we behave, think and feel. Through the direction and nature of our attention, we prove ourselves to be partners in creation, both of the world and of ourselves. In keeping with this, attention is inescapably bound up with value – unlike what we conceive as 'cognitive functions', which are neutral in this respect. Values enter through *the way in which* those functions are exercised: they can be used in different ways for different purposes to different ends. Attention, however, intrinsically is a *way in which*, not a thing: it is intrinsically a relationship, not a brute fact. It is a 'howness', a something between, an aspect of consciousness itself, not a 'whatness', a thing in itself, an object of consciousness. It brings into being a world and, with it, depending on its nature, a set of values.

UNDERSTANDING THE BRAIN

This leads to a fundamental point about any attempt to understand the brain. It is a particularly acute case of the problems encountered in understanding anything. The nature of the attention one brings to bear on anything alters what one finds; what we aim to understand changes its nature with the context in which it lies; and we can only ever understand anything *as* a something.

There is no way round these problems – if they are problems. To attempt to detach oneself entirely is just to bring a special kind of attention to bear which will have important consequences for what we find. Similarly we cannot see something without there being a context, even if the context appears to be that of 'no context', a thing ripped free of its moorings in the lived world. That is just a special, highly value-laden kind of context in itself, and it certainly alters what we find, too. Nor can we say that we do not see things *as* anything at all – that we just see them, full stop. There is always a model by which we are understanding, an exemplar with which we are comparing, what we see, and where it is not identified it usually means that we have tacitly adopted the model of the machine.

Does that mean that all attempts to approach truth – other than to say everything has its truth in its own way – are doomed, that every version of reality has equal value? Certainly not. I will explore these issues later, as they are central to this book. That needs to wait until we have had a look at what the hemispheres actually 'do'.

Such considerations apply to the attempt to understand anything at all. But when we come to look at what we refer to as brain functions, there is a problem of a wholly different order. We are not 'just' looking at things in the world – a lump of rock, or even a person – but the processes whereby the world itself, together with the rock or the person, might be brought into being for us at all, the very foundations of the fact of our experience, including any idea we might have about the nature of the world, and the nature of the brain, and even the idea that this is so. If it is true that attention changes the nature of what we find, how do we decide the most appropriate attention for *that*? One that tries to ignore the inwardness of experience? What possible context is there in which to place the foundations of experience of all contexts whatever? And what kind of a thing are we to see it 'as'? The answer is far from obvious, but in the absence of an attempt to address the question we do not give *no* answer. We answer with the model we understand – the only kind of thing we can ever fully understand, for the simple reason that we made it: the machine.

We cannot look at the world coming into being within the brain, without that qualifying the world in which the brain itself exists; our understanding of the brain's ways of understanding alters our understanding of the brain itself – the process is not unidirectional, but reciprocal. If it turns out that the hemispheres have different ways of construing the world, this is not just an interesting fact about an efficient information-processing system; it tells us something about the nature of reality, about the nature of our experience of the world, and needs to be allowed to qualify our understanding of the brain as well.

For physicians like myself, this is manifested in the astonishing and moving experiences of our patients, both those with discrete neurological lesions and those with what are thought of as more ordinary psychiatric conditions. For them it is not a matter of 'data loss', but of nothing less than the world itself truly having changed. This is why trying to persuade them of an alternative reality is of limited value, unless they have already managed to regain the world in which we are living.

CONCLUSION

In this chapter I have raised a number of questions arising from the structure of the human brain, and done little as yet to answer them. Why are the hemispheres separate? The separation of the hemispheres seems not accidental, but positively conserved, and the degree of separation carefully controlled by the band of tissue that connects them. This suggests that the mind, and the world of experience that it creates, may have a similar need to keep things apart. Why?

Birds and animals, like us, have divided hemispheres. In them the difference seems to have to do with the necessity of attending to the world in two ways at once. Does it in humans? The frontal lobes are particularly highly developed in humans. Their function is to yield distance – necessary for our most characteristically human qualities, whether that be foresight or empathy. As a result we need to be able to be open to whatever there is, and yet, at the same time, to provide a 'map', a version of the world which is simpler, clearer and therefore more useful. This does not, of course, in itself account for the existence of two hemispheres, but could it give a clue as to a way in which the separation of the hemispheres might become particularly useful?

The brain is structurally asymmetrical, which probably indicates asymmetry of function. This has always been thought to be because of language – which after all is a sort of 'map', or version of the world. Is that not, surely, the reason that there is an expansion in the posterior part of the left hemisphere? This account cannot be right for a number of reasons which I will consider in Chapter 3, quite apart from the fact that it does nothing to explain the expansion in the anterior part of the right hemisphere. The answer to the questions I have raised will have to wait until we reach that chapter. But there is something we should consider, as we approach the next chapter, in which we will take a much closer look at what actually goes on in the two hemispheres of the human brain.

Experience is forever in motion, ramifying and unpredictable. In order for us to *know* anything at all, that thing must have enduring properties. If all things flow, and one can never step into the same river twice – Heraclitus's phrase is, I believe, a brilliant evocation of the core reality of the right hemisphere's world – one will always be taken unawares by experience, since nothing being ever repeated, nothing can ever be known. We have to find a way of fixing it as it flies, stepping back from the immediacy of experience, stepping outside the flow. Hence the brain has to attend to the world in two completely different ways, and in so doing to bring two different worlds into being. In the one, we *experience* – the live, complex, embodied, world of individual, always unique beings, forever in flux, a net of interdependencies, forming and reforming wholes, a world with which we are deeply connected. In the other we 'experience' our experience in a special way: a 're-presented' version of it, containing now static, separable, bounded, but essentially fragmented entities, grouped into classes, on which predictions can be based. This kind of attention isolates, fixes and makes each thing explicit by bringing it under the spotlight of attention. In doing so it renders things inert, mechanical, lifeless. But it also enables us for the first time to know, and consequently to learn and to make things. This gives us power.

These two aspects of the world are not symmetrically opposed. They are not equivalent, for example, to the 'subjective' and 'objective' points of view, concepts which are themselves a product of, and already reflect, one particular way of being in the world – which in fact, importantly, already reflect a 'view' of the world. The distinction I am trying to make is between, on the one hand, the way in which we experience the world pre-reflectively, before we have had a chance to 'view' it at all, or divide it up into bits – a world in which what later has come to be thought of as subjective and objective are held in a suspension which embraces each potential 'pole', and their togetherness, together; and, on the other hand, the world we are more used to thinking of, in which subjective and objective appear as separate poles. At its simplest, a world where there is 'betweenness', and one where there is not. These are not different ways of *thinking about* the world: they are different ways of *being in* the world. And their difference is not symmetrical, but fundamentally asymmetrical.

With that in mind, let's turn to the hemispheres for a closer look at what they 'do'.

CHAPTER 2

WHAT DO THE TWO HEMISPHERES 'DO'?

How much neurological and neuropsychological evidence is there that the hemispheres really are all that different? Or, if there are differences, that there are consistent and significant patterns to the differences, rather than just a random carve-up of 'functions' according to the dictates of space? (This 'toy cupboard' model, which is represented by the traditional view that brain functions are just accommodated according to where space can be found or made, is the one invoked to explain the residence of language functions in the left hemisphere.) Surely, it may be said, the really important differences are those between the many further subdivided functional and anatomical areas described by neuroscience within each hemisphere?

Such differences are certainly of huge significance. However to de-scribe (write about) any thing is to select amongst an infinity of possible features: it is inevitably to circum-scribe (draw a line round) what is salient for the purpose. In comparing two cars, for example, it is obviously true – but, for the time being, irrelevant – that there are far greater similarities between the two cars as a whole than there are differences between, say, their engines. But the point of comparing them is to focus on their differences. My interest here, then, is not in the myriad similarities, which go without saying, but precisely in the differences between the hemispheres. There is, however, one very important intrahemispheric rather than interhemispheric regional difference that I will need to refer to, because it cannot, in the nature of things, be disentangled from the larger question; I will deal with this at the end of the chapter, where I hope it will make most sense.

I would also caution against the natural tendency of the analytic approach, having unimpeachably distinguished parts, to see the parts, rather than the systemic whole to which they belong, as of primary significance. Science involves both analysis and synthesis of knowledge. Increasingly we realise that no one 'bit' of the brain can be responsible for anything that we experience: the brain is a dynamic system, and it is to systemic wholes, 'composed' of many *post factum* identifiable parts, that we need to attend. When we divide, we would be best to divide where nature has clearly made a division: between the hemispheres. In what follows, where I refer, as I often do, to regions within the hemisphere, it should be taken for granted that the important activity is not confined to that region alone, but that it acts in concert with many others, principally, though not of course confined to, regions within the same hemisphere.[1]

There are, as it happens, pervasive and consistent differences between the hemispheres, existing at many levels.

Starting once again with the structure, most studies have found that the right hemisphere is longer, wider, and generally larger, as well as heavier, than the left.[2] Interestingly this is true of social mammals in general.[3] The right hemisphere is in fact wider than the left throughout most of its length, only the posterior parieto-occipital region being broader in the left hemisphere.[4] The cerebral hemispheres show a highly consistent right-greater-than-left asymmetry from childhood to adulthood, with the ventricles (spaces within the hemisphere that are filled with cerebrospinal fluid, and form effectively an inverse measure of brain volume) being larger on the left.[5] However, the expansion of the speech areas in the left hemisphere is also very early in origin and is detectable from 31 weeks' gestation, being clearly present during most of the last trimester.[6]

As well as differing in the size and shape of a number of defined brain areas,[7] the hemispheres differ in the number of neurones,[8] neuronal size (the size of individual nerve cells),[9] and the extent of dendritic branching (the number of connective processes put out by each nerve cell) within areas asymmetrically.[10] There is greater dendritic overlap in cortical columns in the right hemisphere, which has been posited as a mechanism for greater interconnectivity compared with the left.[11] The ratio of grey to white matter also differs.[12] The finding that there is more white matter in the right hemisphere, facilitating transfer *across* regions, also reflects its attention to the global picture, where the left hemisphere prioritises local communication, transfer of information *within* regions.

Neurochemically the hemispheres differ in their sensitivity to hormones (for example, the right hemisphere is more sensitive to testosterone),[13] and to pharmacological agents;[14] and they depend on preponderantly different neurotransmitters (the left hemisphere is more reliant on dopamine and the right hemisphere on noradrenaline).[15] Such structural and functional differences[16] at the brain level suggest there may indeed be basic differences in what the two hemispheres *do*. So what does the neuropsychological literature tell us about that?

While it is true that we know a lot about what different, in some cases fairly minutely discriminated, areas within each hemisphere 'do', in the sense that we can answer the question 'what' it is that they appear to help mediate, we have tended to pay less attention to the 'how', the way in which they do this – not in the sense of the mechanism by which they do it, of which we have a rapidly increasing understanding, but in the sense of what *aspect* of a certain 'function' is being addressed. As soon as one starts to look in this way at the question – for example, not where language is, but what *aspects* of language are where – striking differences between the hemispheres emerge.[17]

THE PATHWAYS TO KNOWLEDGE

Brain structure is easy to measure, function more problematic. So let me start by saying something of the ways in which we come to have knowledge of brain functioning, and some of the problems associated with them. This is important because there is a tendency, particularly among non-specialists, to believe that, thanks to modern technology, we can easily 'see' which parts of the brain are involved in almost any human activity.

The first thing to make clear is that, although the brain is often described as if it were composed of *bits* – 'modules' – of one kind or another, which have then to be strung together, it is in fact a single, integrated, highly dynamic system. Events anywhere in the brain are connected to, and potentially have consequences for, other regions, which may respond to, propagate, enhance or develop that initial event, or alternatively redress it in some way, inhibit it, or strive to re-establish equilibrium. There are no bits, only networks, an almost infinite array of pathways. Thus, especially when dealing with complex cognitive and emotional events, all references to localisation, especially within a hemisphere, but ultimately even across hemispheres, need to be understood in that context.

Having said that, how can one make a start? One method is to study subjects with brain lesions. This has certain advantages. When a bit of the brain is wiped out by a stroke, tumour or other injury, we can see what goes missing, although interpretation of the results is not always as straightforward as it might seem.[18] Another is to use temporary experimental hemisphere inactivations. One way in which this is achieved is by the Wada procedure, most commonly carried out prior to neurosurgery in order to discriminate which hemisphere is primarily responsible for speech. This involves injecting sodium amytal or a similar anaesthetic drug into the blood supply of one carotid artery at a time, thus anaesthetising one half of the brain at a time, while the other remains active. Another way is through transcranial magnetic stimulation techniques, which uses an electromagnet to depress (or, depending on the frequency, enhance) activity temporarily in one hemisphere, or at a specific location within the hemisphere. In the past a similar opportunity came from unilateral administration of electroconvulsive therapy (ECT); it was then possible to ask the subject to carry out specific tasks, in the knowledge that one hemisphere was inactivated for about 15–20 minutes following treatment.

Further techniques that can be helpful involve delivering a perceptual stimulus to one hemisphere only. The tachistoscope is a way of delivering a visual stimulus for a few milliseconds only, too short for gaze to be redirected; careful placement of the stimulus enables it to be delivered to one half of the visual field only. Dichotic listening techniques deliver different stimuli to either ear, usually through headphones, and this was one of the ways in which it was first established that in general there is an advantage for the right ear (left hemisphere) in dealing with verbal material. But in the intact brain we can assume that information spreads very quickly to the contralateral hemisphere, so in using these techniques one is looking at small differences in reaction times, or marginal differences in salience.

For this reason a particularly rich resource has been individuals with so-called split brains, patients who, in order to control intractable epilepsy, underwent a procedure called callosotomy, which divides the corpus callosum. This operation is rare nowadays, as most seizures are controllable with modern pharmacological agents, but when it was first carried out, by Sperry and Bogen and their colleagues in California in the 1950s and 1960s, it was revolutionary – both for the patients, who began to lead normal lives, and for neurologists, psychologists and philosophers, who saw a window opened into the workings of the brain. In the case of split-brain subjects, stimuli presented to one ear or to one visual field cannot be transferred across the corpus callosum to the other hemisphere, giving a relatively pure picture of how one hemisphere on its own responds, which is why they are so valuable to researchers. Some particular circumstances make split-brain subjects especially intriguing. If an image is shown to a split-brain subject in the left visual field, he or she will be unable to name what was seen, since the image from the left visual field is sent to the right side of the brain only, and the right hemisphere in most subjects cannot speak. Since interhemispheric communication is largely absent, the speaking left hemisphere cannot name what the right hemisphere has just seen. The person can nonetheless indicate a corresponding object with his or her left hand, since that hand is controlled by the right side of the brain.

Other information comes from EEG recordings, and increasingly from functional neuroimaging, which allows one to see which areas of the brain are preferentially activated while performing a task, and this area is promising. The information from the EEG is instantaneous, and therefore quite precise in time, but harder to localise precisely in the brain. By contrast, functional magnetic resonance imaging (fMRI), the preferred method of imaging now available, gives more precise localisation, but with a three- to five-second time spread. These techniques can be combined. Neuroimaging, including single photon emission computed tomography (SPECT) and positron emission tomography (PET), as well as fMRI, use a variety of techniques to detect where there are changes in the perfusion (blood supply) of the brain, the common principle being that active areas metabolise at a higher rate and therefore require a temporarily increased blood supply. It is worth saying something, however, about the problems associated with neuroimaging studies as a source of information on their own.[19]

Imaging just shows a few peaks, where much of interest goes on elsewhere.[20] One cannot assume that the areas that light up are those fundamentally responsible for the 'function' being imaged, or that areas that do not light up are not involved.[21] And, what is more, one cannot even assume that whatever 'peaks' is of primary importance, since only effortful tasks tend to register – the more expert we are at something the *less* we will see brain activity. For example, people with higher IQs have *lower* cerebral metabolic rates during mentally active conditions;[22] as do those with bigger brain size,[23] which is also correlated with IQ.[24] We have, too, to remember that the activations we visualise in the brain may actually be inhibitory in nature – inhibition may be indistinguishable from activation using current fMRI methods.[25]

That does not nearly exhaust the problems to be surmounted. Small differences in the way the task is presented may make a large difference to the results. Changes in novelty or complexity can mask relevant structures or falsely identify irrelevant ones.[26] The more complex the task, the more widely distributed the networks involved are likely to be, and the harder it will be to know what it is that one is measuring; subtraction paradigms, where two sets of conditions are compared so as to isolate the element of interest, are associated with their own problems.[27]

As if that is not enough, many variables are involved in any experiment involving human beings. Male and female subjects respond differently; not only left and right handedness may make a difference, but more importantly, strongly lateralised handedness (whether right or left) may give a different picture from more mixed handedness; race and age also make differences. Individual cases may be different because the way we experience the world individually is different; even the same brain varies in its response to the same task depending on the context – for example, what's happened previously. In the words of one prominent neuroimaging specialist: 'Some people believe that psychology is just being replaced by brain imaging, but I don't think that's the case at all ... It's the confrontation of all these different methods that creates knowledge.'[28]

For all these reasons I have tried throughout not to rely on neuroimaging only, and as little as possible on any one line of evidence alone. The importance of, wherever possible, linking neuroimaging with evidence from brain lesion studies has recently been emphasised in relation to the concept of 'theory of mind'.[29] But, as I began by pointing out, even brain lesion studies have their limitations.[30]

All in all, it should be clear that anything like complete concurrence of findings is not to be expected; there are bound to be many discrepancies, and overall this is not as precise a science as it may appear. Nonetheless in aggregate we have a mass of information that does suggest consistent differences, and it's at these we need to take a closer look.

In doing so, I will sometimes refer to brain regions illustrated in Figures 2.1 and 2.2, specifically parts of the prefrontal cortex, the diencephalon, basal ganglia, and the limbic system, and, while the argument can be followed without a knowledge of detailed anatomy, the images may help readers not familiar with the area.

I should also say that this is necessarily a very long chapter. I recognise that that may be a little disheartening to the reader, and I could have divided it into several parts. But my hope is that we can get away from looking at separate 'areas of cognition', however much I may have had to carve up the seamless world each hemisphere delivers into recognisable chunks for the purposes of description. In the process of doing so, I have been keenly aware of the artificiality of such divisions, since each inevitably overlaps with many others, and ultimately I believe they form a single, coherent whole. To have cut it up further into separate chapters would have reinforced the tendency I wish to avoid. But the various subhead-

WHAT DO THE TWO HEMISPHERES 'DO'? ♦ 37

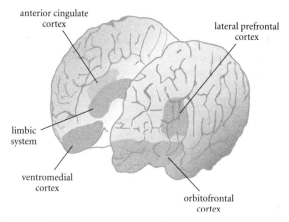

Fig. 2.1 Prefrontal cortex and limbic system.

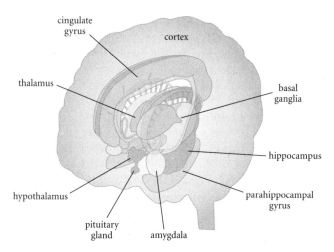

Fig. 2.2 Diencephalon, basal ganglia and limbic system.

ings of this chapter are a compromise which will, I hope, give the process some sense of direction.

BREADTH AND FLEXIBILITY VERSUS FOCUS AND GRASP

I'd like to begin with what we have already touched on, the fundamental importance of attention. If what it is that exists comes into being for each one of us through its interaction with our brains and minds, the idea that we could have a knowledge of it that was not also an expression of ourselves, and dependent on what we brought to the relationship, is untenable. It may seem obvious, though, that the task of the brain – what we have a brain for – is to put us in touch with whatever it is that exists apart from ourselves.

But this conclusion is not quite as obviously right as it seems. Different aspects of the world come into being through the interaction of our brains with whatever it is that exists apart from ourselves, and precisely *which* aspects come into being depends on the nature of our attention. It might turn out that for some purposes, those that involve making use of the world and manipulating it for our benefit, we need, in fact, to be quite selective about what we see. In other words we might need to *know* what is of use to us – but this might be very different from understanding in a broader sense, and certainly might require filtering out some aspects of experience. Without experiencing whatever it is, we would have nothing on which to ground our knowledge, so we have to experience it at some stage; but in order to *know* it, we have to 'process' experience. We have to be able to recognise ('re-cognise') what we experience: to say this is a 'such-and-such', that is, it has certain qualities that enable me to place it in a category of things that I have experienced before and about which I have certain beliefs and feelings. This processing eventually becomes so automatic that we do not so much experience the world as experience our representation of the world. The world is no longer 'present' to us, but 're-presented', a virtual world, a copy that exists in conceptual form in the mind.

Much of our capacity to 'use' the world depends, not on an attempt to open ourselves as much as possible to apprehending whatever it is that exists apart from ourselves, but instead on apprehending whatever I have brought into being for myself, my representation of it. This is the remit of the left hemisphere, and would appear to require a selective, highly focussed attention.

The right hemisphere, as birds and animals show, is 'on the look out'. It has to be open to whatever it is that exists apart from ourselves, as much as possible without preconceptions, not just focussing on what it already knows, or is interested in. This requires a mode of attention that is broader and more flexible than that of the left hemisphere. What actually happens in detail?

The conventional neuropsychological literature distinguishes five types of attention: vigilance, sustained attention, alertness, focussed attention and divided attention. While not identical, vigilance and sustained attention are similar, and they are often treated as one concept. Together with alertness, they form the basis of what has been called the *intensity* axis of attention. The other axis is *selectivity*, made up of the two remaining types, focussed and divided attention.[31] Experiments confirm that the different types of attention are distinct and independent of one another, and subserved by a number of different brain structures distributed extensively over the prefrontal, anterior cingulate, and posterior parietal areas of both hemispheric cortices. Clearly within either hemisphere, and possibly between hemispheres, the system of control processes is complex. However, some broad consistent differences in hemisphere specialisation are striking when one comes to review the available evidence.

Alertness and sustained attention may have the ring of technical 'functions', just the sort of things it's hard to get excited about outside the psychology lab. But, like vigilance, they are the ground of our being in the world, not only at the lowest, vegetative level, but at the highest, spiritual levels ('Brethren, be sober, be vigilant', '*O Mensch, gib acht!*').[32] Without alertness, we are as if asleep, unresponsive to the world around us; without sustained attention, the world fragments; without vigilance, we cannot become aware of anything we do not already know. Looking at the evidence from brain research, it becomes clear that vigilance and sustained attention are grossly impaired in subjects with right-hemisphere lesions, especially right frontal lobe lesions;[33] by contrast, in patients with left-hemisphere lesions (therefore relying on their intact right hemisphere) vigilance is preserved.[34] Patients with right-hemisphere lesions also exhibit what is called perceptuomotor slowing, a sign of diminished alertness, associated with lapses of attention.[35] Studies in both healthy subjects and split-brain patients corroborate the role of the right hemisphere in the 'intensity' aspects of attention;[36] and scanning studies provide further confirmatory evidence of right-hemisphere dominance in alertness and sustained attention.[37] Overall it appears clear that, of the two main axes of attention, *intensity* (alertness, vigilance and sustained attention) is reliant on the right hemisphere.

The other main axis of attention is *selectivity* (focussed and divided attention). Turning to focussed attention first, the story here is quite different. Deficits in focussed attention are more severe with left-hemisphere injury.[38] Although selective attention may be bilateral,[39] it is more typically associated with activity in the left caudate or left anterior cingulate.[40] Healthy subjects show a left-hemisphere preference for choice reactions.[41] And scanning studies suggest focussed attention is associated with activity in the left orbitofrontal cortex and basal ganglia.[42]

As regards divided attention, the evidence is divided. While some studies suggest that both left and right hemispheres are involved,[43] there appears to be a clear primary role for the right hemisphere, especially the right dorsolateral prefrontal cortex.[44]

To sum up, the right hemisphere is responsible for every type of attention except focussed attention. Even where there is divided attention, and both hemispheres appear to be involved, it seems probable that the right hemisphere plays the primary role (possibly that of unifying the divided input – see below). Because it is the right hemisphere that is responsible for attention globally, and because there is a natural tendency for each hemisphere to process preferentially stimuli from the contralateral attentional field, most people, if asked to bisect a line, will do so slightly to the left of the actual midpoint – because doing so equalises the apparent extent of the half-lines as seen from the right hemisphere's point of view.[45] It is lesions in the right inferior parietal lobule that cause the most serious impairment of global attention.[46]

There have been suggestions that the basis for the right-hemisphere predominance for attention may lie in the more sophisticated visuospatial processing of the right hemisphere, but I would be inclined to see that as a consequence of the attentional difference rather than a cause of it.[47]

More specifically there is evidence of left-hemisphere dominance for local, narrowly focussed attention and right-hemisphere dominance for broad, global, and flexible attention.[48] The scope of the right hemisphere's world is broad.[49] Patients with a right-hemisphere lesion (therefore relying on their intact left hemisphere) start with the pieces and put them together to get the overall picture, whereas those with a left-hemisphere lesion (relying on their right hemisphere) prefer a global approach.[50] Patients with right-hemisphere damage don't seem able to adjust the breadth of the 'spotlight' of their attention: they suffer 'an excessive and more or less permanent narrowing of their attentional window'.[51] That's what happens when we have to rely on left-hemisphere attention on its own.

THE NEW VERSUS THE KNOWN

From this it follows that in almost every case what is new must first be present in the right hemisphere, before it can come into focus for the left. For one thing, the right hemisphere alone attends to the peripheral field of vision from which new experience tends to come; only the right hemisphere can direct attention to what comes to us from the edges of our awareness, *regardless of side*.[52] Anything newly entering our experiential world instantly triggers a release of noradrenaline – mainly in the right hemisphere.[53] Novel experience induces changes in the right hippocampus, but not the left.[54] So it is no surprise that phenomenologically it is the right hemisphere that is attuned to the apprehension of anything new.[55]

This difference is pervasive across domains. Not just new experience, but the learning of new information or new skills also engages right-hemisphere attention more than left,[56] even if the information is verbal in nature.[57] However, once the skills have become familiar through practice, they shift to being the concern of the left hemisphere,[58] even for skills such as playing a musical instrument.[59]

If it is the right hemisphere that is vigilant for whatever it is that exists 'out there', it alone can bring us something other than what we already know. The left hemisphere deals with what it knows, and therefore prioritises the expected – its process is predictive. It positively prefers what it knows.[60] This makes it more efficient in routine situations where things are predictable, but less efficient than the right wherever the initial assumptions have to be revised,[61] or when there is a need to distinguish old information from new material that may be consistent with it.[62] Because the left hemisphere is drawn by its expectations, the right hemisphere outperforms the left whenever prediction is difficult.[63] The link between the right hemisphere and what is new or emotionally engaging exists not just in humans, but already in higher mammals: for example, horses perceive new and possibly emotionally arousing stimuli with the left eye.[64]

POSSIBILITY VERSUS PREDICTABILITY

The right hemisphere is, in other words, more capable of a frame shift;[65] and not surprisingly the right frontal lobe is especially important for flexibility of thought, with damage in that area leading to perseveration, a pathological inability to respond flexibly to changing situations.[66] For example, having found an approach that works for one problem, subjects seem to get stuck, and will inappropriately apply it to a second problem that requires a different approach – or even, having answered one question right, will give the same answer to the next and the next. It is the right frontal cortex that is responsible for inhibiting one's immediate response, and hence for flexibility and set-shifting;[67] as well as the power of inhibiting immediate response to environmental stimuli.[68]

It is similar with problem solving. Here the right hemisphere presents an array of possible solutions, which remain live while alternatives are explored.[69] The left hemisphere, by contrast, takes the single solution that seems best to fit what it already knows and latches onto it.[70] V. S. Ramachandran's studies of anosognosia reveal a tendency for the left hemisphere to deny discrepancies that do not fit its already generated schema of things. The right hemisphere, by contrast, is actively watching for discrepancies, more like a devil's advocate.[71] These approaches are both needed, but pull in opposite directions.

This difference is not predicated on any of the old distinctions such as verbal versus visuospatial. It operates equally in the realm of attention to verbal information. In keeping with what we know of its priorities, the left hemisphere actively narrows its attentional focus to highly related words while the right hemisphere activates a broader range of words. The left hemisphere operates focally, suppressing meanings that are not currently relevant. By contrast, the right hemisphere 'processes information in a non-focal manner with widespread activation of related meanings'.[72] Whereas close lexical semantic relationships rely more on the left hemisphere, looser semantic associations rely on the right.[73] Because the right hemisphere makes infrequent or distantly related word meanings available,[74] there is increased right-hemisphere involvement when generating unusual or distantly related words[75] or novel uses for objects.[76] This may be one of many aspects that tend to associate the right hemisphere with a freer, more 'creative' style. The right anterior temporal region is associated with making connections across distantly related information during comprehension,[77] and the right posterior superior temporal sulcus may be selectively involved in verbal creativity.[78] In the 'close' situation, by contrast, the left hemisphere actively *suppresses* the right, to exclude associations which are semantically only distantly related.[79]

The more flexible style of the right hemisphere is evidenced not just in its own preferences, but also at the 'meta' level, in the fact that it can also use the left hemisphere's preferred style, whereas the left hemisphere cannot use the right hemisphere's. For example, although the left hemisphere gains more benefit from a single strong association than several weaker associations, only the right hemisphere can use either equally.[80]

One of the standard psychological tests that is supposed to measure creativity is the Remote Association Test, an expression of the belief that creativity requires the ability to make associations between widely different ideas or concepts.[81] Since efforts of will focus attention and deliberately narrow its range,[82] it may be that cessation of the effort to 'produce something' – relaxation, in other words – favours creativity because it permits broadening of attention, and, with the expansion of the attentional field, engagement of the right hemisphere.[83] (From what has been said it can be seen that relatively more remote or tenuous associations of thought are made more easily by permitting the broader scope of right-hemisphere attention, which may also explain the 'tip of the tongue' phenomenon: the harder we try, the more we recruit narrow left-hemisphere attention, and the less we can remember the word. Once we stop trying, the word comes to us unbidden.)

Since the left hemisphere actually inhibits the breadth of attention that the right hemisphere brings to bear, creativity can increase after a left-hemisphere stroke, and not just in sensory qualities but, as Alajouanine says of one painter he describes, in 'numerous intellectual and affective components'.[84] Certainly there is plenty of evidence that the right hemisphere is important for creativity,[85] which given its ability to make more and wider-ranging connections between things, and to think more flexibly, is hardly surprising.[86] But this is only part of the story. Both hemispheres are importantly involved. Creativity depends on the union of things that are also maintained separately – the precise function of the corpus callosum, both to separate and connect; and interestingly division of the corpus callosum does impair creativity.[87]

INTEGRATION VERSUS DIVISION

In general the left hemisphere is more closely interconnected within itself, and within regions of itself, than the right hemisphere (see p. 33 above).[88] This is all part of the close focus style, but it is also a reflection at the neural level of the essentially *self-referring* nature of the world of the left hemisphere: it deals with what it already knows, the world it has made for itself. By contrast, as I have mentioned, the right hemisphere has a greater degree of myelination, facilitating swift transfer of information between the cortex and centres below the cortex,[89] and greater connectivity in general.[90] Functionally its superior integration is evidenced by EEG measures[91] and by the more diffuse but overlapping somatosensory projections (carrying information on touch, pain and body position) and auditory inputs on the right side of the brain.[92]

At the experiential level it is also better able to integrate perceptual processes, particularly bringing together different kinds of information from different senses.[93] There is evidence from brain-damaged war veterans that confirms the difference between the left hemisphere's focal organisation and the right hemisphere's more profuse and diffusely organised structure, and indicates that this may be why the right hemisphere has the advantage in constructing a richly diverse three-dimensional world in space. We would expect on first principles that having widely different kinds of functions grouped together in the more diffusely organised right hemisphere should lead to a different quality of integration from that characteristic of the more focally organised left hemisphere: there would be a greater convergence of disparate types of information, and 'one might predict *heteromodal* integration to an extent surpassing that possible in a focally organised hemisphere.'[94] In plain English, this means bringing together in consciousness different elements, including information from the ears, eyes, and other sensory organs, and from memory, so as to generate the richly complex, but coherent, world we experience. By contrast, the left hemisphere would be 'inadequate for the more rapid complex syntheses achieved by the [right] hemisphere'.[95]

I mentioned that new stimuli lead to release of noradrenaline in the right hemisphere. Most neurones 'fatigue', that is to say they cease to respond, when continuously stimulated. These noradrenergic neurones do not fatigue, however, but maintain their condition of excitation, so that exploratory attention is held open across a greater expanse of both space and time.[96] The range of the right hemisphere is further increased by the fact that it has a longer working memory, and so is able both to access more information and hold it together at any one time for longer.[97] It is capable of bearing more information in mind and doing so over longer periods, with greater specificity (which also means less susceptibility to degradation over time by memory).[98]

This broader field of attention, open to whatever may be, and coupled with greater integration over time and space, is what makes possible the recognition of broad or complex patterns, the perception of the 'thing as a whole', seeing the wood for the trees.[99] In short the left hemisphere takes a local short-term view, whereas the right hemisphere sees the bigger picture.

THE HIERARCHY OF ATTENTION

There are, then, two widely differing ways of attending to the world. How do they relate to one another?

If whatever is new to experience is more likely to be present in the right hemisphere, this suggests a temporal hierarchy of attention, with our awareness of any object of experience beginning in the right hemisphere, which grounds experience, before it gets to be further processed in the left hemisphere.

This coexists with and is confirmed by a hierarchy of attention at any one moment in time, which also establishes the right hemisphere, not the left, as predominant for attention.[100] Global attention, courtesy of the right hemisphere, comes first, not just in time, but takes precedence in our sense of what it is we are attending to; it therefore guides the left hemisphere's local attention, rather than the other way about.[101] As an illustration, we would normally see the images below as an H (composed of Es) and a 4 (composed of 8s).

```
EEEE            EEEE                        88888888
EEEE            EEEE                     88888 88888
EEEE            EEEE                    88888    88888
EEEE            EEEE                   888888    88888
EEEE            EEEE                   888888    88888
EEEEEEEEEEEEEEEEEEEE                   888888    88888
EEEEEEEEEEEEEEEEEEEE              8888888888888888888888
EEEE            EEEE              8888888888888888888888
EEEE            EEEE                             88888
EEEE            EEEE                             88888
EEEE            EEEE                             88888
EEEE            EEEE                             88888
EEEE            EEEE                             88888
```

The exception to this is in schizophrenia, where the right-hemisphere-dependent ability to see the whole at once is lost; then the figure becomes just a mass of Es and 8s. One of the crucial differences in schizophrenia – and in schizotypy – lies in the mode of attention, whereby the whole is built up from the parts.[102] However, the attentional hierarchy can also be inverted in certain circumstances in normal individuals.[103] When there is a high probability that what we are looking for lies at the local level, our window of attention narrows, in order to optimise performance at this level, 'thus reversing the natural tendency to favour the global aspect'.[104]

Essentially the left hemisphere's narrow focussed attentional beam, which it believes it 'turns' towards whatever it may be, has in reality already been seized by it.[105] It is thus the right hemisphere that has dominance for *exploratory* attentional movements, while the left hemisphere assists focussed *grasping* of what has already been prioritised.[106] It is the right hemisphere that controls where that attention is to be oriented.[107]

We may think that we build up a picture of something by a process of serial scanning – putting the bits together – because this is the way our conscious, verbal, left hemisphere, when asked to work out how it is done after the fact, accounts for it. But in reality we see things first whole: serial attentional processing is not needed. In other words, we do not have to orientate our attention to each feature of an object in turn to understand the overall object; the features are all present without the need to combine the products of focal attention.[108]

Beyond the difference in nature and extent of the attention that the two hemi-spheres give to the world, there is a fascinating and fundamental difference in their orientation. One might think that both hemispheres would take the world as a whole as their concern, or, if it is impossible for both to do so, that there would be a symmetrical and complementary distribution of attention across the whole field. But this is not the case. Since the left visual field, and the perceptions of the left ear, are more available to the right hemisphere, and by the same token the right visual field, and the perceptions of the right ear to the left hemisphere, one would expect, and indeed one finds, a gradient of attention from left to right, or right to left, across the experiential world for either hemisphere. But these gradi-ents are not symmetrical: there is a fundamental *asymmetry* of concern about the whole picture. The right hemisphere is concerned with the whole of the world as available to the senses, whether what it receives comes from the left or the right; it delivers to us a single complete world of experience. The left hemisphere seems to be concerned narrowly with the right half of space and the right half of the body – one part, *the part it uses*.[109]

In split-brain patients, for example, the right hemisphere attends to the entire visual field, but the left hemisphere only to the right.[110] This refusal of the left hemisphere to acknowledge the left half of the world accounts for the fascinating phenomenon of 'hemi-neglect' following a right-hemisphere stroke, after which the individual is completely dependent on the left hemisphere to bring his body and his world into being.[111] Because the concern of the left hemisphere is with the right half of the world only, the left half of the body, and everything lying in the left part of the visual field, fails to materialise (see Figure 2.3). So extreme can this phenomenon be that the sufferer may fail to acknowledge the existence of anyone standing to his left, the left half of the face of a clock, or the left page of a newspaper or book, and will even neglect to wash, shave or dress the left half of the body, sometimes going so far as to deny that it exists at all.

This is despite the fact that there is nothing at all wrong with the primary visual system: the problem is not due to blindness as ordinarily understood. If one temporarily disables the left hemisphere of such an individual through transcranial magnetic stimulation, the neglect improves, suggesting that the problem following right-hemisphere stroke is due to release of the unopposed action of the left hemisphere.[112] But you do not get the mirror-image of the neglect phenomenon after a left-hemisphere stroke, because in that case the still-functioning right hemisphere supplies a whole body, and a whole world, to the sufferer. And, because the right hemisphere alone subserves the extremities of the attentional field (whether left or right), where hemi-neglect results in loss of the left field, there is, extraordinarily enough, also loss of the extreme *right* field.[113]

There is a curious phenomenon of 'stickiness' about the attention exhibited by the left hemisphere, which is related to its relative inflexibility referred to above. Following right-hemisphere damage, the right hemifield seems to exert a magnetic attraction.[114] Patients find their gaze pulled, despite themselves, towards the right.[115] And it has even been suggested that the phenomenon of attentional hemineglect is not so much a matter of disregarding the left side of space, as of being captured by the right side of space, and unable to let go.[116] The left hemisphere has difficulty disengaging;[117] and this seems to be precisely because, instead of familiarity causing it to disattend, it causes it to attend all the *more*.

Fig. 2.3 Templates (left column) copied by patients with neglect (right column).

Patients start off by being attracted towards items on the right, but then become stuck to them, because instead of causing inhibition (negative feedback), as would normally be the case, repeated or familiar stimuli on the right side cause facilitation (positive feedback).[118] A patient of mine who had had a right-hemisphere stroke following rupture of an arteriovenous malformation in his temporoparietal region would become fixated by inanimate objects in his right hemifield: if there was a door hinge to his right, for example, he would find himself waylaid by it as he tried to pass through the doorway, and get 'stuck' inspecting it for protracted periods, unless actively disengaged by one of his carers.

It is probably relevant that it is the right hemisphere that controls conjugate eye movements, that is, that makes the two eyes move together,[119] leading to the interesting thought that it may be the right hemisphere that also keeps the hemispheres together, in the interests of a whole world of experience, rather than allowing the left hemisphere wilfully to go its own way.

In summary, the hierarchy of attention, for a number of reasons, implies a grounding role and an ultimately integrating role for the right hemisphere, with whatever the left hemisphere does at the detailed level needing to be founded on, and then returned to, the picture generated by the right. This is an instance of the right → left → right progression which will be a theme of this book. And it lies at the very foundation of experience: attention, where the world actually comes into being.

But that does not quite complete the picture. There is a further highly significant point to be observed here about the relationship between the hemispheres. It will be remembered that chicks use either eye for different purposes and different views of the world. Chicks using both eyes, however, do not do the splits: they approximate more to the right-hemisphere view.[120] That is in keeping with what we would expect from everything we have heard about the attentional hierarchy. But it may also have to do with the fact that at this stage their hemispheres are relatively independent. For we know that, in the adult birds, the commissures which develop – the bands of nerve tissue, such as the corpus callosum, that connect the two hemispheres – permit the left hemisphere to have an inhibitory effect on the right hemisphere to a greater extent than the right hemisphere has on the left. In doing so they actually succeed in reversing the natural asymmetry: they impose the left-hemisphere view of the world. Only when interhemispheric communication is rendered impossible by severing of the commissures does one see, once again, the natural asymmetry in favour of the right hemisphere's view of the world appear.[121]

THE WHOLE VERSUS THE PART

I have mentioned that the link between the right hemisphere and holistic or *Gestalt* perception is one of the most reliable and durable of the generalisations about hemisphere differences, and that it follows from the differences in the nature of attention.[122]

The right hemisphere sees the whole, before whatever it is gets broken up into parts in our attempt to 'know' it. Its holistic processing of visual form is not based

Fig. 2.4 Emergence of the *Gestalt*.

on summation of parts. On the other hand, the left hemisphere sees part-objects.[123] The best-known example of this process of *Gestalt* perception is the way in which the Dalmatian dog, sniffing the ground in the shade of a tree, suddenly emerges from this mass of dots and splashes (Figure 2.4). The process is not a gradual putting together of bits of information, but an 'aha!' phenomenon – it comes all at once.

The right hemisphere, with its greater integrative power, is constantly searching for patterns in things. In fact its understanding is based on complex pattern recognition.[124]

Split-brain subjects have a complete inability to relate the shape or structure of something they have seen to something they feel with their hand – if the object is felt with their right hand. With the left hand (right hemisphere), however, they perform perfectly.[125] Gazzaniga and LeDoux thought this must be dependent on some sort of tactile or 'manipulatory' advantage of the 'minor' hemisphere, because they were able to show that in a second experiment involving visual–visual integration, involving fitting a broken figure together, the left hemisphere was not so bad (though it was still not as good as the right hemisphere). See Figure 2.5.

But this second test is hardly much of a test of the capacity to generate a sense of the whole. A test of the capacity to generate a sense of the whole would be, precisely, to have a sense of what it would be like in modalities other than those in front of one – to be able to tell from the feel of something what it would look like, never having seen it; or to be able to select by touch alone an object that had been seen – the capacity which the left hemisphere lacks.

Subjects with unilateral brain damage show complementary deficits in drawing skills, depending on whether it is right or left hemisphere function that is compromised. The productions of those with right-hemisphere damage, relying on their

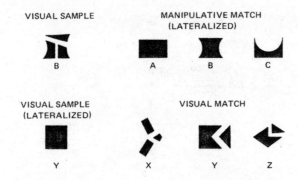

VISUAL SAMPLE   MANIPULATIVE MATCH
(LATERALIZED)

B   A   B   C

VISUAL SAMPLE   VISUAL MATCH
(LATERALIZED)

Y   X   Y   Z

Fig. 2.5 In the first experiment, visual sample B is seen: the right hand and left hand are separately tested for ability to select the required shape by touch alone from A, B or C. In the second, visual sample Y is shown separately to either visual field: the subject then has to match it visually to one of the broken figures X, Y or Z (from Gazzaniga and LeDoux, 1978).

Fig. 2.6 Drawings of a man by a subject with a right parietal lesion, and of a bicycle and a house by a subject with a right parieto-occipital lesion (from Hécaen & Ajuriaguerra, 1952).

left hemisphere, lose overall coherence and integrity, and become so distorted they are barely recognisable: there is no grasp of the *Gestalt*, the whole. For example, if asked to draw a person, subjects with right parieto-occipital lesions 'exhibit considerable difficulty in assembling the various elements correctly, in their repeated attempts putting the limbs in extraordinary positions (arms attached to the neck or to the lower part of the trunk)'. One patient, asked to draw an elephant, 'draws only a tail, a trunk and an ear.' Putting together a model of an elephant is no easier: it 'is done slowly and ends in a complete fiasco. Although, from what he says, he recognises the essential elements, he is incapable of putting them in even approximately the right place or relation to one another.'[126] Figures become almost unbelievably simplified and distorted: a man, just a blob with three sticks for limbs; a bicycle, two small wheels positioned above the (bigger) pedals; a house reduced to a few chaotic lines, with a roof symbolised by an inverted V. See Figure 2.6.

The drawings of those with left-hemisphere damage, by contrast, relying on their right hemisphere, sometimes exhibit relative poverty of detail, because the accent is on the shape of the whole.[127] See Figure 2.7.[128]

It is the same with perception, as with execution. For example, a patient with right-hemisphere damage described by Hécaen and de Ajuriaguerra was unable to

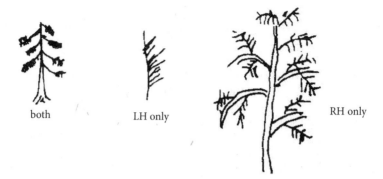

both   LH only   RH only

Fig. 2.7 Tree drawn by the same subject: under normal conditions; with the right hemiphere inactivated; and with the left hemisphere inactivated (from Nikolaenko, 2001).

recognise a drawing of a house, until he saw that whatever it was had a chimney.[129] The whole was inscrutable, but the part gave it away.

But once again, the failures of integrative processing where there is right-hemisphere damage are not confined to one domain or another, and are not part of the old visual/verbal dichotomy: difficulties experienced by patients with right-hemisphere lesions in grasping visuospatial information as a whole are related to difficulties they have in verbal-semantic understanding.[130]

Because of the way in which the left hemisphere is biased towards identification by parts, and the right hemisphere towards the whole picture, they also differ in the way they understand what they experience.

CONTEXT VERSUS ABSTRACTION

For the same reason that the right hemisphere sees things as a whole, before they have been digested into parts, it also sees each thing in its context, as standing in a qualifying relationship with all that surrounds it, rather than taking it as a single isolated entity.[131] Its awareness of the world is anything but abstract.

Anything that requires indirect interpretation, which is not explicit or literal, that in other words requires contextual understanding, depends on the right frontal lobe for its meaning to be conveyed or received.[132] The right hemisphere understands from indirect contextual clues, not only from explicit statement, whereas the left hemisphere will identify by labels rather than context (e.g. iden-tifies that it must be winter because it is 'January', not by looking at the trees).[133]

This difference is particularly important when it comes to what the two hemi-spheres contribute to language. The right hemisphere takes whatever is said within its entire context.[134] It is specialised in pragmatics, the art of contextual under-standing of meaning, and in using metaphor.[135] It is the right hemisphere which processes the non-literal aspects of language,[136] of which more later. This is why the left hemisphere is not good at understanding the higher level meaning of utterances such as 'it's a bit hot in here today' (while the right hemisphere understands 'please open a window', the left hemisphere assumes this is just helpful supply of meteorological data). It is also why the right hemisphere underpins the appreciation of humour, since humour depends vitally on being able to understand the context of what is said and done, and how context changes it. Subjects with right brain damage, like subjects with schizophrenia, who in many respects resemble them, cannot understand implied meaning, and tend to take conversational remarks literally.

The left hemisphere, because its thinking is decontextualised, tends towards a slavish following of the internal logic of the situation, even if this is in contravention of everything experience tells us.[137] This can be a strength, for example in philosophy, when it gets us beyond intuition, although it could also be seen as the disease for which philosophy itself must be the cure; but it is a weakness when it permits too ready a capitulation to theory. The left hemisphere is the hemisphere of abstraction,[138] which, as the word itself tells us, is the process of wresting things from their context. This, and its related capacity to categorise things once they have been abstracted, are the foundations of its intellectual power. A patient with left-hemisphere damage described by Hécaen and de Ajuriaguerra, therefore relying on his right hemisphere only, on being asked to copy a model using pieces of wood appeared 'as if compelled by some bizarre force to place the pieces of wood on top of the model that we were intending him to copy, rather than to one side'. This was thought to signify 'a problem with the ability to produce an abstract representation from a concrete model'.[139]

The left hemisphere can only re-present; but the right hemisphere, for its part, can only give again what 'presences'. This is close to the core of what differentiates the hemispheres. Hughlings Jackson, in many respects the father of modern neuropsychiatry, whose acute observations of patients with brain injury and epilepsy make him still a rich source of insight into hemisphere differences, intuited this as far back as the First World War. A patient of his had lost the power of expression in speech, but retained some automatic understanding of the names of objects, which Jackson presumed to be mediated by his right hemisphere. Although he could instantly pick up a brick on command, according to Jackson he could have no 'memory' of the word *brick*:

> I do not believe that the man who cannot say (nor write) the word brick can be said to have a 'memory' of it (be conscious of the *word itself*). He has no consciousness of it, but of the thing it is a symbol of – a very different thing.[140]

Abstraction is necessary if the left hemisphere is to re-present the world. The left hemisphere operates an abstract visual-form system, storing information that remains relatively invariant across specific instances, producing abstracted types or classes of things; whereas the right hemisphere is aware of and remembers what it is that distinguishes specific instances of a type, one from another.[141] The right hemisphere deals preferentially with actually existing things, as they are encountered in the real world.[142] Because its language roots things in the context of the world, it is concerned with the *relations between* things. Thus the right hemisphere does have a vocabulary: it certainly has a lexicon of concrete nouns and imageable words which it shares with the left hemisphere; but, more than that, perceptual links between words are made primarily by the right hemisphere.[143]

In general abstract concepts and words, along with complex syntax, are left-hemisphere-dependent. But, once again, the right hemisphere's language inferiority depends to a significant degree on positive inhibition by the left hemisphere. If the left hemisphere is sufficiently distracted, or incapacitated, the right hemisphere turns out to have a more extensive vocabulary, including long, unusual and non-imageable words.[144]

The contextual versus abstract distinction is illustrated by the different use of symbols by each hemisphere. In one sense of the word, a symbol such as the rose is the focus or centre of an endless network of connotations which ramify through our physical and mental, personal and cultural, experience in life, literature and art: the strength of the symbol is in direct proportion to the power it has to convey an array of implicit meanings, which need to remain implicit to be powerful. In this it is like a joke that has several layers of meaning – explaining them destroys its power. The other sort of symbol could be exemplified by the red traffic light: its power lies in its use, and its use depends on a 1:1 mapping of the command 'stop' onto the colour red, which precludes ambiguity and has to be explicit. This sort of symbolic function is in the realm of the left hemisphere, while the first type belongs to the realm of the right.[145]

In fact a particularly important difference lies in the right hemisphere's capacity to understand metaphor, which I will discuss in the next chapter. The right temporal region appears to be essential for the integration of two seemingly unrelated concepts into a meaningful metaphoric expression.[146] Fascinatingly, however, clichéd metaphorical or non-literal expressions are dealt with in the left hemisphere: for such an expression, it is seeing the *literal* meaning of the hackneyed phrase that refreshes it, that requires insight (a bit like seeing a joke), and therefore in this case the non-salient (unfamiliar, because non-clichéd) meaning gets to be processed in the right hemisphere.[147]

INDIVIDUALS VERSUS CATEGORIES

At the same time it is the right hemisphere that has the capacity to distinguish specific examples within a category, rather than categories alone: it stores details to distinguish specific instances.[148] The right hemisphere presents individual, unique instances of things and individual, familiar, objects, where the left hemisphere re-presents categories of things, and generic, non-specific objects.[149] In keeping with this, the right hemisphere uses unique referents, where the left hemisphere uses non-unique referents.[150] It is with the right hemisphere that we distinguish individuals of all kinds, places as well as faces.[151] In fact it is precisely its capacity for holistic processing that enables the right hemisphere to recognise individuals.[152] Individuals are, after all, *Gestalt* wholes: that face, that voice, that gait, that sheer 'quiddity' of the person or thing, defying analysis into parts.

Where the left hemisphere is more concerned with abstract categories and types, the right hemisphere is more concerned with the uniqueness and individuality of each existing thing or being. The right hemisphere's role as what Ramachandran has described as the 'anomaly detector' might in fact be seen rather as an aspect of its preference for things as they actually exist (which are never entirely static or congruent – always changing, never the same) over abstract representation, in which things are made to be fixed and *equivalent*, types rather than individuals.

The right hemisphere is concerned with finer discriminations between things, whether living or non-living.[153] Indeed the cerebral principles of categorisation take this into account in a remarkable way. What is general and what is specific are, after all, relative. Thus characterising an object as a car, or a piece of fruit, is general; but as to what variety of fruit (pear), or in particular which kind of pear (comice), or what make of car (Citroën), particularly which model of Citroën (2CV), the matter is more specific.[154] As the more 'subordinate' categories become more individuated they are recognised by the right hemisphere, whereas the left hemisphere concerns itself with the more general, 'superordinate' categories.[155] In keeping with this, despite the well-known right-hemisphere advantage in dealing with the visuospatial, the left hemisphere is superior at identifying simple shapes and figures, which are easily categorised, whereas complex figures, being less typical, more individual, are better processed by the right hemisphere.[156]

In general, then, the left hemisphere's tendency is to classify, where the right hemisphere's is to identify individuals.[157] But of course both hemispheres are involved in recognition according to the grouping of experience – how could it be otherwise? Each hemisphere must be able to make sense of reality by revealing a shape to what otherwise would be an amorphous mass of impressions. But how they do this in practice differs in vital respects which have a direct impact on the nature of the world that each brings into being. The right hemisphere's version is more global and holistic, based on the recognition of similarity with an ideal exemplar, and on where this is positioned in the context of other examples, whereas the left hemisphere identifies single features that would place the object in a certain category in the abstract.[158] As a result, where the left hemisphere utilises abstract categories, the right hemisphere operates more effectively using specific exemplars.[159] Functional imaging of the brain shows that the left hemisphere takes a 'God's eye', or invariant view, in its representation of objects, where the right hemisphere uses stored 'real world' views in order to group experience.[160]

The systematic categorising process of the left hemisphere can sometimes begin to have a life of its own. I have mentioned that networks of dopaminergic neurones are more widely distributed in the left hemisphere than the right. Excess dopaminergic transmission, which occurs in, for example, amphetamine abuse and in high-dose treatment with anti-Parkinsonian drugs, can mimic aspects of schizophrenia because it tends to favour the left hemisphere over the right. In such circumstances, a sort of freewheeling need to collect and categorise, coupled with the left hemisphere's over-riding concern with getting and making, is some-times seen, known as 'punding' – the mechanical and repetitive assembling and disassembling of machines, collecting and categorising of inanimate objects, such as torches, TVs, stones, boxes, and so on.[161] I once had a patient with schizo-phrenia who arranged and rearranged symmetrical structures of carefully collected commercial packaging: the resultant 'sculptures' filled his living room. On one occasion, after he had spent the weekend at his flat, I asked him how he had got on. He replied dryly: 'I moved some things to the right' – a response that has considerable interest in view of the left hemisphere's strong bias to attend to the right side of space, and disattend to the left (there is an asymmetry of hemi-spheric function in schizophrenia, with an abnormal but overactive left hemi-sphere compared with the right). The passion for collecting and organising is seen in other conditions, of course, including Asperger's syndrome, which also shows right-hemisphere deficits.

Don't think, though, that this categorising drive has a life of its own only in people who we regard as ill. It's at work all the time in all of us. As Henry Maudsley put it: we have

> a sufficiently strong propensity not only to make divisions in knowledge where there are none in nature, and then to impose the divisions on nature, making the reality thus conformable to the idea, but to go further, and to convert the gener-alisations made from observation into positive entities, permitting for the future these artificial creations to tyrannise over the understanding.[162]

THE DIFFERENCES IN SAMENESS

The contrast between the differing world views of the two hemispheres is brought into focus in a remarkable way by the issue of sameness and difference. Again, seeing their handling of these as just different 'comparator functions in informa-tion processing' misses the point. They are not 'functions' within a world we already know to have a certain (mechanical) structure: they are themselves part of the foundations of the world in which we try to understand them.

An individual could be seen as a little universe, an infinite number of serial moments, experiences and perceptions (as the left hemisphere would see it), which are of course (at least as far as the right hemisphere is concerned) a single whole. Your wife or husband who left the house this morning may be in a different mood or have a different haircut by the evening, but this doesn't present a problem of identification, because these separate slices of experience, these separate frames of the film, as the left hemisphere would see it, are not really separate at all – they are the different aspects of one unique whole. But with certain right-hemisphere deficits, the capacity for seeing the whole is lost, and subjects start to believe they are dealing with different people. They may develop the belief that a person they know very well is actually being 're-presented' by an impostor, a condition known, after its first describer, as Capgras syndrome.[163] Small perceptual changes seem to suggest a wholly different entity, not just a new bit of information that needs to be integrated into the whole: the significance of the part, in this sense, outweighs the pull of the whole.

Fascinatingly, right-hemisphere deficit syndromes can result in something which looks like the opposite: the belief that someone one knows is duplicated in different places at different times. Not in other words the division of a unique whole, but the mass reproduction of one. 'Something personal and usually alive has been duplicated as if it were a mere item on an assembly line,' according to John Cutting, with loss of uniqueness and familiarity.[164] A patient of mine accused her husband of two-timing because she believed she saw him on several occasions with different women while she was out in the town shopping, at times when she knew he should have been at work. This curious condition is called Fregoli syndrome, after an Italian quick-change artist of the early 1900s.[165] Here the fine discrimination of individuals supplied by the right hemisphere is lost, and different individuals are lumped together and again 're-presented' in a category.[166] It is not the opposite of the Capgras syndrome, but a natural consequence of the same cause: a loss of the sense of a unique whole. Such 'delusional misidentification' applies not only to people, but to objects: another patient of mine began a vendetta against someone who, she believed, had entered her bedroom and subtly changed all her clothes for copies of a slightly inferior quality. It can even apply to places: one individual held that there were eight 'impostor' cities, duplicating his own, and said he had spent the last eight years wandering between them, without finding the real one. There were also eight duplicates of his wife and children, each duplicate living in a separate duplicate city with a double of the patient.[167]

Overall, then, and in keeping with the principle that it is not *what* is done, but *how* it is done, that distinguishes the two hemispheres, one cannot say that one hemisphere deals with single items ('units'), and the other with aggregates. Both deal with 'units' and both deal with aggregates. Thus the right sees individual entities (units), and it sees them as belonging in a contextual whole (an aggregate), from which they are not divided. By contrast the left sees parts (units), which go to make up a something which it recognises by the category to which it belongs (an aggregate). However, the relationship between the smaller unit and the broader aggregate in either case is profoundly different: as is the mode of attention to the world with which it is associated.

THE PERSONAL VERSUS THE IMPERSONAL

Because the right hemisphere sees nothing in the abstract, but always appreciates things in their context, it is interested in the personal, by contrast with the left hemisphere, which has more affinity for the abstract or impersonal.[168] The right hemisphere's view of the world in general is construed according to what is of concern to it, not according to objective impersonal categories, and therefore has a personal quality. This is both its strength and its weakness in relation to the left hemisphere. It deals preferentially with whatever is approaching it, drawing near, into relationship with it.[169] The right temporal lobe deals preferentially with memory of a personal or emotionally charged nature, what is called episodic memory, where the left temporal lobe is more concerned with memory for facts that are 'in the public domain'.[170] Interestingly the right hemisphere's concern with the personal past may be directly linked to something else we will come to, its tendency towards feelings of sadness.[171]

THE LIVING VERSUS THE NON-LIVING

The great neurologist François Lhermitte drew attention thirty-five years ago to an essential difference between the hemispheres, when he described a case which confirmed that the right hemisphere is more concerned with living individuals than man-made objects.[172] This flows naturally from its interest in whatever it is that exists apart from ourselves, and its capacity for empathy – as well as from its capacity to see the whole, where the left hemisphere sees an agglomerate of parts: there is an intuitive relationship between cutting things up and depriving them of life. It is the left hemisphere alone that codes for non-living things,[173] while both hemispheres code for living things, perhaps because the living can be seen as independent individuals (right hemisphere) or as objects of use, prey, 'things', and so on (left hemisphere).[174] However, at least one study has found a clean divide between the hemispheres, the left coding for the non-living, and the right for the living, regardless of the task.[175] Another study concluded that there are 'different brain networks subserving the identification of living and nonliving entities'.[176] Food, however, and musical instruments, presumably because of the intimate way in which they take part in the life of the body, sort with the living rather than the non-living. The body as such is a right-hemisphere entity, whereas body 'parts' are the province of the left hemisphere.[177] In fact when the right hemisphere is no longer available to bring the left side of the body into being, the left hemisphere may substitute only a mechanical structure of inanimate parts down that side. One patient described by Ehrenwald reported that, following a right-hemisphere stroke,

'where the left half of his chest, abdomen and stomach should be, he's got only a wooden plank.' It goes right down to his anus, and is divided into compartments by transverse planks . . . food doesn't follow the usual path from the stomach through the intestines, 'it gets sucked into the compartments of this scaffolding and it falls through the hole at the bottom of the framework'. All this is only on the left side. On the right the organs are all perfectly in place.[178]

And Ehrenwald records that it was not just a delusional *idea*, but a percept: he could *see and feel* the plank.

Not only does the right hemisphere have an affinity with whatever is living, but the left hemisphere has an equal affinity for what is mechanical. The left hemisphere's principal concern is utility. It is interested in what it has made, and in the world as a resource to be used. It is therefore natural that it has a particular affinity for words and concepts for tools, man-made things, mechanisms and whatever is not alive. The left hemisphere codes for tools and machines.[179] References to tools and actions of grasping activate the left hemisphere *even in left-handers*, despite the fact that they habitually use the right hemisphere/left hand to grasp objects and use tools in daily life. And right-hemisphere damage leaves the ability to use simple tools unaltered, whereas left-hemisphere damage renders the sufferer incapable of using a hammer and nail, or a key and a padlock. However, right-hemisphere damage particularly impairs naturalistic actions involving a sequence of steps – for example, making a cup of coffee or wrapping a present.[180]

> Could one go so far as to say that the left side represents science and the right side nature? Although I have myself expressed scepticism over the popular dichotomies associated with the two sides of the brain, I think there is a case for supposing that the left side represents the fruits of human invention, including language, manufacture and a partwise way of representing objects.[181]

So writes Michael Corballis, in the context of a tribute to Roger Sperry, both major contributors to our understanding of the hemispheres, and both alike sceptics of the 'popular dichotomies'. He draws attention to the affinity of the left hemisphere for everything it has itself made ('the fruits of human invention') in contrast to the affinity of the right hemisphere for what exists before and after – and beyond – ourselves, namely nature. I would not accept the term 'science', in the true sense of the word, as applying to the left hemisphere; much of the spirit of empiricism comes from the right hemisphere, as I will suggest when considering scientific discovery during the period of the Renaissance, and science does not always proceed by predictable paths – it is more fortuitous, less controlled, than the left hemisphere thinks, and involves open awareness of what is.[182] Perhaps Corballis would not accept it either, as he does not answer his own question. But if one were to substitute the word 'mechanism' – and, alas, so much science can be mechanistic – I would be in complete agreement.

The right temporal region appears to have areas not only specific for living things, but additionally for all that is specifically human.[183] Such judgments of 'humanness' are separate from the right hemisphere's superior ability to recognise faces.[184]

The right hemisphere prioritises whatever actually *is*, and what concerns us. It prefers existing things, real scenes and stimuli that can be made sense of in terms of the lived world, whatever it is that has meaning and value for us as human beings.[185] It is more able to assimilate information from the environment,[186] without automatically responding to it, and, possibly as a result, the developing right hemisphere is more sensitive to environmental influences.[187]

At the same time the left hemisphere is more at home dealing with distorted, non-realistic, fantastic – ultimately artificial – images.[188] This may be because they invite analysis by parts, rather than as a whole. But it does appear that the left hemisphere has a positive bias towards whatever is bizarre, meaningless or non-existent,[189] though the data here are particularly hard to interpret because most studies have not sufficiently distinguished confounding elements.[190]

The fact that, while things are still 'present' in their newness, as individually existing entities – not 're-presented' as representatives of a category – they belong to the right hemisphere, can be seen in the light of this distinction between the living and the non-living, since as they become over-familiar, inauthentic and therefore *lifeless*, they pass to the left hemisphere.

Because of the right hemisphere's openness to the interconnectedness of things, it is interested in others as individuals, and in how we relate to them. It is the mediator of empathic identification.[191] If I imagine myself in pain I use both hemispheres, but your pain is in my right hemisphere.[192] The same neurones in the right anterior cingulate cortex, an area known to be associated with the appreciation of pain, show activity whether we ourselves are hurt or we witness someone else undergoing a similar painful experience.[193] 'Self-awareness, empathy, identification with others, and more generally inter-subjective processes, are largely dependent upon . . . right hemisphere resources.'[194] When we put ourselves in others' shoes, we are using the right inferior parietal lobe, and the right lateral prefrontal cortex, which is involved in inhibiting the automatic tendency to espouse one's own point of view.[195] In circumstances of right-hemisphere activation, subjects are more favourably disposed towards others and more readily convinced by arguments in favour of positions that they have not previously supported.[196]

In general the right hemisphere is critical for making attributions of the content, emotional or otherwise, of another's mind, and particularly in respect of the affective state of another individual.[197] According to Simon Baron-Cohen, the right hemisphere is engaged even in listening to words describing the mind, such as 'think' and 'imagine'.[198] But the right hemisphere will empathise with, identify with, and aim to imitate only what it knows to be another living being, rather than a mechanism – a point of interest in view of the roles we have seen the two hemispheres play in the division of the world into the animate and the inanimate.[199] When we look at either a real hand or a 'virtual reality' hand grasping an object, we automatically activate the appropriate left-hemisphere areas, as if we too were grasping – but, strikingly, only in the case of the real, living hand do regions in the right temporoparietal area become activated.[200] We have an unconscious, involuntary urge to imitate someone we are watching carrying out an action – so much so that, especially if it's something we've practised ourselves, the empathic entrainment is actually stronger than the voluntary desire to do something we'd like to see happen. But this is true only if we think it is a real person that's acting. If we think it's a computer, we just are not engaged.[201]

The right hemisphere plays an important role in what is known as 'theory of mind', a capacity to put oneself in another's position and see what is going on in that person's mind.[202] This capacity emerges in primates along with self-recognition and self-awareness, and is closely linked to it.[203] It is a capacity that children do not acquire fully until the age of four (though elements are probably present from 12 to 18 months), and which autistic children never acquire.[204] The classic test for theory of mind shows two dolls, Sally and Anne, playing with a marble. They put it away in a box, and leave the room. While Sally is out, Anne returns, plays with the marble and puts it away in a different box. The question is: 'When Sally returns, where will she look for the marble?' Those without capacity for theory of mind indicate the new box where they know the marble to be, not the original one where Sally last saw it placed.[205]

The right hemisphere has by far the preponderance of emotional under-standing.[206] It is the mediator of social behaviour.[207] In the absence of the right hemisphere, the left hemisphere is unconcerned about others and their feelings: 'social intercourse is conducted with a blanket disregard for the feelings, wishes, needs and expectations of others.'[208] Patients with right frontal deficits, but not left frontal deficits, suffer a change of personality whereby they become incapable of empathy.[209]

Considerable interest has been raised by the discovery that there are neurones, nicknamed 'mirror neurones', which are active both when we do something and when we watch others do it.[210] Physiological and behavioural evidence indicated that the left pars opercularis (part of Broca's area), the area of the frontal lobe crit-ical for speech production, contains mirror neurones which are involved in the imitation of finger movements.[211] So absorbing was this finding – which is indeed highly significant, and which I will discuss in the next chapter – that it was until recently thought that mirror neurones were a speciality of the human left hemi-sphere, and their existence has even been put forward as a reason for language's having developed in the left hemisphere, rather than the right.[212] But that seems a bit like putting the cart before the horse, especially since both the left and right pars opercularis equally have mirror neurones, and both hemispheres contribute to the processing of watching and imitating.[213] In fact, which hemisphere is involved on any one occasion has not only to do with what and where the action is that we are copying, but also with how instrumental ('object-directed') that action is. Such actions excite the left hemisphere's system. On the other hand, the predominant contribution to the imitation of actions that are non-instrumental comes from the *right* temporal and frontal lobes.[214]

Mirror neurones are a means of understanding another's intentions, amongst other things, and are not just about copying actions.[215] They form part of our capacity to understand others and empathise with them. For instance, in imitating other people's facial expressions, it is the right pars opercularis, with its mirror neurones, which is the critically important area; and it is this area that appears to be silent in autistic children when carrying out such a task.[216]

EMOTIONAL ASYMMETRY

The affinity of the right hemisphere with emotions and the bodily experience of them is reflected in a range of functional asymmetries. Part of the right frontal pole of the brain, the so-called orbitofrontal cortex of the right hemisphere, is essential to emotional understanding and regulation.[217] It is also where the emotional signif-icance of events is consciously appreciated.[218] The right hemisphere is in general more intimately connected with the limbic system, an ancient subcortical system that is involved in the experience of emotions of all kinds, and with other subcor-tical structures, than is the left hemisphere.[219] The right frontal pole also regulates the hypothalamic-pituitary axis, which is the neuroendocrine interface between the body and emotion,[220] and is essential to our subjective appreciation of the body's physiological condition.[221] It is intimately connected with the unconscious and automatic systems for regulating the body and its level of arousal, for example through the autonomic control of heart rate or neuroendocrine function.[222] As a consequence it is also the right frontotemporal cortex that exerts *inhibitory* control over emotional arousal.[223]

Although there has been much debate about the particular emotional timbre of each hemisphere (of which more shortly), there is evidence that in all forms of emotional perception, regardless of the type of emotion, and in most forms of expression, the right hemisphere is dominant.[224]

EMOTIONAL RECEPTIVITY

It is the right hemisphere that identifies emotional expression: it is faster and more accurate than the left hemisphere in discriminating facial expression of emotion.[225] Specifically the right superior temporal sulcus appears to be involved in recognition of facial emotion.[226] The right hemisphere is the locus of interpretation, not only of facial expression, but of prosody (vocal intonation) and gesture.[227] The superiority for emotional perception is in addition to, and distinct from, the right parietal lobe's known superiority for visuospatial interpretation.[228] Those with right-hemisphere damage have difficulty understanding emotional intonation or implication.[229]

Curiously it seems that the left hemisphere reads emotions by interpreting the lower part of the face. Though the left hemisphere can understand emotional display, it looks not at the eyes, even when directed to do so, but at the mouth.[230] The right hemisphere alone seems to be capable of understanding the more subtle information that comes from the eyes. Empathy is not something one reads in the lower face, where relatively blunt messages – friend or foe – tend to be conveyed. A patient of mine with a right temporoparietal deficit asked me 'What's all this with the eyes?' When I asked what she meant, she explained that she had noticed people apparently communicating coded messages with their eyes, but could not understand what they were, presumably because the part of her brain that would have interpreted it was no longer functioning – further grounds for paranoia in those who have to rely on their left hemisphere to constitute the world.

When it comes to the understanding (and expression) of emotion in language, again, despite left-hemisphere preponderance for language, the right hemisphere is superior.[231] Emotional language may be possible even when speech is lost through a left-hemisphere stroke.[232] It is the right hemisphere that understands the emotional or the humorous aspect of a narrative.[233] Memory for emotional language is in the right hemisphere.[234] Ultimately there is clear evidence that when it comes to recognising emotion, whatever it may be, whether it is expressed in language or through facial expression, it is the right hemisphere on which we principally rely.[235]

The face is the common mediator of two of the most significant aspects of the right hemisphere's world: the uniqueness of the individual and the communication of feeling. The right hemisphere is involved in identifying not just the facial expression of emotion, but the emotion as it relates to an individual face.[236] This begins in children and is the principle medium for the child's growing sense of identity, through interaction with the mother's face.[237] It is also in the right parietotemporal cortex that the child appreciates the mother's voice.[238]

Because of its concern with our embodied selves, our feelings, and the feelings and intentions of others, as well as their uniqueness, it could be anticipated that it is through the right hemisphere that emotional faces are stored in memory.[239] In fact it is the right hemisphere that is principally responsible for our ability to identify and remember faces at all.[240] The capacity would seem to us quite extraordinary if we were not so close to it and so familiar with it. Faces are broadly similar complex three-dimensional structures that have to be distinguished from one another by often minutely differing interrelations amongst the 'parts' of the whole (which, nonetheless, can change with facial expression from second to second), and individually discriminated in differing orientations, at varying distances, in different lighting conditions, often while moving, and in a fraction of a second. It is amazing that we can do it at all. An inability to recognise faces is called prosopagnosia, and follows right-hemisphere lesions.[241]

What the right hemisphere crucially appears to be able to do here is to see the 'configurational' aspects of the whole. In prosopagnosia, this capacity is lacking.[242] In fact, in its absence the left hemisphere has to rely on the laborious process of trying to put the face together from the parts, with the paradoxical effect that it may find it no easier to recognise a face the right way up than upside down, and may even find it easier upside down, because such views force a concentration on the parts.[243]

There is a critical role here for the right middle fusiform gyrus,[244] but latterly it has become clear that the network underlying facial recognition is broadly distributed in the right hemisphere.[245] Right-brain-damaged patients are not only poorer at identifying faces, compared with left-brain-damaged patients, but are poor at assessing such features as the age of a face with which they are not familiar.[246] The right hemisphere is pre-eminent, not only in identifying an individual human face, and in interpreting its emotional expression, but in appreciating its age, sex, and attractiveness.[247]

It was one of Wigan's achievements to have recognised prosopagnosia in 1844,[248] but it took another hundred years for it to be given a name. In 1947 Joachim Bodamer described a patient who reported that faces seemed to him 'strangely flat, white with emphatic dark eyes, as if made from a flat surface, like white oval plates, all alike'.[249] The lack of depth is very interesting for reasons I will come to. Prosopagnosia was linked to right-hemisphere lesions by Sergent and Villemure, who recognised that there was 'an inability to combine the component features into a configurational facial representation that would uniquely define each face'.[250] Putting together the parts could not achieve a unique whole.

It is also remarkable that once again there is a specific defect for recognition of eyes. In some cases, presumably because the left hemisphere, with its interest in the lower part of the face, steps into the breach, subjects with partial prosopagnosia following a right-hemisphere lesion have been able to glean evidence from the mouth area, but were quite unable to use information from the eyes.[251]

The superiority of the right hemisphere for recognising faces is yet another lateralised difference that goes a considerable way down the evolutionary chain – for example, it is even present, believe it or not, in sheep, who can remember individual human and sheep faces after a gap of years, again relying principally on the right hemisphere.[252]

EMOTIONAL EXPRESSIVITY

As well as emotional recognition, the right hemisphere plays a vital role in emotional expression,[253] via the face or the prosody of the voice.[254] The right frontal lobe is of critical importance for emotional expression of virtually every kind through the face and body posture.[255] The one exception to the right hemisphere superiority for the expression of emotion is anger.[256] Anger is robustly connected with left frontal activation.[257] Aggression is motivating and dopamine plays a crucial role in the rewards it offers.[258]

Autistic children, who cannot understand social language, irony and metaphor, and lack capacity for empathy – all mediated by the right frontal region – lack prosodic skill, the ability to convey meaning and feeling through intonation and inflection of the voice.[259]

It is the right hemisphere that mediates spontaneous facial expressions in reaction to humour or other emotions, including smiling and laughter.[260] It is also the right hemisphere that is responsible for the peculiarly human ability to express sadness through tears.[261]

The left half of the face (or 'hemiface'), which is controlled by the right hemisphere, is more involved in emotional expression.[262] Emotions are also more strongly perceived when expressed by the left hemiface:[263] and, intriguingly, the left hemiface is also larger than the right in right-handers.[264] Although facial expression of emotion is a human universal, there are, inevitably, differences in facial expression across cultures; and because of the very fact that the left hemiface displays more complex emotional information, being able to convey mixed feelings, it seems that it may be easier in cross-cultural situations for people to read the relatively simple information conveyed by the *right* hemiface.[265]

This specialisation of the right hemisphere for emotion is a process which begins in pre-human species: chimpanzees and some other non-human primates show, just as we do, right-hemisphere specialisation for facial expression of emotions.[266]

The right hemisphere's affinity for both the perception and expression of emotion appears to be confirmed by the strong universal tendency to cradle infants with their faces to the left, so that they fall within the principal domain of attention of the adult's right hemisphere, and they are exposed to the adult's own more emotionally expressive left hemiface.[267] This preference is known to go back at least 2,000–4,000 years,[268] and even left-handed mothers display the leftward cradling bias.[269] In fact even chimpanzees and gorillas show the same leftward bias for cradling their infants.[270]

DIFFERENCES IN EMOTIONAL AFFINITY

It is the right hemisphere which gives emotional *value* to what is seen, a topic I will return to later, in considering the way in which the hemispheres influence the meaning we find in the experiential world.[271] In the absence of a functioning right hemisphere our world and our selves become emotionally impoverished. The right frontal lobe plays a supremely important part in personality – in who we fundamentally are.[272]

Nonetheless the left hemisphere does play a role in the understanding and expression of emotion. What are the differences?

It seems, for a start, that the left hemisphere specialises in more superficial, social emotions, by contrast with the right hemisphere, which is more directly in touch with primary-process emotionality.[273] Related to this, the left hemisphere may also be more involved in conscious representation of emotion: willed, or forced, emotional expressions, once again principally of the mouth area, are controlled by the left hemisphere.[274] A study on conscious and unconscious processing of emotional facial expression has suggested that the left but not the right amygdala is associated with explicit *representational* content of the observed emotion, whereas the right amygdala is more closely involved with unconscious emotional processing.[275]

It has to be said that, though it is involved with emotion, the left hemisphere remains, by comparison with the right, emotionally relatively neutral,[276] something which is evidenced by its affinity for 'non-emotional', abstract paintings.[277] Emotional stimuli are not incorporated into mood – not adopted personally – when offered to the left hemisphere rather than the right.[278] The whole business seems more conscious, more willed, more deliberate, and that is in keeping with the left hemisphere's need to influence and manipulate, as well as its role in re-presenting experience. In alexithymia, a condition of lack of awareness or capacity to express emotional arousal in words, the problem arises from an inability of the emotionally aware right hemisphere, which can be shown to be experiencing emotional arousal, to communicate it to the left hemisphere.[279]

The literature also suggests that there may be differences in the emotional timbre of the hemispheres, and this is a complex area.[280] Old ideas that the right hemisphere was concerned with so-called 'negative' emotions and the left hemisphere with 'positive' emotions are not substantiated; a prevailing theory is that right-hemisphere emotions are those of 'withdrawal', and left-hemisphere emotions those of 'approach'. Neither seems to me very satisfactory. Some broad agreement exists that the right hemisphere is more in tune with sadness, and less with anger, than the left hemisphere;[281] and that what we call 'positive' emotions rely on both.[282] While the right hemisphere is associated with positive affect in many cases,[283] and may even be the principle source of pleasurable experience,[284] it is in general the left hemisphere that tends to take a more optimistic view of the self and the future.[285] In fact there is evidence, which I shall come to, that it may take an unwarrantedly optimistic view. Once again the right hemisphere's range is more inclusive (it can deal with either), and the left hemisphere's more partial. It seems to me a possibility that those emotions which are related to bonding and empathy, whether we call them 'positive' or 'negative', are preferentially treated by the right hemisphere, as one would expect: such stimuli capture right-hemisphere attention.[286] By the same token, those to do with competition, rivalry and individual self-belief, positive or negative, would be preferentially treated by the left hemisphere.[287]

Another thought-provoking detail about sadness and the right hemisphere involves the perception of colour. Brain regions involved in *conscious identification* of colour are probably left-sided, perhaps because it involves a process of categorisation and naming;[288] however, it would appear that the *perception* of colour in mental imagery under normal circumstances activates only the right fusiform area, not the left,[289] and imaging studies, lesion studies and neuropsychological testing all suggest that the right hemisphere is more attuned to colour discrimination and perception.[290] Within this, though, there are hints that the right hemisphere prefers the colour green and the left hemisphere prefers the colour red (as the left hemisphere may prefer horizontal orientation, and the right hemisphere vertical – a point I shall return to in considering the origins of written language in Chapter 8).[291] The colour green has traditionally been associated not just with nature, innocence and jealousy but with – melancholy: 'She pined in thought, / And with a green and yellow melancholy / She sat like Patience on a monument, / Smiling at grief'.[292]

Is there some connection between the melancholy tendencies of the right hemisphere and the mediaeval belief that the left side of the body was dominated by black bile? Black bile was, of course, associated with melancholy (literally, Greek *melan-*, black + *chole*, bile) and was thought to be produced by the spleen, a left-sided organ. For the same reasons the term *spleen* itself was, from the fourteenth century to the seventeenth century, applied to melancholy; though, as if intuiting that melancholy, passion, and sense of humour all came from the same place (in fact the right hemisphere, associated with the left side of the body), 'spleen' could also refer to each or any of these.

The issue of the relationship between depressive illness and the right hemisphere is complex. Here more than anywhere one has to take into account the influence of the anterior–posterior ('front–back') axis of the brain, as well as the right–left axis. It seems that the polarity of emotional timbre between the two hemispheres is specifically tied to the most highly and lately evolved, most 'human' parts of the brain, the frontal lobes. Left anterior lesions are associated with depression, and right anterior lesions associated with 'undue cheerfulness'.[293] The closer the left-hemisphere lesion lies to the frontal pole, the greater the depressive symptomatology.[294] For those with right-hemisphere lesions the converse is true: the more caudal (the further back) the lesion, the greater the chance of depression.[295] This confluence of evidence suggests that the right frontal pole has a depressive stance compared with either the left frontal pole or its own parieto-occipital cortex.[296] Depression *per se* is probably associated with reduced right posterior activity in addition to increased right frontal activity in most cases,[297] although as one might predict threat monitoring is a right-posterior activity.[298] There is evidence of left-hemisphere over-activity in mania,[299] the polar opposite of depression, and this may also obtain in other mammals.[300]

Lesion studies confirm the relationship between activity of the right frontal lobe and depression,[301] and neuroimaging studies also suggest a correlation between left frontal hypofunction and depression.[302] Greater right than left activation is related to depressed mood.[303] Specifically increased electrical activity in the right-prefrontal region is a marker of depression,[304] and the majority of EEG studies also confirm left frontal hypoactivation.[305] In normal subjects relative right-sided EEG activation at rest predicts greater experience of 'negative' affect: subjects with relatively greater left-frontal activation at rest 'may be able quickly to terminate their reaction, while subjects with right-frontal activation may lack the requisite coping skills to minimise the duration of the negative affective response'.[306] Depressives relatively favour the left visual field and make more eye movements to the left in ways that have been validated to suggest right-hemisphere activation.[307]

Confirmatory evidence comes from treatment for depression. The decreased left anterior functioning found in depression remits, as expected, with the illness. Where the blood flow in the left anterior frontal region is initially more sharply decreased, this predicts a better response to antidepressants.[308] Depression is less likely to resolve or respond to treatment where there are irreversible lesions in the left hemisphere (but not other brain areas).[309]

There is also evidence that the types of depression experienced in right posterior hypoactivity are different from those experienced in left frontal hypoactivity, in ways which are in keeping with the views of the worlds that the two hemispheres bring into being. Thus depression resulting from damage to the right hemisphere has more of indifference or apathy – a global, vague lifelessness – in contrast to the anxious, disturbed depression, accompanied by biological features, resulting from lesions to the left hemisphere.[310] The sort of anxiety that accompanies depressed mood, and could be induced by reading a sad narrative, is known as anxious arousal, and shows greater lateralisation to the right hemisphere. By contrast anxious apprehension, based as it is on a fear of uncertainty and lack of control – preoccupations of the left hemisphere – is accompanied by preferential left hemisphere activation.[311]

In interpreting all neuroimaging studies of emotion, one should bear in mind the strictures of Jaak Panksepp, probably the world's most distinguished neuroscientist of affect and emotion, that we are more likely to be imaging the areas associated with the cognitive content of an affective state than those associated with the pre-cognitive affective state itself.[312]

REASON VERSUS RATIONALITY

Despite the right hemisphere's overwhelmingly important role in emotion, the popular stereotype that the left hemisphere has a monopoly on reason, like the view that it has a monopoly on language, is mistaken. As always it is a question not of 'what', but of 'in what way'.

In fact reasoning is of different kinds, and though linear, sequential argument is clearly better executed by the left hemisphere, some types of reasoning, including deduction, and some types of mathematical reasoning, are mainly dependent on the right hemisphere. More explicit reasoning is underwritten by the left hemisphere, less explicit reasoning (such as is often involved in problem solving, including scientific and mathematical problem solving) by the right hemisphere.[313] There is a relation between the pleasurable 'aha!' phenomenon of insight and the right amygdala, which mediates interactions between emotions and higher frontal cognitive function.[314] In fact an extensive body of research now indicates that insight, whether mathematical or verbal, the sort of problem solving that happens when we are, precisely, not concentrating on it, is associated with activation in the right hemisphere, mainly in the right anterior temporal area, specifically in the right anterior superior temporal gyrus, though where there are high levels of restructuring involved there is also activity in the right prefrontal cortex.[315] Insight is also a perception of the previous incongruity of one's assumptions, which links it to the right hemisphere's capacity for detecting an anomaly.

Problem solving, making reasonable deductions, and making judgments may become harder if we become conscious of the process. Thus rendering one's thought processes explicit, or analysing a judgment, may actually impair performance, because it encourages the left hemisphere's focus on the explicit, superficial structure of the problem.[316]

The evidence is that mathematical skills are divided between the hemispheres. Some studies have shown mathematical performance to be impaired worse in children[317] and in adults[318] with left-hemisphere, than with right-hemisphere, damage. However, in another study left-hemisphere-damaged children were significantly poorer only at written language, while right-hemisphere-damaged children performed worse on written language, reading and maths.[319] The right hemisphere clearly does play a role in arithmetical calculations,[320] and, in general, mathematical calculations activate more strongly on the right.[321] Addition and subtraction activate the right parietal lobe, whereas multiplication activates verbal remembrance of 'times tables' in the left hemisphere.[322] Calculating prodigies appear to use more right-hemisphere-dependent strategies, making use of episodic memory.[323]

The right hemisphere appears to be crucially involved in the process of deductive reasoning, a process which is independent not only of left-hemisphere language areas, but also of right-hemisphere visuospatial areas: for example, even in the absence of any correlated visual input (e.g. where problems are presented acoustically via headphones), different types of reasoning problems evoke activity in the right superior parietal cortex, and bilaterally in the precuneus.[324] That the precuneus is involved is in itself interesting, because the precuneus, a centre that lies deep inside the parietal lobe, is deeply connected both with emotion – it forms part of the limbic system – and the sense of the self. It is one of the brain's most consistently 'hot' spots, with a high resting metabolic rate, and it goes quiet in altered states of consciousness where the sense of self is no longer active, such as sleep, anaesthesia and vegetative states. It seems to play an important role in episodic memory, which is critical for personal identity, and in adopting the first person perspective.[325] And in fact deductive logic is also associated with the right ventromedial prefrontal area of the brain, an area known to be devoted to emotion and feeling.[326] Seeing what follows from a social, emotional understanding of the situation in which one finds oneself in the real world is at least as important, then, as seeing what follows from an abstract proposition.

One finding that might seem at first sight unexpected, but the full significance of which will become apparent only in the next chapter, is that it is the right hemisphere that has the intuitive sense of numbers and their relative size. However, the sense is approximate and does not have precision. The left hemisphere, by contrast, has precision, but it has no intuitive sense of what it is actually doing, other than following rules and manipulating symbols.[327] If one acquires a computational skill leading to a precise answer, it will be most evident in the language in which it was acquired: there is no such language effect in relation to inexact estimation, the intuitive sense of size.[328]

It is worth considering that numbers can either signify *absolutes* – a quantifiable amount, as in statistics – which would suggest an affinity with the left hemisphere, or signify *relations*, which would suggest an affinity with the right hemisphere. For Pythagoras, it was this regularity of proportion or relationship, rather than number in any absolute sense, that underpinned music and beauty – the music of the spheres, the natural harmony of the universe.

THE TWIN BODIES

Emotion is inseparable from the body in which it is felt, and emotion is also the basis for our engagement with the world. Social understanding in the sense of empathic connection, as well as understanding how others feel, what they mean not only by what they say in context, as we have seen, but by their facial expressions, their 'body language' and tone of voice – all this is made possible by the right hemisphere.

In keeping with its capacity for emotion, and its predisposition to understand mental experience within the context of the body, rather than abstracting it, the right hemisphere is deeply connected to the self as *embodied*. Although each side of the brain has both motor and sensory connections with the opposite side of the body, we know that the left hemisphere carries an image only of the contralateral (right) side of the body – when the right hemisphere is incapacitated, the left part of the individual's body virtually ceases to exist for that person. It is only the right parietal lobe that has a whole body image.[329] Importantly this body image is not just a picture. It is not a representation (as it would be if it were in the left hemisphere), or just the sum of our bodily perceptions, or something imagined, but a living image, intimately linked to activity in the world – an essentially affective experience.[330] Which is why disturbances in it lead to profoundly disturbing illnesses, such as body dysmorphia and anorexia nervosa.[331]

More than this, the right and left hemispheres see the body in different ways. The right hemisphere, as one can tell from the fascinating changes that occur after unilateral brain damage, is responsible for our sense of the body as something we 'live', something that is part of our identity, and which is, if I can put it that way, the phase of intersection between our selves and the world at large. For the left hemisphere, by contrast, the body is something from which we are relatively detached, a thing in the world, like other things (*en soi*, rather than *pour soi*, to use Sartre's terms), devitalised, a 'corpse'.[332] As Gabriel Marcel puts it, it is sometimes as if I *am* my body, sometimes as if I *have* a body.[333] Some languages, such as German, see the body in these two senses as so distinct that they have different words for them: *Leib* for the first, *Körper* for the second. Incidentally the German word *Körper*, related to the English 'corpse', came into the language through medicine and theology (the body there being the element left when the soul departed); the word *Leib*, related to *leben/lebendig* (English 'live/alive') referred to the 'bodies' that survived a battle – those who were not *Körper*. In fact even more striking is that the Greek word which subsequently came to indicate the body considered separately from the person, *sōma*, is never used in Homer to refer to the living body, only to a corpse.[334]

The left hemisphere appears to see the body as an assemblage of parts: remember the patient of Ehrenwald's, whose body became rectilinear, compartmentalised, inanimate and hollow (an assemblage of scaffolding) following a right-hemisphere stroke. If the right hemisphere is not functioning properly, the left hemisphere may actually deny having anything to do with a body part that does not seem to be working according to the left hemisphere's instructions. Patients will report that the hand 'doesn't belong to me' or even that it belongs to the person in the next bed, or speak of it as if made of plastic.[335] One patient complained that there was a dead hand in his bed. A male patient thought the arm must belong to a woman in bed with him; a white woman thought hers belonged to 'un petit nègre' in bed with her; another complained that there was a child in the bed, on his left. Yet another was convinced that the nurses had bundled up his arm with the dirty laundry and sent it away to be washed.[336]

One patient believed quite firmly that the paralysed arm belonged to her mother, though in all other respects her conversation was quite normal.[337] The process in her case was, typically, reversed by inhibiting the left hemisphere, by a process called vestibular stimulation:

Examiner: Whose arm is this?
AR (patient): It's not mine.
Examiner: Whose is it?
AR: It's my mother's.
Examiner: How on earth does it happen to be here?
AR: I don't know. I found it in my bed.
Examiner: How long has it been there?
AR: Since the first day. Feel, it's warmer than mine. The other day too, when the weather was colder, it was warmer than mine.

Examiner:	So where is your left arm?
AR:	(*makes an indefinite gesture forwards*) It's under there.
	Immediately after vestibular stimulation [inhibiting the left hemi-sphere], *the examiner asks the patient to show her the patient's left arm.*
AR:	(*points to her own left arm*) Here it is.
Examiner:	(*raises the patient's left arm*) Is this arm yours?
AR:	Why, yes.
Examiner:	Where is your mother's arm?
AR:	(*hesitates*) It is somewhere about.
Examiner:	Where exactly?
AR:	I don't know. Perhaps here, under the bedclothes. (*She looks to her right, under the bedclothes.*)
	Two hours after vestibular stimulation AR is questioned again by the examiner.
Examiner:	(*points to the patient's left arm*) Whose arm is this?
AR:	It's my mother's. It's warmer.
Examiner:	Where is your left arm?
	AR stares silently at the examiner. One hour and a half later, she spontaneously addresses the examiner.
AR:	(*points to her left arm*) My mother's arm is colder than it was this morning. Feel how cold it is.
	On the following morning (30 November), the examiner asks AR again whose is AR's left arm, while pointing to it.
AR:	It's my mother's. It's pretty warm. I found it here. She forgot it when she was discharged from the hospital.
	After vestibular stimulation performed according to the same procedure used the day before, the examiner raises the patient's left arm and asks once again whose arm it is.
AR:	(*touches her left arm*) It's mine.
	Examiner: Where is your mother's arm?
AR:	It must be here, in the corner. (*She looks for her mother's arm under the bedclothes without finding it.*) It's pretty warm. It is a strong arm; my mother was a laundress . . .

This is known as asomatognosia, and it often follows right-hemisphere stroke.[338] A lack of capacity to recognise parts of the embodied self is always associated with right-hemisphere damage, never with left-hemisphere damage.[339] The phenomenon can be replicated by selectively anaesthetising the right hemisphere.[340]

It can also give rise to the belief that the affected part is under alien control. A patient described by Lhermitte showed no concern and was positively euphoric, despite being paralysed down his left side: 'it seemed as if the entire left-hand side of his body had disappeared from his consciousness and from his psychic life'. Three days later, however, this patient reports that from time to time an alien hand, which disturbs and annoys him, comes and places itself on his chest: he says 'this hand presses on my tummy and chokes me'. 'This hand bothers me', he says again, 'it doesn't belong to me, and I'm afraid it might thump me.'

He thought it might belong to the man in the next bed.[341] Another patient came to believe that the left side of his body was 'evil' and controlled by external agents, perhaps by the devil in collusion with his dead father.[342]

There is greater proprioceptive awareness in the right hemisphere than the left: that is to say, the right hemisphere knows better than the left, without having to look, where for example the contralateral hand is and what position it adopts – even though that favours the left hand in right-handers.[343] The right hemisphere is far more closely linked to the physiological changes that occur in the body when we experience emotion.[344] The right hemisphere's superiority in the emotional realm is explicitly linked to this close physiological relationship with the body.[345] This is a further reason why we hold babies to the left: 'the emotional impact of touch, the most basic and reciprocal mode of interaction, is also more direct and immediate if an infant is held to the left side of the body'.[346] Although studies of the effects of stroke on sexual function have shown it to be worse following left-hemisphere stroke, this is confounded by depression, a common sequel of left-hemisphere stroke; if depressed subjects are excluded it appears to be more dependent on the right hemisphere.[347]

Interestingly, when there is right hemisphere damage, there appears to be a removal of the normal integration of self with body: the body is reduced to a compendium of drives that are no longer integrated with the personality of the body's 'owner'. This can result in a morbid and excessive appetite for sex or food, which is out of keeping with the nature of the individual involved.[348]

I drew attention earlier to the fact that the right hemisphere is more intimately connected with the unconscious and automatic systems for regulating the body and its level of arousal, for example through the autonomic control of heart rate or neuroendocrine function (see pp. 58–9 above). There is one exception to this. There are two 'opponent processors' within the autonomic nervous system, the sympathetic and the parasympathetic systems. There is some evidence that, whereas sympathetic nervous control is more influenced by the right hemisphere, control of the parasympathetic nervous system is more under left-hemisphere control.[349] Of the two, the sympathetic is more important for modulating heart rate and blood pressure in response to emotion.[350] It is also more involved with response to the new, the uncertain, and the emotionally demanding, the special domains of the vigilant right hemisphere, whereas the parasympathetic nervous system produces relaxation of autonomic function, appropriate to the familiar, the known and the emotionally more neutral, the special domains of the left hemisphere. But release of the left hemisphere can certainly increase activity inappropriately, and will be associated with sympathetic activity. Perhaps the safest conclusion is that this area remains unclear.

MEANING AND THE IMPLICIT

When we think of meaning we tend to think of language, and the left hemisphere's great contribution to meaning is language, symbol manipulation. So great is it that I will devote the next chapter to examining the significance of this alone. The left hemisphere has a much more extensive vocabulary than the right, and more subtle and complex syntax. It extends vastly our power to map the world and to explore the complexities of the causal relationships between things.

This superiority has nothing to do with a greater affinity for auditory material. For one thing, music is in most respects better appreciated by the right hemisphere (see below). To the extent that there is an auditory superiority for language in the left hemisphere, it is in any case due to its inhibitory effect on the right hemisphere.[351] Rather the superiority for language stems from its nature as the hemisphere of *representation*, in which signs are substituted for experience. If it were not for this, one might have expected sign language, which is visuospatial rather than verbal in nature, to be dealt with in the right hemisphere. But, despite that, sign language is left-hemisphere-mediated;[352] and disturbances of sign language in deaf subjects are also consistently associated with left-hemisphere damage, the resulting deficits being typically analogous to the language problems experienced by hearing subjects with a lesion in the same location.[353] This proves that the specialisation of what is called the auditory cortex is not to do with the processing of auditory material, or even of words themselves. It is to do with the processing of signs, tokens, representations of things, whether these be verbal or visuospatial. And, equally, the supposed visuospatial bias of the right hemisphere is probably not about visuospatial qualities in themselves, but because this is the main route of perception of the external world, of things in and of themselves, as opposed to their signs.

But the left hemisphere is attached to language *per se*: language is where it is at home. It seems to be (in an interesting parallel with the situation regarding numbers mentioned above) actually less concerned about meaning than the right hemisphere, as long as it has control of the form and the system. In conditions of right-hemisphere damage, where the left hemisphere is no longer under constraint from the right, a meaningless hypertrophy of language may result.[354]

Once again the stereotypes are wrong. The left hemisphere may have a lot to do with language, but the right hemisphere plays a vital part in language, too. It uses language not in order to manipulate ideas or things, but to understand what others mean. This 'silent' hemisphere recognises words,[355] and has vocabulary, as discussed above, and even some aspects of syntax.[356] In fact not just language reception, but expression, too, is highly right-hemisphere-dependent: the verbal expression problems of right-hemisphere-damaged patients can be severe, and it has been suggested that they are almost as severe as those of left-hemisphere-damaged patients.[357]

And, as far as comprehension goes, they are in some respects worse. The right hemisphere's particular strength is in understanding meaning as a whole and in context. It is with the right hemisphere that we understand the moral of a story,[358] as well as the point of a joke.[359] It is able to construe intelligently what others mean, determining from intonation, and from pragmatics, not just from summation of meaning units, subject to the combinatorial rules of syntax, as a computer would.[360] It is therefore particularly important wherever non-literal meaning needs to be understood – practically everywhere, therefore, in human discourse, and particularly where irony, humour, indirection or sarcasm are involved.[361] Patients with right-hemisphere damage have difficulty understanding non-literal meaning.[362] They have difficulty with indirect meaning, such as is implied by metaphor[363] and humour.[364] In fact, those with right-hemisphere damage cannot make inferences, an absolutely vital part of understanding the world: they do not understand implicit meanings whatever their kind, but detect explicit meanings only.[365] (Once an inference is made and begins to be more explicit, the process can be transferred from the right superior temporal gyrus to the left.)[366] While syntactical performance is more impaired in left-hemisphere-damaged children, actual lexical understanding is worse impaired by right-hemisphere damage.[367]

The full significance of the left hemisphere's incapacity for, and the right hemisphere's affinity for, metaphor will become clear in the next chapter. While it does, certainly, mean that understanding of the indirect, connotative language of poetry depends on the right hemisphere, the importance of metaphor is that it *underlies all forms of understanding whatsoever*, science and philosophy no less than poetry and art.[368]

The right hemisphere specialises in non-verbal communication.[369] It deals with whatever is implicit, where the left hemisphere is tied to 'more explicit and more conscious processing'.[370] Subtle unconscious perceptions that govern our reactions are picked up by the right hemisphere. For example, it is the area around the fusiform gyrus of the right hemisphere that is dominant for *unconscious* reading of facial expressions.[371] Emotional shifts that are expressed in minute facial changes are mirrored and synchronously matched by the observer's right hemisphere within 300-400 milliseconds, at levels beneath awareness.[372] Looking at the movements of another's eyes and mouth activates the right posterior temporo-occipital cortex.[373] It will be remembered that the left hemisphere does not attend to the eyes: this is one reason why the right hemisphere is better at detecting deceit.[374] Because the right hemisphere picks up subtle clues and meanings, and because it can understand how others are feeling and thinking, we rely on it when we judge whether people are lying.[375] Those with right-hemisphere damage have difficulty distinguishing jokes from lies; by contrast those with left-hemisphere damage are actually better at detecting a lie than normal individuals, another instance of the way in which the hemispheres require separation as much as connection.[376] I am reminded of an observation of John Napier's about the relationship between lying and explicit *versus* implicit communication: 'If language was given to men to conceal their thoughts, then gesture's purpose was to disclose them.'[377]

The realm of all that remains, and has to remain, implicit and ambiguous is extensive, and is crucially important. This is why one feels so hopeless relying on the written word to convey meaning in humanly important and emotionally freighted situations.

Non-verbal behaviour, language, facial expression, intonations and gestures are instrumental in establishing complex contradictory, predominantly emotional relations between people and between man and the world. How frequently a touch by the shoulder, a handshake or a look tell more than can be expressed in a long monologue. Not because our speech is not accurate enough. Just the contrary. It is precisely its accuracy and definiteness that make speech unsuited for expressing what is too complex, changeful and ambiguous.[378]

As we have seen, things that are value-laden for me, because of their place in 'my' world, are salient to the right hemisphere, a consequence of its concern for what has personal meaning. The 'I', here, is a social being, however, not an objectified isolated entity, since the right hemisphere mediates social behaviour in all its ramifications. This is why a right-hemisphere stroke, although not involving speech directly, is in practice more disabling than a left-hemisphere stroke, despite the fact that in a left-hemisphere stroke speech is usually lost. Following a left-hemisphere stroke, despite the difficulties incurred with loss of speech and loss of use of the right hand, the chances of independent living are higher than after a right-hemisphere stroke.[379] It is not just the capacity to interpret emotional signals, in a functional or utilitarian sense, that is mediated by the right hemisphere. While the capacity to interpret other's minds, even to appreciate what they must be thinking and feeling – the capacity that is missing in autism – *is* lost in a right-hemisphere stroke,[380] it is more than that too: it is the capacity positively to empathise. Meaning is more than words.

MUSIC AND TIME

Sometimes it is music. Music, being grounded in the body, communicative of emotion, implicit, is a natural expression of the nature of the right hemisphere. The relationship between language and music is something we will explore in the next chapter: their overlapping functions and origins reveal some vital truths about ourselves. Given that intonation of the voice and the emotional aspects of experience are its special concern, it is to be expected that music would be a largely (though not exclusively) right-hemisphere phenomenon.

There are, however, other respects in which music is a natural candidate for the concerns of the right hemisphere. It is the relations *between* things, more than entities in isolation, that are of primary importance to the right hemisphere. Music consists entirely of relations, 'betweenness'. The notes mean nothing in themselves: the tensions between the notes, and between notes and the silence with which they live in reciprocal indebtedness, are everything. Melody, harmony and rhythm each lie in the gaps, and yet the betweenness is only what it is because of the notes themselves. Actually the music is not *just* in the gaps any more than it is *just* in the notes: it is in the whole that the notes and the silence make together. Each note becomes transformed by the context in which it lies. What we mean by music is not just any agglomeration of notes, but one in which the whole created is powerful enough to make each note live in a new way, a way that it had never done before. Similarly poetry cannot be just any arrangement of words, but one in which each word is taken up into the new whole and made to live again in a new way, carrying us back to the world of experience, to life: poetry constitutes a 'speaking silence'. Music and poetic language are both part of the world that is delivered by the right hemisphere, the world characterised by betweenness. Perhaps it is not, after all, so wide of the mark to call the right hemisphere the 'silent' hemisphere: its utterances are implicit.

But it is not just because it exists in betweenness that music is the concern of the right hemisphere. Its indivisible nature, the necessity of experiencing the whole at any one time, though it is forever unfolding in time, a thing that is ever changing, never static or fixed, constantly evolving, with the subtle pulse of a living thing (remember, even musical instruments are present to the brain as living things), the fact that its communication is by its nature implicit, profoundly emotive, working through our embodied nature – everything about music, in short, makes it the natural 'language' of the right hemisphere. If it is true, as Walter Pater famously said, following Novalis, that all art constantly aspires towards the condition of music, all art aspires to reside in the world that is delivered to us by the right hemisphere.

The relation between music and the body is not by any means confined to voluntary (or apparently voluntary) movements of the limbs, as in dance. We are all aware of the many ways in which music affects us physically through our emotions. Musical phrases act like metaphors emanating from, and enormously expanding the meaning of, movement in and of the body: rising, falling, pulsing, breathing. Many features of music, including obviously syncopations, but also melodic appoggiaturas and enharmonic changes, set up patterns of expectation which are ultimately either confirmed or disappointed;[381] and this process leads to physiological reactions such as alterations in breathing, or changes in heart rate, in blood pressure, and even in temperature, as well as bringing us out in a sweat, bringing tears to our eyes, or making our hair stand on end.[382] Such changes are again mediated through the right hemisphere's vital connection with subcortical centres, with the hypothalamus, and with the body in general.

It has been said that music, like poetry, is intrinsically sad,[383] and a survey of music from many parts of the world would bear that out – not, of course, that there is no joyful music, but that even such music often appears to be joy torn from the teeth of sadness, a sort of holiday of the minor key. It is what we would expect in view of the emotional timbre of the right hemisphere; and there is a stronger affinity between the right hemisphere and the minor key, as well as between the left hemisphere and the major key.[384] The pre-Socratic philosopher Gorgias wrote that 'awe [*phrike*] and tearful pity and mournful desire enter those who listen to poetry', and at this time poetry and song were one.[385]

The relationship between music and emotion is fascinating, and to some degree baffling. Suzanne Langer said that music not only has the power to recall emotions we are familiar with, but to evoke 'emotions and moods we have not felt, passions we did not know before.'[386] Music seems, in other words, to expand the range of possible emotions limitlessly because the emotion experienced is so bound up with the particularity of the work that mediates it, yet the lexicon with which we are obliged to describe the feelings remains frustratingly limited. Thus the 'sadness' of a piece of Bach will be quite different from the 'sadness' of a piece of Mozart, and 'sadness' in the *Matthew Passion* will be different from the sort of 'sadness' we might discern in *The Musical Offering*, and the 'sadness' we experience in one movement of the *Matthew Passion* – the wonderful alto aria *Erbarme dich*, for example – will be of a quite different kind from the 'sadness' of, say, its final chorus, *Wir setzen uns mit Tränen nieder*. This must be what Mendelssohn meant by his otherwise paradoxical pronouncement that 'the thoughts that are expressed to me by music I love are not too indefinite to be put into words, but on the contrary too definite.'[387] Language returns us inevitably to the worn currency of re-presentation, in which the unique qualities of everything that exists are reduced to the same set of terms. As Nietzsche put it: 'Compared with music all communication by words is shameless; words dilute and brutalise; words depersonalise; words make the uncommon common.'[388]

Though speech is principally a left-hemisphere function, the production of words in song is associated with wide activation of the right hemisphere.[389] Following a left hemisphere stroke which leaves the patient unable to speak, he or she may be able to sing the words of songs without difficulty. Damage to the right hemisphere, by contrast, can lead to a condition known as amusia, in which the ability to appreciate and understand, or to perform, music may be lost.[390] Right-hemisphere lesions may leave the understanding of speech relatively unaffected, while the perception of nonverbal sounds (including music) is profoundly disrupted.[391] In such cases, as well as in auditory agnosia (which is commoner following bilateral damage), the perception of timbre, rhythm and complex sounds is badly affected.[392] Most cases of amusia without aphasia, inability to appreciate or perform music, but without impairment of speech comprehension or production, involve right-hemisphere damage.[393] The reverse situation depends on the right hemisphere being spared. A well-known composer and Professor of Music at Moscow Conservatory, Vissarion Shebalin, had a left temporal and parietal stroke with consequent severe aphasia (impairment of language), but carried on composing works of excellent quality – according to Shostakovich indistinguishable from his pre-stroke works.[394] A professional organist and composer who was blind from the age of two had a left middle cerebral artery stroke, with consequent severe aphasia, as well as alexia and agraphia (inability to read or write) in Braille for words – but not for music, and carried on playing and composing unaffected.[395] A composer and conductor who had a left-hemisphere stroke was no longer able to read words, but could read and write music without difficulty.[396]

Melody, tone, timbre and pitch-processing are almost always mediated via the right hemisphere (in non-professional musicians).[397] Rhythm is more widely based. Discriminating rhythm patterns activates broadly distributed networks in temporal, inferior parietal and prefrontal cortex almost exclusively in the right hemisphere.[398] However, some basic, metrical rhythms are mediated by the left hemisphere, particularly by Broca's area;[399] while more complex rhythms, and those with more deviations from the standard pattern, such as syncopations and cross rhythms, are preferentially treated by the right hemisphere.[400] The right hemisphere is more sensitive to harmony,[401] which could be considered essentially a right-hemisphere function.[402] The right hemisphere is also the source of our ability to relate harmony to intonation (the basis for harmonic progression) and to some aspects of rhythm.[403]

But music raises an intriguing problem. All that I have just said applies to the amateur: the professional or highly trained musician appears to use the left hemisphere to a much greater extent in the understanding of music. This has been interpreted by some as suggesting the adoption of a more consciously learned, theoretically based or analytic approach in such trained subjects. This is almost certainly true. It may also be, as Jerre Levy has argued, that the evidence from both successful artists and musicians suggests that their skills are more widely distributed across both hemispheres than is usual ('flying mathematicians' – see p. 12 above).[404] This would be in keeping with the finding that visuospatial attention is more evenly distributed between the hemispheres in musicians, possibly because of their having acquired the skill of reading music, a left–right sequential process like language (thus favouring left-hemisphere processing), but the meaning of which is nonetheless represented visuospatially (possibly favouring right-hemisphere processing). Additionally pianists have to be able to use each hand equally to translate between visuospatial and motor sequences.[405]

The findings of Goldberg and Costa suggest, however, that it may also be a special case of a more generally applicable principle, as we have seen above. While we are gathering new information, the right hemisphere is responsible, but once whatever it is becomes thoroughly 'known', familiar, it is taken over by the left hemisphere.[406] The discovery that the contrapuntal music of J. S. Bach causes a strong right-hemisphere activation even in trained musicians is fascinating. It was explained by the researchers who made the finding on the basis that a range of melodic contours needs to be maintained in awareness simultaneously, requiring the right hemisphere's greater capacity to hold experience in working memory.[407] While that may be right, an alternative explanation might lie in the impossibility of attending to all parts of such music in its entirety, so that it can never be experienced in exactly the same way on different hearings. Because it is never finally captured, it is always new. And the two explanations are perhaps not so different, since the left hemisphere 'capture' that results in inauthenticity is possible only by limiting the scope of what is attended to.

Music – like narrative, like the experience of our lives as we live them – unfolds in time. The movement of time is what makes music what it is. Not just that it has ictus and rhythm; its structure extends through and across time, depending on memory to hold it together.

Time is the context that gives meaning to everything in this world, and conversely everything that has meaning for us in this world, everything that has a place in our lives, exists in time. This is not true of abstractions and re-presentations of entities, but all that *is* is subject to time. The sense of time passing is associated with sustained attention, and even if for that reason alone, it is only to be expected that this arises in the right hemisphere, subserved by the right prefrontal cortex and inferior parietal lobe.[408] The ability to compare duration in time is clearly better performed by the right hemisphere,[409] and relies on the right dorsolateral prefrontal cortex.[410] In fact virtually all aspects of the appreciation of time, in the sense of something lived through, with a past, present and future, are dependent on the right hemisphere, principally the right prefrontal and parietal cortex.[411] The sense of past or future is severely impaired in right-hemisphere damage.[412]

What is called temporal sequencing is an ambiguous concept. Such sequencing, depending on what one means by that, may be right-hemisphere-dependent[413] or, at least where the sequence has no 'real world' meaning, as it would in a narrative, left-hemisphere-dependent[414] – the understanding of narrative is a right-hemisphere skill; the left hemisphere cannot follow a narrative.[415] But sequencing, in the sense of the ordering of artificially decontextualised, unrelated, momentary events, or momentary interruptions of temporal flow – the kind of thing that is as well or better performed by the left hemisphere – is not in fact a measure of the sense of time at all. It is precisely what takes over *when the sense of time breaks down.* Time is essentially an undivided flow: the left hemisphere's tendency to break it up into units and make machines to measure it may succeed in deceiving us that it is a sequence of static points, but such a sequence never approaches the nature of time, however close it gets. This is another instance of how something that does not come into being for the left hemisphere is re-presented by it in non-living, mechanical form, the closest approximation as it sees it, but always remaining on the other side of the gulf that separates the two worlds – like a series of tangents that approaches ever more closely to a circle without ever actually achieving it, a machine that approximates, however well, the human mind yet has no consciousness, a Frankenstein's monster of body parts that never truly lives. A condition called palinopsia, in which there is disturbance and fragmentation of the normal flow of visual experience, or abnormal persistence over time of images, causing visual trails, is caused by posterior right-hemisphere lesions;[416] and similar phenomena – loss of fluidity of motion through time – in other modalities than sight are probably similarly associated with deficits in the right posterior cortex.[417] Under such conditions the right hemisphere ability to perceive flow as a single, unified motion across time is lost. It becomes replaced, in the left hemisphere's timeless, but mechanical world, by the summing of an infinite series of static moments, rather like the succession of frames in a ciné film, known as the *Zeitraffer* phenomenon.

Again it has been suggested that, whereas the right hemisphere is required for the sustained 'monitoring of temporal information', the left hemisphere is more efficient for detection of brief temporal flow interruptions that are decontextualised.[418] In my view this merely confirms the predilection for abstraction, as well as the lack of capacity for perception of temporal flow, in the left hemisphere. The critical point here is that the right hemisphere has an advantage where there is fluency of motion, or flow over time, but the left hemisphere an advantage where there is stasis, or focus on a point in time.[419] There is an ambiguity in the idea of permanence. The left hemisphere seems to accept the permanence of something only if it is static. But things can change – flow – and yet have permanence: think of a river. The right hemisphere perceives that there is permanence even where there is flow. Hence, when it is damaged, living beings have no permanency – the Capgras phenomenon.

Music takes place in time. Yet music also has the capacity to make us stand outside time. As George Steiner put it, 'music is . . . time made free of temporality'.[420] Equally it works through the body, but transports us beyond the world of the merely physical: it is highly particular, and yet seems to speak of things that are universal.[421] Perhaps this going 'through' a thing to find its opposite is an aspect of the right-hemisphere world, in which 'opposites' are not incompatible, an aspect of its roundness, rather than linearity. However, I would say, at the risk of pushing language to or beyond its proper limits, that time itself is (what the left hemisphere would call) paradoxical in nature, and that music does not so much free time from temporality as bring out an aspect that is always present within time, its intersection with a moment which partakes of eternity. Similarly it does not so much use the physical to transcend physicality, or use particularity to transcend the particular, as bring out the spirituality latent in what we conceive as physical existence, and uncover the universality that is, as Goethe spent a lifetime trying to express, always latent in the particular. It is also a feature of music in every known culture that it is used to communicate with the supernatural, with whatever is by definition above, beyond, 'Other than', our selves.[422]

DEPTH

The equivalent of time in the visual realm could be thought of as spatial depth: indeed since Einstein we have come to understand that time and space are aspects of one entity. As it is the right hemisphere that gives 'depth' to our sense of time, in the visual realm it is the right hemisphere that gives us the means of appreciating depth in space,[423] the way in which we stand in relation to others, rather than by categorisation. The right hemisphere has a tendency to deal with spatial relations in terms of the degree of distance, which it can discriminate easily, in contrast with the strategy of the left hemisphere, which tends to be more categorical: 'above', 'below', and so on.[424] There is a parallel here with the sense of time: duration belongs to the right hemisphere, while sequencing ('before', 'after' = 'above', 'below') belongs to the left. The right hemisphere's organisation of space depends more on depth, whether things are nearer or further 'from me'.[425] The right hemisphere is even biased towards what lies further 'from me', an aspect of its broader, wider and deeper attention.[426] The left hemisphere, by comparison, has difficulty with processing depth: as a result, it may get the size of things wrong, sometimes dramatically.[427]

Right-hemisphere deficits cause difficulty in dealing with irregular smoothly curved surfaces, such as are characteristic of living things, in three dimensions, even though the capacity to deal with a predictable rectilinear 3D object like a cube is spared. It has been suggested that this problem in dealing with curved volumes may underlie prosopagnosia,[428] and it might be a contributing factor. One of the features Bodamer's 'Patient S' described was, after all, the lack of depth, the reduction of the face to a 'white oval plate'.[429]

The right hemisphere tends to present the world realistically, with visual detail and in three dimensions, with depth; and an aesthetic sense of the intensity and beauty of visual representations comes largely from the right hemisphere.[430]

The right hemisphere represents objects as having volume and depth in space, as they are experienced; the left hemisphere tends to represent the visual world schematically, abstractly, geometrically, with a lack of realistic detail, and even in one plane (see Figures 2.8 and 2.9).[431]

Drawings of buildings, in individuals with an inactivated right hemisphere, may even be laid out flat with all façades simultaneously visible, as in a child's drawing.[432] One way of putting this is that the left hemisphere is concerned with what it *knows*, where the right hemisphere is concerned with what it *experiences* (see Figure 2.10).

A patient studied by Gazzaniga and LeDoux, who underwent a commissurotomy, could draw a cube normally with either hand prior to the operation, but following the procedure could draw only a poor diagram with his favoured right hand, though the left hand was able to draw a 3-dimensional construct of a cube (see Figure 2.11).[433]

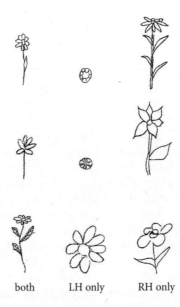

both   LH only   RH only

Fig. 2.8 Flower as drawn by the same subjects: in normal conditions; with right hemisphere inactivated; and with left hemisphere inactivated (from Nikolaenko, 1997).

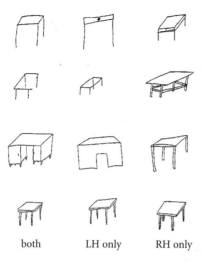

Fig. 2.9 Table as drawn by the same subjects: in normal conditions; with right hemisphere inactivated; and with left hemisphere inactivated (from Nikolaenko, 1997).

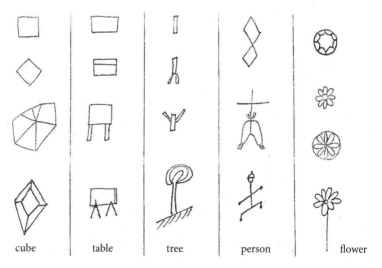

Fig. 2.10 Everyday objects drawn 'according to the left hemisphere', with right hemisphere inactivated (from Nikolaenko, 1997).

CERTAINTY

The left hemisphere likes things that are man-made. Things we make are also more certain: we know them inside out, because we put them together. They are not, like living things, constantly changing and moving, beyond our *grasp*.

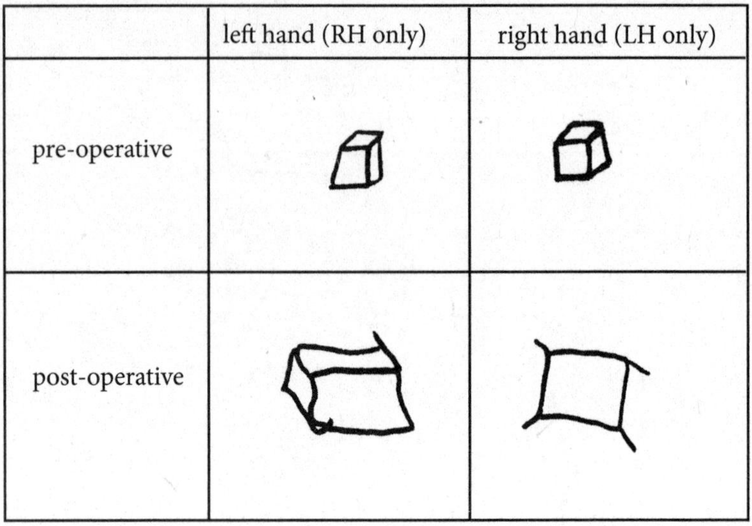

	left hand (RH only)	right hand (LH only)
pre-operative		
post-operative		

Fig. 2.11 Cube drawing before and after commissurotomy. Pre-operatively, the patient could draw a cube with either hand. Post-operatively, however, the preferred right hand performed poorly (from Gazzaniga & LeDoux, 1978).

Because the right hemisphere sees things as they are, they are constantly new for it, so it has nothing like the databank of information about categories that the left hemisphere has. It cannot have the certainty of knowledge that comes from being able to fix things and isolate them. In order to remain true to what is, it does not form abstractions, and categories that are based on abstraction, which are the strengths of denotative language. By contrast, the right hemisphere's interest in language lies in all the things that help to take it beyond the limiting effects of denotation to connotation: it acknowledges the importance of ambiguity. It therefore is virtually silent, relatively shifting and uncertain, where the left hemisphere, by contrast, may be unreasonably, even stubbornly, convinced of its own correctness.[434] As John Cutting puts it, despite 'an astonishing degree of ignorance on the part of the left (supposed major) hemisphere about what its partner, the right (supposed minor) hemisphere, [is] up to, [it] abrogates decision-making to itself in the absence of any rational evidence as to what is going on'.[435]

There are numerous examples of this phenomenon. A split-brain subject, to whose right hemisphere a photograph of a nude in a suggestive pose is projected, becomes flustered and laughs in an embarrassed fashion. When the experimenter asks her why, her verbal left hemisphere has no idea. She therefore makes something plausible up – someone in the room is upsetting her.

But a famous example, reported by Gazzaniga and LeDoux, illustrates the most important point here. The experimenters show a split-brain patient (PS) a picture projected to one or other hemisphere and ask him to pick a card connected with the scene. For example, they show a snow scene to the right hemisphere and ask him to choose an appropriate picture from an array of cards, with either hand. He cannot say what it is that he has seen, because the right hemisphere cannot speak, but he is able with his left hand to go straight to the picture of a shovel. However, since the left hemisphere did not see anything, his right hand chooses at random, and scores no better than chance. Then they make things a bit more interesting. At the same time that they flash a picture of the snow scene to the right hemisphere, they flash a picture of a chicken claw to the left hemisphere. Each hemisphere has knowledge of only one image, and in each case it is different. When they ask PS to choose an appropriate card, again his left hand chooses a shovel (because the right hemisphere has seen the snow), but the right hand chooses a picture of a chicken (because what the left hemisphere has seen is the chicken claw). When asked why his left hand had chosen the shovel, his verbal left hemisphere, which has to respond to the question, but knows nothing of the snow scene, the real reason for choosing the shovel, is not in the least abashed. He explains that he saw a chicken, and of course chose the shovel because 'you need that to clean out the chicken shed'.

The really interesting finding here, as the authors themselves put it, is that 'without batting an eye' the left hemisphere draws mistaken conclusions from the information available to it and lays down the law about what only the right hemisphere can know: 'yet, the left did not offer its suggestion in a guessing vein but rather [as] a statement of fact . . .'[436]

This may be linked to a phenomenon known as confabulation, where the brain, not being able to recall something, rather than admit to a gap in its understanding, makes up something plausible, that appears consistent, to fill it. Thus, for example, in the presence of a right-sided lesion, the brain loses the contextual information that would help it make sense of experience; the left hemisphere, nothing loath, makes up a story, and, lacking insight, appears completely convinced by it.[437] Even in the absence of amnesia, the left hemisphere exhibits a strong tendency to confabulate: it thinks it knows something, recognises something, which it doesn't, a tendency that may be linked to its lack of ability to discriminate unique cases from the generalised categories into which it places them.[438] The left hemisphere is the equivalent of the sort of person who, when asked for directions, prefers to make something up rather than admit to not knowing. This impression is confirmed by Panksepp: 'The linguistically proficient left hemisphere . . . appears predisposed to repress negative emotions, and even chooses to confabulate.'[439] To some extent perhaps we inevitably confabulate stories about our lives, a process overseen by what Gazzaniga calls the left-hemisphere 'interpreter'.[440] However, it is the right hemisphere that makes judgments about the truth or plausibility of these narratives.[441]

The fact is that this habit is far from harmless: it leads the left hemisphere to make poor inferences and some mistaken choices. In one experiment by Gazzaniga's colleagues, split-brain subjects (JW & VP) were asked to guess which colour, red or green, was going to be displayed next, in a series where there were obviously (four times) more green than red.[442] Instead of spotting that the way to get the highest score is to choose green every time (the right hemisphere's strategy), leading to a score of 80 per cent, the left hemisphere chose green at random, but about four times

Fig. 2.12 Is this a duck or a rabbit?

more often than red, producing a score of little better than chance. The problem here, as subsequent research has illuminated, is that the left hemisphere develops a *rule* – a rule that is, however, wrong.[443]

In a similar, earlier experiment in normal subjects, researchers found that, not only does (what we now know to be) the left hemisphere tend to insist on its theory at the expense of getting things wrong, but it will later cheerfully insist that it got it right. In this experiment, the researchers flashed up lights with a similar frequency (4:1) for a considerable period, and the participants again predicted at random in a ratio of 4:1, producing poor results. But after a while, unknown to the subjects, the experimenters changed the system, so that whichever light the subject predicted, that was the light that showed next: in other words, the subject was suddenly bound to get 100 per cent right, because that was the way it was rigged. When asked to comment, the subjects – despite having carried on simply predicting the previously most frequent light 80 per cent of the time – overwhelmingly responded that there was a fixed pattern to the light sequences and that they had finally cracked it. They went on to describe fanciful and elaborate systems that 'explained' why they were always right.[444]

So the left hemisphere needs certainty and needs to be right. The right hemisphere makes it possible to hold several ambiguous possibilities in suspension together without premature closure on one outcome. The right prefrontal cortex is essential for dealing with incomplete information and has a critical role to play in reasoning about incompletely specified situations. The right hemisphere is able to maintain ambiguous mental representations in the face of a tendency to premature over-interpretation by the left hemisphere.[445] The right hemisphere's tolerance of uncertainty is implied everywhere in its subtle ability to use metaphor, irony and humour, all of which depend on not prematurely resolving ambiguities. So, of course, does poetry, which relies on right-hemisphere language capacities. During ambiguous stimulation of perceptual rivalry (the phenomenon of an ambiguous figure that can be seen in one way or another, but not both simultaneously, such as the duck–rabbit above or the Necker cube opposite[446]) right frontal cortex is more active.[447]

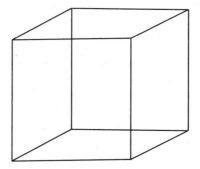

Fig. 2.13 Is this a cube seen from above right, or from below left?

Blurred or indistinct images are not a problem for the right hemisphere, but are for the left, even where the nature of the task would suggest that it should be more problematic for the right hemisphere.[448] One of the most consistent early findings in hemisphere specialisation was that whenever an image is either only fleetingly presented, or presented in a degraded form, so that only partial information is available, a right-hemisphere superiority emerges – even when the material is verbal.[449] In some subtle experimental work Justine Sergent was able to demonstrate this and its converse, namely that when images are presented for longer than usual, thus increasing their certainty and familiarity, a left-hemisphere superiority emerges, even when it comes to face recognition. She makes the interesting observation that letters of the alphabet 'represent a finite set of stimuli that are sharply focussed, familiar and overlearned', whereas visual images 'represent a potentially infinite set of shapes of large visual angle size, with different levels of structure of unequal importance and salience that are most often unfamiliar to subjects'. In doing so she neatly reveals a common thread which unites, on the one hand, the left hemisphere's affinity for what it itself has made (here language), well-worn familiarity, certainty and finitude, and, on the other, the right hemisphere's affinity for all that is 'other', new, unknown, uncertain and unbounded.[450] Again what have to be referred to, in an account such as I am giving in this chapter, left-hemisphere fashion, as separate 'functions' (or areas of concern), should also be seen, right-hemisphere fashion, as aspects of one and the same entity that are only artificially separated in the process of description. The 'functions' are not arbitrarily housed together in this or that hemisphere: they form, in the case of either hemisphere, aspects of two whole ways of being in the world.

Certainty is also related to narrowness, as though the more certain we become of something the less we see. To put this in the context of the neurophysiology of vision: the fovea of the human eye, a tiny region in the retina at the centre of gaze, is the most pronounced of that of all primates. Here resolution is about 100 times that at the periphery.[451] But it is only about 1° across. The part of the visual field that is actually brought into resolution is no more than about 3° across. This is where the narrow focussed beam of left-hemisphere attention is concentrated: what is *clearly* seen.

SELF-AWARENESS AND EMOTIONAL TIMBRE

The right hemisphere is also more realistic about how it stands in relation to the world at large, less grandiose, more self-aware, than the left hemisphere.[452] The left hemisphere is ever optimistic, but unrealistic about its short-comings. When patients who have had a right-hemisphere stroke are offered constructive guidance about their performance it makes little impact.[453] In the words of one researcher into head injury, 'children with right-brain deficit disorder ignore task obstacles, accept impossible challenges, make grossly inadequate efforts, and are stunned by the poor outcomes. These children act fearless because they overlook the dangers inherent in the situation.'[454] A highly intelligent professional described by Stuss was completely unaware of his lack of capacity to do his job after the removal of a tumour in the right prefrontal cortex. When asked to role-play as an occupational health adviser to someone with his problems, he appropriately advised medical retirement, but when asked to apply this insight to his own situation he was completely unable to do so.[455] There are many similar case reports.[456]

Although relatively speaking the right hemisphere takes a more pessimistic view of the self, it is also more realistic about it.[457] There is evidence that (a) those who are somewhat depressed are more realistic, including in self-evaluation; and, see above, that (b) depression is (often) a condition of relative hemisphere asymmetry, favouring the right hemisphere.[458] Even schizophrenics have more insight into their condition in proportion to the degree that they have depressive symptoms.[459] The evidence is that this is not because insight makes you depressed, but because being depressed gives you insight.[460]

Insight into illness generally is dependent on the right hemisphere, and those who have damage to the right hemisphere tend to deny their illness – the well-recognised, and extraordinary phenomenon of anosognosia, in which patients deny or radically minimise the fact that they have, for example, a blatant loss of use of what may be one entire half of the body.[461] A patient with a completely paralysed (left) limb may pointedly refuse to accept that there is anything wrong with it, and will come up with the most preposterous explanations for why he is not actually able to move it on request. This happens to some degree in the majority of cases after a stroke affecting the left side of the body (involving right-hemisphere damage), but practically never after a right-sided stroke (involving left-hemisphere damage). The phenomenon of denial can be temporarily reversed by activating the affected right hemisphere.[462] Equally, denial of illness (anosognosia) can be induced by anaesthetising the right hemisphere.[463]

Note that it is not just a blindness, a failure to see – it's a wilful denial. Hoff and Pötzl describe a patient who demonstrates this beautifully: 'On examination, when she is shown her left hand in the right visual field, she *looks away and says* '*I don't see it.*' She spontaneously hides her left hand under the bedclothes or puts it behind her back. She never looks to the left, even when called from that side.'[464] If forced to confront the affected limb, there is not infrequently a sense of revulsion from it, known as misoplegia: if the examiner puts the patient's own left hand in her right hand, 'she takes hold of it only to drop it immediately with an expression of disgust'.[465]

In right-hemisphere lesions, there is not only denial or indifference in the face of incapacity, but sometimes a disturbance of mood 'reminiscent of the fatuousness of those with frontal lesions: euphoria, joviality, a penchant for feeble puns'. One of the patients reported by Hécaen and de Ajuriaguerra, who had complete hemi-asomatognosia caused by a parietal tumour 'exhibited a surprising joviality, at the same time complaining of a fierce headache'.[466]

Denial is a left-hemisphere speciality: in states of relative right-hemisphere inactivation, in which there is therefore a bias toward the left hemisphere, subjects tend to evaluate themselves optimistically, view pictures more positively, and are more apt to stick to their existing point of view.[467] In the presence of a right-hemisphere stroke, the left hemisphere is 'crippled by naively optimistic forecasting of outcomes'.[468] It is always a winner: winning is associated with activation of the left amygdala, losing with right amygdala activation.[469]

There are links here with the right hemisphere's tendency to melancholy. If there is a tendency for the right hemisphere to be more sorrowful and prone to depression, this can, in my view, be seen as related not only to being more in touch with what's going on, but more in touch with, and concerned for, others. 'No man is an island': it is the right hemisphere of the human brain that ensures that we feel part of the main. The more we are aware of and empathically connected to whatever it is that exists apart from ourselves, the more we are likely to suffer. Sadness and empathy are highly correlated: this can be seen in studies of children and adolescents.[470] There is also a direct correlation between sadness and empathy, on the one hand, and feelings of guilt, shame and responsibility, on the other.[471] Psychopaths, who have no sense of guilt, shame or responsibility, have deficits in the right frontal lobe, particularly the right ventromedial and orbitofrontal cortex.[472]

Perhaps to feel at all is inevitably to suffer. The Greek word *pathe*, feeling, is related to *pathos*, an affliction, and to *paschein*, to suffer: the same roots are in our word 'passion' (and a similar development leads to the German word for passions, *Leidenschaften*, from the root *leiden*, to suffer). This is just one reason to doubt the easy equation between pleasure and happiness, on the one hand, and 'the good', on the other.

> Intrinsically caring for another essentially involves a certain disposition, the disposition to experience sorrow at the other's serious misfortune . . . To be just is to be disturbed by injustice. Pain, suffering, and the loss of pleasure, then, sometimes constitute who we are and what we value. They are essentially woven into our deepest commitments. As reasons flow from our deepest commitments, we will sometimes have non-instrumental reason to suffer.[473]

Once, when Berlioz sobbed at a musical performance a sympathetic onlooker remarked: 'You seem to be greatly affected, *monsieur*. Had you not better retire for a while?' In response, Berlioz snapped: 'Are you under the impression that I am here to enjoy myself?'[474]

When Lear cries, 'Is there any cause in nature that makes these hard hearts?', we could reply, on one level, yes – a defect in the right prefrontal cortex.[475] But that just illuminates the fact that cruelty does not exist in 'nature': only humans with their left prefrontal cortex have the capacity for deliberate malice. But then only humans, with their right prefrontal cortex, are capable of compassion.

MORAL SENSE

Another area where analytic retrospection misleads us as to the nature of what we are seeing, since it reconstructs the world according to left-hemisphere principles, is that of morality. Moral values are not something that we work out rationally on the principle of utility, or any other principle, for that matter, but are irreducible aspects of the phenomenal world, like colour. I agree with Max Scheler,[476] and for that matter with Wittgenstein,[477] that moral value is a form of experience irreducible to any other kind, or accountable for on any other terms; and I believe this perception underlies Kant's derivation of God from the existence of moral values, rather than moral values from the existence of a God. Such values are linked to the capacity for empathy, not reasoning; and moral judgments are not deliberative, but unconscious and intuitive, deeply bound up with our emotional sensitivity to others.[478] Empathy is intrinsic to morality.

Patients with lesions in the ventromedial frontal lobes are impulsive, fail to foresee consequences and are emotionally disengaged from others; in particular the right ventromedial frontal cortex, which has rich interconnections with limbic structures, is critical to every aspect of moral and social behaviour.[479] Moral judgment involves a complex right-hemisphere network, particularly the right ventromedial and orbitofrontal cortex, as well as the amygdala in both hemispheres.[480] Damage in the right prefrontal cortex may lead to frank psychopathic behaviour.

Our sense of justice is underwritten by the right hemisphere, particularly by the right dorsolateral prefrontal cortex.[481] With inactivation of this area, we act more selfishly. This is probably related to the right frontal lobe's capacity to see the other's point of view, and for empathy in general. I will discuss the relation between altruism and the right hemisphere in Chapter 4. The right frontal lobe's capacity to inhibit our natural impulse to selfishness means that it is also the area on which we most rely for self-control and the power to resist temptation.[482]

I think we can also make a connection here with a rather fundamental difference between the hemispheres. The left hemisphere's 'stickiness', its tendency to recur to what it is familiar with, tends to reinforce whatever it is already doing. There is a reflexivity to the process, as if trapped in a hall of mirrors: it only discovers more of what it already knows, and it only does more of what it already is doing. The right hemisphere by contrast, seeing more of the picture, and taking a broader perspective that characteristically includes both its own and the left hemisphere's, is more reciprocally inclined, and more likely to espouse another point of view. One way of thinking of this is in terms of feedback systems. Most biological systems seek homeostasis: if they move too far in one direction, they stabilise themselves by self-correction. This is 'negative feedback', the most familiar example of which is the operation of a thermostat: if the temperature constantly tends to drop, the thermostat triggers a heating system that will act to bring the temperature back to the desired level. However, systems can become unstable and enter a situation in which 'positive feedback' obtains – in other words, a move in one direction, rather than producing a move in the opposite direction, serves to promote further moves in the same direction, and a snow-balling effect occurs. The right hemisphere, then, is capable of freeing us through negative feedback. The left hemisphere tends to positive feedback, and we can become stuck.[483] This is not unlike the difference between the normal drinker and the addict. After a certain point, the normal drinker begins to feel less like another drink. What makes an addict is the lack of an 'off switch' – another drink only makes the next, and the next, more likely. And, interestingly enough, lesions of the frontolimbic systems, mainly in the right hemisphere, are associated with addictive behaviour. Pathological gamblers, for example, have frontal deficits which are mainly right-sided;[484] by contrast, in cocaine addicts, for example, stimulating the right prefrontal cortex reduces craving for cocaine.[485] And denial, a left-hemisphere speciality, is typical of addiction.

THE SELF

Conscious awareness of the self is a surprisingly late development in evolution. The higher apes, such as chimpanzees and orang-utans, are capable of self-recognition, but monkeys are not: they fail the mirror test.[486] The right prefrontal region is critically involved in self-recognition, whether by face or by voice.[487] Imaging studies of self-recognition by face or voice confirm the importance of the right frontal region and the right cingulate cortex.[488] An important correlate of self-awareness in humans is the correct use of the personal pronouns 'I' and 'me', which is lacking in autism, a condition which replicates many right-hemisphere deficits.[489]

Clearly no one hemisphere can on its own constitute the self. The self is a complex concept, but, in brief, the self as intrinsically, empathically inseparable from the world in which it stands in relation to others, and the continuous sense of self, are more dependent on the right hemisphere, whereas the objectified self, and the self as an expression of will, is generally more dependent on the left hemisphere. Some studies in split-brain subjects suggest a right-hemisphere advantage for self-recognition;[490] but others reveal that both hemispheres equally can recognise the self objectively, though the right hemisphere has an advantage for recognising familiar others.[491]

The personal 'interior' sense of the self with a history, and a personal and emotional memory, as well as what is, rather confusingly, sometimes called 'the self-concept', appears to be dependent to a very large extent on the right hemisphere. The self-concept is impaired by right-hemisphere injury, wherever in the right hemisphere it may occur;[492] but the right frontal region is of critical importance here.[493] This could be described as self-experience. The right hemisphere seems more engaged by emotional, autobiographical memories.[494] It is hardly surprising that the 'sense of self' should be grounded in the right hemisphere, because the self originates in the interaction with 'the Other', not as an entity in atomistic isolation: 'The sense of self emerges from the activity of the brain in interaction with other selves.'[495] The right orbitofrontal cortex, the part of the right frontal lobe most crucial for social and empathic understanding, is larger in primates than the left.[496] It is likely that this part of the brain expands during the period of playful interaction between infant and mother in the second half of the first year, and the second year, of life, during which the sense of the self emerges, and indeed the right orbitofrontal cortex is seen by Allan Schore as the crucible of the growing self.[497] The right hemisphere matures earlier than the left, and is more involved than the left in almost every aspect of the development of mental functioning in early childhood, and of the self as a social, empathic being.[498] Social development in the infant takes place independently of language development, another pointer to its right-hemisphere origins.[499]

The relationship between the evolution of a sense of self and the sense of others as beings like oneself, and therefore as evoking empathy and understanding, which I have referred to before as an achievement of the right frontal lobes, is borne out by the close relationship between the development of a sense of self and the development of 'theory of mind' (see p. 57 above). This is, for example, evidenced by the fact that the neuroimaging correlates of both self-awareness and theory of mind lie in the right frontal and right cingulate cortex.[500]

It is also the right hemisphere which is responsible for 'maintaining a coherent, continuous and unified sense of self'.[501] Evidence from patients with dementia is highly suggestive that it is the right hemisphere that 'connects the individual to emotionally salient experiences and memories underlying self-schemas', and which therefore forms 'the glue holding together the sense of self'.[502] The remark is reminiscent of a formulation of Douglas Watt's that 'emotion binds together virtually every type of information the brain can encode ... [it is] part of the glue that holds the whole system together',[503] and indeed, to the degree that that is true, the observation that the right hemisphere binds together the sense of self would follow from this. And as already implied in the brief discussion of the hemispheres and time, it is the right (prefrontal) cortex, in conjunction with its reciprocal connections with other cortical and subcortical structures, which enables human adults to see themselves as just that – selves, with continuous existence over time.[504] Right frontal damage impairs the sense of self over time – self with a narrative, and a continuous flow-like existence.[505]

Sperry and his colleagues hypothesised that it is a right-hemisphere network that gives rise to self-awareness.[506] The right hemisphere is preferentially involved in 'the processing of self-images, at least when self-images are not consciously perceived'.[507] In particular, a right frontoparietal network in the human brain seems critical for distinguishing the self from others.[508] Activation in the right inferior and medial parietal region, namely the anterior precuneus and posterior cingulate cortex, is proportionate to the degree that stimuli are perceived as referring to the self.[509] When subjects look at an image of their own face, activation is seen in the right hemisphere, especially at the right occipitotemporoparietal junction and in the right frontal operculum.[510]

Individuals may neglect or misidentify their own hands and feet when the right hemisphere – but not when the left hemisphere – is damaged or temporarily inactivated.[511] Asomatognosia, the condition in which subjects fail to recognise their embodied self or parts of their own body, is found in nearly 90 per cent of subjects following any right-hemisphere stroke;[512] and, conversely, the condition appears to be associated only with right-hemisphere deficits – Feinberg, who has made a study of the condition, notes that of the 100 cases known to him, not once has it followed left-hemisphere damage.[513]

In keeping with this, those with damage to the right frontotemporal cortex may experience a cognitive detachment from self.[514] When subjects read a first-person narrative, they activate the precuneus and anterior cingulate cortex bilaterally, but also preferentially the right temporo-parietal junction, compared with reading a third-person narrative.[515]

Philosophers spend a good deal of time inspecting and analysing processes that are usually – and perhaps must remain – implicit, unconscious, intuitive; in other words, examining the life of the right hemisphere from the standpoint of the left. It is perhaps then not surprising that the glue begins to disintegrate, and there is a nasty cracking noise as the otherwise normally robust sense of the self comes apart, possibly revealing more about the merits (or otherwise) of the process, than the self under scrutiny. Schizophrenics, like philosophers, have a problem with the sense of the self which ordinary individuals, involved with living, lack. As Wittgenstein once remarked: 'it's strange that in ordinary life we are not troubled by the feeling that the phenomenon is slipping away from us, the constant flux of appearance, but only when we philosophise. This indicates that what is in question here is an idea suggested by a misapplication of our language.'[516] Could this be read as the 'misapplication of language' – in other words, the faulty procedure of seeking truth by standing in the world of the left hemisphere while looking at the world of the right?

One recent elegant experiment underlines the key role played by the right hemisphere in the recognition of the self, and at the same time emphasises the left hemisphere's affinity with public, rather than personal, knowledge. Using the Wada test, each subject was shown a computer-generated picture of the subject's own face morphed with that of a person famous in public life. After the anaesthetic wore off, the subjects were then shown the separate pictures of the famous person and of themselves, and were asked which more closely resembled the picture they had previously seen. Those who had viewed the picture with their right hemisphere chose the picture of themselves: those who had viewed it with their left hemisphere chose the picture of the famous person.[517] In this study nine out of ten cases conformed to this pattern. Although there is one commissurotomy ('split-brain') case reported that appears to suggest the opposite,[518] virtually all other evidence points to the key role of the right hemisphere in self-recognition.[519]

The right frontal region appears to be essential for the determination of self in other modalities, too, such as voice recognition.[520] Damage to the right parietal and medial regions may result in confusions of self with other;[521] damage to the right frontal lobe creates a disturbance of ego boundaries, suggesting 'that the right hemisphere, particularly the right frontal region, under normal circumstances plays a crucial role in establishing the appropriate relationship between the self and the world'.[522] It is this region that is so obviously not functioning properly in schizophrenia, where subjects not only lack empathy, humour, metaphorical understanding, pragmatics, social skills and theory of mind, but crucially mistake the boundaries of self and other, even at times feeling themselves to melt into other individuals or that other beings are invading or occupying their own body space.

Important aspects of self-awareness in the sense of how we are likely to seem or come across to others – akin to insight – also depend on the right hemisphere. The capacity to understand one's self as a human being like others, which is involved in self-awareness, is an aspect of the human ability to identify with others, empathise with them and share their feelings, dependent as we have seen, on the right hemisphere. The right inferior parietal lobule plays a crucial role both in planning[523] and monitoring the outcomes[524] of one's own actions.

It was one of the earliest perceptions that the left hemisphere is the seat of *conscious* self-awareness, certainly for the expression of its selfhood through the conscious will.[525] I have already suggested that the expression of the will, in the sense of the conscious, rational will – grasping and manipulating – may have been responsible for the expansion of the left hemisphere. Nonetheless it turns out that when we are acting 'for ourselves', in the sense of initiating new action rather than following another's lead, the activity is largely in the right hemisphere, though this may be restricted to practical, habitual actions.[526] There is a tendency for independence and motivation to be associated with the right hemisphere, and passivity with the left hemisphere. This is related to its stickiness, described above, its relative inability to shift set, espouse a new way of looking at things, rather than get locked into environmental cues. 'Environmental dependency' syndrome refers to an inability to inhibit automatic responses to environmental cues: it is also known as 'forced utilisation behaviour'. Individuals displaying such behaviour will, for example, pick up a pair of glasses that are not their own and put them on, just because they are lying on the table, involuntarily pick up a pen and paper and start writing, or passively copy the behaviour of the examiner without being asked to, even picking up a stethoscope and pretending to use it. According to Kenneth Heilman, the syndrome, as well as aboulia (loss of will), akinesia (failure to move), and impersistence (inability to carry through an action) are all commoner after right, rather than left, frontal damage.[527] In four out of the five cases of environmental dependency in Lhermitte's classic paper in which the syndrome was first described, the only or principal lesion was in the right frontal lobe. In each case the patient explained that 'you held out objects to me; I thought I had to use them'.[528] However, the situation is far from straightforward, since my reading of further data provided by Lhermitte is that the syndrome is as common after lesions in either frontal lobe;[529] and a lesion in either frontal lobe may, in any case, 'release' behavioural patterns characteristic of the posterior hemisphere on the same side (see below), as much as impair the functioning of the hemisphere as a whole (or indeed the contralateral hemisphere via the corpus callosum). But it would be in keeping with other research that shows forced utilisation behaviour after right-hemisphere damage: one patient not only showed exaggerated responses to external cues (utilization behaviour), and motor impersistence, but a right-handed instinctive grasp reaction, after an infarct in the right thalamus, which was associated with under-perfusion of the entire right cerebral cortex, especially the frontal area.[530]

In reality we are a composite of the two hemispheres, and despite the interesting results of experiments designed artificially to separate their functioning, they work together most of the time at the everyday level. But that does not at all exclude that they may have radically different agendas, and over long time periods and large numbers of individuals it becomes apparent that they each instantiate a way of being in the world that is at conflict with the other.

CODA: THE 'FRONT–BACK' PROBLEM

I mentioned at the beginning of this chapter that there was one intrahemispheric rather than interhemispheric regional difference that I needed to refer to. This involves the relationship of the frontal lobes, the most highly evolved and most distinctively human of all regions of the brain, with the processes going on elsewhere in the brain, including the posterior cortex, which they exist to exert control over. The frontal lobes achieve what they achieve largely through what is normally described as *inhibition* of the posterior part of the same hemisphere. It might be better described, however, especially in the case of the right hemisphere, as *modulation* – the inhibitory effect is 'significantly more pronounced' in the case of the left hemisphere, perhaps in keeping with its less integrated, more black and white, style.[531] This relationship between 'front' and 'back' is another example of paired 'opponent processors' enabling fine modulation of response (see p. 9 above).

What do I mean by modulation? A process that resists, but does not negate. It is best thought of as the imposition of necessary distance, or delay, enabling something new to come forward. In this way it is like the apparently antagonistic relationship of the two hemispheres (a topic which I will explore at length later in the book): it is neither that the products of one hemisphere negate the products of the other, nor that in some bland sense they merely 'complement' one another. Their incompatibility permits instead, in a dialectical synthesis, something new to arise. To take an example: if the right hemisphere's immediacy of association with emotion and the body leads it to prioritise what is close, what is 'mine', the right frontal lobe brings distance and delay to espousing 'my' position. As a result it enables others to stand forth as individuals like 'me'; it enables a broader empathy and the beginnings of altruism. This is not a negation of something by the frontal lobe, but a modulation of it, an 'unpacking', if you like, of something that was there all along, albeit in germ only – something that comes to life only when a degree of necessary distance is interposed. Or to take another example, this time from the left hemisphere. The relative detachment from the body displayed by the left hemisphere, and its tendency to abstraction, normally serve its purposeful striving towards individual gain. The left frontal lobe, however, brings distance, and allows the experience of the peaceful detachment from the material realm and 'emptying out' described by experts in meditation as a mystical experience. Again this is no negation, but an elaboration, of what the left hemisphere affords. There is not likely to be 'a God spot' in the brain, and the area is fraught with problems of terminology and methodology: but there are areas that are often implicated as accompaniments of religious experience.[532] An appropriately cautious and objective review of the literature to date by Michael Trimble concludes that there is a slow accumulation of evidence in favour of religious experience being more closely linked with the 'non-dominant' hemisphere, especially the posterior right hemisphere (temporoparietal region). But, to illustrate my point, the other region that is implicated lies in the left frontal lobe – specifically because of its power to inhibit the posterior left hemisphere (temporoparietal region), the seat of language and of sequential analysis.[533]

CONCLUSION

The literature on brain function is enormously extensive, and increasing geometrically with every passing day. This chapter cannot, in the nature of things, pretend to be an exhaustive review: to achieve that alone would require a team of experts, and a book several times the size of this one. Rather it is designed to highlight the differences between the hemispheres, where there is coherent evidence, and particularly to reverse the entrenched prejudice that, while the right hemisphere may add a bit of colour to life, it is the left hemisphere that does the *serious* business. With the (admittedly hugely important) exception of explicit manipulation involving language and serial analysis, the left hemisphere is not the 'dominant' hemisphere. Language and analysis will form the subject of the next chapter. What I have tried here to convey is the sheer extent, and something of the feel, of our dependence on the right hemisphere, all of which stands in complete contrast to the view of it as the 'silent' hemisphere. This, and the still current soubriquet, the 'minor' hemisphere, should make us think about the way in which we view ourselves. We are so used to focussing on utility and 'function' that the fact that right-hemisphere damage may completely alter the way in which we stand in relation to the world, and fundamentally change our mode of being, has gone until recently virtually unnoticed. Indeed at the risk of appearing to allow the left hemisphere even less to walk away with, I should point out that there is evidence that even those of the highest *verbal*, as well as spatial, ability probably rely to a greater extent on the right hemisphere.[534] Perhaps inevitably following from that, it turns out that those of highest intelligence, whatever their discipline, may do so.[535]

Ultimately if the left hemisphere is the hemisphere of 'what', the right hemisphere, with its preoccupation with context, the relational aspects of experience, emotion and the nuances of expression, could be said to be the hemisphere of 'how'. This perhaps explains why conventional neuroscience, being itself largely a manifestation of left-hemisphere activity, has focussed so much on *what* the brain is doing in which hemisphere, not *in what way* it does it in each hemisphere, thus, in my view, missing the significance of what it is trying to understand.

Before embarking on this chapter, I suggested that there were two ways of being in the world, both of which were essential. One was to allow things to be *present* to us in all their embodied particularity, with all their changeability and impermanence, and their interconnectedness, as part of a whole which is forever in flux. In this world we, too, feel connected to what we experience, part of that whole, not confined in subjective isolation from a world that is viewed as objective. The other was to step outside the flow of experience and 'experience' our experience in a special way: to *re-present* the world in a form that is less truthful, but apparently clearer, and therefore cast in a form which is more useful for manipulation of the world and one another. This world is explicit, abstracted, compartmentalised, fragmented, static (though its 'bits' can be re-set in motion, like a machine), essentially lifeless. From this world we feel detached, but in relation to it we are powerful.

I believe the essential difference between the right hemisphere and the left hemisphere is that the right hemisphere pays attention to the Other, whatever it is that exists apart from ourselves, with which it sees itself in profound relation. It is deeply attracted to, and given life by, the relationship, the betweenness, that exists with this Other. By contrast, the left hemisphere pays attention to the virtual world that it has created, which is self-consistent, but self-contained, ultimately disconnected from the Other, making it powerful, but ultimately only able to operate on, and to know, itself.

However, as I also emphasised at the outset, both hemispheres take part in virtually all 'functions' to some extent, and in reality both are always engaged. I do not wish to leave the impression that it might be a good thing if the entire population had a left-hemisphere stroke. I take it for granted that the contributions made by the left hemisphere, to language and systematic thought in particular, are invaluable. Our talent for division, for seeing the parts, is of staggering importance – second only to our capacity to transcend it, in order to see the whole. These gifts of the left hemisphere have helped us achieve nothing less than civilisation itself, with all that that means. Even if we could abandon them, which of course we can't, we would be fools to do so, and would come off infinitely the poorer. There are siren voices that call us to do exactly that, certainly to abandon clarity and precision (which, in any case, importantly depend on both hemispheres), and I want to emphasise that I am passionately opposed to them. We need the ability to make fine discriminations, and to use reason appropriately. But these contributions need to be made in the service of something else, that only the right hemisphere can bring. Alone they are destructive. And right now they may be bringing us close to forfeiting the civilisation they helped to create.

CHAPTER 3

LANGUAGE, TRUTH AND MUSIC

IN WHAT HAS GONE BEFORE, I HAVE DELIBERATELY FOLLOWED NEUROPSYCHOLOGICAL practice in focussing on a set of discrete tasks or functions, that can be defined and measured, since that is the way we have gathered information about the brain, and it is the way we are used to thinking about it. I now want to look at this material in a different light. I want to draw it together, and suggest that the hemispheric differences are not just a curiosity, with no further significance, a bunch of neuropsychological facts, but actually represent two individually coherent, but incompatible, aspects of the world.

That will lead naturally to an exploration of why it is we have language – for communicating, for thinking, or for what? And what is the role of music? Do the answers to these questions cast any light on the asymmetrical expansions of the left and right hemispheres?

THE NEW AND THE FAMILIAR, AND TWO KINDS OF KNOWING

One of the findings mentioned in the last chapter (see pp. 40 and 75 above) was the important discovery by Goldberg and Costa, confirmed by subsequent research, that new experience of any kind – whether it be of music, or words, or real-life objects, or imaginary constructs – engages the right hemisphere. As soon as it starts to become familiar or routine, the right hemisphere is less engaged and eventually the 'information' becomes the concern of the left hemisphere only.[1]

Understandably this has tended to be viewed as a specialisation in information processing, whereby 'novel stimuli' are preferentially 'processed' by the right hemisphere and routine or familiar ones by the left hemisphere. But this already, like any model, presupposes the nature of what one is looking at (a machine for information processing). What would we find if we were to use a different model? Would perhaps something else emerge?

I want to suggest a different way of looking at the role played by the brain in forming our experience of the world. This involves concerning oneself with the nature of knowledge itself.

We use the word 'know' in at least two importantly different senses. In one sense knowledge is essentially an *encounter* with something or someone, therefore with something 'other' (a truth embodied in the phrase 'carnal knowledge'). We say we know someone in the sense that we have experience of him or her, so that we have a 'feel' for who he or she is, as an individual distinct from others. This kind of knowledge permits a sense of the uniqueness of the other. It is also uniquely 'my' knowledge. If another person were to ask 'what is she like?', you might begin by trying to describe her in a few words ('quick-tempered', 'lively', modified by qualifying phrases such as 'quite', 'a bit', 'very' and so on), but you'd soon be frustrated by the feeling that these general terms didn't really help get it across. You might resort to retelling instances of things she'd said or done. You might get out a photograph – we learn a lot from faces. But if the questioning continued, you'd have to say: 'Look, you'll just have to meet her – I'll introduce you.' It's also 'my' knowledge, not just in the sense that I can't pass it on to you, but in the sense that it's got something of me in it. What I know about her comes from the fact that it was I who encountered her. Another person might allow other aspects of her to come forward and might know her as someone rather different. But it would also be odd if everyone who knew her found her to be someone altogether different. That would imply that there was no stable underlying entity to know. We would expect a consensus of those who knew her to emerge. This is the kind of knowledge we think of first when talking about the living.

Coming on the heels of the last chapter, I hope that some of these points may ring a bell. Certain aspects appear familiar. It's the way we naturally approach knowledge of a *living being*; it's to do with *individuals*, and permits a sense of *uniqueness*; it's 'mine', *personal*, not something I can just hand on to someone else unchanged; and it is not *fixed* or *certain*. It's not easily captured in *words*; the *whole* is not captured by trying to list the *parts* ('quick-tempered', 'lively', etc); it has at least something to do with the *embodied* person (the photograph); it resists *general* terms; it has to be *experienced*; and the knowledge depends on *between-ness* (an encounter). These are all, in fact, aspects of the world 'according to' the right hemisphere.

This kind of knowledge derives from a coming together of one being or thing as a whole with another. But there is another kind of knowledge, a knowledge that comes from putting things together from bits. It is the knowledge of what we call facts.[2] This is not usually well applied to knowing people. We could have a go – for example, 'born on 16 September 1964', 'lives in New York', '5ft 4in tall', 'red hair', 'freckles', and so on. Immediately you get the sense of somebody – who you *don't* actually know. Either it's a read-out from a police database, or it's one of those cheesy magazine profiles of celebrities ('latest book read', etc). What's more, it sounds as though you're describing an inanimate object – 'chest of drawers, two single over three double, bun feet, circa 1870, $30 \times 22 \times 28$in' – or a corpse. It is the only kind of knowledge permitted by science (though some of the very best scientists have used subterfuge to get away with the other kind). It concerns knowledge in the public domain – the local train timetable, the date of the Battle of Trafalgar, and so on. Its virtue is its certainty – it's fixed. It doesn't change from person to person or from moment to moment. Context is therefore irrelevant. But it doesn't give a good idea of the whole, just of a partial reconstruction of aspects of the whole.

This knowledge has its uses. Its great strength is that its findings are repeatable. Its qualities are the inverse of those previously outlined, and they are associated with the left hemisphere: an affinity with the *non-living*; with '*pieces*' of information; *general, impersonal, fixed, certain* and *disengaged.*

Both kinds of knowledge can be brought to bear on the same object, of course. My knowledge of you can be informed by knowing your age, height and place of birth, but that is not in itself at all what I mean by knowing you. These ways of knowing are so different that in many languages other than English they are referred to by different words: the first by, for example, Latin *cognoscere*, French *connaître*, German *kennen*; the second by Latin *sapere*, French *savoir*, German *wissen* – and so on. What I want to suggest is that, just as *wissen* could sometimes be applied to people and living things, *kennen* can be applied to a lot more than our acquaintances. This kind of knowing may help us to understand, rather than simply to amass information about, a host of things in the world, animate and inanimate. In fact there is clear evidence that we used to do this in the past, but have lost the habit or perhaps even the ability (see Part II).

To take one example of an apparently non-living entity that appears to require us to know it in the sense of *kennen* rather than *wissen*, think of a piece of music. The approach to music is like entering into relation with another living individual, and research suggests that understanding music is perceived as similar to knowing a person; we freely attribute human qualities to music, including age, sex, personality characteristics and feelings.[3] The empathic nature of the experience means that it has more in common with encountering a person than a concept or an idea that could be expressed in words.[4] It is important to recognise that music does not *symbolise* emotional meaning, which would require that it be interpreted; it *metaphorises* it – 'carries it over' direct to our unconscious minds. Equally it does not symbolise human qualities: it conveys them direct, so that it acts on us, and we respond to it, as in a human encounter. In other words, knowing a piece of music, like knowing other works of art, is a matter of *kennenlernen*. Coming to us through the right hemisphere, such living creations are seen as being essentially human in nature. In an earlier book I argued that works of art – music, poems, paintings, great buildings – can be understood only if we appreciate that they are more like people than texts, concepts or things.[5] But the perception is ancient: Aristotle, for example, compared tragedy to an organic being.[6]

What Goldberg and Costa may be uncovering is not just something about novelty and familiarity but about two whole ways of knowing in the two hemispheres. To know (in the sense of *kennen*) something is never fully to know it (in the sense of *wissen*) at all, since it will remain for ever changing, evolving, revealing further aspects of itself – in this sense always *new*, though familiar, in the original sense of coming to belong among our chosen ones, those with whom we stand in close relation, our *familia* (in Latin literally our 'household'). To know (in the sense of *wissen*) is to pin something down so that it is repeatable and repeated, so that it becomes familiar in the other sense: routine, inauthentic, lacking the spark of life. I think what one might deduce from their study is that the first apprehension of anything is by the right hemisphere while it remains new, and, I would suggest, while we are still getting to know it (in the sense of *kennen-lernen*); but that it is soon taken over by the left hemisphere, where it becomes familiar, in the sense that it is now known (*gewußt*) and therefore certain (*gewiß*). Knowledge of the whole is all too soon followed by knowledge of the parts.

Jung said that 'all cognition is akin to recognition'.[7] By this he meant that we come to know in the sense of 'cognise' (*wissen*) something only by recognising (*erkennen*) something we already knew (*kennen*). In the process it becomes clear, familiar, where before it was latent, intuitive. This is, I believe, an expression of the same process that Goldberg and Costa describe at the neurological level; the new becomes old. In fact Nietzsche goes further and seizes the nub of the matter, when he expresses a similar idea: 'it is through "knowing" [*erkennen*, re-cognition] that we come to have the feeling that we *already know* [*wissen*] something; thus it means *combating a feeling of newness and transforming the apparently new into something old*.'[8]

As Gregory Bateson says, all knowledge has to be knowledge of distinction, and it is of something other than the self.[9] Equally one might say that all experience is experience of difference. Even at the sensory level we cannot experience anything unless there is a change or difference: our sensory nerves quickly 'fatigue', and we become accustomed, for example, to a smell, or to a sound. Our senses respond to the difference *between* values – to relative, not absolute, values.[10] (It seems that knowledge and perception, and therefore experience, exist only in the relations *between* things. Perhaps indeed everything that exists does so only in relation-ships, like mathematics or music: there are aspects of quantum physics that would support such a view.)

This fact, that knowledge comes from distinctions, implies that we can come to an understanding of the nature of any one thing, whatever it might be, only by comparison with something else we already know, and by observing the similarities and differences. However, just as everything changes its nature, however slightly, when it changes its context, what we choose to compare a thing with determines which aspects of it will stand forward and which will recede. Thus comparing a foot-ball match with a trip to the betting shop brings out some aspects of the experience; comparing it with going to church brings out others. The model we choose to use to understand something determines what we find. If it is the case that our under-standing is an *effect* of the metaphors we choose, it is also true that it is a *cause*: our understanding itself guides the choice of metaphor by which we understand it. The chosen metaphor is both cause and effect of the relationship. Thus how we think about our selves and our relationship to the world is already revealed in the metaphors we unconsciously choose to talk about it. That choice further entrenches our partial view of the subject. Paradoxically we seem to be obliged to understand something – including ourselves – well enough to choose the appropriate model before we can understand it. Our first leap determines where we land.[11]

If we assume a purely mechanical universe and take the machine as our model, we will uncover the view that – surprise, surprise – the body, and the brain with it, is a machine. To a man with a hammer everything begins to look like a nail. But because we can come to know things only in terms of other things we know, every 'explanation', however convincing, is merely a model; a comparison of something with something else. All one can say when trying, for example, to interpret scanning data to understand what the brain is doing when I imitate the action of someone else, is that there appears to be some sort of correlation between whatever it is we observe going on in the brain – say a 'hot spot' on a brain scan, suggesting increased metabolism in my right frontal lobe – with the experience I am having at the same time. The nature of that correlation, however, remains obscure, because it is instantiated in a unique substance, which is the human body – there isn't anything that *that* can be compared with, to get a handle on it, except other living bodies, which does not get us much further. You can compare it with a machine, if you wish; but the analogy is bound to be a poor one in every respect except, of course, whatever it is that the body and a machine have in common, and that is *all* the comparison will reveal (the catch is that to those who have bought into this model as the way to illumination, everything about the body will come to look more and more mechanical, and so the model comes to seem more and more apt: the original choice eventually seems confirmed as a perfect fit). Talk of 'functions' and 'mechanisms' leads us up this particular garden path. The model of the machine is the only one that the left hemisphere likes; remember that it is specialised in dealing with tools and machines. The machine is something that has been put together by the left hemisphere from the bits, so it is understandable purely in terms of its parts; the machine is lifeless and its parts are inert – the tappets don't change their nature with their context.

I want to try to stand back a bit from the question of which 'functions', therefore, the supposedly machine-like hemispheres are performing, and think of them instead more globally as having a disposition, or stance, towards the world – having a 'take' on it, if you like. This is to suggest that they may share some aspects of human mental life, I know; but is that really as strange as it sounds – or any stranger than supposing that all they did was compute like machines? If it is true that consciousness, whatever it is, arises from the sheer complexity of self-interconnected neuronal activity,[12] why should the hemispheres, the two largest and most densely self-interconnected neuronal masses, each amounting to half the brain, and each capable of sustaining conscious life on its own, not have some of the features of normal consciousness? The separated hemispheres in split-brain patients each have a distinct personality, with characteristic tastes and preferences, according to one of those most closely involved with the study of such patients.[13] The unconscious, while not identical with, is certainly more strongly associated with, the right hemisphere (for a fuller discussion of this issue, see pp. 187–8 below). To that extent, it might be expected that the separate hemispheres have distinct personalities and values: as Freud wrote, the unconscious is 'a particular realm of the mind with its own wishful impulses, its own mode of expression and its peculiar mental mechanisms which are not in force elsewhere'.[14]

This is just another model, and like all models it should be taken for what it is, a comparison, not an identification. The most one can hope is that it may allow something to stand forward, something different at any rate from what stands forward in the conventional cognitivist account. Applying a different model, not that of a machine but of a person, to each hemisphere reveals different aspects, and enables us to get a sense of each hemisphere as a whole rather than an assemblage.

WHAT LANGUAGE TELLS US ABOUT THE HEMISPHERES

Since what we think about the world and what we know of it is, whether we like it or not, mediated largely by language, it's worth taking a closer look at the nature of language, and its relationship to the hemispheres. It is likely to tell us a lot about hemisphere differences, about how each hemisphere relates to the world at large, and even about how the hemispheres relate to one another, since it is itself nothing less than a version of the world, a type of experience, which therefore bridges the physical and the abstract, the unconscious and the conscious, the implicit and the explicit.

Language is the province of both hemispheres and, like everything else, has different meanings in either hemisphere. Each uses it differently, and different aspects of it stand out in the use that either hemisphere makes of it.

Let's return to the structure of the brain and take another look at that strange asymmetry in the left parietal region, where language is said to reside. Isn't that *obviously* what it's for? What's the problem with that explanation?

While it is true that the left hemisphere expansion is now associated with language functions,[15] there are difficulties with the belief that it is language that necessitated the expansion.[16] For one thing, fossil records of primitive humans from the earliest periods, long before anthropologists believe language developed,[17] already show this typical pattern of brain asymmetry.[18] Even more striking is the fact that some of the great apes, and possibly other large primates such as baboons, which clearly have no language,[19] already show a similar asymmetry to that of the human brain, with enlargement in the same area of the left hemisphere that in humans is associated with language.[20] The planum temporale, which in humans is certainly associated with language, and is generally larger on the left than on the right, is also larger asymmetrically, also on the left, in orang-utans, gorillas[21] and chimpanzees.[22] And Yakovlevian torque, too, is present not only in fossil humans, but in the great apes.[23]

What is more, now that we know more about the functioning of our own brains, we know that it is not actually true that language is subserved by one hemisphere: its functioning is distributed across the two. If it is true that most syntax and vocabulary, the nitty-gritty of language, are in most subjects housed in the left hemisphere, it is nonetheless the right hemisphere which subserves higher linguistic functions, such as understanding the meaning of a whole phrase or sentence in context, its tone, its emotional significance, along with use of humour, irony, metaphor, and so on. But if it is the right hemisphere that, in linguistic terms, paints the picture, it is still the left hemisphere that holds the 'paint box'. Following a left-hemisphere stroke, the right-hemisphere painter has lost his materials. Hence the old view that the left hemisphere was 'dominant': in its absence no picture is painted – there is no coherent speech. But the argument that language had to be held together in one place, thus explaining the left-hemisphere expansion, just doesn't hold water.

So what *is* this expansion in the left hemisphere about? Perhaps, it has been suggested, it is a consequence of right handedness. But this begs a further question, namely why we should have developed right handedness. The usual assumption is that, man being the tool-making animal, extra skill was needed in the manufacture of such tools, requiring specialisation. But it is not obvious why skill is best acquired in one hand only. Skilful operators could be even more skilful if they could use both hands equally well, and the brain is not subject to some economic regulation that means that the development of one hand must be at the expense of the skill acquisition of the other. It is, however, an evolutionary fact that, for using and making, we have tended strongly to prefer the right hand, which is controlled by the left side of the brain – in fact by part of the brain that is, as it happens, very close to Broca's area, the part of the left hemisphere that has come to subserve the expressive power of syntax and vocabulary, the names of things and how we put them together.

Moreover if we look once again at the higher apes, it also turns out that some of them begin to prefer the right hand to grasp things – despite the fact that, though they may *use* sticks and stones, they are certainly not tool-makers in the human sense.[24] Any asymmetry in their brains is unlikely to be due to the need for brain space to house the complex skills of tool making. Their grasping right hands must be a sign of something else.

Most bizarrely, it would seem that it is *not an expansion at all*. It's just that there is a deliberate *inhibition of expansion* in the corresponding area in the right hemisphere. And we even know the genes that do it. The researcher who found them comments: 'It is safe to assume that the asymmetry that ended up leading to language is unlikely to have appeared because of language ... It is likely to have appeared for some other reason and basically got co-opted by language.'[25]

Lateralisation of brain function, and asymmetry of its structure, occurred without language or tool design. I am not saying that, once hemisphere asymmetry came to accelerate in humans, it had nothing to do with language or handedness: it obviously did.[26] My point is only that these could not have been the drivers, the origin of the phenomenon; the asymmetries associated with language and handedness must be epiphenomena of something else, something more fundamental, more primitive. What was that?

In order to understand this asymmetry better, we need to step back for a moment and ask ourselves why we have language at all. Because the world without it is so unimaginable, and because language is the medium through which we appraise all things, including language itself, it is harder than it may at first seem to bring it into focus. Just what sort of a thing is language? What sort of plan might it form part of, and has it got anything in common with handedness?

Fairly obviously, one might think, language must have developed for communication. But that is not as obvious as it seems. Some 300,000 to 400,000 years ago or longer, *homo heidelbergensis*, the common ancestor of *homo sapiens* and *homo neanderthalensis*, had a large brain and a vocal apparatus comparable to those of modern humans, and, although we cannot be sure of the earliest date such features arose, it may well have been as long ago as about half a million years.[27] However, the evidence suggests that we did not develop the degree of sophisticated symbol manipulation that language requires until a much later point, possibly as little as 40,000 years ago, but at any rate not earlier than a mere 80,000 years ago, when the first cultural artefacts, along with evidence of visual representation, suddenly and profusely arise, and humans began to adopt ritualised burial of the dead.[28] It would seem, then, that for most of human history, despite a large brain and presumably high intelligence,[29] they managed to communicate satisfactorily without language as we understand it. Admittedly they were not civilised in the true meaning of the word. But they survived and thrived as *social* animals, living in groups. How did our ancestors communicate adequately, if not by language?

Addressing these questions necessitates looking at yet another curiosity in what the fossil record tells us.

We know that spoken language is dependent, not only on sufficient brain space to house the dictionary and grammar, but on quite specific features of the vocal apparatus (not just the vocal cords, but the articulatory bits and pieces of the tongue and mouth) enabling us to articulate a wide range of sounds, as well as on a remarkable degree of respiratory control, allowing us to sustain long, fluent, articulated phrases, and to modulate intonation subtly over the length of a single breath. All known languages require these features. Monkeys and apes do not have any such control, which is one of the reasons why attempts to train them to speak have been so unsuccessful. Birds alone can imitate human speech, while our nearest relatives cannot hope to do so: the birds' vocal apparatus, or syrinx (literally, 'flute'), and their sophisticated control of respiration, explains why.[30]

When did humans develop these capacities? It might be thought a hopeless task to assess at what point in human history our ancestors developed the sophisticated control of vocal apparatus and respiration that we now possess. However, some ingenious observations allow a reliable inference to be made. In order to reach the tongue, the nerve which supplies it, the hypoglossal nerve, has to pass through an opening in the base of the skull, called the anterior condylar canal. The amount of work a nerve has to do is reflected in its size; in turn the size of the hole through which it passes indicates the size of the nerve. So by measuring the size of the canal in the base of the skull, we can get a very good idea of how much articulatory work the tongue of the skull's 'owner' had to do. Similar considerations apply to the thoracic vertebral canal in supplying the nerves that control respiration to the muscles of the chest wall. And what we find, as we might expect, is that apes and monkeys have much smaller canals, in relation to the nerves both of articulation and of respiration, than modern humans. But, and here is the thought-provoking oddity, examination of the earliest human skeletons, from long before the time we believe language arose, reveals canal sizes almost indistinguishable from those of modern humans. Why is that?

The most likely answer is a surprise, and requires a bit of a frame shift for most of us. For the explanation of this sophisticated control and modulation of the production of sound, in the absence of language as we know it, has to be that it was for a sort of non-verbal language, one in which there was intonation and phrasing, but no actual words: and what is that, if not music?

There are significant similarities between music and language, suggesting at least a common origin. For example, many subtle aspects of language are mediated by regions of the right hemisphere which also mediate the performance and experience of music. Furthermore these right hemisphere regions are the homologues of areas in the left hemisphere that are involved with language production and comprehension – they are in the 'same' position on the other side of the brain. Music and language have a shared architecture, built out of intonational phrases related by a kind of 'syntax', although the syntax of music has more to do with the overall shape of the whole piece over many minutes (or, in the case of Wagner,[31] hours) than with the specific relationship of rapidly successive elements in a linear progression. In both music and speech, the phrase is the basic unit of structure and function, and both speech phrases and musical phrases have melody and rhythm, which play a crucial role in their expressiveness. There is even a close semantic relationship between music and language: musical phrases convey specific meanings that, if required, we will intuitively associate with specific words.[32]

When it comes to understanding the origins of language, however, there is less agreement, and speculation has followed one of three paths. There are those who believe that music is a useless spin-off, or epiphenomenon, of the development of language; there are those, on the contrary, who believe that language itself developed out of musical communication (a kind of singing); and finally there are those who hold that music and language developed independently but alongside one another, out of a common ancestor, which has been dubbed 'musilanguage'.[33] It seems to me that this last option is hard to distinguish from the 'music came first' position. That is because, while 'musilanguage' may not have been very sophisticated music, it must have been more like music than like referential language, and, for it to have been a 'language' in any sense, it must have relied on what we think of as the musical aspects – the non-verbal aspects – of language, such as pitch, intonation, volume, rhythm and phrasing. The very existence of the concept of 'musilanguage' merely points up how much the musical aspects of language do contribute to meaning, in that they could in themselves provide the basis for communication of meaning.

The evidence of the fossil record is, as I say, that the control of voice and respiration needed for singing apparently came into being long before they would ever have been required by language. But is there any reason, apart from this, why we should adopt the view that music came first?

LANGUAGE OR MUSIC: WHICH CAME FIRST?

There are, if nothing else, some indications on the matter. In the first place, the 'syntax' of music is simpler, less highly evolved, than that of language, suggesting an earlier origin. More importantly, observation of the development of language in children confirms that the musical aspects of language do indeed come first. Intonation, phrasing and rhythm develop first; syntax and vocabulary come only later. Newborns are already sensitive to the rhythms of language;[34] they prefer 'infant-directed speech' – otherwise known as 'baby talk' – which emphasises what is called prosody, the music of speech. In response to this, mothers expand the pitch excursions, broaden the repertoire and raise the overall pitch of their speech, as well as slowing the tempo and emphasising its rhythm, as soon as their child is born.[35] Newborn infants can distinguish the timbre and intonation of their mother's voice, and prefer it to any other;[36] and can distinguish the unique intonation of their 'mother' tongue, which again they prefer to others.[37] These capacities for distinguishing the characteristic inflections of a language, or even of an individual speaker, are not signs of an inborn talent for language as such: they rely on aspects of right-hemisphere holistic processing capable of making fine discriminations in global patterns and having little to do with the analytic processing of language by the left hemisphere.[38] Indeed even primates can iden-tify individual voices, using such features. These processes, then, in newborns have more to do with the activation of areas of the brain which subserve the non-verbal, the musical, aspects of speech. There is a (not wholly reliable) principle that 'ontogeny recapitulates phylogeny', that, in other words, the development of individuals of a species follows a similar course to that taken by the development of the species as a whole: a simple example is the early development by the human embryo of a tail, which it later loses. To the degree that this principle holds here, then music came before language. An observation to this effect was made even by Salomon Henschen: 'The musical faculty is phylogenetically older than language; some animals have a musical faculty—birds in a high degree. It is also ontogenet-ically older, for the child begins to sing earlier than to speak.'[39]

Ultimately music is the communication of emotion, the most fundamental form of communication, which in phylogeny, as well as ontogeny, came and comes first. Neurological research strongly supports the assumption that 'our love of music reflects the ancestral ability of our mammalian brain to transmit and receive basic emotional sounds', the prosody and rhythmic motion that emerge intuitively from entrainment of the body in emotional expression: 'music was built upon the prosodic mechanisms of the right hemisphere that allow us affective emotional communications through vocal intonations.'[40] Presumably such 'mechanisms' were highly important for group survival. They were also likely to have deep roots: 'the deeply emotional stirrings generated by music', writes the influential anthropolo-gist Robin Dunbar, 'suggest to me that music has very ancient origins, long predating the evolution of language.'[41]

This conclusion has not been universally welcomed. There are a number of reasons, but one stands out, at least as far as concerns geneticists. Developments must demonstrate evolutionary advantage. Language, it is reasoned, gives a huge advantage in the power it confers to its possessor: but what has music to do with power – what advantage can it yield? It doesn't apparently put you in a position to deliver a knockout blow to the opposition, and doesn't look like a way of pushing your genes (despite unconvincing appeals to what one might call the 'Tom Jones factor'). So music has been seen as a pointless 'exaptation' of language: that is to say, an adaptation of a skill, originally developed for its competitive advantage in one area, to a quite different purpose.[42] Thus typing could be seen as an exaptation of the digital skill developed for making tools: it was not the pressure to out-publish one's colleagues that caused the skill to develop in the first place, any more than we have legs in order to give employment to tailors. Music has to be, on such an account, an irrelevant spin-off from something with more of a competitive cutting edge – namely, language: Steven Pinker certainly sees it as such, and even suggests that music is as meaningless and self-indulgent as pornography or a taste for fatty food.[43] Nonetheless the evidence does not stack up in favour of music being an exaptation of language – rather the reverse. If language evolved later, it looks like it evolved from music. So the evolutionary problem remains (I hope to offer a possible resolution of the problem in due course).

It is not only geneticists who may have difficulty with the idea. We now tend to think of music as peripheral, if not useless. We are all inclined to raise an eyebrow when our ancestors are referred to as the 'singing Neanderthals'.[44] But in fact many theorists of language, including Rousseau in the eighteenth century, von Humboldt in the nineteenth century and Jespersen in the twentieth, have thought it likely that language developed from music, so that the theories of Mithen and others in the twenty-first century do not come out of the blue.[45]

That we could use non-verbal means, such as music, to communicate is, in any case, hardly surprising. The shock comes partly from the way we in the West now view music: we have lost the sense of the central position that music once occu-pied in communal life, and still does in most parts of the world today. Despite the fact that there is no culture anywhere in the world that does not have music, and in which people do not join together to sing or dance, we have relegated music to the sidelines of life. We might think of music as an individualistic, even solitary experience, but that is rare in the history of the world. In more traditionally struc-tured societies, performance of music plays both an integral, and an integrative, role not only in celebration, religious festivals, and other rituals, but also in daily work and recreation; and it is above all a shared performance, not just something we listen to passively.[46] It has a vital way of binding people together, helping them to be aware of shared humanity, shared feelings and experiences, and actively drawing them together. In our world, competition and specialisation have made music something compartmentalised, somewhere away from life's core. So Oliver Sacks writes:

> This primal role of music is to some extent lost today, when we have a special class of composers and performers, and the rest of us are often reduced to passive

listening. One has to go to a concert, or a church or a musical festival, to recapture the collective excitement and bonding of music. In such a situation, there seems to be *an actual binding of nervous systems* . . .[47]

But if it should turn out that music leads to language, rather than language to music, it helps us understand for the first time the otherwise baffling historical fact that poetry evolved *before* prose.[48] Prose was at first known as *pezos logos*, literally 'pedestrian, or walking, *logos*', as opposed to the usual dancing *logos* of poetry. In fact early poetry was sung: so the evolution of literary skill progresses, if that is the correct word, from right-hemisphere music (words that are sung), to right-hemisphere language (the metaphorical language of poetry), to left-hemisphere language (the referential language of prose).

Music is likely to be the ancestor of language and it arose largely in the right hemisphere, where one would expect a means of communication with others, promoting social cohesion, to arise.

COMMUNICATION WITHOUT LANGUAGE

The predominance of language, and, above all, of the effects of the written word, may itself have contributed to the decline of music in our culture. (I hope in later chapters to show that the culture of the written word tends inevitably towards the predominantly left-hemisphere phenomenon of a competitive, specialised and compartmentalised world.) We may find it initially hard to accept the primacy of music, since we are trapped inside a culture that is so language-determined and language-dependent that we cannot imagine it being any other way. Because the part of communicating that we are aware of lies in the choice of words, we imagine wrongly that that must be where most, or perhaps even all, communication lies. What we are not conscious of, and need for most purposes to remain unconscious of, is that the majority of the messages we communicate are not in words at all. Animals communicate with one another, and even co-operate, without language, so why shouldn't we?

Some animals adopt a form of 'musilanguage', using intonation, not just body language, to communicate with humans: look at the domestic dog. Amongst one another they communicate preferentially by scent, and body language. But they have achieved awareness of the fact that intonation is an important part of human communication. Good vocal communicators as they are, the possibilities for them are limited: they have neither the range of concepts to convey, nor the vocal or respirational apparatus that early humans would have possessed with which to convey them.

In case one is tempted to think that music could never provide a flexible or extensive enough means of communication for hominids, one should remember that the extensive social lives of some of the most intelligent non-human animals, not only bonobos, but aquatic mammals, such as whales and dolphins, down to and including the complex attack manoeuvres of killer whales, are co-ordinated entirely by what one might call 'music' – a 'language' of pitch, intonation and temporal relation.[49] And our pre-lingual children communicate with us – not always, it is true, with desired clarity, but effectively enough. Even left-hemisphere stroke sufferers, who have suddenly and devastatingly lost the use of language, can learn to communicate an array of intentions and meanings, as well as, obviously, emotions, despite the fact that they are at the immense double disadvantage that they did not grow up learning instinctively and intuitively the skill of communicating without words, and that they live in a culture which has organised itself wholly around communication through language.

Perhaps the most striking evidence, though, is that there are extant tribes in the Amazon basin, such as the Pirahã, a hunter-gatherer tribe in Brazil, whose language is effectively a kind of song, possessing such a complex array of tones, stresses, and syllable lengths that its speakers can dispense with their vowels and consonants altogether and sing, hum or whistle conversations.[50]

For our primate ancestors, who clearly had no speech, body language played a vital role in social cohesion, especially in prolonged sessions of mutual grooming. One theory is that singing, a sort of instinctive musical language of intonation, came into being precisely because, with the advent of humans, social groups became too large for grooming to be practical as a means of bonding. Music, on this account, is a sort of grooming at a distance; no longer necessitating physical touch, but a body language all the same. And, the theory goes, referential language was a late evolution from this.[51] It is estimated that even now over 90 per cent of communication between humans is by non-verbal means, through body language and perhaps especially through intonation. Communication, after all, does not only mean the kind of language we use to talk *about* things. Music is communication – but it speaks *to* us, not *about* things. It does not refer (to a third party): it has an 'I–thou' existence, not an 'I–it' existence.

In fact, even without the anthropological evidence, we might well be doubtful that language was needed for communication, if for no other reason than that language, unlike more intuitive, musical, forms of communication, is the perfect medium for concealing, rather than revealing, meaning. The fact that we now communicate mainly through language shouldn't blind us to the equally important fact that we do not need it for most types of communication. Most of our communication goes on without it anyway, whether we like it or not, and language may even make some kinds of communication more problematic.

THOUGHT WITHOUT LANGUAGE

Surely, though, it may be said, even if language isn't strictly necessary for communication, its advent was necessary for humans to become the thinking beings they are, capable of forming concepts, making judgments, taking decisions, solving problems, all that is characteristic of our highest functions? Well, not really – in fact, not at all. The belief that one cannot think without language is yet another fallacy of the introspective process, whereby thinking in words *about* language only serves to confirm the importance of the verbal process. When we consciously introspect, or retrospect, on our own thought processes, and try to construct what happens, how the mind works, we can do so only as we would *under those circumstances* try to achieve the task, consciously, putting it in words. But the mind is not like this. We carry out most mental processes that would normally constitute what we mean by thinking without doing anything consciously, or in language, at all. We make sense of the world, form categories and concepts, weigh and evaluate evidence, make decisions and solve problems, all without language, and without even being consciously aware of the process.

Indeed, many of these things can be achieved satisfactorily only if we do not become too explicitly aware of the process, which would otherwise have a limiting and inhibiting effect. Many examples exist of famous scientific problems that were solved without language. After much cogitation, Kekulé seized the shape of the benzene ring, the foundation of organic chemistry, when the image of a snake biting its tail arose from the embers of his fire; Poincaré, having spent 15 days trying to disprove Fuchsian functions, suddenly saw their reality, as, after a cup of black coffee, 'ideas rose in crowds – I felt them collide until pairs interlocked'; later their relation to non-Euclidean geometry occurred to him at the moment he put his foot on a bus, though he was in the middle of a completely unrelated conversation ('on my return to Caen, for conscience' sake I verified the result at my leisure'). The structure of the periodic table of the elements came to Mendeleyev in a dream. Einstein wrote that 'the words or the language, as they are written or spoken, do not seem to play any role in the mechanism of my thought . . .'[52] Similar points were made by Gauss and Helmholtz. Mathematical thinking, which is principally right-hemisphere-mediated, takes place in three dimensions. Rudolf Arnheim wrote in his classic work, *Visual Thinking*, as powerful today as when it was written in 1969: 'What we need to acknowledge is that perceptual and pictorial shapes are not only translations of thought products but the very flesh and blood of thinking itself.'[53] Note that expression: the 'very flesh and blood of thinking'. I will have more to say about this later in a discussion of language and the body. But the point is this: the fact that we are more aware of those times when we do think explicitly to ourselves in words – and now conceive of all thought as taking place in words – should not deceive us into believing that language is necessary for thought. It could even be an impediment to it. Most forms of imagination, for example, or of innovation, intuitive problem solving, spiritual thinking or artistic creativity require us to transcend language, at least language in the accepted sense of a referential code. Most thinking, like most communication, goes on without language.

What is more, in evolutionary terms, thought, including concept formation, clearly predates language. Quite apart from the already mentioned existence of sophisticated pre-lingual hominids, we know that animals can think and form concepts. Any sentient being living in an environment where it needs to defend itself from predators and find enough to eat must be capable of forming concepts and placing things in categories. Without it, it would be forced to start from scratch with every encounter with friend or foe, with plant or poison, and wouldn't last long. These assumptions are borne out by the evidence of studies demonstrating that indeed categorical perception is not unique to humans, and cannot therefore depend on language.[54] The ability to categorise is in fact almost universal.[55] Pigeons, for example, can categorise different types of leaves, or fish, or people. They can even distinguish a human face in a crowd, and artificial from natural objects.[56]

In fact they have also been shown to be able to categorise cartoon pictures, and to discriminate examples of modern art, for example a Monet from a Picasso.[57] Trained to peck a key that will give access to hempseed in response to one or other type of picture, they were able to choose appropriately, and could even begin to generalise from Monet to Renoir, and from Picasso to Braque. And their discrimination was not based on one dimension, such as colour, or contour, since they were also tested in black and white and out of focus. Similarly pigeons can tell Bach from Hindemith, or Stravinsky.[58] Mind you, carp can tell blues from classical music; even – and I suspect the investigator must have indulged a sense of humour here – Muddy Waters from the *Trout Quintet* (in case you're wondering, they had to press a puck with their snout: a correct choice yielded a food pellet).[59] And animals are more broadly capable of mental representation, of the ability to generalise, and to form categories and reason, though they do not have language.[60] Dogs even understand the apparently arbitrary connections between words and actions or things.

Concept formation, together with the ability to see the relations between things and events, and the ability to link concepts with signs of some kind, presumably physical movements, arose through natural selection, and formed the substrate of language long before the emergence of modern humanity. Forward planning, hitherto thought to be a hallmark of human cognition, is clearly present in birds that have no language (a point worth making since, for example, Irene Pepperberg's African grey parrot, Alex, was able to communicate, plan and reason – but he had quite a vocabulary).[61] Even 'theory of mind', the ability to attribute mental states to others, which has become the shibboleth of complex, multilayered thought – since children are commonly said not to acquire it till about the age of four, and some subjects, particularly those with autism, may never acquire it at all – is intact in human subjects who have lost language,[62] and may be present to a degree in chimpanzees and primates.[63] Clearly, therefore, 'theory of mind' cannot depend on language, either.

Once again, not just animals, but the young of our own species, indicate that it is wrong to assume that meaning depends on language, though our conscious left hemisphere may be unable to conceive of meaning that is not conveyed in words. Meaning, and the ability to communicate meaning, antedates language in human development. What is more such meaning is mediated, not by the left, but by the right hemisphere. The attunement of emotionally expressive facial expressions between mother and baby in the child's early maturing right hemisphere means that, long before the infant either comprehends or speaks a single word, it possesses an extensive repertoire of signals to communicate its internal state.[64]

That thought does not depend on language is also demonstrated by those who have developed aphasia – lost the power of speech. Those that recover are able to describe their experience and we are fortunate to have the description left by Jacques Lordat, a professor of physiology at the University of Montpellier, a man who, somewhat ironically, had made a study of aphasia. In 1843 he published a paper in which he gave a detailed description of an aphasic episode, lasting several weeks, that he himself had experienced following a stroke. Lordat noticed that

> when I wanted to speak I could not find the expressions that I needed ... *the thought was all ready*, but the sounds that had to express it as intermediary were no longer at my disposition ... I was unable to accept ... the theory that verbal signs are necessary, even indispensable for thought.[65]

In fact subjects who have suffered a stroke demonstrate that even complex reasoning and mathematical calculation do not depend on language.[66] Syntactic structure is distinct from logical structure: subjects that have lost their grasp of syntax following a left-hemisphere stroke remain able to use sophisticated thought processes, as complex as the structure of complex syntax, and can calculate and reason perfectly well.[67] Patients with semantic dementia, too, can perform calculations, sometimes exceptionally well.[68]

That we do not need words in order to hold concepts is also demonstrated by some beautiful research carried out amongst tribal peoples with quite differently structured vocabularies from our own. It turns out that, for example, numerical concepts do not depend on the pre-existence of linguistic terms for them. Tribes with limited words for numbers (such as the Amazonian tribe, the Mundurukú, who have no word for a value greater than three) can succeed in arithmetical tasks that involve values as great as 80. Some members of the Mundurukú speak both their own language, with its extremely limited vocabulary for numbers, and Portuguese, in which there are an unlimited range of number words, while others speak only Mundurukú. The two groups of speakers nonetheless perform comparably on calculation tasks (whether or not, in other words, their number vocabulary goes further than '3'), and both groups perform as well as French-speaking controls; and this is the same for adults and children.[69] The idea of 'recursive infinity' – that is, that you can keep adding one indefinitely to get ever larger numbers – comes naturally to us, even when it does not figure in our established symbolic systems, though Chomsky and his colleagues have claimed that it is derived from the recursive property of natural languages.[70] The Oksapmin of Papua New Guinea, who use body-parts as a counting system, quickly adapted the system to a generative counting rule (i.e. being able to count higher and higher, up 'levels' of magnitude clearly too great for there to be an adequate number of body parts) when times changed and money was introduced to their system.[71] It would seem that such key concepts are innate, rather than being culturally imposed as a product of a learnt language, and this is further borne out by research on the way children develop concepts of number.[72]

But, it may be said, surely we need language in order to discriminate, or at any rate to make fine discriminations, among the things we experience: how can we organise experience if we do not have 'labels' for what it is we perceive? This also turns out to be untrue. For example, not having a word for a colour does not mean we can't recognise it. Quechi Indians have only five colour terms, but can differentiate hues as well as any Westerner; and, nearer to home, Germans, who do not have a native word for the colour 'pink', can of course recognise it all the same.[73] However, words can *influence* our perceptions. They can interfere with the way in which we perceive colours – and facial expressions, for that matter – suggesting that colour words can create new boundaries in colour perception, and language can impose a structure on the way we interpret faces.[74] In other words, language is necessary neither for categorisation, nor for reasoning, nor for concept formation, nor perception: it does not itself bring the landscape of the world in which we live into being. What it does, rather, is shape that landscape by fixing the 'counties' into which we divide it, defining *which* categories or types of entities we see there – how we carve it up.

In the process, language helps some things stand forward, but by the same token makes others recede. Observation of child development confirms this:

> It has been suggested that our concepts are determined by the language that we speak (the Sapir–Whorf hypothesis). However, this is no more than a half or quarter truth. Children certainly often get the concept first and then quickly learn the word to describe it, which is the wrong way round from the Sapir–Whorf point of view. Moreover there is evidence that five-month-old babies have a concept, to do with tightness of fit, which they subsequently lose if their native language does not embody the same concept.[75]

The Sapir–Whorf hypothesis has partial truth – if you don't have the word, you are likely to *lose* the concept; but this research demonstrates that the concept can arise without the word, and is therefore not dependent on it. So thinking is *prior* to language. What language contributes is to firm up certain particular ways of seeing the world and give fixity to them. This has its good side, and its bad. It aids consistency of reference over time and space. But it can also exert a restrictive force on what and how we think. It represents a more *fixed version* of the world: it shapes, rather than grounds, our thinking.[76]

Language is not essential, then, to communication or to thinking – and may interrupt or interfere with both. So we return to the question: why did language actually come about, and what is it for?

There may be a clue in the fact that the other conventionally defining human characteristic, apart from language, is tool making, and that this is associated with the development of right-hand skill: interestingly enough with the same area of the left hemisphere as semantics and syntax. But even if the development of right-hand skill had caused the outgrowth of the left petalia (which it can't have done, because the outgrowth long antedates it) that would still leave us with the question of why the process had to be asymmetrical. Unless, that is, the agenda of the two hemispheres are quite different.

LANGUAGE AND THE HAND

The location of grasp in the left hemisphere, close to speech, is not accidental and tells us something. We know from experience that there are many connections between the hand and language. For example, there clearly is a close relationship between spoken language and the wealth of gesture language that often accompanies it. In normal subjects, restricting hand movement produces an adverse effect on the content and fluency of speech.[77] Ramachandran even reports the case of a young woman, who was born without upper limbs. She experiences phantom arms; and the fact that she has phantom arms at all, replicating a number of such findings in the congenitally limbless, is interesting enough (phantoms are usually thought of as being the residual of a limb that is lost, that in other words must have been there originally).[78] But, even though these phantom arms do not, for example, swing by her side as she walks, she cannot stop them gesticulating when she speaks. Even though she has never been able to use an arm or hand, speech activates these areas of her brain.[79]

At the neurophysiological level, too, it turns out that there are similarities between the skills required for speech production and those required for hand movement, specifically movement of the right hand.[80] In fact, according to Marcel Kinsbourne, language develops specifically in relation to 'right-sided action and, particularly, rightward orienting'.[81] It is, according to him, an 'elaboration, extension and abstraction of sensorimotor function', originating in a proto-language formed by the 'utterances that were coincident with and driven by the same rhythm as the movement in question'.[82] As if to confirm the close connection between language and the body, especially pointing and grasping movements of the right hand, babies and young children can be seen to point while they babble, and the child 'always points while naming and does not name without pointing – stretching out the right hand . . . Babbling can also be heard in conjunction with the motor sequences that are sequelae of the orienting response – locomotion, grasp, manipulation.'[83] And the association holds not just for the child: even in the adult, language, gesture, and bodily movement are 'different actualizations of the same process.'[84]

Manipulospatial abilities may have provided the basis of primitive language, and such abilities and referential language require similar neural mechanisms.[85] The syntactic elements of language may well derive from gesture.[86] And not just from gesture, but from the more functional, more manipulative, hand movements: tool making and speech are both 'serial, syntactic and manipulatory behaviours based on complex articulations of biomechanical patterns.'[87] In fact, so strong is the connection that one theory is that referential language may have evolved, not from sounds at all, but actually direct from hand movements – not only that, but specifically from motions to do with *grasping*.[88] The closeness of function is imaged in anatomy by the proximity of the area for speech and the area of the brain designed to promote grasping. As mentioned, Broca's area, the motor speech area of the frontal lobe, involves certain specialised nerves called mirror neurones which are involved in finger movements, and are also activated in watching others carry out hand movements.[89]

This complicity of language and grasping movements of the hand is not just an interesting neurophysiological and neuroanatomical finding. It is intuitively correct, as evidenced by the terms we use to describe linguistic comprehension and expression. It is not an accident that we talk about 'grasping' what someone is saying. The metaphor of grasp has its roots deep in the way we talk about thinking in most languages (e.g. the various Romance derivatives of Latin *com-prehendere*, and cognates of *be-greifen* in Germanic languages). In his fascinating study of the human hand, the German-speaking Hungarian psychologist Géza Révész writes:

> In German the notion of '*handeln*' embraces all meaningful and goal-directed human activities. It characterises unequivocally the total personality of man. This idea is not limited to external manipulation, that is actions which effect changes in the outer world. It also includes inner action, the purposeful activities of the mind. In his mode of manipulation man experiences his real 'I'. Through it he acquires power over physical nature, gathers a rich fund of material from experience, enlarges his range of effectiveness, and develops his capacities ... Impulses, aspirations, wishes, decisions press for realisation, and this takes place chiefly through the mediation of the hand ... If we wish to convey that we have acquired something mental, we say that we have *grasped* it.[90]

He points to words such as *Erfassen, Begriff, begreiflich, Eindruck, Ausdruck, behalten, auslegen, überlegen*. We have them too in English – not just grasp and com*prehend*, but words such as im*press*ion, ex*press*ion, in*tend*, con*tend*, pre*tend* (from Latin *tendere*, to reach with the hand).

Among other things which Révész draws attention to is the fact that, though touch is the first, most basic and most convincing of the senses (the simplest organisms have only tactile hairs or cilia), it can nonetheless provide only a *piecemeal* image of something. Handling something gives one bits of information at a time, and one has to put together the parts: it does not deliver a sense of the whole. He also points out that in distinguishing things with the hand it is a question of *what type of* a thing, and not of *which particular* one.

All of this – this grasping, this taking control, this piecemeal apprehension of the world, this distinguishing of types, rather than of individual things – takes place for most of us with the right hand. And so it is not surprising that hidden in these reflections are clues to the nature of left-hemisphere processes. In all these respects – not just in the taking control, but in the approach to understanding by building it up bit by bit, rather than being able to sense the whole, in the interest in *categories* of things, rather than in individuals – grasp follows a path congenial to the operations of the left hemisphere. It is also through grasping things that we grant things certainty and fixity: when they are either uncertain or unfixed, we say we 'cannot *put our finger* on it', we 'haven't got a *hold* of it'. This too is an important aspect of the world according to the left hemisphere. The idea of 'grasping' implies seizing a thing for ourselves, for use, wresting it away from its context, holding it fast, focussing on it. The grasp we have, our understanding in this sense, is the expression of our will, and it is the means to power. It is what enables us to 'manipulate' – literally to take a handful of whatever we need – and thereby to dominate the world around us.

And, as if to confirm the deep relationship between the left hemisphere and instrumentality, an attitude of grasping and use, it will be remembered that tool use is preferentially represented in the left hemisphere even in a left-handed individual. This is surely a remarkable finding. Even though the individual's brain is so organised that the right hemisphere governs day-to-day actions using the left hand, concepts of tool use preferentially activate not the right hemisphere but the left.[91] And still further evidence, just as remarkable, shows that, again even in left-handers, actions specifically of grasping are associated with left-hemisphere control – the concept is separate, therefore, from control of the hand as such.[92] Meanwhile exploratory, rather than grasping, motions of the hand activate the right superior parietal cortex, *even when the hand that is doing the exploring is the right hand*.[93] These findings from imaging are in keeping with clinical experience. Subjects with right-hemisphere damage tend to grasp anything within reach, or even brandish their right hand about in empty space, as if searching for something to grasp. And this is not just the release of a primitive reflex: unlike those subjects who exhibit a grasp reflex, they are able to loosen their grip immediately, when asked to do so. It is volitional.[94] And the contrast with those with left-hemisphere damage, therefore relying on their right hemisphere, could not be more stark:

> The patient, when asked to copy the examiner's gestures, tries to put his own hands on the examiner's . . . When his hands are brought into action, it seems as if they are seeking not to remain isolated, as if trying 'to find companionship in something that fills up the empty space'.[95]

LANGUAGE AND MANIPULATION

I am not the first to have surmised that referential language originated in something other than the need to communicate. The philosopher Johann Gottfried Herder, who in 1772 published one of the most important and influential essays on the origins of language, noticing that what I would call the 'I–thou' element in communication at the most intuitive level, the empathic force that is present in music, is hardly characteristic of human language, concluded that 'language appears as a natural organ of reason'.[96] That might require qualification, since, as I have emphasised, reasoning goes on without it; but what he points to here is the importance of language primarily as an aid to a certain particular type of cognition. Nearer our own time, the distinguished American neuroscientist Norman Geschwind ventured that language may not, after all, have originated in a drive to communicate – that came later – but as a means of mapping the world.[97] I would agree with that and go further. It is a means of manipulating the world.

Understanding the nature of language depends once again on thinking about the 'howness', not the 'whatness'. The development of denotative language enables, not communication in itself, but a special *kind* of communicating, not thinking itself, but a special *kind* of thinking.

It is certainly not so important for personal communication within a relationship, and may even be a hindrance here. Telephone conversations, in which all non-verbal signals apart from some partially degraded tonal information are lost, are unsatisfactory not only to lovers and friends, but to all for whom personal exchange is important; one would not expect the medium to work well as a means of, for example, conducting therapy sessions, or for any type of interviewing. It is unattuned to the 'I–thou' relationship. Where words come into their own is for transmitting information, specifically about something that is not present to us, something that is removed in space or time, when you and I need to co-operate in doing something about something *else*. It almost unimaginably expands the realm of the 'I–it' (or the 'we–it') relationship.

And what about the role that language plays, now that it exists, in thinking? Once again, language's role is in giving command over the world, particularly those parts that are not present spatially or temporally, a world that in the process is transformed from the 'I–thou' world of music (and the right hemisphere) to the 'I–it' world of words (and the left hemisphere). Words alone make concepts more stable and available to memory.[98] Naming things gives us power over them, so that we can use them; when Adam was given the beasts for his use and to 'have dominion' over them, he was also the one who was given the power to name them. And category formation provides clearer boundaries to the landscape of the world, giving a certain view of it greater solidity and permanence. That may not have begun with humans, but it was obviously given a vast push forward by referential language. Language refines the expression of causal relationships. It hugely expands the range of reference of thought, and expands the capacity for planning and manipulation. It enables the indefinite memorialisation of more than could otherwise be retained by any human memory. These advantages, of memorialisation and fixity, that language brings are, of course, further vastly enhanced when language becomes written, enabling the contents of the mind to be fixed somewhere in external space. And in turn this further expands the possibilities for manipulation and instrumentalisation. The most ancient surviving written texts are bureaucratic records.

Language in summary brings precision and fixity, two very important features if we are to succeed in manipulating the world. And, specifically, though we may not like to recognise this, it is good for manipulating other human beings. We can't easily hide the truth in *non*-verbal communication, but we can in words. We can't easily direct others to carry out our plans without language. We can't act at a distance without language. Language, it would seem, starts out with what look like imperial aspirations.

Of course there is nothing wrong with manipulation in itself, with having designs on things that we can control, change, or make new. These are certainly basic, human characteristics, and they are the absolute foundations of civilisation. In this sense language is, as it is conventionally but simplistically conceived, a vastly precious and important gift.

Reverting to the needs of the frontal lobes, it provides the framework for a virtual representation of reality. Language enables the left hemisphere to represent the world 'off-line', a conceptual version, distinct from the world of experience, and shielded from the immediate environment, with its insistent impressions, feelings and demands, abstracted from the body, no longer dealing with what is concrete, specific, individual, unrepeatable, and constantly changing, but with a disembodied representation of the world, abstracted, central, not particularised in time and place, generally applicable, clear and fixed. Isolating things artificially from their context brings the advantage of enabling us to focus intently on a particular aspect of reality and how it can be modelled, so that it can be grasped and controlled.

But its losses are in the picture as a whole. Whatever lies in the realm of the implicit, or depends on flexibility, whatever can't be brought into focus and fixed, ceases to exist as far as the speaking hemisphere is concerned.

It also shifts the balance towards the concerns of the left hemisphere, which are not always consonant with those of the right. There are many links between language and grasp, and they have a similar agenda. Both sharpen focus on the world: mental grasp, like physical grasp, requires precision and fixity, which language provides, making the world available for manipulation and possession. Was it the drive for power, embodied in the will to control the environment, which accelerated symbol manipulation and the extension of conceptual thought – already present in some apes,[99] and present in our early ancestors – resulting in the expansion of the left hemisphere before language and grasp evolved? In this light, language and grasp can be seen as expressions at the phenomenal level of a deeper lying drive in the left hemisphere: effective manipulation of the world, and beyond that competition with other species, and with one another. Once the capacity for manipulation was established in the left hemisphere, and no doubt especially once the power of abstraction was embedded there with the beginnings of a referential language, the preferential use of the right hand to carry out the literal manipulation of the environment would naturally have followed.

METAPHOR

Language functions like money. It is only an intermediary. But like money it takes on some of the life of the things it represents. It begins in the world of experience and returns to the world of experience – and it does so via metaphor, which is a function of the right hemisphere, and is rooted in the body. To use a metaphor, language is the money of thought.

Only the right hemisphere has the capacity to understand metaphor.[100] That might not sound too important – like it could be a nice thing if one were going to do a bit of lit crit. But that is just a sign of the degree to which our world of discourse is dominated by left-hemisphere habits of mind. Metaphoric thinking is fundamental to our understanding of the world, because it is the *only* way in which understanding can reach outside the system of signs to life itself. It is what links language to life.

The word metaphor implies something that carries you across an implied gap (Greek *meta-* across, *pherein* carry). When I call language metaphorical, I am not thinking only of Keats addressing the Grecian urn – 'Thou still unravish'd bride of quietness, / Thou foster-child of silence and slow time'. Here there are clearly many complex, interacting metaphors, and that this creates something new and different from a factual description of the Sosibios Vase is obvious. This is metaphorical language in a dramatic sense. But there are two other, broader, but related, senses in which language is metaphorical. Speaking metaphorically, one might say that language is open to carry us across to the experiential world at the 'top' and at the 'bottom'.

At the 'top' end, I am talking about any context – and these are not by any means to be found in poetry alone – in which words are used so as to activate a broad net of connotations, which though present to us, remains implicit, so that the meanings are appreciated as a whole, at once, to the whole of our being, conscious and unconscious, rather than being subject to the isolating effects of sequential, narrow-beam attention. As long as they remain implicit, they cannot be hijacked by the conscious mind and turned into just another series of words, a paraphrase. If this should happen, the power is lost, much like a joke that has to be explained (humour is a right-hemisphere faculty).

At the 'bottom' end, I talking about the fact that every word, in and of itself, eventually has to lead us out of the web of language, to the lived world, ultimately to something that can only be pointed to, something that relates to our embodied existence. Even words such as 'virtual' or 'immaterial' take us back in their Latin derivation – sometimes by a very circuitous path – to the earthy realities of a man's strength (*vir-tus*), or the feel of a piece of wood (*materia*). Everything has to be expressed in terms of something else, and those something elses eventually have to come back to the body. To change the metaphor (and invoke the spirit of Wittgenstein) that is where one's spade reaches bedrock and is turned. There is nothing more fundamental in relation to which we can understand *that*.

That is why it is like the relation of money to goods in the real world. Money takes its value (at the 'bottom' end) from some real, possibly living, things – somebody's cows or chickens, somewhere – and it only really has value as and when it is translated back into real goods or services – food, clothes, belongings, car repairs – in the realm of daily life (at the 'top' end). In the meantime it can take part in numerous 'virtual' transactions with itself, the sort of things that go on within the enclosed monetary system.

Let me emphasise that the gap across which the metaphor carries us is one that *language itself creates*. Metaphor is language's cure for the ills entailed on us by language (much as, I believe, the true process of philosophy is to cure the ills entailed on us by philosophising). If the separation exists at the level of language, it does not at the level of experience. At that level the two parts of a metaphor are not similar; they are the *same*. The German thinker Jean Paul (Johann Paul Friedrich Richter) wrote in 1804, in his *Vorschule der Ästhetik*:

Ingenious figures of speech can either give soul to the body or body to the spirit. Originally, when man was still at one with the world, this two-dimensional trope did not yet exist; one did not compare that which showed no resemblance, but one proclaimed identities: metaphors were, as with children, necessary synonyms for body and mind. Just as, in the case of writing, pictures preceded the alphabet, metaphor (insofar as it designated relations and not objects) was the first word in spoken language, and only after losing its original colour could it become a literal sign.[101]

A metaphor asserts a common life that is experienced in the body of the one who makes it, and the separation is only present at the linguistic level. Our sense of the commonality of the two ideas, perceptions or entities does not lie in a *post hoc* derivation of something abstracted from each of them, which is found on subsequent comparison to be similar, or even one and the same thing; but rather on a single concrete, kinaesthetic experience more fundamental than either, and *from* which they in turn are derived. Thus a clash of arguments and a clash of cymbals are not seen to have something in common only after the disembodied idea of a 'clash' is abstracted from the one and from the other, and found – aha! – to be similar; it is rather that these experiences – a clash of arguments and a clash of cymbals, or, for that matter, a clash of swords, or a clash of colours – are felt in our embodied selves as sharing a common nature.

When the metaphor is paraphrased or replaced, whatever had been extralingual, unconscious, and therefore potentially new and alive in the collision of these two entities gets reconstructed, this time in terms only of what is familiar. The point of metaphor is to bring together the whole of one thing with the whole of another, so that each is looked at in a different light. And it works both ways, as the coming together of one thing with another always must. You can't pin one down so that it doesn't move, while the other is drawn towards it: they must draw towards each other. As Max Black says: 'If to call a man a wolf is to put him in a special light, we must not forget that the metaphor makes the wolf seem more human than he otherwise would.'[102] And Bruno Snell, discussing the way in which Homer likens the brave warrior to a rock amidst the crashing waves, the rock then, in turn, being described as 'steadfast' by analogy with human behaviour, writes perceptively:

This peculiar situation, namely that human behaviour is made clear only through reference to something else which is in turn explained by analogy with human behaviour, pertains to all Homeric similes. More than that, it pertains to all genuine metaphors, and in fact to every single case of human understanding. Thus it is not quite correct to say that the rock is viewed anthropomorphically, unless we add that our understanding of rock is anthropomorphic for the same reason that we are able to look at ourselves petromorphically ... *man must listen to an echo of himself before he may hear or know himself.*[103]

Metaphor (subserved by the right hemisphere) comes *before* denotation (subserved by the left). This is a historical truth, in the sense that denotative language, even philosophical and scientific language, is derived from metaphors founded on immediate experience of the tangible world.

> Metaphor is centrally a matter of thought, not just words. Metaphorical language is a reflection of metaphorical thought . . . Eliminating metaphor would eliminate philosophy. Without a very large range of conceptual metaphors, philosophy could not get off the ground. The metaphoric character of philosophy is not unique to philosophic thought. It is true of all abstract human thought, especially science. Conceptual metaphor is what makes most abstract thought possible.[104]

It is also a truth about epistemology, how we understand things. Any one thing can be understood only in terms of another thing, and ultimately that must come down to a something that is experienced, outside the system of signs (i.e. by the body). The very words which form the building blocks of explicit thought are themselves all originally metaphors, grounded in the human body and its experience.

Metaphor *embodies* thought and places it in a living *context*. These three areas of difference between the hemispheres – metaphor, context and the body – are all interpenetrated one with another. Once again it is the right hemisphere, in its concern for the immediacy of experience, that is more densely interconnected with and involved in the body, the ground of that experience. Where the right hemisphere can see that metaphor is the only way to preserve the link between language and the world it refers to, the left hemisphere sees it either as a lie (Locke, expressing Enlightenment disdain, called metaphors 'perfect cheats')[105] or as a distracting ornament; and connotation as a limitation, since in the interests of certainty the left hemisphere prefers single meanings.

For the left hemisphere, consequently, language can come to seem cut off from the world, to be itself the reality; and reality, for its part, comes to seem made up of bits strung together, as the words are strung together by syntax. The left hemisphere is bound to see language like this because it understands things by starting from the observation of 'pieces' and builds them up to make something, and this is the only route it has to understanding both the world and language itself, the medium with which it does its understanding, including its understanding of language.

LANGUAGE ROOTED IN THE BODY

Metaphors, even the simple ones hidden in expressions like feeling 'down', derive from our experience of living as embodied creatures in the everyday world.[106] The body is, in other words, also the necessary *context* for all human experience.

In fact even language, historically and within the story of each living individual as he or she acquires language, demonstrates that it is not a theoretical system or set of procedures, made up of bits strung together by rules or algorithms, but an embodied skill, and its origins lie in the empathic communication medium of music and the right hemisphere, where it is deeply connected with the body.

I mentioned earlier that there were those who believed that language arose, not from music, but from gesture. There is, however, no necessary conflict between such beliefs. Music is deeply gestural in nature: dance and the body are everywhere implied in it. Even when we do not move, music activates the brain's motor cortex.[107] Music is a holistic medium, 'multimodal' as Mithen puts it, not limited to a distinct modality of experience. To the extent that the origins of language lie in music, they lie in a certain sort of gesture, that of dance: social, non-purposive ('useless'). When language began to shift hemispheres, and separate itself from music, to become the referential, verbal medium that we now recognise by the term, it aligned itself with a different sort of gesture, that of grasp, which is, by contrast, individualistic and purposive, and became limited to one modality.

But language, if we attend to it rightly, still trails the clouds of glory from its origins in the right hemisphere. The eighteenth-century German philosopher Herder, in his *Essay on the Origin of Language*, points out that language can help to blind us to the intrinsically synaesthetic nature of experience, but suggests that some of this must, in spite of language, be caught in the word-sounds arising from it:[108]

> We are full of such interconnections of the most different senses . . . in nature all the threads are one single tissue. . . . The sensations unite and all converge in the area where distinguishing traits turn into sounds. Thus, what man sees with his eye and feels by touch can also become soundable.[109]

Yet with the rise of Saussurian linguistics in the twentieth century, it has become fashionable to insist on the arbitrary nature of the sign – a fascinating and counterintuitive move, designed to emphasise the 'freedom' of language as far as possible from the trammels of the body and of the physical world it describes. There is, however, plenty of evidence that the sounds of words are not arbitrary, but evocative, in a synaesthetic way, of the experience of the things they refer to. As has been repeatedly demonstrated, those with absolutely no knowledge of a language can nonetheless correctly guess which word – which of these supposedly arbitrary signs – goes with which object, in what has become known as the 'kiki/bouba' effect ('kiki' suggesting a spiky-shaped object, where 'bouba' suggests a softly rounded object).[110] However much language may protest to the contrary, its origins lie in the body as a whole. And the existence of a close relationship between bodily gesture and verbal syntax implies that it is not just concrete nouns, the 'thing-words', but even the most apparently formal and logical elements of language, that originate in the body and emotion. The deep structure of syntax is founded on the fixed sequences of limb movement in running creatures.[111] This supports evidence that I will examine in Chapter 5 that the very structures and content of thought itself exist in the body *prior* to their utterance in language.

Why do I emphasise this bodily origin of thought and language? Partly because it has been denied in our own age, not by any means only, or even mainly, by de

Saussure and his followers. More than that, the fact of its denial seems to me to form part of a general trend, throughout the last hundred years or so, towards the ever greater repudiation of our embodied being, in favour of an abstracted, cere-bralised, machine-like version of ourselves that has taken hold on popular thinking – even though there may be more recent trends in philosophy that attempt, with widely varying degrees of success, to point away from such conclusions. As Lakoff and Johnson make clear,

> the very structure of reason itself comes from the details of our embodiment. The same neural and cognitive mechanisms that allow us to perceive and move around also create our conceptual systems and modes of reason ... Reason is evolutionary, in that abstract reason builds on and makes use of forms of percep-tual and motor inference present in 'lower' animals ... Reason is thus not an essence that separates us from other animals; rather, it places us on a continuum with them.[112]

The flight of language from the enchantment of the body during the last hundred years represents, I believe, part of a much broader revolt of the left hemi-sphere's way of conceiving the world against that of the right hemisphere, the theme of Part II of this book.

The vehemence of the comparison of music to such useless exaptations as pornography and a taste for fatty food intentionally or unintentionally makes it hard to put forward the case that language, the precious tool of scientific cogni-tion, comes ultimately from the mucky world of emotion and the body. Is that what is being denied? Or is it perhaps that scientific discourse, so heavily dependent on referential language, doesn't like acknowledging those skeletons in the family closet, its embarrassing bodily ancestors, grasp and manipulation? Whatever the motive, language certainly does its best to cover its tracks and deny its parentage.

Take the rise of the Chomskyan theory of universal grammar.[113] The belief that the structures of analytic language are hard-wired into our brains helps to perpet-uate the idea that the brain is a cognitive machine, a computer that is fitted with a *rule-based programme* for structuring the world, rather than its being an inextric-able part of an embodied, living organism that develops implicit, performative, skills through an empathic process of intelligent imitation. While I am not in a position to do full justice to an issue that is still a matter of lively debate among the experts, it is uncontroversial that the existence of a universal grammar such as Chomsky conceived *is* highly debatable. It remains remarkably speculative 50 years after he posited it, and is disputed by many important names in the field of linguistics.[114] And some of the facts are hard to square with it. Languages across the world, it turns out, use a very wide variety of syntax to structure sentences.[115] But more importantly the theory of universal grammar is not convincingly compatible with the process revealed by developmental psychology, whereby chil-dren actually acquire language in the real world. Children certainly evince a remarkable ability to grasp spontaneously the conceptual and psycholinguistic shapes of speech, but they do so in a far more holistic, than analytic, way. They are astonishingly good imitators – note, not copying machines, but *imitators*.

Imitation can certainly be reduced to a matter of copying by rote: breaking an action down into a series of steps, and reproducing them mechanically. Deliberate, explicit copying of single gestures, out of context, would be like this. But it can also be driven by a feeling of attraction which results, by a process that remains mysterious, in our apprehending the whole and trying to feel what that must be like from the inside – by so to speak 'inhabiting' the other person. This is how we imitate someone else's voice, speech patterns or physical mannerisms, their way of talking or walking. I use the term 'attraction' in a sense that makes no necessary judgment about the worth of its object: if imitation can be the sincerest form of flattery, it can also be the sincerest form of mockery. But it does often carry a charge of positive attraction towards its object: we become who we are by imitating the models of people we admire or respect. It is also how we acquire most of our skills, even though at times we may resort to copying by rote. Such imitation is empathic, and involves identification. It plays an important role in human development, not only in skill acquisition – such, precisely, as a child's developing mastery of language – but in the development of values which form part of our individuality. I will return to the topic of imitation in Chapter 7, when I consider the possible ways in which shifts in the history of ideas could come about.

Skills are embodied, and therefore largely intuitive: they resist the process of explicit rule following. The *Chuang Tzu*, a classic of Taoist literature, contains several stories, such as that of Cook Ting cutting up an ox for Lord Wen-hui, designed to illustrate the fact that a skill cannot be formulated in words or rules, but can be learnt only by watching and following with one's eyes, one's hands and ultimately one's whole being: the expert himself is unaware of how he achieves what it is he does.[116] As Dreyfus and Dreyfus put it in their book *Mind Over Machine*: 'an expert's skill has become so much a part of him that he need be no more aware of it than he is of his own body.'[117] Despite powerful suggestions to the contrary, language is *not* an abstraction from life, a game – with its suggestions of autonomy, triviality and definition by rules. No, it is an extension of life. In Wittgenstein's famous phrase: 'to imagine a language means to imagine a form of life' – not a virtual *representation* of life, but a *form* of life.[118]

A child does not acquire the skill of language, any more than the skill of life, by learning rules, but by imitation, a form of empathic identification, usually with his or her parents, or at any rate with those members of the group who are perceived as more proficient. I have suggested that such identification involves an (obviously unconscious) attempt to inhabit another person's body, and this may sound some-what mystical. But imitation is an attempt to be 'like' (in the sense of experiencing what it is 'like' to be) another person, and what it is 'like' to be that person is some-thing that can be experienced only 'from the inside'.[119] Not just the acquisition of language, but the everyday business of language in itself involves just such an inhabiting. Communication occurs because, in a necessarily limited, but nonetheless crucially important, sense, we come to feel what it is like to be the person who is communicating with us. This explains why we pick up another person's speech habits or tics, even against our will (a stammer is a sometimes embarrassing case in point); it explains many of the problems of emotional entrainment in conversation, the countertransference that occurs, not just in therapy, but in ordinary, everyday life, when we experience in our own frames the very feelings that our interlocutor experiences. And empathy is associated with a greater intuitive desire to imitate.[120]

By inhabiting the body of the other: is this how language ('musilanguage') began? Rudolf Laban, who perhaps more closely observed the meaning of bodily movement in performance than anyone that ever lived, has some fascinating observations to make in this regard. In sub-Saharan Africa there is a form of communication using drumbeats which has been dubbed, perhaps somewhat infelicitously, 'rhythmic drum telegraphy'. The technique is widespread, and by it apparently detailed messages can be communicated over long distances. According to Laban, there is no attempt, as the Westerner might imagine, to mimic the sound pattern of words or phrases; that would be rendered pointless by the many different languages spoken by different tribes occupying adjacent territories. Instead 'the reception of these drum or tom-tom rhythms is accompanied by a vision of the drummer's movement, and it is this movement, a kind of dance, which is visualised and understood.'[121] Communication occurs because the listener inhabits the body of the person who drums and experiences what it is that *the drummer* is experiencing. Even if language no longer seems to us in the West to 'body forth' meaning in this way, it may be that at least our understanding of music still shares this inhabiting of the movements of the other – the performer, the singer, perhaps even the composer. Laban again: 'It is . . . interesting to note that orchestral music is produced by the most precise bodily movements of the musicians,' and he suggests that perhaps one of the reasons we like to see, as well as hear, music performed is exactly that we can better inhabit the performer's body, a perception that appears to me intuitively correct.[122]

To recapitulate, then: language originates as an embodied expression of emotion, that is communicated by one individual 'inhabiting' the body, and therefore the emotional world, of another; a bodily skill, further, that is acquired by each of us through imitation, by the emotional identification and intuitive harmonisation of the bodily states of the one who learns with the one from whom it is learnt; a skill moreover that originates in the brain as an analogue of bodily movement, and involves the same processes, and even the same brain areas, as certain highly expressive gestures, as well as involving neurones (mirror neurones) that are activated equally when we carry out an action and when we see another carry it out (so that in the process we can almost literally be said to share one another's bodily experience and inhabit one another's bodies); a process, finally, that anthropologists see as derived from music, in turn an extension of grooming, which binds us together as physically embodied beings through a form of extended body language that is emotionally compelling across a large number of individuals within the group. At the least one can say that it forms bridges, as any mode of communication has to, between individuals, at every stage of its development and practice, historically and individually, and it does so by relying on our common corporeality, within a group – the image of which, furthermore, is the body. We call a group of people 'a body', and its constituents are seen as limbs, or 'members'. Their relationship within the group is not additive merely, as it would be in a mechanical assembly of items, but combinatory, producing a new entity that is more than the sum of its parts. If it were a chemical, one would say that it were a compound, rather than a mixture.

If language began in music, it began in (right-hemisphere) functions which are related to empathy and common life, not competition and division; promoting togetherness, or, as I would prefer, 'betweenness'. By its nature as a means of communication, language is inevitably a shared activity, like music, which begins in the transmission of emotion and promotes cohesion. Human singing is unique: no other creature begins to synchronise the rhythm, or blend the pitch, of its utterances with that of its fellows, in the way that human singing instinctively does. It is not, like birdsong, individualistic in intention and competitive in nature (remember that birdsong, like other instrumental utterances, is grounded in the left hemisphere, not, like human music, in the right). Everything about human music suggests that its nature is sharing, non-competitive. And so it has been argued by a number of anthropologists that the development of musical skill must have been a product, not of individual selection, but of group selection, a process whereby 'reproduction of all genes present in a group is influenced in a similar manner by newly developed behaviours'.[123] Natural selection exploits the difference in individual rates of successful reproduction within the group, but here the whole group would have benefited – in terms of its cohesion as a group – from something the whole group would have evolved.[124]

And indeed referential language too would have to have been a product of group selection if it really had much to do with communication. Either everyone in the group develops it, and the group benefits, so that the members of the group flourish, or it doesn't develop – since it's not much good being a solitary expert communicator if your fellows can't pick up the message. And this makes perfect sense: the advantages of spoken language, such as more efficient hunting, would have benefited all individuals in the group, even if there was a range of development in linguistic skills, since the products of hunting would have been shared. Classical natural selection, by contrast, would have to demand that the skill be positively hidden or kept secret from others – a skill, however, which, by its very nature, is concerned with sharing information. So it looks as if language may have started out, not as the product of ruthless competition, but as another area in which humanity has done better by co-operation and collaboration.[125] Returning to the puzzle of music's (apparent lack of) competitive advantage, we have conventionally been unable to see any advantage because we are used to thinking in terms only of individual pitted against individual, not in terms of the group, in which individuals work together.

This is the argument from utility. Like so many other things that we are so often told are useful to the group – music and dance, a sense of beauty and a sense of awe – language helped make us more effective competitors at the group level, if not at the level of the individual. Ultimately, though, I believe that the great achievement of humankind is not to have perfected utility through banding together to form groups, but to have learnt through our faculty for intersubjective experience, and our related ability to imitate, to transcend utility altogether. We can, through our ability to imitate, make our own choices about the direction we take, mould our thinking and behaviour, and therefore our human future, according to our own values, rather than waiting to be driven by the blind process of genetic competition, which knows only one value, that of utility. We can *choose* to imitate forms of thinking or behaving; and by so doing both speed up our evolution by many orders of magnitude, and shift it away from the blind forces of chance and necessity, in a direction or directions of our own choosing.

It is rather odd to find Dunbar referring to dance as useless: 'dancing, a phenomenon that probably ranks, along with smiling and laughter', he writes, 'as one of the most futile of all human universals'.[126] I say it is odd because he of all people ought to be able to see past its apparent uselessness to the individual, to its supposed usefulness to the group. Perhaps he does, and calls it 'futile' tongue in cheek. But I'd rather agree with him, nonetheless, that smiling, laughter and dance are – gloriously – useless: how many of us really believe that when we dance, laugh, or smile we do so ultimately because of some dreary utility to the group to which we belong? Perhaps there is no end in view. Perhaps these spontaneous behaviours are pointless, with no purpose beyond themselves, other than that they express something beyond *our* selves. Perhaps, indeed, the fact that so many of our distinguishing features are so 'useless' might make one think. Instead of looking, according to the manner of the left hemisphere, for utility, we should consider, according to the manner of the right hemisphere, that finally, through intersubjective imitation and experience, humankind has escaped from something worse even than Kant's 'cheerless gloom of chance': the cheerless gloom of necessity.[127]

Deprived of an explanation in terms of a final cause – the reason that makes sense of a behaviour in terms of its outcome – scientists sometimes think they have accounted for a phenomenon by redescribing it on another level. Thus Dunbar explains our indulging in 'futile' activities by reference to endorphins. Grooming, music, togetherness, love, religion – all turn out mysteriously to release endorphins. 'Sound familiar?', he queries, on one such occasion, pleased with the simplicity of his solution, but aware that it has clocked up a few air miles by now: 'Well, of course it is: it is the endorphin story all over again.'[128] And that is supposed to explain *at last* why we need, enjoy and take comfort in such things. But is this really any different from proudly announcing that, after prolonged research, we have discovered that the reason we dislike being belittled, ignored or hit over the head with a shillelagh is that it causes depletion of endorphins, reduced bioavailability of serotonin, secretion of cortisol or overdrive of the sympathetic nervous system? In the real world, however, we do not choose to engage in activities because they release endorphins, and endorphin release is a blast; it's that when we engage in what, for a myriad complex and subtle reasons, has meaning and importance for us, we are happier, endorphins merely being part of the final common pathway for happiness at the neurochemical level – just as we avoid a mugger not because we'd like to maintain our levels of serotonin as long as possible, but because he's likely to attack us and make life miserable for us, depleted serotonin just being the final common pathway of misery.

So language is a hybrid. It evolved from music and *in this part of its history* represented the urge to communicate; and to the extent that it retains right-hemisphere empathic elements, it still does. Its foundations lie in the body and the world of experience. But referential language, with its huge vocabulary and sophisticated syntax, did not originate in a drive to communicate, and from this point of view, represents something of a hijack. It has done everything it can to repudiate both its bodily origins and its dependency on experience – to become a world unto itself. Despite all that, however, the urge to speak still does not come from Broca's area, where the motor speech act originates. That's evident from the fact that subjects with lesions in Broca's area usually seem desperate to communicate. No, it comes from the anterior cingulate, a deeper lying region profoundly implicated in social motivation. Subjects with damage to this area exhibit akinetic mutism, the lack of desire to communicate despite having perfectly normal speech function. 'This reinforces the conclusion that speech is fundamentally a social act, and it has only been tortuously bent for scientific ends. Parenthetically, dolphins and whales have rich neural expansions in this area of the brain [anterior cingulate], and they do seem to be highly communicative.'[129] It might also be pointed out that these animals, famous for their intelligence and sociability, communicate by music.

Language has done its best to obscure its parentage. It has increasingly abstracted itself from its origins in the body and in the experiential world. It developed its current form to enable us to refer to whatever is *not present* in experience: language helped its *re-presentation*. This had the effect of expanding its usefulness to communication and thinking for some purposes, but reducing it for others. In the process important aspects of language, the denotative elements that enable precision of reference and planning, have taken up residence in the left hemisphere, while other aspects of language, broadly its connotative and emotive functions, have remained in the right hemisphere. And the understanding of language at the highest level, once the bits have been put together, the making sense of an utterance in its context, taking into account whatever else is going on, including the tone, irony, sense of humour, use of metaphor, and so on, belongs once again with the right hemisphere.

The way these aspects of language have sorted is, as we have seen, not random, but in keeping with the overall nature of each hemisphere. Metaphor is the crucial aspect of language whereby it retains its connectedness to the world, and by which the 'parts' of the world which language appears to identify retain their connectedness one to another. Literal language, by contrast, is the means whereby the mind loosens its contact with reality and becomes a self-consistent system of tokens. But, more than this, there is an important shape here which we will keep encountering: something that arises out of the world of the right hemisphere, is processed at the middle level by the left hemisphere and returns finally to the right hemisphere at the highest level.

THE RIGHT FRONTAL EXPANSION

We have talked a lot about the left hemisphere and its world. What of the right hemisphere? At the same time as developing this specialised narrowly focussed view of the world, we cannot afford to lose track of the totality of experience in all its richness. It's all very well having a virtual world, but first and foremost one has to carry on inhabiting the real world of experience, where one's ability to manipulate can be put to effect. Man's success has been not just in manipulating the environment, as the 'tool-making animal', but in creating close-knit societies, the basis of civilisation.

It is the right hemisphere that enables us to do just that, by maintaining its broader remit, and, in light of what the frontal lobe development opens up to us, take it much further. Already specialised in social bonding, it would be the natural place for the relational, empathic skills of man, the 'social animal', to be further developed: and this is exactly what one finds. As I have mentioned, if one looks at the brain's structure, one notices that it is not just the left hemisphere that has an asymmetrical enlargement, but the right, too.

As we have seen, asymmetries similar to those found in the human brain are also found in monkeys and apes, and I have mentioned the existence in them of a left-hemisphere expansion. But it is not just in this that our evolutionary ancestors anticipate us. They have this right frontal petalia, too.

The evidence as to which petalia came first, right or left, is divided.[130] Being frontal, unlike the more posterior left-hemisphere expansion, the right petalia may well have arrived later on the scene. In the human foetus, however, the frontal regions of the right hemisphere develop before the occipital regions of the left hemisphere – does ontogeny here recapitulate phylogeny?[131] In general the right hemisphere matures first, though in the second year of life the left hemisphere overtakes it, with the laying down of the speech and language areas;[132] but there is also evidence that the right hemisphere then continues developing after the left hemisphere has matured, with the more sophisticated emotional and prosodic elements of language developing in the fifth and sixth years of life.[133] If true, there is an interesting parallel here between the developmental history of the hemispheres (right → left → right) and their functional relationship. In any case, a right frontal petalia begins to be found in some of the more social monkeys, such as macaques, and in apes,[134] but reaches its most pronounced in humans – in whose brains it is in fact the most asymmetrical region of all.[135]

If it is even more pronounced than the left petalia, and even more particular to humans, why have we paid so little attention to it? Could that be because we have focussed on the left hemisphere, and what it does, at the expense of the right, and what it does? Until recently everything about the right hemisphere has been shrouded in darkness. It was, after all, considered to be silent; and to the verbal left-hemisphere way of thinking, that means dumb. Is the right frontal lobe responsible for anything that might compare with the achievements, in terms of grasp and denotative language, of the left hemisphere?

We know that it is the right frontal lobe which enables us to achieve all the rest of which language is capable; which makes empathy, humour, irony possible, and helps us to communicate and express not just facts, but our selves. Here language becomes not a tool of manipulation but a means of reaching out to the 'Other'. But it is, of course, not just in the realm of language that its significance lies – far from it.

Indeed, most of the remarkable things about human beings, the things that differentiate us from the animals, depend to a large extent on the right hemisphere, and in particular on the contributions of the region of this right-hemisphere expansion, the right frontal lobe. If asked to name the characteristics that ultimately differentiate humans from animals, the classic answers, reason and language, seem like a poor stab. Plenty of animals show, in their degree, capacity to deduce (deductive reasoning is importantly associated with right-hemisphere function, in any case): crows can reason, even bees have language of a kind. Of course, even the most highly evolved animals are incomparably inferior to ourselves in both respects, but the point is that they do show at least glimmerings of such, utilitarian, functions. But there are many things of which they show no evidence whatsoever: for instance, imagination, creativity, the capacity for religious awe, music, dance, poetry, art, love of nature, a moral sense, a sense of humour and the ability to change their minds. In all of these (though as always both hemispheres undoubtedly play a part), a large part, and in most cases the principal part, is played by the right hemisphere, usually involving the right frontal lobe. Where the left hemisphere's relationship with the world is one of reaching out to grasp, and therefore to *use*, it, the right hemisphere's appears to be one of reaching out – just that. Without purpose. In fact one of the main differences between the ways of being of the two hemispheres is that the left hemisphere always has 'an end in view', a purpose or use, and is more the instrument of our conscious will than the right hemisphere.

CONCLUSION

I suggest that there are two opposing ways of dealing with the world that are both vital but are fundamentally incompatible, and that therefore, even before humans came on the scene, required separate treatment, even neurological sequestration from one another. One tendency, important for being able to get things from the world for one's own purposes, involves isolation of one thing from the next, and isolation of the living being, perceived as subjective, from the world, perceived as objective. The drive here is towards manipulation, and its ruling value is utility. It began in my view by colonising the left hemisphere, and with the increasing capacity for distance from the world mediated by the expansion of the frontal lobes as one ascends the evolutionary tree, resulted in a physical expansion of the area designed to facilitate manipulation of the environment, symbolically and physically, in the higher monkeys and apes. Eventually that expansion became the natural seat of referential language in humans.

The other tendency was centripetal, rather than centrifugal: towards the sense of the connectedness of things, before reflection isolates them, and therefore towards engagement with the world, towards a relationship of 'betweenness' with whatever lies outside the self. With the growth of the frontal lobes, this tendency was enhanced by the possibility of empathy, the seat of which is the right frontal expansion in social primates, including humans.

It may well be that we, and the great apes before us, are not the originators of the asymmetry in hemisphere function – not even the originators of the *nature* of that asymmetry – but inheritors of something much older than ourselves, which we have utilised and developed in peculiarly human ways to peculiarly human ends. It is not just human beings who have found that there are needs, drives or tendencies, which, while equally fundamental, are also fundamentally incompatible: an essentially divisive drive to acquisition, power and manipulation, based on competition, which sets individual against individual, in the service of unitary survival; and an essentially cohesive drive towards co-operation, synergy and mutual benefit, based on collaboration, in the service of the survival of the group. Before the arrival of language or tool making in the left hemisphere, with their need for *Lebensraum*, could have 'driven it out', the higher apes show signs already of having segregated the expression of social emotion, as we have, to the right hemisphere of the brain – kept away from the areas of useful abstraction; and abstraction, just as importantly, kept from exerting its corrosive effect on experience.

Both of these drives or tendencies can serve us well, and each expresses an aspect of the human condition that goes right to the core. It is not inevitable, ultimately, that they should be in conflict; and in fact it is best that they should not be. In some human brains, it appears that they can more closely co-exist, and I will return to that in the conclusion of this book. But the relationship between the hemispheres is not straightforward. Difference can be creative: harmony (and counterpoint) is an example. Here differences cohere to make something greater than either or any of the constituents alone; which is why it would be a mistake to see the divisive tendency as purely negative. Before there can be harmony, there must be difference. The most fundamental observation that one can make about the observable universe, apart from the mysterious fact that it exists at all – prompting the ultimate question of philosophy, why there is something rather than nothing – is that there are at all levels forces that tend to coherence and unification, and forces that tend to incoherence and separation. The tension between them seems to be an inalienable condition of existence, regardless of the level at which one contemplates it. The hemispheres of the human brain, I believe, are an expression of this necessary tension. And the two hemispheres also adopt different stances about their *differences*: the right hemisphere towards cohesion of their two dispositions, the left hemisphere towards competition between them.

Since the right hemisphere is more distinctive of the human condition than the left, it remains a puzzle why it has been neglected. It seems part of what one might call the 'minor hemisphere' syndrome. Yet we know it is the hemisphere on which experience is grounded and which has the broader view, the one that is open to whatever else exists outside the brain. How, then, has this neglect occurred? Is it just that the left hemisphere has control of language and analytic argument, and that therefore whenever scientists (who depend on such methodology to build up a view of anything from the 'bits' of information) look at the brain, they do so only with the left hemisphere, and see only what it sees? Is it just that such means are not capable of understanding the world as it is as a whole, and that therefore the left hemisphere prefers its own version, which at least makes sense to it? Or is there something else going on here?

The sheer vehemence with which the right hemisphere has been dismissed by the representatives of the articulate left hemisphere, despite its overwhelming significance, suggests a possible rivalry. I believe there has been until very recently a blindness among neuroscientists to the contributions made by the right hemisphere. In 1966 R. C. Oldfield wrote that 'a certain conspiracy of silence prevails among neurologists about the lack of anything much for the right hemisphere to do'.[136] Until John Cutting's *The Right Cerebral Hemisphere and Psychiatric Disorders* and his *Principles of Psychopathology*, and Michael Trimble's recent *The Soul in the Brain: The Cerebral Basis of Language, Art, and Belief*,[137] it has not only received little credit, but has been the object of some, at least superficially, inexplicable animus. There would seem to be a partisanship amongst scientists in the left hemisphere's favour, a sort of 'left-hemisphere chauvinism' at work. One sees it even in the language used by the most objective writers to describe the hemisphere differences: for example, the smart left hemisphere's need for precision leads to 'fine' processing, the *lumpen* right hemisphere's to 'coarse' processing. No mention here of the dangers of over-determination, or the virtues of a broader range, of subtlety, ambiguity, flexibility or tolerance.

In this respect, it is perhaps worth reporting the unbiased impression of a 'naïve' reader, the composer Kenneth Gaburo, approaching the neuroscientific literature from outside, who picked up that 'there is something extraordinarily pejorative' in the language used to describe the right hemisphere.[138] Amongst other references to the left hemisphere as 'dominant', and the right hemisphere as 'minor', 'silent', and so on, he refers to the influential paper which Salomon Henschen, one of the giants of the history of neuropathology, and a former Professor of Medicine at Uppsala, contributed to *Brain* in 1926. The situation is indeed worse even than Gaburo implies, since Henschen's actual words are:

> In every case the right hemisphere shows a manifest inferiority when compared with the left, and plays an automatic role only . . . This fact shows the inferiority of the right hemisphere, especially of the right temporal lobe . . . A person who

is not able to understand words after destruction of the left temporal lobe sinks to the level of primitive man . . . The right temporal lobe is, of course, sufficient for the more primitive psychical life; only by using the left temporal lobe can man reach a higher level of psychical development . . . it is evident that the right hemisphere does not reach the same high level of psychical development as the left . . . The question therefore arises if the right hemisphere is a regressing organ . . . it is possible that the right hemisphere is a reserve organ.[139]

Michael Gazzaniga, one of the most distinguished living neuroscientists and hemisphere researchers, carries on the tradition, and his language is in the tradition of Henschen. There are 'shocking differences between the two hemispheres': 'the left hemisphere has many more mental capacities than the right one . . . [The right hemisphere] is a distant second with problem-solving skills . . . It knows precious little about a lot of things.'[140] He once wrote that 'it could well be argued that the cognitive skills of a normal disconnected right hemisphere without language are vastly inferior to the cognitive skills of a chimpanzee.'[141] In a more recent article, he has written: 'A brain system (the right hemisphere) with roughly the same number of neurons as one that easily cogitates (the left hemisphere) is incapable of higher order cognition—convincing evidence that cortical cell number by itself cannot fully explain human intelligence.'[142] Yet when the right hemisphere can be shown to outperform the left at some fairly basic task of prediction, he interprets this as a sign of the intelligence of the *left* hemisphere, on the grounds that animals are also capable of outperforming the human left-hemisphere strategy. In fact the problem is that the left hemisphere just loves a theory, and often this is not helpful in practice – which is why it gets it wrong. Of attention he writes that

> the left-dominant hemisphere uses a 'guided' or 'smart' strategy whereas the right hemisphere does not. This means that the left hemisphere adopts a helpful cognitive strategy in solving the problem whereas the right hemisphere does not possess those extra cognitive skills. But it does not mean that the left hemisphere is always superior to the right hemisphere in attentional orienting.[143]

True enough. In fact, as he knows, since he refers to the fact, the right hemisphere is predominant for attentional orienting, a topic that will be familiar to the reader. What he refers to as a 'smart' and 'helpful' strategy – 'those extra cognitive skills' – are in fact neither smart nor helpful, when compared with the open, undogmatic stance of the right hemisphere. They lead to *less* accuracy, not more. But you might not know that from the language used.

Just as tedious, of course, is the tendency to see what commonly passes for the 'left hemisphere' in pop parlance as wholly without redeeming features. Often, it seems to me, such positions conceal an undercurrent of opposition to reason and the careful use of language, and once words slip their anchors, and reason is discounted – as some quite influential post-modern and feminist critics have advocated – Babel ensues.[144] Doubts about the extent of rationalism, the belief that reason alone can yield all truth, do not make one anti-rational: to decry reason itself is utter folly. Poetry and metaphor, like science, hold no brief for sloppiness, quite the opposite, just as it is reason, not its unfettered disregard, that leads to scepticism about misplaced and excessive rationalism. But language and reason are the children of both hemispheres, not one alone. The work of the left hemisphere needs to be *integrated* with that of the right hemisphere, that is all. The left hemisphere is the Master's most prized counsellor, his valued emissary.

I have already suggested that there is a need for the hemispheres to keep their distance from one another and to be able to inhibit one another. More than that, the concerns of the left hemisphere with getting and using make it by nature *competitive* – it may be remembered that it is confident, unreasonably optimistic, unwitting of what goes on in the right hemisphere, and yet in denial about its own limitations. What if it should turn out – and it does – that the left-hemisphere advantage gained by right handedness has been the result, *not* of an increase of skill in the right hand, but of a *deficit in the left*?[145] There may be another interesting asymmetry here.

Marian Annett, perhaps the greatest living authority on handedness, believes that we may have developed 'over-dependence on the left hemisphere at the expense of right hemisphere skills'. She points to the unexpectedly large number of left-handers amongst artists, athletes, and 'skilled performers of many kinds'.[146] A marked difference between the performance of the two hands in right-handers is associated with a slight improvement in the right hand, but the price for this, according to Annett, is that 'the left hand declines dramatically', a finding that has been corroborated by many other researchers.[147]

This pattern of a specific relative right-hemisphere handicap is borne out at the anatomical level.[148] The planum temporale, as mentioned in the first chapter, is asymmetrical in most human brains, with the left being up to a third bigger than the right. But in cases where, unusually, the two hemispheres develop symmetrically, it's not that the two plana are the same size as the usual right (smaller) planum, but the size of the usual left planum: in other words, they are *both* large. In normal brains of right-handers, therefore, it's not that the left planum is increased, but that the right planum is *decreased*, in size. Recent research to find the gene or genes responsible for brain asymmetry in the language region expected to find a gene which operated on the left hemisphere to cause it to expand. Instead they found genes that acted on the right hemisphere to prevent its expansion: of the 27 genes implicated, most were more highly expressed on the right, and the most important gene was dramatically more so. Christopher Walsh, a professor of neurology at Harvard who led the research, comments: 'We tend to assume teleologically, because of our focus on language being that most beautiful thing, that it must be endowed by some special mechanism in the left hemisphere ... in fact, it may just be normally repressed in the right hemisphere and allowed to take place in the left'.[149]

The 'normal' situation, then, is associated with right-hemisphere losses, both anatomical and functional.[150] The mechanisms inducing human cerebral asymmetry operate by reducing the role of the right hemisphere.[151]

Why? Not to be lateralised at all is a disadvantage, as we have seen.[152] This has to be because there are trade-offs associated with the specialisation of the 'dominant' hemisphere, the one with control of language and grasping. Isolation of left-hemisphere-type function makes it that bit easier for it to do what it has to. It functions more efficiently if it is not having to deal with the conflicting 'version' of the world put forward by the other, so-called 'minor', hemisphere. So the non-dominant hemisphere has to be put at a disadvantage. But take the process too far, and the obvious losses occasioned by hobbling the right hemisphere outweigh the advantage to the left. It is an inverted U-shaped curve. Speed in moving pegs on a board with either hand is a measure of the skill of the contralateral hemisphere: strong right-handers are *slower* than non-right-handers, especially with their left hand.[153] Equally the relatively few strong left-handers, whose brains may mirror those of strong right-handers, are at a disadvantage, too. In fact Annett surmises that the high numbers of left-handers among mathematicians[154] and sports professionals is not so much due to an intrinsic advantage for left-handers as to the absence of strong right-handers (who are at a disadvantage).[155] Those more likely to have anomalous patterns of lateralisation, such as left-handers, and those with dyslexia, schizophrenia, bipolar disorder, and autism, for example (together with their relatives, who may, advantageously, carry some, but not all, of the genes for the condition), are the least likely to show what might be called 'left-hemisphere encapsulation'. In other words, in the normal brain the serial processing that forms the basis of left-hemisphere function is carefully segregated from functions that it might impair, but the corollary of this is that the holistic approach of the right hemisphere is not available to the same extent for language and conceptual thought. In anomalous lateralisation patterns, this segregation no longer occurs, with reciprocal advantages and disadvantages. This would result in some gaining access to particular talents from which the rest of us are debarred ('flying mathematicians'), and some faring worse, and losing the evolutionary advantages of specialisation ('inhibited trapeze artists'). This view is compatible with the available large body of evidence that there are both special talents and handicaps associated with anomalous cerebral organisation in these conditions, and in the relatives of those with such conditions.

This is clearly a huge topic, which deserves more analysis. The point I wish to emphasise here is that the left hemisphere has to 'blot out' the right hemisphere in order to do its job at all. That is surely the import of the functional and anatomical evidence that left hemisphere superiority is based, not on a leap forward by the left hemisphere, but on a 'deliberate' handicapping of the right.

If we are to understand the relation between the hemispheres, and their possible rivalry, we need to compare the two experiential worlds that the hemispheres produce.

CHAPTER 4

THE NATURE OF THE TWO WORLDS

IN THE FIRST CHAPTER I DREW ATTENTION TO THE DIVIDED NATURE OF THE BRAIN AND suggested it had a purpose: perhaps there were things that needed to be kept apart. I also drew attention to the brain's asymmetry, a suggestion that difference did not necessarily involve equality. In the second chapter I looked at what the nature of the differences between the hemispheres might be. In the third chapter I suggested that the hemispheres were not just randomly assorted 'databanks', but had coherent and possibly irreconcilable sets of values, imaged in the left hemisphere's control of manipulation through the right hand, and the evolution of language out of music, with language coming to reside largely in the left hemisphere, and music largely in the right. In this chapter I will look in greater detail at the kinds of world the two hemispheres bring into being, and raise the question whether they really are symmetrical, or whether one takes precedence. To begin with, let's return to attention, where we began our exploration of hemisphere difference.

Our attention is responsive to the world. There are certain modes of attention which are naturally called forth by certain kinds of object. We pay a different sort of attention to a dying man from the sort of attention we'd pay to a sunset, or a carburettor. However, the process is reciprocal. It is not just that what we find determines the nature of the attention we accord to it, but that the attention we pay to anything also determines what it is we find. In special circumstances, the dying man may become for a pathologist a textbook of disease, or for a photojournalist a 'shot', both in the sense of a perceived frozen visual moment and a round of ammunition in a campaign. Attention is a moral act: it creates, brings aspects of things into being, but in doing so makes others recede. What a thing is depends on who is attending to it, and in what way. The fact that a place is special to some because of its great peace and beauty may, by that very fact, make it for another a resource to exploit, in such a way that its peace and beauty are destroyed. Attention has consequences.

One way of putting this is to say that we neither discover an objective reality nor invent a subjective reality, but that there is a process of responsive evocation, the world 'calling forth' something in me that in turn 'calls forth' something in the world. That is true of perceptual qualities, not just of values. If there is no 'real'

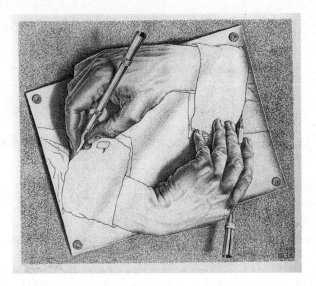

Fig. 4.1 *Drawing Hands*, by M. C. Escher, 1948.

mountain, for example, separate from one created by the hopes, aspirations, reverence or greed of those who approach it, it is equally true that its greenness, or grey-
ness, or stoniness lies not in the mountain or in my mind, but comes from between
us, called forth from each and equally dependent on both; as music arises from
neither the piano nor the pianist's hands, the sculpture neither from hand nor
stone, but from their coming together. And then the hands are part of the lived
body – or, put more conventionally, are the vehicle of the mind, which is in turn
the product of all the other minds that have interacted with it, from Beethoven and
Michelangelo down to every encounter of our daily lives. We are transmitters, not
originators.

Our attention is responsive to the world, but the world is responsive to our
attention. The situation presents a paradox for linear analysis, like M. C. Escher's
hand that draws the hand that draws the hand . . . (see Figure 4.1).

This paradox applies to the problem of how we get to know anything, but is
peculiarly problematic for the special case whereby we are seeking to approach the
very processes whereby knowledge itself comes into being. It is not possible to
discuss the neuropsychological basis of our awareness of the world without
adopting a philosophical position, whether or not one is conscious of doing so.[1]
Not to be aware of doing so is implicitly to have adopted the default standpoint of
scientific materialism. Unfortunately, according to this position, one of the hands
in Escher's picture must come first.

Neuropsychology is inextricably bound up with philosophy. In recent years this
has been increasingly recognised, more by philosophers than neuroscientists, with
one or two important exceptions. Some of these developments are very much to

be welcomed. However, all too often there is a potentially treacherous, because undetected, process at work. What science is actually doing when it delivers its revelations goes unexamined: the scientific process and the meaning of its findings is generally taken for granted. The model of the body, and therefore the brain, as a mechanism is exempted from the process of philosophical scepticism: what it tells us becomes the truth. And, since the brain is equated with the mind, the mind too becomes a mechanism. The philosophical world view is brought into line with that, and reveals – the truth of the mechanical model as applied to brain and mind. As a result, in a spectacular hijack, instead of a mutually shaping process, whereby philosophy interrogates science, and science informs philosophy, the naïve world view of science has tended by default to shape and direct what has been called 'neurophilosophy'.

If the world of the left hemisphere and the world of the right hemisphere are both present to the mind, and form coherent aspects of experience, should we expect to find the resultant incompatibilities reflected in the history of philosophy? The hemispheres have different answers to the fundamental question 'what is knowledge?', as discussed in the last chapter, and hence different 'truths' about the world. So on the face of it, yes. But the default approach of philosophy is that of the left hemisphere, since it is via denotative language and linear, sequential analysis that we pin things down and make them clear and precise, and pinning them down and making them clear and precise equates with seeing the truth, as far as the left hemisphere is concerned. And since the type of attention you bring to bear dictates the world you discover, and the tools you use determine what you find, it would not be surprising if the philosophical vision of reality reflected the tools *it* uses, those of the left hemisphere, and conceived the world along analytic, and purely rationalistic, lines. It would be unlikely for philosophy to be able to get beyond its own terms of reference and its own epistemology; and so the answer to the question whether the history of philosophy would reflect the incompatibilities of the hemispheres is – probably not.

If there were, however, evidence that, despite this, philosophers had increasingly felt compelled to try to give an account of the right hemisphere's reality, rather than the left's, that would be of extraordinary importance. Admittedly, trying to achieve it at all using the conventional tools of philosophy would be a bit like trying to fly using a submarine, all the while making ingenious adaptations to the design to enable one to get a foot or two above the water. The odds against success would be huge, but the attempt alone would be indicative that there was something compelling beyond the normal terms of reference, that forced one to make the attempt. This would be far stronger evidence for the ultimate reality of the right hemisphere's world than any amount of philosophy that confirmed the left hemisphere's reality, which would be only to be expected.

What I shall argue in this chapter is that precisely such a development has in fact occurred in philosophy, and that it has been evident in the work of the most influential philosophers of our age. Such a development seems to me as striking as the developments in mathematics and physics since the 1880s to which it is in some important respects a parallel. It's hardly surprising that scientific method for a long time led to a vision of the universe – the Newtonian universe – which reflected the principles of the scientific method. But when it began to compel conclusions incompatible with the model assumed by its method, a 'paradoxical' universe, that was a more revealing finding. In the late nineteenth-century Georg Cantor struggled with the idea that there was a *necessary* uncertainty and incompleteness to the realm of mathematics. Infinity was no longer tameable by turning it into an abstract concept, giving it a name, and then carrying on as though it were just another number. He came to the realisation that there is not just one 'infinity', but an infinity of infinities, beyond anything we can capture or represent, something that was real, not just taking series 'as far as they will go', but beyond; something Other in nature than the series that tried to reach it, and that could in principle never be reached by any kind of known cognitive process. His contemporary Ludwig Boltzmann introduced time and probability into the timeless and certain realm of physics, showing that no system can be perfect; Kurt Gödel's incompleteness theorems proved that that would always inevitably be the case, that there will always be truths within any system that cannot be proved in terms of that system. Niels Bohr's 'Copenhagen interpretation' of quantum mechanics and Werner Heisenberg's Uncertainty Principle established a universe in which uncertainty is at the core, not just a product of human imperfection, to be remedied in time by advances in learning, but in the very nature of things. Though the insight or intuition that led them to these discoveries came, I suggest, from the right hemisphere, or from both hemispheres working together, in every case their conclusions followed clearly from left-hemisphere processes, the logic of sequential analysis. These transformative developments nonetheless validate the world as given by the right hemisphere, not the left.

To return to philosophy and the brain, we should expect them to illuminate one another: philosophy should help us understand the nature of the brain, and the nature of the brain should help to illuminate philosophical problems. There are three questions in particular worth asking here. Has what we know about the hemispheres anything to offer in illuminating philosophical debate? Equally, does philosophy help make sense of the hemisphere differences we know exist? And what can the answers to both questions tell us about the nature of the brain?

The first question takes us into deep water immediately. Philosophers themselves will be the best judges, and the issues are as extensive and complex as the mind itself. However, some possible areas for discussion naturally suggest themselves.

In Western philosophy for much of the last two thousand years, the nature of reality has been treated in terms of dichotomies: real versus ideal, subject versus object. Over time the meanings of the terms, and sometimes the terms themselves, have changed, and the constant need to transcend such dichotomies has led to modifications and qualifications of the *kind* of realism or idealism, the *type* of objectivism or subjectivism, but the essential issue has remained: how are we to connect the world and our minds? Since our world is brought into being by two hemispheres which constitute reality in profoundly different ways, it might seem likely that some of these dichotomies could be illuminated by the differences between the worlds each of the cerebral hemispheres brings into being.

It has nothing to do with the idea that, for example, one hemisphere might be subjective and the other objective. That's obviously untrue. Rather the point is that philosophy in the West is essentially a left-hemisphere process.[2] It is verbal and analytic, requiring abstracted, decontextualised, disembodied thinking, dealing in categories, concerning itself with the nature of the general rather than the particular, and adopting a sequential, linear approach to truth, building the edifice of knowledge from the parts, brick by brick. While such a characterisation is not true of most pre-Socratic philosophers, particularly Heraclitus, it is at least true of the majority of philosophers since Plato in the West until the nineteenth century, when, for example, Schopenhauer, Hegel and Nietzsche began to question the basis on which philosophy made its advances. Philosophy is naturally given, therefore, to a left-hemisphere version of the world, in which such divides as that between the subject and the object seem especially problematic. But these dichotomies may depend on a certain, naturally dichotomising, 'either/or', view of the world, and may cease to be problematic in the world delivered by the right hemisphere, where what appears to the left hemisphere to be divided is unified, where concepts are not separate from experience, and where the grounding role of 'betweenness' in constituting reality is apparent. The key to such philosophical dichotomies lies not, then, I suggest, in the division between the hemispheres, but within the nature of the left hemisphere itself.

If one had to characterise the left hemisphere by reference to one governing principle it would be that of division. Manipulation and use require clarity and fixity, and clarity and fixity require separation and division. What is moving and seamless, a process, becomes static and separate – *things*. It is the hemisphere of 'either/or': clarity yields sharp boundaries. And so it makes divisions that may not exist according to the right hemisphere. Just as an individual object is neither just a bundle of perceptual properties 'in here', nor just something underlying them 'out there', so the self is neither just a bundle of mental states or faculties, nor, on the other hand, something distinct underlying *them*. It is an aspect of experience that perhaps has no sharp edges.

Heraclitus (like the Oriental philosophers who influenced Greek thought until Plato) was unperturbed by paradox, taking it as a sign that our ordinary ways of thinking are not adequate to the nature of reality. But around the same time that the Platonic mode of discourse, with its insistence on the Law of the Excluded Middle,[3] came into play – as, in other words, thinking became philosophy in the accepted sense – paradox started to emerge as a focus of intellectual disquiet. Some of the most famous are:

The sorites paradox (from Greek *soros*, a heap). Thought to have originated with Eubulides of Miletus (*c.* 350 BC). If one grain of sand is not a heap, and at no stage adding one more grain of sand is going to make the difference between not being a heap and being a heap, how can it ever be that (by, for example, the time 100,000 grains are reached) a heap has come into being?

The Ship of Theseus paradox. Plutarch wrote in his life of Theseus:

> The ship wherein Theseus and the youth of Athens returned had thirty oars, and was preserved by the Athenians down even to the time of Demetrius Phalereus, for they took away the old planks as they decayed, putting in new and stronger timber in their place, insomuch that this ship became a standing example among the philosophers, for the logical question of things that grow; one side holding that the ship remained the same, and the other contending that it was not the same.[4]

The reference to Demetrius Phalereus dates this from about 300 BC. The 'logical question of things that grow' alluded to, known usually as the 'Growing Argument', is the basis of numerous paradoxes, such as Chrysippus' paradox, the point being that, as things grow, at least one particle is added to them or lost by them, and so, according to one interpretation, they cease to be the same entity. In effect all living things present this problem, that of a thing that flows, since they are always in a state of change and self-repair. (As the German philosopher Novalis was to put it 2,000 years later: 'There is no doubt that our body is a moulded river.')[5]

Zeno's paradoxes. Originating with Zeno of Elea (*c.* 450 BC):

- *Achilles and the tortoise.* In a race in which Achilles gives the tortoise a head start, Achilles can never overtake the tortoise, because first he has to reach the point where the tortoise began, then the point the tortoise reached while Achilles reached the tortoise's starting point, and so *ad infinitum.*
- *The dichotomy.* We can never move at all, because first we have to get halfway to where we are going, but before that, a quarter of the way, and before that an eighth, and so *ad infinitum.*
- *The arrow.* An arrow fired at a target cannot move, because, at any one moment, the arrow either is where it *is*, or it is where it is not. If it remains where it is, then it must be standing still, but if it moves where it is not, it can't be there. So it cannot move at all.

The Epimenides paradox. Named after Epimenides of Knossos (*c.* 600 BC), a possibly mythological Cretan seer, who wrote in a light-hearted poem or song that 'Cretans are always liars' – false if true, true if false. It seems that this only started to look like a real problem when examined retrospectively by later Greek writers.

Looked at with an understanding of the different worlds disclosed by the two hemispheres, the development of paradox starts to make sense. There is a sudden obtrusion of the left hemisphere's take on reality, which then conflicts with the right hemisphere's.

Take the sorites paradox. This results from believing that the whole is the sum of the parts, and can be reached by a sequential process of incrementation. It tries to relate two *things*: a grain of sand and a heap, as though their relationship was transparent. It also presupposes that there must either be a heap or not be a heap at any one time: 'either/or' are your only alternatives. That is the left-hemisphere view, and sure enough it leads to paradox. According to the right-hemisphere view, it is a matter of a shift in context, and the coming into being of a *Gestalt*, an entity which has imprecisely defined bounds, and is recognised whole: the heap comes into being gradually, and is a process, an evolving, changing 'thing' (this problem is related to the Growing Argument). Failure to take into account context, inability to understand *Gestalt* forms, an inappropriate demand for precision where none can be found, an ignorance of process, which becomes a never-ending series of static moments: these are signs of left-hemisphere predominance.

Or the Ship of Theseus. Here again the problem is caused by a belief that the whole is the sum of the parts, and disappears as the parts are changed. There is also a belief that there must necessarily come a 'point' in a process where identity changes. The fact that this type of paradox was known as the Growing Argument (*auxanomenos logos*) demonstrates that there is a difficulty here in dealing with all living, changing forms. All, once more, points to a dominance of the left-hemisphere view over that of the right.

Zeno's paradoxes similarly rest on the adoption of the left hemisphere's view that every flowing motion in space or time can be resolved into a series of static moments or points that can then be summed to give back the living whole. The 'seamless' fluidity of motion in space or time is 'reduced' to a series, akin to the series of still frames in a ciné film. This is what happens to subjects who suffer right-hemisphere damage, and develop palinopsia (see p. 76 above). This fragmentation of experience is also what underlies delusional misidentification, another right-hemisphere-deficit syndrome, where the seamlessness, the individual quiddity, of a living being, is broken down into a series of manifestations, taking us back to the Growing Argument: my wife one day is not the same person as my wife the next.[6]

The Cretan liar paradox is a little different, but here, too, the problem is caused by relying on the left hemisphere only to construct the world. It does so by rules, and with precision. Meanwhile, the right hemisphere, like Achilles in real life, overtakes the left-hemisphere tortoise in one effortless stride: right-hemisphere pragmatics mean that we know precisely what Epimenides is getting at. We don't have to get hung up on the rules. In the real world nothing is absolute, and with a lack of pedantry appropriate to the fact that his remark actually comes from a poem, and is probably humorous in intent, since he is well aware that he is a Cretan, we understand that Epimenides has stepped outside the frame for a moment, to take a look at the people he belongs to. In real life one has come across people who take humorous remarks literally, or who laboriously attempt to replace understanding by the application of absolute rules and come up with a paradox, and they are usually somewhere along the Asperger spectrum. It looks like right-hemisphere failure again: misunderstanding of context, lack of humour, lack of flexibility, insistence on the certainty obtained by rules. What this paradox also illuminates is that any enclosed, self-referring system the left hemisphere comes up with, if taken strictly on its *own* terms, self-explodes: there is a member of the system that cannot be accommodated by the system.[7] There is always an escape route from the hall of mirrors, if one looks hard enough.

Paradox means, literally, a finding that is contrary to received opinion or expectation. That immediately alerts us, since the purveyor of received opinion and expectation is the left hemisphere. I called it a sign that our ordinary ways of thinking, those of the left hemisphere, are not adequate to the nature of reality. But – wait! Here it seems that the left hemisphere, with its reliance on the application of logic, is stating the opposite: that it is *reality* that is inadequate to our *ordinary ways of thinking*. Contrary to received opinion, it asserts, arrows do not move, Achilles cannot overtake the tortoise, there can never be a heap of sand, Theseus' ship is not really his ship after all, Epimenides was inevitably talking nonsense. In other words its understanding of paradox is – not that there must be problems in applying this kind of logic to the real world – but that the real world isn't the way we think it is *because logic says so*. This looks like an interesting usurpation, a swapping of roles, with the new dispensation redefining who is Master, and who emissary.[8]

Problems arising from whether we see the world as a process, always in flux, or as a series of static, finished, entities, have inevitably persisted in philosophy. In the Middle Ages it was acknowledged in the distinction between the world seen as *natura naturans*, nature 'naturing', doing what nature does, a process ever evolving, and to that degree unknowable, and *natura naturata*, nature 'natured', a something completed, perfect (which always implies past tense, an arrest of the flow of time), static, knowable. Spinoza was one of the few philosophers, apart from Pascal, between Plato and Hegel to have a strong sense of the right-hemisphere world.[9] For him this distinction, understandably, had a particular importance; he also pre-eminently understood the way in which the universal is attained to only via the particular; 'the more we understand individual things, the more we understand God'.[10]

But the area in which the hemispheres and philosophy can be mutually illuminating that is of chief interest in this book is that of the relationship of the mind to the world. Just because of the immensity of that topic, I want to limit it by moving on to look at things from the other end of the process, and attempt my second question, what philosophy can tell us that will help us understand the hemisphere differences.

Let's return to the main point of hemisphere difference, division *versus* cohesion. Since the notorious Cartesian subject–object divide, philosophy has grappled with the spectre of solipsism. To know something is to encounter something other, and know it as separate from ourselves. If all I am certain of is my own existence (*cogito ergo sum*), how does one ever cross the gap? For the solipsist, there is nothing to encounter, since all we know stems from our own mind alone: according to Wittgenstein, the solipsist is like someone who tries to make the car go faster by pushing against the dashboard from inside. There is a paradox here, too: the position is self-undermining, in that it nonetheless demands another mind, another consciousness that can constitute the solipsist (as Hegel's master needs the slave in order to be a master): to use the term 'I' requires the possibility of there being something which is 'not-I' – otherwise, in place of 'all that is, is mine', we just get the vacuous 'all that is mine, is mine'.[11]

As Louis Sass has demonstrated in relation to the world of the schizophrenic, solipsistic subjectivity on the one hand (with its fantasy of omnipotence) and alienated objectivity on the other (with its related fantasy of impotence) tend to collapse into one another, and are merely facets of the same phenomenon: both imply isolation rather than connection.[12] The attempt to adopt a God's eye view, or 'view from nowhere' in Thomas Nagel's famous phrase, the position pretended by objectivism, is as empty as solipsism, and is ultimately indistinguishable from it in its consequences: the 'view from nowhere' pretends to equate to a 'view from everywhere'.[13] What is different is the 'view from somewhere'. Everything that we know can be known only from an individual point of view, or under one or another aspect of its existence, never in totality or perfection.[14] Equally what we come to know consists not of things, but of relationships, each apparently separate entity qualifying the others to which it is related. But this does not entail that there can be no reliably constituted shared world of experience. Because we do not experience precisely the same world does not mean that we are condemned not to meet in a world at all. We cannot take refuge in fantasies of either omnipotence or impotence. The difficult truth is less grand: that there is a *something* apart from ourselves, which we can influence to *some* degree. And the evidence is that how we do so matters.

DEWEY AND JAMES: CONTEXT AND THE NATURE OF TRUTH

Towards the end of the nineteenth century and in the early twentieth century the American pragmatist philosophers John Dewey and William James, in different ways, began to signal dissatisfaction with the atomistic, rationalistic approach in philosophy and the abstraction that necessarily goes with it. Dewey wrote:

> Thinking is always thinking, but philosophical thinking is, upon the whole, at the extreme end of the scale of distance from the active urgency of concrete situations. It is because of this fact that neglect of context is the besetting fallacy of philosophical thought ... I should venture to assert that the most pervasive fallacy of philosophic thinking goes back to neglect of context ... neglect of context is the greatest single disaster which philosophic thinking can incur.[15]

If the process of philosophy is to understand the world, and in reality things are always embedded in a context of relation with other things that alter them, you are not going to succeed in understanding them if you start by taking them out of context. 'We are not explicitly aware of the role of context just because our every utterance is so saturated with it that it forms the significance of what we say and hear.'[16] Here Dewey refers to the implicit nature of the right hemisphere's world, its insistence on the importance of context and the ultimate importance of right-hemisphere pragmatics in yielding the meaning of 'what we say and hear'. And context implies change and process:

> To see the organism *in* nature, the nervous system in the organism, the brain in the nervous system, the cortex in the brain is the answer to the problems which haunt philosophy. And when thus seen they will be seen to be *in*, not as marbles are in a box but as events are in history, in a moving, growing, never finished process.[17]

Dewey and James addressed the problem of how one can know truth in a world where things vary depending on context, and part of that context is the nature of the mind that does the knowing. 'The qualities never were "in" the organism; they always were qualities of interactions in which both extra-organic things and organisms partake.'[18] James, like Dewey, saw that there was a something other than ourselves, and that therefore, despite the impossibility of a 'detached' objectivity, truth to it was important:

> The much lauded objective evidence is never triumphantly there; it is a mere aspiration or *Grenzbegriff* [limit or ideal notion] marking the infinitely remote ideal of our thinking life . . . [But] when as empiricists we give up the doctrine of objective certitude, we do not thereby give up the quest or hope of truth itself. We still pin our faith on its existence, and still believe that we gain an ever better position towards it by systematically continuing to roll up experiences and think. Our great difference from the scholastic lies in the way we face. The strength of his system lies in the principles, the origin, the *terminus a quo* of his thought; for us the strength is in the outcome, the upshot, the *terminus ad quem*. Not where it comes from but what it leads to is to decide.[19]

This account of James's illuminates the difference between two approaches to knowledge or understanding, those of the two hemispheres. According to the left hemisphere, understanding is built up from the parts; one starts from one certainty, places another next to it, and advances as if building a wall, from the bottom up. It conceives that there is objective evidence of truth for a part outside the context of the whole it goes to constitute. According to the right hemisphere, understanding is derived from the whole, since it is only in the light of the whole that one can truly understand the nature of the parts. One process is pushed from behind (from a *terminus a quo*), the other pulled from in front (towards a *terminus ad quem*). According to the latter vision, that of the right hemisphere, truth is only ever provisional, but that does not mean that one must 'give up the quest or hope of truth itself'.

Dewey was also dissatisfied with the idea that knowledge was a passive process, whereby clear and certain truths were 'out there' to be accessed by a process in which the human mind and imagination did not have to play an active part. His Gifford lectures of 1929, *The Quest for Certainty*, 'claimed that the debate in philosophy had rested, ever since the 1630s [Descartes's era] on too passive a view of the human mind, and on inappropriate demands for geometrical certainty'.[20] He deplored the resultant 'spectator' theory of knowledge, 'the traditional conception, according to which the thing to be known is something which exists prior to and wholly apart from the act of knowing'.[21]

This theme was taken up by the German and French philosophers of the phenomenological tradition. It is with them that things took a remarkable, almost unforeseeable, step, and it is to them that I now turn. My point in doing so should not be misunderstood. It is not to assert that these philosophers are 'right' – though I believe they do reveal important truths about ourselves and the world, known to other traditions, that were until recently completely lost sight of in Western philosophy. There are always different views in philosophy, and argument literally knows no end. There will always be some who remain unconvinced of what these philosophers seem to have seen and tried to convey. No – my point is that these philosophers, none of whom could possibly have had access to what we now know about hemisphere differences, nonetheless each found himself compelled, unawares, to derive the reality and ultimate importance of the right-hemisphere world, even though each started from the premises and tools of philosophy, with their naturally inbuilt bias towards the way of thinking of the left hemisphere.

HUSSERL AND THE IDEA OF INTERSUBJECTIVITY

Edmund Husserl was born in Moravia in 1859, and began by studying mathematics, physics and astronomy, though he became increasingly concerned with the relationship between psychology and philosophy. His main works were published between the turn of the twentieth century and the Second World War (he died in 1938); as with Wittgenstein, his philosophical position evolved dramatically, and his later works grapple with the problems of rationalism in a world partly constituted by human consciousness. He was the first, and perhaps the only, true phenomenologist in the strictest sense, aiming to study consciousness and conscious experience (phenomena) objectively, but nonetheless from a first-person, rather than a third-person, perspective. He used particular kinds of thought experiments, called 'reductions' (nothing whatever to do with reductionism), in a painstaking attempt to get at things as they are in themselves, aiming to transcend all preconceived theoretical frameworks, and the subject–object divide. Since phenomenology has been the major influence on European philosophy in the twentieth century, Husserl, as its founder, is generally seen as one of the most influential thinkers of our age. Heidegger, Merleau-Ponty, Scheler and many others are often called phenomenologists, and Hegel, a century earlier, has been seen as a forerunner.

Though Husserl brought a background in Cartesian philosophy and the methodology of science to bear on mental phenomena, he came to realize that this philosophy and this methodology failed to account for the nature of experience. According to Husserl, the roots of the European crisis of modernism lay in '*verirrenden Rationalismus*' and '*Blindheit für das Transzendentale*':[22] a sort of mad rationalism and a blindness to the transcendental. In his later philosophy, Husserl aimed to transcend the apparent duality of subjective and objective, of realism and idealism, that had so troubled philosophy since Plato: he emphasised the role that empathy, the capacity not just to put oneself in someone else's shoes but, importantly, to feel what they are feeling, plays in constructing the world.[23] He came to the conclusion that there was an objective reality, but that it was constituted by what he called intersubjectivity. This comes about through shared experience, which is made possible for us by our embodied existence alongside other embodied individuals.[24] He distinguished between the two ways in which we know the body: as a material object (*Körper*), alongside other objects in the world, and in that sense alien to us, and the way we experience it as something not just living, but lived (*Leib*), as it were from the inside. When we see others engaged in action in the world, we feel them to be *leibhaft*, as though we shared with them our consciousness of embodied existence.[25]

In this emphasis on the body, the importance of empathy, and intersubjectivity (which forms part of what I mean by 'betweenness'), Husserl is asserting the essential role that the right hemisphere plays in constituting the world in which we live. He, too, emphasises the importance of context: things only are what they are because they find themselves in the surroundings in which they find themselves, and are connected to whatever it is that they are connected to. This raises the spectre of epistemological circularity, since achieving an understanding of any one thing depends on an understanding of the whole; and the tools of language and logical analysis take one away from context, back to the set of familiar concepts that, if one is a philosopher, one is constantly trying to transcend through analysis in language. That was the purpose of what he called the phenomenological reductions. His own approach is linear, but is forced to acknowledge the awkward truth displayed in Escher's hands. The world arises from a circular process that circles and searches its origins, more like a picture that comes into focus all at once, than a linear address to a target: by a right-hemisphere process, in other words, rather than a left.

The fact that empathy with others grounds our experience not just of them, but of ourselves and the world, has been borne out by research in psychology in recent years. One might think, in Cartesian fashion, that we attribute an 'inwardness' to others on the basis that we recognise our own feelings first, link them to outward expressions, utterances and actions that we make contemporaneously with those feelings, and then, when we see those same expressions in others, attribute the same feelings to them by a sort of logical analogy with ourselves. But developmental psychology shows that this is a false assumption. The direction in which it works appears not to be from within our (separate) selves to within (separate) others, but from shared experience to the development of our own inwardness *and* that of others. We do not need to learn to make the link between our selves and others, because although individual we are not initially separated, but intersubjective in our consciousness.[26] As one philosopher of mind, reflecting on the relevance of phenomenology to neuroscience, has put it,

> there is a remarkable convergence between these two traditions, not simply on the topic of intersubjectivity, but on virtually every area of research within cognitive science, as a growing number of scientists and philosophers have discussed. In the case of intersubjectivity, much of the convergence centres on the realization that *one's consciousness of oneself as an embodied individual in the world is founded on empathy* – on one's empathic cognition of others, and others' empathic cognition of oneself.[27]

Again the process is circular (or spiral-like), rather than linear.

The left hemisphere is not impressed by empathy: its concern is with maximising gain for itself, and its driving value is utility. As a result, philosophers in the Anglo-American tradition, more or less untouched by the European phenomenologists, have been nonplussed by altruistic behaviour. They have had to resort to complex logical formulations that defy common sense and experience to explain behaviour that is obviously the product of care as being ultimately selfish (despite the fact that the Prisoner's Dilemma – see below – appears to demonstrate that the rational person should not in fact act selfishly, another paradox that illuminates one of the 'Gödelian' points within the left hemisphere's system). Naturally there are ways of logically taking into account such problems of logic. More and more refined riders, more self-referential loops, are added, reminding one of nothing so much as the epicycles upon epicycles that were added by pre-Keplerian astronomers to planetary orbits in order to 'save the phenomena'. It is like the attempt to describe a living curve using only straight lines: more and more are added, and the curve is ever more approximated, with infinite complexity, the lines never quite reaching their target and always remaining outside the curve – which a free hand could have delineated in one sweep. Or like a complex construction of cogs and wheels to produce a simulacrum of a living person, there being always, however closely, even exquisitely, approaching its goal, something more that it lacks.

The Prisoner's Dilemma is a problem that will be familiar to many readers, originating in an aspect of economic and social modelling known as games theory, and first posed by Flood and Dresher in 1950.[28] It goes like this. The police suspect two individuals, A and B, of a serious crime, but have insufficient evidence to pin it on them. They arrest the suspects and interrogate them separately. Each is told that if he testifies for the prosecution against the other, and the other remains silent, he will go free and his opposite number will receive the maximum sentence of 10 years in jail. In the case where they both remain silent, the police would be able to make only a much lesser charge stick, for which they would each serve six months. If each were to betray the other, each would receive a two-year sentence. Neither prisoner is in a position to know what the other prisoner will do. How should each respond – by remaining silent or betraying the other (defecting)?

Their options are summarised below.

	B is silent	B defects
A is silent	A gets six months B gets six months	A gets 10 years B goes free
A defects	A goes free B gets 10 years	A gets 2 years B gets 2 years

The essence of the problem is that the best outcome for both is where each remains silent, and they each serve six months (top left option). But, if each behaves rationally, they will end up doing worse: each will defect, and they will both end up serving two years (bottom right option). The reason for this is clear. A does not know what B will do, so he weighs up his options. If B is silent, A will do better by defecting: he will go free, instead of serving six months in jail. If, on the other hand, B defects, A will still do better by defecting, since he will get two years instead of 10. So whatever happens he is better off to defect. And, of course, the situation being symmetrical, B will reason similarly: hence they are stuck in the bottom right hand corner of the diagram, while they would both be better off in the top left.

As the game is repeated, various attempts to anticipate what the other may be thinking can be made, affecting the outcome. For example, A may learn from experience that neither can emerge from this trap unless they are prepared to trust and take a risk. So he may behave altruistically in the next round. If B does also, they will both be rewarded. If B does not, A may decide not to be a sucker in the third round, but instead to punish A by defecting next time. Even if B does reciprocate in round two, A may decide to defect in round three, on the expectation that B may carry on reciprocating, to A's advantage. Obviously there are an infinite number of such tangles that can be worked through, but they are worked through only in such artificial settings by computer scientists and philosophers. In the real world we realize that, in a nutshell, we cannot get anywhere unless we are prepared to take a risk and we are prepared to trust. Calculation is unhelpful, and is superseded by a habit of beneficence in most of us for whom the right orbitofrontal cortex, the basis of empathy, is still functioning properly. For highly unempathic individuals, such as psychopaths, in whom this part of the brain is defective, and therefore for whom this aspect of the world is missing, they will devote themselves, like philosophers, to calculation.[29]

Most subjects in the Prisoner's Dilemma prefer mutual co-operation over unilateral defection, even though the dilemma is set up so that it is apparently in their self-interest to defect, regardless of what the other player does.[30] It seems we do not seek simply to maximise our material advantage at the expense of others, and this is not explained by 'selfish' prudential reasoning. Altruism is a necessary consequence of empathy: we feel others' feeling, engage in their being. The great apes are capable of empathy and can be altruistic: for example Binti Jua, a gorilla at Brookfield Zoo in Chicago, saved a young boy who fell into her compound.[31] Dogs that have lived with humans can act in ways that are driven neither by instinct nor by any conceivable self-interest, and would be counted altruistic if they occurred in humans: they cannot be making a calculation of any kind. Why should we not also be capable of acts of love?

> We should remember that in mammals the social bonding mechanisms are based on learning and are certainly more pervasive than the *innate* mechanisms for 'kin recognition'. We can learn to love other animals . . . the acquisition of nurturant behaviour leaves a seemingly indelible print on a creature's way of being in the world.[32]

Altruism in humans extends far beyond anything in the animal world, and also beyond what is called 'reciprocal altruism', in which we behave 'altruistically' in calculated expectation of the favour being reciprocated. It is not a matter of the genes looking after themselves at the expense of the individual, either; human beings co-operate with people with whom they are not genetically related. It is also far more than merely co-operation based on the importance of maintaining one's reputation; we co-operate with, and put ourselves out to help, those we may barely know, those we know we may never meet again, and those who can in no way reward us. The possibility of future reciprocation may, of course, influence decisions, where it operates, but it is not fundamental to the phenomenon.[33]

It is mutuality, not reciprocity, fellow-feeling, not calculation, which is both the motive and the reward for successful co-operation. And the outcome, in utilitarian terms, is not the important point: it is the process, the relationship, that matters. At the neurological level, we know that in experimental situations using the Prisoner's Dilemma, subjects that achieve mutual co-operation with another human individual show activity in areas of the brain associated with pleasure (parts of the mesolimbic dopamine system, including the striatum and the orbitofrontal cortex); they do not, however, in a situation where they achieve the appearances of 'mutual co-operation' with a programmed computer rather than a living person. It is also interesting that when playing with a human partner the majority of the regions showing particular involvement in co-operation are right-sided, whereas with a machine partner they are mainly left-sided (stuff the empathy, we're just both out to win).[34] And in case anyone should think that empathy necessarily means being soft on others, those right-sided regions include the right caudate, an area known to be involved in altruistic punishment of defection.[35]

MERLEAU-PONTY: EMPATHY AND THE BODY

The discussion of empathy obliges me to step out of chronological sequence here, to look at the philosophy of Maurice Merleau-Ponty, since the part played by empathy and the body in the construction of reality is central to his thinking. He was born in 1908, and his major works were published in French between the war years and the 1960s, with translations into English following by ten to twenty years in most cases:

it would be hard to overstate his influence on philosophy, psychology and art criticism from the second half of the twentieth century onwards. He was among the many thinkers that were influenced by Husserl's philosophy of intersubjectivity.

Merleau-Ponty wrote about the reciprocity of communication that 'it is as if the other person's intentions inhabited my body and mine his'.[36] The concept of what may be called the 'lived body', the sense of the body not as something we live inside, not even as an extension of ourselves, but as an aspect of our existence which is fundamental to our being, could be seen as the ultimate foundation of the philosophy of Merleau-Ponty. He recapitulated the view of Henri Bergson that the self-experience of the human being is embedded in the world, with the body as the mediator, and held that the human body is the means whereby consciousness and the world are profoundly interrelated and *engaged* with one another. For Merleau-Ponty the 'object' of perception cannot be viewed in isolation, because it is in reality embedded in a context, the nexus of relations among existing things which gives it meaning within the world. Thus no one object exists independently of others, but reflects a part of whatever else it co-exists with, and in turn is itself similarly reflected there. This is related to a sense of the intrinsic incompleteness of perspective available on any given entity at a given moment. Such partial disclosures, 'takes' or *Abschattungen* (a term of Husserl's, often, rather unhelpfully, translated as 'adumbrations'), are a necessary part of the true experience of any existing thing, which ultimately exists in the totality of possible views. Such partial views do not undermine, but tend to confirm, such a thing's real existence: only the representation of a theoretical ideal could pretend to completeness. Merleau-Ponty emphasised specifically the importance of depth as a foundation for such experience in the lived world, contrasting the different aspects, or *Abschattungen*, of a single whole, which reveal themselves in an object that has depth, with the *parts* that are all that one is left with where the object lacks depth.[37]

That the relations between 'the subject and his body', and in turn between the body and the world, the relations which form the focus of Merleau-Ponty's philosophical concerns, are underwritten by the right hemisphere is knowledge potentially available to anyone who has cared for stroke patients. It becomes obvious when something goes wrong with right-hemisphere functioning. This was remarked nearly 50 years ago in a now classic paper on the apraxias, neurological syndromes in which there is an inability to carry out an action, despite there being no impairment of sensory or motor function. Of these conditions Hécaen and his colleagues wrote: 'It is indeed remarkable that the apraxias expressing an impairment of relations between the subject and his body or between the body and the surrounding space are found in connection with lesions of the minor [i.e. right] hemisphere.'[38] All the same, when the issue is how to *use* an object, at least if the use is straightforward, the lesion is usually in the left hemisphere; but where it is not a question of straightforward use, the right hemisphere tends to be implicated.[39] Constructional apraxias, which depend on the loss of the sense of the whole, are commonest and most severe after right-sided lesions.[40]

For Merleau-Ponty truth is arrived at through engagement with the world, not through greater abstraction from it; the general is encountered through, rather than in spite of, the particular; and the infinite through, rather than in spite of, the finite. In relation to art, Merleau-Ponty's view, which accords with experience, was that the artist did not merely reflect what was there anyway, albeit in a novel way, but actually 'brought into being a truth' about the world that was not there before, perhaps the best example of the universal being manifest through the particular.[41]

It is the rootedness of our thought and language in the body that we share with others which means that despite the fact that all truth is relative, this in no way undermines the possibility of shared truth. It is the right hemisphere's 'primary consciousness', coupled to the body's preconscious awareness of the world, which relates our visceral and emotional experience to what we know about the world.[42] This position has been corroborated more recently by Lakoff and Johnson, and once again the body is the crucial mediator:

The mind is not merely embodied, but embodied in such a way that our concep-tual systems draw largely upon the commonalities of our bodies and of the envir-onments we live in. The result is that much of a person's conceptual system is either universal or widespread across languages and cultures. Our conceptual systems are not totally relative and not *merely* a matter of historical contingency, even though a degree of conceptual relativity does exist and even though histor-ical contingency does matter a great deal ... truth is mediated by embodied understanding and imagination. That does not mean that truth is purely subjec-tive or that there is no stable truth. Rather, our common embodiment allows for common, stable truths.[43]

The grounding role in experience played by empathy, the primacy for Merleau-Ponty of experience over conceptual thought (one of his essays is entitled 'The primacy of perception, and its philosophical consequences'),[44] his insistence on context and on the fundamental role played by the physically instantiated self in the 'lived body' as the prerequisite for being-in-the-world, the lived body as the medium of intersubjective experience, the consequent importance of depth, which is the necessary condition for embodied existence, his emphasis on the work of art as bringing into being something entirely new, not just a redeployment of what already exists, are all, in my view, expressions of the stance or disposition towards the world of the right hemisphere.

HEIDEGGER AND THE NATURE OF BEING

However, it was with the philosophy of Martin Heidegger that this world view reached its most comprehensive ever expression.[45] Here we need to step back a few years. Born in 1889 in southern Germany, he was destined for the priesthood, and his early work was on Aristotle and Duns Scotus; but he began to realise that our treatment of being, as though it were just an attribute of things like other attributes, or, worse, a thing alongside other things, led to a misunderstanding of the world and our selves. His great work *Sein und Zeit* (Being and Time) was published in 1927, and its importance was immediately recognised.

Because our use of a term such as 'being' makes us feel that we understand what being is, it hides the sense of radical astonishment we would have if we could truly understand it, and subverts our attempts to do so. I am reminded of Cantor's perception that treating infinity as just another kind of number stopped us understanding its nature and hence the nature of the world. But just as that did not mean that we should abandon mathematics, Heidegger's insight does not mean that we should abandon language. It just means that we have to be constantly vigilant to undermine language's attempt to undermine our understanding.

While Heidegger has ardent admirers and equally ardent detractors, there is no doubting his importance, despite the difficulty of his writings, in every aspect of modern thought: his influence throughout the humanities has been profound indeed. Heidegger's entire thrust is away from the clear light of analysis, and this has led to misunderstandings. While he has been admired as a wise philosopher-teacher by some, he has been reviled as an obfuscator by others. Those with an interest in tearing down the boundaries of the world of ordinary sense have adopted him as a patron. I believe this attempt by what Julian Young calls 'the "anarcho-existentialists" for whom every reality interpretation is an oppressive power-structure' to annex Heidegger to their cause represents a travesty, an almost total inversion of what he stood for.[46] For Heidegger, the fact that our apprehension of whatever is takes part in the process of that thing becoming what it is, and that therefore there is no single truth about anything that exists, does not mean that any version of a thing is valid or that all versions are equally valid. As Eric Matthews says, talking about Merleau-Ponty's reflections on the art work:

> Because the medium of the resulting work is not conventionally-referring language, whatever meaning it has will not be expressible in any other terms than those of the work itself. It is not an *arbitrary* meaning: because we cannot give a 'correct' translation into some other medium, it does not follow that we can give the work any meaning we care to.[47]

And that does not go just for works of art. Things are not whatever we care to make them. There is a something that exists apart from our own minds, and our attempt to apprehend whatever it is needs to be true to, faithful to, that whatever-it-is-that-exists and at the same time true to ourselves in making that apprehension. No single truth does not mean no truth.

To speak of truth sounds too grand, too filled with the promise of certainty, and we are rightly suspicious of it. But truth will not go away that easily. The statement that 'there is no such thing as truth' is itself a truth statement, and implies that it is truer than its opposite, the statement that 'truth exists'. If we had no concept of truth, we could not state anything at all, and it would even be pointless to act. There would be no purpose, for example, in seeking the advice of doctors, since there would be no point in having their opinion, and no basis for their view that one treatment was better than another. None of us actually lives as though there were no truth. Our problem is more with the notion of a single, unchanging truth.

The word 'true' suggests a relationship between things: being true to someone or something, truth as loyalty, or something that fits, as two surfaces may be said to be 'true'. It is related to 'trust', and is fundamentally a matter of what one *believes* to be the case. The Latin word *verum* (true) is cognate with a Sanskrit word meaning to choose or believe: the option one chooses, the situation in which one places one's trust. Such a situation is not an absolute – it tells us not only about the chosen thing, but also about the chooser. It cannot be certain: it involves an act of faith, and it involves being faithful to one's intuitions.

For Heidegger, Being (*Sein*) is hidden, and things as they truly are (*das Seiende*) can be 'unconcealed' only by a certain disposition of patient attention towards the world – emphatically not by annexing it, exploiting it or ransacking it for congenial meanings, in a spirit of 'anything goes'. Heidegger related truth to the Greek concept of *aletheia*, literally 'unconcealing'. In this concept a number of facets of truth are themselves unconcealed. In the first place it suggests something that pre-exists our attempts to 'dis-cover' it.[48] Then it is an entity defined by a negative – by what it is not; and in opposition to something else (*un*concealing). It is come at by a *process*, a coming into being of something; and that process is also, importantly, part of the truth. It is an act, a journey, not a thing. It has degrees. It is found by removing things, rather than by putting things together. This idea of truth-as-unconcealing contrasts with the idea of truth-as-correctness, which is static, unchanging. Truth as unconcealing is a progress towards something – the something is in sight, but never fully seen; whereas truth as correctness is given as a thing in itself, that can in principle be fully known.

For Heidegger, truth was such an unconcealing, but it was also a concealing, since opening one horizon inevitably involves the closing of others. There is no single privileged viewpoint from which every aspect can be seen.[49] It may be true that, to quote Patricia Churchland, 'it is reasonable to *identify* the blueness of an object with its disposition to scatter ... electromagnetic waves preferentially at about 0.46μm' [emphasis in the original].[50] That is, I suppose, a sort of truth about the colour blue. That is one way in which blue discloses itself. Most of us would think it left rather a lot out. There are also other very important truths about the colour blue that we experience, for example, when we see a canvas by Ingres, or by Yves Klein, or view the sky, or sea, which are closed off by this. It is, in this sense, like the duck–rabbit: we can have only one 'take' on it at a time. We see things by seeing them *as* something. In this sense too we create the world by attending to it in a particular way.

But there is a more important reason why truth has to be concealment. Every thing that purports to be the truth is, according to Heidegger, inevitably an approximation and true things, things that really are, rather than as we may apprehend them, are in themselves ineffable, ungraspable. Thus to see them clearly is to see something at best indistinct to vision – except that to see them distinctly would not be truly to see *them*. To have the impression that one sees things as they truly are, is not to permit them to 'presence' to us, but to substitute something else for them, something comfortable, familiar and *graspable* – what I would call a left-hemisphere *re*-presentation. The inexperienced mariner sees the ice floe; the experienced mariner sees the berg and is awe-struck.

Heidegger's concept of hiddenness does not imply a sort of throwing up of one's hands in the air before the incomprehensible. Just the opposite, as his life's work implies. Hiddenness does *not* mean, in the arts, being beyond approach, nor does it invite a free-for-all; instead it suggests that what is understood by the right hemisphere is likely to be uncomprehended by the left. Heidegger's somewhat gnomic saying, *in der Unverborgenheit waltet die Verbergung* ('in unconcealment dwells hiddenness and safekeeping') appositely draws attention to the simultaneous hiddenness and radiance of truth in works of art. The meaning is present wholly in the work of art: it cannot be extracted from it or dragged into the daylight, but is perfectly projected there where it is. One might compare Wittgenstein: 'The work of art does not aim to convey *something else*, just itself.'[51]

The stance, or disposition, that we need to adopt, according to Heidegger, is one of 'waiting *on*' (*nachdenken*) something, rather than just 'waiting *for*' it; a patient, respectful nurturing of something into disclosure, in which we need already to have some idea of what it is that will be. George Steiner compares it to 'that "bending toward" of spirit and intellect and ear' to be seen in Fra Angelico's *Annunciation* in San Marco.[52] A highly active passivity, in other words. There is a process of responsiveness between man (*Dasein*, literally 'being there', or perhaps 'the being that is *in* the world') and Being, which is well described again by Steiner:

An *Ent-sprechen* is not 'an answer to' (*une réponse à*), but a 'response to', a 'correspondence with', a dynamic reciprocity and matching such as occur when gears, both in quick motion, mesh. Thus, our question as to the nature of philosophy calls not for an answer in the sense of a textbook definition or formulation, be it Platonic, Cartesian, or Lockeian, but for an *Ent-sprechung*, a response, a vital echo, a 're-sponsion' in the liturgical sense of participatory engagement ... For Descartes, truth is determined and validated by certainty. Certainty, in turn, is located in the *ego*. The self becomes the hub of reality and relates to the world outside itself in an exploratory, necessarily exploitative, way. As knower and user, the *ego* is predator. For Heidegger, on the contrary, the human person and self-consciousness are *not* the centre, the assessors of existence. Man is only a privileged listener and respondent to existence. The vital relation to otherness is not, as for Cartesian and positivist rationalism, one of 'grasping' and pragmatic use. It is a relation of audition. We are trying 'to listen to the voice of Being'. It is, or ought to be, a relation of extreme responsibility, custodianship, answerability to and for.[53]

The contrast here being drawn between, on the one hand, the isolated ego, standing in a relation of alienated and predatory exploitation to the world around it, mysteriously leaping from subject to object and back again, retiring with its booty into the cabinet of its consciousness, where it demands certainty of knowledge; and, on the other, a self that is drawn into and inextricably bound up with the world in a relation, not just metaphysical in nature, but of 'being-with' and inside, a relation of care (*Sorge*) and concern, suggesting involvement of the whole experiential being, not just the processes of cognition – this contrast evokes in my view some of the essential differences between the worlds that are brought about for us by the two hemispheres. But that is by no means all.

Since *Dasein* is 'to be there' in the world – the literal, actual, concrete, daily world – to be human at all is to be immersed in the earth, and the quotidian matter-of-factness of the world. The right hemisphere is concerned with the *familiar*, not in the sense of the inauthentically routine, but in the sense of the things that form part of 'my' daily world or *familia*, the household, those I care for.[54] It is not alien from material things, but, quite the opposite, attends to individual things in all their concrete particularity. This is exactly the 'personal sensibility to the grain and substance of physical existence, to the "thingness" and obstinate quiddity of things, be they rock or tree or human presence' that is found in Heidegger.[55] Again this roots existence in the body and in the senses. We do not inhabit the body like some alien Cartesian piece of machine wizardry, but live it – a distinction between the left and right hemisphere understandings of the body. In trying to convey the 'otherness' of a particular building, its sheer existence or *essent* prior to any one act of cognition by which it is partially apprehended, Heidegger speaks of the primal fact of its existence being made present to us in the very smell of it, more immediately communicated in this way than by any description or inspection.[56] The senses are crucial to the 'presence' of being, 'to our apprehension of an *is* in things that no analytic dissection or verbal account can isolate'.[57]

Time is responsible for *Dasein*'s individuality, and is the condition under which existing things are. In *Sein und Zeit* (*Being and Time*) Heidegger insists that we do not live *in* time, as if it were some independent, abstract flow, alien to our being, but live time – much as being-in-the-world is not the same as being in the world like a marble in a box. We live time rather than just conceive it, and similarly we live the body rather than simply derive sensory information through it.[58] Through the experience of time, *Dasein* becomes a 'being towards death': without death existence would be care-less, would lack the power that draws us to one another and to the world. For Heidegger the 'nadir of inauthentic temporality' is time as a sequence of instants (the left-hemisphere mode), which is opposed to the lived time of *Dasein*, and whatever gives it meaning.[59]

Everydayness was an important concept for Heidegger: again it has two meanings, and Heidegger's distinctions once more illuminate hemisphere differences, as hemisphere differences illuminate Heidegger's meaning. To take a famous example of his, the hammer that I use finds its place naturally in a context of the action for which I use it, and becomes almost an extension of myself, so that there is no awareness or focal (left hemisphere) attention to it. It recedes into its context – the lived world of me, my arm, the action of hammering, and the world around in which this takes place (right hemisphere); in Heidegger's terms it is *zuhanden* ('ready-to-hand').[60] By contrast, it stands out, becomes in Heidegger's terms *vorhanden* ('present-at-hand'), only when something goes wrong and interrupts this flow, and draws my attention to it as an object for inspection (left hemisphere). Then it begins to become alien. But the situation is more complex and alive (right hemisphere) than this analytical schema (left hemisphere) makes it appear. Things do not end up 'filed' (left hemisphere) or for that matter 'dwelling' (right hemisphere) in one or other hemisphere, but are constantly moving back and forth, or, to put it more accurately, aspects of them belong to one hemisphere and aspects to the other, and these aspects are continually coming forward and retreating in a process that is dynamic. The business of living calls forth aspects of things in either hemisphere. The routine of daily life, in which things have their familiar place and order (right hemisphere), can dull things into what Heidegger called inauthenticity (left hemisphere), through the very weight of familiarity, and in my terms its left hemisphere re-presentation comes to take the place of the thing itself (broadly the *idea* of the hammer replaces the thing as it is experienced). However, the very alienation inherent in the experience of its sudden *Vorhandenheit*, when the hammer becomes the focus of my attention, allows the possibility of rediscovering the authenticity that had been lost, because the detachment enables us to see it anew as an existing thing, something remarkable, almost with a sense of wonder (in which, for Heidegger, as for many other philosophers, all philosophy begins).

As things become dulled and inauthentic, they become conceptualised rather than experienced; they are taken out of their living context, a bit like ripping the heart out of a living body. Heidegger called this process that of *Gestell*, or framing, a term which suggests the detachment of seeing things as if through a window (as in a famous image of Descartes's),[61] or as re-presented in a picture, or, nowadays, framed by the TV or computer screen.[62] Inherent in it is the notion of an arbitrarily abrupted set of potential relationships, with the context – which ultimately means the totality of Being, all that is – neatly severed at the edges of the frame. Because reality is infinitely ramified and interconnected, because its nature is to hide, and to recede from the approach of logical analysis, language is a constantly limiting, potentially misdirecting and distorting medium. Yet it is necessary to Heidegger as a philosopher. In its tendency to linearity it resists the reticulated web of Heidegger's thought, and his writing espouses images and metaphors of paths that are circuitous and indirect, the *Holzwege*, *Feldweg*, *Wegmarken*, and so on, suggesting threading one's way through woods and fields.[63] It is interesting that Descartes's philosophy was half-baked while he slept in a Bavarian oven, the metaphor of stasis and self-enclosure revealing, philosophy and the body being one, the nature of the philosophy; whereas Heidegger was, according to Steiner, 'an indefatigable walker in unlit places': *solvitur ambulando*.[64] Truth is process, not object.

From the analytic point of view, as Steiner says, one has constantly to attempt to 'jump "outside" and beyond the speaker's own shadow'.[65] One must never also lose sight of the interconnected nature of things, so that Heidegger's project is in this, too, opposed to Descartes, who limited himself to viewing objects singly: 'if one tries to look at many objects at one glance, one sees none of them distinctly'.[66] Heidegger reached naturally towards metaphor, in which more than one thing is kept implicitly (hiddenly) before the mind, since he valued, unusually for a philosopher, the ambiguity of poetic language. He lamented the awful *Eindeutigkeit* – literally the 'one-meaningness', or explicitness – to which in a computer age we tend: both Wittgenstein and Heidegger, according to Richard Rorty, 'ended by trying to work out honourable terms on which philosophy might surrender to poetry'.[67] Wittgenstein's work became increasingly apophthegmatic: he repeatedly struggled with the idea that philosophy was not possible outside of poetry.[68] And Heidegger ultimately found himself, in his last works, resorting to poetry to convey the complexity and depth of his meaning. He saw language as integral to whatever it brings forward, just as the body is to *Dasein*, not as a mere container for thought: 'Words and language are not wrappings in which things are packed for the commerce of those who write and speak.'[69]

There is also inherent in Heidegger's talk of language an understanding that our relationship with language, like the relationship we have with the world which it images, is not a matter of will, bending words like things to our utility, not one of manipulation and direction (as the left hemisphere has it). It is language that speaks in us, he says, not we who speak it.[70] The idea, at first sight paradoxical (once again Heidegger strains to the limit what language can say), incorporates the idea that language connects us to, and in some sense, instantiates, wisdom that we need through painful philosophical discourse, or, as he increasingly came to believe, through poetry, to permit to speak to us; that we need to listen to what emerges from our language, rather than speak through it – which is to impose ideas on it. We need to allow the 'silent' right hemisphere to speak, with its under-standing that is hard to put into the ordinary language of every day, since everyday language already takes us straight back to the particular way of being in the world – that of the left hemisphere – that it is trying to circumvent. When we go towards something in an effort to apprehend it, Heidegger appears to be saying, we are not näively the prime movers. For us to be able to understand anything we have already to be in possession of enough understanding of it to be able to approach it, and indeed we have, yes, already to understand it in some sense before we can 'under-stand' it.[71]

We arrive at the position (which is so familiar from experience) that we cannot attain an understanding by *grasping* it for ourselves. It has already to be in us, and the task is to awaken it, or perhaps to unfold it – to bring it into being within us. Similarly we can never make others understand something unless they already, at some level, understand it.[72] We cannot give them our understanding, only awaken their own, latent, understanding. This is also the meaning of the dark saying that ideas come to us, not we to them. Our role in understanding is that of an open, in one sense active, passivity: 'in insight (*Einblick*), men are the ones that are caught sight of'.[73] The idea is also familiar in Merleau-Ponty: 'it is being that speaks within us, and not we who speak of being'; and again, 'it is not we who perceive, it is the thing that perceives itself yonder'.[74] The idea that the conscious mind is passive in relation to what comes to it through the right hemisphere, and from whatever-it-is-that-exists beyond, is also expressed by Jung: 'Everyone knows nowadays that people "have complexes". What is not so well known, though far more important theoretically, is that complexes can *have us*'.[75]

Philosophy and philosophical discourse is only one way of understanding the world. Most people who instinctively see the world in Heideggerian terms don't become philosophers – philosophers are self-selected as those who feel they can account for, or at any rate sensibly question, reality in the very terms that would need to be transcended if we are to do justice to the right hemisphere's reality. There are notable exceptions, however, Schopenhauer being one of them. As Heidegger and Wittgenstein made terms with poetry, Schopenhauer believed that the mediations of art in general, but particularly music, were more directly able to reveal the nature of reality than was philosophy. He also believed in the importance of compassion and religious enlightenment in doing so. Interestingly, from our point of view, he said that 'philosophical astonishment is therefore at bottom perplexed and melancholy; philosophy, like the overture to *Don Juan* [Mozart's *Don Giovanni*], begins with a minor chord'.[76] In view of the associations of melancholy, music, empathy and religious feeling with the right hemisphere, the observation acquires a new significance, because I believe that, despite appearances, philosophy begins and ends in the right hemisphere, though it has to journey through the left hemisphere on its way (see below).

It is still true that Heidegger, while doing all he can to use language to undermine language, persists in according a primal role to language in Being. It is often asked, why not music? Perhaps the answer is personal: if he had not thought language of primal importance, and himself instinctively seized on language rather than music or the visual arts, as his medium, he would not have been a philosopher. All the same, starting from the modes of operation of the left hemisphere – language, abstraction, analysis – Heidegger remained true to what he perceived was constantly *hidden* by the left hemisphere's view; he did not, for once, let it be swept away, but with extraordinary patience, persistence and subtlety, allowed it to speak for itself, despite the commitment to language, abstraction and analysis, and thus succeeded in transcending them. It is this extraordinary achievement which makes him, in my view, a heroic figure as a philosopher, despite all that might be, and has been, said against the ambivalence of his public role in the Germany of the 1930s.[77]

Although starting from a very different philosophical tradition, and working by a different route, the later Wittgenstein reached many of the same conclusions as Heidegger. There can be no doubting the scrupulosity of Wittgenstein's grapplings with the nature of reality. Yet, like Heidegger, he found that the philosophical process needed to work against itself, and saw himself as bringing philosophy to a standstill. 'If my name survives', he wrote, 'then only as the *terminus ad quem* of the great philosophy of the West. As the name of him who burnt the library of Alexandria'.[78] Like Heidegger, Wittgenstein too emphasised the primacy of context over rules and system building, of practice over theory: 'What one acquires here is not a technique; one learns correct judgments. There are also rules, but they do not form a system, and only experienced people can apply them right. Unlike calculating rules.'[79] He emphasised that it is not just minds that think and feel, but human beings. Like Heidegger, he grasped that truth can hide or deceive as well as reveal. Wittgenstein scholar Peter Hacker writes:

> Every source of truth is also unavoidably a source of falsehood, from which its own canons of reasoning and confirmation attempt to protect it. But it can also become a source of conceptual confusion, and consequently of forms of intellectual myth-making, against which it is typically powerless. Scientism, the illicit extension of the methods and categories of science beyond their legitimate domain, is one such form, and the conception of the unity of the sciences and the methodological homogeneity of the natural sciences and of humanistic studies one such myth. It is the task of philosophy to defend us against such illusions of reason.[80]

Wittgenstein was sceptical of the scientific method for two main reasons: its tendency to 'reduce', and the deceptive clarity of its models. He referred to the 'preoccupation with the method of science ... reducing the explanation of natural phenomena to the smallest possible number of primitive natural laws.'[81] Though 'irresistibly tempted to ask and answer questions in the way science does ... it can never be our job to reduce anything to anything.' (Cf. Joseph Needham: 'nothing can ever be reduced to anything.'[82]) One of his favourite sayings was 'Everything is what it is and not another thing,'[83] an expression of the right hemisphere's passionate commitment to the sheer quiddity of each individual thing, through which alone we approach the universal, and its resistance to the reductionism inevitable in the system building of the left hemisphere.

Despite his respect for the honourable business of the search for clarity, Wittgenstein was wary of the false clarity that scientific thinking, and sometimes the mere business of formulation in language, brings. I referred earlier to the way in which language's particular contribution to thought is to give it clarity and solidity: as his disciple Friedrich Waismann saw, speaking of the mind's own processes, a psychological motive 'thickens, hardens, and takes shape, as it were, only after we express it in words.'[84] We need to struggle towards objectivity, and yet the reality we aim to reveal is itself not precise, so that the artificial precision of our language betrays us.[85] Wittgenstein spoke disparagingly of the 'irritation of *intellect*', the 'tickling of intellect', which he opposed to the religious impulse (he said he could not help 'seeing every problem from a religious point of view').[86] He saw the business of philosophy as opposing the anaesthetic of self-complacent reason: 'Man has to awaken to wonder – and so perhaps do peoples. Science is a way of sending him to sleep again.'[87]

Heidegger would have agreed. The importance of Heidegger for the theme of this book lies not only in his perception that ultimately the world is given by (what we can now see to be) the right hemisphere. He went even further, and appears intuitively to have understood the evolving relationship between the hemispheres, which forms the subject of the second part of this book: namely that, with at times tumultuous upheavals, retrenchments and lurches forward, there has been a nonetheless relentless move towards the erosion of the power of the right hemisphere over recent centuries in the West.

Freud himself, although he knew that the rational understanding, which he called 'secondary process', could never replace the 'primary process' of the unconscious, came to believe that over human history reason had encroached on instinct and intuition.[88] Heidegger saw that there was a fatal continuity between the assertive, predicative, definitional, classificatory idiom of Western metaphysics and that will to rational–technological mastery over life which he calls nihilism. In *The Question Concerning Technology and Other Essays*, he wrote that 'the fundamental event of the modern age is the conquest of the world as picture'.[89] He saw scientific research as bringing a certain type of narrow and decontextualised methodology to bear on nature and on history, which isolated and objectified its subject and was essential to the character of the enterprise. Speaking of vision, and the evolution of the Greek concept of *theoria*, later the Latin *contemplatio*, he sees 'the impulse, already prepared in Greek thinking, of a looking-at that sunders and compartmentalises', and speaks of 'an encroaching advance . . . toward that which is to be grasped by the eye'.[90] It is all too reminiscent of Descartes 'trying to be a spectator rather than an actor in all the comedies that are played out [in the world]'.[91]

Moving forward in time to consider the last two centuries, Heidegger saw the disasters of Western materialism as stemming from a 'forgetting of Being', and the apparently opposed forces of capitalism and communism as merely variants in a common technicity and exploitation of nature. Our attempts to force nature according to our will are futile, he thought, and show no understanding of Being. This might sound like a pious reflection, and one that does not tally with reason. But there is meaning here that even the left hemisphere can understand. The domination and massive despoliation of nature and natural resources, the reduction of the world to commodity, has not led to the happiness it was designed to yield. According to Heidegger, what is everywhere apparently now demanded is tough, instant and, where necessary, violent action; 'the long patient waiting for the gift' has come to look like mere weakness.[92]

SCHELER: THE IMPORTANCE OF VALUE IN CONSTITUTING REALITY

I need also to say something about Heidegger's lesser known contemporary, colleague and friend, Max Scheler, who died young, but was the only person Heidegger believed truly understood him. Heidegger went so far, in fact, as to call Scheler 'the strongest philosophical force in Germany today, nay, in contemporary Europe, and even in contemporary philosophy as such'.[93] Scheler progressed further than Heidegger in certain philosophical directions, particularly the exploration of value and feeling, not as epiphenomena, but as constitutive of the phenomenological world. According to Scheler, values are not themselves feelings, though they reach us through the realm of feeling, much as colours reach us through the realm of sight. Scheler, like other phenomenological philosophers, emphasised the interpersonal nature of experience, particularly the nature of emotion, which he thought transcended the individual, and belonged to a realm in which such boundaries no longer applied. According to Scheler's phenomenology in *The Nature of Sympathy*, which he supported by an examination of child development and linguistics, and which has been corroborated by research since his death in 1928,[94] our early experience of the world is intersubjective and does not include an awareness of self as distinct from other.[95] There is, instead, 'an immediate flow of experiences, undifferentiated as between mine and thine, which actually contains both our own and others' experiences intermingled and without distinction from one another'.[96]

Scheler's view that emotion is irreducible, and plays a grounding role in experience, relates to what has been called the primacy of affect (I will deal with this in the next chapter). In this, as Scheler's translator Manfred Frings notes, he followed Pascal, who, mathematician that he was, famously asserted that the heart has its reasons of which reason knows nothing.[97] But, for Scheler, it was not just any affect, however, that was primary, but that of love itself. For him, man is essentially *ens amans*, a being that loves. In Scheler's paradigm, this attractive power (in the literal sense of the word) is as mysterious and fundamental as the attractive power of gravity in the physical universe.

Value, for Scheler, is a pre-cognitive aspect of the existing world, which is neither purely subjective (i.e. 'whatever I take it to be') nor purely consensual (i.e. 'whatever we agree it to be'). It is not, he asserts, something which we derive, or put together from some other kind of information, any more than we derive a colour, or come to a conclusion about it, by making a calculation. It comes to us in its own right, prior to any such calculation being made. This position is importantly related to two right-hemisphere themes which we have encountered already: the importance of context and of the whole. For example, the same act carried out by two different people may carry an entirely different value, which is why morality can never be a matter of actions or consequences taken out of context, whether that be the broader context or that of the mental world of the individual involved (the weakness of a too rigidly codified judicial system). Hence we judge some things that would out of context be considered weaknesses to be part of what is valuable or attractive in the context of a particular person's character; we do not arrive at a judgment on a person by summing the totality of their characteristics or acts, but judge their characteristics or acts by the 'whole' that we know to be that person.[98] (That is not to deny that there might build up so many incongruent 'parts' that one was no longer able to resist the judgment they invited, with a resulting revolution in the nature of the whole. It's like making mayonnaise: add too much oil too fast and the suspension breaks down.)

Value is not a flavour that is added for some socially useful purpose; it is not a function or consequence of something else, but a primary fact. Scheler referred to the capacity for appreciating value as *Wertnehmung*, a concept which has been translated into the rather less accommodating English language as 'value-ception'. For him this value-ception governs the type of attention that we pay to anything, and by which we learn more about it. Our value-ceptive knowledge of the whole governs our understanding of the parts, rather than the reverse. It is, in fact, one way of breaking into Escher's circle of hands, with which this chapter began.

Scheler also held that values form a hierarchy.[99] Of course one may or may not agree with him here – these are matters of judgment and intuition, rather than argument – but what seems to me significant is that, without knowing anything about hemisphere differences, he perfectly illustrates the polarity of value systems of the two hemispheres. The right hemisphere sees the lower values as deriving their power from the higher ones which they serve; the left hemisphere is reductionist, and accounts for higher values by reference to lower values, its governing values of use and pleasure. Scheler's hierarchy begins with the lowest level, of what he calls *sinnliche Werte*, or values of the senses – whether something is pleasant or unpleasant. Values of utility (or uselessness) are on the same level as those of the senses, since 'nothing can meaningfully be called useful except as a means to pleasure; utility ... in reality has no value except as a means to pleasure.'[100] The next level is that of *Lebenswerte*, 'values of life', or vitality: what is noble or admirable, such as courage, bravery, readiness to sacrifice, daring, magnanimity, loyalty, humility, and so on; or, on the contrary, what is mean (*gemein*), such as cowardice, pusillanimity, self-seeking, small-mindedness, treachery and arrogance.[101] Then comes the realm of the *geistige Werte*, values of the intellect or spirit – principally justice, beauty and truth, with their opposites. The final realm is that of *das Heilige*, the holy. See Figure 4.2.

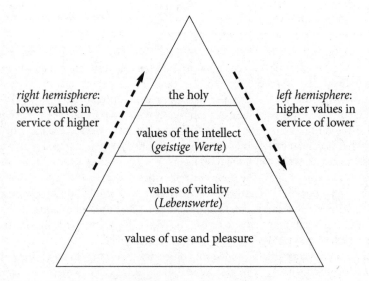

Fig. 4.2 Pyramid of values according to Scheler.

It is relevant to the thesis of this book that there are important qualities which happen to be instrumentally useful, and therefore should be pursued on utilitarian grounds, but that doing so makes no sense, since they cannot be grasped by an effort of will, and the attempt to do so merely drives them further away. This is a point made with great subtlety and elegance by the philosopher Jon Elster, in his brilliant book *Sour Grapes*: as typical of such values he mentions wisdom, humility, virtue, courage, love, sympathy, admiration, faith and understanding.[102] It is yet another Gödelian point of weakness in rationalism (his book is subtitled *Studies in the Subversion of Rationality*). If pursued for their utility, they vanish into nothing. All such values belong to the higher levels of Scheler's hierarchy. The values of the useful and pleasurable, those of the lowest rank, are the only ones to which left-hemisphere modes of operation are applicable – and even these are often self-defeating to pursue (as the paradox of hedonism demonstrates).[103] As things are re-presented in the left hemisphere, it is their use-value that is salient. In the world it brings into being, everything is either reduced to utility or rejected with considerable vehemence, a vehemence that appears to be born of frustration, and the affront to its 'will to power'. The higher values in Scheler's hierarchy, all of which require affective or moral engagement with the world, depend on the right hemisphere.

It is said that the meaning of the Hebrew words translated as 'good and evil', in the Genesis myth of Adam and Eve eating the fruit of the Tree of the Knowledge of Good and Evil, 'mean precisely the useful and the useless, in other words, what is useful for survival and what is not'.[104]

TWO WORLDS

If a left-hemisphere process consistently seems to run up against the limits of its own method and needs to transcend them, that is convincing evidence that the reality it is trying to describe is something Other. The fact that in the twentieth century philosophers, like physicists, increasingly arrived at conclusions that are at variance with their own left-hemisphere methodology, and suggest the primacy of the world as the right hemisphere would deliver it, tells us something important.

Returning from the realm of philosophy to the use of language in everyday experience, we may also be aware of another reality, that of the right hemisphere – yet feel that explicitness forces us towards acknowledging only the world of the left hemisphere. We live, in other words, in two different types of world. There should tend, therefore, to be two meanings to most words that we commonly use to describe our relationship with the world. They will not all be like 'grasp' – willed, self-serving, unidirectional.

Seeing the world

Probably the most important metaphor of our relationship to the world is that of sight. 'Knowing as seeing' is one of the most consistent of all metaphors, and exists in all Indo-European languages, suggesting that it developed early in the Indo-European *Ursprache* (or 'primal' language).[105] It is deeply ingrained in the way we apprehend the world. 'I see', we say, meaning 'I understand.'

In the era of universal CCTV surveillance, mobile phones that 'capture' video, and so on, many people imagine their eyes to be something like the lens of a camera on a moving swivel, perhaps a bit like a film-maker's camera – just as our model of thinking and remembering is that of the computer, with its inert memory banks. The image suggests that we choose where we point our attention; in that respect we see ourselves as supremely active, and self-determining. As to the 'impressions' we receive, we are like a photographic plate, taking a faithful record of the world 'out there'; and in that we pride ourselves on objectivity, being supremely passive. The process is linear, unidirectional, acquisitive, and is the left hemisphere's vision of vision.

But the camera model is just as misleading and restrictive as the computer model. We know that we are neither as active in choosing where we direct our attention, nor as passive in the process of seeing, as this account suggests. There is another story to be told about seeing, and it is one that is better supported by neuroscience. It is also more in keeping with the right hemisphere's view of the world. According to this view, we are already in a relationship with the world, which helps to direct our attention; and which also means that we bring something of ourselves to the process of creating a 'vision' of the world.

Are we active choosers?

Take first the idea that we are active choosers of where we look. On its own the left hemisphere is remarkably entrapped by its vision.[106] Once it sees something, it locks onto it, in a way that has little to do with choice. The world that it would be choosing from is, in any case, provided by the broader attention of the right hemisphere, and often what engages the focus of our attention comes to us pre-consciously, and bypasses any willed action. For example, the eye is 'caught', as we say, by salient words or names that leap out of the page (words which are probably undiscoverable again once we try to find them, and the narrow attentional beam of the left hemisphere comes into play). In practice so-called 'pre-attentional' processing means that before we can have had a chance to read what is there, we notice pre-consciously whatever has a particular affective charge or demand on our attention.[107] So it is clearly not true that we have to attend to something consciously before we can know it: we can only select what to attend to when we know what it is we are dealing with. We know it first, then are drawn to attend, so as to know more – Escher's hands again. The world comes to meet us and acts to attract our gaze. Vitality, life and movement themselves draw the eye. The figure of someone walking by distracts us; it is hard not to succumb even to the television if a set is switched on anywhere in the room, because it portrays life and movement. In a room with a fire, we are drawn to looking at it; in the pre-TV era it was the focus of attention for a social gathering (*focus* is simply the Latin word for 'hearth'), and it functioned as the TV now does to allow closeness without having to 'focus' too explicitly on one another. In this it fulfilled another, social, end.

The difficult bit about the 'stickiness' of the left hemisphere is that once we have already decided what the world is going to reveal, we are unlikely to get beyond it. We are prisoners of expectation.

New experience, as it is first 'present' to the mind, engages the right hemisphere, and as the experience becomes familiar, it gets 're-presented' by the left hemisphere. Not only does the left hemisphere seem to specialise, as Goldberg and Costa observed, in dealing with what is (already) familiar, but whatever it is the left hemisphere deals with is bound to become familiar all too quickly, because there is a tendency for it to keep recurring to what it already knows. This has implications for the kind of knowledge the left hemisphere can have. The essential problem is that the mind can only truly know, in the sense of bring into sharp focus, and 'see clearly', what it has itself made. It therefore knows – in the sense of certain knowledge (*wissen*), the sort of knowledge that enables a thing to be pinned down and used – only what has been re-presented (in the left hemisphere), not what is present as a whole (before the right hemisphere).

In a now famous experiment by Simons and Chabris, subjects were asked to watch a short video clip showing a basketball game in a relatively confined indoor setting.[108] They were asked to count how many times one team took possession of the ball. When asked afterwards, most observers were completely oblivious of the fact that a figure in a grotesque gorilla suit walks into the middle of the *mêlée*, turns to face the camera, beats his chest with his fists, dances a jig, and strolls nonchalantly out the other side of the picture – something so comically blatant on second viewing, once one knows what to expect, that it is hard to believe one could really have missed it. As they and others have neatly and dramatically demonstrated, we see, at least consciously, only what we are attending to in a focussed way (with the conscious left hemisphere). Since what we select to attend to is guided by our expectations of what it is we are going to see, there is a circularity involved which means we experience more and more only what we already know. Our incapacity to see the most apparently obvious features of the world around us, if they do not fit the template we are currently working with (part of what Noë and O'Regan have dubbed 'the grand illusion'),[109] is so entrenched that it is hard to know how we can ever come to experience anything truly new.

Neurocognitivists say that we can re-cognise, and therefore know, something only if we have already got the model of it in our brain.[110] That does perfectly describe left-hemisphere processes: but it would mean that we were forever trapped in the re-presented, no longer alive, world of the left hemisphere's knowledge, forever re-experiencing the familiar, the world forever going stale. We'd be back to the hall of mirrors. It doesn't explain, either, how we could get to know something in the first place – for the model to get into our brain at all. It's Escher's hands again.

The left hemisphere will never help us here. As one researcher has put it, the left hemisphere on its own, for example after a right-hemisphere stroke, just 'sees what it expected to see'.[111] We need, as Heraclitus pointed out, to expect the unexpected: 'he who does not expect will not find out the unexpected, for it is trackless and unexplored'.[112] In other words we must learn to use a different kind of seeing: to be vigilant, not to allow the right hemisphere's options to be too quickly foreclosed by the narrower focussing of the left hemisphere.

It is the task of the right hemisphere to carry the left beyond, to something new, something 'Other' than itself. The left hemisphere's grasp of the world is essentially theoretical, and is self-referring. In that respect it gives validity to the postmodern claim that language is a self-enclosed system of signs – but if, and only if, it is a product of the left hemisphere alone. By contrast, for the right hemisphere there is, as Johnson said of theories about literature, always an appeal open to nature: it is open to whatever is new that comes from experience, from the world at large.[113]

The corollary of this impact of expectation on attention is that the left hemisphere delivers what we know, rather than what we actually experience. This can be seen in its drawing skills. It will even draw the bones it knows to be within the human figure (so-called 'X-ray' drawings), and has a poor grasp of relative scale, spatial relationships and depth.

There is an inevitable relationship between certainty and 're-cognition', the return to something already familiar. Conscious knowledge, the knowledge that characterises left-hemisphere understanding, depends on its object being fixed – otherwise it cannot be known. Thus it is only its re-presentation in consciousness, after it has already become present to the *un*conscious mind, that enables us to know something consciously. There is neurophysiological evidence that conscious awareness lags behind unconscious apprehension by nearly half a second.[114] Chris Nunn, in a recent book on consciousness and the brain, writes that, as a consequence, 'bizarre phenomena can occur like consciously perceiving an object to be of some illusory size, but nevertheless unconsciously adjusting one's grasp correctly in relation to its actual size'.[115] To know something consciously, to be aware of it, requires *memory*. He writes:

> At the most basic level, one cannot sustain attention to anything unless there is some form of memory of what one's attention was doing a moment ago and of what the 'anything' is. [Conscious] attention is thus entirely dependent for its very moment-to-moment existence on intrinsic memory ... Then again, the objects on which attention focuses seem to be available because they have been remembered. They are, in a sense objects extracted from memory that happen to coincide with features of the world 'out there'.

This is a neurocognitive expression of the phenomenological truth that what we know with our conscious left hemisphere is already in the past, no longer 'alive' but re-presented.[116] And it takes us back to Jung: 'all cognition is akin to recognition'.[117]

Amazingly enough, this understanding of the *past* condition of knowledge is embodied in the Greek word, *eidenai*, 'to know', arising at the very moment in cultural history where we were moving towards a more conscious awareness of mental processes.[118] *Eidenai* is related to *idein* ('to see'), and in fact originally meant 'to *have seen*'.

Are we passive receivers?

The second part of the camera image is passive receptivity. But we never just 'see' something in the sense that a photographic plate receives rays of light.[119] In the real world we bring a lot of our selves to the party. And that means gaze alters what it finds.

This used to be expressed in the idea, prevalent in the Ancient World, and again at the Renaissance, of the rays that come from the eye, from a deep source of life and energy within. Homer describes the beams, 'penetrating as the sun', which come from the eye of the eagle. Of the human eye Empedocles wrote that, when it had been created, 'the primeval fire hid itself in the round pupil', protected by delicate membranes from the waters flowing round it.[120] And Plato, in the *Timaeus*, for once seems almost to anticipate the phenomenologists when he writes that a smooth, dense stream of gentle light from the purest fire within us merges with the light from what it sees, so that 'one body' is formed between ourselves and the object of our vision, conveying the 'motions' of what is seen into every part of our own body and soul.[121]

The phrase 'gazing into someone's eyes' goes further, and suggests that something actually emanates from our eyes and enters into the object of our attention, as in the Elizabethan conceit of the dart that comes from the lover's eye, or even more the lovers of Donne's *Extasie* for whom

> Our eye-beames twisted, and did thred
> Our eyes, upon one double string.

In those beams from the lover's eye, one can also sense the profound, reciprocating communication that the eye offers. In looking, in other words, we enter into a reciprocal relationship: the seeing and the seen take part in one another's being. The camera model is merely that of the left hemisphere, whose sequential analytic grasp of things does not reach to reverberative, reciprocal movement, the betweenness of sight. Some famous passages of Husserl were succinctly anticipated by Blake in *The Marriage of Heaven and Hell* when he wrote 'A fool sees not the same tree that a wise man sees.'

Gaze is active all right. Pliny the Elder wrote in his *Natural History* of the basilisk, a sort of venomous reptile that could kill with its gaze, and the belief in such a creature was current until the Renaissance.[122] This embodies a truth about attention. The focussed but detached attention of the surgeon, with intent to care, may easily mimic the focussed but detached attention of the torturer, with intent to control; only the knowledge of the *intention* changes the way in which we understand the act. And, if I am its recipient, it changes my self-experience, too. It is in fact the detachment with which the detailed plans of the extermination camps were developed, often relying on the expertise of engineers, physicians and psychiatrists, that makes the Holocaust so particularly chilling. We say, and we feel, that the human being is reduced to the status of a machine, or of a part in a machine, and in doing so we acknowledge that the object is changed by the way in which it is attended to. Even with a corpse, the mode of attention alters what is found. In China the body, including the dead body, is viewed as an organism: once attacked with a scalpel, however, it reveals itself to be made of apparently divisible parts.[123]

Science must above all divest itself of what will distort. Of course, to abandon ourselves to every personal whim or passion could never lead to any kind of shared truth. But achieving such lack of distortion is a much more subtle process than it may appear. Objectivity *requires* interpretation of what one finds, depends on imagination for its achievement.[124] Detachment has a deeply ambiguous nature. The cool, detached stance of the scientific or bureaucratic mind ultimately may lead where we do not wish to follow. And the relationship implied by the left-hemisphere attention brought to bear through the scientific method, with its implied materialism, is not *no* relationship – merely a disengaged relationship, implying, incorrectly, that the observer does not have an impact on the observed (and is not altered by what he or she observes). The betweenness is not absent, just denied, and therefore of a particular – particularly 'cold' – kind. We cannot know something without it being known to *us* – we cannot see what it would be like if it were not *we* that were knowing it. Thus every thing we apprehend is the way it is because we see it in that way rather than another way. When science adopts a view of its object from which everything 'human' has as far as possible been removed, bringing a focussed, but utterly detached attention to bear, it is merely exercising another human faculty, that of standing back from something and seeing it in this detached, in some important sense denatured, way. There is no reason to see that particular way as privileged, except that it enables us to do certain things more easily, to use things, to have power over things – the preoccupation of the left hemisphere.

The right hemisphere's gaze is intrinsically empathic, by contrast, and acknowledges the *inevitability* of 'betweenness': in fact it is the fact of gaze normally being an empathic process that makes the detached stare so destructive. Merleau-Ponty wrote:

> My eye for me is a certain power of making contact with things, and not a screen on which they are projected . . . The other's gaze transforms me into an object, and mine him, only if both of us withdraw into the core of our thinking nature [left hemisphere], if we both make ourselves into an inhuman gaze, if each of us feels his actions to be not taken up as understood, but observed as if they were an insect's. This is what happens, for instance, when I fall under the eyes of a stranger. But even then the objectification of each by the other's gaze is felt as unbearable only because it takes the place of a possible communication.[125]

Elsewhere Merleau-Ponty refers to the moment of approach when 'vision ceases to be solipsistic' and 'the other turns back upon me the luminous rays in which I had caught him'.[126]

Merleau-Ponty was aware not only of the importance of embodiment in forming the basis of the intersubjective world, but of the ambiguities of vision, with its potential either to alienate and objectify, or alternatively to form the medium of intersubjectivity. One of his best-known works is entitled *The Visible and the Invisible*. If the flesh is viewed as wholly opaque – in other words, if we take into account only the realm of the visible – it acts as an obstacle, something that alienates the viewer from what is seen. But if viewed another way, seen *through* as much as seen, the 'thickness' (*l'épaisseur*, implying something between transparency and opacity) of the flesh, far from being an obstacle, is what enables us to be aware of the other and of ourselves as embodied beings, and becomes the means of communication between the two.[127] (In *L'oeil et l'esprit*, he uses the analogy of something seen through water at the bottom of a pool – and the word used here of the semi-translucent water is again *l'épaisseur*, where again the English translation has to make do with the rather too literal 'thickness').[128] Note that it must retain its *semi*-transparent status, uniting the visible and the invisible: complete transparency would just render it invisible, and once again we become alienated, with no means to communicate.[129]

How we see the world alters not just others, but who *we* are. We need to be careful what we spend our time attending to, and in what way. Participants in a general knowledge quiz were primed in one of three ways, by engaging in activities that made them think about the stereotypes of professors, secretaries or hooligans. Those primed with the professor stereotype scored 60 per cent, those primed with the hooligan stereotype scored only 40 per cent, and those primed with the secretary stereotype scored somewhere in-between.[130] In another test, those primed with 'punk' stereotypes were more rebellious and less conformist than those primed with 'accountant' stereotypes.[131] Similarly, after playing a realistic and aggressive video game, participants, especially young men, became more likely to respond aggressively if provoked.[132] People primed with stereotypes of elderly people (such as 'sentimental', 'grey-haired', 'playing bingo') become more conservative in their opinions; those primed with politician stereotypes become more long-winded. If primed with positive associations of the ageing process (such as wise and experienced), elderly people perform better on memory tests than those primed with negative associations (such as 'senile' or demented).[133] Nurses working with elderly people, who are, if you like, in a state of perpetual priming, performed worse on memory tasks than those who had infrequent contact with old people.[134] Old people primed with negative stereotypes of ageing can even give up the will to live.[135]

What we attend to, and how we attend to it, changes it and changes us. Seeing is not just 'the most efficient mechanism for acquiring knowledge', as scientists tend to see it.[136] It is that, of course, but it is also, and before anything else, the main medium by which we enact our relationship with the world. It is an essentially empathic business.

Mutual gaze, and particularly shared averted gaze towards another object, are highly evolved characteristics. Apart from humans, only some apes and monkeys, where they have had prolonged contact with humans, may be capable of undertaking shared gaze to another object.[137] Dogs are exquisitely sensitive to human attention, especially direction of gaze and expressions of the eyes:[138] they may be able to share attention, and some other mammals are certainly able to follow the direction of gaze, but it is harder to be sure what level of attention is exhibited.[139] Most cats, despite prolonged contact with humans, are unable to understand that you are interested in something else, and do not engage with the direction of your gaze. It's no better if you point: pointing just results in the cat looking at your finger. A dog, however, will understand that you are engaged by an interest that lies in a certain direction and its own gaze is empathically entrained in the same direction. In both shared and mutual gaze, in which we feel a link with the mind of the other individual, the right hemisphere provides the neurological substrate. When we shift our gaze where we see another looking, we do so via the right hemisphere.[140] In humans, mutual gaze, even when it is averted (i.e. when two people are mutually aware of their common attention to the same object), is accompanied by activation of a highly distributed network extending throughout the right hemisphere.[141] The interpretation of faces is the prerogative of the right hemisphere; in looking at the face of one's partner (compared with an unknown face) the right insula increases in activity. Viewing one's own face (by contrast with an unknown face) induces activation in the left prefrontal and superior temporal cortex as well as a more extensive right limbic activation.[142] So it seems that sharing attention, and looking into the eyes of another, as well as recognising the face of someone very close to one, all increase activity in the right hemisphere over and above what would be needed to process faces alone. In fact, shared mental states in general activate the right hemisphere.[143] And all aspects of empathic attention are disrupted in autism: eye contact,[144] the capacity to follow another's gaze,[145] joint or shared attention,[146] and understanding the mind behind the gaze.[147] There may also be deficits of gaze attention in schizophrenia.[148]

It is therefore problematic for science and often philosophy that an abstruse and abstracted language, and an alienating vision, are seen as the proper and only approach to truth. Descartes, according to the philosopher David Levin, '*prefers the distance of vision . . . even when it means dehumanisation*'.[149] But in this he was pursuing the belief that acknowledging our relationship with the world will make it obtrude. In reality it obtrudes more when not acknowledged. The baggage gets on board, as Dennett puts it, without being inspected. In a scientific paper, one may not say 'I saw it happen', but 'the phenomenon was observed'. In Japan, however, science students, who 'observe' phenomena, do so with quite a different meaning, and in quite a different spirit, from their Western counterparts. The word *kansatsu*, which is translated as 'observe', is closer to the meaning of the word 'gaze', which we use only when we are in a state of rapt attention in which we lose ourselves, and feel connected to the other. The syllable *kan* in *kansatsu* contains the nuance that the one who gazes comes to feel a 'one-body-ness' with the object of gaze.[150]

So the eye has a potential to connect and to divide. And in fact even the hand does not have to be as I described it – willed, self-serving, unidirectional. The hand has other modes of being. An outstretched hand can mean other things – can comfort, cure, or quicken (note that the body of Adam, in Michelangelo's famous representation, is vivified by divine communication to his left hand, and thus to the right hemisphere; see Figure 4.3 below).

And since attention is modified by the *in*tention that lies behind it, even grasp can bring to life, when the context changes, as in the image in the church of St Saviour in Khora (see Plate 4), in which the figure of Christ in triumph moves at the Last Day like a whirlwind over the tombs of the dead, grasping them by the arm and wresting them from the sleep of the grave.

The hand is the vehicle of touch, as well as grasp, and therefore the origin of the metaphor of 'tact'. In fact to attend means, precisely, to reach out a hand towards: we reach out – 'ad-tend' – in order to give, as well as to take.

FAUX AMIS

The different ontological status of the two hemispheres impinges on the meaning of all the philosophical terms that are used by us to understand the world, since both hemispheres think they understand them, but do so in different ways, each transforming the concept or experience by the context (that of the left- or right-hemisphere world) in which it finds itself. Like the left-hand and right-hand worlds seen by Alice on either side of the looking glass, each has its own version of reality, in which things superficially look the same but are different. I will conclude the chapter with brief discussions of a few of these *faux amis*, or 'false friends', that arise where the right and left hemispheres understand words differently.

Fig. 4.3 *Creation of Man,* by Michelangelo, from the ceiling of the Sistine Chapel, 1508–12.

'Knowledge' and 'truth' I have discussed – again there are two versions: one purporting to be impersonal, static, complete, a thing, and the other personal, provisional, a matter of degree, a journey. 'Belief' is closely related and has two meanings too.

Belief

Believing is not to be reduced to thinking that such-and-such might be the case. It is not a weaker form of thinking, laced with doubt. Sometimes we speak like this: 'I believe that the train leaves at 6.13', where 'I believe that' simply means that 'I think (but am not certain) that'. Since the left hemisphere is concerned with what is certain, with knowledge of the facts, its version of belief is that it is just absence of certainty. If the facts were certain, according to its view, I should be able to say 'I know that' instead. This view of belief comes from the left hemisphere's disposition towards the world: interest in what is useful, therefore fixed and certain (the train timetable is no good if one can't rely on it). So belief is just a feeble form of knowing, as far as it is concerned.

But belief in terms of the right hemisphere is different, because its disposition towards the world is different. The right hemisphere does not 'know' anything, in the sense of certain knowledge. For it, belief is a matter of care: it describes a *relationship*, where there is a calling and an answering, the root concept of 'responsibility'.[151] Thus if I say that 'I believe in you', it does not mean that I think that such-and-such things are the case about you, but can't be certain that I am right. It means that I stand in a certain sort of relation of care towards you, that entails me in certain kinds of ways of behaving (acting and being) towards you, and entails on you the responsibility of certain ways of acting and being as well. It is an acting 'as if' certain things were true about you that in the nature of things *cannot* be certain. It has the characteristic right-hemisphere qualities of being a betweenness: a reverberative, 're-sonant', 'respons-ible' relationship, in which each party is altered by the other and by the relationship between the two, whereas the relationship of the believer to the believed in the left-hemisphere sense is inert, unidirectional, and centres on control rather than care. I think this is what Wittgenstein was trying to express when he wrote that 'my' attitude towards the other is an 'attitude towards a soul. I am not of the *opinion* that he has a soul.'[152] An 'opinion' would be a weak form of knowledge: that is not what is meant by a belief, a disposition or an 'attitude'.

This helps illuminate belief in God. This is not reducible to a question of a factual answer to the question 'does God exist?', assuming for the moment that the expression 'a factual answer' has a meaning.[153] It is having an attitude, holding a disposition towards the world, whereby that world, as it comes into being for me, is one in which God belongs. The belief alters the world, but also alters me. Is it true that God exists? Truth is a disposition, one of being true to someone or something. One cannot believe in nothing and thus avoid belief altogether, simply because one cannot have *no* disposition towards the world, that being in itself a disposition. Some people choose to believe in materialism; they act 'as if' such a philosophy were true. An answer to the question whether God exists could only come from my acting 'as if' God is, and in this way being true to God, and experiencing God (or not, as the case might be) as true to me. If I am a believer, I have to believe in God, and God, if he exists, has to believe in me.[154] Rather like Escher's hands, the belief must arise reciprocally, not by a linear process of reasoning. This acting 'as if' is not a sort of cop-out, an admission that 'really' one does not believe what one pretends to believe. Quite the opposite: as Hans Vaihinger understood, all *knowledge*, particularly scientific knowledge, is no more than an acting 'as if' certain models were, for the time being, true.[155] Truth and belief, once more, as in their etymology, are profoundly connected.[156] It is only the left hemisphere that thinks there is certainty to be found anywhere.

Will

Our primary being lies in a disposition towards the world – certainly not in a thought, or a whole panoply of thoughts, about the world, not even in a feeling or feelings about the world as such. Willing, like believing, with which I think it shares some properties, is thus better thought of as a matter of a disposition towards the world. The left-hemisphere disposition towards the world is that of use. Philosophy being a hyperconscious cognitive process, it may be hard to get away from the left hemisphere's perspective that will is about control, and must lie in the conscious left hemisphere. But if our disposition towards the world, our relationship with it, alters, will has a different meaning. The disposition of the right hemisphere, the nature of its attention to the world, is one of care, rather than control. Its will relates to a desire or *longing* towards something, something that lies beyond itself, towards the Other.

Evidence from a number of different sources suggests, as discussed in the previous chapter, that the mind arranges experience, grouping things according to similarities, quite without the aid of language, and needs to do so in order to make any sense of it at all. This is clearly evident from the behaviour of birds and vertebrate animals, and must take place at a relatively low subcortical level, since some very rapid automatic reactions are based on a perception of what sort of a thing it is that is being reacted to. We also know that at higher levels both hemispheres take part in the process of identification. There are hints that the way in which they do this differs in some fundamental respects.[157] For the concept of a 'type', too, can have two meanings – having only one 'whatness', it can nonetheless have two 'hownesses'. In one sense, it refers to the category to which something can be reduced, because of a specific feature or features. But a child comes to understand the world, to learn about it, by seeing the shapes – both literally, the visuospatial shapes, and metaphorically, the structures – that stand forward in its experience, using a form of *Gestalt* perception, rather than by applying rules. This is the beginnings of the human faculty for seeing what Wittgenstein in the *Philosophical Investigations* referred to as 'family resemblances', which associate individuals without there necessarily being any one defining feature that all members of the group have in common.[158] It implies a sense of a something that has never yet been seen, and yet that something nonetheless has a meaning in relation to each of the exemplars that is experienced, and it becomes clearer only with more and more experience. So although we often think of a 'type' as a highly reduced phenomenon, 'the lowest common denominator' of a certain set of experiences, it can also be something much greater than any one experience, in fact lying beyond experience itself, and towards which our set of experiences may tend. If Bateson is right that all knowledge is knowledge of difference, this method is the only way to know anything: categorising something leads only to loss of the essential difference.

This is where we come back to the will. Some of the most powerful drivers of human behaviour are such ideal types – not 'character types', which are effectively stereotypes, but something akin to archetypes, that have living power in the imagination and can call us towards them. In his book *De la Mettrie's Ghost* Chris Nunn deals with some of these, using the examples of 'the noble Roman' or 'the saint', which he describes as narratives of a certain way of being that we tell ourselves to make sense of our experience, and which in turn help to shape our responses to experience.[159] These are types, but they have certain qualities that suggest a right hemisphere origin. They are not reductions (downwards), but aspirations (upwards); they are derived from experience, but are not encompassed by it; they have affective meaning for us, and are not simply abstractions; their structure, as Nunn points out, has much in common with narrative; they cannot be derived from or converted into rules or procedures. In fact one of the things that would most surely invalidate them would be a tendency for them to become just that – a set of rules or procedures: 'do this and this, and you will be a saint'.

To my way of thinking they have much in common with Jung's archetypes. He saw these as bridging the unconscious realm of instinct and the conscious realm of cognition, in which each helps to shape the other,[160] experienced through images or metaphors that carry over to us affective or spiritual meaning from an unconscious realm.[161] In their presence we experience a pull, a force of attraction, a longing, which leads us towards something beyond our own conscious experience, and which Jung saw as derived from the broader experience of humankind. An ideal sounds like something by definition disembodied, but these ideals are not bloodless abstractions, and derive from our affective embodied experience.

For even the body has its different 'hownesses': in the realm of utility, on the one hand, it becomes the means by which we act on and manipulate the world; but, on the other, it is also the ultimate metaphor of all experience, including our experience of the highest realms of value. This is recognised by Laban when he notes that bodily 'movement has always been used for two distinct aims: the attainment of tangible values in all kinds of work, and the approach to intangible values in prayer and worship'.[162] The body, thus, holds in itself the dispositions of both hemispheres towards the world.

Familiarity and newness

An archetype may be familiar to us without our ever having come across it in experience. Familiarity is another ambiguous concept. It is not that one or other hemisphere 'specialises in', or perhaps even 'prefers', whatever it may be, but that each hemisphere has its own disposition towards it, which makes one or another aspect of it come forward – and it is that *aspect* which is brought out in the world of that hemisphere. The particular table at which I work, in all its individual given-ness, is familiar to me as part of 'my' world and everything that matters to me (right hemisphere); tables generically are familiar precisely because they are generic (left hemisphere) – in the sense that there is nothing new or strange to come to terms with. Equally the Eiffel Tower is familiar to the man who has spent his life under-neath its shadow (right hemisphere); the Eiffel Tower is familiar as a clichéd icon for Paris (left hemisphere). A piece of music I have passively heard and overheard is familiar to the point of having no life; a piece of music practised and struggled with by a musician is familiar to the point of coming alive. One is emptied of meaning by being constantly *re*-presented; the other is enriched in meaning by being constantly *present* – lived with, and actively incorporated into 'my' life.

Newness, a related concept, is similarly distinct in its hemisphere-specific meanings. In one sense it is precisely the return from left-hemisphere familiarity to right-hemisphere familiarity, from inauthenticity to authenticity. It cannot be willed, though it might be much desired; it requires an (apparently passive) patient openness to whatever is, which allows us to see it as if for the very first time, and leads to what Heidegger called radical 'astonishment' before the world. That concept is also related to Jan Patočka's shakenness: a sort of elemental driving out of the complacency of our customary modes of seeing the world.[163] It is what Wordsworth in particular strove to achieve: in Coleridge's words,

> to excite a feeling analogous to the supernatural, by awakening the mind's atten-tion from the lethargy of custom, and directing it to the loveliness and the wonders of the world before us; an inexhaustible treasure, but for which in conse-quence of the film of familiarity and selfish solicitude we have eyes, yet see not, ears that hear not, and hearts that neither feel nor understand.[164]

It involves reconnection with the world which familiarity had veiled. It is at the furthest remove from the need to shock: it requires looking more carefully at what seems only too familiar, and seeing it perhaps for the very first time.

But there is also a quite different type of novelty, which can be achieved at will, by actively recombining already known elements in bizarre ways, thus breaking the conventions of our shared reality and getting as far as possible from anything that could be described as familiar. This places the already presented 'parts' in disjunc-tive combinations, and fractures the familiar (in the right hemisphere sense). It aims to produce a reaction of shock through its unflinching acceptance of the bizarre or alien. This is the sense in which the modernists aimed, in Pound's phrase, to 'make it new', the sense of 'The Shock of the New'.[165] This type of novelty emanates from the world of the left hemisphere.

Activity and passivity

I described as 'apparently passive' the openness of the right hemisphere to whatever is. That is because, in the absence of an act of will, this is how the left hemisphere sees it. But there is a wise passivity that enables things to come about less by what is done than by what is *not* done, that opens up possibility where activity closes it down.

The dichotomy between activity and passivity comes about from the standpoint of a need for control. Passivity, from this perspective, is loss of control, loss of self-determination, loss of the capacity for effective, that is to say, useful, interaction – a failure of instrumentality. However, this takes no note of all the important states of affairs, beginning with sleep and ending with wisdom, discussed earlier in this chapter that cannot be brought about by an effort of will – where, in fact, an open receptiveness, which permits things to grow, is actually more productive. It is something like what Keats described as 'negative capability', that characteristic of a 'man of achievement', namely, 'when a man is capable of being in uncertainties, mysteries, doubts, without any irritable reaching after fact and reason'.[166] Here the link with the capacity not to force things into certainty, clarity, fixity is made explicit, and again links it to the right hemisphere's domain.

Ultimately we need to unite the ways of seeing that are yielded by both hemispheres. Above all the attention of the left hemisphere needs to be reintegrated with that of the right hemisphere if it is not to prove damaging.

CONCLUSION

I mentioned the importance of the intention behind attention. As may have become clear from the last chapter, the nature of language in the left hemisphere and its relationship with grasp imply the overriding value to it of *use*. The left hemisphere is always engaged in a *purpose*: it always has an end in view, and downgrades whatever has no instrumental purpose in sight. The right hemisphere, by contrast, has no designs on anything. It is vigilant for whatever *is*, without preconceptions, without a predefined purpose. The right hemisphere has a relationship of concern or care (what Heidegger calls *Sorge*) with whatever happens to be.

If one had to encapsulate the principal differences in the experience mediated by the two hemispheres, their two modes of being, one could put it like this. The world of the left hemisphere, dependent on denotative language and abstraction, yields clarity and power to manipulate things that are known, fixed, static, isolated, decontextualised, explicit, disembodied, general in nature, but ultimately lifeless. The right hemisphere, by contrast, yields a world of individual, changing, evolving, interconnected, implicit, incarnate, living beings within the context of the lived world, but in the nature of things never fully graspable, always imperfectly known – and to this world it exists in a relationship of care. The knowledge that is mediated by the left hemisphere is knowledge within a closed system. It has the advantage of perfection, but such perfection is bought ultimately at the price of emptiness, of self-reference. It can mediate knowledge only in terms of a mechanical rearrangement of other things already known. It can never really 'break out' to know anything new, because its knowledge is of its own re-presentations only. Where the thing itself is 'present' to the right hemisphere, it is only 're-presented' by the left hemisphere, now become an *idea* of a thing. Where the right hemisphere is conscious of the Other, whatever it may be, the left hemisphere's consciousness is of itself.

And this brings us finally to the third question I asked at the outset in this chapter: can all this tell us something about the nature of the brain? I think so. That answer is implicit in all that has gone before. There is no such thing as the brain, only the brain according to the right hemisphere and the brain according to the left hemisphere: the two hemispheres that bring everything into being also, inevitably, bring themselves – like Escher's hands. So to some people the brain is a *thing*, and a particular type of thing, a machine; which is only to say that it is something we understand from the bottom up and which exists for a purpose we recognise. To others it is something the nature of which is unique, which we can understand, therefore, only by being content with a degree of *not*-knowing which opens the mind to whatever is, and whose purpose is not so easily determined. In other words, we should expect that some people will be confident that they know precisely what sort of thing the brain is, while others may know 'precious little' about that.[167]

CHAPTER 5

THE PRIMACY OF THE RIGHT HEMISPHERE

IF THE TWO HEMISPHERES PRODUCE TWO WORLDS, WHICH SHOULD WE TRUST IF WE are after the truth about the world? Do we simply accept that there are two versions of the world that are equally valid, and go away shrugging our shoulders? I believe that the relationship between the hemispheres is not equal, and that while both contribute to our knowledge of the world, which therefore needs to be synthesised, one hemisphere, the right hemisphere, has precedence, in that it underwrites the knowledge that the other comes to have, and is alone able to synthesise what *both* know into a usable whole. In this chapter I will explain why I believe that to be the case.

We might be persuaded by the fact that the left hemisphere provides a detailed and precise picture, to suppose that it, rather than its irritatingly imprecise counterpart, gives us the *truth* about the world. And its less engaged stance might be a clue that it is more trustworthy. However, the fact that disengaged attention is in some cases psychopathic tells us that the question has meaning for the value, including the moral value, of the world we experience. It's an important question to decide – but there is a problem in reaching a conclusion here. Each hemisphere attends in a different way; different ways of attending produce different realities, *including about this question of hemisphere difference*. How to break out of the hermeneutic circle?

One way of approaching the question would be to look at the results: to compare the results of adopting a more detached kind of attention to the world with the results of adopting a more engaged kind. Towards the end of this book I will do just that – look at how the assumption that the world is best understood according to the left hemisphere's take, as a mechanism, compares with the assumption that the world is more like a living thing, a connected whole, as the right hemisphere would see it. I will do so without any special pleading, judging the answer according to the values of the left hemisphere, not those of the right. We can after all measure the consequences of the way we look at the world by what happens to it, and what happens to us. However, since attention alters us as well as what we attend to, the very judgment we made might reflect not so much reality as the nature of who we had become or were becoming. It seems hard to step outside this problem, which raises another circularity.

This is why the last chapter looked for indications from philosophy. I began by suggesting that there might be some clues from physics, the other path by which we try to apprehend ultimate reality – if it is indeed another path, and not the same path in another light. There is a tendency for the life sciences to consider a mechanistic universe more 'real', even though physics long ago moved away from this legacy of nineteenth-century materialism, with the rather odd result that the inanimate universe has come to appear animate, to take part in mind, while the animate universe appears inanimate, mindless. Science has to prioritise clarity; detached, narrowly focussed attention; the knowledge of things as built up from parts; sequential analytic logic as the path to knowledge; and the prioritising of detail over the bigger picture. Like philosophy it comes at the world from the left hemisphere's point of view. And the left hemisphere's version of reality works well at the local level, the everyday, on which we are focussed by habit. There Newtonian mechanics rules; but it 'frays at the edges', once one pans out to get the bigger picture of reality, at the subatomic, or at the cosmic, level. Here uncertainty replaces certainty; the fixed turns out to be constantly changing and cannot be pinned down; straight lines are curved: in other words, Einstein's laws account better than Newton's. Straight lines, such as the horizon, are curved if one takes a longer view, and space itself is curved – so that the rectilinearity of the left hemisphere is a bit like the flat-Earther's view: 'that's the way it looks here and now'. I would say that the shape, not just of space and time, but of our apprehension of them, is curved: beginning in the right hemisphere, passing through the realm of the left hemisphere somewhere in the middle, and returning to that of the right hemisphere. Reality has a roundness rather than rectilinearity, a theme I will return to at the end of this book.

In the last chapter I pointed to the fact that in the twentieth century, despite the nature of the philosophic process, themes emerged from philosophical debate which, unknowingly, corroborate the right hemisphere's understanding of the world. These include: empathy and intersubjectivity as the ground of consciousness; the importance of an open, patient attention to the world, as opposed to a wilful, grasping attention; the implicit or hidden nature of truth; the emphasis on process rather than stasis, the journey being more important than the arrival; the primacy of perception; the importance of the body in constituting reality; an emphasis on uniqueness; the objectifying nature of vision; the irreducibility of all value to utility; and creativity as an unveiling (no-saying) process rather than a wilfully constructive process.

Wittgenstein spoke of 'an experience that was, for him, a paradigm of the sense of ultimate value: the sense of wonder at the very existence of the world itself.'[1] Heidegger said that what we call the pre-Socratic philosophers were not philosophers, but thinkers (*Denker*) who had no need of 'philosophy', caught up as they were in the radical astonishment of Being. For Plato, 'the sense of wonder (*thaumazein*) is the mark of the philosopher – philosophy indeed has no other origin';[2] in fact he thought that *theios phobos* (sacred fear) was so profoundly moving and life-altering that the arts, which could summon it up, ought to be under strict censorship to preserve public order. Aristotle wrote that 'it is owing to their wonder that men both now begin, and at first began, to philosophize'.[3]

But already Democritus, a contemporary of Plato, starts to praise *athaumastia* and *athambia*, a refusal to be moved or amazed by anything; 'the Stoic sages regard it as their highest aim not to lose their composure, and Cicero as well as Horace commends the *nil admirari*' – to be astonished at nothing.[4] The mark of the true philosopher becomes not the capacity to see things as they are, and therefore to be awestruck by the fact of Being, but precisely the opposite, to keep cool in the face of existence, to systematise and clarify the world, so that it is re-presented as an object of knowledge. The role of the philosopher, as of the scientist, becomes to demystify.

The sense of awe which motivates philosophy was, however, never lost: even Descartes held that 'wonder [is] the first of all the passions'.[5] But it has also been perceived by many that wonder was not just the origin, but the *aim*, of philosophy. Thus to Goethe it was 'the highest that man can attain'.[6] Wittgenstein saw greater wisdom in mythic than in scientific accounts of the world, which 'leave us with the distinct impression that everything has been accounted for; they give us the illusion of explaining a world that we might do better to wonder at . . . Wittgenstein criticises explanation in order to make way for wonder. Clarity for him was largely in the *service* of awe; his critical energies were directed at unmasking what he saw as the pseudo-explanations that tend to come between us and the world, blinding us to the sheer wonder of its existence'.[7] Similarly Thomas Nagel writes: 'Certain forms of perplexity – for example, about freedom, knowledge, and the meaning of life – seem to me to embody more insight than any of the supposed solutions to those problems'.[8] And most recently Arne Naess put it in these words: 'Philosophy begins *and ends* with wondering – profound wondering'.[9] It is this that twentieth-century philosophy painstakingly regained.

Philosophy shares the trajectory that I have described as typical of the relationship between the hemispheres. It begins in wonder, intuition, ambiguity, puzzlement and uncertainty; it progresses through being unpacked, inspected from all angles and wrestled into linearity by the left hemisphere; but its endpoint is to see that the very business of language and linearity must themselves be transcended, and once more left behind. The progression is familiar: from right hemisphere, to left hemisphere, to right hemisphere again.

This would also be in keeping with other evidence for the primary role of the right hemisphere in yielding the experiential world.

FURTHER EVIDENCE FOR THE PRIMARY ROLE OF THE RIGHT HEMISPHERE

In fact we have already touched on a number of reasons for supposing that the right hemisphere plays a primary, grounding role in the relationship between the hemispheres. There is the *primacy of broad vigilant attention*: though focussed attention may appear to its owner to be under conscious control, in reality it is already spoken for; we direct attention according to what we are aware of, and for that we need broad, right-hemisphere, attention. Then there is the *primacy of wholeness*: the right hemisphere deals with the world before separation, division, analysis has transformed it into something else, before the left hemisphere has *re*-presented it. It is not that the right hemisphere connects – because what it reveals was never separated; it does not synthesise – what was never broken down into parts; it does not integrate – what was never less than whole.

We have also looked at the role the right hemisphere plays in delivering what is new: its *primacy of experience*. What we know had to come into being first for the right hemisphere, since by definition at first it is new, and the right hemisphere delivers what is new as it 'presences' – before the left hemisphere gets to re-present it. And we have the fact that the left hemisphere's most powerful tool, referential language, has its origins in the body and the right hemisphere: a sort of *primacy of means*.

I'd now like to look at some further lines of evidence on the matter.

THE PRIMACY OF THE IMPLICIT

The origins of language in music and the body could be seen as part of a bigger picture, part of a primacy of the implicit. Metaphor (subserved by the right hemisphere) comes *before* denotation (subserved by the left). This is both a historical and an epistemological truth. Metaphorical meaning is in every sense prior to abstraction and explicitness. The very words tell one this: one cannot draw something away (Latin, *abs-* away, *trahere* pull), unless there is something to draw it away from. One cannot unfold something and make it explicit (Latin, *ex-* out, *plicare* fold), unless it is already folded. The roots of explicitness lie in the implicit. As Lichtenberg said, 'Most of our expressions are metaphorical – the philosophy of our forefathers lies hidden in them.'[10]

Metaphor is not just a reflection of what has been, however, but the means whereby the truly new, rather than just the novel, may come about. When a metaphor actually lives in the mind it can generate new thoughts or understanding – it is cognitively real and active, not just a dead historical remnant of a once live metaphor, a cliché.[11]

All understanding, whether of the world or even of ourselves, depends on choosing the right metaphor. The metaphor we choose governs what we see. Even in talking about understanding we cannot escape metaphors. 'Grasping' things, for example, won't get us as far as we would like, because the most important things in life refuse to be grasped in either sense. Like Tantalus' grapes they retreat from the reaching hand.

The paradox of philosophy is that we need to get beyond what can be grasped or explicitly stated, but the drift of philosophy is always and inevitably back towards the explicit. Merleau-Ponty, Heidegger, Scheler, and the later Wittgenstein perceived that explicitness ties us down to what we already know, however much we may carry on 'unfolding' and 'unfolding' it. Implicitly, and at times explicitly, each of them tried to take philosophy beyond the explicit, therefore in one sense beyond itself. In doing so, they illuminated the limits of analytic language ('whereof one cannot speak, thereof one must remain silent'). But the attempt still is worth making, indeed has to be made, and always will, provided only that one respects the limits to what can be achieved. 'For an old psychologist and pied piper like me', wrote Nietzsche, only too aware of the problems of language, '. . . precisely that which would like to stay silent *has to become audible*'.[12]

These philosophers' writings are replete with metaphorical images which not only embody, but themselves express, implicitness. Thus, perhaps echoing Heidegger's circuitous path through the fields (*Feldweg*), Wittgenstein speaks of philosophical inquiry as, not an explicit statement, but a series of perspectives, like a number of discrete walks across a mountain range which will, perhaps, allow an idea of the whole to emerge. Three hundred years before either Heidegger or Wittgenstein, Donne had written: 'On a huge hill, / Cragged, and steep, Truth stands, and hee that will / Reach her, about must, and about must goe . . .'[13] Perhaps it is fitting that a poet should have got there first. This circular, or more accurately, spiral-like, progress is, again, very suggestive.

The biggest problem of explicitness, however, is that it returns us to what we already know. It reduces a unique experience, person or thing to a bunch of abstracted, therefore central, concepts that we could have found already anywhere else – and indeed *had already*. Knowing, in the sense of seeing clearly, is always seeing 'as' a something *already known*, and therefore not present but re-presented. Fruitful ambiguity is forced into being one thing or another. I started this chapter by suggesting that, because of its power to change, attention can also destroy. Many things that are important to us simply cannot withstand being too closely attended to, since their nature is to be indirect or implicit. Forcing them into explicitness changes their nature completely, so that in such cases what we come to think we know 'certainly' is in fact not truly known at all. Too much self-awareness destroys not just spontaneity, but the quality that makes things live; the performance of music or dance, of courtship, love and sexual behaviour, humour, artistic creation and religious devotion become mechanical, lifeless, and may grind to a halt if we are too self-aware.

Those things that cannot sustain the focus of conscious attention are often the same things which cannot be willed, that come only as a by-product of something else; they shrink from the glare of the left hemisphere's world. Some things, like sleep, simply cannot be willed.[14] The frame of mind required to strive for them is incompatible with the frame of mind that permits them to be experienced. As Montaigne wrote:

> Even things I do easily and naturally I cannot do once I order myself to do them with an express and prescribed command. The very parts of my body which have a degree of freedom and autonomy sometimes refuse to obey me if I plan to bind them to obligatory service at a certain time and place.[15]

What's true of making love and going to sleep is also true of things less physical: for example, attempts to be natural, to love, to be wise, or to be innocent and self-unseeing, are self-defeating.[16] The best things in life hide from the full glare of focussed attention. They refuse our will.

It is, however, precisely the left hemisphere's task to bring things into focus, to render the implicit explicit, in order that what is seen may become the object of our will. This is achieved by a certain kind of vision, since only vision, of all the human senses, can give truly detailed information, and give clear pinpointing in space, to guide our grasp. This clarity and fixity of the object is highly amenable to the world view of the left hemisphere: in fact it is only in the case of the left hemisphere, not of the right, that one can speak appropriately of a world 'view' at all. But sight alone of all the senses also allows finely discriminated depth. As long as that depth is preserved, it yields for the right-hemisphere engagement, 'betweenness'. Shorn away, it allows precision-focussing by the left hemisphere, at a point in a two-dimensional plane (one is aware of this two dimensionality particularly when focussing a microscope or telescope). The resulting illusion is of *clarity*, the ability to know something 'just as it is', as though everything about it were revealed through clear vision.

Depth is the sense of a something lying *beyond*. Another way of thinking of this would be more generally in terms of the ultimate importance of context. Context is that 'something' (in reality nothing less than a world) in which whatever is seen inheres, and in which its being lies, and in reference to which alone it can be understood, lying both *beyond* and *around* it. The problem with the 'attentional spotlight', as conventional psychological literature calls it, is that this isolates the object of attention from its context – not just its surroundings, but the depth in which it lives. It opacifies it. Our vision stops at 'the thing itself'. The price is that this sheering away of the context produces something lifeless and mechanical. In a famous passage in the *Meditations*, Descartes speaks of looking from a window and seeing men pass in the street. 'Yet', he reflects, 'do I see any more than hats and coats which could conceal automatons? I *judge* that they are men.'[17] It is not surprising that, shorn by the philosophic stare of all context that might give them meaning, the coats and hats that Descartes sees from his window walking about in the street could be animated by a machine. They have become fully opaque; the observer no longer passes through them to see the living person beneath. He no longer sees what is *implied*. However, the attention of the right hemisphere, concerned as it is with the being in context, permits us to see through them to the reality that lies around and beyond them. It could not make the mistake of seeing the clothes and hats in isolation.

The illusion that, if we can see something clearly, we see it *as it really is*, is hugely seductive. Ruskin, in *Modern Painters*, makes the point that clarity is bought at the price of limitation: 'We never see anything clearly . . . What we call seeing a thing clearly, is only seeing enough of it to *make out what it is*; this point of intelligibility varying in distance for different magnitudes and kinds of things . . .' He gives the example of an open book and an embroidered handkerchief on a lawn. Viewed from a distance of a quarter of a mile, they are indistinguishable; from closer, we can see which is which, but not read the book or trace the embroidery on the handkerchief; as we go nearer, we 'can now read the text and trace the embroidery, but cannot see the fibres of the paper, nor the threads of the stuff'; closer still and we can see the watermark and the threads, 'but not the hills and dales in the paper's surface, nor the fine fibres which shoot off from every thread'; until we take a microscope to it, and so on, *ad infinitum*. At which point do we see it clearly? 'When, therefore, we say, we see the book *clearly*,' Ruskin concludes, 'we mean only that we know it is a book.'[18] Clarity, it seems, describes not a degree of perception, but a type of *knowledge*. To know something clearly is to know it partially only, and to *know* it, rather than to experience it, in a certain way.

With the beginnings of modernity our experience itself becomes increasingly pictorial. As Heidegger writes: 'The world picture does not change from an earlier one into a modern one, but rather the fact that the world becomes picture at all is what distinguishes the essence of the modern age.'[19] This changes the nature of existence.

> Where the world becomes picture . . . the world [is] conceived and grasped as picture. What is, in its entirety, is now taken in such a way that it first is in being and only is in being to the extent that it is set up by man, who represents and sets forth.[20]

Heidegger's animus was directed particularly against the impact of Descartes, who had written that the 'conduct of our life depends entirely on our senses' and 'sight is the noblest and most comprehensive' of them.[21] This is precisely because Descartes was concerned with vision as an instrument of clear, sharply defined knowledge of each thing in isolation – a project impossible to reconcile with understanding based on the implicit, context-bound nature of things as delivered by the right hemisphere, which the left hemisphere only subsequently 'represents and sets forth' as distinct items. It is not by chance that the word 'distinct' implies division.

In order truly to see the thing as it is, attention needs to do something quite different. It needs both to rest on the object and pass *through* the plane of focus. Seeing the thing as it is depends on also seeing through it, to something beyond, the context, the 'roundness' or depth, in which it exists. If the detached, highly focussed attention of the left hemisphere is brought to bear on living things, and not later resolved into the whole picture by right-hemisphere attention, which yields depth and context, it is destructive. We become like insects, as Merleau-Ponty says. It is similar with works of art, which as I have said have more in common with people than things. Explicitness always forces this sheering away, this concentration on the surface, and the loss of transparency – or more correctly semi-transparency. It is the analogue of the joke explained, the metaphor laboriously restated. In such circumstances, the mechanism of the joke, of the metaphor, becomes opaque and obtrudes. Metaphoric meaning depends on this semi-transparency, this being-seen-and-not-being-seen. Kerényi writes of Homeric symbols, for example, that they can be 'seen through', as 'the visible sign of an invisible order . . . not as an element of "symbolism", but as a transparent part of the world.' If they obtruded *as* symbols, they would need to be explicitly decoded, and that would rob them of all their power.[22]

Making things explicit is the equivalent of focussing on the workings, at the expense of the work, the medium at the expense of the message. Once opaque, the plane of attention is in the wrong place, as if we focussed on the mechanics of the play, not on the substance of the play itself; or on the plane of the canvas, not what is seen there.

Depth, as opposed to distance from a surface, never implies detachment. Depth brings us into a relationship, whatever the distance involved, with the other, and allows us to 'feel across' the intervening space. It situates us in the same world as the other. Thus, however distant the figures in a Claude painting, we feel drawn to them and their world; we are taken on a journey into the *depth* of space that surrounds them, as Hazlitt said. Diderot wrote a series of descriptions of seven walks he had taken with a certain Abbé for his companion through the most beautiful, wild scenery, and what they had seen and experienced there; only at the end does he reveal that these were imagined travels within the landscapes of Vernet's paintings.[23] What produces alienation is not depth, but lack of depth. Loss of depth forms an important feature of the Cartesian, objective view of the world, as if it were projected on the surface of the retina, or on the photographic plate. We are rebuffed by the two dimensionality of the plane that stands some distance from us, without depth, a two-dimensional world in which we can no longer stand alongside what becomes the 'object' of our vision. Depth is of great psychological significance, and it is relevant that in schizophrenia, which simulates an overactive left-hemisphere state, there is, as Louis Sass has shown, a perspectival slippage, a loss of grip on the frame of reference.[24] Attention ceases to be paid to, say, the scene pictured on the paper, and is transferred to the plane of the paper itself. There is a loss of precisely the *transparency* that operates when we understand something in the normal way.

A painting is not a thing in the world: nor is it just a representation of the world. In a marvellous phrase of Merleau-Ponty's, we do not *see* paintings, as much as see *according to* them.[25] They are, like people, and the forms of the natural world, neither just objective things, nor mere representations of things: they permit us to see through, and according to, themselves. They have a semi-opaque (or semi-transparent) quality, not disappearing altogether, in which case some reality or other would be seen in their place, a reality which they would no more than represent. No, they have reality of their own. But equally they are not mere things, existing 'out there' independent of us or whatever else it is that exists. We are aware of them but see through them, see the world according to them. To take the example of the Claude painting: we neither allow our eye simply to rest on the pure thing in front of us, a canvas measuring such and such, with so and so patches of blue, green and brown on it, nor do we see straight through it, as though ignorant that we are looking at a painting, and imagining we look through a window. Equally with poetry: language does often function as if it were transparent, when we are reading a piece of prose, and unaware of its facticity. But in poetry the language itself is present to us – semi-transparent, semi-opaque; not a thing, but a living something that allows us to move through it and beyond, though never allowing the language to disappear as though it played no part in the whatever it is beyond language that it yields to us.

Drama, too, can be either completely absorbing or quite alienating, becoming a picture in which we do not participate. In order to absorb, the medium has to be translucent or transparent: we must not focus on the players – or the playwright (Shakespeare completely disappears in his work). That's why bad acting can be so embarrassing. It draws our attention to the fact that the actors are acting, and to how they see themselves; they become like critics whose self-preening causes them to obtrude between us and what they claim to illuminate. The implicit becomes explicit and all is lost.

PRIMACY OF AFFECT

If the implicit grounds the explicit, it would imply that one's feelings are not a reaction to, or a superposition on, one's cognitive assessment, but the reverse: the affect comes first, the thinking later. Some fascinating research confirms that affective judgment is not dependent on the outcome of a cognitive process. We do not make choices about whether we like something on the basis of explicit assessment, a balance sheet, weighing up its parts. We make an intuitive assessment of the whole before any cognitive processes come into play, though they will, no doubt, later be used to 'explain', and justify, our choice. This has been called 'the primacy of affect'.[26] We make an assessment of the whole at once, and pieces of information about specific aspects are judged in the light of the whole, rather than the other way round (though these pieces of information, if there are enough that do not cohere with our idea of the whole, can ultimately cause a shift in our sense of the whole).[27] The implication is that our affective judgment and our sense of the whole, dependent on the right hemisphere, occur before cognitive assessment of the parts, the contribution of the left hemisphere. 'I would anticipate that . . . at some deep and fundamental affective level, the right hemisphere is more in touch with true inner feelings and less able to lie.'[28] Panksepp's suspicion would be supported by the research evidence discussed in Chapter 2. While affect is not of course the same as value, like value it is primary, not just derived from cognitive assessment, as the left hemisphere would have us believe when it retrospectively examines the process; and it was this insight that lay behind Max Scheler's important concept of *Wertnehmung*, pre-cognitive apprehension of the value of something, its meaning for 'me'.[29]

The disposition towards the world comes first: any cognitions are subsequent to and consequent on that disposition, which is in other words 'affect'.[30] Affect may too readily be equated with emotion. Emotions are certainly part of affect, but are only part of it. Something much broader is implied: a way of attending to the world (or not attending to it), a way of relating to the world (or not relating to it), a stance, a disposition, towards the world – ultimately a 'way of being' in the world.

But emotion is very important, and it too is closer to the core of our being than cognition. As Nietzsche wrote, 'thoughts are the shadows of our feelings—always darker, emptier, *simpler*.'[31] Several lines of reasoning from the evidence converge to suggest that the essential core of being is subcortical.[32] Perceptual–cognitive awareness would appear to have developed on the back of affective awareness, which was a 'revolutionary prerequisite', writes Jaak Panksepp: 'From such a vantage, Descartes' faith in his assertion "I think, therefore I am" may be super-seded by a more primitive affirmation that is part of the genetic makeup of all mammals: "I feel, therefore I am." '[33] He later goes on in a footnote: 'the bottom-line statement probably should be "I am, therefore I am." '[34]

Emotion and the body are at the irreducible core of experience: they are not there merely to help out with cognition. Feeling is not just an add-on, a flavoured coating for thought: it is at the heart of our being, and reason emanates from that central core of the emotions, in an attempt to limit and direct *them*, rather than the other way about. Feeling came, and comes, first, and reason emerged from it: 'emotion has taught mankind to reason', as the eighteenth-century French philosopher Vauvenargues put it.[35] Even the prejudice we have in favour of reason cannot itself be justified by reasoning: the virtues of reason are something we can do no more than intuit. In his influential book *Descartes' Error*, Damasio points to the primacy of emotion in neurological terms, when he notes that

> the apparatus of rationality, traditionally presumed to be *neo*cortical, does not seem to work without that of biological regulation, traditionally presumed to be *sub*cortical. Nature appears to have built the apparatus of rationality not just on top of the apparatus of biological regulation, but also *from* it and *with* it.[36]

This observation brings me back to the point I made in Chapter 1, that the struc-ture of the brain gives its history, and helps, partly because of that very fact, towards an understanding of the mind. Nonetheless Damasio does not appear to recognise the phenomenological primacy of emotion or affect: instead he sees emotion as auxiliary, there to play a role in guiding the thinking being that we are, rather than seeing thinking as there to guide the feeling being that we are. 'Emotions', he insists, 'are not a luxury', as though such an idea could ever have occurred to anyone in the light of experience, let alone of the acknowledged primacy of affect. Emotions are not a luxury, Damasio goes on to reassure us, because they are useful *tools*: 'they play a role in communicating meaning to others, and they may also play the cognitive guidance role that I propose . . .'[37] Thus emotions are there to serve as handmaiden to reason, playing a useful role in helping us communicate, or possibly in weighing the products of cognition, but not at the irreducible core of the experience of ourselves.

In the process of trying to rehabilitate feelings by showing that they form, after all, a vital part of the *cognitive* process, Damasio inevitably does so by trying to make them explicit, measurable, quantitative – turning them into speed or an amount of mental associative processes, speed or an amount of motor behaviours – rather than qualitative. He also sees them, as William James did, as an *interpretation* of bodily 'data': in fact he even states that 'regular feeling comes from a "readout" of the body changes'.[38] The inseparability of the body and emotion (not to mention affect) is interpreted in such a way that emotion ends up *derived* from the body by a 'readout', there to *guide* the cognition that is doing the reading. Apparently unaware that he is repeating Descartes' error,[39] he writes: 'I conceptualise the essence of feelings as something you and I can see through a window that opens directly onto a continuously updated image of the structure and state of our body . . .'[40] Once you are able to 'see' your feelings 'through a window' opening onto an 'image' of your body, you have clearly far outstripped Descartes at his own game.

I think part of the difficulty here, which I will return to throughout this book, is that in the context of intellectual discourse we are always obliged to 'look at' the relationship of cognition to affect from the cognitive point of view. Quite what it would mean to treat it from the point of view of affect is less easily said, not easily even imagined: there is no question about it, if we want to *know* about this relationship, rather than be satisfied with intuition, then we are obliged to treat cognition as the path to knowledge. Asking cognition, however, to give a perspective on the relationship between cognition and affect is like asking an astronomer in the pre-Galilean geocentric world whether, in his opinion, the sun moved round the earth or the earth round the sun. To ask the question alone would be enough to label one as mad. But notice what the metaphor reveals: for in time the observation of tiny discrepancies in the model became significant enough to cause a *bouleversement* of the entire known universe. And so cognition eventually did find its own path to its kind of truth: the primacy of affect.

THE PRIMACY OF THE UNCONSCIOUS WILL

Some now famous experimental work by Benjamin Libet, published in 1985, attempted to investigate the conscious will from a neurophysiological point of view. Libet asked subjects to make spontaneous movements of their fingers at will, and recorded what was going on in the brain by monitoring the accompanying electroencephalographic data, recorded by electrodes on the scalp.[41] He confirmed earlier findings of a German neurologist, Hans Kornhuber, who had shown that there is a blip in the trace, known as a 'readiness potential' (*Bereitschaftspotential*), about a second before the movement takes place.[42] But, much to his amazement, he discovered that the conscious urge to move the finger occurred, not before, but approximately 0.2 seconds *after*, the readiness potential. In other words the brain seemed to know in advance that its 'owner' was going to make a decision to carry out an action.

This clearly doesn't square with the common-sense notion that we make a conscious decision to do something, and has cast doubt in some minds on free will, giving rise to an extensive philosophical literature of debate. As Susan Pockett puts it, some of Libet's research results 'seem to deny to consciousness any major role in the conduct of our day-to-day affairs'.[43] Quite so. But as one of the contributors to this debate points out, this is only a problem if one imagines that, for me to decide something, I have to have willed it with the conscious part of my mind.[44] Perhaps my unconscious is every bit as much 'me'. In fact it had better be, because so little of life is conscious at all.

One would have thought that such a conclusion would not be hard to embrace in a post-Freudian era. It certainly would not surprise those who have read the now classic work of Princeton psychologist Julian Jaynes, *The Origin of Consciousness in the Breakdown of the Bicameral Mind*, in which he systematically disabuses the reader of the idea that consciousness is needed for any of the defining features of human mental life.[45] He points out that very little brain activity is in fact conscious (current estimates are certainly less than 5 per cent, and probably less than 1 per cent), and that we take decisions, solve problems, make judgments, discriminate, reason, and so on, without any need for conscious involvement.

Before saying more about the conscious and unconscious mind, it would be helpful to clarify the terms. Adam Zeman is admirably concise in doing so.[46] He distinguishes three principal meanings of the term consciousness: (1) *consciousness as waking state*: 'after a lucid interval, the injured soldier lapsed into unconsciousness'; (2) *consciousness as experience*: 'I became conscious of a feeling of dread, and an overpowering smell of burning rubber'; (3) *consciousness as mind*: 'I am conscious that I may be straining your patience' – in which case, unlike the previous example, one is not reporting on experience as such, but on something one bears in awareness even if not actually thinking about it and experiencing the consequences of such a thought at the time. Consciousness in each of these senses is sustainable by either hemisphere in isolation, though the quality of that consciousness might differ. The major difference between the hemispheres lies in their relationship with the *unconscious* mind, whether that means the dream state (thinking of consciousness in the first sense), or what we experience or bear in mind without being aware of it (the second and third senses). Whatever does not lie in the centre of the attentional field, where we are focussed, is better yielded by the right hemisphere, and the left hemisphere can sometimes show surprising ignorance of it.

Jaynes aligns the right hemisphere with the unconscious mind, and this link has been made by many others.[47] The alignment has to be a matter of degree rather than all or nothing. As one writer puts it, 'the left side is *involved* with conscious response and the right with the unconscious mind'.[48] It is true that processing of pre-conscious information, which includes most of what is encompassed in social understanding, tends to be carried out by the right hemisphere.[49] The attentional system that detects stimuli outside the focus of conscious processing, is 'strongly lateralised to the right hemisphere'.[50] Equally, conscious processing tends to go on in the left hemisphere. This dichotomy can be seen at play even in a realm, such as emotion, with an admittedly strong right-hemisphere bias: the right hemisphere processes unconscious emotional material, whereas the left hemisphere is involved in the conscious processing of emotional stimuli.[51] Certainly the right hemisphere experiences material that the left hemisphere cannot be aware of; [52] and according to Allan Schore, Freud's pre-conscious lies in the right orbitofrontal cortex.[53] Freud wrote of non-verbal, imagistic thinking that it 'is, therefore, only a very incomplete form of becoming conscious. In some way, too, it stands nearer to unconscious processes than does thinking in words, and it is unquestionably older than the latter both ontogenetically and phylogenetically.'[54] Freud may in fact have derived his distinction between the secondary (conscious) process and the primary (unconscious) process from Hughlings Jackson's distinction between the verbal, propositional thought of the left hemisphere and the speechless, 'lower levels of ideation' associated with the right hemisphere.[55] All of this is perhaps in keeping with evidence suggesting that during REM sleep and dreaming there is greatly increased blood flow in the right hemisphere, particularly the temporoparietal region.[56] EEG coherence data also point to the predominance of the right hemisphere in dreaming.[57]

If what we mean by consciousness is the part of the mind that brings the world into focus, makes it explicit, allows it to be formulated in language, and is aware of its own awareness, it is reasonable to link the conscious mind to activity almost all of which lies ultimately in the left hemisphere. One could think of such consciousness as a tree growing on one side of a fence, but with a root system that goes deep down into the ground on both sides of the fence. This type of consciousness is a minute part of brain activity, and must take place at the highest level of integration of brain function, at the point where the left hemisphere (which in reality is in constant communication with the right hemisphere, at the millisecond level) acts as Gazzaniga's 'interpreter'.[58] Not the only one that does the experiencing, mind you, but the one that does the interpreting, the translation into words. (Note the significance of the metaphor. Meaning does not originate with an interpreter – all one can hope for from the interpreter is that in his or her hands the true meaning is not actually lost.)

Why should 'we' not be our unconscious, as well as our conscious, selves? Libet's experiment does not tell us that we do not choose to initiate an action: it just tells us that we have to widen our concept of who 'we' are to include our unconscious selves. The difficulties seem to arise, as so often, because of language, which is principally the left hemisphere's way of construing the world. It will be objected that what we *mean* by words such as 'will', 'intend', 'choose' is that the process is conscious: if it's not conscious, then we did not will it to happen, we did not intend it, it was not our choice. The fact that it is clear to all of us these days that our unconscious wishes, intentions, choices can play a huge part in our lives seems not to be noticed.

If forced to concede this point, the next line of defence is to disown the unconscious, just as in split-brain patients the left hemisphere will disown the actions that are obviously initiated ('chosen', 'intended', 'willed') by the right hemisphere: it was not 'my' will. One does not in fact have to look at split-brain patients to see that the right hemisphere has a will, can intend, mean, will and choose, just as the left hemisphere can. As Hans Vaihinger wrote:

the organic function of thought is carried on for the most part *unconsciously*. Should the product finally enter consciousness also, or should consciousness momentarily accompany the processes of logical thought, this light only penetrates to the shallows, and the actual fundamental processes are carried on in the darkness of the unconscious. The specifically purposeful operations are chiefly, and in any case at the beginning, wholly instinctive and unconscious, even if they later press forward into the luminous circle of consciousness . . .[59]

I want to present some amazing research findings that I hope will confirm not only that this is so, but that, once again, these intentions arise from the right hemisphere and are prior, in every sense – temporally, logically and ontologically – to those of the left hemisphere.

BOTH THOUGHT AND ITS EXPRESSION ORIGINATE IN THE RIGHT HEMISPHERE

The findings in question come from the study of gesture, in itself a sort of language with a subtlety and immediacy that goes beyond the explicitness of words: 'We respond to gestures with an extreme alertness and, one might almost say, in accordance with an elaborate and secret code that is written nowhere, known by none, and understood by all.'[60] There is, incidentally, a hemispheric distinction between expressive gestures, which embody inner emotional states, and instrumental gestures, designed to influence the immediate behaviour of another. As we might expect, expressive gestures activate the right hemisphere, in the region of the superior temporal sulcus, while instrumental ones activate a left-lateralised system associated with language and motor imitation.[61]

But the importance of gesture is that it gives an insight into the genesis of thought. David McNeill has for years painstakingly videotaped human interactions and analysed the relationship between gesture language and what is spoken. The focus of his work is not on hemisphere difference as such, but along the way he lets drop some observations that are pure gold to those who are interested in the topic.[62]

The first point of interest to ourselves is that *gestures slightly anticipate speech*:

The anticipation of speech by gesture is important evidence for the argument that gestures reveal utterances in their primitive form: there is a global-synthetic image taking form at the moment the preparation phase begins, but there is not yet a linguistic structure with which it can integrate.[63]

It will be clear that 'global-synthetic' is a description of the holistic or *Gestalt* nature of thought associated with the right hemisphere. McNeill refers, by contrast, to the 'linear-segmented' nature of verbal utterance – linearity and segmentation being features of the analytic nature of thought in the left hemisphere. So it would appear that the first manifestation of thought is in the 'global-synthetic' form generated by the right hemisphere. Yet the actual stroke phase of the gesture – its expressive part – appears to be deliberately delayed so that it is synchronised with the act of speech, once the left hemisphere has got there, and the two modes of thought have combined.[64]

McNeill reviews evidence for the main hypotheses about the relationship between gesture and speech, and concludes that there is a synthesis of two 'opposite modes of thought'. One is expressed in gesture, and is 'global-synthetic all the way down': it is constructed at the moment of speaking, and is idiosyncratic in nature, rather than forming a systematic code – all features that identify it as right-hemisphere-derived. The other is expressed in words, having 'a linear-segmented hierarchical linguistic structure,'[65] features which identify it as derived from the left hemisphere. But he emphasises that it is the right-hemisphere contribution that has both temporal priority and ontological priority, since thought is originally 'largely imagistic and minimally analytic', whereas by the moment of utterance, it has become 'both imagistic and analytic and is a synthesis of the holistic and analytic functions.'[66] In terms of the thesis of this book, then, the process begins in the realm of the right hemisphere, gets input from the left hemisphere, and finally reaches a synthesis of right with left.

'Gestures do not merely *reflect* thought', writes McNeill, 'but help *constitute* thought . . . Without them thought would be altered or incomplete.'[67] This is reminiscent of Max Black's insistence that paraphrase of metaphor produces 'a loss of cognitive content'; it is not just that literal paraphrase 'may be tiresomely prolix or boringly explicit (or deficient in qualities of style); it fails to be a translation because it fails to give the insight that the metaphor did.'[68] Almost all gestures accompany speech,[69] and though most are made by the right hand[70] – since speech and gesture are so closely combined in and near Broca's area – the metaphoric nature of gesture language, in fact, comes from the right hemisphere, and has to be routed across to the left hemisphere for execution. We can see this in split-brain patients, whose gesture pattern from the right hand (reflecting the disconnected left hemisphere) is abstract and impoverished in the extreme, but becomes rich again when it comes from the left hand (reflecting the disconnected right hemisphere). Fascinatingly, though, this now interferes with fluency of speech, since the global-synthetic form of what one wants to say, expressed with fluency immediately by the left hand, cannot, as it normally would, be transferred across the corpus callosum to become available to the left hemisphere for speech[71] – further evidence, if such were needed, that the richness of thought comes from the right hemisphere and is transferred across to the left hemisphere secondarily for translation into language. Gazzaniga's image of the 'interpreter' again, perhaps more apt than even he realized.

McNeill unearths further evidence of the link between the gestural language that has primacy and its right-hemisphere origins. 'After right-hemisphere damage, speakers show tendencies both to decontextualise speech and *to reduce gesture output*;'[72] and those who do not make gestures tend to give more 'segmented' sequences of information than global descriptions.[73] As mentioned, restricting hand movement limits the content and fluency of speech,[74] and we can now see that this is probably because it inhibits expression of the primary global-synthetic concept of what one wants to say, originating in the right hemisphere.

Perhaps the most striking finding of all is that, *when there is a mismatch between gesture and speech, it is the gesture that carries the day in 100 per cent of cases.* 'In all cases, the affecting element in the stimulus appeared to be the gesture, and it was never the speech.'[75] Where a mathematical speaker made a mistake verbally, his gesture proceeded with the metaphorical meaning correctly, implying that the thought was correct even if the language wasn't, and the gesture conveyed the thought.[76]

McNeill also found that the disconnected left hemisphere could not engage with narrative, for two main reasons: it lacked concreteness and specificity in its relation of the story, and became abstract and generic; and it got time sequences wrong and conflated episodes that were separate in the story because they looked similar (in other words, it categorised them, and therefore put them together, even though in the lived world their meaning was destroyed by being taken out of narrative sequence). In place of a narrative, it produced a highly abstract and disjointed meta-narrative.[77] Narrative forms of thought are associated with the right hemisphere;[78] they are associated with self–other interactions and are heavily affectively charged – and they arise earlier than 'paradigmatic' forms.[79]

Overall McNeill's evidence supports strongly the other arguments that thought, meaning and the urge to communication come first from the relatively unconscious realm of the right hemisphere. If the historical hypothesis that music led to language is correct, then this is yet further demonstration of the primacy of the right hemisphere way of being.[80]

RE-PRESENTATION WAITS ON PRESENTATION

The evidence from McNeill's work is that – temporally, logically and ontologically – the right-hemisphere world grounds that of the left. It forms an illuminating companion, in my view, to Libet's work on the will. In both cases the conscious left hemisphere believes that it is an originator, whereas in fact it is a receiver of something that comes to it from elsewhere.

Similarly I would say that the conscious left hemisphere thinks that it is in control, directing its gaze where it wants, bringing the world into being as it squints here and there as it pleases, while the reality is that it is selecting from a broader world that has already been brought into being for it by the right hemisphere – and often it is not even doing that, since, far more than it realizes, its choices have already been made for it.

This has to be the case since the business of re-presentation has to wait on the phenomenon of presentation. Turning to the neurological and neuropsychological literature again, we can see what happens when the contribution of the right hemisphere to the world is absent. The world loses reality. People who have lost significant right-hemisphere function experience a world from which meaning has been drained, where vitality appears attenuated, and where things themselves seem insubstantial, to lack corporeal solidity. Because of the sense of detachment, such people can begin to doubt the actuality of what they see, wondering if it is in fact all 'play-acting', a pretence, unreal. They can come to think that the hospital, with its doctors and nurses, is an elaborate charade put on for their benefit. This is similar to the delusional misidentification syndromes of Capgras and Fregoli referred to earlier, in which familiar people, things or places are felt to be replaced by copies, or impostors – syndromes which are also associated with right hemisphere deficits. Vié, in a series of papers in 1944, reported some remarkable examples of various kinds of misidentification, including two separate cases of French soldiers who, invalided out of the First World War, maintained that it was all – soldiers, trenches, bombs and all – a theatrical performance.[81] The left-hemisphere world is, after all, virtual – not present, but a representation. In schizophrenia this can easily slip over into a feeling of menace, in which there seems to be something being 'put on' or pretended which is being 'kept from' the individual; the alienation leads to paranoia, coupled with a sort of anxious boredom or 'ennui'. Others exhibit an almost fatuous lack of concern. Interestingly right-hemisphere-damaged individuals may see their own bodies as alien, as mechanical, an assemblage of parts, or a mere thing in the world like other things, rather than an integral aspect of ourselves that we *live*, not just live *in*. An inappropriate sense of detachment, alienation, and estrangement from the self and the world are all characteristic consequences of right-sided, usually temporoparietal, lesions.[82] This condition is similar to aspects of schizophrenia, and it is probable that much of the phenomenology of the acute phase of schizophrenia arises from the fact that important aspects of right-hemisphere function are distorted or attenuated.

Thus it is the right hemisphere that permits a living world to come into being, and it is from this that the re-presented world of the left hemisphere is derived. The difference between the two, what is present and what is represented, is illustrated beautifully by the different concepts of truth that they hold.[83] How would you get an idea of that? Take the following example of a syllogism with a false premise:

1. Major premise: all monkeys climb trees;
2. Minor premise: the porcupine is a monkey;
3. Implied conclusion: the porcupine climbs trees.

Well – does it? As Deglin and Kinsbourne demonstrated, each hemisphere has its own way of approaching this question. At the outset of their experiment, when the intact individual is asked 'Does the porcupine climb trees?', she replies (using, of course, both hemispheres): 'It does not climb, the porcupine runs on the ground; it's prickly, it's not a monkey.' (Annoyingly, there are in fact porcupines that do climb trees, but it seems that the Russian subjects, and their investigators, were unaware of this, and therefore for the purposes of the experiment it must be assumed that porcupines are not arboreal.) During experimental temporary hemisphere inactivations, the left hemisphere *of the very same individual* (with the right hemisphere inactivated) replies that the conclusion is true: 'the porcupine climbs trees since it is a monkey.' When the experimenter asks, 'But is the porcupine a monkey?', she replies that she knows it is not. When the syllogism is presented again, however, she is a little nonplussed, but replies in the affirmative, since 'That's what is written on the card.' When the right hemisphere *of the same individual* (with the left hemisphere inactivated) is asked if the syllogism is true, she replies: 'How can it climb trees – it's not a monkey, it's wrong here!' If the experimenter points out that the conclusion must follow from the premises stated, she replies indignantly: 'But the porcupine is not a monkey!'

In repeated situations, in subject after subject, when syllogisms with false premises, such as 'All trees sink in water; balsa is a tree; balsa wood sinks in water', or 'Northern lights are often seen in Africa; Uganda is in Africa; Northern lights are seen in Uganda', are presented, the same pattern emerges. When asked if the conclusion is true, the intact individual displays a common sense reaction: 'I agree it seems to suggest so, but I know in fact it's wrong.' The right hemisphere dismisses the false premises and deductions as absurd. But the left hemisphere sticks to the false conclusion, replying calmly to the effect that 'that's what it says here.'

In the left-hemisphere situation, it prioritises the system, regardless of experience: it stays within the system of signs. Truth, for it, is coherence, because for it there is no world beyond, no Other, nothing outside the mind, to correspond with. 'That's what it says here.' So it corresponds with itself: in other words, it coheres. The right hemisphere prioritises what it learns from experience: the real state of existing things 'out there'. For the right hemisphere, truth is not mere coherence, but correspondence with something other than itself. Truth, for it, is understood in the sense of being 'true' to something, faithfulness to whatever it is that exists apart from ourselves.

However, it would be wrong to deduce from this that the right hemisphere just goes with what is familiar, adopting a comfortable conformity with experience to date. After all, one's experience to date might be untrue to the reality: then paying attention to logic would be an important way of moving away from false customary assumption. And I have emphasised that it is the right hemisphere that helps us to get beyond the inauthentically familiar. The design of the above experiment specifically tests what happens when one is forced to choose between two paths to the truth in answering a question: using what one knows from experience or following a syllogism where the premises are blatantly false. The question was not whether the syllogism was structurally correct, but what actually was true. But in a different situation, where one is asked the different question 'Is this syllogism structurally correct?', even when the conclusion flies in the face of one's experience, it is the right hemisphere which gets the answer correct, and the left hemisphere which is distracted by the familiarity of what it already thinks it knows, and gets the answer wrong.[84] The common thread here is the role of the right hemisphere as 'bullshit detector'. In the first case (answering the question 'What is true here?') detecting the bullshit involves using common sense. In the second case (answering 'Is the logic here correct?'), detecting the bullshit involves resisting the obvious, the usual train of thought. This illustrates the aspect of the right hemisphere's activity which Ramachandran refers to as the 'devil's advocate'.[85]

THE FUNCTIONING OF THE NERVOUS SYSTEM IS RIGHT-HEMISPHERE CONGRUENT

One further line of evidence merits consideration. I have suggested that the function and structure of the brain act as a metaphor of mind: in other words, that we can learn something about the nature of mental processes by observing the brain. At the same time I have suggested that there is something more fundamental about the world that is brought into being by the right hemisphere, with its betweenness, its mode of knowing which involves reciprocation, a reverberative process, back and forth, compared with the linear, sequential, unidirectional method of building up a picture favoured by the left hemisphere. But surely, it may be said, the nervous system isn't itself like the right hemisphere model. One nerve transmits an impulse to the next, which transmits it in turn to another, or to a muscle fibre, and eventually that results in action. The process is linear, sequential: what's 'reverberative' about that? Surely if *neurones themselves* work in this linear, sequential, unidirectional way – whatever may happen later on in the handling of this 'information' – then the left hemisphere model is fundamental to our being, to our mental processes and therefore to consciousness itself.

Well, as it happens, the way in which neurones behave is *not* linear, sequential, unidirectional: they behave in a reciprocal, reverberative fashion, and not just in the right hemisphere. Here is Marcel Kinsbourne:

> Counter to the traditional image of the brain as a unidirectional information thoroughfare, when cell stations in the brain connect, the traffic is almost always bi-directional. The traffic is not in one direction, with a little feedback, either. Areas interact equally in both directions, directly reciprocally, or indirectly by looping across several cell stations, so that the neural traffic reverberates through its starting point. The forebrain is overwhelmingly an arena of reverberating reciprocal influence.[86]

It seems that this reciprocity, this betweenness, goes to the core of our being. Further than even this, there is fascinating evidence that betweenness and reciprocity exist at the level of cell structure and function *within* the single neurone, even at the molecular level, as the brain comes to understand something and lay down memory traces.[87] Whether it goes on at the atomic and subatomic levels I do not know, but my layman's reading of such literature suggests that it may well do so.

The process of bringing the world into being begins, then, with the right hemisphere. And, as I mentioned in Chapter 2, it is the right hemisphere which develops its functions first, and which remains dominant through at least the first year of life.[88]

Primacy could just mean coming first, in the sense that childhood comes before maturity. But I do not mean only that the right hemisphere starts the process of bringing the world into being. I mean that it does so because it is more in touch with reality, and that it has not just temporal or developmental priority, but ontological supremacy. Whatever the left hemisphere may add – and it adds enormously much – it needs to return what it sees to the world that is grounded by the right hemisphere.

Now we come to the world of the left hemisphere, a virtual world, but one where we are no longer patient recipients, but powerful operators. The values of clarity and fixity are added by the processing of the left hemisphere, which is what makes it possible for us to control, manipulate or use the world. For this, attention is directed and focussed; the wholeness is broken into parts; the implicit is unpacked; language becomes the instrument of serial analysis; things are categorised and become familiar. Affect is set aside, and superseded by cognitive abstraction; the conscious mind is brought to bear on the situation; thoughts are sent to the left hemisphere for expression in words and the metaphors are temporarily lost or suspended; the world is re-presented in a now static and hierarchically organised form. This enables us to have knowledge, to bring the world into resolution, but it leaves what it knows denatured and decontextualised.

This is the world that is familiar to us from the intermediate, or 'classical' period of philosophy, from Plato at least until Kant, once the insights of the pre-Socratic philosophers were lost and before those of the German 'idealists', and later the phenomenologists, were gained. In physics it is that of classical mechanics, the Newtonian universe, and more broadly that vision of nature that began with Democritus and his contemporaries and came to an end with Niels Bohr and his.

The left hemisphere, the mediator of division, is never an endpoint, always a staging post. It is a useful department to send things to for processing, but the things only have meaning once again when they are returned to the right hemisphere.

There needs to be a process of reintegration, whereby we return to the experiential world again. The parts, once seen, are subsumed again in the whole, as the musician's painful, conscious, fragmentation of the piece in practice is lost once again in the (now improved) performance. The part that has been under the spotlight is seen as part of a broader picture; what had to be conscious for a while becomes unconscious again; what needs to be implicit once again retires; the represented entity becomes once more present, and 'lives'; and even language is given its final meaning by the right hemisphere's holistic pragmatics.

So what begins in the right hemisphere's world is 'sent' to the left hemisphere's world for processing, but must be 'returned' to the world of the right hemisphere where a new synthesis can be made. Perhaps an analogy would be the relationship between reading and living. Life can certainly have meaning without books, but books cannot have meaning without life. Most of us probably share a belief that life is greatly enriched by them: life goes into books and books go back into life. But the relationship is not equal or symmetrical. Nonetheless what is in them not only *adds* to life, but genuinely goes back into life and *transforms* it, so that life as we live it in a world full of books is created partly by books themselves.

This metaphor is not perfect, but it makes the point. In one sense a book, like the world according to the left hemisphere, is a selective, organised, re-presented, static, revisitable, boundaried, 'frozen' extract of life. It has taken something infinitely complex, endlessly interrelated, fluent, evolving, uncertain, never to be repeated, embodied and fleeting (because alive) and produced something in a way very different that we can use to understand it. Though obviously far less complex than life itself, it has nonetheless brought into being an aspect of life that was not there before it. So the left hemisphere (like the book), can be seen as taking from the world as delivered by the right hemisphere (unconsidered 'life'), and giving life back enhanced. But, on the shelf, the contents of the book are dead: they come back to life only in the process of being read. No longer static, boundaried, 'frozen', the contents of the book are taken up into the world where nothing is ever fixed or fully known, but always becoming something else.

I take it that there is something that exists outside the mind. One has to have a starting point, and if you do not believe at least *that*, I have nothing to say, not least because, if you are right, you are not there for me to say it to. The relationship of our brains to that something whatever it is that exists apart from ourselves could be of four kinds: (1) no relationship at all – which returns us to solipsism, since my brain would be the sole source of everything I experienced; (2) receptive – in the sense that, perhaps like a radio set, the brain picked up at least something of whatever it was from out there, and that became what is experienced; (3) generative – in the sense that the brain created at least something of the whatever it is that exists apart from ourselves; or (4) reverberative, that is to say, both receptive and generative – both picking up, receiving, perceiving, and in the process making, giving back, creating 'whatever it is that exists apart from ourselves but includes ourselves'. I am simply going to state at this point that I adopt the last of these alternatives. Of course, which is right is a terribly important question for philosophy, but if such a thing is susceptible of proof, I can't prove it. All I can say is that all the evidence available to me as a living, thinking, experiencing human being leads me to that conclusion.

So, given the argument of this book, is it both the hemispheres that are doing this giving and receiving and becoming part of it all out there – or just one? My view is that both the right and left hemispheres are involved in the giving and receiving process out of which the world we experience is created, but, once again, not symmetrically. The right hemisphere appears to be the first bringer into being of the world, but what it brings into being can only inevitably be partial. The idea that our brains are perfectly adapted to bring into being for us everything that may exist in the universe, particularly that they could bring into being everything in the universe at one time, is patently ridiculous. To use the analogy of a radio receiver, it can be tuned into only one wavelength at a time, and there will always be radio waves, not to mention other forms of waves, that it will never be able to pick up. But this filtering, this restriction, imposed on the right hemisphere is not just a limitation in the negative sense, any more than being able to transmit one programme at any one time is a negative quality in a radio. Such limitation is a condition of its functioning at all. From it, something particular is permitted to come into being for us, the world as the right hemisphere delivers it to us.

The left hemisphere in turn grasps, sees, receives only some of what the right hemisphere has received. Its method is selection, abstraction – in a word negation. But this selection, this narrowing, is once again not a diminution, but an increase. By restricting or selecting, something new that was not there before comes into being. The process is like sculpture, in which a thing comes into being through something else being pared away. The paring away can reveal the thing that lives within the stone: but equally that thing, whatever it is, lives only in the stone, not in the paring away on its own. Thus the stone in a sense depends on the sculptor's hand, but not as badly as the sculptor's hand depends on the stone. The world that we experience is a product of both hemispheres, clearly, but not in the same way. The restrictive bringing into being of something by the left hemisphere depends still on its foundation in something that underwrites it in the right hemisphere (and both of them on something that underwrites them both, outside the brain).

It is possible that this biphasic, and essentially apophatic ('no-saying'), structure to the disclosing of whatever it is that exists apart from ourselves was foreseen by Max Scheler. While there is no simple equation between the right hemisphere and Scheler's *Drang*, and the left hemisphere and his *Geist*,[89] I believe this nonetheless illuminates an important element both in how the hemispheres relate to one another, and in how they together relate to whatever it is that exists apart from ourselves. The relationship between the hemispheres is *permissive* only. The right hemisphere can either fail to permit (by saying 'no') or permit (by not saying 'no'), aspects of Being to 'presence' to it. Until they do so, it does not know what they are, and so cannot be involved in their being as such prior to their disclosure. Subsequent to this, the left hemisphere can only fail to permit (by saying 'no'), or permit (by not saying 'no') aspects of what is 'presented' in the right hemisphere to be 're-presented': it does not know what the right hemisphere knows and therefore cannot be involved in its coming into being as such.

This negatory or apophatic mode of creation of whatever-it-is is reflected in our experience that what we *know* about things as they truly are, starting with Being itself, is apophatic in nature: we can *know* only what they are *not*. Its particular significance is that it describes the path taken to truth by the right hemisphere, which sees things whole, and if asked to describe them has to remain 'silent'. It has no way of coming at what this thing is other than by pointing to it, or by unconcealing it, allowing the thing to reveal itself as much as possible (by not saying 'no' to it, but saying 'no' to whatever lies around and obscures it), as a sculptor chisels away the stone to reveal the form inside. Further, because what the left hemisphere has available to it is only what it does not say 'no' to of what 'presences' to the right hemisphere, it has parts of the whole only, fragments which, if it tries to see the whole, it has wilfully to put together again. It has to try to arrive at understanding by putting together the bits and pieces, positively constructing it from the inside, as though the statue were 'put together'. By such a process, a human person becomes like a Frankenstein's monster, rather than a living being – not for nothing one of the originating metaphors of Romanticism.

This idea is not only a philosophical insight that helps us to explain what we know of the worlds brought into being by the two hemispheres at the phenomenological level. Once again we find it instantiated at the neurological level in the functional anatomy of the brain. Remember that the primary function of the corpus callosum is to act as a filter on transmission between the hemispheres,[90] allowing communication to pass, but preponderantly acting to *inhibit* activity, thus shaping the evolution of conscious experience in, primarily, the left hemisphere. But that is not all. The most highly evolved part of the brain, the frontal cortex, achieves what it does largely by negating (or not negating) other brain activity. 'The cortex's job is to prevent the inappropriate response rather than to produce the appropriate one', writes Joseph LeDoux; that is, it pares down from among things that exist, it selects, it does not originate.[91] And one answer to the problem raised for free will by Libet's experiments is that there is time between the unconscious initiation of an action and its execution for the conscious mind to intervene and 'veto' the action. In this sense, it may exert its influence more as 'free won't' than 'free will'.[92]

The frontal lobes are indisputably the parts of the brain that make us most human, that bring about for us all the greatest things we achieve. This negation is therefore hugely creative. When we remember that it is the right hemisphere that succeeds in bringing us in touch with whatever is new by an attitude of receptive openness to what is – by contrast with the left hemisphere's view that it makes new things actively, by wilfully putting them together bit by bit – it seems that here, too, is evidence, if any further were needed, that the right hemisphere is more true to the nature of things.

THE PROCESS OF REINTEGRATION

Ultimately the principle of division (that of the left hemisphere) and the principle of union (that of the right hemisphere) need to be unified: in Hegel's terms, the thesis and antithesis must be enabled to achieve a synthesis on a higher level. Split-brain patients can tell us a little about this level from their experiences outside the lab, in their encounters with life; for they appear to have problems with dreaming and imagination.[93] In the case of dreaming, it may be that it takes place but that the difficulty lies in the left hemisphere having access to it, and therefore being able to report it. But one can see that the generation of the greatest feats of the human spirit require integration of both hemispheric worlds, and split-brain patients do appear to have an impoverished level of imagination and creativity, suggesting, as I believe to be clearly the case, that integrated functioning of both hemispheres is needed for such activity. The form that that integration takes may be far from straightforward, of course. It may be that, in the absence of the intact corpus callosum, it is impossible for either hemisphere to inhibit the other adequately and stop it from interfering for critical periods. Or it may be a failure of reintegration once the separate business is done.

If the left hemisphere vision predominates, its world becomes denatured (in Heidegger's terms, there is 'unworlding' of the world). Then the left hemisphere senses that something is wrong, something lacking – nothing less than life, in fact. It tries to make its productions live again by appealing to what it sees as the attributes of a living thing: novelty, excitement, stimulation. It is the faculty of imagination, however, which comes into being between the two hemispheres, which enables us to take things back from the world of the left hemisphere and make them live again in the right. It is in this way, not by meretricious novelty, that things are made truly new once again.

The right hemisphere needs the left hemisphere in order to be able to 'unpack' experience. Without its distance and structure, certainly, there could be, for example, no art, only experience – Wordsworth's description of poetry as 'emotion recollected in tranquillity' is just one famous reflection of this. But, just as importantly, if the process ends with the left hemisphere, one has only concepts – abstractions and conceptions, not art at all. Similarly the immediate pre-conceptual sense of awe can evolve into religion only with the help of the left hemisphere: though, if the process stops there, all one has is theology, or sociology, or empty ritual: something else. It seems that, the work of division having been done by the left hemisphere, a new union must be sought, and for this to happen the process needs to be returned to the right hemisphere, so that it can live. This is why Nietzsche held that 'in contrast to all those who are determined to derive the arts from a single principle, as the necessary source of life for every work of art, I have kept my gaze fixed on these two artistic deities of the Greeks, Apollo and Dionysos.'[94] According to Nietzsche, these two gods represented the two fundamentally opposed artistic drives (*Kunsttriebe*): one towards order, rationality, clarity, the sort of beauty that comes with perfection, human control of nature, and the celebration of masks, representations or appearances; the other towards intuition, the over-riding of all humanly contrived boundaries, a sense of oneness or wholeness, physical pleasure and pain, and the celebration of nature beyond human control, as she really is. It will be appreciated that this contrast does not correspond neatly to the left hemisphere versus the right hemisphere – more, in neuropsychological terms, to the frontal lobes versus the more ancient, subcortical regions of the limbic system; but since, as I have emphasised, such distinctions carry with them implications for the division of the hemispheres (in that the right hemisphere is more in touch with these ancient and 'primitive' forces, though modulating them importantly in many respects), they have a relevance to the subject of this book.

The left hemisphere knows things the right hemisphere does not know, just as the right knows things of which the left hemisphere is ignorant. But it is only, as I have tried to suggest in earlier chapters, the right hemisphere that is in direct contact with the embodied lived world: the left hemisphere world is, by comparison, a virtual, bloodless affair. In this sense, the left hemisphere is 'parasitic' on the right. It does not itself have life: its life comes from the right hemisphere, to which it can only say 'no' or not say 'no'. This idea lies behind Blake's perception in *The Marriage of Heaven and Hell* that 'Energy is the only life, and is from the Body; and *Reason is the bound or outward circumference of Energy* [emphasis added].' Reason (what Blake calls elsewhere *Ratio*, closer to rationality than reason) draws its very existence from the delimitation of something else in which the life actually inheres. This is not, as Blake may have intended it, to decry the importance of reason, but it is to say something important about its ontological status. Similarly the relationship between the hemispheres entails more than an equal and symmetrical participation of the two: there is an asymmetry between the principles of division (left hemisphere) and unification (right hemisphere), ultimately in favour of union. Heidegger was not alone in seeing that beauty lies in the coming to rest of opposites, that have been sharply distinguished, in the connectedness of a harmonious unity. The need for ultimate unification of *division with union* is an important principle in all areas of life; it reflects the need not just for two opposing principles, but for their opposition ultimately to be harmonised. The relation between union and division is not in this sense, once again, equal or symmetrical.[95]

Thinkers and philosophers of the Romantic tradition have struggled to express this idea in different ways. I introduce the term 'Romantic' here with some trepidation, because to some it suggests the limitations of a circumscribed period of recent Western cultural history, in their minds associated with fantasy and lack of rigour. Unfortunately it is the only term we have to refer to a philosophical, as much as cultural, revolution which heralded the beginnings of a reawareness of the power of metaphorical thought, of the limitations of classical, non-paraconsistent logic, and the adoption of non-mechanistic ways of thinking about the world, which belatedly enabled us to catch up with ideas that have been for centuries, if not millennia, current in Eastern cultures. With the advent of Romanticism, paradox became once more not a sign of error, but, as it had been seen by Western philosophers before Plato, and by all the major schools of thought in the East before and since, as a sign of the necessary limitation of our customary modes of language and thought, to be welcomed, rather than rejected, on the path towards truth. 'Paradox is everything simultaneously good and great', wrote Friedrich Schlegel.[96]

As I say, the Romantics, struggled to express the idea of the unity of union with division.[97] Here is Schlegel again: 'Where philosophy stops, poetry has to begin . . . Whatever can be done while poetry and philosophy are separated has been done and accomplished. So the time has come to unite the two.'[98] Making a slightly different point, but in a similar vein, he wrote: 'It is equally fatal for the mind to have a system and to have none. It will simply have to decide to combine the two.'[99] And Coleridge wrote in his *Biographia Literaria*:

> In order to obtain adequate notions of any truth, we must intellectually separate its distinguishable parts; and this is the technical *process* of philosophy. But

having done so, we must then restore them in our conceptions to the unity in which they actually co-exist; and this is the *result* of philosophy.[100]

Hegel, too, held that union and division have themselves to be unified, suggesting the ultimate priority of the principle of union over that of division, despite the necessary part played by division at one stage of the process. 'Everything', he wrote (with characteristic impenetrability) 'depends on the unity of differentiatedness and non-differentiatedness, or the identity of identity and non-identity.'[101]

The concept of the individual (entity or person, whatever it may be) is therefore an ambiguous concept. On the one hand it can be seen as a part, which has prior existence to the whole in which it resides, and that whole is seen as reached by summing the parts – the individual as a 'unit' in a complex of units, like a block amongst building blocks (left hemisphere point of view). On the other, the individual can itself be seen as a whole, indivisible into parts from which that whole could ever be recreated once dismembered; but nonetheless not itself separate from a greater whole to which it belongs, and which is reflected in it, from which, even, it derives its individuality (right hemisphere point of view). Thus, according to this point of view, the divisive tendency towards individuation exists *within* the tendency to union; individual entities are distinguished, but only within a union which supervenes, and qualifies that distinction. In Romanticism, as I shall suggest later, this sense of individuality, as applied to the human individual, was sustainable, but nonetheless felt to exist within the context of something broader and deeper than itself, towards which it tended. This tending towards something else did not annihilate the individuality of the self, but grounded it.

The system building of the left hemisphere has been very powerful historically, because it is rhetorically powerful. It looks like being a way of integrating, or reintegrating, the disparate facts or entities that the left hemisphere has itself created.

But in fact it creates something very different from the whole that has been lost. I would merely draw attention, following Elster, to the fact that rationalistic systems contain the seeds of their own destruction. In a Gödelian way, there are always elements that arise from *within* the system (rationally conceived goals) that cannot be achieved *by* the system (rational means of pursuit), and that indeed draw our attention to the limits of the system, and point us beyond. Similarly there are tensions between the rational pursuit of certainty and the desire for knowledge, since, as Hegel pointed out, 'immediacy' (the quality of being understandable without the need for any other concept or idea) is not compatible with determinacy, and hence certainty is purchased at the expense of content: 'The more certain our knowledge the less we know.'[102] The more we pinpoint something to be certain of it, the less we actually know of it, the equivalent of the uncertainty principle referred to above.[103]

The difficulty of articulating the deeply felt distinction between, on the one hand, a vision of the world as an assemblage of parts or fragments that need, in order to be understood, to be aggregated into a system (left hemisphere), and the appreciation of individual, or particular, entities that are never separate from the whole to which they belong, and from which unity, paradoxical as it may seem, they derive their individuality (right hemisphere), preoccupied and perplexed the Romantics. In Coleridge's letters, and in his *Biographia Literaria*, one sees him struggling towards a clearer perception of this duality; indeed finding a way of illuminating this deeply felt aspect of the mind's own duality was the battle in which he was engaged for most of his intellectual life. He wrote:

> I can *at times* feel strongly the beauties, you describe, in themselves, & for them-selves—but more frequently *all things* appear little—all the knowledge, that can be acquired, child's play—the universe itself—what but an immense heap of *little* things?—I can contemplate nothing but parts, & parts are all *little*—!—My mind feels as if it ached to behold & know something *great*—something *one & indivis-ible* and it is only in the faith of this that rocks or waterfalls, mountains or caverns give me the sense of sublimity or majesty!—But in this faith *all things* counterfeit infinity! [emphasis in the original].[104]

By contrast, only a few days later he wrote of his

> love of 'the Great', & 'the Whole'.—Those who have been led to the same truths step by step thro' the constant testimony of their senses, seem to me to want a sense which I possess—They contemplate nothing but *parts*—and all *parts* are necessarily little—and the Universe to them is but a mass of *little things*.[105]

By the end of the nineteenth century, Nietzsche had concluded that this vision of a mass of disconnected little things was not just another way of seeing, but an arti-ficial way, imposed on the underlying connectedness of existence for the conven-ience of *knowing*: 'there are no lasting, final units, no atoms, no monads: here too the 'being' of things has been *inserted* by us (for practical, useful, perspectival reasons)'.[106] What he means here by the '"being" of things' is the sense of finished, independently existing entities, rather than an interconnected whole always in the process of becoming: a sense that is imposed on the world by the left hemisphere for 'practical, useful, perspectival reasons', parts and systems being a by-product of the process of 'knowing', left-hemisphere fashion.

'My mind feels as if it ached to behold & know something *great* . . .' In German the feeling of longing for something that exists outside the self to which it feels itself to be connected was crystallised in the word *das Sehnen*, often translated into English as 'longing'. What this concept seems to me to enshrine is the feeling of being connected to something but removed from it. The connection remains despite the distance, and the separation despite the sense of union. Why I bring this up here is that the distinction exists *within* the union, which trumps it. However distinguished, the individual remains part of the whole and is under-standable only in terms of the whole of which it forms a part.

The word *das Sehnen*, longing, is from the same root as *die Sehne*, a tendon. The object of longing is that towards which we 'tend', and 'tendon' is similarly related to the words 'tend' and 'tendency'. In fact the English word 'sinew' is cognate with *die Sehne*, and 'sinew' used to refer to the whole elastic union of muscle and tendon. These images suggest the workings of a joint, such as for example, the elbow. The joint is made possible by the existence of the tendon, an elastic connection that allows the bones that take part in the joint (but do not constitute the joint) to move away from one another and to remain connected, or to move together and remain separate; an image picked up wittily, but nonetheless profoundly, by Donne in his pair of compasses, the image of the two lovers in *A Valediction: forbidding mourning*. The significance of these ideas will become more apparent in Part II.

There is, in summary, then, a force for individuation (left hemisphere) and a force for coherence (right hemisphere): but, wherever the whole is not the same as the sum of the parts, the force for individuation exists within and subject to the force for coherence. In this sense the 'givens' of the left hemisphere need to be once again 'given up' to be reunified through the operations of the right hemisphere. This sense that the rationality of the left hemisphere must be resubmitted to, and subject to, the broader contextualising influence of the right hemisphere, with all its emotional complexity, must surely explain the eminently sane and reasonable philosopher David Hume's assertion that 'Reason is, and ought only to be the slave of the passions, and so never can pretend to any other office than to serve and obey them.'[107] He did not mean that unbridled passion should rule our judgments, but that the rational workings of the left hemisphere (though he could not have known that that was what they were) should be subject to the intuitive wisdom of the right hemisphere (though he equally could not have recognised it as such). If reason arises from feeling, as Vauvenargues says, and should in turn bow to feeling, as Hume here suggests, this perfectly expresses my view that what arises in the left hemisphere does so from the right hemisphere, and needs to be subject to it once more.

REINTEGRATION AS *AUFHEBUNG*

I have expressed this reintegration in terms of a 'return' to the right hemisphere. This risks suggesting that the achievements of the left hemisphere's interventions are lost or nullified, reduced only to a remembrance to be borne in mind when looking at the new whole achieved by the right hemisphere, as though one were looking at the *same* whole as before, only with new eyes. This would be like a child taking a watch to bits and putting it together again. The only significant sense in which the reintegrated watch would now be different would be in the child's newfound knowledge of its constituent parts; an important difference for the child, to be sure, but not effectively altering the watch. Once again we are misled by the metaphor of a mechanism, a watch, that is, at least in one sense, no more than the sum of its parts.

Instead, the pattern I would adopt to explain the way in which this process occurs in the bihemispheric apprehension of the world is that of Hegel's *Aufhebung*. The word, often translated as sublation, literally means a 'lifting up' of something, and refers to the way in which the earlier stages of an organic process, although super-seded by those that come after, are not repudiated by them, even though the later stages are incompatible with the earlier ones. In this sense the earlier stage is 'lifted up' into the subsequent stage both in the sense that it is 'taken up into' or 'subsumed' into the succeeding stage, and in the sense that it remains present in, but trans-formed by, a 'higher' level of the process. In a famous passage near the opening of the Preface to *The Phenomenology of Mind*, Hegel illustrates it by reference to the development of a plant:

> The bud disappears when the blossom breaks through, and we might say that the former is refuted by the latter; in the same way when the fruit comes, the blossom may be explained to be a false form of the plant's existence, for the fruit appears as its true nature in place of the blossom. These stages are not merely differenti-ated; they supplant one another as being incompatible with one another. But the ceaseless activity of their own inherent nature makes them at the same time moments of an organic unity, where they not merely do not contradict one another, but where one is as necessary as the other; and this equal necessity of all moments constitutes alone and thereby the life of the whole.[108]

Thus what is offered by the left hemisphere should be and needs to be *aufge-hoben* by the right hemisphere, not cancelling the left hemisphere's contribution, but taking it further, by drawing it back into the realm of unification (in fact in German *aufgehoben* positively includes the idea of being *preserved*, as well as transformed).

It's not just that Hegel happens to crystallise the relationship of the hemispheres with this concept, or even that the relationship of the hemispheres is an example of dialectical ontology – the nature of existence arising out of opposition or nega-tion. Hegel, along with Heraclitus and Heidegger, has a particular place in the unfolding story of the relationship between the cerebral hemispheres, in that, it seems to me, his philosophy actually tries to express the mind's intuition of its own structure – if you like, the mind cognising itself. His spirit is like an unseen presence in this book, and it is necessary to devote a few pages to his heroic attempts to articulate, in relation to the structure of the mind or spirit (*Geist*), what lies almost beyond articulation, even now that we have knowledge of the structure of the brain.

My choice of the Nietzschean fable of the Master and his emissary suggests that right at the heart of the relationship between the hemispheres I see a power struggle between two unequal entities, and moreover one in which the inferior, dependent party (the left hemisphere) starts to see itself as of primary importance. Hegel, too, spoke of the 'master' and the 'slave', it is true, but let me first clear something out of the way. What most people know of Hegel's treatment of the master/slave relationship is from a passage in *Phenomenology of Spirit* (B, IV, A) entitled 'Lordship and Bondage'. There he is talking about a master and slave in the accepted sense of two persons in a socially defined relationship, and his concern is the paradoxical relationship between an actual master and slave in their quest for mutual 'recognition'. Putting it simply, the slave's recognition of the master is rendered worthless to the master because of the master's contempt for the slave,[109] but the slave is able to gain a more genuine sense of recognition for his skilled work, and is thus enabled after all to achieve a more fulfilled self-consciousness. This is essentially a fable about the futility of social elitism, and does not concern us here.

But there is a far more interesting, and far more profoundly prescient, passage that follows this in *Phenomenology of Spirit* (B, *IV*, B), that on the 'Unhappy Consciousness'. Here he is talking of something quite different, something of immediate relevance to the subject of this book: the inward division of the mind or spirit, which finds itself split into a 'master' subself and a 'slave' subself. The description of the relationship of these two parts of the mind uncannily foresees what neurological research was going to reveal about the workings of the brain, and which forms the subject of this book, except that Hegel is using the term 'master' here to refer to the usurping force that I associate with the left hemisphere – in other words to the emissary turned despot, known as the 'major' hemisphere – and the 'slave' to refer to the true Master, ill-treated by the usurper, which I associate with the right hemisphere, the 'silent' or 'minor' hemisphere.[110]

In a rather dense passage from the same work, Hegel gives such a brilliant exposition of what neurological research appears to indicate that I include it here as the most extraordinary instance of the mind by introspection 'cognising itself'. He gives in the first paragraph what seems to me to be a perfect description of the weaknesses of the approach to the real world made by the left hemisphere so long as it remains unresolved by subsequent engagement of the right hemisphere. In the second paragraph he describes how true knowledge redeems itself by 'returning back into itself' in the right hemisphere (the italics, and of course the interpolations, are mine):

If the specific determination . . . is one that in itself is concrete or actual [as present to the RH], it all the same gets degraded [by the formal understanding of the LH] into something *lifeless* and *inert* [because merely a re-presentation], since it is *merely predicated* of another existing entity, and *not known* as an *immanent living principle* of this existence [which are all LH modes, by contrast with those of the RH]; nor is there any comprehension of how in this entity its *intrinsic* and *peculiar* way of expressing and producing itself takes effect [as the RH would be able to understand, with its ability to appreciate such deep-lying and unique qualities, by contrast with the LH]. This, *the very kernel of the matter*, formal understanding *leaves to others to add later on* [the LH leaves for the RH to reinstitute at a later stage of reintegration, which is why such a reintegration is essential]. Instead of making its way into the *inherent* content of the matter in hand [as the RH would], understanding always takes a *survey* of the whole [from the LH's vantage point on the vertical axis, as if reading a map], assumes a position *above* the particular existence about which it is speaking, i.e., it *does not see it at all*.

Here Hegel has brilliantly seized the difference between the reality of the world as originally perceived by the right hemisphere, and the 'formal understanding' of it by the left. He continues:

True scientific knowledge, on the contrary, demands *abandonment to the very life of the object* [the mode that only the RH can achieve], or, which means the same thing, claims to have before it the inner necessity controlling the object, and to express this only. *Steeping itself in its object* [along the horizontal axis, as the RH does], *it forgets to take that general survey* [as the LH would have done], which is *merely a turning of knowledge away from the content back into itself* [alluding to the inevitably self-referring nature of the LH]. But being sunk into the material in hand, and following the course that such material takes, true knowledge *returns back into itself* [to its origin in the RH], yet not before the content *in its fullness* [as fully 'unpacked' by the LH, its invaluable contribution] is taken into itself, is reduced to the simplicity of being a determinate characteristic, drops to the level of being *one aspect* of an existing entity [not just what the LH sees, but taken alongside, and in the context of, what the RH yields], and *passes over into its higher truth* [as revealed by the final *Aufhebung* of both RH and LH]. By this process *the whole* as such, surveying its entire content, itself *emerges out of the wealth wherein its process of reflection seemed to be lost* [the return to the RH recovers the whole, now made richer by the LH process in which it had threatened to be lost].[111]

What is offered by the right hemisphere to the left hemisphere is offered back again and taken up into a synthesis involving both hemispheres. This must be true of the processes of creativity, of the understanding of works of art, of the development of the religious sense. In each there is a progress from an intuitive apprehension of whatever it may be, via a more formal process of enrichment through conscious, detailed analytic understanding, to a new, enhanced intuitive understanding of this whole, now transformed by the process that it has undergone.

This idea, though difficult, is critically important, because the theme of Part II of this book will be that there has been a tendency for the left hemisphere to see the workings of the right hemisphere as purely incompatible, antagonistic, as a threat to its dominion – the emissary perceiving the Master to be a tyrant. This is an inevitable consequence of the fact that the left hemisphere can support only a mechanistic view of the world, according to which it would certainly be true that the unifying tendency of the right hemisphere would reverse its achievements in delineating individual entities. According to that view, opposition cannot result in sublation, a *negation* of negation, but only negation pure and simple. But this is to see according to 'either/or'; and to see individual entities as atomistic, like billiard balls operating in a vacuum – there being no larger entities, except those that are the sum of the interactions of the individual 'billiard balls'. Nature in fact abhors a vacuum, as we all know, and there is therefore not *nothing* between the 'billiard balls'. Rather than separate entities in a vacuum, we might think of individual entities as dense nodes within some infinitely stretchable or distensible viscous substance, some existential *goo* – neither ultimately separable nor ultimately confounded, though neither without identity nor without the sense of ultimate union.

This idea explains the apparently paradoxical attempt according to the spiritual practices of all traditions to 'annihilate' the self. Why would one want to do such a thing, if the point of creation was to produce the infinite variety embodied in the myriad selves of all the unique existing beings in the created world? Would this not be just to strive to reverse the creative process, and return from Being to Nothing? Instead what I understand by this miscalled 'annihilation' of the self is a sacrifice of the boundaries which once defined the self, not in vitiation of the self, but in its *kenosis*, a transformation whereby it is emptied out into a whole which is larger than itself.[112] So it is that neither the bud nor the blossom is repudiated by, but rather *aufgehoben* in, the fruit.

As I have suggested above, all apparently 'complete' systems, such as the left hemisphere creates, show themselves ultimately, not just by the standards or values of the right hemisphere, but *even in their own terms*, to be incomplete. In addition, whether or not the superstructure holds up, their foundations lie in, and are 'bootstrapped' on, intuition: the premises from which the rational system building begins, and even the rational mode of operation itself, that of the value of reason, cannot be confirmed by the process of rationalistic systematisation, but need ultimately to be intuited. That does not invalidate our intuition in favour of reason, of course, any more than it invalidates other of our intuitions, such as the value of goodness, or of beauty, or of truthfulness, or the existence of God. (Wittgenstein in the *Tractatus* describes each of logic, ethics and aesthetics as transcendental.[113]) But it does mean that they take their origin from the right hemisphere, and cannot transcend their origins except by reverting to the right hemisphere in a process of sublation or *Aufhebung*. However much rationalistic systems give the illusion of completeness – and they can be very hard to escape for those who cannot see their weaknesses – they do in fact conceal within themselves the clue of thread that leads out of the maze.

NECESSARY IGNORANCE

The left hemisphere seems to play a crucial role in determining what comes into being; it is part of the process of creation. Applying linear, sequential analysis forces the implicit into explicitness, and brings clarity; this is crucial in helping bring about an aspect of what is there. But, in doing so, the whole is lost.

Here again we are brought to face the incompatibility of what we need to do. We have to attend openly to the world in order not to miss something new or important that will tend to change the way we look at any one thing; and yet to focus on one thing so that we can see what it is well enough that, once relinquished, it can return to being constitutive of the whole picture in an enriched sense. Again we are made to recognise that to see clearly one aspect is to conceal another aspect: that truth is a concealing as well as an unconcealing. The difficulty is an expression of the fundamental incompatibility involved in mounting the vertical axis at the same time that we go out as far as possible into the world along the horizontal axis.[114] Living seems to force us, like Schrödinger's cat, into some sort of limiting option. It seems that we cannot achieve specificity in observation and at the same time preserve the other characteristics of the object of our attention, much as a light wave (a process) collapses and behaves like a particle (an isolated entity) if it is pinned down by detailed observation.

The right hemisphere needs *not* to know what the left hemisphere knows, for that would destroy its ability to understand the whole; at the same time the left hemisphere cannot know what the right hemisphere knows. From inside its own system, from its own point of view, what it believes it has 'created' appears complete. Just because what it produces is in focus and at the centre of the field of vision, it is more easily seen. This is one reason we are so much more aware of what it contributes to our knowledge of the world.

The left hemisphere cannot deliver anything new direct from 'outside', but it can unfold, or 'unpack', what it is given. Its very strength – and it contains enormous strength, as the history of civilisation demonstrates – lies in the fact that it can render explicit what the right hemisphere has to leave implicit, leave folded in. Yet that is also its weakness. The clarifying explicitness needs to be reintegrated with the sense of the whole, the now unpacked or unfolded whatever-it-may-be being handed back to the domain of the right hemisphere, where it once more lives. This turns out to be a problem, as I shall try to explain in the next chapter.

CHAPTER 6

THE TRIUMPH OF THE LEFT HEMISPHERE

LOOKING BACK OVER THE EVIDENCE I HAVE DISCUSSED IN THE PREVIOUS CHAPTER from philosophy, neurology and neuropsychology, it would appear that there is a good chance that the right hemisphere may be seeing more of the whole picture. Despite the left hemisphere's conviction of its own self-sufficiency, everything about the relationship of the hemispheres to one another and to reality suggests the primacy of the right hemisphere, both in grounding experience (at the bottom level) and in reconstituting left-hemisphere-processed experience once again as living (at the top level). We have also seen that many important aspects of experience, those that the right hemisphere is particularly well equipped to deal with – our passions, our sense of humour, all metaphoric and symbolic understanding (and with it the metaphoric and symbolic nature of art), all religious sense, all imaginative and intuitive processes – are denatured by becoming the object of focussed attention, which renders them explicit, therefore mechanical, lifeless. The value of the left hemisphere is precisely in making explicit, but this is a staging post, an intermediate level of the 'processing' of experience, never the starting point or end point, never the deepest, or the final, level. The relationship between the hemispheres is therefore highly significant for the type of world we find ourselves living in.

The left hemisphere is competitive, and its concern, its prime motivation, is *power*. If the working relationship were to become disturbed, so that the left hemisphere appeared to have primacy or became the end point or final staging post on the 'processing' of experience, the world would change into something quite different. And we can say fairly clearly what that would be like: it would be relatively mechanical, an assemblage of more or less disconnected 'parts'; it would be relatively abstract and disembodied; relatively distanced from fellow-feeling; given to explicitness; utilitarian in ethic; over-confident of its own take on reality, and lacking insight into its problems – the neuropsychological evidence is that these are all aspects of the left hemisphere world as compared with the right.

What do we know of the relationship between the hemispheres in practice, and where could our knowledge, not of hemisphere differences, but of the working *relationship* of the hemispheres come from? There is limited mileage in looking at functional imaging, since its time frames are too large to detect most hemisphere interactions; and the EEG lacks specificity. There is a tendency simply to find, at any one moment in time, that areas in both hemispheres are involved (once again I would emphasise that everything human involves both hemispheres: we do virtually nothing with one hemisphere alone).

Just as what we know about the normal functioning of the brain comes from very particular accidents of nature, or from carefully contrived artificial experiments that highlight what otherwise goes unremarked, so what we know about relations between the hemispheres comes from careful observation of how they operate in highly specialised circumstances that allow their 'working relationship' to come under scrutiny. Some such evidence comes from carefully designed experiments on normal subjects in which the reactions of the hemispheres can be artificially separated and their interactions minutely observed. However, a particularly rich source has been split-brain patients.

My thesis is that the hemispheres have complementary but conflicting tasks to fulfil, and need to maintain a high degree of mutual ignorance. At the same time they need to co-operate. How is this achieved, and what is their working relationship like?

The corpus callosum, and the other subcortical structures, such as the cerebral commissures, which communicate between the hemispheres also have complementary but conflicting roles.[1] They need to share *information*, but at the same time to keep the *worlds* where that information is handled separate. At the beginning of this book I referred to neurological evidence that the corpus callosum is largely inhibitory in function. That sounds competitive, but it might be co-operative, because co-operation requires difference, not more of the same. An action in one hemisphere is not usually best mirrored in the other: it is not co-operation for the surgeon and the assistant both to try to make the incision. In order to achieve many musical effects, whether between the singers in a choir, or the members of a string ensemble, or the two hands of a pianist, especially where there are fugal elements, discords, cross-rhythms and syncopations, it is equally vital for the performer to be sensitive to, and attentive to, one set of experiences, and simultaneously to be taken up in, and express, another, that may appear, at the local level, to be in conflict with it. We must inhibit one in order to inhabit the other. If one thinks of the relationship between the hemispheres as being like that between the two hands of the pianist (whose two hemispheres do indeed have to co-operate, but equally must remain independent), one can see that the task of the corpus callosum has to be as much to do with inhibition of process as it is with facilitation of information transfer, and co-operation requires the correct balance to be maintained.

We looked earlier at neurological evidence, but what of the phenomenological evidence – what actually happens in the world of the patient whose corpus callosum suddenly stops functioning? I mentioned that split-brain patients lead remarkably normal lives. If one met them, went out for a meal with them, or even went on holiday with them, one might never guess that there was anything unusual about them. Under certain laboratory conditions, in which the workings of the two hemispheres can be artificially isolated, we can learn about their independent function; but this apart, split-brain patients have not appeared particularly handicapped. Which invites the question, why ever not?

As far as sharing information goes, most experience of the external world is not confined to one hemisphere, and there is considerable redundancy in the system: 'As we move around the world looking at objects, touching them, hearing sounds, and so forth, most of the information is taken in by both cerebral hemispheres. In addition, both hemispheres are usually able to generate some appropriate behavioural response.'[2] We are not by any means completely reliant on callosal transmission. In fact, for this reason, experimental conditions for testing each hemisphere of a split-brain subject in isolation have to be carefully planned so that stimuli reach one hemisphere alone. And, as with all human beings, most of what each hemisphere knows, it knows in common with its counterpart. Both hemispheres, after all, have been through the same experiences, shared the same body, and indeed still are united in that body: everything below the corpus callosum – the diencephalon, the cerebellum, the brainstem, the spinal cord, and all the rest – and all that the body communicates to them second by second, they continue to share. Furthermore, as Sperry's colleague Joseph Bogen points out, even in normal subjects no connective pathways, even in the corpus callosum, function all the time; and lengthy neurotransmission times across the corpus callosum enforce a degree of interhemispheric independence.[3]

That is just as well because, as I have emphasised, there are good reasons why nature has conserved the great divide between the hemispheres. Each hemisphere has to remain independent, and inevitably remain to some extent ignorant, of what goes on in its counterpart. Inhibition is the other primary function, perhaps the principal function, of the corpus callosum.[4] How does splitting it affect that?

In the long run, not as badly as one might think. By the time the brain is surgically divided, each hemisphere has had years of working with an intact corpus callosum during which to establish its own specialised modes of operation, laid down as memories in the patterns of neuronal connection within either hemisphere. So it is not the establishing, only the functional maintenance, of such specialisation that is impaired.

Nonetheless, in the first months following surgery, split-brain patients reported some rather disconcerting experiences. These took the form of an apparent conflict of will, displayed in so-called intermanual conflict. Such was the case of a man who found himself in the unfortunate position of going to embrace his wife with one arm and pushing her away with the other.[5] Other patients with disruption of the corpus callosum have reported similar experiences, for example:

On several occasions while driving, the left hand reached up and grabbed the steering wheel from the right hand. The problem was persistent and severe enough that she had to give up driving. She reported instances in which the left hand closed doors the right hand had opened, unfolded sheets the right had folded, snatched money the right had offered to a store cashier, and disrupted her reading by turning pages and closing books.[6]

Or: 'I open the closet door. I know what I want to wear. As I reach for something with my right hand, my left comes up and takes something different. I can't put it down if it's in my left hand. I have to call my daughter.'[7] Notice that it is always the left hand that is 'misbehaving': I will return to that shortly.

These symptoms tended to settle with time. In fact split-brain patients manage surprisingly well, in that 'despite having two independent and different cognitive processors, they behave as unified individuals and seldom display signs of hesitation, confusion or dissociation in their day-to-day activities'.[8] This is because, although callosotomy severs the principal means of transfer of information between hemispheres, there are other subcortical tracts that connect them, sharing information and helping inhibit function, even if using some of these 'detours' takes some retraining of the brain.[9]

But the nature of the initial experience following operation bears further consideration, nonetheless. Such stories have been somewhat discounted, perhaps because of the tendency for commentators to rush into speculations about the divisibility of the self. However, Roger Sperry himself, who won a Nobel prize for his work on split brains, wrote, 'both the left and right hemispheres may be conscious simultaneously in different, even in mutually conflicting, mental experiences that run along in parallel.'[10] Such an idea clearly does raise questions about the self and personal identity, questions that have been much discussed, particularly by philosophers in the 1960s and 1970s when the research on split-brain subjects was getting to be known. But my purpose in referring to these experiences here is to suggest that the main evidence of disturbance following the operation was not, as might have been expected, things that no longer happened, but just the opposite – things that couldn't be *prevented* from happening, which, in other words, couldn't be inhibited. In this respect, split-brain subjects are like patients who have suffered a stroke or other neurological injury affecting the pathways through the corpus callosum: there is a problem of compromised interhemispheric inhibition.[11] It is worse for those with callosal agenesis (a common condition, affecting up to 1 per cent of the population, in which the corpus callosum fails to develop),[12] or those with congenital dysfunction of the corpus callosum: they have never had the advantage of living with a functional divide, and so cannot develop the usual interhemispheric inhibition in the first place.[13]

Incompetence of the corpus callosum has been implicated in the genesis of some psychiatric disorders, notably in the psychosis of schizophrenia; and this is in keeping with the fact that cases of psychosis have been found in association with complete and partial agenesis of the corpus callosum.[14] If the main effect of an intact normal corpus callosum is inhibitory, its being compromised will have unpredictable results: either it will prove creatively fruitful, or it will simply be disruptive, by causing premature collapse into unity of elements or processes whose mutual independence needed to be maintained. Research in schizophrenia, using neuropsychological testing, as well as EEG and other measures, demonstrates precisely *a failure of interhemispheric inhibition*. In schizotypy, too, there is known to be intrusion of left-hemisphere modes into right-hemisphere functioning.[15] Many of the phenomena of schizophrenia and of schizotypy – both the potentially creative (flying mathematicians) and the obviously disruptive effects (inhibited trapeze artists, see pp. 12–13) – could be explained by such intrusions, including intrusions of right-hemisphere modes into left-hemisphere functioning, as well as intrusion of left-hemisphere modes into right-hemisphere functioning.

In other words incompetence or agenesis of the corpus callosum leads to a picture of apparently increased interconnectivity of function.[16] This apparently paradoxical finding makes sense if the main purpose of the corpus callosum is to maintain *separation* of the hemispheres.[17]

Independent functioning of the hemispheres is one of the achievements of maturity: children are, relatively speaking, split-brain subjects, with less interhemispheric independence.[18] Babies and young children are less reliant on the corpus callosum: callosal myelination does not even begin until the end of the first year of life, and progresses only slowly thereafter.[19] Pre-adolescent children find it relatively difficult to use their hemispheres separately, which is still further evidence of the inhibitory role played by the corpus callosum in adults.[20] Interhemispheric connectivity grows during childhood and adolescence, with the result that the hemispheres become more independent.[21] It may not be a coincidence that babies and young children are also more reliant on the right hemisphere, which matures earlier than the left, and it may be that it is the increasing importance of left-hemisphere function with age that necessitates the separation, in both hemispheres' interests, of their realms of activity. The Berlin Wall that meets this need would be the increasingly efficient corpus callosum.

All in all, my view is that the corpus callosum does act principally as the agent of hemisphere differentiation rather than integration, though ultimately differentiation may be in the service of integration. This complex, almost paradoxical, function at the very core of the brain, forming a bridge that nonetheless separates the worlds of the hemispheres, is captured with extraordinary prescience in one of the verses of the Hindu spiritual treatise *The Upanishads*: 'In the space within the heart lies the controller of all . . . He is the *bridge* that serves as the *boundary* to keep the different worlds apart.'[22]

THE RELATIONSHIP BETWEEN THE HEMISPHERES

What do we know of the normal working relationship of the hemispheres, in those whose brains have not been artificially split? Is it one of harmony or discord? The question is not simple. Just as inhibition may be maintained in the interests of co-operation, co-operation may be maintained in the interests of competition: where two co-operate, the first may do so in a reciprocal spirit, while the second does so out of self-interest, that self-interest benefitting from the generosity of spirit of the first.

Moreover we have to distinguish between different levels of a relationship. Think of the relationship between two colleagues, who together run a small business. Which relationship are we talking about? At the simplest level one could describe the

business partners' day-to-day mode of working together. So, for example, one could say that they share an office, and, what's more, share a breadth of training and experience in the work that they do, so that both can field enquiries. Each is acknowledged, nonetheless, to have special interests and expertise, and accordingly, where practicable, they split the work along agreed lines, especially where the work is complex; but where it would be quicker or more expedient, because, say, one of them is out of the office and an immediate response is needed, the other will step in and do whatever is required. At this level, and in this sense, the relationship appears pretty balanced and unproblematic.

But that might not be the relationship I'm thinking of. I mean, how do their roles interact, and how does each contribute to the work of the company as a whole? This is a rather different question, and takes us beyond the day-to-day, to something more like 'month-to-month' mode, a middle level.

Here, say, it might turn out that Franny is particularly interested in, and gifted at, bringing in new business; Fred, being a bit more of a backroom type, is better at doing the accounting and IT work. Without new business coming in, the outfit will fold; equally they will hardly survive without proper accountancy and IT support. So each needs the other. However, let's say that Fred has decided that the future lies in developing new and better accounting software systems, that that's what really matters. Anyone, he says to himself, can find the business; it takes someone special to keep the figures balanced, the systems running and ticking over. As a result Fred spends much of his time using the business data to help him develop more sophisticated software, and doesn't prioritise getting the figures ready for Franny's meetings with clients. He is given to feeling superior to Franny, telling himself there's nothing much she does that anyone couldn't do. At the same time Franny resents Fred spending so much of his time on what appear to be technicalities, freeloading on her ability to forge connections and make deals, and then letting her down at the last minute. There is an atmosphere in the office: bad-tempered exchanges, cool silences. And that represents another aspect of their relationship.

But there is a third level to this relationship; not the day-to-day, not even the month-to-month, but the long-term plan, which I just happen to have heard about. Unknown to Franny, Fred has decided he is going to take the company's data, ditch Franny, do a moonlight flit and start up an IT business all of his own.

I'm well aware that hemispheres are not people. Nor is this vignette supposed to sum up the relationship between the cerebral hemispheres. It is designed to do one thing only: to suggest that there would be different answers to the question how the hemispheres relate depending on the level at which we are looking. We need to look at the lowest level, the 'day-to-day' nitty-gritty of how they get through the work together – who answers the telephone. We need also to step back a bit, to the middle level, and look at how their roles complement one another in constructing our world – in theory, and, which may not be the same thing, in practice. And we should not forget to look at the long-term strategy, something that an outsider might know about before one of the partners.

LEVEL ONE

If we start with level one, the 'day-to-day' – or in the case of the hemispheres, millisecond-to-millisecond – relationship, certainly their 'takes' on the world are both necessary to us from moment to moment as living human beings. It is not just that the three-dimensional space in which we move, as beings with bodies, requires bilateral engagement with the environment, and therefore bilateral engagement of the brain; our thinking processes, which define us as humans, involve the need for intuition and conceptualisation together. To the extent that the left hemisphere is the locus of conceptualised knowledge, and to the extent that the right hemisphere embodies intuitive perception, it is clear that both are necessary, and that a balance needs to be kept. Kant's famous formula, *Begriffe ohne Anschauungen sind leer, Anschauungen ohne Begriffe sind blind* ('concepts without intuitions are empty; intuitions without concepts are blind'), applies here.[23] Viewed from the standpoint of utility and task achievement, most ordinary tasks of daily life require 'input' from both spheres; and from the natural standpoint of everyday living, the world that we experience in the ordinary way is a fusion of what each hemisphere delivers. So it's clearly going to be in our best interests for the hemispheres to co-operate.[24]

I mentioned earlier, however, the nonchalance with which the left hemisphere makes up what is going on in the right hemisphere when in reality it has no idea. There is something intriguing about its reluctance to admit ignorance. Some subtle experiments looking at sequences of tasks that would normally call into action the two hemispheres differentially suggest that their mode of interaction is not one in which they co-operate over what each does best, like some parody of an ideal bureaucratic government, but instead is more like the real thing, one of rivalry between departments.[25] The competition between the hemispheres can actually impair performance (which is no doubt why they are able mutually to inhibit one another).

I think it would be a mistake to attribute will to these millisecond-by-millisecond decisions. I do think a hemisphere can have a will, but it needs time to exert it. It is striking, on the one hand, that

a hemisphere assumes control of processing as a result of set or expectation as to the nature of the processing requirements *prior* to actual information processing, and ... it remains in control even if its performance, for whatever reasons, is considerably worse than that which could have been produced by the opposite side of the brain.[26]

It's as if each hemisphere took the view: 'If this letter looks as if it's addressed to me, I'm going to deal with it, even if it turns out on opening it that it was really addressed to you.' There may be good reasons for this approach. For example, if there were excessive time costs in sending the information across to the other side for processing, it might be better to accept the somewhat inferior response because it would come quicker. The mutually inconsistent modes of processing adopted by the hemispheres create a difficulty, requiring something like an umpire for situations in which both cerebral hemispheres have access to the same information at the same time. Such 'umpire decisions' may be made at a very low level, below that of the hemispheres themselves, and there may be a 'metacontrol' switch, as far down as the brainstem, that apportions work between the hemispheres.[27]

From the split-brain patients, as we saw, it is clear that in the intact situation it is the will of the left hemisphere, at a more conscious level, that normally inhibits the will of the right. It would be tempting to suggest that it is also the left hemisphere, on the micro level of millisecond-to-millisecond, that takes the lion's share of the catch. Indeed some of the experimental evidence does appear to support the view that the majority of right-handed people are biased toward the mode of processing favoured by the left hemisphere, provided the stimulus is so arranged as to give them a choice.[28] But other evidence is against it, and it seems that the bias probably gets in at the next level.[29]

LEVEL TWO

So let's move up from the automatic, moment-to-moment responses of the hemispheres, to consider their relationship in the products of consciousness – at the phenomenological level, where their interaction brings into being our world of experience. At this level it is harder to demonstrate neuropsychological fact, precisely because what we are looking at is not just the interaction of neurones but the phenomenological experience of human beings. This takes place over longer periods than those of the neuronal action potential, and at the highest level of integrated awareness. No one knows where that is, if they wanted to image it, or how to measure its neurological correlates; and it is a process that fluctuates, rather than remaining still in one place at one time to be measured. What happens here has largely to be deduced from what we know of the nature, preoccupations, interests, values and typical modes of operation of the two hemispheres individually, as explored earlier in the book. But all the same some ingenious observations can be, and have been, made.

In the discussion of level one, the emphasis was on the necessary inhibition of one hemisphere by the other, since they each need to work separately. However, at a higher level, and over longer time spans, they also need to work together, not just because some important human faculties, such as imagination, appear to depend on the synthesis of the workings of both hemispheres. In the last chapter I described evidence for the primacy of the right hemisphere in constituting our experience of reality, with the need for left hemisphere 'unfolding' of what the right hemisphere understands, so that the now unfolded vision can subsequently be reintegrated with the reality of the right hemisphere. I expressed this in terms of Hegel's *Aufhebung*, the essential point being that something new, that was not present before, comes into being through the process, not negating the earlier stages, but transforming them.

And one of the most significant findings from hemisphere research at the neurological level demonstrates just that. Marie Banich, Director of the Institute of Cognitive Science at Boulder, Colorado, and a leading researcher into hemisphere interaction, writes:

> The major finding to come out of our laboratory since the mid-1980s is that interhemispheric interaction is much more than just a mechanism by which one hemisphere 'photocopies' experiences and feelings for its partner. Interhemispheric interaction has important emergent functions – functions that cannot be derived from the simple sum of its parts . . . the nature of processing when both hemispheres are involved cannot be predicted from the parts.[30]

It is possible to determine which areas of the brain are recruited in order to carry out a task using one hemisphere only, and, by repeating it, this can be determined for each hemisphere on its own. But when both hemispheres co-operate in carrying out the task, it is not just that additional regions come into play, as one might expect, but wholly different regions altogether, many of those that were activated in the single-hemisphere condition remaining inactive, and new areas in different parts of the brain, being recruited.[31]

At a global level we can prefer one or the other hemisphere
But do the hemispheres actually co-operate to bring this situation about? There are some clues at the neurological level to the relationship they have in practice.

It turns out that one or other hemisphere may predominate – its particular cognitive and perceptual style as a whole more greatly influencing our experience of the world – not only during chunks of phenomenological experience (which therefore must last longer than a few milliseconds at a time) but even over very long periods. We can even have, as personalities, characteristic and consistent biases towards one or other hemisphere, certainly for particular kinds of experience, associated with differing degrees of arousal and activation in either hemisphere. This phenomenon is known as 'hemispheric utilisation bias' or 'characteristic perceptual asymmetry'.[32]

Some interesting sidelights on the relationship between the hemispheres can be seen by examining the way in which these individual differences affect competition for the control of visual attention. In experiments where a task is carried out requiring attention to one's non-favoured visual field (the field contralateral to one's non-favoured hemisphere), while irrelevant, distracting information is presented to the favoured visual field, those subjects with a characteristic *left*-hemisphere bias found that the already strong tendency for the left hemisphere to prioritise the right visual field, and downplay the left visual field, was enhanced. This meant that the irrelevant information on the right interfered with the task going on in the left visual field (controlled by the right hemisphere). But for those with a characteristic *right*-hemisphere bias, when conditions were reversed, no such competitive effects were seen: irrelevant information in the right hemisphere's favoured left visual field did not interfere with the subject's ability to attend to the matter in hand going on, now, in the right visual field (the field favoured by the left hemisphere).[33]

This suggests a more even distribution of concern in the right hemisphere than in the left. We know that the right hemisphere 'looks out' for both hemispheres' territory, not just its own, like the left hemisphere. But this goes further: having a 'utilisation bias' in favour of the left hemisphere intensifies this effect, whereas having a similar bias in favour of the right hemisphere does nothing to upset the even-handedness of its concern. This resonates with another well-established research finding: that transfer of information from left hemisphere to right hemisphere takes place more slowly than transfer from right to left.[34] And, be it noted, this is regardless of whether the task is by nature better suited to the right hemisphere or left hemisphere.[35]

Competition between the hemispheres is also revealed by the response to injury. If, following a brain injury, one temporarily disables the other (non-injured) hemisphere by, for example, transcranial magnetic stimulation, this causes an improvement in function in the damaged hemisphere.[36] Similarly, if the individual should suffer a stroke in the 'normal', non-damaged hemisphere, the originally injured hemisphere then improves. This was observed long ago by the distinguished neurophysiologist Brown-Séquard, when he found he was able to reverse a paralysis caused by a lesion in one hemisphere of a frog by inflicting a similar lesion at the same point in the contralateral hemisphere.[37] What is more, such interhemispheric competition appears yet again to be asymmetrical, with the suppressive effect of the left hemisphere on the right being greater than that of the right on the left.[38]

Does this remind you of anything? The finding, perhaps, that once the hemispheres are in touch via the commissures, the left hemisphere is better able to suppress the right than the right is able to suppress the left (see p. 46).

Further information comes from individuals with split brains. Though they have some handicaps, they are at an advantage in at least one respect: there are some tasks they can carry out more swiftly than normal subjects.[39] For example, tasks involving focussed attention usually engage primarily the left hemisphere. But, in split-brain patients, the left hemisphere cannot so effectively inhibit the right, so that both are able to bring focussed attention (the right hemisphere can also yield focussed attention) to bear and both contribute, with the result that the task is carried out in half the time.

In some cases one can see this pattern of hemisphere competition exemplified in individual brain development following an injury. Subjects with early left-hemisphere brain damage, in whom therefore language has to be accommodated in the right hemisphere alongside the normal right-hemisphere synthetic-*Gestalt* faculties, show IQ deficits in their *non-verbal* functions, because the presence of language in the same hemisphere interferes. The direction of influence tends again to be more that of the left hemisphere over the right.

What the stories of the split-brain patients in their first few months after operation also reveal is that it is the left hemisphere, Gazzaniga's interpreter, that is in control, at the conscious level, of the consistent nature of 'our' experience, even though we may have differing views, desires, and values in either hemisphere. In inter-manual conflict, it is never the right hand that is experienced as the rebel, the 'naughty' hand, the one that is 'out of control': it is always the left, that pushes the other way, grabs the wheel, chooses the 'wrong' clothes. 'Of course it is', you may say: 'it's not the right hand that behaves disruptively.' But disruptive of what? Once the script has been written and the play half performed by the left hemisphere, an incursion from the right hemisphere is bound to be disruptive and unwelcome from its point of view. It's the left hemisphere, ignorant of what is going on in the right hemisphere, that both decides what it is that 'I' want, and then judges any interruption from the right hemisphere as contrary to 'my' best interests. But set it in another context, and who knows what might have happened had he actually listened a long while back to his right hemisphere and left his wife rather than embrace her; or – in another patient's story – had she closed the door, driven the other way, worn the flame-coloured dress? At any rate, at least we can deduce that when she says 'I know what I want to wear', she means 'My left hemisphere knows what it wants me to wear, and I am identified with my left hemisphere.'[40]

From the previous chapter one can see that it is essential that what the left hemisphere yields is returned to the realm of the right hemisphere, where it can once again live. Only the right hemisphere is in touch with primary experience, with life; and the left hemisphere can only ever be a staging post, a processing house, along the route – not the final destination. The right hemisphere certainly needs the left, but the left hemisphere depends on the right.[41] Much that marks us out, in the positive sense as well as the negative sense, as human beings requires the intervention of the left hemisphere, *as long as it is acting in concert with the right hemisphere.* Important human faculties depend on a synthesis of their activity. In the absence of such concerted action, the left hemisphere comes to believe its territory actually *is* the world.

Despite the asymmetry in their roles, in favour of the right hemisphere, there is an important opposing asymmetry of power, in favour of the left hemisphere. The Master makes himself vulnerable to the emissary, and the emissary can choose to take advantage of the situation, to ignore the Master. It seems that its nature is such that it is prone to do so, and it may even, mistakenly, see the right hemisphere's world as undoing its work, challenging its 'supremacy'.

The image suggests, of course, that the two hemispheres have wills that may not always be in harmony. How legitimate is it to think of the hemispheres as having wills in this sense? Bogen refers to two 'crucial facts': that 'it takes only one hemisphere to have a mind', and that 'hemispheres can sustain the activity of two separate spheres of consciousness following commissurotomy'.[42] Sperry writes that, in commissurotomy patients,

> each hemisphere can be shown to experience its own private sensations, percepts, thoughts, and memories that are inaccessible to awareness in the other hemisphere. Introspective verbal accounts from the vocal left hemisphere report a

striking lack of awareness in this hemisphere for mental functions that have just been performed immediately before in the right hemisphere. In this respect each surgically disconnected hemisphere appears to have a mind of its own, but each cut off from, and oblivious to, conscious events in the partner hemisphere.[43]

And it is not just like this in surgically disconnected hemispheres. Temporary inactivation of one or other hemisphere, through the Wada test, produces similar results.

Even without such specialised procedures, sometimes the brain of the ordinary subject shows disconnection comparable to that found in split-brain subjects.[44] If there are separate sensations, percepts, thoughts and memories, as well as separate ways of dealing with all of these, it would hardly be surprising if there were separate desires formed, separate wills, to each hemisphere – and we know from the split-brain subjects' experience that this is the case.

But we also know from them, as we know from our own experience of divided will, that, despite all this, there can be only one unified field of consciousness. And how is that?

Sperry makes his own attempt to answer this question, and his solution lies in referring to something that must go on at the top end of the process. He writes: 'The overall, holistic functional effect could thus determine the conscious experience. If the functional impact of the neural activity has a unitary effect in the upper-level conscious dynamics, the subjective experience is unified.'[45] In dealing with these issues it is nigh on impossible to remain within the limits of commonly accepted language use, and I make no claim to be able to solve these issues in a way that avoids the traps of language. But I cannot help finding phrases such as 'the overall, holistic functional effect' unsatisfactory in explanatory terms. It seems to beg every question – what is it, other than a redescription of what it is trying to explain? And in which hemisphere does it, or 'the upper-level conscious dynamics', whatever they may be, lie?

It seems to me more fruitful to think of consciousness not as something with sharp edges that is suddenly arrived at once one reaches the very top of mental functioning, but as a process that is gradual, rather than all-or-nothing, and begins low down in the brain, rising up from below the level of the hemispheres, before it reaches the great divide. It may be that the reverse of Sperry's model applies. The problem then becomes not how two wills can *become* one unified consciousness, but how one field of consciousness can accommodate two wills. These evolve from the higher cognitive levels, because it is here that different worlds are given to consciousness by each hemisphere, with different sets of values and different experiences. As I move from one situation to another, where different contexts and different sets of values change my preferences, my will changes.

Perhaps, then, consciousness is unified at the *lowest* levels, and it is actually only when the process becomes *self*-conscious at the topmost levels, within cognition, that the possibility of separation occurs. Here I would quote Jaak Panksepp:

Most forms of intentionality and deep emotional feelings are not split in any obvious way by a parting of the hemispheres. Only the cognitive interpretations [high-level phenomena] of specific events are affected . . . The unity of an under-lying form of consciousness in split-brain individuals, perhaps their fundamental sense of self, is affirmed by the fact that the disconnected hemispheres can no more easily execute two cognitive tasks simultaneously than can the brains of normal individuals.[46]

The 'fundamental sense of self' here referred to by Panksepp, the core of the self, is affective and deep-lying: its roots lie at a level below the hemispheric divide, a level, however, with which each cognitively aware hemisphere at the highest level is still in touch. The conflicts that exist are the result of differences between the two hemispheres in high-level cognitive processing, and in most cases they become apparent only when, under special circumstances, care is taken to introduce mater-ial to one hemisphere only, and in such a way that it will have no opportunity to descend to a level of the self which can communicate via pathways below the corpus callosum. That would help explain why split-brain patients do not experi-ence any disturbance of the sense of self. So much of our experience, and our sense of our self, comes from low down in the 'tree' of consciousness, below hemispheric level: 'integration' does not need to be achieved. All the corpus callosum has to do is to help maintain moment-to-moment independence of the hemispheres, not integration of the self. This explains why split-brain patients describe not a frag-mentation of the self, but merely some difficulty inhibiting inappropriate conflicts of action.

Panksepp sees consciousness as something that begins very deep indeed, in the so-called peri-aqueductal grey matter in the midbrain, and 'migrates' through higher regions of the brain, especially the cingulate, temporal and frontal regions of the cortex.[47] So he sees it as something that is not all or nothing, but has a continuous existence, transforming itself as it travels upwards, through the branches, to what he calls, by analogy with the forest canopy, the 'cerebral canopy', until in the frontal cortices it becomes high-level cognitive awareness.[48] I like this image of the cerebral 'canopy' because it reminds us that consciousness is not a bird, as it often seems to be in the literature – hovering, detached, coming in at the top level and alighting on the brain somewhere in the frontal lobes – but a tree, its roots deep inside us. It reinforces the nature of consciousness not as an entity, but as a *process*.[49] If, as Thomas Nagel famously put it, consciousness is that which exists 'when there is something it is like to *be* that organism',[50] this identifies that the experience of consciousness is not a 'whatness', but a 'howness' – a 'what it is *like*' – a way of being which distinguishes living things, and is bound to be at least as much a characteristic of the right hemi-sphere (which is excluded from the process of understanding to the very degree that we are focussed on the issue and bent on analysis) as it is of the left (the hemisphere that does the focussing and analysing).[51]

Consciousness is not the same as inwardness, although there can be no inward-ness without consciousness. To return to Patricia Churchland's statement that it is reasonable to *identify* the blueness of an object with its disposition to scatter electromagnetic waves preferentially at about 0.46μm,[52] to see it like this, as though from the outside, excluding the 'subjective' experience of the colour blue – as though to get the inwardness of consciousness out of the picture – requires a very high degree of consciousness and self-consciousness. The polarity between the 'objective' and 'subjective' points of view is a creation of the left hemisphere's analytic disposition. In reality there can be neither absolutely, only a choice between a betweenness which acknowledges itself, and one which denies its own nature. By *identifying* blueness solely with the behaviour of electromagnetic particles one is not avoiding value, not avoiding betweenness, not avoiding one's shadow being cast across the picture. One is using the inwardness of consciousness in a very specialised way to strive to empty itself as much as possible of value, of the self. The paradoxical result is an extremely partial, fragmented version of the colour blue, which is neither value-free nor independent of the self's disposition towards its object.

One of the difficulties in practising philosophy is that we are obliged to bring into the focus of our attention, and therefore make explicit, processes which by their nature are not focussed on, and cannot be made explicit. Any attempt to do so immediately and radically alters what we find. Wittgenstein repeatedly remarks on the way that stopping acting and engaging with the world in order to reflect on it makes things appear alien – we feel 'the phenomenon is slipping away from us' (see p. 89 above). Thus his thrust as a philosopher is to help us get on with things, to 'move about around things and events in the world instead of trying to delineate their essential features'[53] – in other words, to be skilled participants in the life of the world as it flows (right hemisphere), not detached analysts of the process once it stops (left hemisphere). Whether this might undermine the practice of philosophy altogether is a question of which Wittgenstein was, of course, also highly aware.

This has profound implications for our attempts to pin down what consciousness is, since such attempts always and necessarily bring to bear high levels of self-awareness which induce a reflexive condition different from consciousness as understood intuitively. Panksepp, who has written on the subject from the standpoint of a neuroscientist, sees consciousness as ultimately affective in nature, and founded on 'motor processes that generate self-consciousness by being closely linked to body image representations' – in other words, we are first and foremost aware of ourselves through feeling states that lead to action in, and engagement with, the world as embodied beings. He rejects the view that consciousness arises from sensory-perceptual imagery, according to the prevailing cognitive model, based as it is on what we find when we stop acting in the world and introspect on our own thought processes. 'Consciousness', he writes, 'is not simply a sensory-perceptual affair, a matter of mental imagery, as the contents of our mind would have us believe. It is deeply enmeshed with the brain mechanisms that automatically promote action readiness.'[54]

I know that it does not necessarily feel as if the sense of the self comes from lower levels of the nervous system. But I do not think it would 'feel' any different if it did or didn't. The problem is that when we are trying to introspect on ourselves we change the nature of what we are looking at. Our active, embodied engagement with the world is a skill. It is something we learn before we are conscious of it, and consciousness threatens to disrupt it, as it disrupts all skills. In fact what one means by a skill is something intuitive and non-explicit. We do not work out what actions we need to make in order to hammer effectively, and then give instructions consciously to our hands and arms to carry them out in a certain order, with myriads of caveats and qualifications – 'If the hammer glances off too much to the right, aim slightly further to the left; if this does not work, try using slightly less force,' and so on. If we did, we would hammer very badly: instead we just pick up the hammer and strike. As Dreyfus, a Heidegger scholar who has written powerfully about the problems of trying to 'operationalise' skills, particularly more complex skills that require considerable experience, points out, we resort to explicit analysis of the process only when we introspect on what happened – either because something has gone wrong, or because we are complete beginners. Philosophers and psychologists who champion the view that our mental processes are akin to those of a computer 'have yet to notice that we only become aware of our skills when things are not going smoothly or when someone performing an experiment has given us a task in which we have no prior experience or skill. Then we are indeed dependent on analysis.'[55]

Which brings us back to the question of whether 'consciousness is in the left hemisphere'. Obviously much depends on what is meant by 'conscious', and if consciousness is a continuum, it will necessarily be impossible to be clear-cut about it – in fact supposing it to be a clear-cut phenomenon would be one sign of being off track. The most robust distinction that can be made, however, although it is itself far from unproblematic, is that between self-consciousness and consciousness 'pure and simple'. But what is consciousness without self-consciousness? We cannot tell whether another creature has self-consciousness – or, strictly, consciousness at all – so we are obliged to introspect on our own experience. However, such introspection is by definition self-conscious, and so we will not get to know what it is like to be conscious without being self-conscious by this route, either. One can however distinguish between times when one is aware of *oneself as the object of attention* and times when one is simply aware of being. This is the closest I can get to the distinction. It has the double advantage of coinciding with what we normally mean by 'self-consciousness' in everyday parlance; and of pinpointing the abnormality in subjects whose psychopathology, as in many anxiety disorders, especially social phobia, is of excessive self-consciousness. Sufferers describe an uncomfortable sense of being observed, even of there being an 'eye' that observes their 'I' (in the world of schizophrenia this process becomes psychotic, and is experienced as a reality; see Plate 1). Such self-consciousness also has the paralysing effect of rendering awkward and artificial the skills of ordinary social life which have to remain intuitive and unconscious to be effective; so one of the aspects of self-consciousness is the dragging into the centre of awareness of what should remain outside of it.

Most, if not all, of the 'functions' mediated by the right hemisphere fall into this category of what has to remain outside the focus of awareness – implicit, intuitive, unattended to. And so it looks as though *self-consciousness*, at least, comes about when the left hemisphere is engaged in inspecting the life of the right. As far as the right hemisphere activities themselves go, we are conscious most of the time when carrying them out, but we are not focussed on them, and therefore not conscious *of them* – the attention is somewhere else (and they can come and go from consciousness, depending on what else is going on).[56] Many over-learned routines, such as driving a familiar route, are like this. At the time we are not aware of carrying them out, but we would become so immediately if our attention were drawn to it – or if we made a mistake.[57] Many over-learned and routine behaviours must involve the left hemisphere. So clearly not everything in the left hemisphere can be – or ever could have been – in the focus of attention. For one thing, that focus is very small; and, for another, very little of the left hemisphere can be near the top of the cerebral canopy, where awareness mainly is.

The idea that self-consciousness, in the sense of being aware of ourselves doing or being something, is the left hemisphere inspecting the right is supported by a number of observations. The attentional 'spotlight', as we have seen, is a function of the left hemisphere. The casualties in self-consciousness are all right-hemisphere-based, social or empathic skills. And schizophrenic subjects, whose psychopathology depends on a reflexive hyperconsciousness, and who often depict a detached observing eye in their paintings, show a relative hypofunction of the right hemisphere in relation to the left (see Plate 2).

More specifically, the idea that things come into being through an apophatic process (see p. 197) also casts light, I believe, on the problem of the self, and helps to confirm this view. Hume introspected and found no sign of the self, just a string of sense impressions. Fichte thought that was quite natural. The self, he believed, would not emerge in cognition: the more absorbed you are in the process of attending, the less aware you are of yourself as the absorber. It is only when there is some kind of resistance that one becomes aware of the self, 'not as an object but as that which is obtruded upon by some kind of recalcitrant reality'.[58] This is as if things become, in Heidegger's terms, *vorhanden*, separate from us, and we feel ourselves separate from them. In Merleau-Ponty's terms, it has to do with the plane of focus: whether the 'I' is transparent or opaque. I come into being as a self through the experience of resistance, as a lake is bounded by the shore which makes it a lake. These associations with opacity and *Vorhandenheit* again suggest that the self-conscious self emerges only when the focus of left-hemisphere attention is brought to bear on the right-hemisphere world.

What about those who have suffered a left-hemisphere stroke? Clearly they remain conscious. The degree to which they remain *self*-conscious is harder to assess because of the difficulty of reporting on it in an articulate fashion. It is not impossible to imagine ways of circumventing this problem, however, though I am not aware of research addressing the point. I would be surprised if self-consciousness were altogether lacking, and it may be that, if the tree cannot reach the forest canopy on one side of the fence, it will push up on the other in an attempt to do so, with possibly paradoxical results that those who have had left-hemisphere strokes may be more, rather than less, self-conscious, because of the damaging effect of having the attentional spotlight in the same hemisphere as all those things that by their nature need to flee from it; rather as those with left-hemisphere brain damage in childhood develop poorer right-hemisphere skills because of the presence in the same hemisphere of language, with its Gorgon stare.

Panksepp's vision of consciousness as a process that begins in the midbrain and migrates upwards also suggests a possible approach to the so-called binding problem, which refers to the difficulty of knowing how the various modular elements of brain function come to be united in the experience of the self – where in, or by what part of, the brain do the various modules that are identified by cognitive psychology get to be unified?

One answer to this is epistemological: that this is largely a problem created by the model of mind we have espoused. Derived inevitably from the self-conscious, self-reflexive mechanisms of the left hemisphere, our examination of ourselves identifies the parts of a living whole, then wonders how the parts can be put together (the Frankenstein's monster problem). But Panksepp's vision gives a neurological answer to this problem: what look like 'modules' are better seen as branches of a tree – except that, in this tree, Spanish moss also hangs between the branches.

Ramachandran describes experiments which

> flatly contradict the theory that the brain consists of a number of autonomous modules acting as a bucket brigade. Popularised by artificial intelligence researchers, the idea that the brain behaves like a computer, with each module performing a highly specialised job and sending its output to the next module, is widely believed ... But my experiments ... have taught me that this is not how the brain works. Its connections are extraordinarily labile and dynamic. Perceptions emerge as a result of reverberations of signals between different levels of the sensory hierarchy, indeed across different senses.[59]

Experience is not just a stitching together, at the topmost level, of Gazzaniga's 'patchwork' of functions. Experience is already coherent in its wholeness at very low levels in the brain, and what higher levels do is not to put together bits (left-hemisphere fashion) but to permit the growth of a unified whole (right hemisphere fashion). There are known to be highly complex, and complexly interconnected, cortico-subcortical loops involving the basal ganglia, deep-lying nuclei in the brain, way below the corpus callosum, which, as we understand more about them, we realize increasingly are involved, not just in motor co-ordination, as we used to think, but in both the segregation and the integration of motor, affective and cognitive functions. These 'loops' underlie subtle, emotionally laden aspects of experience. Although the cognitive, motor and affective elements are carefully segregated, even within the subthalamic nuclei – relay centres that are minute (only 5–15 mm in diameter) – they are also equally carefully interconnected (even at this very low level there is division *within union*). The processes that are subserved are learned, but have become nonetheless automatic, not under conscious control. Patients with conditions such as Parkinson's disease can now be treated by a procedure known as deep brain stimulation, which involves surgically implanting electrodes in the subthalamic nuclei and stimulating them for brief periods (a painless procedure that is carried out, and indeed must be carried out, with the patient fully conscious). Professor Yves Agid and his team at the Pitié-Salpêtrière in Paris found that by minute variation in the position of the electrode, they caused a patient to change from the impassive, immobile, 'switched-off' Parkinsonian state, to one of severe depression. In video recordings their patient can be seen grimacing, holding her head in her hands, and expressing feelings of sadness, guilt, uselessness, and hopelessness: 'I'm falling down in my head, I no longer wish to live, to see anything, hear anything, feel anything ...' When asked why she was crying and if she felt pain, she responded: 'No, I'm fed up with life, I've had enough ... I don't want to live any more, I'm disgusted with life ... Everything is useless ... worthless: I'm scared in this world.' When asked why she was sad, she replied: 'I'm tired. I want to hide in a corner ... I'm crying over myself, of course ... I'm hopeless, why am I bothering you ...' Less than 90 seconds after stimulation was stopped, the depression disappeared. For the next five minutes she was in a mildly hypomanic state, laughing and joking with the examiner, and playfully pulling his tie. By moving the probe minutely, she became frankly hypomanic, appearing not just cheerful, but being 'over the moon', and restlessly active – all within minutes or seconds.[60]

Experience that is completely 'fused' or unified in its automatic recruitment of cognitive, emotional and motor aspects of being, and which is experienced at the *highest* phenomenological level as an integrated phenomenon, with thoughts about the uselessness of carrying on living, feelings of deep sadness and gestures of despair, is already coherently constituted (and 'ready to go') at this low level in the tree of consciousness. It is not as if moving the electrode caused incoherent experience, such as the motor restrictions of Parkinson's disease, with the cognitions of mania and the affect of depression, parts without relationship that would need to await the highest levels of cortical function for integration. Experiential wholes, that are completely coherent across all realms, and affect us at the most conscious as well as unconscious levels, are already present well below consciousness.

LEVEL THREE

To recap. More than one will (and *a fortiori* more than one set of goals or values) does not mean more than one consciousness: so with one consciousness we can have more than one will, expressive of more than one aim. In Chapters 2 to 4, I suggested that the two hemispheres, as two vast coherent neurological systems, each capable of sustaining consciousness on their own, do have different concerns, goals and values, and that these are therefore likely to be expressed in different wills; and in this chapter I have put forward evidence suggesting that a conflict of wills may be exactly what we find. In Chapter 5, I showed that on a range of both philosophical and neuropsychological grounds the right hemisphere has primacy, and that, though the left hemisphere has a valuable role, its products need to be returned to the realm of the right hemisphere and once more integrated into a new whole, greater than the sum of its parts. Earlier in this chapter I showed that on the first, millisecond-to-millisecond, level, the most obvious fact about the relationship between the hemispheres is that it depends on separation and mutual inhibition, which is coherent with the view of the relationship between the phenomenological worlds of the two hemispheres, according to which each must, for different reasons, remain ignorant of the other. At the second level, that of their more global interaction over longer time periods that form the basis of conscious experience, the evidence is that the relationship is not symmetrical or reciprocal, with the advantage being taken by the left hemisphere.

There is therefore a conflict of asymmetries.

Ontological asymmetry

In favour of the right hemisphere there is what might be called *ontological asymmetry* (the primacy of the right hemisphere's interaction with whatever exists). The right hemisphere is the primary mediator of experience, from which the conceptualised, re-presented world of the left hemisphere derives, and on which it depends. Because, as Blake says, 'Reason is the bound or outward circumference of Energy' (energy being something like Scheler's *Drang*), which, as he puts it, 'is the only Life, and comes from the Body', the left hemisphere does not itself have life, such life as it appears to have coming from reconnecting with the body, emotion and experience through the right hemisphere. It is this primacy of the (right-hemisphere-mediated) interaction with the lived world beyond ourselves over our (left-hemisphere-mediated) re-presentation of it that lies behind Goethe's inversion of the Johannine pronouncement: 'In the beginning was the word [*logos*].' In the mouth of Faust it becomes: '*Im Anfang war die Tat!*' ('In the beginning was the deed').[61]

Asymmetry of function

Also in favour of the right hemisphere is an *asymmetry of function*, which follows from the first asymmetry. In the functioning together of the two hemispheres, the products of the left hemisphere *need* to be returned to the realm of the right hemisphere in order to live. While experience is enriched by the opposite process, whereby the products of the right hemisphere are sent to the left hemisphere for 'unpacking', there is no necessity for that process. One process is literally vital: the other is not.

These two asymmetries indicate where the interhemispheric balance of power ought to lie, and indeed needs to lie: with the right hemisphere. But it does not. There are three other asymmetries which mean that in fact the balance of power is doomed to be dangerously skewed towards the lesser hemisphere, the left. These are an 'asymmetry of means', 'asymmetry of structure' and 'asymmetry of interaction'.

Asymmetry of means
The left hemisphere point of view inevitably dominates, because it is most acces-sible: closest to the self-aware, self-inspecting intellect. Conscious experience is at the focus of our attention, usually therefore dominated by the left hemisphere. It benefits from an *asymmetry of means*. The means of argument – the three Ls, language, logic and linearity – are all ultimately under left-hemisphere control, so that the cards are heavily stacked in favour of our conscious discourse enforcing the world view re-presented in the hemisphere which speaks, the left hemisphere, rather than the world that is present to the right hemisphere. Its point of view is always easily defensible, because analytic; the difficulty lies with those who are aware that this does not exhaust the possibilities, and have nonetheless to use analytic methods to transcend analysis. It is also most easily expressible, because of language's lying in the left hemisphere: it has a voice. But the laws of non-contradiction, and of the excluded middle, which have to rule in the left hemi-sphere because of the way it construes the nature of the world, do not hold sway in the right hemisphere, which construes the world as inherently giving rise to what the left hemisphere calls paradox and ambiguity. This is much like the problem of the analytic versus holistic understanding of what a metaphor is: to one hemisphere a perhaps beautiful, but ultimately irrelevant, lie; to the other the only path to truth.

But even that fact, significant as it is, does not convey the true scale of the distinction, which concerns not just the functional differences at a moment in time, but what happens over much longer periods in the ordinary human brain. The left hemisphere builds systems, where the right does not. It therefore allows elaboration of its own workings over time into systematic thought which gives it permanence and solidity, and I believe these have even become instantiated in the external world around us, inevitably giving it a massive advantage (see Chapter 12). There is something very suggestive about the fact that the predomi-nance of the left hemisphere may result from there being – possibly there having been engineered? – a *deficit* in the right hemisphere.

Let's look first at the way in which the two hemispheres try to know, to get a grasp on the world. Using the familiar information-processing terminology, the left hemisphere favours analytic, sequential 'processing', where the right hemi-sphere favours parallel 'processing' of different streams of 'information' simulta-neously. This is what I have expressed as the left hemisphere's way of building up a picture slowly but surely, piece by piece, brick on brick. One thing is established as (apparently) certain; that forms a platform for adding the next little bit of (apparent) certainty. And so on. The right hemisphere meanwhile tries to take in all the various aspects of what it approaches at once. No part in itself precedes any other: it is more like the way a picture comes into focus – there is an 'aha!' moment when the whole suddenly breaks free and comes to life before us. For it, though, knowledge comes through a relationship, a betweenness, a back and forth rever-berative process between itself and the Other, and is therefore never finished, never certain.

There is a huge disadvantage for the right hemisphere here. If this knowledge has to be conveyed to someone else, it is in fact essential to be able to offer (apparent) certainties: to be able to repeat the process for the other person, build it up from the bits. That kind of knowledge can be handed on, because it is not 'my' knowledge. It is knowledge (*Wissenschaft*), not knowledge (*Erkenntnis*). By contrast, passing on what the right hemisphere knows requires the other party already to have an understanding of it, which can be awakened in them; if they have no such knowledge, they will be easily seduced into thinking that the left hemisphere's kind of knowledge is a substitute.

Sequential analytic 'processing' also makes the left hemisphere the hemisphere *par excellence* of sequential discourse, and that gives it the most extraordinary advantage in being heard. It is like being the Berlusconi of the brain, a political heavyweight who has control of the media. Speech is possible from the right hemisphere, but it is usually very limited. We have seen that thought probably originates in the right hemisphere, but the left hemisphere has most syntax and most of the lexicon, which makes it very much the controller of the 'word' in general. Coupled with its preference for classification, analysis and sequential thinking, this makes it very powerful in constructing an argument. By contrast it is hard for the right hemisphere to be heard at all: what it knows is too complex, hasn't the advantage of having been carved up into pieces that can be neatly strung together, and it hasn't got a voice anyway.

Asymmetry of structure

And then there is an *asymmetry of structure*. There is an asymmetry inherent in this system building, namely the difficulty of escape from a self-enclosed system. The system itself closes off any possible escape mechanisms. The existence of a system of thought dependent on language automatically devalues whatever cannot be expressed in language; the process of reasoning discounts whatever cannot be reached by reasoning. In everyday life we may be willing to accept the existence of a reality beyond language or rationality, but we do so because our mind as a whole can intuit that aspects of our experience lie beyond either of these closed systems. But *in its own terms* there is no way that language can break out of the world language creates – except by allowing language to go beyond itself in poetry; just as *in its own terms* rationality cannot break out of rationality, to an awareness of the necessity of something else, something other than itself, to underwrite its existence – except by following Gödel's logic to its conclusion. Language *in itself* (to this extent the post-modern position is correct) can only refer to itself, and reason can only elaborate, 'unpack' the premises it starts with. But there can be no evidence within reason that yields the premises from which reason must begin, or that validates the process of reasoning itself – those premises, and the leap of faith in favour of reason, have to come from behind and beyond, from intuition or experience.[62]

Once the system is set up it operates like a hall of mirrors in which we are reflexively imprisoned. Leaps of faith from now on are strictly out of bounds. Yet it is only whatever can 'leap' beyond the world of language and reason that can break out of the imprisoning hall of mirrors and reconnect us with the lived world. And the evidence is that this unwillingness to allow escape is not just a passive process, an 'involuntary' feature of the system, but one that appears willed by the left hemisphere. The history of the last 100 years particularly, as I shall attempt to convey in Part II, contains many examples of the left hemisphere's intemperate attacks on nature, art, religion and the body, the main routes to something beyond its power. In other words its behaviour looks suspiciously tyrannical – the Master's emissary become a tyrant.

The left hemisphere, with its rational system-building, makes possible the will to action; it believes it is the one that makes things happen, even makes things live. But nothing in us, actively or positively, make things live – all we can do is permit, or not permit, life, which already exists. It may still seem difficult to understand how a set of relations that are predicated, as I would agree with Scheler (and for that matter with Heidegger) that they are, on *negation* – the power to say 'no' or not say 'no' – can prove to have life and be creative. It seems obvious to the left hemisphere, which is all that we have to 'think' (reason) with, and which remains ignorant of what the right hemisphere knows, that creation must be the result of something positive it does. It *makes* things, as it *makes* things happen, and it thinks it gives life to them. In this it is like a cat pushing a dead mouse about the floor in order to see it move. But we do not have the power to make things live: like the cat, we can only either permit life, or not permit it.

This idea is not as strange, however – or as unusual in the history of philosophy – as it may seem. The act of creation may be one of invention, not in the modern sense of the word, but in its older sense: one of discovery, of finding something that was there, but required liberation into being. The word invention used to mean discovery (Latin *invenire*, to find), and it is only since the seventeenth century that the word has come to take on the grandiose sense of something we make, rather than something we uncover. *Un*-covering, or '*dis*-covering', has built into the very word the act of negation, of saying 'no' to something that conceals. It was Spinoza who first made the point that *omnis determinatio est negatio* – 'all determination [in the sense of the bringing into sharper focus of anything] is negation'. And Hegel, who is here, as so often, in the forefront of modern philosophy, emphasised the creative importance of negation. But the idea is familiar to mainstream science. The Popperian criteria for truth incorporate the notion that we can never prove something to be true; all we can do is prove that the alternatives are *untrue*.

The feeling we have of experience happening – that even if we stop doing anything and just sit and stare, time is still passing, our bodies are changing, our senses are picking up sights and sounds, smells and tactile sensations, and so on – is an expression of the fact that life comes to us. Whatever it is out there that exists apart from us comes into contact with us as the water falls on a particular landscape. The water falls and the landscape resists. One can see a river as restlessly searching out its path across the landscape, but in fact no activity is taking place in the sense that there is no will involved. One can see the landscape as blocking the path of the water so that it has to turn another way, but again the water just falls in the way that water has to, and the landscape resists its path, in the way it has to. The result of the amorphous water and the form of the landscape is a river.

The river is not only passing across the landscape, but entering into it and changing it too, as the landscape has 'changed' and yet not changed the water. The landscape cannot make the river. It does not try to put a river together. It does not even say 'yes' to the river. It merely says 'no' to the water – or does not say 'no' to the water, and, by its not saying 'no' to the water, wherever it is that it does so, it allows the river to come into being. The river does not exist before the encounter. Only water exists before the encounter, and the river actually comes into being in the process of encountering the landscape, with its power to say 'no' or not say 'no'. Similarly there is 'whatever it is that exists apart from ourselves', but 'whatever it is that exists' only comes to be what it is as it finds out in the encounter with ourselves what it is, and we only find out and make ourselves what we are in our encounter with 'whatever it is that exists'.

A problem of time emerges. There is in all descriptions, that are, after all, *re-presentations*, the problem that they begin with something known. They then build on what is known with something else that is known. These could be words or mental images (like photographs, what the French call *clichés* – fixed, frag-mented, two-dimensional). Thus it is that we have the illusion of something being brought into being by being put together. All language is inevitably like this: it substitutes for the experienced ambiguity and uncertainty of the original encounter with something in the process of coming into being, a sequence of apparently fixed, certain pieces of *information*. Information is by definition something fixed, a bunch of facts as we put it. But all the conscious mind can do when it has a bunch of pieces is put the pieces together to try to make something. However, this is no more a way of actually re-enabling the experience itself than living beings are made by stitching together the limbs. Thus the apparent sequence of things causing one another in time is an artefact of the left-hemisphere way of viewing the world. In creation we are not actively putting together something we already know, but finding something which is coming into being through our knowing, at the same time that our knowing depends on its coming into being; as Pushkin says of *Evgeny Onegin*, in the middle of the work itself, that he did not know where it was going, it was an unfinished path, a journey, an exploration, of whatever it was that was coming into being between himself and the imaginative world.

Asymmetry of interaction

Finally there is an *asymmetry of interaction*. It seems to me that the overall way in which the hemispheres relate has critically shifted from a form of what might be called stable dynamic equilibrium to an inequilibrium. When there are two neces-sary but mutually opposed entities in operation together, an imbalance in favour of one can, and often will, be corrected by a shift in favour of the other – a swing of the pendulum. But negative feedback can become positive feedback, and in the left hemisphere there is an inbuilt tendency for it to do so.[63] To return to the image of the pendulum, it would be as if a violent swing of the pendulum shifted the whole clock, which then over-balanced. I believe that we have entered a phase of cultural history in which negative feedback between the products of action of the two hemispheres has given way to positive feedback in favour of the left hemisphere. Despite the primacy of the right hemisphere, it is the left hemisphere that has all the cards and, from this standpoint, looks set to win the game. That is the subject of Part II.

What light does Heidegger cast on the interaction of the hemispheres? According to Heidegger, what were anciently seen as the Apollonian, more rationalistic, and Dionysian, more intuitive, aspects of our being have become grossly unbalanced. Nietzsche claimed that the constant opposition between these two very different tendencies led to a fruitful incitement to further and ever higher levels of life and creativity (which accords with the evidence of the relationship between the two hemispheres at its best). War, as Heraclitus said, is the father of all things. But the war between these tendencies has become, according to Heidegger, no longer creative but merely destructive. We have become 'pre-eminently endowed with the ability to grasp and delimit': the Apollonian has triumphed at the expense of the Dionysian. We are caught up, he believed, in a frenzy of 'forming projects, enclosures, frameworks, division and structuring', destroying ourselves and our environment and turning all into 'resource', something to be merely exploited, Nature turned into 'one gigantic filling station', as he once graphically put it.[64] This is the opposite of the problem the Greeks confronted, for whom the balance lay more towards the Dionysian, and who therefore strove, and needed to strive, towards the Apollonian.

However, from within Heidegger's own philosophy there emerge grounds to suppose that the situation is not beyond remedy. He quoted with approval Hölderlin's lines: *Wo aber Gefahr ist, wächst / Das Rettende auch* ('Where there is danger, that which will save us also grows'). How I understand this in relation to the brain is this.

At the first level, it tells us something about the constant, relatively stable, interrelation of the hemispheres at their best. In a way it is Nietzsche's point about the fruitful relation of the Apollonian and Dionysian. Within the realm of the left hemisphere ('where there is danger') there is also the possibility of an 'unfolding' of what is implicit, which, if returned to the right hemisphere, will lead to something greater and better coming forward ('that which will save us'). This sounds very abstract, but I think it can be made clearer by an example. If we subject a work of art, say, or even the human body, to detached, analytic attention, we lose the sense of the thing itself, and its being in all its wholeness and otherness recedes. But the result of such attention, *provided it is then relinquished*, so that we stand in a state of openness and receptivity before the thing once again, may be a deeper and richer 'presencing'. The work of the left hemisphere done, the thing 'returns' to the right hemisphere positively enriched. The best criticism of works of art produces just this result, and the study of medicine at its best achieves it, too, in relation to the human body. Again it is the analogy of the necessary analysis carried out by the pianist in learning a piece, an analysis that must be forgotten during performance. The 'danger' inherent in the process is the potential arrogance of the left hemisphere, which may not allow the return: it may come to think of itself as all in all.

The left hemisphere can play a vital, irreplaceable role if only it can be restored to its rightful place, and allow itself to be readopted by the right hemisphere. The left hemisphere is a crucial part of the creative process – the unfolding of potential. Becoming is potential, and for Being to emerge from Becoming, it needs to be 'collapsed' into the present, as the wave function 'collapses' under observation, and Schrödinger's cat becomes either dead or alive – the terms on which we exist. But it needs nonetheless to hand its work back to the right hemisphere. It is only out of the unity of division and unity that a new unity comes: so unity melds with its opposite and yet becomes more itself. (It is not, *per contra*, true that out of the unity of division and unity a new *division* comes, nor is it true that out of the *division* of unity and division a new division comes: by remaining divided nothing new comes at all.)

At the second level, it has something to say about the particular danger of the modern world view, in which the hemispheres are, I believe, out of kilter. A state of fallenness, which Heidegger called *Verfallen*, is according to him an inevitable part of existence. But there is a sense in which, as Heidegger believed, this has its positive too, since the very existence of *Verfallen* prompts *Dasein* to awareness of the loss of its authentic self, and to strive harder towards what is authentic. This process is inevitably one of cycles or alternations of direction. The sense of longing and striving for something beyond, which otherwise we could not achieve, is an idea I will return to in Part II, where I will consider the influence of the divided brain on Western culture. In the unfolding story I tell, the left hemisphere comes to be more and more powerful: at the same time problems grow.

CODA: SLEEPWALKING INTO THE ABYSS

Right from his twenties until his death, in the year 1832, at the age of eighty-two, Goethe was obsessed with the legend of Faustus, and worked on what was to become his ultimate epic masterpiece, the long dramatic poem *Faust*, all his life. The legend of Faustus, the learned doctor who, frustrated by the bounds of his knowledge and power, makes a pact with the devil to increase them without limit while he lives, the price of which is his immortal soul, lies deep in the German psyche, and versions of the story go back to the Middle Ages. The myth is clearly a warning against *hubris*. In Goethe's version of the story, Faust is an essentially good man, who has already done much for others through his skills as a physician, before his lust for power and knowledge lead him to do many destructive things. Yet, although Faust comes in the end to realise that there are indeed limits to what humanity can understand or achieve, he is brought back, through his own pain and remorse, to an awareness of the good his knowledge can bring to others: his ultimate moment of happiness, the purpose of his bargain with Mephistopheles, comes through his realisation of what he can do for humanity, not for himself. At the end of the work, God, not the devil, takes his soul; in doing so he acknowledges the truly great value of Faust's endless striving. In this version of the myth, it seems to me, the right hemisphere's desire for understanding something further and beyond and the left hemisphere's means for helping achieve that end – the Master and his emissary working in concert – are seen as ultimately redeemed and redeeming.[65] More explicitly Goethe wrote in midlife a poem, *Der Zauberlehrling* (The Sorcerer's Apprentice), the story of which is familiar to most people from Disney's *Fantasia*, but in which the returning sorcerer – to whom Goethe refers as *der alte Meister*, the old master – is not angry with the foolish apprentice who thought he could do on his own what his master did, but merely bids him understand that he, the Master, alone can conjure spirits safely. If the left hemisphere is hot-headed and rivalrous, the right hemisphere is not: it has an accurate appreciation of what its companion can offer.

But in either story – that of Faust or of the apprentice – there is a saving awareness that things have gone badly wrong. In the story I am to tell, the left hemisphere acts like a sorcerer's apprentice that is blithely unaware that he is about to drown, a Faust that has no insight into his errors and the destruction they have brought about.

Let us remind ourselves of the neurological literature for a moment. Although the left hemisphere does not see and cannot understand what the right hemisphere understands, it is expert at pretending that it does, at finding quite plausible, but bogus, explanations for the evidence that does not fit its version of events. It will be remembered from the experiments of Deglin and Kinsbourne that the left hemisphere would rather believe authority, 'what it says on this piece of paper', than the evidence of its own senses. And remember how it is willing to deny a paralysed limb, even when it is confronted with indisputable evidence? Ramachandran puts the problem with his customary vividness:

> In the most extreme cases, a patient will not only deny that the arm (or leg) is paralysed, but assert that the arm lying in the bed next to him, his own paralysed arm, doesn't belong to him! *There's an unbridled willingness to accept absurd ideas.*

But when the damage is to the left hemisphere (and the sufferer is therefore depending on the right hemisphere), with paralysis on the body's right side,

> they almost never experience denial. Why not? They are as disabled and frustrated as people with right hemisphere damage, and presumably there is as much 'need' for psychological defence, but in fact they are not only aware of the paralysis, but constantly talk about it . . . It is the vehemence of the denial – not a mere indifference to paralysis – that cries out for an explanation.[66]

Again Nietzsche had the measure of it: '"I have done that", says my [veridical episodic right-hemisphere] memory. "I cannot have done that"—says my pride [theory-driven, denial-prone left-hemisphere], and remains adamant. At last—memory yields.'[67]

The left hemisphere is not keen on taking responsibility. If the defect might reflect on the self, it does not like to accept it. But if something or someone else can be made to take responsibility – if it is a 'victim' of someone else's wrongdoing, in other words – it is prepared to do so. Ramachandran carried out an experiment in which a patient with denial of a left arm paralysis received an injection of harmless salt water that she was told would 'paralyse' her (in reality already paralysed) left arm. Once her left hemisphere had someone else to blame for it, it was prepared to accept the existence of the paralysis.[68]

Ramachandran again: 'The left hemisphere is a conformist, largely indifferent to discrepancies, whereas the right hemisphere is the opposite: highly sensitive to perturbation.'[69] Denial, a tendency to conformism, a willingness to disregard the evidence, a habit of ducking responsibility, a blindness to mere experience in the face of the overwhelming evidence of theory: these might sound ominously familiar to observers of contemporary Western life.

A sort of stuffing of the ears with sealing wax appears to be part of the normal left-hemisphere mode. It does not want to hear what it takes to be the siren songs of the right hemisphere, recalling it to what has every right – indeed, a greater right, as I have argued – to be called reality. It is as though, blindly, the left hemisphere pushes on, always along the same track. Evidence of failure does not mean that we are going in the wrong direction, only that we have not gone far enough in the direction we are already headed.

The left hemisphere as a sleepwalker

The popular assumption, aided by the reflections of some respectable neuroscientists, is that the *right* hemisphere might be something like a zombie, or a sleepwalker. It seems to be supposed naïvely that the defining quality of the zombie, that quintessentially uncanny phenomenon, is the lack of the verbalising and rationalising intelligence exemplified by the left hemisphere.

In Chapter 10 I will deal with the phenomenon of the uncanny, of the zombie and its like, phenomena that started to figure in literature, oddly but significantly enough, in the Enlightenment. I will suggest that the uncanny looks extraordinarily like certain aspects of the world according to the *left* hemisphere, in which vitality is absent, and the human is forced to approximate to the mechanical. Zombies have much in common with Frankenstein's monster, after all. They perform like computer simulations of the human. There is no life in their eyes. And Giovanni Stanghellini has explored with subtlety, in his book *Disembodied Spirits and Deanimated Bodies*, the way in which the 'zombie' state is mimicked by schizophrenia, a largely right-hemisphere-*deficit* condition.[70]

So-called 'zombie' states are characterised by dissociation, in which the conscious mind appears cut off from the body and from feeling. That in itself suggests a relative hypofunction of the right hemisphere. Dissociation is, furthermore, the fragmentation of what should be experienced as a whole – the mental separation of components of experience that would ordinarily be processed together, again suggesting a right-hemisphere problem. Core features of dissociation include amnesia for autobiographical information, identity disturbances, depersonalisation and derealisation (lack of the sense of the reality of the phenomenal world, which appears to be a two-dimensional projection). On first principles one would therefore expect this to be a right-hemisphere-deficit condition. And subjects with right-hemisphere damage do in fact report exactly this – a change in, and a foreignness of, the self, which is disconnected from the world, a loss of feeling of belonging in the world. At times they report having become insensible automata, puppets, or mere spectators, devoid of feelings and cut off from the surrounding world (one even reported that her head has been turned into a cone, but with the front part missing; other patients reported feeling themselves to be just a casing, or cover, their 'I' having been separated from them, located outside the body, somewhere nearby and to the left). Subjects almost invariably speak of 'going to another space or place'.[71]

Given all this, it would be extraordinary if dissociation in 'normal' subjects did not involve a disconnection from the right hemisphere, and an interhemispheric imbalance in favour of the left. And this is just what the empirical evidence shows.[72] In fact in dissociation, the hemispheres are more than usually disengaged, with an effective 'functional commissurotomy', or disruption of functioning in the corpus callosum.[73] Activation of the left hemisphere in subjects especially prone to dissociation results in faster than usual inhibition of the right hemisphere, whereas those not prone to dissociation exhibit a balanced interhemispheric inhibition, corroborating the idea that dissociation involves a functional superiority of the left hemisphere over the right hemisphere.[74]

The ultimately dissociative state is hypnosis. Despite popular prejudice that hypnosis is likely to involve the 'release' of the right hemisphere, it has none of the features that one would expect if it really were a state of right-hemisphere predominance. And indeed many imaging studies have now confirmed that there appears to be a predominance of left-sided activation during hypnosis.[75] Being asked to imagine that a brightly coloured picture is black and white, and being hypnotised, so that we really come to believe that the picture *is* black and white, involve different brain states; and the difference is that, in the hypnotic state, there is abnormally increased activation in the left hemisphere.[76] In hypnosis the right hemisphere is *not* activated, even during a typically 'right-hemisphere' task, using overall EEG power as the criterion.[77] In a neuroimaging study exploring the neural correlates of hypnosis, activity decreases in the precuneus, posterior cingulate and right inferior parietal lobule,[78] which is coherent, since as we saw earlier, in Chapter 2, these areas are known to be associated with the sense of individual agency.[79] Furthermore, hypnosis produces an enhancement in *focal* concentration, together with a relative suspension of peripheral awareness, a mode of attention typical of the left hemisphere. It is, according to one source, 'analogous to macular vision: intense and detailed, but restricted', a perfect description of the left hemisphere field of vision.[80] And in keeping with the left-hemisphere hypothesis, more hypnotisable subjects display higher levels of dopaminergic activity (dopamine transmission is more extensive in the left hemisphere).[81]

So if I am right, that the story of the Western world is one of increasing left-hemisphere domination, we would not expect insight to be the key note. Instead we would expect a sort of insouciant optimism, the sleepwalker whistling a happy tune as he ambles towards the abyss.

I now want to turn to the influence of the divided brain on Western culture.

PART TWO

HOW THE BRAIN HAS SHAPED
OUR WORLD

CHAPTER 7

IMITATION AND THE EVOLUTION
OF CULTURE

KNOWING WHAT WE DO ABOUT THE NATURE OF THE DIFFERENT WORLDS EACH
hemisphere brings about, and understanding their relationship, we can, I
believe, begin to see a pattern in the course of Western history. I believe there has
been a succession of shifts of balance between the hemispheres over the last 2,000
years, and the second part of this book will explore this point of view, with the
particular aim of understanding what is happening in the contemporary world.

The history of the West shows times when a move forward in one hemisphere
'releases' a move forward in the other, according to Nietzsche's assertion that
'these two very different drives [the Apollonian and Dionysian] exist side by side,
mostly in open conflict, stimulating and provoking one another to give birth to
ever-new, more vigorous offspring, in whom they perpetuate the conflict inherent
in the opposition between them.'[1] But we have now reached a point where, for
reasons I have suggested, the balance has swung too far – perhaps irretrievably
far – towards the Apollonian left hemisphere, which now appears to believe that
it can do anything, make anything, on its own. Like the emissary in the fable, it
has grown tired of its subservience to the Master, and as a result the survival of the
domain they share is, in my view, in the balance.

In this second part of the book I shall consider what the principal shifts in
Western culture reveal about themselves, specifically within the frame of this
metaphor. I will begin with the rise of the written word, the use of currency, the
origin of drama and some facets of the new kind of civilisation that erupted in
sixth century BC Athens, but will concentrate attention on the regeneration of
Western civilisation in the Renaissance, the upheavals of the Reformation, the rise
of the Enlightenment, the transition to Romanticism, and the emergence of
modernism and post-modernism. All I can hope to do in these chapters is to point
to a few characteristics that have relevance for the topic of this book. It goes
without saying that to deal, in what is no more than a series of inevitably short
chapters, with topics so vast that each would now be considered too great for a
whole lifetime of research, is inevitably to be hugely selective; and there will be
those who think I should not have been so foolhardy as to attempt it at all. To
them, I can only say that I am wholly conscious of the pitfalls, but still feel that,
unless we are quite sure that there could never be an overall pattern to be

discerned, we are obliged, in full knowledge of the temerity of the undertaking, to make the attempt.

I do not propose to deal in any detail with non-Western culture. Partly this is a function of my ignorance; partly the scope of such a book would threaten to be unmanageable. I also wonder if the same cataclysmic changes in the intellectual climate are really to be found outside of the West: I will have some reflections to make towards the end of the book on hemisphere balance in Far Eastern cultures which suggests that the two hemispheres enjoy there a better symbiosis than they do in the West.

But there may have been important shifts in other cultures, possibly coincident, in some cases, with those in the West: Karl Jaspers certainly thought there was a crucial shift in the way we see the world that occurred not only in the West, but in China, and India, at the same time that it occurred in Ancient Greece, between about 800 and 200 BC. He called this a pivotal period, or *Achsenzeit* (sometimes translated 'axial age'), in world history, and in his *The Origin and Goal of History* identified common characteristics between some of the greatest thinkers of the period, including Plato, Buddha and Confucius.[2] This was also the period of Heraclitus, Lao Tzu, the Upanishads, and the Hebrew prophets. Similarly, some of the developments in the West have parallels elsewhere: with regard to the Reformation, one could point to other times and places in which the visual image was proscribed, and where there was a text-based, black-and-white, intolerant fundamentalism, at odds with any richer understanding of myth and metaphor: such tendencies form an important part of the history of some other religions, including Islam.

But there is nothing like the extraordinary divarication of culture that seems to have characterised the history of the West – no equivalent of the Enlightenment, with its insistence on just one, rectilinear, way of conceiving the world, and (because there was no need for it) no Romanticism that aimed to redress it. As Max Weber demonstrated in his histories of Chinese and Indian culture, and of Judaism, it was only in the West that unchecked, acquisitive rationalism in science, capitalism and bureaucracy took hold.[3] 'It is sometimes asked why the Scientific Revolution occurred in the West in the modern era and not, say, in China, or mediaeval Islam, or mediaeval Paris or Oxford,' notes Stephen Gaukroger, at the outset of his magisterial exploration of the rise of science, and of the reasons why, in the West, there has been a 'gradual assimilation of all cognitive values to scientific ones.'[4] He continues,

But it is the Scientific Revolution that requires explanation, not these developments ... [In those other cultures where there have been major scientific advances] science is just one of a number of activities in the culture, and attention devoted to it changes in the same way attention devoted to the other features may change, with the result that there is competition for intellectual resources within an overall balance of interests in the culture. ... [In the West] the traditional balance of interests is replaced by a dominance of scientific concerns, while science itself experiences a rate of growth that is pathological by the standards of earlier cultures, but is ultimately legitimated by the cognitive standing that it takes on. This form of scientific development is exceptional and anomalous.[5]

WHY HAVE THE SHIFTS OF BALANCE OCCURRED?

Some people may reasonably doubt that any such shifts have occurred. At any one period of human history there will, it goes without saying, be many different factors at play, and many, sometimes conflicting, points of view will have been expressed. Individuals, as befits individuals, will fail to conform to an overall pattern. It is in the nature of generalisation that there will be many exceptions, and experts will always disagree with any generalisation, as experts should. Fine-grained analysis is the expert's prerogative. However, the more fine-grained the expert analysis, the more difficult it may be to see an overall pattern: it cannot be other than the view from close up. This will inevitably lead some to the conclusion that no pattern exists, but I believe this to be a mistake. One has to stand back in order to see patterns at all; there is a 'necessary distance' for such pattern recognition to work.

If I am right that there have been shifts in hemisphere balance, why have they come about? To the historian, a multitude of social and economic factors will inevitably be involved in the process whereby many events unfolded which led to such cataclysmic movements in the history of ideas, and I have no doubt that, as always, chance also played an important role. However, such social and economic factors inevitably exist in an inextricably involved dynamic relationship with changes in the way we look at the world, and are indeed simply part of another way of describing the process. Each aspect that we choose to bring into focus makes a different aspect stand forth out of a nexus in which no one element can be said to have caused all the others, since what look like 'elements' are simply facets of the indivisible human condition. If one holds one set of factors steady – say, the economic – then one appears to have accounted for everything in those terms. But hold another set steady – whether social, institutional, intellectual, or of any other kind – and the picture may look equally convincing. The fact is that nothing can in reality be 'held steady' in this way: all is in a constant state of dynamic interaction. And one of the factors in this interaction, I suggest, has been the need to resolve the inherently unstable relationship between the worlds delivered by the two hemispheres.

One does not need to posit drives that are instantiated in the hemispheres. Up to now, the discussion has been of the cerebral hemispheres strictly within the context of the single human individual. In that context, I may sometimes have spoken almost as if they were personalities, with values and goals of their own. As I have argued, that is not as big a distortion as might first appear: they are substantial parts of a living being, which certainly does have values and goals. However, we are now turning to look at the 'battle of the hemispheres', as one might call it, over long periods of history, often, though not invariably, longer than the lifetime of any one brain. It may seem that I am suggesting that there is some cosmic struggle going on behind the scenes here, with the left and right hemispheres slugging it out on a grand scale. Metaphorically speaking that is true. Whether it is more literally the case that there are conflicting forces of a metaphysical nature driving the ways of being in the world represented by the cerebral hemispheres is obviously not a question I can answer, and it does not need to be answered in this book.

Many philosophers and all theologians over the ages have thought that there were forces that acted in and through our minds and bodies, not just individually, but over expanses of time. More recently Freud spoke of the drives (*Triebe*) behind human behaviour, *eros* and *thanatos*, the life and death 'instincts'. Jung too believed there were attractive and propulsive forces that worked over long periods of human history. Nietzsche called the Apollonian and Dionysian tendencies 'drives' (*Triebe*). Scheler spoke of *Drang* and *Geist*. Such forces are conceived as operating through natural processes – invisible, but made visible over the long, long run in their effects, in this case on the human brain, mind and culture, just as the invisible wind is made visible in its effects over millennia on the rock. Are there wills to be seen at work in the hemispheres? One might equally ask, is the gene really selfish? It's a legitimate question. Richard Dawkins' epithet is no idle turn of phrase. It was chosen to do some hard work, conveying a picture of the cosmos, one might even say a philosophical standpoint; while at the same time being comfortably metaphorical, and therefore easy to disown. Officially the gene has nothing to do with any forces that might be driving evolution, a 'neutral' process onto which we tend to project our own moral values. The cerebral hemispheres, being intimately related to the occasioning of mental phenomena, are in a different position from the gene in this respect, but the same question may be asked. To ask questions about the existence of such drives is, I believe, perfectly legitimate, but they simply seek explanation at a different level. Whatever the answer, the picture would look the same.

I am not committed to the view that the brain is the driver of culture, any more than I am to the view that culture is the driver of brain development. They will inevitably mould each other. But one of the constraints on how we see the world has to be the balancing of the options given to us by the two cerebral hemispheres. These constitute relatively stable differences over the length of human history. Cultural shifts can *exploit* such options: but hemisphere differences would still *constrain* the options available to the human mind.

Such shifts as occur in this story need to be accounted for by processes that work in the world as we commonly understand it, and I will outline my thoughts about the means by which such shifts occur shortly. But, however they may occur, one is still left with the question, *why* they occur.

Shifts in culture are hugely important, not just matters of intellectual fashion: it's not simply a question of 'last season the collar was narrow, this season it'll be broad'. Without imputing drives to the hemispheres, one can see that each hemispheric world is complemented by the other, and in a situation where one predominates, the lack of the other will become increasingly apparent. As I hope to demonstrate in the next chapter, it seems that the two hemispheres became more independent of one another's operations at an early point in the history of the West. Greater independence allows each hemisphere to go further in its own direction, with a relative enhancement, or exaggeration, depending on the point of view, of its intrinsic mode of operation. This situation has its dramatic rewards, but is also more unstable than one in which there is less polarisation, and invites divergence from, and subsequent regression towards, the mean position, rather than an enduring equipoise. That divergence is a contributory factor, therefore, to the shifts of balance.

More specifically we know that there is a continual tendency for the authenticity of right hemisphere 'presencing' to be transformed into an inauthentic 're-presenting' in the left; in essence, what was living becomes a cliché. The experience of the inauthenticity of the right hemisphere's world *as it is represented in the left* may then, logically, lead in one of two directions, and I believe we can see them both exemplified in the history that we will be looking at in this part of the book.

In the first, we remain within the realm of homeostasis, of negative feedback, of 'swings of the pendulum'. There is a natural reaction, resulting in a return to the authenticity of the right-hemisphere world itself. This, however, in turn is doomed soon to be co-opted by the left hemisphere and become inauthentic again.

In the second, however, there is not a return to the right-hemisphere world, but on the contrary a rejection of it, since it now comes to be seen as *intrinsically* – rather than *contingently* having become – inauthentic, and therefore as invalid. Instead of a corrective swing of the pendulum, therefore, there is a loss of homeostasis, and the result is positive feedback, whereby the left hemisphere's values simply become further entrenched. This also helps to explain why the left hemisphere necessarily gains ground over time.

Today all the available sources of intuitive life – cultural tradition, the natural world, the body, religion and art – have been so conceptualised, devitalised and 'deconstructed' (ironised) by the world of words, mechanistic systems and theories constituted by the left hemisphere that their power to help us see beyond the hermetic world that it has set up has been largely drained from them. I have referred to the fact that a number of influential figures in the history of ideas, among them Nietzsche, Freud and Heidegger, have noted a gradual encroachment over time of rationality on the natural territory of intuition or instinct. In terms of the evolutionary history of the brain, Panksepp has expressed similar ideas:

> The level of integration between brain areas may be changing as a function of cerebral evolution. One reasonable way for corticocognitive evolution to proceed is via the *active inhibition* of more instinctual subcortical impulses. It is possible that evolution might actually promote the disconnection of certain brain functions from others. For instance, along certain paths of cerebral evolution, perhaps in emerging branches of the human species, there may be an increasing disconnection of cognitive from emotional processes. This may be the path of autism, in its various forms.[6]

It has not been a smooth and even process, however: more like a tug of war in which the players move back and forth, but ground is continually lost by one side. And I agree with them that ultimately the balance has gone further and further towards what we can now see to be the world of the left hemisphere – despite everything we know from Part I suggesting that what it knows must be reintegrated with the broader understanding of the right.

HOW HAVE THE SHIFTS OF BALANCE OCCURRED?

First, I need to make it clear that, despite my pointing in the first few chapters to structural and functional asymmetries that we know took millennia to arise (and even began to arise in other species), I am not suggesting that the major shifts in the history of ideas involved fluctuations in the *structure* of the brain over the tiny time scales of recent history. It is conceivable that, were it possible to scan the brain of pre-Achaean humans – say, in the eighth century BC – one might find some small, but possibly measurable, differences in the structure, or more probably in the functioning, of the brain, compared with the brains of those who lived 1,000 years earlier, or with the modern human brain. But such changes could take place only over very long time scales. As to what is actually happening in the brain when the more recent 'swings', those of the last five hundred years or so, take place, nothing is visible (at least nothing on a scale that we could actually measure). Is there anything going on at the brain level at all?

I think the answer is 'yes'. Our experience of the world helps to mould our brains, and our brains help to mould our experience of the world. Patterns of brain function, if not changes in visible structure, are likely to be involved. But by what processes?

Classical natural selection, which depends on the very slow process of random mutation, with environmental selective pressures then acting over generations to favour certain mutations above others, requires long periods of time. It is just about conceivable that this operated in the ancient Greek situation, since this arose on the back of the incursion of a new population into the central Mediterranean at this time, with a different gene pool. In that sense this change is quite different from those that came afterwards in modern Europe. And the specific migrational factors which apply to ancient Greece do not apply to other contemporary, or earlier civilisations, which may help to account for the very considerable differences between Greek and, say, Egyptian or Mesopotamian cultures (and, still more, of course, Eastern cultures). Genetic shifts might also explain the extraordinary decline which followed the overrunning of the Roman Empire by Goths, Huns and Franks in the fourth and fifth centuries AD, since, however much one may admire aspects of life in what used to be called the Dark Ages, effectively whole ways of thinking and being, whole aspects of the phenomenological world, simply *disappeared* in the West for nearly a thousand years.

But the later evolution of ideas, from the Renaissance on, is simply not susceptible to this kind of argument, because the time periods are far too short, and there aren't any major migrations of population that I'm aware of that might change the European gene pool sufficiently.

There are other aspects to transmission which do not depend on Darwinian natural selection alone. There is, for example, the Baldwinian effect, which acts as an accelerator on the process. This refers to the way in which we do not mate at random, but selectively promote a certain gene or genes by choosing a mate who has also got the characteristics for which the gene or genes encode (an articulate man is more likely to marry an articulate woman). Similarly we alter the environment so that it favours the genes we carry (the articulate develop a society in which articulacy is at a premium, with the result that the inarticulate are – in theory at least – at a reproductive disadvantage compared with the articulate). I can't believe this can be having much of an effect: it's still too slow, and mostly it's not true to the facts of human history to suggest that the characteristics we are talking about in this book made much difference to gene reproduction.

Despite this, there *are* thought to be mechanisms whereby brain capacities and cognitive abilities acquired during a single human lifetime could be transmitted to the next generation. These are known as epigenetic mechanisms, because they do not depend on alterations in the actual sequence of nucleotides in the DNA within the genes, but on factors which influence what is expressed by that same DNA.

Consider this. On the face of it, it's odd that the gene sequence in every cell in the body is the same – a kidney cell, though structurally and functionally different from a muscle cell, is exactly the same in respect of its DNA – and yet each kind of cell gives rise only to its own kind of tissue. This is because only parts of the gene sequence in each case get to be expressed. Similarly, processes such as DNA methylation, alteration of the histone molecules in chromatin (which forms the 'core' round which the double helix spirals), mitochondrial transmission and X-chromosome inactivation modulate expression of parts of the genome, and form possible mechanisms for learnt behaviours to be transmitted. This is because use of certain cell functions by the organism during its lifetime actually alters the structure of that cell, leading to what has been called 'cell memory'. (This is a bit like the way in which the structure of a neuronal connection in the brain changes with use, so as to promote preferential use of the same connection in future, part of a process of 'solidification' of mind by brain which underwrites the phenomenon of memory.) Cultural developments can be transmitted through genetic mechanisms. Just as the structure and functioning of the brain has influenced the evolution of culture, the evolution of culture has had its influence on the brain:

> The relationship resembles one of reciprocating interaction, in which culture is generated and shaped by biological imperatives while the course of genetic evolution shifts in response to cultural innovations . . . [epigenetic rules may] predispose mental development to take certain specific directions in the presence of certain kinds of cultural information.[7]

So certain ways of thinking will shape the individual nervous system, structurally as well as functionally. The presence or absence of stimulation affects the number of synaptic contacts, strengthening some and eliminating others.

(Incidentally, the process of development through stimulation is one of *reduction* and *pruning*; it seems that, even at the level of individual neurones, things are brought into being or not by the system either saying 'no', or not saying 'no'.) The efficiency, rather than just the number, of synaptic connections is altered by adult learning, and this may concern global units (in other words co-operative sets of nerve cells).[8] Such changes throughout the nervous system of an individual could then be epigenetically transmitted to the next generation, culture and the brain shaping one another over relatively short time spans.

Further and beyond any of this, surely ideas do spread by contagion, and no doubt in one sense in competition with one another, concepts solemnised in Dawkins's 'memes', the cultural equivalent of genes. A meme is said to be a repli-cator of cultural information that one mind transmits (verbally or by demonstra-tion) to another mind, examples being 'tunes, ideas, catch-phrases, clothes fashions, ways of making pots or of building arches'[9] and other concepts, ideas, theories, opinions, beliefs, practices, habits, dances and moods, ultimately, and inevitably, including the idea of God – the Dawkins delusion. This is a perfect example, incidentally, of the left hemisphere's way of construing its own history, not least in its way of breaking a culture into atomistic fragments devoid of context, as though snippets of behaviour, feeling or thinking – of experience, in other words – stuck together in large enough numbers, constitute the world in which we live.

Memes are seen mechanistically as 'replicators', like genes engineering perfect *copies* of themselves. In the case of gene replication, variation enters in only by accident, by random mutation caused by errors in transcription, or by interfer-ence with gene structure from environmental sources, such as radiation. The machinery makes a mistake or is handed shoddy materials, but, as long as it remains in this story, it remains a machine. The equivalent for a meme would be my misremembering a tune, or mishearing it in the first place. But 'memes' if they existed would be replicating, unlike genes, within a mind: a mind whose constant interaction with what ever comes to it leaves nothing unchanged or unconnected with something else. We are imitators, not copying machines.

Human imitation is not slavish. It is not a mechanical process, dead, perfect, finished, but one that introduces variety and uniqueness to the 'copy', which above all remains alive, since it becomes instantiated in the context of a different, unique human individual. Imitation is imaginatively entering into the world of the one that is imitated, as anyone who has tried the exercise of imitating an author's style will know. That is perhaps what we mean by style: not a *fashion*, just something superficial, taken up or put off, as it sounds, like a garment, but an essence – *le style, c'est l'homme*. Even to attend to anything so closely that one can capture its essence is not to copy slavishly. To Ruskin it was one of the hardest, as well as one of the greatest human achievements, truly to see, so as to copy and capture the life of, a single leaf – something the greatest artists had managed only once or twice in a life time: 'If you can paint *one* leaf, you can paint the world.'[10] Imitating nature may be like imitating another person's style; one enters into the life. Equally that life enters into the imitator. In imitation one takes up something of another person, but not in an inert, lifeless, mechanical sense; rather in the sense of its being *aufgehoben*, whereby it is taken into ourselves and transformed. If one needs to be convinced that there is no necessary opposition between imagination and imitation, one need only look at the long, rich history of Oriental culture. In fact imitation is imagination's most powerful path into whatever is Other than ourselves.

Imitation is a human characteristic, and is arguably the ultimately most important human skill, a critical development in the evolution of the human brain.[11] It is surely how we came to learn music, and though Chomsky may have distracted our attention from this, it is how we learnt, and learn, language. Only humans, apart from birds, are thought normally to imitate sounds directly,[12] and only humans can truly imitate another's course of action.[13] Other species may adopt the same goal as another individual member of their species, and may succeed in finding their own way to achieve it, but only humans directly imitate the means as well as the end.[14] This may sound like a rather backward step, but it isn't. The enormous strength of the human capacity for mimesis is that our brains let us escape from the confines of our own experience and enter directly into the experience of another being: this is the way in which, through human consciousness, we bridge the gap, share in what another feels and does, in what it is like to be that person. This comes about through our ability to transform what we perceive into something we directly experience.

It is founded on empathy and grounded in the body. In fact imitation is a marker of empathy: more empathic people mimic the facial expressions of those they are with more than others. In an important study of this phenomenon, there was a contrast between the empathy people *said* they felt and the empathy they actually evinced, involuntarily, in their faces and bodies. Individuals who were already established as low in empathy didn't display the same emotion in their faces as high-empathy subjects, but reported in words feeling the same – the feelings their conscious left hemispheres *knew* that they *ought* to feel.[15] As might be expected, there is significantly increased right-sided activity in the limbic system specifically during imitation, compared with mere observation, of emotional facial expressions.[16]

There is even some evidence that we identify projectively with people with whom we share a common purpose – when we are co-operating in a task, for example – to such a degree that we seem to merge identity with them. In ingeniously designed experiments where two participants are sitting next to one another, sharing a combined task, but with functionally independent roles, the two individuals appear spontaneously to function as one agent with a unified action plan.[17] Children eagerly imitate other human beings, but do not imitate mechanical devices that are carrying out the same actions.[18] This is like the finding in adults that we make spontaneous movements signifying our involvement in events we are watching evolve – so long as we believe them to be the result of another's action. Such movements are, however, absent when we believe that (in other respects identical) results have been generated by a computer rather than a living being.[19]

Imitation is non-instrumental. It is intrinsically pleasurable, and babies and small children indulge in it for its own sake.[20] The process is fundamental and hard-wired, and babies as little as forty-five minutes old can imitate facial gestures.[21] It is how we get to know what we know, but also how we become who we are.

> The wonder of mimesis lies in the copy drawing on the character and power of the original, to the point whereby the representation may even assume that character and that power. In an older language, this is 'sympathetic magic'; and I believe it is as necessary to the very process of *knowing* as it is to the constitution and subsequent naturalisation of *identities* . . .[22]

So writes Michael Taussig, in *Mimesis and Alterity*, and he quotes Walter Benjamin:

> Nature creates similarities. One need only think of mimicry. The highest capacity for producing similarities, however, is man's. His gift of seeing resemblances is nothing other than a rudiment of the powerful compulsion in former times to become and behave like something else. Perhaps there is none of his higher functions in which his mimetic faculty does not play a decisive role.[23]

Imitation gives rise, paradoxically as it may seem, to individuality. That is precisely because the process is not mechanical reproduction, but an imaginative inhabiting of the other, which is always different because of its intersubjective betweenness. The process of mimesis is one of intention, aspiration, attraction and empathy, drawing heavily on the right hemisphere, whereas copying is the following of disembodied procedures and algorithms, and is left-hemisphere-based. The distinction is similar to that sometimes claimed between metaphor on the one hand and simile on the other: simile has no interiority. Thus writing of the difference between the earliest humans and *homo sapiens*, Steven Mithen writes: 'We might characterise Early Humans as having a capacity for simile – they could be "like" an animal – but not for metaphor – they could not "become" an animal.'[24] What he is getting at here is empathic identification.

The distinction is explored with subtlety by Thomas Mann, in his commemoration lecture 'Freud and the Future' of 1936, where he speaks thus of imitation in the world of classical antiquity:

> Alexander walked in the footsteps of Miltiades, and in the case of Caesar his ancient biographers were rightly or wrongly convinced that he intended to imitate Alexander. This 'imitation', however, is much more than is conveyed by the word today. It is a mythical identification, a procedure which was specially familiar to the ancient world but has retained its efficacy right into modern times and, spiritually speaking, is open to anyone at any time. Attention has often been drawn to the archaic traits in the figure assumed by Napoleon. He regretted that the modern consciousness did not allow him to give himself out as the son of Jupiter-Ammon, as Alexander had done. But we need not doubt that he

confounded himself mythically with Alexander at the time of his expedition to the East, and later when he had decided on an empire in the West, he declared, 'I *am* Charlemagne'. Be it noted that he did not say, ' I recall Charlemagne', nor 'My position is like Charlemagne's', nor even, 'I am as Charlemagne', but simply 'I *am* he'. This is the mythical formula.[25]

I am reminded here of Bruno Snell, also speaking of the ancient world: 'The warrior and the lion are activated by one and the same force . . . a man who walks "like a lion" betrays an actual kinship with the beast.' Homeric metaphors are 'not only symbols, but the particular embodiments of universal vital forces'. They assign 'a role very similar to that of the beasts also to the natural elements. We have already met with the storm, the wave, the rock . . . above all they are regarded as the conductors of fundamental forces such as are alive also in man.'[26]

Snell's mention of a man who walks like a lion betraying a kinship with the beast is not just poetical, but has a practical meaning. Trackers, in cultures dependent on hunting, learn to 'get inside' the animal they are tracking, to reflect it as much as possible in their own being, what it must have been feeling and thinking as it left its track: this is how they succeed in finding it.[27] Perhaps, when we empathise, we actually *become* the object of our empathy, and share its life; in some sense that goes beyond what language can convey – because it can only convey (unless through poetry) combinations of concepts that reflect our partic-ular world picture here and now. Perhaps we can even do this with natural forms that we now call inanimate, as Wordsworth found that the 'huge and mighty Forms' of mountains

> . . . that do not live
> Like living men mov'd slowly through my mind
> By day and were the trouble of my dreams.[28]

Thus in Japanese thought, 'human beings and every natural thing are one body in total' and there is a 'feeling of love for natural things just as if the natural things were the people themselves'.[29]

We already know from the discovery of the existence of mirror neurones that when we imitate something that we can see, it is as if we are experiencing it. But it goes further than this. Mental representation, in the absence of direct visual or other stimulus – in other words, imagining – brings into play some of the same neurones that are involved in direct perception.[30] It is clear from this that, even when we so much as imagine doing something, never mind actually imitate it, it is, at some level which is far from negligible, as if we are actually doing it ourselves. Imagining something, watching someone else do something, and doing it ourselves share important neural foundations.

Imagination, then, is not a neutral projection of images on a screen. We need to be careful of our imagination, since what we imagine is in a sense what we are and who we become. The word *imago* is related to *imitari*, which means to form after a model, pattern or original. There is ample evidence, some of which I cited earlier, that imitation is extremely infectious: thinking about something, or even just hearing words connected with it, alters the way we behave and how we perform on tasks.[31] This was understood by Pascal, who realized that the path to virtue was imitation of the virtuous, engagement in virtuous habits – the foundation of all monastic traditions.

Let's go back to the question of how humans acquired music and language, since it helps us to understand the revolutionary power of imitation. Music and language are skills, and skills are not like physical attributes – bigger wings, longer legs: not only can they be imitated, which obviously physical characteristics on the whole can't, but in the case of music and language they are reciprocal skills, of no use to individuals on their own, though of more than a little use to a group. An account of the development of skills such as language purely by the competitive force of classical natural selection has to contend not only with the fact that the skills could easily be mimicked by those not genetically related, thus seriously eroding the selective power in favour of the gene, but also with the fact that unless they *were* mimicked they wouldn't be much use. Imitation would itself have a selective advantage: it would enable those who were skilled imitators to strengthen the bonds that tied them to others within the group, and make social groups stable and enduring. Those groups that were most cohesive would survive best, and the whole group's genes would do better, or not, depending on the acquisition of shared skills that promote bonding – such as music, or ultimately language. Those individuals less able to imitate would be less well bound into the group, and would not prosper to the same degree.

The other big selective factor in acquiring skills and fitting in with the group would be flexibility, which comes with expansion of the frontal lobes – particularly the right frontal lobe, which is also the seat of social intelligence. Skills are intuitive, 'inhabited' ways of being and behaving, not analytically structured, rule-based techniques. So it may be that we were selected – not for specific abilities, with specific genes for each, such as the 'language gene(s)' or the 'music gene(s)' – not even 'group selected' for such genes – but individually for the dual skills of flexibility and the power to mimic, which are what is required to develop skills in general.

THE 'IMITATION GENE'

Let us suppose that there were both a gene for imitation and a gene that favoured a particular skill. Let's take an example of the acquisition by human beings at some time in their history of some skill or other – say, swimming. (I know learning to swim was never really like this, but try to put that out of your mind for now.) Suppose there were a gene for swimming, and that being able to swim was for some reason hugely advantageous: those who couldn't swim were going to be left far behind. If swimming turned out to be completely inimitable – either you have the gene for it and can do it, or you can't do it at all – soon there would be only those with the gene for swimming. Outcome: after a number of generations, everyone would be swimming, all with the gene.

Suppose, by complete contrast, swimming turned out to be so easy to imitate that every individual that saw it could learn to swim. The gene for swimming would have no force whatever, and would be in no way subject to selective pressure, and might even die out. Outcome: just the same, but much sooner, everyone would be swimming, by imitation – a quicker mechanism – but mostly without the gene; though a few might, irrelevantly, have the gene that enabled swimming anyway.

Suppose, however, which is more likely than either of these extreme positions, swimming were *partially* imitable, but only partially. There would be some selective pressure in favour of those who had the gene for swimming, and gradually more people would have the gene, and therefore would swim: equally some people would imitate it, and would also swim, though lacking the gene. But because the behaviour was only partially imitable, you would be able to imitate it only if you were a very good imitator. So there would also be a strong selective pressure in favour of those who were very good imitators – those with the gene for imitation – who wouldn't necessarily have the gene for swimming, but would nonetheless be able to swim. Outcome: soon everyone would be swimming, some with the gene for swimming, some with the gene for imitation, and a few with both.

But now suppose that another partially imitable behaviour came along, which had a similar, or even greater, competitive advantage – say, flying. Those with the gene for imitation would have a head start: they would be not only able to swim, but able to fly (and take on the next development, say 'dive'), and would be streets ahead of those who didn't, who would have to have both the genes for flying and for swimming if they were to survive.

Several things follow from this:

- The process that favours the gene for imitation gets started only if the crucial behaviour is partially imitable: if it is either wholly imitable (in which case the gene is irrelevant) or wholly inimitable (in which case the gene is ineffective), it won't get started.
- The behaviours in question have to exert sufficient selective pressure, that is, be sufficiently important to survival. The process will work faster if the behaviours to be imitated exert greater selective pressure.
- The second explosion of learning (in the example, flying) will happen faster than the first (swimming), because it will rely mainly on imitation, and imitation is a faster process than gene transmission. And there will be a tendency for increasing reliance on imitation rather than gene transmission to speed up the process still further when the development of further new skills inevitably comes along.

Now, suppose that for swimming we read 'music', and for flying we read 'language'. Wouldn't it reach a stage where everyone had the gene for imitation, and imitation was all that now mattered, not genetic mechanisms that favoured particular behaviours? I don't think so, because it would always be easier to pick something up if you happened to have the genetic (or epigenetic) mechanisms that made that sort of behaviour more likely. But imitation would always work faster, so that in the end what we chose to imitate would govern which epigenetic mechanisms got selected (e.g. a culture in which we learnt to think and speak of ourselves in more computer-like ways would lead to selection for the 'geek' brain), rather than the genes that got selected dictating what we imitated.

The achievement of imitation – the meta-skill that enables all other skills – may explain the otherwise incomprehensibly rapid expansion of the brain in early hominids, since there would be a sudden take-off in the speed with which we could adapt and change ourselves, and in the range of our abilities. Imitation is how we acquire skills – any skill at all; and the gene for skill acquisition (imitation) would trump the genes for any individual skills. Thus from a gene – the symbol of ruthless competition (the 'selfish gene'), and of the relatively atomistic and oppositional values of the left hemisphere – could arise a skill that would enable further evolution to occur not only more rapidly but in a direction of our own choosing – through empathy and co-operation, the values of the right hemisphere. Genes could free us from genes. The great human invention, made possible by imitation, is that we can choose who we become, in a process that can move surprisingly quickly. As I put it above, we escape the 'cheerless gloom of necessity'. This could also explain the apparent paradox for classical genetics, that communicative skills such as music and language would have to be acquired by individualistic competition, although the skills themselves would be of no use unless the whole group acquired them together. Perhaps we are not the ruthless competitors we have been conditioned to believe ourselves to be by mechanistic models of behaviour. Perhaps, even, the world is not a mechanism.

The overwhelming importance of mimesis points to the conclusion that we had better select good models to imitate, because as a species, not only as individuals, we will become what we imitate. We will pass down the behaviours we have learnt to imitate by epigenetic mechanisms, and for this reason William James, in an inversion of the popular prejudice, saw the human species as having a larger array of apparently instinctual behaviours than any other.[32]

In the mechanical system of cause and effect, causes antedate their effects and, so to speak, push from behind. The logical extension of such systems is closure, in that ultimately what happens is determined by prior events: we go where we are pushed. Human choices appear to be open, but the existence of free will remains hard to argue for, though some have made sophisticated cases based on an understanding of the realms of theoretical physics in which cause and effect cede to probabilities and uncertainties. I am not able to evaluate these properly. Viewed from the phenomenological point of view, however, we feel ourselves to be free, though being pulled, drawn, attracted forward towards and by things that have a sort of magnetic power (such as archetypes), rather than pushed or prodded forward by what's happened. It may be that this is what Nietzsche had in mind when he wrote:

'Action at a distance' cannot be eliminated: *something draws something else closer, something feels drawn*. This is the fundamental fact: compared to this, the mechanistic notion of pressing and pushing is merely a hypothesis based on *sight* and *touch*, even if it does serve as a regulative hypothesis for the world of sight![33]

These important attractors are perhaps best expressed as values, though the word 'values' sounds rather lame to me in the context. Perhaps 'ideals' would be more like it, but this word, too, has its problems and has been discredited in our age. These ideals or values stand outside time, unlike cause and effect. They are less minutely determining than prior causes, in that there is some choice of which attractors one resists, and which one approaches. Speaking in this way does not, I know, obviate questions of cause, which come back in some such guise as 'What caused this person to be attracted to this ideal or set of values?' These are like the questions about predestination and divine grace that have vexed theology since St Augustine.[34]

By values I do not mean the principles by which one might resolve a moral conflict – say, whether to make a purely consequentialist calculus or observe Kantian deontological principles (the view that particular duties are primary, or even absolute, and do not depend on the value of outcomes). What is up for debate there is not the value – say, that of preserving life – but the particular course of action in a dilemma which can best be reconciled with that value. What I mean are the *values themselves* that are at stake: whether, for example, courage or self-sacrifice have value in themselves, irrespective of the outcome, or of any deontological principle. Such values would, however, be excluded from the calculus of an instrumental morality. Values in this sense need to go 'beyond good or evil'. Scheler not only distinguished realms of value, but arranged them hierarchically, from the realm of those that can be appreciated only at the sense level, or in terms of utility, at the bottom, to the realm of the holy at the top.[35] One may or may not be inclined to accept Scheler's particular schema of values, but what is relevant about them to the division of the hemispheres is that the left hemisphere recognises only this lowest rank of value. Other values, which Scheler ranked higher than utility, such as bravery, beauty, intelligence, holiness, require an approach that is not tied exclusively to that tool of utility, sequential analytic logic (which is not the same necessarily as saying that they involve emotion). They have to be apprehended in a different way, which is made possible by the right hemisphere's openness to what is not ultimately justifiable only in logical terms.

In the left-hemisphere world there is, however, a way of accommodating such values: by simply returning them all to the only value it knows, that of utility. Beauty, for example, is a way of ensuring that we select healthy reproductive partners; bravery acts to defend territory in the interests of the gene pool; intelligence leads to power to manipulate the environment, and one's fellow creatures; holiness is an invention designed to promote cohesion of the group; and so on – the arguments will be only too familiar. Those who are not relying solely on their left hemisphere's construal of the world will detect the fraud instantly. It is not that arguments *cannot* be constructed along these lines, although often they need to be remarkably ingenious to 'save the phenomena' – for example, of all the myriad sources of beauty in the world, sexual partners can only form a small part, and even there beauty is not the same as sexual attractiveness. It is just that they fail to convince: back to values – which ultimately lie beyond argument. Rationality is, naturally, reluctant to accept the very possibility of a thing lying beyond rationalistic argument, since the left hemisphere cannot accept the existence of anything that lies outside itself. As always, it is the right hemisphere that is drawn to whatever is Other, what lies beyond.

That being the case, these attractors I speak of will appeal to the right hemisphere. But the weakness of the right hemisphere is the flip side of its strength, that it is embodied, or embedded, in the world. It grounds the natural viewpoint of the self-unreflecting being in the world: it therefore cannot sufficiently, on its own, disengage itself from 'the natural viewpoint'. The 'too, too solid flesh' of everydayness hangs about it. It therefore all too easily lapses: it is constrained by everyday reality, and its viability *depends* on not being unnaturally ruptured from the lived world. The trouble is that the more 'natural' its view seems to it, the less it is really allowing the extraordinary, awe-inspiring fact of the being of anything at all to be present for us. Thus it risks, in its own way, lapsing into the inauthenticity of Heidegger's *Verfallen*.[36] In this state it is the left hemisphere that enables the wilful taking up of an 'unnatural' view. By doing this we are enabled to ascend from the gravity of the earth, on the vertical axis represented by the left hemisphere, and see from a different standpoint. We are able to escape, temporarily, the pull of the earth and see things afresh. In Heidegger's terms, *Dasein* becomes aware of its inauthenticity and strives towards its more authentic self. The swing towards the left hemisphere, therefore, is occasioned by the awareness of inauthenticity. And ultimately it will be the sense of inauthenticity in the world according to the *left* hemisphere which will cause the return of the pendulum, the right hemisphere struggling towards something the power of which it senses from beyond the everyday. Each hemisphere risks inauthenticity from a different source, which is why each is vital to the other. The right hemisphere is at risk from the familiarity entailed in its very *engagement* with the world, as the world 'presences'; the left hemisphere from the familiarity of cliché – *disengaged re-presentation*. Each cultural shift can be seen as a response to the eventual inauthenticity of the world according to one or other of the hemispheres, but for the right hemisphere the route back has to be through engagement with an attractive power beyond itself.

If there is anything in the idea that mimesis itself emerges from classical genetic mechanisms, but then comes to overtake them, or, at any rate, pull alongside of them, can we see a hemisphere shift of a kind here, too – the values of the right hemisphere emerging, almost seamlessly, from those of the left? In the atomistic sense in which an individual is understood by the left hemisphere, development takes place through a line of individuals competing with other lines of individuals via their genes – the survival of the fittest. From this point of view, the group is a potential threat to individuality, tolerated by an amalgam of wary aliens, who concede co-operation within it only for the personal benefit that it yields. From the right hemisphere point of view, whereby an individual's individuality can be understood only within a context (the group), what would look to the left hemisphere like the individual's identity being *lost* in the group becomes merely its being taken up (*aufgehoben*) within the group wherein it belongs. Out of wary opposition arises empathy: out of the world of 'eat or be eaten' comes a shared meal round the fire. A linear striving, my gene against yours, turns into a reverberative process of collaboration, out of which, as in the Prisoner's Dilemma, we all do better – because the 'battle' of the hemispheres is only a battle from the left hemisphere's point of view. From the more inclusive standpoint of the right hemisphere, it is simply another reverberative process, in which something comes into being – as all life does – through the union of separated forces, retaining their separation but within that union, one entity acting with another. If, as Heraclitus said, war is the king and father of all things, peace is the queen and mother.

Not only that, but we progress faster, and in the direction of our choosing. At one level, evolution is really just the survival or otherwise of genes – not even their 'striving', or 'competition', because that suggests intent. Yet Dawkins dubbed the process 'selfish': even the best scientists, it seems, cannot help anthropomorphising. But the characterisation was right, since, if we anthropomorphise genes, much as I have anthropomorphised the hemispheres, they do operate in a selfish or ruthless fashion. Through this process we are 'pushed from behind', and have no say over where we go. Nonetheless, by an *Aufhebung* devoutly to be wished, from all of that emerges a process, that of skill acquisition through mimesis, in which our eyes are opened, in which collaboration plays a part, and where there is a degree of freedom, in that we can choose what we imitate.

The cultural shifts in hemisphere balance that I identify should not, then, I repeat, be thought of as structural shifts in the brain, certainly not at the macro level (we know there are both structural and functional brain changes caused even by individual experience at the microscopic level). They will be functional shifts, which will have been initiated by imitation of beliefs and practices, ways of seeing the world and ways of being in the world which favour one or other of the hemispheres. These might then be given further permanence by epigenetic mechanisms replicating in the next generation the brain changes that go with such habits of mind and brain, and therefore help to encourage and entrench them.

We have, then, become free to choose our own values, our ideals. Not necessarily wisely, of course. This process could be commandeered by the left hemisphere again if it could only persuade us to *imitate* and acquire left-hemisphere ways of being in the world. That is what I believe has happened in recent Western history. In our contemporary world, skills have been downgraded and subverted into algorithms: we are busy imitating machines.

CHAPTER 8

THE ANCIENT WORLD

IN HIS BOOK *FACES: THE CHANGING LOOK OF HUMANKIND*, MILTON BRENER HAS
presented a detailed study of the way in which the portrayal of the human face
evolved in antiquity.[1] Noting that 90 per cent of emotional communication is non-
verbal, and that most of this is expressed through the face (described by Georg
Lichtenberg as 'the most entertaining surface on earth'),[2] he begins by reflecting
that there are virtually no faces in prehistoric art. Its subjects are mainly animals;
where there are humans, there is often only a pelvis, buttocks and breasts, and
almost all figurines are headless; where there is a head, though there may be hair,
there is no face. When faces first begin to appear they are expressionless,
schematic and non-individualised. He makes a case that the earliest drawings, in
their lack of spatial orientation or relationship between parts, repetition of stereotypic abstract patterns, and description of what we know rather than what we see
(for example, the so-called 'X-ray' portrayal of the human being, showing the
bones inside the body) show suggestive points of comparison with the productions of neuropsychiatric patients relying on the left hemisphere alone.[3]
Additionally Brener refers to evidence that subjects with dyslexia and prosopagnosia (inability to recognise individuals by face), both of whom have problems of
right-hemisphere functioning, exhibit a preference for the 'primitive' facial
pattern, found in early art, of inexpressive schematic features.[4]

The importance of the right hemisphere in 'processing' faces and apprehending
facial expressions, in feeling and expressing emotions, including and especially
through the face, in feeling empathy and in appreciating individuality, has been
referred to above (Chapter 2), as has the basis in the right hemisphere for the
capacity for aesthetic enjoyment. The relatively sudden change that came over the
portrayal of the human face in the period beginning in the sixth century BC, and
particularly from the fourth century, in Greece, in which the more abstracted,
stereotypic and inexpressive gaze of Egyptian and early Greek representations of
the face and head gives way to portraiture which is more individualised, varied,
emotionally expressive and empathic, is attributed by Brener to a rapid advancement in functioning of the right hemisphere in Greece at around the same period.
Other evidence for this, according to Brener, would be evolution of a body of
highly expressive poetry rich in metaphor, the evolution of the idea of the

individual as having legitimate claims to be balanced with those of the community at large, and a sense of empathy with others in general, as well as an interest in the natural world – to which I would add a sense of humour based on ironic appreciation of the pathos of man's position in the world as a 'being towards death'.

In support of his thesis, Brener cites the work of Hans-Joachim Hufschmidt, a German scholar who has studied the direction of gaze in 50,000 portrayals of the human face over time.[5] This work, published in 1980, yields a remarkable finding. It seems that early two-dimensional representations tend to show the face either looking straight ahead or looking towards the viewer's right. However, during the period between the sixth century BC and the Hellenistic period, there is a clear shift of orientation, so that the majority of portraits come to face in the opposite direction, towards the viewer's left.

In 1973, Chris McManus and Nick Humphrey had already published in *Nature* the results of a study of approximately 1,400 Western portrait paintings from the sixteenth to twentieth centuries, showing that there is a tendency during this period, also, for the sitter to be portrayed looking to the viewer's left.[6] These findings have since been confirmed by others.[7] The implication appears to be that the focus of interest comes to lie in the viewer's left visual field (preferentially subserved by the right hemisphere), at the same time that the more emotionally expressive left hemiface of the subject (controlled by the subject's right hemisphere) is exposed to view.

The strength of Hufschmidt's research, apart from the enormous scale of his undertaking, is his inclusion of the ancient world. This reveals a distinct shift towards favouring the right hemisphere in the appreciation of representations of the human face from the sixth century BC onwards. According to Brener and Hufschmidt, the tendency was lost again in the Dark Ages, but re-emerged at the Renaissance. Other research has confirmed that the left-facing tendency was strongest in the fifteenth century, and has gradually waned until the twentieth century, when it reverted to the pattern of equal right and left profiles seen before the rise of Greek civilisation.[8] This finding is of considerable interest in view of the thesis of this book, especially in relation to what I see as the rightward shift in the brain that occurred at the time of the Renaissance and the leftward shift that is evidenced in modernism.

The 'natural' tendency, as exhibited by the majority of face profiles drawn by children, is still to face left, even in some cases if they are copying a model that is facing to the right.[9] Self-portraits tend to exhibit the opposite bias, towards the right, which is presumably because painters tend to orientate themselves in front of the mirror so that their image appears in their left visual field, which involves turning the face to the right so that the left side of the face is exposed – appearing in the mirror image as the right side of the face.[10] A study of a long series of self-portraits by the famous German painter Lovis Corinth before and after the right-hemisphere stroke he experienced in 1911, shows that, following the stroke, he reversed both facial orientation and the direction of the light source in his paintings.[11] (In most Western painting since the Renaissance, just as there is a tendency for the face to be turned to the left, there is a tendency for the light source to come from the left side.)[12]

Brener's thesis is original and deserves to be better known: it is one of the very few attempts I am aware of to relate movements in the history of ideas to cerebral lateralisation. While I accept the importance of the sudden standing forth at this time of a wide range of right-hemisphere functions, particularly as exemplified in the visual arts, my own take on this state of affairs is different from Brener's.

Greek civilisation brought many things that we would have to, at one level, associate with a sudden efflorescence of the *left* hemisphere, at least as much as the right: the beginnings of analytic philosophy, the codification of laws, the formalisation of systematic bodies of knowledge. These require the ability to stand back from and detach ourselves from the crowd, from nature and from ourselves, that we may objectify. This is in my view also the basis for the *forging of bridges with others*, and with nature, which classically and according to much of the neuropsychological literature, is mediated by the right hemisphere. To return to a somewhat Hegelian theme of an earlier chapter, union cannot exist without separation and distinction, but separation and distinction are of no use unless they form the prelude to a later, greater, union or synthesis.

I would therefore say that what happened was this. Initially there was a symmetrical, bihemispheric advance at this time – an advance in the functioning of the frontal lobes of both hemispheres. It is the frontal lobes that bring distance (in space) and delay (in time): they enable us to stand back from our world, and from ourselves. But this development, permitting as it does a far greater capacity to speculate, to consider the lessons of the past and to project possible worlds into the future, to build projects and schemes for the better governing of the state and for the increase of knowledge of the world at large, requires the ability to record: to make externalised, therefore more permanent, traces of the mind's workings, to fix, to freeze the constantly passing flow of life on the wing. It requires, therefore, a huge expansion of the realm of the written word, as well as the development of diagrams, formulas and maps; records of observations of nature; and records of the history of people and states. From what has been outlined in connection with re-presentation in the earlier parts of this book, it will be seen that this necessitates reliance on the left hemisphere, not the right. Such standing back is the essence of analytic philosophy, which is a left-hemisphere function – at least philosophy in the West since Plato and up to the time of Kant. The Greeks began this process of standing back; and the beginnings of analytical philosophy, of theorising about the political state, of the development of maps, of the observation of the stars and of the 'objective' natural world, all may be mediated by the left hemisphere; though the urge to do so at all comes from the right.

This 'necessary distance', brought about through the frontal lobes, by the very same token, makes it possible to see oneself as a self like other selves; to stand back and observe the human face objectively, so that it can be portrayed, as Brener shows, in such beautiful detail. It acts as midwife to the expansion of the right-hemisphere functions that Brener points to. The origins of the concept of the individual as distinct from, as well as bonded to, the community arise too at this time, initially through the ability to achieve distance.[13] This standing back enables us to see so much more of whatever is – it unfolds, makes explicit, our understanding; but once this has happened it expands the capacity of the right hemisphere to reintegrate this understanding implicitly. And from this come all the right-hemisphere advances that I agree with Brener characterise this period of Greek history: the rise of certain aspects of the 'self'; empathy with others; imaginative, metaphoric language and art; humour and irony; the discrimination of individual faces, emotional expression, and so on.

In summary, therefore, whereas Brener would see overall a straightforward opposition of the two hemispheres, with a perhaps hard-to-explain advance in right-hemisphere functions at the expense of the left occurring at this time, I would see a rise in bilateral frontal lobe function initially, which both necessitates an advance of the left hemisphere to underwrite the 'distance' involved and, through the creation of necessary distance, enables the right hemisphere to expand its capacity. I do not deny the evidence of right-hemisphere advance, simply relate it differently to the roles of the left hemisphere and frontal lobes.

It might be asked, since my formulation involves *both* hemispheres making advances, why it is necessary to invoke hemisphere differences at all. Why not, after all, drop the whole hemisphere issue and just return to the common-sense view that there was a general advance in knowledge, or imagination, or creativity, in some undifferentiated sense at this time? My response is that this completely fails to engage with the main feature of this advance, namely that it involves moves in two diametrically opposed directions at once – towards greater abstraction from the world and, simultaneously, towards greater empathic engagement with the world. In other words the *differences* between what the hemispheres now 'do' or deliver, as attested by all the data referred to and discussed in the earlier parts of this book, get to be greatly accentuated at this time. A new, undoubtedly fruitful, tension arises from this accentuation of the divergence between the two worlds delivered by the hemispheres. And, since the data that we have on hemisphere difference are derived almost exclusively from Westerners over the last hundred years or so, we do not know whether the same differences to the same degree have always existed or exist elsewhere in the world. All we can say is that they must have arisen at some point in the history of Western man at least; and, since the first place that we see evidence of cultural activity expressive of a relatively independently functioning left hemisphere, and of a relatively independently functioning right hemisphere, is in Greece during this period, it may be that what we are witnessing is a (relative) disconnection or sundering of the hemispheres, and the origins of hemisphere specialisation as we now know it.

This leads me to a consideration of the thesis of Julian Jaynes's remarkable classic, *The Origin of Consciousness in the Breakdown of the Bicameral Mind*.[14] This book, now more than 30 years old, caused a stir when first published and has remained in debate ever since. Jaynes, who was a psychologist at Princeton with an interest in the ancient world, put forward a thesis that consciousness, in the sense of introspective self-awareness, first arose in Homeric Greece. He posits that, when the heroes of the *Iliad* (and the Old Testament) are reported as having heard the voices of the gods (or God) giving them commands or advice, this is not a figurative expression: they literally heard voices. The voices were speaking their own intuitive thoughts, and arose from their own minds, but were perceived as external, because at this time man was becoming newly aware of his own (hitherto unconscious) intuitive thought processes. These intuitive thought processes Jaynes identifies with the workings of the right hemisphere. He compares the phenomenon with the auditory hallucinations experienced in schizophrenia, in which there is some evidence that the speech that 'surfaces' as a hallucination may be arising from the right hemisphere. His contention, which it will be apparent is almost contrary to my own, is that, at this time, there was a breakdown of the previously 'bicameral' mind, a mind with two distinct chambers, or hemispheres, and that it was the relatively sudden, disconcerting access of the left hemisphere to the workings of the right hemisphere that resulted in the phenomena described.

There is much to admire about this imaginative and in some ways eccentric book, but it remains a fact that, while Jaynes's hypothesis continues to be as widely read as ever, it has not been taken up or expanded by psychologists. Perhaps this was inevitable with a hypothesis of such breadth and originality, lying so much outside the mainstream of psychological research. But I think there is at least one other important reason. In keeping with a view more fashionable at the time he was writing, and based on a psychoanalytic interpretation of schizophrenia as a regressive state of unfettered emotionalism, lack of self-awareness and relative disinhibition, he sees schizophrenia as a return to a more ancient, perhaps 'primitive', form of mental functioning, in which the effects of civilisation have not been permitted, as in the rest of us, to overlay the primary processes of mental life with rationalisation, the voices that schizophrenic subjects experience not yet dismissed as simply an aspect of our own thought processes. If there are parallels between the hearing of voices in the ancient world and in schizophrenia, his argument goes, that is because these mental processes are a sign of a more primitive structure and organisation of the mental world (in respect both of phylogeny and of ontogeny). One can see that his argument necessitates this. The inhabitants of the ancient world heard voices, literally, but we no longer do; schizophrenics hear voices and we do not; *ergo*, schizophrenia must involve a regression to a primitive form of mentation.

The problem with this is that all the evidence suggests that schizophrenia is a relatively modern disease, quite possibly existent only since the eighteenth century or thereabouts, and that its principal psychopathological features have nothing to do with regression towards irrationality, lack of self-awareness, and a retreat into the infantile realm of emotion and the body, but entail the exact opposites: a sort of misplaced hyper-rationalism, a hyper-reflexive self-awareness, and a disengagement from emotion and embodied existence. This is awkward for his position.

I believe Jaynes was near to making a breakthrough – did in fact make one – but that, perhaps derailed by the view of schizophrenia outlined above, his conclusion was diametrically opposed to the one he should have drawn. His insight that there was a connection between the voices of the gods and changes in the mental world of those who heard them, that this might have something to do with the brain, and indeed that it concerned the relationship between the hemispheres, remains, in my view, fundamentally correct. However, I believe he got one important aspect of the story back to front. His contention that the phenomena he describes came about because of a *breakdown* of the 'bicameral' mind – so that the two hemispheres, previously separate, now merged – is the precise inverse of what happened. The phenomena came about because of a relative separation of the two chambers, the two hemispheres. Phenomena that were previously uncomplicatedly experienced as part of a relatively unified consciousness now became alien. Intuitions, no longer acted on unselfconsciously, no longer 'transparent', no longer simply subsumed into action without the necessity of deliberation, became objects of consciousness, brought into the plane of attention, opaque, objectified. Where there had been previously no question of whether the workings of the mind were 'mine', since the question would have had no meaning – there being no cut off between the mind and the world around, no possibility of standing back from one's own thought processes to ascribe them to oneself or anyone or anything else – there was now a degree of detachment which enabled the question to arise, and led to the intuitive, less explicit, thought processes being objectified as voices (as they are in schizophrenia), viewed as coming from 'somewhere else'. This interpretation, moreover, has the advantage that it fits with what we know about the tendency in schizophrenia to bring into conscious awareness processes normally left unconscious and intuitive.

Putting it at its simplest, where Jaynes interprets the voices of the gods as being due to the disconcerting effects of the opening of a door between the hemispheres, so that the voices could for the first time be heard, I see them as being due to the closing of the door, so that the voices of intuition now appear distant, 'other'; familiar but alien, wise but uncanny – in a word, divine.

My thesis is that the separation of the hemispheres brought with it both advantages and disadvantages. It made possible a standing outside of the 'natural' frame of reference, the common-sense everyday way in which we see the world. In doing so it enabled us to build on that 'necessary distance' from the world and from ourselves, achieved originally by the frontal lobes, and gave us insight into things that otherwise we could not have seen, even making it possible for us to form deeper empathic connections with one another and with the world at large. The best example of this is the fascinating rise of drama in the Greek world, in which the thoughts and feelings of our selves and of others are apparently objectified, and yet returned to us as our own. A special sort of seeing arises, in which both distance and empathy are crucial.

But the separation also sowed the seeds of left-hemisphere isolationism, allowing the left hemisphere to work unchecked. At this stage in cultural history, the two hemispheres were still working largely together, and so the benefits outweighed by a long way the disadvantages, but the disadvantages became more apparent over time.

For the sake of simplicity, I will deal with the changes in more or less chronological order, beginning with what one might call the archaic period at least as far as the seventh century BC, moving on to consider the changes of the sixth and fifth centuries up to the time of Plato separately, and then dealing with the later period from Plato onwards.

ARCHAIC GREECE

It is not known whether the great Homeric epics, the *Iliad* and the *Odyssey*, were the work of one individual or of several, and their date is also much debated: they clearly draw on an established tradition, and may have been worked on by a number of poets before they reached their written form, possibly around the second half of the eighth century BC. It is equally uncertain whether the composing and writing down of the poems were done by the same person or persons. Whoever it was that composed or wrote them, they are notable for being the earliest works of Western civilisation that exemplify a number of characteristics that are of interest to us. For in their most notable qualities – their ability to sustain a unified theme and produce a single, whole coherent narrative over a considerable length, in their degree of empathy, and insight into character, and in their strong sense of noble values (Scheler's *Lebenswerte* and above) – they suggest a more highly evolved right hemisphere.

That might make one think of the importance to the right hemisphere of the human face. Yet, despite this, there are in Homeric epic few descriptions of faces. There is no doubt about the reality of the emotions experienced by the figures caught up in the drama of the *Iliad* or the *Odyssey*: their feelings of pride, hate, envy, anger, shame, pity and love are the stuff of which the drama is made. But for the most part these emotions are conveyed as relating to the body and to bodily gesture, rather than the face – though there are moments, such as at the reunion of Penelope and Odysseus at the end of the *Odyssey*, when we seem to see the faces of the characters, Penelope's eyes full of tears, those of Odysseus betraying the 'ache of longing rising from his breast'. The lack of emphasis on the face might seem puzzling at a time of increasing empathic engagement, but I think there is a reason for this.

In Homer, as I mentioned in Part I, there was no word for the body as such, nor for the soul or the mind, for that matter, in the living person. The *sōma* was what was left on the battlefield, and the *psuchē* was what took flight from the lips of the dying warrior. In the living person, when Homer wants to speak of someone's mind or thoughts, he refers to what is effectively a physical organ – Achilles, for example, 'consulting his *thumos*'. Although the *thumos* is a source of vital energy within that leads us to certain actions, the *thumos* has fleshly characteristics such as requiring food and drink, and a bodily situation, though this varies. According to Michael Clarke's *Flesh and Spirit in the Songs of Homer*, Homeric man does not *have* a body or a mind: 'rather this thought and consciousness are as inseparable a part of his bodily life as are movement and metabolism'.[15] The body is indistinguishable from the whole person.[16] 'Thinking, emotion, awareness, reflection, will' are undertaken in the breast, not the head: 'the ongoing process of thought is conceived of as if it were precisely identified with the palpable inhalation of the breath, and the half-imagined mingling of breath with blood and bodily fluids in the soft, warm, flowing substances that make up what is behind the chest wall.'[17] He stresses the importance of flow, of melting and of coagulation. The common ground of meaning is not in a particular static thing but in the ongoing *process* of living, which 'can be seen and encapsulated in different contexts by a length of time or an oozing liquid'. These are all images of transition between different states of flux, different degrees of permanence, and allowing the possibility of ambiguity: 'The relationship between the bodily and mental identity of these entities is subtle and elusive.'[18] Here there is no necessity for the question 'is this mind or is it body?' to have a definitive answer. Such forbearance, however, had become impossible by the time of Plato, and remains, according to current trends in neurophilosophy, impossible today.

Words suggestive of the mind, the *thumos* 'family', for example, range fluidly and continuously between actor and activity, between the entity that thinks and the thoughts or emotions that are its products.[19] Here Clarke is speaking of terms such as *is, aiōn, menos*. 'The life of Homeric man is defined in terms of processes more precisely than of things.'[20] *Menos*, for example, refers to force or strength, and can also mean semen, despite being often located in the chest. But it also refers to 'the force of violent self-propelled motion in something non-human', perhaps like Scheler's *Drang*: again more an activity than a thing.[21]

This profound embodiment of thought and emotion, this emphasis on processes that are always in flux, rather than on single, static entities, this refusal of the 'either/or' distinction between mind and body, all perhaps again suggest a right-hemisphere-dependent version of the world. But what is equally obvious to the modern mind is the relative *closeness of the point of view*. And that, I believe, helps to explain why there is little description of the face: to attend to the face requires a degree of detached observation. That there is here a work of art at all, a capacity to frame human existence in this way, suggests, it is true, a degree of distance, as well as a degree of co-operation of the hemispheres in achieving it. But it is the gradual evolution of greater distance in post-Homeric Greek culture that causes the efflorescence, the 'unpacking', of both right and left hemisphere capacities in the service of both art and science.

With that distance comes the term closest to the modern, more disembodied, idea of mind, *nous* (or *noos*), which is rare in Homer. When *nous* does occur in Homer, it remains distinct, almost always intellectual, not part of the body in any straightforward sense: according to Clarke it 'may be virtually identified with a plan or stratagem'.[22] In conformation to the processes of the left hemisphere, it is like the flight of an arrow, directional.[23]

By the late fifth and fourth centuries, separate 'concepts of body and soul were firmly fixed in Greek culture'.[24] In Plato, and thence for the next two thousand years, the soul is a prisoner in the body, as he describes it in the *Phaedo*, awaiting the liberation of death.

Jaynes makes the observation that in Homer 'there is also no concept of will or word for it, the concept developing curiously late in Greek thought. Thus, Iliadic men have no will of their own and certainly no notion of free will.'[25] Here Jaynes seems to me too modern, too little forbearing, in his approach to what has to remain unresolved. For the gods were seen at the implicit level as aligned in some sense with the self, however distinct they may have been at the explicit level. Clarke refers to what he calls a 'double plane of causation': sudden thoughts and emotions are seen both as the intervention of personal deities and at the same time as an aspect of independent human psychology. 'The crux is that the two planes exist in harmony, and the god's intervention need not imply that the mortal man is less fully responsible for his actions.' Similarly poetic skills come from oneself *and* from the gods; and, in general, thought comes from oneself *and* from divine prompting.[26] E. R. Dodds, in *The Greeks and the Irrational*, wrote that in Homer the gods represented 'an interference with human life by nonhuman agencies which put something into a man and thereby influence his thought and conduct',[27] which again makes things seem more cut and dried than, particularly in the light of Clarke's book, I believe they were. So 'my' will was not, at this stage, just the left hemisphere, conscious striving, but also the right hemisphere, intuitive attraction to values and ideals, represented by the voices of the gods.

Christopher Gill provides a subtle analysis of the way in which, in the Homeric era, the sense of the self is intimately bound up with 'interpersonal and communal dialogue' in a shared ethical life,[28] an analysis which provides fascinating confirmation of the view that pre-Hellenistic Greece was much less subject to the effects of left-hemisphere domination than it later came to be. Partly as a consequence of this, what count as 'my' thoughts, beliefs, intentions, etc., do not have to be those which I am consciously aware are mine. The point is excellently made. It is good to bear this in mind while reading the story told by Bruno Snell in his classic *The Discovery of the Mind*, in my view still a fascinating analysis of the degree to which certain concepts were or were not present to the ancient Greek consciousness, and of the evolution of, precisely, the conscious and self-conscious mind during this period.[29]

I have talked of the necessity of seeing from a certain optimal distance. What do we know about how the Greeks did *see* the world? If we look at Greek words for vision, we find a very rich variety. What is striking is how many of them imply the *quality* of experience of the one who sees, or the *quality* of what is seen, as well as the relationship between the eye and what it beholds. The idea of the eye coldly transmitting certain sense data to our perception, of it *apprehending* its object, does not enter the language until late.

Homer uses a great variety of words to denote sight: Snell notes at least nine.[30] When Homer says of an eagle that he looks very sharply – *oxytaton derketai* – he has in mind the beams of the eagle's eye, like the 'sharp' rays of the sun that Homer refers to. *Derkesthai* denotes, therefore, not just an eye as we might say 'registering' something, but a fierce glance that rests on its object. *Paptainein* 'denotes a visual attitude, and does not hinge upon the function of sight as such'. It is a way of looking about inquisitively, carefully, or with fear. *Leussein* is to see something bright, and expresses a 'pride, joy and a feeling of freedom'. As a result this verb is characteristically found in the first person, and 'derives its special significance from a mode of seeing; not the function of sight, but the object seen, and the sentiments associated with the sight, give the word its peculiar quality'.[31] *Theasthai* is to gaze in astonishment with wide open eyes; and *ossesthai*, 'to have a threatening impression', something like 'to suspect'.

Eventually the principal parts of the verb *idein*, to see, were brought together from three different verbs: *horan*, *idein* and *opsesthai*. What is clear is that there was originally no single word to convey the simple function of sight *tout court*. There were originally only words for relations with things, the quality of the experience, how the 'seer' stood towards the 'seen'.[32] In other words sight had not been abstracted yet from its context within the lived world, where it is reverberative, itself alive, an expressive of betweenness – not yet thought of as unidirectional, detached, dead: not yet *observation*.

By contrast *theorein*, the origin of our word 'theory', is a much later word. Here it takes on the meaning we normally associate with seeing, the eye *apprehending* an object. Interestingly it was not originally a verb, but is a back-formation from the word for a spectator, *theoros*. What I take from this is that it is derived from what was thought of as a special situation, one of greater than usual detachment from a 'spectacle'. Words for 'thinking', in the sense of abstract cognition, and words for 'seeing' come to be closely related. The prominence, after the Homeric era, of *theorein* and *noein*, when compared with the earlier terms for seeing, marks a degree of abstraction from what is under consideration. A related distinction, touched on above, arises between aspects of the mind, between *thymos* and *noos*: very broadly *thymos* is instinct, what keeps the body in motion, coupled with emotion, whereas *noos* is reflection, ideas and images. Already, it would appear, the Greeks were making felt distinctions between thought and experience as mediated by the left hemisphere and as mediated by the right.

THOUGHT AND EXPERIENCE IN CLASSICAL GREECE

In or around the sixth century BC a radical change in the way we think about the world seems to have occurred, which is conventionally seen as the beginnings of philosophy (according to Bertrand Russell, 'philosophy begins with Thales').[33] Although many speculations were made over the next few hundred years, obviously leading to differing, sometimes opposed, conclusions, I would venture to say that the starting point in each case was one underlying perception: an intellectual sense of wonder at the sheer fact of existence, and, consequently, a conviction that our normal ways of construing the world are profoundly mistaken. In hindsight, one could call this an awareness of radical inauthenticity, and I believe it stems from the achievement of a degree of distance from the world.

In the light of what we know about the hemispheres, one could predict that this might lead in broadly one of two directions. It could lead to a turning away from the conceptualisation of experience, an attempt to rid perceptual phenomena of their customary accretions of thought, which render the world inauthentically familiar: a return from the re-presentation of reality towards an active openness to the 'presencing' of what is. In other words, a return to the authenticity of the right-hemisphere world. Or it could lead in the opposite direction, to a discrediting of the testimony of the senses, now seen as the root of deception, and a turning further inwards to the contemplation of the contents of the mind alone. In other words, not to a return to the right-hemisphere world, but on the contrary a rejection of it, since it now comes to be seen as *intrinsically* inauthentic, and therefore as invalid.

I believe we see both processes, but that they follow a progression. At first we see an equitable balance, governed by an awareness of the primacy of the right hemisphere, but with time the balance shifts ever further towards the triumph of the left.

The most familiar point of commonality in pre-Socratic philosophy is an attempt to reconcile a sense of the apparent unity of the phenomenal world with its obvious diversity. This suggested that there should be some common originary principle, or *archē*, from which all things came: the multiplicity of appearances, phenomena, being a reflection of the mutability of the primary substance, which underlies everything and could metamorphose between different states. This project could (in my view, falsely) be seen as monistic: I would see it, not as a reduction of the many to the one, but as a way of accounting for division within unity, while at the same time respecting the reality of both.

Russell's 'first philosopher', Thales, like his successors in the Milesian school, of which he was, in the early sixth century, the founder, was a dedicated observer of the natural world: he made discoveries in astronomy – he is said to have correctly predicted an eclipse of the sun in 585 BC – and used mathematics to address problems in engineering. He posited that the primary principle of all things, that from which they originate and to which they return, was water, a conclusion which it is assumed he derived from the obvious transitions of water between solid, liquid and gaseous states, and its omnipresence in living things.

However, Anaximander, Thales' pupil, took things much further. He posited that all things arise from, and ultimately return to, an originary principle that he called the 'unbounded' or the 'indefinite' (*apeiron*). This carries with it the suggestion of something that cannot be qualified, and therefore must be approached apophatically (*apeiron* literally means undefined, or unlimited), and that has neither beginning nor end, and therefore is an endless source, from which things eternally arise and to which they eternally return, forever in process, rather than an *archē* that simply occupies a static point in time, or acts as origin of a chain of causation. Although not accessible to direct perception, the *apeiron* nonetheless accounted for phenomenal aspects of the world. Central to the idea of the *apeiron* is that it must be able to contain within itself, without their mutual annihilation, all opposing principles: no other candidate for the role, as Anaximander rightly saw, such as water, or any other conceivable physical element, could fulfil this condition (for a start, water cannot give rise to dryness). These opposing principles within the *apeiron*, according to Anaximander, are of crucial importance. They balance one another, and it is this giving and taking, this ebb and flow of opposites, that gives rise to all things, since, as he puts it, they 'pay retribution to one another' for their trespasses on each other, according to an inescapable logic in things: 'When things perish, they return whence they come to be, in accordance with necessity, for they give to each other recompense for their injustice according to the ordinance of time'.[34]

In contrast with his pupil Anaximenes, whose candidate for the *archē* was another element (in his case, air), Anaximander yields a number of insights: into the necessary, both productive and destructive, nature of the coming together of opposites; into the primacy of what is neither definite nor finite; and into the nature of the *archē* as process, rather than thing – all, in my view, insights into the right-hemisphere world, though the process of philosophy, reasoning about the causes and nature of the world, and trying to systematise it, may itself come from the left hemisphere.[35]

Though fragments are all that remain to us of Heraclitus, as with the other pre-Socratic philosophers, significantly more of them survive, and those that have survived have a taciturn, apophthegmatic, and often paradoxical, quality that has made them an endlessly rich resource for interpretation over the centuries. This very fact has been held against Heraclitus by those who see understanding as necessarily determinate, transmissible through clarity, a commodity to be exported and imported, rather than something fruitfully undetermined, perhaps inevitably incomplete, requiring an individual process of exploration, and evoked from within us by a response to the suggestive possibility in the text. (Once again let me emphasise that I do not imply that 'anything goes', only that whatever it is that does go is unlikely to be neatly conformable to everyday language.)

Heraclitus' exact dates are unknown, but he flourished in the late sixth century BC. He came from Ephesus, an opulent rival city to the north of Miletus, and he cared little for the philosophy of the Milesians. He had a poor opinion of the *dēmos* (the masses), had no pupils or followers, and, according to Diogenes Laertius, characteristically deposited his book as a dedication in the great temple of Artemis, where the general public would not have had access to it.[36]

Heraclitus held that the nature of things is intrinsically hard to seek out using the tools with which we would normally equip ourselves for the task. Our natural assumptions and our common ways of thinking will lead us astray, and we need to be both wary and indefatigable in our seeking after truth. 'He who does not expect will not find out the unexpected', he wrote, 'for it is trackless and unexplored';[37] the nature of things, and therefore the truthful evocation of them, is such that it 'neither declares nor conceals, but gives a sign'.[38] The Heraclitus scholar Charles Kahn writes that the 'parallel between Heraclitus' style and the obscurity of the nature of things, between the difficulty of understanding him and the difficulty in human perception, is not arbitrary: to speak plainly about such a subject would be to falsify it in the telling, for no genuine understanding would be communicated'.[39] The point is not that the nature of things is contradictory, but that the attempt to render them in language leads inevitably to what we call paradox, and the attempt to avoid paradox therefore distorts.[40]

The hiddenness or necessarily implicit quality of Nature requires a particularly alert flexibility on the part of those who go to approach her. 'Hidden structure is superior to manifest structure';[41] and openness is required by the seeker of wisdom, as well as enquiry into many different things: 'men who love wisdom', he wrote, 'must be good enquirers into many things indeed', for 'Nature loves to hide'.[42] He held that 'one could not reach the ends of the soul though one travelled every way, so deep is its measure [logos]', (possibly 'so deep is what it has to tell us').[43] Heraclitus shared Thales' view that 'all things are full of gods'[44]: for him all things are full of soul, and there is no sharp divide between mind or soul and the world of matter.[45] Bruno Snell says that Heraclitus, who was 'the first writer to feature the new concept of the soul', in speaking of its depth was drawing on a history of archaic poetry containing such words as *bathyphron*, deep-pondering, and *bathymetes*, deep-thinking. 'Concepts like "deep knowledge", "deep thinking", "deep pondering", as well as "deep pain" are common enough in the archaic period. In these expressions, the symbol of depth always points to the infinity of the intellectual and spiritual, which differentiates it from the physical.'[46]

Heraclitus' response to the misleading nature of re-presentation, to the way things seem, is not to go further in that direction, away from phenomena, but to look again at what our experience tells us. In other words, he does not advise a turning inwards in order to discover the nature of reality, but a patient and careful attention to the phenomenal world. Most people, he says, make the mistake of prioritising opinion, their ideas, over experience, over 'things as they encounter them'.[47] Thus 'whatever comes from sight, hearing, learning from experience: this I prefer'. Elsewhere he writes that 'eyes are surer witnesses than ears', in other words that what we experience is more certain than what people *say* about what they experience.[48] But experience is not enough on its own. It needs understanding; and most people are not in a position to understand what they experience: 'eyes and ears are poor witnesses for men if their souls do not understand the language'.[49]

For Heraclitus *logos*, the ultimate reason, cause, meaning, or deep structure of the world, is not some power that lies somewhere behind appearances, as it later would become, but is what Kahn calls a 'phenomenal property', evidenced and experienced in reasoned thought and responses to the world.[50]

If we are enabled to attend to experience, rather than to our pre-conceived ideas about experience, we encounter, according to Heraclitus, the reality of the union of opposites. Appreciating this coming together, wherein all opposing principles are reconciled, was the essence of *sophia* (wisdom, the root of philosophy) for Heraclitus.[51] Opposites define one another and bring one another into existence.[52] His famous pronouncement that 'war is father of all, and king of all', is the most celebrated expression of the creative power of opposition, of the fact that opposites do not cancel one another, but (here he seems to me to be in agreement with Anaximander) are the only way to create something new.[53] Thus, as Heraclitus says, high and low notes are both needed for harmony, and we would have no life without the coming together of male and female.[54] 'They do not understand', he says, 'how a thing agrees, at variance with itself: it is a *harmoniē* like that of the bow or the lyre.'[55] To get near understanding this, one needs to know that *harmoniē* can be understood in each of three senses: a fitting together (as of cut surfaces that are 'true'), a reconciliation (as of warring parties), and an attunement (as of strings or tones); equally one needs to appreciate that the bow and the lyre consist in nothing other than strings that are, and must be, under tension, where the stable complex whole is balanced and efficient not despite, but *because of*, a pulling in opposite directions. Perhaps Heraclitus' most elegant compression of meaning lies in his aphorism: 'the name of the bow (*biós*) is life (*bíos*); its work is death'.[56]

The taut string, its two ends pulling apart under opposing forces, that for bow or lyre is what gives its vital strength or virtue, is the perfect expression of a dynamic, rather than static, equilibrium. This holding of movement within stasis, of opposites in reconciliation, is also imaged in Heraclitus' most famous saying, that 'all things flow'.[57] Stability in the experiential world is always stability provided by a form through which things continue to flow: 'As they step into the same rivers, other and still other waters flow upon them . . . One cannot step twice into the same river'.[58] The river is always different, but always the same. Ultimately, of course, rivers themselves, not just the waters that flow through them, come and go: in this too our bodies are like rivers. But stasis, the opposite of change and flux, is incompatible with life, and leads only to separation, and disintegration: 'even the potion separates unless it is stirred'.[59]

Heraclitus is sometimes included amongst those who thought that the *archē* was one of the elements, in his case fire. This is because of his saying that 'all things are requital for fire, and fire for all things, as goods for gold and gold for goods'.[60] However, if it is to be thought of in this way, it is in Anaximander's sense, as an endless process (requital), rather than as a 'cause', or occupying a point in time. Fire is also unique amongst the elements in not being in any sense a thing or substance, but a pure process, pure phenomenal energy (in fact Heraclitus' meaning may be an intuition of the interchangeability of matter and energy); it also perfectly illustrates the power both to create life and to destroy it. In all this it manages to capture what the *apeiron* has over a substance such as water or air, while not itself being absent from the phenomenal world in the way the *apeiron* has to be.

Heraclitus seems to me to have grasped the essence of the balance between the hemispheres, while remaining aware of the primacy of the right hemisphere's world. I see this in, amongst other things, his insistence on the hidden, implicit, and unbounded nature of the primary reality; in his 'paradoxical' use of language in an attempt to transcend the normally confined (because left-hemisphere-congruent) expressive possibilities of language; in his insistence on the importance of perception, despite the difficulties of truly understanding what it is that we perceive; in his prioritising of experience over our theories about experience; in his insistence that opposites need to be held together, rather than inevitably cancelling one another out; in his sense that all is in the process of change and eternal flux, rather than stasis or completion; and in his sense that all things contain an energy or life. In addition he sees the *logos* as something 'shared', reciprocal, perhaps even reciprocally coming into being, rather than, as he says we tend to see it, something achieved through 'private', isolated thought processes;[61] and he emphasises that things change their nature depending on context (seawater, for example, is life-giving to fish, deadly poison to humans).[62] In one fragment that Kahn regards as authentic but uninterpretable, Heraclitus is remembered for using the term *anchibasiē*, 'stepping near': no better term could be found to characterise the right hemisphere's approach to truth, when contrasted with that of the left hemisphere.[63]

Let us move on to the early fifth century BC, in Elea, a Greek colony on the southern coast of Italy, where Parmenides founded his own school of philosophy. Parmenides was a priest of Apollo: his main work is a poem that survives in fragmentary form, and is explicitly opposed to Heraclitus (and, on different grounds, to Pythagoras). The important message enshrined in its double structure – The Way of Truth *versus* The Way of Belief – is that the phenomenal world is a deception. Thought is all that there is: 'for thought and being are the same thing'.[64] What can be thought must be, and what cannot be thought cannot exist. What follows from logic, however much it flies in the face of experience, must be true. However, contradiction, a conflict within the system of language and reason, is taken as a sure indication of error.

That there is movement is certainly a thought most of us have, and so one would have thought that, by Parmenides' logic, it must be true. But apparently not: motion turns out to be an illusion. 'All that exists' cannot move, because then it would move into the void, where nothing exists – a logical impossibility. (If this is reminiscent of Zeno, that is because Zeno was a pupil of Parmenides.) So everything that *is* remains so, timeless, undifferentiated and unchanging. All is stasis, and the process of becoming is forever banished. The phenomena of movement and change are illusory appearances. In its prioritising of a logical system over truth to phenomena, in its refusal of ambiguity or contradiction, in its achievement of certainty and stasis, this philosophy shows its allegiance to the world of the left hemisphere. Heidegger, it must be said, adopts the view that ultimately Heraclitus and Parmenides were saying the same thing; but he achieves this, it seems to me, by a sort of sleight of hand, rescuing Parmenides' Being by finding it ultimately in the being of all actually existing beings, so that the two are reconciled.[65] If true, it demonstrates only what I have argued for in Part I of this book, that left-hemisphere paths will, if followed far enough, lead inevitably to the world as recognised by the right hemisphere.

As Plato in his dialogues *Parmenides* and *Sophist* reveals, Parmenides' position leads to many unpalatable consequences. Effectively the complete sundering of the worlds of experience and of ideas leads to the consequence that 'we do not participate in knowledge itself'[66] (the opposite of Heraclitus's claim that the *logos* is shared). So philosophers do not participate in knowledge (a self-undermining position) and none of us can partake in the reality of being (another). The impossibility of difference as well as sameness brings all discourse to a halt.[67] None of this would matter so much if self-undermining positions were not expressly excluded by Parmenides (and by Socrates), and if rational discourse was not held by both to be the way to truth.

In the *Theaetetus*, Socrates points out that Parmenides was the only one of 'the wise' to deny that all is change and motion.[68] Yet, despite this, Parmenides had a huge influence both on Plato, and, through him, on the subsequent history of Western philosophy. Plato's belief that knowledge must be unfailing and general led to the position that we cannot know things that are changing or particular. In the left-hemisphere sense of 'knowledge' this is true. For Plato that knowledge then becomes reality: the realm of the Forms, disembodied, ideal and universal abstractions, of which actual, physical sensory objects of experience are but shadows. The need for certainty and clarity, coupled with the law of the excluded middle, blinded us to the possibility of what came to be seen as paradox. From this time forward, Greek philosophy is dominated by the assumptions and modes of operation of the left hemisphere. And by the time of Theophrastus, a pupil of Aristotle writing in the third century BC, Heraclitus's riddling, epigrammatic style had become simply – a sign of mental illness.[69]

The very fact of having a philosophy at all was one of the many changes to be brought about by the advent of necessary distance. Drama, at least as conceived by the Greeks, is another, and as Nietzsche saw it, a demonstration of the necessary balance of Apollo and Dionysus.[70] This distance has nothing to do with the ironising distance, or *Verfremdungseffekt*, espoused by modern dramatists, and indeed works to the opposite end. It enables us to feel powerfully with, and thus to know ourselves in, others, and others in ourselves. 'Man must listen to an echo of himself before he may hear or know himself,' as Snell says; and it is in drama that we find that echo.'[71] The 'process of the tragic chorus is the original phenomenon of drama', wrote Nietzsche, 'this experience of seeing oneself transformed before one's eyes and acting as if one had really entered another body, another character'.[72] In tragedy, we see for the first time in the history of the West the power of empathy, as we watch not just the painful moulding of the will, and of the soul, of men and women (the constant theme of tragedy is *hubris*), but the gods themselves in evolution, moving from their instincts for vengeance and retributory justice towards compassion and reconciliation.

And it is also in drama that opposites that can never be reconciled in the explicit discourse of philosophy come to be, nonetheless, reconciled, through the implicit power of myth.

There was in Athens a special cult of Prometheus, the god of technical skill and intelligence (though not of wisdom).[73] It will be remembered that it was Prometheus who stole fire from heaven and gave it to mortals: in the terms of this book, the emissary taking to himself the power of the Master. It was said that Zeus had planned to destroy humankind, and that Prometheus's gift brought them hope of power to resist. For this crime, Prometheus was chained by Zeus to a rock, where every day his liver would be torn out by a bird of prey only to grow again in time for the next day's torment to begin. In his play *Prometheus Bound*, Aeschylus sympathetically represents Prometheus' fate, although, through the device of the chorus, he is enabled to remain ultimately ambiguous in his stance. He puts into Prometheus' mouth this justification of himself as the deliverer of humanity:

> Before they were like babes, but I roused them to reason and taught them to think . . . though they had eyes to see, they saw in vain; they had ears, but could not hear; but like forms in dreams, they spent their entire lives without purpose and in confusion . . . until I showed them the risings of the stars, and their settings, hard to discern. I invented for them Number, chief of all devices, and how to set down words in writing, Memory's handmaid, and mother of the Muses . . .[74]

It is Prometheus, in other words, who brings numeracy and literacy. Although in Aeschylus' play, Hermes, as the messenger of Zeus (the 'Master's emissary'), is sent to pile on the agony to the unrepentant Prometheus, in some versions of the myth Hermes himself is credited with bringing fire from heaven, and he is in some respects Prometheus's *alter ego*. Like Prometheus, Hermes was associated with the invention of weights and measures, and with literature and the arts. Importantly from the point of view of this book, he was also the god of merchants and trick-sters, corresponding to the Egyptian Thoth, the god of sciences and technology, who was also the god of writing (Plato, in the *Phaedrus*, considered Thoth to have been its inventor, and deplored its advent).[75] Prometheus, too, 'founder of the sacrifice, was a cheat and a thief', writes Kerényi: 'these traits were at the bottom of all the stories that deal with him', the image of those who steal the divinity that lies round about them, 'whose temerity brings immeasurable and unforeseen misfortune upon them'.[76]

Aeschylus, whose works were written in the first part of the fifth century BC, is generally accepted to be the founder of Greek tragedy, and was certainly so desig-nated by A. W. Schlegel: 'Aeschylus is to be considered as the creator of Tragedy; in full panoply she sprung from his head, like Pallas from the head of Jupiter.'[77] What is more, Schlegel considered *Prometheus Bound* to be the essence of tragedy: 'The other productions of the Greek Tragedians are so many tragedies; but this I might say is Tragedy herself.'[78] Ironically it is not certain that Aeschylus himself wrote the play (although the consensus appears to be in favour);[79] but certainly, if tragedy recounts the history of its hero's downfall from the height of glory to the depths of despair through the consequences of *hubris*, this play, along with Milton's *Paradise Lost*, must count as the epitome of tragedy.

Aeschylus was a brave soldier, who fought at Marathon and Salamis, and took part in the rout of the Persians; indeed he was so proud of this that his epitaph referred to his participation at the battle of Marathon, but not to his pre-eminence as a playwright. He was also a man with profound respect for the religious mysteries. He was an initiate at Eleusis, and it shows how seriously the mysteries were taken that, despite the esteem in which he was held, he almost lost his life for having supposedly disclosed aspects of the mysteries in his *Eumenides*.[80] As a youth he tended vines, and, according to Pausanias, on one occasion fell asleep in the vineyard; in his dream, Dionysus, god of wine, appeared to him and exhorted him to write tragedy. The plays he wrote were performed as part of the competitive spectacle at the festivals of Dionysus, which had then not long been established.

Aeschylus was, then, a Dionysian; not just in the technical sense, but in the Nietzschean sense. His intuitive and imaginative art, ambiguous as Dionysus himself, 'the ambiguous god of wine and death', came to him via divine inspiration, announced to him in his sleep, and was inextricably bound to the world of religion and its mysteries. As Sophocles said of him, 'Aeschylus does what is right without knowing it': there cannot be a clearer statement of his debt to the workings of the right hemisphere.[81] Aeschylus' description of the fate of Prometheus is profoundly moving and compassionate, yet also recounts the pain that comes on man from his hubristic attempt to seize and use what belongs to another realm in order to make himself powerful because, as Schlegel puts it, Prometheus is 'an image of *human nature itself*'.[82]

Gnothi seauton: know thyself. These famous words were sculpted over the entrance to the temple of the oracle at Delphi. The oracle itself, speaking through a woman who was in a state of intoxication from breathing the vapours arising from the infusion of sacred herbs, was a way of setting aside the ever too ready grasp on the world of the rationalising intellect, and opening it to the intuitions that arise from interpreting ambiguous utterances in an atmosphere of devotion – a sort of self-revealing Rorschach blot, rather like the Chinese book of poetic, and purportedly divinatory, utterances, the *I Ching*. It seems to me that in Aeschylus' tragedy of Prometheus, the mind is coming to know itself, 'without knowing it': it is the mind (in fact the brain) cognising itself. The tragedy of Prometheus is a tale of two hemispheres. And, in more general terms, the Greek invention, or discovery, of tragedy, based as it is on the ever recurrent theme of downfall through *hubris*, represents the paradox of self-consciousness: the beginnings of the mind coming to know and understand its own nature.

THE WRITTEN WORD

Neither the works of Homer nor those of the great tragedians, Aeschylus, Sophocles and Euripides, would be known if it were not for the existence of written records; and clearly there is no way one can tell the story of the hemispheres in the Ancient World without considering the significance of the history of writing. What is the relationship between writing and the hemispheres?

To answer that question one needs to look at the stages of development in the history of writing from its first beginnings to the present Western (or Latin) alphabet, which is essentially the same as the Greek alphabetic system. By the fourth century in Greece, all the important hemispheric shifts in the process of inscription had already taken place. There are four important elements to the story, and in each one the balance of power is moved further to the left. These are: the move from pictograms to phonograms; the yielding of syllabic phonograms to a phonetic alphabet; the inclusion of vowel signs in the alphabet; and the direction of writing.

From pictograms to phonograms

As far as we know, the first form of written language emerged in the fourth millennium BC. Pictograms, visual representations of the thing referred to, were first used in Sumer around 3300 BC. These gradually gave way to ideograms, which are more schematic diagrams. This represents a shift, perhaps not a great one, but a shift nonetheless, towards abstraction. A much greater shift in the same direction occurred when ideograms in turn were replaced by phonograms. This shift towards arbitrary signs that are no longer even schematically related to the perceptual properties of the thing referred to, only to the sounds made in referring to it, moves writing further into the territory of the left hemisphere. Writing arose in Egypt around the same period as in Sumer, or a little later, about 3100 BC. It appears that there all three forms – pictograms, ideograms and phonograms – were used alongside each other in different contexts throughout.

From phonograms to phonetic alphabet; and the inclusion of vowels

Phonograms, in some languages, represent syllables; in alphabetic languages they represent single phonetic components, originally consonants. Greek is not a syllabic, but a phonemic, language. In a syllabic language such as Chinese, the same syllable may be pronounced with different tones or, as in Hebrew or Arabic, with different vowels; in changing the tone or the vowels one changes the meaning. This has an important implication. As long as language remains syllabic, rather than purely phonemic, it inevitably relies on context for the differentiation between written characters which represent potentially quite different meanings. Knowing how to read and understand a syllabic language involves processes which distinguish it from the reading and understanding of a purely phonemic language such as Greek, Latin or the other modern European languages such as English. Most importantly, meaning emerges from the context, the mind revising the ways in which a syllable or sound can be read (though at lightning speed), as it does with the meaning in poetry, working around an utterance that resolves into focus as a whole, rather than through a unidirectional linear sequence of instructions, where each certainty builds on the last. Less obvious, but no less significant, is the fact that in syllabic languages concepts are put together from syllables which have meaning in themselves. Although modern Western languages are not syllabic, but phonemic, we can get an idea of what this is like if we remain aware of the etymology of English (or German, or other Western) words – if we are sufficiently aware of a word's structure, and of the original meanings of the component parts. In syllabic languages, therefore, meaning is less arbitrary, more clearly rooted in the world out of which it emanates, and retains its metaphoric base to a greater extent. (It is no accident that Heidegger, writing in a phonemic language, so often returns to etymology.) In both these respects syllabic languages favour understanding by the right hemisphere, whereas phonemic languages favour that of the left hemisphere.

The origin of all alphabetic systems as such lies in Proto-Canaanite (2000–1500 BC), with the development of Akkadian phonograms written in cuneiform from

1500 BC. The Greek alphabet, from which, of course, the Latin alphabet was derived, is itself a derivation of the Phoenician alphabet. In fact the Greek alphabet is nearly identical with the Phoenician alphabet, but, fascinatingly, in view of the later change in the direction of writing, *mirror-reversed*.[83] The date at which this occurred is disputed but probably occurred around the ninth century BC or earlier.

The insertion of vowels, which happened for the first time with the Greek alphabet's evolution out of Phoenician, further consolidated a shift in the balance of hemispheric power, removing the last unconscious processing strategies from context-based to sequence-based coding.[84]

The direction of writing

The right hemisphere prefers vertical lines, but the left hemisphere prefers horizontal lines.[85] If lines are vertical, the left hemisphere prefers to read them from the bottom up, whereas the right hemisphere prefers to read from the top down.[86] In almost every culture writing has begun by being vertical. Some, such as the oriental languages, remain vertical: they are also generally read from the top down, and from right to left. In other words, they are read from the maximally right-hemisphere-determined point of view.[87] Although both oriental and Western languages are generally read from the top down, so that at the global level they still conform to the right-hemisphere preference, at the local, sequential level they have drifted in the West towards the left hemisphere's point of view. This process started with the move to phonetics. While 'almost all pictographic writing systems favour a vertical layout . . . practically all systems of writing that depend exclusively on the visual rendition of phonological features of language are horizontally laid out.'[88] So it is that vertical writing began to be replaced by horizontal writing, and disappeared altogether in the West by about 1100 BC. By the eleventh century BC, Greek was being written horizontally, although right to left.

It continued to be written right to left until the seventh century BC. However, at around this time a fascinating change occurred. Between the eighth and sixth centuries, Greek began to be written in what is known as *boustrophedon*, literally 'as the ox ploughs', which is to say going to the end of the line, turning round, and coming back – alternating direction line by line. By the fifth century BC, however, left to right was becoming the norm, and by the fourth century the transition was complete, and all forms of Greek were being written left to right.[89]

Reading left to right involves moving the eyes towards the right, driven by the left hemisphere, and preferentially communicating what is seen to the left hemisphere. And it turns out that, while virtually all syllabic languages are written right to left, almost every phonemic language, such as the Indo-European family of languages, being composed of a linear sequence of independent elements, is written left to right.

Phonemic languages put merely contiguous relationships in the place of contextual relationships, digital in the place of analogical relationships, and sequence in place of form. Moreover the addition of vowels makes an astonishingly clear difference to the direction of writing: according to de Kerckhove, '95% of phono-logical orthographies that include markings of vocalic sounds [e.g. vowels] . . . are written towards the right, whereas almost all the systems that do not include letters for vowels are written towards the left, and have been rendered so almost from the beginning, for over three millennia.'[90]

Given the nature of the Greek language, it was almost inevitable that the direction in which it was written should have changed. 'The Greek system', writes de Kerckhove, 'introduced a level of abstraction that would all but remove the script from the context of its production in oral forms . . . its basic process was the *atomisation* of speech.'[91] It was the Greek philosopher Democritus who was to achieve the same atomisation of the physical universe. We are now so used to hearing speech as a succession of separate building blocks, rather than as an utterance as a whole, that it is hard to imagine that even the separations between words were not regularised in writing, so that all was written continuously, until the Byzantine period.[92]

So by the time we reach the fourth century BC, each of the changes that had taken place in written language favoured a shift of balance inexorably towards the left hemisphere. In this way the history of writing recapitulates the history of language generally: originating in the right hemisphere, but translating itself into the left.

Did the shift in the nature and direction of writing cause a shift towards favouring the left hemisphere, or did some much deeper cognitive shift take place in the Greek world, of which changes in the nature of writing were merely an outward sign or symptom?

I do not think that the very nature of writing required such a shift – something else, deeper lying, must have been responsible. For one thing, it remains a fact that most languages of the non-Western world are structured so as to favour the right hemisphere; but, despite this, these right-hemisphere-prone languages have ceased to be processed by the right hemisphere, and are in fact now processed by the left. Presumably this is because, in a world where Western habits of mind are becoming inescapable, those non-Western cultures have by now inherited the cognitive changes that began in Greece around this time. In the modern world, in other words, language has so far aligned itself with the agenda of the left hemisphere that even those languages that must have started out being processed by the right hemisphere, such as Hebrew and Arabic, and are still read from right to left, are now actually to a large extent processed in the left hemisphere.[93] Similarly, although it is true that pictograms are less strongly lateralised to the left hemisphere than phonograms,[94] it is not true, as once was thought, that *kanji*, a pictographic Japanese script, is better appreciated by the right hemisphere, while *kana*, a Japanese phonographic script, is more easily processed by the left hemisphere: it appears that both scripts are processed principally in the left hemisphere, though in different regions.[95] In Chinese, too, the majority of language processes are, like those of Western alphabetic languages, now subserved by the left hemisphere.[96] However, the effect is not absolute; and, much as there is evidence that reading

Hebrew and Arabic utilises both hemispheres more equally than Western languages,[97] reading Chinese words aloud activates far more widespread networks of the right hemisphere than English, probably because of the subtlety of both visual and tonal demands by Chinese.[98]

One has to accept that Greek, like many other languages, began being written in the opposite direction, the one that favours the right hemisphere (could the mirror reversals of letters that occurred at the point of Greek adoption of the Phoenician alphabet be a sign of things to come?). Why did it change direction, and need to include vowels, unless because it was being processed by the left hemisphere? The inclusion of vowels appears to have been necessitated by the sequential, as opposed to contextual, analytic approach of the left hemisphere, not the other way round. Other languages had managed fine without vowels.

So where Eric Havelock has argued, as has John Skoyles, that it may have been not just literacy, but the structure of the Greek alphabet, which was responsible for the cognitive shifts of Greek culture, I would agree that the relationship is highly significant; but my view is that the nature of the Greek alphabet is more likely to have been an effect than a cause, in other words to have merely consolidated a shift that must have begun in something else.[99]

'Writing is an instrument of power,' writes Claude Hagège; 'it enables the sending of orders to far-off fiefdoms and can determine which laws will prevail.'[100] Certainly that would seem to be true of writing in the Western world, from its origins in Sumer and Egypt. 'Writing is basically a technology,' wrote the great French historian, Fernand Braudel,

> a way of committing things to memory and communicating them, enabling people to send orders and to carry out administration at a distance. Empires and organised societies extending over space are the children of writing, which appeared everywhere at the same time as these political units, and by a similar process . . . [Writing] became established as a means of controlling the society . . . In Sumer, most of the archaic tablets are simply inventories and accounts, lists of food rations distributed, with a note of the recipients. Linear B, the Mycenae-Cretan script which was finally deciphered in 1953, is equally disappointing, since it refers to similar subject matter: so far it has revealed hardly anything but palace accounts. But it was at this basic level that writing first became fixed and showed what it could do, having been invented by zealous servants of state or prince. Other functions and applications would come in due course. Numbers appear in the earliest written languages.[101]

Braudel mentions number as appearing early in written language: in fact the Sumerians were the first to write down numbers, and theirs was the first real empire. Numbers are essential for controlling crops, herds, and people. Perhaps, however, it is not so much that empires are the children of writing, but that both empires and writing, at least as it came into being in the West, are the children of the left hemisphere. Writing does not *have* to have this character; it may do so only in the West. In other cultures, writing may not have originated with the same ominous, utilitarian agenda in view: according to Hagège, 'the origin of Chinese writing appears to have been magicoreligious and divinatory rather than economic and mercantile.'[102] Perhaps, if it is true of writing only in the West that it has this nature, this reflects something about our particular brain development in the West.

MONEY

Be that as it may, there can be no doubt that in Greece writing had much to do with the economic and mercantile. Money has an important function which it shares with writing: it replaces things with signs or tokens, with representations, the very essence of the activity of the left hemisphere. I would suggest that they are aspects of the same neuropsychological development. The same developments that lead to the word being more 'real' (for the left hemisphere) than the reality it signifies occur with money. Richard Seaford asserts that monetary currency necessitates an antithesis of sign and substance, whereby the sign becomes decisive, and implies an ideal substance underlying the tangible reality.[103] It is interesting that, much as Skoyles had seen the alphabet as the prime mover in a new way of thinking, Seaford sees money as being the prime mover of a new kind of philosophy, and one can certainly understand why, given that this formulation of Seaford's bears an uncanny resemblance to Plato's theory of Forms. As the reader will by now imagine, I would not favour seeing either the alphabet or currency as the prime movers, but as epiphenomena, signs of a deeper change in hemisphere balance evidenced in both.

Money changes our relationships with one another in predictable ways. These also clearly reflect a transition from the values of the right hemisphere to those of the left. In Homer, artefacts of gold and silver may be aristocratic gifts, and are associated with deity and immortality, but are not *money*: in fact, significantly, unformed gold and silver, as such, had negative associations.[104] Before the development of currency, there is an emphasis on reciprocity. Gifts are not precise, not calculated, not instantaneously enacted or automatically received, not *required*; the gifts are not themselves substitutable, but unique; and the emphasis is on the value of creating or maintaining a relationship, which is also unique. With trade, all this changes; the essence is competitive: the exchange is instantaneous, based on equivalence, and the emphasis not on relationship, but on utility or profit.[105] As Seaford points out, money is homogeneous, and hence homogenises its objects and its users, eroding uniqueness: it is impersonal, unlike talismanic objects, and weakens the need for bonds, or for trust based on a knowledge of those with whom one is exchanging. It becomes a universal aim, corrupting even death ritual, and threatening other values as it transcends and substitutes for them; and it becomes a universal means, including to divine good will or to political power. It 'breeds an unlimited greed'.[106] The late development of the *polis* brings about these changes and leads to the development of coinage.[107]

So it was not just the alphabet, but currency, which arose in the Greek world. What is more, both arose out of the possibilities offered by trade. Braudel refers to both the alphabet and currency as 'accelerators of change':

The adoption of an alphabet reintroduced writing into a world which had lost it. And once writing was within the grasp of all, it became not only an instrument of command but a tool of trade, of communication and often of demystification ... As for currency, the need for it had been felt before it appeared ... It was in about 685 BC that authentic money (coins made of electrum, a mixture of gold and silver) appeared for the first time in history in Lydia, the rich realm of Croesus ... But most specialists think that a true monetary economy was not in place until the fourth century BC and the achievements of the Hellenistic period. In the eighth and seventh centuries, this stage was still a long way off. Nevertheless, throughout the Aegean, things were stirring. Having been long cut off from the eastern world, Greece now made contact with it again through the cities on the Syrian coast, in particular Al-Mina. The luxury of this area dazzled the Greeks, whose way of life was still modest. Along with artefacts from Phoenicia and elsewhere – ivories, bronzes and pottery – Greece began to import a new style of living. Foreign decorative art came as a contrast to the stiff geometrical style. With works of art came fashions, the first elements of Greek science, superstitions, and possibly the beginnings of Dionysiac cults.[108]

There are several things to note here. First, writing became a tool of command, trade, communication – and 'often of demystification'. Its movement is towards power or the means of power, yes; but also already, for better or worse (and sometimes, undoubtedly, it will be for the better) towards the explicit at the expense of the implicit – the direction of the left hemisphere.

But this passage is fascinating for a completely different reason: the way it charts, if one thinks about the dates, a progression through the Greek world. First, there is the reference to Al-Mina, a trading post at the mouth of the Orontes, probably founded in the ninth century BC, though it had been a point of commerce with the Mycenaean world since the fourteenth century BC. Of this, Braudel elsewhere comments:

It was to be a crucially important colony, representing as it did the first opening up of Greece to Syria, Palestine, the neo-Hittite and Aramaean states, Assyria, Urardhu and all the caravan routes of the continental Middle East. The city was moreover largely populated by Phoenicians. It is not therefore surprising that it is increasingly seen as the city where Greece met the east; it was here that the Greeks became acquainted with the Phoenician alphabet, here too that the orientalising phase of Greek art originated, the first challenge to the geometric style.[109]

From the earliest period, there was cross-fertilisation of the Greek mind with influences from the East (also a significant element in the genesis of pre-Socratic thought).[110] The elements that are here identified – art that was no longer 'in the stiff geometrical style' beloved of the left hemisphere, the 'first elements' of Greek science, namely the deductive method (not the theorising or system-building which came later), 'superstitions' and the 'beginnings of the Dionysiac cults', that is, religious mystery – all speak of influences of the right hemisphere.

But there is something else. Very like writing, which was ambivalently poised between rightward and leftward movement during the period from the seventh to the fifth century, only taking the plunge into being fully rightward-orientated (favouring the left hemisphere) in the fourth century, currency began circulating in the seventh century, but was not much used; it was only really widespread by the fourth century.[111] In terms of hemispheric balance, an early right-hemisphere influence stands in equipoise with influences of the left hemisphere; then seems to give way, at least measured by the two critical areas of writing and currency, by the fourth century to left-hemisphere preponderance – around the time when the world of the pre-Socratic philosophers ceded to the world of Plato.

If one goes right back to the early days of Greek civilisation, to the Mycenaean world which held sway from the middle of the second millennium till about 1100 BC, long before the age of Homer, it becomes clear that very important influences originated from the cross-fertilisation of East and West. The paintings of Mycenae attest to the exchange of the mythology of dread, which had characterised Egyptian culture and art, for one of lightness and mirth. The severely hierarchical relationships that characterised Egyptian art give way to the portrayal of relaxed, equal relationships, not just of man with man, but of men with women, something observed for the very first time in Mycenaean art in Crete.[112] Surely these, it seems to me, represent the most positive aspects of the left hemisphere, in its guise as Lucifer, the bringer of light? Here the left hemisphere appears to be *in harmony with the workings of the right*, which are abundantly evidenced in the fascination with the living animal world in all its particularity, and a lively imagination. 'Plants and animals were painted everywhere on walls and vases', writes Braudel:

> here a spike of grass, there a bunch of crocuses or irises, a spray of lilies against the ochre background of a vase, or the Pompeian red of a wall-painting; reeds arranged in a continuous almost abstract design, a branch of flowering olive, an octopus with tangled arms, dolphins and starfish, a blue flying fish, a circle of huge dragon flies ... Frescoes and pottery all lent themselves to this inventive fantasy. It is remarkable to find the same plant or marine motifs handled in a thousand different ways on so many vases turned out by the potter's wheel and exported by the hundred – as if the artists wanted to relive the pleasure of creation every time.[113]

Mimesis, in the sense of making images and forms with the natural appearance of people, things and events, which Greek art and sculpture went on to perfect, was strikingly absent from the conventional images created by other societies. As Gombrich observes, the 'Egyptian painter distinguished, for instance, between a dark brown for men and a pale yellow for women's bodies. The real flesh tone of the person portrayed obviously mattered as little in this context as the real colour of a river matters to the cartographer.'[114] In such pictures, little or nothing is related to feeling or to individual character, though the figure's importance might be conveyed by size – as would happen again in the religious art of the Dark Ages and early Middle Ages. With Greek art, all this would change as if by a miracle, portraying figures of exceptional beauty and life, figures that invite empathy, and inhabit our world.

The mediator of these benign developments in which both hemispheres partake is the evolution of what I have called 'necessary distance'. It is fundamental to this concept that it is what actually brings one into connection with that from which one is appropriately distanced; it is not a distancing that separates. Necessary distance is what makes empathy possible. It would seem that this is what lies behind the importance of harmony, balance, equipoise, in Greek culture at its best.

This is rather beautifully illustrated by the relationship that later came about between Athenians and their land, on which they still, for some of the year, lived. Although they could be said to be the first city dwellers in the modern sense, there is no implication, as there would be now, of this alienating them from the life of the land – quite the opposite. 'The "citizens" were residents of a territory greater than the city itself . . . Politically [the *polis*] was of a piece with the surrounding territory,' writes Braudel; and he continues, quoting Edouard Will's *Histoire politique du monde hellénistique*, 'the existence of a city was inconceivable without a surrounding territory, the division of which among the citizens was the basis of civic identity.'[115] The Athenians were the originators of the 'prejudice' that 'toil on the land (and the accompanying leisure, whether that of the great landowner or that of everyone in wintertime) was the only activity really worthy of a man.'[116] In times of danger they would retreat to the city; and every spring during the Peloponnesian War, when the Spartans would arrive over the pass above Eleusis, the Athenians, having left their homes in the fields for the high ground of the Pelargicon, the walls surrounding the Acropolis, would 'watch the enemy arriving in the distance'.[117] It was also from these walls that in more peaceful times, as Braudel puts it with gentle humour, the *eupatridae*, the aristocracy, 'could survey their land and their peasants from a convenient distance'.[118] But this distance was the enabler of love, such as those who could never stand back enough from the land to see it at all might never experience. Not only was this expressed in autochthony myths as parental love, but

the passionate love they bore their little homelands verged on the pathological, going well beyond the reasonable. They used the term meaning sexual desire, *himeros*, to refer to it. Nowhere else in world history has this love for the native soil been taken to such extremes, with the result that love could yield only to hatred.[119]

But that takes us to the subsequent period in which the harmony or equipoise was lost.

THE LATER PERIOD

Braudel believed, as did de Selincourt, that 'everything worthwhile [in Greek culture] had been accomplished' by the time Plato and Aristotle came on the scene, in the fourth century. This would certainly be the view of Heidegger, as it had been that of Nietzsche, according to whom the highpoint was the age of Aeschylus, when Apollo and Dionysus were reconciled, the time of the birth of tragedy. In Nietzsche's view, in the end 'the ambiguous god of wine and death yielded the stage to Apollo and the triumph of rationality, to theoretical and practical utilitarianism as well as democracy, which was a contemporary phenomenon', symptoms of the ageing of Greek civilisation, and foreshadowing the depressing spectacle, as he saw it, of the modern Western world.[120] Without necessarily espousing the extreme view of Nietzsche on the role of the Apollonian, this analysis seems to me essentially correct.

However, there were positive developments in the later period. It is only with the continuing evolution of greater distance from one another that we start to focus on the uniqueness of ourselves and others as individuals, which is largely what is expressed in the face. If we describe our own feelings, we are more immediately aware of the sensations and emotional reactions throughout our physical frame than of our own changing facial expressions: for *that* we would need a higher degree of self-consciousness, such as a mirror brings. By contrast, the quasi-mythological characters of Homer's epic are like the characters in Greek tragedy, of archetypal status, not merely individuals: and in the drama the actors wore masks. The lack of description or depiction of the expressive face, in Homer at least, is not a sign of lack of fellow-feeling or empathy – there would have been no difficulty in the quite different process of spontaneously reading or understanding the feelings of others by their faces in daily life – but it is a consequence of the degree of fusion between self and other, the lack of self-consciousness that Gill describes in the archaic era.

In the visual art of sculpture, by contrast with poetry and drama, we are specifically creating an image of something from the 'outside' – a degree of distance is of the essence, and hence we start to see empathy expressed there precisely in the other's *face*. A still further degree of self-consciousness, and systematisation, in the art of understanding faces is implied by physiognomy. Interest in physiognomy implies, all the same, a conscious awareness of the close relationship between soul and body, the idea that one can read something about individuals – their character, their special personal qualities, perhaps even their defects – in the physical qualities of the face. There is a relationship between all individuality and imperfection; all that makes us special could be seen from the left-hemisphere point of view as the falling away from some abstract ideal. Perhaps this is what Aristotle was alluding to when he wrote that 'men are good in but one way, but bad in many'.[121] Reading imperfections in the face as individuality is clearly likely to be a right-hemisphere development, though its systematisation as a sort of science suggests left-hemisphere involvement.

I have alluded to Brener's interesting study of representations of the human face in antiquity. What he shows very convincingly is the painstaking care that started to be shown in sculpture and portraiture, and the degree to which portraiture sought to be faithful: facial expression is so subtle that very minor discrepancies can make enormous differences to interpretation and understanding. An interest in faces depends upon the skill of mimesis and the cognitive capacity for a minutely detailed attention which is always subservient to the whole. Pliny the Elder recorded of Apelles, a famous painter of the fourth century BC, that 'his portraits were such perfect likenesses that, incredible as it may seem, Apion the Grammarian has left it on record that a physiognomist, or *metoposkopos*, as they call them, was able to tell from the portraits alone how long the sitter had to live or had already lived.'[122]

'Physiognomy', writes one recent scholar, 'as a theoretical concern in the philosophy of antiquity starts with Phaedo [of Elis, fourth century BC], flourishes in Aristotle's school, and ends, one might fairly say, with Galen [second century AD].'[123] The great classical text on the subject, Polemon of Laodicea's *Physiognomy*, was written in the second century AD. He was the first to emphasise the eye, which alone takes up a third of the whole book (Book I is devoted to the eye, Book II to 'other parts of the body'). In sculpture, around AD 130, there was a move from the merely painted pupil to an incised and engraved pupil, enlarging the powers of expressive sculpture in stone.[124]

This period from the fourth century BC to the second century AD, as is evident from Brener's detailed analysis, is the high point of the expressiveness of portraiture in both painting and sculpture, with the most extraordinary attention to individual expression and to the realism that underwrites individuality in both Greek, and perhaps particularly Roman, art. Why does it come late, relatively speaking? Hufschmidt shows that in fact the tendency to favour the right hemisphere in interpretation of faces begins around the sixth century BC. But I think an increase in expressiveness was inevitably dependent not just on empathy, but on the development, generation by generation, of a quite specific mimetic skill that took longer to evolve than the empathic sensibility that it expressed, and which one senses to be there in early lyric poetry, in, for example, Alcaeus, Sappho and Anacreon, from the sixth century onwards. The degree of expressiveness one finds in portraiture of the Hellenistic period required an awareness of the huge complexity of independently innervated muscle fibre groups, particularly in the upper half of the face around the eyes – and that simply takes time. It also takes a necessary balance of right and left hemispheres.

Nietzsche's judgment on the Hellenistic era needs to be qualified, then. It also tends to underplay the important role that the left hemisphere, the Apollonian, played in the genesis of the best in Greek culture (which Nietzsche, to be fair, elsewhere acknowledged). Here again Heidegger's perception that the Greeks were essentially still Dionysian explains the redeeming feel of the advent of Apollo in their world, at least at first. But as Nietzsche points out, it is not just Dionysus that is 'ambiguous'. Apollo is an ambiguous figure, too. The derivation of the name of Apollo means 'the luminous one' (in German, *der Scheinende*); as such also the god of *fantasy*, of that which only seems to be the case (*das Scheinende*), rather than of what is.[125]

The great humanistic achievements of poetry, drama, sculpture, architecture, along with empathy, humour and the sense of the individual self, are not the only achievements of Ancient Greece. It also saw the foundation of systematically structured bodies of objective knowledge, products of writing and owed to the advances of the left hemisphere in tandem with the right. These include the development of a legal constitution and a body of laws; philosophy; the invention of the idea of, and the study of, history; the formalisation of geographic knowledge and the study of maps; the structuring of a system of education; the invention of the orders of architecture; systematic description of the human body, and of the animal world; geometry; and theories of physics. In themselves all of these represent enormous advances, and in terms of the thesis of this book demonstrate the power for good that the left hemisphere wields when it acts as the emissary of the right hemisphere, and has not yet come to believe itself the Master.

The right hemisphere is prophetic or 'divinatory', however, and can see where this will lead. Its prophecies are enshrined in the myth of Prometheus. Where did it lead?

In the late fifth century BC, Socrates' pupil Plato was born. Plato's written works date from the early fourth century, and in these dialogues, real or imagined, between Socrates and one of the many who came to him inquiring after truth, Socrates demonstrates to his inquirer the falsity of the premises from which he started, by leading him to a contradiction that follows logically from those premises. Plato's influence on the history of logic, mathematics, and moral and political philosophy cannot be overestimated, despite the fact that his works were lost from view for over a thousand years until the Renaissance, available only in partial reports and commentaries translated into Latin via Arabic. His legacy includes the (left-hemisphere-congruent) beliefs that truth is in principle knowable, that it is knowable through reason alone, and that all truths are consistent with one another.

By the time of Socrates, the Heraclitean respect for the testimony of our senses had been lost. The phenomenal world yields only deception: the *ideas* of things come to be prioritised over things themselves, over whatever it is of which we have direct knowledge. Plato's doctrine of the eternal Forms gives priority to the unchanging categorical type (say, the 'ideal table') over the myriad phenomenal exemplars (actual tables in the everyday world), which are no more than imperfect copies of the ideal form. It is true that Plato's pupil, Aristotle, who was a true scientist, and probably the most brilliant polymath the world has ever known, interested in, as far as possible without preconceptions, observing and understanding the natural world, and ever mindful of the importance of experience, effectively reversed this, finding the universal in and through particular instantiations. But, alas, the spirit of Aristotle did not survive with his works. Instead they became, in an inversion of that spirit, a sort of Holy Writ of the experiential world for 1500 years – rendering his thought about experience, provisional as it was, static, unchanging, and idealised as infallible, until the Renaissance.

There were tendencies in the very fabric of Greek language and thought that inevitably favoured abstraction and idealisation. Snell makes the point that the Greek language, by inventing the definite article, could take an attribute of an existing thing, expressed through an adjective – that it was 'beautiful', say – and turn it into an abstract noun by adding the definite article: so from beautiful (*kalos*) to 'the beautiful' (*to kalon*).[126] In a clever and audacious, one might say hubristic, inversion, the left hemisphere now seems to imply that what is purely conceptual is what is real, and what is experienced, at least by the senses, is downgraded, and amazingly enough actually becomes the 'representation'! Thus in *The Republic*, Plato writes:

> The stars that decorate the sky, though we rightly regard them as the finest and most perfect of visible things, are far inferior, just because they are visible, to the true realities; that is, to the true relative velocities, in pure numbers and perfect figures, of the orbits and what they carry in them, which are perceptible to reason and thought but not visible to the eye . . . We shall therefore treat astronomy, like geometry, as setting us problems for solution, and ignore the visible heavens, if we want to make a genuine study of the subject . . .[127]

This separation of the absolute and eternal, which can be known by *logos* (reason), from the purely phenomenological, which is now seen as inferior, leaves an indelible stamp on the history of Western philosophy for the subsequent two thousand years.

The reliance on reason downgrades not just the testimony of the senses, but all our implicit knowledge. This was the grounds of Nietzsche's view that Socrates, far from being the hero of our culture, was its first degenerate, because Socrates had lost the ability of the nobles to trust intuition: 'Honest men', he wrote, 'do not carry their reasons exposed in this fashion.'[128] Degeneration, by this account, begins relatively late in Greece, with Plato, and involves the inability to trust what is implicit or intuitive. 'What must first be proved is worth little', Nietzsche continues in *The Twilight of the Idols*:

> one chooses dialectic only when one has no other means. One knows that one arouses mistrust with it, that it is not very persuasive. Nothing is easier to erase than a dialectical effect: the experience of every meeting at which there are speeches proves this.

With the loss of the power of intuition,

> rationality was then hit upon as the *saviour*; neither Socrates nor his 'patients' had any choice about being rational: it was *de rigueur*, it was their *last* resort. The fanaticism with which all Greek reflection throws itself upon rationality betrays a desperate situation; there was danger, there was but *one* choice: either to perish or – to be *absurdly rational*.[129]

And if this seems to be just the pardonable excesses of Nietzschean *furor*, the ravings of an inspired madman, consider these words from Panksepp the neuroscientist:

Although language is the only way we can scientifically bridge the chasm between mind and brain, we should always remember that we humans are creatures that can be deceived as easily by logical rigour as by blind faith ... It is possible that some of the fuzzier concepts of folk-psychology may lead us to a more fruitful understanding of the integrative functions of the brain than the rigorous, but constrained, languages of visually observable behavioural acts[130]

(and cf. Friedrich Waismann above, p. 157).

In this later Greek world, truth becomes something proved by argument. The importance of another, ultimately more powerful, revealer of truth, metaphor, is forgotten; and metaphor, in another clever inversion, comes even to be a lie, though perhaps a pretty one. So the statements of truth contained in myth become discounted as 'fictions', that is to say untruths or lies – since, to the left hemisphere, metaphor is no more than this.

Great philosopher that he undoubtedly was, Plato is not quite straightforward in this respect. Even Plato had intuitions he could not dismiss. What is quite moving, even tragic, in the true sense (because it involves Socrates' hubristic trust in his own dialectic powers), is to see Socrates/Plato torn between his own intuitions and the awareness that he is no longer at liberty to trust them. Plato was originally a poet and it was his association with Socrates that impressed on him the need to forsake poetry for dialectic. In *The Republic* Socrates fulminates against the works of

> tragedians and other dramatists – such representations definitely harm the minds of their audiences ... representations at the third remove from reality, and easy to produce without any knowledge of the truth ... all the poets from Homer downwards have no grasp of reality but merely give us a superficial representation ... So great is the natural magic of poetry. Strip it of its poetic colouring, reduce it to plain prose, and I think you know how little it amounts to ... the artist knows little or nothing about the subjects he represents and ... his art is something that has no serious value.

The work of painters and artists of all kinds, including poets are 'far removed from reality', and appeal to 'an element in us equally far removed from reason, a thoroughly unsound combination'. Art is 'a poor child born of poor parents', appeals to 'a low element in the mind', and has 'a terrible power to corrupt even the best characters'. Poets are to be banished from the Republic.[131] All those involved in creative arts deal in deceit: the metaphor is a lie. Calculation (logic) is to be preferred to imagination: denotation to connotation. Being a poet also involves imagining one's way into many things, and 'is unsuitable for our state, because there one man does one job and does not play a multiplicity of rôles': so much for Heraclitus' insight that one needs to inquire into many things, not just one, if one is not to be led astray.[132] Plato's proscriptions on music, like so much else about his Republic, remind one of a Soviet-style totalitarian state. There is no need of a wide harmonic range; most rhythms and modes are outlawed; flutes, harps and 'harpsichords' are banned, as are all 'dirges and laments'; and there will be need only of two kinds of music, the kind that encourages civil orderliness, and the kind that sternly encourages us to war.[133] All has been reduced to utility in the service of the will to power.[134]

But at the same time, Plato himself needs to use myth in order to explain things that resist formulation in language or dialectic: the allegory of the Cave, or the ring of Gyges, for example. In fact Plato appears ambivalent, and gives hints, particularly in the *Symposium*, that the realm of the Forms attracts us in a way that transcends the logical; and that those who have intuited the Form of the Good, and the Form of the Beautiful, are compelled to pursue them, and to try to convey them to others, exactly as I have suggested the ideals towards which the right hemisphere is drawn act upon it, contrasting these with the purely abstracted forms of things which are created by the left hemisphere. While awaiting death in prison, Socrates' *daemon* (conscience) visited him and repeatedly told him to make music.[135] 'Whatever urged these exercises on him', wrote Nietzsche, 'was something similar to his warning voice':

> it was his Apolline insight that, like some barbarian king, he did not understand the noble image of some god and, in his ignorance, was in danger of committing a sin against a deity. The words spoken by the figure who appeared to Socrates in dream are the only hint of any scruples in him about the limits of logical nature; perhaps, he must have told himself, things which I do not understand are not automatically unreasonable. Perhaps there is a kingdom of wisdom from which the logician is banished? Perhaps art may even be a necessary correlative and supplement of science?[136]

But there is no doubt that it is ultimately the left-hemisphere version of the world that Plato puts forward, for the first time in history; puts forward so strongly that it has taken two thousand years to shake it off.

And so it is that perhaps the most profound legacy of the Greeks, their myths, come to be seen as 'myths' as we now use the term, false histories. But here is Malinowski on the true nature of myth:

> These stories live not by idle interest [that is, not as a sort of primitive science, merely to answer intellectual curiosity], not as fictitious or even as true narratives; but are to the natives a statement of a primeval, greater, and more relevant reality, by which the present life, fates, and activities of mankind are determined, the knowledge of which supplies man with the motive for ritual and moral actions, as well as with indications as to how to perform them.[137]

This kind of truth cannot be apprehended directly, explicitly; in the attempt, it becomes flattened to two-dimensionality, even deadened, by the left hemisphere. It has to be metaphorised, 'carried across' to our world, by mythology and by ritual, in which the gods approach us; or as we begin to approach *them*, when we stand back in 'necessary distance' from our world through sacred drama. So Kerényi writes:

In the domain of myth is to be found not ordinary truth but a higher truth, which permits approaches to itself from the domain of *bios* [not just life, but 'the highly characterised life of a human being', perhaps best rendered, despite the apparent chasm of two millennia, as *Dasein*]. These approaches are provided by sacred plays, in which man raises himself to the level of the gods, plays too which bring the gods down from their heights. Mythology, indeed, especially Greek mythology, could in some sense be considered as the play of the gods, in which they approach us.[138]

Eventually myths become a sort of surrogate science, exactly what Malinowski says they are not. And some Platonic myths are of this kind. Thus how did man come to have his current bodily shape? Well, originally he was a head, of course; a head that was spherical – the perfect shape: except that it couldn't control where it went.

Accordingly, that the head might not roll upon the ground with its heights and hollows of all sorts, and have no means to surmount the one or to climb out of the other, they gave it the body as a vehicle for ease of travel; that is why the body is elongated and grew four limbs that can be stretched out or bent, the god contriving thus for its travelling.[139]

This myth tells us a lot about the relation between the mind and body that was already emerging. In fact the process is at work even in the fifth century BC, as this creation myth of Empedocles suggests:

On [the earth] many heads sprung up without necks, and arms wandered bare and bereft of shoulders; eyes strayed up and down in want of foreheads. Solitary limbs wandered seeking for union. But, as divinity was mingled still further with divinity, these things joined together as each might chance, and many other things besides them continually arose.[140]

Fancy that! The mind has now come to believe that the body is an assemblage of separate bits, wandering about aimlessly on their own, and put together by chance. No prizes for guessing which hemisphere that comes from.

THE ROMANS

Most of the great legacy of Rome's literature belongs to the Augustan era, the first century BC, with Virgil, Horace, Ovid, Propertius and Catullus all writing during a period of fifty years of one another. Undoubtedly there is here a remarkable increase in psychological sophistication, and both touching and witty insights into human nature, its potential greatness and its failings. This period saw not just the expansion and codification of jurisprudence, but the establishment of an ideal of reasonableness and of moral rectitude in art and poetry as well. Virgil and Horace were obviously drawn by what one might see as Scheler's *Lebenswerte*: the ideal of the noble Roman emanates from their work. Virgil's attraction to and idealisation of the natural world,[141] the importance of human bonds, both those of *amor* and those of *pietas*, coupled with his sense of pity for the passing of human lives and achievements – *sunt lacrimae rerum et mentem mortalia tangunt*[142] – all suggests an alliance between the right and left hemispheres at this time, in which the right hemisphere primacy is respected. Ovid, a man who in his life had reason enough to contemplate the harsh reverses of fate, called his greatest work the *Metamorphoses*, the title itself suggestive of the Heraclitean flux; and in it once again one sees that standing back from the world which enables the finest spirits both to rise on the vertical axis and to venture out along the horizontal axis into the lived world of the human heart:

> There is no greater wonder than to range
> The starry heights, to leave the earth's dull regions,
> To ride the clouds, to stand on Atlas' shoulders,
> And see, far off, far down, the little figures
> Wandering here and there, devoid of reason,
> Anxious, in fear of death, and so advise them,
> And so make fate an open book . . .

> . . . Full sail, I voyage
> Over the boundless ocean, and I tell you
> Nothing is permanent in all the world.
> All things are fluid; every image forms,
> Wandering through change. Time is itself a river
> In constant movement, and the hours flow by
> Like water, wave on wave, pursued, pursuing,
> Forever fugitive, forever new.
> That which has been, is not; that which was not,
> Begins to be; motion and moment always
> In process of renewal . . .

> Not even the so-called elements are constant . . .

> Nothing remains the same: the great renewer,
> Nature, makes form from form, and, oh, believe me
> That nothing ever dies. . . .[143]

Yet, alongside its great artistic achievements, which undoubtedly result from the co-operation of both hemispheres, Roman civilisation provides evidence of an advance towards ever more rigidly systematised ways of thinking, suggestive of the left hemisphere working alone. In Greece, the Apollonian was never separate from the Dionysian, though latterly the Apollonian may have got the upper hand. Augustus, who presided over the great flourishing of the arts, was the first Emperor; but as the scale of imperial power grew in tandem with the evolution of Roman military and administrative successes, the Apollonian left hemisphere begins to freewheel. The Roman Empire was 'characterised by its towns and cities', writes Braudel:

brought into being by a Roman power which shaped them in its own image, they provided a means of transplanting to far-flung places a series of cultural goods, always identifiably the same. Set down in the midst of often primitive local peoples, they marked the staging-posts of a civilisation of self-promotion and assimilation. That is one reason why these towns were all so alike, faithfully corresponding to a model which hardly changed over time and place.[144]

Even when there is at times a strong input of originality from Rome, for example 'in the taste for realistic detail, for lifelike portraiture, landscape and still life – the original spark must have come from the east';[145] which takes us back to Greece, and the further Eastern origins of Greece's own originality.

In drama there is a possible parallel to this left-hemisphere overdrive, with the influence of Theophrastan character 'types', or as we would say stereotypes, on Roman New Comedy, the fairly predictable sit-com of the era, that replaced the more exuberantly wild, bizarre and ultimately far more imaginative, and intellectually stimulating, Old Comedy, typified among the Greeks by Aristophanes. (Theophrastus was a student of Aristotle: it is said that Aristotle having pronounced to the effect that one swallow doth not a summer make, Theophrastus dutifully applied himself to a treatise on precisely how many swallows it took.)[146]

Rome's greatness depended more on codification, rigidity and solidity than it did on flexibility, imagination and originality. Speaking of law making, Braudel writes:

> Without a doubt, Rome's intelligence and genius came into its own in this area. The metropolis could not maintain contact with its Empire – the rest of Italy, the provinces, the cities – without the legal regulations essential to the maintenance of political, social and economic order. The body of law could only increase over the ages.[147]

At first that brought seductive stability. By the second century AD the Roman Empire, according to Charles Freeman, 'had reached the height of its maturity in that it was relatively peaceful, was able to defend itself and its elites flourished in an atmosphere of comparative intellectual and spiritual freedom'.[148]

But it did not last. It may be that an increasing bureaucracy, totalitarianism and an emphasis on the mechanistic in the late Roman period represents an attempt by the left hemisphere to 'go it alone'. With this in mind, it is worth looking briefly at the development of Roman architecture and sculpture, since as Braudel says, 'the domain in which Rome most rapidly developed its own personality was architecture.'[149] We see its intellectual progress visibly charted there. There is a poetic as well as historical truth in the fact that the imperial vastness of Roman architecture was made possible by the invention of concrete.

'The everyday life of the average man – his whole political, economic, and social life – was transformed during Late Antiquity', writes Hans Peter L'Orange, whose book *Art Forms and Civic Life in the Late Roman Empire* is a classic study of the relationship between the architecture and broader values of this period.[150] His study brings out one after another the features of left-hemisphere dominance so beautifully, and in ways that are so relevant by analogy with our own situation, that I allow him to speak for himself. 'The free and natural forms of the early Empire, the multiplicity and variation of life under a decentralised administration, was replaced by homogeneity and uniformity under an ever-present and increasingly more centralised hierarchy of civil officials.' What he sees as the 'infinite variety of vigorous natural growth' was levelled and regulated, into 'an unchangeable, firmly crystallised order', where individuals were no longer independent in a freely moving harmony with their surroundings, but became an immoveable part in the cadre of the state. L'Orange refers to an increasing standardisation and equalisation of life, related to the militarisation of society, resulting in a replacement in art of organic grouping by 'mechanical coordination'.[151]

This is imaged for L'Orange in the changes in architecture, 'the characteristic transition from organic articulation of a well-differentiated structure to an abstract simplification in great planes and lines . . .' In Classical art and architecture, form had not been something added on by the artist from without or above, but rather brought forth from 'deep within the object itself'. There was an organic beauty which pervaded the whole conception and could be found in its smallest detail: 'in the same way that the individual type of a living being determines the form of each single part of it, so the principle for the whole structure of the classical building is contained within each single element of it.'[152] The phrase reminds one of the way in which, in living forms, the structure of DNA within every cell contains information about the whole organism, or of the fractality of organic forms.[153] Thus, he continues, often on sacred sites the classical temples stand 'with peculiar recalcitrance' beside one another,

> each with its own orientation determined by its god or cult, by sacred portents and signs in the temple ground. Each building defies superior order of axiality, symmetry, or unity of direction ... This organic and autonomous life, this supreme development from within of each part, of each ornament of the building, was lost during the Hellenistic-Roman evolution that followed.

The forms of buildings become 'standardised, subordinated, and symmetrised', subsumed as parts of a bigger complex. In cannibalising older buildings for material, so called *spolia* (the spoils of conquest) are thrown in anywhere, to make weight in the colossal, 'endless flights of monotonously divided walls'; and in a sign of complete lack of sense of part to whole, the bases of columns are even used as capitals.[154]

Things are no better when it comes to the human face. Until the end of the third century, portraiture had sought to convey a lifelike individuality, revealing its subject as situated 'in time, in the very movement of life . . . the play of features in the nervous face . . . the very flash of personality'.[155] Asymmetry played a part in achieving this. Around AD 300, however, a fundamental change took place in the depiction of the face. Portraits in stone begin to show a 'peculiarly abstract', distant gaze, unconcerned with the elusive, changing, complex world in which we live, fixed on eternal abstractions: 'the features suddenly stiffen in an expressive Medusa-like mask'.[156] In portraiture of the period, the richly complex plastic modelling of the face sinks into something symmetrical, regular, crystalline, 'just as the plastic articulation of the building structure disappears into the great continuous wall surfaces'.[157] A technical shift, from the chisel to the running drill, brings with it a harshness and flatness, so that

the body loses its substantiality, it disintegrates: we are anxious lest it shrink to nothing and vanish . . . There is a movement away from lifelike nature to abstract types, from plastic articulation to conceptual generalisation, from the corporeal to the symbolic. A higher meaning is implanted in the object, which more and more is reduced to a shell enclosing this meaningful core, more and more becomes a sign referring to a thought – and, as a sign, always identical, formula-like, stereotype.

'It is', concludes L'Orange, 'as if the natural objects flee from living perception . . .'[158]

This change was to see no reversal until the Renaissance. From now on through the Middle Ages face and body are symbols only: individualistic portraits of the emperors disappear, and they become alike in the same way as the saints.[159] There is a turning away from beauty of proportion, based on the human body; size now represents an idea, the degree of significance we should attach to the figure. Martyrs and ascetics, with their revulsion from the body, replace the classical heroes: all life in the flesh is corrupt. Plotinus' belief that the tangible reality of nature was a beautiful reflection of the Platonic Ideas cedes to a view of the natural world as 'only a jungle of confusion where humans lose their way'.[160] Myth and metaphor are no longer semi-transparent, but an opaque shell of lies which encloses the real truth, an abstraction at its core. Depictions on triumphal arches are no longer of the actual victor and the actual events, but of the generalised, symbolic attributes of the absolute victor: nothing is what it is, but only what it represents.

There is a loss of the sense of the beauty of proportion. In classical sculpture, the figures are separated in order that each body may be seen in itself as a corporeally beautiful whole; while at the same time, by their position, movement and gesture, they are placed in a certain rhythmic reciprocal contact which presents them as an organic, living group. By the third century AD, this classical composition has been 'shattered'. Figures not only lose their corporeal beauty, but no longer exist in organic groupings: a sense of the whole, and the flow of life, are lost.

They overlap and cover one another in such a way that they no longer appear as organic units but rather as parts of entwined tangles of figures . . . the contours of the figures no longer flow rhythmically, but are formed by straight and jagged lines, somewhat spasmodically; characteristic are the abrupt, marionette-like movements.

Towards the end of the third century and into the early fourth century, organic form is replaced by 'a *mechanical* order imposed upon objects from above . . .'[161] The figures are equalised, pressed into symmetrical, horizontal lines, 'just as the soldier to his rank and file . . . in a peculiar way the figures are *immobilised*'. There is an 'infinite repetition of identical elements', made even firmer by symmetry. 'In the whole of conceptual life', L'Orange concludes, 'there is a movement away from the complex towards the simple, from the mobile towards the static, from the dialectic and relative towards the dogmatic and the authoritarian, from the empirical towards theology and theosophy.'[162]

Perhaps the best way of putting it is that there came about a sort of hierarchy of the hemispheres which reversed the natural order. At the more humble, domestic level, the right hemisphere was left relatively undisturbed, while its ambitious, if not grandiose, emissary lorded it over the empire. 'In the domains of painting and sculpture, Roman art slowly distinguished itself from its Greek models', writes Braudel:

> there was indeed a popular art . . . an art not so much Roman as south Italian, which was to contribute something distinctive to Rome. This was a sturdy, realistic kind of art, depicting people and things with verisimilitude . . . It is in the domestic art of the portrait that one finds Roman art par excellence . . . Greek influence occasionally introduced a more pretentious note, but the Roman portrait, whether sculpted or painted, retained from its age-old tradition a very great expressive force and was always comparatively sober in style.[163]

At the local level, a more vibrant and tolerant culture may have prevailed, but increasingly it seems, another culture – strident, intolerant, concerned with abstractions, and with conformity – appears to have taken hold.

In his book *The Closing of the Western Mind*, Charles Freeman puts forward the view that this was a consequence of the rise of Christianity.[164] Once the Emperor Constantine, himself a Christian, decreed religious tolerance of all cults, including Christianity, by the Edict of Milan in 313, he began the process of integrating the Church into the state. In doing so, he also promoted its identification with military success, with secular power, and with wealth. Although this clearly brought a kind of stability for Christians, who for centuries had been subject to persecution, it also led, according to Freeman, to a world which was rigid, less accommodating of difference, more concerned with dogma and less with reason. With the Nicene decree of Theodosius in 381, not only was paganism outlawed, but a certain specific understanding of the nature of the Trinity became orthodoxy: there was no room for disagreement and debate was stifled.

The Greek tradition had been one of tolerance of others' beliefs, an inclusive attitude to the gods, and one could see Constantine's Edict as lying in that tradition. But by the end of the fourth century, such tolerance was a thing of the past, as the dispute between Symmachus and Ambrose over the Altar of Victory demonstrates.[165] For the Greeks spirituality and rationality, *muthos* (*mythos*) and

1 Psychotic subjects experience an all-observing eye that exists on a level with the objects it observes. This page from a Victorian flower album in the Bethlem Royal Hospital Archive (by Barbara Honywood) long antedates the modernism it appears to predict.

2 In this remarkable painting by David Chick, of a psychotic experience, the androgynous subject exists in the plane of the paper, as does the all-observing eye, despite the emphatic perspective (also from the Bethlem archive).

3 *Christ and His Mother*, St Saviour in Khora, Istanbul, early 14th century. The expressive power of these faces has rarely been surpassed, and is startling in its historical context, 150 years before Leonardo. In a reversal of our own values, the artist himself is unknown.

4 *Resurrection of the Dead*, also from St Saviour in Khora, early 14th century. Grasp, the left hemisphere's means of control, is not intrinsically self-serving: it can also reach out to others. The life-giving force here comes from the left side of Christ's body.

5 *Adoration of the Shepherds*, by Domenico Ghirlandaio (1485). For the first time in Western art there are two kinds of perspective, in space and in time, which powerfully draw us into relation with the subject of the painting and make us aware of mortality.

6 *The Ambassadors*, by Hans Holbein the Younger (1533). Human achievement is not denied, but contextualised, by mortality: the anamorphic skull is only properly visible from the side.

7 *Seaport with the Embarkation of the Queen of Sheba*, by Claude Lorrain (1648).
Here light, colour and the texture of the stone surfaces all emphasise the depth of
perspective in both time and space, drawing us into felt relationship with the world.

8 *Landscape with Ascanius Shooting the Stag of Sylvia*, by Claude Lorrain (1682).
There are at least five successive planes of vision here, subtly modulated by colour
and light, and the temple ruins appear already as old as the foundations of the world.

9 Scene from '*The Last of the Mohicans*', by Thomas Cole (1827). The spirit encountered in Claude still presides, though the perspective on the world and the past is now elevated.

10 *The Conflagration*, by Albert Bierstadt (late 19th century). It was not the Enlightenment, but Romanticism, which revealed the beauty and power of light: this study is, like Turner's celebrations of colour and light, far from abstract.

11 Frontispiece to William Blake's poem *Milton* (1804–11). Inspiration, in the form of the spirit of Milton, is shown entering Blake's body at the left tarsus, the cerebral representation of which is close to the right limbic system.

12 *Large Reclining Nude,* by Henri Matisse (1935). Loss of proportion and perspective in modernism emphasises emotional detachment. Like harmony, perspective arrived with the Renaissance, and left with modernism.

13 *The Muse*, by Pablo Picasso (1935). In an amusing portrayal of modernist ennui, the painter is abandoned by his muse, which sleeps like a bored child. The deliberately disrupted perspective is designed to disconcert.

14 *La Lunette d'Approche*, by René Magritte (1963). Is what we take to be real just a representation? The top corner of the right pane shows that representation is in the process of becoming the primary reality.

logos, could coexist without conflict.[166] That *muthoi* could be 'frozen in written form and interpreted to make statements of "truth" (*logoi*)' was alien to the Greeks. But, as Freeman admits, there was resistance to such formulations in early Christianity, as well, and Christians as much as pagans suffered under Theodosius' decree.[167] What Freeman takes to be the contrast between Greek and Christian thought might better be seen, according to some scholars, as the contrast between, on the one hand, the flexibility of a way of thinking which can be found in the rich tradition of the early Christian fathers as well as in the paganism with which it co-existed (where the hemispheres, too, co-operated), and, on the other, a culture marked by a concern with legalistic abstractions, with 'correctness', and the dogmatic certainties of the left hemisphere, whether Greek or Christian, which inexorably replaced them. Thus Mary Beard writes in a review: 'The real problem is in Freeman's stark opposition between the classical and Christian worlds.'[168]

For Freeman's claim is that it was reason that was lost during the ensuing period of late antiquity and the Middle Ages. But it was not. As Beard says, the Christian world was 'positively overflowing with intellectual and rational argument'. It's just that they deployed it on a legalistic framework for divinity, rather than on the movement of the planets. What was lacking was any concern with the world in which we live; their gaze was fixed firmly on theory, abstractions, conceptions, and what we could find only in books. And that was not just something to do with Christianity. It was, after all, Plato who said that we should do astronomy by 'ignoring the visible heavens', who taught that the imperceptible forms of things were more real than the things themselves: and it was also Plato who, in his *Republic*, and still more in his *Laws*, envisaged the first, utterly joyless, authoritarian state, in which what is not compulsory is proscribed. Plato's distaste for emotion, and mistrust of the body and the concrete world make an interesting comparison with the asceticism of Christianity during what we have come to know as the Dark Ages. The passion is for control, for fixity, for certainty; and that comes not with religion alone, but with a certain cast of mind, the cast of the left hemisphere.

This had not been the tradition of Aristotle, however, who, as Heraclitus had recommended, was an enquirer into many things indeed, a true empirical scientist, always the advocate for the incarnate world; and, as Freeman says, he had an 'openness to the provisional nature of knowledge' that made him a great philosopher.[169] But, in the period to come, Aristotle's work too was 'frozen', and paradoxically became an authority, removing the need to enquire, rather than being an inspiration to think for oneself. The striking thing about Greek intellectual life had been the tolerance of opposition: independence of mind, in this sense, began with the Greeks.[170] But it also declined with them, and eventually with the Romans after them, so that Christianity, which is in one sense the most powerful *mythos* in advocacy of the incarnate world, and of the value of the individual, that the world has ever known, also ended up a force for conformity, abstraction, and the suppression of independent thought.

Though the Empire continued to survive in one form or another in the East, it was destroyed in the West. The conditions of intellectual life simply no longer obtained, and knowledge of Greek was lost. There was little in the way of mathematical or scientific advance between 500 and 1100. Not until the tenth century did Greek texts, preserved in Arabic translations, begin to filter back into European consciousness. As learning revived it was very much under the control of the Church, but it is also true that it was largely due to the Church, which preserved and copied texts, and encouraged learning, and whose scholars were open to Greek and Arab ideas, that classical culture made it through from late antiquity to the Renaissance.

The decline of the Roman Empire has been the subject of more controversy than almost any other development in Western history. In his book *The Fall of Rome and the End of Civilization*, Bryan Ward-Perkins lists no fewer than 210 concepts that have been invoked to account for it.[171] His own formulation is that fiscal decline, with its consequences for an army under-funded by taxation, led to civil wars, which further undermined resources, and ultimately to defeat at the hands of the 'barbarians', resulting in a catastrophic collapse of civilisation. I find his argument compelling, though I am no historian. And it does not seem to me to be in conflict with the idea that there was a change in cast of mind – with the influx of a new population that would be inevitable. Only the change of mind had started anyway: it is evident in the fabric of the Empire itself.

CONCLUSION

This chapter has necessarily covered a lot of ground, though it goes without saying that it still only scratches the surface. Let me try to summarise. I see the starting point as an achievement of 'necessary distance', probably through an enhancement of frontal lobe function. Initially this led to a period of unparalleled richness in Greek culture when the left hemisphere and right hemisphere worked in harmony (when, in Nietzsche's terms, there was a union of Apollo with Dionysus, the time of the birth of tragedy). This was marked not by some sort of compromise, a holding back, of both hemispheres in relation to one another, but on the contrary by a going further than had ever been gone before in both directions at once, an unfolding of the potential of each hemisphere such as the Western world had never seen before. However, in philosophy, in attitudes to the phenomenal world, including ways of, literally, seeing it, in a view of the soul and body, in poetry and drama, in architecture and sculpture of the human form and face, and in the evolution of the Greek alphabet and of currency, we see the balance of power shifting always in the same direction, with the left hemisphere (Apollo) gradually coming to win the day.

Out of the history of Greece and Rome come confirmatory and converging lines of evidence that it was through the workings of the emissary, the left hemisphere, that the 'empire' of the mind expanded in the first place; and that, as long as it worked in concert with the Master, the right hemisphere, faithfully bringing back the knowledge and understanding gained by it, and offering them to the right hemisphere so as to bring a (now more complex) world into being, an ability which belongs to the right hemisphere alone, the empire thrived. On the other hand, once the left hemisphere started to believe that its dominion was everything, once the wealth it created began to remain obdurately in its own province, as though it could survive on its own, rather than being returned to the world that only the right hemisphere could bring about, then the empire – not the Roman Empire, which the world could do without, but the empire that the hemispheres between them had created, which we cannot – began to crumble.

CHAPTER 9

———◆———

THE RENAISSANCE AND THE REFORMATION

T HE PERIOD OF PERHAPS SEVEN HUNDRED YEARS THAT USED TO BE KNOWN AS THE Dark Ages, between the fall of Rome in the fifth century and what we now think of as the early Renaissance, in the twelfth, was by no means as lacking in vitality and colour as the name implied. That the term has fallen into disuse may be a recognition of the often remarkable quality of craftsmanship evident in what has survived from the period, or of the fact that it is no longer 'dark' in the sense that we know little about it – modern historiography has seen to that. It might also be due to its pejorative flavour; yet it would surely be a brave person who challenged the idea that the Renaissance was a remarkable, indeed unparalleled, step forward in the history of civilisation, akin to the developments of sixth-century Athens, in comparison with which the 'Dark Ages', whatever their merits, pale, relatively speaking, in significance.

In the next few chapters, I am inevitably going to have to use some much debated terms, such as the Renaissance, the Enlightenment, and Romanticism. To the left hemisphere these look like categories that should be definable; to the right hemisphere they are the products of experience of loose constellations of phenomena, which have a family resemblance. Conventionally, at this point, I should refer to a renewed interest, with the coming of the Renaissance, in the world at large, a thirst for knowledge of the natural world, and the historical world – the broader context in which we live, with the accent on how things are, rather than how they ought in theory to be, or are according to authority: the beginnings of modern science, history and philosophy. In the arts it is usual to speak of the new sense of the importance of harmony, of the relation of part to whole, a new spirit of conception that is both daring and tactful, graceful yet original. In all things, we learn, there was a new sense of the balanced reciprocities of individual and society, and of male and female. It is often said that it is in the Renaissance that the recognisably modern Western world begins. But, of course, it is more complicated than that.

That said, it might well look as if the Renaissance was the next great insurgence of the right hemisphere, perhaps even more pronounced than that of the Ancient World. But that, too, is an over-simplification. Once again there seems to have been a 'standing back', but this time a more self-conscious standing back than in sixth-century BC Athens. After all, from the outset there is a self-conscious retro-spection towards that ancient world, a second level of self-consciousness. In view of the extended metaphor in the first part of the book, in which I related the activity of the frontal lobes to the ability to rise above the terrain, enabling the left hemisphere to see the world laid out as its territory, it is perhaps significant that one of the first great Renaissance writers, Petrarch, is also said to have been the first person to think of climbing a hill for the view, but it is striking that what he reports is, not the utility of the experience, but its beauty. This illustrates a feature of these turning points in Western civilisation, that they begin as symmet-rical. The standing back is, if one can put it that way, in itself 'hemisphere-neutral', a function of the bilateral frontal lobes. But once again the fact of standing back necessitates a sharpening of the division of labour, a demand for abstraction and generalisation, favouring the left hemisphere; and at the same time it generates a leap forward in the right hemisphere's relation with the world around it, to which it now stands in a deepened and enriched relationship, through the achievement of what I have called 'necessary distance'.

Petrarch's 'view' suggests an opening of the eyes: he saw what was there for all to see, but none had seen. This is a Renaissance characteristic, a sudden coming into awareness of aspects of experience that had unaccountably been neglected: in science, a return to looking at things carefully 'as they are' rather than as they were

Fig. 9.1 Bishop blessing annual fair (from mediaeval vellum in Bibliothèque Nationale, Paris). Size represents what we know, not what we see.

known to be; in painting, similarly, to what we see rather than what we know. This is bound up with the important rediscovery of perspective (contrast Figures 9.1 and 9.2). It used to be thought that this was a Renaissance invention, but it is clear that it was understood by late Greek painters, and in particular can be seen in Roman wall paintings. But the faculty had been lost for over 1,000 years, until the time of Giotto, in the late thirteenth and early fourteenth centuries, who is often said to have been the first Renaissance painter to employ perspective. It was taken further in the paintings of Masaccio, after Brunelleschi demonstrated practical perspective in the piazza of the Duomo in Florence in 1415. Alberti, in his *De Pictura* of 1435, gave the first systematic treatise on the geometrical basis of perspective.

In the first part of this book I have referred to the fact that depth relies principally on the right hemisphere. Each hemisphere, however, has its contribution to make to perspective. Perspectival space is also related to individuality, another classic element of the Renaissance world view, since perspective mediates a view of the world from an individual standpoint – one particular place, at one particular time, rather than a God's-eye 'view from nowhere'. Like individuality, however, perspective is understood differently by the two hemispheres. Perspective is, on the one hand, the means of relating the individual to the world and enormously enhancing the sense of the individual as standing within the world, where depth includes and even draws in the viewer through the pull of the imagination; and, on the other, a means of turning the individual into an observing eye, a geometer coolly detached from his object's space. Equally the rise of the sense of the individual as distinct from the society to which he belongs enables both an understanding of others as individuals with feelings exactly like one's own, the grounds of empathy; and, at the same time, a detachment of the individual from the world around him that leads ominously in the direction of autism.

An example, that may stand for many here, of the way in which perspective re-establishes a context in which the viewer stands alongside the depicted subject, is the Adoration scene of Ghirlandaio (see Plate 5), which not only obviously illustrates perspectival depth in a spatial sense but also a sense of perspective in time, since it shows the infant Christ reposing next to a crib, which in this case is a Roman sarcophagus (despite the fact that the Magi are dressed as contemporary

Fig. 9.2 *Ideal City*, attributed to Piero della Francesca, but now thought to be by Luciano Laurana, after 1470.

Florentines – 'our' representatives of the present in the 1,500 year perspective narrated).

The sense of lived time is also a right-hemisphere-derived property, which is analogous to depth and has its own 'perspective'. 'Lived time' is not just an awareness of the fact of time, of the same laws of mutability existing immutably for everyone at all times and in all places, the grounds of the mediaeval moralising *ubi sunt* motif ('Where now is Alexander the Great, the Emperor Clovis?'), the purpose of which was to teach us to scorn all earthly things. I am distinguishing this from a sense of the irreparable loss of particular individuals, and of the rise and fall of particular cultures, irreplaceable as they are, where it is the *value* of the transitory, not its worthlessness, that is celebrated. Seeing one's own age in a broader context of cultural history, which is conventionally a defining aspect of what we call the Renaissance, depends on the contextualising function of the right hemisphere.

In the poems of François Villon, for example, one can see this change in a dramatic form. His *Ballade des dames du temps jadis* (Ballad of the ladies of days gone by) begins in conventional form with a recital of the great beauties of the past, asking where they are, but already in its refrain – *mais où sont les neiges d'antan?** – one can sense a more intimate, personal, melancholic note, that has nothing to do with moralising. The second half of the poem describes with great passion and pity the plight of old men and women, once beautiful and respected for their wit and charm, pushed aside and treated as fools, and ends by describing the 'poor little women', with nothing left to live on, supplanted by young *pucelettes*, asking God why they were born so soon and 'by what right':

> *Nostre Seigneur se taist tout quoi,*
> *Car au tancer il le perdroit†*

In his classic *The Waning of the Middle Ages*, Johan Huizinga wrote of the *danse macabre des femmes* by Villon's contemporary Martial d'Auvergne: 'In lamenting the frailty of the lives of women, it is still the briefness of joy that is deplored, and with the grave tone of the *memento mori* is mixed the regret for lost beauty.'[1]

When one reads this and many other poems of Villon's whose theme is pity for the transience of everything beautiful and good, one has to remind oneself that Villon himself never experienced age, but died, it is thought, in his early thirties: a colourful, picaresque character, he narrowly escaped the gallows. His *Ballade des pendus* (Ballad of the hanged men), his own epitaph, opens with a call across the centuries:

> *Frères humains qui après nous vivez*
> *N'ayez les cuers contre nous endurciz*

---

* 'but where are the snows of yesteryear?'
† 'Our Lord is silent and gives no reply, for if he had to defend himself against reproach he would lose.'

Car, se pitié de nous pauvres avez,
Dieu en aura plus tost de vous merciz.*

This is a new kind of remembering, a remembering that takes into account death, Villon's omnipresent subject, not just as a physical fact, or a moral lesson, or a matter for theological debate, but as a matter of the individual, a matter of the heart.

In these poems there are at least three kinds of remembering with which Villon's art is entrained: remembering the long perspective of the historical past, as peopled by real suffering human beings like himself; a projection forward to a time when he can see himself retrospectively through the eyes of others after he is dead; and the remembrance of his own past and its losses. It puts one in mind of Ronsard, his polished successor, writing, *Quand tu seras bien vieille, au soir à la chandelle,* imagining how his mistress, when she is old and grey, sitting alone by the light of her candle, will remember that *Ronsard me célébrait du temps que j'étais belle.*† Villon is also one of the first writers to appear before the reader as an individual, as, to use Wordsworth's phrase, 'a man speaking to men' – as one might say of Skelton or, particularly, Chaucer in English. In his work, too, we start to see imperfections and failings, not as deplorable lapses from some ideal, but as both what make us individual and at the same time bind us together.

All of this suggests the standing forward of the right hemisphere at this time. It also sets man again in the light of the 'being towards death' that Heidegger saw. Erasmus, like other Renaissance scholars, such as Sir Thomas More, had always on his desk a skull, a *memento mori*; and one of Holbein's greatest and most powerful canvases, *The Ambassadors,* depicts two handsome, clever, self-confident young men, at the height of their powers, surrounded by the symbols of their knowledge, sophistication and prosperity, while across the canvas he has painted in such a way that it could be seen only by someone descending the staircase (apt metaphor!) on which the painting was designed to hang, a grinning skull (see Plate 6).

One of the first great English poets before the Romantic era to enshrine vividly remembered personal scenes of great emotional intensity in his work was Sir Thomas Wyatt, writing in the second quarter of the sixteenth century. In his famous poem about the loss of the love of Anne Boleyn, 'They fle from me that sometime did me seke / With naked fote stalking in my chamber . . .' his memory erupts with extraordinary vividness:

Thancked be fortune, it hath ben otherwise
Twenty tymes better; but ons in speciall,
In thyn arraye after a pleasaunt gyse,
When her lose gowne from her shoulders did fall,

---

* 'Brothers, fellow-men, you who live after we are dead, do not harden your hearts against us; for if you have pity on us poor wretches, God may the sooner have pity on you.'
† 'Ronsard sang my praise in the days when I was beautiful.'

And she me caught in her arms long and small;
Therewithall sweetly did me kysse,
And softely saide, *dere hert, howe like you this?*

In another remarkable, but lesser-known, poem[2] he evokes the pain of love not on his own account but as it strikes the heart of his beloved (an achievement of the right frontal lobe if ever there was one), and speaking partly with her voice:

There was never nothing more me payned,
Nor nothing more me moved,
As when my swete hert her complained
That ever she me loved.
    Alas the while!

And he continues:

She wept and wrong her handes withal.
The teres fell in my nekke;
She torned her face and let it fall;
Scarcely therewith coulde speke.
    Alas the while!

Her paynes tormented me so sore
That comfort had I none,
But cursed my fortune more and more
To se her sobbe and grone:
    Alas the while!

What we are being let into here is something profound about the betweenness of emotional memory. Our feelings are not ours, any more than, as Scheler said, our thoughts are ours. We locate them in our heads, in our selves, but they cross inter-personal boundaries as though such limits had no meaning for them: passing back and forth from one mind to another, across space and time, growing and breeding, but where we do not know. What we feel arises out of what I feel for what you feel for what I feel about your feelings about me – and about many other things besides: it arises from the betweenness, and in this way feeling binds us together, and, more than that, actually unites us, since the feelings are shared. Yet the paradox is that those feelings only arise because of our distinctness, our ability to be separate, distinct individuals, that come, that go, in separation and death.

Drama has come to the fore at those points in history when we have achieved 'necessary distance', when we have been sufficiently detached to be looking at one another, but not yet so detached that we are inappropriately objective about, or alienated from, one another. The plays of Shakespeare constitute one of the most striking testimonies to the rise of the right hemisphere during this period. There is a complete disregard for theory and for category, a celebration of multiplicity and the richness of human variety, rather than the rehearsal of common laws for

personality and behaviour according to type. Shakespeare's characters are so stubbornly themselves, and not the thing that fate, or the dramatic plot, insists they
should be, that their individuality subverts the often stereotyped pattern of their
literary and historical sources: Richard II ill-suited to being king, more a self-
absorbed poet; Macbeth overcome with scruples and visions of guilt, the reluctant
usurper; Antony, love-besotted, his will suborned, hardly the fearless military
commander; and so on. My favourite is the character of Barnardine, a prisoner
awaiting hanging, whose only reason for being introduced into the plot of
Measure for Measure is so that he can get on and be hanged, and his head substituted for that of Claudio; out of a sort of sheer bloody-minded refusal to be an
idea rather than an individual, he will not 'arise and be hanged' when he should,
and there is nothing for it, but a suitable head has to be found somewhere else.
Shakespeare also famously confounded genres, introducing comic scenes into his
tragedies, and characters such as Jacques into his comedies; at every level he
confounded opposites, seeing that the 'web of our life is of a mingled yarn, good
and ill together'. Instead of standing outside or above his creation and telling us
how to judge his characters, Shakespeare emphasises the inevitability of feeling for
and with them, even with Shylock, again inherited with the story line as an a
exemplar of moral corruption. Perhaps most importantly – and this was Maurice
Morgann's brilliant insight – Shakespeare brought into being figures such as
Falstaff, that are incomprehensible in terms of the elements into which they could
be analysed, but form, *Gestalt*-like, new coherent, living wholes.[3] A coward, brag-
gart and buffoon when taken to pieces and the evidence judged in the abstract, he
nonetheless has qualities of bravery and generosity of heart which redeem what
would have been just a catalogue of imperfections, not by 'outweighing' them, but
by transforming them into something else within the quiddity of his being.

One of the most mysterious expressions of the way in which the whole does not
depend on the sum of the parts is in the art of caricature. Here gross distortions
of every part can be compatible with immediate recognition of the whole.
Caricature in the ancient world – and it existed both in Egypt and Greece – was
always the exaggeration of a type, not the caricature of an individual. The first
artist to deploy caricature of an individual, and the originator of the term 'cari-
catura', was Annibale Carracci (1560–1609). 'A good caricature', he said, 'like every
work of art, is more true to life than reality itself.'[4] The genius of caricature is, as
Gombrich and Kris point out, to have revealed that 'similarity is not essential to
likeness'. Carracci portrayed his friends and fellow creatures as animals. There the
artist changes every feature, every single part of the face. 'All he retains is the
striking and individual *expression* which remains unaltered even when it is transferred to another creature. To recognise such similarity in different shapes . . .
gives us all a shock of surprise to which we respond with laughter.' The carica-
turist's work, they comment, 'is still somewhat akin to black magic.'[5]

From the earliest, all the Renaissance arts showed a newfound expressiveness, a
delicacy of feeling which can be heard as early as in the troubadour songs of Adam
de la Halle, or in the love poetry of Christine de Pisan. In the visual arts this was

manifest from Giotto onwards in a preoccupation with the expressive powers of the human face in particular, which can be seen in Masaccio, or Gozzoli, even in grouped scenes, where it might be thought less important. It will be remembered that the researches of Hufschmidt, Grüsser, Latto and others revealed that during the Renaissance there was a peak in left-facing (right-hemisphere-favouring) profiles in portraiture.[6] In keeping with my view that the Renaissance initially involves a standing forth of the right hemisphere, it seems that from the fourteenth century onwards, there begins a tendency for the light source in paintings to be situated in the left visual field. This tendency increased during the Renaissance, and declined from the eighteenth century onwards: during the twentieth century the mediaeval tendency for a non-directional light source returned, a change which was to be

> correlated with the disappearance of apparent depth (illusionary perspective) and the tendency of the artists to remain in the two-dimensional plane. It should be noted that the wall paintings of Pompeii and Herculaneum (earlier than the first century AD) also exhibit a left dominance in light direction, as do the Byzantine mosaics in the churches of Ravenna.[7]

Intriguingly, there appears to have been a marked shift, according to James Hall, in the way the left and right sides of the body were viewed at around this time. The traditional view of the left side as, literally, *sinister* would appear to have softened at the Renaissance, and given way to an intuitive sense of its positive qualities. According to Hall, 'the superior beauty of the left hand was an important component of the courtly love tradition', right at the outset of the Renaissance.[8] As the Renaissance unfolded, the claims of the left side were advanced at the expense of the right: it was seen as the more beautiful side – finer, more gentle, more truthful, more in touch with feeling. The entire left side of the body took on a cast of beauty, truthfulness and fragility.[9] Given that it was centuries too early for these views to be influenced by knowledge of hemisphere differences, it looks like another possible instance of the brain intuitively cognising itself.

In music, there was the astonishing efflorescence of polyphony, with an emphasis on highly expressive melodic lines, and above all, for the first time, complex harmony, including false relations and suspensions, and the relationship of the parts to the whole. Though there is unquestionably much joyful music of the Renaissance, its greatest productions are melancholy in nature: the Requiems and the great devotional works associated with Passiontide, and in the secular realm its lute songs and madrigals celebrating love that is only occasionally requited. They can of course also be very funny, and wit and humour are also prominent features, often self-mocking in nature, of poetry, music and painting in this period.

Melancholy in the sixteenth century was commonly associated with wit, intelligence, wisdom and judiciousness, in a tradition that culminated in, rather than merely being derived from, Burton.[10] In her book on the history of melancholy,

Jennifer Radden notes that for Renaissance writers Aristotle's view[11] that in certain thoughtful temperaments groundless melancholy sometimes ran deep introduced 'a theme emphasising that the fear and sadness of melancholy are *without cause*' [Radden's italics].[12] She notes that 'emphasis on the groundless nature of the fear and sadness of melancholia declined in the eighteenth century. But it returned in nineteenth-century analyses . . .'[13] This 'uncaused' melancholy that is the evidence of a thoughtful nature can be found in Shakespeare, where Antonio in the opening lines of *The Merchant of Venice* is made to say:

In sooth I know not why I am so sad,
It wearies me, you say it wearies you;
But how I caught it, found it, or came by it,
What stuff 'tis made of, whereof it is born,
I am to learn.

I suggest that the melancholy of the period, which is also a feature of its music and poetry, is an aspect of the dominance at the time of the right-hemisphere world, and emphasis on its 'uncausedness' is designed to make the point that it is not merely a limited, explicable reaction to an event, or chain of events, or a state of affairs in the visible world of any kind, but is intrinsic to a certain way of being in the world that was emerging at the time. The fact that this ceased to obtain during the eighteenth century and re-emerged in the nineteenth is consistent with what I shall be contending in later chapters.

William James, the greatest psychologist ever to have studied religion sympathetically, wrote that 'melancholy . . . constitutes an essential moment in every complete religious evolution',[14] and that the 'completest religions' are those in which pessimism has best been developed. There is, at least, a strong connection between religious belief and melancholic temperament in the Renaissance period, as between music and melancholy (the connection between music and religion is a universal in all cultures and at all times: see p. 77 above). I would see these interconnected phenomena as necessarily related, given the right-hemisphere predominance in each of them and the relative prominence of the world 'according to' the right hemisphere at this time. An interesting study could be made of the place of tears in the art and poetry of the period – in the plays of Shakespeare, in the songs of Dowland and his contemporaries, and, with greater detachment, and an almost bizarre 'dryness', in the poems of Donne (see below), of Marvell ('the Tears do come / Sad, slowly dropping like a Gumme'), of Crashaw (whose almost every poem is filled with tears, those 'watery diamonds', those 'portable and compendious oceans') – where they inevitably form implicit, and almost illicit, bridges between secular and religious devotion.

The Renaissance is also the time when not just apparently opposed or contradictory ideas could be entertained together, when not just ambiguity and multiplicity of meaning in language are rife (from the obvious love for puns, 'conceits', and so on, to the whole array of fruitful ambiguities in which Elizabethan poetry inheres and consists), but when emotions are experienced as characteristically mixed. Although Metrodorus anciently said that there is something akin to pleasure in sadness, mixed emotions were not commonly appreciated in the ancient world (Seneca thought the idea quite immoral),[15] and that sadness and pleasure intermingle was hardly accepted till the Renaissance. Snell says that 'not until Sappho are we to read of the bitter-sweet Eros. Homer is unable to say "half-willing, half-unwilling"; instead he says "he was willing, but his *thymos* was not".[16] Renaissance poetry, on the other hand, from Michelangelo's 'la mia allegrezz'è la malinconia'* to the endless madrigals of sweet death and dying, reiterates the union of pleasure and pain, the affinity of sweetness and sadness. Because of its reliance on indirect expression, metaphor and imagery, and its tolerance of the incomplete and unresolved, rather than on explicitness and the resolution of contradictory propositions in the pursuit of clarity and certainty, the epistemology of the right hemisphere is congenial to ambiguity and the union of opposites, where that of the left hemisphere cannot afford to be.

It is worth saying something about the difference between desire and longing here. One of the tics, or tricks, whereby we nowadays dismiss anything that does not fit with the left-hemisphere view of the world, is to label it 'Romantic'. Having done that we feel we have pulled the guts out of it. We have consigned it to a culture-bound view of the world which was relatively short-lived – not more than about fifty years or so – and long *passé*, with for good measure hints of excess, sentimentality and lack of intellectual rigour thrown in. Many of the views or attitudes that are so labelled turn out, however, to have enjoyed a rather more extensive and widespread existence than that would imply, as I hope to show later in this chapter. I would suggest that longing, not necessarily in the form of *die blaue Blume* of the Romantics, is one such concept, surely as ancient as humankind. It is present in Greek verse, beginning with Odysseus's longing – the original *nostalgia* (*nostos* meaning the 'return home' and *algos* 'pain') – for his native Ithaca; it is in the Hebrew psalms – 'like as the hart desireth the waterbrooks, so longeth my soul after thee, O God'; it is in the Anglo-Saxon poems *The Wanderer* and *The Seafarer* – both as a longing for one's home when journeying, and a longing for the sea, when the spring comes to the land-dwellers. It is no exaggeration to say that the Renaissance starts with the deepest of longing, that of courtly love, the awe-struck worship of the unattainable ideal of womanhood, and the longing of the lover for the beloved, and progresses by Arcadian imagery and pastoral, in a searching out of the past, that was also a searching for a lost Golden Age. Longing is at the heart of much of the poetry and music of the high Renaissance, particularly perhaps in England, where the lament for the loss of the old order of the Catholic Church gave rise to some of the most beautifully elegiac music of all time, particularly in the many settings of the *Lamentations* by Tudor composers. One even finds prefigurements of the Romantic longing for what is

* 'I find my happiness in melancholy.'

lost with childhood in a poem such as Vaughan's *The Retreate*, or in the *Centuries* of Traherne.

In Anglo-Saxon, as in Old Saxon, Old High German and Old Norse, from which it derives, the roots of the verb 'to long', in the sense of 'to yearn for', relate to the word meaning 'to seem, or be, or grow long'; hence 'to reach out' or 'extend towards'. The word *langian* in Anglo-Saxon, like its equivalents in each of the other languages, is impersonal in grammatical form, with an accusative of the person who is longing: thus not 'I long for', but, literally, 'it longs me [of]', whatever it might be. This form suggests something about longing that differentiates it from wanting or desiring a thing. Wanting is clear, purposive, urgent, driven by the will, always with its goal clearly in view. Longing, by contrast, is something that 'happens' between us and another thing.[17] It is not directed by will, and is not an aim, with the ultimate goal of acquisition; but instead is a desire for union – or rather it is experienced as a desire for *re*-union. This goes with there not necessarily being a simple explicit vision of what it is that is longed for, which remains in the realms of the implicit or intuitive, and is often spiritual in nature. Spiritual longing and melancholy share these more diffuse and reverberative features, of something that 'happens' or 'comes about' between ourselves and an Other, whatever it may be. In either case it is not necessarily possible to say what the 'cause' (or better, the origin) is – what the melancholy, or the longing, is *about* or *for*. Wanting is clear in its target, and in its separation from the thing that is wanted. Longing suggests instead a distance, but a never interrupted connection or union over that distance with whatever it is that is longed for, however remote the object of longing may be. It is somehow experienced as an elastic tension that is set up between the one that is longing and the object of that longing – the pull, tautness as in a bow string (in German, *die Bogensehne*) holding together the two ends of the bow that are never really separate. It is *die Sehne* and *die Sehnsucht* again.

'Great art is the arrangement of the environment so as to provide for the soul vivid, but transient values', wrote A. N. Whitehead, so that 'something new must be discovered . . . the permanent realization of values *extending beyond its former self*'.[18] Art therefore in its nature constantly impels us to reach out and onward to something beyond itself and beyond ourselves. Whitehead here contrasts the '*transient* values' that the instantiated work of art embodies, with the '*permanent realisation* of values' extending beyond its former self, which is the effect of art. This reaching out to something beyond what humans have made or can make, to something Other than ourselves, by means of art, which they have made, is the mode of the right hemisphere.

It has been said that Castiglione, in his *Book of the Courtier*, perhaps too knowingly advocates the principle *ars est celare artem* (skill lies in hiding one's skill). But is this too self-conscious? This has certainly been interpreted as encouragement to a form of benign deceit, whereby one pretends, especially if one is a gentlemanly courtier, to be able to do something effortlessly which in reality involves learning, and a degree of application. That may be true. However, skill is a process that is acquired – at times by mechanical and explicit methods, certainly

– but increasingly, as one's skill progresses, by intuitive imitation and by unreflective experience, a topic of relevance when one considers the fate of skills in the
twentieth century. It is fatal to the art of skilled practitioners for them to display,
during performance, any hint of the conscious effort that learning their skill
involved (as Hazlitt said of the Indian jugglers): they must have achieved such a
degree of mastery that they can perform intuitively, or the performance will fail.
The technique, in other words, must be transparent: our eye should not be falling
on the performers, but on what they do. That is not deceit, but being respectful of
the nature of skill, a right-hemisphere intuitive process that remains implicit and
embodied – in *that* sense hidden. This, I think, is the true meaning of Castiglione's
advice.

Individuality gives rise to a seeking after originality, a turning away from the
received, communal and conventional patterns of behaviour and thought.[19] If I
am correct that the right hemisphere's orientation is towards experience of the
Other, whatever it is, the world in as much as it exists apart from the mind,
whereas the left hemisphere has its own coherent system derived from what the
right hemisphere makes available to it, but which is essentially closed ('bootstrapping' itself), then both individuality and originality, and the relationship between
them, are going to be different depending on which hemisphere dominates. My
view is that the sense of the importance of individuality and originality come in
essence from the standing back mediated by *both* frontal lobes, and that the consequences are picked up in different ways by either hemisphere. We see ourselves as
separate: in the right-hemisphere case, still in vital connection with the world
around us; in the left-hemisphere case, because of the nature of the closed, self-
contained system in which it operates, isolated, atomistic, powerful, competitive.
Thus once again individuality and originality are not in themselves viewable as the
prerogative of one hemisphere or the other: both exist for each hemisphere but in
radically different ways, with radically different meanings.

The new emphasis on originality and individuality changed the role of the artist
(and incidentally of the artist's patron), which came into focus with the
Renaissance, when the artist for the first time becomes a kind of hero. There are a
number of stories of artists such as Leonardo, Michelangelo and Holbein being
deferred to, or at any rate treated as an equal by, the noble or king for whom they
worked: the Emperor Maximilian got a nobleman to hold the ladder for Dürer,
and Charles V himself (an eccentric and sympathetically melancholic man by
disposition) is said to have stooped to pick up Titian's paintbrush for him.[20] Once
again the heroic status of the artist is not, as commonly supposed, a phenomenon
peculiar to Romanticism. The deference shown is really a deference to the workings of the 'divine' inspiration within the artist, a concept supposed to have been
exploded in our time, but in the terms of this book relating to the implicit, intuitive, unwillable skills that come from the right hemisphere. It is worth looking at
some of the anecdotal literature about artists in the Renaissance, because not only
does it establish the way in which the creative process was envisaged (whether the
stories are apocryphal or not is irrelevant here), but demonstrates incidentally my

point that what we dismiss as Romantic may be less limited in time and place than we imagine. In the Renaissance, the unconscious, involuntary, intuitive and implicit, that which cannot be formalised, or instilled into others by processes governed by rules, and cannot be made to obey the will, was respected and courted. All the qualities that are admired in the artist are those that come from the right hemisphere, including the skill that hides itself. They are all to be found later in Romanticism, it is true; but it will not do to bundle up half of human experience as 'Romantic' with an intention to dismiss it. It may turn out that it is we who have the unusual, more limitingly culture-bound, views.

An important source for considering Renaissance beliefs about the artist is the classic work of Kris and Kurtz, *Legend, Myth, and Magic in the Image of the Artist: A Historical Experiment*, first published in 1934.[21] Many of the Renaissance commonplaces about art and the artist are summed up in Latin apophthegms such as *ars est celare artem*. One such is *poeta nascitur, non fit* – a poet is born, not made. In illustration of this there are stories about how artists from childhood exhibited untutored facility in drawing or painting. One famous such story concerns Giotto, who was supposedly discovered by Cimabue when, passing the place where Giotto, then a shepherd, was tending his flock, he saw the extraordinary lifelike pictures that Giotto, to pass the time, had painted on a rock. The point of the story is that skill is a gift, both in the sense that it comes unasked, and is not therefore the product of effortful learning of rules, and that it is intuitive, in both respects suggesting an origin outside the left hemisphere. This view of the artist was also common in the ancient world: for example, there are stories of Lysippus, Silanion and Erigonos, all confirming that their skills were untaught. The story of Giotto has its equivalents even further afield, and is reminiscent of the story, cited by Kris and Kurtz, of the Japanese painter Maruyama Okyo being discovered by a passing samurai, having painted a pine tree on a paper sack in the village store.[22]

This idea is connected to that of the gift of inspiration. Although inspiration cannot be relied on, not forced or willed into being, it could be indirectly courted by using chance as a way to limit the power of conscious intention, allowing a co-operation between what is given and what comes to be created by the artist. Thus famously Leonardo advised painters to take their starting point from the shape of a chance outline, created by, for example, damp stains on a wall, 'because by indistinct things the mind is stimulated to new inventions'.[23] According to Kris and Kurtz, Leonardo's recommendation is far from unique:

> We become aware of how extraordinarily widespread these connections are when we learn that the eleventh-century Chinese painter Sung-Ti advised Ch'ên Yung-chih to create a picture of a landscape in accordance with the ideas suggested by a tumbledown wall: 'For then', he said, 'you can let your brush follow the play of your imagination and the result will be heavenly and not human.'[24]

The view of the artist's creation as a discovery, rather than an invention, parallels the view of the artist's talent itself as a discovery, not an invention.

Similarly, since the work comes not from conscious effort, but from intuition or inspiration, first ideas are best. Thus it was that Ben Jonson reported that 'the players have often mentioned it as an honour to Shakespeare that in his writing (whatsoever he penned) he never blotted out a line'; to which Jonson rather sharply retorted: 'would he had blotted a thousand'.[25] According to Vasari, Fra Angelico was said never to have reworked any of his paintings, since 'that was how God wanted them'.[26]

Again what must be imitated is not the results of other painters' work, but Nature herself, which is the artist's teacher: *naturam imitandam esse*. This touches on a number of interrelated themes: a preference for what Nature gives, over what humans have made; that the skill comes from Nature, not from what other painters may teach; a reliance on experience over rules. This is not confined to Romantic artists or Western artists at all, but often can be found in oriental views of the artist: according to Kris and Kurtz, for instance, 'Han Kan is reputed to have said that the horses from the Imperial stables, not painters, had been his teachers'.[27] Art is seen as a spiritual revelation of what lies in nature. There is inter-subjectivity, artists entering into their subjects and the subjects into the artists and their art. Apparently 'when Han Kan painted horses, he himself became a horse'.[28] Otto Fischer speaks of 'the Taoist-inspired endeavour to interpret art as the revelation of Being through a human medium . . . Since indeed the aim of Chinese art has been to render visible the life force of Nature, it is understandable that art has had to appear as a spiritual revelation of Nature'.[29]

The artist's copies of nature are not dead, but by embodying the life force of nature come to seem as if themselves living. The story of Zeuxis, that he painted grapes so lifelike that birds would come and peck at them, is well-known, but stories of works of art being mistaken for the living thing come not just from Greece, but from China, Japan, Persia, and Armenia, as well as from many Renaissance sources.[30] Renaissance artists were also fabled to have renounced wealth and material prosperity in the pursuit of their art, living in solitude and drawing their inspiration from nature. Again such stories are paralleled in Greek, Western and Oriental culture.[31]

This gives rise to the myth of the artist as possessor of magic powers. Magic is the way that the left hemisphere sees powers over which it has no control. This is similar to the paranoia which the left hemisphere displays in schizophrenia, in relation to the intuitive actions and thought processes stemming from the right hemisphere, ascribing them to alien forces, or malicious influence. Thus there is the artist as the conduit for something Other than human, the *divino artista*, the artist who is somehow one with God the maker, a metaphor of *deus artifex* himself, as intuitively understood by the right hemisphere, able to make an inanimate block of stone move, or come to life; and there is the flip side of this, the artist as deceiver and trickster, like Prometheus having stolen fire from Heaven, even diabolical, the Arch-deceiver, willing to go to any lengths to secure an accurate imitation of nature. Thus it was rumoured that Michelangelo tortured a young man to death in order to be able to sculpt his likeness. In both cases the myth, God or devil, is related to the artist's ability perfectly to imitate nature.

Such views about the nature of artistic creation, then, are not confined to one place or time, but are common in cultures less left-hemisphere-dominated than our own. And so is another phenomenon that characterises the Renaissance: an appreciation of the beauty of this world, to be seen no longer as something to be resisted or treated as a snare, no longer something from which our eyes were to be averted, but as an indicator of something beyond. It was seen, but seen *through* – what I call semi-transparency. This went hand in hand with the rehabilitation of earthly, embodied, sense-mediated existence, in contrast to the derogation of the flesh in the Middle Ages. For Montaigne, as for Erasmus, the body became present once more as part of us, therefore potentially itself spiritual, to be loved, rather than just seen as a prison of the soul:

> Those who wish to take our two principal pieces apart and to sequester one from the other are wrong. We must on the contrary couple and join them closely together. We must command the soul not to withdraw to its quarters, not to entertain itself apart, not to despise and abandon the body (something which it cannot do anyway except by some monkey-like counterfeit) but to rally to it, take it in its arms and cherish it, help it, look after it, counsel it, and when it strays set it to rights and bring it back home again.[32]

One even begins to find an inversion of the until then usual assumption that the soul might be wiser than the body:

> Forsake not Nature nor misunderstand her:
> Her mysteries are read without faith's eyesight:
> She speaketh in our flesh; and from our senses,
> Delivers down her wisdoms to our reason

wrote Fulke Greville;[33] and in Marvell one finds *A Dialogue between the Soul and Body* in which the last word, literally and metaphorically, goes to the body.[34]

The relationship between ourselves and the world that has depth was a source of endless fascination to the metaphysical poets, particularly Donne, Herbert (e.g. *The Elixir*) and Traherne (e.g. *Shadows in the Water*), who all use images such as the plane of the glass in the window, the flat surface of the mirror, and the reflective surface of a pool of water, to explore imaginative contact with a world *beyond* the plane of vision: seeing, but seeing through. The world is not a brute fact but, like a myth or metaphor, semi-transparent, containing all its meaning within itself, yet pointing to something lying beyond itself.

As I suggested earlier, a sense of depth is intrinsic to seeing things in context. This is true both of the depth of space and the depth of time, but here I would say that it implies, too, a metaphysical depth, a respect for the existence of something at more than one level, as is inevitable in myth or metaphor. It is this respect for context that underlies the sense in the Renaissance of the interconnectedness of knowledge and understanding, the uncovering of answering patterns across different realms, ultimately implying the necessity of the broadest possible context for knowledge. Hence the rise of what came to be dubbed 'Renaissance man', Heraclitus' 'enquirers into many things indeed'.

The return to the historic past, the rediscovery of the Classical world, was not a fact-finding mission, driven by curiosity or utility: its importance lay not just in the increase of knowledge in itself, but in the exemplars of wisdom, virtue, and statecraft that it yielded. It was recognised that human dignity lay in our unique capacity to choose our own destiny, through the models we choose and the ideals towards which we are drawn, not simply through the blind pursuit of reason wherever it might lead. This involved self-knowledge, and the fascination with the unique and different paths taken by different personalities towards their particular goals – hence the importance of the recording of individual lives, and the rise of both true biography (as opposed to hagiography) and autobiography.

One of the most famous and entertaining of Renaissance self-portraits must be that of Aeneas Sylvius Piccolomini, otherwise known as Pope Pius II. This is not only a landmark in the literature of self-exploration (as well as self-promotion), but importantly reveals a love of nature for its own sake, another feature of the new world of the Renaissance seen in Dante and Petrarch, as well as in some of the early German lyric poets, despite Jacob Burckhardt's generalisation that 'the Italians are the first among modern peoples by whom the outward world was seen and felt as something beautiful'.[35] In a characteristic passage Aeneas Sylvius writes:

It was the sweet season of early spring. All the hills about Siena were smiling in their vesture of foliage and flowers, and luxuriant crops were growing up in the fields. The Sienese country immediately around the city is indescribably lovely with its gently sloping hills, planted with cultivated trees or vines or ploughed for grain, overlooking delightful valleys green with pasture land or sown fields, and watered by never-failing streams. There are also thick forests planted by nature or man where birds sing most sweetly and on every hill the citizens of Siena have built splendid country seats . . . Through this region the Pope travelled in happy mood . . .[36]

Elsewhere he writes of a visit to Viterbo:

Masses of flowering broom gave much of the country a golden hue and some of it was covered with other shrubs or various plants that presented purple or white or a thousand other colours to the eye. The world was green in that month of May and not only the meadows but the woods were smiling and birds were singing sweetly . . . Almost every day at dawn he would go out into the country to enjoy the sweet air before it grew hot and to gaze on the green crops and the blossoming flax, then most lovely to see with its sky-blue colour . . .[37]

And it is not just the sweetness, but the grandeur, of nature, its 'lofty cliffs', high and 'inaccessible', its 'unfathomable' crystal clear lakes, that delight him. 'Nature', he says, 'is superior to any art'. The date is May 1463.[38]

THE REFORMATION

In the first chapter of Part II, I suggested that there are two ways in which the inauthenticity of re-presentation, of the left hemisphere's world, can stimulate a response. One is the tendency to redress the loss, through an urgent longing for the vibrancy and freshness of the world that the right hemisphere delivers; the other is quite the opposite – a rejection of it, since that right hemisphere world now comes to be seen as *intrinsically* inauthentic, and therefore as invalid. Instead of a corrective swing of the pendulum, therefore, there is a loss of homeostasis, and the result is positive feedback, whereby the left hemisphere's values simply become further entrenched.

Though we have been focussing on a return to the right hemisphere in the flowering of the Renaissance, with an almost magnetic attraction towards the newly discovered history, writings, arts and monuments of the ancient world, which opened eyes to the vibrancy of a living world beyond the mediaeval 'world-picture', the decline of the Middle Ages yields an example of both processes at work. One can see the second process (a rejection of the right hemisphere's world) in the way in which the decline of metaphoric understanding of ceremony and ritual into the inauthentic repetition of empty procedures in the Middle Ages prompted, not a *revitalisation* of metaphoric understanding, but an outright rejection of it, with the advent of the Reformation. This cataclysmic convulsion is said to have begun with Luther's *Ninety-Five Theses*, which he nailed to the door of the Schloßkirche in Wittenberg in 1517.

In the subsequent unfolding of events, however, Luther could be seen as a somewhat tragic figure. He was himself tolerant, conservative, his concern being for authenticity, and a return to experience, as opposed to reliance on authority. His attitude to the place of images in worship and in the life of the Church was balanced and reasonable: his target was not images themselves (which he actually endorsed and encouraged) but precisely the *functionalist* abuse of images, images which he thought should be reverenced. Yet despite this, he found himself unleashing forces of destruction that were out of his control, forces which set about destroying the very things he valued, forces against which he inveighed finally without effect. Describing the fanaticism of the time, 'I have seen them return from hearing the sermon, as if inspired by an evil spirit', wrote Erasmus, 'the faces of all showing a curious wrath and ferocity.'[39] There are, I think, interesting parallels with the fate of Heidegger, struggling to transcend the Cartesian subjective/objective polarity, committed to the difficult business of authentic encounter with whatever 'is', a process requiring careful and scrupulous attention; but soon hijacked by those who wished to take his 'problematising' of the concept of objective truth as the signal for a free-for-all in which all values are 'merely relative' (interpreted as meaning values have no force), in which there is no longer any 'objective' standard of truth (interpreted as meaning no truth), and in which ultimately an anarchic destruction of everything Heidegger valued and struggled to defend was unleashed in his name. Here too, as in Luther's case, I would say the original impulse, towards authenticity, came from the right hemisphere, but quickly became annexed to the agenda of the left hemisphere. Not by a revolutionary inversion, but by a slippage of meaning which repays attention.

Luther perceived that the inner and outer realms, however one expresses it – the realm of the mind/soul and that of the body, the realm of the invisible and the visible – needed to be *as one*, otherwise the outward show had nothing to say about the inward condition. In other words, the visible world should be a 'presentation', in the literal sense that something 'becomes present' to us in all its actuality, as delivered by the right hemisphere. This perception, which is simply part of, and entirely continuous with, the Renaissance insistence on the seamlessness of the incarnate world, inspired Luther to decry the emptiness that results when the outer and inner worlds are divorced. But his followers took it to mean that the outer world was in itself empty, and that therefore the only authenticity lay in the inner world alone. The result of this is that the outer world becomes seen as merely a 'show', a 're-presentation' of something elsewhere and nowhere – not an image, since an image is a living fusion of the inner and outer, but a mere signifier, as delivered by the left hemisphere. The transition that is made in this important derailment of Luther's intention is not from belief in outer forms to belief in inner forms, but from a view of outer and inner as essentially fused aspects of one and the same thing to the belief that they are separate ('either/or'). Thus it should not be thought that the impetus of the Renaissance was abruptly derailed by a contrary movement of the spirit at the Reformation: there was a seamless transition from one position into its opposite, the one morphed into the other. I shall have more to say about such processes in relation to the otherwise apparently problematic transitions from the Enlightenment to Romanticism, and from Romanticism to modernism, each of which has been seen as an earth-shattering inversion, whereas I would see each as a fluent transition, despite accepting the fundamentally opposed nature of the phenomena in each case.

The Reformation is the first great expression of the search for certainty in modern times. As Schleiermacher put it, the Reformation and the Enlightenment have this in common, that 'everything mysterious and marvellous is proscribed. Imagination is not to be filled with [what are now thought of as] airy images.'[40] In their search for the one truth, both movements attempted to do away with the visual image, the vehicle *par excellence* of the right hemisphere, particularly in its mythical and metaphoric function, in favour of the word, the stronghold of the left hemisphere, in pursuit of unambiguous certainty.

This was not, of course, the first time that iconoclasm had reared its head. In the eastern Roman Empire there had been a period of over 100 years (between 730 and 843) during which, with only one brief hiatus, the Byzantines were forbidden to venerate religious images. Paintings were whitewashed over, and images destroyed. This movement is thought to have been in response to the inroads made by the Arabs, whose religion proscribes religious images, deep into the Empire: they laid siege to Constantinople on three occasions. But such aversion to the visual image at the Reformation, following on, as it did, from the flowering of the Italian Renaissance, the greatest outpouring of religious art in human history, was something quite extraordinary. What is so compelling here is that the motive force behind the Reformation was the urge to regain authenticity, with which one can only be profoundly sympathetic. The path it soon took was that of the destruction of all means whereby the authentic could have been recaptured.

Here I take Joseph Koerner's recent magisterial treatment of Reformation theology, politics and philosophy through their relationship with the visual image, with symbolism, and with the written word, as a major source (there is no comparable work that so intelligently links these different aspects of Reformation culture).[41] The problem of the Reformation was, according to Koerner, one of 'either/or', a 'hatred based on the absolute distinction between truth and falsehood'.[42] Because of the inability to accept the ambiguous or metaphorical, and because of a fear of the power of the imagination, images were objects of terror. Statues had to be reduced to 'mere wood'. In fact the supposed 'idolaters' never had believed they were worshipping statues – that self-serving fiction existed only in the minds of the iconoclasts, who could not understand that divinity could find its place *between* one 'thing' (the statue) and another (the beholder), rather than having to reside, fixed, in the 'thing' itself. Luther himself said as much: 'I believe that there is no person, or certainly very few, who does not understand that the crucifix that stands over there is not my God – for my God is in Heaven – but rather only a sign.'[43]

Decapitation of statues by the Reformers took place because of the confounding of the animate and the inanimate, and the impossibility of seeing that one can live in the other metaphorically. In a world where metaphoric understanding is lost we are reduced to 'either/or', as Koerner says. *Either* the statue is God *or* it is a thing: since it is 'obviously' not God, it must be a thing, and therefore 'mere wood', in which case it has no place in worship. To see that 'mere' wood can partake of the divine requires seeing it as a metaphor, and being able to see that, precisely because it is a *metaphor* rather than a representation, it *is* itself divine. It is not just something non-divine *representing* the divine, it is something divine. This is the difference between the belief that the bread and wine *represent* the body and blood of Christ, and the belief that they *are* in some important sense the body and blood of Christ, metaphors of it. It was the explicit analytical left hemisphere attempt to untangle this that had led, in mediaeval scholastic theology, to an 'either/or', and resulted in the improbable doctrine of transubstantiation: that at the moment of the priest's pronouncing the words of consecration, what had been mere bread and mere wine became suddenly, and literally, the body and blood of Christ. What the right hemisphere had understood intuitively, being comfortable with metaphoric meaning, was forced into the straightjacket of legalistic thinking, and forced to be either literal bread and wine or literal body and blood. At the Reformation this problem re-emerged. To say it was not literally body and blood seemed to Catholic thinking to sell out to the view that it was just a representation, which clearly is inadequate to the reality of metaphoric thinking, in which the body and blood come about not just because of a few words spoken at a specific moment but because of the entire *context* of the mass, including all its words and procedures, the presence and faithful disposition of the congregation, etc. It is contexts, and the disposition of the mind of those who partake in them, another pair of right hemisphere entities, which enable metaphors to work.

What Koerner's book demonstrates at length and in detail is the way in which the Reformation replaces presentation with *re*-presentation (in the terms of this book, replaces the right-hemisphere realm with the left-hemisphere realm). What is experienced by the observer (itself a telling concept) is transposed to the meta-level. One well-known work approved by the Reformers, and emanating from their spirit, appears to deny the possibility that the work of art could be something greater than its transposition into verbal meaning: 'its surfaces support words while its depths are filled only with what words refer to'. In such a canvas, 'the choirboys sing from a hymnal displaying neither the text nor the music of their song, but the biblical command requiring them to sing. Words bathe in the grey light of what seems a useless significance.'[44]

There are several ways in which the Reformation anticipated the hermetic self-reflexivity of post-modernism, perfectly expressed in the infinite regress of self-referral within some of the visual images which Koerner examines (pictures which portray the setting in which the picture stands, and contain therefore the picture itself, itself containing a further depiction of the setting, containing an ever smaller version of the picture, etc). One of Cranach's masterpieces, discussed by Koerner, is in its self-referentiality the perfect expression of left-hemisphere emptiness, and a precursor of post-modernism. There is no longer anything to point to beyond, nothing Other, so it points pointlessly to itself. Rather paradoxically for a movement that began as a revolt against apparently empty structures, it is in fact the structures, not the content, of religion, that come into focus *as* the content. But such is the fate of those who insist on 'either/or', rather than the wisdom of semi-transparency.

In contrast with the brothers van Eyck's marvellous Ghent Altarpiece, *The Adoration of the Lamb*, of 1432, Koerner notes of Göding's Mühlberg Altarpiece (1568), an example of the infinite regress problem, that it 'yearns in just the opposite direction: not toward a real presence materially before it, but toward an infinity endlessly repeated and deferred'.[45] Referring to itself, it leads nowhere. A pietistic image of the lamb of God proclaiming that it is the lamb of God, 'rather than transporting us from signifier to signified ... keeps us shuttling *between* signifiers'.[46] The problem is that the pictorial symbols are merely re-presentations, not *presentations*: they show the 'caricature' lamb of God, or Christ, or God the Father, and refer in shorthand, not, as earlier painting had done, incarnating in each marvellously realised exemplar, the very *experience* of the lamb of God, or Christ, or God the Father. The texts that accompany them are worse still. Koerner again notes inscriptions in engravings – 'I am the way', 'This is the lamb, etc.' – and comments: 'note how, in the woodcut itself, the printed "etc." objectifies the quote'.[47] To my mind it betrays a bored impatience that is the correlative of its lack of content. The phrases have become empty stereotypes, representing nothing other than their own verbal nature, pointers to themselves, rather than being capable of exhibiting meaning that lies elsewhere and beyond. Such pictures as were permitted in the Reformation Church are self-referential, in that what they depict is what is actually going on in the church. In as much, they become redundant: they do not reach out to the Other, but remain stubbornly trapped within a system of signs.

Images become explicit, understood by reading a kind of key, which demonstrates that the image is thought of simply as an adornment, whose only function is to fix a meaning more readily in the mind – a meaning which could have been better stated literally. This anticipates the Enlightenment view of metaphor as an adornment that shows the writer's skill, or entertains, or aids flagging attention, rather than as an indispensable part of understanding. 'Sacrament becomes information-transfer', writes Koerner. 'Its material elements convey not substances, but meanings, and these latter are immutably conveyed regardless of the form they take.' In the twentieth century, too, we have seen liturgical reformers embrace a view that the 'meaning' is independent of the form, one of the most damaging legacies of the Reformation. Continuing the idea that sacrament has been reduced to information transfer, Koerner continues that the 'seeming afterthought, that Christ's words need explaining, completes a scenography of data downloaded from a storage medium. Even the words of sacrament count only if they *mean* something, for all else "serve[s] no purpose".'[48]

This is the era of the triumph of the written word, and words actually acquire the status of things. (I am reminded of Sam Johnson's wise admonition that 'words are the daughters of earth', whereas 'things are the sons of heaven'.) 'In Protestant culture', writes Koerner, '*words acquired the status of things* by their aggressive material inscription.' A compendium of consoling sayings consists mostly of 'sayings about sayings'.[49] It is fascinating that the way to get the meaning across is apparently to repeat the words endlessly, drumming it further and further into the realm of the over-familiar, again the domain of the left hemisphere. For example, the words *verbum Domini manet in aeternum* ('the word of the Lord shall endure for ever' – yet a further element of self-referentiality) became so familiar that it was reduced to the acronym VDMIE. (Note that these acronyms start with Roman bureaucracy (e.g. SPQR) and are, I would say, a hallmark of the bureaucratic mind – look at modern officialdom.) The letters VDMIE were embroidered and reproduced endlessly, ultimately becoming, despite the Reformers, a totemic, apotropaic device, a talisman with the status of an idol, as the reified words in their abbreviated form become the only available 'thing' for the sacred to attach to. As Koerner puts it, 'materialised for display, words become objects of ritual action'; a point also made by Kriss-Rettenbeck: 'the word freezes into an idol'.[50] I would say that the abbreviations, like the impatient reduction to 'etc.' ('the lamb of God, etc.'), betray the boredom and ultimate emptiness that attaches to signifiers that refer only to themselves, that have departed into the realm of the inauthentic through over-familiarity.

Pictures were defaced, often replaced by boards with written texts, and sometimes actually written over: a concrete expression of the triumph of language. To detached observation the rituals of Catholicism, lacking speech, cultivating rather what has to remain imprecise, implicit, but richly metaphorical, became 'senseless and indecipherable'.[51] 'Image-breakers ceaselessly say that images cannot speak': their failing is their silence. They do not use *words*.[52]

These different ways of looking at the world – 'proclamation' of the word versus 'manifestation' of the divine – are aligned with hemisphere differences. As Ricoeur demonstrated, the 'emergence of the word from the numinous is . . . the primordial trait' that differentiates proclamation from manifestation.[53] For 'emergence of the word from the numinous' read the triumph of the left hemisphere over the right.

At this time, according to Koerner, pictures become 'art', moved out of their living context in worship, to an artificial context where they can become allowable and safe, with frames round them (often pictures had literally to be reframed because of the exigencies of smuggling them away from the iconoclasts to safety).

Contexts bring meanings from the whole of our selves and our lives, not just from the explicit theoretical, intellectual structures which are potentially under control. The power-hungry will always aim to substitute explicit for intuitive understanding. Intuitive understanding is not under control, and therefore cannot be trusted by those who wish to manipulate and dominate the way we think; for them it is vital that such contexts, with their hidden powerful meanings that have accrued through sometimes millennia of experience, are eradicated. In terms of the conflict that forms the subject of this book, the left hemisphere, the locus of will to power, needs to destroy the potential for the right hemisphere to have influence through what is implicit and contextual. Hence the Calvinists set about an erasure of the past, involving the destruction of everything that would nourish memory of how things had been – a sort of Red Revolution, 'that will leave nothing in the church whereof any memory will be'.[54]

The body is the ultimate refractory context of experience. There was a revulsion against the representation of Christ's body and his bodily suffering, which was thought to show nothing of importance. A Manichaeism is at work here which rejects the body: 'Christ says that his own flesh is of no use but that the spirit is of use and gives life.'[55] This is related to the more widespread loss of the incarnate nature of metaphor as a whole, and its substitution by simile: in the Eucharist 'this is my body' becomes 'this *signifies* (is like) my body'. But there is another reason for rejecting the body: it is equated with the transient, 'earthly corruption', whereas the word is equated with enduring changelessness, which is in turn how the divine is now seen.

Some further interesting phenomena begin to appear. Rejection of the body, and of embodied existence in an incarnate world, in favour of an invisible, discarnate realm of the mind, naturally facilitates the application of general rules. In other words, abstraction facilitates generalisation. Both retreat from the body and the seeking out and development of general rules are fundamental aspects of the world delivered by the left hemisphere, and they are mutually reinforcing. The Reformers were keen to do away with the concrete instantiations of holiness in any one place or object. The invisible Church being the only church to have any reality, the Church existed literally everywhere, and actual churches became less significant: every place was as good as any other in which to hold a service. The force of this was that every place was as holy as any other, provided the word of God could be proclaimed there, which by definition it could. But holiness, like all other qualities, depends on a distinction being made. In an important sense, if everything and everywhere is holy, then nothing and nowhere is holy. Once freed from having to consider the actual qualities of existing things, places and people, ideas can be applied blanket-fashion; but the plane of interaction between the world of ideas and the world of things which they represent becoming, by the same token, 'frictionless', the wheels of words lose their purchase, and spin uselessly, without force to move anything in the world in which we actually live. A recognisably similar development became familiar in the twentieth century, where the retreat of art into the realm of the idea, into concepts, enabled it to become a commonplace that 'everything is art'; or that, properly considered, everything is as beautiful as everything else; with the inevitable consequence that the meaning of art and the meaning of beauty became eroded, and it has become almost a solecism, seen as betraying a lack of sophisticated (i.e. left-hemisphere) understanding, to interrogate artworks according to such criteria.

I have emphasised the left hemisphere's inclination towards division, as opposed to the apprehension of connectedness made by the right hemisphere. But there are two types of division and two types of union. In Part I, I made a distinction, which is central to the thesis of this book, between two ways of looking at 'parts' and 'aggregates'. In the left-hemisphere view, there is at one level the part or fragment, and, at the other, the generalised abstraction, aggregated from the parts. In the right hemisphere view, there is the individual entity in all its distinctness, at one level, and the whole to which it belongs, at the other. It is, in other words, the special capacity of the right hemisphere both to deliver wholes *and* to deal with particularities: these are not contradictory roles. It is the special capacity of the left hemisphere to derive generalities, but generalities have nothing to do with wholes; they are in fact necessarily built from parts, aspects, fragments, of existing things – things which, in their total selfhood, individuality, or *haeccitas*, could never have been generalised. Every existing entity comes into being only through boundaries, because of distinctions: which is perhaps why the Book of Genesis speaks of God creating by *dividing* – the earth from the heavens, the sea from the dry land, the night from the day, and so on. The drive towards separation and distinction brings individual things into being. By contrast, the drive towards generalisation, with its effective 'democratisation' of its object (of the holy, of art, of the beautiful), has the effect of destroying its object as a living force.

Koerner draws attention to the bureaucratic categorisation that springs up in the Lutheran Church. And, as Max Weber emphasised, in his repeated explorations of the relation between Protestantism, capitalism and bureaucratisation, bureaucratisation (and categorisation, with which it is so closely related) is an instrument of power. Perhaps, more importantly, Protestantism being a manifestation of left-hemisphere cognition is – even though its conscious self-descriptions would deny this – itself inevitably linked to the will to power, since that is the agenda of the left hemisphere. Bureaucratisation and capitalism, though not necessarily themselves the best of bedfellows, and at times perhaps in conflict, are each manifestations of the will to power, and each is linked to Protestantism. Weber held that the cognitive structure of Protestantism was closely associated with capitalism: both involve an exaggerated emphasis on individual agency, and a discounting of what might be called 'communion'. An emphasis on individual agency inevitably manifests itself, as David Bakan has suggested, in self-protection, self-assertion, and self-expansion, whereas communion manifests itself in the sense of being at one with others. 'Agency', he writes, 'manifests itself in isolation, alienation, and aloneness: communion in contact, openness and union. Agency manifests itself in the urge to master: communion in non-contractual co-operation.'[56] Success in material terms became, under Protestantism, a sign of spiritual prowess, the reward of God to his faithful.

As Weber saw, modern capitalism is anti-traditional – desperate, like bureaucratisation, to do away with the past. Tradition is simply the embodied wisdom of previous generations. It should change, as all things subject to the realm of the right hemisphere change, develop and evolve, but it should do so organically: it is not wise to reject it or uproot it altogether and on principle. But to the left hemisphere, tradition represents a challenge to its brave plan to take control, *now*, in the interests of salvation as it conceives it.

Removing the places of holiness, and effectively dispensing with the dimension of the sacred, eroded the power of the princes of the Church, but it helped to buttress the power of the secular state. The capacity for religion to crystallise structures of power and obedience was soon allied under the Reformers to the power of the state. 'Sacred centres thus gave way to centres of attention', writes Koerner, referring to the physical arrangement of the new church interior, in which the focus is no longer the altar, but the pulpit. The Lutheran assembly, despite its emphasis on the word, 'controlled sight more rigorously' than the Roman Catholic Church had ever done.[57] Its emphasis on punishment for departing from the moral law, and its panoptical monitoring of the populace, are imaged in the exalted position of the pulpit, the place of dissemination of the moral law, often situated at a dizzying height over the heads of the masses near the roof of the church, high above the altar, with tiers of seating for the secular hierarchies in the galleries at the next level beneath, each positioned far over the heads of the obedient populace, ranged in geometric order below.

I would note that this geometricity of Reformed churches, the people neatly placed in symmetrical ranks on the floors which are laid out like graph paper (see Figure 9.3), is highly suggestive of left-hemisphere functioning.[58]

Remember that, for the left hemisphere, space is not something lived, experienced through the body, and articulated by personal concerns as it is for the right hemisphere, but something symmetrical, measured and positioned according to abstract measures. And this is something we can all recall from personal experience: in a congregation seated neatly in rows, one feels like an obedient subject, one of the masses, whereas standing in a crowd, as one would

Fig. 9.3 *Sermon in the Hall of the Reformed Community of Stein near Nuremberg*, attributed to Lorenz Strauch, *c.* 1620.

have done in a pre-Reformation church, one is part of a living thing, that *is* that community of living human beings, there and then: one of humanity, not one of 'the people'. This is what Nietzsche is referring to, when he draws attention to the Reformed church's one

> speaking mouth [the preacher] and very many ears [the congregation] . . . Standing at a modest distance behind both groups, with a certain tense supervisory mien, is the state, there in order from time to time to recollect that *it* is the purpose, goal, and model of this odd speaking and listening procedure . . .

the procedure of Reformed religion.[59]

The focus is on immobility and fixity. Where the Roman Church encouraged and incorporated movement, walking and processing, the new Church's chairs are everywhere the most visible feature of the Reformed interior, enforcing stasis and system, and (interestingly, despite its democratic rhetoric) social order and hierarchy.

> Having repudiated pious donation as belonging to a false religion of works, the Lutheran confession discovered in church seating a new, lucrative and . . . continuous resource. People's desire to distinguish themselves in this world by sitting above or before their neighbour funded a church which preached that such distinctions were of no account.[60]

And Ernst Troeltsch takes the point further, emphasising the transfer of power to the state: 'Thus the aim that was realized in Catholicism through a directly divine church order, Lutheranism, in its purely spiritualised form, stripped of every kind of hierarchical or sacerdotal organ, realized through the government and the civil administration, to which, however, precisely for that reason, there accrued a semi-divinity.[61] Instead of, as under the old dispensation, all being equal 'below' the priestly ministrants, representing the power of God, the people of the Reformed Church were thrown back on the petty gradations of secular difference. Significantly one sees in the iconography of the Reformers depictions of princes kneeling, not just before the anonymous priest, but before a particular human individual, Luther, where previously they would have humbled themselves before the anonymous power of the priesthood, representing Divinity.[62]

What I wish to emphasise is the transition, within the Reformation, from what are initially the concerns of the right hemisphere to those of the left hemisphere: how a call for authenticity, and a reaction against the undoubtedly empty and corrupt nature of some practices of the mediaeval Roman Catholic Church, an attempt therefore to return from a form of re-presentation to the true presence of religious feeling, turned rapidly into a further entrenchment of inauthenticity.

Of course the Reformation was not a unitary phenomenon: the Elizabethan settlement was very different from anything in Calvin's Geneva, and that too differed from the circumstances and beliefs of the Puritans who set sail for New England. But there are often common elements, and when we see them we are, in my view, witnessing the slide into the territory of the left hemisphere. These include the preference for what is clear and certain over what is ambiguous or undecided; the preference for what is single, fixed, static and systematised, over what is multiple, fluid, moving and contingent; the emphasis on the word over the image, on literal meaning in language over metaphorical meaning, and the tendency for language to refer to other written texts or explicit meanings, rather than, through the cracks in language, if one can put it that way, to something Other beyond; the tendency towards abstraction, coupled with a downgrading of the realm of the physical; a concern with re-presentation rather than with presentation; in its more Puritanical elements, an attack on music; the deliberate attempt to do away with the past and the contextually modulated, implicit wisdom of a tradition, replacing it with a new rational, explicit, but fundamentally secular, order; and an attack on the sacred that was vehement in the extreme, and involved repeated and violent acts of desecration.

In essence the cardinal tenet of Christianity – the Word is made Flesh – becomes reversed, and the Flesh is made Word.

THE BEGINNINGS OF ENLIGHTENMENT

'I embrace most willingly those of Philosophy's opinions which are most solid, that is to say, most human', wrote Montaigne, but:

> to my mind she is acting like a child when she gets on her high-horse, preaching to us that it is a barbarous match to wed the divine to the earthy, the rational to the irrational, the strict to the permissive, the decent to the indecent . . . A fine thing to get up on stilts, for even on stilts we must ever walk with our legs! And upon the highest throne in the world, we are seated, still, upon our arses.[63]

In his classic analysis of modernity, *Cosmopolis*, the philosopher Stephen Toulmin, a disciple of Wittgenstein, saw two distinct phases to the origins of modernity. One was that of Erasmus, Rabelais, Shakespeare and Montaigne, a tolerant, literary and humanistic phase, in which horizons expanded – literally as well as metaphorically, since this was the age of the explorer, and a fascination with other peoples and their customs, a revelling in difference. The second, a scientific and philosophical phase, he believes turned its back on the earlier phase, in terms more rigid and dogmatic: 'there are good precedents for the suggestion that the 17th century saw a reversal of Renaissance values.'[64] One might think that odd in view of, for example, the received version of Galileo's dispute with the Church – a piece of hagiography that suits the dogma of our own age, that Galileo must have been the champion of reason in the face of irrational bigotry on the part of the Church. In fact his ideas were certainly not dismissed by either the pope or his cardinals, who indeed let him know that they admired his work; and, if it had not been for Galileo's personality, he would not have found himself placed under house arrest, which led to his canonisation in the chronicles of science. As Toulmin points out, the Church did end up becoming less tolerant, but this came about during the Counter-Reformation, a reaction to the excesses of the Reformation, at a time when, as he amply demonstrates, philosophy and science, too, became more inflexible and doctrinaire.

There was, according to Toulmin, a narrowing, not an expansion, of concern, as one moves from the sixteenth century to the seventeenth, from the world of *Pantagruel* to that of *Pilgrim's Progress*, from Shakespeare to Racine, from Montaigne to Descartes – a 'narrowing in the focus of preoccupations, and a closing in of intellectual horizons'. Reason itself became narrower in conception, no longer respecting context, as Aristotle had insisted, when he held that what was reasonable in clinical medicine was different from what was logical in geometrical theory.[65] A universal, timeless theory became the only true subject of philosophy: abstract generalisations and rules for perfection superseded acceptance of the contingency of difference. Toulmin identifies during this period a shift from the reciprocal oral mode to the fixed and unidirectional written mode, from the local and particular to the general, from concrete to abstract, from practical to theoretical, from time-dependent and transitory to timeless and permanent: in each case, where both had been previously held in equilibrium (right hemisphere with left), only the second became acceptable.[66] But, as Aristotle put it, 'that which lasts long is no whiter than that which perishes in a day'.[67]

Something, too, was happening to the self. The sixteenth century was the age of the autobiography and the self-portrait, of the voice of Montaigne, and the self-aware reflections of Dürer: in fact Montaigne, in taking himself for his subject, was consciously thinking of a portrait.[68] It is also the period during which mirrors became a more common part of domestic life. This self-awareness does not (yet) equate with the objectification of the self, but with the achievement, rather, of 'necessary distance', which enhances an understanding of the self as part of a shared world of other, similar, beings. 'Few are more aware of the power of imagination than I am', wrote Montaigne, everyone feels its force, but some are turned upside down by it. It makes such an intense impression on me that I prefer to avoid it altogether rather than try to resist it . . . the very sight of someone else's pain causes me real pain, and my body often takes on the sensations of the person I am with. Another's perpetual cough tickles my lungs and throat. I'm more reluctant to visit those I love and am bound to care for, when they're sick, than those I care less about, and mean less to me. I adopt their disease that troubles me, and make it my own.[69]

Here we find him observing, more than 400 years before the experiments were done, what we know about empathy and mimesis. And he was his own experimental subject. Empathic as he was, he observed himself with detachment.

This optimal relation of the self to others, and the optimal distance from oneself to achieve it, is embodied in the writings of many Renaissance writers, but as time wears on, one can feel it coming under strain. Donne has some fascinating passages, both in his poems and in his *Meditations*, on the eyes and self-exploration; on seeing oneself reflected in other's eyes. As Fanny Burney later trembled more to see the look of horror in her surgeon's eyes when he was operating on her cancerous breast than she did at her own pain, Donne describes in his last illness how he knows himself first through his physician's face:

I observe the physician with the same diligence as he the disease; I see his fears, and I fear with him; I overtake him, I overrun him, in his fear, and I go the faster, because he makes his pace slow; I fear the more, because he disguises his fear, and I see it with the more sharpness, because he would not have me see it.[70]

As the illness progresses, he writes that 'they have seen me and heard me, arraigned me in these fetters and received the evidence; I have cut up mine own anatomy, dissected myself, and they are gone to read upon me . . .'[71] Many of his poems involve the conceit of eyes and self-knowledge. In his poems Donne plays with a more literal sense in which one can be said to see one's own image in the eye of the beloved, the sense in which Plato said that one saw one's soul there: the word 'pupil' comes from the Latin *pupilla*, a doll, referring to the minute inverted image of oneself seen reflected in the eye of another. In *Witchcraft by a Picture*, he not only sees himself 'burning' in his mistress's eye, but 'My picture drown'd in a transparent teare, / When I looke lower I espie . . .' He fancifully chides her for conjuring with his image in order to kill, but then softens:

But now I have drunke thy sweet salt teares,
And though thou poure more I'll depart;
My picture vanish'd, vanish feares,
That I can be endamag'd by that art;
Though thou retaine of mee
One picture more, yet that will bee,
Being in thine owne heart, from all malice free.

His poems suggest to me the precariousness of keeping the hemispheres working together. What I believe Eliot was referring to in his famous formulation of the unified sensibility of the Metaphysical poets, and its 'dissociation' later in the seventeenth century, was the ability to bring together the diverging hemispheric worlds, though I believe that he was wrong to suppose that the Metaphysical poets are part of the 'unification'.[72] The relationship was more complex. Eliot elsewhere likened the analytic meaning of a poem to the meat that the burglar tosses to the dog while he burgles the house.[73] Donne's self-observation certainly made him acutely aware of the ways in which *attention* can be divided:[74] and he himself encourages us to attend in more than one way, teasing and analysing with half of our minds, while he may conjure something completely astonishing at a quite different level. Thus in *The Relique*, a poem in which he imagines his grave being opened and 'he that digs it' seeing the token of his love, a 'bracelet of bright haire about the bone', Donne waylays us with verbal and conceptual play about the religion of love, only at the end to seem to walk off into another realm:

> But now alas,
> All measure, and all language, I should passe,
> Should I tell what a miracle shee was.

And with that the poem just breaks off.

The very fact that Donne and his contemporaries were so aware of two aspects of experience that needed to be brought together was a sign that the 'dissociation' was already established, though in parts of his greatest poems Donne is able to achieve a synthesis. At his best he manages to hold to the remarkable growth in self-awareness while simultaneously respecting the importance of what must remain implicit, subtle, indirect, even hidden, if it is not to be lost altogether. In the end his poems demonstrate, as does the music of J. S. Bach, that, at this point in history, it was still possible lightly to unpick parts of the whole without losing the *Gestalt* – in Donne's case, though, at times only *just*.

And they were aware of it. It is not just Hamlet's 'the times are out of joint', or Ulysses' great speech in *Troilus and Cressida* (Act 1, scene 3): 'Take but degree away, untune that string, / And hark what discord follows. . .' It is Donne, too:

> Then, as mankinde, so is the worlds whole frame
> Quite out of ioynt . . .

> And freely men confesse that this world's spent,
> When in the Planets, and the Firmament
> They seeke so many new; they see that this
> Is crumbled out againe to his Atomis.
> 'Tis all in pieces, all coherence gone;
> All iust supply, and all Relation:
> Prince, Subiect, Father, Sonne, are things forgot,

For euery man alone thinkes he hath got
To be a Phoenix, and that there can be
None of that kinde, of which he is, but he.
This is the worlds condition now . . .

While Shakespeare and Donne would inevitably have had in mind the political and religious upheavals of the age, it is surely something far greater than that, a different sort of power game, that they have intuited. They lament the loss of the relation of part to whole, of individual to community, of the context, the cosmos, to which each single soul belongs – each now standing alone. There is a loss of harmony ('each thing meets in mere oppugnancy', in Ulysses' phrase), the whole has become a heap of bits and pieces ('crumbled out again to its atoms'). And, as Ulysses reminds us, this can have only one ending:

Then every thing include itself in power,
Power into will, will into appetite,
And appetite, an universal wolf
(So doubly seconded with will and power),
Must make perforce an universal prey,
And last eat up himself.

'The scientific revolution only gathered pace in the early seventeenth century, after the flowering of the Renaissance was over', according to Peter Hacker.[75] This would certainly fit with the publication of Galileo's *Dialogue* in 1632. But the spirit does evolve out of that of the Renaissance and the respect for the natural world. The move to phenomenal observation led to the flourishing not only of the arts, but also of the sciences, which were importantly, *not yet distinct* from them.

Francis Bacon's advocacy of empirical method is an important factor in the scientific revolution. He was certainly an enquirer into many things (according to Aubrey, he died trying to create the world's first frozen chicken), but the spirit in which his enquiries were undertaken has been mistaken by some recent commentators. It is true that he did coin the phrase 'knowledge is power', which in retrospect shows signs of less happy things to come; but it is often forgotten that the context in which he wrote those words was actually that of God's foreknowledge of the world he had created, and could therefore only ever be applied by human beings to the knowledge we have of our own creations (machines) – never of Nature herself.[76] There has become current an idea that Bacon advocated putting Nature (personified according to convention as a woman) on the rack. While there is certainly something in Bacon's language that suggests forcing Nature to give up her secrets reluctantly, nowhere does he say that she should be tortured, or put on the rack, an idea that seems to have come from a casual remark by Leibniz in a letter to a colleague, and which was perpetuated by Ernst Cassirer.[77] What Bacon says is that we learn more by *constraining* the conditions under which we make our observations, in other words by carefully designed experiments, than we can do from casual observation of Nature unconstrained – an acknowl-edgment that, in Heraclitus' phrase, 'Nature loves to hide.' He was deeply respectful of Nature, and wrote that 'Nature to be commanded must be obeyed . . . The subtlety of Nature is greater many times over than the subtlety of the senses and understanding.'[78]

It was not long, however, before Descartes, certainly, was saying, in very different spirit, that science will make us 'the lords and masters of nature.'[79] And gone is Bacon's careful recognition that, while observing Nature attentively is essential, she is many times subtler than our senses or our understanding. If Descartes had observed that caveat, he would never have made the fatal mistake of believing 'that I could take it as a general rule that the things we conceive very clearly and very distinctly are all true.'[80] That was the fallacy that was to derail the next three centuries of Western thought.

CONCLUSION

In this necessarily cursory review of a vast topic, I have tried to focus on elements that indicate shifts in our experience and understanding of the world which have meaning in terms of hemisphere discrimination. Once again, one does not find, I submit, a purely random pattern, suggesting no correlation with hemisphere differences. Once again, I believe, in the earlier phases of this movement (however one cares to think of it) in the history of ideas that is called the Renaissance, one sees a fruitful balance in the relation of the hemispheres. This operated to bring about the quintessential Renaissance achievements of perspective, both in spatial depth and in historical and personal time, and of the idea of the individual. For the most part, however, the changes that occurred at around this period do suggest the salience of primarily the right hemisphere's world. One of the defining features of the Renaissance must be its opening of the eyes to experience, initially almost exclusively personal experience, in preference to what is 'known' to be the case, the teachings of scholastic theory and received opinion. There is a corresponding respect for the quiddity of individual things and people, rather than their being seen as members of categories. There was a faithful imitation of, and close attention to, the natural world, and to what other people in other times may have thought or known; and in this breadth of concern, and the insistence on the interconnectedness of things and the importance of the fullest possible context, it again speaks of the right hemisphere's world. This also included the body and the soul equally and inseparably as the context of all living things. In its respect for the body as more than a thing, and an integral part of the whole person; in its rehabilitation of the senses; in its emphasis on spatial depth, and on time as lived, with man becoming the 'being towards death'; in the rekindling of empathy in the arts, including theatre, and a preoccupation with the expressive powers of the human face in particular, in the portraiture that dominates the visual arts of the period; in the sense of the self as an individual, yet integrated by moral and emotional bonds to society; in the newfound expressiveness of all the arts; in the rise of polyphony, with the importance of melody, harmony and the relationship of the parts to the whole; in the rise of wit and pathos, and the predominant emphasis on the links between wisdom and melancholy; in its attraction to exemplars, rather than to categories; in its capacity to accept the *coniunctio oppositorum*, and to relish mixed emotions and the coming together of widely different ideas; in its emphasis on the importance of what must remain implicit, on inborn and intuited skills (as well as on the artist as a semi-divine being), and on the world as never just what it 'seems' to be, but pointing beyond to something Other, a world that is semi-transparent, pregnant with myth and metaphor – in all these respects, it seems to me that the Renaissance started out with a huge expansion of the right hemisphere's way of being in the world, into which, initially, the work of the left hemisphere is integrated. And it is this that accounts for the astonishing fertility and richness, as well as the remarkable breadth of concern, to this day memorialised in the concept of the Renaissance man, of this period.

As the Renaissance progresses, there becomes evident, however, a gradual shift of emphasis from the right hemisphere way of being towards the vision of the left hemisphere, in which a more atomistic individuality characterised by ambition and competition becomes more salient; and originality comes to mean not creative possibility but the right to 'free thinking', the way to throw off the shackles of the past and its traditions, which are no longer seen as an inexhaustible source of wisdom, but as tyrannical, superstitious and *irrational* – and therefore wrong. This becomes the basis of the hubristic movement which came to be known as the Enlightenment.

CHAPTER 10

———◆———

THE ENLIGHTENMENT

T HE ENLIGHTENMENT IS, OF COURSE, THE AGE OF REASON. THIS TERM, SO REDOLENT of clarity, simplicity and harmony, generates confusion, complexity and contradiction at the outset. '*Rational* and *rationality, reason* and *Reason*, remain hotly contested notions, whose users disagree even about the nature of their disagreement,' wrote the philosopher Max Black.[1] One principal distinction underlies most of the others; it is a distinction that has been understood and expressed in language since ancient times, and therefore is likely to have a substrate in the lived world. This is the distinction between, on the one hand, Greek *nous* (or *noos*), Latin *intellectus*, German *Vernunft*, English *reason* (allied to common sense – *sensus communis*, in Vico's sense rather than Kant's) and, on the other, Greek *logos/dianoia*, Latin *ratio*, German *Verstand*, English *rationality*. The first of these – flexible, resisting fixed formulation, shaped by experience, and involving the whole living being – is congenial to the operations of the right hemisphere; the second – more rigid, rarified, mechanical, governed by explicit laws – to those of the left.

The first, what I have called right-hemisphere sense, was traditionally considered to be the higher faculty. There are a number of reasons why this was so. For a start, the edifice of rationality (*logos*), the left-hemisphere type of reason, was weakened by the recognition that (in contravention of the consistency principle) a thing and its opposite may well both be true. But there is one problem that attacks the very root of *logos*. Although constitutive for science and much of philosophy, because of its being based on argumentation and the provision of proof, it cannot constitute – cannot ground – itself according to its own principles of proof and argumentation. The value of rationality, as well as whatever premises it may start from, has to be intuited: neither can be derived from rationality itself. All rationality can do is to provide internal consistency once the system is up and running. Deriving deeper premises only further postpones the ultimate question, and leads into an infinite regress; in the end one is back to an act of intuitive faith governed by reason (*nous*). *Logos* represents, as indeed the left hemisphere does, a closed system which cannot reach outside itself to whatever it is that exists apart from itself. According to Plato, *nous* (reason as opposed to rationality) is characterised by intuition, and according to Aristotle it is *nous* that grasps the first principles through induction. So the primacy of reason (right hemisphere) is due to the fact that rationality (left hemisphere) is founded on it. Once again the right hemisphere is prior to the left.

Kant is commonly held to have reversed these priorities. At first sight this would appear to be the case, since for him *Verstand* (rationality) plays a constitutive role, and is therefore primary, while *Vernunft* (reason) plays a regulatory one, once *Verstand* has done its work. Rationality, according to this formulation, comes first, and reason then operates on what rationality yields, to decide how to use and interpret the products of rationality. However, I do not think that Kant's formulation embodies a reversal as much as an extension. There was something missing from the earlier classical picture that reason is the ground of rationality, namely the necessity for rationality to return the fruits of its operations to reason again. Reason is indeed required to give the intuitive, inductive foundation to rationality, but rationality needs in turn to submit its workings to the judgment of reason at the end (Kant's regulatory role). Thus it is not that A (reason) → B (rationality), but that A (reason) → B (rationality) → A (reason) again. This mirrors the process that I have suggested enables the hemispheres to work co-operatively: the right hemisphere delivers something to the left hemisphere, which the left hemisphere then unfolds and gives back to the right hemisphere in an enhanced form. The classical, pre-Kantian, position focussed on the first part of the process: A (reason) → B (rationality), thus reason is the ground of rationality. My reading of Kant is that it was his perception of the importance of the second part of this tripartite arrangement, namely that B (rationality) → A (reason), the products of rationality must be subject to reason, that led him to what is perceived as a reversal, though it is better seen as an extension of the original formulation.

Reason depends on seeing things in context, a right-hemisphere faculty, whereas rationality is typically left-hemisphere in that it is context-independent, and exemplifies the interchangeability that results from abstraction and categorisation. Any purely rational sequence could in theory be abstracted from the context of an individual mind and 'inserted' in another mind as it stands; because it is rule-based, it could be taught in the narrow sense of that word, whereas reason cannot in this sense be taught, but has to grow out of each individual's experience, and is incarnated in that person with all their feelings, beliefs, values and judgments. Rationality can be an important part of reason, but only part. Reason is about holding sometimes incompatible elements in balance, a right-hemisphere capacity which had been highly prized among the humanist scholars of the Renaissance. Rationality imposes an 'either/or' on life which is far from reasonable.

The Enlightenment is, for all its love of unity, a most self-contradictory phenomenon: it was, one may fairly say, the best of times, it was the worst of times. The highest achievements of the Enlightenment, those for which eighteenth-century culture is widely admired, express the harmony and balance, often accompanied by an ironic, but tolerant, acceptance of human frailty, which, I believe, mark a high point in the co-operation of the right and left hemispheres, with, in my terms the left hemisphere having delivered itself back to the right hemisphere. But built into the foundations of Enlightenment thought are precepts that are bound to lead eventually to a less flexible and humane outlook, that of the left hemisphere alone.

Let us think, not of reason, but of metaphor. Metaphorical understanding has a close relationship with reason, which seems paradoxical only because we have inherited an Enlightenment view of metaphor: namely, that it is either indirectly literal, and can be reduced to 'proper' literal language, or a purely fanciful ornament, and therefore irrelevant to meaning and rational thought, which it indeed threatens to disrupt. It is seen as a linguistic device, not as a vehicle of thought. What the literalist view and the anti-literalist view share is that, ultimately, metaphor can have nothing directly to do with truth. Either it is simply another way of stating literal truth or else it undermines any claim to truth. But as Lakoff and Johnson have shown, 'metaphor is centrally a matter of thought, not just words'.[2] The loss of metaphor is a loss of cognitive content.[3] Thinking cannot be severed from our bodily existence, out of which all metaphors arise.

DESCARTES AND MADNESS

The most influential Enlightenment philosopher, René Descartes, famously attempted to demonstrate precisely the opposite. He saw the body, the senses and the imagination as likely to lead, not only to error, but into the realm of madness. In the *Meditations on First Philosophy* he refers to the 'madmen' who trust their senses and end up imagining 'that their heads are made of earthenware, or that they are pumpkins, or made of glass'.[4]

There is a deep irony involved here. The symptoms he describes are characteristic of delusions that occur in schizophrenia.[5] But schizophrenia is not characterised at all by trusting the senses – rather by an unreasonable mistrust of them. It entails in many cases a wholesale inability to rely on the reality of embodied existence in the 'common-sense' world which we share with others, and leads to a dehumanised view of others, who begin to lose their intuitively experienced identity as fellow humans and become seen as devitalised machines. One's own body becomes no longer the vehicle through which reality is experienced, but instead is seen as just another object, sometimes a disturbingly alien object, in the world that is validated by cognition alone. Sufferers from schizophrenia have been known to see themselves as, for example, copying machines, or to contemplate cutting their wrists to find out whether they contain engine oil.

'To lose one's reason' is the old expression for madness. But an excess of rationality is the grounds of another kind of madness, that of schizophrenia. As Louis Sass argued in his *Madness and Modernism* and in *The Paradoxes of Delusion*,[6] and Giovanni Stanghellini has further emphasised in *Disembodied Spirits and Deanimated Bodies*,[7] schizophrenia is not characterised by a Romantic disregard for rational thinking and a regression into a more primitive, unself-conscious, emotive realm of the body and the senses, but by an excessively detached, hyperrational, reflexively self-aware, disembodied and alienated condition.

Louis Sass has demonstrated, by his comparisons of Wittgenstein's critique of philosophy with Daniel Paul Schreber's detailed accounts of his own psychotic illness (Schreber was the subject of Freud's only study of schizophrenia), that there are extensive similarities between schizophrenia and the state of mind that is brought about when one makes a conscious effort to distance oneself from one's surroundings, refrain from normal action and interaction with them, suspend one's normal assumptions and feelings about them and subject them to a detached scrutiny – an exercise which in the non-mentally ill is normally confined to philosophers. The belief that this will result in a deeper apprehension of reality ignores the fact that the nature of the attention we bring to bear on anything alters what we find there. Adopting a stance that is normally found only in patients suffering from schizophrenia is not obviously a recipe for finding a higher truth.[8]

However, the Cartesian view of the world does just this. Referring to a famous passage from the *Meditations on First Philosophy* in which Descartes describes looking out of his window and seeing what he knows to be people passing by as seeming to him nonetheless like mere machines, wearing hats and coats, the philosopher David Levin comments:

> What could be a greater symptom of madness than to look out of one's window and see (what might, for all one knows, be) machines, instead of real people? The point I want to make is that *this*, this kind of vision, is what the rationality he has embraced leads to. Not by mere chance, not by a momentary caprice, but by the inexorable logic of the rationality to which he is committed . . . Only a philosopher could, or would, talk in this way [with scepticism about the existence of other people]. In 'real life', outside the study, such a way of talking – such a way of *looking* at other people – would be judged mad, a subtle symptom of paranoia.[9]

Descartes held that there was 'absolutely no connection (at least that I can understand)' between 'that curious tugging in the stomach which I call hunger' and the desire to eat.[10] Even pain was a mystery: 'why', he asks, 'should that curious sensation of pain give rise to a particular distress of mind?'[11] This seems to me to display a quite extraordinary lack of intuitive understanding. If there is, in fact, one place at which the relationship between the body and subjective experience can be intuitively understood, it is right there, in sensations such as pain and hunger. But then Descartes was not sure that he had a body at all:

> I can make a probable conjecture that the body exists. But this is only a probability; and despite a careful and comprehensive investigation, I do not yet see how the distinct idea of corporeal nature which I find in my imagination can provide any basis for a necessary inference that some body exists.[12]

Descartes's rationality led him not only to doubt the existence of others, but to see knowledge of his own body as constituted by the intellect, rather than self-evident through intuition: 'Even bodies are not strictly perceived by the senses or the faculty of imagination, but by the intellect alone, and . . . this perception derives not from their being touched or seen but from their being understood.'[13] Thus, by an astonishing inversion, rationality becomes not merely constitutive of reason, but of intuition and the body. However, reason is not only rooted in the body, in *our* bodies, but in the physical and instinctual realm that we share with animals. As Lakoff and Johnson write:

> Reason is evolutionary, in that abstract reason builds on and makes use of forms of perceptual and motor inference present in 'lower' animals . . . Reason is thus not an essence that separates us from other animals; rather, it places us on a continuum with them . . . Reason is not completely conscious, but mostly uncon-scious. Reason is not purely literal, but largely metaphorical and imaginative. Reason is not dispassionate, but emotionally engaged . . . Since reason is shaped by the body, it is not radically free, because the possible human conceptual systems and the possible forms of reason are limited. In addition, once we have learned a conceptual system, it is neurally instantiated in our brains and we are not free to think just anything.[14]

The very basis of abstract thought, both in its concepts and in the manipulation of those concepts, lies in metaphors drawn from the body: 'Reason is imaginative in that bodily inference forms are mapped onto abstract modes of inference by metaphor.'[15]

Descartes is one of the first and greatest exemplars of the left hemisphere's salience in the philosophy of the Enlightenment. If one thinks back to the neuropsychological literature on the appreciation of time, which has formed a significant part of my analysis of the differences between right and left hemi-sphere, and I believe casts light on the process of reason in early Greek paradox, one is struck by the view of time held by Descartes. According to Charles Sherover, Descartes had 'problems with the very idea of temporal continuity, epit-omised in his conviction that each moment is a somehow irreducible real self-enclosed atomic point in the structure of the universe, and is devoid of any sustaining continuity with any other moment.'[16]

A number of aspects of Descartes's philosophical stance can be summarised. Detached from the body, its tiresome emotions and its intimations of mortality, he aspired to be 'a spectator rather than an actor in all the *comedies*' the world displays.[17] All-seeing, but no longer bodily or affectively engaged with the world, Descartes experiences the world as a representation. That has its rewards for Descartes, but it also has some profoundly negative consequences, not just for us, but for him. It is true that it enables him to achieve his prized goals of certainty and fixity, but it does so at the expense of content. Then again: objectification is, sure enough, a means to domination and control, but it succeeds by a strategy from which the ego itself cannot escape. Here is Levin:

> The ego's possibility of mastering, dominating and controlling required, in turn, that objectification – reification – must be given priority, for objectification is the way that the world is brought before us in representation, made available for our

technological mastering, and subjected to our domination. But the final ironic twist in the logic of this process of objectification is that it escapes our control, and we ourselves become its victims, simultaneously reduced to the being-available of mere objects and reduced to the being of a purely inner subjectivity that is no longer recognised as enjoying any truth, any reality.[18]

Each of these facets of Descartes's predicament recapitulates the phenomenology of schizophrenia. The sense of being a passive observer of life, not an actor in it, is related to the passivity phenomena that are a primary characteristic of the condition. Many of the paintings by sufferers show an all-observing eye, detached from the scene it observes, floating in the picture.

Affective non-engagement could be said to be the hallmark of schizophrenia. The sense that the world is merely a representation ('play-acting') is very common, part of the inability to trust one's senses, enhanced by the feeling of unreality that non-engagement brings in its wake – nothing is what it seems. Such an inability to accept the self-evident nature of sensory experience leads to an emptying out of meaning. There is a characteristic combination of omnipotence and impotence, of being all there is and yet nothing at all, which again follows from the lack of betweenness with what *is*, with the shared world of common experience.

My purpose here is not to discount Descartes, but to illuminate the links between his philosophical enterprise and the experience of schizophrenia, which, as John Cutting has shown, appears to be a state in which the sufferer relies excessively on (an abnormally functioning) left hemisphere.[19] I would argue that in all its major predilections – divorce from the body, detachment from human feeling, the separation of thought from action in the world, concern with clarity and fixity, the triumph of representation over what is present to sensory experience, in its reduction of time to a succession of atomistic moments, and in its tendency to reduce the living to the devitalised and mechanical – the philosophy of Descartes belongs to the world as construed by the left hemisphere.

DEVITALISATION AND THE NEED FOR CERTAINTY

As the German philosopher Johann Georg Hamann, one of the Enlightenment's earliest critics, saw, this Cartesian world view would lead to devitalisation, and in social terms, to bureaucratisation. The immediacy with which unnatural detachment induces boredom can be seen from the novelist Alberto Moravia's description of boredom, in his novel of that name:

> Boredom to me consists in a kind of insufficiency, or inadequacy or lack of reality ... yet again boredom might be described as a malady affecting external objects and consisting of a withering process; an almost instantaneous loss of vitality ... The feeling of boredom originates for me in a sense of the absurdity of a reality which is insufficient, or anyhow unable, to convince me of its own effective existence ...[20]

The concept of boredom arose in the eighteenth century. Patricia Spacks, in her informative work on the subject, relates it to 'the dreariness of non-engagement'.[21] (According to Isaiah Berlin, 'Vauvenargues, complained bitterly about the appalling emptiness of life . . . Madame de la Popelinière said that she wished to throw herself out of the window because she felt that life had no meaning and no purpose.')[22] I would connect the rise of the concept of boredom with an essentially passive view of experience; a view of vitality as mediated by novelty, a stimulant force which comes to us from outside, rather as the power supply comes to a computer, and in relation to which we are passive recipients (as the left hemisphere finds itself in relation to what comes to it from the right hemisphere). One might contrast this with the view of vitality, as the Romantics would come to see it, as the result of imagination bringing something into being between ourselves and whatever it is that exists 'out there', in which we act as fashioners of our own experience (as the right hemisphere experiences whatever it is that lies outside the brain).[23] The connection with the left hemisphere is again apparent in the relationship between boredom and the experience of time: no longer a lived narrative, it is static, eternal, unchanging. Boredom is 'a typically modern characteristic of the experience of subjective time', writes Anton Zijderveld,[24] an idea expanded on by Martin Waugh: 'When we are bored, our attitude toward time is altered, as it is in some dreamlike states. Time seems endless, there is no distinction between past, present and future. There seems to be only an endless present.'[25] That sounds oddly like Plato's realm of the ideal Forms.

In his book *The Roots of Romanticism*, Isaiah Berlin lays out what it was about the Enlightenment that Romanticism later came to put in question. He refers to 'the three propositions . . . upon which the whole Western tradition rested': namely, 'that all genuine questions can be answered, that if a question cannot be answered it is not a question'; 'that all these answers are knowable, that they can be discovered by means which can be learnt and taught to other persons'; and 'that all the answers must be compatible with one another'.[26] These tenets could be said to be the foundations of Enlightenment thinking. When Berlin refers to the 'Western tradition', he is speaking of the Western philosophical tradition, that is, that part of Western culture dealing in explicit fashion with the resolution of 'questions' and 'answers'. Although philosophers in the West since the time of Plato had behaved as though these tenets, Berlin's three propositions, were true, there was, until the time of the Enlightenment, enough implicit expression of cultural wisdom through the media of poetry, drama, painting, and, above all, religious ritual – in all of which it is easily perceived as far from true that all questions can be answered, that all answers can be taught, and that all answers are mutually compatible – that these tenets, though important in philosophy, had not come to shape the culture itself. But with the heightened self-awareness of the Enlightenment, these three, obviously false, propositions came to dominate not just academic philosophy, but the business of life itself; or, to look at it another way, in what became known as the age of *les philosophes*, we all became philosophers *malgré nous*.

The necessity for the Enlightenment of certainty and 'transmissibility' creates a problem for the arts, which are intrinsically ambiguous and uncertain, and where creative genius is not 'transmissible'. There is a consequent downgrading of imagination in favour of fancy, and a mistrust of metaphor, as we have noted, which is equated with the lie. There are obvious continuities between the Reformation and the Enlightenment. They share the same marks of left-hemisphere domination: the banishment of wonder; the triumph of the explicit, and, with it, mistrust of metaphor; alienation from the embodied world of the flesh, and a consequent cerebralisation of life and experience. The right hemisphere bid for reason, in which opposites can be held in balance, was swiftly transformed into a move toward left-hemisphere rationality, in which one of the two must exclude, even annihilate, the other. The impulse towards harmony was replaced with the impulse towards singleness and purity.

If one looks at Reynolds' *Discourses*, for example, a hugely influential book in its day, based on a series of lectures delivered to the Royal Academy between 1769 and 1791, one finds him criticising great figures of Renaissance art, such as Bernini, for portraying mixed emotions, something that had once been, and later would again be, considered a sign of genius. (Fortunately, Reynolds, whose writings were a consistent target for Blake, did not stick to his precepts in his own painting.) Where reason respects the implicit, the ambiguous, the unresolved, rationality demands the explicit, the clear and the complete.

The emphasis on 'light' in 'Enlightenment' suggests not just clarity and precision, but of course the banishment of the darker, more 'negative' emotions. The optimism of the Enlightenment is based on the belief that man can control his destiny. Death is correspondingly de-emphasised. From 1681, when Nahum Tate revised it, *King Lear* was for 150 years performed, believe it or not, with a happy ending, and other of Shakespeare's tragedies were performed with comedy resolutions. It is hard not to see in this a degree of denial, especially when one remembers other societies in which art was compulsorily optimistic. This is in keeping with the fact that the left hemisphere sees things literally as lighter, and is more prone to 'positive' emotions. (I put the terms 'positive' and 'negative', in relation to the emotions, in inverted commas, because, even though they have been naturalised in the language to such a degree that it may now be hard to see the inherent bias in the terms, they suggest in typical left-hemisphere fashion that its favoured emotions are more valuable, more productive, even more substantial, than others. Literally they suggest that one set of emotions is based on the absence of the others – 'negative' implying denial, or 'no-saying', to something else that has prior or primary existence. It may be far from true, however, that 'negative' emotions such as sadness are negative in any sense; indeed to be without the capacity for sadness would mean a degree of detachment from the manifestly suffering world around one which bordered on the psychopathic.)

DECEPTIVE CLARITY

In this age vision became more akin to the model of the camera; perspective more the detached process that it initially avoided being in the Renaissance. Vision has become a more alienating process as we have progressed in self-consciousness in the West. Perhaps this was already foreseen in the Renaissance: written on the tomb of one of the first makers of eyeglasses, who died in 1317 and is buried in Santa Maria Maggiore in Rome, are the words: 'God forgive him his sins.'[27] The moral consequences of the discovery of optics are not to be under-estimated (though this is likely to be an effect, rather than a cause, of Western alienation, since, according to Joseph Needham, optics were 'particularly well developed in ancient and medieval China').[28] Writing of the insidious effect of the metaphor of 'reflection' on our understanding of understanding, one modern philosopher writes: 'The source of the turn to the idea of reflection in modern philosophy lies in modern optics. Modern optics is the analogue for the modern conception of the intellect as a source of "reflective" knowledge.'[29] In fact the discoveries of optics were made by the Greeks, though they were later largely lost, and their power to change the way we 'see' the world took a vast leap forward with the Enlightenment. The word 'reflection' first started to be used to refer to thought processes in the seventeenth century. In 1690 Locke defined it as 'that notice which the mind takes of its own operations, and the manner of them', already seeing reflection as the process of self-reflection.[30] As early as 1725, Vico was referring to 'the barbarism of reflection'.[31]

We are used now to the idea that sights – even picturesque sights – are like a quarry that is pursued and 'captured' by the camera, but it may come as a surprise to learn that they were already being talked of in this way in the eighteenth century. According to Thomas Gray, those early tourists would already '*capture* prospects at every ten paces', or '*catch* the diversity of views'.[32] Equally William Gilpin's famous essays on the picturesque advise that the 'first source of amuse-ment to the picturesque traveller, is the *pursuit* of his object – the expectation of new scenes continually opening, and arising to his view'.[33]

The very existence of the idea of the picturesque – nature as like a painting – reveals that nature is thought to require improvement by human hand and eye. Nature now suffered under the Enlightenment in the same way that metaphor had done: from having been something revered because it opened a way out of the realm of the artificial towards a more profound reality, picturesque nature became Locke's perfect cheat, just a pretty deception. Faced with this, the sensible response of the Enlightened mind is not to seek beyond, to find a Nature that *transcends* the picturesque, but instead to do the opposite, to retreat, and to rede-fine Nature in terms of civilised behaviour. Thus when Mrs Elton, in Jane Austen's *Emma*, enthusiastically describes her proposed picnic party in the grounds of Mr Knightley's house, she is firmly put in her place: 'There is to be no form or parade – a sort of gipsy party', gushes Mrs Elton:

'We are to walk about your gardens, and gather the strawberries ourselves, and sit under trees; – and whatever else you may like to provide, it is to be all out of doors – a table spread in the shade, you know. Every thing as natural and simple as possible. Is not that your idea?'

'Not quite. My idea of the simple and the natural will be to have the table spread in the dining-room. The nature and the simplicity of gentlemen and ladies, with their servants and furniture, I think is best observed by meals within doors. When you are tired of eating strawberries in the garden, there shall be cold meat in the house.'

Nature was to be treated with suspicion: observed, perhaps, as a parent might observe with indulgence an unruly child, but needing as much instruction in good manners – how to eat cold meat. Nature yields to artifice, not artifice to nature.

The powerful all-surveying, all-capturing eye achieved its apotheosis in Jeremy Bentham's Panopticon. This was, tellingly, a prison design which enabled prisoners to be under total surveillance while being themselves unaware of when they were being watched, a project about which Bentham was so enthusiastic that he spent much of his time and personal fortune on it. It has become familiar through the writings on modern society of Michel Foucault, with obvious correlates in the present world of technological surveillance, and in this way one could say that Bentham's dream, or nightmare, was prescient.

Bentham, the father of utilitarianism, was an eccentric character. In some ways he prefigures the child-like adults for whom Dickens had so keen an eye. He has many of the features that would suggest a mild degree of autism, and more specifically deficits in right-hemisphere functions. He was socially awkward: according to J. S. Mill, he 'probably never talked to women at all, except for his cook and housemaid', and according to Mill's biographer, Packe, 'courted women with a clumsy jocularity'.[34] He had a peculiarly pedantic way of talking, and referred to his morning walks as 'antejentacular circumgyrations'. With inanimate objects he was more at home, and had pet names for them: his stick was Dapple, and his teapot, through an impish uprising of his much-repressed unconscious, was Dick. Mill wrote of him that

> he had neither internal experience nor external ... He never knew prosperity and adversity, passion nor satiety ... He knew no dejection, no heaviness of heart. He never felt life a sore and a weary burthen. He was a boy to the last ... How much of human nature slumbered in him he knew not, neither can we know. Other ages and other nations were a blank to him for the purposes of instruction. He measured them but by one standard; their knowledge of facts, and their capability to take correct views of utility, and merge all other objects in it ... Knowing so little of human feelings, he knew still less of the influences by which those feelings are formed: all the more subtle workings both of the mind upon itself, and of external things upon the mind, escaped him; and no one, probably, who, in a highly instructed age, ever attempted to give a rule to all human conduct, set out with a more limited conception either of the agencies by which human conduct *is*, or of those by which it *should* be, influenced.[35]

The description is uncannily reminiscent of Balzac's description of Fontenelle, another Enlightenment philosopher (see Chapter 11, n. 18 below).

As Mill suggests, Bentham wished to 'give a rule' to human conduct: he saw himself as a legislator of all that had hitherto gone unlegislated.[36] He was a vehement critic of intuitive wisdom. 'His lifelong distaste for organised religion – which he called "The Jug", short for juggernaut', writes Huw Richards, 'was rapidly supplemented by a contempt for the British common law tradition espoused by Blackstone. He saw both as the product of superstition, deference and ancestor-worship, rather than logic and real human needs.'[37] His great projects were those of classification; and indeed it was he who invented the words *international, codify* and *maximise*. Despite these tendencies to legislate for 'Society', Bentham held, in keeping with his personal temperament and with the world as seen by the left hemisphere, that 'the community is a fictitious body'.[38]

The left-hemisphere preferences that he shows so obviously in some things were evidenced more subtly in others. Rather touchingly, he seems to have cherished all his life the memory of a moment in his youth when a young lady at Bowood, the seat of his patron Lord Lansdowne, had presented him with a flower, and wrote to her at the age of 80 to remind her: 'to the end of his life he could not hear of Bowood without tears swimming in his eyes'. On such occasions he would, however, exclaim, in keeping with the optimistic, future-directed gaze of the left hemisphere: 'Take me forward, I entreat you, to the future – do not let me go back to the past.'[39]

It might be anticipated that Bentham would not look favourably on poetry, and in this he can speak for a number of voices from the mid-seventeenth to the mid-eighteenth centuries. '*Prose*', he wrote, and I would like to suppose that there was here at least some self-mocking humour, 'is where all the lines but the last go on to the margin – poetry is where some of them fall short of it.'[40] However, elsewhere, I have to admit, he wrote in all apparent seriousness that

> prejudice apart, the game of push-pin is of equal value with the arts and sciences of music and poetry. If the game of push-pin furnish more pleasure, it is more valuable than either. Everybody can play at push-pin: poetry and music are relished only by a few. The game of push-pin is always innocent: it were well could the same be always asserted of poetry. Indeed, between poetry and truth there is a natural opposition: false morals and fictitious nature.[41]

Art is by its nature implicit and ambiguous. It is also embodied: it produces embodied creations which speak to us through the senses, even if their medium is language, and which have effects on us physically as embodied beings in the lived world. The Enlightenment is concerned primarily with the intellect, with all that 'transcends' (from the Enlightenment point of view) the limitations of the contingent and the physical, the incarnate and unique. Enlightenment art is, therefore, something of an oxymoron. The two art forms that are least vulnerable to explicitness are music and architecture – not because they are congenial to it, but precisely the opposite, because they are so inherently implicit (though one can ask what a poem or painting is 'about', the question becomes vapid when applied to music or architecture).

Probably for this reason music and architecture are the arts that survived best in this period, being least available to being hijacked into the world of explicitness. Haydn's music is one of the most complete expressions of the Enlightenment spirit in art. In it there is a sense of tension between opposites held beautifully in balance, a lightness and pleasure in symmetry, a sense of decorum, and all being in its place. But it also contains disconcertingly mysterious elements which suggest a world far beyond that of drawing-room order alone.[42] Mozart so clearly displays elements of darkness and perturbation that it may be doubted whether he is really an Enlightenment composer, so much does he prefigure Romanticism, particularly in his later works; but this, too, is made all the more powerful for its restraint, and its relish for bitter-sweet emotions, and, in his operas particularly, for a combination of irony and compassion, so that (like many great artists of all ages – Chaucer, for example, in his treatment of Troilus) he is never superior to his characters, but acknowledges a shared vulnerability. This was also the greatest age of European domestic architecture, though that architecture is largely derived from the principles of the Italian Renaissance architects, above all Palladio. Here, then, is the best side of Enlightenment art.

Poetry was more easily subverted in this age of consummate prose. Poetry was a form of flattering lie: Lord Chesterfield recommended his son to tear a couple of sheets from a book of Latin poetry and take them with him to the 'necessary-house', where, once he had read them, he could 'send them down as a sacrifice to Cloacina' (the goddess of sewers);[43] which led Keats to write of him that he 'would not bathe in the same River with lord C. though I had the upper hand of the stream.'[44] The Enlightenment belief was that there was a finite set of possible true ideas or thoughts, and that they existed in the abstract and were subsequently given embodiment in language. In this way they were certain and known, but they could be made to look new by wearing new clothes. Poetry adorned ideas with decorous clothing that would enable us to take pleasure in the familiar, but it did not bring new experiences. This was what lay behind Pope's famous line in praise of intelligent poetry: 'What oft was thought, but ne'er so well express'd', and he continued: 'Expression is the dress of thought . . .'[45] This later formed the basis of Wordsworth and Coleridge's attack on the Augustans in the Preface to *Lyrical Ballads*, since they saw poetry as the work of the imagination, which is genuinely creative, in the sense that it brings new experiences into being – not as the work of fantasy, which merely recombines what we are already familiar with in a new way. This view is in line with Scheler's perception of the nature of poetry, which I quote at length because I know of no better exposition of this crucial point:

> For this reason poets, and all makers of language having the 'god-given power to tell of what they suffer' [Goethe, *Marienbader Elegie*], fulfil a far higher function than that of giving noble and beautiful expression to their experiences and thereby making them recognisable to the reader, by reference to his own past experience of this kind. For by creating new forms of expression, the poets soar above the prevailing network of ideas in which our experience is confined, as it were, by

ordinary language; they enable the rest of us to *see*, for the first time, in our own experience, something which may answer to these new and richer forms of expression, and by so doing they actually *extend* the scope of our *possible* self-awareness. They effect a real enlargement of the kingdom of the mind and make new discoveries, as it were, within that kingdom. It is they who open up new branches and channels in our apprehension of the stream and thereby show us for the first time *what* we are experiencing. That is indeed the mission of all true art: not to reproduce what is already given (which would be superfluous), nor to create something in the pure play of subjective fancy (which can only be transitory and must necessarily be a matter of complete indifference to other people), but to press forward into the whole of the external world *and* the soul, to see and communicate those objective realities within it which rule and convention have hitherto concealed. The history of art may be seen, therefore, as a series of expeditions against the intuitable world, within and without, to subdue it for our comprehension; and that for a kind of comprehension which no science could ever provide. An emotion, for example, which everyone can now perceive in himself, must once have been wrested by some 'poet' from the fearful inarticulacy of our inner life for this clear perception of it to be possible: just as in commerce things (such as tea, coffee, pepper, salt, etc.), which were once luxuries, are nowadays articles of everyday use in general supply.[46]

The poetry of Dryden and Pope belongs to the best part of the Enlightenment – generous, non-dogmatic, wry in spirit; and elsewhere I have written of Sam Johnson's idiosyncratic refusal to fit his own precepts.[47] But few would suggest that poetry of the Augustan Age is, at least consciously, concerned with presenting authentic experience, so much as representing it pleasingly, casting it in a certain light; not enlarging the kingdom of the mind, and making new discoveries, but tending its gardens and trimming its hedges as neatly and elegantly as possible. Of course great artists will always rebel against the limitations of the medium, which nonetheless are the condition of their mastery, as Goethe famously said.[48] But these are the exceptions. When Reynolds is faced with the uncouth genius of Michelangelo, or Johnson faced with the still more uncouth genius of Shakespeare (or with the sublimity of the Scottish Highlands), and when they are able to recognise it, one feels that they succeed only because of their willingness to jettison all the theoretical baggage of the Enlightenment when faced with the enormity of experience.

SYMMETRY AND STASIS

The classical heroic couplet, with its pointed caesura, allows symmetry to equalise – in fact equality is essential to symmetry; and this punctuated, symmetrically self-referring motion can sometimes be used for deliberately *puncturing* effect:

Here thou, great ANNA! whom three realms obey
Dost sometimes counsel take – and sometimes Tea.[49]

This movement, constantly returning into itself and pausing, contrasts with the earlier, open, turbulent, river-like flow of Milton's syntax, always intimating something further and beyond, that would later be recaptured and transformed in its turn by Wordsworth; just as the ever-changing, growing, flowing form of the music of Bach contrasts with the self-contained perfection of classical form in Haydn. But this constant reining in of both motion and meaning every other line, with its closed, static, self-involved structure, in which rhyme and paronomasia discipline the strayings of the spirit, and bring everything neatly back to symmetry, is evaded in many of Dryden's best lines, such as the end of his elegy on the death of a friend, 'Farewel, too little and too lately known', with its final alexandrine almost sleepwalking beyond the frame of the poem:

Once more, hail and farewel; farewel thou young,
But ah too short, *Marcellus* of our Tongue;
Thy Brows with Ivy, and with Laurels bound;
But Fate and gloomy Night encompass thee around.[50]

or the wonderful crispness of his farewell to the seventeenth century:

All, all, of a piece throughout;
Thy Chase had a Beast in View;
Thy Wars brought nothing about;
Thy Lovers were all untrue.
'Tis well an Old Age is out,
And time to begin a New.[51]

Symmetry is an intriguing concept. In the abstract it is undoubtedly appealing at a very deep level. The word itself means equal measure, and it is a feature of all the ideal typical shapes of 'regular solids' beloved of the Greeks. In mathematics the term refers not just to symmetry about an axis, but to any procedure which one can perform on an object and leave it *unchanged*. It also signifies independence from *contingency* – in other words, universality: if a law obeys symmetry, it is universally applicable. Newtonian mechanics obey symmetry. All these meanings ally it with the realm of stasis, of universals, of simple, ideal forms: the left hemisphere. Oddly, though, symmetry does not appear in the phenomenal world, although it is approximated by living things, which on closer inspection are, however, like the brain, not truly symmetrical, and are constantly moving and changing. And, though it is often stated that animals find symmetry in a mate attractive, humans appear not, in fact, to share such preferences.[52] Even in cases where symmetry is clocked as more healthy, it is *still* experienced as less attractive.[53] In fact symmetry in living faces, because it suggests something mechanical and unreal, borders on the uncanny, a perception that lies behind 'the fearful symmetry' of Blake's tiger. And, as one might expect, in portraiture of the Enlightenment 'faces generally are represented more symmetrically than in any other Western style', according to F. D. Martin. 'That is one of the reasons why this portraiture is, as Wilde puts it, "once seen, never remembered".'[54]

Symmetry – in poetry, in music, in architecture, in prose and in thought – was perhaps the ultimately guiding aesthetic principle of the Enlightenment. There is a relationship between symmetry and two other important Enlightenment qualities, both of them allied to the preferences of the left hemisphere: stasis and equality.

The relationship between the left hemisphere and equality is a consequence of its categorical method. Where one is dealing with individual people or things, when one respects the contingencies of the situation in which they find themselves, and by which they are modified, when one accepts that the things or persons themselves and the context are continually subject to change, no two entities are *ever* equal in any respect. (Cassirer notes that in Arabic there are between five and six thousand terms for 'camel', the category for which we have one.)[55] However, once the items are classified and entered into categories, they become equal: at least *from the standpoint of the categoriser* every member of the category can be substituted by any other member of the category. In that sense there is an equalising drive built into the categorising system. But the categories themselves are nonetheless arranged in a hierarchical taxonomy, which means that, while the individual variations of living things are flattened out, the differences between *categories* become where the inequality resides.

So it is with the left hemisphere and stasis. Because the left hemisphere is dealing with things that are known, they have to have a degree of fixity: if their constantly changing nature is respected, they cannot be known. To the left hemisphere, a thing once known does not change, though it may move, or be moved, atomistically, according to the will, and it must indeed be *made* to move to fit in with the categorisations of the left hemisphere's will. Thus, where the left-hemisphere world obtains, the continual change and the individual differences of actual living things are exchanged for stasis and equality, as the butterfly is skewered, unmoving, a specimen in the collector's cabinet. At the same time, however, the left hemisphere achieves, through this process, power to manipulate, which I would claim has always been its drive. Power inevitably leads to inequality: some categories of things are more useful, and therefore more valued, than others. So the differences inherent in actual individual things or beings are lost, but those derived from the system are substituted. Similarly, though the thing itself no longer changes, manipulation inevitably leads to change: the recalcitrance of the particular is subjected to the Procrustean bed of the category it represents. So the changing, evolving nature of individual things or beings is lost, but those changes demanded by the system are substituted. And change and difference, outlawed at the individual level, return by the back door.

THE PURSUIT OF EQUALITY

The French Revolution and the American Revolution are two of the most important and enduring legacies of the Enlightenment. As Berlin says, they have almost nothing to do with Romanticism:

... the principles in the name of which the French Revolution was fought were principles of universal reason, of order, of justice, not at all connected with the sense of uniqueness, the profound emotional introspection, the sense of the differences of things, dissimilarities rather than similarities, with which the Romantic movement is usually associated.[56]

(However, as I hope to show later, there is a track that leads direct from the Enlightenment to Romanticism – another case of there being a *smooth* transition from one hemisphere's agenda to the (in reality quite opposed) agenda of the other hemisphere, which I have argued for in the case of the Reformation.) The American Revolution, with its famous claims for the individual right to pursue happiness, expresses the left hemisphere's belief that any good – happiness, for example – should be susceptible to the pursuit of the will, aided by rationality. In doing so it has illuminated the paradoxical nature of rationality: that while the rational mind must pursue 'the good', the most valuable things cannot be pursued (the pursuit of happiness has not generally led to happiness). Such valuable things can come only as side effects of something else.

The left hemisphere misunderstands the importance of implicitness. There is therefore a problem for it, that certain logically desirable goals simply cannot be directly pursued, because direct pursuit changes their nature and they flee from approach: thus the direct pursuit of liberty, equality and fraternity – despite being fine ideals – is problematic. The French Revolution famously championed liberty, equality and fraternity. The problem with bringing them to the fore as concepts and going for them explicitly, left-hemisphere fashion, rather than allowing them to emerge as the necessary accompaniment of a certain tolerant disposition towards the world, right-hemisphere fashion, is that they can be only negative entities once they become the province of the left hemisphere. This is because the left hemisphere, despite its view of itself as bringing things about, can *only say 'no' or not say 'no' to what it finds given to it by the right hemisphere* (just as the right hemisphere in turn can only say no or not say no to 'the Other', i.e. whatever it is that exists apart from ourselves: see Chapter 5 above). Thus, since there is no *equality* in the givenness of things as they actually appear to the right hemisphere, equality becomes, for the left hemisphere, a need and a drive to pull down anything that stands out as not equalling 'equality' – the essentially negative sense in which equality was pursued through the mayhem and carnage of the French Revolution. Neither is there any *liberty* in what is given by the right hemisphere, which delivers the world as a living web of interdependencies that require responses, and entail responsibility – not the exhilarating nihilism of 'liberty', in the sense of casting off all constraints. The liberty of the left hemisphere is, as is bound to be the case, an abstract concept, not what experience teaches us through living. This is what Edmund Burke was getting at in his 1775 speech on conciliation with America, when he said that 'abstract liberty, like other mere abstractions, is not to be found'.[57] The left hemisphere's version of liberty is a mere concept, not the freedom which can be experienced only through belonging, within a complex of constraints.

Instead, because it has to positively *do* something (but the only thing it can do is to say 'no'), it is obliged to proceed by negation: to set about eroding and dismantling the structures of naturally evolved traditional communities in which such experience of liberty could be achieved, seeing them as impediments to its own version of an unconstrainedly free society. *Fraternity* too lives in the relationships that are formed in the communities of kinship and society made possible by evolution of the right frontal lobe (not 'Society', a conceptual construct of the left hemisphere). The left hemisphere version of this is a sort of association of labour (*Gesellschaft*, in Tönnies' terms, as opposed to *Gemeinschaft*)[58] and the bureaucratic provision of what is called 'care', at the same time that the network of private and personal bonds and responsibilities in communities, in which fraternal feelings and the actual experience of care are made possible, is eroded.

The American Revolution is a rather different matter; for one thing, it was notably lacking in 'Jacobins'. Its approach was not to do as much as possible to bring into being freedom by an effort of will (the French model), but as little as possible: a *laissez-faire* approach which approximates to Berlin's concept of negative liberty – as few restraints as possible. As such it enjoyed, unlike the French Revolution, the support of Burke. Whatever its rhetoric, its aim was the reduction of formal restrictions on society, while maximising communality, largely in the interests of economic well-being. Democracy as Jefferson saw it, with its essentially local, agrarian, communitarian, organic, structure, was in harmony with the ideals of the right hemisphere. But in time it came to be swept away by the large-scale, rootless, mechanical force of capitalism, a left-hemisphere product of the Enlightenment. What de Tocqueville presciently saw was that the lack of what I would see as right-hemisphere values incorporated in the fabric of society would lead in time to a process in which we became, despite ourselves, subject to bureaucracy and servitude to the State: 'It will be a society which tries to keep its citizens in "perpetual childhood"; it will seek to preserve their happiness, but it chooses to be the sole agent and only arbiter of that happiness.' Society will, he says, develop a new kind of servitude which

> covers the surface of society with a network of small complicated rules, through which the most original minds and the most energetic characters cannot penetrate ... it does not tyrannise but it compresses, enervates, extinguishes, and stupefies a people, till each nation is reduced to be nothing better than a flock of timid and industrious animals, of which government is the shepherd.[59]

This is, as John Passmore puts it, 'Benthamite or Fabian perfection made manifest'.[60]

That this dislocation between the ideal and the reality has tended to obtain wherever societies have most stridently identified themselves with Enlightenment concepts (the 'people's democracies' of the world) is explained at one level perhaps by Elster's paradox that rationality contains the seeds of its own destruction. At another level, it is an expression of the reality that the left hemisphere cannot bring something to life: it can only say 'no' or not say 'no' to what it finds given to it by the right hemisphere. Once again this is Blake's perception that: 'Energy is the only life, and is from the Body; and *Reason is the bound or outward circumference of Energy*' (see p. 200).

The most obvious expression of the necessarily negative force of the left hemisphere's project is the way in which the ideals of liberty, justice and fraternity led to the illiberal, unjust, and far from fraternal, guillotine. Anything that is essentially sacramental, anything that is not founded on rationality, but on bonds of reverence or awe (right-hemisphere terrain), becomes the enemy of the left hemisphere, and constitutes a bar to its supremacy; and so the left hemisphere is committed to its destruction. That there were, as at the Reformation, abuses of power, is not in doubt, and in the case of both priests and monarch, these were sometimes justified by reference to divine authority, an intolerable state of affairs. But, as at the Reformation, it is not the abuse, but the thing abused – not idolatry, but images, not corrupt priests but the sacerdotal and the sacred – that become the targets. The sheer vehemence of the attacks on priests and king during the French Revolution suggest not just a misunderstanding of, but a fear of, their status as metaphors, and of the right hemisphere non-utilitarian values for which they metaphorically act.

The destruction of the sacerdotal power of the Church was a goal of the French Revolution, as it had been of the Reformation. The Reformation, however, had not been nakedly, explicitly, secular: it had purported to replace a corrupt religion with a purified one. All the same its effect had been to transfer power from the sacerdotal base of the Catholic Church to the state, an essential part of the relentless process of secularisation, in the broadest sense – by which I mean the representation of human experience in purely rationalistic terms, necessarily exclusive of the Other, and the insistence that all questions concerning morality and human welfare can and should be settled within those terms – which I would see as the agenda of the left hemisphere. The French Revolution, by contrast, was indeed openly opposed to the Church, but its most daring attack was on the sacramental, necessarily metaphorical, nature of royalty (and by extension the aristocrats, whose authority was reciprocally related to that of the monarchy). At the time of the Reformation, the effigies of saints had sometimes been dragged to the public square and there decapitated by the town's executioner. This not only in itself prefigures the French Revolution, and emphasises the continuity between regicide and the abolition of the sacramental, but also powerfully enacts two other left-hemisphere tendencies that characterise both the Reformation and the Enlightenment, to which we now might turn.

Take the striking picture by Villeneuve reproduced in Figure 10.1. In her book, *The Body in Pieces: The Fragment as a Metaphor of Modernity*, Linda Nochlin comments that 'the imagery – and the enactment – of destruction, dismemberment and fragmentation remained powerful elements in Revolutionary ideology at least until the fall of Robespierre in 1794 and even after'.[61] It will be remembered at the outset that fragmentation is a primary characteristic of left-hemisphere

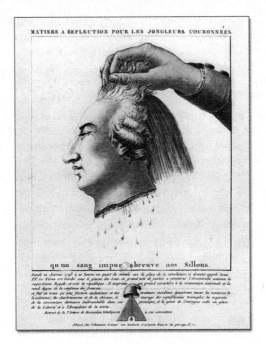

Fig. 10.1 *Matière à réflection pour les jongleurs couronnées*, by Villeneuve, 1793.

perception (see Chapter 2). Nochlin comments on such images of the beheading of the monarch that they represent 'a castration image of unprecedented power and suggestiveness'.[62] Whether or not that is the case, this engraving embodies perfectly the most important aspects of the left hemisphere triumph that it depicts. Immediately one notices the most obvious fact, that it represents the right hand, the left hemisphere's tool, taking ultimate power over the sacramental (note Villeneuve's irreverent reference to *jongleurs couronnées*, as though the mysterious element in kingship were simply a form of sleight of hand). It demonstrates not just the production of a fragment, with its congeniality to left-hemisphere preferences, but specifically the separation of the head from the rest of the body, a metaphor that could be said to go to the very foundations of the left-hemisphere world, with its tendency to reject the physical and retreat into an abstracted, cerebralised world disconnected as far as possible from the demands of the body.[63] Further, at the same time that this particular head is so obviously reduced to an inanimate object, a 'thing' in the hand of the executioner, it appears nonetheless uncannily alive, almost managing a smile of contempt for its tormentor. It may be remembered that inanimate objects are the special territory of the left hemisphere, whereas all that is living belongs in the right hemisphere. The almost living nature of the head, which is nonetheless so clearly an image of the triumph of death, represents with shocking force the triumph of the left hemisphere. (I will deal later with the fascination with the 'uncanny', which derives from the loss of certainty over the distinction between the living and the purely mechanical).

Again, this picture parodies the sacrament that was most central to the world whose abolition it was celebrating, that of the transubstantiation of bread and wine into the living body and blood of Christ. The king was a metaphor of the divine presence, by authority of which he ruled; the *ostensio* of the royal head here parodies the *ostensio* of the sacrament, of the living body, accompanied as it would be by the words *hoc est enim corpus meum*, 'for this is my body' – words which in their jumbled form, *hocus pocus*, became a shorthand for everything that was rejected in the sacramental world (becoming to the Enlightened mind no more than a world of *jongleurs*). Notice also the drops of blood falling from the head as if to confirm the parody, blood that that will be taken up, 'drunk' by so many, not as a sacrament for God's people, but with brutal utilitarianism, through the food for 'the people' that it will help to fertilise – the text below the picture expressing the wish that this 'impure blood' will make fruitful the ploughed fields. Once again the sacramental realm of the right hemisphere is subjugated to the functionalism and utility of the left hemisphere.

As David Freedberg has argued in *The Power of Images*, the need to mutilate an image indicates belief in its power.[64] Koerner makes the point that iconoclasm, in granting so much uncanny power to images, came close to the idolatry it condemned.[65] And again, referring to the treatment of statues before town courts as living criminals, 'in similarly punishing and preserving idols, did not Münster's iconoclasts invest them with the seeming personhood they abhorred? How material did materiality become when, as sometimes occurred, a saint's effigy was decapitated by the town executioner?'[66] Or is it, Koerner says, that they attack representation itself, the wood which represented a saint now representing representation itself? I would say not. The wooden image of the saint stands not for re-presentation but for metaphorical understanding, and it was *that* – metaphorical understanding – that came before the tribunal, was arraigned and executed.

So it was, too, in the age of the Enlightenment, where it was not wooden saints, but kings and dukes that were decapitated. Just as the statue did not have to be either wood or God, the king does not have to be either a mere person, like everyone else, or superhuman. That does not exhaust the possibilities. He acts as a metaphor for what we reverence, for the divine in the human. This metaphoric essence of royalty depends on the accidental qualities of the individual being submerged in the uniqueness of the role, as one expects the particularity of the actor to be lost in his role; except that the actor merely *represents* a king, whereas the royal person *is* a king (the distinction, again, between representation and metaphor). The attack on royalty in the name of utilitarianism depends on exposing the individual as 'just a person' without the qualities that the king holds metaphorically, the implication being that this invalidates his royal nature.

While the Enlightenment, then, was apparently all about enlightening our darkness, it had a dark side of its own. It is 'a mental disorder' wrote Descartes, 'which prizes the darkness higher than the light'.[67] Descartes was rather keen on branding those who saw things differently from himself as mad. Dominated by the left hemisphere, his world is one of comedy and light – he was, after all, the spectator in all the comedies the world displays. But there is madness here, too, which, as I have suggested, approximates the madness of schizophrenia. The successors to the Enlightenment, the Romantics, who I shall argue belonged to a world more dominated by the right hemisphere, saw, instead of comedy and light, tragedy and darkness, their 'madness' approximating that of melancholia and depression. But darkness was not to be banished by a fiat of the Enlightenment, either.

It has become increasingly obvious to historians and social theorists of the last hundred years that the Enlightenment, despite its optimism about itself, was not just a period of uncomplicated progress in human understanding and in society and politics at large. The appeal to reason can lead to sweetness and light, but it can also be used to monitor and control, to constrict and repress, in keeping with my view that the aim of the left hemisphere is power. With time, a dark side to the Enlightenment became too obvious to conceal.

THE UNCANNY

The uncanny was seen by Freud as the repression of something that should not be seen, that should not come into the light. My argument in previous chapters has been that the rise of modern Western man is associated with an accentuation of the difference between the hemispheres, in other words the evolution of a more, rather than less, 'bicameral' mind. The further accentuation of this difference in the Enlightenment, through the striving for an objective, scientific detachment – independent as far as possible of the 'confounding' effects of whatever is personal or intuitive, or whatever cannot be made explicit and rationally defended – led to an entrenchment of this separation. Much as the voices of the gods, from being a naturally integrated part of the world as experienced, came to appear alien to the Ancient Greeks, so at the Enlightenment the promptings of the right hemisphere, excluded from the world of rationalising discourse in the left hemisphere, came to be seen as alien. I believe this is the origin of the rise of the experience of the 'uncanny', the darker side of the age of the Enlightenment.

In her absorbing study of the phenomenon, *The Female Thermometer: Eighteenth-Century Culture and the Invention of the Uncanny*, Terry Castle explores the elements of phantasmagoria, grotesquerie, carnivalesque travesty, hallucinatory reveries, paranoia, and nightmarish fantasy which accompanied Enlightenment.[68] There is an important common element to the classic loci of the uncanny. Citing Freud's famous essay of 1919, 'The "Uncanny"', Castle refers to

> doubles, dancing dolls and automata, waxwork figures, alter egos, and 'mirror selves', spectral emanations, detached body parts ('a severed head, a hand cut off at the wrist, feet that dance by themselves'), the ghastly fantasy of being buried alive, omens, precognition, *déjà vu* . . .[69]

I would argue that these phenomena are related to the experiences of subjects with schizophrenia – living things experienced as mechanisms, or as simulacra of living beings, the living body become an assemblage of apparently independently moving fragments, the self losing its intuitive ipseity, no longer self-evidently unique, but possibly copied, reproduced, or subtly altered; and that, accordingly, the phenomena exemplify the disengaged workings of the left hemisphere, attempting to make sense in its own terms of what comes to it from the right hemisphere, from which it has become alienated. Indeed the experience of the uncanny could be said to be the defining experience of schizophrenia as first described by Kraepelin and Bleuler – what is known in current psychiatric terminology as 'delusional mood', in which the experienced world is bizarrely altered in a way that is hard to define, and appears vaguely sinister and threatening.

Freud was in fact quoting Schelling's formulation when he held that the uncanny is what should have remained hidden, but has been brought to light; in the uncanny, he saw evidence of past experience that had been repressed, a dark secret that is dragged into the light of consciousness. Freud emphasises that the uncanny effect does not proceed automatically from the idea of the supernatural in itself. Children imagine their dolls to be alive, for example, and there are fantastic occurrences in fairy tales, but neither of these are in any sense uncanny. The ghost appears in Hamlet, but however gloomy and terrible it is made to seem, it does not have the quality of the uncanny. In all these cases there is a context that is acknowledged to be removed from that of everyday reality. It is, as Freud says, when the story-teller rejects the possibility of supernatural happenings and 'pretends to move in the world of common reality' that the uncanny occurs. It represents the possibility, terrifying to the rational, left-hemisphere mind, that phenomena beyond what we can understand and control may truly exist. The uncanny takes its force from the context in which it appears. The phenomena of the right hemisphere appear uncanny once they appear in the context of the left-hemisphere world of the rational, the mechanistic, the certain, the humanly controlled. It is notable that some tales of the uncanny attempt to reassure the left hemisphere by revealing at the end, after the thrill of the uncanny has been experienced, that after all there is a rational, perhaps scientific, explanation of the phenomena. Such is the ending, for example, of one of the most famous of the early tales of the uncanny, Ann Radcliffe's *The Mysteries of Udolpho*. In this it is like the popular contemporary presenters of phantasmagoria, who would reveal at the end of the show, to appreciative gasps at their ingenuity, the apparatus of lights, screens, 'magic lanterns', and so on, which were responsible for their effects.

Frankenstein, subtitled *The Modern Prometheus*, Mary Shelley's story of the left hemisphere assembling a living whole – a man – from dead parts and bringing it to life, ends, as we know, rather less obligingly. But that was the message of Romanticism, not of the Enlightenment. In the Enlightenment, the living was thought to be the sum of its parts: and, if so, its parts could be put together to make the living again. For Romanticism, not only was the living not reducible to the mechanical – the world of the right hemisphere irreducible to that of the left – but even the inanimate world came to be seen as alive, the reintegration of the left hemisphere's realm into that of the right.

CHAPTER 11

ROMANTICISM AND THE
INDUSTRIAL REVOLUTION

WHAT IS ROMANTICISM? JUDGING BY THE ATTEMPTS THAT HAVE BEEN MADE TO define it, it is more than a little enigmatic. In fact Isaiah Berlin devotes the whole of the first chapter of *The Roots of Romanticism*, one of the best explorations of the topic, to the mutually incompatible propositions that have been advanced as constituting its essential nature. If he reaches a conclusion it is that, though the Enlightenment could be summed up in the cognitive content of a relatively small number of beliefs, Romanticism never could, because its concern is with a whole disposition towards the world, which involves the holder of that disposition, as well as what beliefs might be held. Not in other words, with a *what*, but with a *how*.

How it came about that the Enlightenment gave place to Romanticism is, too, something of an enigma to historians of ideas, as Berlin goes on to demonstrate. The well-worn phrase 'the Romantic Revolution' conjures a picture of something like that contemporaneous political upheaval, the French Revolution; one would therefore expect to see the established squires and landed gentry of the intellect finding the equivalent of revolting masses at their gates – as though the revolutionaries sprang fully armed from the head of Zeus. In fact what one finds is an almost invisible, seamless transition, and I don't think it was even a revolution in the sense that people consciously reacted against a way of looking at the world that they found to be deficient. Instead it was more like a Romantic *Evolution* than a Revolution – in which the seeds of Romanticism were there in the stuff of Enlightenment. How did this come about?

The answer, it seems to me, is that Romanticism is more inclusive. The best of Enlightenment values were not negated, but *aufgehoben*, by Romanticism, and persist not only into the coming era, but in fact to this day – along with some of the Enlightenment's more damagingly simplistic notions. Simplicity is a laudable aim, but one must not make things any simpler than they are. As always, it was the clashes of theory with experience that showed up the cracks in the edifice of rationalism. If I am correct in my supposition that the right hemisphere is grappling with experience, which is multiple in nature, in principle unknowable in its totality, changing, infinite, full of individual differences, while the left hemisphere sees only a version or representation of that experience, in which, by contrast, the world is single, knowable, consistent, certain, fixed, therefore ultimately finite, generalised across experience, a world that we can master – the Enlightenment world, in other words – it follows that the left hemisphere is a closed system, 'bootstrapping' itself. It cannot, however, shield itself from experience completely – or has not been able to until recently (the subject of the last chapter of this book). Its weakness, therefore, will be exposed when attention is turned to those elements within the system that point to something beyond it.

Since the foundation of Enlightenment thinking is that all truths cohere, are mutually compatible, non-contradictory, ultimately reconcilable, its weak place is where incompatibilities are found; and indeed in general we are, and always have been, liberated into another way of looking at the world wherever irreconcilables are brought into focus. One such point of weakness occurred with the dawning awareness that, as a generalisation, differences are as important as generalities. Montesquieu was aware that the belief that 'man is everywhere different' is as important and as true as the assertion that 'man is everywhere the same'. This perception leads from the premises of the system itself – that generalisation is the route to truth, and that all generalisations should be compatible – straight to a paradox. The idea of individual difference is central to Romanticism, but it is not merely this which makes Montesquieu's point tend towards the Romantic: his very acceptance that a thing and its opposite may be true is in itself a Romantic acceptance. The movement from Enlightenment to Romanticism therefore is *not* from A to not-A, but from a world where 'A and not-A cannot both be true' is necessarily true to one where 'A and not-A can both hold' holds (in philosophical terms this becomes Hegel's thesis, antithesis → synthesis). Thus some elements (a certain kind of idealism, for example) can be found in both Enlightenment and Romanticism, which is how the continuity occurs: to give an example, it is how the French Revolution can be seen itself as a manifestation of the Romantic spirit, while at the same time, as Berlin says, the principles in the name of which it was fought were Enlightenment principles, at odds with the thrust of Romanticism. The progression from Enlightenment to Romanticism can be seen as either seamless (upper arrow) or antithetical (lower arrow), depending on where the emphasis lies:

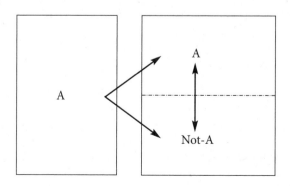

In this chapter I will develop the view that Romanticism is a manifestation of right-hemisphere dominance in our way of looking at the world. Here I am reminded of the fact that the right hemisphere is more inclusive, and can equally use what the left hemisphere uses as well as its own preferred approach, whereas the left hemisphere does not have this degree of flexibility or reciprocity.

Whereas for the Enlightenment, and for the workings of the logical left hemisphere, opposites result in a battle which must be won by 'the Truth', for the Romantics, and for the right hemisphere, it is the coming together of opposites into a fruitful union that forms the basis not only of everything that we find beautiful, but of truth itself. This was perfectly expressed by Hölderlin. He saw that both the essence of beauty and the ground of all philosophy lay in *das Eine in sich selber unterschiedne*, 'the one differentiated in itself'. This great insight of Heraclitus', according to Hölderlin, 'could occur only to a Greek, for it is the essence of beauty, and, before this was discovered, there was no philosophy.'[1]

What were the trigger points for needing to move on – the weaknesses in the left-hemisphere system?

It's true there was this matter of a thing and its opposite both being possible. But there were others, many others. For a start, reason itself proclaimed the fact that reason was insufficient. Montesquieu's perception anticipates Blake's saying that 'to generalise is to be an idiot', being itself a generalisation. It draws attention, in Gödelian fashion, to the truth that every logical system leads to conclusions that cannot be accommodated within it. An earlier mathematician, Pascal, had reached a similar conclusion, uncongenial as it is to the philosophy of Enlightenment. 'The ultimate achievement of reason', he wrote, 'is to recognize that there are an infinity of things which surpass it. It is indeed feeble if it can't get as far as understanding that.'[2] But this had been common knowledge to what Pascal calls 'esprits fins', subtle minds, before the Enlightenment.[3] 'Philosophy never seems to me to have a better hand to play', as Montaigne wrote, 'than when she battles against our presumption and our vanity; when in good faith she acknowledges her weakness, her ignorance and her inability to reach conclusions.'[4]

Then there was the fact that theory was just not compatible with experience. In figures such as Rousseau and the painter David I believe one can trace a smooth evolution from the ideals of the Enlightenment to those of Romanticism (the upper arrow in the diagram above). But in many other figures of the transitional era there is simply a disjunction between what they explicitly held to be true and what implicitly they must, from their actions and judgments, have believed. Just as Reynolds, when faced with the unruly genius of Michelangelo, was magnanimous enough to sweep away the precepts he had outlined for years in his lectures, Johnson jettisoned Enlightenment preconceptions, which he referred to as 'the petty cavils of petty minds', when faced with the reality of Shakespeare's greatness. How to accommodate Shakespeare's flagrant disregard for the classical unities, his tendency, like life itself, to mix comedy and tragedy, his refusal to produce representative types, but instead to produce individuals of flesh and blood ('his story requires Romans or kings, but he thinks only on men')?[5] In fact Pope had already come to the conclusion that his 'Characters are so much Nature herself, that 'tis a sort of injury to call them by so distant a name as Copies of her' – in other words that they were *present*, not re-presented. And he continues: 'every single character in *Shakespeare* is as much an Individual, as those in Life itself'.[6] Johnson paved the way for Carlyle's judgment that Shakespeare's works, like a force of nature, 'grow up withal *un*consciously from the unknown deeps in him; – as the oak-tree grows from the Earth's bosom'. Carlyle refers to the hidden, necessarily implicit meaning of Shakespeare, 'like *roots*, like sap and forces working underground . . . Speech is great; but Silence is greater'.[7]

As the Renaissance was reinvigorated by its recurrence to the world of Ancient Greece and Rome, so the post-Enlightenment world was reinvigorated by its recursion to the Renaissance, particularly by the rediscovery of Shakespeare, a vital element in the evolution of Romanticism, not just, or even especially, in England, but in Germany and France. It yielded evidence of something so powerful that it simply swept away Enlightenment principles before it, as inauthentic, untenable in the face of experience. It was not just his grandeur, his unpredictability, his faithfulness to nature that commended him. In Shakespeare, tragedy is no longer the result of a fatal flaw or error: time and again it lies in a clash between two ways of being in the world or looking at the world, neither of which has to be mistaken. In Shakespeare tragedy is in fact the result of the coming together of opposites. And Maurice Morgann's brilliant essay of 1777 emphasises the importance, in individuality, of the context dependency of personal characteristics, struggling to express the concept of the *Gestalt* nearly two hundred years before its time.[8]

BODY AND SOUL

In case it looks as though I am making a point about art rather than life, let's take an example of life in action. The great Enlightenment philosopher and wit, Nicolas Chamfort, having, with a typically Enlightened superiority to embodied existence, declared that love as it then existed was no more than '*l'échange de deux fantaisies et le contact de deux épidermes*',[9] found himself having to abandon the Court after an unhappy love affair with a very beautiful, but very married, dancer.[10] Sadder still, a passionate enthusiast for the Revolution in theory, he became quickly disillusioned with the reality. Persecuted by the Jacobins he had ardently supported, he ended by shooting himself in the face and stabbing himself in the neck, and, having failed to kill himself, living out his last days in agony.

For the Romantic mind, by contrast, theory was not something abstracted from experience and separate from it (based on representation), but present in the act of perception. There was therefore no question of 'applying' theory to life, since phenomena themselves were the source of 'theory'. Fact and theory, like particular and universal, were not opposites. According to Goethe they 'are not only intimately connected, but . . . interpenetrate one another . . . the particular represents the universal, "*not* as a dream and shadow, but as a momentarily living manifestation of the inscrutable"'.[11] The particular metaphorises the universal. Goethe deplored the tendency for us, like children that go round the back of a mirror to see what's there, to try to find a reality behind the particularity of the archetypal phenomenon.[12]

Chamfort's description of love illustrates another weakness in Enlightenment thinking that paved the way for Romanticism. It was the problem of the explicit, and the things that necessarily fled from it, as if for their lives. Self-knowledge had been the goal of human wisdom since ancient times. Goethe wisely wrote, however, that 'we are, and ought to be, obscure to ourselves, turned outwards, and working upon the world which surrounds us.'[13] We see ourselves, and therefore come to know ourselves, only *indirectly*, through our engagement with the world at large.[14] His observation suggests a consequence of the Enlightenment project which, again in Gödelian fashion, followed from it, but could not be contained within it. The Enlightenment pursuit of certainty and clarity could not be made to stop at the bounds of the self: was not awareness of self the guarantor of rational, intelligent behaviour? As Pope put it, 'the proper subject of mankind is Man'; and, great poet that he was, he may be said to have succeeded in expressing his personal view on the subject admirably. But the searchlight of objective attention cannot be applied to man himself. It does not result in self-knowledge, because the heightened self-consciousness involved cuts one off from large parts of experience, by crucially altering the nature of what it attends to, and thus subverting its very purpose as an instrument of knowledge. Some things have to remain obscure if they are not to be forced to be untrue to their very nature: they are known, and can be expressed, only indirectly.

One of these is embodied existence. It was not just Chamfort, of course. Philosophers have, for the most part, had an antagonistic and unsympathetic relationship to the body – it goes with the territory. Kant described marriage as an agreement between two people as to the 'reciprocal use of each others' sexual organs';[15] Kant also, it may be noted, remained single, and died probably a virgin.[16] Descartes described laughter as that which

> results when the blood coming from the right-hand cavity of the heart through the central arterial vein causes the lungs to swell up suddenly and repeatedly, forcing the air they contain to rush out through the windpipe, where it forms an inarticulate, explosive sound. As the air is expelled, the lungs are swollen so much that they push against all the muscles of the diaphragm, chest and throat, thus causing movement in the facial muscles with which these organs are connected. And it is just this facial expression, together with the inarticulate and explosive sound, that we call 'laughter'.[17]

Well, that's not what I call laughter – although it's hard not to laugh. But what's striking here is not just the sense of disgust, the deliberately disengaged, mechanical attitude taken by Descartes in this anatomy of hilarity. It's that his authoritative manner is not in any way inhibited by the fact that actually he had no idea what he was talking about. His anatomy is a complete work of fantasy. But laughter was to be put in its place, because it was spontaneous, intuitive and unwilled, and represented the triumph of the body. I am reminded of the story that Voltaire, when asked if he had ever laughed, responded: '*je n'ai jamais fait ha! ha!*'[18]

The problem here is not the acknowledgment of the part played in our lives by the flesh – Montaigne and Erasmus had done that with great tact, affection and humour – but the insistence on stopping there, the refusal to see *through* it. Spinoza's appreciation that 'the more capable the body is of being affected in many ways, and affecting external bodies in many ways, the more capable of thinking is the mind',[19] sets the body in its proper relationship with our 'higher parts', in the way that Wittgenstein later was to do when he wrote that 'the human body is the best picture of the human soul'.[20] Philosophy itself is rooted in the body, after all: according to the authors of *Philosophy in the Flesh*, 'real people have embodied minds whose conceptual systems arise from, are shaped by, and are *given meaning through* living human bodies. The neural structures of our brains produce conceptual systems and linguistic structures that cannot be adequately accounted for by formal systems that only manipulate symbols'.[21] There is nothing reductionist here, any more than it is reductionism when Diderot states with marvellous frankness that '*il y a un peu de testicule au fond de nos sentiments les plus sublimes et de notre tendresse la plus épurée*'.[22] On the contrary, it is a warning not to get too carried away with the virtues of abstraction.

The fusion of body with mind, or more properly with spirit or soul, was never more keenly felt than by the Romantics. 'O Human Imagination, O Divine Body', wrote Blake.[23] Wordsworth stretched sense to the limit to express this living union. 'I know no book or system of moral philosophy written with sufficient power to melt into our affections, to incorporate itself with the blood & vital juices of our minds', he wrote of the relative weakness of philosophy compared with poetry: 'these bald & naked reasonings are impotent over our habits, they cannot form them; from the same cause they are equally powerless in regulating our judgments concerning the value of men & things'.[24] I cannot imagine that anyone before him would have thought of speaking of the 'blood and vital juices of the mind'. In the Preface to *Lyrical Ballads*, his poetic manifesto, Wordsworth wrote that personifications of abstract ideas, such as were common in Augustan verse, are 'a *mechanical* device of style', a mechanism which 'writers in metre seem to lay claim to by prescription'. By contrast he wished to keep his reader 'in the company of *flesh and blood*':

> Poetry sheds no tears 'such as angels weep', but natural and human tears; she can boast of no celestial ichor that distinguishes her vital juices from those of prose; the same human blood circulates through the veins of them both.[25]

Here there is a contrast with his lifelong companion and fellow poet Coleridge. Carlyle gives an amusing portrait of Coleridge, his guests falling asleep around the dinner table as he theorised about the endlessly fascinating relationship between 'sum-m-mject' and 'om-m-mject'; but possibly because, precisely, of the abstraction of his approach, Coleridge never managed to find a way of transcending this polarity.[26] By contrast Wordsworth did not need to *talk about* it, because he expressed in the very fabric of his poetry the union of subject and object, the incarnation of the world of images in the lived body. This is something to do with the very movement of his phrases, and their effects on our physical frame, even on our breathing and pulse. Sometimes he actually refers to this synthesis in the poetry itself – he speaks of 'a real solid world / Of images about me';[27] it is in both the sense and the movement of some of his most famous lines: 'felt in the blood, and felt along the heart', 'have hung upon the beatings of my heart', 'and all that mighty heart is lying still'. And, in the most startling expression of his view that Nature was a living, flesh and blood presence, he states with characteristic straightforwardness that the respirations of Nature were so real to him, its breathings so felt in the frame of his being, that he sometimes mistook them for the panting of his dog.[28]

Paradoxically an appreciation of the embodied nature of our experience and understanding of the world could also be said to have emerged seamlessly from the Enlightenment. This is because the Enlightenment had looked to the Classical world for its models of reason, order and justice; but one of the side effects of the return to antiquity which characterised neo-Classicism, and of the Grand Tour in which it manifested itself, was not just the revelation of the palpably beautiful forms of Classical sculpture but the rediscovery of the seductively warm South.

Eichendorff said that Romanticism was the nostalgia of Protestants for the Catholic tradition.[29] There are many levels at which one can read this remark. At one level it could indicate the nostalgia of a people, self-consciously alienated from their traditional culture, for a world in which the traditional culture unreflectively still persists. Unlike history seen as an intellectual realm, a repository of ideas about socio-cultural issues, tradition is an *embodiment* of a culture: not an *idea* of the past, but the past itself embodied. This is no longer available to those who have abandoned the tradition. At another level Eichendorff's remark could be seen as an expression of the love of the cold North for the bodily sensuality of the South. And the past, the South and the body are inextricably linked in Romanticism, as some of Goethe's most famous poems attest, particularly the *Römische Elegien* (originally entitled *Erotica Romana*). But, more than all this, one could see Eichendorff's remark about the nostalgia of Protestants for the Catholic tradition as acknowledging a move, which indeed is what I believe the rise of Romanticism to be, to redress the imbalance of the hemispheres, and to curtail the dominion of the left. The left hemisphere is more closely associated with the conscious will, and could be seen as the administrative arm of the frontal lobes in their important achievement of self-awareness. Any such move, therefore, meets a paradox at the outset: how to succeed in a self-conscious attempt to achieve a state of (relative) unselfconsciousness. This is the topic of Kleist's famous and remarkable essay 'On the Puppet Theatre', a topic I will return to at the end of this book.

A longing for the innocent unself-consciousness of both the historical and personal past is a central theme of Romanticism, which again points away from the world of the left hemisphere to that of the right. It does so not just because of the association of the left hemisphere with excessive self-consciousness. Personal and emotive memory are preferentially stored in the right hemisphere, and childhood, too, is associated with a greater reliance on the right hemisphere. The right hemisphere is particularly important in childhood experience and is preponderant even in *language* development in early childhood;[30] many hand gestures are produced in speech areas of the right hemisphere, which are abandoned in early childhood, as language shifts to the left hemisphere. It is with the right hemisphere that we recall childhood memories,[31] and autobiographical memories of all kinds.[32] As mentioned in Chapter 2, the right hemisphere is more advanced until the second year of life.[33] Given the relatively 'split brain' nature of the child, this is also a peculiarly unalloyed right hemisphere, one that is sheltered from being overwhelmed, as it later will be, by the left. The right hemisphere is more active in children up to the age of four years,[34] and intelligence across the spectrum of cognitive faculties in children (and probably in adults) is related principally to right-hemisphere function.[35] In childhood, experience is relatively unalloyed by re-presentation: experience has 'the glory and the freshness of a dream', as Wordsworth expressed it.[36] This was not just a Romantic insight, but lay behind the evocations of their own childhood by, for example, Vaughan in *The Retreat* and Traherne in his *Centuries*.[37] Childhood represents innocence, not in some moral sense, but in the sense of offering what the phenomenologists thought of as the pre-conceptual immediacy of experience (the world before the left hemisphere has deadened it to familiarity). It was this authentic 'presencing' of the world that Romantic poetry aimed to recapture.

The Romantic acceptance that there is no simple 'fact of the matter' – a reality that exists independently of ourselves and our attitude towards it – brought to the fore the absolutely crucial question of one's disposition towards it, the relationship in which one stands to it. This emphasis on disposition towards whatever it might be, rather than the primacy of the thing itself in isolation or abstraction, explains the otherwise baffling plethora of often contradictory accounts of what Romanticism 'stood for' – Berlin's point, the move from what is said or done to the *spirit* in which it is said or done. How was it that the French Revolution, executed in the name of reason, order, justice, fraternity and liberty, was so unreasonable, disorderly, unjust, unfraternal and illiberal? For the same reason that other grandiose projects originating in the rationalising of the left hemisphere have ended up betraying their ideals. In accordance with the left-hemisphere preoccupation with *what* a thing is, rather than *what manner* of thing it is ('what' rather than 'how'), ideas, concepts, acts become neatly reified (the familiar statuesque figures of Reason, Justice, Liberty and so on), and the way in which they are actualised in the messy human context of the lived world gets to be neglected. Ends come to justify means.

'My thinking is not separate from objects', wrote Goethe:

the elements of the object, the perception of the object, flow into my thinking and are fully permeated by it . . . My perception itself is a thinking, and my thinking a perception. Man knows himself only to the extent that he knows the world; he becomes aware of himself only within the world, and aware of the world only within himself. Every new object, clearly seen, opens up a new organ of perception in us.[38]

This last, perhaps somewhat cryptic, sentence suggests that for us truly to experience something it has to enter into and alter us, and there must be something in us which specifically responds to it as unique.[39] A consequence of this, as Thomas Kuhn recognised, will be that those phenomena with which we have no affinity, and which we are not in some sense ready to see, are often not seen at all.[40] Theory, in the conventional sense of the term, can restrict one's capacity to see things, and the only remedy is to be aware of it.

Understanding, then, is not a discursive explanatory process, but a moment of connection, in which we see through our experience – an *aperçu* or insight.[41] All seeing is 'seeing as'; not that a cognition is added to perception, but that each act of seeing, in the sense of allowing something to 'presence' for us, is in itself necessarily an act of understanding.[42]

> An extremely odd demand is often set forth but never met, even by those who make it: i.e., that empirical data should be presented without any theoretical context, leaving the reader, the student, to his own devices in judging it [the classic demand of Enlightenment science]. This demand seems odd because it is useless simply to look at something. Every act of looking turns into observation, every act of observation into reflection, every act of reflection into the making of associations; thus it is evident that we theorise every time we look carefully at the world.[43]

Theory, in this sense, according to Goethe, is not systematised abstraction after the fact, and separate from experience, but vision that sees something in its context (the 'making of associations') and sees through it.

Reality was not, as Goethe and the Romantics came to see, the fixed and unchanging state of affairs that the left hemisphere assumes. 'The phenomenon must never be thought of as finished or complete', Goethe wrote, 'but rather as evolving, growing, and in many ways as something yet to be determined.'[44] Interestingly, in the light of the last chapter, he noted that '*Vernunft* [reason] is concerned with what is becoming, *Verstand* [rationality] with what has already become ... [Reason] rejoices in whatever evolves; [rationality] wants to hold everything still, so that it can utilise it'.[45] That we take part in a changing world, and that the world evokes faculties, dimensions, and characteristics in us, just as we bring aspects of the world into existence, is perhaps the most profound perception of Romanticism.

This was not an idea or theory, but, for the Romantics, an incarnate reality. One can see it in the paintings and feel it in the poetry of the period. It is related to the sense of depth which is everywhere conveyed in its art.

DEPTH

The great art of the period is landscape art, and the chief influence on landscape art in the period was undoubtedly Claude Lorrain. Despite his having died long before the birth of Romanticism, he appears to have prefigured the vision of the Romantics; one can see in him – and in contrast with his more Cartesian compatriot, contemporary and friend, Nicolas Poussin – a route direct from the Renaissance to Romanticism, a sort of high road of the right hemisphere which the Enlightenment left untouched. A highly skilled intuitive craftsman more than an intellectual, but none the less for that a genius of the imagination, he seems better than anyone to have seen the significance of the relationship between two of the defining preoccupations of the Renaissance: retrospection to a Classical past and observation of nature. In his paintings one experiences the mind as profoundly engaged with the world, the human spirit as drawn out almost limitlessly by the very magnitude of the expanses of space and time. Constable thought him 'the most perfect landscape painter the world ever saw'.[46] Turner idolised him and obsessively reinvented his idiom; it was his greatest ambition to paint something worthy of comparison with Claude's *Seaport with the Embarkation of the Queen of Sheba*, that might hang beside it in the National Gallery in London – an ambition which, incidentally, he realised.[47] Keats was inspired to some of his greatest lines by one of Claude's paintings, the one that came to be called *The Enchanted Castle*.[48]

The subjects of Claude's paintings are not the tiny figures whose history forms their pretext, but the depth, spatial and temporal, of our relationship with the world, for which colour, light and texture act as visual metaphors. In Claude's paintings there is a deep perspective, enhanced sometimes by the steeply angled buildings which often form part of the foreground, particularly of his harbour scenes, and by an extraordinary ability to use variations in light and colour to suggest not just distance as such, but a succession, or progression, of distances, each giving place to the next, by which the viewer is inexorably drawn into the imagined scene.

Light is usually transitional, too, not the full, supposedly 'all-revealing' light of enlightenment, but the half-light of dawn or dusk. The first Romantic poetry is revealed by its similar settings – William Collins's *Ode to Evening*, with its 'hamlets brown, and dim-discover'd spires', the twilit opening of Gray's *Elegy*, the sonnets of William Lisle Bowles, or Young's *Night Thoughts* – but also its transitional seasons, Keats's *Ode to Autumn*, Shelley's 'West Wind, thou breath of Autumn's being', and so on. In terms of the hemispheres, half-light and transitional states have a multitude of affinities with complexity, transience, emotional weight, dream states, the implicit and the unconscious, rather than clarity, simplicity, fixity, detachment, the explicit and full consciousness. The temporal perspective is also immense: the buildings of, for example, Claude's *Landscape with Ascanius shooting the Stag of Sylvia* or the *Seaport with the Embarkation of the Queen of Sheba* (see Plates 7 and 8) already have what seems to be centuries, if not millennia, of wear upon them.

Evocation of depth is both the means by which we are drawn into a felt relationship with something remote (rather than just observing it, which would be the effect of a flat plane), and, at the same time and inseparably, the incontestable evidence of separation from it. Distance in time and place not only expands the soul, but inevitably enters it into a state of awareness of separation and loss – the primal condition of the Romantics.

In this process, space often acts as a metaphor for time. One sees this in the very earliest works of Romanticism, for example in the works of Thomas Gray. His 'Ode on a Distant Prospect of Eton College', where he had spent his school days, is not so much a distant prospect in space, but in time, for which it here acts as a metaphor – a view into the past. His elevated standpoint allows him to look down on his former self ('Lo, in the vale of years beneath'), as he sees the lack of self-awareness in the schoolboys contrasted with his own painful knowledge of what is to come ('Alas, regardless of their doom the little victims play!'). The elevated position not only represents distance but a higher degree of self-consciousness. Similarly Wordsworth's famous retrospective lines from 'Tintern Abbey' – 'Five years have past; five summers with the length of five long winters . . .' – are written from a vantage point in the valley above Tintern from which he can look down on

> These hedge-rows, hardly hedge-rows, little lines
> Of sportive wood run wild: these pastoral farms,
> Green to the very door; and wreaths of smoke
> Sent up, in silence, from among the trees!

which represent not just personal, but cultural, memories of innocent unself-consciousness, the loss of cultural innocence entailed in his being part of a world that is too self-aware, the loss that Gray had evoked in the 'Elegy in a Country Churchyard'.

In the opening of Book VIII of his long autobiographical poem *The Prelude*, Wordsworth depicts a country fair taking place in the valley below him as he sits on the side of Helvellyn, the voices of the country folk, laughing and talking, coming up to him in snatches. Again his elevated view is an image of self-consciousness, a level of self-awareness that he cannot now lose, forever separated from the simple pleasures of rusticity by his awareness that true pleasure belongs only to those who are not self-aware. The evocation of their voices carrying echoingly up to his seat above conveys perfectly the combination of closeness and distance, of something recaptured, but also forever lost. How to be unself-reflectingly simple down there, and yet in a position to appreciate the simplicity at the same time?

There is an ambiguous condition here, in which one is taken back to another world, as one is in Claude's canvases, and yet from which one is excluded. The same distance that connects sunders. The bitterness and the sweetness are aspects of the same experience, and come into being to the same extent at the same time on the same terms. It is this ambiguous condition that gives rise to the mixed emotions, the 'pleasurable melancholy' of the Romantics – not, as seems often to be assumed (shades of Seneca, see above p. 307), a self-indulgent pleasure in pain for its own sake. That error arises from 'either/or' thinking (it must be pleasure or it must be pain), coupled with sequential analysis (if both are present, one must give rise to the other, presumably pain to pleasure). The option that both emotions might be caused at the very same moment by the very same phenomenon is excluded.

Something similar appears to lie behind a common misunderstanding of the sublime, another core Romantic phenomenon. Vast distances evoked by visual depth, grand objects and perspectives, become of great significance, because of their metaphoric power to express a sense of ineffability, which is experienced physically and emotionally as much as conceptually. Ten years before Burke wrote his famous *Philosophical Enquiry into the Origin of Our Ideas of the Sublime and Beautiful*, his lesser known contemporary John Baillie wrote that 'every Person upon seeing a grand Object is affected with something which as it were extends his very Being, and expands it to a kind of *Immensity*.'[49] What I would draw attention to here is the clear expression of the fact that, rightly beheld, the sublime expands and extends, not dwarfs, the being of the beholder. But the same depth that unites is also the evidence of separation. To the degree that one is united with something greater than oneself, one feels the expansion of soul that Baillie refers to; to the degree that one is aware of the separation, one feels one's smallness. This is intrinsic to the experience of awe.

The breakthrough in Romantic thinking to the essential connectedness of things enabled them to see that those who are in awe of any great object – whether it be God, or the vastness, beauty and complexity of nature – do not set themselves apart from it; they feel something that is Other, certainly, but also something of which they partake. Because of the empathic connection or betweenness – of which depth here is a metaphor – they both share in the character of the Other and feel their separateness from it. Reverence is no abasement, they understood, but with as much truth an exaltation: a sense of belonging to something greater than oneself, which for the Romantics was the phenomenal world, and what one could see *through* it.

Depth and height become symbols of profundity: the essential element in the sublime is not merely something large but whose limits, like a mountain top that is lost in cloud, are unknown. 'The notion of depth', writes Berlin, 'is something with which philosophers seldom deal. Nevertheless', he continues,

it is a concept perfectly susceptible to treatment and indeed one of the most important categories we use. When we say that a work is profound or deep, quite apart from the fact that this is obviously a metaphor, I suppose from wells, which are profound and deep – when one says that someone is a profound writer, or that a picture or a work of music is profound, it is not very clear what we mean, but we certainly do not wish to exchange these descriptions for some other term such as 'beautiful' or 'important' or 'construed according to rules' or even 'immortal' . . . According to the romantics – and this is one of their principal contributions to understanding in general – what I mean by depth, although they

do not discuss it under that name, is inexhaustibility, unembraceability . . . There
is no doubt that, although I attempt to describe what . . . profundity consists in,
as soon as I speak it becomes quite clear that, no matter how long I speak, new
chasms open. No matter what I say I always have to leave three dots at the end . . .
I am forced in my discussion, forced in description, to use language which is in
principle, not only today but for ever, inadequate for its purpose . . . You have no
formula that will by deduction lead you to all [the 'vistas' opened by profound
sayings].[50]

In the chapter on the Renaissance I emphasised the broader and deeper
perspective on both time and space, that characterised the era. If one looks at the
engravings of Ancient Roman architecture in the influential *Speculum Romanae
Magnificentiae* (The Mirror of Rome's Magnificence) of the Frenchman Antonio
Lafréri, an engraver working in Rome and active in the mid-sixteenth century (see
Figure 11.1), one sees there an unbroken line that directly connects them in spirit,
not just with Claude's architectural studies in the next century, but to such iconic
early Romantic works of 200 years later as Piranesi's *Vedute di Roma* series,
Barbault's *Vues des Plus Beaux Restes des Antiquités Romaines*, and even the
Carceri d'Invenzione, so much in keeping with the spirit of Horace Walpole and de
Quincey. 250 years later, Ducros is painting with a remarkably similar eye (see
Figure 11.2). And there is a clear link between Claude's landscapes and those of
Romantic landscape artists such as Richard Wilson in England or Thomas Cole in
America (see Plate 9).

Fig. 11.1 *The Coliseum*, by Antonio Lafréri, *c.* 1550.

Fig. 11.2 *The Coliseum*, by Louis Ducros, late 18th century.

Paradoxically it was not the Enlightenment, but Romanticism, which revealed the beauty and power of light. In Claude the Romantics found their exemplar. Constable's cloud studies, and the shimmering, deliquescent landscapes of Turner, which were so eagerly studied by the Impressionists, are essentially celebrations of light and colour. And yet it is profoundly mistaken, as often happens, to see them as proto-abstracts, abstracts in all but name. Abstracts are by definition disengaged – abstracted – from the world. They do not contain light: light, like depth and texture, exists only in experience, not in the realm of thought. A painting such as Bierstadt's *Conflagration* makes the point beautifully (see Plate 10). In one sense close to the abstract, it is about as far from abstract as can be imagined, and even achieves a sublimity through light, depth and colour that his more conventional landscapes sometimes miss, by their too explicit designs on the viewer.

It is notable that it is at times when, according to my view, there has been a period of 'release' of the right hemisphere – the Renaissance and Romanticism – that there has been an interest in the long view, and the high view, of life: the view that brings distance. This might be related to the right hemisphere's having a generally broader view, which one knows is the case, but it might be more than that. If one is aware of the uniqueness of individual people and things, and at the same time affectively engaged with them, one is inevitably forced to confront separation and loss. This is expressed metaphorically in an evocation of distance in space and time, and therefore with landscapes viewed from above, and from a distance, both in painting and in poetry. An affective relationship with 'the Other' over distances of time and space provides the wherewithal to understand ourselves as part of a three-dimensional world – not just three-dimensional in the spatial sense, but with temporal and emotional depth, too, a world in which we move inexorably towards death. The seeing oneself in other places, and other times, and yet still not turning away from the chasm that yawns between, such an important feature of the world of the Romantics, with its ability to fuse separation with connection, is foreseen in Donne's famous image of the compasses, and of the lovers' souls stretched out between them, like a jeweller's sheet of 'gold to ayery thinnesse beate': that poem too was about not just love and lovers' separations, but the ultimate separation (that according to Donne is not a separation) of death.

MELANCHOLY AND LONGING

In both the Renaissance and Romanticism, there is a captivation by the past, including the classical past (think of Shelley's *Ozymandias*), in contrast to the Enlightenment accent on the future. Even the elegy for lost youth, which seems so quintessentially Romantic, is there in the Renaissance time and again: as in Sir Walter Ralegh's:

> Like truthless dreams, so are my joys expir'd,
> And past return are all my dandled days;
> My love misled, and fancy quite retir'd,
> Of all which pass'd the sorrow only stays . . .

or in Chidiock Tichborne's 'Elegy':

> The spring is past, and yet it hath not sprung,
> The fruit is dead, and yet the leaves are green,
> My youth is gone, and yet I am but young,
> I saw the world, and yet I was not seen,
> My thread is cut, and yet it was not spun,
> And now I live, and now my life is done.

There is similarly an emphasis on the individual or unique, rather than the general, and on the fleeting, rather than the fixed and unchanging. This has seemed to post-Romantic sensibilities culture-bound and perhaps self-indulgent. It is, in fact, however, only in a world where things are interchangeably replaceable or remain unaltered – the realm of Ideas or representations, that of the left hemisphere – that one could afford to take any other point of view.

Just as in the Renaissance the uncaused nature of melancholy seems to have been emphasised, so that it did not risk being confused with, and reduced to, a reaction to specific circumstances, so one finds it again emphasised in Romanticism. '*Ich weiß nicht, was soll es bedeuten, / Daß ich so traurig bin*', begins Heine's *Die Lorelei*; and so complains Lermontov: '*Chto zhe mne tak bol'no i tak trudno? / Zhdu l' chevo? Zhalyeyu li o chyom?*'* And in each case the beauty of the

---

* Heine: 'I know not what it should mean that I am so sad'; Lermontov: 'What is it that pains and troubles me? Am I hoping – or grieving – for something?' (from '*Vykhozhu odin ya na dorogu*').

expansive natural scene around the poet – in Heine's case the peacefully flowing Rhine and the sunset on the mountain tops, in Lermontov's the solemn wonder of the heavens over the steppe, sleeping in their blue stillness – is contrasted with the sadness that is so hard to fathom. Later Tennyson was to write 'Tears, idle tears, / I know not what they mean, / Tears from the depth of some divine despair . . .' As Tennyson's comments on the composition of this poem make clear, it was not an expression of woe, but of longing.[51] It was associated with distance across time and space: 'it is so always with me now; it is the distance that charms me in the landscape, the picture and the past, and not the immediate to-day in which I move'.[52] As a child he was already haunted by what he called the passion of the past.[53] Distance produces a something that is neither in the subject nor the object, but in what arises between them, and it is intrinsically melancholic. Hazlitt wrote:

> When I was a boy, I lived within sight of a range of lofty hills, whose blue tops blending with the setting sun had often tempted my longing eyes and wandering feet. At last I put my project in execution, and on a nearer approach, instead of glimmering air woven into fantastic shapes, found them huge lumpish heaps of discoloured earth . . . Distance of time has much the same effect as distance of place . . . It is not the little, shimmering, almost annihilated speck in the distance, that rivets our attention and 'hangs upon the beatings of our hearts': it is the interval that separates us from it, and of which it is the trembling boundary, that excites all this coil and mighty pudder in the breast. Into that great gap in our being 'come thronging soft desires' and infinite regrets.[54]

It is not on the resoundingly obvious fact of Romantic melancholy that I wish to focus, but on the meaning, in hemisphere terms, of the condition. I touched on this in the chapter on the Renaissance – the difference between wanting and longing. The first is an impulsion, the second an attraction. Wanting is a drive, such as the left hemisphere experiences, or possibly embodies, in which one is impelled, as it were 'from behind', towards something which is inert, and from which one is isolated, something not participating in the process except through the fact of its existence. In longing, one is drawn 'from in front' towards something from which one is already not wholly separate, and which exerts an influence through that 'division within union'. The first is like a hydraulic force (like Freud's model of drives), a mechanical pressure; the second is more like a magnetic field, an electric attraction (as Jung's model of archetypes would suggest). The first is unidirectional; the second bidirectional – there is a 'betweenness'. The first is linear; the second, as the concept of a 'field' suggests, holistic, round in shape. The first has a clear view of its target; the second intuits its 'Other'. The first is a simple, in the sense of unmixed, force – one either wants or does not want. Longing, by contrast, is full of mixed emotions. Think of the typical targets of longing: home, sometimes conflated with death, as in Eichendorff's poem '*Aus der Heimat hinter den Blitzen rot*', so wonderfully set to music by Schumann, which, in its painful ambiguity, demonstrates how bitter-sweet longing is. Or for the loved one, as in almost all of Heine's poems: '*Im wunderschönen Monat Mai . . . Da hab' ich ihr gestanden / Mein Sehnen und Verlangen*'; or for example in Goethe's '*Nur wer die Sehnsucht kennt, / weiss was ich leide!*' Or – shades of the early Renaissance – for the eternal ideal of womanhood, '*das Ewig-Weibliche*', as Goethe described it, which '*zieht uns hinan*' ('draws us on and upwards' – in German the idea of *anziehen* includes the idea of drawing something 'home', as we say). Or for the warm South, as in Goethe's '*Kennst du das Land, wo die Zitronen blühn?*' Or for childhood, or the past, in practically every poet from Wordsworth to Hardy, and beyond. Ultimately though, it is for something that has no name. It is a movement of faith in a state of uncertainty: as Shelley put it, 'The devotion to something afar / From the sphere of our sorrow'.

Although the term was coined only in the eighteenth century, nostalgia was not invented then. In Plato's *Symposium* it is the basis of the fable that Aristophanes tells of the origins of love, of the divided creature that longs to be reunited with its other half. And at the other end of the time spectrum, it is in Bellow's portrait of Allan Bloom, the original of Ravelstein in his novel of that name, who 'thought – no, he saw – that every soul was looking for its peculiar other, longing for its complement'. It is also the core emotion of Oriental poetry. 'Nostalgia for the past is a key to the understanding of Japanese poetry,' writes Donald Keene.[55] For over a thousand years, almost all short poems in Japanese consisted of evocation of the seasons,

> either directly or as revealed by characteristic phenomena such as mist, haze, fog, and so on . . . the moon, unless qualified by another seasonal word, was always the moon in autumn . . . Japanese poets have been unusually sensitive to the changes that accompany the seasons . . . Summer and winter poems . . . were accorded only half the space given to spring and autumn poems [cf. English Romanticism] . . . the mood is more often bittersweet than either tragic or joyous. Rarely is there a suggestion of the happiness of love; the poets wrote most often about the unresponsiveness of the beloved, the failure of the beloved to pay a promised visit, even the acceptance of death as the only resolution of an unhappy affair, as if joy were unseemly.[56]

It is incidentally not just in eighteenth-century Germany and England that empathy with nature developed – that is in any case clear from Renaissance poetry; it was already an important element in the sensibility of tenth-century Japan, in for example the important anthology of the *Kokinshū* poets.[57] In other words many of the features of Romanticism are in fact potentially universals, part of the structure of the human mind and brain, not just aspects of a culture-bound syndrome. In other cultures what we label Romantic is seen as the 'natural' viewpoint, to which the left-hemisphere world of rationalistic mechanism and materialism appears as the culture-bound syndrome.

Keene draws attention to the place of mist, haze, fog and moonlight in Japanese poetry. The Romantics, too, had a predilection for whatever can be only partly discerned – for unfinished sketches, for the half-light of dawn, for scenes by twilight or moonlight, for music heard afar off, for mountains whose tops are obscured by mist that comes and goes. In Chapter 2 I referred to the consistent finding that whenever an image is either only fleetingly presented, or presented in a degraded form, so that only partial information is available, a right-hemisphere superiority emerges.[58] One way of looking at Romanticism is to see it as the wooing, by whatever means can be brought to bear, of the world as delivered by the right hemisphere.

Another way of looking at it is that in the process of completing, or attempting to complete, through imagination the fragmentary impression, one becomes in part the creator of what one perceives. Importantly, only *in part*: if the thing were either wholly given, so that we played no part at all, or wholly our invention, there would be no betweenness, nothing to be shared. As Wordsworth suggested, we '*half* create' and *half* perceive the world we inhabit.[59] This reciprocal, evolving process between the world and our minds again suggests the right hemisphere's role here: 'something evermore about to be'.

Further, one could say that the sublime is more truly present when only partially visible than when explicit, and subject to the full glare of consciousness: it is our re-presentations of natural beauty – as of the erotic, or of the divine – that are limiting, so that, by another 'paradox' (as the left hemisphere would see it) limited information is less limiting, more capable of permitting them to presence to us.

However, these are not distinct 'reasons' which just coincidentally happen together to mean that such half-perceived images are likely to recruit the right hemisphere: they are all inseparable aspects of one 'world', the coherent world of the right hemisphere, just as its opposites – clarity of information, detachment of the observer from the observed, and the triumph of the re-presented over the present – are not unconnected 'facts', but all aspects of the coherent world of the left hemisphere.

THE PROBLEM OF CLARITY AND EXPLICITNESS

The light of day is associated with full consciousness, and therefore has an affinity with the more conscious explicit processes of the left hemisphere: hence Diderot's praise of Richardson, that in the psychological subtlety of his novels he 'lights the depths of the cavern with his torch',[60] through his willingness to explore the less explicit reaches of the affective, unconscious mind. The Romantics perceived that one might learn more from half-light than light. If it is true that wisdom can be approached only by indirect and hidden paths, this may once again have more than a Romantic application: Homer made night the time of the entire creative process,[61] Hegel believed that (for more than one reason) the owl of Minerva, the goddess of wisdom, flew only at dusk,[62] Heidegger was 'an indefatigable walker in unlit places'.[63] Certainly Kant and Bentham, with their daily walks by which you could set your watch, or Fontenelle, who never walked at all if he could help it, would have thought it mighty odd that de Quincey spent months of his life walking at night through the gas-lit streets of London and Edinburgh, or through the moonlit lanes of Dartmoor and the Lake District. Walking in the Quantock hills at night was in fact part of the highly suspect behaviour that led Pitt's Home Secretary, the Duke of Portland, to place Wordsworth and Coleridge under surveillance in 1797 (the government agent set to follow them on their walks thought he had been found out when he heard Coleridge refer to a certain 'Spy Nozy' – viz., Spinoza).[64]

'Vision', writes the neurobiologist Semir Zeki, 'just happens to be the most efficient mechanism for acquiring knowledge and it extends our capacity to do so almost infinitely.'[65] Quite so: but the very qualities that made that efficient mechanism the instrument of the Enlightenment made it suspect to the Romantics. Herder, in his *Sculpture*, one of the first important Romantic treatises on art, wrote that 'the living, embodied truth of the three-dimensional space of angles, of form and volume, is not something we can learn through sight', for great sculpture is

> *physically present, tangible truth.* The beautiful line that constantly varies its course is never forcefully broken or contorted, but rolls over the body with beauty and splendour; it is never at rest but always moving forward ... Sight destroys beautiful sculpture rather than creating it; it transforms it into planes and surfaces, and rarely does it not transform the beautiful fullness, depth, and volume of sculpture into a mere play of mirrors . . . Consider the lover of art sunk deep in contemplation who circles restlessly around a sculpture. What would he not do to transform his sight into touch, to make his *seeing* into a form of touching that *feels* in the dark?[66]

'A thousand viewpoints are not sufficient' to prevent the living form being reduced by sight, when unaided by the other senses, to a two-dimensional diagram, what Herder calls a 'pitiful polygon'. This fate is avoided only when the viewer's 'eye becomes his hand'.[67] This synaesthesia, whereby the eye, no longer the isolated tool of the intellect, must bring the *whole* of the viewer's body in contact with the *whole* of the body viewed, often emerges, in defiance of language, as the sensibility of Romanticism develops, and is memorably expressed by Goethe in his *Römische Elegien*, when he writes of lying in bed in Rome with his mistress:

> *Und belehr' ich mich nicht, indem ich des lieblichen Busens*
> *Formen spähe, die Hand leite die Hüften hinab?*
> *Dann versteh' ich den Marmor erst recht: ich denk' und vergleiche,*
> *Sehe mit fühlendem Aug', fühle mit sehender Hand.**

Art is brought into the most intimate proximity with the living, breathing human form: his mistress a work of art, the work of art his mistress. And the work of art not only becomes itself a living creature, it can be appreciated only by the whole

---

* 'And am I not instructing myself by observing the forms of her lovely bosom, guiding my hand down over her hips? Then at last I truly understand the marble: I think and compare, see with a feeling eye, feel with a seeing hand': Goethe, *Römische Elegien*, V, lines 7–10.

embodied self, by a sort of love which partakes of *eros*.[68] Goethe's eroticism here, though playful, is not misplaced. One of the first and greatest art historians, J. J. Winckelmann, famed for his part in the establishment of neoclassical taste, was nonetheless swept off his feet by his encounters with Greek sculpture, as Reynolds had been by Michelangelo. Confronted by the genius of Greek sculpture, he is impassioned with a rapture somewhere between the erotic and the divine. The Apollo Belvedere becomes for him 'a beautiful, youthful embodiment of the deity [which] awakened tenderness and love, which could transport the soul into a sweet dream of ecstasy, the state of human bliss sought by all religions . . .'[69] In this 'image of the most beautiful god', Winckelmann writes, the 'muscles are subtle, blown like molten glass into scarcely visible undulations and more apparent to the touch than to sight.'[70]

As his rapturous description (see n. 69) reaches its climax, Winckelmann's imagination turns to the myth of Pygmalion, the statue that was so much loved that it came to life: 'My chest seems to expand with veneration and to heave like those I have seen swollen as if by the spirit of prophecy, and I feel myself transported to Delos and to the Lycian groves, places Apollo honoured with his presence – for my figure seems to take on life and movement, like Pygmalion's beauty . . .'[71] In a reversal of the Enlightenment tendency to reduce the living to the inanimate (to regard it under the view afforded by the left hemisphere), here the inanimate is brought to life (returned to the right hemisphere's world). And, significantly, the process is reciprocal, not unidirectional. Winckelmann gives life to the statue, but the statue brings Winckelmann to a renewed sense of life – so much so that his expression here is ambiguous: is 'my figure' here Apollo's, or Winckelmann's? He repeatedly refers to the image of Pygmalion, in relation to the 'great Greek artists' seeking 'to overcome the hard objectivity of matter and, if it had been possible, to animate it'.[72] Herder's essay is actually entitled *Sculpture: Some Observations on Shape and Form from Pygmalion's Creative Dream*.

Hegel praised Winckelmann for transcending the narrow concerns of the art world of his time and having 'managed to open up in the field of art a new medium and whole new way of looking at things for the human spirit'.[73] Herder, too, saw Winckelmann's description of the Apollo as a heroic attempt to overcome the dominance of sight, and to enter into a more profound relation to sculptural form, as a lover would with his beloved.[74] He praises Winckelmann for making the object of his admiration a living presence through his sensitivity to the movement that is everywhere implied in contour. The essence of sculpture resides in that 'beautiful elliptical line' which encircles the entire form, a line which, like Hogarth's line of beauty, cannot be inscribed on a flat surface – something more like 'a fine wire' twisting around an object and curving through three dimensional space, so that the object is constituted as an integral whole.[75]

As Enlightenment thinking begins to recede, there is, as Hall notes, a renewed sense of the special status of the left side. In his justly famous passage describing the antique sculpture of Laocoon, the Trojan priest who, with his two sons, was killed by sea-serpents in an act of divine retribution, Winckelmann wrote: 'The left side, into which the serpent pours forth its venom with a furious strike, is where, because of its proximity to the heart, Laocoon appears to suffer most intensely, and this part of the body can be called a wonder of art.'[76]

All the qualities and values that Herder and Winckelmann evoked in their description of sculpture, unknown, of course, to them, rely on the phenomenological world of the right hemisphere. Herder points to the importance of an unbroken continuity, which dismisses as inadequate any mere focus on parts; a never-resting evolution, that defies stasis; an insistence on depth, volume, fullness and the complex curvature of living surfaces, transcending the rectilinear flatness of the single plane of vision; a commitment to the work of art, imaged in the urgent recruitment of *Einfühlung* (empathy, lit. 'feeling in') mediated by the hand, rather than the detached coolness of the eye. Both Herder and Winckelmann, despite his classicism (and Goethe, too, despite his), intuit powerfully that these values lie at the core of our response to the art of the Ancient World. For it is not just a matter of sculpture: with the obvious exception of the issues of hand and eye, these same values could all be applied to, say, the poetry of Homer. And not just to the Ancient World, either: one could say the same of Miltonic verse, or the music of J. S. Bach. Though arising in the context of a Romantic response to sculpture, what is revealed is neither purely sculptural, nor purely Romantic, but obtains wherever art is a living presence. And, later in the *Römische Elegien*, as if to demonstrate this point, Goethe even manages to bring the composition of poetry – so far, one might think, from the business of sculpture – as close synaesthetically to the business of sculptural *eros* as it is possible to get, relating how he gently counts out the pulse of the hexameters with his fingers on the back of his beloved, while, overcome with sleep, she lies resting in his arms.[77]

The problem with sight, as Herder notes, is its tendency to meet our approach with the cool rebuff of a planar surface, an image, a representation, rather than with the palpable immediacy of the thing itself as it 'presences' to us – the 'physically present, tangible truth'. Because of this tendency to sap the life from the embodied original and substitute a product of the mind, Wordsworth spoke of what he called 'the tyranny of the eye',

> When that which is in every stage of life
> The most despotic of our senses gain'd
> Such strength in me as often held my mind
> In absolute dominion . . .[78]

He is here speaking of the loss of what Heidegger calls authenticity: what had once been a source of wonder became part of the everyday. This is also what I believe Blake had in mind when he wrote:

> This Life's dim Windows of the Soul
> Distorts the Heavens from Pole to Pole
> And leads you to Believe a Lie
> When you see with, not thro', the Eye.[79]

We need to see *through* the eye, through the image, past the surface: there is a fatal tendency for the eye to replace the depth of reality – a depth which implies the vitality, the corporeality and the empathic resonance of the world – with a planar *re*-presentation, that is, a picture. In doing so, the sublime becomes merely the picturesque.

In art there needs to be a certain balance between the facticity of the medium and the something that is seen through the medium, what I have referred to in shorthand as *semi*-transparency. A too great emphasis on the sound and feel of words as 'things' separate from their meaning, or alternatively on the meaning as something separate from the sound and feel of the words in which it exists, destroys poetry. Similarly with painting: but there the tendency for 're-presentation', being dependent on the eye, is greatest. We rush to the 'meaning' too quickly in its subject matter (this is not a reason for rejecting representation in art, a quite different issue – just for being on one's guard for the substitution of representation for the whole, form and matter together). Here again distance results in seeing indistinctly, which allows other aspects of the painting – its 'music' – to come forward. 'There is an impression', wrote Delacroix, 'which results from a certain arrangement of colours, light effects, shadows, etc. It is what one might call the music of the painting. Before you even know what the picture represents, you enter a cathedral, and you find yourself at too great a distance to know what it represents, and often you are rapt by this magical harmony . . .'[80]

The Romantics were constantly aware of the difficulty inherent in remaining with the presence rather than substituting the representation. The truth of this perception, obvious in art, must apply to our apprehension of reality at large, and therefore just as much to the realm of science. Goethe, whose scientific writings are fascinating and too little known today, warned against the tendency immediately to reduce observation to conception, thus losing the power of the object in all its newness to help us break out of the otherwise unbreachable defences of our conceptual systems. He wrote that the student of nature 'should form to himself a method in accordance with observation, but he should be careful not to reduce observation to a mere concept, to substitute words for this concept, and to proceed to treat these words as if they were objects'.[81] In general language is the route by which this conceptualisation occurs: 'how difficult it is to refrain from replacing the thing with its sign; to keep the object (*Wesen*) alive before us instead of killing it with the word.'[82]

Language, a principally left-hemisphere function, tends, as Nietzsche said, to 'make the uncommon common': the general currency of vocabulary returns the vibrant multiplicity of experience to the same few, worn coins.[83] Poetry, however, by its exploitation of non-literal language and connotation, makes use of the right hemisphere's faculty for metaphor, nuance and a broad, complex field of association to reverse this tendency. 'Poetry', in Shelley's famous formulation, 'lifts the veil from the hidden beauty of the world, and makes familiar objects be as if they were not familiar . . . It creates anew the universe, after it has been annihilated in our minds by the recurrence of impressions blunted by reiteration.'[84]

However, poetry, like other manifestations of the imagination, has the typical right hemisphere resistance to explicit approach. Wordsworth speaks movingly, in recollecting the moments of inspiration in his childhood: 'the hiding-places of my power / Seem open; I approach, and then they close'.[85] The right hemisphere has to use subterfuge and indirection to achieve its aims. Berlin's account of why Romanticism relies on what he calls symbols, but I would call metaphors, conveys perfectly the stranglehold that the left hemisphere has on the means of communication of the right:

> I wish to convey something immaterial and I have to use material means for it. I have to convey something which is inexpressible and I have to use expression. I have to convey, perhaps, something unconscious and I have to use conscious means. I know in advance that I shall not succeed, and therefore all I can do is to get nearer and nearer in some asymptotic approach; I do my best, but it is an agonising struggle in which, if I am an artist, or indeed for the German romantics any kind of self-conscious thinker, I am engaged for the whole of my life.[86]

In doing so, they were redeeming the inauthenticity of the familiar.

The deadening effect of the familiar – the inauthentic, in phenomenological terms – is the trap of the left hemisphere. Breaking out of it requires the work of the imagination – not fantasy which makes things novel, but imagination that actually makes them new, alive once more. A defining quality of the artistic process, perhaps its *raison d'être*, is its implacable opposition to the inauthentic. However, there is an absolute distinction, even an antithesis, here being made between two ways of responding to the experience of the inauthentic. In one, the inauthentic is seen as that which is too familiar, in the left-hemisphere sense, which is to say too often presented, therefore in fact never more than re-presented (in other words, a worn-out resource). In the other, inauthenticity is seen as resulting precisely from a loss of familiarity, in the right-hemisphere sense, which is to say never being present at all – we are no longer 'at home' with it, have become in fact alienated from it. In one, the thing itself is perceived as exhausted, and needs to be replaced; in the other, the problem lies not in the thing itself, which we have barely begun to explore, but in our selves and our ability to see it for what it really is. As a result, the responses are different at all levels. In the first case, the solution is seen as lying in a conscious attempt to produce novelty, something never seen before, to invent, to 'be original'. In the second, the solution, by contrast, is to make the everyday appear to us anew, to be seen again as it is in itself, therefore to discover rather than to invent, to see what was there all along, rather than put something new in its place, original in the sense that it takes us back to the origin, the ground of being. This is the distinction between fantasy, which presents something novel *in the place of* the too familiar thing, and imagination, which clears away everything between us and the not familiar enough thing so that we see *it* itself, new, as it is. Wordsworth, the most original of poets, was mocked for the insistent return of his gaze to what had been seen a thousand times before in an attempt to see it for the first time. It is in this context that one can appreciate Steiner's aphorism that 'originality is antithetical to novelty'.[87]

Through his special use of language, particularly linguistic connectors, prepositions and conjunctions, to convey the experience of 'betweenness', his use of double negatives to present a thing and its opposite to the mind at once, and, most importantly of all, to allow, painfully, something to come into being out of an almost luminous absence or emptiness, Wordsworth brings about poetic formulations that are often the counterparts of the positions that I believe Heidegger strove laboriously to express in discursive prose.[88] (Heidegger gravitated more and more in his later work towards the poetry of Hölderlin to illustrate his meaning: I believe that if he had been familiar with Wordsworth he might have found in him much of value.)

Retrospection towards a realm that is lost is at the centre of Wordsworth's poetry, and yet much of his work is about how this loss can be healed. The whole of *The Prelude*, the autobiographical *tour de force* which in my opinion contains much of his greatest work, is in one sense an exercise in retrospection. Like Tennyson after him, Wordsworth appears to have been naturally inclined to a sense of the past: his first few poems as a young man are all about memory. 'My soul will cast the backward view', he wrote; another poem dwells on the 'memory of departed pleasures', and in a third he wrote: 'for only then, when memory is hushed, am I at rest'.[89] One might be forgiven for thinking these were the thoughts of age, but they all come from poems he wrote before he was even eighteen years old.

However, as he matures, and certainly by the time of the 1805 Prelude, he begins to see memory as no longer inert and unidirectional, but as something that *lives*, and that at times has the power to revivify us now. In *The Prelude* he famously refers to such moments as 'spots of time . . . Which with distinct preeminence retain / A vivifying Virtue', by which 'our minds / Are nourished and invisibly repair'd'.[90]

The extraordinarily restorative quality of the relationship between Wordsworth and nature is in some ways implicitly, and even at times explicitly, related to the sustaining and comforting relationship between mother and child; and it is of more than passing interest that this, like virtually every other aspect of Wordsworth's achievement, depends on the right hemisphere, through the operation of what in psychoanalytic terms is known as the maternal 'comforting substrate'.[91] One of these 'spots of time' occurred when, only five years old, and hardly able to hold his horse's bridle, he was riding on the lonely fells. Separated from his companion, he lost his way, and found himself by a hangman's gibbet. His eye having fallen on the place where the name of the murderer was still to be seen carved in the turf:

> forthwith I left the spot
> And, reascending the bare Common, saw

A naked Pool that lay beneath the hills,
The Beacon on the summit, and more near,
A Girl who bore a Pitcher on her head
And seem'd with difficult steps to force her way
Against the blowing wind. It was, in truth,
An ordinary sight: but I should need
Colours and words that are unknown to man
To paint the visionary dreariness
Which, while I look'd all round for my lost guide,
Did at that time invest the naked Pool,
The Beacon on the lonely Eminence,
The woman, and her garments vex'd and toss'd
By the strong wind . . .[92]

He carries on to describe how the memory of this scene has changed, has given a
radiance to his subsequent experience of these lonely fells, and continues:

Oh! Mystery of Man, from what a depth
Proceed thy honours! I am lost, but see
In simple childhood something of the base
On which thy greatness stands, but this I feel,
That from thyself it is that thou must give,
Else never canst receive. The days gone by
Come back upon me from the dawn almost
Of life: the hiding-places of my power
Seem open; I approach, and then they close;
I see by glimpses now; when age comes on,
May scarcely see at all, and I would give,
While yet I may, as far as words can give,
A substance and a life to what I feel:
I would enshrine the spirit of the past
For future restoration . . .[93]

The visionary power, so restorative, is something he cannot control and is not
even predictable. Wordsworth is at pains to point out how ordinary, even bleak,
the scene is that brings such power. And with age it happens less often.

When it does occur, it is not just that this happens unbidden. It is not even that
the attempt to make it happen is counterproductive: 'I approach, and then they
close'. It is that Wordsworth needs to be positively *looking away*. In the famous
passage from Book I of the *Prelude* when he describes birds-nesting on a crag
('Oh! When I have hung / Above the raven's nest, by knots of grass / And half-inch
fissures in the slippery rock/ But ill sustain'd'), or from Book V, where the
'Winander boy' calls to the owls across the lake ('in that silence, while he hung /
Listening, a gentle shock of mild surprise / Has carried far into his heart the
voice / Of mountain torrents'), the vision happens while Wordsworth is intent on

something else – more than that, while his senses are on the stretch, but focussed on something other than the scene that enters into the heart.[94] The vision comes as a by-product. De Quincey tells a story of Wordsworth, during the time of the Peninsular War, walking out at night to meet the mail coach from Keswick that would bring eagerly awaited news. Lying full stretch on the road so that he could put his ear to it and pick up the distant rumbling that would indicate the approach of the mail, his eye happened to chance on a bright star glittering between the brow of Seat Sandal and Helvellyn, and struck him suddenly 'with a pathos and a sense of the infinite, that would not have arrested me under other circumstances.'[95] The vision comes because of an effort made and then relaxed. So Wordsworth describes at the opening of Book XII of *The Prelude* how inspiration requires both the effort by which the mind 'aspires, grasps, struggles, wishes, craves' and the stillness of the mind which 'fits him to receive it, when unsought' – despite the effort, it still only comes unsought.[96] It is a bit like the process of memory itself, whereby we struggle to recapture, say, a name, which only later comes unbidden once we turn away. It is as if the effort opened the windows of the soul, but the explicit intention obscured Wordsworth's sight, as if falling on the blind spot at the centre of the field of vision. It is only when our intentions are fixed on something else that we can see things as they really are.

I believe that what Wordsworth is actually doing here is talking about the relationship between the two hemispheres. Narrowly focussed attention is the province of the left hemisphere, and an increase in stress, fear and excitement actually inhibits the spread of neuronal recruitment in a manner that favours this very closely targeted kind of attention within the left hemisphere. Yet while the left hemisphere is preoccupied with its quarry, like Eliot's dog with its meat (see p. 326 above), the right hemisphere is actually freed, its vigilance also in a state of enhancement, to see the scene afresh, once more authentic, not overlaid by the familiarity that the left hemisphere would normally bring to the scene. The left hemisphere would have pre-digested it, as it were, into another picturesque scene of mountains, lakes or starry skies. The initial effort of close attention is needed, but, its work done, it must give way to an open receptivity, a sort of *active* passivity.

There is a combination of factors at work that points to the right hemisphere being the mediator of the revivifying power he refers to, apart from the unwilled nature of the experience, its reciprocal nature, and its paradoxical apparent emptiness. The feeling of guilt and awe that hangs over many of the 'spots of time' scenes suggests an association with the right hemisphere on which our religious sense appears to depend. Similarly the sense of ultimate meaning which pervades the spots of time is known to occur in some kinds of specifically right-temporal-lobe seizures, and therefore may have an origin in this region of the brain. Other factors that are also suggestive of the association include the importance of large visual masses and forms ('huge and mighty forms that do not live / Like living men mov'd slowly through my mind / By day and were the trouble of my dreams'), and the fact that these experiences are so much associated with childhood, in which, as I have mentioned, the right hemisphere plays a particularly important role in all forms of understanding.

How to recapture this in adulthood? Wordsworth's answer is given in his entire life's work: in and through poetry, which with its reliance on metaphor and implicit meaning allows the right hemisphere to circumvent the ordinary processes of everyday language which inevitably return us to the familiar, and reduce the numinous to the quotidian. There is always a paradox involved, in that he is trying to reproduce the unself-consciousness that permits experience of the numinous, the condition of such unself-consciousness being that it cannot be consciously reproduced. In revisiting his childhood self and trying to bring him to life he is intently focussed on a being whose essential importance to the poet is that he was completely unself-aware.

In the Tintern Abbey ode, the constant reference to the theme of return, the carefully placed iterations ('again I hear . . . Once again / Do I behold . . . The day is come when I again repose'), the movement of the verse itself, wandering and returning, like the river it images

How oft, in spirit, have I turned to thee,
O sylvan Wye! Thou wanderer through the woods,
How often has my spirit turned to thee![97]

all evoke a sense of change within unchangingness, like the river that is always moving but always the same, like Donne's compasses that always circle the same place and return.

SELF-CONSCIOUSNESS AND REPRESENTATION

There is a lack of self-consciousness to Wordsworth that is essential to his genius, and which enabled him to write his greatest as well as his worst lines. This is a characteristic he shares with both Blake and Keats (and later with Hopkins and Hardy). These three Romantic geniuses, very different, highly individual poets as they are, share what John Bayley, in describing Keats, refers to as his 'unmisgiving' quality, a point later taken up by Christopher Ricks in *Keats and Embarrassment*.[98] The lack of misgiving explains their combination of greatness and at times insouciant foolishness: they make themselves vulnerable in order to become the conduit of something greater than themselves. The explicit, self-conscious workings of the left hemisphere constantly oppose this condition, and therefore need to be stilled.

The very titles of Blake's major works, *Songs of Innocence and Experience* and *The Marriage of Heaven and Hell*, allude to the reality that, in the lived world of the right hemisphere, opposites are not 'in opposition'. Blake's visionary poetry nonetheless dramatises in various forms a battle between two powerful forces that adopt different guises: the single-minded, limiting, measuring, mechanical power of what Blake called Ratio, the God of Newton, and the myriad-minded, liberating power of creative imagination, the God of Milton. This opposition persists despite the right hemisphere's unification of opposites, for the same reason that a tolerant society cannot necessarily secure the co-operation of the intolerant who would undermine it, and may ultimately find itself in the paradoxical situation of having to be intolerant of them. I commented earlier that Aeschylus's *Prometheus Bound*, 'doing right without knowing it', displays the mind unwittingly cognizing itself. Unconsciously it gives voice to the right hemisphere's prophecy of where the revolt of the left hemisphere would lead. Blake too voices, without being aware of it, the brain's struggle to ward off domination by the left hemisphere. For instance, in 'There is No Natural Religion' he writes:

Conclusion. If it were not for the Poetic or Prophetic Character the Philosophic & Experimental would soon be at the ratio of all things, and stand still, unable to do other than repeat the same dull round over again [to reach outside the known one needs the right hemisphere: the left hemisphere can only repeat the known].

Application. He who sees the Infinite [looks outward to the ever-becoming with the right hemisphere] in all things sees God. He who sees the Ratio only [looks at the self-defined world brought into being by the left hemisphere] sees himself only [the left hemisphere is self-reflexive].

Therefore God becomes as we are, that we may be as he is [through the right hemisphere gives us access to imagination/metaphor, the bridge whereby the divine reaches us, and liberates us from ourselves].

Blake, too, saw himself as inspired by a return to a great figure of the pre-Augustan era, not so much in his case Shakespeare or Michelangelo (though he was undoubtedly indebted to both), but to the spirit of Milton, which, with characteristic specificity and a wonderful refusal to be nonplussed, he believed had entered his body through the instep of his left foot:

Then first I saw him in the Zenith as a falling star
Descending perpendicular, swift as the swallow or swift:
And on my left foot falling on the tarsus, enter'd there . . .[99]

– thereby gaining literally direct access to the right hemisphere. And so thunderstruck was he by the experience that fortunately he illustrated the event (see Plate 11).

Romanticism in fact demonstrates, in a multitude of ways, its affinity for everything we know from the neuropsychological literature about the workings of the right hemisphere. This can be seen in its preferences for the individual over the general, for what is unique over what is typical ('typical' being the true meaning of the word 'Classical'), for apprehension of the 'thisness' of things – their particular *way* of being as the *ultima realitas entis*, the final form of the thing exactly as it, and only it, is, or can be – over the emphasis on the 'whatness' of things; in its appreciation of the whole, as something different from the aggregate of the parts into which the left hemisphere analyses it by the time it appears in self-conscious awareness; in its preference for metaphor over simile (evident in the contrast between Romantic and Augustan poetry), and for what is indirectly expressed over the literal; in its emphasis on the body and the senses; in its emphasis on the personal rather than the impersonal; in its passion for whatever is seen to be living, and its perception of the relation between what Wordsworth called the 'life of the mind' and the realm of the divine (Blake: 'all living things are holy'); in its accent on involvement rather than disinterested impartiality; in its preference for the betweenness which is felt across a three-dimensional world, rather than for seeing what is distant as alien, lying in another plane; in its affinity for melancholy and sadness, rather than for optimism and cheerfulness; and in its attraction to whatever is provisional, uncertain, changing, evolving, partly hidden, obscure, dark, implicit and essentially unknowable in preference to what is final, certain, fixed, evolved, evident, clear, light and known.

As the nineteenth century advanced, one sees a mixed picture, a transitional phase. There is a divide between the inspired Tennyson who wrote

I heard no sound where I stood
But the rivulet on from the lawn
Running down to my own dark wood;
Or the voice of the long sea-wave as it swell'd
Now and then in the dim-gray dawn;
But I look'd, and round, all round the house I beheld
The death-white curtain drawn;
Felt a horror over me creep,
Prickle my skin and catch my breath,
Knew that the death-white curtain meant but sleep,
Yet I shudder'd and thought like a fool of the sleep of death . . .[100]

and the Tennyson of fairyland. But, with some exceptions, painters were quicker than poets to succumb to fancy or academicism.

Hopkins is a case of particular interest: almost everything about him suggests a right-hemisphere predominance. He was a priest, who suffered from depression. He had a fascination with the thisness of things, what, following Duns Scotus, he called *haeccitas* (sometimes *haeceitas*):

Each mortal thing does one thing and the same:
Deals out that being indoors each one dwells;
Selves—goes itself; myself it speaks and spells,
Crying Whát I do is me: for that I came.[101]

In his 'Comments on the Spiritual Exercises of St. Ignatius Loyola', Hopkins refers to

that taste of myself, of I and me above and in all things, which is more distinctive than the taste of ale or alum, more distinctive than the smell of walnutleaf or camphor, and is incommunicable by any means to another man (as when I was a child I used to ask myself: What must it be to be someone else?) . . . searching nature I taste *self* at but one tankard, that of my own being.[102]

This is reminiscent of Heidegger capturing the very 'essent' of a thing through the smell.[103] Hopkins coined the term *inscape* to represent this unique quality of a thing, person, place or event, and *instress* to represent the energy that sustained it, something akin to authentic *Dasein*. He was a passionate observer of things as they are: 'moonlight hanging or dropping on treetops like a blue cobweb', 'drops of rain hanging on rails etc. seen with only the lower rim lighted like nails (of fingers)', 'soft chalky look with more shadowy middles of the globes of cloud on a night with a moon faint or concealed'.[104] He was so captivated by the sound and feel of words, their 'thingness', clang and touch, that, although he never loses the sense, he sometimes comes close to doing so. He was hyper-alert to the meanings of words according to their etymology, again like Heidegger, and through them revealed important connections.[105] He had a love for all that is wild, and untouched by humanity: 'What would the world be, once bereft / Of wet and wildness?'[106] He had a highly developed sense of awe, and of guilt ('poor, tortured, Gerard Manley Hopkins', as Robert Graves called him, only to dismiss him).[107] He realized the importance of the leap of intuition, as opposed to the unbroken line of rationality: 'it is a happy thing that there is no royal road to poetry', he wrote, 'one cannot reach Parnassus except by flying thither'.[108] He saw that the ground of beauty was sameness within difference, and difference within sameness; and stressed the importance of the relationship between things over the things themselves.[109] And he was subject to sudden inspiration in which many of his greatest poems came to him: 'I shall shortly have some sonnets to send you, five or more. Four of these came like inspirations unbidden and against my will.'[110]

Inspiration is something we cannot control, towards which we have to exhibit what Wordsworth called a 'wise passiveness'.[111] As the nineteenth century wore on, this lack of control fitted ill with the confident spirit engendered by the Industrial Revolution, and this lack of predictability with the need, in accord with the Protestant ethic, for 'results' as the reward for effort. Imagination was something that could not be relied on: it was transitory, fading from the moment it revealed itself to consciousness (in Shelley's famous phrase, 'the mind in creation is a fading coal'), recalcitrant to the will. In response to this, 'the Imaginative', a product of active fantasy, rather than of the receptive imagination, began to encroach on the realm of imagination itself: it's there, for example, in the self-conscious mediaevalising of the Victorians. This 're-presentation' of something which had once been 'present' suggests that once more the territory of the right hemisphere is being colonised by the left. One sees it in visual terms, in the extraordinary attention to detail at the expense of the overall composition, a loss of the sense of the whole (the vision of the left hemisphere superseding that of the right), to be seen in the Pre-Raphaelites, and to some extent in Victorian painting in general, and reaching a sort of apotheosis in the obsessively detailed pictures of the schizophrenic Richard Dadd. As Peter Conrad pointed out, Henry James's judgment on *Middlemarch*, just or not, that it was 'a treasure house of detail, but ... an indifferent whole', picks up a central feature of Victorian art and literature.[112]

THE SECOND REFORMATION

In the first part of the book, I referred to the German so-called 'idealist' philosophers of the late eighteenth and early nineteenth centuries, and therefore of the Romantic age, and their view that one had to combine reason with imagination, system-building with perception of individuality, consistency with contradiction, analysis with a sense of the whole. What is striking is the degree of enthusiasm for, and active participation in, science that they had exhibited. Goethe is another conspicuous example: in fact he believed his scientific work to be more important than his poetry. With his discovery in 1784 of the intermaxillary bone in the human foetal skull, a vestigial remnant of a bone to be found in the skull of apes and thought to be missing in humans, he demonstrated to his own satisfaction, long before Darwin, that all living things were related and that their forms evolved from the same stem.

Though they were primarily philosophers and poets, they saw the world as a living unity, in which the metaphysical and the material were not to be separated, but where, nonetheless, different contexts demanded appropriately different approaches. In an exploration of the spirit of Goethe's age, one historian writes, in words that echo Nietzsche on Apollo and Dionysus:

> For even rationality cannot get by without imagination, but neither can imagination without rationality. The marriage of the two is, however, of such a peculiar kind, that they carry on a life and death struggle, and yet it is only together that they are able to accomplish their greatest feats, such as the higher form of conceptualising that we are accustomed to call reason.[113]

But this marriage was not to last. A sort of second Reformation was on the way. The Reformation of the sixteenth century could be seen as having involved a shift away from the capacity to understand metaphor, incarnation, the realm that bridges this world and the next, matter and spirit, towards a literalistic way of thinking – a move away from imagination, now seen as treacherous, and towards rationalism. In the middle of the nineteenth century in Germany, there arose a new intellectual movement, which, as one of its protagonists Ludwig Feuerbach indeed acknowledged, had its roots in the Reformation. It too had difficulty with the idea that the realms of matter and spirit interpenetrated one another: if a thing was not to be wholly disembodied, just an idea, it had to be wholly material. Gone was the understanding of the complex, often apparently paradoxical nature of reality, an acceptance of the *coniunctio oppositorum*: we were back to the realm of 'either/or'. It too embraced a sort of literalism, and mistrusted imagination. This philosophy, known as materialism, was explicitly based on a view that science is the only foundation for knowing and understanding the world.

The origins of this scientific materialism, or 'positivism', lay in the French Enlightenment. Auguste Comte had asserted that science was not only our sole source of genuine knowledge about the world, but that it was the only way to understand humanity's place in the world, and the only credible view of the world as a whole. He saw societies and cultures passing through three stages: a theological phase, where religious perspectives dominate, ceding to a stage of philosophical analysis, inevitably shaped by metaphysical assumptions, which in turn gives way to the 'positive', scientific stage, in which these are jettisoned, and we achieve 'objective' knowledge. According to Richard Olson, throughout the early years of the nineteenth century, every major tradition of natural science strove to extend its ideas, methods, practices, and attitudes to social and political issues of contemporary concern.[114] As Aristotle had warned, each kind of knowledge has its proper context: it cannot be assumed that what is rational for the geometer is rational for the physician, or for the politician. But the left hemisphere does not respect context. Comte's wishes came to be realised, and the analytic strategies associated with mechanics generally led to a presumption that society could be treated as an aggregate of individual units – not a society in fact, but the prototype of the 'masses' – with the society's well-being reduced to a sum of individual pleasures and pains.

Feuerbach was the foremost of the apostate group known as the young Hegelians. Where Hegel had been at pains to preserve the (right hemisphere's) ultimate unity of spirit and matter, without either simply collapsing into the other, Feuerbach and his fellow materialists saw only the (left hemisphere) alternatives: matter or ideal. In rejecting the ideal as an empty representation, they were compelled to accept only matter. In a striking parallel with the Reformation, however, the first impulse was towards *authenticity*. The young Hegelians wished to rescue the realm of sensory experience, what can be seen and touched, from what they saw as subjection to the realm of concepts and ideas, and more generally experience from a representation of experience, and religion from mere theology. Experience was not the same as ideas about experience, true enough. But as with the ideologues of the Reformation, they ended by destroying the bridge between the two realms, and reducing the complexity of existence to something simple and clear. Whereas at the Reformation it had been the Word, in this case it was Matter.

Reality was what science could deal with, and *only* that was real. Karl Vogt proclaimed that thought, the secretion of the brain, could be changed, like other bodily secretions, by diet: 'since belief is only a property of the body's atoms, a change in beliefs depends only on the way in which the atoms of the body are substituted'.[115] He seems not to have noticed that this applies to the belief in materialism, too. How were we to decide which placement of atoms was the one to embrace, assuming that is something one could do to a placement of atoms? But these questions were not answered. By driving a wedge between the realm of sensory experience and the realm of ideas, the whole realm of ideas became suspect. Ideas were what led us to believe that things we could not see with our eyes and touch with our hands – like God – were real, whereas they must, so went the logic, be our own inventions. Worse, endowed with such independent existence, they kept us in a state of indignity and humility.

The denial of the divine was as important to them as the elevation of matter. This was itself, of course, an idea; and, if it could be said to be true, so was the idea of its truth. But there is more than a little of the Promethean about the material-ists. When one of their number, Ludwig Büchner, emerged from a period of personal crisis it was with the proclamation: 'No longer do I acknowledge any human authority over me.'[116] No *human* authority, notice. The unwillingness to acknowledge any authority was, in another parallel with the Reformation, at the very core of materialism: but these reformers, like those before them, had to acknowledge *some* sort of authority, even if it were the authority of reason (which is something in itself we can only intuit). So the materialists, too, had to have a superhuman authority: and this new divinity was science. Both scientific materi-alism and the dialectical materialism of Engels and Marx emerged from the view that science was the only authority.

In 1848, revolution spread across Europe, and its reverberations were felt most strongly in France and Germany. 'For the scientific materialists, and to some extent for Marx as well, opposition to groundless authority was the task and natural science was its justification.'[117] Speaking in 1853, Lyon Playfair, one of the keenest evangelists for scientific materialism in nineteenth-century Britain, declared that 'science is a religion and its philosophers are the priests of nature': T. H. Huxley, Darwin's 'bulldog', described his talks as lay sermons.[118] This was part of a broad shift whereby, according to Gaukroger, the West's sense of its own superiority shifted seamlessly in the early nineteenth century from its religion to its science.[119] In doing so it swapped one religion for another; but these 'priests of nature' did not honour nature herself so much as the human capacity to control nature, and to make it apparently graspable by rationalism alone: the left hemi-sphere reflecting on itself. It is interesting that Marx called Prometheus, opposed as he was to 'all divine and earthly Gods who do not acknowledge human self-consciousness as the highest divinity . . . the most eminent saint and martyr in the philosophic calendar'.[120] It is an uncomfortable fact that Hitler, too, was later to write that the Aryan is 'the Prometheus of mankind from whose bright forehead the divine spark of genius has sprung at all times, forever kindling anew that fire of knowledge which illumined the night of silent mysteries and thus caused man to climb the path to mastery over the other beings of this earth.'[121] In sweeping away the past, it seems that the concept of hubris, which the Greeks had under-stood as lying at the heart of all tragedy, was lost.

By contrast, in the ancient world, according to Kerényi, 'vulnerability was an attribute of the gods, just as it is characteristic of human existence'.[122] (The core *mythos* of Christianity, for that matter, is the vulnerability of the divine, God suffering alongside his creation.) But this admission is not possible to the Promethean left hemisphere. 'Prometheus, founder of the sacrifice, was a cheat and a thief', he writes, 'these traits were at the bottom of all the stories that deal with him.' Under his tutelage, men became stealers of the divinity that lies round about them, 'whose temerity brings immeasurable and unforeseen misfortune upon them'.[123]

The left hemisphere's lack of concern for context leads to two important consequences, each of which makes its version of reality more dangerous and simultaneously more difficult to resist. The appropriateness or otherwise of applying scientism to one field of human experience rather than another – Aristotle's perception – is disregarded, since to understand that would require a sense of context, and of what is reasonable, both of which, from the left-hemisphere point of view, are unnecessary intrusions by the right hemisphere on its absolute, non-contingent nature, the source of its absolute power. At the same time, science preached that it was exempt from the historicisation or contextualisation that was being used to undermine Christianity in the nineteenth century,[124] a way of enabling science to criticise all other accounts of the world and of human experience while rendering itself immune to criticism. This doctrine of the infallibility of science is also a result of the Enlightenment failure to understand the contextual nature of all thought, what Dewey called 'the dogma of immaculate conception of philosophical systems'.[125] None of this would have been possible without its development of its own *mythos*, which in the twentieth century was to become the dominating *mythos* of our culture. The key features of it are all in place, however, by the mid-nineteenth century.

First there was the myth of the unity of science – the left hemisphere's view that there is one logical path to knowledge, irrespective of context; whereas in reality science is, to quote Gaukroger again, 'a loose grouping of disciplines with different subject matters and different methods, tied in various ways each of which work for some purposes but not for others'.[126] Then there was the myth of the sovereignty of the scientific method – of the left hemisphere's planned, relentless progress following a sequential path to knowledge. In fact we know that, though scientific method plays its part, the greatest advances of science are often the result of chance observations, the obsessions of particular personalities, and intuitions that can be positively inhibited by too rigid a structure, method or world view.[127] Technological advances, too, have been less often the foreseen consequences of systematic method than the results of local enthusiasts or skilled artisans attempting empirically to solve a local problem, and many have been frankly serendipitous by-products of an attempt to achieve something quite different. And there are things that are simply beyond scientific knowledge, where it is a category error to suppose that they can be understood in this fashion. The left hemisphere's hubris is affronted by this idea, and when the great German physiologist Emil DuBois-Reymond, the discoverer of the neuronal action potential, drew attention to the proper limits of scientific understanding with his declaration: *ignorabimus* ('[there are things which] we shall never know'), its reaction was – and remains – one of indignation.

Then there was the myth of science as above morality, oddly coupled with an uncritical acceptance of the idea that science is the only sure foundation for decency and morality – the left hemisphere in characteristic denial, since we know that despite its many successes in alleviating human suffering, it has a far from unblemished record in this respect, with its methods of research, as well as the perhaps unintended, but nonetheless foreseeable, consequences of its actions, and sometimes its very aims (in collaboration with corrupt regimes) being at times manifestly harmful. And, in further denial, there is the myth of its brave stand against the forces of dogma, usually in the form of the Church, encapsulated in grossly simplified tales, designed to convey the message that science alone is without preconception.[128]

THE INDUSTRIAL REVOLUTION

But it is the Industrial Revolution which enabled the left hemisphere to make its most audacious assault yet on the world of the right hemisphere – or perhaps one should say that the left hemisphere's most daring assault *was* the Industrial Revolution. It goes without saying that this move is of the profoundest consequence for the story of this book, and underwrites the defining characteristics of the modern world, which will form the subject of the next and final chapters.

It is notable that when the left hemisphere takes a step forward it does so – in keeping with its competitive, confident, manner, and its belief in its unassailable rightness (the clarity of Truth) – in a manner which is absolute and intolerant, and sweeps opposition aside: the Reformation, the Cromwellian Revolution, the French Revolution, the rise of scientific materialism (where it met opposition, it did so as much as a consequence of the peculiarly aggressive tone of its proponents as of anything it claimed). The Industrial Revolution, slicing its way through the landscape and sweeping away cultural history, is no exception. The boldness of its move goes beyond even that, however.

If the right hemisphere delivers 'the Other' – experience of whatever it is that exists apart from ourselves – this is not the *same* as the world of concrete entities 'out there' (it is certainly more than that), but it does encompass most of what we would think of as actually existing things, at least before we come to think of them at all, as opposed to the concepts of them, the abstractions and constructions we inevitably make from them, in conscious reflection, which forms the contribution of the left hemisphere. But what if the left hemisphere were able to externalise and make concrete its own workings – so that the realm of actually existing things apart from the mind consisted to a large extent of its own projections? Then the ontological primacy of right-hemisphere experience would be outflanked, since it would be delivering – not 'the Other', but what was already *the world as processed by the left hemisphere*. It would make it hard, and perhaps in time impossible, for the right hemisphere to escape from the hall of mirrors, to reach out to something that truly was 'Other' than, beyond, the human mind.

In essence this was the achievement of the Industrial Revolution. It is not just that this movement was obviously, colossally, man's most brazen bid for power over the natural world, the grasping left hemisphere's long-term agenda. It was also the creating of a world in the left hemisphere's own likeness. The mechanical production of goods ensured a world in which the members of a class were not just approximate fits, because of their tiresome authenticity as individuals, but truly identical: equal, interchangeable members of their category. They would be free from the 'imperfections' that come from being made by living hands. The subtle variations of form that result from natural processes would be replaced by invariant forms, as well as by largely 'typical' forms, in other words the shapes which the left hemisphere recognises: perfect circles, rectilinear forms such as the straight line, the rectangle, the cube, the cylinder. (Delacroix wrote that 'it would be worthy to investigate whether straight lines exist only in our brains'; as Leonard Shlain has pointed out, straight lines exist nowhere in the natural world, except perhaps at the horizon, where the natural world ends.)[129] Such regular shapes are not produced by natural processes and are inimical to the body, which is after all a source of constant variation, change, and evolution of form, both in itself, and in everything it goes to create. Thus as far as possible evidence of the body would be eliminated from what is made. It would above all make tools, mechanisms, the sort of inanimate objects preferentially dealt with by the left hemisphere, and it would make machines that make machines, self-propagating parodies of life that lack all the qualities of the living. Its products would be certain, perfect in their way, *familiar* in the 'iconic' sense (preferred by the left hemisphere), not in the sense of 'special things that have value for me' (preferred by the right): identical entities, rectilinear in shape, endlessly reproducible, mechanistic in nature, certain, fixed, man-made.

Is it over-stated to say that this would lead to a position where the pre-reflectively experienced world, the world that the right hemisphere was to deliver, became simply 'the world as processed by the left hemisphere'? I do not think so. I would contend that a combination of urban environments which are increasingly rectilinear grids of machine-made surfaces and shapes, in which little speaks of the natural world; a worldwide increase in the proportion of the population who live in such environments, and live in them in greater degrees of isolation; an unprecedented assault on the natural world, not just through exploitation, despoliation and pollution, but also more subtly, through excessive 'management' of one kind or another, coupled with an increase in the virtuality of life, both in the nature of work undertaken, and in the omnipresence in leisure time of television and the internet, which between them have created a largely insubstantial replica of 'life' as processed by the left hemisphere – all these have to a remarkable extent realised this aim, if I am right that it is an aim, in an almost unbelievably short period of time. Heisenberg, in the 1950s, wrote that technology no longer appears

> as the product of a conscious human effort to enlarge material power, but rather like a biological development of mankind in which *the innate structures of the human organism are transplanted in an ever-increasing measure into the environment* of man.[130]

I could hardly believe my eyes when I came across this passage, because it expresses precisely my contention that the innate structures of the left hemisphere are, through technology, being incarnated in the world it has come to dominate.

But the left hemisphere would appear to be unsatisfied with this, because it still leaves possible exits from the maze, from the hall of mirrors, unbarred. Through the fact of our embodied nature, through art and through religion, the right hemisphere might still be able to make a comeback. And so we now need to take a look not just at the evolution of the world of things, but of the world of ideas in the twentieth century, to see how the left hemisphere has effectively closed off the escape routes. This is where the 'asymmetry of interaction' that I alluded to at the end of Part I comes into play, where the situation, until now evidencing a series of ever more violent swings between the hemispheres, goes out of kilter, and results in a possibly final triumph of the left-hemisphere world.

CHAPTER 12

THE MODERN AND POST-MODERN WORLDS

VIRGINIA WOOLF'S OFTEN QUOTED REMARK THAT 'ON OR ABOUT DECEMBER 1910 human character changed' is memorable for its playful specificity. It is usual to refer that specificity to Roger Fry's controversial exhibition 'Manet and the Post-Impressionists', which had opened in November 1910 at the Grafton Galleries in London. However, the change she meant was very far from specific: it was indeed all-encompassing. 'All human relations have shifted', she continued, 'those between masters and servants, husbands and wives, parents and children. And when human relations change there is at the same time a change in religion, conduct, politics and literature.'[1] Pretty comprehensive, then: even Roger Fry could not be expected to have taken the credit for that.

The specificity of the date she gives for the beginning of the modern era, of the era of Modern-*ism* – for it is to that self-proclaiming consciousness of radical change that she refers – is designed to suggest not so much the swiftness of the transition, as the abruptness of the disjunction, between what had gone before and what was to come after. As I hope to show later, that disjunction was not as great as it might appear. The change had already been long in process: what was sudden was the revelation of the consequences. It was less an avalanche after unexpected snow than a landslide following years of erosion.

The changes were, right enough, though, changes that affected all aspects of life: as she says, not just art, but the ways in which we conceived the world in which we lived, related to one another, and even saw ourselves in relation to the cosmos at large. Modernity was marked by a process of social disintegration which clearly derived from the effects of the Industrial Revolution, but which could also be seen to have its roots in Comte's vision of society as an aggregation of essentially atomistic individuals. The drift from rural to urban life, again both a consequence of the realities of industrial expansion and of the Enlightenment quest for an ideal society untrammelled by the fetters of the past, led to a breakdown of familiar social orders, and the loss of a sense of belonging, with far-reaching effects on the life of the mind. The advances of scientific materialism, on the one hand, and of bureaucracy on the other, helped to produce what Weber called the disenchanted world. Capitalism and consumerism, ways of conceiving human relationships based on little more than utility, greed, and competition, came to supplant those based on felt connection and cultural continuity. The state, the representative of the organising, categorising and subjugating forces of systematic conformity, was beginning to show itself to be an overweening presence even in democracies. And there were worrying signs that the combination of an adulation of power and material force with the desire, and power (through technological advance) to subjugate, would lead to the abandonment of any form of democracy, and the rise of totalitarianism.

The effects of abstraction, bureaucratisation and social dislocation on personal identity have been themes of sociology since Max Weber and Émile Durkheim, and their effects on consciousness in modernity have been explored in works such as *The Homeless Mind*, by Peter Berger and colleagues.[2] Pervasive rationalistic, technical and bureaucratic ways of thinking have emptied life of meaning by destroying what Berger calls the 'sacred canopy' of meanings reflecting collective beliefs about life, death and the world in which we live. The resultant *anomie*, or loss of all bearings, the demise of any shared structure of values, leads to a sort of existential angst.

In his book on the subject, *Modernity and Self-identity*,[3] Anthony Giddens describes the characteristic disruption of space and time required by globalisation, itself the necessary consequence of industrial capitalism, which destroys the sense of belonging, and ultimately of individual identity. He refers to what he calls 'disembedding mechanisms', the effect of which is to separate things from their context, and ourselves from the uniqueness of place, what he calls 'locale'. Real things and experiences are replaced by symbolic tokens; 'expert' systems replace local know-how and skill with a centralised process dependent on rules. The result is an abstraction and virtualisation of life. He sees a dangerous form of positive feedback, whereby theoretical positions, once promulgated, dictate the reality that comes about, since they are then fed back to us through the media, which form, as much as reflect, reality. The media also promote fragmentation by a random juxtaposition of items of information, as well as permitting the 'intrusion of distant events into everyday consciousness', another aspect of decontextualisation in modern life adding to loss of meaning in the experienced world.[4]

The 'homeless' mind: attachment to place runs deep in us. In neurological terms, the evolutionary roots of the integrated emotional system involved in the formation of social attachments may lie in more ancient and primitive animal attachments to place.[5] Some animals bond as much with their nest sites as with their mothers.[6] 'Belonging' comes from the same Old English word *langian* which forms the root of 'longing'. It means a sense of powerful emotional attachment to 'my place', where I am 'at home', and implies a sense of permanence. In the last hundred years this has come increasingly under attack from at least three of the defining features of modernity: mobility, which ensures a permanently changing population, who do not necessarily have any prior attachment to the place where they now find themselves; an extreme pace of change in the physical environment, fuelled by consumption, the need for convenience of transport, exploitation of the natural world, the transformation of agriculture from an ancient culture into a business, and increasing urbanisation, all of which results in the familiar scene quickly becoming alien; and the fragmentation of social bonds within communities, for a host of reasons, devastatingly and meticulously captured in a work such as Robert Putnam's *Bowling Alone*, leaving us feeling less and less as if we belong anywhere.[7]

Thus our attachments, the web of relations which give life meaning, all come to be disrupted. Continuities of space and time are related: the loss of sense of place threatens identity, whether personal, or cultural, over time – the sense of a place not just where we were born and will die, but where our forefathers did, and our children's children will. Continuities of time are disrupted as the traditions that embody them are disrupted or discarded, ways of thinking and behaving change no longer gradually and at a pace that the culture can absorb, but radically, rapidly and with the implicit, and at times explicit, aim of erasing the past. And, as Putnam demonstrates, the sense of community – the ultimate attachment, connectedness with one another – also weakens radically.

The changes that characterise modernism, the culture of modernity, then, are far deeper and wider than their manifestation in art. They represent, I believe, a world increasingly dominated by the left hemisphere, and increasingly antagonistic to what the right hemisphere might afford.

In his account of the scientific revolution of the seventeenth century, Toulmin sees a relationship between social, religious and political conflict, on the one hand, and the hungering for certainty that was exhibited in the science and philosophy of the age. Though he makes the perhaps understandable assumption that the first was the cause of the second, he himself cannot avoid noticing evidence that the second was, to a greater extent, the cause of the first. For the previous age of the humanists had been just as wracked by uncertainties in the social sphere, as in religion and politics, but a different attitude towards certainty had prevailed amongst its thinkers and writers. It was the hunger for certainty in the later period, representing in my view a shift towards the left hemisphere's values, priorities and modes of being, that led to a hardening of positions on all sides, to the relative intransigencies of both scientism and the Counter-Reformation, and to conflict.

When we come to the twentieth century, Toulmin identifies, I believe rightly, a still greater demand for certainty:

The ideas of 'strict rationality' modelled on formal logic, and of a universal 'method' for developing new ideas in any field of natural science, were adopted in the 1920s and 1930s with *even greater* enthusiasm, and in an *even more extreme* form, than had been the case in the mid-17th century ... The Vienna Circle program was ... even more formal, exact, and rigorous than those of Descartes or Leibniz. Freed from all irrelevant representation, content, and emotion, the mid-20th-century *avant garde* trumped the 17th-century rationalists in spades.[8]

And here again he makes, *mutatis mutandis*, the same assumption: that the demand for certainty was a response to the unrest in Europe occasioned by Fascism and Stalinism. I rather doubt that. For one thing the intellectual changes can be seen well before the rise of totalitarianism. What if Fascism and Stalinism were facets of the same mental world as modernism, both of them expressions of the deep structure of the left hemisphere's world?

MODERNISM AND THE LEFT HEMISPHERE

I will return to that question in due course. First let's see if there is any more direct evidence of a growing domination of the culture by left-hemisphere ways of conceiving the world. What would we expect to see?

Let me briefly recap. In cases where the right hemisphere is damaged, we see a range of clinically similar problems to those found in schizophrenia. In either group, subjects find it difficult to understand context, and therefore have problems with pragmatics, and with appreciating the 'discourse elements' of communication. They have similar problems in understanding tone, interpreting facial expressions, expressing and interpreting emotion, and understanding the presuppositions that lie behind another's point of view. They have similar problems with *Gestalt* perception and the understanding and grasping of wholes. They have similar problems with intuitive processing, and similar deficits in understanding metaphor. Both exhibit problems with appreciating narrative, and both tend to lose a sense of the natural flow of time, which becomes substituted by a succession of moments of stasis.[9] Both report experiencing the related *Zeitraffer* phenomenon in visual perception (something that can sometimes be seen represented in the art works of schizophrenic subjects). Both appear to have a deficient sense of the reality or substantiality of experience ('it's all play-acting'), as well as of the uniqueness of an event, object or person. Perhaps most significantly they have a similar lack of what might be called common sense. In both there is a loss of the stabilising, coherence-giving, framework-building role that the right hemisphere fulfils in normal individuals. Both exhibit a reduction in pre-attentive processing and an increase in narrowly focussed attention, which is particularistic, over-intellectualising and inappropriately deliberate in approach. Both rely on piecemeal decontextualised analysis, rather than on an intuitive, spontaneous or global mode of apprehension. Both tend to schematise – for example, to scrutinise the behaviour of others, rather as a visitor from another culture might, to discover the 'rules' which explain their behaviour. The living become machine-like: as if to confirm the primacy of the left hemisphere's view of the world, one schizophrenic patient described by Sass reported that 'the world consists of tools, and . . . everything that we glance at has some utilization'.[10] From neuroimaging, too, there is evidence that schizophrenics show abnormal patterns of brain activation, often showing excessive left-hemisphere activation in situations where one would expect more activation of the right hemisphere. This goes across a whole range of activities: for example, even the sense of smell appears to be abnormally lateralised. There is a decrease in expected right-hemisphere activation in limbic connections to the rhinencephalon (smell brain) and right orbitofrontal cortex, and an increase in left hemisphere activity during olfaction.[11] When one considers how critical the sense of smell is for infant–mother bonding, and social bonding of all kinds, and the part it plays in grounding our world in intuition and the body, one appreciates that, tiny as this piece of the jigsaw may be, it is not insignificant.[12] The right hemisphere is not functioning normally, and the left hemisphere takes its place. And, as it happens, drugs that help stabilise schizophrenia act to reduce dopaminergic activity, a form of neurotransmission on which the left hemisphere is dependent to a greater extent than the right.[13]

There are, then, remarkable similarities between individuals with schizophrenia and those whose right hemisphere is not functioning normally. This is hardly surprising since there is a range of evidence suggesting that just such an imbalance in favour of the left hemisphere occurs in schizophrenia.[14] If that is what happens in individuals, could a culture dominated by left-hemisphere modes of apprehension begin to exhibit such features?

Odd as it may sound, there is striking and substantial evidence of precisely that.

MODERNISM AND SCHIZOPHRENIA: THE CORE PHENOMENOLOGY

The influential psychologist Louis Sass has written widely about the culture of modernism, its art, its writings and its philosophy, in connection with the phenomenology of schizophrenia. In *The Paradoxes of Delusion: Wittgenstein, Schreber, and the Schizophrenic Mind*,[15] Sass considers the parallels between the role of detached, introspective observation in philosophy, as discussed by Wittgenstein, and the reports of Daniel Paul Schreber, a provincial German judge who in middle age developed psychotic symptoms which he recorded in his *Memoirs of My Nervous Illness*.[16] The importance of Sass's work is that it demonstrates how the nature of attention alters what it finds; and specifically that when we cease to act, to be involved, spontaneous and intuitive, and instead become passive, disengaged, self-conscious, and stare in an 'objective' fashion at the world around us, it becomes bizarre, alien, frightening – and curiously similar to the mental world of the schizophrenic. Sass explores the idea that 'madness . . . is the end-point of the trajectory [that] consciousness follows when it separates from the body and the passions, and from the social and practical world, and turns in upon itself'.[17] For Sass, as for Wittgenstein, there is a close relation between philosophy and madness. The philosopher's 'predilection for abstraction and alienation – for detachment from body, world and community',[18] can produce a type of seeing and experiencing which is, in a literal sense, pathological.

In Wittgenstein's own words, 'staring is closely bound up with the whole puzzle of solipsism'.[19] Over-awareness itself alienates us from the world and leads to a belief that only we, or our thought processes, are real. If this seems curiously reminiscent of Descartes's finding that the only reliable truth was that his own thought processes guaranteed that he, at least, existed, that is not accidental. The detached, unmoving, unmoved observer feels that the world loses reality, becomes merely 'things seen'. Attention is focussed on the field of consciousness itself, not on the

394 • THE MASTER AND HIS EMISSARY

world beyond, and we seem to experience *experience*. In the *Philosophical Investigations*, Wittgenstein actually notes that when this kind of staring attention takes over, others appear to lack consciousness, to be automata rather than minds (as Descartes had also found). This is a common experience in schizophrenia and a core experience of Schreber's. There is a lack of seeing *through*, to whatever there is beyond.

Engagement reverses this process. Wittgenstein's own 'anti-philosophy' is seen as an attempt to restore sanity to the philosophical mind caught up in the hyperconsciousness of metaphysical thought. He noted that when we act or interact – even, perhaps, if all we do is to walk about in our surroundings rather than sit still and stare at them – we are obliged to reckon with the 'otherness' of things. As Sass puts it, 'the very weight of the object, the resistance it offers to the hand, testify to its existence as something independent of will or consciousness'; moving an object 'confirms one's own experience of activity and efficacy'.[20] One is reminded of Johnson's response to Berkeley's idealism by kicking a stone, and saying: 'I refute it thus.'

In his ground-breaking work *Madness and Modernism*, Sass goes on to draw a multitude of closely argued parallels between the reported experiences of schizophrenics and the world picture of modernism and post-modernism.[21] His purpose is not to pass a value judgment, simply to point out the parallels, in the literature, the visual arts and the critical discourse about art of this era, with every aspect of the core phenomenology of schizophrenia. His argument is compelling and illuminating, but it has a fascinating broader significance. What Sass picks up in modern culture and identifies with schizophrenia may in fact be the over-reliance on the left hemisphere in the West, which I believe has accelerated in the last hundred years. In fact Sass himself discusses this possibility (along with several others) in an appendix called 'Neurobiological Considerations'.

Although the phenomenology of schizophrenia comprises an array of symptoms and experiences, these relate to a group of core disturbances in the relationship between the self and the world. Perhaps the single most important one is what Sass calls hyperconsciousness. Elements of the self and of experience which normally remain, and *need* to remain, intuitive, unconscious, become the objects of a detached, alienating attention; and levels of consciousness multiply, so that there is an awareness of one's own awareness, and so on. The result of this is a sort of paralysis, in which even everyday 'automatic' actions such as moving one leg in front of another in order to walk, can become problematic. 'I am not sure of my own movements any more', says one patient. 'It's very hard to describe this but at times I'm not sure about even simple actions like sitting down. It's not so much thinking out what to do, it's the doing of it that sticks me . . .' Another says: 'People just do things, but I have to watch first to see how you do things . . .' And another: 'I have to do everything step by step, nothing is automatic now. Everything has to be considered . . .'[22] This goes with an inability to trust one's own body or one's intuitions. Everything gets dragged into the full glare of consciousness. Ulrich, the antihero of Robert Musil's novel *The Man Without Qualities*, describes being so aware of 'the leaps that the attention takes, the exertion of the eye-muscles, the pendulum movements of the psyche' occurring at every moment, that just keeping one's body vertical in the street is a tremendous effort. This puts one in mind of the psychologist Chris Frith's identification of the core abnormality in schizophrenia as 'an awareness of automatic processes which are normally carried out below the level of consciousness'.[23]

Associated with this is what Sass calls a loss of 'ipseity', a loss in other words of the pre-reflective, grounding sense of the self.[24] The self has to be constructed 'after the fact' from the products of observation, and its very existence comes into doubt. This gives rise to a reflexivity, whereby attention is focussed on the self and its body, so that parts of the self come to appear alien. There is a loss of the pre-reflective sense of the body as something living and lived, a loss of the immediate physical and emotional experience which grounds us in the world, since bodily states and feelings fall under the spotlight of awareness, and are deprived of their normal compelling immediacy and intimacy. Emotions lose their normal *directedness* towards action, towards other beings, arising from a personal past and directed towards a personal future, in a coherent world of other beings.

There is a veering between two apparently opposite positions which are in reality aspects of the same position: omnipotence and impotence. Either there is no self; or all that the observing eye sees is in fact part of the self, with the corollary that there is no world apart from the self. Whether there is no self, or everything is embraced in the self, the result is the same, since both conditions lack the normal sense we have of ourselves as defined by an awareness that there exists something apart from ourselves. This position is associated, in schizophrenia, with a subjectivisation of experience: a withdrawal from the external world and a turning of attention inward towards a realm of fantasy. The world comes to lack those characteristics – the ultimate *unknowability* of aspects of the world that exceed our grasp, and the recalcitrance of a realm separate from our fantasy – that suggest a reality that exists apart from our will. At the same time, the world and other people in it are objectified, become objects. In a term borrowed from Heidegger, Sass sees an 'unworlding' of the world: a loss of the sense of the overarching context that gives coherence to the world, which becomes fragmented and lacking in meaning.

Although there may be some variations in the terms used, there is little dispute, following the work of Louis Sass, Giovanni Stanghellini, Josef Parnas, Dan Zahavi and others, that these clearly interrelated phenomena – hyperconsciousness, loss of ipseity and 'unworlding' – are fundamental to the experience of subjects with schizophrenia.[25]

THE RELATIONSHIP BETWEEN SCHIZOPHRENIA AND MODERNIST ART

I mentioned the relationship between such experiences and the condition of the introspective philosopher: but, as in the Enlightenment, where increased self-consciousness brought what needed to remain intuitive into the glare of reason, with the result that we all became *philosophes malgré nous*, the relationship between schizophrenia and modern thought goes further than philosophy proper, into the culture at large. Sass identifies the same phenomena that characterise schizophrenia in the culture at large. 'I used to cope with all this internally, but my intellectual parts became the whole of me', says one patient. Compare Kafka, who speaks for the alienated modern consciousness, noting in his diary how introspection 'will suffer no idea to sink tranquilly to rest but must pursue each one into consciousness, only itself to become an idea, in turn to be pursued by renewed introspection'.[26] The process results in a hall of mirrors effect in which the effort at introspection becomes itself objectified. All spontaneity is lost. Disorganisation and fragmentation follow as excessive self-awareness disrupts the coherence of experience. The self-conscious and self-reflexive ponderings of modern intellectual life induce a widely recognisable state of alienated inertia. What is called reality becomes alien and frightening.

The disintegrating stare that Wittgenstein noticed is a characteristic of schizophrenia. 'Persons in the schizophrenia spectrum', writes Sass elsewhere, 'often seem to move in on the stimulus field in the sense of engaging in a kind of fixed, penetrating, over-focused stare that dissolves the more commonly recognised Gestalts in favour of their component parts.'[27] But it is also a feature of modernism, and, for all of us, it has the effect of bringing about wilfully the fragmented world of the left hemisphere. According to Susan Sontag, it is the mode positively invited in the viewer by modernist art. 'Traditional art invites a look', she wrote. '[Modernist art] engenders a stare'.[28] The stare is not known for building bridges with others, or the world at large: instead it suggests alienation, either a need to control, or a feeling of terrified helplessness.

The effect of hyperconsciousness is to produce a flight from the body and from its attendant emotions. Schizophrenics describe an emptying out of meaning – each word 'an envelope emptied of content', as one patient puts it, with thought become so abstract as to attain a sort of ineffable vacuity. They may feel themselves entirely emptied of emotion, except for a pervasive feeling of anxiety or nausea in the face of the sheer existence of things. Bizarre, shocking and painful ideas or actions may be welcomed as a way of trying to relieve this state of numbed isolation. So it is, too, in modernism: Sass compares Antonin Artaud (who himself suffered from schizophrenia): 'I can't even find anything that would correspond to feelings', and suggests that the 'theatre of cruelty', which Artaud originated, was a response to this devitalised condition. 'I wanted a theatre', he told Anaïs Nin, 'that would be like a shock treatment, galvanise, shock people into feeling.'[29] These sentiments are reminiscent of the explanations given by patients who harm themselves, so as to relieve the numbness of no-feeling. The patient etherised upon a table in the opening of 'Prufrock' seems prophetic of the anaesthetised state of modernism, in which everything physical and emotional is cut off.

Sass points to a dehumanisation, a disappearance of the active self, in modernism. There is, in its place, a certain fragmentation and passivisation, a loss of the self's unity and capacity for effective action: either an impersonal subjectivism, such as one finds in Virginia Woolf's *The Waves* – 'subjectivity without a subject', as he puts it; or alternatively the most extreme kind of objectivism, refusing all empathy, stripping the world of value, as in Robbe-Grillet's 'The Secret Room'. This 'story' consists of a series of static descriptions of a woman's corpse. Its cold, clinical detachment expresses better than any purely abstract art the triumph of alienation over natural human feeling, over in fact the body and all that it implies. One could say that the stabbed corpse stands in here for the body in general, and its fate at the hands of modernism. His description of the woman's flesh and bloody wounds in terms of geometry, the fragmented manner and the disruption of time sequence, all contribute to a sense of unreality, despite Robbe-Grillet's manifesto of describing what 'simply *is*'. Being is not so simple.

Robbe-Grillet's story and a number of others are carefully compared by Sass with characteristic schizophrenic discourse. The parallels include lack of a cohesive narrative line, dissolution of character, neglect of conventional space–time structure, loss of comprehensible causal relations, and disruption of the symbol–referent relationship – or, as I would say, the all-important sense of metaphor. Most interestingly schizophrenics emphasise the static, and downplay emotional and dynamic, aspects of the world, evoking a universe more dominated by objects than by processes and actions. This parallels the preferences of the left hemisphere for inanimate things, for stasis, over what is living and evolving.

In modernism the disruption of narrative, with formal devices drawing attention away from the inherent temporality of language, empties human action and intention of the meaning they have in a world to which we respond, and which responds to us. According to Heidegger, 'care' is only possible within temporality, in which we are directed towards our own future, and that of others who share our mortality, a care which is grounded in a coherent past. All of this, coupled with the forcible alienation caused by the bringing into awareness of what is required to remain latent, results in a detachment and irony that are inimical to pathos, a subversive disengagement and spirit of mockery towards life and art. Here is Walter Benjamin:

> The art of storytelling is coming to an end . . . It is as if something that seemed inalienable to us, the securest among our possessions, were taken from us: the ability to exchange experiences. One reason for this phenomenon is obvious: experience has fallen in value. And it looks as if it is continuing to fall into bottomlessness.[30]

If one had to sum up these features of modernism they could probably be reduced to these: an excess of consciousness and an over-explicitness in relation to what needs to remain intuitive and implicit; depersonalisation and alienation from the body and empathic feeling; disruption of context; fragmentation of experience; and the loss of 'betweenness'. Each of these is in fact to some degree implied in each of the others; and there is a simple reason for that. They are aspects of a single world: not just the world of the schizophrenic, but, as may by now be clear, the world according to the left hemisphere.

The problem of an unstable alternation between subjectivism and objectivism that Sass identifies in modernism (either polarity being at odds with a world in which there is still what I call betweenness) is associated with a derealisation and 'unworlding of the world', just as it is in schizophrenia. The world is either robbed of its substantiality, its 'otherness', its ontological status as an entity having any independence from the perceiving subject; or alternatively seen as alien, devoid of human resonance or significance. In either case the ego is passivised. In the one case it is little more than an impotent observer of inner experiences, sensations, images, and so on (derealisation); in the other it is transformed into a machine-like entity in a world of static neutral objects (unworlding). Instead of one consistent inhabited viewpoint, there arises an obvious perspectivism, or relativism, an uncertainty and multiplicity of points of view. This has the effect of either, on the one hand, drawing attention to the presence of a particular perspective, thereby displaying a recognition of its limitedness, or alternatively attempting to transcend such limits by inhabiting a variety of perspectives. This goes with the belief that there is no true world, because everything is, as Nietzsche famously said, but 'a perspectival appearance whose origin lies in us'.[31] Though this is something Nietzsche recognised in the modern mind, he did not welcome it: in fact he dreaded its consequences, speaking of that 'great blood-sucker, the spider scepticism' and warning that our excessive self-consciousness will destroy us.[32] We are the 'Don Juans of cognition', he said, whose 'knowledge will take its revenge on us, as ignorance exacted its revenge in the Middle Ages.'[33]

There is what Sass calls an aesthetic self-referentiality in modernism, the work of art become 'a form of drama in which consciousness watches itself in action' (Valéry);[34] either emptying itself of external attachments or representational content, so that the formal elements become themselves the content; or exploiting representational or narrative conventions self-consciously and without context, so that they themselves become the focus of the work. In other words there is a shift of the plane of attention to the surface, whether of the canvas – Greenberg's famous 'flatness' of modernist painting – or of the written medium, to the mechanics of the process of creation, as in the *Verfremdungseffekt*, in which we no longer suspend our disbelief, but have disbelief thrust upon us. (Schizophrenics experience, precisely, a loss of visual depth. One patient describes the external world as 'like a two-dimensional transparency, something like an architect's drawing or plan'.) Attention is focussed on the medium, not on the world beyond that medium, which is effectively denied. The self-reflexive tropes of postmodernist literature and criticism concentrate attention on language, and undercut the possibility of existence beyond language. As Erich Heller says of Nietzsche's portrait of the 'last philosopher': 'Nothing speaks to him any more – except his own speech; and, deprived of any authority from a divinely ordered universe, it is only about speech that his speech can speak with a measure of philosophical assurance.'[35]

SELF-REFERENTIALITY AND THE LOSS OF MEANING

Ultimately there is nothing less than an emptying out of meaning. The influential contemporary neuroscientist Michael Gazzaniga has referred to the left hemisphere as 'the interpreter', the locus of self-consciousness, of conscious volition, and of rationality, which since the Enlightenment we have seen as being our defining qualities as human beings.[36] An interpreter is not an originator, however, but a facilitator, and should be involved in mediating *between* parties. The more we rely on the left hemisphere alone, the more self-conscious we become; the intuitive, unconscious unspoken elements of experience are relatively discounted, and the interpreter begins to interpret – itself. The world it puts into words for us is the world that words themselves (the left hemisphere's building blocks) have created. Hence there is Nietzsche's 'speech about speech'. The condition is a lonely, self-enwrapped one: 'nothing speaks to him any more'. The left hemisphere, isolating itself from the ways of the right hemisphere, has lost access to the world beyond words, the world 'beyond' our selves. It is not just that it no longer sees through the two-dimensional surface of the canvas to the world behind, through the window to the world beyond the pane, focussing instead on the plane before its eyes: it no longer sees through the representation of the world that is left hemisphere 'experience' at all, to a world that is 'Other' than itself. Man himself keeps getting into the picture, as Heidegger says of the modern era.

The interpreter's task is to look for meaning. But that meaning can only come to the representational world by allowing a betweenness with the world it represents – as words need their real world referents to have meaning. Constantly searching for meaning, but not finding any, it is oppressed, as the schizophrenic is oppressed, by an unresolved and irresoluble sense of meaningfulness without a focus, a sense that '*something* is going on'. Everything, just as it is, seems to have meaning, but what it is is never clear. The more one stares at things the more one freights them with import. That man crossing his legs, that woman wearing that blouse – it can't just be accidental. It has a particular meaning, is intended to convey something; but I am not let in on the secret, which every one else seems to understand. Notice that the focus of paranoia is a loss of the normal betweenness – something that should be being conveyed from others to myself, is being kept from me. The world comes to appear threatening, disturbing, sinister. When implicit meaning is not understood, as Wittgenstein surmised, paranoia is the result: 'Mightn't we imagine a man who, never having had any acquaintance with music, comes to us and hears someone playing a reflective piece of Chopin and is convinced that this is a language and people merely want to keep the meaning secret from him?'[37]

It may seem paradoxical that the other thing that happens when one is fixated by aspects of the environment and stares at them is precisely the opposite of this freighting with an excessive sense of meaning: they lose meaning completely. They lose their place in the order of things, which gives them their meaning, and become alien. The stare can either freight something with meaning or empty it completely of meaning, but these are not as opposed as they seem: cut loose from the context that would normally give things their meaning implicitly – no longer having 'resonance' for us – they mean everything or nothing, whatever we care to put on them, rather as the subject has to be either omnipotent or impotent. In an

early scene in his novel *La Noia* (translated into English as *Boredom*), Alberto
Moravia describes staring at a tumbler till it no longer seems to have a purpose or
a context, is no longer something with which, as he says, 'I feel I have some sort
of relationship', and becomes

> an absurd object – then from that very absurdity springs boredom . . . Boredom to
> me consists in a kind of insufficiency, or inadequacy or lack of reality . . . yet again
> boredom might be described as a malady affecting external objects and consisting
> of a withering process; an almost instantaneous loss of vitality . . . The feeling of
> boredom originates for me in a sense of the absurdity of a reality which is insuffi-
> cient, or anyhow unable, to convince me of its own effective existence . . .[38]

Devitalisation leads to boredom, and boredom, in turn, to sensationalism. The
high stimulus society in which we live is represented through advertising as full
of vibrancy and vitality, but, as advertisers know only too well, its condition is one
of boredom, and the response to boredom. Since the rise of capitalism in the
eighteenth century, when according to Patricia Spacks boredom as such began, an
'appetite for the new and the different, for fresh experience and novel excitements'
has lain at the heart of successful bourgeois society, with its need above all to
be getting and spending money.[39] Use of the word 'boredom' and reports of the
experience have escalated dramatically during the twentieth century.[40] It has
infested the places of desire and further saps vitality: by 1990, 23 per cent of French
men and 31 per cent of French women already reported being bored while making
love – '*l'atrophie du désir*.'[41] There is a vicious cycle between feelings of boredom,
emptiness and restlessness, on the one hand, and gross stimulation and sensationalism on the other: in fact Wordsworth makes the point in the Preface to *Lyrical
Ballads*. So Anton van Zijderveld, in his excellent study of cliché, notes that 'it can
be observed that speech becomes gross and hyperbolic, music loud and nervous,
ideas giddy and fantastic, emotions limitless and shameless, actions bizarre and
foolish, whenever boredom reigns.'[42] Modernist art from Dadaism to the present
day has its share of artworks that illustrate Zijderveld's point. Scheler speaks of our
' "culture" of entertainment' as a collection of 'extremely merry things, viewed by
extremely sad people who do not know what to do with them.'[43] Zijderveld
connects the phenomenon with advertising and the exigencies of a mass market.
Of course he is right. But like Scheler I would prefer to see a little beyond such
formulations in socioeconomic terms, valid as they clearly are in their own way.

I would relate both the boredom and sense of devitalisation, and the associated
demand for stimulation, to the needs of an 'unplugged' left hemisphere.[44]
Disconnected from the grounding effects of the right hemisphere, which could lead
it out of itself and back to what I have called 'the Other', it can find nothing except
what it already knows. Newness would come from the imagination, which recon-
nects us with whatever it is that exists apart from ourselves: all that is open to the
left hemisphere acting alone is novelty (*The Shock of the New* should really have
been entitled, were it not ambiguous, *The Shock of the Novel*). Crude sensationalism

is its stock in trade. The left hemisphere, with its orientation towards what is life-less and mechanical, appears desperate to shock us back to life, as if animating Frankenstein's corpse. When the Austrian experimental artist Hermann Nitsch crucifies a dead lamb, he reminds us that he is flogging a dead horse.

In Erich Fromm's study *On Disobedience*, he describes modern man as *homo consumens*: concerned with things more than people, property more than life, capital more than work. He sees this man as obsessed with the structures of things, and calls him 'organisation man', flourishing, if that is the right word, as much under the bureaucracy of communism as under capitalism. There is a close rela-tionship between the mentality that results in bureaucratic organisation and the mentality of capitalism. Socialism and capitalism are both essentially materialist, just different ways of approaching the lifeless world of matter and deciding how to share the spoils. To that extent one might say that their antipathy represents little more than a farmyard scrap between two dogs over a bone. These preferences – for things more than people, status or property more than life, and so on – align with those of the left hemisphere, and what I want to explore here is the close rela-tion between a concern for materiality and a simultaneous impulse towards abstraction.

REPRESENTATION: WHEN THINGS ARE REPLACED BY CONCEPTS,
AND CONCEPTS BECOME THINGS

Once we can no longer hold together what the left hemisphere calls – because it separates them – spirit and matter, things become simultaneously more abstract and more purely 'thing-like': the Cartesian divorce. If one thinks about an arche-typal piece of modernist art, such as Duchamp's urinal, or Carl André's pile of bricks, one is struck by the fact that as a work of art each is at the same time unusually concrete and unusually abstract. The realms just do not cohere, or, as in what I would call a true work of art, interpenetrate. Again one is reminded of schizophrenia. Asked to describe what a Rorschach blot resembles, a schizo-phrenic patient may either describe the literal characteristics of the blot – the very disposition and quality of the strokes on the page – or declare that it represents some vague concept such as 'motherhood', or 'democracy'.[45]

That the left hemisphere is concerned with abstraction has been a theme of the first part of the book, but it also has a preference for inanimate *things*, particularly as they have *use* for us. There is no paradox involved: materialists, as I suggested earlier, are not people who overvalue, but who undervalue, matter. They see it only under Scheler's lowest realm of value: that of utility and sensation. The abstraction is reified, the concept becomes a thing 'out there'. The world in our time has *become* a 'world picture', according to Heidegger: not a new world picture, but rather 'the fact that the world becomes picture at all is what distin-guishes the essence of the modern age'.[46]

In his book *The Philosopher's Gaze: Modernity in the Shadows of the Enlightenment* the philosopher D. M. Levin writes that re-presentation, the left hemisphere's role, is the characteristic state of modernity. The process of re-presenting a thing not only distances us from it, and substitutes an abstraction, a token, for the thing itself; it also objectifies, and reifies it, so as to bring it under control. What 'presences' is not accepted *as* it presences, but, he writes,

> subjected to a certain delay, a certain postponement, a certain deferral, so that the ego-logical subject can give what is presencing *to itself*, can, in other words, make *itself* the giver of what it receives. In this way, the subject exercises maximum epistemic control. We might say that the emblem of such an attitude – the correlate in the realm of vision – is the stare.[47]

As he points out, even worse is that

> the final ironic twist in the logic of this process of objectification is that it escapes our control, and we ourselves become its victims, simultaneously reduced to the being-available of mere objects and reduced to the being of a purely inner subjectivity that is no longer recognised as enjoying any truth, any reality.[48]

Levin's point that this enables the mind actually to believe that it creates the world and then gives the world to itself, is a perfect formulation of the process whereby the left hemisphere, interposes a simulacrum between reality and our consciousness – like *trompe l'oeil* shutters in front of a window, bearing an exact replica of the view – and then interprets its own creation as the reality. This nightmare of claustrophobia is taken further by Magritte, who painted many pictures designed precisely to dislocate our intuitive sense of the relationship between the representation and the thing represented. In his painting of 1963, *La lunette d'approche* (see Plate 14), the view, from a partly open window, of sea, sky and clouds, appears to be on the surface of the glass, and beyond the open window is just an empty blackness (on closer inspection the upper right-hand window reveals that the representation is actually becoming the reality).

The whole process is reminiscent of the wonderful image of Borges and Casares, in their short story 'On Exactitude in Science', of a vast map, 1:1 scale, that is exactly co-extensive with the terrain it 'covers', both metaphorically and literally.[49] The piece builds on an idea of Lewis Carroll's in *Sylvie and Bruno Concluded*, where a map is referred to as having 'the scale of a mile to the mile'. As one of Carroll's characters remarks, noting some practical difficulties with this map, 'we now use the country itself, as its own map, and I assure you it does nearly as well.'

The normal relationship of reality to representation has been reversed. At the beginning of this book, I summarised the left hemisphere's role as providing a map of the world. That map now threatens to replace the reality.

My contention is that the modern world is the attempt by the left hemisphere to take control of everything it knows so that it is the giver to itself of what it sees. If it is Gazzaniga's interpreter, it is, finally and self-referentially, its *own* interpreter (a role hitherto, according to William Cowper, reserved for God).

Ultimately this process of re-presentation affects our sense of our own identity. Again Borges, much of whose writing in one form or another unknowingly explores the relationship between the worlds of the two hemispheres, has the measure of it:

> The other one, the one called Borges, is the one things happen to. I walk through the streets of Buenos Aires and stop for a moment, perhaps mechanically now, to look at the arch of an entrance hall and the grillwork on the gate; I know of Borges from the mail and see his name on a list of professors or in a biographical dictionary. I like hourglasses, maps, eighteenth-century typography, the taste of coffee and the prose of Stevenson; he shares these preferences, but in a vain way that turns them into the attributes of an actor . . . Besides I am destined to perish, definitively, and only some instant of myself can survive in him. Little by little, I am giving over everything to him, though I am quite aware of his perverse custom of falsifying and magnifying things. Spinoza knew that all things long to persist in their being; the stone eternally wants to be a stone and the tiger a tiger . . . Years ago I tried to free myself from him and went from the mythologies of the suburbs to the games with time and infinity, but those games belong to Borges now and I shall have to imagine other things. Thus my life is a flight and I lose everything and everything belongs to oblivion, or to him.
>
> I do not know which of us has written this page.[50]

Boredom and anxiety are different manifestations of the same underlying condition.[51] Kafka said that his deepest feelings towards other people were indifference and fear. According to Elias Canetti, that makes him a representative modern man.[52] One might think that this had much to do with Kafka's particular character, and there is no doubt that Kafka had a somewhat schizoid personality – such personalities lack warmth, find it difficult to engage with the world or other people, and tend to combine indifference with a state of chronic anxiety. In fact a remarkable number of the leading figures of modernism displayed schizoid or schizotypal features: Nietzsche, de Nerval, Jarry, Strindberg, De Chirico, Dali, Wittgenstein, Kafka, Bartok, Stravinsky, Webern, Stockhausen and Beckett are just a few that spring to mind. (By contrast a remarkable number of Romantic artists – and indeed artists of all times other than the modern – exhibited the contrasting features of affective conditions such as melancholia or bipolar (manic-depressive) disorder.)[53] Canetti's point, however, is that Kafka's indifference and fear are part of the modern condition. Fromm describes modern man as lonely, bored, anxious and passive.[54] This combination of anxiety or fear with boredom and indifference is also remarkably like the emotional range of the schizophrenic subject, where apathy and indifference are varied mainly by paranoia. Both schizophrenia and the modern condition, I suggest, deal with the same problem: a freewheeling left hemisphere.

RISE IN ILLNESSES CHARACTERISED BY RIGHT-HEMISPHERE DEFICITS

One line of thought suggests that, if there is a shift in the way we, as a culture, look at the world – a change in the mental world that we all share, reinforced by constant cues from the environment, whether intellectual, social or material – that might make the expression of psychopathological syndromes that also involve such shifts more common. Put simply, if a culture starts to mimic aspects of right-hemisphere deficit, those individuals who have an underlying propensity to over-reliance on the left hemisphere will be less prompted to redress it, and moreover will find it harder to do so. The tendency will therefore be enhanced. Though we need to be cautious in how we interpret the evidence, it is nonetheless a matter of interest that schizophrenia has in fact increased in tandem with industrialisation and modernity.

In England schizophrenia was rare indeed, if it existed at all, before the eighteenth century, but increased dramatically in prevalence with industrialisation.[55] Similar trends can be observed in Ireland, Italy, the United States, and elsewhere.[56] However, even at the end of the nineteenth century schizophrenia appears to have been relatively rare compared with the first half of the twentieth century, when it steeply increased.[57] There are, however, very considerable problems involved in studies of the prevalence of schizophrenia,[58] and for methodological reasons, it is not clear whether the rates of schizophrenia are at present continuing to rise, or have reached a plateau, or are maybe even falling – on that point, studies can be found to support almost any conclusion. What is beyond reasonable doubt, however, since it has been established by repeated research over at least half a century, is that schizophrenia increased *pari passu* with industrialisation; that the form in which schizophrenia exists is more severe and has a clearly worse outcome in Western countries; and that, as recent research confirms, prevalence by country increases in proportion to the degree that the country is 'developed', which in practice means Westernised.[59] Descriptions of melancholia, or of manic-depressive (now called bipolar) disorder, are immediately recognisable in accounts from ancient Egypt, Greece and Rome, yet there are no descriptions of schizophrenia.

That it may be reinforced or promoted by the nature of the environment in the broadest sense – both physical and psycho-social – would appear to be confirmed by research. After controlling for all confounding factors, mental health is better in rural than non-rural populations and deteriorates in tandem with population density.[60] City dwelling is associated with higher rates of depression, certainly, but even more with schizophrenia, in the genesis, or expression, of which it is the most potent environmental factor.[61] The relative risk of developing schizophrenia in an urban rather than a rural setting is nearly double, and the evidence suggests that it is more likely that the urban environment causes psychosis than that high-risk individuals migrate to urban areas.[62] The concept of 'social defeat' has been developed as an explanation of the high levels of schizophrenia in immigrant populations, particularly those from the West Indies into Britain.[63] It is acknowledged that urban environments are more competitive. This is in part a reflection of capitalist culture, which is always most strongly expressed in cities for a host of obvious reasons. It is also because the kind of social order that would have valued an individual for anything other than their earning power has been lost. It's a culture, if that is still the right word for it, of 'winners' and 'losers'.

If I am right in detecting that the left hemisphere world has come to predominate, with that of the right hemisphere receding in importance, other illnesses reflecting such an imbalance might also have become more prevalent. Have they?

Anorexia nervosa is by its nature an attack on the flesh, on embodied being – and it increased in prevalence during the twentieth century. Looking for explanations in terms of the social environment, it has been attributed in the popular press to the emphasis on the glamour of thinness. While this may have played a part in triggering episodes of illness in some cases (more typically in bulimia nervosa), this misconstrues the nature of the illness. Cases of what is called 'holy anorexia' can be traced for centuries, although not with the frequency we see now, a classic example being that of St Catherine of Siena; and the drive in such cases appears to be a desire for purification, and mortification of the flesh. Although anorexia is increasing rapidly in South Africa, it is still rare in contemporary West Africa, though even there cases exist. When subjects in such a context are asked to explain their motivation, they attribute their anorexia to a spiritual desire for purification and atonement, meaning abjuration of the flesh.[64] Contemporary sufferers in the West often speak in similar terms, though not usually using overtly religious language: they speak of purification, a hatred of the body, a desire ultimately to 'disappear'. The body image, dependent on the right parietal lobe is grossly distorted, to a psychotic degree, so that patients on the point of death through starvation may still see themselves as fat. Often the sense of the self – who one is at all – is lost. Anorexia is also in many cases associated with other forms of deliberate self-harm, such as cutting or burning, a condition which is also on the increase in the West, and is the most blatant form of attack on the body. Both anorexia and episodes of self-harm are used to numb feelings, although sometimes self-harm can be used to recall the sense of being alive at all, the experience of *something* in the body, in a state of otherwise total dissociation from feelings and from physical existence.

We would expect, on the basis of the psychopathology, with its distortions of body image, deliberate attacks on the body through starvation and other methods, loss of self-identity, numbing of feelings, desire for perfection, and need to be delivered from the contradictions and ambiguities of embodied existence, that this condition should be associated with over-reliance on the left hemisphere at the expense of the right. And this is exactly what research suggests – not just imaging and EEG studies, but lesion studies, and tests of cognitive function.[65] Particularly striking is the case of a patient with a long history of anorexia nervosa who had a total and virtually instantaneous recovery after a left-hemisphere stroke affecting motor and sensory function of the right side of her body. Prior to the stroke, she wrote, 'anorexia controlled my life and influenced things which I did or did not do . . . relationships – lost interest in them. Only interested in anorexia.' After the stroke she reported that 'I have no feelings of guilt. I no longer count calories. I am relaxed about eating/around food. I can eat out in restaurants now.'[66]

Multiple personality disorder is another dissociative disorder, which has features of hypnotic suggestibility. It is also a characteristically modern condition, hitting popular consciousness in the 1950s, and first incorporated into DSM (the Diagnostic and Statistical Manual of Mental Disorders) in 1980, although a small number of case reports of so-called 'double personality' aroused a good deal of interest in the late nineteenth century.[67] It also clearly involves, albeit unconsciously, the most blatant abdication of responsibility ('it wasn't me – it was my other half!'). This too is likely to be a right-hemisphere-deficit syndrome. Ramachandran describes a patient with a right-hemisphere stroke who was 'halfway between anosognosia [denial of disability, which we have seen is a left-hemisphere speciality] and multiple personality disorder syndrome' as a result of two lesions, one affecting the right frontal lobe and the other the right cingulate.[69] EEG studies support the idea of right-hemisphere dysfunction coupled with relative left hemisphere overactivation in multiple personality disorder.[69] Left-hemisphere hyperactivation fits with the fact that multiple personality disordered patients exhibit first-rank symptoms of schizophrenia, and describe being the passive victims of a controlling force, since schizophrenia is another condition in which there is a failure to integrate left-hemisphere and right-hemisphere processes, with a dysfunctional right hemisphere and an overactive left hemisphere, giving rise to the sense of alien control.[70] Although examination of epileptic patients with two distinct personalities has led to the suggestion that multiple personalities might represent the differing personalities of the two hemispheres, this model clearly cannot account for the majority of patients who have not just dual, but literally 'multiple' personalities, in some cases over a hundred.[71] They must be able to dissociate a multitude of different parts within the fragmented 'whole' of their selfhood – a process which by its nature suggests a key role for the left hemisphere.

Anorexia nervosa, multiple personality disorder and deliberate self-harm are linked by 'dissociation': there is a sense of being cut off – and often a craving to be cut off – from one's feelings, and from embodied existence, a loss of depth of emotion and capacity for empathy, a fragmentation of the sense of self; and these features also characterise what is known as 'borderline' personality disorder. Once again, this may be a condition whose prevalence is increasing. Though it is possible in retrospect to see elements of the clinical picture in descriptions of behaviour going back to ancient Greece, the condition was first described only in 1938.[72] Yet it has grown in the space of 70 years to become 'certainly one of the commonest psychiatric diagnoses'.[73] Here too there is evidence of right-hemisphere dysfunction, with many regions of the right hemisphere appearing underactive.[74] There is even evidence of alterations in structural brain asymmetry in borderline personality disorder, with strong leftward deviations in the parietal region, especially marked in those who demonstrate clear dissociative states.[75]

Then there is autism, a condition which has hugely advanced in prevalence during the last fifty years. While it may be that some of the rise is due to greater awareness of the condition, it is unlikely that this explains the very large increase. Autism, and Asperger's syndrome, which is often thought of as a type of high-functioning autism, were first described in 1943 and 1944 respectively. The research was quite independent, despite the temporal proximity: Asperger was not aware of Kanner's paper, describing the first case histories of classic autism, when he wrote his own. Since that time rates have steadily climbed, and continue to climb. Again, both these conditions are marked by clinical features strongly suggestive of right-hemisphere hypofunction, and the resulting picture is one of left-hemisphere dominance. There is in autism an inability to tell what another is thinking (lack of 'theory of mind'); a lack of social intelligence – difficulty in judging nonverbal features of communication, such as tone, humour, irony; an inability to detect deceit, and difficulty understanding implicit meaning; a lack of empathy; a lack of imagination; an attraction to the mechanical; a tendency to treat people and body parts as inanimate objects; an alienation from the self (autistic children often fail to develop the first-person perspective and speak of themselves as 'he' or 'she'); an inability to engage in eye contact or mutually directed gaze; and an obsession with detail.[76] All these features will be recognisable as signs of left hemisphere predominance.

I am not, of course, suggesting that the deficits at the neurological level, in any of these conditions, including schizophrenia, are confined to the right hemisphere only, or that the pattern of right hemisphere deficits in each condition is the same – manifestly it is not. One of the many factors that might modulate the clinical picture would be which areas of the right hemisphere were functioning abnormally, and in what way, as well as precisely what is happening in the left hemisphere at the same time: the brain is a dynamic system, and change in any one place causes changes elsewhere. But if we look at the clinical picture in each of these conditions and ask ourselves which aspects of the phenomenological world of the sufferer are distorted or absent, and in what way, and correlate that with the findings at the neurological level, I believe the deficits reveal a repeated pattern of hypofunction of the normal right hemisphere, and an exaggerated reliance on the provisions of the left.

THE SELF-PERPETUATING NATURE OF THE LEFT HEMISPHERE WORLD

The development of mass technological culture, urbanisation, mechanisation and alienation from the natural world, coupled with the erosion of smaller social units and an unprecedented increase in mobility, have increased mental illness, at the same time that they have made the 'loner' or outsider the representative of the modernist era. His apprehension of life has become fragmentary, and the welter of disparate information and surrogate experiences, taken out of context, with which we are deluged intensifies the sense of fragmentation. Increasing virtuality and distance from other human lives tends to induce a feeling of an alien, perhaps hostile environment. Social isolation leads to exaggerated fear responses, violence and aggression,[77] and violence and aggression often lead, in turn, to isolation. Structures which used to provide the context from which life derived its meaning have been powerfully eroded, and 'seepage' from one context into another produces bizarre, sometimes surreal, juxtapositions which alter the nature of our attention to them, facilitating irony, distance and cynicism at the expense of empathy. In this way the experience of life in the twentieth and twenty-first centuries reproduces many of the experiences until now confined to schizophrenics. At the same time people with schizoid or schizotypal traits will be attracted to, and be deemed especially suitable for, employment in the areas of science, technology and administration which have, during the last hundred years, been immensely influential in shaping the world we live in, and are, if anything, even more important today.

Thus a culture with prominent 'schizoid' characteristics attracts to positions of influence individuals who will help it ever further down the same path. And the increasing domination of life by both technology and bureaucracy helps to erode the more integrative modes of attention to people and things which might help us to resist the advances of technology and bureaucracy, much as they erode the social and cultural structures that would have facilitated other ways of being, so that in this way they aid their own replication.

THE PROBLEM OF ART IN THE MODERN WORLD

I commented at the beginning of this chapter that the disjunction between modernism and what preceded it was not as great as it seemed. The movement known as Aestheticism which emerged at the end of the nineteenth century has been seen as the last flowering of Romanticism. By now effete and etiolated, Romanticism, it is believed, finally expired, to be replaced by the counter-Romantic distancing ironies of Absurdism and the Dadaist movement, and by the beginnings of modernism in Russia and France. The idea suggests a revolution: a time-expired idea or set of ideas embodied in a culture is overthrown by the new more vigorous growth of an opposing movement. I suggested that this was not the case in the Reformation, the Enlightenment or the Romantic 'Revolution', but that instead in each case there was not a discontinuity, but a continuity, whereby a slippage occurred in the balance between the hemispheres.

Aestheticism was an extension of the self-consciousness of Victorian art, and a precursor of the self-consciousness of modernism. It conceptualised 'the Imaginative', as the Enlightenment had cultivated 'Phansie', in the place of imagination. The left hemisphere 'creates' newness by recombining in a novel fashion what is already known, not as imagination does, by allowing something that we thought we knew to be truly revealed for the first time. It is like those children's books with pages split into three, in which you can invent a new animal by putting together the head of a camel, the body of a seal and the legs of a goat. It produced, by the reliable contrivances of inversion or random juxtaposition, the novelty of the artificial, the bizarre, the unnatural and the obscurely menacing: Gerard de Nerval, with his green hair, taking a lobster for a walk on a string; the perverse self-indulgent world of Huysman's *À Rebours* ('Against Nature'); or de Lautréamont in *Les Chants de Maldoror* (from '*mal d'aurore*', an 'evil dawn') speaking of the 'chance encounter of a sewing-machine and an umbrella on a dissecting-table'.

The Aesthetes' creed of 'art for art's sake', while it sounds like an elevation of the value of art, in that it denies that it should have an ulterior purpose beyond itself – so far, so good – is also a devaluation of art, in that it marginalises its relationship with life. In other words it sacrifices the betweenness of art with life, instead allowing art to become self-reflexively fulfilled. There is a difference between the forlorn business of creating 'art for art's sake', and art nonetheless having to be judged solely 'as art', not as for another purpose. In the process of creation, the artist's plane of focus needs to be somewhere beyond and through the work of art, not just on its being art, otherwise it becomes less than art. In viewing the art work, we too are carried beyond the work of art, precisely because the artist was not focussed on the art as such, but in something beyond it; and that is part of its greatness, by which, as it might seem paradoxically, we come to judge the work of art solely on its merits as a work of art – not, in other words, for some ulterior purpose for which art is being *used*. We come to see not the work of art, but the *world according to the art work*, as Merleau-Ponty says, necessitating that it is neither opaque nor wholly transparent, but 'semi-transparent'. To take a couple of examples: Duccio, in painting a Madonna and Child, was not producing 'art for art's sake'; nor was Degas, in painting *L'Absinthe*, his famous portrait of absinthe drinkers in a Paris café. If either had focussed on the plane of the wooden panel, or the canvas, itself, and the 'pure' business of aesthetics, they could not have produced the great works these represent. Duccio was taken up in the spirit of devotion to his divine subject; Degas in the pity of the human scene before him. Yet one need not share Duccio's religious beliefs to appreciate the work of art; and indeed seen as a 'work of art', rather than as an object of devotion, those beliefs become certainly not irrelevant, but secondary. The work could have been the product of sincere piety, or alternatively of pure aesthetic manipulation, and yet a poor work of art. Similarly, the social commentary in *L'Absinthe* is scarcely irrelevant, but cannot itself form the basis of a judgment on its artistic worth. It seems that while works cannot be *created* for art's sake, they must be *judged* for art's sake, not for some ulterior purpose. The plane of the focus of attention for the creator and the viewer are different; we are allowed to regard artists and their work in a way that they must not regard themselves. Put that way it is not that different from any human relationship: I might regard Mother Teresa in a way that would worry me if I believed it was also the way she saw herself.

As, with the advance of modernism, art became ever more self-conscious, it encountered further problems. Alienation, fragmentation, decontextualisation: the defining features of the modern world were as problematic for art as they were for society, since art, like society, derives its meaning and power from connection, cohesion, context. The predicament of art in the modern period could be said to be how to respond to this challenge. And its problem is made more intractable by a different sort of deracination – more than just the severance from place, or even from history, but the inevitably consequent severance from the roots of all meaning in shared values and experiences, the vast implicit realm from which imagination draws its power. Once this rupture has occurred, it can no more be remedied by a conscious effort of the will than a flower plucked from the plant can be made to grow again by being stuck back on the stalk.

Many artists saw that the modern world was fragmented, incoherent, decontextualised and alien, a world where the implicit and intuitive had been lost. But art itself cannot succeed if it too is fragmented, incoherent, decontextualised and alien, nor if it becomes explicit and discursive – if it becomes *about* its own plight. I have argued that a work of art is more like a living being than a thing. That our encounter with that being matters and means something depends on the fact that any living being is in itself whole and coherent, and forms part of a larger context in which we too are involved and engaged. If it is itself experienced as fragmented, incoherent, decontextualised and alien it ceases to live. It also becomes merely opaque – the eye rests on the wrong plane, the plane of the work itself, rather than passing through it. The work of art no longer succeeds in letting us see the world anew, as Merleau-Ponty had suggested, but obtrudes itself as the focus of our attention.

In response to this dilemma modernist art has tended to diverge. The reaction of one influential strand to the experience of a world as seen by the left hemisphere was to adopt the features of that world in the work itself. By doing so it constantly risked, and only by chance at times evaded, triviality. It became itself recruited to the left hemisphere's campaign. Others (and I believe they have been the minority, at least in the visual arts and music), including artists as various as Egon Schiele, Marc Chagall, and Stanley Spencer, have grappled with this conundrum and been impelled to truly imaginative, intuitive solutions, creating often idiosyncratic works of great power. Many great artists such as Picasso or Matisse, Stravinsky or Schoenberg, move uneasily between these positions, at times their intuitions leading them (as happened with great artists in the age of the Enlightenment) gloriously to sweep away the precepts of modernism itself.

Few artists of the period have escaped the problem entirely; many have not escaped it at all. But this fact is carefully obscured, I believe, by two tendencies in the criticism of modernism (themselves both modernist tendencies). The first is a willingness to accept an explicit manifesto or message (again, as in the Enlightenment) as a substitute for imaginative experience: this is often an apparently coded message, which thereby flatters the decoder. We seem to see art, where we have nothing more than a text. The other tendency complements it: in the *absence* of a message we tend to 'stare' at it *until it is freighted with meaning*. It's rather like the projections we make into a Rorschach blot. We mistake our lonely monologue for a dialogue. Tristan Tzara, one of the founders of Dadaism, rather gave the game away when he proclaimed, at the outset of modernism, that art had become 'a private affair – the artist produces it for himself', and judgment had become completely subjective.[78]

The field of modernism is vast: the term has been applied to a bewildering array of different groups, cliques, and movements within poetry, the novel, drama, cinema, the visual arts, architecture, and music, and it has been applied to politics and sociology. There are common features, however. One might start by considering the self-conscious vision of itself as modern, in the sense not of building on the past while taking it in a new direction, but of sweeping it away altogether. Its inception was therefore marked by a series of explicit manifestos demanding a grand new beginning that involved destruction of what had gone before, and a breaking of the mould as an end in itself. There was a sense that man, too, was capable of being refashioned by a transformation of society and art according to a theoretical ideal, refashioned in a new image. There was a glorification of the power of science and technology, an exultation – as in the Enlightenment, but more shrill – at the triumph of man over nature, now assured by industrial might. An unfaltering belief in the future complemented an uncompromising scorn for the past. Above all there was a belief – more than that, an intoxicating self-excitement – in the sheer power of the human will, in our power to shape our destiny. It is not, I think, by accident that the age of modernism also saw the rise of totalitarian ideologies in Russia, Germany and Italy.

Nazism is 'the very epitome of the modern', writes the historian of modernism, Modris Eksteins; 'the modernism of Nazism was unmistakable ... political extremism was in lockstep in the modern era with cultural adventurism.' He notes that the close ties between Marinetti's Futurism and Mussolini's Fascism have never been doubted; and, he goes on, there is a fascination with the unleashing of demonic power, the 'uncompromising shredding of the past'.[79] Cultural Revolution and totalitarianism are spiritual allies.

The 'profound kinship' between modernism and fascism is explored at length, and with tact and subtlety, by Roger Griffin in his book *Modernism and Fascism*.[80] 'War is the world's only hygiene,'[81] declared the Futurists. The resonances there are unfortunate, but not, I think, insignificant. An admiration for what is powerful rather than beautiful, a sense of alienated objectivity rather than engagement or empathy, and an almost dogmatic trampling on all taboos, lies at the heart of the modernist enterprise. The Futurists espoused a culture of youth and violence: 'we want no part of it, the past,' they cried. Their call for a novelty 'however daring, however violent',[82] sits uneasily close to the pervasive modernist (and post-modernist) concern, from its very inception to the present day, with a strangeness sometimes bordering on the perverse, and a fascination with the amoral restless-ness of modern urban life. One might not want to go as far as Paul Virilio does, when he makes the direct connection between the German Expressionists (who did call for murder) and Ilse Koch, the 'Bitch of Buchenwald', who turned pris-oners skins into *art brut* (the Russian poet Mayakovsky also called for skulls to be turned into ashtrays). Not all modernist art, clearly, leads to the bloodbaths of Hermann Nitsch or the mutilations of Rudolf Schwarzkogler. But one can surely agree with Virilio that the unanchored re-presentation of reality as art, however dislocated or disturbing – an extension of the aesthetic creed, art for art's sake – which is endemic in modernism is part of a much more profound failure of compassion and an erosion of pity.[83] Pity may in fact be the only taboo left for modernism, after what Ortega called the 'ban on all pathos' in modern art.[84]

At the same time, obviously and worryingly, totalitarian movements have had none of the characteristics that would lend themselves to making good art. If there is anything in the idea that modernist art partakes of the same nature as Leninism, Fascism or Stalinism there is clearly a difficulty here. Lenin is reported to have said: 'I'm no good at art, art for me is something like an intellectual appendix. And when its use as propaganda, which we need at the moment, is over, we shall cut it out, as useless – snip, snip.'[85] This was the era of which Nadezhda Mandelstam wrote that those with voices had their 'tongues . . . cut out, and with the stump that remained they were forced to glorify the tyrant.'[86] According to Martin Sixsmith, suicide was 'an astoundingly common outcome' for poets and writers in the years after 1917 (e.g. Mayakovsky, Esenin): 'the Kremlin was bent on wiping out originality – imagination was no longer needed or welcome.'[87] Later the Nazis and Stalinists discouraged imagination, which was decadent and useless, and, as with Leninism, glorified art only where it might have a political purpose beyond art.

As modernism progresses, alienation, through shock and novelty, become defences against the boredom and inauthenticity of modernity. The inauthenticity against which modernism reacted is not in doubt. But there are, as I suggested in Chapter 7, two directions in which, under such circumstances, one might go. One can see the problem as a *contingent* loss of the authenticity of the right-hemisphere world and try to re-engage the right hemisphere, by patiently clearing away the adhesions of familiarity overlying one's subject; or one can see the right hemisphere's world as *intrinsically* inauthentic and try to sweep it away altogether. Newness (seeing afresh what one thought of as familiar, as though for the first time – the patient process of Romanticism) and novelty (deliberately disturbing the representation of reality in an attempt to 'shock' oneself into something that feels unfamiliar) are contrary concepts. Viktor Shklovsky's call, in his essay 'Art as Technique', to 'make it strange' could represent either. It has usually been interpreted as the second, but I do not think this is what he had in mind, as his delight in Tolstoy – and in the novels of Sterne – would suggest. He noted that Tolstoy 'describes an object as if he were seeing it for the first time, an event as if it were happening for the first time', and wanted to recapture that authenticity. Indeed, although his essay was taken as a manifesto by the Formalists, it is clear that what he is talking about is not sensationalism, shock tactics or bizarre distortions at all – in fact, the opposite. 'Habitualisation', he writes,

> devours works, clothes, furniture, one's wife, and the fear of war . . . art exists that one may recover the sensation of life; it exists to make one feel things, to make the stone *stony*. The purpose of art is to impart the sensation of things as they are perceived and not as they are known. . . .'[88]

As one sees from the examples of tactful obliqueness, metaphor and subtly inverted point of view which he chooses in that essay, his belief is that by the *implicit*, and by an indirectness that borders on indirection, one can make something that the explicit had deadened to total inauthenticity come to life again: as 'perceived and not as . . . *known*'. I would therefore make an important distinction between Shklovsky and the majority of those who espoused the slogan of 'make it new'. But Shklovsky's more subtle understanding, representing the right hemisphere's bid to take back to authenticity what had become exhausted by over-familiarity, was not to prevail.

Steiner's *mot*, that 'originality is antithetical to novelty' (see p. 375 above), puts its finger on a huge problem for the willed, self-conscious nature of modernist art, and art since modernism. For there is no polarity between the tradition and originality. In fact originality as an artist (as opposed to as a celebrity or a showman) can only exist within a tradition, not for the facile reason that it must have something by 'contrast' with which to be original, but because the roots of any work of art have to be intuitive, implicit, still coming out of the body and the imagination, not starting in (though they may perhaps later avail themselves of) individualistic cerebral striving. The tradition gets taken up – *aufgehoben* – into the whole personality of the artist and is for *that* reason new, rather than novel by an effort of will. There's a fear that without novelty there is only banality; but the pay-off is that it is precisely the striving for novelty that leads to banality. We confuse novelty with newness. No one ever decided not to fall in love because it's been done before, or because its expressions are banal. They are both as old as the hills and completely fresh in every case of genuine love. Spiritual texts present the same problem, that they can use only banalities, which mean something totally different from the inside of the experience. Language makes the uncommon common. It can never create experience of something we do not know – only release something in us that is already there.

Fig. 12.1 *Turin Spring*, by Giorgio de Chirico, 1914.

In subtle ways, disengagement is discernible at the outset of modernism. For example, de Chirico's paintings are undoubtedly visionary, but the light that had drawn one into connection with the world becomes in his paintings harsh, mordant, giving rise to abnormally sharp contrast; shadows are irrational, surfaces flattened, objects juxtaposed without being brought into relation, producing an effect that is threatening and disconcerting (see Figure 12.1). Perspective, that had been used to engage, here becomes the concomitant of a steeply angled geometricity that appears alien. Increasingly perspective is deliberately disrupted, and the depth of the painted field replaced by the surface of the canvas (see Plates 12 and 13).

When Kazimir Malevich in 1913 exhibited his black square, in 1915 his black circle, and in 1917 his white square ('White on White') he was, of course, making a statement – though using art to 'make a statement' is itself another aspect of left hemisphere domination. But he was also, by adopting such simple geometric forms, especially in black and white, adopting what we now know to be left-hemisphere preferences. Cubism in turn replaced the subtle softness of textured living surfaces, exactly what we need our right temporoparietal regions to interpret, by dislocated, abstracted surfaces, composed of rectilinear shapes, represented from a multitude of viewpoints (which therefore cannot be inhabited), intersecting randomly, and destroying the sense of depth. The demand that all surfaces of an object be represented in a single plane again goes straight back to the left hemisphere's tendency to represent schematically: there is a deliberate emphasis on fragmentation, and simplification into the regular shapes of cylinders, cubes, or spheres which the left hemisphere prefers. Viewed from a neuropsychological standpoint, modernist art appears to mimic the world as it would appear to someone whose right hemisphere was inactivated: in other words, it brings into being the world of the left hemisphere.

Even the *Zeitraffer* phenomenon, discussed in Chapter 2, which follows a breakdown in the integrated flow of movement in time and space brought about by the right hemisphere, is there from the outset. The *Technical Manifesto of Futurist Painting* published in 1910 declares: 'on account of the persistency of an image upon the retina, moving objects constantly multiply themselves'.[89] That this was quite untrue (provided one's right hemisphere is intact) did not prevent it being accepted as obvious. It became the job of painting to reproduce this deficit. In the novel, similarly, the flow of narrative, which both images the right hemisphere's continuous appreciation of time and its understanding of the meaning of human action, became disrupted; the flow of time was replaced by static scenes and dislocated sequence, tending to disrupt character and meaningful action, reproducing the world as experienced by those with right-hemisphere deficits. 'Freedom' from context, which only the right hemisphere can provide, is intrinsic to the character of modernist art. Above all, art in the modernist age becomes theoretical, conceptual – even if, in some cases, its ostensible theory or concept is that one should be intuitive.

One would expect the human face and body, both highly dependent on the right hemisphere for their appreciation and expression, to suffer in characteristic ways. It will be remembered that subjects with right hemisphere brain damage cannot gauge the proper relationship of what come to be seen as body 'parts'; there is an impairment of proprioception – the unreflective awareness of where the 'parts' are; and they lose a sense of intuitive 'ownership', so that the body seems to be motivated by an alien force, or alternatively an inanimate object. The left side, particularly the left hand, may be disowned.[90] In an essay entitled 'Some simple reflections on the body', Paul Valéry wrote that the body

> at times takes on a sudden charge of impulsive energies that make it 'act' in response to some interior mystery, and at other times seems to become the most crushing and immovable weight . . . The thing itself is formless: all we know of it by sight is the few mobile parts that are capable of coming within the conspic-uous zone of the space which makes up this *My Body*, a strange asymmetrical space in which distances are exceptional relations. I have no idea of the spatial relations between 'My Forehead' and 'My Foot', between 'My Knee' and 'My Back' . . . This gives rise to strange discoveries. My right hand is generally unaware of the left. To take one hand in the other is to take hold of an object that is *not-I*. These oddities must play a part in sleep and, *if such things as dreams exist*, must provide them with infinite combinations . . . *[The body] has no past* [emphases in the original].[91]

Here, in addition to exhibiting a failure of the sense of the relation of the parts of the body, an impairment of proprioception (he can only be aware of the position of his body 'parts' if he can see them), a sense of the body as acting in an alien manner, and the feeling that his left hand is not his, Valéry confirms the left hemi-sphere view by insisting that 'the body has no past' – a quite bizarrely counterin-tuitive notion that nonetheless indicates the left hemisphere's lack of sense of lived time; by suggesting that the unconscious life of dreams may not exist at all; and reporting the body as asymmetrical (true from the left hemisphere vantage point, less so, if true at all, from the right). And, believe it or not, this is the *least* objec-tified of three 'bodies' that, according to Valéry, we possess: it's the one we experi-ence – the other two being the body 'which others see', and the body known to science. We see the same in the visual representation of the body in the art of the period. The figures are distorted and dislocated: faces become barely recognisable as such, with deliberate disruption of the capacity for subtle expression. The de-animation of the body reaches its most disturbing apotheosis in the bizarrely distorted and dismembered marionettes of Hans Bellmer, but is obvious in main-stream artists such as Picasso (see Figure 12.2).

The list of names of the main movements in modernism could be seen, from the neuropsychological point of view, as a catalogue of left-hemisphere modes of apprehension. This is not a value judgment on the individual works of art produced, some of which were extraordinarily powerful, even beautiful – merely a reflection on the process that has affected our view of the world during the modern period. Some, such as *Cubism*, I have already mentioned. *Pointillism* reduces *Gestalt* figures to a mass of discrete particles, and the continuity of lines and surfaces to a

Fig. 12.2 *Woman in a Red Armchair,* by Pablo Picasso, 1932.

series of discrete dots (in this anticipating mechanical, digital reproduction, though pointillism draws attention to the disjunctions, where technology aims to hide them): this is the way the left hemisphere represents continuous flow. *Dadaism* and its off-shoots, *Absurdism* and *Surrealism,* express the value of total disjunction, random juxtaposition and the emptying out of meaning: as will be remembered, the left hemisphere has an advantage in processing such non-*Gestalt* and meaningless phenomena. *Abstract* painting similarly favours left-hemisphere processing. *Collage* represents the concept of the whole as composed of independent pieces. *Minimalism* emphasises the simple forms that are preferred by the left hemisphere. *Functionalism* preaches that utility is the over-riding consideration in form. One of its most famous proponents, Le Corbusier, famously reduced the rich concept of 'home' to that of *une machine à habiter.* Another, Mies van der Rohe, declared an outright refusal of all local colour: only the abstract and universal were to be admitted. Modernism in general openly rejected the unique specifics of time and place, and of concern for the context of different peoples at different times for different purposes, in favour of timeless universalities. The abstract shapes of modernist art and sculpture, too, resist any attempt at contextualisation. *Futurism* declares the left hemisphere's preference for the future over the past. Perhaps above all the revolutionary zeal and the opposition to every kind of authority on principle confirm that we are in the left hemisphere's world.

MODERNIST MUSIC

Walter Pater's aphorism that all art aspired to the condition of music alluded to the fact that music is the least explicit of all the arts (and the one most directly attuned to our embodied nature). In the twentieth century, by contrast, art has aspired to the condition of language, the most explicit and abstracted medium available to us. What the artist, whether painter, sculptor, or installation artist, has written about his or her creation is as important as the thing itself, and is often displayed next to the work of art, as if guiding the understanding of the onlooker – as if in fact the work could not speak for itself. Written material often obtrudes (as, incidentally, it does in the paintings of schizophrenics) within the frame of the artwork itself, as it never had before, except during the Reformation, and to a greater extent. Similarly performances of contemporary music are prefaced by a text written by the composer explaining his or her intentions, aspirations, and experiences during the composition.

Music is the most physically compelling of the arts. The tension in the intervals between successive tones (melody), co-occurring tones (harmony) and stresses (rhythm) are immediately and involuntarily conveyed as the relaxation and tension of muscular tone in the physical frame, and have manifestly direct effects on respiration and heart rate. Its origins lie in dance and song. It has direct effects also on physical, as well as mental, well-being: for example, it alleviates anxiety, depression and pain in patients with physical illnesses.[92] Under certain circumstances it can be essential to maintaining health. At a Benedictine monastery in the South of France,

> chanting was curtailed in the mid-1960s as part of the modernisation efforts associated with the Second Vatican Council. The results could not have been more disastrous. The monks had been able to thrive on only about four hours sleep per night, provided they were allowed to chant. Now they found themselves listless and exhausted, easily irritated, and susceptible to disease. Several doctors were called in, but none was able to alleviate the distress of the monastic community. Relief came finally, but only when Alfred Tomatis convinced the abbot to reinstate chanting. As he recalled: 'I was called by the Abbot in February, and I found that 70 of the 90 monks were slumping in their cells like wet dishrags . . . I reintroduced chanting immediately. By November, almost all of them had gone back to their normal activities, that is their prayers, their few hours of sleep, and the legendary Benedictine work schedule.' The decisive factor, it seems, had been a simple matter of sound.[93]

Yet since the twentieth century music has aspired to, and attained, a high level of abstraction.[94] Its appeal has become very largely cerebral and highly self-conscious, with a structure which may be so complex as to be imperceptible from within the experience of the work, or alternatively chaotic, or even aleatory. As Schoenberg put it: 'how the music *sounds* is not the point.'[95] Schoenberg, it might also be noted, started out composing music of which the sound very obviously was the point. Melodic line has largely been abandoned in avant-garde music, and its harmonic structures are hard to appreciate intuitively, even if they are appreciable conceptually. Though the analytic left hemisphere may add to the experience of music, the same principle applies here as everywhere: the products of the left hemisphere's work need to be returned to the right hemisphere where they can live. It is in this no different from the process of musical performance, which may represent hours of effortful analysis, and piecemeal labour behind the scenes, all of which has to be forgotten when it is transmuted into the living work once again. Mathematics needs to be taken up into the living frame if it is to work in music – as it is in the music of J. S. Bach, for example: it needs, in a word, to be embodied. Music is, of all the arts, the one that is most dependent on the right hemisphere; of all aspects of music, only rhythm is appreciated as much by the left hemisphere, and it may not be accidental that, while contemporary art music has become the preserve of a few devotees (in a way that was never previously true of new music in its time), popular music in our age has become dominated by, and almost reduced to, rhythm and little else.

In 1878, Nietzsche could see the beginnings of the process, and wrote prophetically:

> our ears have become increasingly intellectual. Thus we can now endure much greater volume, much greater 'noise', because we are much better trained than our forefathers were to listen for the *reason in it*. All our senses have in fact become somewhat dulled because we always inquire after the reason, what 'it means', and no longer for what 'it is' . . . our ear has become coarsened. Furthermore, the ugly side of the world, originally inimical to the senses, has been won over for music . . . Similarly, some painters have made the eye more intellectual, and have gone far beyond what was previously called a joy in form and colour. Here, too, that side of the world originally considered ugly has been conquered by artistic understanding. What is the consequence of this? The more the eye and ear are capable of thought, the more they reach that boundary line where they become asensual. *Joy is transferred to the brain; the sense organs themselves become dull and weak. More and more, the symbolic replaces that which exists.*[96]

'The symbolic replaces that which exists': surely the perfect expression of the triumph of theory and abstraction over experience and incarnation, of representation over 'presencing', in other words of the left hemisphere, there at the core of music and the other arts. And he continues that 'the vast majority, which each year is becoming ever more incapable of understanding meaning, even in the sensual form of ugliness . . . is therefore learning to reach out with increasing pleasure for that which is intrinsically ugly and repulsive, that is, the basely sensual'.

The problem of modernism, as Sass points out, is one of excessive self-consciousness. The question of what style to espouse, and with it the need to make a conscious decision to be something never before seen or heard, began to be more and more oppressive from the period of the later Romantics onwards – composers not just being intuitively drawn to imitate something they had heard elsewhere, as in the past, but deliberately inventing themselves and their art, rather than discovering it. This resulted, perhaps inevitably, in the decision to abandon our intuitive sense of harmony, melody and tonality.

It may seem unjustifiable to speak of an intuitive sense of harmony, melody or tonality, since these are now widely believed to be purely culturally determined, with the implication that they could be refashioned at will. But that is not the case at all. Music, of course, evolves, and what constitutes harmony, for example, has changed slowly over the course of time. The dominant seventh was considered a discord until the nineteenth century, and even the major third was once – in *organum*, therefore until the fourteenth century – considered a discord. (This is in itself fascinating, because it shows that the 'melancholy' minor third was accepted before the more 'optimistic' major third.) But generally there is intercultural understandability. Mongolian music, for example, does not sound harmonically incomprehensible, and certainly not unpleasant, to the Western ear. The acceptability and emotional meaning of music is not purely culture-bound. In fact it is almost universal.[97] For example, Norwegians acculturated to a Western musical tradition make precisely the same associations between particular emotions and particular musical intervals as are made in Ancient Indian music – a radically different musical tradition.[98] This would accord with most Westerners' experience of Indian music, acknowledged as it is to be complex and based on different musical principles from our own.

Studies of adults from different cultures, and from different generations, studies in preverbal infants and even studies in animals and birds, show remarkable agreement in what is perceived as consonant and pleasurable, and what is seen as dissonant and disagreeable.[99] Specifically there are universal natural preferences at the physiological level for harmony over dissonance.[100] Harmony causes changes in the autonomic nervous system, with a slowing of the heart.[101] Dissonance activates areas of the brain associated with noxious stimuli, and harmony areas associated with pleasurable experience.[102] Babies as young as four months old prefer consonance to dissonance, and infants already associate the minor key with sadness.[103] In terms of the hemispheres, the right hemisphere is more sensitive to harmony, more involved in the processing of it, and more sensitive to the distinctions between consonance and dissonance.[104] And there is a specific right hemisphere link with processing consonance, and a left hemisphere link with processing dissonance.[105]

The appreciation of harmony is inherently complex. It is the last aspect of musicality to develop, beginning around the age of six, and reaching maturity only by puberty. Harmony in music is an analogue of perspective in painting. Each produces what is experienced as 'depth': each is right-hemisphere-dependent. They developed together at the same time in the Renaissance; and, similarly, they declined together with modernism, harmony becoming more precarious as painters such as Picasso started deliberately disorienting the viewer through manipulation of perspective.

Bach's music is full of discords, and one would have to be musically deaf not to appreciate them – in both senses of the word 'appreciate', because such moments are especially to be relished, as are the wonderful passing dissonances and 'false relations' in the music of, for example, Byrd and his contemporaries. But they are introduced to be resolved. The same element that adds relish to the dish makes it inedible if it comes to predominate. The passing discords so frequent in Bach are *aufgehoben* into the wider consonance as they move on and resolve. Context is once again absolutely critical – in fact nowhere can context be more important than in music, since music is pure context, even if the context is silence. Thus, in harmony as elsewhere, a relationship between expectation and delay in fulfilment is at the core of great art; the art is in getting the balance right, something which Bach consummately exemplifies.

There is an enormously subtle range of emotional expression over the entire range of the harmonic, with the tiniest changes making enormous differences in meaning. But we cannot make the same subtle discriminations of emotional timbre between discords, because the human nervous system, and the mammalian nervous system from which it derives, appreciates discord as distress, so that all threatens quickly to become merely angst-ridden, and the emotional range is inevitably reduced. The sound of modernist music tends to be intrinsically alien, minatory, which is why it is used in films to convey a sense of some frightening 'other world' (for example, at points where such an effect was required in the film *2001*, Ligeti replaced Strauss).

The left hemisphere plays an important part in rhythm perception, though more complex rhythms are right-hemisphere-dependent[106] and rhythmic skills are preserved in total left-hemisphere ablation. Despite Plato's assertion that rhythm comes mainly from the mind, which possibly reflects more on Plato than it does on rhythm, there are again limits to what the human frame can experience and what the human brain can appreciate. Honegger is supposed to have said:

> I myself remain very sceptical about these rhythmic refinements. They have no significance except on paper. They are not felt by the listener . . . After a performance of Stravinsky's *Symphony in Three Movements* the players in the orchestra all remarked: 'One has no time to listen or appraise. One is too busy counting eighth notes.'[107]

Many composers, as might be imagined, have found themselves ambivalent about the process. Tippett lamented the loss of melody, described by Haydn as 'that which is most difficult to produce – the invention of a fine melody is a work of genius', and by Mozart as 'the essence of music: I should liken one who invents melodies to a noble racehorse, and a mere contrapuntist to a hired post-hack'.[108] Hindemith was sceptical of serial music, likening it to one of 'those sickeningly wonderful merry-go-rounds on fairgrounds and in amusement parks . . . the idea is, of course, to disturb the customer's feeling of gravitational attraction by combining at any given moment so many different forms of attraction that his sense of location cannot adjust itself fast enough'.[109] The lack of tonal centres destroys the listener's anchor point for hierarchies of intervals. Although the composer may understand where he is going, the listener simply cannot, because we do not have sufficient short-term memory to cope with this degree of apparent formlessness.

Yet composers such as Benjamin Britten, Arvo Pärt and Philip Glass, as well as more recently Morten Lauridsen, John Tavener, and James MacMillan, have found their own way to producing at times hauntingly beautiful music that is intuitively, rather than purely theoretically, grounded, expressive rather than rationalistic. For them modernism has been a way of continuing, while at the same time expanding and enlarging, the possibilities of what, for want of a better term, we are obliged to call the Romantic. And jazz, less self-conscious about self-invention, less insistent on escaping the idioms of melody, harmony and rhythm – though treating them with a freedom that can be exhilarating (if sometimes pushing the bounds of the perceptible) – seems to me one of the great creations of the modernist era.

THE SUCCESSES OF MODERNISM

Most theories of beauty from Plato to Nietzsche and beyond share the same concept of beauty: an organic whole which shows harmony between the parts. Western and Eastern concepts of beauty, despite their having evolved largely independently, are remarkably consonant.[110] This will hardly surprise any Westerner familiar with Oriental art in all, or any, of its forms. Despite individual exceptions there is general agreement across cultures. This is why translations of poetry and fiction sell widely in many languages, why exhibitions of Japanese art, concerts of Indian, Indonesian or Japanese music, and even performances of oriental drama in the West are so successful; and why Western art galleries are popular attractions for large numbers of visitors from the East, and performances of Shakespeare, and concerts of Western music or ballet, are in demand in China and Japan, where some of the best performers of classical European music now originate. Even the completely untutored, indigenous populations of places such as Papua New Guinea, who have had no exposure to classical Western music, appreciate and understand intuitively the emotional import of the music of Mozart. None of this would be possible without the existence of non-socially constructed values that enable the apprehension of beauty and the understanding of its expression through art. There is a developing acceptance by psychology and the social sciences that human universals clearly do exist.[111]

In music there is an intuitive language, the dialects of which are literally as widespread as, and older than, the human race. That is not just my intuition, but what the research demonstrates. Modernism experimented, unsuccessfully in my view, with abandoning it. In the visual arts, the ways in which humanity has used colour and form are nowhere near as cohesive, but aesthetic preferences, if not representational techniques and skills, are generally shared. Again deliberate attempts to reverse or abandon these are interesting mainly as experiments. But the conventions of language itself – not the language of music or visual art – are something one simply cannot reverse, at least not for long, if language is one's medium. This has had a protective effect on poetry within modernism. The attempt was made to abandon them, and figures such as Kurt Schwitters, mainly known for his collage art, wrote Dadaist 'poems' consisting only of nonsense syllables and sounds, but this was not to prove a fruitful departure. Even Eliot's *The Waste Land*, a collection of fragments, at times randomly collated, its elaborate spoof footnotes suggesting that meaning is not in the words themselves, but needs further decoding in order to be unlocked, was something of a dead end, an interesting culturohistorical document, like Joyce's *Finnegan's Wake*, rather than powerful poetry – although its borrowings make it gleam in places like a magpie's nest.

In music and the visual arts the formal conventions embodied intuitive wisdom that could not be discarded without loss of meaning. However, the very stuff of language, unlike notes or colours in themselves, has meaning and intuitive power that is relatively resistant to the abandonment of conventions. This puts it in a special category. As a result, the era of modernism, starting in France in the mid-nineteenth century with figures such as Baudelaire, Verlaine, Mallarmé, Rimbaud, and carried forward by later figures such as Ponge, and in the English-speaking world by such figures as Hardy, Frost, Yeats, Eliot, Auden, Stevens, and latterly Larkin, has proved exceptionally rich, with powerful and original poetry, comparable with that of any age, being written not just by the great names, but by many lesser known figures who may not have established reputations, but who have written one or two truly great poems. This seems to me to apply more to the modern era than to any other in literary history. As Philip Larkin wrote in the preface to his superb *Oxford Book of Twentieth Century Verse*, surely one of the most rewarding anthologies ever compiled, 'Looking at what I have chosen, I see that it represents a much greater number of poets than are to be found in the volumes corresponding to this one for the nineteenth and eighteenth centuries.' I take this to be a direct result of the relative freedom of modernism. Minor poets in a received style relatively rarely produce other than acceptable conventional poetry. Where intuition, however, is relatively untrammelled by such conventions, there may be much dross, but there will also often be sapphires to be found in the mud.

Finally it seems to me that one of the great achievements of modernism has been in cinema. Some of the same considerations apply here as apply in the case of poetry. The very stuff, the 'vocabulary', of visual imagery has meaning and intuitive power, and though there might be something called abstract art, an abstract film (Derek Jarman's *Blue* notwithstanding) is as unlikely a creation as an abstract poem. The contribution of modernism has been liberating here, too, unleashing intuition rather than, as I would claim of modernist art and music, starting out by declaring the means of intuitive expression out of bounds. And here, too, alongside the Tarkovskys, Polanskis and Paradzhanovs, the great poets of cinema (Tarkovsky being one of the few artists of whom one can genuinely use the term Shakespearean), there are many lesser figures who have produced great works.

POST-MODERNISM

With post-modernism, meaning drains away. Art becomes a game in which the emptiness of a wholly insubstantial world, in which there is nothing beyond the set of terms we have in vain used to 'construct' meaning, is allowed to speak for its own vacuity. The set of terms are now seen simply to refer to themselves. They have lost transparency; and all conditions that would yield meaning have been ironised out of existence.

Subjects with schizophrenia display what Sass describes as 'a distinctive combination of superiority and impotence'.[112] This, too, he sees as a characteristic of the modernist stance, but it is perhaps most evident in post-modernism. In post-modern literary criticism, the impotence is obvious: if reality is a construct without any objective existence, and if words have no referent, we are all absolutely impotent to say or do anything that has meaning, raising the question why the critic wrote in the first place. Why would any solipsist write? The attempt to convince another of one's point of view explodes the solipsist's position. Nonetheless an intrinsically superior attitude of the critic towards the authors that form his or her subject is evident. Where the author thought he was doing something important, even profound – was, in Wordsworth's phrase, 'a man speaking to men' – the critic can reveal that he was really playing a word game, the rules of which reflected socially constructed norms of which the author was unaware. The author becomes a sort of puppet, whose strings are pulled by social forces behind the scenes. He is 'placed'. Meanwhile the work of art gets to be 'decoded', as if the value of the work lay in some message of which the author was once more unaware, but which we in our superiority can now reveal.

This coded-message model, which 'has very much the status of an axiom in most versions of structuralism',[113] is the perfect expression of the left hemisphere trying to understand right-hemisphere language. Aware that there is more going on here than meets the eye, the left hemisphere sets about making things explicit, in an attempt to discover what it is; but meanwhile is not really aware of the 'this-ness' of the work of art, in which the real 'meaning' lies, at all. Instead its supposed decoding is a demonstration of its own cleverness. But 'literary value', as Severin Schroeder writes, 'cannot be reduced to the things that are described and the opinions that are conveyed; it is always a matter of *how* certain things are presented and expressed. And this How cannot be reduced to another What.'[114] That How, the uniqueness of the work of art that is akin to the uniqueness of a person, is appreciable only by the right hemisphere.

The advice to a critic has to be that given to every doctor by Hippocrates: 'above all, do no harm'. Be careful not to import something that will obscure the view; a patient, tactful approach to the otherness of the work, however, might yield a glimpse of something rare.

Separating words from their referents in the real world, as post-modernism does, turns everything into a nothing, life itself into a game. But the coupling of emotionally evocative material with a detached, ironic stance is in fact a power game, one that is being played out by the artist with his or her audience. It is not so much a matter of playfulness, with its misplaced suggestion of innocence, as a grim parody of play. It is familiar to psychiatrists because of the way that psychopaths use displays of lack of feeling – a jokey, gamesy, but chilling, indifference to subjects that spontaneously call forth strong human emotions – to gain control of others and make them feel vulnerable. So where, for example, performance artists display material that would normally call forth strong emotional reactions, and then undercut, or ironise it, this is a form of coercive self-aggrandisement. If others show their revulsion, their vulnerability is made obvious – they have been manipulated, and they appear naïve, at a disadvantage; if they do not, they have been forced to be untrue to their feelings and dissemble, like the playground victim that smiles timidly and fatuously at his tormentors, thus tacitly confirming the bully's power.

The trend in criticism towards a superiority born of the ability to read the code is perhaps first seen in the culture of psychoanalysis, which, writes Sass, claims to reveal 'the all-too-worldly sources of our mystical, religious, or aesthetic leanings, and to give its initiates a sense of knowing superiority'.[115] It is closely allied to all forms of reductionism. Reductionism, like disengagement, makes people feel powerful. When the eighteenth-century purveyors of phantasmagoria revealed the apparatus that had given rise to those spectacular effects, they were also revealed as the clever ones who know, and the audience were asked temporarily to enjoy the feeling of being in the presence of a greater intelligence. Their readiness to believe had made dupes of them. They had allowed themselves to be moved, where they should, if they had known, been serenely unmoved, permitting perhaps a knowing smile to play about their lips. It's hard not to feel that there is a degree of *Schadenfreude* about it, as in the older brother who tells his younger sister she is adopted; or the psychopath who manipulates people's feelings of compassion to rob them. Of course good psychoanalysis carefully eschews the superior position, but the point that it is built into the structure, and that one needs to be constantly vigilant not to succumb to it, remains valid.

The knowing superiority of reductionism is also clear in modern scientific discourse. Reductionism is an inescapable consequence of a purely left-hemisphere vision of the world, since the left hemisphere sees everything as made up from fundamental building blocks, the nature of which is assumed to be obvious, or at least knowable in principle in isolation from whatever it is they go to make up. Its model is simple, and it has ramified into popular culture, where it has been adopted unreflectively as the 'philosophy' of our age. Within that culture it has had a corrosive effect on higher values, inducing a sort of easy cynicism, and encouraging a mechanistic view of the human.

At the intellectual level it is brought into focus by the debate about the nature of consciousness. In a bold inversion, Nick Humphrey claims, in his book *Seeing Red*, that it is those who are sceptical of the idea that we can explain consciousness reductively who are really feeling smug and superior. Such scepticism 'taps straight into people's sense of their own metaphysical importance', he writes, and 'allows people the satisfaction of being insiders with secret knowledge'.[116] Those are hard claims to refute, and he might have a point. Equally some people might feel that the same charges could be levelled at those neuroscientists who believe in the power of their intellect to reveal the 'true' nature of consciousness, of which the rest of us remain ignorant.

When one comes to Humphrey's own explanation of consciousness, one is naturally curious to know what paraphernalia he is going to reveal behind the phantasmagoria. He claims two things. The first is in line with many other accounts of consciousness: that it is the consequence of re-entrant circuits in the brain, creating a 'self-resonance'. Sensory responses, he writes, 'get *privatised*' and 'eventually the whole process becomes closed off from the outside world in an internal loop within the brain . . . a feedback loop'.[117] The perfect image of the hermetic world of the left hemisphere: consciousness is the projection of a representation of the world 'outside' onto the walls of that closed-off room. His particular contribution in this book, though, is to go further and imagine that a genetic development occurred whose 'effect is to give the conscious Self just the extra twist that leads the human mind to form an exaggeratedly grandiose view of its own nature'. The self and its experience 'becomes reorganized precisely so as to impress the subject with its *out-of-this-world* qualities'. If 'those who fall for the illusion, tend to have longer and more productive lives', then evolution has done its work. The sense we have of consciousness, then, as hard to get to the bottom of is just a 'deliberate trick' played by the 'illusionist' in our genes, to make us better at surviving.[118]

One could point out that, while this certainly might offer a sort of explanation of *why* consciousness, with its sense of something beyond our grasp (what Humphrey describes as its 'out-of-this-world' qualities), exists as it does, it gets no nearer to *what*, or *what sort of a thing*, it is, or how it comes about – thus tending to confirm the sceptic's view. But that is to set the bar rather high, since nobody has ever got near to explaining what consciousness is, despite references to re-entrant circuits, positive feedback, mental representations that are illusions, and gene wizardry. His attempt to discount our intuition that there might be something here that lies beyond what materialism alone can account for is definitely ingenious. As a strategy for accommodating a mind-boggling difficulty into the existing paradigm without having actually to alter the paradigm, it is in fact spectacular. In that respect, it reminds one of the explanation given by Philip Gosse, the Victorian father of marine biology and a biblical Fundamentalist, for the existence of fossils in rock dating back millions of years, long before, according to the Bible, living things had been created. They were, he said, suggestions of life that never really existed, put there by God to test our faith. As with Gosse's explanation, it's hard to know what sort of evidence might be allowed to count against Humphrey's belief, though similarly his account might give rise to some incredulity in more sceptical minds.

Some of those who are sceptical, but are cited by Humphrey as examples of the self-deluding conviction that consciousness takes quite some explaining, are the philosophers Stuart Sutherland ('Consciousness is a fascinating but elusive phenomenon; it is impossible to specify what it is, what it does, or why it evolved. Nothing worth reading has been written about it'); Thomas Nagel ('Certain forms of perplexity – for example, about freedom, knowledge, and the meaning of life – seem to me to embody more insight than any of the supposed solutions to these problems'); Nakita Newton ('Phenomenal consciousness itself is *sui generis*. Nothing else is like it *in any way at all*'); Jerry Fodor ('Nobody has the slightest idea how anything material could be conscious. Nobody even knows what it would be like to have the slightest idea about how anything material could be conscious'); and Colin McGinn ('Isn't it perfectly evident to you that . . . [the brain] is just the wrong kind of thing to give birth to [phenomenal consciousness]? You might as well assert that numbers emerge from biscuits or ethics from rhubarb.')[119] Although I do not completely agree with the last, I believe the fundamental point is valid. To these one could continue to add: I have cited Wittgenstein above, whose view is similar to Nagel's, but their position is really in a long line of what has conventionally been considered wise scepticism about the absolute power of human understanding, including Montaigne, the Buddha, Socrates and St Paul.[120]

The point here is that scientific materialism, despite its apparent opposition to the post-modernist stance, shows similar left-hemisphere origins. They share a sense of superiority, born of the conviction that others are taken in by illusions, to which those in the know have the explanation. It is there, beautifully revealed in that impotent, self-enclosed, boot-strapping circuitry, 'the whole process . . . closed off from the outside world in an internal loop within the brain'. It is an example of positive feedback, and it is just this that the left hemisphere, being cut off from reality, its self-reflections reverberating endlessly round its mirrored walls, exemplifies. The structure of scientific realism, like post-modernism, reflects its left-hemisphere origins.

Some aspects of the post-modern condition, it may be objected, surely have an affinity with the workings of the right hemisphere. In stark contrast to the Enlightenment, it could be said that our own age lacks conviction and embraces whatever is unclear, indeterminate, fluid and unresolved. If the Enlightenment demonstrated its reliance on left-hemisphere modes of being by its optimism and certainty, its drive towards clarity, fixity and finality, why do I claim that post-modernism is also an expression of left-hemisphere functioning?

The difference depends on the level of consciousness. In the Enlightenment, although the process of alienation of the observing subject was well under way, there was as yet little doubt that there existed a world for it to observe. Its construction of the world as clear, orderly, fixed, certain and knowable, was inevitably a simulacrum substituted for the ever-changing and evolving, never graspable actuality of experience, but it was nonetheless taken for a reality – as though the frescoes on the wall of an eighteenth-century dining room were taken for the world outside.

A couple of hundred years and another level of self-consciousness later, the observing subject is not just aware, but aware of its own awareness. It is no longer an option to ignore the fact that all cannot be made to agree, that all is not fixed, certain and knowable, and that all is not necessarily going to end up being redeemed by human control. The post-modern revolt against the silent, static, contrived, lifeless world displayed in the fresco on the wall is not because of its artificiality – the fact that it is untrue to the living world outside – but because of its 'pretence' that there exists a world outside to be true to. The contrast is not between the fixity of the artificial and the fluidity of the real, but between the fixity and the chaos of two kinds of artificiality.

Post-modern indeterminacy affirms not that there is a reality, towards which we must carefully, tentatively, patiently struggle; it does not posit a truth which is nonetheless real because it defies the determinacy imposed on it by the self-conscious left-hemisphere interpreter (and the only structures available to it). On the contrary, it affirms that there *is* no reality, no truth to interpret or determine. The contrast here is like the difference between the 'unknowing' of a believer and the 'unknowing' of an atheist. Both believer and atheist may quite coherently hold the position that any assertion about God will be untrue; but their reasons are diametrically opposed. The difference is not in what is said, but in the disposition each holds toward the world. The right hemisphere's disposition is tentative, always reaching painfully (with 'care') towards something which it knows is beyond itself. It tries to open itself (not to say 'no') to something that language can allow only by subterfuge, to something that reason can reach only in transcending itself; *not*, be it noted, by the abandonment of language and reason, but rather through and beyond them. This is why the left hemisphere is not its enemy, but its valued emissary. Once, however, the left hemisphere is convinced of its own importance, it no longer 'cares'; instead it revels in its own freedom from constraint, in what might be called, in a phrase of Robert Graves's, the 'ecstasy of chaos'.[121] One says 'I do not know,' the other 'I know – that there is nothing to know.' One believes that one cannot know: the other 'knows' that one cannot believe.

CONCLUSION

———◆———

THE MASTER BETRAYED

All the miseries of man but prove his greatness. They are the miseries of a great lord, the miseries of a king that is dispossessed – Pascal[1]

ARE THERE DRIVES BEHIND THE DIFFERENCES I HAVE OUTLINED BETWEEN THE hemispheres? The hemispheres appear to stand in relation to one another in terms that ask for human understanding and the application of human values – just as the competition of genes appears 'selfish'. Putting it in such human terms, it appears essential for the creation of full human consciousness and imagination that the right hemisphere places itself in a position of vulnerability to the left. The right hemisphere, the one that believes, but does not know, has to depend on the other, the left hemisphere, that knows, but doesn't believe. It is as though a power that has an infinite, and therefore intrinsically uncertain, potential Being needs nonetheless to submit to be delimited – needs stasis, certainty, fixity – in order to Be. The greater purpose demands the submission. The Master needs to trust, to believe in, his emissary, knowing all the while that that trust may be abused. The emissary knows, but knows wrongly, that he is invulnerable. If the relationship holds, they are invincible; but if it is abused, it is not just the Master that suffers, but both of them, since the emissary owes his existence to the Master.

WHAT WOULD THE LEFT HEMISPHERE'S WORLD LOOK LIKE?

Let us try to imagine what the world would look like if the left hemisphere became so far dominant that, at the phenomenological level, it managed more or less to suppress the right hemisphere's world altogether. What would that be like?[2]

We could expect, for a start, that there would be a loss of the broader picture, and a substitution of a more narrowly focussed, restricted, but detailed, view of the world, making it perhaps difficult to maintain a coherent overview. The broader picture would in any case be disregarded, because it would lack the appearance of clarity and certainty which the left hemisphere craves. In general, the 'bits' of anything, the parts into which it could be disassembled, would come to seem more important, more likely to lead to knowledge and understanding, than the whole, which would come to be seen as no more than the sum of the parts. Ever more narrowly focussed attention would lead to an increasing specialisation and technicalising of knowledge. This in turn would promote the substitution of information, and information gathering, for knowledge, which comes through experience. Knowledge, in its turn, would seem more 'real' than what one might call wisdom, which would seem too nebulous, something never to be grasped. One would expect the left hemisphere to keep doing refining experiments on detail, at which it is exceedingly proficient, but to be correspondingly blind to what is not clear or certain, or cannot be brought into focus right in the middle of the visual field. In fact one would expect a sort of dismissive attitude to anything outside of its limited focus, because the right hemisphere's take on the whole picture would simply not be available to it.

Knowledge that came through experience, and the practical acquisition of embodied skill, would become suspect, appearing either a threat or simply incomprehensible. It would be replaced by tokens or representations, formal systems to be evidenced by paper qualifications. The concepts of skill and judgment, once considered the summit of human achievement, but which come only slowly and silently with the business of living, would be discarded in favour of quantifiable and repeatable processes. Expertise, which is what actually makes an expert (Latin *expertus*, 'one who is experienced'), would be replaced by 'expert' knowledge that would have in fact to be based on theory, and in general one would expect a tendency increasingly to replace the concrete with the theoretical or abstract, which would come to seem more convincing. Skills themselves would be reduced to algorithmic procedures which could be drawn up, and even if necessary regulated, by administrators, since without that the mistrustful tendencies of the left hemisphere could not be certain that these nebulous 'skills' were being evenly and 'correctly' applied.

There would be an increase in both abstraction and reification, whereby the human body itself and we ourselves, as well as the material world, and the works of art we made to understand it, would become simultaneously more conceptual and seen as mere things. The world as a whole would become more virtualised, and our experience of it would be increasingly through meta-representations of one kind or another; fewer people would find themselves doing work involving contact with anything in the real, 'lived' world, rather than with plans, strategies, paperwork, management and bureaucratic procedures. In fact, more and more work would come to be overtaken by the meta-process of documenting or justifying what one was doing or supposed to be doing – at the expense of the real job in the living world. Technology would flourish, as an expression of the left hemisphere's desire to manipulate and control the world for its own pleasure, but it would be accompanied by a vast expansion of bureaucracy, systems of abstraction and control. The essential elements of bureaucracy, as described by Peter Berger and his colleagues (see p. 390 above), show that they would thrive in a world dominated by the left hemisphere. The authors list them as: the necessity of procedures that are known, and in principle knowable; anonymity; organisability; predictability; a concept of justice that is reduced to mere equality; and explicit abstraction. There is a complete loss of the sense of uniqueness. All of these features are identifiable as facilitated by the left hemisphere.

So much for the tendencies towards abstraction. But there would also be the tendencies towards reification. Increasingly the living would be modelled on the mechanical. This would also have effects on the way the bureaucracies would deal with human situations and with society at large. When we deal with a machine, there are three things we want to know: how much it can do, how fast it can do it, and with what degree of precision. These qualities summarise what distinguishes a good machine from a bad one: it is more productive, faster and more precise than a less good one. However, changes in scale, speed and precision in the real world all change the quality of the experience, and the ways in which we interact with one another: increasing them no longer gives a clearly positive outcome – it can even be very damaging. In human affairs, increasing the amount or extent of something, or the speed with which something happens, or the inflexible precision with which it is conceived or applied, can actually destroy. But since the left hemisphere is the hemisphere of What, quantity would be the only criterion that it would understand. The right hemisphere's appreciation of How (quality) would be lost. As a result considerations of quantity might come actually to replace considerations of quality altogether, and without the majority of people being aware that anything had happened.

Numbers, which the left hemisphere feels familiar with and is excellent at manipulating (though, it may be remembered, it is less good at understanding what they mean), would come to replace the response to individuals, whether people, places, things or circumstances, which the right hemisphere would have distinguished. 'Either/or' would tend to be substituted for matters of degree, and a certain inflexibility would result.

Berger and colleagues emphasise that consciousness changes its nature in a world geared to technological production. It adopts a number of qualities which again are clearly manifestations of the world according to the left hemisphere, and therefore in such a world technology could be expected to flourish and, in turn, further to entrench the left hemisphere's view of the world – just as bureaucracy would be both a product of the left hemisphere and a reinforcement of it in the external world. In a society dominated by technology, Berger and colleagues predict what they refer to as: 'mechanisticity', which means the development of a system that permits things to be reproduced endlessly, and enforces submergence of the individual in a large organisation or production line; 'measurability', in other words the insistence on quantification, not qualification; 'componentiality', that is to say reality reduced to self-contained units, so that 'everything is analysable into constituent components, and everything can be taken apart and put together again in terms of these components'; and an 'abstract frame of reference', in other words loss of context.[3] The philosopher Gabriel Marcel speaks of the difficulty in maintaining one's integrity as a unique, individual subject, in a world where a combination of the hubris of science and the drive of technology blots out the awe-inspiring business of conscious human existence, what he refers to as 'the mystery of being', and replaces it with a set of technical problems for which they purport to have solutions. He warns that in such circumstances we would be too easily persuaded to accept the role thrust upon us, to become an object, no longer a subject, and would connive at our own annihilation.[4]

Philosophically, the world would be marked by fragmentation, appearing to its inhabitants as if a collection of bits and pieces apparently randomly thrown together; its organisation, and therefore meaning, would come only through what we added to it, through systems designed to maximise utility. Because the mechanical would be the model by which everything, including ourselves and the natural world, would be understood, people in such a society would find it hard to understand the higher values in Scheler's hierarchy except in terms of ultimate utility, and there would be a derogation of such higher values, and a cynicism about their status. Morality would come to be judged at best on the basis of utilitarian calculation, at worst on the basis of enlightened self-interest.

The left hemisphere prefers the impersonal to the personal, and that tendency would in any case be instantiated in the fabric of a technologically driven and bureaucratically administered society. The impersonal would come to replace the personal. There would be a focus on material things at the expense of the living. Social cohesion, and the bonds between person and person, and just as importantly between person and place, the context in which each person belongs, would be neglected, perhaps actively disrupted, as both inconvenient and incomprehensible to the left hemisphere acting on its own. There would be a depersonalisation of the relationships between members of society, and in society's relationship with its members. Exploitation rather than co-operation would be, explicitly or not, the default relationship between human individuals, and between humanity and the rest of the world. Resentment would lead to an emphasis on uniformity and equality, not as just one desirable to be balanced with others, but as the ultimate desirable, transcending all others. As a result individualities would be ironed out and identification would be by categories: socioeconomic groups, races, sexes, and so on, which would also feel themselves to be implicitly or explicitly in competition with, resentful of, one another. Paranoia and lack of trust would come to be the pervading stance within society both between individuals, and between such groups, and would be the stance of government towards its people.

Such a government would seek total control – it is an essential feature of the left hemisphere's take on the world that it can grasp it and control it. Talk of liberty, which is an abstract ideal for the left hemisphere, would increase for Machiavellian reasons, but individual liberty would be curtailed. Panoptical control would become an end in itself, and constant CCTV monitoring, interception of private information and communication, the norm. Measures such as a DNA database would be introduced apparently in response to exceptional threats and exceptional circumstances, against which they would in reality be ineffective, their aim being to increase the power of the state and diminish the status of the individual. The concept of the individual depends on uniqueness; but according to the left hemisphere's take on reality, individuals are simply interchangeable ('equal') parts of a mechanistic system, a system it needs to control in the interests of efficiency. Thus it would be expected that the state would not only take greater power directly, but play down individual responsibility, and the sense of individual responsibility would accordingly decline.

Family relationships, or skilled roles within society, such as those of priests, teachers and doctors, which transcend what can be quantified or regulated, and in fact depend on a degree of altruism, would become the object of suspicion. The left hemisphere misunderstands the nature of such relationships, as it misunderstands altruism as a version of self-interest, and sees them as a threat to its power. We might even expect there to be attempts to damage the trust on which such relationships rely, and, if possible, to discredit them. In any case, strenuous efforts would be made to bring families and professions under bureaucratic control, a move that would be made possible, presumably, only by furthering fear and mistrust.

In such a society people of all kinds would attach an unusual importance to being in control. Accidents and illnesses, since they are beyond our control, would therefore be particularly threatening and would, where possible, be blamed on others, since they would look like a threat to one's capacity to control one's life. The left hemisphere, as will be remembered, is in any case not quick to take responsibility, and sees itself as the passive victim of whatever it is not conscious of having willed. In the Renaissance, as in the nineteenth century, when the right hemisphere was in the ascendant, death was omnipresent in life and literature, was openly spoken of, and was seen as part of the fabric of life itself, in recognition of which alone life could have meaning. According to the left-hemisphere view, death is the ultimate challenge to its sense of control, and, on the contrary, robs life of meaning. It would therefore have to become a taboo, while, at the same time sex, the power of which the right hemisphere realises is based on the implicit, would become explicit and omnipresent. There would be a preoccupation, which might even reach to be an obsession, with certainty and security, since the left hemisphere is highly intolerant of uncertainty, and death would become the ultimate unspeakable.

Reasonableness would be replaced by rationality, and perhaps the very concept of reasonableness might become unintelligible. There would be a complete failure of common sense, since it is intuitive and relies on both hemispheres working together. Anger and aggressive behaviour would become more evident in our social interactions, since of all emotional states these are the most highly characteristic of the left hemisphere, and would no longer be counterbalanced by the empathic skills of the right hemisphere. One would expect a loss of insight, coupled with an unwillingness to take responsibility, and this would reinforce the left hemisphere's tendency to a perhaps dangerously unwarranted optimism. There would be a rise in intolerance and inflexibility, an unwillingness to change track or change one's mind.

The sense of autonomy is complexly related to both hemispheres, but crucially dependent on contributions from the right hemisphere.[5] An equivalent to what is called 'forced utilisation behaviour' in individuals might be seen: an increasing passivisation and suggestibility (if it's there, you must use it, do it). There would be a lack of will-power in the sense of self-control and self-motivation, but not of will in the sense of acquisitive greed and desire to manipulate. In relation to culture, we would expect people to become increasingly passive. They would see themselves as 'exposing' themselves before culture, like a photographic plate to light, or even think of themselves as '*being* exposed' to such things.

We could expect a rise in the determination to carry out procedures by rote, and perhaps an increasing efficiency at doing so, without this necessarily being accompanied by an understanding of what they mean.

We would expect there to be a resentment of, and a deliberate undercutting of the sense of awe or wonder: Weber's 'disenchanted' world. Religion would seem to be mere fantasy. The right hemisphere is drawn forward by exemplars of the qualities it values, where the left hemisphere is driven forward by a desire for power and control: one would expect, therefore, that there would develop an intolerance of, and a constant undercutting, ironising, or deconstructing of such exemplars, in both life and in art. Pathos, the characteristic mode of the right hemisphere, would become impossible, perhaps shameful. It would become hard to discern value or meaning in life at all; a sense of nausea and boredom before life would be likely to lead to a craving for novelty and stimulation.

Experiences or things that we would normally see as having a natural, organically evolving, flowing, structure, would come to seem composed of a succession of frames, a sum of an infinite series of 'pieces'. This would include the passage of historical or cultural, as well as personal, time, and organically flowing shapes or forms, and ultimately the development, growth and decay of all things that are alive. This corresponds to the *Zeitraffer* phenomenon. It is coupled with the loss of the sense of uniqueness (see discussion in Chapter 2). Repeatability would lead to an over-familiarity through endless reproduction.

As a culture, we would come to discard tacit forms of knowing altogether. There would be a remarkable difficulty in understanding non-explicit meaning, and a downgrading of non-verbal, non-explicit communication. Concomitant with this would be a rise in explicitness, backed up by ever increasing legislation, de Tocqueville's 'network of small complicated rules'. As it became less possible to rely on a shared and intuitive moral sense, or implicit contracts between individuals, such rules would become ever more burdensome. There would be a loss of tolerance for, and appreciation of the value of, ambiguity. We would tend to be over-explicit in the language we used to approach art and religion, accompanied by a loss of their vital, implicit and metaphorical power.

We would become, like Descartes, spectators rather than actors in all the 'comedies' the world displays. Art would become conceptual, having lost the capacity for eliciting the metaphorical power of its incarnate qualities. Visual art would lack a sense of depth, and distorted or bizarre perspectives would become the norm. Music would be reduced to little more than rhythm; art music would attempt to transcend it, but harmony and melody would be lacking. Dance would become solipsistic, rather than communal. Above all, the word and the idea would come to dominate. Cultural history and tradition, and what can be learnt from the past, would be confidently dismissed in preparation for the systematic society of the future, put together by human will. The body would come to be viewed as a machine, and the natural world as a heap of resource to be exploited. Wild and unre-presented nature, nature not managed and submitted to rational exploitation for science or the 'leisure industry', would be seen as a threat, and consequently brought under bureaucratic control as fast as possible. Language would become diffuse, excessive, lacking in concrete referents, clothed in abstraction, with no overall feel for its qualities as a metaphor of mind. Technical language, or the language of bureaucratic systems, devoid of any richness of meaning, and suggesting a mechanistic world, would increasingly be applied across the board, and might even seem unremarkable when applied to descriptions of the human world, and human beings, even the human mind itself.

This is what the world would look like if the emissary betrayed the Master. It's hard to resist the conclusion that his goal is within sight.

COULD THE LEFT HEMISPHERE SUCCEED ACCORDING TO ITS OWN CRITERIA?

I promised earlier that I would look at the results of adopting the more disengaged stance towards the world of the left hemisphere and assess them by the standards of the left hemisphere itself, not those of the right by which it was undoubtedly likely to be found wanting. What has happened to the world so far, and to ourselves, through treating the world as a mechanism? Does the evidence to date suggest that the left hemisphere could succeed in realising its own purpose, the maximisation of happiness? Following the left hemisphere's path has already involved the destruction and despoliation of the natural world, and the erosion of established cultures, on a scale which I scarcely need to emphasise; but this has been justified in terms of its utility in bringing about human happiness. Is a greater capacity to control and manipulate the world for our benefit leading to greater happiness? If not, it is hard indeed to see what its justification could be.

I am aware that, if one adopts the left hemisphere's view, what I am about to say will be difficult to accept, but the fact remains that increases in material well-being have little or nothing to do with human happiness. Obviously poverty is an ill, and everyone needs their basic material needs to be met, and, for most of us, a little more than that. But, if observation and experience of life are not enough to convince us that, beyond that, there is little, if any, correlation between material well-being and happiness, objective data demonstrate it. Over the last twenty-five years, levels of satisfaction with life have actually declined in the US, a period during which there has been an enormous increase in prosperity; and there may even have been a significant inverse relationship between economic growth and happiness there.[6] Since those blessed with employment spend much of their life at work, the quality of that experience matters. According to Putnam, in 1955 in the US, 44 per cent of all workers enjoyed their working hours more than anything else they did; by 1999 only 16 per cent did. Of course that might be because we are now enjoying ourselves more outside of work, but that clearly isn't the case, since overall levels of satisfaction have declined. In Britain the story is the same. According to Gallup poll data, throughout the 1950s the British were happier than they are today, despite now being three times richer in real terms. In 1957, 52 per cent of the population considered themselves 'very happy', compared with 36 per cent today. Most countries studied show either a decrease or at least no change in well-being despite an increase in prosperity; and no relationship can be found between happiness and economic growth.[7] The main determinants of happiness, as one might have expected, are not economic in nature. As two researchers in the area remark, with some restraint, given the huge increases in material prosperity over the last half century for which robust data exist, 'the intriguing lack of an upward trend in happiness data deserves to be confronted by economists.'[8]

Perhaps the most remarkable example is that of Japan. In 1958, Japan was one of the poorest countries in the world, comparable with India and Brazil as they then were, with an average income in real terms about one-eighth of that enjoyed in the USA in 1991. Over the last 40 years or more, Japan has enjoyed an astounding, and unprecedented, increase in per capita income, of about 500 per cent in real terms. Yet a repeated finding is that levels of happiness among the Japanese have not changed at all, and the latest data, before the current global economic crisis, showed a slight downturn.[9]

More recent evidence in Europe displays the same effect. The so-called Euro-Barometer surveys of satisfaction with life, covering fifteen European countries during the decade to 2000, shows four clusters, in each of which the consensus trend is horizontal or slightly negative.[10] The hedonic treadmill makes sure of that: modern consumers everywhere are in a 'permanent state of unfulfilled desire'.[11] As usual Sam Johnson got there about a couple of centuries before the research: 'Life is a progress from want to want, not from enjoyment to enjoyment.'[12]

Geoffrey Miller, a psychologist who has specialised in research into happiness, has found that

> a person's age, sex, race, income, geographic location, nationality, and education level have only trivial correlations with happiness, typically explaining less than 2% of the variance. An important exception is that hungry, diseased, oppressed people in developing nations tend to be slightly less happy – but once they reach a certain minimum standard of calorie intake and physical security, further increases in material affluence do not increase their happiness very much.[13]

Even in the affluent West, happiness reaches a plateau at an average national income that is remarkably low compared with most people's aspirations, variably estimated as between $10,000–$20,000 (£7,500–£15,000) per annum.[14]

So what does make a difference to happiness? 'The single most common finding from a half century's research on the correlates of life satisfaction, not only in the United States but around the world', writes Robert Putnam in *Bowling Alone*, 'is that happiness is best predicted by' – let's guess: if not wealth, then health? No, not that either, but – 'the breadth and depth of one's social connections'.[15]

Even now, rates of depression do differ markedly between cultures, probably by as much as 12-fold, and such differences in rates of depression appear to be linked to the degree of stability and interconnectedness within a culture.[16] Even being uprooted from your own culture, provided you take with you the way of thinking and being that characterises the more integrated social culture from which you come, is not as disruptive to happiness and well-being as becoming part of a relatively fragmented culture. For example, rates of psychological disturbance in Mexican immigrants to the USA start at a low level, but increase in proportion to the time spent in the US. The lifetime prevalence of any mental disorder in one large study was 18 per cent for Mexican immigrants with less than thirteen years in the US, 32 per cent for those with more than thirteen years, but only for those born in the US did it approximate, at 49 per cent, the national rate for the whole US.[17]

Over recent years, urbanisation, globalisation and the destruction of local cultures has led to a rise in the prevalence of mental illness in the developing world.[18] A massive study involving data regarding nearly 40,000 people across North America, Western Europe, the Middle East, Asia, and the Pacific Rim found that depression is being experienced more often, and at younger ages, with more severe and more frequent episodes, in younger birth cohorts generation by generation, and in the USA had doubled since the Second World War.[19]

In a demonstration of the integrity of mind and body, it is not just mental health, but physical health that suffers when we are not socially integrated. 'Social connectedness' predicts lower rates of colds, heart attacks, strokes, cancer, depression, and premature death of all sorts.[20] In fact the positive effects of social integration rival the detrimental effects of smoking, obesity, high blood pressure and physical inactivity.[21] According to Putnam, 'statistically speaking, the evidence for the health consequences of social connectedness is as strong today as was the evidence for health consequences of smoking at the time of the first surgeon general's report on smoking.'[22] The protective effect of community is demonstrated by the interesting case of Roseto, a close-knit community of Italian immigrants in Pennsylvania, with largely traditional cultural ties – both the formal ones of churches and clubs, and the informal ones that form the fabric of traditional Italian daily life. This community attracted medical attention in the 1940s because of a mysterious anomaly: here was a rate of heart attack less than half the national average, *despite having higher than average risk factors*. After the relationship with social connectedness was discovered, it was predicted that once the mobile younger generation moved away and 'began to reject the tight-knit Italian folkways, the heart attack rate would begin to rise'. By the 1980s this prediction had come true.[23]

All this, one can't help feeling, would be understood easily enough by the right hemisphere, even if it remains opaque to the left hemisphere. Happiness and fulfilment are by-products of other things, of a focus elsewhere – not the narrow focus on getting and using, but a broader empathic attention. We now see ourselves in largely mechanistic terms, as happiness-maximising machines, and not very successful ones at that. Yet we are capable of other values, and of genuine altruism and, in another Gödelian moment, the Prisoner's Dilemma demonstrates that altruism can be, incidentally, useful and rational. In the real, practical, everyday world what I have called the 'return to the right hemisphere' is of ultimate importance.

I do not underestimate the importance of the left hemisphere's contribution to all that humankind has achieved, and to all that we are, in the everyday sense of the word; in fact it is because I value it, that I say that it has to find its proper place, so as to fulfil its critically important role. It is a wonderful servant, but a very poor master. Just as those who believe that religions are mistaken, or even that they have proved to be a greater source of harm than good, must recognise that they have given rise to many valuable and beautiful things, I must make it clear that even the Enlightenment, though I have emphasised its negative aspects, manifestly gave rise to much that is of enduring beauty and value. More than that, the right hemisphere, though it is not dependent on the left hemisphere in the same way that the left is on the right, nonetheless *needs* it in order to achieve its full potential, in some sense to become fully itself. Meanwhile the left hemisphere is dependent on the right hemisphere both to ground its world, at the 'bottom' end, and to lead it back to life, at the 'top'; but it appears to be in denial about this.

I have referred to the fact that a number of thinkers have observed, often with a sense of unease, that over history intuition has lost ground to rationality; but in general their unease has been tempered by the feeling that this must be in a good cause. I also referred to Panksepp, who posits an evolutionary process involving the disconnection of cognitive from emotional processes. That might appear to be true, and even confirmed by my interpretation. But the reason it may look like what is happening is, I suggest, because we have already fallen for the left hemisphere's propaganda – that what it does is more *highly evolved* than what the right hemisphere does. This shift is not about evolution, nor even about emotion *versus* cognition: it is about two modes of being, each with its cognitive and emotional aspects, and each operating at a very high level. It is not about something more evolved competing with something more primitive: in fact the losing party in this struggle, the right hemisphere, is not only more closely in touch with emotion and the body (therefore with the neurologically 'inferior' and more ancient regions of the central nervous system) but also has the most sophisticated and extensive, and quite possibly most lately evolved, representation in the prefrontal cortex, the most highly evolved part of the brain.

It seems, then, that, even in its own terms, the left hemisphere is bound to fail. That will, however, not stop it from persisting in its current path. And the task of opposing this trend is made more difficult by the fact that two of the main sources of non-materialistic values, which might therefore have led to resistance, are both prime targets of the process that the left hemisphere has set in motion. We have no longer a consistent coherent tradition in the culture, which might have passed on, in embodied and intuitive form, the fruits of experience of our forebears, what used to form the communal wisdom – perhaps even common sense, to which modernism and post-modernism are implacably opposed. The historic past is continually under threat of becoming little more than a heritage museum, whereby it becomes reconstructed according to the stereotypes of the left hemisphere. And the natural world used to be another source of contact with something that still lay outside the realm of the self-constructed, but that is on the retreat, and many people in any case lead lives almost completely devoid of contact with it.

THE LEFT HEMISPHERE'S ATTEMPTS TO BLOCK OUR EXIT FROM ITS HALL OF MIRRORS

The left hemisphere is nonetheless subject to paranoia. Internally reflective, or self-reflexive, as the surfaces of its world are, there are points of weakness, potential escape routes from the hall of mirrors, that the left hemisphere fears it may never take hold of completely. These points of weakness in the self-enclosed system are three rather important, indissolubly interlinked, aspects of human existence: the body, the soul and art (which relies on body and soul coming together). Although the left hemisphere plays a part in realising each of these realms of experience, the right hemisphere plays the crucial grounding role in each of them: the 'lived' body, the spiritual sense, and the experience of emotional resonance and aesthetic appreciation are all principally right-hemisphere-mediated. What is more they each have an immediacy which bypasses the rational and the explicitness of language, and therefore leads directly to territory potentially outside of the left hemisphere's sphere of control. These areas therefore present a serious challenge to its dominion, and they have evoked a determined response from the left hemisphere in our age.

THE BODY

Although it might seem that we overvalue the body and physical existence in general, this is not what I deduce from our preoccupation with exercise, health and diet, with 'lifestyles', concerned though this is with the body and its needs and desires. Nor does it follow from the fact that the body was never so much on display, here or in cyberspace. The body has become a thing, a thing we possess, a mechanism, even if a mechanism for fun, a bit like a sports car with a smart sound system. That mechanistic view derives from the nineteenth-century scientific world picture, which has lingered with us longer in biology and the life sciences than in physics. The body has become an object in the world like other objects, as Merleau-Ponty feared. The left hemisphere's world is ultimately narcissistic, in the sense that it sees the world 'out there' as no more than a reflection of itself: the body becomes just the first thing we see out there, and we feel impelled to shape it to our sense of how it 'should' be.

In his too little known book *Symbol and Metaphor in Human Experience*, Martin Foss writes:

> The body is not so much an obstacle to life, but an instrument to life, or, as Aristotle rightly put it, a potential for the soul . . . but indeed life and soul are more than the body and its functions. Soul transcends body and makes one even

forget the body. It is the meaning of the body to be transcended and forgotten in the life for which it serves. It is the most essential characteristic of the body that it *disappears as an independent thing* the more it fulfils its service, and that we get aware of the body as such only if something is wrong, if some part does not serve, that is in sickness or tiredness.[24]

In this the body performs like a work of art. Just as Merleau-Ponty says that we do not see works of art, but see *according* to them, so that although they are vital for what we see, it is equally vital that they become transparent in the process, we live in the world according to the body, which needs its transparency, too, if it is to allow us to be fully alive. Merleau-Ponty called this the necessary transparency of the flesh. The current tendency for flesh to remain opaque, in the explicitness of pornography, for example, bids to rob sex of much of its power, and it is interesting that pornography in the modern sense began in the Enlightenment, part of its unhappy pursuit of happiness, and its too ready equation of happiness with pleasure. Like most answers to boredom, pornography is itself characterised by the boredom it aims to dispel: both are a result of a certain way of looking at the world.

Undoubtedly greater openness has brought its benefits, and mechanistic science very clearly has too, and these should not be under-estimated. But they have eroded, along with much else, the power of the body in our lives, by reducing it to a machine. Such a tendency to see the body as an assemblage of parts, or an illness as a series of discrete issues, without reference to the whole (including often vitally important emotional, psychological and spiritual issues), limits the effectiveness of much Western medicine, and drives people to seek alternative treatments which might in other ways be less powerful to help. It is significant that the 'normal' scientific materialist view of the body is similar to that found in schizophrenia. Schizophrenic subjects routinely see themselves as machines – often robots, computers, or cameras – and sometimes declare that parts of them have been replaced by metal or electronic components. This goes with a lack of transparency of the flesh. No spirit is seen there: 'body and soul don't belong together – there's no unity', as one patient eloquently puts it. This results in the body becoming 'mere' matter. As a result, other human beings, too, appear no more than things, because they are walking bodies. Another patient described by R. D. Laing 'perceived the actions of his wife – a vivacious and lively woman – as those of a kind of robot, an "it" devoid of inner life. If he told his wife a joke and she ("it") laughed, this showed no real feeling, but only her "conditioned" or mechanical nature.'[25] It's hard not to think of Descartes, looking from his window on the world, and seeing not people, but walking machines.

There has, in my view, been a tendency to discount and marginalise the importance of our embodied nature, as though it were something incidental about us, rather than essential to us: our very thinking, never mind our feeling, is bound up with our embodied nature, and must be, and this needs to be acknowledged.[26] So does the converse: that the material world is not wholly distinct from consciousness in some way that remains elusive.

Everything about the body, which in neuropsychological terms is more closely related to and mediated by the right hemisphere than the left, makes it a natural enemy of the left hemisphere, the hemisphere of ideal re-presentation rather than embodied fact, of rationalism rather than intuition, of explicitness rather than the implicit, of what is static rather than what is moving, of what is fixed rather than what is changing. The left hemisphere prefers what it has itself made, and the ultimate rebuff to that is the body. It is the ultimate demonstration of the recalcitrance of reality, of its not being subject to our control. The left hemisphere's optimism is at odds with recognising the inevitable transience of the body, and its message that we are mortal. The body is messy, imprecise, limited – an object of scorn, therefore, to the fastidiously abstracted left hemisphere, with its fantasies of human omnipotence. As Alain Corbin has argued, we have become more cerebral, and retreated more and more from the senses – especially from smell, touch and taste – as if repelled by the body; and sight, the coolest of the senses, and the one most capable of detachment, has come to dominate all.[27]

The left hemisphere's assault on our embodied nature is not just an assault on *our* bodies, but on the embodied nature of the world around us. Matter is what is recalcitrant to the will. The idea that the 'material' world is not just a lump of resource, but reaches into every part of the realm of value, including the spiritual, that through our embodied nature we can commune with it, that there are responses and responsibilities that need to be respected, has largely been lost by the dominant culture. Fortunately, plenty of people still care about the natural world, and there would undoubtedly be an outcry if national parks were targeted for industrialisation; but even here I am afraid that too much of the discussion would be in terms that are reductionist – those of 'the environment' – and the arguments, if they are to carry any weight, would have to be made in terms of jobs saved or 'recreational' benefit (the benefit being to the economy, principally), and appeals made to 'biodiversity', or the 'viability of the biomass'. The natural world has been commodified, as has art.

THE SPIRIT

The left hemisphere's attack on religion was already well under way by the time of the Reformation, and was taken further by the Enlightenment. With the rise of Romanticism, there was, it is true, as might be expected with a shift of equilibrium towards the right hemisphere, a growth in religious feeling and a sense of the transcendental. Romanticism was in itself a reaffirmation of the importance of the transcendental; affirming, not so much religion, as a sense of the holy, in what is best thought of as a form of panentheism (by contrast with pantheism, which equates God with the sum of things, panentheism sees God as *in* all things).[28] But in the West religion has declined in force in the twentieth century, withering away under the advances of capitalism as the state was advertised to do under Marxism. In early twentieth-century Russia, however, it was still a living power that called forth an intemperate reaction. When the Stalinists replaced the cathedral of Our Lady of Kazan in Moscow with a public lavatory, the left hemisphere (never subtle when it comes to metaphoric thinking) pissed on religion, as it had pissed on art when Marcel Duchamp exhibited his notorious urinal (interestingly one of the charges against the Puritan Cromwell was that his troops used religious buildings as lavatories). The persistence of this left-hemisphere metaphor, such as it is, of urine and faeces in modern art would be remarkable, if one did not know that the left hemisphere lacks metaphorical subtlety and is highly conventional.[29]

When we decide not to worship divinity, we do not stop worshipping: we merely find something else less worthy to worship. As Nietzsche put it:

Did one not finally have to sacrifice everything comforting, holy, healing, all hope, all faith concealed in harmony, in a future bliss and justice? Did one not have to sacrifice God himself and out of cruelty against oneself worship stone, stupidity, gravity, fate, nothingness? To sacrifice God for nothingness – this paradoxical mystery of the ultimate act of cruelty was reserved for the generation which is even now arising: we all know something of it already.[30]

The Western Church has, in my view, been active in undermining itself. It no longer has the confidence to stick to its values, but instead joins the chorus of voices attributing material answers to spiritual problems. At the same time the liturgical reform movement, as always convinced that religious truths can be literally stated, has largely eroded and in some cases completely destroyed the power of metaphoric language and ritual to convey the numinous. Meanwhile there has been, as expected, a parallel movement towards the possible rehabilitation of religious practices as *utility*. Thus 15 minutes Zen meditation a day may make you a more effective money broker, or improve your blood pressure, or lower your cholesterol.

I have tried to convey in this book that we need metaphor or *mythos* in order to understand the world. Such myths or metaphors are not dispensable luxuries, or 'optional extras', still less the means of obfuscation: they are fundamental and essential to the process. We are not given the option not to choose one, and the myth we choose is important: in the absence of anything better, we revert to the metaphor or myth of the machine. But we cannot, I believe, get far in understanding the world, or in deriving values that will help us live well in it, by likening it to the bike in the garage. The 2,000-year old Western tradition, that of Christianity, provides, whether one believes in it or not, an exceptionally rich *mythos* – a term I use in its technical sense, making no judgment here of its truth or otherwise – for understanding the world and our relationship with it. It conceives a divine Other that is not indifferent or alien – like James Joyce's God, refined out of existence and 'paring his fingernails' – but on the contrary engaged, vulnerable because of that engagement, and like the right hemisphere rather than the left, not resentful (as the Old Testament Yahweh often seemed) about the Faustian fallings away of its creation, but suffering alongside it. At the centre of this *mythos* are the images of incarnation, the coming together of matter and spirit, and of resurrection, the redemption of that relationship, as well as of a God that submits to suffer for that process. But any mythos that allows us to approach a spiritual Other, and gives us something other than material values to live by, is more valuable than one that dismisses the possibility of its existence.

In an age in which conventional religion does not appeal to many it may be through art that ultimate meanings can be conveyed. I believe art does play an invaluable role in conveying spiritual meaning. Schumann once said of Bach's chorale prelude *Ich ruf' zu dir* – chosen by Andrei Tarkovsky to open his extraordinary poetical exploration of the relationship between mind and the incarnate world, *Solaris* – that if a man had lost all his faith, just hearing it would be enough to restore it. Whether we put it in those terms or not, there is no doubt that here, as in Bach's great *Passions*, something powerful is being communicated that is of a spiritual, not just emotional, nature. Something similar could be said of the extraordinary depiction of Christ and his mother in the ancient church of St Saviour in Khora in Istanbul (see Plate 3).

ART

Here I must speak for myself, since these matters are nothing if not personal. When I think of such works of art, and compare Tracey Emin's unmade bed, or even, I am afraid, so much other post-modern art, just as when I think of Bach and compare him with Stockhausen, I feel we have lost not just the plot, but our sense of the absurd.[31] We stand or sit there solemnly contemplating the genius of the artwork, like the passive, well-behaved bourgeois that we are, when we should be calling someone's bluff. My bet is that our age will be viewed in retrospect with amusement, as an age remarkable not only for its cynicism, but for its gullibility. The two conditions are not as far apart as they may seem.

The left hemisphere having mechanised the body, and ironised the soul, it seems to me, has here set about neutralising or neutering the power of art. As I suggested in the last chapter, there is little evidence that tastes in art are purely social constructions. Though one could hardly expect a universally uncritical acceptance of every innovation, it was not the norm, until the advent of modernism, for people to find new styles of music unpleasant or incomprehensible. The first listeners to Monteverdi's great choral works were enrapt; Handel had to keep the place of rehearsal of his coronation anthems secret because of a fear that too many people wished to attend, and there being a consequent threat to public order. Liszt and Chopin were mobbed and swooned over, more like today's pop idols than their successors in contemporary art music. Music has been neutered indeed.

What about the great music of the past? That cannot exactly be abolished, and the success of the left hemisphere's drive to impede the composition of new music might be undermined by the sheer power of such music to convince us that there is something beyond the self-enclosed, self-invented space of the left hemisphere's world. But it need not worry. Here the commodification of art that Adorno predicted has continued apace, taming and trivialising it, and turning it into mere utility for relaxation or self-improvement.[32]

It's odd what's happened to beauty. Beauty is not just whatever we agree to call it, nor does it go away if we ignore it. We can't remake our values at will. There may of course be shifts in art theory, but that is distinct from beauty itself, and we cannot rid ourselves of the value of beauty by a decision in theory. In this, beauty is like other transcendental ideals, such as goodness. Societies may dispute what is to be considered good, but they cannot do away with the concept. What is more the concept is remarkably stable over time. Exactly what is to be considered good may shift around the edges, but the core remains unchanged. Similarly, exactly what is to be called beautiful may vary a little over time, but the core concepts of beauty remain, which is why we have no difficulty in appreciating the beauty of mediaeval or ancient art despite the passage of centuries. Art theory can pronounce the death of beauty, but in doing so it revives memories of King Canute.

Nonetheless beauty has been effectively airbrushed out of the story of art, like a public figure that has fallen from favour in a brutal regime. Beauty is rarely mentioned in contemporary art critiques: in a reflection of the left hemisphere's values, a work is now conventionally praised as 'strong' or 'challenging', in the rhetoric of power, the only rhetoric in all our relations with the world and with one another that we are now permitted. It has become somehow unsophisticated to talk of beauty – or of pathos, which relies on a belief that there is a reality from which, however painful and incomprehensible it may be, we cannot isolate ourselves. Pathos, which in modernism is replaced by *Angst*, becomes in post-modernism just a joke. In its place there is a sort of ironic jocularity, or 'playful-ness' – except that suggests a sort of innocence and joy that are totally inappropriate to the facts. Once again the words of Nietzsche come to mind, in this case his own later reflections on his early masterpiece, *The Birth of Tragedy*:

> those things which gave rise to the death of tragedy – Socratism in ethics, the dialectics, *smugness and cheerfulness of theoretical man* – might not this very Socratism be a sign of decline, of exhaustion, of sickness, of the anarchic disso-lution of the instincts? And might not the 'Greek cheerfulness' of later Hellenism be simply the red flush across the evening sky? Might not the Epicurean will to *oppose* pessimism be mere prudence on the part of someone who is sick? And science itself, our science . . . is scientific method perhaps no more than fear of and flight from pessimism? A subtle defence against – *truth*? Or, to put it in moral terms, is it something like cowardice and insincerity?[33]

Purely intellectualised, consciously derived art is congenial to the age, because it is easy, and therefore democratic. It can be made to happen on a whim, without the long experience of apprenticeship leading to skill, and without the necessity for intuition, both of which are in part gifts, and therefore unpredictable and undemocratic. Skills have been de-emphasised in art, as elsewhere in the culture.

The atomistic nature of our individuality is made clear in Warhol's tongue-in-cheek ambition for us each to be 'famous for fifteen minutes'. We've all got to be as creative as one another: to accept that some people will always be exceptional is uncomfortable for us. Instead of seeing great art as an indication of what humanity can achieve, it comes to be seen as an expression of what another being, a potential competitor, has achieved. But a society is, or should be, an organic unity, not an assemblage of bits that strive with one another. It is as if every organ in the body wanted to be the head.

I would see interesting parallels with the Reformation, the last time there was a major assault on art, though its target then was somewhat different: not 'the beautiful', but 'the holy'. There are, I believe, parallels that merit exploration between the Reformation and the modernist insistence on art being 'challenging'. This was the defence of the new religion, that people had become complacent and comfortable with the old ways. The reformers cut away the basis of religious worship, in metaphors, rituals, music and works of art, and replaced them with ideas, theories and statements. But complacency and inauthenticity were never far away, and the Church was soon once again open to abuse as a vehicle of wealth and status. The problem, as Luther realized, lay not in the statues, the icons, and the rituals themselves, but in the way they were understood. They had lost their transparency as metaphors, which are always incarnate and therefore must be left to act on us intuitively – neither just material or just immaterial, but bridges between the two realms. Nonetheless, they were destroyed and swept away, in the mistaken belief that religious meaning had better not have to do with the material realm at all.

Art, too, can be abused in a variety of ways – can easily become glib, too comforting, or used to announce wealth or status – and therefore become inauthentic. And so we are involved in doing away with incarnate works of art: metaphor and myth have been replaced by the symbolic, or worse, by a concept. We have an art of ideas, theories, and statements – or of resounding emptiness, that we are invited to fill with our own meanings. And the belief that the power of art could ever lie in a theory about art, or a statement about art of any kind – whether that be a protest against the commodification of art or even a statement that art cannot make a statement – does nothing to rescue the situation, but compounds it, and contributes to the demise of art. After all that, the new art is just as capable as the old of being glib, too comforting, or an announcement of wealth or status.

In the Reformation, though the attack was on the very concept of holiness, it is noteworthy that it did not need to attack holiness directly. It contented itself with attacking the shared acceptance in the culture of what *was* holy: shrines, icons, statues – even most of the saints (*die Heiligen*, the holy ones) were dispensed with. The democratic insistence that worship had nothing to do with place, since religion is anywhere and everywhere, as long as it is in the subjective experience of the participant, struck at the root of the holy: the reformers didn't even need to say 'everything and everywhere is equally *holy*' (which would have had the same effect – that therefore nothing was especially holy). They did not have to say it because, so successful were they, the very terms had moved on. People no longer believed in the holy at all: that was for the foolish and old, those who had not heard, or could not hear, the news.

So it is with ourselves. The art of the past is 'placed', ironised, or rendered absurdly incongruous. And if art can be anywhere or anything – literally a pile of garbage, perhaps – this aims to abolish the beautiful, without needing even to say 'everything and everywhere is equally beautiful'.

I have talked here as though the beautiful were confined to art, but it is of course present in each of the realms that the left hemisphere wishes to neutralise: in the realm of the body, too, and of the spirit, as well as in nature, and in any living culture. Our relationship with the beautiful is different from our relationship with things we desire. Desire is unidirectional, purposive, ultimately acquisitive. In the special case of living beings, desire can be mutual, of course, so when I say 'unidirectional' I do not mean, obviously, that it cannot be reciprocated. I mean that it is a movement towards a goal, like an arrow flying from a bow. In the reciprocated situation, there are two unidirectional lines of flow, in opposite directions, like arrows that pass in mid-air. Our relationship with what is beautiful is different. It is more like longing, or love, a betweenness, a reverberative process between the beautiful and our selves, which has no ulterior purpose, no aim in view, and is non-acquisitive. Beauty is in this way distinguished from erotic pleasure or any other interest we may have in the object. This is surely what Leibniz meant by beauty being a 'disinterested love'.[34] In fact, so central is this idea that one finds it also in Kant, who spoke of beauty as a 'disinterested pleasure',[35] and in Burke, who saw it as a form of 'love [that is] different from desire'.[36]

What ultimately unites the three realms of escape from the left hemisphere's world which it has attacked in our time – the body, the spirit and art – is that they are all vehicles of love. Perhaps the commonest experience of a clearly transcendent power in most people's lives is the power of *eros*, but they may also experience love through art or through spirituality. Ultimately, these elements are aspects of the same phenomenon: for love is the attractive power of the Other, which the right hemisphere experiences, but which the left hemisphere does not understand and sees as an impediment to its authority.

Through these assaults of the left hemisphere on the body, spirituality and art, essentially mocking, discounting or dismantling what it does not understand and cannot use, we are at risk of becoming trapped in the I–it world, with all the exits through which we might rediscover the I–thou world being progressively blocked off.

IS THERE ROOM FOR HOPE?

My theme may seem pessimistic. I do think that there are, nonetheless, reasons for hope. As will be obvious, I think we need, for one thing, urgently to move on from our current, limiting preconceptions about the nature of physical existence, spiritual life and art, and there are some small indications that this may be happening. Art and religion should not become part of the betrayal.

Another reason for hope lies in the fact that, however much the left hemisphere sees progress as a straight line, it is rarely so in the real world. The very circularity of things as they really are, rather than as the left hemisphere conceives them, might be a reason for hope.

Linear progression versus circular
At the end of Part I, I spoke of the progress of the sleepwalking left hemisphere, always going further in the same direction, 'ambling towards the abyss'. The tendency to keep on progressing, inflexibly, always in the one direction may have to do with a subtle feature of the 'shape' of the world as seen by the left hemisphere, compared with that experienced by the right hemisphere. It has often been said that the left hemisphere is the hemisphere of 'linear processing'; its cognitive style is sequential, hence its propensity to linear analysis, or to mechanical construction, taking the bits apart, or putting them together, one by one. This is in keeping with its phenomenological world being one of getting, of utility – of always having an end in view: it is the reaching of the right hand towards its object, or the flying of the arrow from the bow. Its progress is unidirectional, ever onward and outwards, through a rectilinear, Newtonian space, towards its goal.

This incidentally coheres with its mechanistic view of living organisms, and not simply because machines tend to be rectilinear, while living beings are not. Think of something as basic as classical conditioning, whereby a stimulus (ringing a bell, previously associated with the provision of food) produces a 'conditioned response' in Pavlov's dog (salivation). This is thought of as a linear process, the arrow hitting its target. Thus the dog is reduced to a machine. But a slightly different way of thinking of this would be that there is a context to everything, context being a circular, concentric concept, rather than a linear one. If one imagines Pavlov's dog, in a different experiment, having repeated experience of the bell being rung after it has started eating, rather than just before it gets food, one would have to say that, when the dog hears the bell in the absence of food, it experiences an association (a mini-context) in which these two events tend to co-occur. It would have as much reason to start to salivate when it heard the bell, but in doing so it would appear less mechanical, less as though its behaviour were *caused* by the bell. The dog is reduced to a mechanism by the temporal sequencing, an essential part of the concept of causation, and by the stripping away of the context to focus on a sequence. Imagine the smell of alcohol to an alcoholic. Does the smell cause the alcoholic to take a drink – or set up a set of associations, a surrounding context, in which wanting, and having, a drink are part? The dog, too, is appreciating associations or contexts (a right-hemisphere function), not just acting like a left-hemisphere machine: we know, for example, that the sound of its master's voice evokes to a dog an image of its master's face, not because the voice 'causes' the face but because they are part of a whole experience.[37] Perhaps all cause and effect might be thought of in this way. A bat striking a ball necessitates the ball flying off suddenly at great speed in a certain direction. But equally the ball flying off suddenly at great speed in a certain direction necessitates the bat striking it in a certain way. One could say that the bat and the ball have a sort of stickiness, a tendency for their movements to cohere in a certain kind of context.

Be that as it may, the left hemisphere loves straight lines, not curves or circles. It can approximate a curve, however closely, only by the expedient of laying ever more tangents. No straight lines are to be found in the natural world. Everything that really exists follows a series of curved shapes to which the logical products of the human mind can only ever approach tangentially – flow, once again, reduced to a series of points. Leonard Shlain has pointed out that the only apparently straight line in the natural world is that of the horizon; but of course that too turns out to be a section of a curve.[38] Even space, it turns out, is curved. Rectilinearity, as Ruskin had similarly demonstrated of clarity, is illusory, and can only be approximated, like clarity, by narrowing the breadth, and limiting the depth, of the perceptual field. Straight lines are prevalent wherever the left hemisphere predominates, in the late Roman Empire (whose towns and roads are laid out like grids), in Classicism (by contrast with the Baroque, which had everywhere celebrated the curve), in the Industrial Revolution (the Victorian emphasis on ornament and Gothicism being an ultimately futile nostalgic pretence occasioned by the functional brutality and invariance of the rectilinear productions of machines) and in the grid-like environment of the modern city, where that pretence has been dropped.

By contrast the shape that is suggested by the processing of the right hemisphere is that of the circle, and its movement is characteristically 'in the round', the phrase we use to describe something that is seen as a whole, and in depth. Circular motion accommodates, as rectilinearity does not, the coming together of opposites. Cognition in the right hemisphere is not a process of something coming into being through adding piece to piece in a sequence, but of something that is out of focus coming into focus, as a whole. Everything is understood within its penumbra of significances, in its context – all that encircles it. There are strong affinities between the idea of wholeness and roundedness. The movement of the right hemisphere is not the unidirectional, instrumental gesture of grasp, but the musical, whole-bodied, socially generative, movement of dance, which is never in a straight line towards something, but always ultimately returns to its origins. In Shakespeare's comedies the values of community – a community that pre-existed and will outlast, and serves to ground and to contextualise, the individual life – are often celebrated at the end of the play in the ring-dance. Whereas the melancholy Jaques in *As You Like It* accentuates the tragedy of the individual life, working its inevitable way through the seven ages of man to be ultimately 'sans everything', the other characters teasingly aim to help him see beyond this to the bigger picture that suggests that the part, whose trajectory is linear, is taken up into the whole, whose path is in the round.

The images of movement within stasis, and of stasis within movement, are reflected in the circle, as they are in the movement of water, ever flowing, and ever the same; and in the stars that circle and always return. Dante sees this movement as the result of the gravitational effect of love, love 'that moves the sun and the other stars'. To Shakespeare this movement is also the movement of human life – 'our little life is *rounded* with a sleep'. Sir Walter Ralegh speaks of his love occupying a position in his mind 'yeven as the center in each perfait *rovnde*'.[39] To Donne his love for his mistress means that when he is away from her he moves so that he is always in conjunction with her, never more distant, but like the arm of the compasses *circling* its centre point. For Donne, the love of God, too, meant that the created world circled the divine Being: 'God himselfe who had that omni-sufficiency in himselfe, conceived a conveniency for his glory, to draw a Circumference about the Center, Creatures about himselfe'.[40]

Roundness and the image of the sphere come and go with the influence of the right hemisphere. They were central to Romanticism. I have mentioned Blake's 'Reason is the bound or outward circumference of Energy' before: it suggests not just the idea that 'Energy', the vital force of life, is like a sphere, but that reason is always just on the outside, never on the inside – always approximating, however nearly, the circumference, with ever more tangents. Shelley speaks of the phenomenological world as a sphere: 'The devotion to something afar / From the *sphere* of our sorrow'. The idea of the roundness of the phenomenological world is in some of Wordsworth's most famous and mysteriously pregnant lines: 'the *round* earth and the living air', 'rolled *round* in earth's diurnal course', phrases which convey much more than the banal fact that the earth is a sphere and that it rotates.[41] Van Gogh went as far as to say that 'life is probably *round*';[42] and it was Jaspers who gave it as his view that '*jedes Dasein scheint in sich rund*': every *Dasein* seems in itself to be round.[43]

The individual life was seen in the past as more than just a line leading to – what? Its shape had the qualities of a circle: *in my end is my beginning, and in my beginning is my end*. Like many complex and apparently paradoxical dispositions to the world, this belief is better expressed in music than in words. Guillaume de Machaut's rondeau *Ma fin est mon commencement, et mon commencement ma fin*, written in the mid-fourteenth century, is not only remarkable for its beauty, but images its spiritual meaning in the form of the piece, in that the second voice part is the reverse of the first part, and the third is a palindrome. Reverting to an earlier discussion, this is something that is not merely clever, but is appreciable by the listener and taken up (*aufgehoben*) into the whole, where it adds to the meaning. The text expresses a truth about life in this world as well as in the next, death being a gateway to life; for our relationship with the world leads us constantly back to what was already known, but never before by us understood, circling and searching our own origins.

This reflected the shape of the cosmos, the universe, and ultimately of the Divine. The idea that God is a sphere whose centre is everywhere and circumference nowhere has a long history. It is at least as early as the *Corpus Hermeticum*, a body of early Christian texts from Hellenic Egypt dating back to the third century. After an interval of a thousand years, it was picked up by a thirteenth-century bishop, Alain de Lille, and is found throughout the Hermetic tradition in the

Renaissance, notably in Nicholas of Cusa in the fifteenth century and Giordano Bruno in the sixteenth, who wrote of 'an infinite sphere whose centre is everywhere and whose circumference is nowhere', an idea that was given its most famous expression by Pascal in the seventeenth century.[44]

To the early Greeks, the sphere was the perfect shape, expressive of eternity and divinity. Aristotle's universe consisted, in fact, of fifty-five nested spheres. After more than a millennium, the sphere once again became important in the early Renaissance, with the publication in around 1230 of the *Tractatus de Sphaera*, or *Sphaera Mundi*, a compilation of ancient texts by Johannes de Sacrobosco ('John of Holywood'), which was still in use until the end of the seventeenth century. Spheres first began to figure prominently in painting during the Renaissance, both for symbolic reasons and because of a fascination with depicting the curved lucency of the surface. The idea that the spheres of the heavens gave rise through their movements to an inaudible music probably originated with Pythagoras, and was based on his understanding of the mathematical proportions underlying harmonic intervals; in the Renaissance this idea was much elaborated by Kepler's *Harmonice Mundi*, published in 1610.

With the Enlightenment, however, interest in the sphere waned. It was left to the Romantic poets to intuit its importance, until the phenomenologists came on the scene: not just Jaspers (see above), but, for example, Kierkegaard, who conceived of four value-laden 'spheres of existence', and Heidegger, who spoke of the 'sphere of the real'.[45] In view of what I have said above about longing and its parallels with gravity in the physical universe, it is pleasing that Copernicus thought of gravity as a 'natural inclination . . . to combine the parts in the form of a sphere and thus contribute to their unity and wholeness', what Arthur Koestler refers to as 'the nostalgia of things to become spheres'.[46]

Ultimately these intuitions accord with the cyclical views of history and the universe in most cultures other than in the West (until Vico – see p. 504, n. 31), for example in Hindu cosmology – but indeed the myth of the eternal return is a cultural universal.[47] Even in the Christian West it is a curious fact that representations of the cosmos, long before there was any idea of the roundness of the earth or the curvature of space, tend to be represented in the curved roundness of the ceiling of the apse, or of the dome of the church, or of the tympanum over the great west door, rarely on the flatness of a wall.

The glint in the maiden's eye

Similarly in the fruitfulness of opposition, of dialectical growth – what Nietzsche, like Heraclitus, simply calls war – there is hope, since the worse it gets, the better it gets. He quotes, as having long been his motto, *Increscunt animi, virescit volnere virtus*: 'The spirit grows, [and] strength is restored, by wounding.'[48] And the obvious inauthenticity of the left-hemisphere world we have come to inhabit may in itself lead us to seek to change it. In the past that would appear to have been the most important factor, and I hope I may be wrong in seeing the present situation as different. In any case, understanding the nature of the problem has to be the first step towards change. Change, however, would require a willingness to accept being seen as naïve for not getting caught up in the dialectic of the clever ironies, on the one hand, or of scientific materialism, on the other.

Now, says Hegel, that 'the oracles . . . no longer speak to men', and 'the statues have become stone corpses' (there is much in that phrase alone), the remnants of the past, the glories of its art, history and culture, are like 'beautiful fruit broken off a tree; a kindly fate has passed those works on to us, much as a girl might offer us such fruit'.[49] The tree, and the earth in which it grew, and the climate in which the fruit ripened, are no longer available to us except as a 'veiled remembrance', something we represent to ourselves by picturing it. Yet, Hegel says, the knowing-ness with which we now have to recapture this, is like the 'glint of self-awareness' in the eye of the beautiful maiden who offers us the fruit; it is the same Nature that produced those fruit, but 'at a higher level', and it can add as well as take away.

The contrast is like that between the country folk at the fair which Wordsworth sees from Helvellyn, and Wordsworth's poem on the subject, which, though it lacks an unrecapturable quality of the 'self unseeing' that is still available to its subject, is itself a great work at a higher level of self-awareness, which the country folk could not achieve. Of what the ancients were happily unconscious, we are necessarily conscious, Hegel seems to say, but we see more: perhaps as the inno-cence of the adult, where it is achieved, is greater than the innocence of a child, though bought at the cost of much painful awareness.

But such innocence is rare. Age has a chance of bringing it only if we are very lucky or very disciplined. Wordsworth's achievement, like that of Blake and Keats, is that he retains a degree of innocence despite his experience, an innocence which all three evidence in what one might call their vulnerability. Through it alone they are enabled to achieve an inspired quality which could be mistaken by the foolish, at times, for foolishness. The price of their achievement is that they must make themselves open, even to ridicule, rather than shelter behind a self-protective carapace of ironic knowingness and cynicism.[50]

Excessive self-consciousness, like the mental world of schizophrenia, is a prison: its inbuilt reflexivity – the hall of mirrors – sends the mind ever back into itself. Breaking out of the prison presents a problem, since self-consciousness cannot be curbed by a conscious act of will, any more than we can succeed in trying *not* to think of little green apples. The apple of knowledge, once eaten, cannot become once more 'unbitten in the palm'. Nonetheless conscious reflec-tion, the root of the problem, may itself provide the antidote to its own effects. Heidegger, Wittgenstein, and Merleau-Ponty, all of them critics of reflection, embodied in their writing a reflective attempt to surmount reflection. Hölderlin's lines once again come to mind: 'Where there is danger, that which will save us also grows' (see p. 232).

This is because philosophy does not answer our questions but shakes our belief that there are answers to be had; and in doing so it forces us to look beyond its own system to another way of understanding. One of the reasons reading Heidegger is at the same time so riveting and such a painful experience is that he never ceases to struggle to transcend the Cartesian divisions which analytic language entails, in order to demonstrate that there is a path, a way through the forest, the travelling of which is in itself the goal of human thinking. Though we can emerge into a 'clearing', we cannot hope to reach the clear light of the Empyrean, which as Hölderlin's devastating poem *Hyperions Schicksalslied* makes plain, is reserved only for the gods. Perhaps inevitably Heidegger's last writings are in the form of poems. Wittgenstein also saw the true process of philosophy as a way of transcending or healing the effects of philosophy in the philosophical mind: philosophy is itself a disease, as Karl Kraus said of psychoanalysis, for which it purports to be the cure.[51] Merleau-Ponty, more explicitly than either, held out the hope that we could learn to see things again by a process of *surréflexion*, hyper-reflection, which would help to redress the distorting effects of consciousness by making us conscious of them. This idea had already occurred to the Romantics. At the end of his famous essay 'On the Puppet Theatre', Kleist offers the possibility that the crippling effects of self-consciousness may be transcended through a form of still further heightened consciousness, by which we might regain a form of innocence.

> 'Grace appears purest in that human form which has either no consciousness or an infinite one, that is, in a puppet or in a god.'
> 'Therefore', I said, somewhat bewildered, 'we would have to eat again from the Tree of Knowledge in order to return to the state of innocence?'
> 'Quite right', he answered. 'And that's the last chapter in the history of the world.'[52]

With that his essay closes. In this last phrase Kleist may be warning us, as Hölderlin does, that what we crave can be had only in another world, where there are gods. But his essay also confirms that we can move only onward, not backward, and that by doing so we might transcend our situation and in this way return to something lost. Perhaps the very emptiness of self-reflection, what Vico called 'the barbarism of reflection', may push us towards the necessary leap of faith that alone will allow us to escape. After all, even the emptying out of consciousness achieved by Zen is not a random gift but achieved by years of consciously embraced self-discipline.

Reflection, self-reflection, *surréflexion*: what we are talking about clearly has something to do with the plane of vision that we adopt. Gombrich writes that 'the true miracle of the language of art is not that it enables the artist to create the illusion of reality. It is that under the hands of a great master the image becomes *translucent*.'[53] I have used the language of transparency and translucency – of 'seeing through' – repeatedly: because as Gombrich says of the work of art, as Jean Paul says of metaphor, as Kerényi says of myth, and as Merleau-Ponty says of the body, our vision must not stop there at the bounds of the 'thing' – but neither must it be replaced by something else. It is the function of such translucent, or semi-transparent, beings to remain transparent rather than draw attention to themselves, because in doing so they achieve their goal. But talk of transparency, and seeing through, could easily suggest a false line of thought. Water is distinct from ice, but in the ice cube it is present: not as a fly might be trapped there, but *in the very ice*. It *is* the ice. And yet when the ice cube is gone, the water remains. Although we see water in the ice, we do so not because it is there separately, to be seen behind or apart from the cube. Body and soul, metaphor and sense, myth and reality, the work of art and its meaning – in fact the whole phenomenological world, is just what it is and no more, not one thing hiding another; and yet the hard thing is the seemingly easy business, just 'seeing what it is'. The reality is not *behind* the work of art: to believe so would be, as Goethe put it in an image I referred to earlier, like children going round the back of the mirror. We see it *in – through* – the mirror. Similarly, he says, we experience the universal in, or through, the particular, the timeless in, or through, the temporal.

What we might learn from Oriental culture

These ideas would be more intuitively understandable within an Oriental culture. Another reason for hope is that we are probably more open to the remaining cultures of the world that have not yet been completely submerged by the West, though for the same reasons we are increasingly prone to influence them to become more like our own. The pattern of psychological differences between Oriental people and Westerners suggests the possibility of a different relationship between the hemispheres. It is striking, for example, that the Japanese language does not have an established method for composing abstract nouns, and has no definite or indefinite articles, considered to be a crucial step in the emergence of abstract nouns in Greek.[54] The Japanese have nothing that corresponds to the Platonic Idea, and in fact no abstractions in general: they have never developed the dichotomy between the phenomenological world and the world of ideas.[55] Nakamura writes:

> The Japanese are willing to accept the phenomenal world as Absolute because of their disposition to lay a greater emphasis upon intuitive sensible concrete events, rather than upon universals. This way of thinking with emphasis upon the fluid, arresting character of observed events regards the phenomenal world itself as Absolute and rejects the recognition of anything existing over [and above] the phenomenal world.[56]

The sharp dichotomy in our culture between the ways of being of the two hemispheres, which began in Ancient Greece, does not appear to exist, or, at any rate, to exist in the same way, in Oriental culture: their experience of the world is still effectively grounded in that of the right hemisphere.

The Japanese also preserve a healthy scepticism about language, and this goes hand in hand with the rejection of a reality that must, or ever could, be arrived at purely by reason. In Zen Buddhism, according to Soiku Shigematsu, the abbot of Shogenji temple, 'a word is a finger that points at the moon. The goal of Zen pupils is the moon itself, not the pointing finger. Zen masters, therefore, will never stop cursing words and letters.'[57] In general the Japanese place far more emphasis on individual existing things than on generalities, are more intuitive, and less cognitive, when compared with Westerners, and are not so easily swayed by logic or system-building.[58] Understanding comes, according to Ogyu Sorai, a Japanese Confucian of the early eighteenth century, through knowing as many individual things as possible: 'Learning consists in widening one's information, absorbing extensively anything and everything one comes upon.'[59] This attitude would have been immediately comprehensible in the Renaissance in the West, but was lost as the systematising and specialisation of knowledge, through which observation of nature becomes more markedly subjugated to theory-building, became increasingly important with the Enlightenment.

The recognition of absolute significance within the phenomenal world relates to the traditional Japanese love of nature.[60] *Shizen*, the Japanese word for nature, also links it clearly to the right-hemisphere way of being. Its derivation means 'of itself', 'spontaneously'(it is in fact an adverb, not a noun), as opposed to whatever is brought about through calculation or by will.[61] It is all that is 'just as it is'. Everything about the Japanese attitude to nature, expressed both in mythology and in everyday life, suggests an attitude of mutual trust, dependence and interrelationship between man and nature. While *shizen* does, of course, refer to the natural world of grass, trees and forest, it also means the land and the landscape, as well as the 'natural self' considered as a physical, spiritual and moral being, something perhaps akin to *Dasein*: thus, though there is a distinction between man, with his will, and nature, the opposition between man and nature implied in the West is absent in Japanese.

A reverent attitude toward *shizen*, now absent in the West, is characteristic even of the Japanese scientific education system. The term *shizen* implies that nature is the root of life in a spiritual or religious sense.[62] A famous Japanese anthropologist Iwata argues that among the Japanese as well as most southeast Asian people, whether the people are formally Buddhists or Christians, there exists an intuition of animism. Everything surrounding human life, including mountains, hills, rivers, plants, trees, animals, fish and insects, has its own spirit (*kami*), and these spirits communicate with one another as well as with those who live there. Apparently most Japanese are familiar with such spirits, and experience them: natural things cannot, therefore, be seen by them merely as objects, as in Western science.[63] We should be careful before we patronise or dismiss any element of this sophisticated culture, in which there have been high standards of education and literacy for centuries during which half our populations could barely sign their name.

What Oriental cultures also emphasise is the value of what is fleeting, something that has been appreciated in the West only rarely, that is to say during the Renaissance and in the Romantic period. The impermanence of nature (*shizen*) is seen as the Buddhahood, or essence of the divine.[64] In the West, with our recording apparatus of every kind, we value what we can grasp and hold. But life and everything living refuses this approach. It changes as we hold it. Japanese temples are seen as still the same temple though they are rebuilt every 20 years: presumably the Japanese would have had no problem answering the paradox of the Ship of Theseus (see p. 138 above), because they naturally see the world as a process rather than a collection of things – like Heraclitus' river, always changing, but always itself.

Why do we in the West think that ultimate value lies only in the immutable, in what is eternally the same? The idea emerges with Parmenides, and Plato gave wider currency to this view of the world derived from the left hemisphere, where all is static, known, unchanging. But once again at the Renaissance and in Romanticism one does see intuitions in the West that life, and everything of value, lies not in a static state of being, as understood by the left hemisphere, but in becoming, as understood by the right hemisphere. To take just one example, at the end of Spenser's great masterpiece, *The Faerie Queene*, in the so-called 'Cantos of Mutabilitie', we see Spenser divided between his loyalty to the abstract principle that what is fixed and eternally unchanging must be 'right', and his imaginative intuition in favour of mutability, the individuality of created beings, the variety of the created world, the liberation that comes from unpredictability, which his work everywhere attests. He reconciles the two when he puts into the mouth of Nature, after the suspense of a long silence in which she appears to be deep in thought, deliberating her verdict, these words:

> . . . all things stedfastnes doe hate
> And changed be: yet being rightly wayd
> They are not changed from their first estate;
> But by their change their being doe dilate:
> And turning to themselues at length againe,
> Doe worke their owne perfection so by fate . . .

In this formulation Spenser suggests, through the *persona* of Nature herself, that, though things change, they thereby 'dilate' their being, becoming in some sense more themselves, and return eventually into themselves, so working 'their own perfection'. This is the expression of the mysterious circular motion that the right hemisphere descries in things, whereby there is movement within stasis, and stasis within movement. It also suggests the process whereby things 'dilate' their being by their contact with the left hemisphere, provided they are then returned to the right. Nietzsche was vehement in setting 'against the *value* of what remains eternally the same (see the naivety of *Spinoza*, also of *Descartes*), the value of the shortest and most fleeting, the seductive flash of gold on the belly of the snake *vita*.'[65]

If it were true, as one might surmise, that cerebral organisation in Oriental peoples is different from that in Westerners, without the same polarisation of the hemispheres, it might suggest another way in which we could consciously set about influencing the hemispheric balance. What scientific evidence could there be of that?

Hardly surprisingly there is in fact much evidence that East Asians and Westerners perceive the world and think about it in very different ways. In general, East Asians have a more holistic approach. For example, if asked to group objects, East Asians make comparatively little use of categories.[66] They are more likely to attend to the broad perceptual and conceptual field, noticing relationships and changes, and grouping objects according to family resemblances, based on an appreciation of the whole, rather than on membership of a category. Westerners are significantly more likely to give one-dimensional, rule-based responses, based on individual components of the stimuli.[67] East Asians also rely less on formal logic, instead focussing on relations among objects and the context in which they interact. They use more intuitive modes compared with Americans of European origin.[68] They see events as arising from an entire context, and tend to think in a much less linear, and more global way, about causation. By contrast Westerners tend to focus exclusively on the object as cause, and are therefore often mistaken. Westerners are more analytic, and pay attention primarily to isolated objects, and the categories to which they belong. They tend to use rules, including formal logic, to understand their behaviour.[69] These effects remain when language is controlled for.[70]

East Asians use a more 'dialectical' mode of reasoning: they are more willing to accept, to entertain, or even seek out contradictory perspectives on the same issue. They see the world in which they live as complex, containing inherently conflicting elements. Where Chinese students try to retain elements of opposing perspectives by seeking to synthesise them, American students try to determine which is correct so that they can reject the other. Presented with evidence for two opposing positions, Easterners are more likely to reach a compromise, whereas the fact of opposition tends to make Westerners adhere to one position more strongly. Westerners adopt a more 'either/or' approach. In one experiment, Chinese volunteers particularly liked proverbs, whether Chinese or American, that presented an apparent contradiction, such as the Chinese saying 'too humble is half proud'. US participants preferred proverbs without contradictions, such as 'half a loaf is better than no bread'.[71]

Westerners are inclined to attend to some focal object, analyzing its attributes and categorizing it in an effort to find out what rules govern its behaviour. Their attention is drawn by the constant features of entities in isolation. East Asians attend to the whole context, including background and global aspects of a scene, whereas American students focus on a few discrete objects salient in the foreground. In one study, Japanese volunteers who saw a cartoon of underwater life later remembered it as an integrated scene, such as a pond with a large school of fish and a clump of seaweed, where their US counterparts mostly recalled a few fish that they had seen in the foreground.[72]

It has often been noted that these cognitive differences are reflected in the differences between Western and Oriental society. Similarly with art: Oriental art emphasises the field, and tends correspondingly to de-emphasize individual objects, including people, by comparison with Western art.[73] Further, a study of photographic scenes from small, medium, and large cities in Japan and the United States demonstrated, by both subjective and objective measures, that Japanese scenes were more ambiguous and contained more elements than American scenes. In a further twist, both Japanese and American participants primed with Japanese scenes attended more to contextual information than did those primed with American scenes.[74] This last finding, in particular, is fascinating, and tends to confirm my view that the brain creates its own projections in the outer world, which in turn help to influence the workings of the brain in a mutually rein-forcing, and self-perpetuating, way. This would suggest that the nature of the modern Western urban environment may be exaggerating the tendencies that the left hemisphere has projected there, as well as suggesting one reason why the natural environment is felt to have such a healing influence.

Eastern cultures, and in particular the Japanese, have been characterised as 'inter-dependent'; in other words, individuals are less seen in isolation than they are in the West, instead forming part of an interconnected social web. For them, the sense of the self (as we saw for the right hemisphere) develops through understanding its influence on others. Self-improvement in such cultures has far less to do with getting what one wants, and far more to do with confronting one's own shortcom-ings, in the interests of harmony, at home, at work, and amongst friends.[75] Westerners perform better on tasks with independent demands than on tasks with interdependent demands.[76] East Asians make stronger efforts to justify their choices if they have been made on behalf of a friend, Westerners if made for themselves.[77]

The Japanese word for self, *jibun*, implies a share of something which is both separate and not separate, individual and yet still shared. It is a common Western misconception that Japanese culture does not value the individual.[78] On the contrary, originality, self-direction, and autonomy are all highly prized.[79] In fact, if anything the Japanese have a more highly developed sense of private self-consciousness than their American counterparts, with at least as much concern for hidden thoughts, feelings, and motives.[80] But they are also more sensitive to their obligation to belong, rather than seeking only to feel good because of unique qualities that make one stand apart from others.

Emphasis on high self-esteem as a sign of mental health is a relatively recent, Western phenomenon, and is far from being an unmixed good. Having low self-esteem, certainly in the West, is an obvious cause of anxiety and depression; but high self-esteem is positively correlated with a tendency to be unrealistic, to take offence too easily, and to become violent and demanding if one's needs are not met.[81] Whereas in America students seek positive self-regard, the Japanese are more self-critical, an attitude which they sense to have a natural wisdom.[82] The need for positive self-regard, as it is currently conceptualized, is not a universal, but rooted in significant aspects of North American culture.[83] People in the West characteristically over-estimate their abilities, exaggerate their capacity to control essentially uncontrollable events, and hold over-optimistic views of the future. In fact, so much does our happiness depend on such illusions, that, in the West, lacking them is even correlated with psychiatric problems.[84]

This is not true in Japan, where self-worth is not predicated on thinking highly of yourself, but on being a good citizen and member of your social group. Although the Japanese report being proud and happy to be associated with a prestigious college or organisation, they do not hold unrealistically positive opinions about the group to which they belong. Although they set higher standards for themselves, and aspire to higher personal goals, than, for example, Canadian students, they more rarely feel depressed about their failures to measure up. In the West, failure tends to lead to discouragement; in the East, to a determination to do better.[85] The espousal of unrealistic expectations in the absence of a readiness to make sacrifices may be one of the most significant factors in the escalating rates of depression in developed, and developing, countries referred to above.

Beliefs about the left and right sides of the body in China make an interesting contrast with those in the West. Though there were some interesting exceptions in Roman culture, where the left hand was associated with healing and religion,[86] in general we have associated what is on the left with what is *sinister* or *gauche*, associations reinforced by the holy scriptures of Christianity and Islam.[87] This may have to do with the fact that danger is more likely to be apprehended by the left visual field (see Chapter 2), since the right hemisphere is more vigilant; or with the fact that the left hand is weaker; or with the fact that left-handedness is disproportionately represented among those with mental impairment. It might simply reflect the prejudices of the verbal left hemisphere: why is there in many cultures deliberate mutilation or restriction of the left hand or arm, as for example among the Nuer people of the Southern Sudan?[88] There are occasional exceptions: for example, among the Zuñi Indians of North America the left and right sides are personified as brother gods, of which the left is the elder and wiser; but generally the associations are opposite.[89]

However, among the ancient Chinese the left was *yang* and therefore superior, the right *yin* and inferior. The Chinese honour both hands: the ideogram for 'right' consists of 'hand' plus 'mouth' (the hand for eating); the 'left' consists of 'hand' plus 'square', which in China symbolises the arts, particularly religious and magic arts. Chinese people generally educate themselves to be right-handed and right-footed, but as regards eyes and ears, they prefer the left side. The right hand prevails over the left hand, but the left ear and eye over the right. Archers aimed at the enemy's left eye.[90]

Can imaging tell us anything about the differences between East Asian and Western minds? Not much, perhaps, as yet. In terms of structure, cerebral asymmetries in Chinese populations are apparently similar to those of North Americans, though slightly less marked.[91] Some structural differences in the left frontal and bilateral temporal lobes have been detected, which would appear from fMRI evidence to be involved with language production.[92] Chinese speakers activate more strongly in the right temporoparietal region than American English and Spanish speakers, with language function displaying less asymmetry overall in the Chinese.[93] However, the majority of Chinese in Hong Kong (mostly Cantonese-speaking Chinese) have, at least structurally speaking, asymmetrical cerebral hemispheres similar to those of Europeans.[94]

What, if anything, can we deduce from all of this? I think there is by now enough consistent evidence, from a variety of sources, and of a variety of types, for us to accept something which seems intuitively likely: that there are differences between the way in which Westerners and East Asians see the world, and that these have something to do with the balance of the hemispheres. More specifically, in the case of every single difference listed above, it takes the same form, a greater reliance in the West on the left hemisphere, and there is not even a single difference suggesting a greater reliance on the right. It would be tedious to go through them all again here, as there are so many, but to any reader who has got this far I hope they will be obvious. This merely confirms what the great biologist and scholar of Chinese history of science, Joseph Needham, repeatedly observed – that there was a fondness for *particles* in Western thought, to which the Chinese were 'perennially averse'.[95] What this does not, of course, demonstrate is that East Asian culture relies on the right hemisphere, and Western culture on the left. We both rely on each. What the evidence suggests, if reviewed in greater detail than I have here, is that the East Asian cultures use strategies of both hemispheres more evenly, while Western strategies are steeply skewed towards the left hemisphere. In other words, the emissary appears to work in harmony with the Master in the East, but is in the process of usurping him in the West.

What one also has to accept is that, just as the marked difference between the performance of the two hands in right-handers is associated with a slight improvement in the right hand, but the price for this is that 'the left hand declines dramatically',[96] there *are* slight advantages in being so skewed towards the left hemisphere. In some tasks, the rather unbalanced take on things that it offers does increase efficiency. For example, lack of interest in context makes one worse in some respects, but better where context needs to be ignored. Like schizophrenics, Westerners are better than East Asians at learning arbitrary rules for categorisation: they are less distracted by common sense.[97] But the price is that they lose dramatically in other respects. One interesting observation is that Asian Americans approximate more closely to the US model:[98] being exposed to Western patterns of thought leaves them somewhere between the two positions. Provided one can rely on a reciprocal process, this would suggest the possibility of acculturating ourselves in the West to a more balanced way of using our brains, if we are willing to learn from the East – and if we can do so before its cultures are Westernised beyond redemption.

Of course there is a wealth of wisdom in Western culture itself, and it has unequalled strengths, as well as never before seen weaknesses, of its own. But we are increasingly alienated from its history, and, for reasons I have surmised, as things are now, learning from our past seems to present huge problems for us. One possibility is that music, which brought us together before language existed, might even now prove effective in regenerating commonality, avoiding the need for words that have been devalued, or for which we have become too cynical.[99] Let's not forget that it was with music that Orpheus once moved stones. But such a renaissance would require a complete change in our attitude to what we are doing in art, and where it is going. It would require a return to something as patient, attentive, skilled and beautiful as the work of the surgeon in James Kirkup's poem 'A Correct Compassion', who '. . . with a curious nervous elegance laid bare / The root of life', and puts his 'finger on its beating heart'.

Ultimately what we cannot afford to keep deferring is a regrounding of both art and science in the lived world. Both need to be more human, and more humane. In science this means moving away as far as possible from the worn-out mode of scientific materialism with its reductive language. The words we use to describe human processes are highly influential for the way we conceive ourselves, and therefore for our actions and, above all, for the values to which we hold. With a rising interest in neuroscience, we have an opportunity, which we must not squander, to sophisticate our understanding of ourselves, but we can only do so if we first sophisticate the language we use, since many current users of that language adopt it so naturally that they are not even aware of how it blinds them to the very possibility that they might be dealing with anything other than a machine.

CONCLUSION

As Richard Strauss's opera *Ariadne auf Naxos* opens, we see the preparations for the entertainment of a mysterious man of wealth, who has commissioned a serious opera from a young composer. A *commedia dell'arte* troupe has also been engaged to perform: such players are called *maschere*, 'masked ones', and represent stock characters from low life. As the various actors and musicians prepare behind the scenes, the young composer, whose opera concerns the tragic plight of Ariadne abandoned by her lover Theseus, is horrified to learn that these inter-lopers are to perform their tawdry burlesque on the theme of infidelity immedi-ately after his own heart-rending work. What an outrage! But that is as nothing to what he learns a few minutes before the performers are due on stage. At the last minute, their patron changes his plan, and now insists that, for lack of time, both are to be performed simultaneously. Their plots are 'with a few trifling alterations' to be 'served up together'. The resulting farrago, sometimes moving, sometimes comic, always incongruous, forms the second part of Strauss's opera.

At the time Hugo von Hofmannsthal was writing the libretto for *Ariadne*, he was also reading Milton, certainly *L'Allegro* and *Il Penseroso*, his meditations on the comic and tragic muses.[100] But the fact that the structure of *Ariadne* seems so like the brain cognising itself makes one wonder if he was influenced uncon-sciously by his reading of *Paradise Lost*. For *Paradise Lost* seems to me precisely that – a profound self-exploration of the divided human brain: the relationship between two unequal powers, one of which grounds the being of the other, and indeed needs the other for its fulfilment, and which therefore has to make itself vulnerable to that other; who, through blindness and vanity, rejects the union that would have brought about the *Aufhebung* of both, and prefers instead a state of war without end. The fallout from this war is that man and woman, Adam and Eve and their offspring, are turned out of paradise.

In the opening pages of this book, I wrote that I believed it to be profoundly true that the inner structure of our intellect reflects the structure of the universe. By 'profoundly' I meant not just true by definition, as would be the case for those who believe that the universe is in any case a creation of our brains. I think it goes further than that. I believe our brains not only dictate the shape of the experience we have of the world, but are likely themselves to reflect, in their structure and functioning, the nature of the universe in which they have come about.

What the neuropsychological data I have considered in this book exhibit are some underlying tendencies – tendencies that can, however, be ultimately highly revealing. Overall a picture develops from a mass of small details, not necessarily by summing them all, left-hemisphere fashion, but perhaps by seeing the pattern, as the Dalmatian emerges from the blur of splashes and dots, right-hemisphere fashion.[101] If I am wrong, the picture I discern in the dots and splashes will simply not be recognised by others; if there is any truth in it, it may awaken thoughts. As Karl Popper put it, 'bold ideas, unjustified anticipations and speculative thought, are our only means for interpreting nature: our only *organon*, our only instrument for grasping her.'[102] Or, perhaps, reaching out a hand to her.

I would also like to put in a word for uncertainty. In the field of religion there are dogmatists of no-faith as there are of faith, and both seem to me closer to one another than those who try to keep the door open to the possibility of something beyond the customary ways in which we think, but which we would have to find, painstakingly, for ourselves. Similarly as regards science, there are those who are certain, God knows how, of what it is that patient attention to the world reveals, and those who really do not care, because their minds are already made up that science cannot tell them anything profound. Both seem to me profoundly mistaken. Though we cannot be certain what it is our knowledge reveals, this is in fact a much more fruitful position – in fact the only one that permits the possibility of belief. And what has limited the power of both art and science in our time has been the absence of belief in anything except the most diminished version of the world and our selves. Certainty is the greatest of all illusions: whatever kind of fundamentalism it may underwrite, that of religion or of science, it is what the ancients meant by *hubris*. The only certainty, it seems to me, is that those who believe they are certainly right are certainly wrong. The difference between scientific materialists and the rest is only this: the intuition of the one is that mechanistic application of reason will reveal everything about the world we inhabit, where the intuition of the others leads them to be less sure. Virtually every great physicist of the last century – Einstein, Bohr, Planck, Heisenberg, Bohm, amongst many others – has made the same point. A leap of faith is involved, for scientists as much as anyone. According to Max Planck, 'Anybody who has been seriously engaged in scientific work of any kind realizes that over the entrance to the gates of the temple of science are written the words: *Ye must have faith*. It is a quality which the scientist cannot dispense with.' And he continued: 'Science cannot solve the ultimate mystery of nature. And that is because, in the last analysis, we ourselves are part of nature and therefore part of the mystery that we are trying to solve.'[103]

In a famous passage Lessing wrote:

The true value of a man is not determined by his possession, supposed or real, of Truth, but rather by his sincere exertion to get to what lies behind the Truth. It is not possession of the Truth, but rather the pursuit of Truth by which he extends his powers and in which his ever-growing perfectibility is to be found. Possession makes one *passive, indolent, vain* – If God held enclosed in his right hand all truth, and in his left hand the ever-living striving for truth, although with the qualification that I must for ever err, and said to me 'choose', I should humbly choose the left hand and say 'Father, give! pure truth is for thee alone.'[104]

Lessing, like Goethe, wrote a *Faust*, though only fragments remain. In his poem, too, Faust is redeemed by his endless striving. Note, incidentally, that it is the left hand, the servant of the right hemisphere, that contains the ever-living striving for truth.

In this book certainty has certainly not been my aim. I am not so much worried by the aspects that remain unclear, as by those which appear to be clarified, since that almost certainly means a failure to see clearly. I share Wittgenstein's mistrust of deceptively clear models: and, as Waismann said, 'any psychological explanation is ambiguous, cryptic and open-ended, for we ourselves are many-layered, contradictory and incomplete beings, and this complicated structure, which fades away into indeterminacy, is passed on to all our actions.'[105] I am also sympathetic to those who think that sounds like a cop-out. But I do think that things as they exist in practice in the real world, rather than as they exist in theory in our representations, are likely to be intrinsically resistant to precision and clarification. That is not our failure, but an indication of the nature of what we are dealing with. That does not mean we should give up the attempt. It is the striving that enables us to achieve a better understanding, but only as long as it is imbued with a tactful recognition of the limits to human understanding. The rest is hubris.[106]

If it could eventually be shown definitively that the two major ways, not just of thinking, but of being in the world, are *not* related to the two cerebral hemispheres, I would be surprised, but not unhappy. Ultimately what I have tried to point to is that the apparently separate 'functions' in each hemisphere fit together intelligently to form in each case a single coherent entity; that there are, not just currents here and there in the history of ideas, but consistent ways of being that persist across the history of the Western world, that are fundamentally opposed, though complementary, in what they reveal to us; and that the hemispheres of the brain can be seen as, at the very least, a metaphor for these. One consequence of such a model, I admit, is that we might have to revise the superior assumption that we understand the world better than our ancestors, and adopt a more realistic view that we just see it differently – and may indeed be seeing less than they did.

The divided nature of our reality has been a consistent observation since humanity has been sufficiently self-conscious to reflect on it.[107] That most classical representative of the modern self-conscious spirit, Goethe's Faust, famously

462 • THE MASTER AND HIS EMISSARY

declared that 'two souls, alas! dwell in my breast' ('*Zwei Seelen wohnen, ach! in meiner Brust*').[108] Schopenhauer described two completely distinct forms of experience ('*zwei völlig heterogene Weisen gegebene Erkenntniß*');[109] Bergson referred to two different orders of reality ('*deux réalités d'ordre différent*').[110] Scheler described the human being as a citizen of two worlds ('*Bürger zweier Welten*') and said that all great European philosophers, like Kant, who used the same formulation, had seen as much.[111] What all these point to is the fundamentally divided nature of mental experience. When one puts that together with the fact that the brain is divided into two relatively independent chunks which just happen broadly to mirror the very dichotomies that are being pointed to – alienation versus engagement, abstraction versus incarnation, the categorical versus the unique, the general versus the particular, the part versus the whole, and so on – it seems like a metaphor that might have some literal truth. But if it turns out to be 'just' a metaphor, I will be content. I have a high regard for metaphor. It is how we come to understand the world.

NOTES

PREFACE TO THE NEW EXPANDED EDITION

1. Kosslyn & Miller, 2013.
2. Marinsek, Turner & Gazzaniga et al, 2014, p. 7.
3. Gazzaniga, 1983, p. 536.
4. Barbey, Colom & Paul et al., 2014.
5. Simpson, 1963, p. 82.
6. ibid., p. 84.
7. Planck, 1936, p. 5.
8. Thoreau, 1906, p. 373.

INTRODUCTION: THE MASTER AND HIS EMISSARY

1. Hellige, 1993, p. 168.
2. Ramachandran, 2005, p. 279, n. 4.
3. Crow, 2006, p. 793.
4. Many others in the field are similarly convinced that the issue is important. John Cutting, author of the most comprehensive study ever made of the right hemisphere and its functions in relation to psychiatric illness (Cutting, 1990), writes that 'the single greatest advance in neuropsychology in the last 50 years has been the discovery of hemisphere differences in every aspect of human life' (Cutting, 2009). Marcel Kinsbourne, despite his justified aversion to 'dichotomania', has for decades done more than most neuroscientists to pursue the differences between the hemispheres. Claude Braun, another distinguished neuroscientist with an interest in hemisphere differences, writes that 'the vast database of animal research [and] human neuropsychiatric research . . . both clearly establish numerous important and spectacular specialisations of the right hemisphere' (Braun, 2007, p. 398). Elkhonon Goldberg has consistently championed the view that there are important differences in hemisphere function (see p. 482, n. 16 below). Robert Ornstein, having written a book about hemisphere differences, *The Psychology of Consciousness*, in the 1970s, became so frustrated with the vulgarisations that for 20 years he concentrated his research on other matters and gave hemisphere research up as a bad job. He has now returned to it, and admits that he was 'bowled over' on returning to the literature in the 1990s to find how much evidence had come forward that 'the division of the mind is profound' (Ornstein, 1997, pp. 3–4).
5. 'In the intact brain, it is rarely the case that one hemisphere can perform a task normally whereas the other hemisphere is completely unable to perform the task at all. Instead, both hemispheres often have considerable ability to perform a task, even though they may go about it *in different ways* [emphasis added] . . . In this sense, having two cerebral hemispheres is akin to having two reasonably complete "brains" whose differences, compared with their many similarities, are likely to start out being subtle. Although many hemispheric asymmetries are very subtle, the range of tasks showing hemispheric asymmetry is quite broad and spans such diverse domains as motor performance, language, spatial processing and emotion. Thus far, it has not been possible to identify any single information-processing dichotomy that could account for anything close to this entire range of hemispheric asymmetries . . . Whatever links there might be between the various hemispheric asymmetries, they would seem to be determined in some other way or according to some other principle' (Hellige, 1993, pp. 335–6).
6. I adopt a position closer to Schopenhauer's belief that the world exists 'between' something independent of the mind and the mind that apprehends it than to the (in some ways similar, but relatively adynamic) relationship suggested by Kant's view that, as Tanner puts it, 'our experiences are the result of a collaboration between us and a basic reality of which we can know nothing, except that it must exist' (Tanner, 1999, p. 6).
7. To some extent this aspiration has been realised: see Schore, 1997.
8. C. Jung, 1953–79, vol. 10, p. 12.
9. Our brains are 'organs of unique and curious historiography, for whereas in our bodies earlier somatic structures have been superseded by later ones, our brains have retained, without replacing, certain modified forms of the stages of our own evolution' (Fraser, 1989, p. 3).
10. Sherrington, 1906.
11. Kinsbourne, 1988. I agree with Sperry that 'the left-right dichotomy in cognitive mode is an idea with which it is very easy to run wild'. As he says, 'qualitative shifts in mental control may involve up-down, front-back, or various

other organisational changes as well as left-right differences' (Sperry 1982, p. 1225), thus confirming that in his view opponent pairs are involved in shifts of mental control. But the 'left–right' dichotomy is different in kind from the 'up–down' and 'front-back' dichotomies in several important respects, which neither Kinsbourne nor Sperry mention. The cortex and subcortical regions are functionally distinct and incomparable, and run in series rather than in parallel. The cortex arises out of and exists to modulate the 'input' from the more ancient regions that lie below: the relationship between the frontal and posterior regions of the cerebral cortex has a similar structure, in that the frontal lobes developed from, and exist to modulate the action of, the posterior cortex. By contrast, the hemispheres are evolutionary twins: they display a remarkable degree of apparent overlap or redundancy of function, and run in parallel rather than in series. Each on its own can sustain something remarkably like a normal human mind, which certainly cannot be said of any of the other paired entities on its own. I believe the 'front-back' and 'up-down' shifts may be particularly important in understanding both normal functioning and psychopathology at the individual level; only the hemispheres, however, are capable singly of underwriting nothing less than a version of reality, and displaying the rivalry that in this book forms my focus of attention. And as I hope to show, the left–right opposition is itself already inextricably involved, in a far from straightforward way, with the other two dimensions.

12. Ornstein, 1997, p. 16.
13. Sergent, 1982.
14. Laeng, Chabris & Kosslyn, 2003, p. 313.
15. Descartes, 1984–91a, p. 118.
16. The complexities of handedness have been dealt with superlatively well by Chris McManus (in McManus, 2002, to which the interested reader is referred).
17. Language is lateralised to the left in about 96% of right-handed subjects (Rasmussen & Milner, 1977). Although this study was based on a sample of subjects with epilepsy, the finding has been confirmed in normal subjects: see Pujol, Deus, Losilla et al., 1999.
18. Pujol, Deus, Losilla et al., 1999.
19. Valéry, 1957, 'Au sujet d'*Eurêka*', vol. 1, pp. 857–8. In fact he is speaking of Edgar Allan Poe: '*Dans la système de Poe . . . l'univers est construit sur un plan dont la symétrie profonde est, en quelque sorte, présente dans l'intime structure de notre esprit.*' Poe had himself written in *Eureka*: 'the sense of the symmetrical is an instinct which may be depended on with an almost blindfold reliance. It is the poetical essence of the Universe.'
20. Pasteur, 1874 (1 juin; in Pasteur, 1922, p. 361): '*L'univers est un ensemble dissymétrique et je suis persuadé que la vie, telle qu'elle se manifeste à nous, est fonction de la dissymétrie de l'univers ou des conséquences qu'elle entraîne.*' Pasteur's belief that asymmetry distinguishes whatever is living has been confirmed in our time: see, for example, Geschwind & Galaburda, 1985.
21. Very roughly indeed, and I cannot now remember where.
22. For a discussion of Hegel's treatment of 'master' and 'slave', and its relevance to the neuropsychology of the cerebral hemispheres, see pp. 204–5 below.

PART 1: THE DIVIDED BRAIN

CHAPTER 1: ASYMMETRY AND THE BRAIN

1. The source for this is one Avianus Vindicianus, a friend of St. Augustine who was proconsul of Africa in around AD 360–70 (Green, 2003). His tract *De Semine*, preserved in MS no.1342–50 of the Royal Library at Brussels (folio 48r–52v), probably represents the views of Greek physicians of the third century BC. These ideas are often mistakenly attributed to Diocles of Carystus, a known Athenian physician from the fourth century BC, on the basis of the earlier work of the Dutch scholar, Gert-Jan Lokhorst, who published three papers in the 1980s to this effect (Lokhorst, 1982a, 1982b, 1985). However, he later revised his views (see Lokhorst 1996); and from this it would seem that Avianus's sources cannot be earlier than the third century BC. After Avianus there is little until modern times to suggest any view other than the naïve one that the hemispheres are symmetrical, apart from an annotated drawing of the brain from the early fifteenth century preserved in Trinity College, Cambridge (MS. 0.2.40, fol. 57v), which suggests that the right hemisphere is warmer than the left: 'the rygth syde hoot ande dry, the leyft syde cold and drey' (Clarke & Dewhurst, 1972, p. 21). I have no idea where that came from, but it has a sort of metaphorical aptness.
2. Wigan, 1844, p. 271. Wigan sees the hemispheres as like the two eyes: despite their duality, they normally deliver only one object of vision, not two; and, though each eye is sufficient on its own, there are some things that two do better than one. But, as with eyes, the two hemispheres must be identical. He does not therefore distinguish between the two hemispheres, although he says that 'in the healthy brain one of the two hemispheres is almost always superior in power, and exercises control over the volitions of its fellow'. He sees all psychiatric disorders in terms of a moral conflict of wills, the will of the healthy hemisphere, whichever it might be, striving to compensate for the depraved will of the diseased one.
3. Jäncke & Steinmetz, 2003, p. 204; Banich, 2003, p. 262.
4. Conti & Manzoni, 1994; Saron, Foxe, Simpson et al., 2002.
5. Meyer, Röricht, Gräfin von Einsiedel et al., 1995; Röricht, Irlbacher, Petrow et al., 1997; Höppner, Kunesch, Buchmann et al., 1999.
6. Cook, 1984; Hoptman & Davidson, 1994; Chiarello & Maxfield, 1996.
7. Saron, Foxe, Schroeder et al., 2003; Allison, Meador, Loring et al., 2000; Tootell, Mendola, Hadjikhani et al., 1998.
8. Meyer, Röricht, Gräfin von Einsiedel et al., 1995; Bloom & Hynd, 2005.
9. Jäncke & Steinmetz, 2003, pp. 210–11.
10. Hopkins & Marino, 2000; Aboitiz, Scheibel & Zaidel, 1992.
11. Friedman & Polson, 1981.

12. Mind and brain are aspects of the same entity, but completely distinct types of phenomena. The difference is similar to what I take Sartre to mean by his distinction between our inward experience of the body (*pour soi*), and the fact of the body as a 'thing' (*en soi*).
13. Cf. Roger Scruton on time: Scruton, 1997, p. 367.
14. Descartes, 1984–91b, 'Meditation VI', p. 56 (trans. adapted): '... *me non tantum adesse meo corpori ut nauta adest navigio, sed illi arctissime esse conjunctum et quasi permixtum, adeo ut unum quid cum illo componam.*'
15. I said that the fundamental problem in explaining the experience of consciousness is that there is nothing else remotely like it to compare it with, since it is itself the ground of all experience. If it were not for this, a helpful analogy for the relationship I believe I see between mind and brain might be the relationship of a wave to water. The wave exists in the water: that's what we mean by a wave. Does the water cause the wave? No. Is it the movement of the water, then, that causes the wave? No, not that either: the movement of the water just *is* the wave. Similarly the relationship of mind and brain. Does the brain cause the mind? No. Is it the changing states of the brain that cause the mind? No: the changing brain states *are* the mind – *once the brain experiences them*. And that is where the analogy ends, because there is no inwardness to a wave. All the same, the analogy continues to have its uses: the forces of wind and gravitation that end up instantiated as a wave in water do not depend on water for their being, only for their expression at that moment as a wave. They exist apart from – in a sense, above and behind – the water in which they are instantiated, and would carry on existing if the water were not there, though then they would be deprived of their form of expression as that particular wave. Similarly, I believe, it may be that consciousness does not depend on a brain for its existence: just, in the absence of a brain, it is deprived of its expression as that particular mind. Another metaphor, far from original, but none the less useful, is that of the TV set. The TV set is proximally causative of the phenomena that appear on the screen: damage the electronic circuitry, and the picture's gone, or at any rate distorted – true enough. But the TV set is only mediative; it does not itself gives rise to the programme you watch. And you couldn't tell which it does – originate the programme or transmit it – by inspecting the workings: the TV set would look much the same whichever. It is true that we might be able to say from looking at the type of constituent parts in it whether there was anything there that we recognised could in itself generate programmes from scratch, or whether, on the contrary, there is something there which, from what we know of electronic components, appears to pick up electromagnetic waves and turn them into pictures. But that is only possible because we make all the parts of any machine, and set up the system. So we know by definition what sort of a thing a cathode ray tube or plasma screen is, and what it is *for*, what it does. But there is no such state of affairs with a neurone. We didn't make them and we don't know what sort of things they are, or what they are capable of doing. In trying to understand them we have, fatally, already to decide what sort of things they might be in order to know what to compare them with, which kind of model to apply. Apply the machine model and that begs the question entirely.
16. Semendeferi, Lu, Schenker et al., 2002; Schoenemann, Sheehan & Glotzer, 2005.
17. Allen, Damasio, Grabowski et al., 2003.
18. Cf. Pascal: 'When we're too young, our judgment isn't sound, and it's the same when we're too old. If we don't think enough about something – or if we think too much – we're inflexible and get stuck. If we take a look at our work as soon as we've done it, we're not able to be objective; but if we wait too long, we can't get into it any more. It's like looking at pictures from too near or too far away. There is only one place that's exactly right: the others are either too far, too near, too high or too low. In the art of painting it's perspective that determines where that point should be. But who's to say where it is when it comes to truth and morality?': 1976, §381 (Lafuma §21); trans. I. McG. ('*Si on est trop jeune on ne juge pas bien, trop vieil de même. Si on n'y songe pas assez, si on y songe trop, on s'entête et on s'en coiffe. Si considère son ouvrage incontinent après l'avoir fait on en est encore tout prévenu, si trop longtemps après on n'y entre plus. Ainsi les tableaux vus de trop loin et de trop près. Et il n'y a qu'un point indivisible qui soit le véritable lieu. Les autres sont trop près, trop loin, trop haut ou trop bas. La perspective l'assigne dans l'art de la peinture, mais dans la vérité et dans la morale qui l'assignera?*') Similar ideas, foreign to the invariance of Cartesianism, are expressed in (1976) §71(Lafuma §38) and §69 (Lafuma §723). In this and all subsequent quotations from Pascal, the notation of the *Pensées* is that of Léon Brunschvicg, though in each case I have also given the notation proposed by Louis Lafuma for ease of reference to other editions.
19. Marc Dax died in 1837. His series of observations, originally made in 1836, were published by his son Gustave in 1863, following Broca's publication of similar findings in the case of 'Tan' in 1861 and prior to Broca's classic paper of 1865: G. Dax, 1863; M. Dax, 1865; Broca, 1861a, 1861b, 1861c, 1865.
20. Wernicke, 1874.
21. Heschl, 1878; Eberstaller, 1884.
22. Geschwind & Levitsky, 1968. Subsequent studies have suggested that the difference may be due to the fact that the posterior angulation of the right Sylvian fissure takes off more steeply and anteriorly than the left, shortening the planum (Loftus, Tramo, Thomas et al., 1993). The issue of how to define the planum remains unresolved (Honeycutt, Musick, Barta et al., 2000), but a recent study which compared three different definitions of the planum found a leftward asymmetry according to each (Zetzsche, Meisenzahl, Preuss et al., 2001).
23. LeMay & Kido, 1978; LeMay, 1984, 1977; Chiu & Damasio, 1980.
24. Yakovlev & Rakić, 1966; Weinberger, Luchins, Morihisa et al., 1982; Bilder, Wu, Bogerts et al., 1999; Barrick, Mackay, Prima et al., 2005; Good, Johnsrude, Ashburner et al., 2001.
25. D'A. W. Thompson, 1917.
26. Kertesz, Polk, Black et al., 1992. As did Witelson & Kigar (1988), they found that brain asymmetries of structure were generally related to function, although, as the authors point out, phylogenetic correlations between the structure and function of an organ overall should not lead to the expectation that such correlations will be demonstrated in every individual case. For a review of the relationship between anatomical and functional asymmetry in the human brain, see Toga & Thompson, 2003.
27. Jäncke & Steinmetz, 2003, p. 201; Maguire, Gadian, Johnsrude et al., 2000.
28. Amunts, Jäncke, Mohlberg et al., 2000; Amunts, Schlaug, Schleicher et al., 1996; Melsbach, Wohlschläger, Spiess et al., 1996; Snyder, Bilder, Wu et al., 1995.

29. Maguire, Gadian, Johnsrude et al., 2000.
30. Nottebohm, 1970.
31. Jäncke & Steinmetz, 2003, p. 216. See also LeMay & Culebras, 1972, and Hopkins & Marino, 2000.
32. Rogers & Andrew, 2002.
33. Glick, Meibach, Cox et al., 1979; Sandhu, Cook & Diamond, 1986.
34. Rogers, 2000.
35. Hoffman, Robakiewicz, Tuttle et al., 2006.
36. Rogers & Kaplan, 2006; Rogers, 2000.
37. Rogers, Zucca & Vallortigara, 2004.
38. Dharmaretnam & Rogers, 2005.
39. Bugnyar, Stöwe & Heinrich, 2004.
40. Evans, Evans & Marler, 1993; Rogers, 2000; Lippolis, Bisazza, Rogers et al., 2002; Lippolis, Westman, McAllan et al., 2005.
41. Rogers, 2006.
42. Fabre-Thorpe, Fagot, Lorincz et al., 1993.
43. McGrew & Marchant, 1999.
44. Crow, Crow, Done et al., 1998.
45. Rogers, Zucca & Vallortigara, 2004.
46. Güntürkün, Diekamp, Manns et al., 2000.
47. Csermely, 2004.
48. Robins & Rogers, 2006.
49. Vallortigara, Rogers, Bisazza et al., 1998.
50. Bisazza, Cantalupo, Capocchiano et al., 2000; Rogers & Workman, 1989; Halpern, Güntürkün, Hopkins et al., 2005.
51. See, e.g., Fernández-Carriba, Loeches, Morcillo et al., 2002a; Ventolini, Ferrero, Sponza et al., 2005.
52. Rogers, 2000; Vallortigara, 1992.
53. Dharmaretnam & Andrew, 1994.
54. Hoffman, Robakiewicz, Tuttle et al., 2006.
55. Ventolini, Ferrero, Sponza et al., 2005.
56. Denenberg, Garbanati, Sherman et al., 1978.
57. Andrew & Rogers, 2002.
58. Johnsgard, 1981.
59. Corballis, 2003. See also R.H. Bauer, 1993; Nottebohm, 1977; Ehret, 1987; Fitch, Brown, O'Connor et al., 1993; Holman & Hutchison, 1994; and Hook-Costigan & Rogers, 1998, all cited by Corballis.
60. Hunt, 2000; Hunt, Corballis & Gray, 2001; Hunt & Gray, 2004; Rutledge & Hunt, 2004.
61. Rogers, 2000.
62. Kahn & Bingman, 2004.
63. Rogers, 2002.
64. Yamazaki, Aust, Huber et al., 2007; Laeng, Zarrinpar & Kosslyn, 2003; Lux, Marshall, Ritzl et al., 2004. Also see: Halpern, Güntürkün, Hopkins et al., 2005.

CHAPTER 2: WHAT DO THE TWO HEMISPHERES 'DO'?

1. As if to make the point, a recent article on the lateralisation of memory explicitly states, having reviewed the literature, that what makes the difference is the hemisphere, not the site within it: 'lesion site within the hemisphere does not seem to explain much of the laterality findings, if any at all' (Braun, Delisle, Guimond et al., 2009, p. 127). However such a strong claim is unusual, and in most cases the point is clearly relative, not absolute.
2. This was first noted in the mid-nineteenth century (Thurman, 1866). Since then, the finding has been repeatedly confirmed, by amongst others, Crichton-Browne, 1880; Bonin, 1962; Hadziselimovic & Cus, 1966; Galaburda, LeMay, Kemper et al., 1978; Weis, Haug, Holoubek et al., 1989; LeMay, 1982; Schwartz, Creasey, Grady et al., 1985; Kertesz, Polk, Black et al., 1992; Zilles, Dabringhaus, Geyer et al., 1996; and H. Damasio, 2005, p. 82.
3. Kolb, Sutherland, Nonneman et al., 1982; Diamond, Johnson & Ingham, 1975.
4. At least in both Caucasians and East Asians: Wang, He, Tong et al., 1999.
5. Giedd, Snell, Lange et al., 1996.
6. Chi, Dooling & Gilles, 1977b; Witelson & Pallie, 1973.
7. Galaburda, 1995.
8. Galaburda, Aboitiz, Rosen et al., 1986.
9. Hayes & Lewis, 1993.
10. Scheibel, Paul, Fried et al., 1985.
11. Seldon, 1982.
12. Allen, Damasio, Grabowski et al., 2003; Gur, Turetsky, Matsui et al., 1999; Gur, Packer, Hungerbühler et al., 1980; Galaburda, 1995. While the findings of Pujol and colleagues are at variance (Pujol, López-Sala, Deus et al., 2002), it should be pointed out that in that paper they make a number of findings that are not in keeping with the research consensus.
13. Lewis & Diamond, 1995.
14. Glick, Carlson, Drew et al., 1987.
15. Glick, Ross & Hough, 1982; Tucker & Williamson, 1984; Wagner, Burns, Dannals et al., 1983. Alteration of the prenatal environment can result in changes in the hemisphere asymmetry of neuroendocrine control: see, e.g., Fride & Weinstock, 1988.
16. For an overview see Davidson & Hugdahl, 1995, and their subsequent volume, Davidson & Hugdahl, 2003.

17. I use the words 'do' and 'function' for the moment because they are part of the language commonly used in talking about the brain. I place them in inverted commas because I believe they are misleading, since they already presuppose a model, and therefore prejudge the nature of the brain they are trying to help us understand.
18. This is better than looking at brains which have abnormal structure from birth, because such brains will have had the opportunity to reorganise themselves during the first decade of life, the period of maximum plasticity, with the result that their organisation will be atypical and can give us only limited information about the brain in general. With time, it is true, there may be adaptations even in the adult brain following an insult, but they are necessarily far more limited. But brain lesions do have consequences for the non-lesioned areas. The brain is a dynamic system: particularly at the time the lesion is occurring, inferences are unreliable. This caveat applies to neuroscientist Jill Bolte-Taylor's fascinating account of her own left-hemisphere stroke (http://www.ted.com/index.php/talks/jill_bolte_taylor_s_powerful_stroke_of_insight.html, accessed 28 April 2009).
19. See, e.g., Devinsky & D'Esposito, 2004.
20. 'Trying to surmise the brain activation pattern of a cognitive task based on functional neuroimaging data may be like Noah trying to surmise the landscape of Mesopotamia after the Great Flood by staring at the peak of Mount Ararat protruding above the water' (Goldberg, 2001, p. 55).
21. Cacioppo, Berntson, Lorig et al., 2003. Areas that show activity may be doing so in *response* to activity somewhere else in the brain which is not showing up, but is the primary link with the activity in which we are interested. Metabolic activity may be great in one part of the system, e.g. in the basal ganglia, because this is a regulatory constituent of a system whose other parts (neocortex) are where the activity we are interested in measuring is really going on. One proponent of positron emission tomography (PET), a type of functional metabolic imaging, writes of the pitfalls: 'The assumption is that areas with increased or decreased metabolic activity are in some ways dysfunctional (areas with normal metabolic rates might also be dysfunctional) . . . It is known that changes in experimental conditions . . . can lead to large changes in the patterns of regional metabolic activity. (With this in mind I must note that special and unusual conditions are unavoidable concomitants of all PET studies) . . . These uncertainties can be illustrated by analogy with the fuel consumption and electrical activity in an automobile. In a car a variety of functional changes can result in similar levels of fuel consumption. A total lack of fuel use is consistent with mechanical failure, but could also result from a sick or vacationing driver who never starts the car. Increased fuel consumption could be found in a high-performance sports car, a poorly tuned old clunker, or an ordinary car moving at normal speed with an emergency brake on. A change in electrical patterns could be due to the use of windshield wipers or defrosters, the activation by loss of oil of an indicator light, or use of the audio system' (Wexler, 1988, pp. 68–71).
22. Parks, Loewenstein, Dodrill et al., 1988; Haier, Siegel, Nuechterlein et al., 1988; Carly, Golding & Hall, 1995.
23. Yoshii, Barker, Chang et al., 1988; Hatazawa, Brooks, di Chiro et al., 1987; Haier, Chueh, Touchette et al., 1995.
24. McDaniel, 2005.
25. Seidenwurm & Devinsky, 2006.
26. ibid.
27. Cacioppo, Berntson, Lorig et al., 2003.
28. Stanislas Dehaene, leading neuroimaging researcher and Professor of Experimental Cognitive Psychology at the Collège de France, quoted in Holt, 2008, pp. 44–5.
29. Griffin, Friedman, Ween et al., 2006.
30. As one prominent neurologist puts it, 'the same alterations of behaviour can emerge from lesions at different sites in the brain and . . . lesions at apparently the same sites in different individuals may lead to different behavioural manifestations' (Trimble, 2007, p. 62).
31. van Zomeren & Brouwer, 1994.
32. The first is from the service of Compline (taken from 1 Peter 5:8): 'Brethren, be sober, be vigilant; because your adversary the devil, as a roaring lion, walketh about, seeking whom he may devour: whom resist, steadfast in the faith'; the second from Nietzsche's poem of the same title (lit. 'Man, beware!'), memorably set to music by Mahler in his Third Symphony.
33. For evidence relating to right hemisphere lesions in general, see Jerison, 1977; Dimond, 1979a; and Rueckert & Grafman, 1996. For right frontal lesions, see, e.g., Wilkins, Shallice & McCarthy, 1987.
34. Korda & Douglas, 1997.
35. de Renzi & Faglioni, 1965; Benson & Barton, 1970; Howes & Boller, 1975; Nakamura & Taniguchi, 1977; Tartaglione, Bino, Manzino et al., 1986; Sturm & Büssing, 1986. Almost all studies have suggested that patients with right hemisphere lesions are slower than those with left hemisphere lesions, although in one study slowing has been associated with lesions of the left dorsolateral prefrontal cortex (Godefroy, Lhullier & Rousseaux, 1996). For the association of perceptuomotor slowing with lapses of attention, see Rousseaux, Fimm & Cantagallo, 2002.
36. Studies in healthy subjects include: Heilman & van den Abell, 1979; Sturm, Reul & Willmes, 1989; and R. Whitehead, 1991. For evidence from split-brain patients, see, e.g., Dimond, 1979b.
37. Lewin, Friedman, Wu et al., 1996; Pardo, Fox & Raichle, 1991; Sturm, de Simone, Krause et al., 1999. Patients with Alzheimer's disease exhibiting right parietal hypometabolism have problems with vigilance: see Parasuraman, Greenwood, Haxby et al., 1992.
38. Benton & Joynt, 1959; Dee & van Allen, 1973; Sturm & Büssing, 1986.
39. Salmaso & Denes, 1982.
40. For evidence of left caudate involvement, see Godefroy & Rousseaux, 1996 and Godefroy, Lhullier & Rousseaux, 1996; for evidence of left anterior cingulate involvement, see Rousseaux, Godefroy, Cabaret et al., 1996.
41. Bisiach, Mini, Sterzi et al., 1982; Jansen, Sturm & Willmes, 1992.
42. Corbetta, Miezin, Dobmeyer et al., 1991.
43. Godefroy & Rousseaux, 1996; Godefroy, Lhullier & Rousseaux, 1996; d'Esposito, Detre, Alsop et al., 1995.
44. Vohn, Fimm, Weber et al., 2007; Nestor, Parasuraman, Haxby et al., 1991; Corbetta, Miezin, Dobmeyer et al., 1991.
45. Bultitude & Aimola Davies, 2006.

46. Çiçek, Gitelman, Hurley et al., 2007.
47. 'Several studies have suggested that consequences of lesions of the right and left cerebral hemispheres are not equivalent – some of the attention components such as tonic arousal or vigilance being more specifically impaired by right-hemispheric (and most often anterior) lesions; others such as focussed or divided attention (non-spatial) being more severely altered following left injuries' (Rousseaux, Fimm & Cantagallo, 2002, pp. 289–90); and see Sturm, Fimm, Cantagallo et al., 2002, p. 370. Both Jerison and Dimond have suggested that the two hemispheres have different types of attention systems, along similar lines (Jerison, 1977; Dimond, 1979a). Posner suggests that the system subserving sustained attention is closely linked to the spatial attention system in the posterior part of the right hemisphere, and sees this as going some way to explain right hemisphere dominance in sustained attention (Posner, 1995; Posner & Petersen, 1990).
48. Ivry & Robertson, 1998; Kitterle, Christman & Hellige, 1990; Kitterle & Selig, 1991; Sergent, 1982; Robertson, Lamb & Knight, 1988; Robertson & Lamb, 1991; van Kleeck, 1989.
49. Mesulam, 2000; Deouell, Ivry & Knight, 2003.
50. Delis, Robertson & Efron, 1986; Delis, Kiefner & Fridlund, 1988; Siéroff, 1990, 1994; Halligan & Marshall, 1994.
51. Leclercq, 2002, p. 16.
52. See Schutz, 2005 for an overview; also Posner & Raichle, 1994.
53. Edelman & Tononi, 2000; Goldberg, 2001; Mesulam, 2000.
54. Tang, 2003.
55. Goldberg & Costa, 1981; Goldberg, Podell & Lovell, 1994; Rogers, 2000; Regard & Landis, 1988; Feinstein, Goldin, Stein et al., 2002; Goldberg, 1990, 2001; Treyer, Buck & Schnider, 2003; Kimura, 1963; Gordon & Carmon, 1976; Cotton, Tzeng & Hardyck, 1980; Persinger & Lalonde, 2000; Martin, Wiggs & Weisberg, 1997; Henson, Shallice & Dolan, 2000; Gold, Berman, Randolph et al., 1996; Shadmehr & Holcomb, 1997; Haier, Siegel, MacLachlan et al., 1992; Berns, Cohen & Mintun, 1997; Raichle, Fiez, Videen et al., 1994; Tulving, Markowitsch, Craik et al., 1996; Cutting, 1997, p. 67.
56. Gardner, 1974; Sperry, 1985.
57. Mills, Coffey-Corina & Neville, 1993; Thal, Marchman, Stiles et al., 1991.
58. Goldberg, 2001.
59. Bever & Chiarello, 1974.
60. Podell, Lovell, Zimmerman et al., 1995; Phelps & Gazzaniga, 1992.
61. Brownell, Potter, Bihrle et al., 1986; Molloy, Brownell & Gardner, 1990.
62. Metcalfe, Funnell & Gazzaniga, 1995.
63. Federmeier & Kutas, 1999.
64. Larose, Richard-Yris, Hausberger et al., 2006.
65. Coulson, 2001; Rausch, 1977; Cacioppo, Petty & Quintanar, 1982. Neuroimaging tends to show the same right frontal role in set-shifting: see, e.g., Aron, Fletcher, Bullmore et al., 2003; Nagahama, Okada, Katsumi et al., 2001; Rubia, Smith, Brammer et al., 2003.
66. Heilman, 2005, p. 151; Razani, Boone, Miller et al., 2001; Jones-Gotman & Milner, 1977; Ruff, Allen, Farrow et al., 1994.
67. Vanderhasselt, De Raedt, Baeken et al., 2006.
68. Konishi, Nakajima, Uchida et al., 1999.
69. Richards & Chiarello, 1997.
70. Brownell, Simpson, Bihrle et al., 1990; Tucker & Williamson, 1984.
71. Ramachandran, 1994.
72. Yochim, Kender, Abeare et al., 2005, p. 132. See also Chiarello, 1988; Beeman, Friedman, Grafman et al., 1994; Coney & Evans, 2000.
73. Chiarello, 1991, 1998; Chiarello, Burgess, Richards et al., 1990.
74. Burgess & Lund, 1998.
75. Seger, Desmond, Glover et al., 2000; Yamaguchi, Yamagata & Kobayashi, 2000.
76. Posner, 1995; Diggs & Basili, 1987.
77. Jung-Beeman, Bowden, Haberman et al., 2004.
78. Mashal, Faust, Hendler et al., 2007.
79. Chiarello, Senehi & Nuding, 1987; Nakagawa, 1991.
80. Beeman, Friedman, Grafman et al., 1994.
81. Mednick, 1962.
82. Contreras & Llinas, 2001.
83. Heilman, 2005, pp. 117–18; E. A. Easterbrook, 1959; Eysenck, 1995.
84. Alajouanine, 1948, p. 235.
85. Harnad, 1972. One of the problems in measuring creativity is that creative individuals may have abnormal lateralisation, so that what we are measuring in terms of right and left hemisphere function may not correspond with the normal situation. There is a 'strong' association between better left ear (right hemisphere) localisation and creativity (Weinstein & Graves, 2002); and there is further evidence of the association between schizotypy, the right hemisphere and creativity (Poreh, Whitman & Ross, 1993–94; Zanes, Ross, Hatfield et al., 1998). But schizotypy is mainly notable for abnormal lateralisation and over-reliance on the left hemisphere (Platek & Gallup, 2002; Goodarzi, Wykes & Hemsley, 2000; Nunn & Peters, 2001). This is an area complicated, not least, by widely differing meaning of terms. But it has to be said that virtually all the qualities listed by Walter Cannon as the hallmarks of the creative mind are features of right hemisphere function (Cannon, 1965: and see Heilman, 2005, pp. 174–5).

86. Bowden & Beeman, 1998.
87. Bremer 1958; Bogen & Bogen, 1988; Bogen & Bogen, 1999.
88. Scheibel, Paul, Fried et al., 1985; Gur, Packer, Hungerbühler et al., 1980.
89. Gur, Packer, Hungerbühler et al., 1980.
90. Tucker, Roth & Bair, 1986. Its enormous power to integrate information over wide areas is due not only to more and longer-ranging white matter connections, but, at least according to Schutz, to a larger posterior association cortex (whose function is to integrate different kinds of experience), denser association fibres (whose function is to form connections between areas), greater interconnection of temporal lobe neuronal columns and larger integrative structures in the parietal lobe and the area round the Sylvian fissure, than the left hemisphere (see Schutz, 2005: I have not succeeded in verifying all of these findings from the literature).
91. Liotti & Tucker, 1994.
92. Semmes, Weinstein, Ghent et al., 1960; Teuber, Battersby & Bender, 1960; Milner, 1975.
93. Chapanis, 1977; Goldberg & Costa, 1981; Semmes, 1968; Tucker, 1992.
94. Semmes, 1968, pp. 23–4.
95. Levy-Agresti & Sperry, 1968, p. 1151.
96. Tucker & Williamson, 1984.
97. Kirsner, 1980.
98. Kirsner & Brown, 1981; Kirsner, 1980; Marsolek, Schacter & Nicholas, 1996; Marsolek, Squire, Kosslyn et al., 1994; Metcalfe, Funnell & Gazzaniga, 1995.
99. Navon, 1977; Nebes, 1978; Christman, 1997; Beeman, Bowden & Gernsbacher, 2000; Broadbent, 1977; Hellige, 1995; Young & Ratliff, 1983; E. Zaidel, 1985.
100. Mangun, Luck, Plager et al., 1994.
101. Navon, 1977.
102. For schizotypy, see Goodarzi, Wykes & Hemsley, 2000. For schizophrenia, see Bemporad, 1967; Place & Gilmore, 1980; Reich & Cutting, 1982.
103. Kinchla, Solis-Macias & Hoffman, 1983.
104. Leclercq, 2002, p. 16.
105. Delis, Robertson & Efron, 1986; Fink, Halligan, Marshall et al., 1996; van Kleeck, 1989.
106. Gitelman, Alpert, Kosslyn et al., 1996; Desmedt, 1977; Goebel, Linden, Sireteanu et al., 1997.
107. Fimm, Willmes & Spijkers, 2006; Heber, Valvoda & Kuhlen, 2008.
108. LaBerge, 1983; Humphreys, Riddoch & Quinlan, 1985.
109. There is a vast literature on this phenomenon, but see, e.g., Ratcliff, 1982.
110. Berlucchi, Mangun & Gazzaniga, 1997.
111. It has been suggested by Siéroff (1994, p. 145) that it is the preference for local rather than global processing by the left hemisphere that underlies the phenomenon of left hemispatial neglect in right hemisphere lesions (see Leclercq, 2002, pp. 16–17).
112. Oliveri, Rossini, Traversa et al., 1999.
113. Ellis, Jordan & Sullivan, 2006.
114. Rastelli, Funes, Lupiáñez et al., 2008; Siéroff, Decaix, Chokron et al., 2007.
115. de Renzi, Gentilini, Faglioni et al., 1989; Kinsbourne, 1993b.
116. Marshall & Halligan, 1989. For a contrary view, see Bartolomeo & Chokron, 1999.
117. Loetscher & Brugger, 2007.
118. Bartolomeo, Chokron & Siéroff, 1999.
119. de Renzi, 1988.
120. Vallortigara, 2000; Tommasi & Vallortigara, 2001; Vallortigara, Regolin, Bortolomiol et al., 1996.
121. Güntürkün & Böhringer, 1987; Güntürkün, Hellmann, Melsbach et al., 1998. See also Hellige, 1993, p. 175: 'The notion of two hemispheres that are in a mutually inhibitory relationship to each other is also consistent with the hypothesis that in rats and chicks the less emotional left hemisphere normally inhibits the more emotional right hemisphere.'
122. See, for example, Yoshida, Yoshino, Takahashi et al., 2007; Evert & Kmen, 2003; Fink, Marshall, Halligan et al., 1999a; van Kleeck, 1989. For findings in brain-damaged patients, see: Ferman, Primeau, Delis et al., 1999; Schatz, Ballantyne & Trauner, 2000. For neuroimaging, see: Heinze, Hinrichs, Scholz et al., 1998; Iidaka, Yamashita, Kashikura et al., 2004; Lux, Marshall, Ritzl et al., 2004. This area, like many others in neuropsychology, is made more complicated by the fact that key terms are used in different ways by different researchers. A case in point is a recent paper which, contrary to a vast body of research pointing to the opposite conclusion, claims to demonstrate that there is a dominance for global attention in the left hemisphere. However, the experimental conditions do not include any stimulus that forms a whole that is in any way distinguishable from a meaningless assemblage of parts; attention is specifically directed to the local level by the nature of the task; and the stimuli are all simple, stereotypic geometric shapes, of the kind that are automatically preferred by the left hemisphere (Wang, Zhou, Zhuo et al., 2007).
123. See, e.g., Bradshaw & Nettleton, 1981; 1983; Stillings, Feinstein, Garfield et al., 1987; Anderson, 1990; TenHouten, 1991. The idea is taken further by John Cutting (1997 passim, especially pp. 157–63) who provides an illuminating analysis of delusions and abnormal experiences in organic syndromes.
124. E. Zaidel, 1985; Walsh & Darby, 1999.
125. Nebes 1971a, 1971b, 1972, 1973, 1974; Milner & Taylor, 1972; Gazzaniga & LeDoux, 1978.
126. '. . . d'autres éprouvent de considérables difficultés à assembler correctement les divers éléments, donnant au cours de leurs nombreux essais des positions extraordinaires aux membres (bras attachés au cou ou à la partie inférieure du tronc . . .) . . . Dans le dessin sur ordre d'un éléphant, ne dessine qu'une queue, une trompe et une oreille . . . le

puzzle (modèle éléphant) aboutit à un échec total et est exécuté avec lenteur. Bien qu'il reconnaisse les éléments essentiels (verbalisation à mesure), il est incapable de les disposer à leur place même approximative et les uns par rapport aux autres' (trans. I. McG.) Hécaen & de Ajuriaguerra, 1952, pp. 237, 229 & 231 respectively.

127. McFie, Piercy & Zangwill, 1950; Ettlinger, Warrington & Zangwill, 1957; McFie & Zangwill, 1960; Warrington, James & Kinsbourne, 1966.

128. Nikolaenko, 2001; see also Nikolaenko, 2004.

129. Hécaen & de Ajuriaguerra, 1952, p. 224.

130. Benowitz, Moya & Levine, 1990.

131. See, e.g., Kinsbourne, 1982; Kinsbourne, 1988, p. 145; Federmeier & Kutas, 1999.

132. Alexander, Benson & Stuss, 1989.

133. Blakeslee, 1980; Deglin, 1976.

134. Heilman, Scholes & Watson, 1975.

135. See, e.g., Foldi, 1987; Bottini, Corcoran, Sterzi et al., 1994. There is some confusion over what is meant by metaphor. Obviously there is metaphoric content to almost everything we say – language is essentially metaphoric in nature, at the simplest level. If the chosen 'metaphor' for an experiment designed to distinguish between the hemispheres is so bland, obvious or banal that it requires no imagination, presents no novel thought, and does not bring together disparate meanings, little is likely to be discovered. We know that unfamiliar phrases activate the right hemisphere, while familiar ones activate the left hemisphere (Bottini, Corcoran, Sterzi et al., 1994; Eviatar & Just, 2006; Mashal, Faust & Hendler, 2005; Mashal, Faust, Hendler et al., 2007). So when it comes to metaphor, it is in keeping with this that poetic phrases, such as 'rain clouds are pregnant ghosts', are understood by the right hemisphere, while clichés, such as 'babies are angels', are processed by the left hemisphere (Schmidt, DeBuse & Seger, 2007). Specifically, it is not just the novelty inherent in metaphor, but the combination of novelty with the bringing together of disparate ideas that involves the right hemisphere (Mashal & Faust, 2008). Although two recent studies, bravely aiming to repudiate a consensus built on thirty years of research, have purported to demonstrate that it is the *left* hemisphere that is principally involved in the appreciation of metaphor, they have only demonstrated what we already know, that the left hemisphere has a predilection for cliché. As long as a phrase is comfortably familiar, the phrase will activate the left hemisphere only. The metaphors used in one of these studies (Rapp, Leube, Erb et al., 2004) were 'very simple statements', such as 'the alarm clock is a torturer'. Reference to 'torture' is a used, and overused, way of expressing displeasure – 'it was torture having to drag myself out of bed this morning'. This phrase is not essentially different from 'babies are angels'. Bottini and colleagues, who found a right hemisphere pre-eminence, used phrases that still required the bringing together of two distinct ideas, e.g. 'the policeman who didn't give straight answers was jumping ditches'. Rapp and colleagues justified using such simple phrases by referring to the fact that the right hemisphere is known to be involved in understanding more complex sentences. Maybe, but there is nothing whatever complex about the sentences, as sentences, in the Bottini examples – the only thing that is 'complex' about them is that they require seeing the connection between two disparate ideas. That is the essence of metaphor, and it turns out to be beyond the capacity of the left hemisphere. The other study (Stringaris, Medford, Giampietro et al., 2007) was similarly unlikely to test true metaphorical understanding: indeed the paradigm 'metaphor' they report using – 'some surgeons are butchers' – is hardly a metaphor at all; probably, if anything, less so than 'babies are angels'. But when the metaphor is of the kind encountered in poetry, rather than cliché, it is clearly the right hemisphere that is involved (Faust & Mashal, 2007).

136. Foldi, Cicone & Gardner, 1983; Kaplan, Brownell, Jacobs et al., 1990.

137. Deglin & Kinsbourne, 1996.

138. See Cutting, 1997, pp. 185; Kosslyn, 1987; Goldberg, 1990; Hécaen & Albert, 1978.

139. '. . . *comme poussé par une force bizarre à placer sur le modèle que nous lui proposions les pièces de bois, et non à côté . . . un trouble de la faculté de réaliser une copie abstraite à partir d'un modèle concret'* (trans. I. McG.): Hécaen & de Ajuriaguerra, 1952, p. 224.

140. Jackson, 1915, p. 97; in Jackson, 1932, vol. 2, pp. 140–41.

141. Marsolek, 1995.

142. Warrington & Taylor, 1973; Deglin, 1976.

143. Shibahara & Lucero-Wagoner, 2002. For reviews of right hemisphere language, see Beeman & Chiarello, 1998; Joanette, Goulet & Hannequin, 1990.

144. Querné, Eustache & Faure, 2000; Hutner & Liederman, 1991; Querné & Faure, 1996; Landis & Regard, 1998.

145. Gloning, Gloning & Hoff, 1968; Goldberg, 1990.

146. Pobric, Mashal, Faust et al., 2008; Sotillo, Carretié, Hinojosa et al., 2005.

147. Mashal, Faust, Hendler et al., 2008. See the philosopher Jean Paul (Richter) quoted on p. 117: 'metaphor . . . was the first word in spoken language, and only after losing its original colour could it become a literal sign'.

148. Marsolek, 1995.

149. See Brown & Kosslyn, 1993; Kosslyn, 1987; Grossman, 1988; also Cutting, 1997, pp. 64 & 185–6 for further discussion; and pp. 154–9, where Cutting gives examples from the analysis of delusions and anomalous experiences of organic patients.

150. For this whole area, see Cutting, 1997, esp. pp. 154–60 & 188. Also Warrington & McCarthy, 1987; Gardner, 1974; Pallis, 1955; Bornstein, Sroka & Munitz, 1969; Bornstein & Kidron, 1959; Landis, Cummings, Benson et al., 1986.

151. Bourgeois, Christman & Horowitz, 1998; Pallis, 1955.

152. Marsolek, Schacter & Nicholas, 1996; Brown & Kosslyn, 1993; Farah, 2003.

153. Blakeslee, 1980; Deglin, 1976; Marsolek, 1995.

154. Laeng, Zarrinpar & Kosslyn, 2003; Bornstein, 1963; Gloning, Gloning, Hoff et al., 1966; Lhermitte, Chain, Escourolle et al., 1972; see Cutting, 1997, p. 153 for fuller discussion.

155. Laeng, Zarrinpar & Kosslyn, 2003; Grossman, 1981.
156. Umiltà, Bagnara & Simion, 1978. See also Blakeslee, 1980; Deglin, 1976.
157. Pallis, 1955; Bornstein, Sroka & Munitz, 1969; McCarthy & Warrington, 1990; Sergent, Ohta & MacDonald, 1992; Lhermitte, Chain, Escourolle et al., 1972.
158. Laeng, Chabris & Kosslyn, 2003; Laeng, Shah & Kosslyn, 1999; Laeng, Zarrinpar & Kosslyn, 2003; Seger, Poldrack, Prabhakaran et al., 2000; Koivisto & Laine, 1999.
159. Burgund & Marsolek, 2000; Marsolek, 1999; Yamazaki, Aust, Huber et al., 2007.
160. Vuilleumier, Henson, Driver et al., 2002. See also Zaidel & Kosta, 2001; Kosslyn, Koenig, Barrett et al., 1989; Laeng, Chabris & Kosslyn, 2003.
161. See, for example, Fernandez & Friedman, 1999.
162. Maudsley, 1867 (cited in Radden, 2000, p. 27).
163. Capgras & Reboul-Lachaux, 1923.
164. Cutting, 2009. See Förstl, Almeida, Owen et al., 1991; Silva, Leong, Wine et al., 1992; Silva, Leong & Wine, 1993; Ellis, 1994.
165. Courbon & Fail, 1927.
166. Phelps & Gazzaniga, 1992; Metcalfe, Funnell & Gazzaniga, 1995.
167. Thompson, Silk & Hover, 1980.
168. Luria, 1973; van Lancker, 1991; Wallace & Canter, 1985.
169. This is how I would interpret the group of experiences that Cutting himself characterises by the phrase 'self-as-doer' (Cutting, 1997, p. 158). I believe my interpretation is closer to the phenomenon illustrated here.
170. See Tulving, Kapur, Craik et al., 1994; Cimino, Verfaellie, Bowers et al., 1991; Phelps & Gazzaniga, 1992; Metcalfe, Funnell & Gazzaniga, 1995; Markowitsch, Calabrese, Neufeld et al., 1999; Markowitsch, Calabrese, Haupts et al., 1993; Markowitsch, Calabrese, Fink et al., 1997; Markowitsch, 1995. Although the concept of 'self memory' is complex and covers a range of brain activities not confined to one region or one hemisphere alone, true recall of personal experience is consistently more associated with the right hemisphere. The general findings regarding the right prefrontal cortex are impressively consistent. A review by Nyberg et al. (1996) summarizes results of those comparisons in which the PET image corresponding to a semantic reference task was subtracted from an episodic target task. In 25 of the 26 relevant subtractions, the right prefrontal cortex was preferentially involved in the episodic task . . . The right frontal blood flow, uncovered by PET, is most closely associated with task instructions, more specifically the requirement to think back to some specific, previous personal episode . . . We interpret the blood flow in the right prefrontal cortex as signifying neural correlates of the intent to become autonoetically aware of a previous experience' (Wheeler, Stuss & Tulving, 1997, pp. 340–41). Objective data about the self, or imagined (fabricated) autobiographical memories are less strongly lateralised to the right hemisphere, though the relative reliance on verbal constructs (left-hemisphere-dependent) versus imagery, entailed in the task, may also exert an influence here (Conway, Pleydell-Pearce, Whitecross et al., 2003). The distinction that matters seems to be whether or not the episode is re-experienced in the process of recall; clearly recall of some autobiographical information can become little more than objective recall of facts (Wheeler, Stuss & Tulving, 1997). There is thus a distinction between episodic and autobiographical memory (see Gilboa, 2004 for an overview of this complex area). Imaging, as Gilboa demonstrates (op. cit.), is associated with its own set of problems, but so are all artificial laboratory based tests of memory, where, unlike most naturalistic situations, an effort of deliberate registering is involved, usually of information that has no part to play, as yet, in the sense of the continuing self over time. This may explain the distinction that underlies the HERA (Hemispheric Encoding/Retrieval Asymmetry) model (see Tulving, Kapur, Craik et al., 1994), which posits that encoding of memory causes left frontal, and recall of episodic information causes right frontal, activation: the committal to memory, by a conscious effort of will, of information of little personal relevance in the laboratory setting is a wholly different sort of process from the recognition of something that may now form part of one's recognisable experience.
171. Schiffer, Zaidel, Bogen et al., 1998.
172. Lhermitte, Chedru & Chain, 1973.
173. Gainotti, 2002; also Martin, Wiggs, Ungerleider et al., 1996; Perani, Cappa, Bettinardi et al., 1995; Perani, Schnur, Tettamanti et al., 1999; Perani, Cappa, Bettinardi et al., 1995; Mummery, Patterson, Hodges et al., 1998; Damasio, Grabowski, Tranel et al., 1996 (erratum appears in Nature, 1996, 381(6595), p. 810), and comment by Caramazza, 1996.
174. See also Perani, Cappa, Bettinardi et al., 1995; Mummery, Patterson, Hodges et al., 1998; Mummery, Patterson, Hodges et al., 1996.
175. 'Living things (irrespective of task) increased activation in the right middle frontal and right fusiform gyri. Non-living things (irrespective of task) increased activation in the same left posterior middle temporal area seen for tools and inanimate objects by Martin et al. (1996), Damasio et al. (1996), Mummery et al. (1996) and Mummery et al. (1998)' (Price & Friston, 2002, p. 437, commenting on the findings of Cappa, Perani, Schnur et al., 1998).
176. Perani, Schnur, Tettamanti et al., 1999, p. 293.
177. See also Gainotti, 2000; Gainotti & Silveri, 1996.
178. '«À la place de la moitié gauche de la poitrine, du ventre et de l'estomac on lui a mis une planche.» Elle descend jusqu'à l'anus, et est divisée en compartiments par des planches transversales . . . les aliments ne suivent pas le trajet normal de l'estomac et de l'intestin, « ils sont aspirés dans les compartiments de cet échafaudage et ils tombent par le trou sur le bas de l'échafaudage ». Tout cela n'existe que du côté gauche. À droite les organes sont parfaitement en place' (trans. I. McG.). Hécaen & de Ajuriaguerra, 1952, pp. 73–4, referring to Ehrenwald, 1931.
179. Gainotti, 2002; Perani, Cappa, Bettinardi et al., 1995; Martin, Wiggs, Ungerleider et al., 1996; linked by Gainotti (2002, p. 419) to the generation of action words and the observation of actions, concluding that 'the categories of man-made objects may be chiefly subserved by the fronto-parietal regions of the left hemisphere, because

knowledge of these categories is at least in part based on the handling, manual use or, in any case, physical contact and concrete utilization of objects' (quoting Gainotti, Silveri, Daniele et al., 1995). Gainotti (2002) makes the point that the dorsal system of visual processing of the left hemisphere, being involved in action planning, 'could have critically contributed (through processes of concrete utilisation and of physical contact) to building the semantic representation of non-living things' (p. 413), while the ventral system, relying on the interomesial and inferior parts of the temporal lobes, contributes to our sense of living things. 'These data are consistent with an exclusive involvement of the ventral stream of visual processing in tasks concerning living categories and a greater involvement of the dorsal stream in those concerning man-made objects' (p. 416). According to Price & Friston, 2002, 'manipulable relative to natural word generation enhanced activation in the left posterior middle temporal cortex' (p. 436). See also Mummery, Patterson, Hodges et al., 1996; Martin, Wiggs, Ungerleider et al., 1996; Damasio, Grabowski, Tranel et al., 1996. The topic is discussed in Cutting, 1997, pp. 153–4.

180. Hartmann, Goldenberg, Daumüller et al., 2005; Schwartz, Buxbaum, Montgomery et al., 1999.
181. Corballis, 1998, p. 1085.
182. Meyers, 2008. And see pp. 327–8 below.
183. Gainotti, Barbier & Marra, 2003; Giovanello, Alexander & Verfaellie, 2003; Rakison & Poulin-Dubois, 2001; Borgo & Shallice, 2001; Caramazza & Shelton, 1998; Mendez & Perryman, 2002.
184. Mendez & Lim, 2004.
185. Cutting, 1997, pp. 186–8; D. W. Zaidel, 1985, 1987; Vitkovitch & Underwood, 1991; Wapner, Judd & Gardner, 1978; Drews, 1987; Foldi, 1987; Wapner, Hamby & Gardner, 1981; Brownell, Potter, Michelow et al., 1984; Gardner, Brownell, Wapner et al., 1983; Joanette, Goulet & Hannequin, 1990.
186. Nicholls & Cooper, 1991.
187. Joseph, 1988b.
188. Laeng, Shah & Kosslyn, 1999; Zaidel & Kasher, 1989.
189. See Cutting's analysis of delusions and anomalous experiences in organic patients (Cutting, 1997, pp. 162–3). I would say that this series also gives evidence of the generally minatory tone of left hemisphere experience, of something happening that is strange, threatening and hard to pin down, which is the essence of paranoia and of the so-called 'delusional mood' of schizophrenia. See also Yin, 1970; Warrington & Taylor, 1973; R. Jung, 1974; D. W. Zaidel, 1987; van Kleeck & Kosslyn, 1989. There is a left hemisphere advantage, not just for nonsense images but for attending to nonsense syllables, which increases as depression and schizophrenia are treated. The left hemisphere advantage for real words *decreases* as depression and schizophrenia are treated (Wexler, 1986).
190. Some such confounders are the right hemisphere advantage for whatever is new, and whatever is visually complex. A good case in point is the study by Vogt & Magnussen (2005). This shows that while all images are, in naïve subjects, better processed in the right hemisphere, this is more strongly the case for realistic images, less strongly for abstract ones, which is in keeping with what one might expect. However, in trained painters, the realistic images were better processed in the left hemisphere (perhaps comparable with the findings of different lateralisation in professional and amateur musicians, see below), while processing of the abstract paintings was lateralised more strongly to the right than in the naïve subjects. This might have to do with the fact that such complex abstract paintings may be seen as a concept – another 'abstract' – by naïve viewers, whereas to the more engaged attention of the professional they remain 'new', because they never become reduced to a concept (and thus over-familiar) – they are viewed differently on every approach. But the results are also skewed by the fact that the realistic paintings were, unfortunately, in black and white, which tends to favour the left hemisphere (Barnett, 2008), while the abstract ones were in colour, which tends to favour the right hemisphere (Njemanze, Gomez & Horenstein, 1992; Mendola, Rizzo, Cosgrove et al., 1999; Pallis, 1955).
191. Shamay-Tsoory, Tomer, Berger et al., 2003; Rankin, Gorno-Tempini, Allison et al., 2006; Spinella, 2002.
192. Jackson, Brunet, Meltzoff et al., 2006.
193. Morrison, Lloyd, di Pellegrino et al., 2004; Hutchison, Davis, Lozano et al., 1999.
194. Decety & Chaminade, 2003, p. 591.
195. Ruby & Decety, 2001; Wraga, Souheil, Shephard et al., 2001; Decety, Chaminade, Grezes et al., 2002; Chaminade & Decety, 2002; Ruby & Decety, 2003.
196. Drake & Bingham, 1985; Drake, 1991.
197. Shamay-Tsoory, Tomer, Berger et al., 2005; Ohnishi, Moriguchi, Matsuda et al., 2004.
198. Baron-Cohen, Ring, Moriarty et al., 1994; Baron-Cohen, Tager-Flusberg & Cohen, 2000.
199. Legerstee, 1991; Meltzoff, 1995.
200. Perani, Fazio, Borghese et al., 2001.
201. Prinz, 2005a, 2005b, 2002.
202. For evidence from brain-damaged patients that 'theory of mind' depends on the right hemisphere, see: Happé, Brownell & Winner, 1999; Siegal, Carrington & Radel, 1996; Shamay-Tsoory, Tomer, Berger et al., 2005; Molloy, Brownell & Gardner, 1990; Stone, Baron-Cohen, Calder et al., 2003 (right hemisphere damage was the predominant factor); Stone, Baron-Cohen & Knight, 1998; Shammi & Stuss, 1999; Stuss, Gallup & Alexander, 2001 (again right hemisphere lesions were of predominant significance); Griffin, Friedman, Ween et al., 2006; Griffin & Baron-Cohen, 2002; and Winner, Brownell, Happé et al., 1998. For functional imaging evidence that the right hemisphere plays a preponderant role in 'theory of mind', see Baron-Cohen, Ring, Moriarty et al., 1994; Brunet, Sarfati, Hardy-Baylé et al., 2000; Shallice, 2001; Blakemore & Decety, 2001; McCabe, Houser, Ryan et al., 2001; and Vogeley, Bussfeld, Newen et al., 2001. The last two also demonstrate the closeness of association between 'theory of mind' and the sense of the self. A study by Gallagher and colleagues (2000) suggests both hemispheres contribute, though there is a special role for the right middle frontal gyrus. While most of the above evidence implicates the right frontal region, Saxe and Wexler (2005) demonstrate a role for the right posterior cortex. See also p. 477, n. 380, p. 510, n. 14 &

p. 512, n. 76 below; subjects with autism spectrum disorders have problems with 'theory of mind' that replicate right hemisphere deficits (Gunter, Ghaziuddin & Ellis, 2002; Ellis & Gunter, 1999).
203. Gallup, 1982; de Waal, 1996, 1998; Povinelli, Nelson & Boysen, 1990, 1992; Povinelli, Parks & Novak, 1991.
204. Gopnik & Meltzoff, 2006; Ritblatt, 2000.
205. Baron-Cohen, Leslie & Frith, 1985.
206. Voeller, 1986. There is a vast literature on this topic. For reviews of cerebral asymmetry and emotion, see, e.g., Davidson, 1984; Silberman & Weingartner, 1986; Tucker, 1981; Davidson, 1988; Borod, 1992. See also Cutting, 1997, pp. 65–6, 186–8 & 438–42; Sperry, Zaidel & Zaidel, 1979; Deglin, 1976.
207. Mychack, Kramer, Boone et al., 2001.
208. Schutz, 2005.
209. Miller, Chang, Mena et al., 1993; Edwards-Lee, Miller, Benson et al., 1997; Perry, Rosen, Kramer et al., 2001.
210. Rizzolatti, Fogassi, Gallese et al., 2001.
211. Wohlschläger & Bekkering, 2002.
212. Corballis, 2002a.
213. Aziz-Zadeh, Koski, Zaidel et al., 2006; Molnar-Szakacs, Iacoboni, Koski et al., 2005.
214. Biermann-Ruben, Kessler, Jonas et al., 2008.
215. Iacoboni, Molnar-Szakacs, Gallese et al., 2005.
216. Dapretto, Davies, Pfeifer et al., 2006.
217. Roberts, Beer, Werner et al., 2004.
218. Barbas, Saha, Rempel-Clower et al., 2003.
219. Joseph, 1982; Tucker, 1981; Tucker, 1992; Bear 1983; Pribram, 1981.
220. Sullivan & Gratton, 2002.
221. Craig, 2002.
222. Heilman, Schwartz & Watson, 1978; Levy, Heller, Banich et al., 1983; Heilman & van den Abell, 1979; Lane, Novelly, Cornell et al., 1988; Wittling & Pflüger, 1990.
223. Kinsbourne & Bemporad, 1984.
224. Borod, 1992; Borod, Bloom, Brickman et al., 2002; Heilman, Scholes & Watson, 1975; Borod, Koff & Caron, 1983; Borod & Caron, 1980; Heilman & Bowers, 1990; Snow, 2000; Alpers, 2008.
225. Suberi & McKeever, 1977; Landis, Assal & Perret, 1979; Ley & Bryden, 1979; Etcoff, 1984a; Borod, Welkowitz, Alpert et al., 1990; Habib, 1986; Strauss & Moscovitch, 1981.
226. Narumoto, Okada, Sadato et al., 2001.
227. Blonder, Bowers & Heilman, 1991.
228. Bryden, 1982; Etcoff, 1986.
229. Blonder, Bowers & Heilman, 1991; Borod, 1993; Breitenstein, Daum & Ackermann, 1998; Ross, Thompson & Yenkosky, 1977.
230. Prodan, Orbelo, Testa et al., 2001; Gazzaniga & Smylie, 1990.
231. Cicero, Borod, Santschi et al., 1999; Borod, Andelman, Obler et al., 1992; Ely, Graves & Potter, 1989; Joanette & Goulet, 1988; Shapiro & Danly, 1985; Tompkins & Mateer, 1985; Sim & Martinez, 2005.
232. The Victorian neurologist Sir William Gowers recounted the case of a patient who could not even utter the word 'no' until, in distressed exasperation, one day he blurted out: 'I can't say "no" '. See review by 'A. M.' (Adolf Meyer) of Liepmann's 'Das Krankheitsbild der Apraxie ('motorischen Asymbolie') auf Grund eines Falles von einseitiger Apraxie' (Meyer, 1904b, p. 282).
233. Tucker, Watson & Heilman, 1977; Wechsler, 1973.
234. Nagae & Moscovitch, 2002.
235. Bryden, Ley & Sugarman, 1982; Erhan, Borod, Tenke et al., 1998; Hatta & Ayetani, 1985; Safer & Leventhal, 1977; Stirling, Cavill & Wilkinson, 2000; Strauss & Moscovitch, 1981; Graves, Landis & Goodglass, 1981.
236. Etcoff, 1984b; Bowers, Blonder, Feinberg et al., 1991. The right posterior cortex is particularly involved in facial processing as such (Lezak, 1976).
237. Saxby & Bryden, 1985; de Schonen, Gil de Diaz & Mathivet, 1986; Nelson, 1987. For a fuller discussion, see Schore, 1994.
238. Ross, 1983.
239. Suberi & McKeever, 1977.
240. See Cutting, 1997, p. 153; Sergent, Ohta & MacDonald, 1992; de Renzi & Spinnler, 1966; Warrington & James, 1967; Milner, 1968/2003; Levy, Trevarthen & Sperry, 1972; Bruyer, 1986; Ellis, 1983; Ellis, Jeeves, Newcombe et al., 1986; Landis, Cummings, Christen et al., 1986.
241. Sergent & Villemure, 1989; de Renzi, Perani, Carlesimo et al., 1994; Uttner, Bliem & Danek, 2002.
242. Joubert, Felician, Barbeau et al., 2003; Behrmann, Avidan, Marotta et al., 2005; Nunn, Postma & Pearson, 2001; Levine & Calvanio, 1989; Sergent & Signoret, 1992; Barton, Press, Keenan et al., 2002.
243. Farah, Wilson, Drain et al., 1995; Yin, 1969; de Gelder & Rouw, 2000.
244. Schiltz, Sorger, Caldara et al., 2006.
245. Rossion, Caldara, Seghier et al., 2003.
246. de Renzi, Bonacini & Faglioni, 1989.
247. Burt & Perrett, 1997; Luh, Rueckert & Levy, 1991; Butler, Gilchrist, Burt et al., 2005; Butler & Harvey, 2005; Parente & Tommasi, 2008; Deglin, 1976.
248. Wigan, 1844, pp. 128–9.
249. Bodamer, 1947, p. 18; as translated in Ellis & Florence, 1990, p. 88.
250. Sergent & Villemure, 1989, p. 975.
251. Caldara, Schyns, Mayer et al., 2005; Bukach, Bub, Gauthier et al., 2006.

252. Broad, Mimmack & Kendrick, 2000.
253. Sackeim, Greenberg, Weiman et al., 1982; Lee, Loring, Dahl et al., 1993.
254. Borod, Welkowitz, Alpert et al., 1990; Bloom, Borod, Obler et al., 1990; Heilman, Bowers, Speedie et al., 1984; Heilman, Blonder, Bowers et al., 2000.
255. Kolb & Milner, 1981.
256. Indersmitten & Gur, 2003.
257. Harmon-Jones & Allen, 1998; Harmon-Jones, 2004, 2007.
258. Couppis & Kennedy, 2008.
259. Simmons & Baltaxe, 1975.
260. Ross & Mesulam, 1979; Ross, 1993; Borod, Koff & Buck, 1986; Dopson, Beckwith, Tucker et al., 1984.
261. Sackeim, Greenberg, Weiman et al., 1982; Davidson & Fox, 1989; Lee, Loring, Meador et al., 1990; Luciano, Devinsky & Perrine, 1993.
262. Borod, Haywood & Koff, 1997; Hugdahl, Iversen & Johnsen, 1993; Moreno, Borod, Welkowitz et al., 1990.
263. Borod, Kent, Koff et al., 1988; Borod, Koff, Yecker et al., 1998.
264. Keleş, Dıyarbakırlı, Tan et al., 1997; Dane, Gümüstekin, Polat et al., 2002; Dane, Ersöz, Gümüstekin et al., 2004.
265. Indersmitten & Gur, 2003.
266. Fernández-Carriba, Loeches, Morcillo et al., 2002b; Hauser, 1993.
267. Vauclair & Donnot, 2005. 80% of right- and left-handed mothers cradle babies with their head to the left. Males have no preference, but when they become fathers, 80% cradle to the left (Sieratzki & Woll, 1996). The preference is specific to babies, as opposed to inanimate objects, and is therefore not simply a matter of convenience: Almerigi, Carbary & Harris, 2002. See also Saling & Tyson, 1981; Dagenbach, Harris & Fitzgerald, 1988; Manning & Denman, 1994; Turnbull & Lucas, 2000. It was suggested by Salk (1973) that the preference related to proximity of the baby's head to the maternal heart, but overall evidence would suggest that it is because of right hemisphere attention (Harris, Almerigi, Carbary et al., 2001). A study of deaf subjects shows that it is not related to auditory prosody (Turnbull, Rhys-Jones & Jackson, 2001).
268. Grüsser, 1983; 99 out of 103 mother and child sculptures dating from the period between 1900 BC and 0 BC showed the leftward cradling bias (Grüsser, Selke & Zynda, 1988).
269. See, e.g., Salk, 1973. Dagenbach and colleagues (Dagenbach, Harris & Fitzgerald, 1988) give an overview of the literature, suggesting that cradling bias is not related to handedness.
270. See, e.g., Manning & Chamberlain, 1991.
271. R. M. Bauer, 1982; Borod, Koff, Lorch et al., 1985; Cicone, Wapner & Gardner, 1980.
272. Stuss & Benson, 1983; Stuss, Gow & Hetherington, 1992.
273. Liotti & Tucker, 1994; Ross, Homan & Buck, 1994.
274. Gazzaniga & Smylie, 1990; Zaidel, Chen & German, 1995.
275. Morris, Ohman & Dolan, 1998.
276. Cutting, 1997, p. 186; Ross, Homan & Buck, 1994.
277. Coney & Bruce, 2004.
278. Grijalva, 1982.
279. Paul, Lautzenhiser, Brown et al., 2006; Richter, Möller, Spitzer et al., 2006; Spalletta, Ripa, Bria et al., 2006; Hoppe & Bogen, 1977.
280. Gainotti, 1972; Gasparrini, Satz, Heilman et al., 1978; de Bonis, Dellatolas & Rondot, 1985; Terzian & Cecotto, 1959; Perria, Rosadini & Rossi, 1961; Gainotti, 1969.
281. Asthana & Mandal, 2001; Robinson & Price, 1982; Schiffer, Zaidel, Bogen et al., 1998.
282. Adolphs, Jansari & Tranel, 2001.
283. Tucker, 1988.
284. Persinger, Richards & Koren, 1994.
285. Silberman & Weingartner, 1986; Killgore, 2002; Babinski, 1922; Denny-Brown, Meyer & Horenstein, 1952; Hécaen, de Ajuriaguerra & Massonet, 1951. Affective facial stimuli are judged more positively by the left hemisphere than the right (Davidson, Mednick, Moss et al., 1987). The association of positive emotion with the left hemisphere is especially true in women (van Strien & van Beek, 2000). And depressed subjects appear to have increased reliance on the right hemisphere (Emerson, Harrison, Everhart et al., 2001: and see pp. 63–4 below).
286. Brosch, Sander & Scherer, 2007.
287. For example, the right hemisphere is biased towards recognition of the female face, which is less likely to be the focus of competition, and more that of social bonding, than the male face (Parente & Tommasi, 2008). This is supported by evidence that while both males and females attend to angry faces with the left hemisphere (Harmon-Jones & Allen, 1998; Harmon-Jones, 2004; d'Alfonso, van Honk, Hermans et al., 2000), females will attend to principally male angry faces when the right hemisphere is suppressed, but female angry faces when the left hemisphere is suppressed (Brüne, Bahramali, Hennessy et al., 2006).
288. Chao & Martin, 1999; Corbetta, Miezin, Dobmeyer et al., 1991. It is hard to see how any deductions about lateralisation could be made from the study of Lueck and colleagues (Lueck, Zeki, Friston et al., 1989), since it was based on three subjects, two of whom were actually left-handed, and the hemisphere differences were very small.
289. Howard, ffytche, Barnes et al., 1998; Kosslyn, Thompson, Costantini-Ferrando et al., 2000.
290. Njemanze, Gomez & Horenstein, 1992; Mendola, Rizzo, Cosgrove et al., 1999; Clapp, Kirk, Hausman, 2007; Levy & Trevarthen, 1981; Barnett, 2008; Pirot, Pulton & Sutker, 1977; Davidoff 1976; Hannay, 1979; Scotti & Spinnler, 1970; Pennal, 1977; Pallis, 1955.
291. Pettigrew, 2001; Hart, Partridge & Cuthill, 2000. 'There are hints from many sources that the left hemisphere may innately prefer red over green, just as it may prefer horizontal over vertical. I have already discussed the language-horizontal connection. The connection between the left hemisphere and red is also indirect, but is

supported by a remarkable convergence of observations from comparative neurology, which has shown appropriate asymmetries between both the hemispheres and even between the eyes (cone photoreceptor differences between the eyes of birds are consistent with a greater sensitivity to movement and to red on the part of the right eye (Hart, 2000)) and from introspective studies over the millennia in three great religions that have all converged in the same direction on an association between action, heat, red, horizontal, far etc and the right side of the body (i.e. the left cerebral hemisphere, given the decussation between cerebral hemisphere and output) compared with inaction, cold, green, vertical, near etc and the left side/right hemisphere respectively' (Pettigrew, 2001, p. 94). Pettigrew refers to an engaging Tibetan painting illustrating his point (Parfionovitch, Meyer & Dorje, 1992).
292. Viola, in Shakespeare's *Twelfth Night*, Act II, Scene iv, lines 111–16.
293. Starkstein & Robinson, 1988, p. 28.
294. Robinson & Benson, 1981; Robinson & Szetela, 1981; Robinson, Kubos, Starr et al., 1984; Lipsey, Robinson, Pearlson et al., 1983; Starkstein & Robinson, 1988.
295. Robinson, Kubos, Starr et al., 1984; Finset, 1988.
296. Evidence of the connection between the right frontal lobe and depression can come from the most surprising sources. There is a fascinating monograph in the British Library (BM X.529/66791) which was privately printed in 1984 by Gordon H. Wright, an anatomist with a family history of schizophrenia, who noted a connection between depression and infection of the left paranasal sinuses. Apparently in 1/80 brains there is a so-called foramen of Powiesnik which allows communication between these sinuses and the uncus (entorhinal cortex), specifically in the area of the amygdala.
297. Deldin, Keller, Gergen et al., 2001; Keller, Nitschke, Bhargava et al., 2000; Banich, Stolar, Heller et al., 1992; Liotti & Tucker, 1992.
298. Nitschke, Heller & Miller, 2000.
299. 'A review of reported cases reveals that most focal lesions associated with secondary mania involve the diencephalic region and that the majority of lateralized lesions are on the right side' (Cummings & Mendez, 1984). This has been borne out by many subsequent studies: Robinson, Boston, Starkstein et al., 1988; Cutting, 1990; Kulisevsky, Berthier & Pujol, 1993; Cummings, 1997; Vuilleumier, Ghika-Schmid, Bogousslavsky et al., 1998; Braun, Larocque, Daigneault et al., 1999; Blumberg, Stern, Martinez et al., 2000; Carran, Kohler, O'Connor et al., 2003; Dodson, 2004. In one case a patient was scanned before and after a right hemisphere infarct: 'comparison of pre- and poststroke SPECT scans demonstrated a unique pattern of left orbitofrontal hyperperfusion, with extensive right frontal hypoperfusion only after the stroke, during the manic episode' (Mimura, Nakagome, Hirashima et al., 2005, p. 263). Not all researchers are in agreement, however: see, e.g., Bearden, Hoffman & Cannon, 2001; Caligiuri, Brown, Meloy et al., 2004. A patient scanned during an episode of mania induced by deep brain stimulation showed clear activation of the right dorsolateral prefrontal and inferior temporal cortex, as well as of the left anterior cingulate cortex, and deactivation of the left insula (Ulla, Thobois, Lemaire et al., 2006); and similar findings have been made in similar experimental conditions, with activations in the left thalamus, but also in the right middle and inferior temporal gyrus, right inferior parietal gyrus and right inferior frontal gyrus, and deactivation in the left posterior middle temporal and occipital gyrus, left middle frontal gyrus, bilateral cuneus and right medial prefrontal/anterior cingulate gyrus (Mallet, Schüpbach, N'Diaye et al., 2007). See also Chapter 6, n. 60.
300. Robinson, 1979.
301. See, e.g., Finset, 1988; Starkstein & Robinson, 1989; Lauterbach, Jackson, Wilson et al., 1997; Robinson, Starr, Lipsey et al., 1985.
302. Henriques & Davidson, 1991; Bench, Friston, Brown et al., 1992; Greenwald, Kramer-Ginsberg, Krishnan et al., 1998; Lee, Loring, Meador et al., 1988.
303. Davidson, 1992; Davidson, 1993; Heller, 1990; Schwartz, Davidson & Maer, 1975.
304. Schaffer, Davidson & Saron, 1983; Jacobs & Snyder, 1996.
305. Debener, Beauducel, Nessler et al., 2000.
306. Davidson, 1988, pp. 17–18.
307. See Kinsbourne, 1988.
308. Navarro, Gastó, Lomeña et al., 2004.
309. Iosifescu, Renshaw, Lyoo et al., 2006.
310. Kinsbourne & Bemporad, 1984; Finset, 1988.
311. Heller, Nitschke, Etienne et al., 1997; Nitschke, Heller, Palmieri et al., 1999.
312. Panksepp, 1998, p. 310; where he cites George, Ketter, Kimbrell et al., 1996. A further reason for caution is that different intensities of experience might have opposite brain correlates: thus, while 'mild to moderate negative experiences (such as an experimentally induced negative affect or even a more clinical anxious state) might result in right hemisphere processing activation (and an attentional bias to the left ear) . . . an intense experience (such as . . . pure major depression) might interfere with right hemisphere processing, with eventual damage if some critical point is reached': Gadea, Gomez, Gonzalez-Bono et al., 2005, p. 136. See also Rotenberg, 2004, for an interesting thesis on the relationship between overactivity and *hypo*function of the right hemisphere.
313. See Poincaré: '. . . [creative] mathematical work is not simply mechanical . . . it could not be done by a machine, however perfect. It is not merely a question of applying rules, of making the most combinations possible according to certain fixed laws. The combinations so obtained would be exceedingly numerous, useless and cumbersome. The true work of the inventor consists in choosing among these combinations so as to eliminate the useless ones or rather to avoid the trouble of making them, and the rules which must guide this choice are extremely fine and delicate. It is almost impossible to state them precisely; they are felt rather than formulated . . . the subliminal self is in no way inferior to the conscious self; it is not purely automatic; it is capable of discernment; it has tact, delicacy; it knows how to choose, to divine. What do I say? It knows better how to divine than the conscious self, since it succeeds where that has failed. In a word, is not the subliminal self superior to the conscious self?' (Poincaré, 1908 (trans. F. Maitland), quoted in Ghiselin, 1992, p. 28).

314. Parsons & Osherson, 2001.
315. Bowden & Jung-Beeman, 2003; Kounios, Fleck, Green et al., 2008; Sandkühler & Bhattacharya, 2008.
316. Lane & Schooler, 2004; Dodson, Johnson & Schooler, 1997; Wilson & Schooler, 1991; Schooler & Engstler-Schooler, 1990.
317. Ashcraft, Yamashita & Aram, 1992.
318. Jackson & Warrington, 1986.
319. Aram & Ekelman, 1988.
320. Langdon & Warrington, 1997.
321. Dehaene, Piazza, Pinel et al., 2003.
322. Cohen, Dehaene, Chochon et al., 2000; Dehaene & Cohen, 1997.
323. Pesenti, Zago, Crivello et al., 2001.
324. Knauff, Fangmeier, Ruff et al., 2003.
325. See Cavanna & Trimble, 2006 for an excellent review of the functions of the precuneus.
326. Parsons & Osherson, 2001; Houde, Zago, Crivello et al., 2001. However it should be pointed out that this evidence is from scanning data only.
327. Dehaene, 1997; Funnell, Colvin & Gazzaniga, 2007.
328. Spelke & Tsivkin, 2001.
329. Joseph, 1988b; Boll, 1974.
330. Schilder, 1999.
331. See p. 405 below.
332. See Cutting, 1997, pp. 277–83, for a full discussion of the distinction between the left hemisphere's 'body' and the right hemisphere's 'body'.
333. Marcel, 1949.
334. This observation is attributed to Aristarchus, and is cited in Apollodorus, *Lexicon Homericum*, §254.
335. Cutting, 1990, p. 190.
336. Hécaen & de Ajuriaguerra, 1952, pp. 72–3. Compare Roth, 1949, describing a patient who complained bitterly that there was another man's arm in bed with him; another patient kept searching for her hand – 'it feels as if someone has stolen it' (p. 91: note that the arm is 'stolen', not just 'missing').
337. Bisiach, Rusconi & Vallar, 1991.
338. Feinberg, Haber & Leeds, 1990; Feinberg, 2000; Breen, Caine & Coltheart, 2001.
339. See p. 89 below.
340. Meador, Loring, Feinberg et al., 2000.
341. '*Il semblait que toute la moitié gauche de son corps eût disparu de sa conscience et de sa vie psychique . . . ce malade déclare qu'une main étrangère vient se poser de temps en temps sur sa poitrine, ce qui le gêne et l'agace: « cette main, dit-il, m'appuie sur le ventre et m'étouffe ». « Cette main m'agace, dit-il encore, elle n'est pas à moi et j'ai peur qu'elle ne me donne un coup de poing.*' (trans. I. McG.): Hécaen & de Ajuriaguerra, 1952, p. 72.
342. Nightingale, 1982.
343. Goble, Lewis & Brown, 2006.
344. Yokoyama, Jennings, Ackles et al., 1987; McFarland & Kennison, 1989; Spence, Shapiro & Zaidel, 1996; Angrilli, Mauri, Palomba et al., 1996; Yoon, Morillo, Cechetto et al., 1997; Wittling & Pflüger, 1990; Wittling, 1995; Meadows & Kaplan, 1994; Heilman, Schwartz & Watson, 1978.
345. Spence, Shapiro & Zaidel, 1996.
346. Sieratzki & Woll, 2005.
347. Coslett & Heilman, 1986; see commentary in Kimura, Murata, Shimoda et al., 2001.
348. In relation to sex, see Braun, Daigneault, Gaudelet et al., 2008. In relation to food, see Regard & Landis, 1997. The evidence appears to be that right hemisphere lesions cause a grossly excessive increase in a variety of activities, whereas a left hemisphere lesion causes either no significant change, or a mild decrease in the activity: Braun, 2007.
349. Wittling, Block, Schweiger et al., 1998; Wittling, Block, Genzel et al., 1998; Dütsch, Burger, Dörfler et al., 2007; Previc, 1996. Wada testing of epileptic subjects confirms this pattern (Yoon, Morillo, Cechetto et al., 1997; Zamrini, Meador, Loring et al., 1990). A paper by van Honk and colleagues found that the left hemisphere governs sympathetic drive, but unfortunately the experiment involved only exposure to angry faces, and the one emotion that is definitely left-hemisphere-mediated is that of anger (van Honk, Hermans, d'Alfonso et al., 2002). Braun reviews the human and animal literature and agrees that this effect does occur, but suggests that the preponderant effect, which evolves some time later, and which he accepts might represent a later compensatory effect, is in the opposite direction (Braun, 2007).
350. Wittling, Block, Schweiger et al., 1998.
351. Hugdahl, Law, Kyllingsbaek et al., 2000.
352. Bellugi, Poizner & Klima, 1983.
353. Bellugi, Poizner & Klima, 1989.
354. Yamadori, Mori, Tabuchi et al., 1986; Frey & Hambert, 1972; Arseni & Dănăilă, 1977; Braun, Dumont, Duval et al., 2004.
355. The right hemisphere processes language, though less efficiently than the left: see, e.g., Ellis, Young & Anderson, 1988; and Skarratt & Lavidor, 2006.
356. Cutting, 1997, p. 67; Chernigovskaya & Deglin, 1986; Drews, 1987.
357. Diggs & Basili, 1987.
358. Nichelli, Grafman, Pietrini et al., 1995.
359. Coulson & Wu, 2005.
360. Haggard & Parkinson, 1971; Carmon & Nachshon, 1973; Wymer, Lindman & Booksh, 2002; Blakeslee, 1980; and see Cutting, 1997, pp. 184–7.

361. Shamay-Tsoory, Tomer & Aharon-Peretz, 2005.
362. Kaplan, Brownell, Jacobs et al., 1990.
363. Winner & Gardner, 1977; Anaki, Faust & Kravetz, 1998a, 1998b; Brownell, Simpson, Bihrle et al., 1990.
364. Shammi & Stuss, 1999; Gardner, Ling, Flamm et al., 1975; Wapner, Hamby & Gardner, 1981; Brownell, Michel, Powelson et al., 1983; Bihrle, Brownell, Powelson et al., 1986; Dagge & Hartje, 1985.
365. Beeman, 1993.
366. Virtue, Haberman, Clancy et al., 2006.
367. Aram, Ekelman, Rose et al., 1985.
368. See p. 118 below.
369. Benowitz, Bear, Rosenthal et al., 1983.
370. Happaney, Zelazo & Stuss, 2004.
371. Hoshiyama, Kakigi, Watanabe et al., 2003.
372. Dimberg, Thunberg & Elmehed, 2000.
373. Pelphrey, Morris, Michelich et al., 2005.
374. Prodan, Orbelo, Testa et al., 2001.
375. Fabbro, Gran & Bava, 1993; Stuss, Gallup & Alexander, 2001. This capacity has led Julian Keenan and colleagues to see the right hemisphere as the basis of Machiavellian scheming, what they call the 'dark side of consciousness' (Keenan, Rubio, Racioppi et al., 2005). However this is not borne out by the evidence they cite. One paper they refer to suggests that lie-*detection*, not lying, is better in left-handers (Porter, Campbell, Stapleton et al., 2002), and another has nothing to say about lying at all (Stuss, Gallup & Alexander, 2001). The imaging paper by Spence and colleagues shows that lying activated regions bilaterally, if anything more in the left hemisphere – there is no suggestion of rightward inclination at any point (Spence, Farrow, Herford et al., 2001). One paper reports a case of pathological lying, but this is associated with *loss* of right thalamic function (Modell, Mountz & Ford, 1992). Another reports that an individual who tended to have seizures when he lied was found to have a meningioma impinging on the right medial temporal lobe, in proximity to the right anterior cingulate (Sellal, Chevalier & Collard, 1993). It is hard to know what conclusions can reliably be drawn from this (especially as he did not lie when he had seizures, but had seizures when he lied); but if any are to be drawn, it is surely relevant that this region is known to be activated in emotional conflict. We know from previous research that the anterior cingulate is involved in conflicting response tendencies (Carter, Macdonald, Botvinick et al., 2000); that the degree of right anterior cingulate activation is in fact proportional to the degree of response conflict, and inversely related to left dorsolateral prefrontal activation (MacDonald, Cohen, Stenger et al., 2000); and that in general conflicting emotions are dealt with by the right hemisphere (Davidson, Ekman, Saron et al., 1990). This is precisely what the paper by Langleben and colleagues, which they also cite, demonstrates: that the conflict involved in lying – both the emotional conflict (manifest in guilt and anxiety) and the cognitive conflict (having to inhibit the 'prepotent' or natural response) – induces activity in the right anterior cingulate (Langleben, Schroeder, Maldjian et al., 2002). None of this to me suggests that the right hemisphere is involved in the 'dark' side of consciousness. Finally, the paper by Ganis and colleagues reveals only that the right hemisphere is involved in the episodic memory retrieval tasks required by the task paradigm, lying about events in one's life (Ganis, Kosslyn, Stose et al., 2003). What, however, was significant, in my view, was that, as Ganis and colleagues report, 'specifically, we did not predict modulation of activation in the primary motor cortex (close to the hand and mouth representations)' (p. 835). In other words, for no apparent reason, lying activated the 'grasp' regions of the left hemisphere.
376. Winner, Brownell, Happé et al., 1998; Barnacz, Johnson, Constantino et al., 2004; Etcoff, Ekman, Magee et al., 2005. One further intriguing connection with the right hemisphere is that, when engaged in deceit, a subject's true emotional state is often disclosed through the upper, rather than lower, part of the face – which we know the left hemisphere cannot read (Prodan, Orbelo, Testa et al., 2001). See p. 59 above.
377. Napier, 1980, p. 166.
378. Rotenberg. & Arshavsky, 1987, p. 371.
379. Ween, Alexander, d'Esposito et al., 1996; Schutz, 2005.
380. For evidence linking the right hemisphere and 'theory of mind', see n. 202 above. For the link between autism, right hemisphere deficits and 'theory of mind', see Brownell, Griffin, Winner et al., 2000; Ozonoff & Miller, 1996; Sabbagh, 1999; and Stone, Baron-Cohen & Knight, 1998.
381. Sloboda & Juslin, 2001.
382. Sloboda, 1991, 1998; Panksepp, 1995; Panksepp & Bernatsky, 2002; Krumhansl, 1997; Goldstein, 1980.
383. I owe this perception to Professor Alwyn Lishman.
384. Suzuki, Okamura, Kawachi et al., 2008.
385. Gorgias, *Encomium*, §9.
386. Langer, 1942, p. 222.
387. Mendelssohn, letter to Marc-André Souchay dated 5 October 1842 (Mendelssohn-Bartholdy, 1864, pp. 269–70).
388. Nietzsche, 1968, §810, p. 428.
389. Jeffries, Fritz & Braun, 2003.
390. Russell & Golfinos, 2003; Nicholson, Baum, Kilgour et al., 2003.
391. Fujii, Fukatsu, Watabe et al., 1990.
392. Marin & Perry, 1999.
393. ibid.
394. Luria, Tsvetkova & Futer, 1965.
395. Signoret, van Eeckhout, Poncet et al., 1987.
396. Judd, Gardner & Geschwind, 1983.

397. Alcock, Wade, Anslow et al., 2000; Peretz, 1990; Lechevalier, 1997; McKinnon & Schellenberg, 1997; Matteis, Silvestrini, Troisi et al., 1997; Platel, Price, Baron et al., 1997; O'Boyle & Sanford, 1988; Perry, Zatorre & Evans, 1996; Perry, Zatorre, Petrides et al., 1999a, 1999b.

398. Roland, Skinhøj & Lassen, 1981.

399. Lechevalier, 1997; Platel, Price, Baron et al., 1997.

400. Popescu, Otsuka & Ioannides, 2004; Sakai, Hikosaka, Miyauchi et al., 1999; Peretz, 1990; Roland, Skinhøj & Lassen, 1981.

401. Evers, Dannert, Rodding et al., 1999; Preisler, Gallasch & Schulter, 1989; Passynkova, Neubauer & Scheich, 2007.

402. Tramo & Bharucha, 1991; Preisler, Gallasch & Schulter, 1989.

403. Tramo & Bharucha, 1991.

404. J. Levy, 1988.

405. See Patston, Hogg & Tippett, 2007 for discussion; also Patston, Kirk, Rolfe et al., 2007.

406. Goldberg & Costa, 1981.

407. Vollmer-Haase, Finke, Harje et al., 1998.

408. Harrington, Haaland & Knight, 1998.

409. Buchtel, Rizzolatti, Anzola et al., 1978; Bertoloni, Anzola, Buchtel et al., 1978; Mohl & Pfurtscheller, 1992.

410. Jones, Rosenkranz, Rothwell et al., 2004.

411. Maquet, Lejeune, Pouthas et al., 1996; Bueti, Bahrami & Walsh, 2008; Koch, Oliveri, Carlesimo et al., 2002; Koch, Oliveri, Torriero et al., 2003; Pastor, Day, Macaluso et al., 2004; Danckert, Ferber, Pun et al., 2007; Funnell, Corballis & Gazzaniga, 2003; Stagno & Gates, 1991; Alexander, Cowey & Walsh, 2005; Lacruz, Artieda, Pastor et al., 1991; Battelli, Cavanagh, Martini et al., 2003; Rao, Mayer & Harrington, 2001. But see also Cutting, 1997, pp. 198–220, esp. p. 216 ff., for an extensive survey of the literature to that date, as well as Cutting, 1999, pp. 217–18.

412. Becchio & Bertone, 2006.

413. Husain, Shapiro, Martin et al., 1997; Battelli, Cavanagh, Intriligator et al., 2001; Battelli, Pascual-Leone & Cavanagh, 2007.

414. Mills & Rollman, 1980; Swisher & Hirsh, 1972; Carmon & Nachshon, 1971; Nicholls, 1994; Brown & Nicholls, 1997.

415. Hough, 1990; Schneiderman, Murasugi & Saddy, 1992.

416. Cummings, 1997; Ritsema & Murphy, 2007; Bender, Feldman & Sobin, 1968 (in 11 out of 12 cases the abnormal features were in the left visual field, and in 11 out of 12 cases there was pathology demonstrated in the right posterior region); Michel & Troost, 1980 (in two out of three cases there was a right posterior mass); Müller, Büttner, Kuhn et al., 1995 (3 cases of palinopsia, all with lesions in the posterior right hemisphere).

417. Schwartz, Assal, Valenza et al., 2005.

418. Okubo & Nicholls, 2008; Nicholls, Schier, Stough et al., 1999; Elias, Bulman-Fleming & McManus, 1999.

419. Corballis, 1996; Corballis, Boyd, Schulze et al., 1998.

420. Steiner, 1989, p. 27.

421. See Schopenhauer: 'It is just this universality that belongs uniquely to music, together with the most precise distinctness, that gives it that high value . . . Accordingly, music, if regarded as an expression of the world, is in the highest degree a universal language that is related to the universality of concepts much as these are related to the particular things. Yet its universality is by no means that empty universality of abstraction, but is of quite a different kind; it is united with thorough and unmistakable distinctness' (Schopenhauer, 1969, vol. 1, p. 262). '*Gerade diese ihr ausschließlich eigene Allgemeinheit, bei genauester Bestimmtheit, giebt ihr den hohen Werth . . . Die Musik ist demnach, wenn als Ausdruck der Welt angesehn, eine im höchsten Grad allgemeine Sprache, die sich sogar zur Allgemeinheit der Begriffe ungefähr verhält wie diese zu den einzelnen Dingen. Ihre Allgemeinheit ist aber keineswegs jene leere Allgemeinheit der Abstraktion, sondern ganz anderer Art und ist verbunden mit durchgängiger deutlicher Bestimmtheit*' (Schopenhauer, *Die Welt als Wille und Vorstellung*, I, iii, §52, 1960, vol. 1, p. 365).

422. Nettl, 1983.

423. Durnford & Kimura, 1971; Nikolaenko & Egorov, 1998 (trans. N. N. Nikolaenko).

424. Banich & Federmeier, 1999; Hellige & Michimata, 1989; Kosslyn, Koenig, Barrett et al., 1989; Laeng, 1994; Rybash & Hoyer, 1992.

425. Kosslyn, 1987; Kinsbourne, 1993b.

426. Drago, Foster, Webster et al., 2007; Roth, Lora & Heilman, 2002.

427. Grossman, 1988; Menshutkin & Nikolaenko, 1987 (trans. N. N. Nikolaenko).

428. Laeng & Caviness, 2001.

429. Bodamer, 1947 (see p. 60 above).

430. The treatment of this subject is bedevilled by some of the same problems alluded to previously in discussing bizarre and abstract images. Lesion studies are likely to be most informative, but unfortunately few lesion patients are asked about their ability to appreciate beauty, and the few that may report spontaneously on the matter are likely to be overlooked, since failure to appreciate beauty may be treated as an aspect of depression. The only lesion study I am aware of to make that distinction is that of Habib, which suggests loss of the sense of visual beauty following a right temporal lesion (Habib, 1986). One is therefore mainly reliant here on imaging data, with all its attendant problems, particularly in such a spectacularly complex area. A few of the undoubted difficulties in knowing what it is that one is measuring here are outlined in a paper by Nadal and colleagues (Nadal, Munar, Capó et al., 2008). Additionally the tendency to use abstract patterns, or modernist paintings, in such studies alone skews the data, since, as discussed, the right hemisphere has a tendency to prefer images that have meaning in the real world, and the left hemisphere those that do not. One way round this is to compare an image in its original proportions with the same image subtly changed in proportion. This strategy demonstrates that the right insula

and amygdala are the principle areas involved in judgments of beauty, according to such universally held criteria as the golden ratio: see Di Dio, Macaluso & Rizzolatti, 2007. Alternatively, using abstract or modernist paintings, the image can be compositionally interfered with or noise-filtered: where altered versions are compared with the more beautiful originals (much as in Di Dio et al., 2007), the originals are preferred to altered or filtered versions, in each case activating the right hemisphere (lingual and fusiform gyri): see Vartanian & Goel, 2004. Incidentally it is beauty which drives the unconscious creative processes of mathematics, associated with the right hemisphere, as most mathematicians from Pythagoras to Hofstadter will attest. Poincaré wrote that '. . . It may be surprising to see emotional sensibility invoked à propos of mathematical demonstrations which, it would seem, can interest only the intellect. This would be to forget the feeling of mathematical beauty, of the harmony of numbers and forms, of geometric elegance. This is a true aesthetic feeling that all real mathematicians know, and surely it belongs to emotional sensibility . . . The useful combinations are precisely the most beautiful, I mean those best able to charm this special sensibility that all mathematicians know, but of which the profane are so ignorant as often to be tempted to smile at it.' Poincaré, 1908 (trans. F. Maitland), quoted in Ghiselin, 1992, p. 29.

431. Nikolaenko, Egorov & Freiman, 1997.
432. ibid.; Nikolaenko 2003; Egorov & Nikolaenko, 1992.
433. Gazzaniga & LeDoux, 1978.
434. See Cutting, 1999, p. 236; Cutting, 1997, p. 187; Rausch, 1985; Brownell, Potter, Bihrle et al., 1986; Deglin, 1976; Henson, Rugg, Shallice et al., 2000. Evidence from right hemisphere lesions and from split-brain subjects confirms that the left hemisphere is over-confident and the right hemisphere correspondingly tentative: Kimura, 1963; Phelps & Gazzaniga, 1992.
435. Cutting, 1997, pp. 65 & 68.
436. Gazzaniga & LeDoux, 1978, pp. 148–9.
437. Schnider, Gutbrod, Hess et al., 1996; Nebes, 1974; and, more generally, Drake & Bingham, 1985.
438. Schacter, Curran, Galluccio et al., 1996; Curran, Schacter, Norman et al., 1997.
439. Panksepp, 2003, p. 10.
440. Gazzaniga, 1998.
441. Gardner, Brownell, Wapner et al., 1983.
442. Wolford, Miller & Gazzaniga, 2000.
443. Unturbe & Corominas, 2007.
444. Yellott, 1969.
445. Goel, Tierney, Sheesley et al., 2007.
446. The Necker cube is attributed to a Swiss crystallographer, Louis Albert Necker, who in 1832 described the way in which the structure of crystals appeared to reverse spontaneously. Although the duck–rabbit was made famous by Wittgenstein, it was first discussed by the American psychologist, Joseph Jastrow ('The mind's eye', *Popular Science Monthly*, 1899, 54, pp. 299–312), who in turn derived it from a German popular magazine called *Fliegende Blätter* (1892). See http://socrates.berkeley.edu/~kihlstrm/JastrowDuck.htm (accessed 28 April 2009).
447. Lumer, Friston & Rees, 1998.
448. Cowin & Hellige, 1994.
449. Hellige, 1976; Hellige & Webster, 1979; Hellige, 1980; Bradshaw, Hicks & Rose, 1979; Sergent & Bindra, 1981.
450. Sergent, 1982, p. 254.
451. Ballard, 2002.
452. Stuss, 1991b; Wheeler, Stuss & Tulving, 1997; Stuss, Picton & Alexander, 2001. Evidence that the right hemisphere is better at telling truth from falsehood, at least in others, has been presented above, as has evidence that it is better at jettisoning premises that are totally at variance with experience. There may, of course, be situations in which it is positively advantageous to entertain hypotheses that run completely counter to experience, and I believe this is one of the distinctive contributions that the left hemisphere makes to, particularly scientific, creativity.
453. Ramachandran, 1995; Gordon, Drenth, Jarvis et al., 1978; Rausch, 1985.
454. Schutz, 2005, p. 16, citing Rourke, 1989, and Johnson & Myklebust, 1967.
455. Stuss 1991a, Stuss 1991b.
456. See, for example, Schacter, Glisky, and McGlynn, 1990. As Wheeler, Stuss & Tulving put it: 'The whole picture is one of a dissociation between knowledge and the realization of personal relevance of that knowledge' (1997, p. 348).
457. Persinger & Makarec, 1991; Lazure & Persinger, 1992; Ahern, Herring, Tackenberg et al., 1994; Bear & Fedio, 1977. It was observed as long ago as the late nineteenth century that there was a difference in the emotional timbre of auditory hallucinations, depending on the side from which they appeared to arise. For example, Magnan reported that four patients with a chronic psychotic illness involving auditory hallucinations experienced unpleasant, critical and hostile remarks in their left ear, and soothing, even flattering remarks in their right (Magnan, 1883).
458. See pp. 63–4 above.
459. See, e.g., David, 2004, esp. pp. 365 & 370.
460. Alloy & Abramson, 1988; Iqbal, Birchwood, Chadwick et al., 2000; Ghaemi & Rosenquist, 2004, esp. pp. 110–11; Haaga & Beck, 1995.
461. See Adair, Schwartz & Barrett, 2003; Bisiach, Vallar, Perani et al., 1986; Feinberg, Roane, Kwan et al., 1994; Starkstein, Fedoroff, Price et al., 1992; Meador, Loring, Feinberg et al., 2000. First described in a classic paper by the French neurologist Babinski (1914), this phenomenon is as striking as it is common: Cutting estimates that it occurs in the majority of cases of right hemisphere stroke involving left hemiplegia, that is to say, paralysis of the left side of the body (Cutting, 1978). Insight into illness is lost (anosognosia) when the right hemisphere, especially the right parietal lobe, is damaged and insight increases *pari passu* with performance on the Wisconsin Card

Sorting Test, which is thought to be a test of principally right frontal functioning (Morgan & David, 2004) and with tests of specifically right parietal lobe function (McEvoy, Hartman, Gottlieb et al., 1996; Flashman & Roth, 2004). It has been hypothesised that unawareness of (bodily) illness results from an interaction between frontal lobe impairment which compromises the ability to self-monitor, self-correct and draw proper inferences, and parietal lobe dysfunction which affects the complex integration of sensory input (Benson & Stuss, 1990; Ellis & Small, 1993). Bilateral superior and middle frontal gyri volumes are smaller where there is poor insight in psychosis (Flashman & Roth, 2004). There are specifically right-sided deficits in the frontal and parietal lobes of Alzheimer's patients who lack awareness of illness (Reed, Jagust & Coulter et al., 1993; Starkstein, Vazquez, Migliorelli et al., 1995; Derouesne, Thibault, Lagha-Pierucci et al., 1999). For overviews, see Prigatano, 1991, 1994; Heilman, 1991.

462. Bisiach, Rusconi & Vallar, 1991. Ramachandran & Rogers-Ramachandran (1996) provide further experimental evidence for the findings of Bisiach and colleagues. In their patient, stimulation of the right hemisphere also caused an increase in REM sleep, corroborating other evidence that REM sleep may be a right-hemisphere phenomenon (see p. 188 below).

463. Meador, Loring, Feinberg et al., 2000.

464. 'À l'examen, quand on lui montre sa main gauche dans le champ visuel droit, elle détourne le regard et déclare: « Je ne la vois pas ». Spontanément elle cache sa main gauche sous la couverture ou la place derrière son dos. Elle ne regarde jamais à gauche, même lorsqu'on l'appelle par ce côté' (trans. I. McG.): Hécaen & de Ajuriaguerra, 1952, p. 80, referring to Hoff & Pötzl, 1935.

465. '. . . elle la saisit pour l'abandonner aussitôt avec des signes de dégoût' (trans. I. McG.): ibid., p. 80.

466. '. . . troubles de l'humeur rappelant la moria des frontaux: euphorie, jovialité, tendance aux calembours faciles. Une de nos malades hémiasomatognosique totale par tumeur pariétale, bien que se plaignant d'une céphalée extrêmement vive, manifeste ainsi une jovialité surprenante' (trans. I. McG.): ibid., p. 63.

467. Drake & Bingham, 1985; see also Cutting, 1997, p. 184; Ahern, Herring, Tackenberg et al., 1994; Bear & Fedio, 1977.

468. Schutz, 2005, p. 11.

469. Zalla, Koechlin, Pietrini et al., 2000.

470. See, e.g., Rothbart, Ahadi & Hershey, 1994. Children and adolescents with psychopathic tendencies have difficulty recognising sad faces (Blair, Colledge, Murray et al., 2001; Blair & Coles, 2000) and sad vocal tones (Stevens, Charman & Blair, 2001). Reparative behaviour and sadness are highly correlated in childhood (Cole, Barrett & Zahn-Waxler, 1992).

471. Zahn-Waxler & Robinson, 1995.

472. Narayan, Narr, Kumari et al., 2007.

473. Yarnell, 2001, p. 454.

474. Lebrecht, 1985, p. 118. I am reminded of Wittgenstein's reported verdict on life: 'I don't know why we are here, but I'm pretty sure that it is not in order to enjoy ourselves.'

475. King Lear, Act III, Scene vi, lines 34–5.

476. See p. 159 below.

477. See p. 207 below.

478. Greene, Nystrom, Engell et al., 2004; Haidt, 2001.

479. Tranel, Bechara & Denburg, 2002; Tranel, 1994; A. R. Damasio, 1994a, 1994b; Damasio, Tranel & Damasio, 1990; Barrash, Tranel & Anderson, 2000; Bechara, Damasio, Damasio et al., 1994; Bechara, Tranel & Damasio, 2000; Eslinger, 1998.

480. Moll, de Oliveira-Souza & Eslinger, 2003; Moll, de Oliveira-Souza, Bramati et al., 2002; Greene, Nystrom, Engell et al., 2004. For more detailed analysis, see Mendez, 2006.

481. Knoch, Pascual-Leone, Meyer et al., 2006.

482. Knoch & Fehr, 2007; Alonso-Alonso & Pascual-Leone, 2007.

483. See pp. 46, 231–2 & 390.

484. Regard, Knoch, Gütling et al., 2003; Clark, Manes, Antoun et al., 2003.

485. Camprodon, Martínez-Raga, Alonso-Alonso et al., 2007.

486. Lethmate & Dücker, 1973; Gallup, Wallnau & Suarez, 1980; Povinelli, Rulf, Landau et al., 1993; Kitchen, Denton & Brent, 1996; Lin, Bard & Anderson, 1992.

487. Keenan, McCutcheon, Freund et al., 1999.

488. Sugiura, Kawashima, Nakamura et al., 2000.

489. Imbens-Bailey & Pan, 1998.

490. Keenan, Wheeler, Platek et al., 2003; Preilowski, 1977.

491. Uddin, Rayman & Zaidel, 2005.

492. Vanderhaeghen, 1986.

493. Craik, Moroz, Moscovitch et al., 1999.

494. Schiffer, Zaidel, Bogen et al., 1998.

495. Decety & Chaminade, 2003.

496. Falk, Hildebolt, Cheverud et al., 1990.

497. Schore, 1994, p. 125. Schore notes incidentally that the right orbitofrontal cortex is larger in infant rats, though other areas of frontal cortex are larger on the left (van Eden, Uylings & van Pelt, 1984).

498. Trevarthen, 1996; Thatcher, Walker & Giudice, 1987; Schenkenberg, Dustman & Beck, 1971; D. C. Taylor, 1969; Chi, Dooling & Gilles, 1977a; Crowell, Jones, Kapuniai et al., 1973; Geschwind & Galaburda, 1987; Giannitrapani, 1967; Hellige, 1993; Tucker, 1986. As far as structure goes, Trevarthen notes (1996, p. 582): 'The right hemisphere is more advanced than the left in surface features from about the 25th [gestational] week and this advance persists until the left hemisphere shows a post-natal growth spurt starting in the second year.' On structure, see also Rosen & Galaburda, 1985.

499. Bretherton & Bates, 1984.
500. McCabe, Houser, Ryan et al., 2001; Vogeley, Bussfeld, Newen et al., 2001.
501. Devinsky, 2000.
502. Miller, Seeley, Mychack et al., 2001, p. 821.
503. Watt, 1998.
504. Wheeler, Stuss & Tulving, 1997.
505. Stuss & Alexander, 2000; Stuss, Gallup & Alexander, 2001; Stuss, 1991b; Stuss, Picton & Alexander, 2001.
506. Sperry, Zaidel & Zaidel, 1979.
507. Théoret, Kobayashi, Merabet et al., 2004, p. 57.
508. Decety & Sommerville, 2003. See also Uddin, Molnar-Szakacs, Zaidel et al., 2006; Uddin, Kaplan, Molnar-Szakacs et al., 2005; and Feinberg & Keenan, 2005.
509. Lou, Luber, Crupain et al., 2004.
510. Sugiura, Watanabe, Maeda et al., 2005.
511. Feinberg, Haber & Leeds, 1990; and Meador, Loring, Feinberg et al., 2000.
512. Paysant, Beis, Le Chapelain et al., 2004.
513. Feinberg, Haber & Leeds, 1990; Feinberg, 2000; Breen, Caine & Coltheart, 2001.
514. Wheeler, Stuss & Tulving, 1997.
515. Vogeley, Bussfeld, Newen et al., 2001.
516. Wittgenstein, 1971, p. 83.
517. Keenan, Nelson, O'Connor et al., 2001.
518. Turk, Heatherton, Kelley et al., 2002.
519. See, e.g., Keenan, McCutcheon & Pascual-Leone, 2001; Sugiura, Kawashima, Nakamura et al., 2000; Platek, Keenan, Gallup et al., 2004; Kelley, Macrae, Wyland et al., 2002.
520. Nakamura, Kawashima, Sugiura et al., 2001.
521. Decety & Sommerville, 2003.
522. Feinberg & Keenan, 2005, p. 675.
523. Blakemore, Rees & Frith, 1998; Farrer, Franck, Georgieff et al., 2003; den Ouden, Frith, Frith et al., 2005; Ogawa, Inui & Sugio, 2006.
524. Hamilton & Grafton, 2008.
525. For discussion, see Cutting, 1997, pp. 372–3. See also Dandy, 1930 and Serafetinides, Hoare & Driver, 1965.
526. Chaminade & Decety, 2002; Coslett & Heilman, 1989. Yet according to other evidence, for the right hemisphere to initiate an action it must be 'overlearned, habitual actions like actual object-use' (Cutting, 1999, p. 234; Rapcsak, Ochipa, Beeson et al., 1993).
527. Heilman, 2002; Heilman & van den Abell, 1979; Coslett & Heilman, 1989; Coslett, Bowers & Heilman, 1987.
528. Lhermitte, 1983.
529. Lhermitte, Pillon & Serdaru, 1986; Lhermitte, 1986.
530. Hashimoto, Yoshida & Tanaka, 1995.
531. Friston, 2003, p. 183.
532. See d'Aquili & Newberg, 1993; d'Aquili & Newberg, 1999; and Newberg, d'Aquili & Rause, 2001.
533. Trimble, 2007. This is also in keeping with Fenwick (1996), who associates religious experience principally with the right temporal lobe.
534. Gorynia & Müller, 2006.
535. O'Boyle & Benbow, 1990.

CHAPTER 3: LANGUAGE, TRUTH AND MUSIC

1. Goldberg & Costa, 1981; see also Pribram, 1981; and Regard & Landis, 1988.
2. Note that 'facts', like data, imply something that is finished, completed, given that *factum* and *datum* are both past participles.
3. Watt & Ash, 1998.
4. Davies, 2001.
5. McGilchrist, 1982.
6. Aristotle, *Poetics*, 1450B, 1459A.
7. C. Jung, 1953–79, vol. 10, p. 287.
8. Nietzsche, 2003, §34 [244], p. 14 (translation adapted; emphasis in original): ' *"Erkennen" ist der Weg, um es uns zum Gefühl zu bringen, daß wir bereits etwas wissen: also die Bekämpfung eines Gefühls von etwas Neuem und Verwandlung des anscheinend Neuen in etwas Altes.*' In German, *erkennen* also carries the implication of knowing something 'inside out'.
9. Bateson, 1979.
10. See, for example, Ratliff, 1965.
11. When one describes man as a wolf any 'human traits that can without undue strain be talked about in "wolf-language" will be rendered prominent, and any that cannot will be pushed into the background. The wolf-metaphor suppresses some details, emphasises others – in short, *organises* our view of man. Suppose I look at the night sky through a piece of heavily smoked glass on which certain lines have been left clear. Then I shall see only the stars that can be made to lie on the lines previously prepared upon the screen, and the stars I do see will be seen as organised by the screen's structure. We can think of a metaphor as such a screen and the system of "associated commonplaces" of the focal word as the network of lines upon the screen . . .' If I describe a battle as a game of chess, 'the chess vocabulary filters and transforms: it not only selects, it brings forward aspects of the battle that might not be seen at all through another medium' (Black, 1962, pp. 41–2).

482 • NOTES TO pp. 98–102

12. See, e.g., Kinsbourne, 1993a, pp. 43–50.
13. E. Zaidel, 1995; see also Kaplan & Zaidel, 2001, p. 158: 'Each hemisphere can function as an independent cognitive unit, complete with its own perceptual, motoric and linguistic abilities'.
14. Freud, 1960b, p. 212.
15. One research group has suggested that there may be no necessary connection between language dominance and brain torque in individual subjects who have abnormalities of brain lateralisation (Kennedy, O'Craven, Ticho et al., 1999). However, other research suggests that torque is indeed linked specifically to size of the planum temporale, which is known to be intimately involved with language function (Barrick, Mackay, Prima et al., 2005). Whichever position one adopts, the relationship between brain structure and function in unusual individual cases would not form a reliable basis for generalisation about the species, given the remarkable extent of brain plasticity in development. For example, individuals with hugely attenuated cerebral cortices secondary to hydrocephalus sometimes function virtually normally; this does nothing to invalidate the relationship between brain structure and function in general.
16. I am not the first to have questioned whether language is the core difference between the hemispheres. For example, the prominent neurologist and neuropsychologist Elkhonon Goldberg, whose research has been an important influence for me as for others, writes: 'The basic facts linking language to the left hemisphere are not in dispute. The question arises, however, whether the close association with language is the central attribute of the left hemisphere or a special case, a consequence of a more fundamental principle of brain organisation' (Goldberg, 2001, p. 41). He goes on to draw attention to the research suggesting that animals who do not have language may show hemisphere specialisation, and concludes that 'the fundamental principle of brain organisation' between the two hemispheres is that the right hemisphere deals with novel information, and the left with familiar information.
17. See, e.g., Wynn, 1998.
18. *Homo erectus* endocasts demonstrate the same left parietal and right frontal petalia typical of humans: Wynn, 2002.
19. The linguistic capacities of even extensively trained apes are best regarded as non-existent. See, e.g., Bodamer & Gardner, 2002; Premack, 1986; Terrace, Petitto, Sanders et al., 1979.
20. Cantalupo & Hopkins, 2001; Pilcher, Hammock & Hopkins, 2001; Cain & Wada, 1979.
21. LeMay & Geschwind, 1975.
22. Gannon, Holloway, Broadfield et al., 1998.
23. LeMay, 1976. Endocast analysis (of siamang gibbon brains) supports previous work on anthropoids where a left occipital petalia was most commonly observed, followed by a right frontal petalia (Falk, Redmond, Guyer et al., 2000).
24. Whether or not there is conclusive evidence for right-handedness in chimpanzees is not critical to my argument, though evidence suggests it exists (Hopkins, Cantalupo, Freeman et al., 2005; Hopkins & Fernández-Carriba, 2000; Byrne & Byrne, 1991, 1993; R. W. Byrne, 1995; McGrew & Marchant, 1992; McGrew, Marchant, Wrangham et al., 1999; Marchant & McGrew, 1996). Chimpanzees appear to have a handedness distribution midway between that for the expected ('unbiased') norm and that for humans, which is right-shifted (see Annett, 2006: esp. figure 2, p. 105). See also Hopkins, 1995; Hopkins & Cantalupo, 2003; Hopkins, Fernández-Carriba, Wesley et al., 2001; Hopkins, Wesley, Izard et al., 2004. In fact there does appear to be a 'rightwards drift' for interacting with the environment in a wide range of species (see McManus, 2002, p. 215). Although individual members of other species may show a paw preference, this is usually random, and therefore tends to be equally distributed between left and right in any one species, roughly half of whom will have a preference for the right paw, and half for the left. It is first with primates that this begins not to be true: primates begin to show the typical human pattern of a general preference for the right hand. However, primates do not have language. Of course they are able to communicate socially, but they do this without using words, without language as we understand it. What is more, even sustained human attempts to teach primates to communicate using a symbolic language of any kind have resulted in at best very limited success, as with Washoe, a chimpanzee who after years of training eventually mastered around 130 symbols, without any recognisable syntax, compared with the complex syntax of human language and its average vocabulary of about 75,000 words (Oldfield, 1966, p. 341).
25. Christopher Walsh, Bullard Professor of Neurology at Harvard, discussing the research (C. Walsh, 2005).
26. Thus Toga and Thompson conclude, with some discretion, 'clearly, brain asymmetry, language laterality and handedness are interrelated, but in a complex way' (Toga & Thompson, 2003, p. 38).
27. Kay, Cartmill & Balow, 1998; MacLarnon & Hewitt, 1999; Johanson & Edgar, 1996.
28. See Tattersall, 2004, p. 25: 'It is this leap to symbolic manipulation in the mind that most truly marks us off from other forms of life on Earth; and the ability to do this is evidently something that arose rather abruptly, as a by-product of something else, rather than through a process of gradual fine-tuning over the generations.' The earliest known symbolic object, an ochre plaque bearing geometrical engravings, is almost 80,000 years old, and comes from the Blombos cave in Southern Africa (Henshilwood, d'Errico, Yates et al., 2002). The earliest pierced shells, suggesting symbolic body ornamentation, arose at around the same time in the same region, along with evidence of trade in valued materials and the mining of flints (McBrearty & Brooks, 2003). See also Mithen, 1998a, 1998b; Noble & Davidson, 1996; Milo & Quiatt, 1993.
29. Overall the correlation between brain size and intelligence remains robust across species and within human populations. See the most comprehensive meta-analysis of investigations of the relation of brain size to IQ to date: McDaniel, 2005.
30. See, e.g., Suthers & Zollinger, 2004.
31. These long, long musical 'sentences' of Wagner's are, however, paralleled in language by the extraordinarily long sentences of his admirer, Thomas Mann, in which one has to keep subjects and subordinate clauses in mind for minutes at a time, while one waits for the verb, or for the principal clause to conclude.
32. Koelsch, Kasper, Sammler et al., 2004.
33. See S. Brown, 2000b.

34. Sansavini, Bertoncini & Giovanelli, 1997.
35. Cooper & Aslin, 1990.
36. Mehler, Bertoncini, Barrière et al., 1978; DeCasper & Fifer, 1980; Alegria & Noirot, 1978. What is more, they are sensitive to the musical aspects of speech even before they are born: if a mother repeats a short story twice a day for the last six and half weeks of her pregnancy, her newborn child will prefer hearing it to one she did not (DeCasper & Spence, 1986). 'The womb is an acoustic filter that preserves the intonations of a mother's speech': I am indebted to Vaneechoutte & Skoyles (1998) here, and in the discussion of 'the linguistic wars', for an interesting and thought-provoking survey of this area.
37. Mehler, Jusczyk, Lambertz et al., 1988.
38. Bogen, 1985; van Lancker & Canter, 1982.
39. Henschen, 1926.
40. Panksepp & Bernatsky, 2002, p. 136.
41. Dunbar, 2004, p. 132. See also Mithen, 2005; and Livingstone, 1973.
42. Gould & Lewontin, 1979.
43. 'Cheesecake packs a sensual wallop unlike anything in the natural world because it is a brew of megadoses of agreeable stimuli which we concocted for the express purpose of pressing our pleasure buttons. Pornography is another pleasure technology. In this chapter I will suggest that the arts are a third . . . I suspect that music is auditory cheesecake' ('The Meaning of Life', in Pinker, 1997, pp. 525–32).
44. Mithen, 2005.
45. See Rousseau, 1966; von Humboldt, 1988; and Jespersen, 1922.
46. I notice the obverse of this as a Western psychiatrist asking people every day about their interests and hobbies. Whenever people mention music, I ask them whether they sing or play an instrument, and long ago learnt to expect that hardly any will mean other than that they like to listen to recorded music.
47. Sacks, 2006 (emphasis added).
48. This was first suggested by Vico in his *Scienza Nuova* in 1725, and later by Herder, Rousseau, Humboldt and many other theorists, and is confirmed in the case of Greek literature by, for example, Dover and colleagues (Dover, Bowie, Griffin et al., 1997, p. 10). It has also been specifically claimed in relation to Hebrew, Latin, Arabic, Old Icelandic, English, Spanish and German: e.g. Mazari (2006, p. 62). Benedetto Croce not only endorsed the view, but went so far as to say that 'language is always poetry, and . . . prose (science) is a distinction, not of aesthetic form, but of content, that is, of logical form' (Croce, 1922, p. 329).
49. Ford, 1989, 1991.
50. Everett, 2005.
51. See Dunbar, 2004.
52. Henri Poincaré, 'Mathematical Creation', in Ghiselin, 1985, pp. 25–6; Albert Einstein, 'A letter to Jacques Hadamard', in Ghiselin, 1985, p. 32.
53. Arnheim, 1977, p. 134.
54. Aust, Apfalter & Huber, 2005; Kuhl & Miller, 1978; Kluender, Diehl & Killeen, 1987.
55. Categorisation is species-specific, 'but the ability to categorise and to learn categories is remarkably general across taxa': Finkel, 1988, p. 63.
56. Hernstein, Loveland & Cable, 1976.
57. Cerella, 1980; Matsukawa, Inoue & Jitsumori, 2004; Watanabe, Sakamoto & Wakita, 1995.
58. Porter & Neuringer, 1984.
59. Chase, 2001.
60. Greenfield, 1991; Griffin, 1992; Herman, Richards & Wolz, 1984; Matsuzawa, 1991.
61. Raby, Alexis, Dickinson et al., 2007. For Alex, see Pepperberg, 2005.
62. Varley & Siegal, 2000.
63. Premack & Woodruff, 1978; Tomasello, Call & Hare, 2003; Byrne & Whiten, 1992; Call & Tomasello, 2008.
64. Schore, 1994, pp. 87–8; Izard, 1991.
65. Lordat, J., *Analyse de la parole pour servir à la théorie de divers cas d'alalie et de paralalie (de mutisme et d'imperfection du parler) que les nosologistes ont mal connus* ('Analysis of speech as a contribution to a theoretical understanding of different cases of alalia and paralalia (mutism and imperfection of speech) poorly recognised by nosologists'): emphasis added. This essay is discussed in Hécaen & Dubois, 1969, pp. 140–41, and cited by Prins & Bastiaanse, 2006.
66. Varley, Klessinger, Romanowski et al., 2005; Bloom & Keil, 2001; Brannon, 2005; Rossor, Warrington & Cipolotti, 1995; Cappelletti, Butterworth & Kopelman, 2001.
67. Varley, Klessinger, Romanowski et al., 2005.
68. Remond-Besuchet, Noël, Seron et al., 1999.
69. Pica, Lemer, Izard et al., 2004. See also Gordon, 2004; Dixon, 1980. Warlpiri-speaking Australian children, who also lack number words, can match a series of tones to a series of sticks as well as their English-speaking coevals, the significance of which finding is that it eliminates visual memory as a possible explanation (Butterworth, Reeve, Reynolds et al., 2008).
70. Hauser, Chomsky & Fitch, 2002.
71. Saxe & Moylan, 1982.
72. Hartnett & Gelman, 1998.
73. von Wattenwyl & Zollinger, 1978. The degree to which the German word *rosa* might be considered foreign is, of course, open to debate, but the point is made by Heinrich Zollinger: 'The English term orange but not the term pink has a German counterpart. Many Germans, even those who speak English, do not know what pink means . . .' (1988, p. 159).

74. Roberson & Davidoff, 2000; and see Lupyan, 2005.

75. Nunn, 2005, p. 202, n. 2. Also see Hespos & Spelke, 2004. The concept of tightness of fit is present in Korean, but not in English: as a result, Korean children learn to see this as a joint at which to 'carve' the natural world, where English children lose the distinction.

76. As Bloom & Keil conclude, in a concise review, to which the reader is recommended, of the strengths and weaknesses of the various positions adopted by language experts: 'It is a tool for the expression and storage of ideas. It is not a mechanism that gives rise to the capacity to generate and appreciate these ideas in the first place' (Bloom & Keil, p. 364). An interesting sidelight on the fixative properties of language is that if one names explicitly the aspects of a visual scene, one is less likely to be blind to subtle or slow visual changes in it: words fix the features of an evolving process (Simons, 1996).

77. Rauscher, Krauss & Chen, 1996; Rimé, Schiaratura, Hupet et al., 1984.

78. Detailed phantom limbs occur in subjects with congenital limb deficiency: Melzack, Israel, Lacroix et al., 1997; Saadah & Melzack, 1994.

79. Ramachandran, 1993.

80. Here again I am indebted to Vaneechoutte & Skoyles (1998) for a recent discussion of this and related issues. The structure of language may emerge from, and may even be viewed as a special case of, the structure of action (Studdert-Kennedy, 1983, p. 5), adapting the neural substrate of the left hemisphere evolved in primates for right-handed manipulation and bimanual coordination to vocalisation (Moscovitch, 1983). See also Lieberman, 1984, 1991; and Calvin, 1989.

81. Kinsbourne, 1978, p. 553.

82. ibid., pp. 553 & 558.

83. ibid., p. 559.

84. Sarles, 1985, p. 200.

85. Gazzaniga & LeDoux, 1978; LeDoux, Wilson & Gazzaniga, 1977.

86. See, e.g., Hewes, 1973; Corballis, 1992; Armstrong, Stokoe & Wilcox, 1994; Stokoe, 2000; Feyereisen & de Lannoy, 1991.

87. E. Bruner, 2003, p. 38. See also Bradshaw, 1988, 1997.

88. Corballis, 1992; see also further thoughts in Corballis, 2002b, 2003.

89. Wohlschläger & Bekkering, 2002.

90. Révész, 1958, pp. 15–19.

91. Frey, Funnell, Gerry et al., 2005.

92. Gonzalez, Ganel & Goodale, 2006.

93. Stoeckel, Weder & Binkofski, 2004.

94. '. . . ces sujets tendaient à saisir avec cette main [la droite] tout ce qui était à leur portée ou même l'agitaient dans l'espace vide comme à la recherche de quelque chose. À la différence de ce qui se passe chez les sujets présentant un grasping-reflex, ils étaient capables de relâcher immédiatement l'étreinte dès l'ordre donné' (trans. I. McG.): Hécaen & de Ajuriaguerra, 1952, p. 64.

95. '. . . le malade, prié d'imiter les gestes des mains de l'observateur, tente de mettre ses propres mains contre celles de celui-ci . . . Lorsque les mains entrent en action, il semble qu'elles cherchent à ne pas rester isolées, à « trouver une compagnie dans quelque chose qui remplit l'espace»' (trans. I. McG.): ibid., p. 224.

96. Herder, 1966: 'So little did nature create us as severed blocks of rock, as egotistic monads! . . . the plucked chord performs its natural duty: it sounds! It calls for an echo from one that feels alike, even if none is there, even if it does not hope or expect that such another might answer . . . I cannot conceal my amazement that philosophers – people, that is, that look for clear concepts – ever conceived of the idea that the origin of human language might be explained from these outcries of the emotions . . . Children, like animals, utter sounds of sensation. But is not the language they learn from other humans a totally different language?' (pp. 128, 87 & 99 respectively).

97. Geschwind, 1985, pp. 272–3. A similar point has also been made more recently by Jerison, 1985; and Burling emphasises that we would understand the origins of language better by observing the way primates think than the way they communicate (Burling, 1993).

98. Vygotsky, 1962; Clark & Karmiloff-Smith, 1993; Rumelhart, Smolensky, McClelland et al., 1986.

99. 'Some inkling of the power of planning ahead seems to be possessed by chimpanzees, whose tool-modifying activities suggest that they occupy the grey area within the spectrum of tool-using and tool-making – a stage of dawning comprehension': Napier, 1980, p. 113. For an overview, see Cheney & Seyfarth, 1990.

100. See p. 49 above.

101. Quoted in Biese, 1893, p. 12.

102. Black, 1962, p. 44.

103. Snell, 1960, pp. 200–1 (emphasis added).

104. Lakoff & Johnson, 1999, pp. 123 & 129.

105. Locke, 1849, III, x, §34: '. . . all the artificial and figurative application of words eloquence hath invented, are for nothing else but to insinuate wrong ideas, move the passions, and thereby mislead the judgment; and so indeed are perfect cheats . . .' (p. 370).

106. Lakoff & Johnson, 1980, 1999. It is perhaps significant that the functions the conscious left hemisphere associates with itself – optimism, control, consciousness, rationality – are all expressed by means of the spatial metaphor 'up', since it is also keen on winning (not just in individual experience, but in the battle of the hemispheres, as I shall try to suggest); and being in the 'up' position means being physically on top of your opponent – in a word, winning. Examples are (optimism) being upbeat, lifting one's spirits; (control) having control over, ranking above; (consciousness) waking up, but falling asleep; (rationality) rising above one's feelings, but breaking down in tears.

107. Janata & Grafton, 2003.
108. 'I know of more than one instance where an individual . . . could not but associate, by a direct and rapid impulse, this particular sound with that particular colour, this particular phenomenon with that particular dark and quite different feeling, where a comparison through slow reason could detect no relationship whatever.' Herder, 1966, pp. 139–40.
109. Herder, 1966, pp. 140–43.
110. B. Berlin, 1992, 2005; Ramachandran & Hubbard, 2001.
111. Vowles, 1970.
112. Lakoff & Johnson, 1999, p. 4.
113. Chomsky, 1957, 1988.
114. See, e.g., Botha, 1989; Harris, 1993; Tomasello, 1995; Allott, 1995; Bates & Goodman, 1997.
115. Reviewed by Aitchison, 1996.
116. *Chuang Tzu*, 1964, ch. 3, 'The Secret of Caring for Life', pp. 46–9.
117. Dreyfus & Dreyfus, 1986, p. 30.
118. Wittgenstein, 1967b, Part I, §19, p. 8.
119. Nagel, 1979b.
120. Chartrand & Bargh, 1999.
121. Laban, 1960, p. 86.
122. ibid., p. 97. I am sure Laban is right; but I suspect the ultimate difference is that we attend in a much more intense way because of being present at the birth of something, with all the uncertain expectancy of such an event, rather than, as in listening to recorded music, attending its memorial service.
123. Vaneechoutte & Skoyles, 1998.
124. S. Brown, 2000a.
125. S. Brown, 2000b. See also Scherer, 1991. For a general discussion of these issues, see Morley, 2003.
126. Dunbar, 2004, p. 131.
127. For 'the cheerless gloom of chance', see Kant, 1891, p. 15. For the sheer exuberance of human nature, and its refusal to be limited by what is necessary, see William James (1979): 'Man's chief difference from the brutes lies in the exuberant excess of his subjective propensities . . . Had his whole life not been a quest for the superfluous, he would never have established himself as inexpugnably as he has done in the necessary' (p. 104).
128. Dunbar, 2004, p. 128.
129. Panksepp, 1998, p. 334.
130. Falk, Redmond, Guyer et al., 2000; Holloway & de LaCoste-Lareymondie, 1982; E. Bruner, 2003; Broadfield, Holloway, Mowbray et al., 2001.
131. Ornstein, 1997, p. 149.
132. Geschwind & Galaburda, 1985; Chi, Dooling & Gilles, 1977b.
133. Simonds & Scheibel, 1989; Thatcher, Walker & Giudice, 1987.
134. Macaques exhibit a right frontal petalia, involving both the orbital and dorsolateral areas of the frontal lobe, with a possible associated left occipital development (Cheverud, Falk, Hildebolt et al., 1990; Cheverud, Falk, Vannier et al., 1990; Falk, Hildebolt, Cheverud et al., 1990). Great apes show both right frontal and left occipital petalia (Pilcher, Hammock & Hopkins, 2001), though according to Bruner they 'present specific patterns, more marked in Gorilla with a [left occipital] dominance' (E. Bruner, 2003, p. 33).
135. 'The most statistically significant difference [in the entire brain] was located in the right frontal pole and a number of other significant peaks were located in the right superior and middle frontal gyri, particularly in mid-dorsolateral frontal cortex, confirming previous findings that this lobe extends further anteriorly and laterally in the right hemisphere than in the left' (Watkins, Paus, Lerch et al., 2001, p. 869).
136. Oldfield, 1966, p. 352.
137. Trimble, 2007.
138. Gaburo, 1979–80, p. 218.
139. Henschen, 1926, pp. 112, 115, 116 & 119.
140. Gazzaniga, 1998, p. 191.
141. Gazzaniga, 1983, p. 536.
142. Gazzaniga, 2000, p. 1315.
143. ibid, p. 1302.
144. For those who think that this is restricted to notorious cases such as '. . . why is it not as illuminating and honest to refer to Newton's laws as "Newton's rape manual" as it is to call them "Newton's mechanics"?' (Harding, 1986, p. 113), see Patai & Koertge, 2003.
145. The degree of human right handedness is related to weakness of the left hand rather than strength of the right hand (Annett, 1998; Kilshaw & Annett, 1983). There is a clear parallel with the variability in size of the left and right plana temporalia (Galaburda, Corsiglia, Rosen et al., 1987); in symmetrical brains, large plana were found in both cerebral hemispheres, but in asymmetrical ones it was because the right planum was smaller, not because the left planum was greater. The mechanisms inducing human cerebral asymmetry operate by reducing the role of the right hemisphere (Annett & Manning, 1990).
146. Annett, 1998, 1978.
147. Annett, 1998. See also Annett & Manning, 1989; McManus, Shergill & Bryden, 1993; Palmer & Corballis, 1996; Resch, Haffner, Parzer et al., 1997.
148. See n. 145 above.
149. Sun, Patoine, Abu-Khalil et al., 2005; C. Walsh, 2005.
150. Galaburda, Corsiglia, Rosen et al., 1987.

---

151. Annett & Manning, 1990.
152. See p. 26.
153. Kilshaw & Annett, 1983.
154. Annett & Kilshaw, 1982; Benbow, 1986.
155. Annett, 1991.

CHAPTER 4: THE NATURE OF THE TWO WORLDS

1. On this point, at least, I am in agreement with Dan Dennett: 'There is no such thing as philosophy-free science; there is only science whose philosophical baggage is taken on board without examination' (1995, p. 21).

2. In an unpublished study of the degree subjects undertaken by university students who then went on to be admitted to the Bethlem Royal & Maudsley Hospital in London during a psychotic episode, I found that a subsequent diagnosis of schizophrenia was most strongly associated with having chosen to study engineering, followed closely by philosophy (p > 0.001). The abstract, impersonal, sequentialist approach of philosophy distinguishes it from all other humanities subjects (e.g. literature, history), which were the commonest choices amongst those who were subsequently diagnosed with an affective psychosis.

3. That a statement is either true or false, and that if false, its denial must be true. This tenet of Western philosophy since Plato is, as Pascal saw, a poor guide: 'Contradiction is a bad indicator of truth. Plenty of things that are certain are mutually contradictory; plenty of things that are false contain no inconsistency. Contradiction is not a sign of falsehood, nor the lack of contradiction a sign of truth': 1976, §384 (Lafuma §177); trans. I. McG. ('Contradiction est une mauvaise marque de vérité. Plusieurs choses certaines sont contredites. Plusieurs fausses passent sans contradiction. Ni la contradiction n'est marque de fausseté ni l'incontradiction n'est marque de vérité.')

4. Plutarch, 'Life of Theseus', §22–3 (trans. J. Dryden), in Plutarch, 2001, vol. 1, pp. 13–14.

5. Novalis, 1967, p. 541.

6. Capgras syndrome, difference in sameness, is like the dichotomy paradox: a real unity becomes fragmented. Fregoli syndrome, sameness in difference, is like the Achilles paradox: with the loss of unity, the attempt is made to recapture it by summing parts, but necessarily fails.

7. Cf. Russell's paradox: the set of all sets that are not members of themselves leads inexorably to a contradiction. If such a set were a member of itself, it would nonetheless have to be excluded – thereby no longer being a member of itself; but if it were not a member of itself, it would have to be included – thereby becoming a member of itself.

8. 'Why should not logicians, more than anyone, realize the places where hard-edged, clean logic will necessarily run into trouble in dealing with this chaotic and messy universe?', writes Douglas Hofstadter. He carries on by quoting Marvin Minsky, the famous artificial intelligence researcher: 'Logic doesn't apply to the real world . . . This is one of the difficulties that artificial intelligence workers are facing. They are coming to realize that no intelligence can be based on reasoning alone; or rather that isolated reasoning is impossible, because reasoning depends on a prior setting-up of a system of concepts, percepts, classes, categories – call them what you will – in terms of which all situations are understood [context, in other words – I. McG.].' Hofstadter & Dennett, 1982, p. 343.

9. I have referred to this aspect of Pascal's thought throughout the notes. In the matter of flux, Pascal warned: 'Individual things break down and are transformed at every moment: he [man] only sees them in passing . . .': 1976, §72 (Lafuma §199); trans. I. McG. ('Les choses en particulier se corrompent et se changent à chaque instant: il ne les voit qu'en passant . . .')

10. Spinoza, 1947, V, Proposition 24, p. 269 (the translation here preferred is that of Boyle: see Spinoza, 1910, p. 214). For a full discussion of the evolution of these concepts from the Middle Ages onwards, see Mittelstrass, 1988.

11. These ideas have been illuminatingly explored by Louis Sass (1994).

12. Sass, 1994.

13. Nagel, 1986.

14. 'Bias for impartiality is as much a bias as is partisan prejudice, though it is a radically different quality of bias . . . One can only see from a certain standpoint, but this fact does not make all standpoints of equal value. A standpoint which is nowhere in particular and from which things are not seen at a special angle is an absurdity. But one may have affection for a standpoint which gives a rich and ordered landscape rather than for one from which things are seen confusedly and meagrely.' Dewey, 1931, p. 216.

15. ibid., pp. 219, 206 & 212 respectively.

16. ibid., p. 204.

17. Dewey, 1929, p. 241.

18. ibid., p. 212.

19. James, 1979.

20. Toulmin, 1990, p. 10.

21. Dewey, 1988, p. 164.

22. Husserl, 1970, p. 290 (1962, p. 337), quoted in Levin, 1999, p. 61. Sass's thesis that modernism has many of the features of schizophrenia (discussed below, p. 393 ff.) makes an interesting parallel, since he demonstrates that a key element in schizophrenia is not irrationality, but an excessive and misplaced rationalism.

23. Since this is involuntarily absent in subjects with schizophrenia, and voluntarily suspended by philosophers, it may account for the difficulty both have in apprehending the reality of the world.

24. What he called 'intersubjective phenomenology' in the fifth Cartesian Meditation (Husserl, 1995).

25. Husserl, 1952.

26. Gallagher & Meltzoff, 1996, pp. 225–6; Trevarthen, 1979; Aitken & Trevarthen, 1997; Trevarthen & Aitken, 2001.

27. Evan Thompson (2001, p. 2: emphasis in original). Here he refers specifically to Francisco Varela and Shaun Gallagher: Varela, 1996; Gallagher, 1997; Petitot, Varela, Pachoud et al., 1999.

28. See Poundstone, 1992.
29. As so often, I agree with rational-choice theorist Jon Elster: 'Do real people act on the calculations that make up many pages of mathematical appendixes in leading journals? I do not think so' (2007, p. 5).
30. Hayashi, Ostrom, Walker et al., 1999; Kiyonari, Tanida & Yamagishi, 2000.
31. de Waal, 2006a, p. 3. For discussion of animals, empathy and morality, see de Waal, 2006b.
32. Panksepp, 1998, p. 258.
33. Human altruism is sometimes described in terms of 'strong reciprocity' (Fehr, Fischbacher & Gächter, 2002; Gintis, 2000). Strong reciprocity is 'a combination of altruistic rewarding, which is a predisposition to reward others for cooperative, norm-abiding behaviours, and altruistic punishment, which is a propensity to impose sanctions on others for norm violations. Strong reciprocators bear the cost of rewarding or punishing even if they gain no individual economic benefit whatsoever from their acts. In contrast, reciprocal altruists, as they have been defined in the biological literature, reward and punish only if this is in their long-term self-interest' (Fehr & Fischbacher, 2003, p. 785).
34. Rilling, Gutman, Zeh et al., 2002; de Quervain, Fischbacher, Treyer et al., 2004.
35. See n. 34 above. An example of altruistic punishment is the schoolteacher staying behind after school to supervise detention because he or she believes that punishment in this case is good for society, even at cost to the punisher.
36. Merleau-Ponty, 1962, p. 185.
37. Merleau-Ponty, 1969, as discussed by Murata, 1998, p. 298: 'Only something that appears in depth can have "aspects" in the true sense, because without depth there can be no "aspects" nor "sides," but only parts.'
38. Hécaen, de Ajuriaguerra & Angelergues, 1963, p. 227.
39. Haaland & Flaherty, 1984.
40. Sunderland, Tinson & Bradley, 1994; Benton, 1967; Benton & Fogel, 1962; Black & Bernard, 1984; Black & Strub, 1976; Mack & Levine, 1981; Piercy, Hécaen & de Ajuriaguerra, 1960; Piercy & Smyth, 1962; Villa, Gainotti & De Bonis, 1986.
41. Matthews, 2002, p. 136.
42. Edelman, 1989.
43. Lakoff & Johnson, 1999, p. 6.
44. Merleau-Ponty, 1964c.
45. 'From a neuropsychological point of view, *Being and Time* is a prescient account of right hemisphere functions' (Cutting, 1999, p. 290).
46. J. Young, 2004, p. 59.
47. Matthews, 2002, p. 139.
48. It is perhaps suggestive that even the concept of invention means literally 'finding', as in the phrase 'the Invention of the Cross' (L *invenire* to find), rather than 'making up' (putting things together).
49. An idea wonderfully imaged in the Japanese Zen garden, Ryoan-ji, in which, from any one viewpoint, there is always at least one of the 15 stones that cannot be seen.
50. Churchland, 1986, p. 326.
51. Wittgenstein, 1984, p. 58e.
52. Steiner, 1978, p. 130.
53. ibid., pp. 29–31.
54. van Lancker, 1991.
55. Steiner, 1978, p. 34.
56. Heidegger, 1959, p. 33.
57. Steiner, 1978, p. 41.
58. See, e.g., Heidegger, 1999, pp. 458–72.
59. See, e.g., ibid., p. 420 ff: and Inwood, 1999, p. 221.
60. See, e.g., Heidegger, 1999, pp. 98–107.
61. See p. 181.
62. Heidegger, 1977, pp. 3–35.
63. *Holzweg* refers to a loggers' path in woodland, and has at least two contrary associations: the positive one, of a path to a *clearing* in the woods, and the negative one, of a path that goes nowhere, with the word being used in colloquial German to suggest being on the wrong track, or 'barking up the wrong tree'.
64. On this topic, Poincaré, like many others, found that a walk or journey enabled unconscious processes to yield insight into, for example, mathematical problems: see Poincaré, 1908.
65. Steiner, 1978, p. 12.
66. Descartes, 1984–91d, 'Rule IX', p. 33. Descartes's spirit is in total opposition to that of Goethe, who warned that *'zur Einsicht in den geringsten Teil ist die Übersicht des Ganzen nötig'* ('to have insight into the smallest detail one must have an overview of the whole'): Goethe, 1989, 'Betrachtungen über Farbenlehre und Farbenbehandlung der Alten', p. 552 (trans. I. McG.).
67. Rorty, 1989, p. 26.
68. *'Ich glaube meine Stellung zur Philosophie dadurch zusammengefaßt zu haben, indem ich sagte: Philosophie dürfte man eigentlich nur dichten'* (*Vermischte Bemerkungen*, vol. 8, p. 483; emphasis in original): 'I think I summarised my position on philosophy, when I said that really one should write philosophy only as poetry' (trans. I. McG.). As the phrasing suggests, this is a considered view which sums up repeated formulations of the idea in the *Nachlass*.
69. Heidegger, 1959, pp. 13–14.
70. Heidegger, 1971, pp. 189–210.

71. 'Understanding arises neither through talking at length [*vieles Reden*] nor through busily hearing something "all around". Only he who already understands can listen [*zuhören*].' Heidegger, 1999, p. 210.

72. Compare: '*Il y a de certaines choses qu'on n'entend jamais, quand on ne les entend pas d'abord*' ('Some things are such that if you do not understand them immediately, you never will'), Mme de Sévigné, lettre du 14ᵉ mai 1686 au comte de Bussy-Rabutin (Sévigné, 1846, p. 534); and 'If you have not already got it in you, you cannot receive it', from the *Chuang Tzu*, in J. Needham, 1954–98, vol. 2 (1956), p. 85.

73. Heidegger, 1977, p. 47.

74. Merleau-Ponty, 1968, pp. 194 & 185 respectively; cited by Levin, 1999, p. 208.

75. C. Jung, 1953–79, vol. 8, p. 200.

76. Schopenhauer, 1969, vol. 2, supplements to First Book, Part 2, ch. 17, 'On man's need for metaphysics'. The original reads: '*Das philosophische Erstaunen ist demnach im Grunde ein bestürztes und betrübtes: die Philosophie hebt, wie die Ouvertüre zum Don Juan, mit einem Mollakkord an*' (*Die Welt als Wille und Vorstellung*, II, Ergänzungen zum Ersten Buch, ii, 17, 'Über das metaphysische Bedürfniß des Menschen', 1960, vol. 2, p. 222).

77. For an unbiased account, see J. Young, 1998.

78. Wittgenstein, 1997, 2003.

79. Wittgenstein, 1967b, Part II, xi, p. 227.

80. Hacker, 2001, p. 73.

81. Wittgenstein, 1958, p. 18.

82. From 'A biologist's view of Whitehead's philosophy' (1941), in J. Needham, 1943, p. 183.

83. Wittgenstein, 1967a, p. 27. The phrase, however, has a history: it is first recorded in a sermon by Joseph Butler (1729, Preface, p xxix).

84. Waismann, 1994, p. 112. For Waismann I am indebted to Louis Sass (2001).

85. 'The difficulty of psychology is precisely that our ordinary concepts are too rigid; we need something looser, more indefinite. This brings out the fundamental character of the mental; everything is equivocal, indefinite, floating. In order to describe the mental we need a *language* that is just as flexible; which, of course, runs counter to our usual ways of thinking.' Yet 'there really is something like digging down to deeper layers, becoming more truthful, struggling passionately, while things become clearer and clearer. There is undoubtedly such a process of plumbing the depths in which one penetrates to one's innermost motives. So things are not entirely subjective: there *is* truth after all. And yet! When we want to put our finger on it, it will not stand up; when we look more closely at it, it looks different again. It is an interpretation and yet something more than an interpretation, knowledge and yet not quite knowledge: what are we dealing with?' (Waismann, 1994, p. 136).

86. Sass, 2001, p. 284; Drury, 1984, p. 79.

87. Wittgenstein, 1984, p. 5e.

88. E.g.: 'The *psychical* modifications that go along with the process of civilisation are striking and unambiguous. They consist in a progressive displacement of instinctual aims and a restriction of instinctual impulses. Sensations which were pleasurable to our ancestors have become indifferent or even intolerable to ourselves; there are organic grounds for the changes in our ethical and aesthetic ideals. Of the psychological characteristics of civilisation two appear to be the most important: a strengthening of the intellect, which is beginning to govern instinctual life, and an internalisation of the aggressive impulses, with its consequent advantages and perils' (Freud, 1960f, pp. 214–15); 'It is impossible to overlook the extent to which civilisation is built upon a renunciation of instinct, how much it presupposes precisely the non–satisfaction ... of instincts' (Freud, 1960a, p. 97); '[The *Weltanschauung* of science] asserts that there are no sources of knowledge of the universe other than the intellectual working-over of carefully scrutinised observations – in other words, what we call research – and alongside of it no knowledge derived from revelation, intuition or divination. It seems as though this view came very near to being generally recognised in the course of the last few centuries that have passed' (Freud, 1960c, p. 159); '[Civilisation] displaces instinctual aims and brings it about that people become antagonistic to what they had previously tolerated' (Freud, 1960c, p. 179).

89. Heidegger, 1977, p. 134.

90. ibid., p. 164.

91. Descartes, 1984–91a, Part III, p. 125.

92. See J. Young, 2004, p. 11.

93. Heidegger, 'In Memoriam Max Scheler', a eulogy on the death of Max Scheler delivered at the University of Marburg on 21 May 1928 (1984, p. 50).

94. See n. 26 above; as well as the thesis put forward by Peter Hobson (2004).

95. Scheler, 1954, pp. 244–52.

96. ibid., p. 246.

97. '*Le coeur a ses raisons que la raison ne connaît point*': Pascal, 1976, §277 (Lafuma §224).

98. 'People should not worry so much about what they do as about who they are. If they and their ways are good, then their deeds are radiant. If you are righteous, then what you do will also be righteous. We should not think that holiness is based on what we do but rather on what we are, for it is not our works which sanctify us but we who sanctify our works' (Meister Eckhart, 'The Talks of Instruction', 1994, p. 7). The position is also that of St. Augustine contra Pelagius. In the realm of art, it is the argument of Maurice Morgann's famous *Essay on the Dramatic Character of Sir John Falstaff* (see pp. 304 & 355 below): we do not build up the man from his actions, but understand him whole first (by Scheler's value-ception) and judge his actions in the light of who he is, rather than the other way round. This redeeming of apparent imperfection by the whole is the subject of my *Against Criticism* (1982).

99. Scheler, 1973.

100. Scheler, 1998, pp. 124–5. It is a perverse inversion, a product of modern humanity's *ressentiment*, according to Scheler, that has placed pleasure below utility, with the result that the means of pleasure can now be acquired only by those who, paradoxically, value utility more highly. Consequently nobody wins.

101. Scheler, 1998, p. 127.
102. See pp. 180–81 below: Elster, 1983.
103. First formulated by Henry Sidgwick in the *Methods of Ethics*, it is most succinctly expressed by Victor Frankl: '... happiness ... cannot be pursued; it must ensue, and it only does so as the unintended side effect of one's personal dedication to a cause greater than oneself or as the by-product of one's surrender to a person other than oneself' (1984, p. 17).
104. Watts, 1963, p. 9. See also Wilber, 2001, p. 30.
105. Sweetser, 1990.
106. See pp. 45 & 86 above.
107. Goodale & Milner, 1995.
108. Simons & Chabris, 1999.
109. Noë & O'Regan, 2000; Noë, 2002; Kovács, Papathomas, Yang et al., 1996.
110. Ito, 2000.
111. Schutz, 2005, p. 11.
112. Heraclitus, fr. VII (Diels 8, Marcovich 11), in Kahn, 1979 (Kahn's translation).
113. 'There is always an appeal open from criticism to nature': Johnson, 1963, p. 110.
114. Libet, 1989.
115. Nunn, 2005, p. 195.
116. 'The external world is really there around us. That its existence is normally veiled is due not to existence but to our eyes. The habitual way of consciousness makes us look at things mechanically and think them dead. If only this mechanical view is abandoned, then existence is exposed in its nakedness. ... Zen is not, in my view, philosophy or mysticism. It is simply a practice of readjustment of nervous activity. That is, it restores the distorted nervous system to its normal functioning.' Sekida, 1975, pp. 103 & 211.
117. See p. 97: C. Jung, vol. 9ii, p. 287.
118. Snell, 1960, 'Homer's View of Man', pp. 1–22.
119. 'We are not cameras. We do not traverse the world as blank slates, on which the environment presses its information' (Kinsbourne, 2003).
120. Empedocles, §84, lines 8–11 (trans. B. Snell).
121. 'So much of fire as would not burn, but gave a gentle light, [the gods] formed into a substance akin to the light of every-day life; and the pure fire which is within us and related thereto they made to flow through the eyes in a stream smooth and dense, compressing the whole eye, and especially the centre part, so that it kept out everything of a coarser nature, and allowed to pass only this pure element. When the light of day surrounds the stream of vision, then like falls upon like, and they coalesce, and one body is formed by natural affinity in the line of vision, wherever the light that falls from within meets with an external object. And the whole stream of vision, being similarly affected in virtue of similarity, diffuses the motions of what it touches or what touches it over the whole body, until they reach the soul, causing that perception which we call sight.' Plato, *Timaeus* (trans. B. Jowett).
122. Pliny, 1991, Bk. 8, §78 (pp. 117–18).
123. Bray, 1993, vol. 1, pp. 728–54; J. Needham, 1954–98, vol. 2 (1956), pp. 85–93.
124. David Boyle, writing about the deceptive objectivity of precise data, comments on statistics on soil erosion provided by 22 different sources which varied 8,000-fold: 'The scary part is that all the figures were probably correct, but the one thing that they failed to provide was objective information. For that you need interpretation, quality, imagination' (Boyle, 2001, p. 42).
125. Merleau-Ponty, 1962, p. 361.
126. Merleau-Ponty, 1968, p. 78.
127. 'The thickness of flesh', Merleau-Ponty wrote, 'between the seer and the thing is constitutive for the thing of its visibility as for the seer of his corporeity; it is not an obstacle between them, it is their means of communication' (1968, p. 135). '*C'est que l'épaisseur de chair entre le voyant et la chose est constitutive de sa visibilité à elle comme de sa corporéité à lui; ce n'est pas un obstacle entre lui et elle, c'est leur moyen de communication*' (1964a, p. 178).
128. Merleau-Ponty, 1964b, p. 70.
129. I think this is also what the philosopher A. N. Whitehead is getting at when he describes the way sense perception works – both making us aware of the body and taking us beyond it. But he emphasises the potential treacherousness of vision in this regard. It is the sense that, par excellence, enables detachment and objectivity; it, more than any other sense, allows disengagement from the body. As a result Whitehead stresses the importance of both the presence and the non-presence of the body: 'The peculiarity of sense-perception is its dual character, partly irrelevant to the body and partly referent to the body. In the case of sight, the irrelevance to the body is at its maximum ... In the other modes of sensation the body is more prominent. ... The current philosophic doctrines, mostly derived from Hume, are defective by reason of their neglect of bodily reference.' However, he continues, 'even in visual experience we are also aware of the intervention of the body. We know directly that we see *with our eyes*. That is a vague feeling, but extremely important' (A. N. Whitehead, 1934, pp. 63–4 & 75).
130. Dijksterhuis & van Knippenberg, 1998.
131. Pendry & Carrick, 2001.
132. Anderson & Dill, 2000.
133. B. Levy, 1996.
134. Dijksterhuis, Aarts, Bargh et al., 2000.
135. Levy, Ashman & Dror, 1999–2000.
136. Zeki, 1999, p. 4.
137. Emery, 2000; Emery, Lorincz, Perrett et al., 1997. It is possible that some birds reared by humans may be capable of joint attention (Pepperberg & McLaughlin, 1996).

138. Kaminski, 2009, pp. 103–7; Call, Bräuer, Kaminski et al., 2003; Virányi, Topál, Gácsi et al., 2004.
139. Dogs may have a greater capacity than some primates to understand and share human attention: see Udell & Wynne, 2008; Miklósi, Polgárdi, Topál et al., 1998. A number of domesticated species can follow the direction of gaze (Tomasello, Call & Hare, 1998), e.g. goats (Kaminski, Riedel, Call et al., 2005) and dolphins (Tschudin, Call, Dunbar et al., 2001).
140. Okada, Sato & Toichi, 2006.
141. Wicker, Michel, Henaff et al., 1998. In both averted and direct mutual gaze, in addition to the expected ventral occipito-temporal region of the right hemisphere, areas including the occipital part of the fusiform gyrus, the right parietal lobule, the right inferior temporal gyrus and both middle temporal gyri are also activated. In both conditions there is an increase in activity in the right superior parietal lobule, right precentral gyrus and right inferior frontal gyrus, as well as the right amygdala, right pulvinar and bilateral mediodorsal thalamic nuclei. See also Kingstone, Friesen & Gazzaniga, 2000.
142. Kircher, Senior, Phillips et al., 2001.
143. Decety & Chaminade, 2003.
144. Kanner, 1943.
145. Leekam, Hunnisett & Moore, 1998.
146. Charman, Swettenham, Baron-Cohen et al., 1997.
147. Baron-Cohen, Campbell, Karmiloff-Smith et al., 1995; Baron-Cohen, Wheelwright & Jolliffe, 1997; Leekam, Baron-Cohen, Perrett et al., 1997.
148. Rosse, Kendrick, Wyatt et al., 1994.
149. Levin, 1999, p. 47 (emphasis in original).
150. Kawasaki, 1992, quoted by Ogawa, 1998, p. 153.
151. Belief, like faith and truth, etymologically implies a relation of loyalty, and has the same root as love (and as the German words *Glauben* and *Liebe*).
152. Wittgenstein, 1967b, Part II, iv, p. 178.
153. 'Wittgenstein argued that a truly religious belief should not be understood as a kind of empirical claim, a botched attempt to speak objective truths. Rather it is "something like a passionate commitment to a system of reference . . . a way of living, or a way of assessing life. It's passionately seizing hold of *this* interpretation." ' Sass, 2001, p. 282, referring to Wittgenstein, 1984, p. 64e.
154. The inevitable reciprocity of such relations is imaged in Meister Eckhart's 'the eye with which I see God is the same eye with which God sees me . . . one vision or seeing, and one knowing and loving' (1957, p. 288).
155. Vaihinger, 1935.
156. See p. 151 above.
157. Laeng, Zarrinpar & Kosslyn, 2003.
158. Wittgenstein, 1967b, Part I, §67, p. 32.
159. Nunn, 2005, p. 195.
160. C. Jung, 1953–79, vol. 8, p. 271.
161. ibid., vol. 9i, p. 267.
162. Laban, 1960, p. 4.
163. Jan Patočka (1907–77) was an important Czech phenomenological philosopher, active in the Charter 77 human rights movement. He spoke of the 'solidarity of the shaken', at one level an affirmation of the power and determination of those who have suffered great political oppression, but at another a recognition of the resolve born of a different kind of suffering, in those for whom the comfortable familiarity of the apparently known no longer disguises the sheer 'awe-full-ness' of Being – what Rudolf Otto called the *mysterium tremendum et fascinans* (Otto, 1923). Thus Andrew Shanks writes of 'those who have been shaken, especially by the experience of great historic trauma, out of life "within a lie" – or, in general, out of the unquestioned prejudices of their culture – into a genuinely open-minded thoughtfulness. This is not the thoughtfulness of scholarly expertise; but, rather, that other sort of thoughtfulness (to be found at all different levels of scholarly sophistication or articulacy) which may also be described as a fundamental openness to transcendence' (Shanks, 2000, p. 5).
164. Coleridge, 1965, vol. II, ch. xiv, p. 169.
165. Though not the sense of Shklovsky's call 'to make it strange', which is more akin to the right hemisphere sense – see pp. 412–13 below.
166. '. . . several things dove-tailed in my mind, and at once it struck me what quality went to form a Man of Achievement, especially in Literature, and which Shakespeare possessed so enormously – I mean Negative Capability, that is, when a man is capable of being in uncertainties, mysteries, doubts, without any irritable reaching after fact and reason – Coleridge, for instance, would let go by a fine isolated verisimilitude caught from the Penetralium of mystery, from being incapable of remaining content with half-knowledge. This pursued through volumes would perhaps take us no further than this, that with a great poet the sense of Beauty overcomes every other consideration, or rather obliterates all consideration': Keats, letter to George and Thomas Keats dated 21/27(?) December 1817 (2002, pp. 41–2).
167. Again Pascal seems to me to put his finger on it: one cannot begin by assuming one understands one part of this conundrum – say, a neurone – and building up from there to an understanding of an aggregation of such parts: 'the parts of the world are all so interrelated and linked to one another that I think it is impossible to know one without knowing the others, and without the whole . . . Since everything, then, is both a cause of, and is caused by, something else, supporting and being supported, mediate and immediate, and all is held together by a natural though imperceptible bond which draws together the most distant and different entities, I maintain that it is impossible to know the parts without knowing the whole, and equally to know the whole without having an intimate knowledge of the parts . . . Who would not think, seeing us compose everything of mind and body, that this

mixture would be quite intelligible to us? Yet it is what we understand the least. Of all objects of nature, none is more astonishing to man than himself; for he cannot conceive what the body is, still less what the mind is – and least of all how a body should be united to a mind. That is the hardest thing for him, and yet at the same time it is his very being. *Modus quo corporibus adhaerent spiritus comprehendi ab homine non potest, et hoc tamen homo est* (St. Augustine, *City of God*, xxi, 10: The manner in which the spirit is united with the body cannot be understood by man; and yet this is what man is)': 1976, §72 (Lafuma §199); trans. I. McG. ('*Mais les parties du monde ont toutes un tel rapport et un tel enchaînement l'une avec l'autre que je crois impossible de connaître l'une sans l'autre et sans le tout ... Donc toutes choses étant causées et causantes, aidées et aidantes, médiates et immédiates et toutes s'entretenant par un lien naturel et insensible qui lie les plus éloignées et les plus différentes, je tiens impossible de connaître les parties sans connaître le tout, non plus que de connaître le tout sans connaître particulièrement les parties ... Qui ne croirait, à nous voir composer toutes choses d'esprit et de corps, que ce mélange-là nous serait bien compréhensible? C'est néanmoins la chose que l'on comprend le moins. L'homme est à lui-même le plus prodigieux objet de la nature, car il ne peut concevoir ce que c'est que corps et encore moins ce que c'est qu'esprit, et moins qu'aucune chose comment un corps peut être uni avec un esprit. C'est là le comble de ses difficultés et cependant c'est son propre être: modus quo corporibus adhaerent spiritus comprehendi ab homine non potest, et hoc tamen homo est.*')

CHAPTER 5: THE PRIMACY OF THE RIGHT HEMISPHERE

1. Wittgenstein, 1993, pp. 36–44: from Sass, 2001, p. 284.
2. Plato, *Theaetetus*, 155^{d}2 ff.
3. Aristotle, *Metaphysics*, A 2, 982^{b}11 ff.
4. Snell, 1960, p. 42. Democritus, along with Leucippus, is often thought of as the first scientific materialist. He also appears to have been the first person to believe he had a 'theory of everything', which led to his being branded by Montaigne and Pascal as impudent and over-reaching (Montaigne, 'An apology for Raymond Sebond', *Essais*, Bk. II:12 (1993, p. 545); Pascal, 1976, §72 (Lafuma §199).
5. Descartes, 1984–91e, Part II, §53, p. 350. The opening words of Whitehead's *Nature and Life* are: 'Philosophy is the product of wonder' (A. N. Whitehead, 1934, p. 9). And Einstein once said: 'The fairest thing we can experience is the mysterious. It is the fundamental emotion which stands at the cradle of true art and true science. He who knows it not and can no longer wonder, no longer feel amazement, is as good as dead, a snuffed-out candle' (Einstein, 1940, p. 5).
6. Eckermann, 1970, conversation of 18 February 1829, p. 296.
7. Sass, 2001, p. 284.
8. Nagel, 1986, p. 4.
9. Naess, 2002, p. 3 (emphasis added).
10. '*Unsere meisten Ausdrücke sind metaphorisch, es steckt in denselben die Philosophie unserer Vorfahren*': Lichtenberg, 1967–72, *Sudelbuch D (1773–5)*, §515, vol. 1, p. 308.
11. See Lakoff & Johnson, 1999, pp. 82–5; Kemper, 1989; Gibbs & O'Brien, 1990; Nayak & Gibbs, 1990; Gentner, 1982; and Gentner & Gentner, 1983.
12. Nietzsche, 1990, p. 31.
13. Donne, 'Satyre III', lines 79–81.
14. Cf. Pascal: '*Car il ne faut pas se méconnaître: nous sommes automates autant qu'esprit*' (1976, §252, Lafuma §821).
15. Montaigne, 'On presumption', *Essais*, Bk. II:17 (1993, p. 738).
16. See Leslie Farber (1976) and Jon Elster (1983, see p. 161 above) for further exploration of this paradox.
17. Descartes, 1984–91b, 'Meditation II', p. 21 (emphasis in original).
18. Ruskin, 1904, vol. 4, Part V, ch. iv, §4, pp. 60–61 (emphasis in original).
19. Heidegger, 1977, p. 130.
20. ibid., p. 129.
21. Descartes, 1984–91c,'Discourse I: Light', p. 152.
22. Kerényi, 1962, p. 115. Elsewhere he writes of the ritual nature of 'the festal world of Homer', which 'rests on a special knowledge in the poet, a *knowing* which is a *state of being* exactly corresponding to the transparency of the world. The transparency of the world allows the divine figures of nature to shine through for the poet ...' (ibid., p. 144).
23. Diderot, 1995, vol. 2, pp. 86–123.
24. See p. 393 ff. below.
25. Merleau-Ponty, 1964c, p. 164.
26. R. B. Zajonc, 1980; Zajonc, Pietromonaco & Bargh, 1982; and R. B. Zajonc, 1984. Also see Jaak Panksepp: 'to the best of our knowledge, the affective essence of emotion is subcortically and precognitively organised' (1998, p. 26) and 'the normal flow of motivational events in the brain' is one in which 'emotions and regulatory feelings have stronger effects on cognitions than the other way round' (ibid., p. 166).
27. See pp. 159–60 above.
28. Panksepp, 1998, p. 334.
29. The primacy of affect leads me to differ on one point from the analysis of John Cutting, whose exposition of the relationship between the two hemispheres and the two primary major illnesses of schizophrenia and depression forms the core of his *magnum opus* the *Principles of Psychopathology*, as well as his subsequent works, *Psychopathology and Modern Philosophy*, and *The Living, the Dead, and the Never-Alive*. His insight that the world of the schizophrenic subject is the consequence of over-reliance on the left hemisphere, constructing a world the affectless nature of which derives from the relative absence of contribution from a normal right hemisphere, and whose apparent cognitive

distortions are a consequence of the unnatural salience of what the left hemisphere brings into being, is brilliant. I would also accept the general outline of his account of depression as a condition in which there is over-reliance on the world of the right hemisphere; but my problem is with the view that the depressed affect, the mood disturbance, is consequent on the cognitive distortions that come about when the right hemisphere is alone responsible for bringing the world into being, without the countervailing contribution normally made by the left. The cognitive distortions that are undoubtedly present in depression must be, in my view, a consequence, not a cause, of the primary disturbance, which is a disturbance of affect. In short, we believe the world is a crock of shit because we are depressed; we are not depressed because we believe the world is a crock of shit. In the end I think this comes down to the primacy of affect, and applies to the left hemisphere/schizophrenia case as well: in other words, schizophrenia does not result in an affective disengagement from the world because the schizophrenic mind sees the world as mechanical, alien and lifeless: it sees the world as mechanical, alien and lifeless because it has disengaged affectively from the world. The primacy of affect in this case is less obvious, because the whole point is that, in schizophrenia, affect is absent – but the primacy of the *effect of its absence* applies nonetheless.

30. 'Behind every thought there is an affective-volitional tendency, which holds the answer to the last "why" in the analysis of thinking': Vygotsky, 1986, p. 252.

31. Nietzsche, 2001, III, §179, p. 137 (emphasis added).

32. Panksepp, 1998, p. 308.

33. ibid., p. 309.

34. ibid., p. 420, n. 34. To which I can only add that that, too, is grounded on the ultimate declaration of being, once made by the Judaeo-Christian Yahweh, though it might as well have been Heidegger's *Sein*, if *Sein* were to be more forthcoming about itself: 'I AM THAT I AM'.

35. '*Les passions ont appris aux hommes la raison*': Vauvenargues, 1859, §154, p. 389.

36. A. R. Damasio, 1994a, p. 128.

37. ibid., p. 130. Cf. ibid., p. xiii: 'at their best, feelings point us in the proper direction, take us to the appropriate place in a decision-making space, where we have to make a moral judgment'.

38. ibid., p. 157.

39. For problems associated with seeing oneself, let alone seeing one's own feelings, never mind 'through a window', see especially Chapters 6, 8 & 14 of the current work. For further discussion of Damasio, see my review of *Descartes' Error* in *Cognitive Neuropsychiatry*, 1996, *1(2)*, pp. 171–9; from his reactions to which I would not anticipate immediate assent from Damasio in what I have to say here, or anywhere else.

40. A. R. Damasio, 1994a, p. xiv. As Panksepp points out (1998, p. 341), 'animals with essentially no neocortex remain behaviourally, and probably internally, as emotional as ever, indeed more so'. See also: Panksepp, Normansell, Cox et al., 1994.

41. Libet, 1985 (with open peer commentary, pp. 539–58; and Libet's reply, 'Theory and evidence relating cerebral processes to conscious will', pp. 558–66).

42. Kornhuber & Deecke, 1965.

43. Pockett, 2002, p. 144.

44. 'Libet's results seems to be in tension with our commonsense picture only because they suggest positing volitions that initially are not conscious': Rosenthal, 2002, p. 219.

45. Jaynes, 1976. Lakoff & Johnson (1999) make the same point about the low levels of conscious activity needed for most mental life, however sophisticated (p. 13).

46. Zeman, 2001.

47. See Joseph, 1992.

48. Mlot, 1998 (emphasis added).

49. Barchas & Perlaki, 1986.

50. Corbetta & Shulman, 2002, p. 208.

51. Wexler, Warrenburg, Schwartz et al., 1992.

52. Galin, 1974; Joseph, 1992.

53. Schore, 2003.

54. Freud, 1960d, p. 14.

55. Fullinwider, 1983, p. 158.

56. Meyer, Ishikawa, Hata et al., 1987. See also Gabel, 1988; and Ramachandran & Rogers-Ramachandran, 1996, which demonstrates that stimulation of the right hemisphere can cause an increase in REM sleep.

57. Bolduc, Daoust, Limoges et al., 2003; Goldstein, Stoltzfus & Gardocki, 1972.

58. Gazzaniga, 2000. Gazzaniga's highly influential paper merits further discussion. He is of the school that sees 'the cortical arena as a patchwork of specialized processes' (p. 1293: note that the metaphor of patchwork discloses that he sees the processes as stitched together, essentially unrelated in nature, however interconnected they may be); and sees language as having ousted the perceptual functions that were previously in its place in the left hemisphere, but making up for it by outsourcing the work to the right hemisphere on its behalf, so that it is now dependent on the right hemisphere to carry on covering for both (hence the importance of the corpus callosum in keeping the hemispheres in touch). His interpreter, first proposed in an earlier paper (1998), is 'a device that allows us to construct theories about the relationship between perceived events, actions and feelings' (2000, p. 1293), and in so doing to create the 'illusion' of the self. It will be apparent that I do not agree with the fragmented, patchwork view of hemisphere functions (typical itself of the left hemisphere's piecemeal approach); nor with the view that the division of labour between the hemispheres is a matter of domestic economy and efficiency, reminiscent of Adam Smith's division of labour (typical of the left hemisphere's disposition towards the world as resource to be utilised); nor the view that the left hemisphere invents the unified self by a *theory* about the relationship between events, actions and feelings (again typical of the left hemisphere view that it is the creator of our experience, and that any unity we may

experience is an illusion created by the excellent job it has done in putting the bits together cognitively). This is what I meant when I said that relying on the left hemisphere (as we have to) to assess the relationship between the hemispheres is like asking a pre-Galilean geocentric astronomer whether the earth moves round the sun.

59. Vaihinger, 1935, p. 7.
60. Sapir, 1927.
61. Gallagher & Frith, 2004.
62. McNeill, 1992.
63. ibid., p. 25. Later work by McNeill confirms that 'the onset of a gesture movement . . . often precedes and *never* [emphasis in original] follows the semantically related speech' (McNeill, 2000, p. 326, n. 6). See also Kendon, 1972, 1980; Morrel-Samuels & Krauss, 1992; and Nobe, 2000.
64. McNeill, 1992, p. 26.
65. ibid., pp. 35 & 245.
66. ibid., p. 248.
67. ibid., p. 245; and see p. 259 for elaboration of this.
68. Black, 1962, p. 46.
69. McNeill, 1992, p. 23.
70. ibid., p. 331; but not so according to Miller & Franz, who found that the majority are synchronised bimanual gestures, and the minority that are one-handed are evenly divided between the hands (Miller & Franz, 2005).
71. McNeill, 1992, p. 343 ff.
72. McNeill, 2000, p. 326, n. 7 (emphasis added).
73. Miller & Franz, 2005; Iverson, 1999.
74. Rauscher, Krauss & Chen, 1996; Rimé, Schiaratura, Hupet et al., 1984.
75. McNeill, 1992, p. 137.
76. ibid., pp. 167 & 269.
77. ibid., pp. 345–52.
78. EEG activity over the right hemisphere predominates in reading stories and over the left hemisphere in reading a scientific textbook: Ornstein, Herron, Johnstone et al., 1979. And see Vitz, 1990.
79. J. Bruner, 1986.
80. One nice detail of embryology is that the right cerebral hemisphere develops gyral complexity earlier than the left: see, e.g., Chi, Dooling & Gilles, 1977a.
81. According to one, it was ' ". . . make-believe. It's not a real war, just an experiment." If a soldier next to him got wounded, it was just that he injured himself while throwing a grenade. And the flattened houses? "It's a local custom each year to pay certain communes to put on some real shooting on their land" ' ('«. . . *une fantasmagorie. Ce n'est pas une guerre réelle, mais une guerre d'expérience.* » *Un soldat à côté de lui a été blessé, c'est qu'il s'est blessé lui-même en lançant une grenade. Des maisons détruites?* « *C'est une coutume de payer chaque année certaines communes pour des tirs réels sur leur terroire.* »' (trans. I. McG.): Vié, 1944c, p. 248, reporting a paper by Demay & Renaux, 1919. See also Vié, 1944a, 1944b, for further examples.
82. Cutting, 1990; Hécaen & de Ajuriaguerra, 1952; Dobrokhotova & Bragina, 1977. See also p. 405–6 below.
83. Deglin & Kinsbourne, 1996. Inactivation of either hemisphere was the result of the administration of electro-convulsive therapy (ECT) to that hemisphere: ECT has been shown to be a reliable method of hemisphere inactivation, producing predictable neurological signs indicative of inactivation of the treated hemisphere for a period of 30–40 minutes following treatment (see, e.g., Kriss, Blumhardt, Halliday et al., 1978).
84. Goel & Dolan, 2003.
85. See p. 41 above.
86. Kinsbourne, 2003.
87. Forming a new memory requires new synapses to be formed or existing synaptic connections to be strengthened. This is done in two stages. First, an experience alters certain receptors (known as AMPA receptors) at the synapse, privileging that synapse so that it communicates preferentially. Second, new proteins are synthesized that help the memory persist. Synaptic signals that trigger memories cause mRNA that codes for certain proteins to be transported from the nucleus to the synapse. The proteins that are created, called Arc proteins, having played their part at the synapse, travel back to the nucleus in a loop, an important mechanism for coordinating the changes that subserve the laying down of long-term memory. This sending out of emissaries that later report back to the centre at cellular level is a remarkable image of the process of memory itself as experienced. See Rao, Pintchovski, Chin et al., 2006.
88. See above, p. 88; also Decety & Chaminade, 2003.
89. According to Scheler, the cosmos, and beyond that the human world, is formed by the relationship between *Sein* and forces which he refers to as *Drang* and *Geist*, which stand in a permissive relationship – either saying 'no' or not saying 'no' – to one another. The interested reader is referred to Scheler's metaphysics (2008); particularly Chapter 7, pp. 323–67. My views on the complex relationship between the hemispheres and Scheler's *Geist* and *Drang* can be found in McGilchrist, 2009. In essence I believe that, while the right hemisphere has both *Drang* and *Geist*, the left hemisphere has *Geist* only.
90. Mikels & Reuter-Lorenz, 2004; Banich, 1998.
91. LeDoux, 1999, p. 165.
92. The phrase 'free won't' is from Douglas Hofstadter (1985), quoted in Nunn, 2005, p. 39.
93. Bogen, 2000.
94. Nietzsche, 1999, §16, p. 76.
95. Cf. (p. 39) divided attention, where, though both hemispheres are involved, the right hemisphere may play the primary role; and (p. 46) the part played by the right hemisphere in conjugate eye movements.
96. 'Critical Fragments', §48, in F. Schlegel, 1991, p. 6.

97. Many other examples exist. For example, the German philosopher Novalis wrote: 'Up to now our thinking was either purely mechanical – *discursive* – atomistic – or purely intuitive – dynamic. Perhaps now the time for union has come?' (*Logological Fragments*, I, §10, in Novalis, 1997, p. 49).
98. 'Ideas', §48 & §108, in F. Schlegel, 2003, pp. 263 & 265.
99. '*Athenaeum* Fragments', §53, in F. Schlegel, 2003, p. 247.
100. Coleridge, 1965, vol. II, ch. xiv, p. 171.
101. 'With what must science begin?', in Hegel, 1969, vol. I, Bk. i, §112: '. . . [die] Einheit des Unterschieden- und des Nichtunterschiedenseyns, – oder [die] Identität der Identität und Nichtidentität'.
102. Scruton, 1997, p. 152. Similarly Claude Lévi-Strauss, quoted by Staude, 1976: 'The work of the painter, the poet and the composer and the myths and symbols of primitive man [should] seem to us if not as a superior form of knowledge, at any rate as the most fundamental form of knowledge, and the only one that we all have in common; knowledge in the scientific sense is merely the sharpened edge of this other knowledge. More penetrating it may be, because its edge has been sharpened on the hard stone of fact, but this *penetration has been acquired at the price of a great loss of substance*' (p. 303: emphasis added).
103. See p. 136 above.
104. Coleridge, 1956–71, vol. 1, p. 349.
105. ibid., p. 354.
106. Nietzsche, 2003, §11 [73], p. 212 (emphasis in original).
107. Hume, 1986, 'Of the Influencing Motives of the Will', p. 22.
108. Hegel, 1949, p. 68.
109. Groucho Marx's famous *mot* about not wanting to belong to any club that would have him for a member wittily inverts the perspective, but has a similar structure.
110. For a fuller treatment see Shanks, forthcoming.
111. Hegel, 1949, pp. 112–13.
112. For a discussion of kenosis in neuropsychological terms, see Teske, 1996.
113. Wittgenstein, 2001, §6.13 & §6.421, pp. 78 & 86.
114. See p. 21 above.

CHAPTER 6: THE TRIUMPH OF THE LEFT HEMISPHERE

1. Hellige, 1993, pp. 336–7.
2. ibid., p. 168.
3. Ringo, Doty, Demeter et al., 1994.
4. According to Chiarello & Maxfield (1996), inhibition may be of three main kinds: isolation, interference and suppression. Isolation is inhibition of communication, and enables one hemisphere to be cut off from the other to prevent crosstalk that might interfere. Interference is precisely the failure to inhibit communication, which consequently 'inhibits' successful function. Suppression is the active inhibition of the homologous area of the contralateral hemisphere: this is the subject of Norman Cook's *The Brain Code* (1986).
5. Gazzaniga, 1970.
6. Baynes, Tramo, Reeves et al., 1997, p. 1160.
7. Ferguson, Rayport & Corrie, 1985, p. 504.
8. Sergent, 1983b.
9. Sergent, 1983a, 1986 & 1990.
10. Sperry, 1974, p. 11. See also Joseph, 1988a.
11. Boroojerdi, Diefenbach & Ferbert, 1996; Boroojerdi, Hungs, Mull et al., 1998; Schnider, Benson & Rosner, 1993.
12. Cioni, Bartalena & Boldrini, 1994.
13. Rothwell, Colebatch, Britton et al., 1991; Meyer, Röricht, Gräfin von Einsiedel et al., 1995; Meyer, Röricht & Woiciechowsky, 1998.
14. Swayze, Andreasen, Ehrhardt et al., 1990; Lewis, Reveley, David et al., 1988; Filteau, Pourcher, Bouchard et al., 1991; Velek, White, Williams et al., 1988; Degreef, Lantos, Bogerts et al., 1992; MacPherson, Holgate & Gudeman, 1987.
15. Goodarzi, Wykes & Hemsley, 2000.
16. David, 1987; Merrin, Floyd & Fein, 1989. Studies of the ability to inhibit motor-evoked potentials are in agreement with these findings: Boroojerdi, Töpper, Foltys et al., 1999; Höppner, Kunesch, Großmann et al., 2001.
17. This position would appear to be supported by a recent review of callosotomy: 'Synchronization and relay of information to inform one hemisphere about the activities of the other hemisphere is a critical function. Another, perhaps more important, function of the corpus callosum is to allow one hemisphere to control and inhibit homologous areas in the other hemisphere, providing a critical pathway for the development of specialized hemispheric functions' (Devinsky & Laff, 2003, p. 615).
18. Chicoine, Proteau & Lassonde, 2000.
19. Galin, Johnstone, Nakell et al., 1979; Salamy, 1978.
20. Merola & Liederman, 1985.
21. Quinn & Geffen, 1986; Liederman, Merola & Hoffman, 1986.
22. *The Upanishads*, 1953, p. 27: *Brihad-aranyaka*, iv, 4, 22 (emphasis added).
23. So quoted and translated by Friedrich Max Müller in *The Science of Thought*, Longman's, Green & Co., London, 1887, p. 143. There are numerous versions, though Kant (*Critique of Pure Reason*, A51, B75) actually wrote '*Gedanken ohne Inhalt sind leer, Anschauungen ohne Begriffe sind blind*' (1977b, vol. 3, p. 98). In either case the point is made, though *Anschauungen* normally suggests something closer to perceptions: thus 'thoughts without content are empty, perceptions without concepts are blind'.

24. The necessary equipoise between the hemispheres may have been intuited by Pascal: 'Nature has placed us so well in the centre, that if we adjust one side of the balance, we also alter the other. This makes me believe that there are springs in our brain which are so adjusted that if you touch one, you also touch its contrary': 1976, §70 (Lafuma §519); trans. I. McG. ('*La nature nous a si bien mis au milieu que si nous changeons un côté de la balance nous changeons aussi l'autre. Cela me fait croire qu'il y a des ressorts dans notre tête qui sont tellement disposés que qui touche l'un touche aussi le contraire*.') This was allied to the ambivalent status of reason: 'It is equally excessive to shut reason out and to let nothing else in': 1976, §253 (Lafuma §183); trans. I. McG. ('*2 excès: exclure la raison, n'admettre que la raison*').

25. See Galin & Ornstein, 1972; Levy, Trevarthen & Sperry, 1972; Bogen & Bogen, 1969; and TenHouten, 1985.

26. Levy & Trevarthen, 1976, p. 300.

27. 'The tonic and/or phasic status of the several modulatory systems of the brainstem seem fully capable of apportioning their effects to favour one or the other hemisphere in gaining ascendancy in metacontrol' (Kavcic, Fei, Hu et al., 2000, p. 81).

28. Hellige, Jonsson & Michimata, 1988.

29. Hellige, Taylor & Eng, 1989.

30. Banich, 2003, pp. 269–70; Banich & Karol, 1992.

31. Marzi, Perani, Tassinari et al., 1999.

32. Levy, Heller, Banich et al., 1983; Kim & Levine, 1991, 1992; Kim, Levine & Kertesz, 1990; Levine, Banich & Koch-Weser, 1984; Levy, 1990. See also Boles, 1998, for the view that local perceptual asymmetries are more likely than global ones.

33. Spencer & Banich, 2005.

34. Marzi, Bisiacchi & Nicoletti, 1991; Bisiacchi, Marzi, Nicoletti et al., 1994; Brown, Larson & Jeeves, 1994; Saron & Davidson, 1989.

35. Larson & Brown, 1997.

36. Oliveri, Rossini, Traversa et al., 1999; Vuilleumier, Hester, Assal et al., 1996; Lomber & Payne, 1996; Hilgetag, Théoret & Pascual-Leone, 2001.

37. Brown-Séquard, 1890.

38. Kinsbourne, 1993b; Oliveri, Rossini, Traversa et al., 1999.

39. Luck, Hillyard, Mangun et al., 1989, 1994.

40. Outside of the literature on commissurotomy, it is not, in fact, always the left hand that behaves disruptively. There are, albeit rare, cases that show the reverse. Bleuler (1902) described the case of a patient with GPI ('general paralysis of the insane'), a consequence of tertiary syphilis, whose right hand 'grabbed at ropes, chopped things with an axe, sowed seeds, and slung away unwanted invisible objects with great vigour. Sometimes it would seize hold of the blankets or the pillow and try to yank them away, and once upset the patient's dinner. When this happened, the sane left hand readjusted the bedclothes, wiped the patient's mouth, and gave every appearance of remaining in contact with reality. The consciousness associated with the delirious right hand had full command of language; the rational consciousness corresponding to the patient's left-handed activities seemed occasionally able to speak, but was considerably more limited in this respect' (Davidson & Hugdahl, 1995, p. 17; and see commentary in Meyer, 1904a). Similarly Liepmann (1900) described a patient in whom 'the entire callosum was very atrophic' (A. Meyer, 1904b, p. 284) and who, additionally had a cyst in the rostral part of the callosum. Following a left hemisphere stroke, he developed aggressive and out of control behaviour with his right hand, which nonetheless completely suppressed the calm and reasonable activity of his, normally functioning, left hand. 'When asked to pick up and show the use of some objects before him, he blundered in every attempt, acted perversely, and made odd movements with the right arm. *When the right arm was held* and he had to use the left, he correctly picked out cards which he could not do with the right; movements of the foot could be imitated with the left but not with the right foot. When the right side was inhibited the appearance of dementia was stopped and the patient could be examined. There evidently existed *motor confusion and perplexity on the habitually used right side and inability to spontaneously use the left capable side*. The right side would at once fumble and distract hopelessly' (A. Meyer, 1904b, p. 277, emphasis in the original).

41. The relationship has thought-provoking similarities with that described by Meister Eckhart between God and the human soul.

42. Bogen, 1985, p. 38.

43. Sperry, 1985, pp. 14–15.

44. Landis, Graves & Goodglass, 1981.

45. Sperry, 1985, pp. 22–3.

46. Panksepp, 1998, p. 307. See also Lambert, 1991; Pashler, Luck, Hillyard et al., 1994.

47. Panksepp, 1998, p. 312. See also p. 421, n. 45: 'There are powerful interconnections between the mesencephalic areas implicated in the generation of the primal SELF and the frontal cortex.'

48. Panksepp, 1998, p. 314; see also Passingham, 1993; Mantyh, 1982.

49. Another advantage of the idea that consciousness is not an all-or-nothing entity but a graduated process is that it accommodates the possibility of degrees of consciousness in other sentient beings.

50. Nagel, 1979b, p. 166.

51. '[T]he analogical form of the English expression "what is it like?" is misleading. It does not mean "what (in our experience) it *resembles*", but rather "how it is for the subject himself" ' (Nagel, 1979b, p. 170, n. 6).

52. See p. 151 above.

53. van der Merwe & Voestermans, 1995.

54. Panksepp, 1998, p. 303.

55. Dreyfus & Dreyfus, 1986, pp. 147–8.

56. As Thomas Nagel writes: 'I do not wish to claim that the line between conscious and unconscious mental activity is a sharp one. It is even possible that the distinction is partly relative, in the sense that a given item of mental

activity may be assignable to consciousness or not, depending on what other mental activities of the same person are going on at the same time, and whether it is connected with them in a suitable way' (Nagel, 1979a, p. 157).

57. Not quite immediately, if one story of Diana Duff Cooper is to be believed. She was deep in conversation when her passenger remarked on a near miss, to which she is said to have replied: 'Oh my God, am I driving?'

58. I. Berlin, 1999, p. 94.

59. Ramachandran, 2005, p. 56.

60. Bejjani, Damier, Arnulf et al., 1999; and (hypomanic episode) communication re unsubmitted work. Later Agid & colleagues were able reliably to induce hypomania in two patients who consented to have functional imaging contemporaneously, showing mainly widespread activations in the right hemisphere (Mallet, Schüpbach, N'Diaye et al., 2007: see Chapter 2, n. 299). Others have found that stimulation of the subthalamic nuclei can induce mania post-operatively (see, e.g., Kulisevsky, Berthier, Gironell et al., 2002; Romito, Raja, Daniele et al., 2002; Herzog, Reiff, Krack et al., 2003), but this is less significant than Agid's finding that minute displacements of the electrode can induce episodes of integrated affective, cognitive and motor states with acute onset and cessation related to stimulation.

61. Goethe, *Faust*, Part I, line 1237.

62. Since this applies to the structure of reason itself, it applies *a fortiori* to the practical business of science, which is why reductionism could succeed only within a self-enclosed system. Thus Einstein: 'the supreme task of the physicist is the discovery of the most general elementary laws from which the world-picture can be deduced logically. But there is no logical way to the discovery of these elemental laws. There is only the way of intuition, which is helped by a feeling for the order lying behind the appearance, and this *Einfühlung* [literally, empathy or 'feeling one's way in'] is developed by experience' ('Preface', Planck, 1933, p. 12); and Planck himself: '. . . empiricism is unassailable on the fundamental ground of pure logic; and its conclusions are equally impregnable. But if we look at it purely from the viewpoint of knowledge it leads into a blind alley, which is called solipsism. In order to escape from this *impasse* there is no other way open but to jump the wall at some part of it, and preferably at the beginning. This can be done only by introducing, once and for all, a metaphysical hypothesis which has nothing to do with the immediate experience of sense-perceptions or the conclusions logically drawn from them' (Planck, 1933, p. 128).

63. See p. 489, n. 106.

64. Heidegger, 1966, p. 50.

65. According to Max Planck, the aim of science – *knowledge* – 'is an incessant struggle towards a goal which can never be reached. Because the goal is of its very nature unattainable. It is something that is essentially metaphysical and as such is always again and again beyond each achievement. . . . it is just this striving forward that brings us to the fruits which are always falling into our hands and which are the unfailing sign that we are on the right road and that we are ever and ever drawing nearer to our journey's end. But that journey's end will never be reached, because it is always the still far thing that glimmers in the distance and is unattainable. It is not the possession of truth, but the success which attends the seeking after it, that enriches the seeker and brings happiness to him. This is an acknowledgment made long ago by thinkers of deepest insight . . .' (Planck, 1933, p. 83).

66. Ramachandran, 2005, pp. 131–2 (emphasis added).

67. Nietzsche, 1973, §68, p. 72.

68. Ramachandran, 2005, p. 151.

69. ibid., p. 141; and see Fink, Marshall, Halligan et al., 1999b.

70. Stanghellini, 2004.

71. Dobrokhotova & Bragina, 1977.

72. Spitzer, Willert, Grabe et al., 2004.

73. Krystal, Bremner, Southwick et al., 1998.

74. Spitzer, Willert, Grabe et al., 2004.

75. Maquet, Faymonville, Degueldre et al., 1999; Jasiukaitis, Nouriani & Spiegel, 1996; Jasiukaitis, Nouriani, Hugdahl et al., 1997; Aleksandrowicz, Urbanik & Binder, 2006.

76. Kosslyn, Thompson, Costantini-Ferrando et al., 2000.

77. Edmonston & Moscovitz, 1990.

78. Rainville, Hofbauer, Paus et al., 1999.

79. Ruby & Decety, 2001.

80. Spiegel & Spiegel, 1987, p. 23. And they continue: 'It is perhaps no accident that tunnel vision ... is associated with the high hypnotisability of hysterics. One responsive hypnotic subject informed us that she experienced tunnel vision every time she entered the hypnotic state.'

81. Spiegel, 1991.

PART 2: HOW THE BRAIN HAS SHAPED OUR WORLD

CHAPTER 7: IMITATION AND THE EVOLUTION OF CULTURE

1. Nietzsche, 1999, §1, p. 14. Nietzsche goes on to say that the opposition is bridged only by art, until by a 'metaphysical miracle of the Hellenic "Will", they appear paired and, in this pairing, finally engender a work of art which is Dionysiac and Apolline in equal measure: Attic tragedy'.

2. Jaspers, 1949 (trans. 1953).

3. Weber, 1951, 1952, 1958.

4. Gaukroger, 2006, p. 11.

5. ibid., p. 18.
6. Panksepp, 1998, pp. 426–7, n. 19 (emphasis added).
7. Lumsden, 1988, pp. 17 & 20.
8. Changeux, 1988.
9. Dawkins, 1976, p. 192.
10. Ruskin, 1904, vol. 5, Part VI, ch. v, §2, p. 39 (emphasis in original).
11. Hayek, 1978, p. 241.
12. Thorpe, 1967, pp. 1–12. However bats and marine mammals are also known to imitate sounds on occasion, and recently an elephant was discovered to be imitating the distant sound of a truck: see Poole, Tyack, Stoeger-Horwath et al., 2005.
13. This is a complex area, and opinions differ partly because the definition of imitation differs. Until recently it was accepted that only humans imitate: there is evidence, however, that apes, and possibly even monkeys, are capable of imitation, rather than just emulation. For a helpful summary, see Hurley & Chater, 2005, pp. 13–22.
14. Hurley, 2004.
15. Sonnby-Borgström, 2002.
16. Carr, Iacoboni, Dubeau et al., 2003.
17. Prinz, 2005a.
18. Meltzoff, 1995.
19. Prinz, 2005a, 2005b.
20. 'Human infants derive joy in matching *per se*': Andrew Meltzoff, quoted by Melser (2004, p. 59).
21. Meltzoff & Moore, 1983.
22. Taussig, 1993, pp. xiii–xiv (emphasis added).
23. Benjamin, 1986, p. 332. Similarly Adorno wrote: 'The human is indissolubly linked with imitation: a human being only becomes human at all by imitating other human beings' (2005, p. 154).
24. Mithen, 2005, p. 318, n. 30.
25. The passage is quoted, at greater length, by Kerényi ('The mythological strain in Greek religion', in Kerényi, 1962, p. 29), who describes it as a 'wonderful realisation' of the relationship between myth and *bios*.
26. Snell, 1960, 'From myth to logic', pp. 202–3. Snell actually speaks (correctly) of similes, though the force of what he says is clearly that they work like metaphors.
27. Maxwell, 2006.
28. *The Prelude (1805)*, Bk. I, lines 425–7.
29. Ogawa, 1998, p. 147.
30. Le Bihan, Turner, Zeffiro et al., 1993.
31. See p. 167 above.
32. James, 1990, p. 737.
33. Nietzsche, 2003, §34 [247], p. 15 (emphasis in original).
34. The best expression that I know on this subject is that of Schopenhauer, often quoted as '*Der Mensch kann was er will, aber er kann nicht wollen was er will*'. The passage is from Schopenhauer, 1962, p. 563: '*Ich kann tun, was ich will: ich kann, wenn ich will, alles, was ich habe, den Armen geben und dadurch selbst einer werden – wenn ich will! – Aber ich vermag nicht, es zu wollen; weil die entgegenstehenden Motive viel zuviel Gewalt über mich haben, als daß ich es könnte*' ('I can do as I will: I can, if I will, give everything that I have to the poor, and thereby become one of them myself – if I will! – but I cannot will it, since countervailing motives have much too much power over me, for me to be able to do so': trans. I. McG.)
35. See p. 160 above.
36. See p. 233 above. This suspension of the natural attitude is part of what Husserl meant by *epoche*, and is a good example of the Master and the emissary working in harmony: the left hemisphere is involved in facilitating the process of phenomenology, despite the fact that the aim of that process is to regain the right hemisphere's apprehension of the world.

CHAPTER 8: THE ANCIENT WORLD

1. Brener, 2000.
2. '*Die unterhaltendste Fläche auf der Erde für uns ist die vom menschlichen Gesicht*': Lichtenberg, 1967–72, *Sudelbuch F (1776–1779)*, §88, vol. 1, p. 473.
3. A recent paper comparing the productions of an autistic child painter and early cave paintings gives some incidental support to Brener's thesis that primitive art shows a paucity of right-hemisphere function (Humphrey, 1998).
4. Pontius, 1976, 1983 & 1984; Farah, 1994.
5. Hufschmidt, 1980, 1983.
6. McManus & Humphrey, 1973; see also Humphrey & McManus, 1973. Research comparing profile direction with other indications such as the relationship of the painter to the sitter confirms that the reason for favouring the left-facing profile is almost certainly the more emotionally engaging nature of the image: for example, family portraits are more likely to evince the leftward-facing, right hemisphere bias than professional portraits (Nicholls, Clode, Wood et al., 1999). Remarkably enough, portraits of scientists actually evince a rightwards-facing, left hemisphere bias (ten Cate, 2002).
7. For example, Conesa, Brunold-Conesa & Miron, 1995. Of the two advantages attendant on the leftward orientation, it seems likely that an inclination to place the focus of interest in the viewer's left visual hemifield (right hemisphere) predominates, since it is more probable that we have intuitive experience of a greater emotional

sensitivity in one half of the experiential world than that we have subliminal recognition of the expressive advantage of the left hemiface. Some evidence would appear to bear this out in a manner that is germane to the thesis of this book. Images used in advertising, which are aimed not at the empathic right hemisphere, but at the 'grasping' left hemisphere, show a *rightward* bias of the profile, which is apparently consistent over time from the beginnings of pictorial advertising in the Victorian period to the present day (Burkitt, Saucier, Thomas et al., 2006).

8. Grüsser, Selke & Zynda, 1988. There is some support for these conclusions in subsequent research, e.g. Latto, 1996.

9. Shanon, 1979; Jensen, 1952a, 1952b.

10. Latto, 1996; Nicholls, Clode, Wood et al., 1999.

11. R. Jung, 1975. It should be pointed out that he was unusual in demonstrating such a change so clearly following right-hemisphere stroke. Most other painters who have had right-hemisphere strokes have evinced sometimes remarkable changes in style (though some evinced none at all), without altering the direction of profile. For a survey, see Bäzner & Hennerici, 2007.

12. Coles, 1974; Grüsser, Selke & Zynda, 1988.

13. For the different points in the history of the Ancient world that have been put forward as candidates in this development, see, for example, Christopher Pelling, in the preface to Pelling, 1990, p. v.

14. Jaynes, 1976.

15. Clarke, 1999, p. 115.

16. ibid., p. 119.

17. ibid., pp. 74–5.

18. ibid., p. 77.

19. ibid., p. 68.

20. ibid., pp. 114–15.

21. ibid., pp. 110–11.

22. ibid., pp. 121–2.

23. ibid., p. 123.

24. ibid., p. 287.

25. Jaynes, 1976, pp. 70–71.

26. Clarke, 1999, pp. 277–8.

27. Dodds, 1951, p. 28.

28. Gill, 1996.

29. Snell, 1960. In referring to Snell, I am aware that his writings suffer from the fact that they were written some 60–70 years ago, and that they have inevitably and rightly been taken as classics to be reckoned with and criticised. Gill, for example, objects to Snell's philosophical standpoint and his presupposition, according to Gill, of the 'post-Cartesian conception of self and the post-Kantian conception of morality' (Gill, 1996, p. 41). He sees Snell taking 'modern ideas about personality and selfhood as being normative, and [classifies] ancient Greek ideas as relatively "primitive" or "developed" by reference to this norm' (ibid., p. 3). This is, I believe, too harsh and simplistic. In his introduction to *The Discovery of the Mind*, Snell writes: 'Since the turn of the eighteenth century our growing awareness of evolutionary patterns may have contributed to the elimination of such rationalist concepts as the ageless, unchanging "spirit". Yet a proper understanding of the origins of Greek thought remains difficult because all too frequently we measure the products of early Greece by the fixed standards of our own age . . . we are quick to forget how radically the experience of Homer differs from our own' (Snell, 1960, p. 5). Whether or not Snell is in fact guilty of being normative, and thoughtlessly applying modern conceptions and standards (and in my reading he does so very much less than Gill would seem to imply), I have no interest in making value judgments of this kind.

30. The discussion of 'seeing' words is in Snell, 1960, pp. 1–5.

31. Snell compares the German *schauen*, as in Goethe's '*Zum sehen geboren, zum schauen bestellt*' (*Faust*, Part II, v, lines 11288–9).

32. Snell, 1960, 'Homer's View of Man', pp. 1–22.

33. Russell, 1946, p. 25.

34. Most of what we know of Anaximander comes down to us from Aristotle and his pupil Theophrastus. This fragment of Anaximander is all that remains to us of his treatise *On Nature*, and it does so only as reported by the philosopher Simplicius of Cilicia, writing 11 centuries later. The translation here is adapted from that of W. K. C. Guthrie.

35. Although I see Anaximenes as having taken a retrograde step, by concluding, more along the lines of Thales, that a physical element could be a candidate for the *archē*, I grant that from the standpoint of scientific materialism this could be seen as a step forward, in that at least we are back in the realm of the empirically testable, and the idea is more reductive in intent.

36. Diogenes Laertius, 1964, IX, §5.

37. Heraclitus, fr. VII, Diels 18 (I use Kahn's notation (1979), but give Diels's numbers for reference. Translations from Heraclitus are Kahn's unless otherwise stated).

38. ibid., fr. XXXIII, Diels 93.

39. Kahn, 1979, p. 124. Similar points have been made about Heidegger, who learnt so much from Heraclitus, and were indeed made by Heidegger about himself.

40. Kahn quotes Hölscher: '*Paradox ist seine Rede, weil seine Wahrheit paradox ist*': Hölscher, 1968, p. 141.

41. Heraclitus, fr. LXXX, Diels 54.

42. ibid., fr. IX, Diels 35; fr. X, Diels 123.

43. ibid., fr. XXXV, Diels 45 (translation adapted from Snell).

44. Aristotle, *De Anima*, I.5, 411ᵃ7.

44. Aristotle, *De Anima*, I.5, 411^{a}7.

45. Kahn, 1979, pp. 128–30.

46. Snell, 1960, pp. 17–18.

47. Heraclitus, fr. IV, Diels 17.

48. ibid., fr. XIV, Diels 55; fr. XV, Diels 101a. In a deliberately provocative (because probably aimed at the astronomers of the Milesian school) expression of the primacy of phenomena, he is even reported to have said that 'the sun is the size of a human foot', and that 'the sun is new every day': ibid., fr. XLVII, Diels 3; fr. XLVIII, Diels 6.

49. ibid., fr. XVI, Diels 107.

50. Kahn, 1979, p. 102.

51. ibid., p. 21.

52. Heraclitus, fr. XLIX, Diels 126.

53. ibid., fr. LXXXIII, Diels 53.

54. ibid., fr. LXXXI, Diels A22.

55. ibid., fr. LXXVIII, Diels 51.

56. ibid., fr. LXXIX, Diels 48.

57. Known to us from Plato's report: *Cratylus*, 401d.

58. Heraclitus, fr. L, Diels 12; fr. LI, Diels 91.

59. ibid., fr. LXXVII, Diels 125.

60. ibid., fr. XL, Diels 90.

61. ibid., fr. III, Diels 2.

62. ibid., fr. LXX, Diels 61.

63. Kahn, 1979, Appendix I, p. 289. The fragment in question is included in the *corpus* by Diels (122), though not by Kahn. The conversation on *Gelassenheit* in Heidegger's late *Feldweg-Gesprächen* originally bore the title '*Anchibasie*'; he suggests that we should understand the term as *in-die-Nähe-hinein-sich-einlassen* ('letting oneself into a tentative closeness with' whatever it may be).

64. Parmenides, 1898, fr. DK B3 (trans. A. Fairbanks).

65. Heidegger, 1959. I am also aware of Peter Kingsley's view (2001) that Parmenides is a misunderstood mystic. I am in no position to evaluate his position authoritatively, though I note that it has generally not been well received by those who are.

66. Plato, *Parmenides*, 134c (trans. S. Scolnicov).

67. Plato, *Sophist*, 259e.

68. Plato, *Theaetetus*, 152e.

69. According to Diogenes Laertius (1964, IX, §6), Theophrastus blamed the 'half-finished' nature of Heraclitus' work, and its apparent 'inconsistencies' on melancholia (Θεόφραστος δέ φησιν ὑπὸ μελαγχολίας τὰ μὲν ἡμιτελῆ, τὰ δ' ἄλλοτε ἄλλως ἔχοντα γράψαι): I am grateful to Edward Hussey and Chris Pelling for help in interpretation of the phrase ἄλλοτε ἄλλως. Heraclitus became known as 'the melancholy philosopher', probably on the basis of Theophrastus' comments, and Democritus as 'the laughing philosopher', a tradition that may begin with his essay *Peri euthumies*, 'On cheerfulness' (Diogenes Laertius, 1964, IX, §13). For whatever reason, the tradition persisted, with notable treatments in literature by Juvenal, Rabelais and Burton, and in painting by Bramante, Rubens, and (in an interesting portrait of himself painting his self-portrait) Rembrandt. There is, if nothing else, an appropriateness, in terms of hemisphere asymmetry, since Heraclitus' philosophy is, as I have suggested, expressive of the right hemisphere's understanding of the world, and Democritus' philosophy of the left hemisphere's.

70. Drama is 'the Apolline embodiment of Dionysiac insights and effects': Nietzsche, 1999, §8, p. 44.

71. Snell, 1960, pp. 200–1.

72. Nietzsche, 1999, §8, p. 43.

73. Prometheus' name means 'forethought', which might seem to suggest the frontal lobes. However, as Aeschylus has him say, 'I caused men no longer to foresee their death . . . I planted firmly in their hearts blind hopefulness' (*Prometheus Bound*, lines 249–51, trans. P. Vellacott): the combination of foresight with inability to foresee death, a state of optimistic denial, could only be left frontal. His name could also signify 'cunning', which again would go with representing the capacities of the left frontal lobe. Born a Titan, he realised that the Olympians would win in the struggle of the Titans and the Olympians, and sided with the Olympians, thus initially evading the punishment meted out by Zeus to the other Titans. His greatest punishment, which however *he did not foresee*, the punishment that Zeus stored up for him, was to see humankind suffer, to suffer so badly that they would rather desire death than life, and yet to be powerless to help them. For Prometheus, empathy is his nemesis, the punishment he didn't foresee; for that other Promethean figure, Faust, empathy (at least according to Goethe's version of the myth) is his salvation, the reward he had not foreseen.

74. Aeschylus, *Prometheus Bound*, I, lines 443–4, 447–50 & 457–61 (trans. I. McG.).

75. Hagège, 1988, p. 74.

76. Kerényi, 1991, p. xxii.

77. A. W. Schlegel, 1886, p. 79.

78. ibid., p. 93.

79. Mark Griffith, in the introduction to his edition of *Prometheus Bound* (1983), writes: 'it has certainly been regarded as Aeschylean since the third century BC, and no doubts as to its authenticity are recorded from ancient authors or in the *scholia* to the play. Most modern scholars have seen no good reason to doubt the traditional ascription . . .' (p. 32).

80. The story of Aeschylus being put on trial for profaning the mysteries may, however, not be reliable: Lefkowitz, 1981, p. 68.

81. A. W. Schlegel, 1886, p. 95.

82. ibid., p. 93.
83. Skoyles, 1988.
84. de Kerckhove, 1988a.
85. Miller, Liu, Ngo et al., 2000.
86. Amengual, Drago, Foster et al., 2008.
87. While Chinese script continues to be written from right to left, in the construction of an individual graph the general rule is, as one might expect, given the different nature of the exercise, left before right (Sir Geoffrey Lloyd, personal communication).
88. de Kerckhove & Lumsden, 1988, p. 5.
89. Naveh, 1988.
90. de Kerckhove & Lumsden, 1988, pp. 5–6; see also de Kerckhove, 1988b, pp. 156–7.
91. de Kerckhove, 1988b, pp. 169–70 (emphasis added).
92. ibid.
93. Babkoff & Ben-Uriah, 1983; Eviatar, 1997; Faust, Kravetz & Babkoff, 1993; Lavidor, Ellis & Pansky, 2002; Vaid, 1988.
94. Nakamura, Oga, Okada et al., 2005.
95. See, e.g., Tokunaga, Nishikawa, Ikejiri et al., 1999; Thuy, Matsuo, Nakamura et al., 2004.
96. Chee, Tan & Thiel, 1999; Chee, Weekes, Lee et al., 2000; Tan, Spinks, Gao et al., 2000; Tan, Liu, Perfetti et al., 2001; Kuo, Yeh, Duann et al., 2001.
97. Eviatar & Ibrahim, 2007.
98. Tan, Feng, Fox et al., 2001.
99. See Havelock, 1963; Skoyles, 1984, 1985.
100. Hagège, 1988, p. 75.
101. Braudel, 2001, pp. 76 & 78.
102. Hagège, 1988, p. 77.
103. Seaford, 2004, esp. pp. 136–46.
104. ibid., pp. 30–33.
105. ibid., pp. 68–9.
106. ibid., pp. 149–65.
107. ibid., p. 67.
108. Braudel, 2001, p. 264.
109. ibid., p. 246.
110. See West, 1971; and West, 1997.
111. The earliest coins date from the late seventh century or early sixth century, according to Seaford, 2004, p. 129 ff.
112. Braudel, 2001, p. 146 ff.
113. ibid., pp. 147–8.
114. Gombrich, 1977, p. 103.
115. Braudel, 2001, p. 265.
116. ibid., p. 271.
117. ibid., p. 265.
118. ibid., p. 266.
119. ibid., p. 268. The demand that such love should be 'reasonable', and is otherwise pathological, revives memories of Fontenelle, which otherwise seem so far from Braudel's spirit.
120. Braudel, op. cit., pp. 287–8.
121. Aristotle, *Nicomachean Ethics*, II. 6, 1106^{b}35 (trans. W. D. Ross). It is impossible not to be reminded of the opening of Tolstoy's *Anna Karenina*: 'Happy families are all alike; every unhappy family is unhappy in its own way'.
122. Pliny, *Natural History*, Bk. 35, §88, cited by Elsner, 2007, p. 203 (equivalent passage is at Pliny, 1991, p. 333).
123. Boys-Stones, 2007, p. 111.
124. Elsner, 2007, p. 216.
125. Nietzsche, 1999, §1, p. 16.
126. Snell, 1960, p. 229.
127. Plato, *Republic*, 529d–530c (trans. H. D. P. Lee).
128. Dreyfus & Dreyfus, 1986, p. 202.
129. Nietzsche, 1954, aphorisms 5, 6 & 10, pp. 476–8 (emphasis in original).
130. Panksepp, 1998, p. 335.
131. Plato, *Republic*, 595b, 599a, 600d, 601a, 602b, 603a, 605a,b.
132. ibid., 397d–e.
133. ibid., 398–400.
134. Cf. Lenin's words about the arts in relation to the state, p. 412 below.
135. Plato, *Phaedo*, 60^{e}5 ff.
136. Nietzsche, 1999, §14, p. 71.
137. Malinowski, 1926, p. 39.
138. Kerényi, 1962, p. 28.
139. Plato, *Timaeus*, 44d–e (trans. F. M. Cornford).
140. Empedocles, fr. 57–9, as trans. in Burnet, 1892, p. 214.
141. Geikie, 1912; Fairclough, 1930.
142. Virgil, *The Aeneid*, I, line 462. This is a hard line to translate: Fagles gives 'the world is a world of tears, and the burdens of mortality touch the heart', but that misses the idea that there are tears *for* passing things and what

they mean to humanity (compassion, not just misery), which other translators have tried to capture, none quite satisfactorily.

143. Ovid, *Metamorphoses*, XV, lines 160–66, 194–204, 250 & 264–7 (trans. R. Humphries).

144. Braudel, 2001, pp. 338–9.

145. ibid., p. 344.

146. Aristotle does so pronounce at *Nicomachean Ethics*, 1098ª15.

147. Braudel, 2001, pp. 351–2.

148. Freeman, 2002, p. 77.

149. Braudel, 2001, p. 344.

150. L'Orange, 1965, p. 3.

151. ibid., pp. 3–8.

152. ibid., pp. 9–11.

153. Fractality is the property of forms as diverse as plants, river systems, coast lines, snowflakes and blood vessels that dictates that their form at higher levels of magnification replicates their form at lower levels. Although the term is modern, and derives from the mathematics of Benoît Mandelbrot in the mid-1970s, Leibniz may already have intuited, possibly on the basis of microscope findings, that nature is fractal: see Leibniz, 1992, §67–8, pp. 25–6, and commentary on pp. 41 & 234 ff. Elsewhere in this aphoristic late work, Leibniz relates his description of these worlds within worlds that formed part of his monadology to two further concepts of relevance for the theme of this book: the way that each body mirrors its environing universe, and each soul mirrors its environing body (and consequently the entire universe) (§61–2); and the way in which 'all bodies are in a perpetual flux, like rivers, and some parts enter into them and some pass out continually' (§71–2).

154. L'Orange, 1965, pp. 11 & 14–15.

155. ibid., p. 106.

156. ibid., p. 110.

157. ibid., p. 18.

158. ibid., pp. 22–4.

159. ibid., pp. 24–5.

160. ibid., p. 30.

161. ibid., pp. 88–9.

162. ibid., pp. 100 & 128–9.

163. Braudel, 2001, pp. 345–7.

164. Freeman, 2002.

165. Lançon, 2000, p. 93 ff.

166. Freeman, 2002, p. 67.

167. ibid., p. 137.

168. Beard, 2002.

169. Freeman, 2002, p. 21.

170. Lloyd, 1987, p. 57.

171. Ward-Perkins, 2005, p. 32.

CHAPTER 9: THE RENAISSANCE AND THE REFORMATION

1. Huizinga, 1972, p. 142. Of the *danse macabre*, which became a feature of French literature, art and even public performance from the thirteenth century onward, he writes: 'Three young noblemen suddenly meet three hideous dead men, who tell them of their past grandeur and warn them of their own near end' (ibid., p. 140). Martial took it further by applying it, in true Renaissance fashion, to women as well as men.

2. Wyatt, no. 38 in The Egerton MS.

3. Morgann, 1963.

4. Quoted in Godfrey, 1984, p. 11.

5. Gombrich & Kris, 1940, pp. 10–12 (emphasis added).

6. See pp. 258–9 above.

7. Grüsser, Selke & Zynda, 1988, p. 278. For Pompeii and Herculaneum, see Kraus & von Matt, 1977. The effects appear to be modified by hand preference: e.g. Hans Holbein the Younger and Leonardo da Vinci, both left-handers.

8. Hall, 2008, p. 211. This may also explain why we wear wedding rings on the left hand, as there was believed to be a vein that carried blood direct from the ring finger of the left hand to the heart. Clearly there are a number of possible reasons why the left hand came to be preferred, one being that it was less involved with the ordinary practicalities of doing and getting. But this may do no more than redescribe the phenomenon at another level, and one is still in need of an explanation of why it arose when it did.

9. Hall, 2008, p. 222.

10. See, e.g., Klibansky, Saxl & Panofsky, 1964, p. 233; Screech, 1983, pp. 22–4. In fact the connection between wisdom and melancholy, like all right hemisphere truths, is ancient: 'In much wisdom is much grief; and he that increaseth knowledge increaseth sorrow' (Ecclesiastes 1:18).

11. Aristotle, 'Problems Connected with Thought, Intelligence, and Wisdom', in *Problems II*, xxx, (trans. W. S. Hett, 1965, p. 165).

12. Radden, 2000, p. 57.

13. ibid., p. 12.

14. James, 1912, p. 24.

15. '*Illud nullo modo probo, quod ait Metrodorus, esse aliquam cognatam tristitiae voluptatem*' ('I do not in the least accept what Metrodorus says, that there is a certain pleasure akin to sadness'): so Seneca on Metrodorus, in his *Epistles* (XCIX). For discussion, see Marcus Wilson (1997, p. 53).
16. Snell, 1960, p. 19.
17. 'Happen', too, incorporates this sense of non-origination, since it derives from 'hap', meaning chance, the neglected positive of a meaning still present in the negative 'mishap'.
18. A. N. Whitehead, 1926, pp. 290–91.
19. Burckhardt, 1955, the second part of which is entitled 'The Development of the Individual', esp. pp. 80–84 & 279.
20. van Mander, 1936, p. 430; Ridolfi, 1914–24, vol. 1, p. 180.
21. Kris & Kurz, 1979.
22. ibid., p. 27.
23. In Richter, 1952, pp. 181–2: the passages, which are worth reading in their entirety, for their unwitting description of the right hemisphere's ability to extract a face or other meaningful form from highly degraded information, are to be found in M. S. Bibl. Nat. 203822 *verso*, and Vat. Libr. *Trattato della Pintura* (Codex Urbinas 1270) 66.
24. Kris & Kurz, 1979, p. 46; for Sung-Ti, see Giles, 1905, p. 100.
25. Jonson, 'De Shakespeare Nostrati. Augustus in Haterium', 1951.
26. Vasari, 1987, vol. 1, p. 206.
27. Kris & Kurz, 1979, p. 17; for Han Kan, see Giles, 1905, p. 58.
28. Kris & Kurz, 1979, p. 129; for Han Kan, see Ku Teng, 1932.
29. Kris & Kurz, 1979, p. 128; Fischer, 1912.
30. The story of Zeuxis comes from Pliny's *Natural History* of the first century AD (Bk. 35, §65, in Pliny 1991, p. 330) though Zeuxis lived in the fifth century BC.
31. 'Chinese painters are said to have lived for weeks on end in the mountains and forests, among animals, or even in the water, in order to lose themselves completely in nature. Mi Fei called an oddly shaped rock his brother; Fan K'uan (circa 1000 AD) lived in the mountains and forests, often spending the whole day upon a crag and gazing about him, just to drink in the beauty of the countryside. Even when there was snow on the ground, he would wander to and fro by moonlight, staring determinedly ahead, to achieve inspiration. Kao K'o-ming (tenth century AD) loved darkness and silence: he used to roam about in the wild and spend days on end contemplating the beauty of the peaks and woods, oblivious of himself. When he reached home again he retired to a room where he would not be disturbed and allowed his soul to pass beyond the bounds of this world. In this condition he produced his pictures . . . It is related of Ku-Chün-chih (fifth century AD) that he erected a kind of platform in his house, which he used as his workshop. He would climb up to this loft, draw up the ladder behind him, and then was not seen again by his wife and children for many a long day. Hsin Ch'ang (fifteenth century AD) was incapable of painting when anyone's presence disturbed him.' Shades of Montaigne's tower, the original ivory tower. Kris & Kurz, 1979, pp. 113–14 & 127–8; for Mi Fei, Fan K'uan and Kao K'o-ming, see Giles, 1905, pp. 86, 99 & 115; for Ku-Chün-chih and Hsin Ch'ang, see ibid., pp. 25 & 152.
32. Montaigne, 'On presumption', *Essais*, Bk. II:17 (1993, p. 738). See also Screech, 1983, p. 115.
33. Greville, 'Chorus Quintus Tartarorum', from *Mustapha*.
34. One sees something of the same in the visual arts, with the 'choice' theme, which had been a common *topos* in Greek and Roman mythological thinking, gaining prominence in Renaissance art. I agree with Hall (2008, p. 129) that it suggests an antipathy to moral absolutism which is highly characteristic of the Renaissance. More than that, the choices of the flesh are often rendered subversively eloquent: e.g. Raphael's *Allegory of Virtue and Pleasure*, or Titian's *Sacred and Profane Love*.
35. Burckhardt, 1965, p. 178. Later in the same passage, in fact, Burckhardt acknowledges that 'in the fifteenth century, the great masters of the Flemish school, Hubert and Jan van Eyck, suddenly lifted the veil from nature. Their landscapes are not merely the fruit of an endeavour to reflect the real world in art, but have, even if expressed conventionally, a certain poetical meaning – in short, a soul. Their influence on the whole art of the West is undeniable, and extended to the landscape-painting of the Italians, but without preventing the characteristic interest of the Italian eye for nature from finding its own expression' (p. 181). Later Kenneth Clark was to write that 'Hubert van Eyck has painted in the *Adoration of the Lamb* the first great modern landscape . . . As in a landscape by Claude, our eye floats over the flowery lawns into a distance of golden light' (1949, p. 15). The classic study of the topic, apart from a passage in Humboldt's *Cosmos*, is that of Alfred Biese (1905); in 1882 he had published a volume on the development of a feeling for nature in the Ancient world (*Die Entwicklung des Naturgefühls bei den Griechen und Römern*), although it has to be admitted that, for a fascinating topic, it is rather a dull read.
36. Piccolomini, 1988, p. 148.
37. ibid., pp. 251–2.
38. ibid., pp. 308–9.
39. See Huizinga, 1957, p. 177.
40. Schleiermacher, 1893, p. 126: '. . . *alles übernatürliche und wunderbare ist proskribiert, die Phantasie soll nicht mit leeren Bildern angefüllt werden*' ('Über die Bildung zur Religion', 1958, p. 82).
41. Koerner, 2004.
42. ibid., p. 12.
43. Luther, 1883–1986, vol. 10, i, p. 31; quoted by Koerner, 2004, pp. 99–100.
44. Koerner, 2004, p. 26.
45. ibid., p. 436.
46. ibid., p. 279.
47. ibid.

48. ibid., p. 151 (emphasis in original).
49. ibid., p. 283 (emphasis added).
50. ibid., p. 289; Kriss-Rettenbeck, 1963, p. 3.
51. ibid., p. 47.
52. ibid., p. 136.
53. Ricoeur, 1978, p. 21; see also Ashbrook, 1984.
54. Koerner, 2004, p. 58.
55. ibid., p. 138.
56. Bakan, 1966, p. 15.
57. Koerner, 2004, pp. 420–21.
58. See, e.g., Koerner (ibid.), figs. 209 & 201; ('graph paper') 209, 82 & 83.
59. Cited at Koerner, 2004, p. 429.
60. ibid., p. 415–16.
61. ibid., p. 413.
62. ibid., fig. 211.
63. Montaigne, 'On Experience', *Essais*, Bk. III:13 (1993, pp. 1265–9). Translation adapted: Screech translates '*mets sur ses ergots*' (which I have translated 'gets on her high-horse') more closely as 'starts crowing out *ergo*'.
64. Toulmin, 1990, pp. 23–4.
65. ibid., p. 21.
66. ibid., pp. 30–34.
67. Aristotle, *Nicomachean Ethics*, 1096^{b}4.
68. Screech, 1983, p. 6.
69. Montaigne, 'Of the power of the imagination', *Essais*, Bk. I:21 (trans. I. McG.).
70. Donne, *Devotions*, 'Meditation VI'.
71. Donne, *Devotions*, 'Meditation IX'.
72. Eliot, 1950, p. 247.
73. Eliot, 1975, p. 93.
74. In one of his sermons Donne writes: 'I throw my selfe down in my Chamber, and I call in, and invite God and his Angels thither, and when they are there, I neglect God and his Angels, for the noise of a Flie, for the ratling of a Coach, for the whining of a doore . . . A memory of yesterdays pleasures, a feare of tomorrows dangers, a straw under my knee, a noise in mine eare, a light in mine eye, an any thing, a nothing, a fancy, a Chimera in my braine, troubles me in my prayer' ('*Preached at the funerals of Sir* William Cokayne *Knight, Alderman of* London, *December* 12. 1626', *Sermons*, vol. I, LXXX, 1640: in Donne, 1953–62, vol. 7, pp. 264–5). One should not imagine, though, that Donne and his contemporaries were the first to notice such things. For example, the following comes from St. Nilus of Sinai in the fifth century: 'Although our outward aspect is appropriate to prayer, for we kneel and appear to those who see us to be praying; in our thought we imagine something pleasant, graciously talk with friends, angrily abuse enemies, feast with guests, build houses for our relatives, plant trees, travel, trade, are forced against our will into priesthood, organize with great circumspection the affairs of the churches placed in our care, and go over most of it in our thoughts, consenting to any thought that comes along' (Kadloubovsky & Palmer, 1954, p. 145).
75. Hacker, 2001, p. 46.
76. Bacon, 1859, 'Of Heresies', p. 253.
77. Pesic, 1999; Mathews, 1996.
78. Bacon, 1858, Bk. I, aphorisms III & X, pp. 47–8.
79. Descartes, 1984–91a, Part VI, pp. 142–3.
80. ibid., Part IV, p. 127.

CHAPTER 10: THE ENLIGHTENMENT

1. Black, 1983, p. 20.
2. Lakoff & Johnson, 1999, pp. 123 & 129.
3. Black, 1962, p. 46.
4. Descartes, 1984–91b, 'Meditation I', p. 13.
5. McGilchrist & Cutting, 1995.
6. Sass, 1992, 1994.
7. Stanghellini, 2004.
8. 'Schizophrenics very often hold beliefs which are as rigid, all-pervasive, and unconnected with reality, as are the best dogmatic philosophies. However, such beliefs come to them naturally whereas a "critical" philosopher may sometimes spend his whole life in attempting to find arguments which create a similar state of mind' (Feyerabend, 1975, p. 45n).
9. Levin, 1999, pp. 37–42 (emphasis in original).
10. Descartes, 1984–91b, 'Meditation VI', p. 53.
11. ibid., p. 52.
12. ibid., p. 51.
13. ibid., 'Meditation II', p. 22.
14. Lakoff & Johnson, 1999, pp. 4–5.
15. ibid., p. 77.
16. Sherover, 1989, p. 281. See Descartes, 1984–91b: 'it does not follow from the fact that I existed a little while ago that I must exist now, unless there is some cause which as it were creates me afresh at this moment . . . it is quite

clear to anyone who attentively considers the nature of time that the same power and action are needed to preserve anything at each individual moment of its duration as would be required to create that thing anew if it were not yet in existence' ('Meditation III', p. 33); 'there is no relation of dependence between the present time and the immediately preceding time' ('Objections and Replies', Second Set, Axiom II, p. 116); and 'this can be plainly demonstrated from my explanation of the independence of the divisions of time ... the individual moments can be separated from those immediately preceding and succeeding them, which implies that the thing which endures may cease to be at any given moment' ('Objections and Replies', Fifth Set, §9, p. 255).

17. Descartes, 1984–91a, p. 125 (emphasis added). With greater wisdom, Bacon had written of Pythagoras, who made a similar claim: 'In this theatre of man's life, it is reserved only for God and Angels to be lookers on' (1857, p. 421).
18. Levin, 1999, pp. 52–3.
19. Cutting, 1997.
20. Moravia, 1999, p. 5.
21. Spacks, 1995, p. 20.
22. I. Berlin, 1999, p. 30.
23. 'The human mind is capable of being excited without the application of gross and violent stimulants ... one being is elevated above another in proportion as he possesses this capability. For a multitude of causes unknown to former times are now acting with a combined force to blunt the discriminating powers of the mind and, unfitting it for all voluntary exertion, to reduce it to a state of almost savage torpor. The most effective of these causes are the great national events which are daily taking place and the increasing accumulation of men in cities, where the uniformity of their occupations produces a craving for extraordinary incident, which the rapid communication of intelligence hourly gratifies' (Wordsworth, 1973, pp. 24–5).
24. Zijderveld, 1979, p. 77.
25. Waugh, 1975, p. 541.
26. I. Berlin, 1999, pp. 21–2.
27. Trevor-Roper, 1970, p. 52.
28. J. Needham, 1969, p. 17.
29. Verene, 1997, p. 70.
30. Locke, 1849, II, i, §4, p. 54.
31. Vico, 1988, §1106, p. 424. Vico developed a cyclical theory of history, in which there were *ricorsi*, or recurrent phases. He described three ages of man: the first is the age of the gods, in which he follows the divine; the second the age of heroes, in which he follows noble human exemplars; and the third the age of men, in which he pursues narrowly his own interests. (Note that this follows a slow decline down Scheler's pyramid of values, from *das Heilige* to *die Lebenswerte*, and thence to the merely *sinnliche Werte*.) The barbarism of reflection, characteristic of the third age, the age of men, makes humans more inhuman than had the barbarism of the senses. It is, when ill used, 'the mother of falsehood' (ibid., §817, p. 312), opposing the poetic imagination, and leading to Descartes's world of abstraction and alienation. Vico is a hugely sympathetic figure, whose observations represent a penetrating critique of modern Western thought since the Enlightenment. He lamented the lack of wisdom exhibited by the Cartesian philosophy of his time, and complained that the scholars of the day, 'although they may become extremely learned in some respects, their culture on the whole (and the whole is really the flower of wisdom) is incoherent' (1990, p. 77). His thought is known to many through his influence on James Joyce, but more significant is his impact on thinkers as diverse as Horkheimer, Croce, Collingwood, Heidegger, Habermas, Gadamer, Benjamin, Ricoeur, and Auerbach. He was the subject of a classic study by Isaiah Berlin (1976). See also Price, 1999.
32. Gray, 1935, vol. 3, pp. 1107 & 1079.
33. Gilpin, 1808, p. 47.
34. Packe, 1954, p. 16.
35. Mill, 2003, p. 66 (emphasis in original).
36. On reading Helvétius, who gave the opinion that legislation was the most important of earthly pursuits, he gasped: 'And have I indeed a genius for legislation? I gave myself the answer, fearfully and tremblingly – Yes' (Bowring, 1838–43, p. 27).
37. Richards, 2005.
38. Bentham, 2003, p. 18.
39. Packe, 1954, p. 16 (citing Bentham's *Memoirs*).
40. Bentham, letter to Lord Holland dated 31 October 1808 (1838–43, vol. 10, p. 442).
41. Bentham, 'The Rational of Reward' (1825) (1838–43, vol. 2, p. 253).
42. See Kramer (2005) for a perceptive examination of these aspects of Haydn's music.
43. Stanhope, letter dated 11 December 1747 (1901, vol. 1, p. 192).
44. Keats, letter to Charles Dilke dated 4 March 1820 (2002, p. 429).
45. Pope, 'An Essay on Criticism', lines 298 & 318.
46. Scheler, 1954, pp. 252–3 (emphases in original).
47. McGilchrist, 1982.
48. '*In der Beschränkung zeigt sich erst der Meister,/ Und das Gesetz nur kann uns Freiheit geben*': Goethe, 'Natur und Kunst', lines 13–14.
49. Pope, 'The Rape of the Lock', canto III, lines 7–8.
50. Dryden, 'To the memory of Mr Oldham', lines 21–5.
51. Dryden, concluding chorus of 'The Secular Masque', lines 93–8.
52. There is a 'biological trend away from perfect symmetry in primates consequent to adaptive evolutionary alteration favouring functional asymmetry in the brain, perception, and face': Zaidel & Deblieck, 2007, pp. 423–31. See also Zaidel & Cohen, 2005; and Swaddle & Cuthill, 1995.

53. Zaidel, Aarde & Baig, 2005.
54. Martin, 1965, p. 11. He had noticed that in cleaning the famous portrait of Lucrezia Panciatichi by Bronzino one could see that an eighteenth-century restorer had touched up the eyes to make them more equal.
55. Cassirer, 1948, p. 135: 'Hammer-Purgstall [see Joseph von Hammer-Purgstall, 'Das Kamel', in *Denkschriften der Kaiserlichen Akademie der Wissenschaft: Philosophisch-Historische Classe 6*, 1855, pp. 1–84 and *Classe 7*, 1856, pp. 1–104] has written a paper in which he enumerates the various names for the camel in Arabic. There are no less than five to six thousand terms used in describing a camel; yet none of these gives us a general biological concept. All express concrete details concerning the shape, the size, the colour, the age, and the gait of the animal . . .'. In 'the Bakairi language – an idiom spoken by an Indian tribe in Central Brazil – Karl von den Steinen [*Unter den Naturvölkern Zentral-Brasiliens*, p. 81] relates that each species of parrot and palm tree has its individual name, whereas there exists no name to express the genus "parrot" or "palm"'. While reasonable scepticism has been expressed about the number of terms here claimed for camel, and the absence of a single term for 'camel', the OED states that the term 'camel', coming to us from Greek *kamelos*, via Latin *camel(l)us*, 'if of Semitic origin' may come, not from an Arabic term for a camel, but from the Arabic *jamala* 'to bear', presumably suggesting a pack animal (including, therefore, but not confined to, what we call a camel).
56. I. Berlin, 1999, p. 7.
57. Burke, 1881, p. 178.
58. Tönnies, 1887.
59. de Tocqueville, 2003, pp. 723–4.
60. Passmore, 1970, p. 267.
61. Nochlin, 1994, p. 10.
62. ibid., p. 11.
63. When Descartes' body was exhumed in 1666 to be returned from Sweden to France, his head was stolen, and subsequently bought and sold several times before ending up in a museum, *Le Musée de l'Homme* in Paris. His body is buried with another head in the church of St. Germain-des-Prés (Verene, 1997, p. 20). Who says God does not have a sense of humour? Fascinatingly, in another parable of what happens when you separate mind from body, the great utilitarian Jeremy Bentham's dissected and embalmed body, at his request, was (and is) displayed at University College, London, as an 'Auto-Icon' – man become his own representation. But the plan didn't go as expected – his head 'shrivelled ghoulishly and extremely fast. A few years later, the college decided to replace it with a waxwork. The original was placed between his legs, from where it has occasionally been stolen' (Boyle, 2001, p. 17).
64. Freedberg, 1989, pp. 378–428.
65. Koerner, 2004, p. 93.
66. ibid, p. 109.
67. Descartes, 1984–91d, 'Rule IX', p. 33 (the translation here preferred is that of Haldane & Ross: see Descartes, 1911, vol. 1, p. 29).
68. Castle, 1995.
69. ibid., pp. 4–5. The passage Castle quotes in brackets is based on Freud, 1960e, p. 244.

CHAPTER 11: ROMANTICISM AND THE INDUSTRIAL REVOLUTION

1. '*Das große Wort, das* ἕν διαφέρον ἑαυτῷ (*das Eine in sich selber unterschiedne*) *des Heraklit, das konnte nur ein Grieche finden, denn es ist das Wesen der Schönheit, und ehe das gefunden war, gab's keine Philosophie*': Hölderlin, 2008, p. 109 (trans. I. McG.). Hölderlin is thinking of Heraclitus fr. LXXVIII, Diels 51: 'They do not comprehend how a thing agrees at variance with itself: it is an attunement (or 'fitting together', *harmoniē*) turning back on itself, like that of the bow and the lyre' (Kahn, 1979, p. 195 ff.). See p. 270 above, and discussion in Ankersmit, 2005, pp. 386–9.
2. '*La dernière démarche de la raison est de reconnaître qu'il y a une infinité des choses qui la surpassent. Elle n'est que faible si elle ne va jusqu'à connaître cela*': Pascal, 1976, §267 (Lafuma §188); trans. I. McG.
3. 'So the reason that some subtle minds are not rationalistic is that they simply cannot apply themselves to the principles of rationalism; but what makes the rationalists incapable of such subtlety is that they do not see what is there in front of them, and, being used to the crude, cut and dried, principles of rationalism, and to never reasoning until they are certain of their principles, they're lost when it comes to the subtleties, where you can't lay your hands on the principles in this way. Such principles are scarcely to be seen at all; they are sensed rather than seen; it is well-nigh impossible to get anyone to understand them if they do not sense them for themselves. They are so fine and so numerous that you must have a very delicate and very acute sense to perceive them, and without for the most part being able to demonstrate them in sequence, as one would analytically, because such principles are not to be had, and because there would be no end to such an undertaking. You've got to see it just like that, at one glance, and (at least to a degree) without going through any reasoning process. So it is rare that the rationalists achieve subtlety and that subtle minds are rationalistic, because the rationalists want to treat matters of intuition rationalistically, and make fools of themselves, wanting to start with definitions and then move on to principles, which is not the way to deal with this kind of reasoning. Not that the mind does not do so, but it does it implicitly, naturally, and without artifice; for it is beyond man's wit to say how, and even to intuit it belongs only to a few': Pascal, 1976, §1 (Lafuma §512); trans. I. McG. ('*Ce qui fait donc que certains esprits fins ne sont pas géomètres, c'est qu'ils ne peuvent du tout se tourner vers les principes de Géométrie: mais ce qui fait que des géomètres ne sont pas fins, c'est qu'ils ne voient pas ce qui est devant eux, et qu'étant accoutumés aux principes nets et grossiers de Géométrie, à ne raisonner qu'après avoir bien vu et manié leurs principes, ils se perdent dans les choses de finesse, où les principes ne se laissent pas ainsi manier. On les voit à peine: on les sent plutôt qu'on ne les voit: on a des peines infinies à les faire sentir à ceux qui ne les sentent pas d'eux-mêmes: ce sont choses tellement délicates et si nombreuses, qu'il faut un sens bien délicat et bien net pour les sentir, et sans pouvoir le plus souvent les démontrer par ordre comme en Géométrie, parce qu'on n'en possède pas ainsi les principes, et que ce serait une chose infinie de l'entreprendre. Il faut tout d'un coup voir la chose d'un seul regard, et*

non par progrès de raisonnement, au moins jusqu'à un certain degré. Et ainsi il est rare que les géomètres soient fins, et que les fins soient géomètres; à cause que les géomètres veulent traiter géométriquement les choses fines, et se rendent ridicules, voulant commencer par les définitions, et ensuite par les principes, ce qui n'est pas la manière d'agir en cette sorte de raisonnement. Ce n'est pas que l'esprit ne le fasse; mais il le fait tacitement, naturellement, et sans art; car l'expression en passe tous les hommes, et le sentiment n'en appartient qu'à peu.')
4. Montaigne, 'On presumption', *Essais*, Bk. II:17 (1993, p. 721).
5. Johnson, 1963, p. 109.
6. Pope, 1963, pp. 44–5.
7. Carlyle, 1935, p. 409 (emphases in original).
8. Morgann, 1963.
9. 'The exchange of two whims and the contact of two skins': Chamfort, 1923, §359, p. 127.
10. Arnaud, 1992, pp. 101–5.
11. See Cassirer, 1950, pp. 145–6, quoting Goethe (trans. Cassirer): *'Das ist die wahre Symbolik wo das Besondere das Allgemeinere repräsentiert, nicht als Traum und Schatten, sondern als lebendig augenblickliche Offenbarung des Unerforschlichen'* (Goethe, 1991, §314, p. 775).
12. Eckermann, 1970, conversation of 18 February 1829, p. 296.
13. Quoted in Amiel, 1898: entry for 3 February 1862, p. 83. I have been unable to trace the source of this quotation in Goethe, and so, it would appear, have the editors of the *édition intégrale* of Amiel's *Journal Intime* (see vol. 4, p. 521).
14. See p. 272.
15. Scruton, 1986, p. 392.
16. Kuehn, 2001.
17. Descartes, 1984–91e, Part II, §124, p. 371.
18. Or so it is said. Balzac in his essay *Théorie de la démarche* (*Theory of demeanour*), published in 1833, attributes it to Fontenelle, another Enlightenment philosopher, saying only that Voltaire took his lead from Fontenelle. According to Balzac, Fontenelle boasted that he not only never laughed, but never wept tears, and in fact never became impassioned at all; never raised his voice or even spoke in a carriage for fear of having to do so; and had a colleague deliver his lectures for him. He never entered into argument, but simply lay back, closed his eyes and thought of the Collège de France. He never ran, and avoided walking by being carried wherever possible. According to Balzac, he never loved anyone, and had no vices or virtues. *'Cette petite machine délicate,'* he wrote, *'tout d'abord condamnée à mourir, vécut ainsi plus de cent ans'*: 'this delicate little *piece of machinery*, from the outset condemned to die, by this means lived to be more than a hundred' (Balzac, 1853, pp. 75–8). In fact, by another of the ironies meted out to Enlightenment philosophers, he died less than a month short of his perfect century (if, of course, he had not already done so). How prescient was Montaigne when he wrote: 'There are those who, from an uncouth insensibility, hold (as Aristotle says) bodily pleasures in disgust. I know some who do it from ambition. Why do they not also give up breathing, so as to live on what is theirs alone, rejecting the light of day because it is free and costs them neither ingenuity nor effort? . . . I suppose they think about squaring the circle while lying with their wives!' Montaigne, 'On Experience', *Essais*, Bk. III:13 (1993, pp. 1265–9 & 1257).
19. Spinoza, 1947, IV, Appendix § 27, p. 249.
20. Wittgenstein, 1967b, Part II, iv, p. 178.
21. Lakoff & Johnson, 1999, p. 6.
22. 'Underlying our most sublime sentiments and our purest tenderness there is a little of the testicle': Diderot, lettre à Étienne Noël Damilaville, 3 novembre 1760 (1955–70, vol. III, p. 216; trans. I. McG.).
23. Blake, *Jerusalem*, ch. I, plate 24, line 23.
24. Wordsworth, 1974, vol. 1, p. 103.
25. Wordsworth, 1973, pp. 26 & 29 (emphasis added).
26. Carlyle, 1897–9, p. 55.
27. Wordsworth, *The Prelude (1805)*, Bk. VIII, lines 604–5.
28. ibid., Bk. IV, lines 172–80.
29. I. Berlin, 1999, p. 16.
30. Luria, 1980. Until the age of four or five, dendritic systems of the language areas of the right hemisphere are more exuberant than those on the left: see Simonds & Scheibel, 1989.
31. Horowitz, 1983; Ardila, 1984.
32. Cimino, Verfaellie, Bowers et al., 1991; Markowitsch, Calabrese, Neufeld et al., 1999; Markowitsch, Calabrese, Haupts et al., 1993; Markowitsch, Calabrese, Fink et al., 1997; Markowitsch, 1995; Phelps & Gazzaniga, 1992; Metcalfe, Funnell & Gazzaniga, 1995; Tulving, Kapur, Craik et al., 1994.
33. Trevarthen, 1996.
34. Chiron, Jambaque, Nabbout et al., 1997.
35. O'Boyle & Benbow, 1990; and see Gorynia & Müller, 2006.
36. Wordsworth, 'Ode on Intimations of Immortality From Recollections of Early Childhood'.
37. Henry Vaughan's 'The Retreat', a paean to childhood, contains an anticipation of Blake's 'To see a world in a grain of sand, / And a heaven in a wild flower, / Hold infinity in the palm of your hand, / And eternity in an hour': '. . . on some gilded cloud, or flower, / My gazing soul would dwell an hour, / And in those weaker glories spy / Some shadows of eternity'; and Thomas Traherne anticipates Wordsworth: 'All appeared new, and strange at first, inexpressibly rare and delightful and beautiful . . . My knowledge was Divine. I knew by intuition those things which, since my Apostasy, I collected again by the highest reason. My very ignorance was advantageous. I seemed as one brought into the Estate of Innocence . . . The corn was orient and immortal wheat, which never should be reaped, nor ever was sown. I thought it had stood from everlasting to everlasting . . . The green trees when I saw them first through one of the gates transported and ravished me, their sweetness and unusual beauty made my heart to leap,

and almost mad with ecstasy, they were such strange and wonderful things . . .' (Traherne, 2007, 'The Third Century', §2–3, pp. 151–2).

38. Goethe, 1988, 'Significant help given by an ingenious turn of phrase', p. 39. In relation to 'Man knows himself only to the extent that he knows the world; he becomes aware of himself only within the world, and aware of the world only within himself', cf. Snell: 'Man must listen to an echo of himself before he may hear or know himself' (p. 272 above); and Matthews: 'my awareness of myself as a subject necessarily presupposes awareness of other things as objects . . . awareness of our own subjectivity is possible only if we are also aware of a world that transcends it. Subject and object of experience are inseparably bound up together; our being is "being-in-the-world" '(2002, pp. 89–90).

39. There is a similarity here with Plotinus: 'For one must come to the sight with a seeing power made akin and like to what is seen. No eye ever saw the sun without becoming sun-like . . .' (1966, Sixth Tractate, §9).

40. Kuhn, 1970, p. 24.

41. A. Zajonc, 1998, p. 26.

42. Brady, 1998, p. 88.

43. Goethe, 1988, p. 159.

44. Goethe, 1989, 'Bedingungen unter welchen die Farbenerscheinung zunimmt', §217, p. 85: 'Bei allem diesen lassen wir niemals aus dem Sinne, daß diese Erscheinung nie als eine fertige, vollendete, sondern immer als eine werdende, zunehmende, und in manchem Sinn bestimmbare Erscheinung anzusehen sei' (trans. I. McG.).

45. Goethe, 1991, §555, p. 821: 'Die Vernunft ist auf das Werdende, der Verstand auf das Gewordene angewiesen . . . Sie erfreut sich am Entwickeln; er wünscht alles festzuhalten, damit er es nutzen könne' (trans. I. McG.).

46. Constable, 1970, pp. 52–3.

47. His Dido Building Carthage hangs, under the terms of his will, in the same room. In a perfect articulation of the way in which Romantic paintings evoked depth in both time and space, Turner repeatedly expressed a wish to be buried in the painting (see Thornbury, 1862, vol. 1, pp. 299–300).

48. The canvas was originally known as Landscape with Psyche outside the Palace of Cupid. According to Colvin, the lines in the 'Ode to a Nightingale' which speak of having 'charm'd magic casements, opening on the foam / Of perilous seas, in faery lands forlorn', were inspired by the painting, which Keats certainly knew, if only through an engraving, and which he elsewhere mentions in a letter to his friend J. H. Reynolds (letter to Reynolds dated 25 March 1818 (2002, p. 110); Colvin, 1917, pp. 264–5). For further discussion see Jack (1967) and Levey (1988).

49. Baillie, 1967, p. 32.

50. I. Berlin, 1999, pp. 102–4.

51. Frederick Locker-Lampson recalled the poet's comment: 'He told me that he was moved to write "Tears, idle Tears" at Tintern Abbey; and that it was not real woe, as some people might suppose; "it was rather the yearning that young people occasionally experience for that which seems to have passed away from them for ever". That in him it was strongest when he was quite a youth' (Tennyson, Hallam Lord, 1897, vol. 2, p. 73).

52. Quoted by Knowles, p. 170.

53. '. . . for oft/On me, when boy, there came what then I called,/Who knew no books and no philosophies,/In my boy-phrase "The Passion of the Past" ' (Tennyson, 'The Ancient Sage', lines 216–19).

54. Hazlitt, 1824, vol. 2, pp. 220–23. Hazlitt here half-quotes '. . . hung upon the beatings of my heart' from the Tintern Abbey ode (line 54), and Claudio's 'come thronging soft and delicate desires' from Much Ado About Nothing (Act I, Scene i, line 287). That Wordsworth's poem is an archetype of Romantic retrospection is evidenced by Tennyson's inspiration occurring at Tintern Abbey, and Hazlitt's almost involuntary recurrence to its lines here.

55. Keene, 1988, p. 38.

56. ibid., pp. 38–42.

57. ibid., p. 43.

58. See p. 83 above.

59. Wordsworth's famous lines from the Tintern Abbey ode referring to 'the mighty world / Of eye, and ear, – both what they half create, / And what perceive', were themselves half-created, half-remembered from a phrase in Edward Young's Night Thoughts, where Young speaks of our 'senses, which . . . half create the wondrous world they see' (Bk. VI, lines 420 & 427).

60. Diderot, 'Éloge de Richardson', Journal étranger (janvier 1762): 'C'est lui qui porte le flambeau au fond de la caverne' (1821, p. 8).

61. Russell & Konstan, 2005, p. 79.

62. Hegel, 1896, p. xxx.

63. Steiner, 1978, p. 18.

64. Coleridge, 1965, vol. I, ch. x, p. 106.

65. Zeki, 1999, p. 4.

66. Herder, 2002, pp. 40–41 (emphasis in the original).

67. ibid.

68. Herder, 1878c.

69. Winckelmann, 2006, p. 199. And later, even more rapturously, Winckelmann writes again of the Apollo Belvedere: 'An eternal springtime, like that of the blissful Elysian Fields, clothes the alluring virility of mature years with a pleasing youth and plays with a soft tenderness upon the lofty structure of his limbs . . . Scorn sits upon his lips, and the displeasure that he contains within swells the nostrils of his nose and spreads upward to his proud brow. But the tranquillity that hovers over him in a blissful stillness remains undisturbed, and his eyes are full of sweetness, as if he were among the Muses as they seek to embrace him. . . . A brow of Jupiter, gravid with the goddess of wisdom, and eyebrows whose motions declare his will; eyes of the queen of the gods, arched with grandeur, and a mouth whose shape infused desire in the beloved Branchos. His soft hair plays about his divine head like the tender, waving tendrils of the noble grapevine stirred, as it were, by a gentle breeze: it seems anointed with the oil of the gods

and bound at the crown of his head with lovely splendour by the Graces. In gazing upon this masterpiece of art, I forget all else, and I myself adopt an elevated stance, in order to be worthy of gazing upon it . . . My chest seems to expand with veneration and to heave like those I have seen swollen as if by the spirit of prophecy, and I feel myself transported to Delos and to the Lycian groves, places Apollo honoured with his presence – for my figure seems to take on life and movement, like Pygmalion's beauty. How is it possible to paint and describe it!' (ibid., pp. 333–4).

70. ibid., p. 203.
71. ibid., p. 334.
72. ibid., p. 199.
73. Hegel, 1970, p. 92.
74. Herder, 1878b, p. 65–6; Herder, 1878a, p. 12.
75. ibid., p. 64.
76. Winckelmann, 2006, p. 314.
77. Goethe, *Römische Elegien*, V, lines 13–18.
78. Wordsworth, 1933, Bk. XI, lines 173–6.
79. Blake, 'The Everlasting Gospel', d, lines 103–6. He almost repeats the phrase in one of his most famous passages of prose: ' "What", it will be Question'd, "When the Sun rises, do you not see a round disk of fire somewhat like a Guinea?" O no, no, I see an Innumerable company of the Heavenly host crying "Holy, Holy, Holy, is the Lord God Almighty". I question not my Corporeal or Vegetative Eye any more than I would Question a Window concerning a Sight. I look thro' it & not with it' (1972, p. 617).
80. '*Il y a une impression qui résulte de tel arrangement de couleurs, de lumières, d'ombres, etc. C'est ce qu'on appellerait la musique du tableau. Avant même de savoir ce que le tableau représente, vous entrez dans une cathédrale, et vous vous trouvez placé à une distance trop grande du tableau pour savoir ce qu'il représente, et souvent vous êtes pris par cet accord magique . . .*' (Delacroix, 1923, 'Réalisme et idéalisme', vol. 1, pp. 23–4; trans. I. McG.). This idea was echoed later by Baudelaire: 'The right way to tell if a picture is melodious is to look at it from far enough away that one cannot make out the subject or the lines' (1975–6, vol. 2, p. 425: '*La bonne manière de savoir si un tableau est mélodieux est de le regarder d'assez loin pour n'en comprendre ni le sujet ni les lignes*'; trans. I. McG.).
81. Goethe, 1989, 'Verhältnis zur Philosophie', §716, p. 215: '*[Der Physiker] soll sich eine Methode bilden, die dem Anschauen gemäß ist; er soll sich hüten, das Anschauen in Begriffe, den Begriff in Worte zu verwandeln, und mit diesen Worten, als wären's Gegenstände, umzugehen und zu verfahren*' (trans. I. McG.).
82. Goethe, 1988, p. 311.
83. See p. 74 above.
84. Shelley, 1972, pp. 33 & 56.
85. Wordsworth, *The Prelude (1805)*, Bk. XI, lines 336–7.
86. I. Berlin, 1999, p. 102.
87. Steiner, 1989, p. 27.
88. I have discussed these aspects of Wordsworth's style at greater length elsewhere (1982).
89. From 'Extract from the Conclusion of a Poem', 'An Evening Walk', and 'Calm is all Nature as a Resting Wheel', respectively.
90. Wordsworth, *The Prelude (1805)*, Bk. XI, lines 258–65.
91. Horton, 1995.
92. Wordsworth, *The Prelude (1805)*, Bk. XI, lines 302–16.
93. ibid., Bk. XI, lines 329–43.
94. ibid., Bk. I, lines 341–50, and Bk. V, lines 404–13. This second passage is an astonishing evocation of *depth* through language: 'And when it chanced / That pauses of deep silence mock'd his skill, / Then sometimes, in that silence, while he hung / Listening, a gentle shock of mild surprise / Has carried far into his heart the voice/ Of mountain torrents; or the visible scene / Would enter unawares into his mind/ With all its solemn imagery, its rocks, / Its woods, and that uncertain Heaven, receiv'd/ Into the bosom of the steady Lake'. In fact I would say that the whole intent of the last image is to compare the realm of the imaginative mind ('the heart') with the depth of the lake, itself imaged in the vastness of the landscape which can be 'received' into its 'bosom' (heart) – therefore intensifying the sense of vastness and strangeness evoked by the phrase '*far* into his heart'.
95. de Quincey, 1851, vol. I, ch. xii, 'William Wordsworth', pp. 308–9.
96. Wordsworth, *The Prelude (1805)*, Bk. XII, lines 12–14.
97. Wordsworth, 'Lines Composed a Few Miles above Tintern Abbey', lines 55–7.
98. Bayley, 1962; Ricks, 1974.
99. Blake, *Milton*, 'Book the First', §15, lines 47–9. As in Bernini's St. Teresa in the Roman church of Santa Maria in Vittoria, the mystical and spiritual are closely allied to – at least have no other available imagery than – the erotic: Blake's original illustration (now partly obscured by a later sense of propriety) clearly shows him with phallus erect.
100. Tennyson, 'Maud', xiv, stanza 4.
101. Hopkins, 'As kingfishers catch fire', lines 5–8.
102. Hopkins, 1963, pp. 145–6.
103. Heidegger, 1959, p. 33: 'You can, as it were, smell the being of this building in your nostrils. The smell communicates the being of this essent far more immediately and truly than any description or inspection could ever do.'
104. Hopkins, 1963, pp. 90–91; and see pp. 106–10 for further instances.
105. See, for example, his superb unfolding of the word 'horn' in a diary entry for 24 September 1863 (1963, pp. 89–90).
106. Hopkins, 'Inversnaid', lines 13–14.
107. Graves, 1956, p. 141. But then Graves was consumed with rage about poets who enjoyed greater popularity than himself, such as 'sick, muddle-headed, sex-mad D. H. Lawrence' (ibid.).

108. Hopkins, 1963, p. 91.
109. ibid., 'On the Origin of Beauty: a Platonic Dialogue', pp. 92–104.
110. Hopkins, letter to Robert Bridges dated 1st September 1885 (1970, p. 288n).
111. Wordsworth, 'Expostulation and Reply', line 24.
112. Conrad, 1973, p. 1.
113. Korff, 1923, vol. 1, p. 28: '*Denn auch der Verstand kommt nicht ohne Phantasie, die Phantasie aber nicht ohne Verstand aus. Aber die Ehe zwischen ihnen ist doch eine so eigentümliche, daß sie sich gegenseitig auf den Tod befehden und doch nur miteinander, nämlich als die höhere Form der Ideenbildung, die wir Vernunft zu nennen pflegen, ihre größte Leistungen zu vollbringen imstande sind*' (trans. I. McG.).
114. Olson, 2008.
115. '*da der Glaube nur eine Eigenschaft der Körperatome ist, so hängt eine Veränderung des Glaubens nur von der Art und Weise der Ersetzung der Körperatome ab*': Vogt, 1851, p. 5.
116. Büchner, 1885, p. 194; quoted in Gregory, 1977, p. 9.
117. Gregory, 1977, p. 9.
118. Hedley Brooke, 1991, p. 31.
119. Gaukroger, 2006, p. 11.
120. '*. . . gegen alle himmlischen und irdischen Götter, die das menschliche Selbstbewußtsein nicht als die oberste Gottheit anerkennen . . . der vornehmste Heilige und Märtyrer im philosophischen Kalender*': Marx, 1968, p. 262 (trans. K. Merz).
121. Hitler, 1943, p. 290.
122. Kerényi, 1991, p. 31.
123. ibid., p. xxii.
124. Gaukroger, 2006, pp. 11–12.
125. Dewey, 1931, p. 220. As Dewey remarks (ibid., p. 217), 'Newton may have supposed that he was thinking God's thoughts after him, but so far as he thought, he thought Newton's thoughts.'
126. Gaukroger, 2006, p. 16.
127. See p. 472, n. 182.
128. For accounts, see Hedley Brooke, 1991, and Gaukroger, 2006.
129. Shlain, 2001, p. 33, citing Delacroix. Arnheim also quotes Delacroix as writing, in his *Journal*, that straight lines 'never occur in nature; they exist only in the brain of man. Where men do employ them, the elements gnaw them away' (Arnheim, 1954, p. 175). There is certainly a passage in Delacroix, where, speaking of architecture, he wrote that: '*Tout y est idéalisé par l'homme. La ligne droite elle-même est de son invention, car elle n'est nulle part dans la nature*' (Delacroix, 1893, entry of 20 September 1852, vol. 2, pp. 121–2). That is the key: that it is idealised, conceptual, lacking a counterpart in the real world. It has been pointed out that at the microscopic level there are straight lines in crystals: but even there they exist only over very short distances, and all depends on the level at which one chooses to inspect them (in other words, the straightest line in nature is as jagged as a coastline, if viewed sufficiently accurately). With typical forthrightness Blake wrote: 'They say there is no Strait Line in Nature; this Is a Lie, like all that they say. For there is Every Line in Nature'; but he added: 'A Machine is not a Man nor a Work of Art; it is destructive of Humanity & of Art' (1972, 'Public Address: additional passages', p. 603).
130. '*. . . [erscheint dann die Technik] fast nicht mehr als das Produkt bewußter menschlicher Bemühung um die Ausbreitung der materiellen Macht, sondern eher als ein biologischer Vorgang im Großen, bei dem die im menschlichen Organismus angelegten Strukturen in immer weiterem Maße auf die Umwelt des Menschen übertragen werden . . .*' (Heisenberg, 1955, p. 15; 1958, pp. 19–20). The translation here is that of Hannah Arendt (1958, p. 153: emphasis added).

CHAPTER 12: THE MODERN AND POST-MODERN WORLDS

1. Woolf, 1924, pp. 4–5, first read to the Heretics in Cambridge in May 1924, under the title 'Character in Fiction'.
2. Berger, Berger & Kellner, 1974.
3. Giddens, 1991.
4. ibid., p. 27.
5. Panksepp, 1998, p. 262.
6. ibid., pp. 248 & 402, n. 7. See also Panksepp & DeEskinazi, 1980.
7. Putnam, 2000.
8. Toulmin, 1990, p. 159 (emphasis in original).
9. Sass, 1992, pp. 159–60.
10. ibid., p. 168.
11. Moberg & Turetsky, 2006; Clark, Kopala, Hurwitz et al., 1991; Bertollo, Cowen & Levy, 1996; Moberg, Agrin, Gur et al., 1999.
12. Indeed for the relation between the sense of smell and empathy, see Spinella, 2002.
13. It is particularly relevant that the current version of the dopamine hypothesis of schizophrenia, the most widely espoused theory of the genesis of schizophrenia, proposes an interaction between a posterior dopamine *hyper*activity and a frontal dopamine *hypo*activity, which, on the basis that the frontal lobe inhibits posterior activity in the same hemisphere, compounds the effect of a preponderant, though aberrant, left hemisphere in schizophrenia: Laruelle, Kegeles & Abi-Dargham, 2003; Abi-Dargham, 2004.
14. This appears to be the underlying tendency. It is yet more pronounced during the acute phase, is attenuated or reversed by medication, and relatively remits or reverses in the so-called 'negative' syndrome, though in that case

the clinical picture is also marked by overwhelming bilateral frontal deficits. A well-substantiated intellectual asymmetry, with a relative superiority of verbal skills to spatial skills, is commoner in schizophrenics (see, e.g., Heinrichs & Zakzanis, 1998; Amminger, Schlögelhofer, Lehner et al., 2000). It is also present in the relatives of schizophrenics, and 'represents a putative endophenotype of schizophrenia' (Kravariti, Toulopoulou, Mapua-Filbey et al., 2006). This may well be related to the fact that schizophrenics attend selectively to the right ear (left hemisphere) (Hugdahl, Rund, Lund et al., 2003). Auditory and visual hallucinations in schizophrenia tend to occur more commonly in the right hemifield of attention (Bracha, Cabrera, Karson et al., 1985; Nayani & David, 1996; Sommer, Aleman & Kahn, 2003). Functional neuroimaging evidence is complex, and does not yield a clear picture. Several factors contribute to this, including the heterogeneity of clinical sub-syndromes, the difficulty in reliably and adequately distinguishing acute from chronic subjects, and such factors as the effects of illness staging, drug treatment (both current status and the effects of chronicity of treatment) and handedness. But perhaps the most important consideration is that, since it is now widely accepted that schizophrenia involves abnormal cerebral lateralisation (neither the normal asymmetry nor a simple reversal of the normal asymmetry) one would expect *some*, but crucially not all, of the functions normally associated with one hemisphere to be associated in schizophrenia with the contralateral hemisphere (and it is likely that the way in which aspects of brain functioning co-segregate within either hemisphere in schizophrenia may differ between individuals, exacerbating the problem). Knowing which is which presents a very serious methodological challenge. For this reason, I believe comparison of the detailed clinical findings in schizophrenia with those in non-schizophrenic subjects with partial or total inactivation of one hemisphere (whether experimentally induced or as a consequence of brain pathology) gives more reliable evidence of what the phenomenology of schizophrenia represents in terms of hemisphere asymmetry of function than does functional neuroimaging of subjects with schizophrenia. Having said all of that, some neuroimaging findings, which need to be interpreted with caution, would tend to confirm that, in the acute syndrome at least, there is overactivation of an abnormal left hemisphere, which then partially remits with treatment (Sheppard, Gruzelier, Manchanda et al., 1983; Gur, Resnick, Alavi et al., 1987; Gur, Resnick & Gur, 1989; Gur, Mozley, Resnick et al., 1995; Gur & Chin, 1999; Rotenberg, 1994; Bogerts, 1997). But, for example Russell and colleagues (Russell, Early, Patterson et al., 1997) found hyperperfusion in the right, not left, temporal lobe. A useful review of the complex and sometimes heterogeneous findings in this area can be found in Gruzelier, 1999. The acute disturbances of schizophrenia are also due to dysfunction of the right hemisphere, leading to left-hemisphere prepotency, but persistent or chronic abnormalities leading to the withdrawn or negative picture suggest, in addition, hypoactivation of the left hemisphere (Mendrek, Laurens, Kiehl et al., 2004) which may account for the overlap between depressive features and some aspects of the chronic syndrome. Impairments in emotional behaviour in patients with chronic schizophrenia are similar to those found in right-hemisphere brain damage patients, and they display the deficits in appreciating metaphor and humour suggestive of right frontal deficits (Hunca-Bednarska & Kucharska-Pietura, 2002). There is a specific deficit in right-hemisphere attentional functions in schizophrenia, which is separate from a general impairment in facial processing (Kucharska-Pietura, David, Dropko et al., 2002); but such patients do show separate impairments in recognising facial stimuli, vocal stimuli and emotion (Kucharska-Pietura, David, Masiak et al., 2005). Ultimately, given the likelihood of abnormal lateralisation in schizophrenia (see, e.g., Tiihonen, Katila, Pekkonen et al., 1998), it is perhaps safest to rely on the resemblances of the clinical picture to hemisphere deficit states in normal subjects. The findings in schizophrenia are related to others in the schizophrenia/autism spectrum, such as hypoactivation of the so-called 'face area' in the right fusiform gyrus, which has repeatedly been reported in adults with autistic spectrum disorder while looking at faces (Toal, Murphy & Murphy, 2005; for a review see Critchley, Daly, Bullmore et al., 2000). Similarly there are suggestions of an asymmetry in favour of the left hemisphere in schizotypy, with low scores on right, but not left, hemisphere language tasks significantly predicting high scores on positive schizotypal symptomatology scales (Nunn & Peters, 2001). There is particular impairment of normal right hemisphere function (Platek & Gallup, 2002). But schizotypy, too, may be associated with abnormal lateralisation.

15. Sass, 1994.
16. Schreber, 1903.
17. Sass, 1994, p. 12.
18. ibid., p. x.
19. Rees, 1968, quoted in Sass, op. cit., p. 35.
20. Sass, 1994, p. 35.
21. Sass, 1992.
22. All quotations from patients with schizophrenia in this chapter are taken from Sass, 1992, unless otherwise stated.
23. Frith, 1979, p. 233.
24. See Sass & Parnas, 2003, 2007.
25. See Stanghellini, 2004; Parnas, 2000; Parnas & Sass, 2001; Sass & Parnas, 2003; Sass & Parnas, 2001; Zahavi & Parnas, 1999.
26. Kafka, 1949, p. 202.
27. Sass, 2004, p. 71, citing Goodarzi, Wykes & Hemsley, 2000 (see p. 213 above).
28. Sontag, 1978, pp. 15–16.
29. See Sass, 1992, p. 238 (and p. 187). The quotation from Artaud is from Nin, 1966, p. 229.
30. Benjamin, 1969, p. 84.
31. Nietzsche, 1968, §15, pp. 14–15.
32. Nietzsche, 1973 [1886], §209, p. 120.
33. 'Der Don Juan der Erkenntniß': Nietzsche, 1970, Bk. IV, §327, p. 234. In Hollingdale's translation: 'The Don Juan of knowledge – no philosopher or poet has yet discovered him. He does not love the things he knows, but has

spirit and appetite for and enjoyment of the chase and intrigues of knowledge – up to the highest and remotest stars of knowledge! – until at last there remains to him nothing of knowledge left to hunt down except the absolutely *detrimental*; he is like the drunkard who ends by drinking absinthe and *aqua fortis*. Thus in the end he lusts after Hell – it is the last knowledge that *seduces* him. Perhaps it too proves a disillusionment, like all knowledge! And then he would have to stand to all eternity transfixed to disillusionment and himself become a stone guest, with a longing for a supper of knowledge which he will never get! – for the whole universe has not a single morsel left to give this hungry man' (1997, p. 161).

34. Sypher, 1962, p. 123.
35. Heller, 1988, p. 157. The passage he refers to is in Nietzsche, 1977, p. 47: '*Den letzten Philosophen nenne ich mich, denn ich bin der letzte Mensch. Niemand redet mit mir als ich selbst, und meine Stimme kommt wie die eines Sterbenden zu mir . . .*': 'I call myself the last philosopher, for I am the last man. No one speaks to me but myself, and my voice comes to me as from one dying . . .' (trans. I. McG.)
36. Gazzaniga, 1998.
37. Wittgenstein, 1967c, §161, p. 29e.
38. Moravia, 1999, p. 5.
39. Plumb, 1982, p. 316.
40. Klapp, 1986, p. 32. See also Healy, 1984.
41. Spacks, 1995, p. 3.
42. Zijderveld, 1979, p. 84.
43. Scheler, 1998, p. 126.
44. Psychopaths, who have right frontal deficits, show little alteration in heart rate, blood pressure, respirations, or galvanic skin responses when they are subjected to fear, stress, or unpleasant pictures (Intrator, Hare, Stritzke et al., 1997; Raine, Buchsbaum & LaCasse, 1997; Levenston, Patrick, Bradley et al., 2000); and, consequently, seek constant *stimulation*.
45. See Sass, 1992, p. 165.
46. Heidegger, 1977, pp. 129–30.
47. Levin, 1999, p. 54.
48. ibid., pp. 52–3.
49. The story in its entirety, which is feigned to be an excerpt from an old travel book by 'JA Suarez Miranda, *Viajes de varones prudentes* [Travels of Praiseworthy Men], libro iv, cap. xlv, Lerida, 1658', is as follows: '. . . In that Empire, the craft of Cartography attained such Perfection that the Map of a Single province covered the space of an entire City, and the Map of the Empire itself an entire Province. In the course of Time, these Extensive maps were found somehow wanting, and so the College of Cartographers evolved a Map of the Empire that was of the same Scale as the Empire and that coincided with it point for point. Less attentive to the Study of Cartography, succeeding Generations came to judge a map of such Magnitude cumbersome, and, not without Irreverence, they abandoned it to the Rigours of sun and Rain. In the western Deserts, tattered Fragments of the Map are still to be found, Sheltering an occasional Beast or beggar; in the whole Nation, no other relic is left of the Discipline of Geography' (Borges, 1975).
50. Borges, 1964, 'Borges and I', pp. 246–7 (trans. J. E. Irby).
51. Healy, 1984, p. 69.
52. Canetti, 1974, p. 48.
53. See, for example, Jamison, 1993; as well as Post, 1994.
54. Fromm, 1984.
55. Ellard, 1987; Scull, 1979; Hare, 1983, 1988.
56. Tuke, 1894; Tagliavini, 1985; Grob, 1973.
57. Jablensky, 1986.
58. See, e.g., Suvisaari, Haukka, Tanskanen et al., 1999.
59. Saha, Chant, Welham et al., 2005.
60. Weich, Twigg & Lewis, 2006.
61. van Os, 2004; Pedersen & Mortensen, 2001.
62. Krabbendam & van Os, 2005.
63. See, e.g., Selten & Cantor-Graae, 2005; Selten & Cantor-Graae, 2007.
64. See, e.g., Bennett, Sharpe, Freeman et al., 2004; Morgan, Marsden & Lacey, 2000; Bhadrinath, 1990; Rampling, 1985.
65. See Uher, Murphy, Friederich et al., 2005, which shows that the right parietal cortex is underactive in anorexic patients compared with either bulimic patients or normals. An underactive right parietal cortex was also found by Grunwald and colleagues (Grunwald, Weiss, Assmann et al., 2004). A systematic review of 54 case reports revealed that eating disorders are associated with right frontal and temporal lobe damage (Uher & Treasure, 2005). Anorexics display an atypical left hemisphere preponderance in cognitive function (Maxwell, Tucker & Townes, 1984). The same bias towards the left hemisphere may obtain in bulimia nervosa (Wu, Hagman, Buchsbaum et al., 1990).
66. Dusoir, Owens, Forbes et al., 2005.
67. Harrington, 1987, p. 108.
68. Ramachandran, 2005, p. 282, n. 12.
69. Flor-Henry, Tomer, Kumpula et al., 1990.
70. Kluft, 1987; Mesulam, 1981.
71. Ahern, Herring, Tackenberg et al., 1993.
72. Stern, 1938.
73. *American Psychiatric Press Review of Psychiatry*, 1989, p. 8.

74. de la Fuente, Goldman, Stanus et al., 1997.
75. Irle, Lange & Sachsse, 2005; Irle, Lange, Weniger et al., 2007.
76. See Chapter 2 above for discussion of these deficits in relation to the right hemisphere. Apart from these deficits, autistic subjects exhibit other typical right hemisphere neuropsychological deficits: individuals with autism cannot differentiate meanings by context (Frith & Snowling, 1983; Happé, 1997; Jolliffe & Baron-Cohen, 1999); they attend to local, not global, 'information' (Jolliffe & Baron-Cohen, 1997; Shah & Frith, 1993); and they tend to have difficulty using personal pronouns appropriately, especially 'I' and 'me', a faculty which is associated with self-recognition, and is right-hemisphere-mediated (Imbens-Bailey & Pan, 1998). Subjects with autism or Asperger's syndrome show deficits in theory of mind, which are associated with right-hemisphere dysfunction (Gunter, Ghaziuddin & Ellis, 2002; Ellis & Gunter, 1999). Subjects with autistic spectrum disorders show white matter deficits in the corpus callosum and the right hemisphere (Waiter, Williams, Murray et al., 2005). Because of the likelihood of anomalous dominance, however, scanning data need to be interpreted with caution.
77. Agis-Balboa, Pinna, Pibiri et al., 2007.
78. Tzara, 1951.
79. Eksteins, 2008.
80. Griffin, 2007, p. 1. Some have made the, to me not unreasonable, connection between the bureaucratic mentality of Nazism, which saw people as mere *Stücke* (inanimate bits and pieces), and a surrender to what in terms of this book would be left-hemisphere modes of being: Portele, 1979.
81. Marinetti, 1909.
82. Boccioni, U., Carrà, C., Russolo, L. et al., 1910a.
83. Virilio, 2003, pp. 41–2.
84. Ortega y Gasset, 1968, p. 47.
85. From the conversation with the artist Yuri Annenkov (2005); '– Я, знаете, в искусстве не силен, - сказал Ленин, вероятно позабыв о своей статье и о фразе Карла Маркса, - искусство для меня, это... что-то вроде интеллектуальной слепой кишки, и, когда его пропагандная роль, необходимая нам, будет сыграна, мы его – дзык, дзык! – вырежем. За ненужностью.' I am grateful to Dmitri Smirnov and Martin Sixsmith for help in tracking down and translating this passage.
86. Mandelstam, 1999, p. 204.
87. Martin Sixsmith, 'Challenging the Silence', broadcast on BBC Radio 4, 14 August 2006.
88. Shklovsky, 1988, p. 12.
89. Boccioni, U., Carrà, C., Russolo, L. et al., 1910b.
90. For a discussion of all these phenomena, see pp. 66–9 & 89 above.
91. Valéry, 1964, p. 36; original: 1957, 'Réflexions simples sur le corps', vol. 1, p. 927.
92. Cassileth, Vickers & Magill, 2003; Cepeda, Carr, Lau et al., 2006; Siedliecki & Good, 2006.
93. Gioia, 2006, p. 100.
94. A few examples include Iannis Xenakis, who was drawn to electro-acoustic and computerised musical composition through a prior interest in probability calculus and set theory, which led to his founding, in Paris in 1966, the Centre d'Études de Mathématiques et Automatiques Musicales. Edgard Varese became obsessed with mathematics at the time of composing *Intégrales* (1925), writing in the programme note for its New York premiere: 'there is more musical fertility in the contemplation of the stars – preferably through a telescope – and in the high poetry of certain mathematical exposition than in the most sublime gossip of human passions'. Amongst contemporary musicians, the American composer Elliott Carter read mathematics at Annapolis University, Pierre Boulez studied applied mathematics before turning to composition, and György Ligeti discovered fractal geometry in the early 1980s, after which his music was influenced by the complex, many-layered structure of this branch of mathematics. Karlheinz Stockhausen, who displayed many characteristics of a schizotypal personality, used confessedly inappreciable mathematical series to structure his works.
95. Adorno, 1973, p. 87.
96. Nietzsche, 1996, §217, pp. 129–30 (emphasis added).
97. Balkwill, Thompson & Matsunaga, 2004; Balkwill & Thompson, 1999; Ilie & Thompson, 2006.
98. Mithen, 2005, p. 91; Oelman & Loeng, 2003.
99. Tramo, Cariani, Delgutte et al., 2001; Tramo, 2001.
100. Tramo, Cariani, Delgutte et al., 2001.
101. Evers, Dannert, Rodding et al., 1999.
102. Blood, Zatorre, Bermudez et al., 1999; Blood & Zatorre, 2001; Koelsch, Fritz, von Cramon et al., 2006.
103. Zentner, 1996; Zentner & Kagan, 1998; Trainor & Heinmiller, 1998.
104. See above (p. 75); and Wieser & Mazzola, 1986.
105. Passynkova, Neubauer & Scheich, 2007.
106. See above (pp. 74–5).
107. Pleasants, 1955, p. 135.
108. Re Haydn and Mozart: from Hadden, 1902, p. 169. Re Tippett: personal communication from composer David Matthews.
109. Pleasants, 1955, p. 108.
110. See Paul, 1988, p. 15; Paul, 1985.
111. D. E. Brown, 1991.
112. Sass, 1985, p. 76.
113. Schroeder, 2001, p. 211.
114. ibid., p. 225.
115. Sass, 2001, p. 284.

116. Humphrey, 2006, p. 3.
117. ibid., pp. 121–2.
118. ibid., pp. 127–8.
119. Quoted by Humphrey, ibid., pp. 2, 4, 80 & 132: Sutherland, 1989; Nagel, 1986, p. 4; Newton, 2001, p. 48 (emphasis in Newton); Fodor, 1992, p. 5; McGinn, 1993.
120. For Wittgenstein, see p. 157 above. Montaigne's most famous saying was, after a lifetime of learning, *que sçais-je?* The saying that 'the more you know, the more you know that you don't know' is attributed both to the Buddha and to Socrates. St. Paul wrote: 'And if any man think that he knoweth any thing, he knoweth nothing yet as he ought to know' (1 Corinthians 8: 2).
121. The poem is both beautiful and relevant, and in its entirety reads: 'When the immense drugged universe explodes / In a cascade of unendurable colour / And leaves us gasping naked, / This is no more than the ecstasy of chaos: / Hold fast, with both hands, to that royal love / Which alone, as we know certainly, restores / Fragmentation into true being' (Graves, 1968, 'Ecstasy of Chaos').

CONCLUSION: THE MASTER BETRAYED

1. *'Toutes ces misères-là [de l'homme] même prouvent sa grandeur. Ce sont misères de grand seigneur, misères d'un roi dépossédé'*: Pascal, 1976, §398 (Lafuma §116); trans. I. McG.
2. In this section I do not repeat the references to the neuropsychological literature, which are given in Part I of this book (especially throughout Chapter 2).
3. Berger, Berger & Kellner, 1974, esp. p. 44 ff.
4. Marcel, 1962.
5. See discussion at pp. 87–91.
6. See, e.g., Blanchflower & Oswald, 2004; Kenny, 1999.
7. Inglehart & Klingemann, 2000; Easterlin, 1995. Though such findings have been disputed by some, they have been robustly defended: see, for example, Easterlin, 2005.
8. Blanchflower & Oswald, 2004, p. 1380.
9. Easterlin, 2005.
10. Christoph & Noll, 2003.
11. Hamilton, 2003, p. 87.
12. Boswell, 1851, p. 511.
13. G. Miller, 2008.
14. Layard (2005, p. 34) quotes $20,000 (£13,000); G. Easterbrook (2003, p. 170) quotes a figure of only $10,000 (£6,500).
15. Putnam, 2000, p. 333; Argyle, 1987; Myers & Diener, 1995; Veenhoven, 1996.
16. Weissman, Bland, Canino et al., 1996.
17. Vega, Kolody, Aguilar-Gaxiola et al., 1998.
18. Kleinman & Cohen, 1997.
19. Cross-National Collaborative Group, 1992.
20. Putnam, 2000, p. 326.
21. See, e.g., House, Landis & Umberson, 1988.
22. Putnam, 2000, p. 327.
23. ibid., p. 329; Egolf, Lasker, Wolf et al., 1992.
24. Foss, 1949, p. 83.
25. Laing, 1965, p. 49, as cited by Sass, 1992, p. 102.
26. See e.g. pp. 120, 149 & 332–4 above.
27. Corbin, 1988.
28. Cf. probably the greatest of all Romantic painters, Caspar David Friedrich: 'One in everything and everything in one, God's image in leaves and stones, God's spirit in men and beasts . . . the Divine is everywhere, even in a grain of sand' (quoted in Barber, 2008, p. 392). Panentheism is a long tradition, however, not in any sense confined to Romanticism, evident in Christianity from the early Desert Fathers onwards, in many other religions, perhaps especially Buddhism, and reaching a high level of intellectual sophistication in the philosophy of A. N. Whitehead (1926, 1934).
29. A far from complete list of artists using urine or faeces, apart from Marcel Duchamp and Chris Ofili, who made himself famous by using elephant faeces in a portrayal of the Virgin Mary, would have to include the names of Piero Manzoni, Gilbert & George, Stuart Brisley, Cornelius Kolig, Wim Delvoye, Adrian Searle, Santiago Sierra, Kiki Smith, John Miller, Patty Chang, Knut Amsel, Richard Long, Graham Durward, Jonathan Monk, Julia Morrison, Mike Kelley, Paul McCarthy (in his case, inflatable) . . . One might think it would be difficult for music to be subjected to the same treatment, but one would be wrong. Daniel Barenboim gives this example: 'the most extraordinary example of offensive usage of music, because it underlines some kind of association which I fail to recognise, was shown to me one day when watching the television in Chicago and seeing a commercial of a company called American Standard. And it showed a plumber running very, very fast in great agitation, opening the door to a toilet and showing why this company actually cleans the toilet better than other companies. And you know what music was played to that? The Lacrimosa from Mozart's *Requiem*' (BBC Reith Lecture, 'The Neglected Sense', broadcast 14 April 2006).
30. Nietzsche, 1973, §55, p. 63.
31. In the case of the Khora mosaic, one of the greatest achievements of all time, the name of the artist is unknown. In much modern art, in reflection of the left hemisphere's world, one sees not art without a name, but a name without art.

32. Commercial radio stations now break it up into small pieces that will not demand concentration and market it as an anodyne aid to relaxation. In this way it soon becomes fragmented, dismembered, and trivialised by context (or the lack of it), and rendered inauthentic through mechanical repetition. It is turned into a life-style aid. Similarly the great visual works of art of the past suffer from over-reproduction on a million table mats and T-shirts; again there seems to be a worry that they will be valued *only* if they can become a commodity, and perhaps understood at all *only* if they can demonstrate utility. This worry appears to have afflicted the custodians of one of the world's great collections of paintings, London's Tate Gallery. They have produced a series of leaflets with titles such as 'The Calming Collection', 'The First Date Collection', 'The Happily Depressed Collection', or 'The I've Just Split Up Collection'. It includes 'The I Have a Big Meeting Collection', which helpfully advises, like the packet insert that comes with a laxative: 'For maximum effect we recommend you experience this Collection twenty-four hours prior to a meeting. Whatever the reasons for your meeting, we are here to help you look good and to ooze confidence. Let's start by putting you in the mood. Look at *Harvest Home* by John Linnell. You can almost breathe the fresh air from that golden afternoon. Fill your lungs with greatness . . .' And so on. Another recommendation from this 'Collection' is *The Battle of Camperdown*, a late eighteenth-century painting of a famous sea battle between the English and the Dutch, in which hundreds died and thousands were wounded: 'Meetings are often like that. No one said it was going to be easy. But the painting still depicts the moment of victory. Bravery is the name of the game. Off you go' (Quoted in Humphrys, 2006, pp. 127–31.)
33. Nietzsche, 1999, §4, p. 1 (emphases in original).
34. Leibniz, 1996, Bk. II, ch. xx, §5, p. 163 (conventional pagination); the phrase in German is '*uneigennützige und nicht nach Lohn haschende Liebe*' (1904, p. 140); and in the original French, '*l'amour désintéressé ou non mercenaire*' (1845, p. 105). The point he makes, which is different from that made here by Kant, is that, although one takes pleasure in and is fulfilled by beauty, the focus is not on one's own pleasure and fulfilment; in this it is like the benevolent love, rather than concupiscent desire, one might experience for a living being.
35. Kant, 1952, Part I, Section I, Bk. I, i, §5, p. 210 (conventional pagination): 'taste in the beautiful may be said to be the one and only disinterested and *free* delight; for, with it, no interest, whether of sense or reason, extorts approval' (emphasis in the original). The original reads: '*Man kann sagen: daß, unter allen diesen drei Arten des Wohlgefallens, das des Geschmacks am Schönen einzig und allein ein uninteressiertes und freies Wohlgefallen sei; denn kein Interesse, weder das der Sinne, noch das der Vernunft, zwingt den Beifall ab*' (1977c, p. 123). The point is that one's judgment is not reducible to an argument arising purely from sensual or rational considerations.
36. Burke, 1990, p. 57. Burke's point is different again, though closer to that of Leibniz: 'I likewise distinguish love, by which I mean that satisfaction which arises to the mind upon contemplating any thing beautiful, of whatsoever nature it may be, from desire or lust; which is an energy of the mind, that hurries on to the possession of certain objects, that do not affect us as they are beautiful, but by means altogether different. We shall have a strong desire for a woman of no remarkable beauty; while the greatest beauty in men, or in other animals, though it causes love, yet excites nothing at all of desire . . .'
37. Adachi, Kuwahata & Fujita, 2007.
38. See p. 387 above.
39. Dante (*Paradiso*, xxxiii, line 145, the last line of the *Divine Comedy*; trans. J. D. Sinclair), Shakespeare (*Tempest*, Act IV, Scene I, lines 157–8), Ralegh ('The 11th: and last booke of the Ocean to Scinthia', line 433).
40. Donne, 1953–62, vol. 4, p. 330.
41. Pregnancy, both literally and metaphorically, also being a state of roundedness . . . The quotation from Shelley is from his 'One word is too often profaned'; those from Wordsworth are from the Tintern Abbey ode and 'A slumber did my spirit seal'.
42. van Gogh, referred to in Bachelard, 1969, p. 232. But the whole passage, which comes from a letter to Émile Bernard dated 23 June 1888 (2003, p. 370), is interesting for its talk of the 'hemisphere' – presumably half a world – that we now know, and the 'other half of our life' revealed by religion, and to be revealed one day by science: 'Science demonstrates that the earth as a whole is round, something nobody nowadays disputes. For all that, people still persist in thinking that *life is flat* and runs from birth to death. But life, too, is probably round, and much greater in scope and possibilities than the hemisphere we now know. Future generations will probably be able to enlighten us on this very interesting subject, and then science itself – with all due respect – may reach conclusions that are more or less in keeping with Christ's sayings about the other half of our life' (emphasis in original).
43. Jaspers, 1947, p. 50.
44. See Nicholas of Cusa, 1985, Bk. II, ch. xii, p. 93; Bruno, 1879–91, Bk. II, ch. ix, vol. 1, p. 291; Pascal, 1976, §72 (Lafuma §199): '*C'est une sphère infinie dont le centre est partout, la circonférence nulle part*'. In his annotations to the first volume of Nicholas of Cusa's *De Docta Ignorantia*, Jasper Hopkins traces the image of God as an infinite sphere to Meister Eckhart, but acknowledges that its history does not originate with him. For discussion of the metaphor and its history, see Harries, 1975. He refers to Borges's opinion that 'it may be that universal history is the history of the different intonations given a handful of metaphors' (Borges, 1964, 'The fearful sphere of Pascal', p. 192; trans. A. Kerrigan).
45. In the case of Kierkegaard, it begins with his differentiation of the aesthetic and ethical spheres in 1843 (1987, 1983); he explicitly describes three spheres in *Stages on Life's Way* in 1845 (1988), and refines his analysis to essentially four spheres in 1846 (1992); Heidegger, 1999, p. 246.
46. Koestler, 1964, p. 199.
47. Eliade, 1971.
48. Nietzsche, 1990, p. 31; quoting, without acknowledgment, the second-century Roman author, Aulus Gellius (*Noctes Atticae*, Bk. 18, section xi, §4), himself quoting, and championing, the earlier Roman poet Furius Antias (*c.* 100 BC).
49. 'So trust in the eternal laws of the Gods is silenced, and the oracles, who knew in every situation what was to be done, no longer speak to men. The statues have become stone corpses from which the living soul has flown; the

faith that used to animate the hymns of praise has passed away. The tables of the gods are bare of spiritual food and drink, the games and festivals no longer occasions of joyful communion with the divine. The works of the muse lack the power of Spirit, which drew its self-conviction from the ruinous crushing of gods and men. They have already become just what they are for us — beautiful fruit broken off the tree; a kindly fate has passed those works on to us, much as a girl might offer us such fruit. The actual life-world in which they exist is no longer there, neither the tree that bore them, nor the earth, nor the elements which constituted their substance, nor the climate that produced their particular character, nor the succession of seasons which determined their growth. In similar fashion Fate does not preserve for us the living world of those works of art, nor the spring and summer of that ethical life in which they bloomed and ripened, but only a veiled remembrance of all that reality. When we enjoy them, therefore, it is not an act of worship, through which our conscious life might attain its complete truth and be satisfied to the full, but an outer act, as if wiping off some drop of rain or speck of dust from these fruits. In place of the inner elements of the original ethical reality, a reality that environed, created and inspired these works, we construct, in prolix detail, a mere exoskeleton out of the dead elements of its outward existence, — philology, historiography, etc. All this we do, not in order to enter into its actual life, but only so as to represent it ideally or pictorially (*vorstellen*). But just as the maiden who hands us the plucked fruits is more than the Nature that produced them in the first place — the Nature which granted the specific conditions and context for them, tree, air, light, and so on — since she brings all this together at a higher level in the glint of self-awareness in her eye, and her gesture in offering the gifts; so too the Spirit of the fate which presents us with those works of art is more than the ethical life realized in the actual world of that nation. For it is the *recollective inwardizing* (*Er-Innerung*) in *us*, of the spirit which in them was still only *outwardly* manifested; — it is the spirit of the tragic fate which gathers all those individual gods and attributes of the divine substance into the one Pantheon, into the Spirit which is itself conscious of itself as Spirit.' Hegel, *The Phenomenology of Mind* (trans. Baillie, pp. 753–4; in *Phenomenology of Spirit* (trans. Miller), pp. 455–6): translation adapted and synthesised, in Hegelian fashion, from Baillie, Miller, and in particular the translation of Andrew Shanks, to whose work *Trans-Metaphysical Theology* the interested reader is referred for a thought-provoking interpretation of the passage: 'in other words, the worse it gets, the better it gets, as the widely shared experience of alienation opens up the possibility of a truly fresh start': Shanks, forthcoming).
50. In the spirit of Erasmus's great work countering dogmatic certainties, *In Praise of Folly*, Wittgenstein wrote: 'How hard I find it to see what is *right in front of my eyes*! . . . Our greatest stupidities may be very wise . . . Don't *for heaven's sake*, be afraid of talking nonsense! But you must pay attention to your nonsense . . . It's only by thinking even more crazily [*verrückter*] than philosophers do that you can solve their problems . . . Never stay up on the barren heights of cleverness, but come down into the green valleys of silliness': Wittgenstein, 1984, pp. 39, 56, 75 & 76.
51. See, e.g., Wittgenstein, 1967b, Part I, §133, p. 51; ibid., §309, p. 103. He also saw that the roots of many problems in philosophy lie in the way we are enthralled by language: 'These problems are solved, not by adducing further information, but by putting together what we have known all along. Philosophy is a battle against the bewitchment of our intellect through language' (ibid., §109, trans. I. McG.); in the original: '*Diese Probleme werden gelöst, nicht durch Beibringen neuer Erfahrung, sondern durch Zusammenstellung des längst Bekannten. Die Philosophie ist ein Kampf gegen die Verhexung unsres Verstandes durch die Mittel unserer Sprache*'.
52. Kleist, 1982, p. 244. I am here following a train of thought set out by Sass in *Madness and Modernism*, where he says something very similar: his point, it seems to me, cannot be bettered.
53. Gombrich, 1977, p. 389 (emphasis added).
54. In not having definite or indefinite articles, of course, it is hardly alone: cf., among Indo-European languages, Russian.
55. Kawasaki, 2002. I am indebted to Kawasaki at various points in what follows.
56. Nakamura, 1993, pp. 533 & 350.
57. Shigematsu, 1981, p. 3.
58. Nakamura, 1993, pp. 530–36.
59. ibid., p. 537.
60. ibid., p. 355.
61. Kawasaki, 2002.
62. Ogawa, 1998.
63. Iwata, 1989: see Ogawa, 1998, p. 158.
64. 'The impermanence of grass, trees and forests is verily the Buddhahood. The impermanence of the person's body and mind is verily the Buddhahood. The impermanence of the (land) country and scenery is verily the Buddhahood.' Nakamura, 1993, p. 352.
65. Nietzsche, 2003, §9 [26], p. 145 (emphasis in original).
66. Gutchess, Yoon, Luo et al., 2006.
67. Norenzayan, Smith, Kim et al., 2002; Chiu, 1972.
68. Norenzayan, Smith, Kim et al., 2002.
69. Nisbett, Peng, Choi et al., 2001.
70. Ji, Zhang & Nisbett, 2004.
71. Peng & Nisbett, 1999.
72. Masuda & Nisbett, 2001.
73. Nisbett & Masuda, 2003.
74. Miyamoto, Nisbett & Masuda, 2006.
75. Markus & Kitayama, 1991.
76. Kitayama, Duffy, Kawamura et al., 2003.
77. Hoshino-Browne, Zanna, Spencer et al., 2005; Kitayama, Snibbe, Markus et al., 2004.

78. M. Miller, 1997.
79. Tafarodi, Marshall & Katsura, 2004.
80. Gudykunst, Yang & Nishida, 1987.
81. Baumeister, Smart & Boden, 1996.
82. Heine, Lehman, Markus et al., 1999.
83. ibid.
84. S. E. Taylor, 1989; Goffman, 1967.
85. Heine, Lehman, Ide et al., 2001.
86. In ancient Rome although the right hand was preferred for skilled work, the left hand was preferred for extraordinary activities such as religious ritual (Guillaumont, 1985). Virgil (*Moretum*, line 25) states that *laeva ministerio, dextra est intenta labori*: the left hand is for performing rites, the right for work (*ministerium* has the sense both of a skilled art and a religious observance). This superiority of the left hand in the religious domain in ancient Rome influenced Latin Christian arts, which is why St. Peter was always depicted on Christ's left hand; in Byzantine art the opposite rule applied, and he was depicted on Christ's right hand. The Roman priest pours out with his left hand the libation that causes the earth to open. Roman physicians or other makers of medicaments, in order to render certain plants efficacious, must pluck them with the left hand. Animals, also, should be caught with the left hand in order to subdue them and make them harmless. The left horn of a bull and the left hoof of a black ass are compelling charms. Tisiphone brandishes her snakes in her left hand. The Furies carry their torches in their left hands. Medea gathers with her left hand the ingredients of her magic brew. Remedies applied with the left hand and to the left side of the organ or the body, and even the application of the left hand alone, will effect a cure (Frothingham, 1917; Ouspenski, 1976). In Greek εὐώνυμος ('honoured', lit. 'of good name') and ἀριστερός (root ἄριστος, 'best') are two of the words for *left*, though Lloyd says these are euphemistic (Lloyd, 1991).
87. Fabbro, 1994; Tan, 1998.
88. Evans-Pritchard, 1956, p. 234 ff. (where other examples are given). In this regard, Hall mentions the Jewish custom of *teffilin* (Hall, 2008, p. 45).
89. Lloyd, 1991.
90. Granet, 1999, 1973: see Lloyd, 1992.
91. Wang, He, Tong et al., 1999.
92. Kochunov, Fox, Lancaster et al., 2003.
93. Valaki, Maestu, Simos et al., 2004.
94. Robertson-Dunn, Metreweli & Brown, 1996.
95. J. Needham, 1969, p. 17. See also ibid., p. 224: 'Atomism in the physico-chemical sense never played any role of importance in traditional Chinese scientific thinking, which was wedded to the ideas of the continuum and action at a distance'.
96. See p. 131 above.
97. Masuda & Nisbett, 2001.
98. Norenzayan, Smith, Kim et al., 2002.
99. If that sounds too 'Romantic' (in that old putdown), think of the inspiring example of *El Sistema*, the youth music programme in Venezuela, and its many offshoots in other countries, a programme that gave rise to the much-lauded Simon Bolivar Orchestra, and has drawn thousands of poverty-stricken urban youngsters away from disillusionment and a life of crime. Who would have thought that music might have the power to bring so many back to life, inspire them to change their values and behaviour, and create such infectious social good-will, determination, and a sense of belonging?
100. Lewis, 1972.
101. See p. 47 above. Also: 'we should remember that insightful observation of the systematic patterns in nature (whether easily visible or not) remains our second highest calling. In the final accounting, that is the most lovely aspect of science' (Panksepp, 1998, p. 341).
102. Popper, 1980, p. 280.
103. Planck, 1933, pp. 214 & 217.
104. 'Nicht die Wahrheit, in deren Besitz irgend ein Mensch ist, oder zu sein vermeint, sondern die aufrichtige Mühe, die er angewandt hat, hinter die Wahrheit zu kommen, macht den Wert des Menschen. Denn nicht den Besitz, sondern durch die Nachforschung der Wahrheit erweitern sich seine Kräfte, worin allein seine immer wachsende Vollkommenheit bestehet. Der Besitz macht ruhig, träge, stolz — Wenn Gott in seiner Rechten alle Wahrheit und in seiner Linken den einzigen immer regen Trieb nach Wahrheit, obschon mit dem Zusatze, mich immer und ewig zu irren, verschlossen hielte, und spräche zu mir: wähle! Ich fiele ihm mit Demut in seine Linke und sagte: Vater gib! Die reine Wahrheit ist ja doch nur für dich allein! . . .': Lessing, 1979, vol. 8, pp. 32–3; trans. H. B. Garland (1937, p. 174). Cf. Heraclitus fr. LV, Diels 78: 'Human nature has not the insights that the divine has'; and Goethe, 1991, 'Naturwissenschaft', §1033: '*das schönste Glück des denkenden Menschen ist, das Erforschliche erforscht zu haben, und das Unerforschliche ruhig zu verehren*' ('the greatest good fortune for a man of thought is to have fathomed what can be fathomed, and peacefully to respect what is unfathomable'; trans. I. McG.).
105. Waismann, 1994, p. 134.
106. Thus the philosopher Wolfgang Blankenburg on the important, and much misunderstood, concept of common sense: 'We should not allow ourselves to interpret the concept's evanescent quality and lack of contours merely negatively. We may be tempted to do so for the sake of greater conceptual clarity. While such clarity is often a desirable goal, it will in the present case make our concept dissolve into nothing. The very "sponginess" of the concept, rather, is connected with its richness and vitality. We should not presume that its vagueness signifies lack of clarity on our part. It says at the same time something about the peculiarity of the matter itself. It withdraws from our efforts to conceptualise it unambiguously as an object. However, we must not simply yield to this

withdrawal. In our very striving to overcome this resistance, we should take heed of it. We should take this withdrawal as an indication of the *mode of Being* of common sense itself' (Blankenburg & Mishara, 2001, pp. 304–5).

107. Such divisions have intuitively been connected with right and left. In a survey of the significance attached to the terms right and left across many cultures, Sir Geoffrey Lloyd comments that, though they may vary in the moral or affective significance attached to them, they 'tend to be used as the symbols of opposite spiritual categories': Lloyd, 1992, p. 39.

108. Goethe, *Faust*, Part I, line 1112.

109. Schopenhauer, *Die Welt als Wille und Vorstellung*, I, ii, §19, 1960, vol. 1, pp. 163–4.

110. Bergson, 1908, 'De la multiplicité des états de conscience: l'idée de durée', p. 74.

111. Scheler, 1976, 'Die Formen des Wissens und die Bildung', p. 95. Kant said as much, but never used the exact phrase (though see, e.g., 1977a, p. 89). Similar formulations have been made by Hans-Georg Gadamer and Nikolai Hartmann. The expression is often misunderstood to have something to do with dualism, which is far from the intention of any of these philosophers; in separating mind and matter one is cutting through the human world in the wrong direction.

BIBLIOGRAPHY

Abdullaev, Y. G. & Posner, M. I., 'Time course of activating brain areas in generating verbal associations', *Psychological Science*, 1997, *8(1)*, pp. 56–9

Abi-Dargham, A., 'Do we still believe in the dopamine hypothesis? New data bring new evidence', *International Journal of Neuropsychopharmacology*, 2004, *7(suppl. 1)*, pp. s1–5

Aboitiz, F., Scheibel, A. B. & Zaidel, E., 'Morphometry of the Sylvian fissure and the corpus callosum, with emphasis on sex differences', *Brain*, 1992, *115(5)*, pp. 1521–41

Adachi, I., Kuwahata, H. & Fujita, K., 'Dogs recall their owner's face upon hearing the owner's voice', *Animal Cognition*, 2007, *10(1)*, pp. 17–21

Adair, J. C., Schwartz, R. L. & Barrett, A. M., 'Anosognosia', in Heilman, K. M. & Valenstein, E. (eds.), *Clinical Neuropsychology*, 4th edn., Oxford University Press, Oxford, 2003, pp. 185–214

Adolphs, R., Jansari, A. & Tranel, D., 'Hemispheric perception of emotional valence from facial expressions', *Neuropsychology*, 2001, *15(4)*, pp. 516–24

Adorno, T., *Philosophy of Modern Music*, trans. A. G. Mitchell & W. V. Blomster, Seabury Press, New York, 1973

Adorno, T., *Minima Moralia: Reflections on a Damaged Life*, Verso Books, London, 2005 [1974]

Aeschylus, *Prometheus Bound*, ed. M. Griffith, Cambridge University Press, Cambridge, UK, 1983

Agis-Balboa, R. C., Pinna, G., Pibiri, F. et al., 'Down-regulation of neurosteroid biosynthesis in corticolimbic circuits mediates social isolation-induced behavior in mice', *Proc eedings of the National Academy of Sciences of the USA*, 2007, *104(47)*, pp. 18736–41

Ahern, G. L., Herring, A. M., Tackenberg, J. N. et al., 'The association of multiple personality and temporolimbic epilepsy: intracarotid amobarbital test observations', *Archives of Neurology*, 1993, *50(10)*, pp. 1020–25

——, 'Affective self-report during the intracarotid sodium amobarbital test', *Journal of Clinical and Experimental Neuropsychology*, 1994, *16(3)*, pp. 372–6

Aitchison, J., *The Seeds of Speech: Language Origin and Evolution*, Cambridge University Press, Cambridge, UK, 1996

Aitken, K. J. & Trevarthen, C., 'Self/other organization in human psychological development', *Development and Psychopathology*, 1997, *9(4)*, pp. 653–77

Alajouanine, T., 'Aphasia and artistic realization', *Brain*, 1948, *71(3)*, pp. 229–41

Alcock, K. J., Wade, D., Anslow, P. et al., 'Pitch and timing abilities in adult left-hemisphere-dysphasic and right-hemisphere damaged subjects', *Brain and Language*, 2000, *75(1)*, pp. 47–65

Alegria, J. & Noirot, E., 'Neonate orientation behaviour towards human voice', *International Journal of Behavioral Development*, 1978, *1(4)*, pp. 291–312

Aleksandrowicz, J. W., Urbanik, A. & Binder, M., 'Imaging of hypnosis with functional magnetic resonance', *Psychiatria Polska*, 2006, *40(5)*, pp. 969–83

Alexander, I., Cowey, A. & Walsh, V., 'The right parietal cortex and time perception: back to Critchley and the Zeitraffer phenomenon', *Cognitive Neuropsychology*, 2005, *22(3–4)*, pp. 306–15

Alexander, M. P., Benson, D. F. & Stuss, D. T., 'Frontal lobes and language', *Brain and Language*, 1989, *37(4)*, pp. 656–91

Allen, J. S., Damasio, H., Grabowski, T. J. et al., 'Sexual dimorphism and asymmetries in the gray-white composition of the human cerebrum', *NeuroImage*, 2003, *18(4)*, pp. 880–94

Allison, J. D., Meador, K. J., Loring, D. W. et al., 'Functional MRI cerebral activation and deactivation during finger movement', *Neurology*, 2000, *54(1)*, pp. 135–42

Allott, R., 'Language instinct? Gradualistic natural selection is not a good enough explanation', 1995, http:www.PERCEPP.COM/PINKER.HTM (ACCESSED 21 MARCH 2009)

Alloy, L. B. & Abramson, L. Y., 'Depressive realism: four theoretical perspectives', in Alloy, L. B. (ed.), *Cognitive Processes in Depression*, Guilford Press, New York, 1988, pp. 223–65

Almerigi, J. B., Carbary, T. J. & Harris, L. J., 'Most adults show opposite-side biases in the imagined holding of infants and objects', *Brain and Cognition*, 2002, *48(2–3)*, pp. 258–63

Alonso-Alonso, M. & Pascual-Leone, A., 'The right brain hypothesis for obesity', *Journal of the American Medical Association*, 2007, *297(16)*, pp. 1819–22

Alpers, G. W., 'Eye-catching: right hemisphere attentional bias for emotional pictures', *Laterality*, 2008, *13(2)*, pp. 158–78

Amengual, A. M., Drago, V., Foster, P. S. et al., 'Vertical scanning biases and their possible influence on reading direction: celtic wisdom or folly?', *Journal of the International Neuropsychological Society*, 2008, *14(1)*, pp. 102–9

American Psychiatric Press Review of Psychiatry, vol. 8, American Psychiatric Publishing (APPI), Arlington VA, 1989

Amiel, H.-F., *Amiel's Journal: The Journal Intime of Henri-Frédéric Amiel*, trans. M. A. Ward ('Mrs. Humphrey Ward'), Macmillan, London, 1898

Amminger, G. P., Schlogelhofer, M., Lehner, T. et al., 'Premorbid performance IQ deficit in schizophrenia', *Acta Psychiatrica Scandinavica*, 2000, *102(6)*, pp. 414–22

Amunts, K., Jancke, L., Mohlberg, H. et al., 'Interhemispheric asymmetry of the human motor cortex related to handedness and gender', *Neuropsychologia*, 2000, *38(3)*, pp. 304–12

Amunts, K., Schlaug, G., Schleicher, A. et al., 'Asymmetry in the human motor cortex and handedness', *NeuroImage*, 1996, *4(3, pt. 1)*, pp. 216–22

Anaki, D., Faust, M. & Kravetz, S., 'Cerebral hemisphere asymmetries in processing lexical metaphors' (1), *Neuropsychologia*, 1998a, *36(4)*, pp. 353–62

——, 'Cerebral hemisphere asymmetries in processing lexical metaphors' (2), *Neuropsychologia*, 1998b, *36(7)*, pp. 691–700

Anderson, C. A. & Dill, K. E., 'Video games and aggressive thoughts, feelings, and behavior in the laboratory and in life', *Journal of Personality and Social Psychology*, 2000, *78(4)*, pp. 772–90

Anderson, J. R., *Cognitive Psychology and its Implications*, Freeman, New York, 1990

Andrew, R. J. & Rogers, L. J., 'The nature of lateralisation in tetrapods', in Andrew, R. J. & Rogers, L. J. (eds.), *Comparative Vertebrate Lateralisation*, Cambridge University Press, Cambridge, UK, 2002, pp. 94–125

Angrilli, A., Mauri, A., Palomba, D. et al., 'Startle reflex and emotion modulation impairment after a right amygdala lesion', *Brain*, 1996, *119(6)*, pp. 1991–2000

Ankersmit, F. R., *Sublime Historical Experience*, Stanford University Press, Stanford CA, 2005

Annenkov, Y., *The Journal of My Encounters: A Cycle of Tragedies*, subtitled *Memoirs of Prominent Figures in Russian Culture: A. Blok, A. Akhmatova, S. Yesenin and others* [in Russian], Vagreus Publishing, Moscow, 2005

Annett, M., *A Single Gene Explanation of Right and Left Handedness and Brainedness*, Lanchester Polytechnic, Coventry, 1978

——, 'Right hemisphere costs of right-handedness', in Stein, J. F. (ed.), *Vision and Visual Dyslexia*, vol. 13, *Vision and Visual Dysfunction*, Macmillan, London, 1991, pp. 84–93

——, 'Handedness and cerebral dominance: the right shift theory', *Journal of Neuropsychiatry*, 1998, *10(4)*, pp. 459–69

——, 'The distribution of handedness in chimpanzees: estimating right shift in Hopkins' sample', *Laterality*, 2006, *11(2)*, pp. 101–9

Annett, M. & Kilshaw, D., 'Mathematical ability and lateral asymmetry', *Cortex*, 1982, *18(4)*, pp. 547–68

Annett, M. & Manning, M., 'The disadvantages of dextrality for intelligence', *British Journal of Psychology*, 1989, *80(2)*, pp. 213–26

——, 'Reading and a balanced polymorphism for laterality and ability', *Journal of Child Psychology and Psychiatry*, 1990, *31(4)*, pp. 511–29

Aram, D. M. & Ekelman, B. L., 'Scholastic aptitude and achievement among children with unilateral brain lesions', *Neuropsychologia*, 1988, *26(6)*, pp. 903–16

Aram, D. M., Ekelman, B. L., Rose, D. F. et al., 'Verbal and cognitive sequelae following unilateral lesions acquired in early childhood', *Journal of Clinical and Experimental Neuropsychology*, 1985, *7(1)*, pp. 55–78

Ardila, A., 'Right prefrontal syndrome', in Ardila, A. & Ostrosky-Solis, F. (eds.), *The Right Hemisphere: Neurology and Neuropsychology*, Gordon & Breach, New York, 1984, pp. 171–93

Arendt, H., *The Human Condition*, University of Chicago Press, Chicago, 1958

Argyle, M., *The Psychology of Happiness*, Methuen, London, 1987

Aristotle, *Metaphysics*, trans. W. D. Ross, 2 vols., Clarendon Press, Oxford, 1924

——, *Problems II*, trans. W. S. Hett, Heinemann, London, 1965

——, *De Anima*, trans. H. Lawson-Tancred, Penguin, Harmondsworth, UK, 1986

——, *Poetics*, trans. M. Heath, Penguin, Harmondsworth, UK, 1996

——, *Nicomachean Ethics*, trans. W. D. Ross, Oxford University Press, Oxford, 1998

Armstrong, D. F., Stokoe, W. C. & Wilcox, S. E., 'Signs of the origins of syntax', *Current Anthropology*, 1994, *35(4)*, pp. 349–68

Arnaud, C., *Chamfort: A Biography*, trans. D. Dusinberre, University of Chicago Press, Chicago, 1992

Arnheim, R., *Visual Thinking*, University of California Press, Berkeley CA, 1977 [1969]

——, *Art and Visual Perception*, Faber & Faber, London, 1954

Aron, A. R., Fletcher, P. C., Bullmore, E. T. et al., 'Stop-signal inhibition disrupted by damage to right inferior frontal gyrus in humans', *Nature Neuroscience*, 2003, *6(2)*, pp. 115–16

Arseni, C. & D#aban#abail#aba, L., 'Logorrhoea syndrome with hyperkinesia', *European Neurology*, 1977, *15(4)*, pp. 183–7

Ashbrook, J. B., 'Neurotheology: the working brain and the work of theology', *Zygon: Journal of Religion & Science*, 1984, *19(3)*, pp. 331–50

Ashcraft, M. H., Yamashita, T. S. & Aram, D. M., 'Mathematics performance in left and right brain-lesioned children and adolescents', *Brain and Cognition*, 1992, *19(2)*, pp. 208–52

Asthana, H. S. & Mandal, M. K., 'Visual-field bias in the judgment of facial expression of emotion', *Journal of Genetic Psychology*, 2001, *128(1)*, pp. 21–9

Aulus Gellius, *Noctes Atticae*, ed. P. K. Marshall, Clarendon Press, Oxford, 1968

Aust, U., Apfalter, W. & Huber, L., 'Pigeon categorization: classification strategies in a non-linguistic species', in Grialou, P., Longo, G. & Okada, M. (eds.), *Images and Reasoning*, Keio University Press, Tokyo, 2005, vol. 1, pp. 183–204

Aziz-Zadeh, L., Koski, L., Zaidel, E. et al., 'Lateralization of the human mirror neuron system', *Journal of Neuroscience*, 2006, *26(11)*, pp. 2964–70

Babinski, J., 'Contribution a l'étude des troubles mentaux dans l'hémiplégie organique cérébrale (anosognosie)', *Revue Neurologique*, 1914, *27*, pp. 845–8

——, 'Réflexes de défense', *Brain*, 1922, *45*, pp. 149–84

Babkoff, H. & Ben-Uriah, Y., 'Lexical decision time as a function of visual field and stimulus probability', *Cortex*, 1983, *19(1)*, pp. 13–30

Bachelard, G., *The Poetics of Space*, trans. M. Jolas, Beacon Press, Boston MA, 1969 [*La Poétique de l'Espace* 1958]

Bacon, Sir Francis, *The Advancement of Learning* [1605], in *The Works*, vol. 3, trans. and ed. J. Spedding, R. L. Ellis & D. D. Heath, Longman, London, 1857, pp. 253–491

——, *Novum Organon* [1620], in *The Works*, vol. 4, trans. and ed. J. Spedding, R. L. Ellis & D. D. Heath, Longman, London, 1858, pp. 39–248

——, *Meditations Sacrae* [1597], in *The Works*, vol. 7, trans. and ed. J. Spedding, R. L. Ellis & D. D. Heath, Longman, London, 1859, pp. 227–42

Baillie, J., *An Essay on the Sublime*, Kraus, New York, 1967 [1747]

Bakan, D., *The Duality of Human Existence: an Essay on Psychology and Religion*, Rand McNally, Chicago, 1966

Balkwill, L.-L. & Thompson, W. F., 'A cross-cultural investigation of the perception of emotion in music: psychophysical and cultural cues', *Music Perception*, 1999, *17(1)*, pp. 43–64

Balkwill, L.-L., Thompson, W. F. & Matsunaga, R., 'Recognition of emotion in Japanese, Western, and Hindustani music by Japanese listeners', *Japanese Psychological Research*, 2004, *46(4)*, pp. 337–49

Ballard, D. H., 'Our perception of the world has to be an illusion', *Journal of Consciousness Studies*, 2002, *9(5–6)*, pp. 54–71

Balzac, H. de, *Théorie de la démarche*, Didier, Paris, 1853 [1833]

Banich, M. T., 'The missing link: the role of interhemispheric interaction in attentional processing', *Brain and Cognition*, 1998, *36*, pp. 128–57

——, 'Interaction between the hemispheres and its implications for the processing capacity of the brain', in Hugdahl, K. & Davidson, R. J. (eds.), *The Asymmetrical Brain*, Massachusetts Institute of Technology Press, Cambridge MA, 2003, pp. 261–302

Banich, M. T. & Federmeier, K. D., 'Categorical and metric spatial processes distinguished by task demands and practice', *Journal of Cognitive Neuroscience*, 1999, *11(2)*, pp. 153–66

Banich, M. T. & Karol, D. L., 'The sum of the parts does not equal the whole: evidence from bihemispheric processing', *Journal of Experimental Psychology: Human Perception and Performance*, 1992, *18(3)*, pp. 763–84

Banich, M. T., Stolar, N., Heller, W. et al., 'A deficit in right-hemisphere performance after induction of a depressed mood', *Neuropsychiatry, Neuropsychology and Behavioral Neurology*, 1992, *5(1)*, pp. 20–27

Barbas, H., Saha, S., Rempel-Clower, N. et al., 'Serial pathways from primate prefrontal cortex to autonomic areas may influence emotional expression', *BMC Neuroscience*, 2003, *4*, p. 25

Barber, J., *The Road from Eden: Studies in Christianity and Culture*, Academica Press, Palo Alto CA, 2008

Barbey, A. K., Colom, R. & Paul, E. J. et al., 'Architecture of fluid intelligence and working memory revealed by lesion mapping', *Brain Structure and Function*, 2014, *219(2)*, pp. 485–94

Barchas, P. R. & Perlaki, K. M., 'Processing of preconsciously acquired information measured by hemispheric asymmetry and selection accuracy', *Behavioral Neuroscience*, 1986, *100(3)*, pp. 343–9

Barnacz, A. L., Johnson, A., Constantino, P. et al., 'Schizotypal personality traits and deception: the role of self-awareness', *Schizophrenia Research*, 2004, *70(1)*, pp. 115–16

Barnett, K. J., 'Colour knowledge: the role of the right hemisphere in colour processing and object colour knowledge', *Laterality*, 2008, *13(5)*, pp. 456–67

Baron-Cohen, S., Campbell, R., Karmiloff-Smith, A. et al., 'Are children with autism blind to the mentalistic significance of the eyes?', *British Journal of Developmental Psychology*, 1995, *13(4)*, 379–98

Baron-Cohen, S., Leslie, A. M. & Frith, U., 'Does the autistic child have a "theory of mind"?', *Cognition*, 1985, *21(1)*, pp. 37–46

Baron-Cohen, S., Ring, H., Moriarty, J. et al., 'Recognition of mental state terms: clinical findings in children with autism and a functional neuroimaging study of normal adults', *British Journal of Psychiatry*, 1994, *165(5)*, pp. 640–49

Baron-Cohen, S., Tager-Flusberg, H. & Cohen, D. J. (eds.), *Understanding Other Minds: Perspectives from Developmental Cognitive Neuroscience*, Oxford University Press, Oxford, 2000

Baron-Cohen, S., Wheelwright, S. & Jolliffe, T., 'Is there a "language of the eyes"? Evidence from normal adults, and adults with autism or Asperger syndrome', *Visual Cognition*, 1997, *4(3)*, pp. 311–31

Barrash, J., Tranel, D. & Anderson, S. W., 'Acquired personality disturbances associated with bilateral damage to the ventromedial prefrontal region', *Developmental Neuropsychology*, 2000, *18(3)*, pp. 355–81

Barrick, T. R., Mackay, C. E., Prima, S. et al., 'Automatic analysis of cerebral asymmetry: an exploratory study of the relationship between brain torque and planum temporale asymmetry', *NeuroImage*, 2005, *24(3)*, pp. 678–91

Bartolomeo, P. & Chokron, S., 'Left unilateral neglect or right hyperattention?', *Neurology*, 1999, *53(9)*, pp. 2023–7

Bartolomeo, P., Chokron, S. & Sieroff, E., 'Facilitation instead of inhibition for repeated right-sided events in left neglect', *NeuroReport*, 1999, *10(16)*, pp. 3353–7

Barton, J. J., Press, D. Z., Keenan, J. P. et al., 'Lesions of the fusiform face area impair perception of facial configuration in prosopagnosia', *Neurology*, 2002, *58(1)*, pp. 71–8

Bates, E. & Goodman, J., 'On the inseparability of grammar and the lexicon: evidence from acquisition, aphasia and real-time processing', *Language and Cognitive Processes*, 1997, *12(5–6)*, pp. 507–84

Bateson, G., *Mind and Nature – A Necessary Unity*, Ballantine Books, New York, 1979

Battelli, L., Cavanagh, P., Intriligator, J. et al., 'Unilateral right parietal damage leads to bilateral deficit for high-level motion', *Neuron*, 2001, *32(6)*, pp. 985–95

Battelli, L., Cavanagh, P., Martini, P. et al., 'Bilateral deficits of transient visual attention in right parietal patients', *Brain*, 2003, *126(10)*, pp. 2164–74

Battelli, L., Pascual-Leone, A. & Cavanagh, P., 'The "when" pathway of the right parietal lobe', *Trends in Cognitive Sciences*, 2007, *11(5)*, pp. 204–10

Baudelaire, C., 'Salon de 1846', *OEuvres complètes*, ed. C. Pichois, 2 vols., Gallimard, Paris, 1975–6

Bauer, R. H., 'Lateralization of neural control for vocalization by the frog (*Rana pipiens*)', *Psychobiology*, 1993, *21(3)*, pp. 243–8

Bauer, R. M., 'Visual hypoemotionality as a symptom of visual-limbic disconnection in man', *Archives of Neurology*, 1982, *39(11)*, pp. 702–8

Baumeister, R. F., Smart, L. & Boden, J. M., 'Relation of threatened egotism to violence and aggression: the dark side of high self-esteem', *Psychological Bulletin*, 1996, *103(1)*, pp. 5–33

Bayley, J., 'Keats and reality', *Proceedings of the British Academy*, 1962, *48*, pp. 91–125

Baynes, K., Tramo, M. J., Reeves, A. G. et al., 'Isolation of a right hemisphere cognitive system in a patient with anarchic (alien) hand sign', *Neuropsychologia*, 1997, *35(8)*, pp. 1159–73

Bäzner, H. & Hennerici, M. G., 'Painting after right-hemisphere stroke – case studies of professional artists', in Bogousslavsky, J. & Hennerici, M. G. (eds.), *Neurological Disorders in Famous Artists – Part 2, Frontiers of Neurology and Neuroscience*, Karger, Basel, 2007, vol. 22, pp. 1–13

Bear, D. M., 'Hemispheric specialization and the neurology of emotion', *Archives of Neurology*, 1983, *40(4)*, pp. 195–202

Bear, D. M. & Fedio, P., 'Quantitative analysis of interictal behaviour in temporal lobe epilepsy', *Archives of Neurology*, 1977, *34(8)*, pp. 454–67

Beard, M., 'Did Christianity destroy rational thought for 1000 years?', in *The Independent*, London, 14 September 2002

Bearden, C. E., Hoffman, K. M. & Cannon, T. D., 'The neuropsychology and neuroanatomy of bipolar affective disorder: a critical review', *Bipolar Disorders*, 2001, *3(3)*, pp. 106–50

Becchio, C. & Bertone, C., 'Time and neglect: abnormal temporal dynamics in unilateral spatial neglect', *Neuropsychologia*, 2006, *44(14)*, pp. 2775–82

Bechara, A., Damasio, A. R., Damasio, H. et al., 'Insensitivity to future consequences following damage to human prefrontal cortex', *Cognition*, 1994, *50(1–3)*, pp. 7–15

Bechara, A., Tranel, D. & Damasio, H., 'Characterization of the decision-making deficit of patients with ventromedial prefrontal cortex lesions', *Brain*, 2000, *123(11)*, pp. 2189–2202

Beeman, M., 'Semantic processing in the right hemisphere may contribute to drawing inferences from discourse', *Brain and Language*, 1993, *44(1)*, pp. 80–120

Beeman, M. J., Bowden, E. M. & Gernsbacher, M. A., 'Right and left hemisphere cooperation for drawing predictive and coherence inferences during normal story comprehension', *Brain and Language*, 2000, *71(2)*, pp. 310–36

Beeman, M. & Chiarello, C., *Right Hemisphere Language Comprehension: Perspectives from Cognitive Neuroscience*, Lawrence Erlbaum, Mahwah NJ, 1998

Beeman, M., Friedman, R. B., Grafman, J. et al., 'Summation priming and coarse semantic coding in the right hemisphere', *Journal of Cognitive Neuroscience*, 1994, *6(1)*, pp. 26–45

Behrmann, M., Avidan, G., Marotta, J. J. et al., 'Detailed exploration of face-related processing in congenital prosopagnosia: 1. Behavioral findings', *Journal of Cognitive Neuroscience*, 2005, *17(7)*, pp. 1130–49

Bejjani, B.-P., Damier, P., Arnulf, I. et al., 'Transient acute depression induced by high-frequency deep-brain stimulation', *New England Journal of Medicine*, 1999, *340(19)*, pp. 1476–80

Bellugi, U., Poizner, H. & Klima, E. S., 'Brain organization for language: clues from sign aphasia', *Human Neurobiology*, 1983, *2(3)*, pp. 155–70

——, 'Language, modality and the brain', *Trends in Neurosciences*, 1989, *12(10)*, pp. 380–88

Bemporad, J. R., 'Perceptual disorders in schizophrenia', *American Journal of Psychiatry*, 1967, *123(8)*, pp. 971–6

Benbow, C. P., 'Physiological correlates of extreme intellectual precocity', *Neuropsychologia*, 1986, *24(5)*, pp. 719–25

Bench, C. J., Friston, K. J., Brown, R. G. et al., 'The anatomy of melancholia – focal abnormalities of cerebral blood flow in major depression', *Psychological Medicine*, 1992, *22(3)*, pp. 607–15

Bender, M. B., Feldman, M. & Sobin, A. J., 'Palinopsia', *Brain*, 1968, *9(2)*, pp. 321–38

Benjamin, W., 'The Storyteller', *Illuminations*, trans. H. Zohn, ed. H. Arendt, Schocken, New York, 1969, pp. 83–109

——, 'On the mimetic faculty', in *Reflections: Essays, Aphorisms, Autobiographical Writings*, trans. E. Jephcott, ed. P. Demetz, Schocken Books, New York, 1986, pp. 333–6

Bennett, D., Sharpe, M., Freeman, C. et al., 'Anorexia nervosa among female secondary school students in Ghana', *British Journal of Psychiatry*, 2004, *185(4)*, pp. 312–17

Benowitz, L. I., Bear, D. M., Rosenthal, R. et al., 'Hemispheric specialization in nonverbal communication', *Cortex*, 1983, *19(1)*, pp. 5–11

Benowitz, L. I., Moya, K. L. & Levine, D. N., 'Impaired verbal reasoning and constructional apraxia in subjects with right hemisphere damage', *Neuropsychologia*, 1990, *28(3)*, pp. 231–41

Benson, D. F. & Barton, M. I., 'Disturbances in constructional ability', *Cortex*, 1970, *6(1)*, pp. 19–46

Benson, D. F. & Stuss, D. T., 'Frontal lobe influences on delusions: a clinical perspective', *Schizophrenia Bulletin*, 1990, *16(3)*, pp. 403–11

Bentham, J., *The Works of Jeremy Bentham*, ed. J. Bowring, William Tait, Edinburgh, 1838–43

——, *An Introduction to the Principles of Morals and Legislation*, in M. Warnock (ed.), *Utilitarianism and On Liberty, including Mill's 'Essay on Bentham' and selections from the writings of Jeremy Bentham and John Austin*, Blackwell, Oxford, 2003

Benton, A. L., 'Constructional apraxia and the minor hemisphere', *Confinia Neurologica*, 1967, *29*, pp. 1–16

Benton, A. L. & Fogel, M. L., 'Three-dimensional constructional praxis: a clinical test', *Archives of Neurology*, 1962, *7(4)*, pp. 347–54

Benton, A. L. & Joynt, R. J., 'Reaction time in unilateral cerebral disease', *Confinia Neurologica*, 1959, *19*, pp. 247–56

Berger, P. L., Berger, B. & Kellner, H., *The Homeless Mind: Modernization and Consciousness*, Penguin, Harmondsworth, UK, 1974

Bergson, H., *Essai sur les données immédiates de la conscience*, ed. F. Alcan, Librairies Félix Alcan et Guillaumin Réunies, Paris, 1908 [1889]

Berlin, B., *The Principles of Ethnobiological Classification*, Princeton University Press, Princeton NJ, 1992

——, ' "Just another fish story?" Size-symbolic properties of fish names', in Minelli, A., Ortalli, G. & Singa, G. (eds.), *Animal Names*, Istituto Veneto di Scienze, Lettre ed Arti, Venice, 2005, pp. 9–21

Berlin, I., *Vico and Herder: Two Studies in the History of Ideas*, Hogarth Press, London, 1976

——, *The Roots of Romanticism*, Princeton University Press, Princeton NJ, 1999

Berlucchi, G., Mangun, G. R. & Gazzaniga, M. S., 'Visuospatial attention and the split brain', *News in Physiological Sciences*, 1997, *12(5)*, pp. 226–31

Berns, G. S., Cohen, J. D. & Mintun, M. A., 'Brain regions responsive to novelty in the absence of awareness', *Science*, 1997, *276(5316)*, pp. 1272–5

Bertollo, D. N., Cowen, M. A. & Levy, A. V., 'Hypometabolism in olfactory cortical projection areas of male patients with schizophrenia: an initial positron emission tomography study', *Psychiatry Research*, 1996, *60(2–3)*, pp. 113–16

Bertoloni, G., Anzola, G. P., Buchtel, H. A. et al., 'Hemispheric differences in the discrimination of the velocity and duration of a simple visual stimulus', *Neuropsychologia*, 1978, *16(2)*, pp. 213–20

Bever, T. G. & Chiarello, R. J., 'Cerebral dominance in musicians and nonmusicians', *Science*, 1974, *185(150)*, pp. 537–9

Bhadrinath, E. R., 'Anorexia nervosa in adolescents of Asian extraction', *British Journal of Psychiatry*, 1990, *156(4)*, pp. 565–8

Biermann-Ruben, K., Kessler, K., Jonas, M. et al., 'Right hemisphere contributions to imitation tasks', *European Journal of Neuroscience*, 2008, *27(7)*, pp. 1843–55

Biese, A., *Die Philosophie des Metaphorischen*, Leopold Voss, Hamburg and Leipzig, 1893

——, *The Development of the Feeling for Nature in the Middle Ages and Modern Times*, Routledge, London, 1905 [*Die Entwickelung des Naturgefühls im Mittelalter und in der Neuzeit*, 1888]

Bihrle, A. M., Brownell, H. H., Powelson, J. A. et al., 'Comprehension of humorous and nonhumorous materials by left and right brain-damaged patients', *Brain and Cognition*, 1986, *5(4)*, pp. 399–411

Bilder, R. M., Wu, H., Bogerts, B. et al., 'Cerebral volume asymmetries in schizophrenia and mood disorders: a quantitative magnetic resonance imaging study', *International Journal of Psychophysiology*, 1999, *34(3)*, pp. 197–205

Birchwood, M., Iqbal, Z., Chadwick, P. et al., 'Cognitive approach to depression and suicidal thinking in psychosis. 2. Testing the validity of a social ranking model', *British Journal of Psychiatry*, 2000, *177(6)*, pp. 522–8

Bisazza, A., Cantalupo, C., Capocchiano, M. et al., 'Population lateralisation and social behaviour: a study with sixteen species of fish', *Laterality*, 2000, *5(3)*, pp. 269–84

Bisiacchi, P., Marzi, C. A., Nicoletti, R. et al., 'Left-right asymmetry of callosal transfer in normal human subjects', *Behavioural Brain Research*, 1994, *64(1–2)*, pp. 173–8

Bisiach, E., Mini, M., Sterzi, R. et al., 'Hemispheric lateralisation of the decisional stage in choice reaction times to visual unstructured stimuli', *Cortex*, 1982, *18(2)*, pp. 191–7

Bisiach, E., Rusconi, M. L. & Vallar, G., 'Remission of somatoparaphrenic delusion through vestibular stimulation', *Neuropsychologia*, 1991, *29(10)*, pp. 1029–31

Bisiach, E., Vallar, G., Perani, D. et al., 'Unawareness of disease following lesions of the right hemisphere: anosognosia for hemiplegia and anosognosia for hemianopia', *Neuropsychologia*, 1986, *24(4)*, pp. 471–82

Black, F. W. & Bernard, B. A., 'Constructional apraxia as a function of lesion locus and size in patients with focal brain damage', *Cortex*, 1984, *20(1)*, pp. 111–20

Black, F. W. & Strub, R. L., 'Constructional apraxia in patients with discrete missile wounds of the brain', *Cortex*, 1976, *12(3)*, pp. 212–20

Black, M., 'Metaphor', in *Models and Metaphors: Studies in Language and Philosophy*, Cornell University Press, Ithaca NY, 1962, pp. 22–47

——, *The Prevalence of Humbug and Other Essays*, Cornell University Press, Ithaca NY & London, 1983

Blair, R. J. R. & Coles, M., 'Expression recognition and behavioural problems in early adolescence', *Cognitive Development*, 2000, *15(4)*, pp. 421–34

Blair, R. J. R., Colledge, E., Murray, L. et al., 'A selective impairment in the processing of sad and fearful expressions in children with psychopathic tendencies', *Journal of Abnormal Child Psychology*, 2001, *29(6)*, pp. 491–8

Blake, W., *Complete Writings*, ed. Sir Geoffrey Keynes, Oxford University Press, Oxford, 1972

Blakemore, S. J. & Decety, J., 'From the perception of action to the understanding of intention', *Nature Reviews Neuroscience*, 2001, *2(8)*, pp. 561–7

Blakemore, S. J., Rees, G. & Frith, C. D., 'How do we predict the consequences of our actions? A functional imaging study', *Neuropsychologia*, 1998, *36(6)*, pp. 521–9

Blakeslee, T. R., *The Right Brain*, Macmillan, London, 1980

Blanchflower, D. G. & Oswald, A. J., 'Well-being over time in Britain and the USA,' *Journal of Public Economics*, 2004, *88*, pp. 1359–86

Blankenburg, W. & Mishara, A. L., 'First steps toward a psychopathology of "common sense" ', *Philosophy, Psychiatry, & Psychology*, 2001, *8(4)*, pp. 303–15

Bleuler, E., 'Halbseitiges Delirium', *Psychiatrisch-Neurologische Wochenschrift*, 1902, *34*, pp. 361–7

Blonder, L. X., Bowers, D. & Heilman, K. M., 'The role of the right hemisphere in emotional communication', *Brain*, 1991, *114(3)*, pp. 1115–27

Blood, A. J. & Zatorre, R. J., 'Intensely pleasurable responses to music correlate with activity in brain regions implicated in reward and emotion', *Proceedings of the National Academy of Sciences of the USA*, 2001, *98(20)*, pp. 11818–23

Blood, A. J., Zatorre, R. J., Bermudez, P. et al., 'Emotional responses to pleasant and unpleasant music correlate with activity in paralimbic brain regions', *Nature Neuroscience*, 1999, *2(4)*, pp. 382–7

Bloom, J. S. & Hynd, G. W., 'The role of the corpus callosum in interhemispheric transfer of information: excitation or inhibition?', *Neuropsychology Review*, 2005, *15(2)*, pp. 59–71

Bloom, P. & Keil, F. C., 'Thinking through language', *Mind & Language*, 2001, *16(4)*, pp. 351–67

Bloom, R. L., Borod, J. C., Obler, L. K. et al., 'A preliminary characterization of lexical emotional expression in right and left brain-damaged patients', *International Journal of Neuroscience*, 1990, *55(2–4)*, pp. 71–80

Blumberg, H. P., Stern, E., Martinez, D. et al., 'Increased anterior cingulate and caudate activity in bipolar mania', *Biological Psychiatry*, 2000, *48(11)*, pp. 1045–52

Boccioni, U., Carrà, C., Russolo, L. et al., 'Manifesto of the Futurist Painters', *Poesia*, Milan, 1910a (11 February)

——, 'Technical Manifesto of Futurist Painting', *Poesia*, Milan, 1910b (10 April)

Bodamer, J., 'Die Prosop-Agnosie', *Archiv für Psychiatrie und Nervenkrankheiten*, 1947, *179*, pp. 6–53

Bodamer, M. D. & Gardner, R. A., 'How cross-fostered chimpanzees (*Pan troglodytes*) initiate and maintain conversations', *Journal of Comparative Psychology*, 2002, *116(1)*, pp. 12–26

Bogen, J. E., 'The dual brain: some historical and methodological aspects', in Benson, D. F. & Zaidel, E. (eds.), *The Dual Brain: Hemispheric Specialization in Humans*, Guilford Press, New York, 1985, pp. 27–43

——, 'Split-brain basics: relevance for the concept of one's other mind', *Journal of the American Academy of Psychoanalysis*, 2000, *28(2)*, pp. 341–69

Bogen, J. E. & Bogen, G. M., 'The other side of the brain: III. The corpus callosum and creativity', *Bulletin of the Los Angeles Neurological Society*, 1969, *34(4)*, pp. 191–220

——, 'Creativity and the corpus callosum', *Psychiatric Clinics of North America*, 1988, *11(3)*, pp. 293–301

——, 'Split-brains: interhemispheric exchange in creativity', in Runco, M. A. & Pritzker, R. (eds.), *Encyclopedia of Creativity*, Academic Press, San Diego CA, 1999, pp. 571–5

Bogerts, B., 'The temporolimbic system theory of positive schizophrenic symptoms', *Schizophrenia Bulletin*, 1997, *23(3)*, pp. 423–35

Bolduc, C., Daoust, A. M., Limoges, E. et al., 'Hemispheric lateralization of the EEG during wakefulness and REM sleep in young healthy adults', *Brain and Cognition*, 2003, *53(2)*, pp. 193–6

Boles, D. B., 'Relationships among multiple task asymmetries. II. A large-sample factor analysis', *Brain and Cognition*, 1998, *36(3)*, pp. 268–89

Boll, T. J., 'Right and left cerebral hemisphere damage and tactile perception: performance of the ipsilateral and contralateral sides of the body', *Neuropsychologia*, 1974, *12(2)*, pp. 235–8

Bonin, G. von, 'Anatomical asymmetries of the cerebral hemispheres', in Mountcastle, V. B. (ed.), *Interhemispheric Relations and Cerebral Dominance*, Johns Hopkins Press, Baltimore MD, 1962, pp. 1–6

Borges, J. L., *Labyrinths: Selected Stories and Other Writings*, trans. various hands, ed. D. A. Yates, New Directions, New York, 1964

——, *A Universal History of Infamy*, trans. N. T. de Giovanni, Penguin, Harmondsworth, UK, 1975 [*Historia universal de la infamia*, 1935]

Borgo, F. & Shallice, T., 'When living things and other "sensory quality" categories behave in the same fashion: a novel category specificity effect', *Neurocase*, 2001, *7(3)*, pp. 201–20

Bornstein, B., 'Prosopagnosia', in Halpern, L. (ed.), *Problems of Dynamic Neurology*, University of Hadassah, Jerusalem, 1963, pp. 283–318

Bornstein, B. & Kidron, D. P., 'Prosopagnosia', *Journal of Neurology, Neurosurgery, & Psychiatry*, 1959, *22(2)*, pp. 124–31

Bornstein, B., Sroka, H. & Munitz, H., 'Prosopagnosia with animal face agnosia', *Cortex*, 1969, *5(2)*, pp. 164–9

Borod, J. C., 'Interhemispheric and intrahemispheric control of emotion: a focus on unilateral brain damage', *Journal of Consulting and Clinical Psychology*, 1992, *60(3)*, pp. 339–48

——, 'Cerebral mechanisms underlying facial, prosodic, and lexical emotional expression: a review of neuropsychological studies and methodological issues', *Neuropsychology*, 1993, *7*, pp. 445–63

Borod, J. C., Andelman, F., Obler, L. K. et al., 'Right hemisphere specialization for the identification of emotional words and sentences: evidence from stroke patients', *Neuropsychologia*, 1992, *30(9)*, pp. 827–44

Borod, J. C., Bloom, R. L., Brickman, A. M. et al., 'Emotional processing deficits in individuals with unilateral brain damage', *Applied Neuropsychology*, 2002, *9(1)*, pp. 23–36

Borod, J. C. & Caron, H. S., 'Facedness and emotion related to lateral dominance, sex and expression type', *Neuropsychologia*, 1980, *18(2)*, pp. 237–41

Borod, J. C., Haywood, C. S. & Koff, E., 'Neuropsychological aspects of facial asymmetry during emotional expression: a review of the normal adult literature', *Neuropsychology Review*, 1997, *7(1)*, pp. 41–60

Borod, J. C., Kent, J., Koff, E. et al., 'Facial asymmetry while posing positive and negative emotions: support for the right hemisphere hypothesis', *Neuropsychologia*, 1988, *26(5)*, pp. 759–64

Borod, J. C., Koff, E. & Buck, R., 'The neuropsychology of facial expression: data from normal and braindamaged adults', in Blanck, P. D., Buck, R. & Rosenthal, R. (eds.), *Nonverbal Communication in the Clinical Context*, Pennsylvania State University Press, Philadelphia PA, 1986, pp. 196–222

Borod, J. C., Koff, E. & Caron, H. S., 'Right hemisphere specialisation for the expression and appreciation of emotion: a focus on the face', in Perecman, E. (ed.), *Cognitive Processing in the Right Hemisphere*, Academic Press, New York, 1983, pp. 83–110

Borod, J. C., Koff, E., Lorch, M. P. et al., 'Channels of emotional expression in patients with unilateral brain damage', *Archives of Neurology*, 1985, *42(4)*, pp. 345–8

Borod, T. C., Koff, E., Yecker, S. et al., 'Facial asymmetry during emotional expression: gender, valence, and measurement technique', *Neuropsychologia*, 1998, *36(11)*, pp. 1209–15

Borod, J. C., Welkowitz, J., Alpert, M. et al., 'Parameters of emotional processing in neuropsychiatric disorders: conceptual issues and a battery of tests', *Journal of Communication Disorders*, 1990, *23(4–5)*, pp. 247–71

Boroojerdi, B., Diefenbach, K. & Ferbert, A., 'Transcallosal inhibition in cortical and subcortical cerebral vascular lesions', *Journal of the Neurological Sciences*, 1996, *144(1–2)*, pp. 160–70

Boroojerdi, B., Hungs, M., Mull, M. et al., 'Interhemispheric inhibition in patients with multiple sclerosis', *Electroencephalography and Clinical Neurophysiology*, 1998, *109(3)*, pp. 230–37

Boroojerdi, B., Töpper, R., Foltys, H. et al., 'Transcallosal inhibition and motor conduction studies in patients with schizophrenia using transcranial magnetic stimulation', *British Journal of Psychiatry*, 1999, *175(4)*, pp. 375–9

Boswell, J., *Life of Samuel Johnson*, ed. J. W. Croker, John Murray, London, 1851

Botha, R. P., *Challenging Chomsky: The Generative Garden Game*, Blackwell, Oxford, 1989

Bottini, G., Corcoran, R., Sterzi, R. et al., 'The role of the right hemisphere in the interpretation of figurative aspects of language: a positron emission tomography activation study', *Brain*, 1994, *117(6)*, pp. 1241–53

Bourgeois, M. J., Christman, S. & Horowitz, I. A., 'The role of hemispheric activation in person perception: evidence for an attentional focus model', *Brain and Cognition*, 1998, *38(2)*, pp. 202–19

Bowden, E. M. & Beeman, M. J., 'Getting the right idea: semantic activation in the right hemisphere may help solve insight problems', *Psychological Science*, 1998, *9(6)*, pp. 435–40

Bowden, E. M. & Jung-Beeman, M., 'Aha! Insight experience correlates with solution activation in the right hemisphere', *Psychonomic Bulletin & Review*, 2003, *10(3)*, pp. 730–37

Bowers, D., Blonder, L. X., Feinberg, T. et al., 'Differential impact of right and left hemisphere lesions on facial emotion and object imagery', *Brain*, 1991, *114(6)*, pp. 2593–609

Bowring, J., *Memoirs of Bentham*, in Bentham, J., *The Works of Jeremy Bentham*, ed. J. Bowring, William Tait, Edinburgh, 1838–43, vol. 10

Boyle, D., *The Tyranny of Numbers*, HarperCollins, London, 2001

Boys-Stones, G., 'Physiognomy and ancient psychological theory', in Swain, S. (ed.), *Seeing the Face, Seeing the Soul*, Oxford University Press, Oxford, 2007, pp. 19–124

Bracha, H. S., Cabrera, F. J., Karson, C. N. et al., 'Lateralization of visual hallucinations in chronic schizophrenia', *Biological Psychiatry*, 1985, *20(10)*, pp. 1132–6

Bradshaw, G. J., Hicks, R. E. & Rose, B., 'Lexical discrimination and letter-string identification in the two visual fields', *Brain and Language*, 1979, *8(1)*, pp. 10–18

Bradshaw, J. L., 'The evolution of human lateral asymmetries: new evidence and second thoughts', *Journal of Human Evolution*, 1988, *17(6)*, pp. 615–37

——, *Human Evolution. A Neuropsychological Perspective*, Taylor & Francis, London, 1997

Bradshaw, J. L. & Nettleton, N. C., 'The nature of hemispheric specialization in man', *Behavioral and Brain Sciences*, 1981, *4(1)*, pp. 51–91

——, *Human Cerebral Asymmetry*, Prentice-Hall, Englewood Cliffs NJ, 1983

Brady, R. H., 'The idea in nature: rereading Goethe's organics', in Seamon, D. & Zajonc, A. (eds.), *Goethe's Way of Science: a Phenomenology of Nature*, State University of New York Press, New York, 1998, pp. 83–111

Brannon, E. M., 'The independence of language and mathematical reasoning', *Proceedings of the National Academy of Sciences of the USA*, 2005, *102(9)*, pp. 3177–8

Braudel, F., *The Mediterranean in the Ancient World*, trans. S. Reynolds, Penguin, Harmondsworth, UK, 2001 [*Les mémoires de la Méditerranée* 1998]

Braun, C. M. J., 'The evolution of hemispheric specialisation of antagonistic systems of management of the body's energy sources', *Laterality*, 2007, *12(5)*, pp. 397–427

Braun, C. M. J., Daigneault, R., Gaudelet, S. et al., 'Diagnostic and Statistical Manual of Mental Disorders, Fourth Edition symptoms of mania: which one(s) result(s) more often from right than left hemisphere lesions?', *Comprehensive Psychiatry*, 2008, *49(5)*, pp. 441–59

Braun, C. M. J., Delisle, J., Guimond, A. et al., 'Post unilateral lesion response biases modulate memory: crossed double dissociation of hemispheric specialisations', *Laterality*, 2009, *14(2)*, pp. 122–64

Braun, C. M. J., Desjardins, S., Gaudelet, S. et al., 'Psychic tonus, body schema and the parietal lobes: a multiple lesion case analysis', *Behavioural Neurology*, 2007, *18(2)*, pp. 65–80

Braun, C. M. J., Dumont, M., Duval, J. et al., 'Speech rate as a sticky switch: a multiple lesion case analysis of mutism and hyperlalia', *Brain and Language*, 2004, *89(1)*, pp. 243–52

Braun, C. M. J., Larocque, C., Daigneault, S. et al., 'Mania, pseudomania, depression, and pseudodepression resulting from focal unilateral critical lesions', *Neuropsychiatry, Neuropsychology and Behavioral Neurology*, 1999, *12(1)*, pp. 35–51

Bray, F., 'Chinese Medicine', in Bynum, W. F. & Porter, R. (eds.), *Companion Encyclopaedia of the History of Medicine*, Routledge & Kegan Paul, London, 1993, vol. 1, pp. 728–54

Breen, N., Caine, D. & Coltheart, M., 'Mirrored-self misidentification: two cases of focal onset dementia', *Neurocase*, 2001, *7(3)*, pp. 239–54

Breitenstein, C., Daum, I. & Ackermann, H., 'Emotional processing following cortical and subcortical brain damage: contribution of the fronto-striatal circuitry', *Behavioural Neurology*, 1998, *11(1)*, pp. 29–42

Bremer, F., 'Physiology of the corpus callosum', *Research Publications of the Association for Research in Nervous and Mental Disease*, 1958, *36*, pp. 424–48

Brener, M., *Faces: The Changing Look of Humankind*, University Press of America, Lanham MD, 2000

Bretherton, I. & Bates, E., 'The development of representation from 10–28 months', in Emde, R. N. & Harmon, R. J. (eds.), *Continuities and Discontinuities in Development*, Plenum Press, New York, 1984, pp. 229–61

Broad, K. D., Mimmack, M. L. & Kendrick, K. M., 'Is right hemisphere specialisation for face discrimination specific to humans?', *European Journal of Neuroscience*, 2000, *12(2)*, pp. 731–41

Broadbent, D. E., 'The hidden preattentive process', *American Psychologist*, 1977, *32(2)*, pp. 109–18

Broadfield, D. C., Holloway, R. L., Mowbray, K. et al., 'Endocast of Sambungmacan 3 (Sm 3): a new *homo erectus* from Indonesia', *The Anatomical Record*, 2001, *262(4)*, pp. 369–79

Broca, P., 'Perte de la parole, ramollissement chronique et destruction partielle du lobe antérieur gauche du cerveau', *Bulletin de la Société d'Anthropologie de Paris*, 1861a, *2*, pp. 235–8

——, 'Remarques sur le siège de la faculté du langage articule, suivies d'une observation d'aphémie', *Bulletin de la Société Anatomique*, 1861b, *36*, pp. 330–57

——, 'Sur le principe des localisations cérébrales', *Bulletin de la Société d'Anthropologie de Paris*, 1861c, *2*, pp. 190–204

——, 'Sur le siège de la faculté du langage articulé', *Bulletin de la Société d'Anthropologie de Paris*, 1865, *6*, pp. 377–93

Brosch, T., Sander, D. & Scherer, K. R., 'That baby caught my eye . . . attention capture by infant faces', *Emotion*, 2007, *7(3)*, pp. 685–9

Brown, D. E., *Human Universals*, McGraw-Hill, New York, 1991

Brown, H. D. & Kosslyn, S. M., 'Cerebral lateralization', *Current Opinion in Neurobiology*, 1993, *3(2)*, pp. 183–6

Brown, S., 'Evolutionary models of music: from sexual selection to group selection', in Thompson, N. S & Tonneau, F. (eds.), *Perspectives in Ethology* 13: *Evolution, Culture, and Behavior*, Plenum Press, New York, 2000a, pp. 231–81

——, 'The "musilanguage" model of music evolution', in Wallin, N. L., Merker, B. & Brown, S. (eds.), *The Origins of Music*, Massachusetts Institute of Technology Press, London, 2000b, pp. 271–300

Brown, S. & Nicholls, M. E., 'Hemispheric asymmetries for the temporal resolution of brief auditory stimuli', *Perception and Psychophysics*, 1997, *59(3)*, pp. 442–7

Brown, W. S., Larson, E. B. & Jeeves, M., 'Directional asymmetries in interhemispheric transmission time: evidence from visual evoked potentials', *Neuropsychologia*, 1994, *32(4)*, pp. 439–48

Brownell, H. H., Griffin, R., Winner, E. et al., 'Cerebral lateralization and theory of mind', in Baron-Cohen, S., Tager-Flusberg, H. & Cohen, D. J. (eds.), *Understanding Other Minds: Perspectives from Developmental Cognitive Neuroscience*, Oxford University Press, Oxford, 2000, pp. 306–33

Brownell, H. H., Michel, D., Powelson, J. et al., 'Surprise but not coherence: sensitivity to verbal humor in right-hemisphere patients', *Brain and Language*, 1983, *18(1)*, pp. 20–27

Brownell, H. H., Potter, H. H., Bihrle, A. M. et al., 'Inference deficits in right brain-damaged patients', *Brain and Language*, 1986, *27(2)*, pp. 310–21

Brownell, H. H., Potter, H. H., Michelow, D. et al., 'Sensitivity to lexical denotation and connotation in brain-damaged patients: a double dissociation?', *Brain and Language*, 1984, *22(2)*, pp. 253–65

Brownell, H. H., Simpson, T. L., Bihrle, A. M. et al., 'Appreciation of metaphoric alternative word meanings by left and right brain-damaged patients', *Neuropsychologia*, 1990, *28(4)*, pp. 375–83

Brown-Séquard, C.-E., 'Have we two brains or one?', *The Forum*, 1890, *9*, pp. 627–43

Brüne, M., Bahramali, H., Hennessy, M. et al., 'Are angry male and female faces represented in opposite hemispheres of the female brain? A study using repetitive transcranial magnetic stimulation (rTMS)', *Journal of Integrative Neuroscience*, 2006, *5(2)*, pp. 187–97

Bruner, E., 'Fossil traces of the human thought: paleoneurology and the evolution of the genus *Homo*', *Rivista di Antropologia (Journal of Anthropological Sciences)*, 2003, *81*, pp. 29–56

Bruner, J., *Actual Minds, Possible Worlds*, Harvard University Press, Cambridge MA, 1986

Brunet, E., Sarfati, Y., Hardy-Baylé, M.-C. et al., 'A PET investigation of the attribution of intentions with a nonverbal task', *NeuroImage*, 2000, *11(2)*, pp. 157–66

Bruno, G., *De innumerabilibus, immenso et infigurabili* [1591], in *Opera Latine Conscripta*, ed. F. Fiorentino, 3 vols., Naples & Florence, 1879–91

Bruyer, R. (ed.), *The Neuropsychology of Face Perception and Facial Expression*, Lawrence Erlbaum, Hillsdale NJ, 1986

Bryden, M. P., *Laterality: Functional Asymmetry in the Intact Brain*, Academic Press, New York, 1982

Bryden, M. P., Ley, R. G. & Sugarman, J. H., 'A left ear advantage for identifying the emotional quality of tonal sequences', *Neuropsychologia*, 1982, *20(1)*, pp. 83–7

Büchner, L., *Der neue Hamlet, Poesie und Prosa aus Papieren eines verstorbenen Pessimisten*, Schabelitz, Zürich, 1885

Buchtel, H. A., Rizzolatti, G., Anzola, G. P. et al., 'Right hemispheric superiority in discrimination of brief acoustic duration', *Neuropsychologia*, 1978, *16(5)*, pp. 643–7

Bueti, D., Bahrami, B. & Walsh, V., 'Sensory and association cortex in time perception', *Journal of Cognitive Neuroscience*, 2008, *20(6)*, pp. 1054–62

Bugnyar, T., Stöwe, M. & Heinrich, B., 'Ravens, *Corvus corax*, follow gaze direction of humans around obstacles', *Proceedings of the Royal Society of London, Series B: Biological Sciences*, 2004, *271(1546)*, pp. 1331–6

Bukach, C. M., Bub, D. N., Gauthier, I. et al., 'Perceptual expertise effects are not all or none: spatially limited perceptual expertise for faces in a case of prosopagnosia', *Journal of Cognitive Neuroscience*, 2006, *18(1)*, pp. 48–63

Bultitude, J. H. & Aimola Davies, A. M., 'Putting attention on the line: investigating the activationorientation hypothesis of pseudoneglect', *Neuropsychologia*, 2006, *44(10)*, pp. 1849–58

Burckhardt, J., *The Civilization of the Renaissance in Italy*, trans. S. G. C. Middlemore, Phaidon, London, 1965 [1878]

Burgess, C. & Lund, K., 'Modeling cerebral asymmetries in high-dimensional space', in Beeman, M. & Chiarello, C. (eds.), *Right Hemisphere Language Comprehension: Perspectives from Cognitive Neuroscience*, Lawrence Erlbaum, Mahwah NJ, 1998, pp. 215–44

Burgund, E. D. & Marsolek, C. J., 'Viewpoint-invariant and viewpoint-dependent object recognition in dissociable neural subsystems', *Psychonomic Bulletin & Review*, 2000, *7(3)*, pp. 480–89

Burke, E., *Select Works*, ed. E. J. Payne, Clarendon Press, Oxford, 1881

——, *A Philosophical Enquiry into the Origin of Our Ideas of the Sublime and Beautiful*, Oxford University Press, Oxford, 1990 [1757]

Burkitt, J. A., Saucier, D. M., Thomas, N. A. et al., 'When advertising turns "cheeky"!', *Laterality*, 2006, *11(3)*, pp. 277–86

Burling, R., 'Primate calls, human language, and nonverbal communication', *Current Anthropology*, 1993, *34(1)*, pp. 25–53

Burnet, J., *Early Greek Philosophy*, A. & C. Black, London & Edinburgh, 1892.

Burt, D. M. & Perrett, D. I., 'Perceptual asymmetries in judgements of facial attractiveness, age, gender, speech and expression', *Neuropsychologia*, 1997, *35(5)*, pp. 685–93

Butler, J., *Fifteen Sermons Preached at the Rolls Chapel*, 2nd edn., 'To which is added a PREFACE', J. & J. Knapton, London, 1729

Butler, S., Gilchrist, I. D., Burt, D. M. et al., 'Are the perceptual biases found in chimeric face processing reflected in eye-movement patterns?', *Neuropsychologia*, 2005, *43(1)*, pp. 52–9

Butler, S. H. & Harvey, M., 'Does inversion abolish the left chimeric face processing advantage?', *NeuroReport*, 2005, *16(18)*, pp. 1991–3

Butterworth, B., Reeve, R., Reynolds, F. et al., 'Numerical thought with and without words: evidence from indigenous Australian children', *Proceedings of the National Academy of Sciences of the USA*, 2008, *105(35)*, pp. 13179–84

Byrne, R. W., 'The smart gorilla's recipe book', *Natural History*, 1995, *104(10)*, pp. 12–15

Byrne, R. W. & Byrne, J. M., 'Hand preferences in the skilled gathering tasks of mountain gorillas (*Gorilla g. berengei*)', *Cortex*, 1991, *27(4)*, pp. 521–46

——, 'Complex leaf-gathering skills of mountain gorillas (*Gorilla g. berengei*): variability and standardization', *American Journal of Primatology*, 1993, *31(4)*, pp. 241–61

Byrne, R. W. & Whiten, A., 'Cognitive evolution in primates: evidence from tactical deception', *Man*, 1992, *27(3)*, pp. 609–27

Cacioppo, J. T., Berntson, G. G., Lorig, T. S. et al., 'Just because you're imaging the brain doesn't mean you can stop using your head: a primer and set of first principles', *Journal of Personality and Social Psychology*, 2003, *85(4)*, pp. 650–61

Cacioppo, J. T., Petty, R. E. & Quintanar, L. R., 'Individual differences in relative hemispheric alpha abundance and cognitive responses to persuasive communications', 1982, *43(3)*, pp. 623–36

Cain, D. P. & Wada, J. A., 'An anatomical asymmetry in the baboon brain', *Brain, Behavior and Evolution*, 1979, *16(3)*, pp. 222–6

Caldara, R., Schyns, P., Mayer, E. et al., 'Does prosopagnosia take the eyes out of face representations? Evidence for a defect in representing diagnostic facial information following brain damage', *Journal of Cognitive Neuroscience*, 2005, *17(10)*, pp. 1652–66

Caligiuri, M. P., Brown, G. G., Meloy, M. J. et al., 'A functional magnetic resonance imaging study of cortical asymmetry in bipolar disorder', *Bipolar Disorders*, 2004, *6(3)*, pp. 183–96

Call, J., Bräuer, J., Kaminski, J. et al., 'Domestic dogs (*Canis familiaris*) are sensitive to the attentional state of humans', *Journal of Comparative Psychology*, 2003, *117(3)*, pp. 257–63

Call, J. & Tomasello, M., 'Does the chimpanzee have a theory of mind? 30 years later', *Trends in Cognitive Sciences*, 2008, *2(5)*, pp. 187–92

Calvin, W. H., *The Cerebral Symphony: Seashore Reflections on the Structure of Consciousness*, Bantam, New York, 1989

Camprodon, J. A., Martínez-Raga, J., Alonso-Alonso, M. et al., 'One session of high frequency repetitive transcranial magnetic stimulation (rTMS) to the right prefrontal cortex transiently reduces cocaine craving', *Drug and Alcohol Dependence*, 2007, *86(1)*, pp. 91–4

Cannon, W., *The Way of an Investigator*, Hafner, New York, 1965

Cantalupo, C. & Hopkins, W. D., 'Asymmetric Broca's area in great apes', *Nature*, 2001, *414(6863)*, p. 505

Capgras, J. & Reboul-Lachaux, J., 'L'illusion des « sosies » dans un délire systématisé chronique', *Bulletin de la Société Clinique de Médicine Mentale*, 1923, *11*, pp. 6–16

Cappa, S. F., Perani, D., Schnur, T. et al., 'The effects of semantic category and knowledge type on lexicalsemantic access: a PET study', *NeuroImage*, 1998, *8(4)*, pp. 350–59

Cappelletti, M., Butterworth, B. & Kopelman, M., 'Spared numerical abilities in a case of semantic dementia', *Neuropsychologia*, 2001, *39(11)*, pp. 1224–39

Caramazza, A., 'The brain's dictionary', *Nature*, 1996, *380(6574)*, pp. 485–6

Caramazza, A. & Shelton, J. R., 'Domain-specific knowledge systems in the brain: the animate-inanimate distinction', *Journal of Cognitive Neuroscience*, 1998, *10(1)*, pp. 1–34

Carly, P. G., Golding, S. J. J. & Hall, B. J. D., 'Interrelationships among auditory and visual cognitive tasks: an event-related potential (ERP) study', *Intelligence*, 1995, *2(3)*, pp. 297–327

Carlyle, T., *Life of Sterling*, in the *Centenary Edition of the Works of Carlyle*, Chapman and Hall, London, 1897–99, vol. 11

——, 'The hero as poet', in Nichol Smith, D. (ed.), *Shakespeare Criticism: a Selection*, Oxford University Press, Oxford, 1935

Carmon, A. & Nachshon, I., 'Effects of unilateral brain damage on the perception of temporal order', *Cortex*, 1971, *7(4)*, pp. 411–18

——, 'Ear asymmetry in perception of emotional nonverbal stimuli', *Acta Psychologica (Amsterdam)*, 1973, *37(6)*, pp. 351–7

Carr, L., Iacoboni, M., Dubeau, M.-C. et al., 'Neural mechanisms of empathy in humans: a relay from neural systems for imitation to limbic areas', *Proceedings of the National Academy of Sciences of the USA*, 2003, *100(9)*, pp. 5497–502

Carran, M. A., Kohler, C. G., O'Connor, M. J. et al., 'Mania following temporal lobectomy', *Neurology*, 2003, *61(6)*, pp. 770–74

Carter, C. S., Macdonald, A. M., Botvinick, M. et al., 'Parsing executive processes: strategic vs. evaluative functions of the anterior cingulate cortex', *Proceedings of the National Academy of Sciences of the USA*, 2000, *97(4)*, pp. 1944–8

Cassileth, B. R., Vickers, A. J. & Magill, L. A., 'Music therapy for mood disturbance during hospitalization for autologous stem cell transplantation: a randomized controlled trial', *Cancer*, 2003, *98(12)*, pp. 2723–9

Cassirer, E., *An Essay on Man*, Yale University Press, New Haven CT, 1948

——, *The Problem of Knowledge*, trans. W. H. Woglom & C. W. Hendel, Yale University Press, New Haven CT, 1950

Castle, T., *The Female Thermometer: Eighteenth-Century Culture and the Invention of the Uncanny*, Oxford University Press, Oxford, 1995

Cavanna, A. E. & Trimble, M. R., 'The precuneus: a review of its functional anatomy and behavioural correlates', *Brain*, 2006, *129(3)*, pp. 564–83

Cepeda, M. S., Carr, D. B., Lau, J. et al., 'Music for pain relief ', *Cochrane Database Systematic Reviews*, 2006, issue 2. Art. No.: CD004843

Cerella, J., 'The pigeon's analysis of pictures', *Pattern Recognition*, 1980, *12(1)*, pp. 1–6

Chamfort, N., *Maximes et Pensées, Caractères et Anecdotes*, ed. A. van Bever, Crès et Cie., Paris, 1923 [1795]

Chaminade, T. & Decety, J., 'Leader or follower? Involvement of the inferior parietal lobule in agency', *NeuroReport*, 2002, *13(15)*, pp. 1975–8

Changeux, J.-P., 'Learning and selection in the nervous system', in de Kerckhove, D. & Lumsden, C. J (eds.), *The Alphabet and the Brain: the Lateralization of Writing*, Springer-Verlag, Berlin, 1988, pp. 43–50

Chao, L. L. & Martin, A., 'Cortical regions associated with perceiving, naming, and knowing about colors', *Journal of Cognitive Neuroscience*, 1999, *11(1)*, pp. 25–35

Chapanis, L., 'Language deficits and cross-modal sensory perception', in Segalowitz, S. J. & Gruber, F. A. (eds.), *Language Development and Neurological Theory*, Academic Press, New York, 1977, pp. 107–20

Charman, T., Swettenham, J., Baron-Cohen, S. et al., 'Infants with autism: an investigation of empathy, pretend play, joint attention, and imitation', *Developmental Psychology*, 1997, *33(5)*, pp. 781–9

Chartrand, T. L. & Bargh, J. A., 'The chameleon effect: the perception-behavior link and social interaction', *Journal of Personality and Social Psychology*, 1999, *76(6)*, pp. 893–910

Chase, A. R., 'Music discriminations by carp (*Cyprinus carpio*)', *Animal Learning & Behavior*, 2001, *29(4)*, pp. 336–53

Chee, M. W., Tan, E. W. & Thiel, T., 'Mandarin and English single word processing studied with functional magnetic resonance imaging', *Journal of Neuroscience*, 1999, *19(8)*, pp. 3050–68

Chee, M. W., Weekes, B., Lee, K. M. et al., 'Overlap and dissociation of semantic processing of Chinese characters, English words, and pictures: evidence from fMRI', *NeuroImage*, 2000, *12(4)*, pp. 392–403

Cheney, D. L. & Seyfarth, R. M., *How Monkeys See the World: Inside the Mind of Another Species*, University of Chicago Press, Chicago, 1990

Chernigovskaya, T. V. & Deglin, V. L., 'Brain functional asymmetry and neural organization of linguistic competence', *Brain and Language*, 1986, *29(1)*, pp. 141–53

Cheverud, J. M., Falk, D., Hildebolt, C. et al., 'Heritability and association of cortical petalias in rhesus macaques *Macaca mulatta*', *Brain, Behavior and Evolution*, 1990, *35(6)*, pp. 368–72

Cheverud, J. M., Falk, D., Vannier, M. et al., 'Heritability of brain size and surface features in rhesus macaques *Macaca mulatta*', *Journal of Heredity*, 1990, *81(1)*, pp. 51–7

Chi, J. G., Dooling, E. C. & Gilles, F. H., 'Gyral development of the human brain', *Annals of Neurology*, 1977a, *1(1)*, pp. 86–93

——, 'Left-right asymmetries of the temporal speech areas of the human fetus', *Archives of Neurology*, 1977b, *34(6)*, pp. 346–8

Chiarello, C., 'Semantic priming in the intact brain: separate roles for the right and left hemispheres?', in Chiarello, C. (ed.), *Right Hemisphere Contributions to Lexical Semantics*, Springer-Verlag, Heidelberg, 1988

——, 'Interpretation of word meanings by the cerebral hemispheres: one is not enough', in Schwanenflugel, P. J. (ed.), *The Psychology of Word Meanings*, Lawrence Erlbaum, Hillsdale NJ, 1991, pp. 251–78

——, 'On codes of meaning and the meaning of codes: semantic access and retrieval within and between hemispheres', in Beeman, M. & Chiarello, C. (eds.), *Right Hemisphere Language Comprehension: Perspectives from Cognitive Neuroscience*, Lawrence Erlbaum, Mahwah NJ, 1998, pp. 141–60

Chiarello, C., Burgess, C., Richards, L. et al., 'Semantic and associative priming in the cerebral hemispheres: some words do, some words don't . . . sometimes, some places', *Brain and Language*, 1990, *38(1)*, pp. 75–104

Chiarello, C. & Maxfield, L., 'Varieties of interhemispheric inhibition, or how to keep a good hemisphere down', *Brain and Cognition*, 1996, *30(1)*, pp. 81–108

Chiarello, C., Senehi, J. & Nuding, S., 'Semantic priming with abstract and concrete words: differential asymmetry may be post-lexical', *Brain and Language*, 1987, *31(1)*, pp. 43–60

Chicoine, A. J., Proteau, L. & Lassonde, M., 'Absence of interhemispheric transfer of unilateral visuomotor learning in young children and individuals with agenesis of the corpus callosum', *Developmental Neuropsychology*, 2000, *18(1)*, pp. 73–94

Chiron, C., Jambaque, I., Nabbout, R. et al., 'The right brain hemisphere is dominant in human infants', *Brain*, 1997, *120(6)*, pp. 1057–65

Chiu, H. D. & Damasio, A. R., 'Human cerebral asymmetries evaluated by computed tomography', *Journal of Neurology, Neurosurgery, & Psychiatry*, 1980, *43(10)*, pp. 873–8

Chiu, L., 'A cross-cultural comparison of cognitive styles in Chinese and American children', *International Journal of Psychology*, 1972, *7(4)*, pp. 235–42

Chomsky, N. A., *Syntactic Structures*, Mouton, The Hague, 1957

——, *Language and Problems of Knowledge*, Massachusetts Institute of Technology Press, Cambridge MA, 1988

Christman, S., *Cerebral Asymmetries in Sensory and Perceptual Processing*, Elsevier, Amsterdam, 1997

Christoph, B. & Noll, H.-H., 'Subjective well-being in the European Union during the 90s', *Social Indicators Research*, 2003, *64*, pp. 521–46

Chuang Tzu: The Basic Writings, trans. Burton Watson, Columbia University Press, New York, 1964

Churchland, P. S., *Neurophilosophy: Towards a Unified Science of the Mind-Brain*, Massachusetts Institute of Technology Press, Cambridge MA, 1986

Çiçek, M., Gitelman, D., Hurley, R. S. et al., 'Anatomical physiology of spatial extinction', *Cerebral Cortex*, 2007, *17(12)*, pp. 2892–8

Cicero, B. A., Borod, J. C., Santschi, C. et al., 'Emotional versus nonemotional lexical perception in patients with right and left brain damage', *Neuropsychiatry, Neuropsychology and Behavioral Neurology*, 1999, *12(4)*, pp. 255–64

Cicone, M., Wapner, W. & Gardner, H., 'Sensitivity to emotional expressions and situations in organic patients', *Cortex*, 1980, *16(1)*, pp. 145–8

Cimino, C. R., Verfaellie, M., Bowers, D. et al., 'Autobiographical memory: influence of right hemisphere damage on emotionality and specificity', *Brain and Cognition*, 1991, *15(1)*, pp. 106–18

Cioni, G., Bartalena, E. & Boldrini, A., 'Callosal agenesis: postnatal sonographic findings', in Lassonde, M. & Jeeves, M. A. (eds.), *Callosal Agenesis: a Natural Split Brain?*, Plenum Press, New York, 1994, pp. 69–77

Clapp, W., Kirk, I. J., Hausmann, M., 'Effects of memory load on hemispheric asymmetries of colour memory', *Laterality*, 2007, *12(2)*, pp. 139–53

Clark, A. & Karmiloff-Smith, A., 'The cognizer's innards: a psychological and philosophical perspective on the development of thought', *Mind & Language*, 1993, *8(4)*, pp. 487–519

Clark, C., Kopala, L., Hurwitz, T. et al., 'Regional metabolism in microsmic patients with schizophrenia', *Canadian Journal of Psychiatry*, 1991, *36(9)*, pp. 645–50

Clark, K., *Landscape Into Art*, John Murray, London, 1949

Clark, L., Manes, F., Antoun, N. et al., 'The contributions of lesion laterality and lesion volume to decisionmaking impairment following frontal lobe damage', *Neuropsychologia*, 2003, *41(11)*, pp. 1474–83

Clarke, E. & Dewhurst, K., *An Illustrated History of Brain Function*, University of California Press, Berkeley CA, 1972

Clarke, M., *Flesh and Spirit in the Songs of Homer*, Oxford University Press, Oxford, 1999

Cohen, L., Dehaene, S., Chochon, F. et al., 'Language and calculation within the parietal lobe: a combined cognitive, anatomical and fMRI study', *Neuropsychologia*, 2000, *38(10)*, pp. 1426–40

528 ◆ BIBLIOGRAPHY

Cole, P.M., Barrett, K. C. & Zahn-Waxler, C., 'Emotion displays in two-year-olds during mishaps', Child Development, 1992, 63(2), pp. 314–24

Coleridge, S. T., Collected Letters of Samuel Taylor Coleridge, ed. E. L. Griggs, 6 vols., Clarendon Press, Oxford, 1956–71

——, Biographia Literaria, ed. G. Watson, Dent, London, 1965 [1817]

Coles, P. R., 'Profile orientation and social distance in portrait painting', Perception, 1974, 3(3), pp. 303–8

Colvin, S., John Keats: His Life and Poetry, His Friends, Critics, and After-Fame, Macmillan, London, 1917

Conesa, J., Brunold-Conesa, C. & Miron, M., 'Incidence of the half-left profile pose in single-subject portraits', Perceptual and Motor Skills, 1995, 81(3, pt. 1), pp. 920–22

Coney, J. & Bruce, C., 'Hemispheric processes in the perception of art', Empirical Studies of the Arts, 2004, 22, pp. 181–200

Coney, J. & Evans, K. D., 'Hemispheric asymmetries in the resolution of lexical ambiguity', Neuropsychologia, 2000, 38(3), pp. 272–82

Conrad, P., The Victorian Treasure-House, Collins, London, 1973

Constable, J., John Constable's Discourses, ed. R. B. Beckett, Suffolk Records Society, Ipswich, UK, 1970

Conti, F. & Manzoni, T., 'The neurotransmitters and postsynaptic actions of callosally projecting neurons', Behavioural Brain Research, 1994, 64(1–2), pp. 37–53

Contreras, D. & Llinas, R., 'Voltage-sensitive dye imaging of neocortical spatiotemporal dynamics to afferent activation frequency', Journal of Neuroscience, 2001, 21(23), pp. 9403–13

Conway, M. A., Pleydell-Pearce, C. W., Whitecross, S. E. et al., 'Neurophysiological correlates of memory for experienced and imagined events', Neuropsychologia, 2003, 41(3), pp. 334–40

Cook, N. D., 'Homotopic callosal inhibition', Brain and Language, 1984, 23(1), pp. 116–25

——, The Brain Code: Mechanisms of Information Transfer and the Role of the Corpus Callosum, Methuen, London, 1986

Cooper, R. P. & Aslin, R. N., 'Preference for infant-directed speech in the first month after birth', Child Development, 1990, 61(5), pp. 1584–95

Corballis, M. C., 'On the evolution of language and generativity', Cognition, 1992, 44(3), pp. 197–226

——, 'Hemispheric interactions in temporal judgments about spatially separated stimuli', Neuropsychology, 1996, 10(1), pp. 42–50

——, 'Sperry and the age of Aquarius: science, values and the split brain', Neuropsychologia, 1998, 36(10), pp. 1083–7

——, From Hand to Mouth: The Origins of Language, Princeton University Press, Princeton NJ, 2002a ——, 'Laterality and human speciation', in The Speciation of Modern Homo Sapiens, Proceedings of the British Academy, vol. 106, Oxford University Press, Oxford, 2002b, pp. 137–52

——, 'From mouth to hand: gesture, speech, and the evolution of right-handedness', Behavioral and Brain Sciences, 2003, 26(2), pp. 199–260

Corballis, M. C., Boyd, L., Schulze, A. et al., 'Role of the commissures in interhemispheric temporal judgments', Neuropsychology, 1998, 12(4), pp. 519–25

Corbetta, M., Miezin, F. M., Dobmeyer, S. et al., 'Selective and divided attention during visual discriminations of shape, color, and speed: functional anatomy by positron emission tomography', Journal of Neuroscience, 1991, 11(8), pp. 2383–402

Corbetta, M. & Shulman, G. L., 'Control of goal-directed and stimulus-driven attention in the brain', Nature Reviews Neuroscience, 2002, 3(3), pp. 201–15

Corbin, A., The Foul and the Fragrant: Odour and the French Social Imagination, Harvard University Press, Cambridge, MA, 1988 [Le miasme et la jonquille: l'odorat et l'imaginaire social aux XVIIIe et XIXe siècles 1982]

Coslett, H. B., Bowers, D. & Heilman, K. M., 'Reduction in cerebral activation after right hemisphere stroke', Neurology, 1987, 37(6), pp. 957–62

Coslett, H. B. & Heilman, K. M., 'Male sexual function: impairment after right hemisphere stroke', Archives of Neurology, 1986, 43(10), pp. 1036–9

——, 'Hemihypokinesia after right hemisphere stroke', Brain and Cognition, 1989, 9(2), pp. 267–78

Cotton, B., Tzeng, O. J. & Hardyck, C., 'Role of cerebral hemispheric processing in the visual half-field stimulus-response compatibility effect', Journal of Experimental Psychology: Human Perception and Performance, 1980, 6(1), pp. 13–23

Coulson, S., Semantic Leaps: Frame-Shifting and Conceptual Blending in Meaning Construction, Cambridge University Press, Cambridge, UK, 2001

Coulson, S. & Wu, Y. C., 'Right hemisphere activation of joke-related information: an event-related brain potential study', Journal of Cognitive Neuroscience, 2005, 17(3), pp. 494–506

Couppis, M. H. & Kennedy, C. H., 'The rewarding effect of aggression is reduced by nucleus accumbens dopamine receptor antagonism in mice', Psychopharmacology, 2008, 197(3), pp. 449–56

Courbon, P. & Fail, G., 'Syndrome d''illusion de Frégoli'' et schizophrénie', Bulletin de la Société Clinique de Médecine Mentale, 1927, 15, pp. 121–5

Cowin, E. L. & Hellige, J. B., 'Categorical versus coordinate spatial processing: effects of blurring and hemispheric asymmetry', Journal of Cognitive Neuroscience, 1994, 6(2), pp. 156–64

Craig, A. D., 'How do you feel? Interoception: the sense of the physiological condition of the body', Nature Reviews Neuroscience, 2002, 3(8), pp. 655–66

Craik, F. I. M., Moroz, T. M., Moscovitch, M. et al., 'In search of the self: a positron emission tomography study', Psychological Science, 1999, 10(1), pp. 26–34

Crichton-Browne, J., 'On the weight of the brain and its component parts in the insane', Brain, 1880, 2, pp. 42–67

Critchley, H. D., Daly, E. M., Bullmore, E. T. et al., 'The functional neuroanatomy of social behaviour: changes in cerebral blood flow when people with autistic disorder process facial expressions', Brain, 2000, 123(11), pp. 2203–12

Croce, B., Aesthetic as Scienze of Expression and General Linguistic, trans. D. Ainslie, Macmillan, London, 1922 [Estetica come scienza dell' espressione e linguistica generale, 1902]

Cross-National Collaborative Group, 'The changing rate of major depression. Cross-national comparisons', *Journal of the American Medical Association*, 1992, *268(21)*, pp. 3098–3105

Crow, T. J., 'March 27, 1827 and what happened later – the impact of psychiatry on evolutionary theory', *Progress in Neuro-Psychopharmacology and Biological Psychiatry*, 2006, *30(5)*, pp. 785–96

Crow, T. J., Crow L. R., Done D. J. et al., 'Relative hand skill predicts academic ability: global deficits at the point of hemispheric indecision', *Neuropsychologia*, 1998, *36(12)*, pp. 1275–82

Crowell, D. H., Jones, R. H., Kapuniai, L. E. et al., 'Unilateral cortical activity in newborn humans: an early index of cerebral dominance?', *Science*, 1973, *180(82)*, pp. 205–8

Csermely, D., 'Lateralisation in birds of prey: adaptive and phylogenetic considerations', *Behavioural Processes*, 2004, *67(3)*, pp. 511–20

Cummings, J. L., 'Neuropsychiatric manifestations of right hemisphere lesions', *Brain and Language*, 1997, *57(1)*, pp. 22–37

Cummings, J. L. & Mendez, M. F., 'Secondary mania with focal cerebrovascular lesions', *American Journal of Psychiatry*, 1984, *141(9)*, pp. 1084–7

Curran, T., Schacter, D. L., Norman, K. A. et al., 'False recognition after a right frontal lobe infarction: memory for general and specific information', *Neuropsychologia*, 1997, *35(7)*, pp. 1035–49

Cutting, J., 'Study of anosognosia', *Journal of Neurology, Neurosurgery, & Psychiatry*, 1978, *41(6)*, pp. 548–55

——, *The Right Cerebral Hemisphere and Psychiatric Disorders*, Oxford University Press, Oxford, 1990

——, *Principles of Psychopathology*, Oxford University Press, Oxford, 1997

——, *Psychopathology and Modern Philosophy*, Forest Publishing, Scaynes Hill, UK, 1999

——, 'Scheler, phenomenology and psychopathology', *Philosophy, Psychiatry & Psychology*, 2009, *16(2)*

d'Alfonso, A. A., van Honk, J., Hermans, E. et al., 'Laterality effects in selective attention to threat after repetitive transcranial magnetic stimulation at the prefrontal cortex in female subjects', *Neuroscience Letters*, 2000, *280(3)*, pp. 195–8

d'Aquili, E. G. & Newberg, A. B., 'Religious and mystical states: a neurophysiological model', *Zygon: Journal of Religion & Science*, 1993, *28(2)*, pp. 177–99

d'Aquili, E. & Newberg, A., *The Mystical Mind: Probing the Biology of Religion*, Fortress Press, Minneapolis MN, 1999

d'Esposito, M., Detre, J. A., Alsop, D. C. et al., 'The neural basis of the central executive system of working memory', *Nature*, 1995, *378(6554)*, pp. 279–81

Dagenbach, D., Harris, L. J. & Fitzgerald, H. E., 'A longitudinal study of lateral biases in parents' cradling and holding of infants', *Infant Mental Health*, 1988, *9(3)*, pp. 218–34

Dagge, M. & Hartje, W., 'Influence of contextual complexity on the processing of cartoons by patients with unilateral lesions', *Cortex*, 1985, *21(4)*, pp. 607–16

Damasio, A. R., *Descartes' Error: Emotion, Reason and the Human Brain*, Grosset/Putnam, New York, 1994a

——, 'Descartes' error and the future of human life', *Scientific American*, 1994b, *271(4)*, p. 144

Damasio, A. R., Tranel, D. & Damasio, H., 'Individuals with sociopathic behavior caused by frontal damage fail to respond autonomically to social stimuli', *Behavioural Brain Research*, 1990, *41(2)*, pp. 81–94

Damasio, H., *Human Brain Anatomy in Computerized Images*, Oxford University Press, Oxford, 2nd edn., 2005

Damasio, H., Grabowski, T. J., Tranel, D. et al., 'A neural basis for lexical retrieval', *Nature*, 1996, *380(6574)*, pp. 499–505 (erratum appears in *Nature*, *381(6595)*, p. 810)

Danckert, J., Ferber, S., Pun, C. et al., 'Neglected time: impaired temporal perception of multisecond intervals in unilateral neglect', *Journal of Cognitive Neuroscience*, 2007, *19(10)*, pp. 1706–20

Dandy, W. E., 'Changes in our conceptions of localization of certain functions in the brain', *American Journal of Physiology*, 1930, *93*, pp. 643–7

Dane, S., Ersöz, M., Gümüstekin, K. et al., 'Handedness differences in widths of right and left craniofacial regions in healthy young adults', *Perceptual and Motor Skills*, 2004, *98(2)*, pp. 1261–4

Dane, S., Gümüstekin, K., Polat, P. et al., 'Relations among hand preference, craniofacial asymmetry, and ear advantage in young subjects', *Perceptual and Motor Skills*, 2002, *95(2)*, pp. 416–22

Dapretto, M., Davies, M. S., Pfeifer, J. H. et al., 'Understanding emotions in others: mirror neuron dysfunction in children with autism spectrum disorders', *Nature Neuroscience*, 2006, *9(1)*, pp. 28–30

David, A. S., 'Tachistoscopic tests of colour naming and matching in schizophrenia: evidence for posterior callosal dysfunction?', *Psychological Medicine*, 1987, *17(3)*, pp. 621–30

——, 'The clinical importance of insight: an overview', in Amador, X. & David, A. (eds.), *Insight and Psychosis*, 2nd edn., Oxford University Press, Oxford, 2004, pp. 359–92

Davidoff, J., 'Hemispheric sensitivity differences in the perception of colour', *Quarterly Journal of Experimental Psychology*, 1976, *28(3)*, pp. 387–94

Davidson, R. J., 'Affect, cognition and hemispheric specialisation', in Izard, C. E., Kagan, J. & Zajonc, R. B. (eds.), *Emotions, Cognition, and Behavior*, Cambridge University Press, Cambridge, UK, 1984, pp. 320–65

——, 'Cerebral asymmetry affective style and psychopathology', in Kinsbourne, M. (ed.), *Cerebral Hemisphere Function in Depression*, American Psychiatric Press, Washington DC, 1988, pp. 1–22

——, 'Anterior cerebral asymmetry and the nature of emotion', *Brain and Cognition*, 1992, *20(1)*, pp. 125–51

——, 'Parsing affective space: perspectives from neuropsychology and psychophysiology', *Neuropsychology*, 1993, *7(4)*, pp. 464–75

Davidson, R. J., Ekman, P., Saron, C. D. et al., 'Approach-withdrawal and cerebral asymmetry: emotional expression and brain physiology. I', *Journal of Personality and Social Psychology*, 1990, *58(2)*, pp. 330–41

Davidson, R. J. & Fox, N. A., 'Frontal brain asymmetry predicts infants' response to maternal separation', *Journal of Abnormal Psychology*, 1989, *98(2)*, pp. 127–31

Davidson, R. J. & Hugdahl, K. (eds.), *Brain Asymmetry*, Massachusetts Institute of Technology Press, Cambridge MA, 1995

——, *The Asymmetrical Brain*, Massachusetts Institute of Technology Press, Cambridge MA, 2003

Davidson, R. J., Mednick, D., Moss, E. et al., 'Ratings of emotion in faces are influenced by the visual field to which stimuli are presented', *Brain and Cognition*, 1987, *6(4)*, pp. 403–11

Davies, S., 'Philosophical perspectives on music's expressiveness', in Juslin, P. N. & Sloboda, J. A. (eds.), *Music and Emotion: Theory and Research*, Oxford University Press, Oxford, 2001, pp. 23–44

Dawkins, R., *The Selfish Gene*, Oxford University Press, Oxford, 1976

Dax, G., 'Observations tendant à prouver la coïncidence constante des dérangements de la parole avec une lésion de l'hémisphère gauche du cerveau', *Comptes rendus hebdomadaires des séances de l'Académie des sciences*, 1863, *61*, p. 534

Dax, M., 'Lésions de la moitié gauche de l'encéphale coïncidant avec l'oubli des signes de la pensée (lu à Montpellier en 1836)', *Gazette hebdomadaire de médecine et de chirurgie*, 2me série, 1865, *2*, pp. 259–62

de Bonis, M., Dellatolas, G. & Rondot, P., 'Mood disorders in left and right brain-damaged patients: comparison between ratings and self-ratings on the same adjective mood scale. Some methodological problems', *Psychopathology*, 1985, *18(5–6)*, pp. 286–92

de Gelder, B. & Rouw, R., 'Paradoxical configuration effects for faces and objects in prosopagnosia', *Neuropsychologia*, 2000, *38(9)*, pp. 1271–9

de Kerckhove, D., 'Critical brain processes involved in deciphering the Greek alphabet', in de Kerckhove, D. & Lumsden, C. J. (eds.), *The Alphabet and the Brain: the Lateralization of Writing*, Springer-Verlag, Berlin, 1988a, pp. 401–21

——, 'Logical principles underlying the layout of Greek orthography', in de Kerckhove, D. & Lumsden, C. J. (eds.), *The Alphabet and the Brain: the Lateralization of Writing*, Springer-Verlag, Berlin, 1988b, pp. 153–72

de Kerckhove, D. & Lumsden, C. J. (eds.), *The Alphabet and the Brain: the Lateralization of Writing*, Springer-Verlag, Berlin, 1988

de la Fuente, J.-M., Goldman, S., Stanus, E. et al., 'Brain glucose metabolism in borderline personality disorder', *Journal of Psychiatric Research*, 1997, *31(5)*, pp. 531–41

de Quervain, D. J.-F., Fischbacher, U., Treyer, V. et al., 'The neural basis of altruistic punishment', *Science*, 2004, *305(5688)*, pp. 1254–8

de Quincey, T., *Literary Reminiscences*, Ticknor, Reed & Fields, Boston MA, 1851

de Renzi, E., 'Oculomotor disturbances in hemispheric disease', in Johnston, C. W. & Pirozzolo, F. J. (eds.), *Neuropsychology of Eye Movements*, Lawrence Erlbaum, Hillsdale NJ, 1988, pp. 177–91

de Renzi, E., Bonacini, M. G. & Faglioni, P., 'Right posterior brain-damaged patients are poor at assessing the age of a face', *Neuropsychologia*, 1989, *27(6)*, pp. 839–48

de Renzi, E. & Faglioni, P., 'The comparative efficiency of intelligence and vigilance tests in detecting hemispheric cerebral damage', *Cortex*, 1965, *1*, pp. 410–33

de Renzi, E., Gentilini, M., Faglioni, P. et al., 'Attentional shift towards the rightmost stimuli in patients with left visual neglect', *Cortex*, 1989, *25(2)*, pp. 231–7

de Renzi, E., Perani, D., Carlesimo, G. A. et al., 'Prosopagnosia can be associated with damage confined to the right hemisphere – an MRI and PET study and a review of the literature', *Neuropsychologia*, 1994, *32(8)*, pp. 893–902

de Renzi, E. & Spinnler, H., 'Facial recognition in brain-damaged patients. An experimental approach', *Neurology*, 1966, *16(2)*, pp. 145–52

de Schonen, S., Gil de Diaz, M. & Mathivet, E., 'Hemispheric asymmetry in face processing in infancy', in Ellis, H. D., Jeeves, M. A., Newcombe, F. et al. (eds.), *Aspects of Face Processing*, Nijhoff, Dordrecht, Netherlands, 1986, pp. 199–209

de Tocqueville, A., *Democracy in America*, trans. Reeve, H. & Plaag, E. W., Barnes & Noble, New York, 2003 [*De la démocratie en Amérique* 1835–40]

de Waal, F., *Good-Natured: The Origins of Right and Wrong in Humans and Other Animals*, Harvard University Press, Cambridge MA, 1996

——, *Chimpanzee Politics: Power and Sex among Apes*, Johns Hopkins University Press, Baltimore MD, 1998

——, *Our Inner Ape: A Leading Primatologist Explains Why We Are Who We Are*, Riverhead, New York, 2006a

——, *Primates and Philosophers: How Morality Evolved*, Princeton University Press, Princeton NJ, 2006b

Debener, S., Beauducel, A., Nessler, D. et al., 'Is resting anterior EEG alpha asymmetry a trait marker for depression?', *Neuropsychobiology*, 2000, *41(1)*, pp. 31–7

DeCasper, A. J. & Fifer, W. P., 'Of human bonding: newborns prefer their mothers' voices', *Science*, 1980, *208(4448)*, pp. 1174–6

DeCasper, A. J. & Spence, M. J., 'Prenatal maternal speech influences newborns' perception of speech sounds', *Infant Behavior and Development*, 1986, *9(2)*, pp. 133–50

Decety, J. & Chaminade, T., 'When the self represents the other: a new cognitive neuroscience view on psychological identification', *Consciousness and Cognition*, 2003, *12(4)*, pp. 577–96

Decety, J., Chaminade, T., Grezes, J. et al., 'A PET exploration of the neural mechanisms involved in reciprocal imitation', *NeuroImage*, 2002, *15(1)*, pp. 265–72

Decety, J. & Sommerville, J. A., 'Shared representations between self and other: a social cognitive neuroscience view', *Trends in Cognitive Sciences*, 2003, *7(12)*, pp. 527–33

Dee, H. L. & van Allen, M. W., 'Speed of decision-making processes in patients with unilateral cerebral disease', *Archives of Neurology*, 1973, *28(3)*, pp. 163–6

Deglin, V. L., 'Our split brain', *Unesco Courier*, 1976, *29(1)*, pp. 4–31

Deglin, V. L. & Kinsbourne, M., 'Divergent thinking styles of the hemispheres: how syllogisms are solved during transitory hemisphere suppression', *Brain and Cognition*, 1996, *31(3)*, pp. 285–307

Degreef, G., Lantos, G., Bogerts, B. et al., 'Abnormalities of the septum pellucidum on MR scans in first episode schizophrenic patients', *American Journal of Neuroradiology*, 1992, *13(3)*, pp. 835–40

Dehaene, S., *The Number Sense: How the Mind Creates Mathematics*, Oxford University Press, Oxford, 1997, pp. 177–85

Dehaene, S. & Cohen, L., 'Cerebral pathways for calculation: double dissociation between rote verbal and quantitative knowledge of arithmetic', *Cortex*, 1997, *33(2)*, pp. 219–50

Dehaene, S., Piazza, M., Pinel, P. et al., 'Three parietal circuits for number processing', *Cognitive Neuropsychology*, 2003, *20(3-6)*, pp. 487-506

Delacroix, E., *Journal de Eugène Delacroix*, ed. P. Flat & R. Piot, Plon, Nourrit et Cie., Paris, 1893

——, *Œuvres littéraires*, ed. É. Faure, Crès et Cie., Paris, 1923

Deldin, P. J., Keller, J., Gergen, J. A. et al., 'Cognitive bias and emotion in neuropsychological models of depression', *Cognition and Emotion*, 2001, *15(6)*, pp. 787-802

Delis, D. C., Kiefner, M. G. & Fridlund, A. J., 'Visuospatial dysfunction following unilateral brain damage: dissociations in hierarchical and hemispatial analysis', *Journal of Clinical and Experimental Neuropsychology*, 1988, *10(4)*, pp. 421-31

Delis, D. C., Robertson, L. C. & Efron, R., 'Hemispheric specialisation of memory for visual hierarchical stimuli', *Neuropsychologia*, 1986, *24(2)*, pp. 205-14

den Ouden, H. E., Frith, U., Frith, C. et al., 'Thinking about intentions', *NeuroImage*, 2005, *28(4)*, pp. 787-96

Denenberg, V. H., Garbanati, J., Sherman, D. A. et al., 'Infantile stimulation induces brain lateralization in rats', *Science*, 1978, *201(4361)*, pp. 1150-52

Dennett, D., *Darwin's Dangerous Idea: Evolution and the Meanings of Life*, Simon & Schuster, New York, 1995

Denny-Brown, D., Meyer, J. S. & Horenstein, S., 'The significance of perceptual rivalry resulting from parietal lesion', *Brain*, 1952, *75(4)*, pp. 433-71

Deouell, L. Y., Ivry, R. B. & Knight, R. T., 'Electrophysiologic methods and transcranial magnetic stimulation in behavioral neurology and neuropsychology', in Feinberg, T. E. & Farah, M. J. (eds.), *Behavioral Neurology and Neuropsychology*, 2nd edn., McGraw-Hill, New York, 2003, pp. 105-34

Derouesne, C., Thibault, S., Lagha-Pierucci, S. et al., 'Decreased awareness of cognitive deficits in patients with mild dementia of the Alzheimer type', *International Journal of Geriatric Psychiatry*, 1999, *14(12)*, pp. 1019-30

Descartes, R., *The Philosophical Works of Descartes*, 2 vols., trans. E. S. Haldane & G. R. T. Ross., Cambridge University Press, Cambridge, UK, 1911

——, *Discourse on the Method of Rightly Conducting the Reason and Seeking for Truth in the Sciences*, in *The Philosophical Writings of Descartes*, 3 vols., trans. J. Cottingham, R. Stoothoff & D. Murdoch, Cambridge University Press, Cambridge, UK, 1984-91a [*Discours de la méthode* 1637], vol. 1, pp. 109-51

——, *Meditations on First Philosophy*, in *The Philosophical Writings of Descartes*, 3 vols., trans. J. Cottingham, R. Stoothoff & D. Murdoch, Cambridge University Press, Cambridge, UK, 1984-91b [*Meditationes de prima philosophia* 1641], vol. 2, pp. 1-62

——, *Optics*, in *The Philosophical Writings of Descartes*, 3 vols., trans. J. Cottingham, R. Stoothoff & D. Murdoch, Cambridge University Press, Cambridge, UK, 1984-91c [*La Dioptrique* 1637], vol. 1. pp. 152-75

——, *Rules for the Direction of the Mind*, in *The Philosophical Writings of Descartes*, 3 vols., trans. J. Cottingham, R. Stoothoff & D. Murdoch, Cambridge University Press, Cambridge, UK, 1984-91d [*Regulae ad directionem ingenii* 1684], vol. 1, pp. 7-78

——, *The Passions of the Soul*, in *The Philosophical Writings of Descartes*, 3 vols., trans. J. Cottingham, R. Stoothoff & D. Murdoch, Cambridge University Press, Cambridge, UK, 1984-91e [*Les passions de l'âme* 1649], vol. 1, pp. 325-404

Desmedt, J. E., 'Active touch exploration of extrapersonal space elicits specific electrogenesis in the right cerebral hemisphere of intact right-handed man', *Proceedings of the National Academy of Sciences of the USA*, 1977, *74(9)*, pp. 4037-40

Devinsky, O., 'Right cerebral hemisphere dominance for a sense of corporeal and emotional self ', *Epilepsy & Behavior*, 2000, *1(1)*, pp. 60-73

Devinsky, O. & D'Esposito, M., *Neurology of Cognitive and Behavioral Disorders*, Oxford University Press, Oxford, 2004, pp. 52-67

Devinsky, O. & Laff, R., 'Callosal lesions and behavior: history and modern concepts', *Epilepsy & Behavior*, 2003, *4(6)*, pp. 607-17

Dewey, J., *Experience and Nature*, 2nd edn., Open Court, Chicago, 1929

——, *Context and Thought*, University of California Publications in Philosophy, vol. 12(3), University of California Press, Berkeley CA, 1931, pp. 203-24

——, *The Quest for Certainty* [1929], in Boydston, J. A. (ed.), *The Later Works, 1925-1953*, vol. 4, Southern Illinois University Press, Carbondale IL, 1988

Dharmaretnam, M. & Andrew, R. J., 'Age-specific and stimulus-specific use of right and left eyes by the domestic chick', *Animal Behaviour*, 1994, *48(6)*, pp. 1395-406

Dharmaretnam, M. & Rogers, L. J., 'Hemispheric specialization and dual processing in strongly versus weakly lateralized chicks', *Behavioural Brain Research*, 2005, *162(1)*, pp. 62-70

Diamond, M. C., Johnson, R. E. & Ingham, C. A., 'Morphological changes in the young, adult and aging rat cerebral cortex, hippocampus and diencephalon', *Behavioral Biology*, 1975, *14(2)*, pp. 163-74

Diderot, D., *Œuvres de Denis Diderot: Mélanges de littérature et de philosophie*, ed. J.-A. Naigeon, Brière, Paris, 1821

——, *Correspondance*, ed. G. Roth, Éditions de Minuit, Paris, 1955-70

——, in *Diderot on Art*, trans. & ed. J. Goodman, Yale University Press, New Haven CT, 1995

Di Dio, C., Macaluso, E. & Rizzolatti, G., 'The golden beauty: brain response to classical and renaissance sculptures', *PLoS ONE*, 2007, *2(11)*, p. e1201

Diggs, C. C. & Basili, A. G., 'Verbal expression of right cerebrovascular accident patients: convergent and divergent language', *Brain and Language*, 1987, *30(1)*, pp. 130-46

Dijksterhuis, A., Aarts, H., Bargh, J. A. et al., 'Past contact, stereotype strength, and automatic behavior', *Journal of Experimental Social Psychology*, 2000, *36*, pp. 531-44

Dijksterhuis, A. & van Knippenberg, A., 'The relation between perception and behavior, or how to win a game of trivial pursuit', *Journal of Personality and Social Psychology*, 1998, *74(4)*, pp. 865-77

Dimberg, U., Thunberg, M. & Elmehed, K., 'Unconscious facial reactions to emotional facial expressions', *Psychological Science*, 2000, *11(1)*, pp. 86-9

Dimond, S. J., 'Disconnection and psychopathology', in Gruzelier, J. H. & Flor-Henry, P. (eds.), *Hemisphere Asymmetries of Function in Psychopathology*, Elsevier, Amsterdam, 1979a, pp. 35–47

——, 'Performance by split-brain humans on lateralised vigilance tasks', *Cortex*, 1979b, *15(1)*, pp. 43–50

Diogenes Laertius, *Lives of the Philosophers*, trans. & ed. H. S. Long, Oxford University Press, Oxford, 1964

Dixon, R. M. W., *The Languages of Australia*, Cambridge Language Surveys, series ed. W. S. Allen, Cambridge University Press, Cambridge, UK, 1980

Dobrokhotova, T. A. & Bragina, N. N., 'Functional asymmetry and psychopathology in focal brain disorders', Meditsina, Moscow, 1977 (in Russian)

Dodds, E. R., *The Greeks and the Irrational*, University of California Press, Berkeley CA, 1951

Dodson, C. S., Johnson, M. K. & Schooler, J. W., 'The verbal overshadowing effect: why descriptions impair face recognition', *Memory and Cognition*, 1997, *25(2)*, pp. 129–39

Dodson, M. J., 'Vestibular stimulation in mania: a case report', *Journal of Neurology, Neurosurgery, & Psychiatry*, 2004, *75(1)*, pp. 168–9

Donne, J., *Poetical Works*, ed. H. J. C. Grierson, Oxford University Press, Oxford, 1912

——, *The Sermons of John Donne*, 10 vols., ed. G. R. Potter & E. M. Simpson, California University Press, Berkeley CA, 1953–62

——, *Devotions upon Emergent Occasions*, ed. A. Raspa, McGill-Queen's University Press, Montreal, 1975

Dopson, W. G., Beckwith, B. E., Tucker, D. M. et al., 'Asymmetry of facial expression in spontaneous emotion', *Cortex*, 1984, *20(2)*, pp. 243–51

Dover, K. J., Bowie, E. L., Griffin, J. & West, M. L., *Ancient Greek Literature*, Oxford University Press, Oxford, 1997

Drago, V., Foster, P. S., Webster, D. G. et al., 'Lateral and vertical attentional biases in normal individuals', *International Journal of Neuroscience*, 2007, *117(10)*, pp. 1415–24

Drake, R. A., 'Processing persuasive arguments: recall and recognition as a function of agreement and manipulated activation asymmetry', *Brain and Cognition*, 1991, *15(1)*, pp. 83–94

Drake, R. A. & Bingham, B. R., 'Induced lateral orientation and persuasibility', *Brain and Cognition*, 1985, *4(2)*, pp. 156–64

Drews, E., 'Qualitatively different organisational structures of lexical knowledge in the left and right hemisphere', *Neuropsychologia*, 1987, *25(2)*, pp. 419–27

Dreyfus, H. & Dreyfus, S., *Mind Over Machine: The Power of Human Intuition and Expertise in the Era of the Computer*, Free Press, New York, 1986

Drury, M. O'C., 'Some notes on conversation with Wittgenstein', and 'Conversations with Wittgenstein', in Rhees, R. (ed.), *Recollections of Wittgenstein*, Oxford University Press, Oxford, 1984, pp. 76–171

Dryden, J., *Poetry and Prose*, ed. D. Nichol Smith, Clarendon Press, Oxford, 1925

Dunbar, R., *The Human Story: A New History of Mankind's Evolution*, Faber, London, 2004

Durnford, M. & Kimura, D., 'Right hemisphere specialisation for depth perception reflected in visual field differences', *Nature*, 1971, *231(5302)*, pp. 394–5

Dusoir, H., Owens, C., Forbes, R. B. et al., 'Anorexia nervosa remission following left thalamic stroke', *Journal of Neurology, Neurosurgery, & Psychiatry*, 2005, *76(1)*, pp. 144–5

Dütsch, M., Burger, M., Dörfler, C. et al., 'Cardiovascular autonomic function in poststroke patients', *Neurology*, 2007, *69(24)*, pp. 2249–55

Easterbrook, E. A., 'The effect of emotion on cue utilization and the organization of behavior', *Psychological Review*, 1959, *66(3)*, pp. 183–201

Easterbrook, G., *The Progress Paradox: How Life Gets Better While People Feel Worse*, Random House, New York, 2003

Easterlin, R. A., 'Will raising the incomes of all increase the happiness of all?', *Journal of Economic Behavior and Organization*, 1995, *27(1)*, pp. 35–48

——, 'Feeding the illusion of growth and happiness: a reply to Hagerty and Veenhoven', *Social Indicators Research*, 2005, *74(3)*, pp. 429–43

Eberstaller, O., 'Zur Oberflächen-Anatomie der Grosshirn-Hemisphären', *Wiener Medizinische Blätter*, 1884, *7*, pp. 644–6

Eckermann, J. P., *Conversations with Goethe*, ed. J. K. Moorhead, trans. J. Oxenford, Dent, London, 1970

Edelman, G. M., *The Remembered Present*, Basic Books, New York, 1989

Edelman, G. & Tononi, G., *A Universe of Consciousness: How Matter Becomes Imagination*, Basic Books, New York, 2000

Edmonston, W. E. & Moscovitz, H. C., 'Hypnosis and lateralized brain functions', *International Journal of Clinical and Experimental Hypnosis*, 1990, *38(1)*, pp. 70–84

Edwards-Lee, T., Miller, B. L., Benson, D. F. et al., 'The temporal variant of frontotemporal dementia', *Brain*, 1997, *120(6)*, pp. 1027–40

Egolf, B., Lasker, J., Wolf, S. et al., 'The Roseto effect: a fifty-year comparison of mortality rates', *American Journal of Epidemiology*, 1992, *125(6)*, pp. 1089–92

Egorov, A. Y. & Nikolaenko, N. N., 'Functional brain asymmetry and visuo-spatial perception in mania, depression and psychotropic medication', *Biological Psychiatry*, 1992, *32(5)*, pp. 399–410

Ehrenwald, H., 'Anosognosie und Depersonalisation', *Nervenarzt*, 1931, *4*, pp. 681–8

Ehret, G., 'Left hemisphere advantage in the mouse brain for recognizing ultrasonic communication calls', *Nature*, 1987, *325(6101)*, pp. 249–51

Einstein, A., *The World As I See It*, trans. A. Harris, Watts & Co., London, 1940 [1953]

——, 'A letter to Jacques Hadamard', in Ghiselin, B. (ed.), *The Creative Process*, University of California Press, Berkeley CA, 1992, p. 32

Eksteins, M., 'Drowned in eau de vie', *London Review of Books*, London, 21 February 2008, pp. 23–4

Eliade, M., *The Myth of the Eternal Return: or, Cosmos and History*, Bollingen, New York, 1971

Elias, L. J., Bulman-Fleming, M. B. & McManus, I. C., 'Visual temporal asymmetries are related to asymmetries in linguistic perception', *Neuropsychologia*, 1999, *37(11)*, pp. 1243–9

Eliot, T. S., 'The metaphysical poets', in *Selected Essays*, Harcourt Brace, New York, 1950, pp. 241–50
——, 'The use of poetry and the use of criticism', in Kermode, F. (ed.), *Selected Prose of T. S. Eliot*, Harcourt Brace, New York, 1975, pp. 79–96
Ellard, J., 'Did schizophrenia exist before the eighteenth century?', *Australia and New Zealand Journal of Psychiatry*, 1987, *21(3)*, pp. 306–18
Ellis, A. W., Jordan, J. L. & Sullivan, C. A., 'Unilateral neglect is not unilateral: evidence for additional neglect of extreme right space', *Cortex*, 2006, *42(6)*, pp. 861–8
Ellis, A. W., Young, A. W. & Anderson, C., 'Modes of word recognition in the left and right cerebral hemispheres', *Brain and Language*, 1988, *35(2)*, pp. 254–73
Ellis, H. D., 'The role of the right hemisphere in face perception', in Young, A. W. (ed.), *Functions of the Right Cerebral Hemisphere*, Academic Press, London, 1983, pp. 33–64
——, 'The role of the right hemisphere in the Capgras delusion', *Psychopathology*, 1994, *27(3–5)*, pp. 177–85
Ellis, H. D. & Florence, M., 'Bodamer's (1947) paper on prosopagnosia', *Cognitive Neuropsychology*, 1990, *7(2)*, pp. 81–105
Ellis, H. D. & Gunter, H. L., 'Asperger syndrome: a simple matter of white matter?', *Trends in Cognitive Sciences*, 1999, *3(5)*, pp. 192–200
Ellis, H. D., Jeeves, M. A., Newcombe, F. et al. (eds.), *Aspects of Face Processing*, Martinus Nijhoff, Dordrecht, Netherlands, 1986
Ellis, S. J. & Small, M., 'Denial of illness in stroke', *Stroke*, 1993, *24(5)*, pp. 757–9
Elsner, J., 'Physiognomics: art and text', in Swain, S. (ed.), *Seeing the Face, Seeing the Soul*, Oxford University Press, Oxford, 2007, pp. 203–22
Elster, J., *Sour Grapes: Studies in the Subversion of Rationality*, Cambridge University Press, Cambridge, UK, 1983
——, *Explaining Social Behavior: More Nuts and Bolts for the Social Sciences*, Cambridge University Press, Cambridge, UK, 2007
Ely, P. W., Graves, R. G. & Potter, S. M., 'Dichotic listening indices of right hemisphere semantic processing', *Neuropsychologia*, 1989, *27(7)*, pp. 1007–15
Emerson, C. S., Harrison, D. W., Everhart, D. E. et al., 'Grip strength asymmetry in depressed boys', *Neuropsychiatry, Neuropsychology and Behavioral Neurology*, 2001, *14(2)*, pp. 130–34
Emery, N. J., 'The eyes have it: the neuroethology, function and evolution of social gaze', *Neuroscience and Biobehavioral Reviews*, 2000, *24(6)*, pp. 581–604
Emery, N. J. & Clayton, N. S., 'Comparing the complex cognition of birds and primates', in Rogers, L. J. & Kaplan, G. (eds.), *Comparative Vertebrate Cognition*, Kluwer, Dordrecht, Netherlands, 2004, pp. 3–55
Emery, N. J., Lorincz, E. N., Perrett, D. I. et al., 'Gaze following and joint attention in rhesus monkeys (*Macaca mulatta*)', *Journal of Comparative Psychology*, 1997, *111(3)*, pp. 286–93
Empedocles, *Fragments*, in Burnet, J. (trans. & ed.), *Early Greek Philosophy*, A. & C. Black, London, 1892
Erhan, H., Borod, J. C., Tenke, C. E. et al., 'Identification of emotion in a dichotic listening task: event-related brain potential and behavioral findings', *Brain and Cognition*, 1998, *37(2)*, pp. 286–307
Eslinger, P. J., 'Neurological and neuropsychological bases of empathy', *European Neurology*, 1998, *39(4)*, pp. 193–9
Etcoff, N. L., 'Perceptual and conceptual organization of facial emotions: hemispheric differences', *Brain and Cognition*, 1984a, *3(4)*, pp. 385–412
——, 'Selective attention to facial identity and facial emotion', *Neuropsychologia*, 1984b, *22(3)*, pp. 281–95
——, 'The neuropsychology of emotional expression', in Goldstein, G. & Tarter, R. E. (eds.), *Advances in Clinical Neuropsychology*, Plenum Press, New York, 1986, vol. 3, pp. 127–79
Etcoff, N. L., Ekman, P., Magee, J. J. et al., 'Lie detection and language comprehension', *Nature*, 2000, *405(6783)*, p. 139
Ettlinger, G., Warrington, E. & Zangwill, O. L., 'A further study of visual-spatial agnosia', *Brain*, 1957, *80(3)*, pp. 335–61
Evans, C. S., Evans, L. & Marler, P., 'On the meaning of alarm calls – functional reference in an avian vocal system', *Animal Behaviour*, 1993, *46(1)*, pp. 23–38
Evans-Pritchard, E. E., *Nuer Religion*, Oxford University Press, Oxford, 1956
Everett, D. L., 'Cultural constraints on grammar and cognition in Pirahã: another look at the design features of human language', *Current Anthropology*, 2005, *46(4)*, pp. 621–46
Evers, S., Dannert, J., Rodding, D. et al., 'The cerebral haemodynamics of music perception: a transcranial Doppler sonography study', *Brain*, 1999, *122(1)*, pp. 75–85
Evert, D. L. & Kmen, M., 'Hemispheric asymmetries for global and local processing as a function of stimulus exposure duration', *Brain and Cognition*, 2003, *51(1)*, pp. 115–42
Eviatar, Z., 'Language experience and right hemisphere tasks: the effects of scanning habits and multilingualism', *Brain and Language*, 1997, *58(1)*, pp. 157–73
Eviatar, Z. & Ibrahim, R., 'Morphological structure and hemispheric functioning: the contribution of the right hemisphere to reading in different languages', *Neuropsychology*, 2007, *21(4)*, pp. 470–84
Eviatar, Z. & Just, M. A., 'Brain correlates of discourse processing: an fMRI investigation of irony and conventional metaphor comprehension', *Neuropsychologia*, 2006, *44(12)*, pp. 2348–59
Eysenck, H. L., *Genius*, Cambridge University Press, Cambridge, UK, 1995
Fabbro, F., 'Left and right in the Bible from a neuropsychological perspective', *Brain and Cognition*, 1994, *24(2)*, pp. 161–83
Fabbro, F., Gran, B. & Bava, A., 'Hemispheric asymmetry for the auditory recognition of true and false statements', *Neuropsychologia*, 1993, *31(8)*, pp. 865–70
Fabre-Thorpe, M., Fagot, J., Lorincz, E. et al., 'Laterality in cats: paw preference and performance in a visuomotor activity', *Cortex*, 1993, *29(1)*, pp. 15–24
Fairbanks, A., *The First Philosophers of Greece*, Kegan Paul, Trench, Trubner & Co., London, 1898
Fairclough, H., *Love of Nature among the Greeks and Romans*, Longmans, Green & Co., London, 1930
Falk, D., Hildebolt, C., Cheverud, J. et al., 'Cortical asymmetries in frontal lobes of rhesus monkeys (*Macaca mulatta*)', *Brain Research*, 1990, *512(1)*, pp. 40–45

Falk, D., Redmond, J. C., Guyer, J. et al., 'Early hominid brain evolution: a new look at old endocasts', *Journal of Human Evolution*, 2000, *38(5)*, pp. 695–717

Farah, M. J., 'Specialisation within visual object recognition: clues from prosopagnosia and alexia', in Farah, M. J. & Ratcliff, G. (eds.), *The Neuropsychology of High-Level Vision*, Lawrence Erlbaum, Hillsdale NJ, 1994, pp. 133–46

——, 'Disorders of visual-spatial perception and cognition', in Heilman, K. M. & Valenstein, E. (eds.), *Clinical Neuropsychology*, 4th edn., Oxford University Press, Oxford, 2003, pp. 146–60

Farah, M. J., Wilson, K. D., Drain, H. M. et al., 'The inverted face inversion effect in prosopagnosia: evidence for mandatory, face-specific perceptual mechanisms', *Vision Research*, 1995, *35(14)*, pp. 2089–93

Farber, L., *Lying, Despair, Jealousy, Envy, Sex, Suicide, Drugs and the Good Life*, Basic Books, New York, 1976

Farrer, C., Franck, N., Georgieff, N. et al., 'Modulating the experience of agency: a positron emission tomography study', *NeuroImage*, 2003, *18(2)*, pp. 324–33

Faust, M., Kravetz, S. & Babkoff, H., 'Hemispheric specialization or reading habits: evidence from lexical decision research with Hebrew words and sentences', *Brain and Language*, 1993, *44(3)*, pp. 254–63

Faust, M. & Mashal, N., 'The role of the right cerebral hemisphere in processing novel metaphoric expressions taken from poetry: a divided visual field study', *Neuropsychologia*, 2007, *45(4)*, pp. 860–70

Federmeier, K. D. & Kutas, M., 'Right words and left words: electrophysiological evidence for hemispheric differences in meaning processing', *Cognitive Brain Research*, 1999, *8(3)*, pp. 373–92

Fehr, E. & Fischbacher, U., 'The nature of human altruism', *Nature*, 2003, *425(6960)*, pp. 785–91

Fehr, E., Fischbacher, U. & Gächter, S., 'Strong reciprocity, human cooperation, and the enforcement of social norms', *Human Nature*, 2002, *13*, pp. 1–25

Feinberg, T. E., *Altered Egos: How the Brain Creates the Self*, Oxford University Press, Oxford, 2000

Feinberg, T. E., Haber, L. D. & Leeds, N. E., 'Verbal asomatognosia', *Neurology*, 1990, *40(9)*, pp. 1391–4

Feinberg, T. E. & Keenan, J. P., 'Where in the brain is the self?', *Consciousness and Cognition*, 2005, *14(4)*, pp. 661–78

Feinberg, T. E., Roane, D. M., Kwan, P. C. et al., 'Anosognosia and visuoverbal confabulation', *Archives of Neurology*, 1994, *51(5)*, pp. 468–73

Feinstein, J. S., Goldin, P. R., Stein, M. B. et al., 'Habituation of attentional networks during emotional processing', *NeuroReport*, 2002, *13(10)*, pp. 1255–8

Fenwick, P., 'The neurophysiology of religious experience', in Bhugra, D. (ed.), *Psychiatry and Religion: Context, Consensus and Controversies*, Routledge & Kegan Paul, London, 1996, pp. 167–77

Ferguson, S. M., Rayport, M. & Corrie, W. S., 'Neuropsychiatric observations on behavioral consequences of corpus callosum section for seizure control', in Reeves, A. G. (ed.), *Epilepsy and the Corpus Callosum*, Plenum Press, New York, 1985, pp. 501–14

Ferman, T. J., Primeau, M., Delis, D. et al., 'Global-local processing in schizophrenia: hemispheric asymmetry and symptom-specific interference', *Journal of the International Neuropsychological Society*, 1999, *5(5)*, pp. 442–51

Fernandez, H. H. & Friedman, J. H., 'Punding on L-dopa', *Movement Disorders*, 1999, *14(5)*, pp. 836–8

Fernández-Carriba, S., Loeches, A., Morcillo, A. et al., 'Asymmetry in facial expression of emotions by chimpanzees', *Neuropsychologia*, 2002a, *40(9)*, pp. 1523–33

——, 'Functional asymmetry of emotions in primates: new findings in chimpanzees', *Brain Research Bulletin*, 2002b, *57(3–4)*, pp. 561–4

Feyerabend, P., *Against Method*, New Left Books, New York, 1975

Feyereisen, P. & de Lannoy, J.-D., *Gestures and Speech: Psychological Investigations*, Cambridge University Press, Cambridge, UK, 1991

Filteau, M. J., Pourcher, E., Bouchard, R. H. et al., 'Corpus callosum agenesis and psychosis in Andermann syndrome', *Archives of Neurology*, 1991, *48(12)*, pp. 1275–80

Fimm, B., Willmes, K. & Spijkers, W., 'The effect of low arousal on visuo-spatial attention', *Neuropsychologia*, 2006, *44(8)*, pp. 1261–8

Fink, G. R., Halligan, P. W., Marshall, J. C. et al., 'Where in the brain does visual attention select the forest and the trees?', *Nature*, 1996, *382(6592)*, pp. 626–8

Fink, G. R., Marshall, J. C., Halligan, P. W. et al., 'Hemispheric asymmetries in global/local processing are modulated by perceptual salience', *Neuropsychologia*, 1999a, *37(1)*, pp. 31–40

——, 'The neural consequences of conflict between intention and the senses', *Brain*, 1999b, *122(3)*, pp. 497–512

Finkel, L. H., 'Neuronal group selection: a basis for categorisation by the nervous system', in de Kerckhove, D. & Lumsden, C. J. (eds.), *The Alphabet and the Brain: The Lateralization of Writing*, Springer-Verlag, Berlin, 1988, pp. 51–70

Finset, A., 'Depressed mood and reduced emotionality after right-hemisphere brain damage', in Kinsbourne, M. (ed.), *Cerebral Hemisphere Function in Depression*, American Psychiatric Press, Washington DC, 1988, pp. 49–64

Fischer, O., 'Die chinesische Kunsttheorie: ein Versuch', *Repertorium für Kunstwissenschaft*, 1912, *35(2)*, pp. 143–96

Fitch, R. H., Brown, C. P., O'Connor, K. et al., 'Function lateralization for auditory temporal processing in male and female rats', *Behavioral Neuroscience*, 1993, *107(5)*, pp. 844–50

Flashman, L. A. & Roth, R. M., 'Neural correlates of unawareness of illness in psychosis', in Amador, X. & David, A. (eds.), *Insight and Psychosis*, 2nd edn., Oxford University Press, Oxford, 2004, pp. 157–76

Flor-Henry, P., Tomer, R., Kumpula, I. et al., 'Neurophysiological and neuropsychological study of two cases of multiple personality syndrome and comparison with chronic hysteria', *International Journal of Psychophysiology*, 1990, *10(2)*, pp. 151–61

Fodor, J., 'The big idea: can there be a science of mind?', *Times Literary Supplement*, London, 3 July 1992, p. 5

Foldi, N. S., 'Appreciation of pragmatic interpretations of indirect commands: comparison of right and left hemisphere brain-damaged patients', *Brain and Language*, 1987, *31(1)*, pp. 88–108

Foldi, N. S., Cicone, M. & Gardner, H., 'Pragmatic aspects of communication in brain-damaged patients', in Segalowitz, S. J. (ed.), *Language Functions and Brain Organisation*, Academic Press, New York, 1983, pp. 51–86

Ford, J. K. B., 'Acoustic behaviour of resident killer whales (*Orcinus orca*) off Vancouver Island, British Columbia', *Canadian Journal of Zoology*, 1989, *67*, pp. 727–45

——, 'Vocal traditions among resident killer whales (*Orcinus orca*) in coastal waters of British Columbia', *Canadian Journal of Zoology*, 1991, *69*, pp. 1454–83

Förstl, H., Almeida, O. P., Owen, A. M. et al., 'Psychiatric, neurological and medical aspects of misidentification syndromes: a review of 260 cases', *Psychological Medicine*, 1991, *21(4)*, pp. 905–10

Foss, M., *Symbol and Metaphor in Human Experience*, University of Nebraska Press, Lincoln NE, 1949

Frankl, V., *Man's Search for Meaning*, Washington Square Press, New York, 1984

Fraser, J. T., 'The many dimensions of time and mind: an epistemic jigsaw puzzle game', in Fraser, J. T. (ed.), *Time and Mind: Interdisciplinary Issues*, vol. 6 ('The Study of Time'), International Universities Press, Madison CT, 1989, pp. 1–14

Freedberg, D., *The Power of Images: Studies in the History and Theory of Response*, Chicago University Press, Chicago, 1989

Freeman, C., *The Closing of the Western Mind*, Vintage Books, New York, 2002

Freud, S., *Civilisation and Its Discontents*, in *The Standard Edition of the Complete Psychological Works of Sigmund Freud*, trans. & ed. J. Strachey et al., vol. 21, The Hogarth Press, London, 1960a [*Das Unbehagen in der Kultur* 1930]

——, *Introductory Lectures on Psycho-Analysis*, in *The Standard Edition of the Complete Psychological Works of Sigmund Freud*, trans. & ed. J. Strachey et al., vol. 15, The Hogarth Press, London, 1960b [*Vorlesungen zur Einführung in die Psychoanalyse* 1917]

——, *New Introductory Lectures on Psycho-analysis*, in *The Standard Edition of the Complete Psychological Works of Sigmund Freud*, trans. & ed. J. Strachey et al., vol. 22, The Hogarth Press, London, 1960c [*Neue Vorlesungen zur Einführung in die Psychoanalyse* 1933]

——, *The Ego and the Id*, in *The Standard Edition of the Complete Psychological Works of Sigmund Freud*, trans. & ed. J. Strachey et al., vol. 19, The Hogarth Press, London, 1960d [*Das Ich und das Es* 1923]

——, 'The "Uncanny" ', in *The Standard Edition of the Complete Psychological Works of Sigmund Freud*, trans. & ed. J. Strachey et al., vol. 17, pp. 217–56, The Hogarth Press, London, 1960e ['Das Unheimliche' 1919]

——, *Why War?*, in *The Standard Edition of the Complete Psychological Works of Sigmund Freud*, trans. & ed. J. Strachey et al., vol. 22, The Hogarth Press, London, 1960f [*Warum Krieg?* 1933]

Frey, S. H., Funnell, M. G., Gerry, V. E. et al., 'A dissociation between the representation of tool-use skills and hand dominance: insights from left- and right-handed callosotomy patients', *Journal of Cognitive Neuroscience*, 2005, *17(2)*, pp. 262–72

Frey, T. S. & Hambert, G., 'Neuropsychiatric aspects of logorrhoea', *Nordsk Psykiatrisk Tidsskrift*, 1972, *26(3)*, pp. 158–173 [English summary]

Fride, E. & Weinstock, M., 'Prenatal stress increases anxiety related behaviour and alters cerebral lateralization of dopamine activity', *Life Sciences*, 1988, *42(10)*, pp. 1059–65

Friedman, A. & Polson, M. C., 'The hemispheres as independent resource systems: limited-capacity processing and cerebral specialization', *Journal of Experimental Psychology: Human Perception and Performance*, 1981, *7(5)*, pp. 1031–58

Friston, K. J., 'Characterizing functional asymmetries with brain mapping', in Hugdahl, K. & Davidson, R. J. (eds.), *The Asymmetrical Brain*, Massachusetts Institute of Technology Press, Cambridge MA, 2003, pp. 161–86

Frith, C. D., 'Consciousness, information processing and schizophrenia', *British Journal of Psychiatry*, 1979, *134(3)*, pp. 225–35

Frith, U. & Snowling, M., 'Reading for meaning and reading for sound in autistic and dyslexic children', *British Journal of Developmental Psychology*, 1983, *1(4)*, pp. 329–42

Fromm, E., *On Disobedience and Other Essays*, Routledge & Kegan Paul, London, 1984

Frothingham, A. L., 'Ancient orientation unveiled. Part III: the left as the place of honor in Roman and Christian art', *Journal of the Archaeological Institute of America*, 1917, *21(3)*, pp. 313–36

Fujii, T., Fukatsu, R., Watabe, S. et al., 'Auditory sound agnosia without aphasia following a right temporal lobe lesion', *Cortex*, 1990, *26(2)*, pp. 263–8

Funnell, M. G., Colvin, M. K. & Gazzaniga, M. S., 'The calculating hemispheres: studies of a split-brain patient', *Neuropsychologia*, 2007, *45(10)*, pp. 2378–86

Funnell, M. G., Corballis, P. M. & Gazzaniga, M. S., 'Temporal discrimination in the split brain', *Brain and Cognition*, 2003, *53(2)*, pp. 218–22

Gabel, S., 'The right hemisphere in imagery, hypnosis, rapid eye movement sleep and dreaming: empirical studies and tentative conclusions', *Journal of Nervous and Mental Disease*, 1988, *176(6)*, pp. 323–31

Gaburo, K., 'Brain: . . . half a whole', *Perspectives of New Music*, 1979–80, *18(1–2)*, pp. 215–56

Gadea, M., Gomez, C., Gonzalez-Bono, E. et al., 'Increased cortisol and decreased right ear advantage (REA) in dichotic listening following a negative mood induction', *Psychoneuroendocrinology*, 2005, *30(2)*, pp. 129–38

Gainotti, G., 'Réactions "catastrophiques" et manifestations d'indifférence au cours des atteintes cérébrales', *Neuropsychologia*, 1969, *7*, pp. 195–204

——, 'Emotional behaviour and hemispheric side of lesion', *Cortex*, 1972, *8(1)*, pp. 41–55

——, 'What the locus of brain lesion tells us about the nature of the cognitive defect underlying category-specific disorders: a review', *Cortex*, 2000, *36(4)*, pp. 539–59

——, 'The relationships between anatomical and cognitive locus of lesion in category-specific disorders', in Forde, E. M. E. & Humphreys, G. W. (eds.), *Category Specificity in Brain and Mind*, Psychology Press, Hove, UK, 2002, pp. 403–26

Gainotti, G., Barbier, A. & Marra, C., 'Slowly progressive defect in recognition of familiar people in a patient with right anterior temporal atrophy', *Brain*, 2003, *126(4)*, pp. 792–803

Gainotti, G. & Silveri, M. C., 'Cognitive and anatomical locus of lesion in a patient with a category-specific semantic impairment for living beings', *Cognitive Neuropsychology*, 1996, *13(3)*, pp. 357–90

Gainotti, G., Silveri, M. C., Daniele, A. et al., 'Neuroanatomical correlates of category-specific semantic disorders: a critical survey', *Memory*, 1995, *3(3–4)*, pp. 247–64

Galaburda, A. M., 'Anatomic basis of cerebral dominance', in Davidson, R. J. & Hugdahl, K. (eds.), *Brain Asymmetry*, Massachusetts Institute of Technology Press, Cambridge MA, 1995, pp. 51–73

Galaburda, A. M., Aboitiz, F., Rosen, G. D. et al., 'Histological asymmetry in the primary visual cortex of the rat: implications for mechanisms of cerebral asymmetry', *Cortex*, 1986, *22(1)*, pp. 151–60

Galaburda, A. M., Corsiglia, J., Rosen, G. D. et al., 'Planum temporale asymmetry, reappraisal since Geschwind and Levitsky', *Neuropsychologia*, 1987, *25(6)*, pp. 853–68

Galaburda, A. M., LeMay, M., Kemper, T. L. et al., 'Right-left asymmetrics in the brain', *Science*, 1978, *199(4331)*, pp. 852–6

Galin, D., 'Implications for psychiatry of left and right cerebral specialization: a neurophysiological context for unconscious processes', *Archives of General Psychiatry*, 1974, *31(4)*, pp. 572–83

Galin, D., Johnstone, J., Nakell, L. et al., 'Development of the capacity for tactile information transfer between hemispheres in normal children', *Science*, 1979, *204(4399)*, pp. 1330–32

Galin, D. & Ornstein, R., 'Lateral specialisation of cognitive mode: an EEG study', *Psychophysiology*, 1972, *9(4)*, pp. 412–28

Gallagher, H. L. & Frith, C. D., 'Dissociable neural pathways for the perception and recognition of expressive and instrumental gestures', *Neuropsychologia*, 2004, *42(13)*, pp. 1725–36

Gallagher, H. L., Happé, F., Brunswick, N. et al., 'Reading the mind in cartoons and stories: an fMRI study of "theory of mind" in verbal and nonverbal tasks', *Neuropsychologia*, 2000, *38(1)*, pp. 11–21

Gallagher, S., 'Mutual enlightenment: recent phenomenology and cognitive science', *Journal of Consciousness Studies*, 1997, *4(3)*, pp. 195–214

Gallagher, S. & Meltzoff, A. N., 'The earliest sense of self and others: Merleau-Ponty and recent developmental studies', *Philosophical Psychology*, 1996, *9(2)*, pp. 211–33

Gallup, G. G., Jnr., 'Self-awareness and the emergence of mind in primates', *American Journal of Primatology*, 1982, *2(3)*, pp. 237–48

Gallup, G. G., Jnr., Wallnau, L. B. & Suarez, S. D., 'Failure to find self-recognition in mother-infant and infant-infant rhesus monkey pairs', *Folia Primatologica (Basel)*, 1980, *33(3)*, pp. 210–19

Ganis, G., Kosslyn, S. M., Stose, S. et al., 'Neural correlates of different types of deception: an fMRI investigation', *Cerebral Cortex*, 2003, *13(8)*, pp. 830–36

Gannon, P. J., Holloway, R. L., Broadfield, D. C. et al., 'Asymmetry of chimpanzee planum temporale: humanlike pattern of Wernicke's brain language area homolog', *Science*, 1998, *279(5348)*, pp. 220–22

Gardner, H., *The Shattered Mind*, Knopf, New York, 1974

Gardner, H., Brownell, H. H., Wapner, W. et al., 'Missing the point: the role of the right hemisphere in the processing of complex linguistic materials', in Perecman, E. (ed.), *Cognitive Processing in the Right Hemisphere*, Academic Press, New York, 1983, pp. 169–91

Gardner, H., Ling, P. K., Flamm, L. et al., 'Comprehension and appreciation of humorous material following brain damage', *Brain*, 1975, *98(3)*, pp. 399–412

Garland, H. B., *Lessing: the Founder of Modern German Literature*, Bowes & Bowes, Cambridge, 1937

Gasparrini, W. G., Satz, P., Heilman, K. M. et al., 'Hemispheric asymmetries of affective processing as determined by the Minnesota Multiphasic Personality Inventory', *Journal of Neurology, Neurosurgery, & Psychiatry*, 1978, *41(5)*, pp. 470–73

Gaukroger, S., *The Emergence of a Scientific Culture: Science and the Shaping of Modernity, 1210–1685*, Oxford University Press, Oxford, 2006

Gazzaniga, M. S., *The Bisected Brain*, Appleton-Century-Crofts, New York, 1970

——, 'Right hemisphere language following brain bisection: a twenty year perspective', *American Psychologist*, 1983, *38(5)*, pp. 525–37

——, 'Brain and conscious experience', *Advances in Neurology*, 1998, *77*, pp. 181–92

——, 'Cerebral specialization and interhemispheric communication: does the corpus callosum enable the human condition?', *Brain*, 2000, *123(7)*, pp. 1293–326

Gazzaniga, M. S. & LeDoux, J. E., *The Integrated Mind*, Plenum Press, New York, 1978

Gazzaniga, M. S. & Smylie, C. S., 'Hemispheric mechanisms controlling voluntary and spontaneous facial expressions', *Journal of Cognitive Neuroscience*, 1990, *2(3)*, pp. 239–45

Geikie, Sir Archibald, *The Love of Nature Among the Romans*, John Murray, London, 1912

Gentner, D., 'Are scientific analogies metaphors?', in Miall, D. S. (ed.), *Metaphor: Problems and Perspectives*, Harvester Press, Brighton, UK, 1982, pp. 106–32

Gentner, D. & Gentner, D. R., 'Flowing waters or teeming crowds: mental models of electricity', in Gentner, D. & Stevens, A. L. (eds.), *Mental Models*, Lawrence Erlbaum, Hillsdale NJ, 1983, pp. 99–129

George, M. S., Ketter, T. A., Kimbrell, T. A. et al., 'What functional imaging has revealed about the brain basis of mood and emotion', in Panksepp, J. (ed.), *Advances in Biological Psychiatry*, vol. 2, JAI Press, Greenwich CT, 1996, pp. 63–113

Geschwind, N., 'Implications for evolution, genetics, and clinical syndromes', in Glick, S. D. (ed.), *Cerebral Lateralization in Nonhuman Species*, Academic Press, Orlando FL, 1985, pp. 247–76

Geschwind, N. & Galaburda, A. M., 'Cerebral lateralization. Biological mechanisms, associations, and pathology: I. A hypothesis and a program for research', *Archives of Neurology*, 1985, *42(5)*, pp. 428–59

——, *Cerebral Lateralization: Biological Mechanisms, Associations, and Pathology*, Massachusetts Institute of Technology Press, Boston MA, 1987

Geschwind, N. & Levitsky, W., 'Human brain: left-right asymmetries in temporal speech region', *Science*, 1968, *161(837)*, pp. 186–7

Ghaemi, S. N. & Rosenquist, K. J., 'Insight in mood disorders: an empirical and conceptual review', in Amador, X. & David, A. (eds.), *Insight and Psychosis*, 2nd edn., Oxford University Press, Oxford, 2004, pp. 101–15

Ghiselin, B. (ed.), *The Creative Process*, University of California Press, Berkeley CA, 1992

Giannitrapani, D., 'Developing concepts of lateralization of cerebral functions', *Cortex*, 1967, *3*, pp. 353–70

BIBLIOGRAPHY • 537

Gibbs, R. W. & O'Brien, J. E., 'Idioms and mental imagery: the metaphorical motivation for idiomatic meaning', *Cognition*, 1990, *36(1)*, pp. 35–68

Giddens, A., *Modernity and Self-Identity: Self and Society in the Late Modern Age*, Stanford University Press, Stanford CA, 1991

Giedd, J. N., Snell, J. W., Lange, N. et al., 'Quantitative magnetic resonance imaging of human brain development: ages 4–18', *Cerebral Cortex*, 1996, *6(4)*, pp. 551–60

Gilboa, A., 'Autobiographical and episodic memory – one and the same? Evidence from prefrontal activation in neuroimaging studies', *Neuropsychologia*, 2004, *42(10)*, pp. 1336–49

Giles, H. A., *An Introduction to the History of Chinese Pictorial Art*, Kelly & Walsh, Shanghai, 1905

Gill, C., *Personality in Greek Epic, Tragedy, and Philosophy*, Clarendon Press, Oxford, 1996

Gilpin, W., *Three Essays: on Picturesque Beauty; on Picturesque Travel; and on Sketching Landscape: with a Poem on Landscape Painting*, Caldwell & Davies, London, 1808

Gintis, H., 'Strong reciprocity and human sociality', *Journal of Theoretical Biology*, 2000, *206(2)*, pp. 169–79

Gioia, T., *Healing Songs*, Duke University Press, Durham NC, 2006

Giovanello, K. S., Alexander, M. & Verfaellie, M., 'Differential impairment of person-specific knowledge in a patient with semantic dementia', *Neurocase*, 2003, *9(1)*, pp. 15–26

Gitelman, D. R., Alpert, N. M., Kosslyn, S. et al., 'Functional imaging of human right hemispheric activation for exploratory movements', *Annals of Neurology*, 1996, *39(2)*, pp. 174–9

Glick, S. D., Carlson, K. L., Drew, K. L. et al., 'Functional and neurochemical asymmetry in the corpus striatum', in Ottoson, D. (ed.), *Duality and Unity of the Brain*, Macmillan, London, 1987, pp. 3–16

Glick, S. D., Meibach, R. C., Cox, R. D. et al., 'Multiple and interrelated asymmetries in rat brain', *Life Sciences*, 1979, *25(4)*, pp. 395–400

Glick, S. D., Ross, D. A. & Hough, L. B., 'Lateral asymmetry of neurotransmitters in human brain', *Brain Research*, 1982, *234(1)*, pp. 53–63

Gloning, I., Gloning, K., Hoff, H. et al., 'Zur Prosopagnosie', *Neuropsychologia*, 1966, *4(2)*, pp. 113–32

Gloning, I., Gloning, K. & Hoff, H., *Neuropsychological Symptoms and Syndromes in Lesions of the Occipital Lobe and the Adjacent Areas*, Gauthier-Villars, Paris, 1968

Goble, D. J., Lewis, C. A. & Brown, S. H., 'Upper limb asymmetries in the utilization of proprioceptive feedback', *Experimental Brain Research*, 2006, *168(1–2)*, pp. 307–11

Godefroy, O., Lhullier, C. & Rousseaux, M., 'Non-spatial attention disorders in patients with frontal or posterior brain damage', *Brain*, 1996, *119(1)*, pp. 191–202

Godefroy, O. & Rousseaux, M., 'Divided and focussed attention in patients with lesions of the prefrontal cortex', *Brain and Cognition*, 1996, *30(2)*, pp. 155–74

Godfrey, R., *English Caricature 1620 to the Present*, Victoria and Albert Museum, London, 1984

Goebel, C., Linden, D. E. J., Sireteanu, R. et al., 'Different attention processes in visual search tasks investigated with functional Magnetic Resonance Imaging', *NeuroImage*, 1997, *5(4, pt. 2)*, p. S81

Goel, V. & Dolan, R. J., 'Explaining modulation of reasoning by belief', *Cognition*, 2003, *87(1)*, pp. B11–22

Goel, V., Tierney, M., Sheesley, L. et al., 'Hemispheric specialization in human prefrontal cortex for resolving certain and uncertain inferences', *Cerebral Cortex*, 2007, *17(10)*, pp. 2245–50

Goethe, J. W. von, *Faust: der Tragödie erster Teil and Faust: der Tragödie zweiter Teil*, Reclam, Leipzig, 1976–77

——, *Goethe: Scientific Studies*, trans. & ed. D. Miller, Suhrkamp, New York, 1988

——, *Zur Farbenlehre* [1810], in *Sämtliche Werke*, vol. 10., ed. K. Richter, Carl Hanser Verlag, Munich, 1989

——, *Maximen und Reflektionen* [1833], in *Sämtliche Werke*, vol. 17, ed. K. Richter, Carl Hanser Verlag, Munich, 1991

Goffman, E., *Interaction Ritual: Essays on Face-to-Face Behavior*, Doubleday, Garden City NY, 1967

Gold, J. M., Berman, K. F., Randolph, C. et al., 'PET validation of a novel prefrontal task: delayed response alternation (DRA)', *Neuropsychology*, 1996, *10(1)*, pp. 3–10

Goldberg, E., 'Associative agnosias and the functions of the left hemisphere', *Journal of Clinical and Experimental Neuropsychology*, 1990, *12(4)*, pp. 467–84

——, *The Executive Brain: Frontal Lobes and the Civilized Mind*, Oxford University Press, Oxford, 2001

Goldberg, E. & Costa, L. D., 'Hemispheric differences in the acquisition and use of descriptive systems', *Brain and Language*, 1981, *14(1)*, pp. 144–73

Goldberg, E., Podell, K. & Lovell, M., 'Lateralization of frontal lobe functions and cognitive novelty', *Journal of Neuropsychiatry and Clinical Neurosciences*, 1994, *6(4)*, pp. 371–8

Goldstein, A., 'Thrills in response to music and other stimuli', *Physiological Psychology*, 1980, *8(1)*, pp. 126–9

Goldstein, L., Stoltzfus, N. W. & Gardocki, J. F., 'Changes in interhemispheric amplitude relationships in the EEG during sleep', *Physiology & Behavior*, 1972, *8(5)*, pp. 811–15

Gombrich, E. H., *Art and Illusion: A study in the psychology of pictorial representation*, Phaidon Press, London, 1977 [1960]

Gombrich, E. H. & Kris, E., *Caricature*, Penguin, Harmondsworth, UK, 1940

Gonzalez, C. L., Ganel, T. & Goodale, M. A., 'Hemispheric specialization for the visual control of action is independent of handedness', *Journal of Neurophysiology*, 2006, *95(6)*, pp. 3496–501

Good, C. D., Johnsrude, I., Ashburner, J. et al., 'Cerebral asymmetry and the effects of sex and handedness on brain structure: a voxel-based morphometric analysis of 465 normal adult human brains', *NeuroImage*, 2001, *14(3)*, pp. 685–700

Goodale, M. A. & Milner, A. D., *The Visual Brain in Action*, Oxford University Press, Oxford, 1995

Goodarzi, M. A., Wykes, T. & Hemsley, D. R., 'Cerebral lateralisation of global-local processing in people with schizotypy', *Schizophrenia Research*, 2000, *45(1–2)*, pp. 115–21

Gopnik, A. & Meltzoff, A. N., 'Minds, bodies, and persons: young children's understanding of the self and others as reflected in imitation and theory of mind research', in Parker, S. T., Mitchell, R. W. & Boccia, M. L. (eds.), *Self-Awareness in Animals and Humans: Developmental Perspectives*, Cambridge University Press, Cambridge, UK, 2006, pp. 166–86

Gordon, E. E., Drenth, V., Jarvis, L. et al., 'Neurophysiologic syndromes in stroke as predictors of outcome', *Archives of Physical Medicine and Rehabilitation*, 1978, *59(5)*, pp. 399–403

Gordon, H. W. & Carmon, A., 'Transfer of dominance in speed of verbal response to visually presented stimuli from right to left hemisphere', *Perceptual and Motor Skills*, 1976, *42(3)*, pp. 1091–1100

Gordon, P., 'Numerical cognition without words: evidence from Amazonia', *Science*, 2004, *306(5695)*, pp. 496–9

Gorynia, I. & Müller, J., 'Hand skill and hand-eye preference in relation to verbal ability in healthy adult male and female right-handers', *Laterality*, 2006, *11(5)*, pp. 415–35

Gould, S. J. & Lewontin, R. C., 'The spandrels of San Marco and the Panglossian paradigm: a critique of the adaptationist program', *Proceedings of the Royal Society of London, Series B: Biological Sciences*, 1979, *205(1161)*, pp. 581–98

Granet, M., 'Right and left in China', in Needham, R., (ed.), *Right and Left: Essays on Dual Symbolic Classification*, University of Chicago Press, Chicago, 1973, pp. 43–58

——, *La pensée chinoise*, Albin Michel, Paris, 1999 [1934]

Graves, R., 'These be your gods, O Israel!', *The Clark Lectures 1954–1955*, in *The Crowning Privilege: Collected Essays on Poetry*, Doubleday, New York, 1956, pp. 119–42

——, *Poems, 1965–1968*, Cassell, London, 1968

Graves, R., Landis, T. & Goodglass, H., 'Laterality and sex differences for visual recognition of emotional and non-emotional words', *Neuropsychologia*, 1981, *19(1)*, pp. 95–102

Gray, T., in *Correspondence of Thomas Gray*, P. Toynbee & L. Whibley (eds.), Clarendon Press, Oxford, 1935

Green, C. D., 'Where did the ventricular localization of mental faculties come from?', *Journal of the History of the Behavioral Sciences*, 2003, *39(2)*, pp. 131–42

Greene, J. D., Nystrom, L. E., Engell, A. D. et al., 'The neural bases of cognitive conflict and control in moral judgment', *Neuron*, 2004, *44(2)*, pp. 389–400

Greenfield, P. M., 'Language, tools and brain: the ontogeny and phylogeny of hierarchically organized sequential behaviour', *Behavioral and Brain Sciences*, 1991, *14(4)*, pp. 531–95

Greenwald, B. S., Kramer-Ginsberg, E., Krishnan, K. R. et al., 'Neuroanatomic localisation of magnetic resonance imaging signal hyperintensities in geriatric depression', *Stroke*, 1998, *29(3)*, pp. 613–17

Gregory, F., *Scientific Materialism in Nineteenth-Century Germany*, Reidel, Dordrecht, Netherlands, 1977

Greville, Fulke, Baron Brooke, *Selected Poetry of Fulke Greville*, ed. T. Gunn, Faber & Faber, London, 1968

Griffin, D. R., *Animal Minds*, University of Chicago Press, Chicago, 1992

Griffin, R., *Modernism and Fascism*, Palgrave Macmillan, Basingstoke, UK, 2007

Griffin, R. & Baron-Cohen, S., 'The intentional stance: developmental and neurocognitive perspectives', in Brook, A. & Ross, D. (eds.), *Daniel Dennett*, Cambridge University Press, Cambridge, UK, 2002, pp. 83–116

Griffin, R., Friedman, O., Ween, J. et al., 'Theory of mind and the right cerebral hemisphere: refining the scope of impairment', *Laterality*, 2006, *11(3)*, pp. 195–225

Grijalva, L. R., 'Emotional asymmetries reported by dichotically presented depressive and neutral somatic statements', University of Alaska, Anchorage AK (M. S. dissertation), 1982

Grob, G. N., *Mental Institutions in America*, Free Press, New York, 1973

Grossman, M., 'A bird is a bird is a bird: making reference within and without superordinate categories', *Brain and Language*, 1981, *12(2)*, pp. 313–31

——, 'Drawing deficits in brain-damaged patients' freehand pictures', *Brain and Cognition*, 1988, *8(2)*, pp. 189–205

Grunwald, M., Weiss, T., Assmann, B. et al., 'Stable asymmetric interhemispheric theta power in patients with anorexia nervosa during haptic perception even after weight gain: a longitudinal study', *Journal of Clinical and Experimental Neuropsychology*, 2004, *26(5)*, pp. 608–20

Grüsser, O.-J., 'Mother–child holding patterns in Western art: a developmental study', *Ethology and Sociobiology*, 1983, *4(2)*, pp. 89–94

Grüsser, O.-J., Selke, T. & Zynda, B., 'Cerebral lateralisation and some implications for art, aesthetic perception and artistic creativity', in Rentschler, I., Herzberger, B. & Epstein, D. (eds.), *Beauty and the Brain: Biological Aspects of Aesthetics*, Birkhauser Verlag, Basel, 1988, pp. 257–93

Gruzelier, J. H., 'Functional neuropsychophysiological asymmetry in schizophrenia: a review and reorientation', *Schizophrenia Bulletin*, 1999, *25(1)*, pp. 91–120

Gudykunst, W. B., Yang, S.-M. & Nishida, T., 'Cultural differences in self-consciousness and self-monitoring', *Communication Research*, 1987, *14(1)*, pp. 7–34

Guillaumont, F., '*Laeva prospera*: remarques sur la droite et la gauche dans la divination romaine', in Bloch, R. (ed.), *D'Héraclès à Poséidon: Mythologie et Protohistoire*, Librairie Droz, Geneva, 1985, pp. 159–77

Gunter, H. L., Ghaziuddin, M. & Ellis, H. D., 'Asperger syndrome: tests of right hemisphere functioning and interhemispheric communication', *Journal of Autism and Developmental Disorders*, 2002, *32(4)*, pp. 263–81

Güntürkün, O. & Böhringer, P. G., 'Lateralization reversal after intertectal commissurotomy in the pigeon', *Brain Research*, 1987, *408(1–2)*, pp. 1–5

Güntürkün, O., Diekamp, B., Manns, M. et al., 'Asymmetry pays: visual lateralization improves discrimination success in pigeons', *Current Biology*, 2000, *10(17)*, pp. 1079–81

Güntürkün, O., Hellmann, B., Melsbach, G. et al., 'Asymmetries of representation in the visual system of pigeons', *NeuroReport*, 1998, *9(18)*, pp. 4127–30

Gur, R. C., Packer, I. K., Hungerbühler, J. P. et al., 'Differences in the distribution of gray and white matter in human cerebral hemispheres', *Science*, 1980, *207(4436)*, pp. 1226–8

Gur, R. C., Turetsky, B. I., Matsui, M. et al., 'Sex differences in brain gray and white matter in healthy young adults: correlations with cognitive performance', *Journal of Neuroscience*, 1999, *19(10)*, pp. 4065–72

Gur, R. E. & Chin, S., 'Laterality in functional brain imaging studies of schizophrenia', *Schizophrenia Bulletin*, 1999, *25(1)*, pp. 141–56

Gur, R. E., Mozley, P. D., Resnick, S. M. et al., 'Resting cerebral glucose metabolism in first-episode and previously treated patients with schizophrenia relates to clinical features', *Archives of General Psychiatry*, 1995, *52(8)*, pp. 657–67

Gur, R. E., Resnick, S. M., Alavi, A. et al., 'Regional brain function in schizophrenia: I. A positron emission tomography study', *Archives of General Psychiatry*, 1987, *44(2)*, pp. 119–25

Gur, R. E., Resnick, S. M. & Gur, R. C., 'Laterality and frontality of cerebral blood flow and metabolism in schizophrenia: relationship to symptom specificity', *Psychiatry Research*, 1989, *27(3)*, pp. 325–34

Gutchess, A. H., Yoon, C., Luo, T. et al., 'Categorical organization in free recall across culture and age', *Gerontology*, 2006, *52(5)*, pp. 314–23

Haaga, D. A. & Beck, A. T., 'Perspectives on depressive realism: implications for cognitive theory of depression', *Behaviour Research and Therapy*, 1995, *33(1)*, pp. 41–8

Haaland, K. Y. & Flaherty, D., 'The different types of limb apraxia errors made by patients with left vs right hemisphere damage', *Brain and Cognition*, 1984, *3(4)*, pp. 370–84

Habib, M., 'Visual hypoemotionality and prosopagnosia associated with right temporal lobe isolation', *Neuropsychologia*, 1986, *24(4)*, pp. 577–82

Hacker, P. M. S., 'Wittgenstein and the autonomy of humanistic understanding', in Allen, R. & Turvey, M. (eds.), *Wittgenstein, Theory and the Arts*, Routledge, London, 2001, pp. 39–74

Hadden, J. C., *Haydn*, J. M. Dent, London, 1902

Hadziselimovic, H. & Cus, H., 'The appearance of internal structures of the brain in relation to configuration of the human skull', *Acta Anatomica*, 1966, *63(3)*, pp. 289–99

Hagège, C., 'Writing: the invention and the dream', in de Kerckhove, D. & Lumsden, C. J. (eds.), *The Alphabet and the Brain: the Lateralization of Writing*, Springer-Verlag, Berlin, 1988, pp. 72–83

Haggard, M. P. & Parkinson, A. M., 'Stimulus and task factors as determinants of ear advantages', *Quarterly Journal of Experimental Psychology*, 1971, *23(2)*, pp. 168–77

Haidt, J., 'The emotional dog and its rational tail: a social intuitionist approach to moral judgment', *Psychological Review*, 2001, *108(4)*, pp. 814–34

Haier, R. J., Chueh, D., Touchette, P. et al., 'Brain size and cerebral glucose metabolic rate in nonspecific mental retardation and Down syndrome', *Intelligence*, 1995, *20(2)*, pp. 191–210

Haier, R. J., Siegel, B. V., MacLachlan, A. et al., 'Regional glucose metabolism changes after learning a complex visuospatial/motor task: a positron emission tomographic study', *Brain Research*, 1992, *570(1–2)*, pp. 134–43

Haier, R. J., Siegel, B. V., Nuechterlein, K. H. et al., 'Cortical glucose metabolic rate correlates of abstract reasoning and attention studied with positron emission tomography', *Intelligence*, 1988, *12(2)*, pp. 199–217

Hall, J., *The Sinister Side: How Left-Right Symbolism Shaped Western Art*, Oxford University Press, Oxford, 2008

Halligan, P. W. & Marshall, J. C., 'Toward a principled explanation of unilateral neglect', *Cognitive Neuropsychology*, 1994, *11(2)*, pp. 167–206

Halpern, M. E., Güntürkün, O., Hopkins, W. D. et al., 'Lateralization of the vertebrate brain: taking the side of model systems', *Journal of Neuroscience*, 2005, *25(45)*, pp. 10351–7

Hamilton, A. F. de C. & Grafton, S. T., 'Action outcomes are represented in human inferior frontoparietal cortex', *Cerebral Cortex*, 2008, *18(5)*, pp. 1160–68

Hamilton, C., *Growth Fetish*, Allen & Unwin, Crow's Nest NSW, 2003

Hannay, H. J., 'Asymmetry in reception and retention of colors', *Brain and Language*, 1979, *8(2)*, pp. 191–201

Happaney, K., Zelazo, P. D. & Stuss, D. T., 'Development of orbitofrontal function: current themes and future directions', *Brain and Cognition*, 2004, *55(1)*, pp. 1–10

Happé, F., 'Central coherence and theory of mind in autism: reading homographs in context', *British Journal of Developmental Psychology*, 1997, *15(1)*, pp. 1–12

Happé, F., Brownell, H. & Winner, E., 'Acquired "theory of mind" impairments following stroke', *Cognition*, 1999, *70(3)*, pp. 211–40

Harding, S., *The Science Question in Feminism*, Cornell University Press, Ithaca NY, 1986

Hare, E. H., 'Was insanity on the increase?', *British Journal of Psychiatry*, 1983, *142(5)*, pp. 439–55

——, 'Schizophrenia as a recent disease', *British Journal of Psychiatry*, 1988, *153(4)*, pp. 521–31

Harmon-Jones, E., 'Contributions from research on anger and cognitive dissonance to understanding the motivational functions of asymmetrical frontal brain activity', *Biological Psychology*, 2004, *67(1–2)*, pp. 51–76

——, 'Trait anger predicts relative left frontal cortical activation to anger-inducing stimuli', *International Journal of Psychophysiology*, 2007, *66(2)*, pp. 154–60

Harmon-Jones, E. & Allen, J. J., 'Anger and frontal brain activity: EEG asymmetry consistent with approach motivation despite negative affective valence', *Journal of Personality and Social Psychology*, 1998, *74(5)*, pp. 1310–16

Harnad, S. R., 'Creativity, lateral saccades and the nondominant hemisphere', *Perceptual and Motor Skills*, 1972, *34(2)*, pp. 653–4

Harries, K., 'The infinite sphere: comments on the history of a metaphor', *Journal of the History of Philosophy*, 1975, *13(1)*, pp. 5–15

Harrington, A., *Medicine, Mind, and the Double Brain*, Princeton University Press, Princeton NJ, 1987

Harrington, D. L., Haaland, K. Y. & Knight, R. T., 'Cortical networks underlying mechanisms of time perception', *Journal of Neuroscience*, 1998, *18(3)*, pp. 1085–95

Harris, L. J., Almerigi, J. B., Carbary, T. J. et al., 'Left-side infant holding: a test of the hemispheric arousal-attentional hypothesis', *Brain and Cognition*, 2001, *46(1–2)*, pp. 159–65

Harris, R. A., *The Linguistic Wars*, Oxford University Press, Oxford, 1993

Hart, N. S., Partridge, J. C. & Cuthill, I. C., 'Retinal asymmetry in birds', *Current Biology*, 2000, *10(2)*, pp. 115–17

Hartmann, K., Goldenberg, G., Daumüller, M. et al., 'It takes the whole brain to make a cup of coffee: the neuropsychology of naturalistic actions involving technical devices', *Neuropsychologia*, 2005, *43(4)*, pp. 625–37

540 • BIBLIOGRAPHY

Hartnett, P. M. & Gelman, R., 'Early understandings of numbers: paths or barriers to the construction of new understandings?', *Learning and Instruction*, 1998, *8(4)*, pp. 341–74
Hashimoto, R., Yoshida, M. & Tanaka, Y., 'Utilization behavior after right thalamic infarction', *European Neurology*, 1995, *35(1)*, pp. 58–62
Hatazawa, J., Brooks, R. A., di Chiro, G. et al., 'Glucose utilization rate versus brain size in humans', *Neurology*, 1987, *37(4)*, pp. 583–8
Hatta, T. & Ayetani, N., 'Ear differences in evaluating emotional tones of unknown speech', *Acta Psychologica (Amsterdam)*, 1985, *60(1)*, pp. 73–82
Hauser, M. D., 'Right hemisphere dominance for the production of facial expression in monkeys', *Science*, 1993, *261(5120)*, pp. 475–7
Hauser, M. D., Chomsky, N., Fitch, W. T., 'The faculty of language: what is it, who has it, and how did it evolve?', *Science*, 2002, *298(5598)*, pp. 1569–79
Havelock, E. A., *Preface to Plato*, Harvard University Press, Cambridge MA, 1963
Hayashi, N., Ostrom, E., Walker, J. et al., 'Reciprocity, trust, and the sense of control: a cross-societal study', *Rationality and Society*, 1999, *11(1)*, pp. 27–46
Hayek, F. A., *New Studies in Philosophy, Politics, Economics and the History of Ideas*, Routledge & Kegan Paul, London, 1978
Hayes, T. L. & Lewis, D. A., 'Hemispheric differences in layer III pyramidal neurons of the anterior language area', *Archives of Neurology*, 1993, *50(5)*, pp. 501–5
Hazlitt, W., *Table Talk, Or, Original Essays on Men and Manners*, Colburn, London, 1824
Healy, S. D., *Boredom, Self and Culture*, Farleigh Dickinson University Press, Rutherford NJ, 1984
Heber, I. A., Valvoda, J. T. & Kuhlen, T., 'Low arousal modulates visuospatial attention in three-dimensional virtual space', *Journal of the International Neuropsychological Society*, 2008, *14(2)*, pp. 309–17
Hécaen, H. & Albert, M. L., *Human Neuropsychology*, Wiley, New York, 1978
Hécaen, H. & de Ajuriaguerra, J., *Méconnaissances et hallucinations corporelles: intégration et désintégration de la somatognosie*, Masson & Cie., Paris, 1952
Hécaen, H., de Ajuriaguerra, J. & Angelergues, R., 'Apraxia and its various aspects', in Halpern, L. (ed.), *Problems of Dynamic Neurology*, Grune & Stratton, New York, 1963, pp. 217–30
Hécaen, H., de Ajuriaguerra, J. & Massonet, J., 'Les troubles visuoconstructifs par lésions pariéto-occipitales droites. Rôle des perturbations vestibulaires', *L'Encéphale*, 1951, *40*, pp. 122–79
Hécaen, H. & Dubois, J., *La naissance de la neuropsychologie du langage 1825–1865 (textes et documents)*, Flammarion, Paris, 1969
Hedley Brooke, J., *Science and Religion: Some Historical Perspectives*, Cambridge University Press, Cambridge, UK, 1991
Hegel, G. W. F., *The Philosophy of Right*, trans. S. W. Dyde, George Bell, London, 1896 [*Grundlinien der Philosophie des Rechts* 1820]
——, *The Phenomenology of Mind*, trans. J. B. Baillie, George Allen & Unwin, London, 1949 [*Phänomenologie des Geistes* 1807]
——, *The Science of Logic*, trans. A.V. Miller, George Allen & Unwin, London, 1969 [*Wissenschaft der Logik* 1812]
——, *Vorlesungen über die Ästhetik I*, in *Werke*, vol. 13, ed. E. Moldenhauer & K. M. Michel, Suhrkamp, Frankfurt am Main, 1970 [1835]
——, *Phenomenology of Spirit*, trans. A. V. Miller, Clarendon Press, Oxford, 1977 [*Phänomenologie des Geistes* 1807]
Heidegger, M., *An Introduction to Metaphysics*, trans. R. Manheim, Yale University Press, New Haven CT, 1959 [*Einführung in die Metaphysik* 1935]
——, *Discourse on Thinking*, trans. J. M. Anderson & E. H. Freund, Harper & Row, New York, 1966 [*Gelassenheit* 1959]
——, *Poetry, Language, Thought*, trans. A. Hofstadter, Harper & Row, New York, 1971 [compiled from various German sources]
——, *The Question Concerning Technology and Other Essays*, trans. W. Lovitt, Harper & Row, New York, 1977 [title essay 'Die Frage nach der Technik', 1949]
——, *The Metaphysical Foundations of Logic*, trans. M. Heim, Indiana University Press, Bloomington IN, 1984 [*Metaphysische Anfangsgründe der Logik im Ausgang von Leibniz* 1978]
——, *Being and Time*, trans. J. Macquarrie & E. Robinson, Blackwell, Oxford, 1999 [*Sein und Zeit* 1926]
Heilman, K., 'Anosognosia: possible neuropsychological mechanisms', in Prigatano, G. & Schacter, D. (eds.), *Awareness of Deficit After Brain Injury*, Oxford University Press, Oxford, 1991, pp. 53–62
——, *Matter of Mind: a Neurologist's View of Brain-Behavior Relationships*, Oxford University Press, Oxford, 2002
Heilman, K. M., *Creativity and the Brain*, Psychology Press, New York, 2005
Heilman, K. M., Blonder, L. X., Bowers, D. et al., 'Neurological disorders and emotional dysfunction', in Borod, J. (ed.), *The Neuropsychology of Emotion*, Oxford University Press, Oxford, 2000, pp. 367–412
Heilman, K. M. & Bowers, D., 'Neuropsychological studies of emotional changes induced by right and left hemisphere lesions', in Stein, N., Leventhal, B. & Trabasso, T. (eds.), *Psychological and Biological Approaches to Emotion*, Lawrence Erlbaum, Hillsdale NJ, 1990, pp. 97–113
Heilman, K. M., Bowers, D., Speedie, L. et al., 'Comprehension of affective and nonaffective prosody', *Neurology*, 1984, *34(7)*, pp. 917–21
Heilman, K. M., Scholes, R. & Watson, R. T., 'Auditory affective agnosia: disturbed comprehension of affective speech', *Journal of Neurology, Neurosurgery, & Psychiatry*, 1975, *38(1)*, pp. 69–72
Heilman, K. M., Schwartz, H. D. & Watson, R. T., 'Hypoarousal in patients with the neglect syndrome and emotional indifference', *Neurology*, 1978, *28(3)*, pp. 229–32
Heilman, K. M. & van den Abell, T., 'Right hemispheric dominance for mediating cerebral activation', *Neuropsychologia*, 1979, *17(3–4)*, pp. 315–21

Heine, S. J., Lehman, D. R., Ide, E. et al., 'Divergent consequences of success and failure in Japan and North America: an investigation of self-improving motivations and malleable selves', *Journal of Personality and Social Psychology*, 2001, *81(4)*, pp. 599–615

Heine, S. J., Lehman, D. R., Markus, H. R. et al., 'Is there a universal need for positive self-regard?', *Psychological Review*, 1999, *106(4)*, pp. 766–94

Heinrichs, R. & Zakzanis, K., 'Neurocognitive deficit in schizophrenia: a quantitative review of the evidence', *Neuropsychology*, 1998, *12(3)*, pp. 426–45

Heinze, H. J., Hinrichs, H., Scholz, M. et al., 'Neural mechanisms of global and local processing: a combined PET and ERP study', *Journal of Cognitive Neuroscience*, 1998, *10(4)*, pp. 485–98

Heisenberg, W., *Das Naturbild der heutigen Physik*, Rowohlt, Hamburg, 1955; trans. A. J. Pomerans, *The Physicist's Conception of Nature*, Harcourt Brace, New York, 1958

Heller, E., *The Importance of Nietzsche*, University of Chicago Press, Chicago, 1988

Heller, W., 'The neuropsychology of emotion: developmental patterns and implications for psychopathology', in Stein, N. L., Leventhal, B. & Trabasso, T. (eds.), *Psychological and Biological Approaches to Emotion*, Lawrence Erlbaum, Hillsdale NJ, 1990, pp. 167–211

Heller, W., Nitschke, J. B., Etienne, M. A. et al., 'Patterns of regional brain activity differentiate types of anxiety', *Journal of Abnormal Psychology*, 1997, *106(3)*, pp. 376–85

Hellige, J. B., 'Changes in same-different laterality patterns as a function of practice and stimulus quality', *Perception and Psychophysics*, 1976, *20(5)*, pp. 267–73

——, 'Effects of perceptual quality and visual field of probe stimulus presentation on memory search for letters', *Journal of Experimental Psychology: Human Perception and Performance*, 1980, *6(4)*, pp. 639–51

——, *Hemispheric Asymmetry: What's Right and What's Left*, Harvard University Press, Cambridge MA, 1993

——, 'Hemispheric asymmetry for components of visual information processing', in Davidson, R. & Hugdahl, K. (eds.), *Brain Asymmetry*, Massachusetts Institute of Technology Press, Cambridge MA, 1995, pp. 99–121

Hellige, J. B., Jonsson, J. E. & Michimata, C., 'Processing from LVF, RVF, and bilateral presentations: examinations of meta-control and interhemispheric interaction', *Brain and Cognition*, 1988, *7(1)*, pp. 39–53

Hellige, J. B. & Michimata, C., 'Categorization versus distance: hemispheric differences for processing spatial information', *Memory and Cognition*, 1989, *17(6)*, pp. 770–76

Hellige, J. B., Taylor, A. K. & Eng, T. L., 'Interhemispheric interaction when both hemispheres have access to the same stimulus information', *Journal of Experimental Psychology: Human Perception and Performance*, 1989, *15(4)*, pp. 711–22

Hellige, J. B. & Webster, R., 'Right hemisphere superiority for initial stages of letter processing', *Neuropsychologia*, 1979, *17(6)*, pp. 653–60

Helliwell, J. F., 'How's life? Combining individual and national variables to explain subjective well-being', *Economic Modelling*, 2003, *20(2)*, pp. 331–60

Henriques, J. B. & Davidson, R. J., 'Left frontal hypoactivation in depression', *Journal of Abnormal Psychology*, 1991, *100(4)*, pp. 535–45

Henschen, S. E., 'On the function of the right hemisphere of the brain in relation to the left in speech, music and calculation', *Brain*, 1926, *49(1)*, pp. 110–23

Henshilwood, C. S., d'Errico, F., Yates, R. et al., 'Emergence of modern human behavior: Middle Stone Age engravings from South Africa', *Science*, 2002, *295(5558)*, pp. 1278–80

Henson, R. N. A., Rugg, M. D., Shallice, T. et al., 'Confidence in recognition memory for words: dissociating right prefrontal roles in episodic retrieval', *Journal of Cognitive Neuroscience*, 2000, *12(6)*, pp. 913–23

Henson, R., Shallice, T. & Dolan, R., 'Neuroimaging evidence for dissociable forms of repetition priming', *Science*, 2000, *287(5456)*, pp. 1269–72

Herder, J. G., *Die Plastik von 1770*, in *Sämtliche Werke*, 33 vols., ed. B. Suphan, Weidmannsche Buchhandlung, Berlin, 1878a, vol. 8

——, *Viertes Wäldchen* [1769–72], in *Sämtliche Werke*, 33 vols., ed. B. Suphan, Weidmannsche Buchhandlung, Berlin, 1878b, vol. 4

——, *Zum Sinn des Gefühls* [1769], in *Sämtliche Werke*, 33 vols., ed. B. Suphan, Weidmannsche Buchhandlung, Berlin, 1878c, vol. 8

——, 'Essay on the Origin of Language', in *Two Essays on the Origin of Language: Jean-Jacques Rousseau & Johann Gottfried Herder*, trans. J. H. Moran & A. Gode, University of Chicago Press, Chicago, 1966 [*Abhandlung über den Ursprung der Sprache* 1772]

——, *Sculpture: Some Observations on Shape and Form from Pygmalion's Creative Dream*, trans. & ed. J. Gaiger, University of Chicago Press, Chicago, 2002 [*Plastik: Einige Wahrnehmungen über Form und Gestalt aus Pygmalions bildendem Traume* 1778]

Herman, L. M., Richards, D. G. & Wolz, J. P., 'Comprehension of sentences by bottlenosed dolphins', *Cognition*, 1984, *16(2)*, pp. 129–219

Hernstein, R. J., Loveland, D. H. & Cable, C., 'Natural concepts in pigeons', *Journal of Experimental Psychology: Animal Behavior Processes*, 1976, *2(4)*, pp. 285–302

Herzog, J., Reiff, J., Krack, P. et al., 'Manic episode with psychotic symptoms induced by subthalamic nucleus stimulation in a patient with Parkinson's disease', *Movement Disorders*, 2003, *18(11)*, pp. 1382–4

Heschl, R. L., *Über die vordere quere Schläfenwindung des menschlichen Grosshirns*, Braumüller, Vienna, 1878

Hespos, S. J. & Spelke, E. S., 'Conceptual precursors to language', *Nature*, 2004, *430(6998)*, pp. 453–6

Hewes, G. W., 'Primate communication and the gestural origin of language', *Current Anthropology*, 1973, *14(1–2)*, pp. 5–11 [commentary pp. 12–24]

Hilgetag, C. C., Théoret, H. & Pascual-Leone, A., 'Enhanced visual spatial attention ipsilateral to rTMS-induced "virtual lesions" of human parietal cortex', *Nature Neuroscience*, 2001, *4(9)*, pp. 953–7

Hitler, A., *Mein Kampf*, trans. R. Manheim, Houghton Mifflin, Boston MA, 1943

Hobson, P., *The Cradle of Thought: Exploring the Origins of Thinking*, Oxford University Press, Oxford, 2004

Hoff, H. & Pötzl, O., 'Über ein neues parieto-occipitales Syndrom. Seelenlähmung des Schauens, Störung des Körperschemas, Wegfall des zentralen Sehens', *Jahrbuch für Psychiatrie und Neurologie*, 1935, *52*, pp. 173–218

Hoffman, A. M., Robakiewicz, P. E., Tuttle, E. M. et al., 'Behavioural lateralisation in the Australian magpie (*Gymnorhina tibicen*)', *Laterality*, 2006, *11(2)*, pp. 110–21

Hofstadter, D. R., *Metamagical Themas*, Basic Books, New York, 1985

Hofstadter, D. R. & Dennett, D. C., *The Mind's I: Fantasies and Reflections on Self and Soul*, Bantam Books, New York, 1982

Hölderlin, F., *Hyperion, or the Hermit in Greece*, trans. R. Benjamin, Archipelago, New York, 2008

Holloway, R. L. & de LaCoste-Lareymondie, M. C., 'Brain endocast asymmetry in pongids and hominids: some preliminary findings on the paleontology of cerebral dominance', *American Journal of Physical Anthropology*, 1982, *58(1)*, pp. 101–10

Holman, S. D. & Hutchison, J. B., 'Is sexual-aggressive vocal communication related to asymmetric mechanisms in the brain?', *Aggressive Behavior*, 1994, *20(3)*, pp. 223–34

Hölscher, U., *Anfängliches Fragen: Studien zur frühen griechischen Philosophie*, Vandenhoeck & Ruprecht, Göttingen, 1968

Holt, J., 'Numbers Guy: are our brains wired for math?', *The New Yorker*, New York, 3 March 2008, pp. 42–7

Honeycutt, N. A., Musick, A., Barta, P. E. et al., 'Measurement of the planum temporale (PT) on magnetic resonance imaging scans: temporal PT alone and with parietal extension', *Psychiatry Research*, 2000, *98(2)*, pp. 103–16

Hook-Costigan, M. A. & Rogers, L. J., 'Lateralized use of the mouth in production of vocalizations by marmosets', *Neuropsychologia*, 1998, *36(12)*, pp. 1265–73

Hopkins, G. M., in Gardner, W. H. & MacKenzie, N. H. (eds.), *The Poems of Gerard Manley Hopkins*, Oxford University Press, Oxford, 4th edn., 1970

——, *Poems and Prose*, ed. W. H. Gardner, Penguin, Harmondsworth, UK, 1963

Hopkins, W. D., 'Hand preferences for a coordinated bimanual task in 110 chimpanzees (*Pan troglodytes*): cross-sectional analysis', *Journal of Comparative Psychology*, 1995, *109(3)*, pp. 291–7

Hopkins, W. D. & Cantalupo, C., 'Does variation in sample size explain individual differences in hand preferences in chimpanzees (*Pan troglodytes*)? An empirical study and reply to Palmer (2002)', *American Journal of Physical Anthropology*, 2003, *121(4)*, pp. 378–84

Hopkins, W. D., Cantalupo, C., Freeman, H. et al., 'Chimpanzees are right-handed when recording bouts of hand use', *Laterality*, 2005, *10(2)*, pp. 121–30

Hopkins, W. D. & Fernández-Carriba, S., 'The effect of situational factors on hand preferences for feeding in 177 captive chimpanzees (*Pan troglodytes*)', *Neuropsychologia*, 2000, *38(4)*, pp. 403–9

Hopkins, W. D., Fernandez-Carriba, S., Wesley, M. J. et al., 'The use of bouts and frequencies in the evaluation of hand preferences for a coordinated bimanual task in chimpanzees (*Pan troglodytes*): an empirical study comparing two different indices of laterality', *Journal of Comparative Psychology*, 2001, *115(3)*, pp. 294–9

Hopkins, W. D. & Marino, L., 'Asymmetries in cerebral width in nonhuman primate brains as revealed by magnetic resonance imaging (MRI)', *Neuropsychologia*, 2000, *38(4)*, pp. 493–9

Hopkins, W. D., Wesley, M. J., Izard, M. K. et al., 'Chimpanzees (*Pan troglodytes*) are predominantly right-handed: replication in three populations of apes', *Behavioral Neuroscience*, 2004, *118(3)*, pp. 659–63

Hoppe, K. D. & Bogen, J. E., 'Alexithymia in twelve commissurotomized patients', *Psychotherapy and Psychosomatics*, 1977, *28(1–4)*, pp. 148–55

Höppner, J., Kunesch, E., Buchmann, J. et al., 'Demyelination and axonal degeneration in corpus callosum assessed by analysis of transcallosally mediated inhibition in multiple sclerosis', *Clinical Neurophysiology*, 1999, *110(4)*, pp. 748–56

Höppner, J., Kunesch, E., Großmann, A. et al., 'Dysfunction of transcallosally mediated motor inhibition and callosal morphology in patients with schizophrenia', *Acta Psychiatrica Scandinavica*, 2001, *104(3)*, pp. 227–35

Hoptman, M. J. & Davidson, R. J., 'How and why do the two cerebral hemispheres interact?', *Psychological Bulletin*, 1994, *116(2)*, pp. 195–219

Horowitz, M. J., *Image Formation and Psychotherapy*, Jason Aronson, New York, 1983

Horton, P. C., 'The comforting substrate and the right brain', *Bulletin of the Menninger Clinic*, 1995, *59(4)*, pp. 480–86

Hoshino-Browne, E., Zanna, A. S., Spencer, S. J. et al., 'On the cultural guises of cognitive dissonance: the case of easterners and westerners', *Journal of Personality and Social Psychology*, 2005, *89(3)*, pp. 294–310

Hoshiyama, M., Kakigi, R., Watanabe, S. et al., 'Brain responses for the subconscious recognition of faces', *Neuroscience Research*, 2003, *46(4)*, pp. 435–42

Houde, O., Zago, L., Crivello, F. et al., 'Access to deductive logic depends on a right ventromedial prefrontal area devoted to emotion and feeling: evidence from a training paradigm', *NeuroImage*, 2001, *14(6)*, pp. 1486–92

Hough, M. S., 'Narrative comprehension in adults with right and left hemisphere brain-damage: theme organization', *Brain and Language*, 1990, *38(2)*, pp. 253–77

House, J. S., Landis, K. R. & Umberson D., 'Social relationships and health', *Science*, 1988, *241(4865)*, pp. 540–45

Howard, R. J., ffytche, D. H., Barnes, J. et al., 'The functional anatomy of imagining and perceiving colour', *NeuroReport*, 1998, *9(6)*, pp. 1019–23

Howes, D. & Boller, F., 'Simple reaction time: evidence for focal impairment from lesions of the right hemisphere', *Brain*, 1975, *98(2)*, pp. 317–32

Hufschmidt, H.-J., 'Das Rechts-Links-Profil im kulturhistorischen Längsschnitt', *Archiv für Psychiatrie und Nervenkrankheiten*, 1980, *229(1)*, pp. 17–43

——, 'Über die Linksorientierung der Zeichnung und die optische Dominanz der rechten Hirnhemisphäre', *Zeitschrift für Kunstgeschichte*, 1983, *46(3)*, pp. 287–94

Hugdahl, K., Iversen, P. M. & Johnsen, B. H., 'Laterality for facial expressions: does the sex of the subject interact with the sex of the stimulus face?', *Cortex*, 1993, *29(2)*, pp. 325–31

Hugdahl, K., Law, I., Kyllingsbaek, S. et al., 'Effects of attention on dichotic listening: an 150-PET study', *Human Brain Mapping*, 2000, *10(2)*, pp. 87–97

Hugdahl, K., Rund, B. R., Lund, A. et al., 'Attentional and executive dysfunctions in schizophrenia and depression: evidence from dichotic listening performance', *Biological Psychiatry*, 2003, *53(7)*, pp. 609–16

Huizinga, J., *Erasmus and the Age of Reformation*, Harper & Row, New York, 1957 [*Erasmus 1924*]

——, *The Waning of the Middle Ages*, Penguin, Harmondsworth, UK, 1972 [*Herfsttij der Middeleeuwen 1919*]

Hume, D., *A Treatise of Human Nature*, ed. E. C. Mossner, Penguin, Harmondsworth, UK, 1986 [1739–40]

Humphrey, N., 'Cave art, autism and the human mind', *Cambridge Archaeological Journal*, 1998, *8(2)*, pp. 165–91

——, *Seeing Red: a Study in Consciousness*, Harvard University Press, Cambridge MA, 2006

Humphrey, N. K. & McManus, I. C., 'Status and the left cheek', *New Scientist*, 1973, *59*, pp. 437–9

Humphreys, G. W., Riddoch, M. J. & Quinlan, P. T., 'Interactive processes in perceptual organisation: evidence from visual agnosia', in Posner, M. I. & Marin, O. S. (eds.), *Attention and Performance*, vol. 11, Lawrence Erlbaum, Hillsdale NJ, 1985, pp. 301–18

Humphrys, J., *Beyond Words*, Hodder & Stoughton, London, 2006

Hunca-Bednarska, A. & Kucharska-Pietura, K., 'Emotional behavior in schizophrenia and unilateral brain damage – expression and verbalisation of emotions. Cerebral hemispheric asymmetry. Part II', *Psychiatria Polska*, 2002, *36(3)*, pp. 435–48

Hunt, G. R., 'Human-like, population-level specialisation in the manufacture of pandanus tools by New Caledonian crows *Corvus moneduloides*', *Proceedings of the Royal Society of London, Series B: Biological Sciences*, 2000, *267(1441)*, pp. 403–13

Hunt, G. R., Corballis, M. C. & Gray, R. D., 'Laterality in tool manufacture by crows – neural processing and not ecological factors may influence "handedness" in these birds', *Nature*, 2001, *414(6865)*, p. 707

Hunt, G. R. & Gray, R. D., 'Direct observations of pandanus-tool manufacture and use by a New Caledonian crow (*Corvus moneduloides*)', *Animal Cognition*, 2004, *7(2)*, pp. 114–20

Hurley, S., 'Imitation, media violence, and freedom of speech', *Philosophical Studies*, 2004, *117(1–2)*, pp. 165–218

Hurley, S. & Chater, N., 'The importance of imitation', in Hurley, S. & Chater, N. (eds.), *Perspectives on Imitation: From Neuroscience to Social Science*, vol. 1, *Mechanisms of Imitation and Imitation in Animals*, Massachusetts Institute of Technology Press, Cambridge MA, 2005, pp. 1–52

Husain, M., Shapiro, K., Martin, J. et al., 'Abnormal temporal dynamics of visual attention in spatial neglect patients', *Nature*, 1997, *385(6612)*, pp. 154–6

Husserl, E., *Ideen zu einer reinen Phänomenologie und phänomenologischen Philosophie, II*, Nijhoff, The Hague, 1952 [1913]

——, *Die Krisis der Europäischen Wissenschaften und die transzendentale Phänomenologie*, in Biemel, W. (ed.), *Gesammelte Werke*, vol. 6, Nijhoff, The Hague, 1962 [1936]

——, *The Crisis of European Sciences and Transcendental Phenomenology*, trans. D. Carr, Northwestern University Press, Evanston IL, 1970 [*Die Krisis der europäischen Wissenschaften und die transzendentale Phänomenologie: Eine Einleitung in die phänomenologische Philosophie 1936*]

——, *Cartesian Meditations: An Introduction to Phenomenology*, trans. D. Cairns, Kluwer Academic, Dordrecht, Netherlands, 1995 [1960, from *Husserliana* 1950]

Hutchison, W. D., Davis, K. D., Lozano, A. M. et al., 'Pain-related neurons in the human cingulate cortex', *Nature Neuroscience*, 1999, *2(5)*, pp. 403–5

Hutner, N. & Liederman, J., 'Right hemisphere participation in reading', *Brain and Language*, 1991, *41(4)*, pp. 475–95

Iacoboni, M., Molnar-Szakacs, I., Gallese, V. et al., 'Grasping the intentions of others with one's own mirror neuron system', *PLoS Biology*, 2005, *3(3)*, p. e79

Iidaka, T., Yamashita, K., Kashikura, K. et al., 'Spatial frequency of visual image modulates neural responses in the temporo-occipital lobe: an investigation with event-related fMRI', *Cognitive Brain Research*, 2004, *18(2)*, pp. 196–204

Ilie, G. & Thompson, W. F., 'A comparison of acoustic cues in music and speech for three dimensions of affect', *Music Perception*, 2006, *23(4)*, pp. 319–29

Imbens-Bailey, A. & Pan, B. A., 'The pragmatics of self- and other-reference in young children', *Social Development*, 1998, *7(2)*, pp. 219–33

Indersmitten, T. & Gur, R. C., 'Emotion processing in chimeric faces: hemispheric asymmetries in expression and recognition of emotions', *Journal of Neuroscience*, 2003, *23(9)*, pp. 3820–25

Inglehart, R. & Klingemann, H.-D., 'Genes, culture, democracy, and happiness', in Diener, E. & Suh, E. M. (eds.), *Culture and Subjective Well-being*, Massachusetts Institute of Technology Press, Cambridge MA, 2000, pp. 165–83

Intrator, J., Hare, R., Stritzke, P. et al., 'A brain imaging (single photon emission computerized tomography) study of semantic and affective processing in psychopaths', *Biological Psychiatry*, 1997, *42(2)*, pp. 96–103

Inwood, M, *A Heidegger Dictionary*, Blackwell, Oxford, 1999

Iosifescu, D. V., Renshaw, P. F., Lyoo, I. K. et al., 'Brain white-matter hyperintensities and treatment outcome in major depressive disorder', *British Journal of Psychiatry*, 2006, *188(2)*, pp. 180–85

Irle, E., Lange, C. & Sachsse, U., 'Reduced size and abnormal asymmetry of parietal cortex in women with borderline personality disorder', *Biological Psychiatry*, 2005, *57(2)*, pp. 173–82

Irle, E., Lange, C., Weniger, G. et al., 'Size abnormalities of the superior parietal cortices are related to dissociation in borderline personality disorder', *Psychiatry Research*, 2007, *156(2)*, pp. 139–49

Ito, M., 'Neurobiology: internal model visualised', *Nature*, 2000, *403(6766)*, pp. 153–4

Iverson, J. M., 'How to get to the cafeteria: gesture and speech in blind and sighted children's spatial descriptions', *Developmental Psychology*, 1999, *35(4)*, pp. 1132–42

Ivry, R. B. & Robertson, L. C., *The Two Sides of Perception*, Massachusetts Institute of Technology, Cambridge MA, 1998

Iwata, K., *Kami to Kami: Animizumu Uchu no Tabi* (*Spirits and Gods: Travel in the Universe of Animism*), Kodansha, Tokyo, 1989

Izard, C. E., *The Psychology of Emotions*, Plenum Press, New York, 1991

Jablensky, A., 'Epidemiology of schizophrenia: a European perspective', *Schizophrenia Bulletin*, 1986, *12(1)*, pp. 52–73

Jack, I., *Keats and the Mirror of Art*, Clarendon Press, Oxford, 1967

Jackson, J. H., 'On the nature of the duality of the brain: Part III', *Brain*, 1915, *38(1–2)*, pp. 96–103

——, *Selected Writings of John Hughlings Jackson*, 2 vols., ed. J. Taylor, Hodder & Stoughton, London, 1932

Jackson, M. & Warrington, E. K., 'Arithmetic skills in patients with unilateral cerebral lesions', *Cortex*, 1986, *22(4)*, pp. 611–20

Jackson, P. L., Brunet, E., Meltzoff, A. N. et al., 'Empathy examined through the neural mechanisms involved in imagining how I feel versus how you feel pain', *Neuropsychologia*, 2006, *44(5)*, pp. 752–61

Jacobs, G. D. & Snyder, D., 'Frontal brain asymmetry predicts affective style in men', *Behavioral Neuroscience*, 1996, *110(1)*, pp. 3–6

James, W., *Varieties of Religious Experience*, Longmans, Green & Co., London, 1912

——, *The Works of William James: The Will to Believe*, Harvard University Press, Cambridge MA, 1979

——, *The Principles of Psychology*, Great Books, Chicago, 1990 [1890]

Jamison, K., *Touched With Fire: Manic-Depressive Illness and the Artistic Temperament*, Free Press, Old Tappan NJ, 1993

Janata, P. & Grafton, S. T., 'Swinging in the brain: shared neural substrates for behaviors related to sequencing and music', *Nature Neuroscience*, 2003, *6(7)*, pp. 682–7

Jäncke, L. & Steinmetz, H., 'Anatomical brain asymmetries and their relevance for functional asymmetries', in Hugdahl, K. & Davidson, R. J. (eds.), *The Asymmetrical Brain*, Massachusetts Institute of Technology Press, Cambridge MA, 2003, pp. 187–230

Jansen, C., Sturm, W. & Willmes, K., 'Sex-specific "activation"-dominance of the left hemisphere for choice reactions: an experimental study regarding lateralisation of attention functions', *Zeitschrift für Neuropsychologie*, 1992, *3(1)*, pp. 44–51

Jasiukaitis, P., Nouriani, B., Hugdahl, K. et al., 'Relateralizing hypnosis: or, have we been barking up the wrong hemisphere?', *International Journal of Clinical and Experimental Hypnosis*, 1997, *45(2)*, pp. 158–77

Jasiukaitis, P., Nouriani, B. & Spiegel, D., 'Left hemisphere superiority for event-related potential effects of hypnotic obstruction', *Neuropsychologia*, 1996, *34(7)*, pp. 661–8

Jaspers, K., *Von der Wahrheit* (*Philosophische Logik*, vol. 1), Piper Verlag, Munich, 1947

——, *Vom Ursprung und Ziel der Geschichte*, Piper, München/Artemis, Zürich, 1949; *The Origin and Goal of History*, trans. M. Bullock, Routledge & Kegan Paul, London, 1953

——, *Nietzsche*, trans. C. F. Wallraff & F. J. Schmitz, Johns Hopkins University Press, Baltimore MD, 1997

Jaynes, J., *The Origin of Consciousness in the Breakdown of the Bicameral Mind*, Houghton Mifflin, Boston MA, 1976

Jeffries, K. J., Fritz, J. B. & Braun, A. R., 'Words in melody: an H(2)15O PET study of brain activation during singing and speaking', *NeuroReport*, 2003, *14(5)*, pp. 749–54

Jensen, B. T., 'Left-right orientation in profile drawing', *American Journal of Psychology*, 1952a, *65(1)*, pp. 80–83

——, 'Reading habits and left-right orientation in profile drawing by Japanese children', *American Journal of Psychology*, 1952b, *65(2)*, pp. 306–7

Jerison, H. J., 'Vigilance: biology, psychology, theory and practice', in Mackie, R. R. (ed.), *Vigilance (NATO conference series)*, Plenum Press, New York, 1977, pp. 27–40

——, 'On the evolution of the mind', in Oakley, D. (ed.), *Brain and Mind*, Methuen, London, 1985, pp. 1–31

Jespersen, O., *Language, its Nature, Development and Origin*, Allen & Unwin, London, 1922

Ji, L. J., Zhang, Z. & Nisbett, R. E., 'Is it culture or is it language? Examination of language effects in cross-cultural research on categorization', *Journal of Personality and Social Psychology*, 2004, *87(1)*, pp. 57–65

Joanette, Y. & Goulet, P., 'Word naming in right brain-damaged subjects', in Chiarello, C. (ed.), *Right Hemisphere Contributions to Lexical Semantics*, Springer-Verlag, New York, 1988, pp. 1–18

Joanette, Y., Goulet, P. & Hannequin, D., *Right Hemisphere and Verbal Communication*, Springer-Verlag, New York, 1990

Johanson, D. & Edgar, B., *From Lucy to Language*, Weidenfeld & Nicolson, London, 1996

Johnsgard, P., *The Plovers, Sandpipers and Snipes of the World*, University of Nebraska Press, Lincoln NE, 1981

Johnson, D. & Myklebust, H., *Learning Disabilities: Educational Principles and Practices*, Grune and Stratton, New York, 1967

Johnson, S., *Preface to 'The Plays of William Shakespeare'* [1765], in Nichol Smith, D. (ed.), *Eighteenth Century Essays on Shakespeare*, Clarendon Press, Oxford, 1963, pp. 112–61

Jolliffe, T.-D. & Baron-Cohen, S., 'Are people with autism and Asperger syndrome faster than normal on the Embedded Figures Test?', *Journal of Child Psychology and Psychiatry*, 1997, *38(5)*, pp. 527–34

——, 'A test of central coherence theory: linguistic processing in high-functioning adults with autism or Asperger syndrome: is local coherence impaired?', *Cognition*, 1999, *71(2)*, pp. 149–85

Jones, C. R., Rosenkranz, K., Rothwell, J. C. et al., 'The right dorsolateral prefrontal cortex is essential in time reproduction: an investigation with repetitive transcranial magnetic stimulation', *Experimental Brain Research*, 2004, *158(3)*, pp. 366–72

Jones-Gotman, M. & Milner, B., 'Design fluency: the invention of nonsense drawings after focal cortical lesions', *Neuropsychologia*, 1977, *15(4–5)*, pp. 653–74

Jonson, B., *Timber, or Discoveries: being Observations on Men and Manners*, J. M. Dent, London, 1951 [1641]

Joseph, R., 'The neuropsychology of development: hemispheric laterality, limbic language, and the origin of thought', *Journal of Clinical Psychology*, 1982, *38(1)*, pp. 4–33

——, 'Dual mental functioning in a split-brain patient', *Journal of Clinical Psychology*, 1988a, *44(5)*, pp. 770–79

——, 'The right cerebral hemisphere: emotion, music, visual-spatial skills, body-image, dreams, and awareness', *Journal of Clinical Psychology*, 1988b, *44(5)*, pp. 630–73

——, *The Right Brain and the Unconscious*, Plenum Press, New York, 1992

Joubert, S., Felician, O., Barbeau, E. et al., 'Impaired configurational processing in a case of progressive prosopagnosia associated with predominant right temporal lobe atrophy', *Brain*, 2003, *126(11)*, pp. 2537–50

Judd, T., Gardner, H. & Geschwind, N., 'Alexia without agraphia in a composer', *Brain*, 1983, *106(2)*, pp. 435–57

Jung, C., *The Collected Works of CG Jung* (Bollingen Series XX), 20 vols., trans. R. F. C. Hull, ed. H. Read, M. Fordham & G. Adler, Princeton University Press, Princeton NJ, 1953–79

Jung, R., 'Neuropsychologie und Neurophysiologie des Kontur- und Formsehens in Zeichnung und Malerei', in Wieck, H. H. (ed.), *Psychopathologie Musischer Gestaltungen*, Schattauer, Stuttgart, 1974, pp. 29–88

——, 'Compensation of visual neglect of the left side in right hemispheric lesions', in Zülch, K. J., Creuzfeld, O. & Galbraidt, C. J. (eds.), *Cerebral Localization*, Springer-Verlag, Berlin, 1975, pp. 302–5

Jung-Beeman, M., Bowden, E. M., Haberman, J. et al., 'Neural activity when people solve verbal problems with insight', *PLoS Biology*, 2004, *2(4)*, p. E97

Kadloubovsky, E. & Palmer, G. E. H. (trans. & ed.), *Early Fathers From the Philokalia*, Faber & Faber, London, 1954

Kafka, F., *The Diaries of Franz Kafka 1914–1923*, ed. M. Brod, trans. M. Greenberg, Schocken, New York, 1949

Kahn, C. H., *The Art and Thought of Heraclitus*, Cambridge University Press, Cambridge, UK, 1979

Kahn, M. C. & Bingman, V. P., 'Lateralisation of spatial learning in the avian hippocampal formation', *Behavioral Neuroscience*, 2004, *118(2)*, pp. 333–44

Kaminski, J., 'Dogs (*Canis familiaris*) are adapted to receive human communication', in Berthoz, A. & Christen, Y. (eds.), *Neurobiology of 'Umwelt'*, Springer-Verlag, Berlin, 2009, pp. 103–7

Kaminski, J., Riedel, J., Call, J. et al., 'Domestic goats (*Capra hircus*) follow gaze direction and use social cues in an object choice task', *Animal Behaviour*, 2005, *69(1)*, pp. 11–18

Kanner, L., 'Autistic disturbances of affective contact', *The Nervous Child*, 1943, *2*, pp. 217–50

Kant, I., 'The natural principle of the political order considered in connection with the idea of a universal cosmopolitical history', in Hastie, B. D. (trans. & ed.), *Principles of Politics*, T. & T. Clarke, Edinburgh, 1891 [1784]

——, *The Critique of Judgment*, trans. J. C. Meredith, Oxford University Press, Oxford, 1952 [*Kritik der Urteilskraft* 1790]

——, *Grundlegung zur Metaphysik der Sitten* [1785], in *Werke*, ed. W. Weischedel, Suhrkamp, Frankfurt am Main, 1977a, vol. 7

——, *Kritik der reinen Vernunft* [1781], in *Werke*, ed. W. Weischedel, Suhrkamp, Frankfurt am Main, 1977b, vols. 3–4

——, *Kritik der Urteilskraft* [1790], in *Werke*, ed. W. Weischedel, Suhrkamp, Frankfurt am Main, 1977c, vol. 10

Kaplan, J. A., Brownell, H. H., Jacobs, J. R. et al., 'The effects of right hemisphere damage on the pragmatic interpretation of conversational remarks', *Brain and Language*, 1990, *38(2)*, pp. 315–33

Kaplan, J. T. & Zaidel, E., 'Error monitoring in the hemispheres: the effect of lateralized feedback on lexical decision', *Cognition*, 2001, *82(2)*, pp. 157–78

Kavcic, V., Fei, R., Hu, S. et al., 'Hemispheric interaction, metacontrol, and mnemonic processing in split-brain macaques', *Behavioural Brain Research*, 2000, *111(1–2)*, pp. 71–82

Kawasaki, K., 'Kansatsu no kenkyu' [An epistemological study on 'kansatsu' believed to be a precise equivalent for 'observation'], *Nihon Rika Kyoiku Gakkai Kenkyu Kiyo* [Bulletin of the Society of Japanese Teaching], 1992, 33, pp. 71–80

——, 'A cross-cultural comparison of Japanese and English linguistic assumptions influencing pupil learning of science', *Canadian and International Education*, 2002, *31(1)*, pp. 19–51

Kay, R. F., Cartmill, M. & Balow, M., 'The hypoglossal canal and the origin of human vocal behavior', *Proceedings of the National Academy of Sciences of the USA*, 1998, *95(9)*, pp. 5417–19

Keats, J., *Selected Letters of John Keats*, ed. R. Gittings & J. Mee, Oxford University Press, Oxford, 2002

Keenan, J. P., McCutcheon, B., Freund, S. et al., 'Left hand advantage in a self-face recognition task', *Neuropsychologia*, 1999, *37(12)*, pp. 1421–5

Keenan, J. P., McCutcheon, N. B. & Pascual-Leone, A., 'Functional magnetic resonance imaging and event related potentials suggest right prefrontal activation for self-related processing', *Brain and Cognition*, 2001, *47(1–2)*, pp. 87–91

Keenan, J. P., Nelson, A., O'Connor, M. et al., 'Self-recognition and the right hemisphere', *Nature*, 2001, *409(6818)*, p. 305

Keenan, J. P., Rubio, J., Racioppi, C. et al., 'The right hemisphere and the dark side of consciousness', *Cortex*, 2005, *41(5)*, pp. 695–704

Keenan, J. P., Wheeler, M., Platek, S. M. et al., 'Self-face processing in a callosotomy patient', *European Journal of Neuroscience*, 2003, *18(8)*, pp. 2391–5

Keene, D., *The Pleasures of Japanese Literature*, Columbia University Press, New York, 1988

Keles, P.,   S., Tan, M. et al., 'Facial asymmetry in right- and left-handed men and women', *International Journal of Neuroscience*, 1997, *91(3–4)*, pp. 147–59

Keller, J., Nitschke, J. B., Bhargava, T. et al., 'Neuropsychological differentiation of depression and anxiety', *Journal of Abnormal Psychology*, 2000, *109(1)*, pp. 3–10

Kelley, W. M., Macrae, C. N., Wyland, C. L. et al., 'Finding the self: an event-related fMRI study', *Journal of Cognitive Neuroscience*, 2002, *14(5)*, pp. 785–94

Kemper, S., 'Priming the comprehension of metaphors', *Metaphor and Symbolic Activity*, 1989, *4(1)*, pp. 1–17

Kendon, A., 'Some relationships between body motion and speech: an analysis of an example', in Siegman, A. & Pope, B. (eds.), *Studies in Dyadic Communication*, Pergamon, Elmsford NY, 1972, pp. 177–210

——, 'Gesticulation and speech: two aspects of the process of utterance', in Key, M. R. (ed.), *The Relationship of Verbal and Nonverbal Communication*, Mouton, The Hague, 1980, pp. 207–28

Kennedy, D. N., O'Craven, K. M., Ticho, B. S. et al., 'Structural and functional brain asymmetries in human *situs inversus totalis*', *Neurology*, 1999, *53(6)*, pp. 1260–65

Kenny, C., 'Does growth cause happiness, or does happiness cause growth?', *Kyklos*, 1999, *52(1)*, pp. 3–26

Kerényi, C., *The Religion of the Greeks and Romans*, Thames & Hudson, London, 1962

——, *Prometheus: Archetypal Image of Human Existence*, trans. R. Manheim, Bollingen Series LXV(I), Princeton University Press, Princeton NJ, 1991 [*Prometheus: Die menschliche Existenz in Griechischer Deutung* 1959]

Kertesz, A., Polk, M., Black, S. E. et al., 'Anatomical asymmetries and functional laterality', *Brain*, 1992, *115(2)*, pp. 589–605

Kierkegaard, S., *Fear and Trembling*, trans. & ed. H.V. & E.H. Hong, Princeton University Press, Princeton NJ, 1983 [*Frygt og Bæven* 1843]

——, *Either/Or*, trans. & ed. H.V. & E.H. Hong, Princeton University Press, Princeton NJ, 1987 [*Enten–Eller* 1843]

——, *Stages on Life's Way*, trans. & ed. H.V. & E.H. Hong, Princeton University Press, Princeton NJ, 1988 [*Stadier På Livets Vej* 1845]

——, *Concluding Unscientific Postscript to Philosophical Fragments*, trans. & ed. H.V. Hong and E.H. Hong, Princeton University Press, Princeton NJ, 1992 [*Afsluttende uvidenskabelig Efterskrift til de philosophiske Smuler* 1846]

Killgore, W. D., 'Laterality of lesions and trait-anxiety on working memory performance', *Perceptual and Motor Skills*, 2002, *94(2)*, pp. 551–8

Kilshaw, D. & Annett, M., 'Right- and left-hand skill, I: effects of age, sex and hand preference showing superior skill in left-handers', *British Journal of Psychology*, 1983, *74(2)*, pp. 253–68

Kim, H. & Levine, S. C., 'Sources of between-subjects variability in perceptual asymmetries: a meta-analytic review', *Neuropsychologia*, 1991, *29(9)*, pp. 877–88

——, 'Variations in characteristic perceptual asymmetry: modality specific and modality general components', *Brain and Cognition*, 1992, *19(1)*, pp. 21–47

Kim, H., Levine, S. C. & Kertesz, S., 'Are variations among subjects in lateral asymmetry real individual differences or random error in measurement? Putting variability in its place', *Brain and Cognition*, 1990, *14(2)*, pp. 220–42

Kimura, D., 'Right temporal-lobe damage: perception of unfamiliar stimuli after damage', *Archives of Neurology*, 1963, *8(3)*, pp. 264–71

Kimura, M., Murata, Y., Shimoda, K. et al., 'Sexual dysfunction following stroke', *Comprehensive Psychiatry*, 2001, *42(3)*, pp. 217–22

Kinchla, R. A., Solis-Macias, V. & Hoffman, J., 'Attending to different levels of structure in a visual image', *Perception and Psychophysics*, 1983, *33(1)*, pp. 1–10

Kingsley, P., *In the Dark Places of Wisdom*, Duckworth, London, 2001

Kingstone, A., Friesen, C. K. & Gazzaniga, M. S., 'Reflexive joint attention depends on lateralized cortical connections', *Psychological Science*, 2000, *11(2)*, pp. 159–66

Kinsbourne, M., 'Evolution of language in relation to lateral action', in Kinsbourne, M. (ed.), *Asymmetrical Function of the Brain*, Cambridge University Press, Cambridge, UK, 1978, pp. 553–65

——, 'Hemispheric specialization and the growth of human understanding', *American Psychologist*, 1982, *37(4)*, pp. 411–20

——, 'Hemispheric interactions in depression', in Kinsbourne, M. (ed.), *Cerebral Hemisphere Function in Depression*, American Psychiatric Press, Washington DC, 1988, pp. 133–62

——, 'Integrated cortical field model of consciousness', in Marsh, J. (ed.), *Experimental and Theoretical Studies of Consciousness*, John Wiley & Sons, London, 1993a, pp. 43–50

——, 'Orientational bias model of unilateral neglect: evidence from attentional gradients within hemispace', in Robertson, I. H. & Marshall, J. C. (eds.), *Unilateral Neglect: Clinical and Experimental Studies*, Lawrence Erlbaum, Hove, UK, 1993b, pp. 63–86

——, 'The multimodal mind: how the senses combine in the brain', *Semioticon*, 2003, http:WWW.SEMIOTICON.COM/VIRTUALS/MULTIMODALITY2/TALKS/KINSBOURNE.HTM (ACCESSED 28 APRIL 2009)

Kinsbourne, M. & Bemporad, B., 'Lateralization of emotion: a model and the evidence', in Fox, N. A. & Davidson, R. J. (eds.), *The Psychobiology of Affective Development*, Lawrence Erlbaum, Hillsdale NJ, 1984, pp. 259–91

Kircher, T. T., Senior, C., Phillips, M. L. et al., 'Recognising one's own face', *Cognition*, 2001, *78(1)*, pp. B1–15

Kirsner, K., 'Hemisphere-specific processes in letter-matching', *Journal of Experimental Psychology: Human Perception and Performance*, 1980, *6(1)*, pp. 167–79

Kirsner, K. & Brown, H., 'Laterality and recency effects in working memory', *Neuropsychologia*, 1981, *19(2)*, pp. 249–61

Kitayama, S., Duffy, S., Kawamura, T. et al., 'Perceiving an object and its context in different cultures: a cultural look at New Look', *Psychological Science*, 2003, *14(3)*, pp. 201–6

Kitayama, S., Snibbe, A. C., Markus, H. R. et al., 'Is there any "free" choice? Self and dissonance in two cultures', *Psychological Science*, 2004, *15(8)*, pp. 527–33

Kitchen, A., Denton, D. & Brent, L., 'Self-recognition and abstraction abilities in the common chimpanzee studied with distorting mirrors', *Proceedings of the National Academy of Sciences of the USA*, 1996, *93(14)*, pp. 7405–8

Kitterle, F. L., Christman, S. & Hellige, J. B., 'Hemispheric differences are found in the identification, but not the detection, of low versus high spatial frequencies', *Perception and Psychophysics*, 1990, *48(4)*, pp. 297–306

Kitterle, F. L. & Selig, L. M., 'Visual field effects in the discrimination of sine-wave gratings', *Perception and Psychophysics*, 1991, *50(1)*, pp. 15–18

Kiyonari, T., Tanida, S. & Yamagishi, T., 'Social exchange and reciprocity: confusion or a heuristic?', *Evolution and Human Behavior*, 2000, *21(6)*, pp. 411–27

Klapp, O. E., *Overload and Boredom: Essays on the Quality of Life in the Information Society*, Greenwood, New York, 1986

Kleinman, A. & Cohen, A., 'Psychiatry's global challenge', *Scientific American*, 1997, *276(3)*, pp. 86–9

Kleist, H. von, 'On the Marionette Theater', trans. C.-A. Gollub, in Willson, A. L. (ed.), *German Romantic Criticism*, Continuum, New York, 1982, pp. 238–44

Klibansky, R., Saxl, F. & Panofsky, E., *Saturn and Melancholy*, Nelson, London, 1964

Kluender, K. R., Diehl, R. L. & Killeen, P. R., 'Japanese quail can learn phonetic categories', *Science*, 1987, *237(4819)*, pp. 1195–7

Kluft, R. P., 'First-rank symptoms as a diagnostic clue to multiple personality disorder', *American Journal of Psychiatry*, 1987, *144(3)*, pp. 293–8

Knauff, M., Fangmeier, T., Ruff, C. C. et al., 'Reasoning, models, and images: behavioral measures and cortical activity', *Journal of Cognitive Neuroscience*, 2003, *15(4)*, pp. 559–73

Knoch, D. & Fehr, E., 'Resisting the power of temptations: the right prefrontal cortex and self-control', *Annals of the New York Academy of Sciences*, 2007, *1104*, pp. 123–34

Knoch, D., Pascual-Leone, A., Meyer, K. et al., 'Diminishing reciprocal fairness by disrupting the right prefrontal cortex', *Science*, 2006, *314(5800)*, pp. 829–32

Knowles, Sir James, 'Aspects of Tennyson', *Nineteenth Century*, 1893, *33*, pp. 164–88

Koch, G., Oliveri, M., Carlesimo, G. A. et al., 'Selective deficit of time perception in a patient with right prefrontal cortex lesion', *Neurology*, 2002, *59(10)*, pp. 1658–9

Koch, G., Oliveri, M., Torriero, S. et al., 'Underestimation of time perception after repetitive transcranial magnetic stimulation', *Neurology*, 2003, *60(11)*, pp. 1844–6

Kochunov, P., Fox. P, Lancaster, J. et al., 'Localized morphological brain differences between English-speaking Caucasians and Chinese-speaking Asians: new evidence of anatomical plasticity', *NeuroReport*, 2003, *14(7)*, pp. 961–4

Koelsch, S., Fritz, T., von Cramon, D. Y. et al., 'Investigating emotion with music: an fMRI study', *Human Brain Mapping*, 2006, *27(3)*, pp. 239–50

Koelsch, S., Kasper, E., Sammler, D. et al., 'Music, language and meaning: brain signatures of semantic processing', *Nature Neuroscience*, 2004, *7(3)*, pp. 302–7

Koerner, J., *The Reformation of the Image*, Chicago University Press, Chicago, 2004

Koestler, A., *The Sleepwalkers*, Penguin, Harmondsworth, UK, 1964

Koivisto, M. & Laine, M., 'Strategies of semantic categorization in the cerebral hemispheres', *Brain and Language*, 1999, *66(3)*, pp. 341–57

Kolb, B. & Milner, B., 'Performance of complex arm and facial movements after focal brain lesions', *Neuropsychologia*, 1981, *19(4)*, pp. 491–503

Kolb, B., Sutherland, R. J., Nonneman, A. J. et al., 'Asymmetry in the cerebral hemispheres of the rat, mouse, rabbit, and cat: the right hemisphere is larger', *Experimental Neurology*, 1982, *78(2)*, pp. 348–59

Konishi, S., Nakajima, K., Uchida, I. et al., 'Common inhibitory mechanism in human inferior prefrontal cortex revealed by event-related functional MRI', *Brain*, 1999, *122(5)*, pp. 981–91

Korda, R. J. & Douglas, J. M., 'Attention deficits in stroke patients with aphasia', *Journal of Clinical and Experimental Neuropsychology*, 1997, *19(4)*, pp. 525–42

Korff, H. A., *Geist der Goethezeit: Versuch einer ideellen Entwicklung der klassisch-romantischen Literaturgeschichte*, Weber, Leipzig, 1923

Kornhuber, H. H. & Deecke, L., 'Hirnpotentialänderungen bei Willkürbewegungen und passiven Bewegungen des Menschen: Bereitschaftspotential und reafferente Potentiale', *Pflügers Archiv–European Journal of Physiology*, 1965, *284*, pp. 1–17

Kosslyn, S. M., 'Seeing and imagining in the cerebral hemispheres: a computational approach', *Psychological Review*, 1987, *94(2)*, pp. 148–75

Kosslyn, S. M., Koenig, O., Barrett, A. et al., 'Evidence for two types of spatial representations: hemispheric specialization for categorical and coordinate relations', *Journal of Experimental Psychology: Human Perception and Performance*, 1989, *15(4)*, pp. 723–35

Kosslyn, S. M. & Miller, G. W., 'There is no left-brain/right-brain divide', *Time*, 29 November 2013

Kosslyn, S. M., Thompson, W. L., Costantini-Ferrando, M. F. et al., 'Hypnotic visual illusion alters color processing in the brain', *American Journal of Psychiatry*, 2000, *157(8)*, pp. 1279–84

Kounios, J., Fleck, J. I., Green, D. L. et al., 'The origins of insight in resting-state brain activity', *Neuropsychologia*, 2008, *46(1)*, pp. 281–91

Kovács, I., Papathomas, T. V., Yang, M. et al., 'When the brain changes its mind: intraocular grouping during retinal rivalry', *Proceedings of the National Academy of Sciences of the USA*, 1996, *93(26)*, pp. 15508–11

Krabbendam, L. & van Os, J., 'Schizophrenia and urbanicity: a major environmental influence – conditional on genetic risk', *Schizophrenia Bulletin*, 2005, *31(4)*, pp. 795–9

Kramer, L., 'The kitten and the tiger: Tovey's Haydn', in Clark, C. (ed.), *The Cambridge Companion to Haydn*, Cambridge University Press, Cambridge, UK, 2005, pp. 239–48

Kraus, T. H. & von Matt, L., *Pompeji und Herkulaneum*, Dumont, Cologne, 1977

Kravariti, E., Toulopoulou, T., Mapua-Filbey, F. et al., 'Intellectual asymmetry and genetic liability in first-degree relatives of probands with schizophrenia', *British Journal of Psychiatry*, 2006, *188(2)*, pp. 186–7

Kris, E. & Kurz, O., *Legend, Myth, and Magic in the Image of the Artist: A Historical Experiment*, trans. A. Laing & L. M. Newman, Yale University Press, New Haven CT, 1979 [*Die Legende vom Künstler: ein geschichtlicher Versuch* 1934]

Kriss, A., Blumhardt, L. D., Halliday, A. M. et al., 'Neurological asymmetries immediately after unilateral ECT', *Journal of Neurology, Neurosurgery, & Psychiatry*, 1978, *41(12)*, pp. 1135–44

Kriss-Rettenbeck, L., *Bilder und Zeichen religiösen Volksglaubens*, Callwey, Munich, 1963

Krumhansl, C. L., 'An exploratory study of musical emotions and psychophysiology', *Canadian Journal of Experimental Psychology*, 1997, *51(4)*, pp. 336–52

Krystal, J. H., Bremner, J. D., Southwick, S. M. et al., 'The emerging neurobiology of dissociation: implications for treatment of posttraumatic stress disorder', in Bremner, J. D. & Marmar, C. R. (eds.), *Trauma, Memory, and Dissociation*, American Psychiatric Press, Washington DC, 1998, pp. 321–63

Kucharska-Pietura, K., David, A. S., Dropko, P. et al., 'The perception of emotional chimeric faces in schizophrenia: further evidence of right hemisphere dysfunction', *Neuropsychiatry, Neuropsychology and Behavioral Neurology*, 2002, *15(2)*, pp. 72–8

Kucharska-Pietura, K., David, A. S., Masiak, M. et al., 'Perception of facial and vocal affect by people with schizophrenia in early and late stages of illness', *British Journal of Psychiatry*, 2005, *187(6)*, pp. 523–8

Kuehn, M., *Kant: A Biography*, Cambridge University Press, Cambridge, UK, 2001

Kuhl, P. K. & Miller, J. D., 'Speech perception by the chinchilla: identification function for synthetic VOT stimuli', *Journal of the Acoustical Society of America*, 1978, *63(3)*, pp. 905–17

Kuhn, T. S., *The Structure of Scientific Revolutions*, University of Chicago Press, Chicago, 1970

Kulisevsky, J., Berthier, M. L., Gironell, A. et al., 'Mania following deep brain stimulation for Parkinson's disease', *Neurology*, 2002, *59(9)*, pp. 1421–4

Kulisevsky, J., Berthier, M. L. & Pujol, J., 'Hemiballismus and secondary mania following a right thalamic infarction', *Neurology*, 1993, *43(7)*, pp. 1422–4

Kuo, W. J., Yeh, T. C., Duann, J. R. et al., 'A left-lateralized network for reading Chinese words: a 3 T fMRI study', *NeuroReport*, 2001, *12(18)*, pp. 3997–4001

Ku Teng, 'Su Tung P'o als Kunstkritiker', *Ostasiatische Zeitschrift*, 1932, *8*, pp. 104–10

L'Orange, H. P., *Art Forms and Civic Life in the Late Roman Empire*, Princeton University Press, Princeton NJ, 1965

Laban, R., *The Mastery of Movement*, 2nd edn., Macdonald & Evans, London, 1960

LaBerge, D., 'Spatial extent of attention to letters and words', *Journal of Experimental Psychology: Human Perception and Performance*, 1983, *9(3)*, pp. 371–9

Lacruz, F., Artieda, J., Pastor, M. A. et al., 'The anatomical basis of somaesthetic temporal discrimination in humans', *Journal of Neurology, Neurosurgery & Neuropsychiatry*, 1991, *54(12)*, pp. 1077–81

Laeng, B., 'Lateralization of categorical and coordinate spatial functions: a study of unilateral stroke patients', *Journal of Cognitive Neuroscience*, 1994, *6(3)*, pp. 189–203

Laeng, B. & Caviness, V. S., 'Prosopagnosia as a deficit in encoding curved surface', *Journal of Cognitive Neuroscience*, 2001, *13(5)*, pp. 556–76

Laeng, B., Chabris, C. F. & Kosslyn, S. M., 'Asymmetries in encoding spatial relations', in Hugdahl, K. & Davidson, R. J. (eds.), *The Asymmetrical Brain*, Massachusetts Institute of Technology Press, Cambridge MA, 2003, pp. 303–39

Laeng, B., Shah, J. & Kosslyn, S., 'Identifying objects in conventional and contorted poses: contributions of hemisphere-specific mechanisms', *Cognition*, 1999, *70(1)*, pp. 53–85

Laeng, B., Zarrinpar, A. & Kosslyn, S. M., 'Do separate processes identify objects as exemplars versus members of basic-level categories? Evidence from hemispheric specialization', *Brain and Cognition*, 2003, *53(1)*, pp. 15–27

Laing, R. D., *The Divided Self*, Penguin, Harmondsworth, UK, 1965

Lakoff, G. & Johnson, M., *Metaphors We Live By*, University of Chicago Press, Chicago, 1980

——, *Philosophy in the Flesh: The Embodied Mind and its Challenge to Western Thought*, Basic Books, New York, 1999

Lambert, A. J., 'Interhemispheric interaction in the split-brain', *Neuropsychologia*, 1991, *29(10)*, pp. 941–8

Lançon, B., *Rome in Late Antiquity: Everyday Life and Urban Change, AD 312–609*, Routledge, London, 2000

Landis, T., Assal, G. & Perret, E., 'Opposite cerebral hemispheric superiorities for visual associative processing of emotional facial expressions and objects', *Nature*, 1979, *278(5706)*, pp. 739–40

Landis, T., Cummings, J. L., Benson, D. F. et al., 'Loss of topographic familiarity: an environmental agnosia', *Archives of Neurology*, 1986, *43(2)*, pp. 132–6

Landis, T., Cummings, J. L., Christen, L. et al., 'Are unilateral right posterior cerebral lesions sufficient to cause prosopagnosia? Clinical and radiological findings in six additional patients', *Cortex*, 1986, *22(2)*, pp. 243–52

Landis, T., Graves, R. & Goodglass, H., 'Dissociated awareness of manual performance on two different visual associative tasks: a "split-brain" phenomenon in normal subjects?' *Cortex*, 1981, *17(3)*, pp. 435–40

Landis, T. & Regard, M., 'The right hemisphere's access to lexical meaning: a function of its release from left hemisphere control?', in Chiarello, C. (ed.), *Right hemisphere contributions to lexical semantics*, Springer-Verlag, New York, 1988, pp. 33–46

Lane, R. D., Novelly, R., Cornell, C. et al., 'Asymmetric hemispheric control of heart rate', *Psychophysiology*, 1988, *25(4)*, p. 464

Lane, S. M. & Schooler, J. W., 'Skimming the surface: verbal overshadowing of analogical retrieval', *Psychological Science*, 2004, *15(11)*, pp. 715–19

Langdon, D. W. & Warrington, E. K., 'The abstraction of numerical relations: a role for the right hemisphere in arithmetic?', *Journal of the International Neuropsychological Society*, 1997, *3(3)*, pp. 260–68

Langer, S., *Philosophy in a New Key: A Study in the Symbolism of Reason, Rite, and Art*, Harvard University Press, Cambridge MA, 1942

Langleben, D. D., Schroeder, L., Maldjian, J. A. et al., 'Brain activity during simulated deception: an event-related functional magnetic resonance study', *NeuroImage*, 2002, *15(3)*, pp. 727–32

Larose, C., Richard-Yris, M.-A., Hausberger, M. et al., 'Laterality of horses associated with emotionality in novel situations', *Laterality*, 2006, *11(4)*, pp. 355–67

Larson, E. B. & Brown, W. S., 'Bilateral field interactions, hemispheric specialization and evoked potential interhemispheric transmission time', *Neuropsychologia*, 1997, *35(5)*, pp. 573–81

Laruelle, M., Kegeles, L. S. & Abi-Dargham, A., 'Glutamate, dopamine and schizophrenia: from pathophysiology to treatment', *Annals of the New York Academy of Sciences*, 2003, *1003*, pp. 138–58

Latto, R., 'Turning the other cheek: profile direction in self-portraiture', *Empirical Studies of the Arts*, 1996, *14(1)*, pp. 89–98

Lauterbach, E. C., Jackson, J. G., Wilson, A. N. et al., 'Major depression after left posterior globus pallidus lesions', *Neuropsychiatry, Neuropsychology and Behavioral Neurology*, 1997, *10(1)*, pp. 9–16

Lavidor, M., Ellis, A. W. & Pansky, A., 'Case alternation and length effects in lateralised word recognition: studies of English and Hebrew', *Brain and Cognition*, 2002, *50(2)*, pp. 257–71

Layard, R., *Happiness*, Allen Lane, London, 2005

Lazure, C. L. & Persinger, M. A., 'Right hemisphericity and low self-esteem in high school students: a replication', *Perceptual and Motor Skills*, 1992, *75(3, pt. 2)*, p. 1058

Le Bihan, D., Turner, R., Zeffiro, T. A. et al., 'Activation of human primary visual cortex during visual recall: a magnetic resonance imaging study', *Proceedings of the National Academy of Sciences of the USA*, 1993, *90(24)*, pp. 11802–5

Lebrecht, N., *The Book of Musical Anecdotes*, Free Press, New York, 1985

Lechevalier, B., 'Perception of musical sounds: contributions of positron emission tomography', *Bulletin of the Academy of National Medicine*, 1997, *181(6)*, pp. 1191–9

Leclercq, M., 'Theoretical aspects of the main components and functions of attention', in Leclercq, M. & Zimmerman, P. (eds.), *Applied Neuropsychology of Attention*, Psychology Press, London, 2002, pp. 3–55

LeDoux, J., *The Emotional Brain*, Phoenix, London, 1999

LeDoux, J. E., Wilson, D. H. & Gazzaniga, M. S., 'Manipulo-spatial aspects of cerebral lateralization: clues to the origin of lateralization', *Neuropsychologia*, 1977, *15(6)*, pp. 743–50

Lee, G. P., Loring, D. W., Dahl, J. L. et al., 'Hemispheric specialization for emotional expression', *Neuropsychiatry, Neuropsychology and Behavioral Neurology*, 1993, *6(3)*, pp. 143–8

Lee, G. P., Loring, D. W., Meador, K. J. et al., 'Severe behavioral complications following intracarotid sodium amobarbital injection: implications for hemispheric asymmetry of emotion', *Neurology*, 1988, *38(8)*, pp. 1233–6

——, 'Hemispheric specialization for emotional expression: a re-examination of results from intracarotid administration of sodium amobarbital', *Brain and Cognition*, 1990, *12(2)*, pp. 267–80

Leekam, S., Baron-Cohen, S., Perrett, D. I. et al., 'Eye direction detection: a dissociation between geometric and joint attention skills in autism', *British Journal of Developmental Psychology*, 1997, *15(1)*, pp. 77–95

Leekam, S. R., Hunnisett, E. & Moore, C., 'Targets and cues: gaze following in children with autism', *Journal of Child Psychology and Psychiatry*, 1998, *39(7)*, pp. 951–62

Lefkowitz, M., 'Aeschylus', in *The Lives of the Greek Poets*, Duckworth, London, 1981, pp. 67–74

Legerstee, M., 'The role of person and object in eliciting early imitation', *Journal of Experimental Child Psychology*, 1991, *51(3)*, pp. 423–33

Leibniz, G. W., *Nouveaux essais sur l'entendement humain* [publ. posth. 1764], in *Œuvres de Leibniz*, ed. M. A. Jacques, Paris, Charpentier, 1845

——, *Neue Abhandlungen über den menschlichen Verstand*, trans. & ed. C. Schaarschmidt, Dürr, Leipzig, 1904 [publ. posth. 1764]

——, *G. W. Leibniz's Monadology*, ed. N. Rescher, Routledge, London, 1992

——, *New Essays on Human Understanding*, trans. & ed. P. Remnant & J. Bennett, Cambridge University Press, Cambridge, UK, 1996 [publ. posth. 1764]

LeMay, M., 'Morphological cerebral asymmetries of modern man, fossil man and nonhuman primate', *Annals of the New York Academy of Sciences*, 1976, *280*, pp. 349–66

——, 'Asymmetries of the skull and handedness: phrenology revisited', *Journal of the Neurological Sciences*, 1977, *32(2)*, pp. 243–53

——, 'Morphological aspects of human brain asymmetry: an evolutionary perspective', *Trends in Neurosciences*, 1982, *5(8)*, pp. 273–5

——, 'Radiological, developmental and fossil asymmetries', in Geschwind, N. & Galaburda, A. M. (eds.), *Cerebral Dominance: the Biological Foundations*, Harvard University Press, Cambridge MA, 1984, pp. 26–42

LeMay, M. & Culebras, A., 'Human brain – morphologic differences in the hemispheres demonstrable by carotid arteriography', *New England Journal of Medicine*, 1972, *287(4)*, pp. 168–70

LeMay, M. & Geschwind, N., 'Hemispheric differences in the brains of great apes', *Brain, Behavior and Evolution*, 1975, *11(1)*, pp. 48–52

LeMay, M. & Kido, D. K., 'Asymmetries of the cerebral hemispheres on computed tomograms', *Journal of Computer Assisted Tomography*, 1978, *2(4)*, pp. 471–6

Lessing, G. E., *Anti-Goeze: Eine Duplik* [1778], in *Werke*, ed. H. G. Göpfert, Hanser Verlag, Munich, 1979, vol. 8

Lethmate, J. & Dücker, G., 'Untersuchungen zum Selbsterkennen im Spiegel bei Orang-Utans und einigen anderen Affenarten', *Zeitschrift für Tierpsychologie*, 1973, *33(3)*, pp. 248–69

Levenston, G. K., Patrick, C. J., Bradley, M. M. et al., 'The psychopath as observer: emotion and attention in picture processing', *Journal of Abnormal Psychology*, 2000, *109(3)*, pp. 373–85

Levey, M., ' "The Enchanted Castle" by Claude: subject, significance and interpretation', *The Burlington Magazine*, 1988, *130(1028)*, pp. 812–20

Levin, D. M., *The Philosopher's Gaze: Modernity in the Shadows of the Enlightenment*, University of California Press, Berkeley CA, 1999

Levine, D. N. & Calvanio, R., 'Prosopagnosia: a defect in visual configural processing', *Brain and Cognition*, 1989, *10(2)*, pp. 149–170

Levine, S. C., Banich, M. T. & Koch-Weser, M., 'Variations in patterns of lateral asymmetry among dextrals', *Brain and Cognition*, 1984, *3(3)*, pp. 317–34

Levy, B., 'Improving memory in old age through implicit self-stereotyping', *Journal of Personality and Social Psychology*, 1996, *71(6)*, pp. 1092–107

Levy, B., Ashman, O. & Dror, I., 'To be or not to be: the effects of aging stereotypes on the will to live', *Omega*, 1999–2000, *40(3)*, pp. 409–20

Levy, J., 'Cerebral asymmetry and aesthetic experience', in Rentschler, I., Herzberger, B. & Epstein, D. (eds.), *Beauty and the Brain: Biological Aspects of Aesthetics*, Birkhauser Verlag, Basel, 1988, pp. 219–42

——, 'Regulation and generation of perception in the asymmetric brain', in Trevarthen, C. (ed.), *Brain Circuits and Functions of the Mind: Essays in Honor of Roger W. Sperry*, Cambridge University Press, Cambridge, UK, 1990, pp. 231–48

Levy, J., Heller, W., Banich, M. T. et al., 'Are variations among right-handed individuals in perceptual asymmetries caused by characteristic arousal differences between hemispheres?', *Journal of Experimental Psychology: Human Perception and Performance*, 1983, *9(3)*, pp. 329–59

Levy, J. & Trevarthen, C., 'Metacontrol of hemispheric function in human split-brain patients', *Journal of Experimental Psychology: Human Perception and Performance*, 1976, *2(3)*, pp. 299–312

——, 'Color-matching, color-naming and color-memory in split-brain patients', *Neuropsychologia*, 1981, *19(4)*, pp. 523–41

Levy, J., Trevarthen, C. & Sperry, R. W., 'Perception of bilateral chimeric figures following hemispheric deconnexion', *Brain*, 1972, *95(1)*, pp. 61–78

Levy-Agresti, J. & Sperry, R. W., 'Differential perceptual capacities in major and minor hemispheres', *Proceedings of the National Academy of Sciences of the USA*, 1968, *61(3)*, p. 1151

Lewin, J. S., Friedman, L., Wu, D. et al., 'Cortical localisation of human sustained attention: detection with functional MR using a visual vigilance paradigm', *Journal of Computer Assisted Tomography*, 1996, *20(5)*, pp. 695–701

Lewis, D. & Diamond, M. C., 'The influence of gonadal steroids on the asymmetry of the cerebral cortex', in Davidson, R. J. & Hugdahl, K. (eds.), *Brain Asymmetry*, Massachusetts Institute of Technology Press, Cambridge MA, 1995, pp. 31–50

Lewis, H. B., 'Hofmannsthal and Milton', *Modern Language Notes*, 1972, *87(5)*, pp. 732–41

Lewis, S. W., Reveley, M. A., David, A. S. et al., 'Agenesis of the corpus callosum and schizophrenia: a case report', *Psychological Medicine*, 1988, *18(2)*, pp. 341–7

Ley, R. G. & Bryden, M. P., 'Hemispheric differences in processing emotions and faces', *Brain and Language*, 1979, *7(1)*, pp. 127–38

Lezak, M., *Neuropsychological Assessment*, Oxford University Press, Oxford, 1976

Lhermitte, F., ' "Utilization behaviour" and its relation to lesions of the frontal lobes', *Brain*, 1983, *106(2)*, pp. 237–55

——, 'Human autonomy and the frontal lobes. Part II: Patient behavior in complex and social situations: the "environmental dependency syndrome" ', *Annals of Neurology*, 1986, *19(4)*, pp. 335–43

Lhermitte, F., Chain, F., Escourolle, R. et al., 'Étude anatomoclinique d'un cas de prosopagnosie', *Revue Neurologique*, 1972, *126(5)*, pp. 329–46

Lhermitte, F., Chedru, F. & Chain, F., 'À propos d'un cas d'agnosie visuelle', *Revue Neurologique*, 1973, *128(5)*, pp. 301–22

Lhermitte, F., Pillon, B. & Serdaru, M., 'Human autonomy and the frontal lobes. Part I: Imitation and utilization behavior: a neuropsychological study of 75 patients', *Annals of Neurology*, 1986, *19(4)*, pp. 326–34

Libet, B., 'Unconscious cerebral initiative and the role of conscious will in voluntary action', *Behavioral and Brain Sciences*, 1985, *8(4)*, pp. 529–39

——, 'Conscious subjective experience vs unconscious mental functions: a theory of the cerebral processes involved', in Cotterill, R. (ed.), *Models of Brain Function*, Cambridge University Press, Cambridge, UK, 1989, pp. 35–43

Lichtenberg, G. C., *Schriften und Briefe*, ed. W. Promies, Carl Hanser Verlag, Munich, 1967–72

Lieberman, P., *The Biology and Evolution of Language*, Harvard University Press, Cambridge MA, 1984

——, *Uniquely Human: The Evolution of Speech, Thought, and Selfless Behavior*, Harvard University Press, Cambridge MA, 1991

Liederman, J., Merola, J. L. & Hoffman, C., 'Longitudinal data indicate that hemispheric independence increases during early adolescence', *Developmental Neuropsychology*, 1986, *2(3)*, pp. 183–201

Liepmann, H., 'Das Krankheitsbild der Apraxie ('motorischen Asymbolie') auf Grund eines Falles von einseitiger Apraxie', *Monatsschrift für Psychiatrie und Neurologie*, 1900, 8, pp. 15–44

Lin, A. C., Bard, K. A. & Anderson, J. R., 'Development of self-recognition in chimpanzees (*Pan troglodytes*)', *Journal of Comparative Psychology*, 1992, *106(2)*, pp. 120–27

Liotti, M. & Tucker, D. M., 'Right hemisphere sensitivity to arousal and depression', *Brain and Cognition*, 1992, *18(2)*, pp. 138 51

——, 'Emotion in asymmetric corticolimbic networks', in Davidson, R. J. & Hugdahl, K. (eds.), *Human Brain Laterality*, Oxford University Press, Oxford, 1994, pp. 389–424

Lippolis, G., Bisazza, A., Rogers, L. J. et al., 'Lateralisation of predator avoidance responses in three species of toads', *Laterality*, 2002, *7(2)*, pp. 163–83

Lippolis, G., Westman, W., McAllan, B. M. et al., 'Lateralisation of escape responses in the striped-faced dunnart, *Sminthopsis macroura* (*Dasyuridae: Marsupialia*)', *Laterality*, 2005, *10(5)*, pp. 457–70

Lipsey, J. R., Robinson, R. G., Pearlson, G. D. et al., 'Mood change following bilateral hemisphere brain injury', *British Journal of Psychiatry*, 1983, *143(3)*, pp. 266–73

Livingstone, F. B., 'Did the australopithecines sing?', *Current Anthropology*, 1973, *14(1–2)*, pp. 25–9

Lloyd, G. E. R., *The Revolutions of Wisdom: Studies in the Claims and Practice of Ancient Greek Science*, University of California Press, Berkeley CA, 1987

——, 'Right and left in Greek philosophy', *Methods and Problems in Greek Science: Selected Papers*, Cambridge University Press, Cambridge, UK, 1991

——, *Polarity and Analogy: Two Types of Argumentation in Early Greek Thought*, Bristol Classical Press, Bristol, UK, 1992

Locke, J., *An Essay Concerning Human Understanding*, W. Tegg & Co., London, 1849 [1690]

Loetscher, T. & Brugger, P., 'A disengagement deficit in representational space', *Neuropsychologia*, 2007, *45(6)*, pp. 1299–1304

Loftus, W. C., Tramo, M. J., Thomas, C. E. et al., 'Three-dimensional quantitative analysis of hemispheric asymmetry in the human superior temporal region', *Cerebral Cortex*, 1993, *3(4)*, pp. 348–55

Lokhorst G.-J.C., 'An ancient Greek theory of hemispheric specialization', *Clio Medica*, 1982a, *17(1)*, pp. 33–8

——, 'The oldest printed text on hemispheric specialization', *Neurology*, 1982b, *32(7)*, p. 762

——, 'Hemisphere differences before 1800', *Behavioral and Brain Sciences*, 1985, *8(4)*, p. 64

——, 'The first theory about hemispheric specialization: fresh light on an old codex', *Journal of the History of Medicine*, 1996, *51(3)*, pp. 293–312

Lomber, S. G. & Payne, B. R., 'Removal of two halves restores the whole: reversal of visual hemineglect during bilateral cortical or collicular inactivation in the cat', *Visual Neuroscience*, 1996, *13(6)*, pp. 1143–56

Lou, H. C., Luber, B., Crupain, M. et al., 'Parietal cortex and representation of the mental self ', *Proceedings of the National Academy of Sciences of the USA*, 2004, *101(17)*, pp. 6827–32

Luciano, D., Devinsky, O. & Perrine, K., 'Crying seizures', *Neurology*, 1993, *43(10)*, pp. 2113–17

Luck, S. J., Hillyard, S. A., Mangun, G. R. et al., 'Independent hemispheric attentional systems mediate visual search in split-brain patients', *Nature*, 1989, *342(6249)*, pp. 543–5

——, 'Independent attentional scanning in the separated hemispheres of split-brain patients', *Journal of Cognitive Neuroscience*, 1994, *6(1)*, pp. 84–91

Lueck, C. J., Zeki, S., Friston, K. J. et al., 'The colour centre of the cerebral cortex in man', *Nature*, 1989, *340(6232)*, pp. 386–9

Luh, K. E., Rueckert, L. M. & Levy, J., 'Perceptual asymmetries for free viewing of several types of chimeric stimuli', *Brain and Cognition*, 1991, *16(1)*, pp. 83–103

Lumer, E. D., Friston, K. J. & Rees, G., 'Neural correlates of perceptual rivalry in the human brain', *Science*, 1998, *280(5371)*, pp. 1930–34

Lumsden, C. J., 'Gene-culture coevolution: culture and biology in Darwinian perspective', in de Kerckhove, D. & Lumsden, C. J. (eds.), *The Alphabet and the Brain: The Lateralization of Writing*, Springer-Verlag, Berlin, 1988, pp. 17–42

Lupyan, G., 'Carving nature at its joints and carving joints into nature: how labels augment category representations', in Cangelosi, A., Bugmann, G. & Borisyuk, R. (eds.), *Modelling Language, Cognition and Action: Proceedings of the 9th Neural Computation and Psychology Workshop*, World Scientific, Singapore, 2005, pp. 87–96

Luria, A. R., *The Working Brain*, Allen Lane, London, 1973

——, *Higher Cortical Functions in Man*, Basic Books, New York, 1980

Luria, A. R., Tsvetkova, L. S. & Futer, D. S., 'Aphasia in a composer', *Journal of the Neurological Sciences*, 1965, *2(3)*, pp. 288–92

Luther, M., *Werke: Kritische Gesamtausgabe*, 97 vols., Böhlau, Weimar, 1883–1986

Lux, S., Marshall, J. C., Ritzl, A. et al., 'A functional magnetic resonance imaging study of local/global processing with stimulus presentation in the peripheral visual hemifields', *Neuroscience*, 2004, *124(1)*, pp. 113–20

MacDonald, A. W., Cohen, J. D., Stenger, V. A. et al., 'Dissociating the role of the dorsolateral prefrontal and anterior cingulate cortex in cognitive control', *Science*, 2000, *288(5472)*, pp. 1835–8

Mack, J. L. & Levine, R. N., 'The basis of visual constructional disability in patients with unilateral cerebral lesions', *Cortex*, 1981, *17(4)*, pp. 515–31

MacLarnon, A. M. & Hewitt, G. P., 'The evolution of human speech: the role of enhanced breathing control', *American Journal of Physical Anthropology*, 1999, *109(3)*, pp. 341–63

MacPherson, R. I., Holgate, R. C. & Gudeman, S. K., 'Midline central nervous lipomas in children', *Canadian Association of Radiologists Journal*, 1987, *38(4)*, pp. 264–70

Magnan, V., 'Des hallucinations bilatérales de caractère différent suivant le côté affecté', *Archives de Neurologie*, 1883, 6, pp. 336–55

Maguire, E. A., Gadian, D. G., Johnsrude, I. S. et al., 'Navigation-related structural change in the hippocampi [sic] of taxi drivers', *Proceedings of the National Academy of Sciences of the USA*, 2000, *97(8)*, pp. 4398–403

Malcolm, S. R. & Keenan, J. P., 'Hemispheric asymmetry and deception detection', *Laterality*, 2005, *10(2)*, pp. 103–10

Malinowski, B., *Myth in Primitive Psychology*, Kegan Paul, Trench, Trubner, London, 1926

Mallet, L., Schüpbach, M., N'Diaye, K. et al., 'Stimulation of subterritories of the subthalamic nucleus reveals its role in the integration of the emotional and motor aspects of behavior', *Proceedings of the National Academy of Sciences of the USA*, 2007, *104(25)*, pp. 10661–6

Mandelstam, N., *Hope Against Hope: A Memoir*, trans. M. Hayward, Modern Library, New York, 1999

Mangun, G. R., Luck, S. J., Plager, R. et al., 'Monitoring the visual world: hemispheric asymmetries and subcortical processes in attention', *Journal of Cognitive Neuroscience*, 1994, *6(3)*, pp. 267–75

Manning, J. T. & Chamberlain, A. T., 'Left-side cradling and brain lateralization', *Ethology and Sociobiology*, 1991, *12(3)*, pp. 237–44

Manning, J. T. & Denman, J., 'Lateral cradling preferences in humans (*Homo sapiens*): similarities within families', *Journal of Comparative Psychology*, 1994, *108(3)*, pp. 262–5

Mantyh, P. W., 'Forebrain projections to the peri-aqueductal gray in the monkey, with observations in the cat and rat', *Journal of Comparative Neurology*, 1982, *206(2)*, pp. 146–58

Maquet, P., Faymonville, M. E., Degueldre, C. et al., 'Functional neuroanatomy of hypnotic state', *Biological Psychiatry*, 1999, *45(3)*, pp. 327–33

Maquet, P., Lejeune, H., Pouthas, V. et al., 'Brain activation induced by estimation of duration: a PET study', *NeuroImage*, 1996, *3(2)*, pp. 119–26

Marcel, G.-H., *Being and Having*, trans. K. Farrer, Dacre Press, London, 1949 [*Être et avoir* 1935]

——, *The Mystery of Being*, 2 vols., trans. G. S. Fraser (vol. 1) & R. Hague (vol. 2), Harvill Press, London, 1950–1951 [*Mystère de l'Être* 1951]

——, *Man Against Mass Society*, trans. G. S. Fraser, Henry Regnery, Chicago, 1962 [*Les Hommes contre l'humain* 1951]

Marchant, L. F. & McGrew, W. C., 'Laterality of limb function in wild chimpanzees of Gombe National Park: comprehensive study of spontaneous activities', *Journal of Human Evolution*, 1996, *30(5)*, pp. 427–43

Marin, O. S. M. & Perry, D. W., 'Neurological aspects of music perception and performance', in Deutsch, D. (ed.), *The Psychology of Music*, 2nd edn., Academic Press, New York, 1999, pp. 653–724

Marinetti, F., 'Manifeste de Futurisme', *Le Figaro*, Paris, 20 February 1909

Marinsek, N., Turner, B. O., Gazzaniga, M. et al., 'Divergent hemispheric reasoning strategies: reducing uncertainty versus resolving inconsistency', *Frontiers in Human Neuroscience*, 2014, *8*, 839

Markowitsch, H. J., 'Which brain regions are critically involved in the retrieval of old episodic memory?', *Brain Research: Brain Research Reviews*, 1995, *21(2)*, pp. 117–27

Markowitsch, H. J., Calabrese, P., Fink, G. R. et al., 'Impaired episodic memory retrieval in a case of probable psychogenic amnesia', *Psychiatry Research*, 1997, *74(2)*, pp. 119–26

Markowitsch, H. J., Calabrese, P., Haupts, M. et al., 'Searching for the anatomical basis of retrograde amnesia', *Journal of Clinical and Experimental Neuropsychology*, 1993, *15(6)*, pp. 947–67

Markowitsch, H. J., Calabrese, P., Neufeld, H. et al., 'Retrograde amnesia for world knowledge and preserved memory for autobiographic events', *Cortex*, 1999, *35(2)*, pp. 243–52

Markus, H. & Kitayama, S., 'Culture and the self: implications for cognition, emotion, and motivation', *Psychological Review*, 1991, *98(2)*, pp. 224–53

Marshall, J. C. & Halligan, P. W., 'Does the midsagittal plane play any privileged role in "left" neglect?', *Cognitive Neuropsychology*, 1989, *6(4)*, pp. 403–22

Marsolek, C. J., 'Abstract visual-form representations in the left cerebral hemisphere', *Journal of Experimental Psychology: Human Perception and Performance*, 1995, *21(2)*, pp. 375–86

——, 'Dissociable neural subsystems underlie abstract and specific object recognition', *Psychological Science*, 1999, *10(2)*, pp. 111–18

Marsolek, C. J., Schacter, D. L. & Nicholas, C. D., 'Form-specific visual priming for new associations in the right cerebral hemisphere', *Memory and Cognition*, 1996, *24(5)*, pp. 539–56

Marsolek, C. J., Squire, L. R., Kosslyn, S. M. et al., 'Form-specific explicit and implicit memory in the right cerebral hemisphere', *Neuropsychology*, 1994, *8(4)*, pp. 588–97

Martin, A., Wiggs, C. L., Ungerleider, L. G. et al., 'Neural correlates of category-specific knowledge', *Nature*, 1996, *379(6566)*, pp. 649–52

Martin, A., Wiggs, C. L. & Weisberg, J., 'Modulation of human medial temporal lobe activity by form, meaning and experience', *Hippocampus*, 1997, *7(6)*, pp. 587–93

Martin, F. D., 'Spiritual asymmetry in portraiture', *British Journal of Aesthetics*, 1965, *5*, pp. 6–13

Marx, K., *Die Differenz der demokritischen und epikureischen Naturphilosophie* [1841], in *Marx-Engels-Werke*, Dietz Verlag, Berlin, 1968, vol. 40

Marzi, C. A., Bisiacchi, P. & Nicoletti, R., 'Is interhemispheric transfer of visuomotor information asymmetric? Evidence from a meta-analysis', *Neuropsychologia*, 1991, *29(12)*, pp. 1163–77

Marzi, C. A., Perani, D., Tassinari, G. et al., 'Pathways of interhemispheric transfer in normals and in a split-brain subject: a positron emission tomography study', *Experimental Brain Research*, 1999, *126(4)*, pp. 451–8

Mashal, N. & Faust, M., 'Right hemisphere sensitivity to novel metaphoric relations: application of the signal detection theory', *Brain and Language*, 2008, *104(2)*, pp. 103–12

Mashal, N., Faust, M. & Hendler, T., 'The role of the right hemisphere in processing nonsalient metaphorical meanings: application of principal components analysis to fMRI data', *Neuropsychologia*, 2005, *43(14)*, pp. 2084–100

Mashal, N., Faust, M., Hendler, T. et al., 'An fMRI investigation of the neural correlates underlying the processing of novel metaphoric expressions', *Brain and Language*, 2007, *100(2)*, pp. 115–26

——, 'Hemispheric differences in processing the literal interpretation of idioms: converging evidence from behavioral and fMRI studies', *Cortex*, 2008, *44(7)*, pp. 848–60

——, 'An fMRI study of processing novel metaphoric sentences', *Laterality*, 2009, *14(1)*, pp. 30–54

Masuda, T. & Nisbett, R. E., 'Attending holistically versus analytically: comparing the context sensitivity of Japanese and Americans', *Journal of Personality and Social Psychology*, 2001, *81(5)*, pp. 922–34

Mathews, N., *Francis Bacon: The History of a Character Assassination*, Yale University Press, New Haven CT, 1996

Matsukawa, A., Inoue, S. & Jitsumori, M., 'Pigeon's recognition of cartoons: effects of fragmentation, scrambling, and deletion of elements', *Behavioural Processes*, 2004, *65(1)*, pp. 25–34

Matsuzawa, T., 'Nesting cups and metatools in chimpanzees', *Behavioral and Brain Sciences*, 1991, *14(4)*, pp. 570–71

Matteis, M., Silvestrini, M., Troisi, E. et al., 'Transcranial doppler assessment of cerebral flow velocity during perception and recognition of melodies', *Journal of the Neurological Sciences*, 1997, *149(1)*, pp. 57–61

Matthews, E., *The Philosophy of Merleau-Ponty*, Acumen, Chesham, UK, 2002

Maudsley, H., *The Physiology and Pathology of the Mind*, Appleton, New York, 1867

Maxwell, I., *Animal Tracks ID and Techniques*, Flame Lilly Press, 2006

Maxwell, J. K., Tucker, D.M. & Townes, B.D., 'Asymmetric cognitive function in anorexia nervosa', *International Journal of Neuroscience*, 1984, *24(1)*, pp. 37–44

Mazari, R., *Arabic in Chains*, Schiler Verlag, Berlin, 2006

McBrearty, S. & Brooks, A. S., 'The revolution that wasn't: a new interpretation of the origin of modern human behavior', *Journal of Human Evolution*, 2003, *39(5)*, pp. 453–563

McCabe, K., Houser, D., Ryan, L. et al., 'A functional imaging study of cooperation in two-person reciprocal exchange', *Proceedings of the National Academy of Sciences of the USA*, 2001, *98(20)*, pp. 11832–5

McCarthy, R. A. & Warrington, E. K., *Cognitive Neuropsychology*, Academic Press, London, 1990

McDaniel, M. A., 'Big-brained people are smarter: a meta-analysis of the relationship between in vivo brain volume and intelligence', *Intelligence*, 2005, *33*, pp. 337–46

McEvoy, J. P., Hartman, M., Gottlieb, D. et al., 'Common sense, insight, and neuropsychological test performance in schizophrenia patients', *Schizophrenia Bulletin*, 1996, *22(4)*, pp. 635–41

McFarland, R. A. & Kennison, R., 'Asymmetry in the relationship between finger temperature changes and emotional state in males', *Biofeedback and Self Regulation*, 1989, *14(4)*, pp. 281–90

McFie, J., Piercy, M. F. & Zangwill, O. L., 'Visual-spatial agnosia associated with lesions of the right cerebral hemisphere', *Brain*, 1950, *73(2)*, pp. 167–90

McFie, J. & Zangwill, O., 'Visual constructive disabilities associated with lesions of the left cerebral hemisphere', *Brain*, 1960, *83(2)*, pp. 243–60

McGilchrist, I., *Against Criticism*, Faber, London, 1982

——, 'A problem of symmetries', *Philosophy, Psychiatry, & Psychology*, 2009, *16(2)*

McGilchrist, I. & Cutting, J., 'Somatic delusions in schizophrenia and the affective psychoses', *British Journal of Psychiatry*, 1995, *167(3)*, pp. 350–61

McGinn, C., 'Consciousness and cosmology: hyperdualism ventilated', in Davies, M. & Humphreys, G. W. (eds.), Consciousness, Blackwell, Oxford, 1993, pp. 155–77

McGrew, W. C. & Marchant, L. F., 'Chimpanzees, tools and termites: hand preference or handedness?', Current Anthropology, 1992, 33(1), pp. 114–19

——, 'Laterality of hand use pays off in foraging success for wild chimpanzees', Primates, 1999, 40(3), pp. 509–13

McGrew, W. C., Marchant, L. F., Wrangham, R. W. et al., 'Manual laterality in anvil use: wild chimpanzees cracking strychnos fruits', Laterality, 1999, 4(1), pp. 79–87

McKinnon, M. C. & Schellenberg, E. G., 'A left-ear advantage for forced-choice judgments of melodic contour', Canadian Journal of Experimental Psychology, 1997, 51(2), pp. 171–5

McManus, C., Right Hand, Left Hand: the Origins of Asymmetry in Brains, Bodies, Atoms and Cultures, Harvard University Press, Cambridge MA., 2002

McManus, I. C. & Humphrey, N. K., 'Turning the left cheek', Nature, 1973, 243(5405), pp. 271–2

McManus, I. C., Shergill, S. & Bryden, M. P., 'Annett's theory that individuals heterozygous for the right shift gene are intellectually advantaged: theoretical and empirical problems', British Journal of Psychology, 1993, 84(4), pp. 517–37

McNeill, D., Hand and Mind: What Gestures Reveal about Thought, University of Chicago Press, Chicago, 1992

——, 'Catchments and contexts: non-modular factors in speech and gesture production', in McNeill, D. (ed.), Language and Gesture, Cambridge University Press, Cambridge, UK, 2000, pp. 312–28

Meador, K. J., Loring, D. W., Feinberg, T. E. et al., 'Anosognosia and asomatognosia during intracarotid amobarbital inactivation', Neurology, 2000, 55(6), pp. 816–20

Meadows, M. E. & Kaplan, R. F., 'Dissociation of autonomic and subjective responses to emotional slides in right hemisphere damaged patients', Neuropsychologia, 1994, 32(7), pp. 847–56

Mednick, S. A., 'The associative basis of the creative process', Psychological Review, 1962, 69(3), pp. 220–32

Mehler, J., Bertoncini, J., Barrière, N. et al., 'Infant recognition of mother's voice', Perception, 1978, 7(5), pp. 491–7

Mehler, J., Jusczyk, P., Lambertz, G. et al., 'A precursor of language acquisition in young infants', Cognition, 1988, 29(2), pp. 143–78

Meister Eckhart, Meister Eckhart: A Modern Translation, ed. R. B. Blakney, Harper Torchbooks, New York, 1957

——, The Selected Works of Meister Eckhart, trans. O. Davies, Penguin, Harmondsworth, UK, 1994

Melsbach, G., Wohlschläger, A., Spiess, M. et al., 'Morphological asymmetries of motoneurons innervating upper extremities: clues to the anatomical foundations of handedness?', International Journal of Neuroscience, 1996, 86(3–4), pp. 217–24

Melser, D., The Act of Thinking, Massachusetts Institute of Technology Press, Cambridge MA, 2004

Meltzoff, A. N., 'Understanding the intentions of others: re-enactment of intended acts by 18-month-old children', Developmental Psychology, 1995, 31(5), pp. 838–50

Meltzoff, A. N. & Moore, M. K., 'Newborn infants imitate adult facial gestures', Child Development, 1983, 54(3), pp. 702–9

Melzack, R., Israel, R., Lacroix, R. et al., 'Phantom limbs in people with congenital limb deficiency or amputation in early childhood', Brain, 1997, 120(9), pp. 1603–20

Mendelssohn-Bartholdy, F., Letters of Felix Mendelssohn Bartholdy from 1833 to 1847, trans. G. Wallace, ed. P. Mendelssohn-Bartholdy & C. Mendelssohn-Bartholdy, Leypoldt & Holt, New York, 1864

Mendez, M. F., 'What frontotemporal dementia reveals about the neurobiological basis of morality', Medical Hypotheses, 2006, 67(2), pp. 411–18

Mendez, M. F. & Lim, G. T., 'Alterations of the sense of "humanness" in right hemisphere predominant frontotemporal dementia patients', Cognitive and Behavioral Neurology, 2004, 17(3), pp. 133–8

Mendez, M. F. & Perryman, K. M., 'Neuropsychiatric features of frontotemporal dementia: evaluation of consensus criteria and review', Journal of Neuropsychiatry and Clinical Neurosciences, 2002, 14(4), pp. 424–9

Mendola, J. D., Rizzo, J. F., Cosgrove, G. R. et al., 'Visual discrimination after anterior temporal lobectomy in humans', Neurology, 1999, 52(5), pp. 1028–37

Mendrek, A., Laurens, K. R., Kiehl, K. A. et al., 'Changes in distributed neural circuitry function in patients with first-episode schizophrenia', British Journal of Psychiatry, 2004, 185(3), pp. 205–14

Menshutkin, V. V. & Nikolaenko, N. N., 'The role of the right hemisphere in size constancy', Fiziologiia Cheloveka (Human Physiology), 1987, 13(2), pp. 324–6

Merleau-Ponty, M., Phenomenology of Perception, trans. C. Smith, Routledge & Kegan Paul, London, 1962 [Phénoménologie de la perception 1945]

——, Le visible et l'invisible, Gallimard, Paris, 1964a

——, L'oeil et l'esprit, Gallimard, Paris, 1964b

——, The Primacy of Perception and Other Essays on Phenomenology, Psychology, the Philosophy of Art, History and Politics, ed. J. M. Edie, Northwestern University Press, Evanston IL, 1964c

——, The Visible and the Invisible, trans. A. Lingis, Northwestern University Press, Evanston IL, 1968 [Le visible et l'invisible 1964]

——, La prose du monde, Gallimard, Paris, 1969

Merola, J. L. & Liederman, J., 'Developmental changes in hemispheric independence', Child Development, 1985, 56(5), pp. 1184–94

Merrin, E. L., Floyd, T. C. & Fein, G., 'EEG coherence in unmedicated schizophrenic patients', Biological Psychiatry, 1989, 25(1), pp. 60–66

Mesulam, M.-M., 'Dissociative states with abnormal temporal lobe EEG: multiple personality and the illusion of possession', Archives of Neurology, 1981, 38(3), pp. 176–81

——, 'Behavioral neuroanatomy: large-scale net-works, association cortex, frontal syndromes, the limbic system and hemispheric specialization', in Mesulam, M.-M. (ed.), Principles of Behavioral and Cognitive Neurology, Oxford University Press, Oxford, 2000, pp. 1–120

Metcalfe, J., Funnell, M. & Gazzaniga, M. S., 'Right-hemisphere memory superiority: studies of a split-brain patient', *Psychological Science*, 1995, *6(3)*, pp. 157–64

Meyer, A. ['A. M.'], review of Bleuler, E, 'Halbseitiges Delirium', *Psychiatrisch-Neurologische Wochenschrift*, 1902, *34*, pp. 361–367, in *Psychological Bulletin*, 1904a, *1(7–8)*, pp. 285–6

——, review of Liepmann, H., 'Das Krankheitsbild der Apraxie ('motorischen Asymbolie') auf Grund eines Falles von einseitiger Apraxie', *Monatsschrift für Psychiatrie und Neurologie*, 1900, *8*, pp. 15–44, in *Psychological Bulletin*, 1904b, *1(7–8)*, pp. 277–85

Meyer, B.-U., Röricht, S., Gräfin von Einsiedel, H. et al., 'Inhibitory and excitatory interhemispheric transfers between motor cortical areas in normal subjects and patients with abnormalities of the corpus callosum', *Brain*, 1995, *118(2)*, pp. 429–40

Meyer, B.-U., Röricht, S. & Woiciechowsky, C., 'Topography of fibers in the human corpus callosum mediating interhemispheric inhibition between the motor cortices', *Annals of Neurology*, 1998, *43(3)*, pp. 360–9

Meyer, J. S., Ishikawa, Y., Hata, T. et al., 'Cerebral blood flow in normal and abnormal sleep and dreaming', *Brain and Cognition*, 1987, *6(3)*, pp. 266–294

Meyers, M. A., *Happy Accidents: Serendipity in Modern Medical Breakthroughs*, Arcade, New York, 2008

Michel, E. M. & Troost, B. T., 'Palinopsia: cerebral localization with CT', *Neurology*, 1980, *30(8)*, pp. 887–9

Mikels, J. A. & Reuter-Lorenz, P. A., 'Neural gate keeping: the role of interhemispheric interactions in resource allocation and selective filtering', *Neuropsychology*, 2004, *18(2)*, pp. 328–39

Miklósi, Á., Polgárdi, R., Topál, J. et al., 'Use of experimenter-given cues in dogs', *Animal Cognition*, 1998, *1(2)*, pp. 113–21

Mill, J. S., 'Essay on Bentham', in *Utilitarianism and On Liberty, including Mill's 'Essay on Bentham' and selections from the writings of Jeremy Bentham and John Austin*, ed. M. Warnock, Blackwell, Oxford, 2003, pp. 52–87

Miller, B. L., Chang, L., Mena, I. et al., 'Progressive right frontotemporal degeneration: clinical, neuropsychological and SPECT characteristics', *Dementia*, 1993, *4(3–4)*, pp. 204–13

Miller, B. L., Seeley, W. W., Mychack, P. et al., 'Neuroanatomy of the self: evidence from patients with frontotemporal dementia', *Neurology*, 2001, *57(5)*, pp. 817–21

Miller, G., 'The third culture', http:www.EDGE.ORG/3RD_CULTURE/STORY/86.HTML (ACCESSED 4 NOVEMBER 2008)

Miller, K. & Franz, E. A., 'Bimanual gestures: expressions of spatial representations that accompany speech process', *Laterality*, 2005, *10(3)*, pp. 243–65

Miller, M., 'Views of Japanese selfhood: Japanese and Western perspectives', in Allen, D. & Malhotra, A. (eds.), *Culture and Self: Philosophical and Religious Perspectives, East and West*, Westview, Boulder CO, 1997, pp. 145–62

Miller, S. M., Liu, G. B., Ngo, T. T. et al., 'Interhemispheric switching mediates perceptual rivalry', *Current Biology*, 2000, *10(7)*, pp. 383–92

Mills, D. L., Coffey-Corina, S. A. & Neville, H. J., 'Language acquisition and cerebral specialization in 20-month-old infants', *Journal of Cognitive Neuroscience*, 1993, *5(3)*, pp. 317–34

Mills, L. & Rollman, G. B., 'Hemispheric asymmetry for auditory perception of temporal order', *Neuropsychologia*, 1980, *18(1)*, pp. 41–8

Milner, B., 'Visual recognition and recall after right temporal-lobe excision in man', *Neuropsychologia*, 1968, *6(3)*, pp. 191–209 (reprinted in *Epilepsy & Behavior*, 2003, *4(6)*, pp. 799–812)

——, *Hemispheric Specialization and Interactions*, Massachusetts Institute of Technology Press, Cambridge MA, 1975

Milner, B. & Taylor, L., 'Right-hemisphere superiority in tactile pattern-recognition after cerebral commissurotomy: evidence for nonverbal memory', *Neuropsychologia*, 1972, *10(1)*, pp. 1–15

Milo, R. G. & Quiatt, D., 'Glottogenesis and anatomically modern *Homo sapiens*: the evidence for and implications of a late origin of vocal language', *Current Anthropology*, 1993, *34(5)*, pp. 569–98

Mimura, M., Nakagome, K., Hirashima, N. et al., 'Left frontotemporal hyperperfusion in a patient with post-stroke mania', *Psychiatry Research*, 2005, *139(3)*, pp. 263–7

Mithen, S. J., 'A creative explosion? Theory of mind, language and the disembodied mind of the Upper Palaeolithic', in Mithen, S. J. (ed.), *Creativity in Human Evolution and Prehistory*, Routledge & Kegan Paul, London, 1998a, pp. 165–92

——, *The Prehistory of the Mind: A Search for the Origins of Art, Religion and Science*, Phoenix, London, 1998b

——, *Singing Neanderthals: the Origin of Music, Language, Mind and Body*, Phoenix, London, 2005

Mittelstrass, J., 'Nature and science in the Renaissance', in Woolhouse, R. S. (ed.), *Metaphysics and Philosophy of Science in the Seventeenth and Eighteenth Centuries*, Kluwer, Dordrecht, Netherlands, 1988, pp. 17–44

Miyamoto, Y., Nisbett, R. E. & Masuda, T., 'Culture and the physical environment. Holistic versus analytic perceptual affordances', *Psychological Science*, 2006, *17(2)*, pp. 113–19

Mlot, C., 'Unmasking the emotional unconscious', *Science*, 1998, *280(5366)*, p. 1006

Moberg, B. & Turetsky, P., 'Olfaction and psychosis', in Brewer, W. J., Castle, D. & Pantelis, C. (eds.), *Olfaction and the Brain*, Cambridge University Press, Cambridge, UK, 2006, pp. 296–321

Moberg, R., Agrin, R., Gur, R. E. et al., 'Olfactory dysfunction in schizophrenia: a qualitative and quantitative review', *Neuropsychopharmacology*, 1999, *21(3)*, pp. 325–40

Modell, J. G., Mountz, J. M. & Ford, C. V., 'Pathological lying associated with thalamic dysfunction demonstrated by [99mTc] HMPAO SPECT', *Journal of Neuropsychiatry and Clinical Neurosciences*, 1992, *4(4)*, pp. 442–6

Mohl, W. & Pfurtscheller, G., 'The role of the right parietal region in a movement time estimation task', *NeuroReport*, 1992, *2(6)*, pp. 309–12

Moll, J., de Oliveira-Souza, R., Bramati, I. E. et al., 'Functional networks in emotional moral and nonmoral social judgments', *NeuroImage*, 2002, *16(3, pt. 1)*, pp. 696–703

Moll, J., de Oliveira-Souza, R. & Eslinger, P. J., 'Morals and the human brain: a working model', *NeuroReport*, 2003, *14(3)*, pp. 299–305

Molloy, R., Brownell, H. H. & Gardner, H., 'Discourse comprehension by right-hemisphere stroke patients: deficits of prediction and revision', in Joanette, Y. & Brownell, H. H. (eds.), *Discourse Ability and Brain Damage: Theoretical and Empirical Perspectives*, Springer-Verlag, New York, 1990, pp. 113–30

Molnar-Szakacs, I., Iacoboni, M., Koski, L. et al., 'Functional segregation within pars opercularis of the inferior frontal gyrus: evidence from fMRI studies of imitation and action observation', *Cerebral Cortex*, 2005, *15(7)*, pp. 986–94

Montaigne, M. de, *The Complete Essays*, trans. M. A. Screech, Penguin, Harmondsworth, UK, 1993 [1580–95]

Moravia, A., *Boredom*, trans. A. Davidson, New York Review of Books Publications, New York, 1999 [*La Noia* 1960]

Moreno, C. R., Borod, J. C., Welkowitz, J. et al., 'Lateralization for the expression and perception of facial emotion as a function of age', *Neuropsychologia*, 1990, *28(2)*, pp. 199–209

Morgan, J. F., Marsden, P. & Lacey, J. H., ' "Spiritual starvation?" A case series concerning Christianity and eating disorders', *International Journal of Eating Disorders*, 2000, *28(4)*, pp. 476–80

Morgan, K. D. & David, A. S., 'Neuropsychological studies of insight in patients with psychotic disorders', in Amador, X. & David, A. (eds.), *Insight and Psychosis*, 2nd edn., Oxford University Press, Oxford, 2004, pp. 177–93

Morgann, M., *An Essay on the Dramatic Character of Sir John Falstaff* [1777], in Nichol Smith, D. (ed.), *Eighteenth Century Essays on Shakespeare*, Clarendon Press, Oxford, 1963, pp. 203–83

Morley, I., 'The evolutionary origins and archaeology of music: or an investigation into the prehistory of human musical capacities and behaviours, using archaeological, anthropological, cognitive and behavioural evidence', Ph.D. thesis, Faculty of Archaeology and Anthropology, Cambridge University, Cambridge, UK, October 2003

Morrel-Samuels, P. & Krauss, R. M., 'Word familiarity predicts temporal asynchrony of hand gestures and speech', *Journal of Experimental Psychology: Learning, Memory and Cognition*, 1992, *18(3)*, pp. 615–22

Morris, J. S., Ohman, A. & Dolan, R. J., 'Conscious and unconscious emotional learning in the human amygdala', *Nature*, 1998, *393(6684)*, pp. 467–70

Morrison, I., Lloyd, D., di Pellegrino, G. et al., 'Vicarious responses to pain in anterior cingulate cortex: is empathy a multisensory issue?', *Cognitive, Affective and Behavioral Neuroscience*, 2004, *4(2)*, pp. 270–78

Moscovitch, M., 'Stages of processing and hemispheric differences in language in the normal subject', in Studdert-Kennedy, M. (ed.), *The Psychobiology of Language*, Massachusetts Institute of Technology Press, Cambridge MA, 1983, pp. 88–104

Müller, T., Büttner, T., Kuhn, W. et al., 'Palinopsia as sensory epileptic phenomenon', *Acta Neurologica Scandinavica*, 1995, *91(6)*, pp. 433–6

Mummery, C. J., Patterson, K., Hodges, J. R. et al., 'Generating "tiger" as an animal name or a word beginning with T: differences in brain activation', *Proceedings of the Royal Society of London, Series B: Biological Sciences*, 1996, *263(1373)*, pp. 989–95

——, 'Functional neuroanatomy of the semantic system: divisible by what?', *Journal of Cognitive Neuroscience*, 1998, *10(6)*, pp. 766–77

Murata, J., 'Colors in the life-world', *Continental Philosophy Review*, 1998, *31*, pp. 293–305

Mychack, P., Kramer, J. H., Boone, K. B. et al., 'The influence of right frontotemporal dysfunction on social behavior in frontotemporal dementia', *Neurology*, 2001, *56(11, suppl. 4)*, pp. S11–15

Myers, D. G. & Diener, E., 'Who is happy?', *Psychological Science*, 1995, *6(1)*, pp. 10–19

Nadal, M., Munar, E., Capó, M. A. et al., 'Towards a framework for the study of the neural correlates of aesthetic preference', *Spatial Vision*, 2008, *21(3–5)*, pp. 379–96

Naess, A., *Life's Philosophy: Reason and Feeling in a Deeper World*, University of Georgia Press, Athens GA, 2002

Nagae, S. & Moscovitch, M., 'Cerebral hemispheric differences in memory of emotional and non-emotional words in normal individuals', *Neuropsychologia*, 2002, *40(9)*, pp. 1601–7

Nagahama, Y., Okada, T., Katsumi, Y. et al., 'Dissociable mechanisms of attentional control within the human prefrontal cortex', *Cerebral Cortex*, 2001, *11(1)*, pp. 85–92

Nagel, T., 'Brain bisection and the unity of consciousness', in *Mortal Questions*, Cambridge University Press, Cambridge, UK, 1979a, pp. 147–64

——, 'What is it like to be a bat?', in *Mortal Questions*, Cambridge University Press, Cambridge, UK, 1979b, pp. 165–80

——, *The View from Nowhere*, Oxford University Press, Oxford, 1986

Nakagawa, A., 'Role of anterior and posterior attention networks in hemispheric asymmetries during lexical decisions', *Journal of Cognitive Neuroscience*, 1991, *3(4)*, pp. 313–21

Nakamura, H., *Ways of Thinking of Eastern Peoples: India-China-Tibet-Japan*, University of Hawaii Press, Honolulu, 1993 [1964]

Nakamura, K., Kawashima, R., Sugiura, M. et al., 'Neural substrates for recognition of familiar voices: a PET study', *Neuropsychologia*, 2001, *39(10)*, pp. 1047–54

Nakamura, K., Oga, T., Okada, T. et al., 'Hemispheric asymmetry emerges at distinct parts of the occipitotemporal cortex for objects, logograms and phonograms: a functional MRI study', *NeuroImage*, 2005, *28(3)*, pp. 521–8

Nakamura, R. & Taniguchi, R., 'Reaction time in patients with cerebral hemiparesis', *Neuropsychologia*, 1977, *15(6)*, pp. 845–8

Napier, J., *Hands*, George Allen & Unwin, London, 1980

Narayan, V. M., Narr, K. L., Kumari, V. et al., 'Regional cortical thinning in subjects with violent antisocial personality disorder or schizophrenia', *American Journal of Psychiatry*, 2007, *164(9)*, pp. 1418–27

Narumoto, J., Okada, T., Sadato, N. et al., 'Attention to emotion modulates fMRI activity in human right superior temporal sulcus', *Cognitive Brain Research*, 2001, *12(2)*, pp. 225–31

Navarro, V., Gastó, C., Lomeña, F. et al., 'Prognostic value of frontal functional neuroimaging in late-onset severe major depression', *British Journal of Psychiatry*, 2004, *184(4)*, pp. 306–11

Naveh, J., 'The origin of the Greek alphabet', in de Kerckhove, D. & Lumsden, C. J. (eds.), *The Alphabet and the Brain: the Lateralization of Writing*, Springer-Verlag, Berlin, 1988, pp. 84–91

Navon, D., 'Forest before trees: the precedence of global features in visual perception', *Cognitive Psychology*, 1977, *9(3)*, pp. 353–83

Nayak, N. P. & Gibbs, R. W., 'Conceptual knowledge in the interpretation of idioms', *Journal of Experimental Psychology: General*, 1990, *119(3)*, pp. 315–30

Nayani, T. H. & David, A. S., 'The auditory hallucination: a phenomenological survey', *Psychological Medicine*, 1996, *26(1)*, pp. 177–89

Nebes, R. D., 'Handedness and the perception of part-whole relationship', *Cortex*, 1971a, *7(4)*, pp. 350–56

——, 'Superiority of the minor hemisphere in commissurotomized man for the perception of part-whole relations', *Cortex*, 1971b, *7(4)*, pp. 333–49

——, 'Dominance of the minor hemisphere in commissurotomized man on a test of figural unification', *Brain*, 1972, *95(3)*, pp. 633–8

——, 'Perception of spatial relationships by the right and left hemispheres in commissurotomized man', *Neuropsychologia*, 1973, *11(3)*, pp. 285–9

——, 'Hemispheric specialization in commissurotomized man', *Psychological Bulletin*, 1974, *81(1)*, pp. 1–14

——, 'Direct examination of cognitive function in the right and left hemispheres', in Kinsbourne, M. (ed.), *Asymmetrical Function of the Brain*, Cambridge University Press, Cambridge, UK, 1978, pp. 99–137

Needham, J., *Time: The Refreshing River (Essays & Addresses, 1932–1942)*, George Allen & Unwin, London, 1943

——, *Science and Civilisation in China*, Cambridge University Press, Cambridge, UK, 1954–98

——, *The Grand Titration: Science and Society in East and West*, George Allen & Unwin, London, 1969

Needham, R. (ed), *Right and Left: Essays on Dual Symbolic Classification*, University of Chicago Press, Chicago, 1973

Nelson, C. A., 'The recognition of facial expressions in the first two years of life: mechanisms of development', *Child Development*, 1987, *58(4)*, pp. 889–909

Nestor, P. G., Parasuraman, R., Haxby, J. V. et al., 'Divided attention and metabolic brain dysfunction in mild dementia of the Alzheimer's type', *Neuropsychologia*, 1991, *29(5)*, pp. 379–87

Nettl, B., *The Study of Ethnomusicology: Twenty-Nine Issues and Concepts*, University of Illinois Press, Champaign IL, 1983

Newberg, A., d'Aquili, E. & Rause, V., *Why God Won't Go Away*, Ballantine Books, New York, 2001

Newton, N., 'Emergence and the uniqueness of consciousness', *Journal of Consciousness Studies*, 2001, *8(9–10)*, pp. 47–59

Nichelli, P., Grafman, J., Pietrini, P. et al., 'Where the brain appreciates the moral of a story', *NeuroReport*, 1995, *6(17)*, pp. 2309–13

Nicholas of Cusa, *De Docta Ignorantia*, trans. J. Hopkins, Banning Press, Minneapolis MN, 1985 [1440]

Nicholls, M. E., Clode, D., Wood, S. J. et al., 'Laterality of expression in portraiture: putting your best cheek forward', *Proceedings of the Royal Society of London, Series B: Biological Sciences*, 1999, *266(1428)*, pp. 1517–22

Nicholls, M. E. & Cooper, C. J., 'Hemispheric differences in the rates of information processing for simple non-verbal stimuli', *Neuropsychologia*, 1991, *29(7)*, pp. 677–84

Nicholls, M. E. R., 'Hemispheric asymmetries for temporal resolution: a signal detection analysis of threshold and bias', *Quarterly Journal of Experimental Psychology. A. Human Experimental Psychology*, 1994, *47(2)*, pp. 291–310

Nicholls, M. E. R., Schier, M., Stough, C. K. K. et al., 'Left hemisphere advantage for brief temporal events: psychophysical and electrophysiologic support for a left hemisphere temporal processing advantage', *Neuropsychiatry, Neuropsychology and Behavioral Neurology*, 1999, *12(1)*, pp. 11–16.

Nicholson, K. G., Baum, S., Kilgour, A. et al., 'Impaired processing of prosodic and musical patterns after right hemisphere damage', *Brain and Cognition*, 2003, *52(3)*, pp. 382–9

Nietzsche, F., in *The Portable Nietzsche*, trans. W. Kaufmann, Viking, New York, 1954

——, *The Will to Power*, trans. W. Kaufmann, Vintage, New York, 1968 [*Der Wille zur Macht*: nearest German compilation 1906]

——, *Morgenröthe: Gedanken über die moralischen Vorurtheile*, in *Werke: Kritische Gesamtausgabe*, ed. G. Colli & M. Montinari, Walter de Gruyter & Co., Berlin, Section 5, vol. 1, 1970 [1881]

——, *Beyond Good and Evil*, trans. R. J. Hollingdale, Penguin, Harmondsworth, UK, 1973 [*Jenseits von Gut und Böse* 1886]

——, 'Oedipus. Reden des letzten Philosophen mit sich selbst. Ein Fragment aus der Geschichte der Nachwelt', *Fragmente II (1872–74)*, in *Werke: Kritische Gesamtausgabe*, ed. G. Colli & M. Montinari, Walter de Gruyter & Co., Berlin, Section 3, vol. 4, 1977, pp. 47ff

——, *Twilight of the Idols and The Anti-Christ*, trans. R. J. Hollingdale, Penguin, Harmondsworth, UK, 1990 [*Götzen-Dämmerung oder Wie man mit dem Hammer philosophiert* 1888 and *Der Antichrist* 1895]

——, *Human, All Too Human*, trans. M. Faber & S. Lehmann, University of Nebraska Press, Lincoln NE, 2nd edn. (revised), 1996 [*Menschliches, Allzumenschliches – Ein Buch für freie Geister* 1878]

——, *Daybreak: Thoughts on the Prejudices of Morality*, trans. R. J. Hollingdale, ed. M. Clark & B. Leiter, Cambridge University Press, Cambridge, UK, 1997 [*Morgenröthe: Gedanken über die moralischen Vorurtheile* 1881]

——, *The Birth of Tragedy and other writings*, ed. R. Geuss & R. Spiers, trans. R. Spiers, Cambridge University Press, Cambridge, UK, 1999 [*Die Geburt der Tragödie aus dem Geiste der Musik* 1872]

——, *The Gay Science*, trans. J. Nauckhoff, ed. B. Williams, Cambridge University Press, Cambridge, UK, 2001 [*Die fröhliche Wissenschaft* 1882]

——, in Bittner, R. (ed.), *Writings from the Late Notebooks*, trans. K. Sturge, Cambridge University Press, Cambridge, UK, 2003

Nightingale, S., 'Somatoparaphrenia: a case report', *Cortex*, 1982, *18(3)*, pp. 463–7

Nikolaenko, N. N., *Tvorchestvo i Mozg [Creativity and the Brain]*, Psicologia Press, St. Petersburg, 2001

——, 'Representation activity of the right and left hemispheres of the brain', *Acta Neuropsychologica*, 2003, *1(1)*, pp. 34–47

——, 'Visual hemifield preferences: the cerebral hemispheres and the relationship to affective disorder', *Acta Neuropsychologica*, 2004, *2(4)*, pp. 371–92

Nikolaenko, N. N. & Egorov, A. Y., 'The role of the right and left cerebral hemispheres in depth perception', *Fiziologiia Cheloveka (Human Physiology)*, 1998, *24(6)*, pp. 21–31

Nikolaenko, N. N., Egorov, A. Y. & Freiman, E. A., 'Representation activity of the right and left hemispheres of the brain', *Behavioural Neurology*, 1997, *10(1)*, pp. 49–59

Nin, A., *The Diary of Anaïs Nin: 1931–1934*, ed. G. Stuhlmann, Swallow Press, New York, 1966

Nisbett, R. E. & Masuda, T., 'Culture and point of view', *Proceedings of the National Academy of Sciences of the USA*, 2003, *100(19)*, pp. 11163–70

Nisbett, R. E., Peng, K., Choi, I. et al., 'Culture and systems of thought: holistic versus analytic cognition', *Psychological Review*, 2001, *108(2)*, pp. 291–310

Nitschke, J. B., Heller, W. & Miller, G. A., 'Anxiety, stress and cortical brain function', in Borod, J. C. (ed.), *The Neuropsychology of Emotion*, Oxford University Press, Oxford, 2000, pp. 298–319

Nitschke, J. B., Heller, W., Palmieri, P. A. et al., 'Contrasting patterns of brain activity in anxious apprehension and anxious arousal', *Psychophysiology*, 1999, *36(5)*, pp. 628–37

Njemanze, P. C., Gomez, C. R. & Horenstein, S., 'Cerebral lateralization and color perception: a transcranial Doppler study', *Cortex*, 1992, *28(1)*, pp. 69–75

Nobe, S., 'Where do *most* spontaneous representational gestures actually occur with respect to speech?', in McNeill, D. (ed.), *Language and Gesture*, Cambridge University Press, Cambridge, UK, 2000, pp. 186–98

Noble, W. & Davidson, I., *Human Evolution, Language and Mind: A Psychological and Archaeological Inquiry*, Cambridge University Press, Cambridge, UK, 1996

Nochlin, L., *The Body in Pieces: the Fragment as a Metaphor of Modernity*, Thames & Hudson, London, 1994

Noë, A, 'Is the visual world a grand illusion?', *Journal of Consciousness Studies*, 2002, *9(5–6)*, pp. 1–12

Noë, A. & O'Regan, J. K., 'Perception, attention and the Grand Illusion', *Psyche*, 2000, *6(15)*, *uri*http:PSYCHE.CS.MONASH.EDU.AU/V6/PSYCHE-6-15-NOE.HTML/*URI* (ACCESSED 28 APRIL 2009)

Norenzayan, A., Smith, E. E., Kim, B. J. et al., 'Cultural preferences for formal versus intuitive reasoning', *Cognitive Science*, 2002, *26(5)*, pp. 653–84

Nottebohm, F., 'The ontogeny of bird song', *Science*, 1970, *167(3920)*, pp. 950–56

——, 'Asymmetries in neural control of vocalization in the canary', in Harnad, S., Doty, R. W., Goldstein, L. et al. (eds.), *Lateralization in the Nervous System*, Academic Press, New York, 1977, pp. 23–44

Novalis [Friedrich Leopold, Freiherr von Hardenberg], 'Aus den Fragmentensammlungen', *Gesammelte Werke*, Sigbert Mohn Verlag, Gütersloh, Germany, 1967

——, *Philosophical Writings*, trans. & ed. M. M. Stoljar, State University of New York Press, Albany NY, 1997

Nunn, C., *De la Mettrie's Ghost*, Macmillan, London, 2005

Nunn, J. & Peters, E., 'Schizotypy and patterns of lateral asymmetry on hemisphere-specific language tasks', *Psychiatry Research*, 2001, *103(2–3)*, pp. 179–92

Nunn, J. A., Postma, P. & Pearson, R., 'Developmental prosopagnosia: should it be taken at face value?', *Neurocase*, 2001, *7(1)*, pp. 15–27

Nyberg, L., Cabeza, R. & Tulving, E., 'PET studies of encoding and retrieval: the HERA model', *Psychonomic Bulletin & Review*, 1996, *3(2)*, pp. 135–48

O'Boyle, M. W. & Benbow, C. P., 'Enhanced right hemisphere involvement during cognitive processing may relate to intellectual precocity', *Neuropsychologia*, 1990, *28(2)*, pp. 211–16

O'Boyle, M. W. & Sanford, M., 'Hemispheric asymmetry in the matching of melodies to rhythm sequences tapped in the right and left palms', *Cortex*, 1988, *24(2)*, pp. 211–21

Oelman, H. & Loeng, B., 'A validation of the emotional meaning of single intervals according to classical Indian music theory', *Proceedings of the 5th Triennial ESCOM Conference*, Hanover University of Music and Drama, Hanover, 2003, pp. 393–6

Ogawa, K., Inui, T. & Sugio, T., 'Separating brain regions involved in internally guided and visual feedback control of moving effectors: an event-related fMRI study', *NeuroImage*, 2006, *32(4)*, pp. 1760–70

Ogawa, M., 'A cultural history of science education in Japan: an epic description', in Cobern, W. W. (ed.), *Socio-Cultural Perspectives on Science Education: An International Dialogue*, Kluwer, Dordrecht, Netherlands, 1998, pp. 139–61

Ohnishi, T., Moriguchi, Y., Matsuda, H. et al., 'The neural network for the mirror system and mentalizing in normally developed children: an fMRI study', *NeuroReport*, 2004, *15(9)*, pp. 1483–7

Okada, T., Sato, W. & Toichi, M., 'Right hemispheric dominance in gaze-triggered reflexive shift of attention in humans', *Brain and Cognition*, 2006, *62(2)*, pp. 128–33

Okubo, M. & Nicholls, M. E. R., 'Hemispheric asymmetries for temporal information processing: transient detection versus sustained monitoring', *Brain and Cognition*, 2008, *66(2)*, pp. 168–75

Oldfield, R. C., 'Things, words and the brain', *Quarterly Journal of Experimental Psychology*, 1966, *18(4)*, pp. 340–53

Oliveri, M., Rossini, P. M., Traversa, R. et al., 'Left frontal transcranial magnetic stimulation reduces contralesional extinction in patients with unilateral right brain damage', *Brain*, 1999, *122(9)*, pp. 1731–9

Olson, R. G., *Science and Scientism in Nineteenth-Century Europe*, University of Illinois Press, Chicago, 2008

Ornstein, R., *The Right Mind: Making Sense of the Hemispheres*, Harcourt Brace, New York, 1997

Ornstein, R., Herron, J., Johnstone, J. et al., 'Differential right hemisphere involvement in two reading tasks', *Psychophysiology*, 1979, *16(4)*, pp. 398–401

Ortega y Gasset, J., *The Dehumanization of Art and Other Essays on Art, Culture and Literature*, trans. H. Weyl, Princeton University Press, Princeton NJ, 1968

Otto, Rudolf, *The Idea of the Holy*, trans. J. W. Harvey, Humphrey Milford, London, 1923 [*Das Heilige* 1917]

Ouspenski, B. A., 'La "droite" et la "gauche" dans l'art des icônes', in Lotman, Y. M. & Ouspenski, B. A. (eds.), *Travaux sur les systèmes de signes*, Éditions Complexe, Brussels, 1976, pp. 168–74

Ovid, *Metamorphoses*, trans. R. Humphries, Indiana University Press, Bloomington IN, 1955

Ozonoff, S. & Miller, J. N., 'An exploration of right-hemisphere contributions to the pragmatic impairments of autism', *Brain and Language*, 1996, *52(3)*, pp. 411–34

Packe, M. St. J., *The Life of John Stuart Mill*, Secker & Warburg, London, 1954

Pallis, C. A., 'Impaired identification of faces and places with agnosia for colours', *Journal of Neurology, Neurosurgery, & Psychiatry*, 1955, *18(3)*, pp. 218–24

Palmer, R. E. & Corballis, M. C., 'Predicting reading ability from handedness measures', *British Journal of Psychology*, 1996, *87(4)*, pp. 609-20

Panksepp, J., 'The emotional sources of "chills" induced by music', *Music Perception*, 1995, *13(2)*, pp. 171-208

——, *Affective Neuroscience: the Foundations of Human and Animal Emotions*, Oxford University Press, Oxford, 1998

——, 'At the interface of the affective, behavioral, and cognitive neurosciences: decoding the emotional feelings of the brain', *Brain and Cognition*, 2003, *52(1)*, pp. 4-14

Panksepp, J. & Bernatsky, G., 'Emotional sounds and the brain: the neuro-affective foundations of musical appreciation', *Behavioural Processes*, 2002, *60(2)*, pp. 133-55

Panksepp, J. & DeEskinazi, F. G., 'Opiates and homing', *Journal of Comparative and Physiological Psychology*, 1980, *94(4)*, pp. 650-63

Panksepp, J., Normansell, L., Cox, J. F. et al., 'Effects of neonatal decortication on the social play of juvenile rats', *Physiology & Behavior*, 1994, *56(3)*, pp. 429-43

Parasuraman, R., Greenwood, P. M., Haxby, J. V. et al., 'Visuospatial attention in dementia of the Alzheimer type', *Brain*, 1992, *115(3)*, pp. 711-33

Pardo, J. V., Fox, P. T. & Raichle, M. E., 'Localization of a human system for sustained attention by positron emission tomography', *Nature*, 1991, *349(6304)*, pp. 61-4

Parente, R. & Tommasi, L., 'A bias for the female face in the right hemisphere', *Laterality*, 2008, *13(4)*, pp. 374-86

Parfionovitch, Y., Meyer, F. & Dorje, G., *Tibetan Medical Paintings*, Serindia Publications, New York, 1992

Parks, R. W., Loewenstein, D. A., Dodrill, K. L. et al., 'Cerebral metabolic effects of a verbal fluency test – a PET scan study', *Journal of Clinical and Experimental Neuropsychology*, 1988, *10(5)*, pp. 565-75

Parmenides, *Fragments*, trans. & ed. A. Fairbanks, in Fairbanks, A., *The First Philosophers of Greece*, Kegan Paul, Trench, Trubner & Co., London, 1898

Parnas, J., 'The self and intentionality in the pre-psychotic stages of schizophrenia: a phenomenological study', in Zahavi, D. (ed.), *Exploring the Self: Philosophical and Psychopathological Perspectives on Self-experience*, Benjamins, Amsterdam, 2000, pp. 115-48

Parnas, J. & Sass, L. A., 'Self, solipsism and schizophrenic delusions', *Philosophy, Psychiatry, & Psychology*, 2001, *8(2-3)*, pp. 101-20

Parsons, L. M. & Osherson, D., 'New evidence for distinct right and left brain systems for deductive versus probabilistic reasoning', *Cerebral Cortex*, 2001, *11(10)*, pp. 954-65

Pascal, B., *Pensées*, édition Brunschvicg, Garnier Flammarion, Paris, 1976 [1670]

Pashler, H., Luck, S. J., Hillyard, S. A. et al., 'Sequential operation of disconnected cerebral hemispheres in split-brain patients', *NeuroReport*, 1994, *5(17)*, pp. 2381-4

Passingham, R., *The Frontal Lobes and Voluntary Action*, Oxford University Press, Oxford, 1993

Passmore, J., *The Perfectibility of Man*, Duckworth, London, 1970

Passynkova, N., Neubauer, H. & Scheich, H., 'Spatial organization of EEG coherence during listening to consonant and dissonant chords', *Neuroscience Letters*, 2007, *412(1)*, pp. 6-11

Pasteur, L., 'Observations sur les forces dissymetriques', *Comptes rendus de l'Académie des sciences*, 1874, *78*, pp. 1515-18

——, *Dissymétrie Moléculaire*, in *Œuvres de Pasteur*, vol. 1, ed. R. Vallery-Radot, Masson et Cie., Paris, 1922

Pastor, M. A., Day, B. L., Macaluso, E. et al., 'The functional neuroanatomy of temporal discrimination', *Journal of Neuroscience*, 2004, *24(10)*, pp. 2585-91

Patai, D. & Koertge, N., *Professing Feminism: Education and Indoctrination in Women's Studies*, Lexington Books, Lanham MD, 2003

Patston, L. L. M., Hogg, S. L. & Tippett, L. J., 'Attention in musicians is more bilateral than in non-musicians', *Laterality*, 2007, *12(3)*, pp. 262-72

Patston, L. L., Kirk, I. J., Rolfe, M. H. et al., 'The unusual symmetry of musicians: musicians have equilateral interhemispheric transfer for visual information', *Neuropsychologia*, 2007, *45(9)*, pp. 2059-65

Paul, G., *Der Mythos von der modernen Kunst und die Frage nach der Beschaffenheit einer zeitgemässen Ästhetik*, Steiner, Wiesbaden, 1985

——, 'Philosophical theories of beauty and scientific research on the brain', in Rentschler, I., Herzberger, B. & Epstein, D. (eds.), *Beauty and the Brain: Biological Aspects of Aesthetics*, Birkhäuser, Basel, 1988, pp. 15-27

Paul, L. K., Lautzenhiser, A., Brown, W. S. et al., 'Emotional arousal in agenesis of the corpus callosum', *International Journal of Psychophysiology*, 2006, *61(1)*, pp. 47-56

Paysant, J., Beis, J. M., Le Chapelain, L. et al., 'Mirror asomatognosia in right lesions stroke victims', *Neuropsychologia*, 2004, *42(7)*, pp. 920-25

Pedersen, C. B. & Mortensen, P. B., 'Evidence of a dose-response relationship between urbanicity during upbringing and schizophrenia risk', *Archives of General Psychiatry*, 2001, *58(11)*, pp. 1039-46

Pelling, C. (ed.), *Characterization and Individuality in Greek Literature*, Oxford University Press, Oxford, 1990

Pelphrey, K. A., Morris, J. P., Michelich, C. R. et al., 'Functional anatomy of biological motion perception in posterior temporal cortex: an fMRI study of eye, mouth and hand movements', *Cerebral Cortex*, 2005, *15(12)*, pp. 1866-76

Pendry, L. & Carrick, R., 'Doing what the mob do: priming effect on conformity', *European Journal of Social Psychology*, 2001, *31(1)*, pp. 83-92

Peng, K. & Nisbett, R. E., 'Culture, dialectics, and reasoning about contradiction', *American Psychologist*, 1999, *54(9)*, pp. 741-54

Pennal, B. E., 'Human cerebral asymmetry in color discrimination', *Neuropsychologia*, 1977, *15(4-5)*, pp. 563-8

Pepperberg, I., 'Insights into vocal imitation in Grey parrots (*Psittacus erithacus*)', in Hurley, S. & Chater, N. (eds.), *Perspectives on Imitation: From Neuroscience to Social Science*, vol. 1, *Mechanisms of Imitation and Imitation in Animals*, Massachusetts Institute of Technology Press, Cambridge MA, 2005, pp. 243-62

Pepperberg, I. M. & McLaughlin, M. A., 'Effects of avian-human joint attention on allospecific vocal learning by grey parrots (*Psittacus erithacus*)', *Journal of Comparative Psychology*, 1996, *110(3)*, pp. 286–97

Perani, D., Cappa, S. F., Bettinardi, V. et al., 'Different neural systems for the recognition of animals and man-made tools', *NeuroReport*, 1995, *6(12)*, pp. 1637–41

Perani, D., Fazio, F., Borghese, N. A. et al., 'Different brain correlates for watching real and virtual hand actions', *NeuroImage*, 2001, *14(3)*, pp. 749–58

Perani, D., Schnur, T., Tettamanti, M. et al., 'Word and picture-making: a PET study of semantic category effects', *Neuropsychologia*, 1999, *37(3)*, pp. 293–306

Peretz, I., 'Processing of local and global musical information in unilateral brain damaged patients', *Brain*, 1990, *113(4)*, pp. 1185–1205

Perria, L., Rosadini, G. & Rossi, G. F., 'Determination of side of cerebral dominance with amobarbital', *Archives of Neurology*, 1961, *4*, pp. 173–81

Perry, D. W., Zatorre, R. J. & Evans, A. C., 'Co-variation of CBF during singing with vocal fundamental frequency', *NeuroImage*, 1996, *3(3)*, p. S315

Perry, D. W., Zatorre, R. J., Petrides, M. et al., 'Localization of cerebral activity during simple singing', *NeuroReport*, 1999a, *10(16)*, pp. 3453–8

——, 'Localization of cerebral activity during simple singing', *NeuroReport*, 1999b, *10(18)*, pp. 3979–84

Perry, R. J., Rosen, H. R., Kramer, J. H. et al., 'Hemispheric dominance for emotions, empathy and social behaviour: evidence from right and left handers with frontotemporal dementia', *Neurocase*, 2001, *7(2)*, pp. 145–60

Persinger, M. A. & Lalonde, C. A., 'Right to left hemispheric shift in occipital electroencephalographic responses to repeated Kimura figures', *Perceptual and Motor Skills*, 2000, *91(1)*, pp. 273–8

Persinger, M. A. & Makarec, K., 'Greater right hemisphericity is associated with lower self-esteem in adults', *Perceptual and Motor Skills*, 1991, *73(3, pt. 2)*, pp. 1244–6

Persinger, M. A., Richards, P. M. & Koren, S. A., 'Differential ratings of pleasantness following right and left hemispheric application of low energy magnetic fields that stimulate long-term potentiation', *International Journal of Neuroscience*, 1994, *79(3–4)*, pp. 191–7

Pesenti, M., Zago, L., Crivello, F. et al., 'Mental calculation in a prodigy is sustained by right prefrontal and medial temporal areas', *Nature Neuroscience*, 2001, *4(1)*, pp. 103–7

Pesic, P., 'Wrestling with Proteus: Francis Bacon and the "torture" of nature', *Isis*, 1999, *90(1)*, pp. 81–94

Petitot, J., Varela, F. J., Pachoud, B. et al. (eds.), *Naturalizing Phenomenology: Issues in Contemporary Phenomenology and Cognitive Science*, Stanford University Press, Stanford CA, 1999

Pettigrew, J. D., 'Searching for the switch: neural bases for perceptual rivalry alternations', *Brain and Mind*, 2001, *2(1)*, pp. 85–118

Phelps, E. A. & Gazzaniga, M. S., 'Hemispheric differences in mnemonic processing: the effects of left hemisphere interpretation', *Neuropsychologia*, 1992, *30(3)*, pp. 293–7

Pica, P., Lemer, C., Izard, V. et al., 'Exact and approximate arithmetic in an Amazonian indigene group', *Science*, 2004, *306(5695)*, pp. 499–503

Piccolomini, Aeneas Sylvius, Pope Pius II, *Secret Memoirs of a Renaissance Pope: The Commentaries of Aeneas Sylvius Piccolomini, Pius II*, trans. F. A. Gragg, The Folio Society, London, 1988

Piercy, M., Hécaen, H. & de Ajuriaguerra, J., 'Constructional apraxia associated with unilateral cerebral lesions – left and right sided cases compared', *Brain*, 1960, *83(2)*, pp. 225–42

Piercy, M. & Smyth, V. O. G., 'Right hemisphere dominance for certain non-verbal intellectual skills', *Brain*, 1962, *85(4)*, pp. 775–90

Pilcher, D. L., Hammock, E. A. & Hopkins, W. D., 'Cerebral volumetric asymmetries in non-human primates: a magnetic resonance imaging study', *Laterality*, 2001, *6(2)*, pp. 165–79

Pinker, S., *How the Mind Works*, Norton, New York, 1997

Pirot, M., Pulton, T. W. & Sutker, L. W., 'Hemispheric asymmetry in reaction time to color stimuli', *Perceptual and Motor Skills*, 1977, *45(3, pt. 2)*, pp. 1151–5

Place, E. J. S. & Gilmore, G. C., 'Perceptual organization in schizophrenia', *Journal of Abnormal Psychology*, 1980, *89(3)*, pp. 409–18

Planck, M., *Where is Science Going?* (with a preface by Albert Einstein), trans. J Murphy, Allen & Unwin, London, 1933

——, 'Report on the 25th General Assembly of the Kaiser Wilhelm Association for the Advancement of the Sciences', 10–11 January 1936

Platek, S. M. & Gallup, G. G., Jnr., 'Self-face recognition is affected by schizotypal personality traits', *Schizophrenia Research*, 2002, *57(1)*, pp. 81–5

Platek, S. M., Keenan, J. P., Gallup, G. G., Jnr. et al., 'Where am I? The neurological correlates of self and other', *Brain Research: Cognitive Brain Research*, 2004, *19(2)*, pp. 114–22

Platel, H., Price, C., Baron, J.-C. et al., 'The structural components of music perception: a functional anatomical study', *Brain*, 1997, *120(2)*, pp. 229–43

Plato, *Cratylus*, in *The Dialogues of Plato*, trans. B. Jowett, Clarendon Press, Oxford, 1871, vol. 1

——, *Timaeus*, trans. F. M. Cornford, Oxford University Press, Oxford, 1941

——, *Phaedo*, trans. R. Hackforth, Cambridge University Press, Cambridge, UK, 1955

——, *Sophist*, in *The Sophist and The Statesman*, trans. A. E. Taylor, ed. R. Klibansky & E. Anscombe, Nelson, London, 1961

——, *Republic*, trans. H. D. P. Lee, Penguin, Harmondsworth, UK, 1963

——, *Theaetetus*, trans. J. McDowell, Clarendon Press, Oxford, 1973

——, *Parmenides*, trans. S. Scolnicov, University of California Press, Berkeley CA, 2003

Pleasants, H., *The Agony of Modern Music*, Simon & Schuster, New York, 1955

Pliny the Elder, *Natural History: a selection*, trans. & ed. J. F. Healy, Penguin, Harmondsworth, UK, 1991

Plotinus, *Enneads*, vol. 1, trans. A. H. Armstrong, Harvard University Press, Cambridge MA, 1966

Plumb, J. H., 'The Acceptance of Modernity', in Brewer, J., McKendrick, N. & Plumb, J. H. (eds.), *The Birth of a Consumer Society: the Commercialisation of Eighteenth-Century England*, Europa, London, 1982, pp. 316–34

Plutarch, *Lives*, 2 vols., trans. J. Dryden, Random House, New York, 2001

Pobric, G., Mashal, N., Faust, M. et al., 'The role of the right cerebral hemisphere in processing novel metaphoric expressions: a transcranial magnetic stimulation study', *Journal of Cognitive Neuroscience*, 2008, *20(1)*, pp. 170–81

Pockett, S., 'On subjective back-referral and how long it takes to become conscious of a stimulus: a reinterpretation of Libet's data', *Consciousness and Cognition*, 2002, *11(2)*, pp. 144–61

Podell, K., Lovell, M., Zimmerman, M. et al., 'The Cognitive Bias Task and lateralized frontal lobe functions in males', *Journal of Neuropsychiatry and Clinical Neurosciences*, 1995, *7(4)*, pp. 491–501

Poincaré, H., 'La création mathématique', *Science et Méthode*, Flammarion, Paris, 1908

Pontius, A. A., 'Dyslexia and specifically distorted drawings of the face – a new subgroup with prosopagnosia-like signs', *Experientia*, 1976, *32(11)*, pp. 1432–5

——, 'Links between literacy skills and accurate spatial relations in representations of the face: comparison of preschoolers, school children, dyslexics, and mentally retarded', *Perceptual and Motor Skills*, 1983, *57(2)*, pp. 659–66

——, 'Representation of spatial relations on the specific test, Draw-A-Person-With-Face-In-Front, as indicative of literacy skills in Australian Aboriginals and "Westerners"', *Perceptual and Motor Skills*, 1984, *59(1)*, pp. 275–84

Poole, J. H., Tyack, P. L., Stoeger-Horwath, A. S. et al., 'Animal behaviour: elephants are capable of vocal learning', *Nature*, 2005, *434(7032)*, pp. 455–6

Pope, A., *Preface to 'The Works of Shakespear'* [1725], in Nichol Smith, D. (ed.), *Eighteenth Century Essays on Shakespeare*, Clarendon Press, Oxford, 1963, pp. 47–62

——, *Poetical Works*, ed. H. Davis, Oxford University Press, Oxford, 1978

Popescu, M., Otsuka, A. & Ioannides, A. A., 'Dynamics of brain activity in motor and frontal cortical areas during music listening: a magnetoencephalographic study', *NeuroImage*, 2004, *21(4)*, pp. 1622–38

Popper, K. R., *The Logic of Scientific Discovery*, Routledge & Kegan Paul, London, 1980

Poreh, A. M., Whitman, R. D. & Ross, T., 'Creative thinking abilities and hemispheric asymmetry in schizotypal college students', *Current Psychology: Research & Reviews*, 1993–94, *12(4)*, pp. 344–52

Portele, G., 'Gestalttheorie und Wissenschaftstheorie: Plädoyer für eine alternative Wissenschaft', *Gestalt Theory*, 1979, *1(1)*, pp. 26–38

Porter, D. & Neuringer, A., 'Music discriminations by pigeons', *Journal of Experimental Psychology: Animal Behavior Processes*, 1984, *10(2)*, pp. 138–48

Porter, S., Campbell, M. A., Stapleton, J. et al., 'The influence of judge, target, and stimulus characteristics on the accuracy of detecting deceit', *Canadian Journal of Behavioural Science*, 2002, *34(3)*, pp. 172–85

Posner, M. I., 'Attention in cognitive neuroscience: an overview', in Gazzaniga, M. S. (ed.), *The Cognitive Neurosciences*, Massachusetts Institute of Technology Press, Cambridge MA, 1995, pp. 615–24

Posner, M. I. & Petersen, S. E., 'The attention system of the human brain', *Annual Review of Neuroscience*, 1990, *13(1)*, pp. 25–42

Posner, M. I. & Raichle, M., *Images of Mind*, Scientific American Library, New York, 1994

Post, F., 'Creativity and psychopathology: a study of 291 world-famous men', *British Journal of Psychiatry*, 1994, *165(2)*, pp. 22–34

Poundstone, W., *Prisoner's Dilemma*, Doubleday, New York, 1992

Povinelli, D. J., Nelson, K. E. & Boysen, S. T., 'Inferences about guessing and knowing by chimpanzees (*Pan troglodytes*)', *Journal of Comparative Psychology*, 1990, *104(3)*, pp. 203–10

——, 'Comprehension of role reversal in chimpanzees: evidence of empathy?', *Animal Behaviour*, 1992, *43(4)*, pp. 633–40

Povinelli, D. J., Parks, K. A. & Novak, M. A., 'Do rhesus monkeys (*Macaca mulatta*) attribute knowledge and ignorance to others?', *Journal of Comparative Psychology*, 1991, *105(4)*, pp. 318–25

Povinelli, D. J., Rulf, A. B., Landau, K. R. et al., 'Self-recognition in chimpanzees (*Pan troglodytes*): distribution, ontogeny, and patterns of emergence', *Journal of Comparative Psychology*, 1993, *107(4)*, pp. 347–72

Preilowski, B., 'Self-recognition as a test of consciousness in left and right hemisphere of "split-brain" patients', *Activitas Nervosa Superior (Prague)*, 1977, *19(suppl 2)*, pp. 343–4

Preisler, A., Gallasch, E. & Schulter, G., 'Hemispheric asymmetry and the processing of harmonies in music', *International Journal of Neuroscience*, 1989, *47(1–2)*, pp. 131–40

Premack, D., *Gavagai, or the Future History of the Animal Language Controversy*, Massachusetts Institute of Technology Press, Cambridge MA, 1986

Premack, D. & Woodruff, G., 'Does the chimpanzee have a theory of mind?', *Behavioral and Brain Sciences*, 1978, *1(4)*, pp. 515–26

Previc, F. H., 'Nonright-handedness, central nervous system and related pathology, and its lateralization: a reformulation and synthesis', *Developmental Neuropsychology*, 1996, *12(4)*, pp. 443–515

Pribram, K. H., 'Emotions', in Filskov, S. B. & Boll, T. J. (eds.), *Handbook of Clinical Neuropsychology*, Wiley, New York, 1981, pp. 102–34

Price, C. J. & Friston, K. J., 'Functional imaging studies of category specificity', in Forde, E. M. E. & Humphreys, G. W. (eds.), *Category Specificity in Brain and Mind*, Psychology Press, Hove, UK, 2002, pp. 427–47

Price, D. W., *History Made, History Imagined*, University of Illinois Press, Champaign IL, 1999

Prigatano, G., 'Disturbances of self-awareness of deficit after traumatic brain injury', in Prigatano, G. & Schacter, D. (eds.), *Awareness of Deficit After Brain Injury*, Oxford University Press, Oxford, 1991, pp. 111–26

——, 'Individuality, lesion location and psychotherapy after brain injury', in Christiansen, A.-L. & Uzzell, B. P. (eds.), *Brain Injury and Neuropsychological Rehabilitation: International Perspectives*, Laurence Erlbaum, Hillsdale NJ, 1994, pp. 173–86

Prins, R. & Bastiaanse, R., 'The early history of aphasiology: from the Egyptian surgeons (c. 1700 BC) to Broca (1861)', *Aphasiology*, 2006, *20(8)*, pp. 762–91

Prinz, W., 'Experimental approaches to imitation', in Meltzoff, A. & Prinz, W. (eds.), *The Imitative Mind: Development, Evolution, and Brain Bases*, Cambridge University Press, Cambridge, UK, 2002, pp. 143–63

——, 'An ideomotor approach to imitation', in Hurley, S. & Chater, N. (eds.), *Perspectives on Imitation: From Neuroscience to Social Science*, vol. 1, *Mechanisms of Imitation and Imitation in Animals*, Massachusetts Institute of Technology Press, Cambridge MA, 2005a, pp. 141–56

——, 'Construing selves from others', in Hurley, S. & Chater, N. (eds.), *Perspectives on Imitation: From Neuroscience to Social Science*, vol. 2, *Imitation, Human Development, and Culture*, Massachusetts Institute of Technology Press, Cambridge MA, 2005b, pp. 180–81

Prodan, C. I., Orbelo, D. M., Testa, J. A. et al., 'Hemispheric differences in recognizing upper and lower facial displays of emotion', *Neuropsychiatry, Neuropsychology and Behavioral Neurology*, 2001, *14(4)*, pp. 206–12

Pujol, J., Deus, J., Losilla, J. M. et al., 'Cerebral lateralization of language in normal left-handed people studied by functional MRI', *Neurology*, 1999, *52(5)*, pp. 1038–43

Pujol, J., López-Sala, A., Deus, J. et al., 'The lateral asymmetry of the human brain studied by volumetric magnetic resonance imaging', *NeuroImage*, 2002, *17(2)*, pp. 670–79

Putnam, R. D., *Bowling Alone: The Collapse and Revival of American Community*, Simon & Schuster, New York, 2000

Querné, L., Eustache, F. & Faure, S., 'Interhemispheric inhibition, intrahemispheric activation, and lexical capacities of the right hemisphere: a tachistoscopic, divided visual-field study in normal subjects', *Brain and Language*, 2000, *74(2)*, pp. 171–90

Querné, L. & Faure, S., 'Activating the right hemisphere by a prior spatial task: equal lexical decision accuracy in left and right visual fields in normal subjects', *Brain and Cognition*, 1996, *32(2)*, pp. 142–5

Quinn, K. & Geffen, G., 'The development of tactile transfer of information', *Neuropsychologia*, 1986, *24(6)*, pp. 793–804

Raby, C. R., Alexis, D. M., Dickinson, A. et al., 'Planning for the future by western scrub-jays', *Nature*, 2007, *445(7130)*, pp. 919–21

Radden, J. (ed.), *The Nature of Melancholy: from Aristotle to Kristeva*, Oxford University Press, Oxford, 2000

Raichle, M. E., Fiez, J. A., Videen, T. O. et al., 'Practice-related changes in human brain functional anatomy during nonmotor learning', *Cerebral Cortex*, 1994, *4(1)*, pp. 8–26

Raine, A., Buchsbaum, M. & LaCasse, L., 'Brain abnormalities in murderers indicated by positron emission tomography', *Biological Psychiatry*, 1997, *42(6)*, pp. 495–508

Rainville, P., Hofbauer, R. K., Paus, T. et al., 'Cerebral mechanisms of hypnotic induction and suggestion', *Journal of Cognitive Neuroscience*, 1999, *11(1)*, pp. 110–25

Rakison, D. H. & Poulin-Dubois, D., 'Developmental origin of the animate-inanimate distinction', *Psychological Bulletin*, 2001, *127(2)*, pp. 209–28

Ralegh, Sir Walter, *Poems*, ed. A. M. C. Latham, Routledge & Kegan Paul, London, 1951

Ramachandran, V. S., 'Behavioral and magnetoencephalographic correlates of neural plasticity in the adult human brain', *Proceedings of the National Academy of Sciences of the USA*, 1993, *90(22)*, pp. 10413–20

——, 'Phantom limbs, neglect syndromes, repressed memories, and Freudian psychology', *International Review of Neurobiology*, 1994, *37*, pp. 291–333

——, 'Anosognosia in parietal lobe syndrome', *Consciousness and Cognition*, 1995, *4(1)*, pp. 22–51

——, *Phantoms in the Brain: Human Nature and the Architecture of the Mind*, HarperCollins, London, 2005

Ramachandran, V. S. & Hubbard, E. M., 'Synaesthesia: a window into perception, thought and language', *Journal of Consciousness Studies*, 2001, *8(12)*, pp. 3–34

Ramachandran, V. S. & Rogers-Ramachandran, D., 'Denial of disabilities in anosognosia', *Nature*, 1996, *382(6591)*, p. 501

Rampling, D., 'Ascetic ideals and anorexia nervosa', *Journal of Psychiatric Research*, 1985, *19(2–3)*, pp. 89–94

Rankin, K. P., Gorno-Tempini, M. L., Allison, S. C. et al., 'Structural anatomy of empathy in neurodegenerative disease', *Brain*, 2006, *129(11)*, pp. 2945–56

Rao, S. M., Mayer, A. R. & Harrington, D. L., 'The evolution of brain activation during temporal processing', *Nature Neuroscience*, 2001, *4(3)*, pp. 317–23

Rao, V., Pintchovski, S., Chin, J. et al., 'AMPA receptors regulate transcription of the plasticity-related immediate-early gene Arc', *Nature Neuroscience*, 2006, *9(7)*, pp. 887–95

Rapcsak, S. Z., Ochipa, C., Beeson, P. M. et al., 'Praxis and the right hemisphere', *Brain and Cognition*, 1993, *23(2)*, pp. 181–202

Rapp, A. M., Leube, D. T., Erb, M. et al., 'Neural correlates of metaphor processing', *Brain Research: Cognitive Brain Research*, 2004, *20(3)*, pp. 395–402

Rasmussen, T. & Milner, B., 'The role of early left-brain injury in determining lateralization of cerebral speech functions', *Annals of the New York Academy of Sciences*, 1977, *299*, pp. 355–69

Rastelli, F., Funes, M. J., Lupiáñez, J. et al., 'Left visual neglect: is the disengage deficit space- or objectbased?' *Experimental Brain Research*, 2008, *187(3)*, pp. 439–46

Ratcliff, G., 'Disturbances of spatial orientation associated with cerebral lesions', in Potegal, M. (ed.), *Spatial abilities: development and physiological foundations*, Academic Press, New York, 1982, pp. 301–31

Ratliff, F., *Mach Bands: Quantitative Studies on Neural Networks in the Retina*, Holden-Day, San Francisco, 1965

Rausch, R., 'Cognitive strategies in patients with unilateral temporal lobe excisions', *Neuropsychologia*, 1977, *15(3)*, pp. 385–95

——, 'Differences in cognitive function with left and right temporal lobe dysfunction', in Benson, D. F. & Zaidel, E. (eds.), *The Dual Brain*, Guilford Press, New York, 1985, pp. 247–61

Rauscher, F. H., Krauss, R. M. & Chen, Y., 'Gesture, speech and lexical access: the role of lexical movements in speech production', *Psychological Science*, 1996, *7(4)*, pp. 226–31

562 ◆ BIBLIOGRAPHY

Razani, J., Boone, K. B., Miller, B. L. et al., 'Neuropsychological performance of right- and left-frontotemporal dementia compared to Alzheimer's disease', *Journal of the International Neuropsychological Society*, 2001, *7(4)*, pp. 468–80

Reed, B. R., Jagust, W. J. & Coulter, L. et al., 'Anosognosia in Alzheimer's disease: relationships to depression, cognitive function, and cerebral perfusion', *Journal of Clinical and Experimental Neuropsychology*, 1993, *15(2)*, pp. 231–44

Rees, R. (ed.), 'Wittgenstein's notes for lectures on "private experience" and "sense data" ', *Philosophical Review*, 1968, *77*, pp. 271–320

Regard, M., Knoch, D., Gütling, E. et al., 'Brain damage and addictive behavior: a neuropsychological and electroencephalogram investigation with pathologic gamblers', *Cognitive and Behavioral Neurology*, 2003, *16(1)*, pp. 47–53

Regard, M. & Landis, T., 'Beauty may differ in each half of the eye of the beholder', in Rentschler, I., Herzberger, B. & Epstein, D. (eds.), *Beauty and the Brain: Biological Aspects of Aesthetics*, Birkhauser Verlag, Basel, 1988, pp. 243–56

——, ' "Gourmand syndrome": eating passion associated with right anterior lesions', *Neurology*, 1997, *48(5)*, pp. 1185–90

Reich, S. S. & Cutting, J., 'Picture perception and abstract thought in schizophrenia', *Psychological Medicine*, 1982, *12(1)*, pp. 91–6

Remond-Besuchet, C., Noël, M.-P., Seron, X. et al., 'Selective preservation of exceptional arithmetical knowledge in a demented patient', *Mathematical Cognition*, 1999, *5(1)*, pp. 41–63

Resch, F., Haffner, J., Parzer, P. et al., 'Testing the hypothesis of the relationships between laterality and ability according to Annett's right-shift theory: findings in an epidemiological sample of young adults', *British Journal of Psychology*, 1997, *88(4)*, pp. 621–35

Révész, G., *The Human Hand: A Psychological Study*, trans. J. Cohen, Routledge & Kegan Paul, London, 1958 [*De menschelijke hand* 1942]

Richards, H., 'The "uneventful life" that embraced philosophy and science as well as penal reform and fridges', *Times Higher Education Supplement*, London, 9 September 2005

Richards, L. & Chiarello, C., 'Activation without selection: parallel right-hemisphere roles in language and intentional movement?', *Brain and Language*, 1997, *57(1)*, pp. 151–78

Richter, I. A. (ed.), *Selections from the Notebooks of Leonardo da Vinci*, Oxford University Press, Oxford, 1952

Richter, J., Möller, B., Spitzer, C. et al., 'Transcallosal inhibition in patients with and without alexithymia', *Neuropsychobiology*, 2006, *53(2)*, pp. 101–7

Ricks, C., *Keats and Embarrassment*, Clarendon Press, Oxford, 1974

Ricoeur, P., in Reagan, C. & Stewart, D. (eds.), *The Philosophy of Paul Ricoeur*, Beacon Press, Boston MA, 1978

Ridolfi, C., *Le Maraviglie dell'Arte*, ed. D. von Hadeln, Grote, Berlin, 1914–24

Rilling, J. K., Gutman, D., Zeh, T. et al., 'A neural basis for social cooperation', *Neuron*, 2002, *35(2)*, pp. 395–405

Rimé, B., Schiaratura, L., Hupet, M. et al., 'Effects of relative immobilisation on the speaker's nonverbal behaviour and on the dialogue imagery level', *Motivation and Emotion*, 1984, *8(4)*, pp. 311–25

Ringo, J. L., Doty, R. W., Demeter, S. et al., 'Time is of the essence: a conjecture that hemispheric specialization arises from interhemispheric conduction delay', *Cerebral Cortex*, 1994, *4(4)*, pp. 331–43

Ritblatt, S. N., 'Children's level of participation in a false-belief task, age, and theory of mind', *Journal of Genetic Psychology*, 2000, *161(1)*, pp. 53–64

Ritsema, M. E. & Murphy, M. A., 'Palinopsia from posterior visual pathway lesions without visual field defects', *Journal of Neuro-Ophthalmology*, 2007, *27(2)*, pp. 115–17

Rizzolatti, G., Fogassi, L., Gallese, V. et al., 'Neurophysiological mechanisms underlying the understanding and imitation of action', *Nature Reviews Neuroscience*, 2001, *2(9)*, pp. 661–70

Roberson, D. & Davidoff, J., 'The categorical perception of colors and facial expressions: the effect of verbal interference', *Memory and Cognition*, 2000, *28(6)*, pp. 977–86

Roberts, N. A., Beer, J. S., Werner, K. H. et al., 'The impact of orbital prefrontal cortex damage on emotional activation to unanticipated and anticipated acoustic startle stimuli', *Cognitive, Affective and Behavioral Neuroscience*, 2004, *4(3)*, pp. 307–16

Robertson, L. C. & Lamb, M. R., 'Neuropsychological contributions to theories of part/whole organisation', *Cognitive Psychology*, 1991, *23(2)*, pp. 299–330

Robertson, L. C., Lamb, M. R. & Knight, R. T., 'Effects of lesions of temporal-parietal junction on perceptual and attentional processing in humans', *Journal of Neuroscience*, 1988, *8(10)*, pp. 3757–69

Robertson-Dunn, D., Metreweli, C. & Brown, B., 'Cerebral asymmetry in the Chinese', *International Journal of Neuroradiology*, 1996, *2*, pp. 347–52

Robins, A. & Rogers, L. J., 'Complementary and lateralized forms of processing in *Bufo marinus* for novel and familiar prey', *Neurobiology of Learning and Memory*, 2006, *86(2)*, pp. 214–27

Robinson, R. G., 'Differential behavioral and biochemical effects of right and left hemispheric cerebral infarction in the rat', *Science*, 1979, *205(4407)*, pp. 707–10

Robinson, R. G. & Benson, D. F., 'Depression in aphasic patients: frequency, severity and clinical-pathological correlations', *Brain and Language*, 1981, *14(2)*, pp. 282–91

Robinson, R. G., Boston, J. D., Starkstein, S. E. et al., 'Comparison of mania and depression after brain injury: causal factors', *American Journal of Psychiatry*, 1988, *145(2)*, pp. 172–8

Robinson, R. G., Kubos, K. L., Starr, L. B. et al., 'Mood disorders in stroke patients: importance of location of lesion', *Brain*, 1984, *107(1)*, pp. 81–93

Robinson, R. G. & Price, T. R., 'Post-stroke depressive disorders: a follow-up study of 103 patients', *Stroke*, 1982, *13(5)*, pp. 635–41

Robinson, R. G., Starr, L. B., Lipsey, J. R. et al., 'A two-year longitudinal study of post-stroke mood disorders. In-hospital prognostic factors associated with six-month outcome', *Journal of Nervous and Mental Disease*, 1985, *173(4)*, pp. 221–6

Robinson, R. G. & Szetela, B., 'Mood change following left hemispheric brain injury', *Annals of Neurology*, 1981, *9(5)*, pp. 447–53

Rogers, L. J., 'Evolution of hemisphere specialisation: advantages and disadvantages', *Brain and Language*, 2000, *73(2)*, pp. 236–53

——, 'Lateralization in vertebrates: its early evolution, general pattern and development', in Slater, P. J. B., Rosenblatt, J., Snowdon, C. et al. (eds.), *Advances in the Study of Behavior*, vol. 31, Academic Press, New York, 2002, pp. 107–62

——, 'Cognitive and social advantages of having a lateralized brain', in Malashichev, Y. B. & Deckel, A. W. (eds.), *Behavioral and Morphological Asymmetries in Vertebrates*, Landes Bioscience, Austin TX, 2006, pp. 129–39

Rogers, L. J. & Andrew, R. J., *Comparative Vertebrate Lateralization*, Cambridge University Press, Cambridge, UK, 2002

Rogers, L. J. & Kaplan, G., 'An eye for a predator: lateralization in birds, with particular reference to the Australian magpie', in Malashichev, Y. B. & Deckel, A. W. (eds.), *Behavioral and Morphological Asymmetries in Vertebrates*, Landes Bioscience, Austin TX, 2006, pp. 47–57

Rogers, L. J. & Workman, L., 'Light exposure during incubation affects competitive behaviour in domestic chicks', *Applied Animal Behaviour Science*, 1989, *23*, pp. 187–98

Rogers, L. J., Zucca, P. & Vallortigara, G., 'Advantages of having a lateralized brain', *Proceedings of the Royal Society of London, Series B: Biological Sciences*, 2004, *271(suppl. 6)*, pp. S420–2

Roland, P. E., Skinhøj, E. & Lassen, N. A., 'Focal activation of human cerebral cortex during auditory discrimination', *Journal of Neurophysiology*, 1981, *45(6)*, pp. 1139–51

Romito, L. M., Raja, M., Daniele, A. et al., 'Transient mania with hypersexuality after surgery for high frequency stimulation of the subthalamic nucleus in Parkinson's disease', *Movement Disorders*, 2002, *17(6)*, pp. 1371–4

Roricht, S., Irlbacher, K., Petrow, E. et al., 'Normwerte transkallosal und kortikospinal vermittelter Effekte einer hemispharenselektiven elektromyographischer magnetischen Kortexreizung beim Menschen', *Zeitschrift für Elektroenzephalographie, Elektromyographie und Verwandte Gebiete*, 1997, *28*, pp. 34–8

Rorty, R., *Contingency, Irony, Solidarity*, Cambridge University Press, Cambridge, UK, 1989

Rosen, G. D. & Galaburda, A. M., 'Development of language: a question of asymmetry and deviation', in Mehler, J. & Fox, R. (eds.), *Neonate Cognition: Beyond the Blooming, Buzzing Confusion*, Lawrence Erlbaum, Hillsdale NJ, 1985, pp. 307–25

Rosenthal, D. M., 'The timing of conscious states', *Consciousness and Cognition*, 2002, *11(2)*, pp. 215–20

Ross, E. D., 'Right-hemisphere lesions in disorders of affective language', in Kertesz, A. (ed.), *Localization in Neuropsychology*, Academic Press, New York, 1983, pp. 493–508

——, 'Nonverbal aspects of language [review]', *Neurologic Clinics*, 1993, *11(1)*, pp. 9–23

Ross, E. D., Homan, R. W. & Buck, R., 'Differential hemispheric lateralization of primary and social emotions', *Neuropsychiatry, Neuropsychology and Behavioral Neurology*, 1994, *7(1)*, pp. 1–19

Ross, E. D. & Mesulam, M. M., 'Dominant language functions of the right hemisphere? Prosody and emotional gesturing', *Archives of Neurology*, 1979, *36(3)*, pp. 144–8

Ross, E. D., Thompson, R. D. & Yenkosky, J., 'Lateralisation of affective prosody in the brain and callosal integration of hemispheric language functions', *Brain and Language*, 1977, *56(1)*, pp. 27–54

Rosse, R. B., Kendrick, K., Wyatt, R. J. et al., 'Gaze discrimination in patients with schizophrenia: preliminary report', *American Journal of Psychiatry*, 1994, *151(6)*, 919–21

Rossion, B., Caldara, R., Seghier, M. et al., 'A network of occipito-temporal face-sensitive areas besides the right middle fusiform gyrus is necessary for normal face processing', *Brain*, 2003, *126(11)*, pp. 2381–95

Rossor, M. N., Warrington, E. K. & Cipolotti, L., 'The isolation of calculation skills', *Journal of Neurology*, 1995, *242(2)*, pp. 78–81

Rotenberg, V. S., 'An integrative psychophysiological approach to brain hemisphere functions in schizophrenia', *Neuroscience and Biobehavioral Reviews*, 1994, *18(4)*, pp. 487–95

——, 'The peculiarity of the right-hemisphere function in depression: solving the paradoxes', *Progress in Neuro-Psychopharmacology and Biological Psychiatry*, 2004, *28(1)*, pp. 1–13

Rotenberg, V. S. & Arshavsky, V. V., 'The two hemispheres and the problem of psychotherapy', *Dynamische Pychiatrie/Dynamic Psychiatry*, 1987, *20(5–6)*, pp. 369–77

Roth, H. L., Lora, A. N. & Heilman, K. M., 'Effects of monocular viewing and eye dominance on spatial attention', *Brain*, 2002, *125(9)*, pp. 2023–35

Roth, M., 'Disorders of the body image caused by lesions of the right parietal lobe', *Brain*, 1949, *72(1)*, pp. 89–111

Rothbart, M. K., Ahadi, S. A. & Hershey, K. L., 'Temperament and social behavior in childhood', *Merrill-Palmer Quarterly*, 1994, *40(1)*, pp. 21–39

Rothwell, J. C., Colebatch, J., Britton, T. C. et al., 'Physiological studies in a patient with mirror movements and agenesis of the corpus callosum', *Journal of Physiology*, 1991, *438(1)*, p. 34P

Rourke, B. P., *Nonverbal Learning Disabilities: The Syndrome and the Model*, Guilford Press, New York, 1989

Rousseau, J.-J., 'Essay on the origin of languages which treats of melody and musical imitation', in *Two Essays on the Origin of Language: Jean-Jacques Rousseau & Johann Gottfried Herder*, trans. J. H. Moran & A. Gode, University of Chicago Press, Chicago, 1966, pp. 1–74 [*Essai sur l'origine des langues* 1781]

Rousseaux, M., Fimm, B. & Cantagallo, A., 'Attention disorders in cerebrovascular diseases', in Leclercq, M. & Zimmerman, P. (eds.), *Applied Neuropsychology of Attention*, Psychology Press, London, 2002, pp. 280–304

Rousseaux, M., Godefroy, O., Cabaret, M. et al., 'Analyse et évolution des déficits cognitifs après rupture des anévrysmes de l'artère communicante antérieure', *Revue Neurologique*, 1996, *152(11)*, pp. 678–87

Rubia, K., Smith, A. B., Brammer, M. J. et al., 'Right inferior prefrontal cortex mediates response inhibition while mesial prefrontal cortex is responsible for error detection', *NeuroImage*, 2003, *20(1)*, pp. 351–8

Ruby, P. & Decety, J., 'Effect of subjective perspective taking during simulation of action: a PET investigation of agency', *Nature Neuroscience*, 2001, *4(5)*, pp. 546–50

——, 'What you believe versus what you think they believe: a neuroimaging study of conceptual perspective-taking', *European Journal of Neuroscience*, 2003, *17(11)*, pp. 2475–80

Rueckert, L. & Grafman, J., 'Sustained attention deficits in patients with right frontal lesions', Neuropsychologia, 1996, 34(10), pp. 953–63

Ruff, R. M., Allen, C. C., Farrow, C. E. et al., 'Figural fluency: differential impairment in patients with left versus right frontal lobe lesions', Archives of Clinical Neuropsychology, 1994, 9(1), pp. 41–55

Rumelhart, D. E., Smolensky, P., McClelland, J. L. et al., 'Schemata and sequential thought processes in PDP [parallel distributed processing] models', in McClelland, J. L. & Rumelhart, D. E. (eds.), Parallel Distributed Processing, vol. 2, Massachusetts Institute of Technology Press, Cambridge MA, 1986, pp. 7–57

Ruskin, J., Modern Painters, 6 vols., George Allen, London, 1904 [1843–60]

Russell, B., History of Western Philosophy, George Allen & Unwin, London, 1946

Russell, D. A. & Konstan, D., Heraclitus: Homeric Problems, Society of Biblical Literature, Atlanta GA, 2005

Russell, J. M., Early, T. S., Patterson, J. C. et al., 'Temporal lobe perfusion asymmetries in schizophrenia', Journal of Nuclear Medicine, 1997, 38(4), pp. 607–12

Russell, S. M. & Golfinos, J. G., 'Amusia following resection of a Heschl gyrus glioma: case report', Journal of Neurosurgery, 2003, 98(5), pp. 1109–12

Rutledge, R. & Hunt, G. R., 'Lateralised tool use in New Caledonian crows', Animal Behaviour, 2004, 67(2), pp. 327–32

Rybash, J. M. & Hoyer, W. J., 'Hemispheric specialization for categorical and coordinate spatial representations: a reappraisal', Memory and Cognition, 1992, 20(3), pp. 271–6

Saadah, E. S. & Melzack, R., 'Phantom limb experiences in congenital limb-deficient adults', Cortex, 1994, 30(3), pp. 479–85

Sabbagh, M. A., 'Communicative intentions and language: evidence from right-hemisphere damage and autism', Brain and Language, 1999, 70(1), pp. 29–69

Sackeim, H. A., Greenberg, M. S., Weiman, A. L. et al., 'Hemispheric asymmetry in the expression of positive and negative emotions: neurologic evidence', Archives of Neurology, 1982, 39(4), pp. 210–18

Sacks, O., 'The power of music', Brain, 2006, 129(10), pp. 2528–32

Safer, M. A. & Leventhal, H., 'Ear differences in evaluating emotional tones of voice and verbal content', Journal of Experimental Psychology: Human Perception and Performance, 1977, 3(1), pp. 75–82

Saha, S., Chant, D., Welham, J. et al., 'A systematic review of the prevalence of schizophrenia', PLoS Medicine, 2005, 2(5), p. e141

Sakai, K., Hikosaka, O., Miyauchi, S. et al., 'Neural representation of a rhythm depends on its interval ratio', Journal of Neuroscience, 1999, 19(22), pp. 10074–81

Salamy, A., 'Commissural transmission: maturational changes in humans', Science, 1978, 200(4348), pp. 1409–11

Saling, M. M. & Tyson, G., 'Lateral cradling preferences in nulliparous females', Journal of Genetic Psychology, 1981, 139, pp. 309–10

Salk, L., 'The role of the heartbeat in the relations between mother and infant', Scientific American, 1973, 228(5), pp. 24–9

Salmaso, D. & Denes, G., 'Role of the frontal lobes on an attention task: a signal detection analysis', Perceptual and Motor Skills, 1982, 54(3, pt. 2), pp. 1147–50

Sandhu, S., Cook, P. & Diamond, M. C., 'Rat cerebral cortical estrogen receptors: male-female, right-left', Experimental Neurology, 1986, 92(1), pp. 186–96

Sandkühler, S. & Bhattacharya, J., 'Deconstructing insight: EEG correlates of insightful problem solving', PLoS ONE, 2008, 3(1), p. e1459

Sansavini, A., Bertoncini, J. & Giovanelli, G., 'Newborns discriminate the rhythm of multisyllabic stressed words', Developmental Psychology, 1997, 33(1), pp. 3–11

Sapir, E., 'The unconscious patterning of behavior in society', in Dummer, E. S. (ed.), The Unconscious: A Symposium, Knopf, New York, 1927, pp. 114–42

Sarles, H. B., Language and Human Nature, University of Minnesota Press, Minneapolis MN, 1985

Saron, C. D. & Davidson, R. J., 'Visual evoked potential measures of interhemispheric transfer time in humans', Behavioral Neuroscience, 1989, 103(5), pp. 1115–38

Saron, C. D., Foxe, J. J., Schroeder, C. E. et al., 'Complexities of interhemispheric communication in sensorimotor tasks revealed by high-density event-related potential mapping', in Hugdahl, K. & Davidson, R. J. (eds.), The Asymmetrical Brain, Massachusetts Institute of Technology Press, Cambridge MA, 2003, pp. 341–408

Saron, C. D., Foxe, J. J., Simpson, G. V. et al., 'Interhemispheric visuomotor activation: spatiotemporal electrophysiology related to reaction time', in Zaidel, E. & Iacoboni, M. (eds.), The Parallel Brain: the Cognitive Neuroscience of the Corpus Callosum, Massachusetts Institute of Technology Press, Cambridge MA, 2002, pp. 171–219

Sass, L. A., 'Time, space, and symbol: a study of narrative form and representational structure in madness and modernism', Psychoanalysis and Contemporary Thought, 1985, 8, pp. 45–85

——, Madness and Modernism: Insanity in the Light of Modern Art, Literature and Thought, Harvard University Press, Cambridge MA, 1992

——, The Paradoxes of Delusion: Wittgenstein, Schreber, and the Schizophrenic Mind, Cornell University Press, Ithaca NY, 1994

——, 'Wittgenstein, Freud and the nature of psychoanalytic explanation', in Allen, R. & Turvey, M. (eds.), Wittgenstein, Theory and the Arts, Routledge, London, 2001, pp. 253–95

——, 'Schizophrenia: a disturbance of the thematic field', in Embree, L. (ed.), Gurwitsch's Relevancy for Cognitive Science (Contributions to Phenomenology), Springer-Verlag, Dordrecht, Netherlands, 2004, pp. 59–78

Sass, L. A. & Parnas, J., 'Phenomenology of self-disturbances: some research findings and directions', Philosophy, Psychiatry, & Psychology, 2001, 8(4), pp. 347–56

——, 'Schizophrenia, consciousness, and the self', Schizophrenia Bulletin, 2003, 29(3), pp. 427–44

——, 'Explaining schizophrenia: the relevance of phenomenology', in Chung, M. C., Fulford, K. W. M. & Graham, G. (eds.), Reconceiving Schizophrenia, Oxford University Press, Oxford, 2007, pp. 63–95

Saxby, L. & Bryden, M. P., 'Left visual-field advantage in children for processing visual emotional stimuli', Developmental Psychology, 1985, 21(2), pp. 253–61

Saxe, G. B. & Moylan, T., 'The development of measurement operations among the Oksapmin of Papua New Guinea', *Child Development*, 1982, *53(5)*, pp. 1242–8

Saxe, R. & Wexler, A., 'Making sense of another mind: the role of the right temporo-parietal junction', *Neuropsychologia*, 2005, *43(10)*, pp. 1391–9

Schacter, D. L., Curran, T., Galluccio, L. et al., 'False recognition and the right frontal lobe: a case study', *Neuropsychologia*, 1996, *34(8)*, pp. 793–808

Schacter, D. L., Glisky, E. L. & McGlynn, S. M., 'Impact of memory disorder on everyday life: awareness of deficits and return to work', in Tapper, D. & Cicerone, K. (eds.), *The Neuropsychology of Everyday Life*, Kluwer, Boston MA, 1990, pp. 231–57

Schaffer, C. E., Davidson, R. J. & Saron, C., 'Frontal and parietal electroencephalogram asymmetry in depressed and non-depressed subjects', *Biological Psychiatry*, 1983, *18(7)*, pp. 753–62

Schatz, A. M., Ballantyne, A. O. & Trauner, D. A., 'A hierarchical analysis of block design errors in children with early focal brain damage', *Developmental Neuropsychology*, 2000, *17(1)*, pp. 75–83

Scheibel, A. B., Paul, L. A., Fried, I. et al., 'Dendritic organization of the anterior speech area', *Experimental Neurology*, 1985, *87(1)*, pp. 109–17

Scheler, M., *The Nature of Sympathy*, trans. P. Heath, Routledge & Kegan Paul, London, 1954

——, *Formalism in Ethics and Non-Formal Ethics of Values: A New Attempt toward the Foundation of an Ethical Personalism*, trans. M. S. Frings & R. L. Funk, Northwestern University Press, Evanston IL, 1973 [1913–16]

——, *Späte Schriften*, in ed. M. Frings, *Gesammelte Werke*, vol. 9, Francke Verlag, Bern, 1976

——, *Ressentiment*, trans. L. B. Coser & W. W. Holdheim, Marquette University Press, Milwaukee WI, 1998 [1915]

——, *The Constitution of The Human Being*, trans. J. Cutting, Marquette University Press, Milwaukee WI, 2008

Schenkenberg, T., Dustman, R. E. & Beck, E. C., 'Changes in evoked responses related to age, hemisphere and sex', *Electroencephalography and Clinical Neurophysiology*, 1971, *30(2)*, pp. 163–4

Scherer, K. R., 'Emotion expression in speech and music', in Sundberg, J., Nord, L. & Carlson, R. (eds.), *Music, Language, Speech and Brain*, MacMillan Press, Basingstoke, UK, 1991, pp. 146–56

Schiffer, F., Zaidel, E., Bogen, J. et al., 'Different psychological status in the two hemispheres of two splitbrain patients', *Neuropsychiatry, Neuropsychology and Behavioral Neurology*, 1998, *11(3)*, pp. 151–6

Schilder, P., *The Image and Appearance of the Human Body*, Routledge, London, 1999

Schiltz, C., Sorger, B., Caldara, R. et al., 'Impaired face discrimination in acquired prosopagnosia is associated with abnormal response to individual faces in the right middle fusiform gyrus', *Cerebral Cortex*, 2006, *16(4)*, pp. 574–86

Schlegel, A. W., *Lectures on Dramatic Art and Literature*, lecture VI, trans. J. Black, 2nd edn., George Bell & Sons, London, 1886, pp. 78–95

Schlegel, F., *Philosophical Fragments*, trans. P. Firchow, University of Minnesota Press, Minneapolis MN, 1991

——, *Athenaeum Fragments*, in Bernstein, J. M. (ed.), *Classic and Romantic German Aesthetics*, Cambridge University Press, Cambridge, UK, 2003, pp. 246–60

Schleiermacher, F., *On Religion: Speeches to its Cultured Despisers*, trans. J. Oman, Kegan Paul, Trench, Trubner & Co., London, 1893 [*Über die Religion* 1799]

——, *Über die Religion: Reden an die Gebildeten unter ihren Verächtern*, Felix Meiner, Hamburg, 1958 [1799]

Schmidt, G. L., DeBuse, C. J. & Seger, C. A., 'Right hemisphere metaphor processing? Characterizing the lateralization of semantic processes', *Brain and Language*, 2007, *100(2)*, pp. 127–41

Schneiderman, E. I., Murasugi, K. G. & Saddy, J. D., 'Story arrangement ability in right-brain damaged patients', *Brain and Language*, 1992, *43(1)*, pp. 107–20

Schnider, A., Benson, F. & Rosner, L. J., 'Callosal disconnection in multiple sclerosis', *Neurology*, 1993, *43(6)*, pp. 1243–5

Schnider, A., Gutbrod, K., Hess, C. W. et al., 'Memory without context: amnesia with confabulations after infarction of the right capsular genu', *Journal of Neurology, Neurosurgery, & Psychiatry*, 1996, *61(2)*, pp. 186–93

Schoenemann, P. T., Sheehan, M. J. & Glotzer, L. D., 'Prefrontal white matter volume is disproportionately larger in humans than in other primates', *Nature Neuroscience*, 2005, *8(2)*, pp. 242–52

Schooler, J. W. & Engstler-Schooler, T. Y., 'Verbal overshadowing of visual memories: some things are better left unsaid', *Cognitive Psychology*, 1990, *22(1)*, pp. 36–71

Schopenhauer, A., *The World as Will and Representation*, 2 vols., trans. E. F. Payne, Dover, New York, 1969 [*Die Welt als Wille und Vorstellung* 1819]

——, *Die Welt als Wille und Vorstellung*, in *Sämtliche Werke*, ed. Wolfgang, Freiherr von Löhneysen, Cotta-Insel-Verlag, Stuttgart/Frankfurt am Main, 1960, vols. 1 & 2 [1819]

——, *Preisschrift über die Freiheit des Willens*, in *Sämtliche Werke*, ed. Wolfgang, Freiherr von Löhneysen, Cotta-Insel-Verlag, Stuttgart/Frankfurt am Main, 1962, vol. 3 [1819]

Schore, A. N., *Affect Regulation and the Origin of the Self: the Neurobiology of Emotional Development*, Lawrence Erlbaum, Hillsdale NJ, 1994

——, 'A century after Freud's project: is a rapprochement between psychoanalysis and neurobiology at hand?', *Journal of the American Psychoanalytic Association*, 1997, *45(3)*, pp. 807–40

——, *Affect Regulation and the Repair of the Self*, Norton, New York, 2003

Schreber, D. P., *Denkwürdigkeiten eines Nervenkranken*, Oswald Mutze, Leipzig, 1903

Schroeder, S., 'The coded-message model of literature', in Allen, R. & Turvey, M. (eds.), *Wittgenstein, Theory and the Arts*, Routledge, London, 2001, pp. 210–228

Schutz, L. E., 'Broad-perspective perceptual disorder of the right hemisphere', *Neuropsychology Review*, 2005, *15(1)*, pp. 11–27

Schwartz, G. E., Davidson, R. J. & Maer, F., 'Right hemisphere lateralization for emotion in the human brain: interactions with cognition', *Science*, 1975, *190(4211)*, pp. 286–8

Schwartz, M., Creasey, H., Grady, C. L. et al., 'Computed tomographic analysis of brain morphometrics in 30 healthy men, aged 21 to 81 years', *Annals of Neurology*, 1985, *17(2)*, pp. 146–57

Schwartz, M. F., Buxbaum, L. J., Montgomery, M. W. et al., 'Naturalistic action production following right hemisphere stroke', *Neuropsychologia*, 1999, *37(1)*, pp. 51–66

Schwartz, S., Assal, F., Valenza, N. et al., 'Illusory persistence of touch after right parietal damage: neural correlates of tactile awareness', *Brain*, 2005, *128(2)*, pp. 277–90

Scotti, G. & Spinnler, H., 'Colour imperception in unilateral hemisphere-damaged patients', *Journal of Neurology, Neurosurgery, & Psychiatry*, 1970, *33(1)*, pp. 22–8

Screech, M. A., *Montaigne and Melancholy*, Penguin, Harmondsworth, UK, 1983

Scruton, R., *Sexual Desire: a Philosophical Investigation*, Weidenfeld & Nicolson, London, 1986

——, *Modern Philosophy*, Arrow, London, 1997

Scull, A. T., *Museums of Madness: The Social Organization of Insanity in Nineteenth-Century England*, Allen Lane, London, 1979

Seaford, R., *Money and the Early Greek Mind: Homer, Philosophy, Tragedy*, Cambridge University Press, Cambridge, UK, 2004

Seger, C. A., Desmond, J. E., Glover, G. H. et al., 'Functional magnetic resonance imaging evidence for righthemisphere involvement in processing unusual semantic relationships', *Neuropsychology*, 2000, *14(3)*, pp. 361–9

Seger, C. A., Poldrack, R. A., Prabhakaran, V. et al., 'Hemispheric asymmetries and individual differences in visual concept learning as measured by functional MRI', *Neuropsychologia*, 2000, *38(9)*, pp. 1316–24

Seidenwurm, D. J. & Devinsky, O., 'Neuroradiology in the humanities and social sciences', *Radiology*, 2006, *239(1)*, pp. 13–17

Sekida, K., *Zen Training: Methods and Philosophy*, Weatherhill, New York, 1975

Seldon, H. L., 'Structure of human auditory cortex: III. Statistical analysis of dendritic trees', *Brain Research*, 1982, *249(2)*, pp. 211–21

Sellal, F., Chevalier, Y. & Collard, M., ' "Pinocchio syndrome": a peculiar form of reflex epilepsy?', *Journal of Neurology, Neurosurgery, & Psychiatry*, 1993, *56(8)*, p. 936

Selten, J.-P. & Cantor-Graae, E., 'Social defeat: risk factor for schizophrenia?', *British Journal of Psychiatry*, 2005, *187(2)*, pp. 101–2

——, 'Hypothesis: social defeat is a risk factor for schizophrenia?', *British Journal of Psychiatry*, 2007, *191(suppl. 51)*, pp. s9–s12

Semendeferi, K., Lu, A., Schenker, N. et al., 'Humans and great apes share a large frontal cortex', *Nature Neuroscience*, 2002, *5(3)*, pp. 272–6

Semmes, J., 'Hemispheric specialisation: a possible clue to mechanism', *Neuropsychologia*, 1968, *6(1)*, pp. 11–26

Semmes, J., Weinstein, S., Ghent, L. et al., *Somatosensory Changes After Penetrating Brain Wounds in Man*, Harvard University Press, Cambridge MA, 1960

Serafetinides, E. A., Hoare, R. D. & Driver, M. V., 'Intracarotid sodium amylobarbitone and cerebral dominance for speech and consciousness', *Brain*, 1965, *88(1)*, pp. 107–30

Sergent, J., 'The cerebral balance of power: confrontation or cooperation?', *Journal of Experimental Psychology: Human Perception and Performance*, 1982, *8(2)*, pp. 253–72

——, 'Role of the input in visual hemispheric asymmetries', *Psychological Bulletin*, 1983a, *93(3)*, pp. 481–512

——, 'Unified response to bilateral hemispheric stimulation in a split-brain patient', *Nature*, 1983b, *305(5937)*, pp. 800–2

——, 'Subcortical coordination of hemisphere activity in commissurotomized patients', *Brain*, 1986, *109(2)*, pp. 357–69

——, 'Furtive incursions into bicameral minds: integrative and coordinating role of subcortical structures', *Brain*, 1990, *113(2)*, pp. 537–68

Sergent, J. & Bindra, D., 'Differential hemispheric processing of faces: methodological considerations and reinterpretation', *Psychological Bulletin*, 1981, *89(3)*, pp. 541–54

Sergent, J., Ohta, S. & MacDonald, B., 'Functional neuroanatomy of face and object processing: a positron emission tomography study', *Brain*, 1992, *115(1)*, pp. 15–36

Sergent, J. & Signoret, J. L., 'Varieties of functional deficits in prosopagnosia', *Cerebral Cortex*, 1992, *2(5)*, pp. 375–88

Sergent, J. & Villemure, J.-G., 'Prosopagnosia in a right hemispherectomized patient', *Brain*, 1989, *112(4)*, pp. 975–95

Sévigné, Marie de Rabutin-Chantal, marquise de, *Lettres de Mme de Sévigné*, ed. M. Suard, Firmin Didot frères, Paris, 1846

Shadmehr, R. & Holcomb, H. H., 'Neural correlates of motor memory consolidation', *Science*, 1997, *277(5327)*, pp. 821–5

Shah, A. & Frith, U., 'Why do autistic individuals show superior performance on the block design task?', *Journal of Child Psychology and Psychiatry and Allied Disciplines*, 1993, *34(8)*, pp. 1351–64

Shallice, T., ' "Theory of mind" and the prefrontal cortex', *Brain*, 2001, *124(2)*, pp. 247–8

Shamay-Tsoory, S. G., Tomer, R. & Aharon-Peretz, J., 'The neuroanatomical basis of understanding sarcasm and its relationship to social cognition', *Neuropsychology*, 2005, *19(3)*, pp. 288–300

Shamay-Tsoory, S. G., Tomer, R., Berger, B. D. et al., 'Characterisation of empathy deficits following prefrontal brain damage: the role of the right ventromedial prefrontal cortex', *Journal of Cognitive Neuroscience*, 2003, *15(3)*, pp. 324–37

——, 'Impaired "affective theory of mind" is associated with right ventromedial prefrontal damage', *Cognitive and Behavioral Neurology*, 2005, *18(1)*, pp. 55–67

Shammi, P. & Stuss, D. T., 'Humour appreciation: a role of the right frontal lobe', *Brain*, 1999, *122(4)*, pp. 657–66

Shanks, A., *God and Modernity: A New and Better Way to Do Theology*, Routledge, London, 2000

——, *Trans-Metaphysical Theology*, forthcoming

Shanon, B., 'Graphological patterns as a function of handedness and culture', *Neuropsychologia*, 1979, *17(5)*, pp. 457–65

Shapiro, B. E. & Danly, M., 'The role of the right hemisphere in the control of speech prosody in propositional and affective contexts', *Brain and Language*, 1985, *25(1)*, pp. 19–36

Shelley, P. B., *A Defence of Poetry*, Blackwell, Oxford, 1972

Sheppard, G., Gruzelier, J., Manchanda, R. et al., '15-O positron emission tomographic scanning in predominantly never-treated acute schizophrenic patients', *Lancet*, 1983, *2(8365–66)*, pp. 1448–52

Sherover, C. M., 'Res cogitans: the Time of Mind', in Fraser, J. T (ed.), Time and Mind: Interdisciplinary Issues, vol. 6 ('The Study of Time'), International Universities Press, Madison CT, 1989, p. 281

Sherrington, C. S., The Integrative Action of the Nervous System, Yale University Press, New Haven CT, 1906

Shibahara, N. & Lucero-Wagoner, B., 'Hemispheric asymmetry in accessing word meanings: concrete and abstract nouns', Perceptual and Motor Skills, 2002, 94(3, pt. 2), pp. 1292–1300

Shigematsu, S., Zen Forest, Weatherhill, New York, 1981

Shklovsky, V., 'Art as Technique', in Lemon, L. T. & Reis, M. J. (trans. & ed.), Russian Formalist Criticism, University of Nebraska Press, Lincoln NE, 1965, pp. 3–24

Shlain, L., Art & Physics: Parallel Visions in Space, Time and Light, HarperCollins Perennial, New York, 2001

Siedliecki, S. L. & Good, M., 'Effect of music on power, pain, depression and disability', Journal of Advanced Nursing, 2006, 54(5), pp. 553–62

Siegal, M., Carrington, J. & Radel, M., 'Theory of mind and pragmatic understanding following right hemisphere damage', Brain and Language, 1996, 53(1), pp. 40–50

Sieratzki, J. S. & Woll, B., 'Why do mothers cradle babies on their left?', Lancet, 1996, 347(9017), pp. 1746–8

——, 'Cerebral asymmetry: from survival strategies to social behaviour', Behavioral and Brain Sciences, 2005, 28(4), pp. 613–14

Sieroff, E., 'Focussing on/in visual-verbal stimuli in patients with parietal lesions', Cognitive Neuropsychology, 1990, 7(5–6), pp. 519–94

——, 'Les mécanismes attentionnels', in Seron, X. & Jeannerod, M. (eds.), Neuropsychologie humaine, Mardaga, Liège, 1994, pp. 127–51

Siéroff, E., Decaix, C., Chokron, S. et al., 'Impaired orienting of attention in left unilateral neglect: a componential analysis', Neuropsychology, 2007, 21(1), pp. 94–113

Signoret, J. L., van Eeckhout, P., Poncet, M. et al., 'Aphasie sans amusie chez un organiste aveugle: alexieagraphie verbale sans alexie-agraphie musicale en braille', Revue Neurologique, 1987, 143(3), pp. 172–81

Silberman, E. K. & Weingartner, H., 'Hemispheric lateralisation of functions related to emotion', Brain and Cognition, 1986, 5(3), pp. 322–53

Silva, J. A., Leong, G. B. & Wine, D. B., 'Misidentification delusions, facial misrecognition, and right brain injury', Canadian Journal of Psychiatry, 1993, 38(4), pp. 239–41

Silva, J. A., Leong, G. B., Wine, D. B. et al., 'Evolving misidentification syndromes and facial recognition deficits', Canadian Journal of Psychiatry, 1992, 37(8), pp. 574–6

Sim, T.-C. & Martinez, C., 'Emotion words are remembered better in the left ear', Laterality, 10(2), 2005, pp. 149–59

Simmons, J. Q. & Baltaxe, C., 'Language patterns of adolescent autistics', Journal of Autism & Childhood Schizophrenia, 1975, 5(4), pp. 333–51

Simonds, R. J. & Scheibel, A. B., 'The postnatal development of the motor speech area: a preliminary study', Brain and Language, 1989, 37(1), pp. 42–58

Simons, D. J., 'In sight, out of mind: when object representations fail', Psychological Science, 1996, 7(5), pp. 301–5

Simons, D. J. & Chabris, C. F., 'Gorillas in our midst: sustained inattentional blindness for dynamic events', Perception, 1999, 28(9), pp. 1059–74

Simpson, G. G., 'Biology and the nature of science', Science, 1963, 139(3550), pp. 81–8

Skarratt, P. A. & Lavidor, M., 'Magnetic stimulation of the left visual cortex impairs expert word recognition', Journal of Cognitive Neuroscience, 2006, 18(10), pp. 1749–58

Skoyles, J. R., 'Alphabet and the Western mind', Nature, 1984, 309(5967), pp. 409–10

——, 'Did ancient people read with their right hemispheres?: a study in neuropalaeographology', New Ideas in Psychology, 1985, 3(3), pp. 243–52

——, 'Right hemisphere literacy in the ancient world', in de Kerckhove, D. & Lumsden, C. J. (eds.), The Alphabet and the Brain: the Lateralization of Writing, Springer-Verlag, Berlin, 1988, pp. 362–80

Sloboda, J. A., 'Music structure and emotional response: some empirical findings', Psychology of Music, 1991, 19(2), pp. 110–20

——, 'Does music mean anything?', Musicae Scientiae, 1998, 2(1), pp. 21–31

Sloboda, J. A. & Juslin, P. N., 'Psychological perspectives on music and emotion', in Juslin, P. N. & Sloboda, J. A. (eds.), Music and Emotion: Theory and Research, Oxford University Press, Oxford, 2001, pp. 71–104

Snell, B., The Discovery of the Mind, Harper & Row, New York, 1960 [Die Entdeckung des Geistes: Studien zur Entstehung des europäischen Denkens bei den Griechen 1946]

Snow, D., 'The emotional basis of linguistic and non-linguistic intonation: implications for hemispheric specialisation', Developmental Neuropsychology, 2000, 17(1), pp. 1–28

Snyder, P. J., Bilder, R. M., Wu, H. et al., 'Cerebellar volume asymmetries are related to handedness: a quantitative MRI study', Neuropsychologia, 1995, 33(4), pp. 407–19

Sommer, I. E., Aleman, A. & Kahn, R. S., 'Left with the voices or hearing right? Lateralization of auditory verbal hallucinations in schizophrenia', Journal of Psychiatry and Neuroscience, 2003, 28(3), pp. 217–18

Sonnby-Borgström, M., 'Automatic mimicry reactions as related to differences in emotional empathy', Scandinavian Journal of Psychology, 2002, 43(5), pp. 433–43

Sontag, S., Styles of Radical Will, Dell, New York, 1978

Sotillo, M., Carretié, L., Hinojosa, J. A. et al., 'Neural activity associated with metaphor comprehension: spatial analysis', Neuroscience Letters, 2005, 373(1), pp. 5–9

Spacks, P. M., Boredom: the Literary History of a State of Mind, University of Chicago Press, Chicago, 1995

Spalletta, G., Ripa, A., Bria, P. et al., 'Response of emotional unawareness after stroke to antidepressant treatment', American Journal of Geriatric Psychiatry, 2006, 14(3), pp. 220–27

Spelke, E. S. & Tsivkin, S., 'Language and number: a bilingual training study', Cognition, 2001, 78(1), pp. 45–88

Spence, S. A., Farrow, T. F., Herford, A. E. et al., 'Behavioural and functional anatomical correlates of deception in humans', *NeuroReport*, 2001, *12(13)*, pp. 2849–53

Spence, S., Shapiro, D. & Zaidel, E., 'The role of the right hemisphere in the physiological and cognitive components of emotional processing', *Psychophysiology*, 1996, *33(2)*, pp. 112–22

Spencer, K. M. & Banich, M. T., 'Hemispheric biases and the control of visuospatial attention: an ERP study', *BMC Neuroscience*, 2005, 6, p. 51

Sperry, R., 'Some effects of disconnecting the cerebral hemispheres', *Science*, 1982, *217(4566)*, pp. 1223–6

Sperry, R. W., 'Lateral specialization in the surgically separated hemispheres', in Schmitt, F. O. & Worden, F. G. (eds.), *Neuroscience 3rd Study Program*, Massachusetts Institute of Technology Press, Cambridge MA, 1974, pp. 5–19

——, 'Consciousness, personal identity and the divided brain', in Benson, D. F. & Zaidel, E. (eds.), *The Dual Brain: Hemispheric Specialization in Humans*, Guilford Press, New York, 1985, pp. 11–26

Sperry, R. W., Zaidel, E. & Zaidel, D., 'Self recognition and social awareness in the deconnected minor hemisphere', *Neuropsychologia*, 1979, *17(2)*, pp. 153–66

Spiegel, D., 'Neurophysiological correlates of hypnosis and dissociation', *Journal of Neuropsychiatry*, 1991, *3(4)*, pp. 440–45

Spiegel, H. & Spiegel, D., *Trance and Treatment: Clinical Uses of Hypnosis*, American Psychiatric Press, Washington DC, 1987 [1978]

Spinella, M., 'A relationship between smell identification and empathy', *International Journal of Neuroscience*, 2002, *112(6)*, pp. 605–12

Spinoza, B., *Ethics*, trans. W. H. White, Hafner, New York, 1947 [1677]

——, *Ethics: and De Intellectus Emendatione*, trans. A. Boyle, Dent, London 1963 [1677]

Spitzer, C., Willert, C., Grabe, H.-J. et al., 'Dissociation, hemispheric asymmetry, and dysfunction of hemispheric interaction: a transcranial magnetic stimulation approach', *Journal of Neuropsychiatry and Clinical Neurosciences*, 2004, *16(2)*, pp. 163–9

Stagno, S. J. & Gates, T. J., 'Palinopsia: a review of the literature', *Behavioural Neurology*, 1991, *4(2)*, pp. 67–74

Stanghellini, G., *Disembodied Spirits and Deanimated Bodies: the Psychopathology of Common Sense*, Oxford University Press, Oxford, 2004

Stanhope, P. D., 4th Earl of Chesterfield, *The Letters of the Earl of Chesterfield to his Son*, ed. C. Strachey & A. Calthrop, Dunne, London, 1901

Starkstein, S. E., Fedoroff, J. P., Price, T. R. et al., 'Anosognosia in patients with cerebrovascular lesions: a study of causative factors', *Stroke*, 1992, *23(10)*, pp. 1446–53

Starkstein, S. E. & Robinson, R. G., 'Lateralised emotional response following stroke', in Kinsbourne, M. (ed.), *Cerebral Hemisphere Function in Depression*, American Psychiatric Press, Washington DC, 1988, pp. 23–47

——, 'Affective disorders and cerebral vascular disease', *British Journal of Psychiatry*, 1989, *154(2)*, pp. 170–82

Starkstein, S. E., Vazquez, S., Migliorelli, R. et al., 'A single-photon emission computed tomographic study of anosognosia in Alzheimer's disease', *Archives of Neurology*, 1995, *52(4)*, pp. 415–20

Staude, J. R., 'From depth psychology to depth sociology: Freud, Jung, and Lévi-Strauss', *Theory and Society*, 1976, *3(3)*, pp. 303–38

Steiner, G., *Martin Heidegger*, Viking, New York, 1978

——, *Real Presences*, Faber, London, 1989

Stern, A., 'Psychoanalytic investigation of and therapy in the borderline group of neuroses', *Psychoanalytic Quarterly*, 1938, 7, pp. 467–89

Stevens, D., Charman, T. & Blair, R. J., 'Recognition of emotion in facial expressions and vocal tones in children with psychopathic tendencies', *Journal of Genetic Psychology*, 2001, *162(2)*, pp. 201–11

Stillings, N. A., Feinstein, M. H., Garfield, J. et al., *Cognitive Science: an Introduction*, Massachusetts Institute of Technology Press, Cambridge MA, 1987

Stirling, J., Cavill, J. & Wilkinson, A., 'Dichotically presented emotionally intoned words produce laterality differences as a function of localisation task', *Laterality*, 2000, *5(4)*, pp. 363–71

Stoeckel, M. C., Weder, B. & Binkofski, F., 'Left and right superior parietal lobule in tactile object discrimination', *European Journal of Neuroscience*, 2004, *19(4)*, pp. 1067–72

Stokoe, W. C., 'Gesture to sign (language)', in McNeill, D. (ed.), *Language and Gesture*, Cambridge University Press, Cambridge, UK, 2000, pp. 388–99

Stone, V. E., Baron-Cohen, S., Calder, A. et al., 'Acquired theory of mind impairments in individuals with bilateral amygdala lesions', *Neuropsychologia*, 2003, *41(2)*, pp. 209–20

Stone, V. E., Baron-Cohen, S. & Knight, R. T., 'Frontal lobe contributions to theory of mind', *Journal of Cognitive Neuroscience*, 1998, *10(5)*, pp. 640–56

Strauss, E. & Moscovitch, M., 'Perception of facial expressions', *Brain and Language*, 1981, *13(2)*, pp. 308–32

Stringaris, A. K., Medford, N. C., Giampietro, V. et al., 'Deriving meaning: distinct neural mechanisms for metaphoric, literal, and non-meaningful sentences', *Brain and Language*, 2007, *100(2)*, pp. 150–62

Studdert-Kennedy, M. (ed.). *The Psychobiology of Language*, Massachusetts Institute of Technology Press, Cambridge MA, 1983

Sturm, W. & Büssing, A., 'Einfluss der Aufgabenkomplexität auf hirnorganische Reaktionsbeeinträchtigungen – Hirnschädigungs- oder Patienteneffekt?', *European Archives of Psychiatry and Neurological Sciences*, 1986, *235(4)*, pp. 214–20

Sturm, W., de Simone, A., Krause, B. J. et al., 'Functional neuroanatomy of intrinsic alertness: evidence for a fronto-parietal-thalamic-brainstem network in the right hemisphere', *Neuropsychologia*, 1999, *37(7)*, pp. 797–805

Sturm, W., Fimm, B., Cantagallo, A. et al., 'Computerized training of specific attention deficits in stroke and traumatic brain-injured patients: a multicentric efficacy study', in Leclercq, M. & Zimmerman, P. (eds.), *Applied Neuropsychology of Attention*, Psychology Press, London, 2002, pp. 365–80

Sturm, W., Reul, J. & Willmes, K., 'Is there a generalised right hemisphere dominance for mediating cerebral activation? Evidence from a choice reaction experiment with lateralised simple warning stimuli', *Neuropsychologia*, 1989, *27(5)*, pp. 747–51

Stuss, D. T., 'Disturbance of self-awareness after frontal system damage', in Prigatano, G. P. & Schacter, D. L. (eds.), *Awareness of Deficit after Brain Injury: Clinical and Theoretical Issues*, Oxford University Press, Oxford, 1991a, pp. 66–83

——, 'Self, awareness, and the frontal lobes: a neuropsychological perspective', in Strauss, J. & Goethals, G. R. (eds.), *The Self: Interdisciplinary Approaches*, New York, Springer-Verlag, 1991b, pp. 255–78

Stuss, D. T. & Alexander, M. P., 'Executive functions and the frontal lobes: a conceptual view', *Psychological Research*, 2000, *63(3–4)*, pp. 289–98

Stuss, D. T. & Benson, D. F., 'Emotional concomitants of psychosurgery', in Heilman, K. M. & Satz, P. (eds.), *Advances in Neuropsychology and Behavioral Neurology*, vol. 1: *Neuropsychology of Human Emotion*, Guilford Press, New York, 1983, pp. 111–40

Stuss, D. T., Gallup, G. G., Jnr. & Alexander, M. P., 'The frontal lobes are necessary for "theory of mind" ', *Brain*, 2001, *124(2)*, pp. 279–86

Stuss, D. T., Gow, C. A. & Hetherington, C. R., ' "No longer Gage": frontal lobe dysfunction and emotional changes [review]', *Journal of Consulting and Clinical Psychology*, 1992, *60(3)*, pp. 349–59

Stuss, D. T., Picton, T. W. & Alexander, M. P., 'Consciousness, self-awareness and the frontal lobes', in Salloway, S., Malloy, P. & Duffy, J. (eds.), *The Frontal Lobes and Neuropsychiatric Illness*, American Psychiatric Press, Washington DC, 2001, pp. 101–9

Suberi, M. & McKeever, W. F., 'Differential right hemispheric memory storage of emotional and nonemotional faces', *Neuropsychologia*, 1977, *15(6)*, pp. 757–68

Sugiura, M., Kawashima, R., Nakamura, K. et al., 'Passive and active recognition of one's own face', *NeuroImage*, 2000, *11(1)*, pp. 36–48

Sugiura, M., Watanabe, J., Maeda, Y. et al., 'Cortical mechanisms of visual self-recognition', *NeuroImage*, 2005, *24(1)*, pp. 143–9

Sullivan, R. M. & Gratton, A., 'Behavioral effects of excitotoxic lesions of ventral medial prefrontal cortex in the rat are hemisphere-dependent', *Brain Research*, 2002, *927(1)*, pp. 69–79

Sun, T., Patoine, C., Abu-Khalil, A. et al., 'Early asymmetry of gene transcription in embryonic human left and right cerebral cortex', *Science*, 2005, *308(5729)*, pp. 1794–8

Sunderland, A., Tinson, D. & Bradley, L., 'Differences in recovery from constructional apraxia after right and left hemisphere stroke?', *Journal of Clinical and Experimental Neuropsychology*, 1994, *16(6)*, pp. 916–20

Sutherland, S., *The International Dictionary of Psychology*, Crossroad, London, 1989

Suthers, R. A. & Zollinger, S. A., 'Producing song: the vocal apparatus', *Annals of the New York Academy of Sciences*, 2004, *1016*, pp. 109–29

Suvisaari, J. M., Haukka, J. K., Tanskanen, A. J. et al., 'Decline in the incidence of schizophrenia in Finnish cohorts born from 1954 to 1965', *Archives of General Psychiatry*, 1999, *56(8)*, pp. 733–40

Suzuki, M., Okamura, N., Kawachi, Y. et al., 'Discrete cortical regions associated with the musical beauty of major and minor chords', *Cognitive, Affective and Behavioral Neuroscience*, 2008, *8(2)*, pp. 126–31

Swaddle, J. P. & Cuthill, I. C., 'Asymmetry and human facial attractiveness: symmetry may not always be beautiful', *Proceedings of the Royal Society of London, Series B: Biological Sciences*, 1995, *261(1360)*, pp. 111–16

Swayze, V. W., Andreasen, N. C., Ehrhardt, J. C. et al., 'Developmental abnormalities of the corpus callosum in schizophrenia', *Archives of Neurology*, 1990, *47(7)*, pp. 805–8

Sweetser, E., *From Etymology to Pragmatics: Metaphorical and Cultural Aspects of Semantic Structure*, Cambridge University Press, Cambridge, UK, 1990

Swisher, L. & Hirsh, I. J., 'Brain damage and the ordering of two temporally successive stimuli', *Neuropsychologia*, 1972, *10(2)*, pp. 137–52

Sypher, W., *Loss of the Self in Modern Literature and Art*, Random House, New York, 1962

Tafarodi, R. W., Marshall, T. C. & Katsura, H., 'Standing out in Canada and Japan', *Journal of Personality*, 2004, *72(4)*, pp. 785–814

Tagliavini, A., 'Aspects of the history of psychiatry in Italy in the second half of the nineteenth century', in Bynum, W. F., Porter, R. & Shepherd, M. (eds.), *The Anatomy of Madness: Essays in the History of Psychiatry*, vol. 2, Tavistock, London, 1985, pp. 175–96

Tan, L. H., Feng, C. M., Fox, P. T. et al., 'An fMRI study with written Chinese', *NeuroReport*, 2001, *12(1)*, pp. 83–8

Tan, L. H., Liu, H. L., Perfetti, C. A. et al., 'The neural system underlying Chinese logograph reading', *NeuroImage*, 2001, *13(5)*, pp. 836–46

Tan, L. H., Spinks, J. A., Gao, J. H. et al., 'Brain activation in the processing of Chinese characters and words: a functional MRI study', *Human Brain Mapping*, 2000, *10(1)*, pp. 16–27

Tan, U., 'Right and left in the Koran (Qur'an)', *Perceptual and Motor Skills*, 1998, *86(3, pt. 2)*, pp. 1343–6

Tang, A. C., 'A hippocampal theory of cerebral lateralization', in Hugdahl, K. & Davidson, R. J. (eds.), *The Asymmetrical Brain*, Massachusetts Institute of Technology Press, Cambridge MA, 2003, pp. 37–68

Tanner, M., *Schopenhauer*, Routledge, London, 1999

Tartaglione, A., Bino, G., Manzino, M. et al., 'Simple reaction-time changes in patients with unilateral brain damage', *Neuropsychologia*, 1986, *24(5)*, pp. 649–58

Tattersall, I., 'What happened in the origin of human consciousness?', *The Anatomical Record Part B: The New Anatomist*, 2004, *276(1)*, pp. 19–26

Taussig, M., *Mimesis and Alterity: A Particular History of the Senses*, Routledge & Kegan Paul, London, 1993

Taylor, D. C., 'Differential rates of cerebral maturation between sexes and between hemispheres: evidence from epilepsy', *Lancet*, 1969, *2(7612)*, pp. 140–42

Taylor, S. E., *Positive Illusions: Creative Self-Deception and the Healthy Mind*, Basic Books, New York, 1989
ten Cate, C., 'Posing as a professor: laterality in posing orientation for portraits of scientists', *Journal of Nonverbal Behavior*, 2002, *26(3)*, pp. 175–92
TenHouten, W. D., 'Cerebral-lateralization theory and the sociology of knowledge', in Benson, D. F. & Zaidel, E. (eds.), *The Dual Brain: Hemispheric Specialization in Humans*, Guilford Press, New York, 1985, pp. 341–58
——, 'Mind, self, image, emotion and brain in the thought of George Herbert Mead', *Journal of Mental Imagery*, 1991, *15*, pp. 157–9
Tennyson, Alfred, Lord, *Poems*, Oxford University Press, Oxford, 1910
Tennyson, Hallam, Lord, *Alfred Lord Tennyson: A Memoir*, Macmillan, New York, 1897
Terrace, H. S., Petitto, L. A., Sanders, R. J. et al., 'Can an ape create a sentence?', *Science*, 1979, *206(4421)*, pp. 891–902
Terzian, H. & Cecotto, C., 'Su un nuovo metodo per la determinazione e lo studio della dominanza emisferica', *Giornale di Psichiatria e di Neuropatologia*, 1959, *87*, pp. 889–923
Teske, J. A., 'The spiritual limits of neuropsychological life', *Zygon: Journal of Religion & Science*, 1996, *31(2)*, pp. 209–34
Teuber, H. L., Battersby, W. S. & Bender, M. B., *Visual Field Defects after Penetrating Missile Wounds of the Brain*, Harvard University Press, Cambridge MA, 1960
Thal, D. J., Marchman, V., Stiles, J. et al., 'Early lexical development in children with focal brain injury', *Brain and Language*, 1991, *40(1)*, pp. 491–527
Thatcher, R. W., Walker, R. A. & Giudice, S., 'Human cerebral hemispheres develop at different rates and ages', *Science*, 1987, *236(4805)*, pp. 1110–13
Théoret, H., Kobayashi, M., Merabet, L. et al., 'Modulation of right motor cortex excitability without awareness following presentation of masked self-images', *Brain Research: Cognitive Brain Research*, 2004, *20(1)*, pp. 54–7
Thompson, D'A. W., *On Growth and Form*, Cambridge University Press, Cambridge, UK, 1917
Thompson, E., 'Empathy and consciousness', *Journal of Consciousness Studies*, 2001, *8(5–7)*, pp. 1–32
Thompson, M. I., Silk, K. R. & Hover, G. L., 'Misidentification of a city: delimiting criteria for Capgras syndrome', *American Journal of Psychiatry*, 1980, *137(10)*, pp. 1270–72
Thoreau, H. D., *Journal*, entry for 5 August 1851; in B. Torrey (ed.), *The Writings of Henry David Thoreau: Journal*, Houghton Mifflin, Boston & New York, 1906, vol. 2
Thornbury, W., *The Life of J.M.W. Turner, R.A.*, Hurst & Blackett, London, 1862
Thorpe, W. H., 'Animal vocalisation and communication', in Millikan, C. H. & Darley, F. L. (eds.), *Brain Mechanisms Underlying Speech and Language*, Grune & Stratton, New York, 1967, pp. 1–12
Thurman, J., 'On the weight of the brain and the circumstances affecting it', *Journal of Mental Science*, 1866, *12*, pp. 1–43
Thuy, D. H., Matsuo, K., Nakamura, K. et al., 'Implicit and explicit processing of kanji and kana words and non-words studied with fMRI', *NeuroImage*, 2004, *23(3)*, pp. 878–89
Tiihonen, J., Katila, H., Pekkonen, E. et al., 'Reversal of cerebral asymmetry in schizophrenia measured with magnetoencephalography', *Schizophrenia Research*, 1998, *30(3)*, pp. 209–19
Toal, F., Murphy, D. G. M. & Murphy, K. C., 'Autistic-spectrum disorders: lessons from neuroimaging', *British Journal of Psychiatry*, 2005, *187(5)*, pp. 395–7
Toga, A. W. & Thompson, P. M., 'Mapping brain asymmetry', *Nature Reviews Neuroscience*, 2003, *4(1)*, pp. 37–48
Tokunaga, H., Nishikawa, T., Ikejiri, Y. et al., 'Different neural substrates for kanji and kana writing: a PET study', *NeuroReport*, 1999, *10(16)*, pp. 3315–19
Tomasello, M., 'Language is not an instinct', *Cognitive Development*, 1995, *10(1)*, pp. 131–56
Tomasello, M., Call, J. & Hare, B., 'Five primate species follow the visual gaze of conspecifics', *Animal Behaviour*, 1998, *55(4)*, pp. 1063–9
——, 'Chimpanzees understand psychological states – the question is which ones and to what extent', *Trends in Cognitive Sciences*, 2003, *7(4)*, pp. 153–6
Tommasi, L. & Vallortigara, G., 'Encoding of geometric and landmark information in the left and right hemispheres of the avian brain', *Behavioral Neuroscience*, 2001, *115(3)*, pp. 602–13
Tompkins, C. A. & Mateer, C. A., 'Right hemisphere appreciation of prosodic and linguistic indications of implicit attitude', *Brain and Language*, 1985, *24(2)*, pp. 185–203
Tönnies, F., *Gemeinschaft und Gesellschaft*, Fues's Verlag, Leipzig, 1887
Tootell, R. B., Mendola, J. D., Hadjikhani, N. K. et al., 'The representation of the ipsilateral visual field in human cerebral cortex', *Proceedings of the National Academy of Sciences of the USA*, 1998, *95(3)*, pp. 818–24
Toulmin, S., *Cosmopolis: the Hidden Agenda of Modernity*, University of Chicago Press, Chicago, 1990
Traherne, T., *Centuries of Meditations*, Cosimo, New York, 2007
Trainor, L. J. & Heinmiller, B. M., 'The development of evaluative responses to music: infants prefer to listen to consonance over dissonance', *Infant Behavior and Development*, 1998, *21(1)*, pp. 77–88
Tramo, M. J., 'Biology and music: music of the hemispheres', *Science*, 2001, *291(5501)*, pp. 54–6
Tramo, M. J. & Bharucha, J. J., 'Musical priming by the right hemisphere post-callosotomy', *Neuropsychologia*, 1991, *29(4)*, pp. 313–25
Tramo, M. J., Cariani, P. A., Delgutte, B. et al., 'Neurobiological foundations for the theory of harmony in Western tonal music', *Annals of the New York Academy of Sciences*, 2001, *930*, pp. 92–116
Tranel, D., ' "Acquired sociopathy": the development of sociopathic behavior following focal brain damage', in Fowles, D. C., Sutker, P. & Goodman, S. H. (eds.), *Progress in Experimental Personality and Psychopathology Research*, vol. 17, Springer-Verlag, New York, 1994, pp. 285–311
Tranel, D., Bechara, A. & Denburg, N. L., 'Asymmetric functional roles of right and left ventromedial prefrontal cortices in social conduct, decision-making, and emotional processing', *Cortex*, 2002, *38(4)*, pp. 589–612
Trevarthen, C., 'The tasks of consciousness: how could the brain do them?', *Brain and Mind: Ciba Foundation Symposium 69*, Elsevier, Amsterdam, 1979, pp. 187–215

——, 'Lateral asymmetries in infancy: implications for the development of the hemispheres', *Neuroscience and Biobehavioral Reviews*, 1996, *20(4)*, pp. 571–86

Trevarthen, C. & Aitken, K. J., 'Infant intersubjectivity: research, theory, and clinical applications', *Journal of Child Psychology and Psychiatry*, 2001, *42(1)*, pp. 3–48

Trevor-Roper, P., *The World Through Blunted Sight*, Thames & Hudson, London, 1970

Treyer, V., Buck, A. & Schnider, A., 'Subcortical loop activation during selection of currently relevant memories', *Journal of Cognitive Neuroscience*, 2003, *15(4)*, pp. 610–18

Trimble, M. R., *The Soul in the Brain: The Cerebral Basis of Language, Art, and Belief*, Johns Hopkins University Press, Baltimore MD, 2007

Tschudin, A., Call, J., Dunbar, R. I. et al., 'Comprehension of signs by dolphins (*Tursiops truncatus*)', *Journal of Comparative Psychology*, 2001, *115(1)*, pp. 100–5

Tucker, D. M., 'Lateral brain function, emotion, and conceptualization', *Psychological Bulletin*, 1981, *89(1)*, pp. 19–46

——, 'Neural control of emotional communication', in Blanck, P., Buck, R. & Rosenthal, R. (eds.), *Nonverbal Communication in the Clinical Context*, Cambridge University Press, Cambridge, UK, 1986, pp. 258–307

——, 'Neuropsychological mechanisms of affective self-regulating', in Kinsbourne, M. (ed.), *Cerebral Hemisphere Function in Depression*, American Psychiatric Press, Washington DC, 1988, pp. 99–131

——, 'Developing emotions and cortical networks', in Gunnar, M. R. & Nelson, C. A. (eds.), *Minnesota Symposium on Child Psychology*, vol. 24, *Developmental Behavioral Neuroscience*, Lawrence Erlbaum, Hillsdale NJ, 1992, pp. 75–128

Tucker, D. M., Roth, D. L. & Bair, T. B., 'Functional connections among cortical regions: topography of EEG coherence', *Electroencephalography and Clinical Neurophysiology*, 1986, *63(3)*, pp. 242–50

Tucker, D. M., Watson, R. T. & Heilman, K. M., 'Discrimination and evocation of affectively intoned speech in patients with right parietal disease', *Neurology*, 1977, *27(10)*, pp. 947–50

Tucker, D. M. & Williamson, P. A., 'Asymmetric neural control systems in human self-regulation [review]', *Psychological Review*, 1984, *91(2)*, pp. 185–215

Tuke, D. H., 'Increase of insanity in Ireland', *Journal of Mental Science*, 1894, *40*, pp. 549–58

Tulving, E., Kapur, S., Craik, F. I. et al., 'Hemispheric encoding/retrieval asymmetry in episodic memory: positron emission tomography findings [review]', *Proceedings of the National Academy of Sciences of the USA*, 1994, *91(6)*, pp. 2016–20

Tulving, E., Markowitsch, H. J., Craik, F. E. et al., 'Novelty and familiarity activations in PET studies of memory encoding and retrieval', *Cerebral Cortex*, 1996, *6(1)*, pp. 71–9

Turk, D. J., Heatherton, T. F., Kelley, W. M. et al., 'Mike or me? Self-recognition in a split-brain patient', *Nature Neuroscience*, 2002, *5(9)*, pp. 841–2

Turnbull, O. H. & Lucas, M. D., ' "Tell me, where is [this] fancy bred?": the cardiac and cerebral accounts on the lateral cradling bias', in Mandal, M. K., Bulman-Fleming, M. B. & Tiwari, G. (eds.), *Side Bias: A Neuropsychological Perspective*, Kluwer, Dordrecht, Netherlands, 2000, pp. 267–87

Turnbull, O. H., Rhys-Jones, S. L. & Jackson, A. L., 'The leftward cradling bias and prosody: an investigation of cradling preferences in the deaf community', *Journal of Genetic Psychology*, 2001, *162(2)*, pp. 178–86

Tzara, T. [Samy Rosenstock], 'Dada Manifesto 1918', in *The Dada Painters and Poets*, ed. R. Motherwell, Wittenborn, Schultz, New York, 1951, p. 76–81

Uddin, L. Q., Kaplan, J. T., Molnar-Szakacs, I. et al., 'Self-face recognition activates a frontoparietal "mirror" network in the right hemisphere: an event-related fMRI study', *NeuroImage*, 2005, *25(3)*, pp. 926–35

Uddin, L. Q., Molnar-Szakacs, I., Zaidel, E. et al., 'rTMS to the right inferior parietal lobule disrupts self–other discrimination', *Social Cognitive and Affective Neuroscience*, 2006, *1(1)*, pp. 65–71

Uddin, L. Q., Rayman, J. & Zaidel, E., 'Split-brain reveals separate but equal self-recognition in the two cerebral hemispheres', *Consciousness and Cognition*, 2005, *14(3)*, pp. 633–40

Udell, M. A. R. & Wynne, C. D. L., 'A review of domestic dogs' (*Canis familiaris*) human-like behaviors: or why behavior analysts should stop worrying and love their dogs', *Journal of the Experimental Analysis of Behavior*, 2008, *89(2)*, pp. 247–61

Uher, R., Murphy, T., Friederich, H.-C. et al., 'Functional neuroanatomy of body shape perception in healthy and eating-disordered women', *Biological Psychiatry*, 2005, *58(12)*, pp. 990–97

Uher, R. & Treasure, J., 'Brain lesions and eating disorders', *Journal of Neurology, Neurosurgery, & Psychiatry*, 2005, *76(6)*, pp. 852–7

Ulla, M., Thobois, S., Lemaire, J. J. et al., 'Manic behaviour induced by deep-brain stimulation in Parkinson's disease: evidence of substantia nigra implication?', *Journal of Neurology, Neurosurgery, & Psychiatry*, 2006, *77(12)*, pp. 1363–6

Umiltà, C., Bagnara, S. & Simion, F., 'Laterality effects for simple and complex geometrical figures and nonsense patterns', *Neuropsychologia*, 1978, *16(1)*, pp. 43–9

Unturbe, J. & Corominas, J., 'Probability matching involves rule-generating ability: a neuropsychological mechanism dealing with probabilities', *Neuropsychology*, 2007, *21(5)*, pp. 621–30

Upanishads, trans. S. Radhakrishnan, Allen & Unwin, London, 1953

Uttner, I., Bliem, H. & Danek, A., 'Prosopagnosia after unilateral right cerebral infarction', *Journal of Neurology*, 2002, *249(7)*, pp. 1432–59

Vaid, J., 'Asymmetries in tachistoscopic word recognition: scanning effects re-examined', *International Journal of Neuroscience*, 1988, *42(3–4)*, pp. 253–8

Vaihinger, H., *The Philosophy of 'As If'*, trans. C. K. Ogden, 2nd edn., Routledge & Kegan Paul, London, 1935 [*Die Philosophie des Als Ob* 1911]

Valaki, C. E., Maestu, F., Simos, P. G. et al., 'Cortical organization for receptive language functions in Chinese, English, and Spanish: a cross-linguistic MEG study', *Neuropsychologia*, 2004, *42(7)*, pp. 967–79

Valéry, P., *Œuvres*, ed. J. Hytier, Gallimard, Paris, 1957

——, *Aesthetics*, trans. R. Manheim, Routledge & Kegan Paul, London, 1964

Vallortigara, G., 'Right hemisphere advantage for social recognition in the chick', *Neuropsychologia*, 1992, *30(9)*, pp. 761–8
——, 'Comparative neuropsychology of the dual brain: a stroll through animals' left and right perceptual worlds', *Brain and Language*, 2000, *73(2)*, pp. 189–219
Vallortigara, G., Regolin, L., Bortolomiol, G. et al., 'Lateral asymmetries due to preferences in eye use during visual discrimination learning in chicks', *Behavioural Brain Research*, 1996, *74(1–2)*, pp. 135–43
Vallortigara, G., Rogers, L. J., Bisazza, A. et al., 'Complementary right and left hemifield use for predatory and agonistic behaviour in toads', *NeuroReport*, 1998, *9(14)*, pp. 3341–4
van der Merwe, W. L. & Voestermans, P. P., 'Wittgenstein's legacy and the challenge to psychology', *Theory & Psychology*, 1995, *5(1)*, p. 38
van Eden, C. G., Uylings, H. B. & van Pelt, J., 'Sex-difference and left-right asymmetries in the prefrontal cortex during postnatal development in the rat', *Brain Research*, 1984, *314(1)*, pp. 146–53
van Gogh, V., *The Letters of Vincent van Gogh*, trans. A. Pomerans, Penguin, Harmondsworth, UK, 2003
van Honk, J., Hermans, E. J., d'Alfonso, A. A. et al., 'A left-prefrontal lateralized, sympathetic mechanism directs attention towards social threat in humans: evidence from repetitive transcranial magnetic stimulation', *Neuroscience Letters*, 2002, *319(2)*, pp. 99–102
van Kleeck, M. H., 'Hemispheric differences in global versus local processing of hierarchical visual stimuli by normal subjects: new data and a meta-analysis of previous studies', *Neuropsychologia*, 1989, *27(9)*, pp. 1165–78
van Kleeck, M. H. & Kosslyn, S. M., 'Gestalt laws of perceptual organization in an embedded figures task: evidence for hemispheric specialization', *Neuropsychologia*, 1989, *27(9)*, pp. 1179–86
van Lancker, D., 'Personal relevance and the human right hemisphere', *Brain and Cognition*, 1991, *17(1)*, pp. 64–92
van Lancker, D. R. & Canter, G. J., 'Impairment of voice and face recognition in patients with hemispheric damage', *Brain and Cognition*, 1982, *1(2)*, pp. 185–95
van Mander, C., *Dutch and Flemish Painters*, trans. C. van de Wall, McFarlane, Warde, McFarlane, New York, 1936
van Os, J., 'Does the urban environment cause psychosis?', *British Journal of Psychiatry*, 2004, *184(4)*, pp. 287–8
van Strien, J. W. & van Beek, S., 'Ratings of emotion in laterally presented faces: sex and handedness effects', *Brain and Cognition*, 2000, *44(3)*, pp. 645–52
van Zomeren, A. H. & Brouwer, W. H., *Clinical Neuropsychology of Attention*, Oxford University Press, Oxford, 1994
Vanderhaeghen, C. E., 'Self-concept and brain damage', *Journal of General Psychology*, 1986, *113(2)*, pp. 139–45
Vanderhasselt, M. A., De Raedt, R., Baeken, C. et al., 'The influence of rTMS over the right dorsolateral prefrontal cortex on intentional set switching', *Experimental Brain Research*, 2006, *172(4)*, pp. 561–5
Vaneechoutte, M. & Skoyles, J. R., 'The memetic origin of language: modern humans as musical primates', *Journal of Memetics – Evolutionary Models of Information Transmission*, 1998, *2*, pp. 84–117; also available online at http:USERS.UGENT.BE/~MVANEECH/ORILA.FIN.HTML (ACCESSED 21 MARCH 2009)
Varela, F. J., 'Neurophenomenology: a methodological remedy for the hard problem', *Journal of Consciousness Studies*, 1996, *3(4)*, pp. 330–50
Varley, R. A., Klessinger, N. J. C., Romanowski, C. A. J. et al., 'Agrammatic but numerate', *Proceedings of the National Academy of Sciences of the USA*, 2005, *102(9)*, pp. 3519–24
Varley, R. & Siegal, M., 'Evidence for cognition without grammar from causal reasoning and "theory of mind" in an agrammatic aphasic patient', *Current Biology*, 2000, *10(12)*, pp. 723–6
Vartanian, O. & Goel, V., 'Neuroanatomical correlates of aesthetic preference for paintings', *NeuroReport*, 2004, *15(5)*, pp. 893–7
Vasari, G., *Lives of the Artists*, trans. G. Bull, Penguin, Harmondsworth, UK, 1987 [*Le Vite delle più eccellenti pittori, scultori, ed architettori* 1550]
Vauclair, J. & Donnot, J., 'Infant holding biases and their relations to hemispheric specializations for perceiving facial emotions', *Neuropsychologia*, 2005, *43(4)*, pp. 564–71
Vaughan, H., *The Complete Poems*, ed. A. Rudrum, Penguin, Harmondsworth, UK, 1976
Vauvenargues, Luc de Clapiers, marquis de, *Réflexions et Maximes* [1746], in *Œuvres de Vauvenargues*, ed. D.-L. Gilbert, Furne et Cie., Paris, 1859
Veenhoven, R., 'Developments in satisfaction-research', *Social Indicators Research*, 1996, *37*, pp. 1–46
Vega, W. A., Kolody, B., Aguilar-Gaxiola, S. et al., 'Lifetime prevalence of DSM-III-R psychiatric disorders among urban and rural Mexican Americans in California', *Archives of General Psychiatry*, 1998, *55(9)*, pp. 771–8
Velek, M., White, L. E., Williams, J. P. et al., 'Psychosis in a case of corpus callosum agenesis', *Alabama Medicine*, 1988, *58(6)*, pp. 27–9
Ventolini, N., Ferrero, E. A., Sponza, S. et al., 'Laterality in the wild: preferential hemifield use during predatory and sexual behaviour in the black-winged stilt (*Himantopus himantopus*)', *Animal Behaviour*, 2005, *69(5)*, pp. 1077–84
Verene, D. P., *Philosophy and the Return to Self-Knowledge*, Yale University Press, New Haven CT, 1997
Vico, G.-B., *The New Science of Giambattista Vico*, trans. T. G. Bergin & M. H. Fisch, Cornell University Press, Ithaca NY, 1988 [1725]
——, *On the Study Methods of Our Time*, trans. E. Gianturco, Cornell University Press, Ithaca NY, 1990 [1709]
Vié, J., 'Étude psychopathologique des méconnaissances systématiques', *Annales Médico-Psychologiques (Paris)*, 1944a, *102(2, pt. 1)*, pp. 1–18
——, 'Le substratum morbide et les stades évolutifs des méconnaissances systématiques', *Annales Médico-Psychologiques (Paris)*, 1944b, *102(1, pt. 5)*, pp. 440–55
——, 'Les méconnaissances systématiques, étude séméiologique', *Annales Médico-Psychologiques (Paris)*, 1944c, *102(1, pt. 3)*, pp. 229–52
Villa, G., Gainotti, G. & De Bonis, C., 'Constructive disabilities in focal brain-damaged patients: influence of hemispheric side, locus of lesion and coexistent mental deterioration', *Neuropsychologia*, 1986, *24(4)*, pp. 497–510
Virányi, Z., Topál, J., Gácsi, M. et al., 'Dogs respond appropriately to cues of humans' attentional focus', *Behavioural Processes*, 2004, *66(2)*, pp. 161–72

Virgil, *The Aeneid*, trans. R. Fagles, Penguin, Harmondsworth, UK, 2007a

——, *The Eclogues, Georgics and Moretum of Virgil*, ed. G. Stuart, Kessinger, Whitefish MT, 2007b

Virilio, P., *Art and Fear*, Continuum, London, 2003

Virtue, S., Haberman, J., Clancy, Z. et al., 'Neural activity of inferences during story comprehension', *Brain Research*, 2006, *1084(1)*, pp. 104–14

Vitkovitch, M. & Underwood, G., 'Hemispheric differences in the processing of pictures of typical and atypical semantic category members', *Cortex*, 1991, *27(3)*, pp. 475–80

Vitz, P. C., 'The use of stories in moral development', *American Psychologist*, 1990, *45(6)*, pp. 709–20

Voeller, K. K., 'Right-hemisphere deficit syndrome in children', *American Journal of Psychiatry*, 1986, *143(8)*, pp. 1004–9

Vogeley, K., Bussfeld, P., Newen, A. et al., 'Mind reading: neural mechanisms of theory of mind and selfperspective', *NeuroImage*, 2001, *14(1, pt. 1)*, pp. 170–81

Vogt, C., *Untersuchungen über Thierstaaten*, Literarische Anstalt, Frankfurt am Main, 1851

Vogt, S. & Magnussen, S., 'Hemispheric specialization and recognition memory for abstract and realistic pictures: a comparison of painters and laymen', *Brain and Cognition*, 2005, *58(3)*, pp. 324–33

Vohn, R., Fimm, B., Weber, J. et al., 'Management of attentional resources in within-modal and cross-modal divided attention tasks: an fMRI study', *Human Brain Mapping*, 2007, *28(12)*, pp. 1267–75

Vollmer-Haase, J., Finke, K., Harje, W. et al., 'Hemispheric dominance in the processing of JS Bach fugues: a transcranial Doppler sonography (TCD) study with musicians', *Neuropsychologia*, 1998, *36(9)*, pp. 857–67

von Humboldt, W., *On Language: the Diversity of Human Language Structure and its Influence on the Mental Development of Mankind*, Cambridge University Press, Cambridge, UK, 1988 [1836]

von Wattenwyl, A. & Zollinger, H., 'The color lexica of two American Indian languages: Quechi and Misquito', *International Journal of American Linguistics*, 1978, *44(1)*, pp. 56–68

Vowles, D., 'Neuroethology, evolution and grammar', in Aronson, R., Tobach, E., Lehrman, D. et al. (eds.), *Development and Evolution of Behavior: Essays in Memory of TC Schneirla*, W. H. Freeman & Co., San Francisco, 1970, pp. 194–215

Vuilleumier, P., Ghika-Schmid, F., Bogousslavsky, J. et al., 'Persistent recurrence of hypomania and prosopoaffective agnosia in a patient with right thalamic infarct', *Neuropsychiatry, Neuropsychology and Behavioral Neurology*, 1998, *11(1)*, pp. 40–44

Vuilleumier, P., Henson, R. N., Driver, J. et al., 'Multiple levels of visual object constancy revealed by event-related fMRI of repetition priming', *Nature Neuroscience*, 2002, *5(5)*, pp. 491–9

Vuilleumier, P., Hester, D., Assal, G. et al., 'Unilateral spatial neglect recovery after sequential strokes', *Neurology*, 1996, *46(1)*, pp. 184–9

Vygotsky, L. S., *Thought and Language*, trans. A. Kozulin, Massachusetts Institute of Technology Press, Cambridge MA, 1986

Wagner, H. N., Jnr., Burns, H. D., Dannals, R. F. et al., 'Imaging dopamine receptors in the human brain by positron emission tomography', *Science*, 1983, *221(4617)*, pp. 1264–6

Waismann, F., 'Will and motive', in Waismann, F., Schaechter, J. & Schlick, M. (eds.), *Ethics and the Will: Essays*, trans. H. Kaal, Kluwer, Dordrecht, Netherlands, 1994, pp. 53–137

Waiter, G. D., Williams, J. H., Murray, A. D. et al., 'Structural white matter deficits in high-functioning individuals with autistic spectrum disorder: a voxel-based investigation', *NeuroImage*, 2005, *24(2)*, pp. 455–61

Wallace, G. L. & Canter, G. J., 'Effects of personally relevant language materials on the performance of severely aphasic individuals', *Journal of Speech and Hearing Disorders*, 1985, *50(4)*, pp. 385–90

Walsh, C., 'Gene clue to brain asymmetry revealed on right side', *Focus Online*, 2005, http:FOCUS.HMS.HARVARD.EDU/2005/JUN10_2005/NEUROSCIENCE.SHTML (ACCESSED 7 DECEMBER 2008)

Walsh, K. & Darby, D., *Neuropsychology, a Clinical Approach*, 4th edn., Churchill, Livingstone, New York, 1999

Wang, B., Zhou, T. G., Zhuo, Y. et al., 'Global topological dominance in the left hemisphere', *Proceedings of the National Academy of Sciences of the USA*, 2007, *104(52)*, pp. 21014–19

Wang, Y. X., He, G. X., Tong, G. H. et al., 'Cerebral asymmetry in a selected Chinese population', *Australasian Radiology*, 1999, *43(3)*, pp. 321–4

Wapner, W., Hamby, S. & Gardner, H., 'The role of the right hemisphere in the apprehension of complex linguistic materials', *Brain and Language*, 1981, *14(1)*, pp. 15–33

Wapner, W., Judd, T. & Gardner, H., 'Visual agnosia in an artist', *Cortex*, 1978, *14(3)*, pp. 343–64

Ward-Perkins, B., *The Fall of Rome and the End of Civilization*, Oxford University Press, Oxford, 2005

Warrington, E. K. & James, M., 'An experimental investigation of facial recognition in patients with unilateral cerebral lesions', *Cortex*, 1967, *3*, pp. 317–26

Warrington, E. K., James, M. & Kinsbourne, M., 'Drawing disability in relation to laterality of cerebral lesion', *Brain*, 1966, *89(1)*, pp. 53–82

Warrington, E. K. & McCarthy, R. A., 'Categories of knowledge: further fractionations and an attempted integration', *Brain*, 1987, *110(5)*, pp. 1273–96

Warrington, E. K. & Taylor, A. M., 'The contribution of the right parietal lobe to object recognition', *Cortex*, 1973, *9(2)*, pp. 152–64

Watanabe, S., Sakamoto, J. & Wakita, M., 'Pigeons' discrimination of paintings by Monet and Picasso', *Journal of the Experimental Analysis of Behavior*, 1995, *63(2)*, pp. 165–74

Watkins, K. E., Paus, T., Lerch, J. P. et al., 'Structural asymmetries in the human brain: a voxel-based statistical analysis of 142 MRI scans', *Cerebral Cortex*, 2001, *11(9)*, pp. 868–77

Watt, D., 'Affective neuroscience and extended reticular thalamic activating system (ERTAS) theories of consciousness', *Association for the Scientific Study of Consciousness Electronic Seminar*, 1998, http:COGNET.MIT.EDU/POSTERS/TUCSON3/WATT.HTML (ACCESSED 27 APRIL 2009)

Watt, R. J. & Ash, R. L., 'A psychological investigation of meaning in music', *Musicae Scientiae*, 1998, *2*, pp. 33–54

Watts, A., *The Two Hands of God*, Rider & Co., London, 1963

Waugh, M., 'Boredom in psychoanalytic perspective', *Social Research*, 1975, *42*, pp. 538–50

Weber, M., *The Religion of China: Confucianism and Taoism*, trans. H. Gerth, Free Press, Glencoe IL, 1951 [*Konfuzianismus und Taoismus* 1915].

——, *Ancient Judaism*, trans. H. Gerth & D. Martindale, Free Press, Glencoe IL, 1952 [*Das antike Judentum* 1911–13]

——, *The Religion of India: The Sociology of Hinduism and Buddhism*, trans. H. Gerth & D. Martindale, Free Press, New York, 1958 [*Hinduismus and Buddhismus* 1916–17]

Wechsler, A. F., 'The effect of organic brain disease on recall of emotionally charged versus neutral narrative texts', *Neurology*, 1973, *23(2)*, pp. 130–35

Ween, J. E., Alexander, M. P., d'Esposito, M. et al., 'Factors predictive of stroke outcome in a rehabilitation setting', *Neurology*, 1996, *47(2)*, pp. 388–92

Weich, S., Twigg, L. & Lewis, G., 'Rural/non-rural differences in rates of common mental disorders in Britain: prospective multilevel cohort study', *British Journal of Psychiatry*, 2006, *188(1)*, pp. 51–7

Weinberger, D. R., Luchins, D. J., Morihisa, J. et al., 'Asymmetrical volumes of the right and left frontal and occipital regions of the human brain', *Annals of Neurology*, 1982, *11(1)*, pp. 97–100

Weinstein, S. & Graves, R. E., 'Are creativity and schizotypy products of a right hemisphere bias?', *Brain and Cognition*, 2002, *49(1)*, pp. 138–51

Weis, S., Haug, H., Holoubek, B. et al., 'The cerebral dominances: quantitative morphology of the human cerebral cortex', *International Journal of Neuroscience*, 1989, *47(1–2)*, pp. 165–8

Weissman, M. M., Bland, R. C., Canino, G. J. et al., 'Cross-national epidemiology of major depression and bipolar disorder', *Journal of the American Medical Association*, 1996, *276(4)*, pp. 293–9

Wernicke, C., *Der aphasische Symptomencomplex: eine psychologische Studie auf anatomischer Basis*, Max Cohn & Weigert, Breslau, 1874

West, M. L., *Early Greek Philosophy and the Orient*, Oxford University Press, Oxford, 1971

——, *The East Face of Helicon: West Asiatic Elements in Early Poetry and Myth*, Oxford University Press, Oxford, 1997

Wexler, B. E., 'Alterations in cerebral laterality during acute psychotic illness', *British Journal of Psychiatry*, 1986, *149(2)*, pp. 202–9

——, 'Regional brain dysfunction in depression', in Kinsbourne, M. (ed.), *Cerebral Hemisphere Function in Depression*, American Psychiatric Press, Washington DC, 1988, pp. 65–78

Wexler, B. E., Warrenburg, S., Schwartz, G. E. et al., 'EEG and EMG responses to emotion-evoking stimuli processed without conscious awareness', *Neuropsychologia*, 1992, *30(12)*, pp. 1065–79

Wheeler, M. A., Stuss, D. T. & Tulving, E., 'Toward a theory of episodic memory: the frontal lobes and autonoetic consciousness [review]', *Psychological Bulletin*, 1997, *121(3)*, pp. 331–54

Whitehead, A. N., *The Concept of Nature*, Cambridge University Press, Cambridge, UK, 1920

——, *Science and the Modern World*, Cambridge University Press, Cambridge, UK, 1926

——, *Nature and Life*, Cambridge University Press, Cambridge, UK, 1934

Whitehead, R., 'Right hemisphere processing superiority during sustained visual attention', *Journal of Cognitive Neuroscience*, 1991, *3(4)*, pp. 329–34

Wicker, B., Michel, F., Henaff, M. A. et al., 'Brain regions involved in the perception of gaze: a PET study', *NeuroImage*, 1998, *8(2)*, pp. 221–7

Wieser, H.-G. & Mazzola, G., 'Musical consonances and dissonances: are they distinguished independently by the right and left hippocampi?', *Neuropsychologia*, *24(6)*, 1986, pp. 805–12

Wigan, A. L., *A New View of Insanity: The Duality of the Mind Proved by the Structure, Functions and Diseases of the Brain, and by the Phenomena of Mental Derangement, and Shown to be Essential to Moral Responsibility*, Longman, London, 1844

Wilber, K., *No Boundary: Eastern and Western Approaches to Personal Growth*, Shambhala, Boston MA, 2001

Wilkins, A. J., Shallice, T. & McCarthy, R., 'Frontal lesions and sustained attention', *Neuropsychologia*, 1987, *25(2)*, pp. 359–65

Wilson, M., 'The subjugation of grief in Seneca's *Epistles*', in Braund, S. M. & Gill, C. (eds.), *The Passions in Roman Thought and Literature*, Cambridge University Press, Cambridge, UK, 1997, pp. 48–67

Wilson, T. D. & Schooler, J. W., 'Thinking too much: introspection can reduce the quality of preferences and decisions', *Journal of Personality and Social Psychology*, 1991, *60(2)*, pp. 181–92

Winckelmann, J. J., *History of the Art of Antiquity*, trans. H. F. Mallgrave, Getty Research Institute, Los Angeles, 2006 [*Geschichte der Kunst des Alterthums* 1764]

Winner, E., Brownell, H., Happé, F. et al., 'Distinguishing lies from jokes: theory of mind deficits and discourse interpretation in right hemisphere brain-damaged patients', *Brain and Language*, 1998, *62(1)*, pp. 89–106

Winner, E. & Gardner, H., 'The comprehension of metaphor in brain-damaged patients', *Brain*, 1977, *100(4)*, pp. 717–29

Witelson, S. F. & Kigar, D. L., 'Asymmetry in brain function follows asymmetry in anatomical form: gross, microscopic, postmortem and imaging studies', in Boller, F. & Grafman, J. (eds.), *Handbook of Neuropsychology*, Elsevier, Amsterdam, 1988, vol. 1, pp. 111–41

Witelson, S. F. & Pallie, W., 'Left hemisphere specialization for language in the newborn: neuroanatomical evidence of asymmetry', *Brain Research*, 1973, *96(3)*, pp. 641–6

Wittgenstein, L., *The Blue and Brown Books*, ed. R. Rhees, Blackwell, Oxford, 1958

——, *Lectures and Conversations on Aesthetics, Psychology, and Religious Belief*, University of California Press, Berkeley CA, 1967a

——, *Philosophical Investigations*, ed. G. E. M. Anscombe & R. Rhees, trans. G. E. M. Anscombe, 3rd edn., Blackwell, Oxford, 1967b [*Philosophische Untersuchungen* 1953]

——, *Zettel*, ed. G. E. M. Anscombe & G. H. von Wright, trans. G. E. M. Anscombe, Blackwell, Oxford, 1967c

——, *Philosophical Remarks*, ed. R. Rhees, trans. R. Hargreaves & R. White, Blackwell, Oxford, 1971 [*Philosophische Bemerkungen 1964*]

——, *Culture and Value*, ed. G. H. von Wright & H. Nyman, trans. P. Winch, University of Chicago Press, Chicago, 1984 [*Vermischte Bemerkungen 1977*]

——, 'A lecture on ethics', in Klagge, J. C. & Nordmann, A. (eds.), *Ludwig Wittgenstein: Philosophical Occasions 1912–1951*, Hackett, Indianapolis IN, 1993, pp. 36–44

——, *Denkbewegungen: Tagebücher 1930–1932/1936–1937*, ed. I. Somavilla, Haymon, Innsbruck, 1997

——, *Tractatus Logico-Philosophicus*, trans. D. F. Pears & B. F. McGuiness, Routledge & Kegan Paul, London, 2001 [1922; *Logisch-philosophische Abhandlung 1921*]

——, *Movements of Thought: Diaries 1930–1932, 1936–1937*, trans. A. Nordmann, in Klagge, J. C. & Nordmann, A. (eds.), *Ludwig Wittgenstein: Public and Private Occasions*, Rowman & Littlefield, Lanham MD, 2003, pp. 3–255

Wittling, W., 'Brain asymmetry in the control of autonomic-physiologic activity', in Davidson, R. J. & Hugdahl, K. (eds.), *Brain Asymmetry*, Massachusetts Institute of Technology Press, Cambridge MA, 1995, pp. 305–357

Wittling, W., Block, A., Genzel, S. et al., 'Hemispheric asymmetry in parasympathetic control of the heart', *Neuropsychologia*, 1998, 36(5), pp. 461–8

Wittling, W., Block, A., Schweiger, E. et al., 'Hemisphere asymmetry in sympathetic control of the human myocardium', *Brain and Cognition*, 1998, 38(1), pp. 17–35

Wittling, W. & Pflüger, M., 'Neuroendocrine hemispheric asymmetries: salivary cortisol secretion during lateralized viewing of emotion-related and neutral films', *Brain and Cognition*, 1990, 14(2), pp. 243–65

Wohlschläger, A. & Bekkering, H., 'Is human imitation based on a mirror-neurone system? Some behavioural evidence', *Experimental Brain Research*, 2002, 143(3), pp. 335–41

Wolford, G., Miller, M. B. & Gazzaniga, M. S., 'The left hemisphere's role in hypothesis formation', *Journal of Neuroscience*, 2000, 20: RC64, pp. 1–4

Woolf, V., 'Mr Bennett and Mrs Brown', The Hogarth Press, London, 1924

Wordsworth, W., *The Prelude, or Growth of a Poet's Mind (text of 1805)*, ed. E. de Selincourt, Oxford University Press, Oxford, 1933

——, *The Poetical Works of William Wordsworth*, 5 vols., ed. E. de Selincourt & H. Darbishire, Oxford University Press, Oxford, 1940–49

——, 'Preface to *Lyrical Ballads*', in *Lyrical Ballads 1805*, ed. D. Roper, Collins, London, 1973

——, *The Prose Works of William Wordsworth*, ed. W. J. B. Owen & J. W. Smyser, 3 vols., Oxford University Press, Oxford, 1974

Wraga, M., Souheil, J., Shephard, J. et al., 'Mental rotation of self versus objects: an fMRI study', *Proceedings of the Eighth Annual Meeting of the Cognitive Neuroscience Society* (New York, 2001), Cognitive Neuroscience Society, Andover MA, 2001, p. 133

Wu, J. C., Hagman, J., Buchsbaum, M. S. et al., 'Greater left cerebral hemispheric metabolism in bulimia assessed by positron emission tomography', *American Journal of Psychiatry*, 1990, 147(3), pp. 309–12

Wyatt, Sir Thomas, *The Collected Poems*, ed. K. Muir, Routledge & Kegan Paul, London, 1949

Wymer, J. H., Lindman, L. S. & Booksh, R. L., 'A neuropsychological perspective of aprosody: features, function, assessment, and treatment', *Applied Neuropsychology*, 2002, 9(1), pp. 37–47

Wynn, T., 'Did *Homo erectus* speak?', *Cambridge Archaeological Journal*, 1998, 8(1), pp. 78–81

——, 'Archaeology and cognitive evolution', *Behavioral and Brain Sciences*, 2002, 25(3), pp. 389–402

Yakovlev, P. I. & Raki#aac, P., 'Patterns of decussation of bulbar pyramids and distribution of pyramidal tracts on two sides of the spinal cord', *Transactions of the American Neurological Association*, 1966, 91, pp. 366–7

Yamadori, A., Mori, E., Tabuchi, M. et al., 'Hypergraphia: a right hemisphere syndrome', *Journal of Neurology, Neurosurgery, & Psychiatry*, 1986, 49(10), pp. 1160–64

Yamaguchi, S., Yamagata, S. & Kobayashi, S., 'Cerebral asymmetry of the "top-down" allocation of attention to global and local features', *Journal of Neuroscience*, 2000, 20(9), RC72: pp. 1–5

Yamazaki, Y., Aust, U., Huber, L. et al., 'Lateralized cognition: asymmetrical and complementary strategies of pigeons during discrimination of the "human concept" ', *Cognition*, 2007, 104(2), pp. 315–44

Yarnell, P. H., 'The intrinsic goodness of pain, anguish and the loss of pleasure', *The Journal of Value Inquiry*, 2001, 35, pp. 449–54

Yellott, J. I., 'Probability learning with noncontingent success', *Journal of Mathematical Psychology*, 1969, 6, pp. 541–75

Yin, R. K., 'Looking at upside-down faces', *Journal of Experimental Psychology*, 1969, 81(1), pp. 141–5

——, 'Face recognition by brain-injured patients: a dissociable entity?', *Neuropsychologia*, 1970, 8(4), pp. 395–402

Yochim, B. P., Kender, R., Abeare, C. et al., 'Semantic activation within and across the cerebral hemispheres: what's left isn't right', *Laterality*, 2005, 10(2), pp. 131–48

Yokoyama, K., Jennings, R., Ackles, P. et al., 'Lack of heart rate changes during an attention-demanding task after right hemisphere lesions', *Neurology*, 1987, 37(4), pp. 624–30

Yoon, B. W., Morillo, C. A., Cechetto, D. F. et al., 'Cerebral hemispheric lateralization in cardiac autonomic control', *Archives of Neurology*, 1997, 54(6), pp. 741–4

Yoshida, T., Yoshino, A., Takahashi, Y. et al., 'Comparison of hemispheric asymmetry in global and local information processing and interference in divided and selective attention using spatial frequency filters', *Experimental Brain Research*, 2007, 181(3), pp. 519–29

Yoshii, F., Barker, W. W., Chang, J. Y. et al., 'Sensitivity of cerebral glucose metabolism to age, gender, brain volume, brain atrophy, and cerebrovascular risk factors', *Journal of Cerebral Blood Flow and Metabolism*, 1988, 8(5), pp. 654–61

Young, A. W. & Ratcliff, G., 'Visuospatial abilities of the right hemisphere', in Young, A. W. (ed.), *Functions of the Right Cerebral Hemisphere*, Academic Press, London, 1983, pp. 1–31

Young, E., *Night Thoughts*, ed. S. Cornford, Cambridge University Press, Cambridge, UK, 1989

Young, J., *Heidegger, Philosophy, Nazism*, Cambridge University Press, Cambridge, UK, 1998
——, *Heidegger's Philosophy of Art*, Cambridge University Press, Cambridge, UK, 2004
Zahavi, D. & Parnas, J., 'Phenomenal consciousness and self awareness: a phenomenological critique of representational theory', in Gallagher, S. & Shear, J. (eds.), *Models of the Self*, Imprint Academic, Thorverton, UK, 1999, pp. 253–70
Zahn-Waxler, C. & Robinson, J., 'Empathy and guilt: early origins of feelings of responsibility', in Tangney, J. P. & Fischer, K. W. (eds.), *Self-conscious Emotions*, Guilford Press, New York, 1995, pp. 143–73
Zaidel, D. W., 'Hemifield tachistoscopic presentations and hemispheric specialization in normal subjects', in Benson, D. F. & Zaidel, E. (eds.), *The Dual Brain*, Guilford Press, New York, 1985, pp. 143–55
——, 'Hemispheric asymmetry in memory for pictorial semantics in normal subjects', *Neuropsychologia*, 1987, *25(3)*, pp. 487–95
Zaidel, D. W., Aarde, S. M. & Baig, K., 'Appearance of symmetry, beauty, and health in human faces', *Brain and Cognition*, 2005, *57(3)*, pp. 261–3
Zaidel, D. W., Chen, A. C. & German, C., 'She is not a beauty even when she smiles: possible evolutionary basis for a relationship between facial attractiveness and hemispheric specialization', *Neuropsychologia*, 1995, *33(5)*, pp. 649–55
Zaidel, D. W. & Cohen, J. A., 'The face, beauty, and symmetry: perceiving asymmetry in beautiful faces', *International Journal of Neuroscience*, 2005, *115(8)*, pp. 1165–73
Zaidel, D. W. & Deblieck, C., 'Attractiveness of natural faces compared to computer constructed perfectly symmetrical faces', *International Journal of Neuroscience*, 2007, *117(4)*, pp. 423–31
Zaidel, D. W. & Kasher, A., 'Hemispheric memory for surrealistic versus realistic paintings', *Cortex*, 1989, *25(4)*, pp. 617–41
Zaidel, D. W. & Kosta, A., 'Hemispheric effects of canonical views of category members with known typicality levels', *Brain and Cognition*, 2001, *46(1–2)*, pp. 311–16
Zaidel, E., 'Language in the right hemisphere', in Benson, D. & Zaidel, E. (eds.), *The Dual Brain: Hemispheric Specialization in Humans*, Guilford Press, New York, 1985, pp. 205–31
——, 'Interhemispheric transfer in the split brain: long term status following complete cerebral commissurotomy', in Davidson, R. H. & Hugdahl, K. (eds.), *Brain Asymmetry*, Massachusetts Institute of Technology Press, Cambridge MA, 1995, pp. 491–532
Zajonc, A., 'Goethe and the science of his time', in Seamon, D. & Zajonc, A. (eds.), *Goethe's Way of Science: a Phenomenology of Nature*, State University of New York Press, Albany NY, 1998, pp. 15–30
Zajonc, A. B., 'Feeling and thinking: preferences need no inferences', *American Psychologist*, 1980, *35*, pp. 151–75
——, 'On the primacy of affect', in Scherer, K. R. & Ekman, P. (eds.), *Approaches to Emotion*, Lawrence Erlbaum, Hillsdale NJ, 1984, pp. 259–70
Zajonc, R. B., Pietromonaco, P. & Bargh, J., 'Independence and interaction of affect and cognition', in Clark, M. S. & Fiske, S. (eds.), *Affect and Cognition: the 17th Annual Carnegie Symposium on Cognition*, Lawrence Erlbaum, Hillsdale NJ, 1982, pp. 211–27
Zalla, T., Koechlin, E., Pietrini, P. et al., 'Differential amygdala responses to winning and losing: a functional magnetic resonance imaging study in humans', *European Journal of Neuroscience*, 2000, *12(5)*, pp. 1764–70
Zamrini, E. Y., Meador, K. J., Loring, D. W. et al., 'Unilateral cerebral inactivation produces differential left/right heart rate responses', *Neurology*, 1990, *40(9)*, pp. 1408–11
Zanes, J., Ross, S., Hatfield, R. et al., 'The relationship between creativity and psychosis-proneness', *Personality and Individual Difference*, 1998, *24(6)*, pp. 879–81
Zeki, S., *Inner Vision: An Exploration of Art and the Brain*, Oxford University Press, Oxford, 1999
Zeman, A., 'Consciousness', *Brain*, 2001, *124(7)*, pp. 1263–89
Zentner, M. R., 'Infants' preferences for consonance vs. dissonance and for major vs. minor in music', *Infant Behavior and Development*, 1996, *19 (suppl. 1)*, p. 836
Zentner, M. R. & Kagan, J., 'Infants' perception of consonance and dissonance in music', *Infant Behavior and Development*, 1998, *21(3)*, pp. 483–92
Zetzsche, T., Meisenzahl, E. M., Preuss, U. W. et al., 'In-vivo analysis of the human planum temporale (PT): does the definition of PT borders influence the results with regard to cerebral asymmetry and correlation with handedness?', *Psychiatry Research*, 2001, *107(2)*, pp. 99–115
Zijderveld, A. C., *On Clichés: the Supersedure of Meaning by Function in Modernity*, Routledge & Kegan Paul, London, 1979
Zilles, K., Dabringhaus, A., Geyer, S. et al., 'Structural asymmetries in the human forebrain and the forebrain of non-human primates and rats', *Neuroscience and Biobehavioral Reviews*, 1996, *20(4)*, pp. 593–605
Zollinger, H., 'Biological aspects of color naming', in Rentschler, I., Herzberger, B. & Epstein, D. (eds.), *Beauty and the Brain: Biological Aspects of Aesthetics*, Birkhauser Verlag, Basel, 1988, pp. 149–64

INDEX

578 ◆ INDEX